Poetry Criticism

Guide to Gale Literary Criticism Series

For criticism on	Consult these Gale series
Authors now living or who died after December 31, 1999	**CONTEMPORARY LITERARY CRITICISM (CLC)**
Authors who died between 1900 and 1999	**TWENTIETH-CENTURY LITERARY CRITICISM (TCLC)**
Authors who died between 1800 and 1899	**NINETEENTH-CENTURY LITERATURE CRITICISM (NCLC)**
Authors who died between 1400 and 1799	**LITERATURE CRITICISM FROM 1400 TO 1800 (LC)** **SHAKESPEAREAN CRITICISM (SC)**
Authors who died before 1400	**CLASSICAL AND MEDIEVAL LITERATURE CRITICISM (CMLC)**
Authors of books for children and young adults	**CHILDREN'S LITERATURE REVIEW (CLR)**
Dramatists	**DRAMA CRITICISM (DC)**
Poets	**POETRY CRITICISM (PC)**
Short story writers	**SHORT STORY CRITICISM (SSC)**
Literary topics and movements	**HARLEM RENAISSANCE: A GALE CRITICAL COMPANION (HR)** **THE BEAT GENERATION: A GALE CRITICAL COMPANION (BG)** **FEMINISM IN LITERATURE: A GALE CRITICAL COMPANION (FL)** **GOTHIC LITERATURE: A GALE CRITICAL COMPANION (GL)**
Asian American writers of the last two hundred years	**ASIAN AMERICAN LITERATURE (AAL)**
Black writers of the past two hundred years	**BLACK LITERATURE CRITICISM (BLC)** **BLACK LITERATURE CRITICISM SUPPLEMENT (BLCS)**
Hispanic writers of the late nineteenth and twentieth centuries	**HISPANIC LITERATURE CRITICISM (HLC)** **HISPANIC LITERATURE CRITICISM SUPPLEMENT (HLCS)**
Native North American writers and orators of the eighteenth, nineteenth, and twentieth centuries	**NATIVE NORTH AMERICAN LITERATURE (NNAL)**
Major authors from the Renaissance to the present	**WORLD LITERATURE CRITICISM, 1500 TO THE PRESENT (WLC)** **WORLD LITERATURE CRITICISM SUPPLEMENT (WLCS)**

ISSN 1052-4851

Poetry Criticism

Excerpts from Criticism of the Works of the Most Significant and Widely Studied Poets of World Literature

Volume 89

Michelle Lee
Project Editor

GALE
CENGAGE Learning™

Detroit • New York • San Francisco • New Haven, Conn • Waterville, Maine • London

GALE
CENGAGE Learning

Poetry Criticism, Vol. 89

Project Editor: Michelle Lee

Editorial: Dana Barnes, Thomas Burns, Elizabeth Cranston, Kathy D. Darrow, Kristen Dorsch, Jeffrey W. Hunter, Jelena O. Krstović, Thomas J. Schoenberg, Noah Schusterbauer, Lawrence J. Trudeau, Russel Whitaker

Data Capture: Frances Monroe, Gwen Tucker

Indexing Services: Factiva, Inc.

Rights and Acquisitions: Matt Derda, Timothy Sisler, Sara Teller

Composition and Electronic Capture: Gary Leach

Manufacturing: Rhonda Dover

Associate Product Manager: Marc Cormier

For product information and technology assistance, contact us at **Gale Customer Support, 1-800-877-4253.** For permission to use material from this text or product, submit all requests online at **www.cengage.com/permissions.** Further permissions questions can be emailed to **permissionrequest@cengage.com**

While every effort has been made to ensure the reliability of the information presented in this publication, Gale, a part of Cengage Learning, does not guarantee the accuracy of the data contained herein. Gale accepts no payment for listing; and inclusion in the publication of any organization, agency, institution, publication, service, or individual does not imply endorsement of the editors or publisher. Errors brought to the attention of the publisher and verified to the satisfaction of the publisher will be corrected in future editions.

Gale
27500 Drake Rd.
Farmington Hills, MI, 48331-3535

LIBRARY OF CONGRESS CATALOG CARD NUMBER 81-640179

ISBN-13: 978-0-7876-9886-7
ISBN-10: 0-7876-9886-5

ISSN 1052-4851

Printed in the United States of America
1 2 3 4 5 6 7 12 11 10 09 08

Contents

Preface vii

Acknowledgments ix

Literary Criticism Series Advisory Board xi

Preface

*P*oetry Criticism (*PC*) presents significant criticism of the world's greatest poets and provides supplementary biographical and bibliographical material to guide the interested reader to a greater understanding of the genre and its creators. Although major poets and literary movements are covered in such Gale Literary Criticism series as *Contemporary Literary Criticism (CLC)*, *Twentieth-Century Literary Criticism (TCLC)*, *Nineteenth-Century Literature Criticism (NCLC)*, *Literature Criticism from 1400 to 1800 (LC)*, and *Classical and Medieval Literature Criticism (CMLC)*, *PC* offers more focused attention on poetry than is possible in the broader, survey-oriented entries on writers in these Gale series. Students, teachers, librarians, and researchers will find that the generous excerpts and supplementary material provided by *PC* supply them with the vital information needed to write a term paper on poetic technique, to examine a poet's most prominent themes, or to lead a poetry discussion group.

Scope of the Series

PC is designed to serve as an introduction to major poets of all eras and nationalities. Since these authors have inspired a great deal of relevant critical material, *PC* is necessarily selective, and the editors have chosen the most important published criticism to aid readers and students in their research. Each author entry presents a historical survey of the critical response to that author's work. The length of an entry is intended to reflect the amount of critical attention the author has received from critics writing in English and from foreign critics in translation. Every attempt has been made to identify and include the most significant essays on each author's work. In order to provide these important critical pieces, the editors sometimes reprint essays that have appeared elsewhere in Gale's Literary Criticism Series. Such duplication, however, never exceeds twenty percent of a *PC* volume.

Organization of the Book

Each *PC* entry consists of the following elements:

- The **Author Heading** cites the name under which the author most commonly wrote, followed by birth and death dates. Also located here are any name variations under which an author wrote, including transliterated forms for authors whose native languages use nonroman alphabets. If the author wrote consistently under a pseudonym, the pseudonym will be listed in the author heading and the author's actual name given in parenthesis on the first line of the biographical and critical introduction. Uncertain birth or death dates are indicated by question marks. Single-work entries are preceded by the title of the work and its date of publication.

- The **Introduction** contains background information that introduces the reader to the author and the critical debates surrounding his or her work.

- The list of **Principal Works** is ordered chronologically by date of first publication and lists the most important works by the author. The first section comprises poetry collections and book-length poems. The second section gives information on other major works by the author. For foreign authors, the editors have provided original foreign-language publication information and have selected what are considered the best and most complete English-language editions of their works.

- Reprinted **Criticism** is arranged chronologically in each entry to provide a useful perspective on changes in critical evaluation over time. All individual titles of poems and poetry collections by the author featured in the entry are printed in boldface type. The critic's name and the date of composition or publication of the critical work are given at the beginning of each piece of criticism. Unsigned criticism is preceded by the title of the source in which it appeared. Footnotes are reprinted at the end of each essay or excerpt. In the case of excerpted criticism, only those footnotes that pertain to the excerpted texts are included.

- Critical essays are prefaced by brief **Annotations** explicating each piece.

- A complete **Bibliographical Citation** of the original essay or book precedes each piece of criticism.

- An annotated bibliography of **Further Reading** appears at the end of each entry and suggests resources for additional study. In some cases, significant essays for which the editors could not obtain reprint rights are included here. Boxed material following the further reading list provides references to other biographical and critical sources on the author in series published by Gale.

Cumulative Indexes

A **Cumulative Author Index** lists all of the authors that appear in a wide variety of reference sources published by Gale, including *PC*. A complete list of these sources is found facing the first page of the Author Index. The index also includes birth and death dates and cross references between pseudonyms and actual names.

A **Cumulative Nationality Index** lists all authors featured in *PC* by nationality, followed by the number of the *PC* volume in which their entry appears.

A **Cumulative Title Index** lists in alphabetical order all individual poems, book-length poems, and collection titles contained in the *PC* series. Titles of poetry collections and separately published poems are printed in italics, while titles of individual poems are printed in roman type with quotation marks. Each title is followed by the author's last name and corresponding volume and page numbers where commentary on the work is located. English-language translations of original foreign-language titles are cross-referenced to the foreign titles so that all references to discussion of a work are combined in one listing.

Citing *Poetry Criticism*

When citing criticism reprinted in the Literary Criticism Series, students should provide complete bibliographic information so that the cited essay can be located in the original print or electronic source. Students who quote directly from reprinted criticism may use any accepted bibliographic format, such as University of Chicago Press style or Modern Language Association (MLA) style. Both the MLA and the University of Chicago formats are acceptable and recognized as being the current standards for citations. It is important, however, to choose one format for all citations; do not mix the two formats within a list of citations.

The examples below follow recommendations for preparing a bibliography set forth in *The Chicago Manual of Style,* 14th ed. (Chicago: The University of Chicago Press, 1993); the first example pertains to material drawn from periodicals, the second to material reprinted from books:

Linkin, Harriet Kramer. "The Language of Speakers in *Songs of Innocence and of Experience.*" *Romanticism Past and Present* 10, no. 2 (summer 1986): 5-24. Reprinted in *Poetry Criticism.* Vol. 63, edited by Michelle Lee, 79-88. Detroit: Thomson Gale, 2005.

Glen, Heather. "Blake's Criticism of Moral Thinking in *Songs of Innocence and of Experience.*" In *Interpreting Blake,* edited by Michael Phillips, 32-69. Cambridge: Cambridge University Press, 1978. Reprinted in *Poetry Criticism.* Vol. 63, edited by Michelle Lee, 34-51. Detroit: Thomson Gale, 2005.

Suggestions are Welcome

Readers who wish to suggest new features, topics, or authors to appear in future volumes, or who have other suggestions or comments are cordially invited to call, write, or fax the Associate Product Manager:

Associate Product Manager, Literary Criticism Series
Gale
27500 Drake Road
Farmington Hills, MI 48331-3535
1-800-347-4253 (GALE)
Fax: 248-699-8054

Acknowledgments

The editors wish to thank the copyright holders of the criticism included in this volume and the permissions managers of many book and magazine publishing companies for assisting us in securing reproduction rights. Following is a list of the copyright holders who have granted us permission to reproduce material in this volume of *PC*. Every effort has been made to trace copyright, but if omissions have been made, please let us know.

COPYRIGHTED MATERIAL IN *PC*, VOLUME 89, WAS REPRODUCED FROM THE FOLLOWING PERIODICALS:

American Poetry Review, v. 27, September-October, 1998 for "A Marriage Between Writers: *Birthday Letters* as Memoir and as Poetry" by Alan Williamson. Reproduced by permission of the author.—*ANQ,* v. 19, winter, 2006. Copyright © 2006 by Helen Dwight Reid Educational Foundation. Reproduced with permission of the Helen Dwight Reid Educational Foundation, published by Heldref Publications, 1319 18th Street, NW, Washington, DC 20036-1802.—*Criticism,* v. 47, fall, 2005. Copyright © 2005 by Wayne State University Press. Reproduced with permission of the Wayne State University Press.—*Eighteenth Century Life,* v. 13, November, 1989. Copyright © 1989 by Duke University Press. All rights reserved. Used by permission of the publisher.—*Explicator,* v. 53, winter, 1995. Copyright © 1995 by Helen Dwight Reid Educational Foundation. Reproduced with permission of the Helen Dwight Reid Educational Foundation, published by Heldref Publications, 1319 18th Street, NW, Washington, DC 20036-1802.—*GLQ,* v. 11, 2005. Copyright © 2005 by Duke University Press. All rights reserved. Used by permission of the publisher.—*Hollins Critic,* v. 34, October, 1997. Copyright © 1997 by Hollins College. Reproduced by permission.—*Horn Book Magazine,* v. 81, May, 2005. Copyright © 2005 by the Horn Book, Inc., Boston, MA, www.hbook.com. All rights reserved. Reproduced by permission.—*Journal of Modern Literature,* v. 23, summer, 2000; v. 28, winter, 2005. Copyright © 2000, 2005 by Indiana University Press. Both reproduced by permission.—*Poetry,* v. 183, 2004 for "Stare at the Monster" by Michael Hofmann. Copyright © 2004 by Modern Poetry Association. Reproduced by permission of the author.—*Raritan,* v. 21, spring, 2002. Copyright © 2002 by *Raritan: A Quarterly Review*. Reproduced by permission.—*Religion and the Arts,* v. 5, 2001. Copyright © 2001 by Koninklijke Brill, Leiden, The Netherlands. Courtesy of Brill Academic Publishers.—*Shakespeare in Southern Africa,* v. 13, 2001. Copyright © 2001 by Rhodes University, Institute for the Study of English in Africa. Reproduced by permission.—*Shakespeare Quarterly,* v. 54, 2003. Copyright © 2003 by the Johns Hopkins University Press. Reproduced by permission.—*South Carolina Review,* v. 38, spring, 2006. Copyright © 2006 by Clemson University. Reproduced by permission.—*Studia Neophilologica,* v. 66, 1994 for "Venus Reconsidered: The Goddess of Love in *Venus and Adonis*" by A. D. Cousins. Reproduced by permission of Taylor & Francis, Ltd., http//:www.informaworld.com, and the author.—*Studies in Eighteenth-Century Culture,* v. 33, 2004. Copyright © 2004 by the American Society for Eighteenth-Century Studies. All rights reserved. Reproduced by permission.—*Studies in English Literature, 1500-1900,* v. 41, summer, 2001; v. 42, winter, 2002; v. 44, summer, 2004. Copyright © 2001, 2002, 2004 by William Marsh Rice University. All reproduced by permission.—*Twentieth Century Literature,* v. 45, spring, 1999; v. 50, spring, 2004; v. 51, winter, 2005. Copyright © 1999, 2004, 2005 by Hofstra University Press. All reproduced by permission.—*Upstart Crow,* v. 21, 2001. Copyright © 2001 by Clemson University. Reproduced by permission.—*Virginia Quarterly Review,* v. 80, spring, 2004. Copyright © 2004 by the *Virginia Quarterly Review*, The University of Virginia. Reproduced by permission of the publisher.

COPYRIGHTED MATERIAL IN *PC*, VOLUME 89, WAS REPRODUCED FROM THE FOLLOWING BOOKS:

Anderson, Nathalie. From "Ted Hughes and the Challenge of Gender," in *The Challenge of Ted Hughes.* Edited by Keith Sagar. St. Martin's Press, 1994. Copyright © 1994 by the MacMillan Press Ltd. Reprinted by permission of St. Martin's Press, LLC.—Brown, Sarah Annes. From *The Metamorphosis of Ovid: From Chaucer to Ted Hughes.* Duckworth, 1999. Copyright © 1999 by Sarah Annes Brown. Reproduced by permission of Gerald Duckworth & Co. Ltd.—Cahoon, Leslie. From "Haunted Husbands: Orpheus's Song (Ovid, *Metamorphoses* 10-11) in Light of Ted Hughes's *Birthday Letters*," in *Defining Genre and Gender in Latin Literature: Essays Presented to William S. Anderson on His Seventy-Fifth Birthday.* Edited by William W. Batstone and Garth Tissol. Peter Lang, 2005. Copyright © 2005 by Peter Lang Publishing, Inc., New York. All rights reserved. Reproduced by permission.—Churchwell, Sarah. From "'Your Sentence Was Mine Too': Reading Sylvia Plath in Ted Hughes's *Birthday Letters*," in *Literary Couplings: Writing Couples, Collaborators, and*

Gale Literature Product Advisory Board

The members of the Gale Literature Product Advisory Board—reference librarians from public and academic library systems—represent a cross-section of our customer base and offer a variety of informed perspectives on both the presentation and content of our literature products. Advisory board members assess and define such quality issues as the relevance, currency, and usefulness of the author coverage, critical content, and literary topics included in our series; evaluate the layout, presentation, and general quality of our printed volumes; provide feedback on the criteria used for selecting authors and topics covered in our series; provide suggestions for potential enhancements to our series; identify any gaps in our coverage of authors or literary topics, recommending authors or topics for inclusion; analyze the appropriateness of our content and presentation for various user audiences, such as high school students, undergraduates, graduate students, librarians, and educators; and offer feedback on any proposed changes/enhancements to our series. We wish to thank the following advisors for their advice throughout the year.

Stephen Duck
1705?-1756

English poet.

INTRODUCTION

Best known for *The Thresher's Labour,* a long poem about the brutally monotonous and difficult work performed by seasonal farm workers, published in *Poems on Several Subjects* (1730), Duck has been a literary and social curiosity for critics and readers ever since his own time. Transformed from agricultural laborer to literary celebrity as a result of being "discovered" by a local clergyman, he ultimately received the patronage of Queen Caroline enabling him to devote himself to writing poetry. Duck is of particular interest to modern scholars because his career reveals much about social attitudes toward working-class writers and their works in the eighteenth century. He inspired many later working-class poets, notably Robert Burns and John Clare, with his example.

BIOGRAPHICAL INFORMATION

Duck was born in Charlton St. Peter, in Wiltshire, England, to poor parents who were farm workers, mostly on land owned by others. Duck attended the local charity school until he was thirteen and then left to work as an itinerant day laborer, principally a thresher. He married a woman named Ann when he was nineteen and around that time also became interested in furthering his education. He invested in some books on arithmetic, studying them, along with the Bible, in the evenings when his work was done. With his friend John Lavington, he eventually built up a small library that included, among other volumes, the works of John Milton, Seneca, Ovid, William Shakespeare, and Samuel Butler, as well as issues of *The Spectator.* Duck began to compose poetry, modeling it on his reading and burning his pieces when he finished them. He eventually came to the attention of the Rev. Stanley who, fascinated by Duck's "primitivism," self-education, and poetic ambitions, introduced him to numerous wealthy and influential patrons; one of these, Lord Maclesfield, read Duck's poems to Queen Caroline, who in turn invited the author to live at court and work as her gardener. While he was on his way to court, Duck's wife died, leaving him a widower with three children. Expected to participate in the public life of the court, Duck became more and more estranged from his background as he advanced through his various royal appointments—yeoman of the Guard, Queen's librarian, and master of Duck Island at St. James Park. He married Sarah Big, the Queen's housekeeper, in 1735 and was installed that same year in a house in Richmond Gardens. Having published his first collection of poetry, *Poems on Several Subjects* in 1730, Duck continued to write, but his poetry, as critics have noted, lost its naturalness and organic quality in favor of a more formal, courtly style. While he was certainly considered a phenomenon of success, many commentators, including Alexander Pope and Jonathan Swift, disparaged his humble beginnings and his rustic poetry. Still, his poems were popular with the reading public and there were numerous pirated editions of his first collection. Left without a patron after Queen Caroline died, Duck took holy orders in 1746 and, with the help of influential friends, became preacher at Kew Chapel, attracting huge crowds of curious churchgoers. Some biographers have speculated that Duck suffered from depression and despair as a result of the extreme change in his circumstances; whether or not this was true, he apparently drowned himself in a local river in the spring of 1756.

MAJOR WORKS

Commentators agree that Duck's early poem, *The Thresher's Labour,* written in 1729 or 1730 while he was still employed as a thresher, is his masterpiece. Written in the georgic style, it is characterized by abundant realistic detail and sometimes-rough versification, and is a vivid, unadorned evocation of agricultural labor as well as a tribute to the dignity of the worker. Duck's tone is humble throughout, notably in his dedication to his patron, but the poem also reflects the workers' complaints about their situation in general and about the demanding field master in particular. Focusing on summer and fall, when the bulk of the itinerant workers' labor is performed, the poem suggests the pleasant natural rhythms of the outdoor life as well as the painful monotony of farm work. The poem also treats the theme of economic exploitation as the vast wealth of the farmowner is attained through the deadening hard work of the laborers. His later poems, written after he came to live at court, are considered inferior in style and theme to *The Thresher's Labour,* and critics note that his abandonment of his old way of life, the source of his poetic inspiration, led Duck to produce poetry that reads almost like a parody of his earlier style. Many of his later compositions are occasional and commemorative. For example, *The Vision* (1737) is an elegy on the death of Queen Caroline, *Every Man in His Own Way* (1741) is a reply to a friend's letter suggesting he end his poetic career, and *Caesar's Camp* (1755) is a patriotic celebration of England's agricultural wealth and national standing, ending with a tribute to the infamous Duke of Cumberland.

CRITICAL RECEPTION

Critical assessment of Duck's poetry has always been intertwined with commentary about his life. Rose Mary Davis, one of the first twentieth-century scholars to write a detailed study of Duck and his work, readily acknowledged the psychological and sociological questions presented by Duck's life, writing "one wonders whether his life as protégé of royalty brought out the best that was in him any more than his life as a farm-laborer had done." Other critics have analyzed Duck's role in other social contexts: Linda Zionkowski, for instance, explores the effects of the expanding book trade in eighteenth-century England on the publication of his poetry, while Moira Ferguson and E. P. Thompson compare *The Thresher's Labour* with *The Woman's Labour* (1739), Mary Collier's sharp response to Duck's passages disparaging women workers in his poem. Jennifer Batt compares two contemporary biographical accounts of Duck, noting the extent to which fact, legend, and reportage are intertwined in the pieces. More recently, the elements of Duck's style have received closer critical scrutiny. Bridget Keegan asserts that in *The Thresher's Labour* Duck made a notable contribution to the eighteenth-century debate about the nature and purpose of georgic poetry, adding that the "multiplication of speaking voices in the poem argues a sophistication that most critics have been unwilling to acknowledge." Similarly, Peggy Thompson analyzes Duck's use of the heroic couplet, noting that it sometimes undermines his intent, while James Mulholland writes about Duck's transformation of the pastoral form that enabled him "to reconcile his dual status as an agrarian and as a poet." Focusing on the narrative and descriptive aspects of Duck's style, Steve Van-Hagen suggests that Duck's verse partakes of both pastoral and georgic but in fact remains "generically distinct" due to his gift for evoking the sights and sounds of physical labor, while at the same time preserving the dignity of the laborer.

PRINCIPAL WORKS

Poetry

Poems on Several Subjects (also published as *Poems on Several Occasions* and *Curious Poems on Several Occasions*) 1730; revised and enlarged editions published 1732, 1733, 1736, and 1753

Royal Benevolence: A Poem 1730

To His Royal Highness the Duke of Cumberland, on His Birth-Day, April the 15th, 1732 1732

A Poem on the Marriage of His Serene Highness the Prince of Orange, with Ann Princess-Royal of Great Britain 1733-34

Truth and Falsehood: A Fable 1734

A Poem on Her Majesty's Birth-Day 1735

The Vision: A Poem on the Death of Her Most Gracious Majesty Queen Caroline 1737

Alrick and Isabel; or, The Unhappy Marriage: A Poem 1740

Every Man in His Own Way: An Epistle to a Friend 1741

An Ode on the Battle of Dettingen, Humbly Inscrib'd to the King 1743

Caesar's Camp; or, St. George's Hill 1755

The Thresher's Labour by Stephen Duck and The Woman's Labour by Mary Collier (edited by Moira Ferguson) 1985

CRITICISM

Rose Mary Davis (essay date 1926)

SOURCE: Davis, Rose Mary. "The Thresher." In *Stephen Duck, the Thresher-Poet*, pp. 1-39. Orono, Maine: The University Press, 1926.

[*In the following excerpt from her detailed study of Duck, Davis presents an overview of the poet's life, his rise to fame, and the reception of his poetry up to the time he secured the patronage of Queen Caroline.*]

The eighteenth century was an age of verse-writers; and the writing of the verse was by no means confined to such persons as we would today dignify by the name of poets, but rather as Havens points out in his *Influence of Milton* ". . . any person interested in literature was likely to publish a long, ambitious poem,—an epic, a satire, or a treatise on religion, gardening, or the art of doing something that the author had never done." Continuing, he notes that interest in poetry had permeated all social levels and all occupations: "clergymen, lawyers, physicians, university fellows, or country gentlemen," and adds that "a considerable number were produced by cobblers, tailors, carpenters, by threshers like Stephen Duck and milkwomen like Ann Yearsley, and even by children of thirteen or fifteen years. Chatterton and Burns showed what boys and ploughmen might do; while Southey's *Lives of Uneducated Poets* indicates that there were many others who won temporary success in a field where today they would probably not venture." He quotes Saintsbury to the effect that "Poetry has hardly ever received more, and rarely so much honour" and that "for anybody who would give it [the eighteenth century] verse after its own manner it had not infrequent rewards, dignities . . . and almost always praise, if not pudding, given in the most liberal fashion."[1] In *Nature's Simple Plan* Tinker takes a similar stand in disputing the charge against the eighteenth century of "chilling poets into silence." If this was the case, he believes it was not wilful or conscious: "England awaited the advent of a poet with impatience and even sought for poetic genius in the most unlikely places."[2]

A contemporary statement, confirming this view appears in the works of the Reverend Joseph Spence, who believed that in the period one might "easily distinguish a greater Propensity, than seems to have been usual in other Ages, towards rewarding such as have particularly deserved it: and this goes so far, that I myself can have the Pleasure at present of reckoning two or three, in the little circle of my own most intimate Friends, who have been rais'd purely by their literary Merit and good Character from inconsiderable or no Circumstances, to considerable, or at least very easy ones."[3]

Not all the comment of the time, however, reflects such a complacent view. The poet, Edward Young, in 1730 seems to be regretting the literary tendencies of the proletarian classes:

> His hammer this, and that his trowel quits,
> And wanting sense for tradesmen, serve for wits:
> By thriving men subsists each other trade;
> Of ev'ry broken craft a writer's made:[4]

The author of an article abstracted from the *Grubstreet Journal,* in the *Gentleman's Magazine* for 1731 sees no cause for rejoicing in the fact that ". . . nothing has increased their society so much as Poetry. We are taught it at school; if not, believe we are born Poets. Every Corner abounds with its Professors; the Bellman nightly salutes his Master and Mistress; the Marshal, his Gentlemen soldiers every Christmas; Every street rings with Ballads, the Royal Palace resounds with Odes, and every Churchyard with its productions."[5]

Richard West, writing to Horace Walpole in January 1736-7, gives his view of the situation: "Poetry, I take it, is as universally contagious as the small-pox; every one catches it once in their life at least, and the sooner the better; for methinks an old rhymester makes as ridiculous a figure as Socrates dancing at fourscore. But I can never agree with you that most of us succeed alike;" and later in the same letter, he continues: "It is a difficult matter to account why but certain it is that all people from the duke's coronet to the thresher's flail are desirous to be poets[6]. . . ."

Undoubtedly these comments were largely inspired by the success and prominence of Stephen Duck, the thresher poet, who, beginning life as a farm laborer, attracted so much attention from persons of distinction that he was brought to court in 1730, given a house to live in, and awarded an annual pension by Queen Caroline, consort of George II. Moreover, numerous attempts, usually less successful, to emulate Duck's success, were made by other persons of the laboring classes. That poetical aspiration among the lower orders still persisted, even twenty odd years later at the time of Duck's death, is indicated in a passage from *The Adventurer* for December 11, 1753: "They who have attentively considered the history of mankind, know that every age has its peculiar character . . . THE present age, if we consider chiefly the stage of our own country, may be stiled with great propriety THE AGE OF AUTHORS; for, perhaps, there never was a time, in which men of all degrees of ability, of every kind of education, of every profession and employment, were posting with ardour so general to the press. The province of writing was formerly left to those, who by study, or appearance of study, were supposed to have gained knowledge unattainable to the busy part of mankind; but in these enlightened days, every man is qualified to instruct every other man, and he that beats the anvil or guides the plough, not contented with supplying corporal necessities, amuses himself in the hours of leisure with providing intellectual pleasures for his countrymen." Further on in the same article, the suggestion previously quoted from the *Grubstreet Journal* is repeated, i. e., that these aspiring toilers should be urged back into the occupations for which they were obviously better fitted: "It is, indeed, of more importance to search out the cure, than the cause of this intellectual malady; and he would deserve well of his country, who, instead of amusing himself with conjectural speculations, should find means of persuading the peer to inspect his steward's accounts, or repair the rural mansion of his ancestors, who could replace the tradesman behind his counter, and send back the farmer to the mattock and the flail."[7] The reference to the thresher's flail indicates that, even at this late date. Duck's origin had by no means been forgotten.

There is little to excite admiration in Duck's poetry; and one's first thought is to look for an explanation of his success in the social and artistic theories of the age; Tinker, working apparently on this assumption, seems to seek it in the beginnings of Romantic primitivism. He suggests that Thomas Gray may have had Duck in mind when he wrote of the "mute inglorious Milton."[8] Except for a possible trace of this attitude in Spence, however, it is very difficult to discover it in any contemporary comment on Duck. The poetic efforts of the thresher seem to have aroused interest for three reasons: such a poet was a curiosity[9]; he was a worthy and pious man who, both because of his excellent character and his poetic gifts which had flowered in spite of, and not because of his homely environment, deserved a better fate than that of a thresher[10]; and finally he evidently had a winning personality which inspired confidence and made friends for him among all classes with whom he came in contact.

In regard to Duck's parents,[11] all record seems to be silent. Andrew Kippis, in an article on Duck in the 1793 edition of *Biographia Britannica,* states that the names of his parents cannot be ascertained, and that his biographers do not mention the place or county of his birth, but that "it is well known he was a native of Wiltshire."[12] The Reverend H. B. M. Smith, present vicar of Charlton, Wiltshire, has informed me in a letter that there are "no entries of the name of Duck in the parish Registers here, which were very imperfectly kept at that time." There is ample corroboration of the statement that Duck was born at Charlton, on the River Avon, near Marlborough, Wiltshire,[13] but about the date there seems to be room for question. The account of Duck by Leslie Stephen in the *Dictionary of National Biography* [*D. N. B.*] gives the year as 1705, but the only original source to which this date can be traced is the account of Duck's life prefixed to the pirated *Poems on Several Subjects.* At the beginning of this account, which Duck in the *Preface* to the first authorized collections of his works brands as "very false" and "by a Person who seems to have had as little Regard for Truth, as he had for Honesty, when he stole my Poems,[14]" we are told that the poet was born in 1705 near the seat of Peter Bathurst, Esq., at Clarendon Park in the County of Wilts "of Parents remarkable only for their Honesty and Industry.[15]" This edition, which is dated 1730, is signed at the end of the poems "Stephen Duck, Ann. Aetat. 25."[16] It may be mentioned in passing that Duck's statement as to the falsity of this account need not apply to every item of it. It probably reflected the rumour of the day.[17]

The authorized source for information about Duck's early life is the *Full and Authentick Account of Stephen Duck, the Wiltshire Poet* by Joseph Spence. It was published as a pamphlet in 1731 in the form of "a letter to a member of Parliament," (who may have been Henry Rolle of Stevenstone, North Devon),[18] and was later revised and prefixed to the various editions of Duck's *Poems on Several Occasions.* In neither version does Spence have anything to say of the place or date of Duck's birth. Several writers, notably the *Supplement* to the 1766 edition of *Biographia Brittanica,* imply the possibility of a date as early as 1700 and suggest that Duck was born about the beginning of the century.[19]

To the fact that he was born of agricultural parents, we have Duck's own testimony. In the poem called **"Gratitude, a Pastoral,"** Duck, speaking in the character of Colin, says:

O You, Menalcas, know my abject Birth,
Born in a Cot, and bred to till the Earth . . .[20].

Of his childhood and early education, Spence remarks:

My Friend *Stephen* had originally no other Teaching than what enabled him to read and write English, nor that any otherwise than at a Charity-School[21]. . . . About his Fourteenth Year, he was taken from this School; and work'd with his Father, at Day-Labour, for Two or Three Months. After that his Father took a little Farm, and kept *Stephen* constantly at work; and that generally in the Field. This lasted for about three Years: when his Father being forc'd to quit the Farm again, poor *Stephen* went to Service. He had then several little Revolutions in his Fortunes: liv'd sometimes with one Farmer, and sometimes with another: in low Employments always; generally as a Thresher: Which you know was his Post when he came to be talk'd of and to be sent for by some Persons of Distinction, who added very much to the Character that had been giv'n of him.[22]

The gossiping and unreliable chronicler already referred to tells us that Duck had "a small Share of Reading and Writing bestowed on him, with very little or no Grammar," and that before he reached Syntaxis, his mother reeived a complaint from the schoolmaster: *"That he took his Learning too fast, even faster than the Master could give it to him."* His mother thereupon "removed her Son from School to the Plow, lest he might become too fine a Gentleman for the Family that produced him."[23]

The Dictionary of National Biography says that at fourteen the boy was employed as an agricultural laborer at 4s 6d a week. The statement on the title-page of the pirated *Poems on Several Subjects* states that this was his wage when he was "lately a poor Thresher;" and one might infer that the *Dictionary* accepted as authentic the material contained in this very dubious source.

The next important event in Duck's career was his marriage, which, if we accept 1705 as the correct date of his birth, took place when he was only nineteen. A correspondent in *Notes and Queries* for 1869, signing himself "E. W.," has copied the following entries from the parish registers of Charlton, near Pewsey (Pewsey is also near Marlborough):

Stephen Duck and Ann his wife married 22d June, 1724

Erney Duck baptized 1725

Wm. Duck baptized 1725[24]

Ann Duck baptized 1729

Ann Duck buried 1730[25]

The last item probably refers to Mrs. Duck, as she is known to have died in that year.

The unauthorized account speaks as follows with regard to Duck's first helpmate: ". . . our Poet is to be unhappily number'd amongst those Men, whose *Learning* and *fine Parts* are not able to give their Yoke-mates that *Satisfaction* and *Content,* which a weak Mind with a vigorous Constitution is generally apt to do. However, he has had three Children born to him in Wedlock." Speaking in a later passage of the thresher's first literary efforts, he tells us that Stephen "went on writing and burning, and his Wife continually scolding, because he neglected his Labour." When he tried to scan his lines, she would "run out and raise the whole Neighborhood, telling the People, *That her Husband dealt with the Devil, and was going mad because he did nothing all day but talk to himself, and tell his Fingers.*"[26] The unreliable source of this story does not prevent its repetition by Robert Southey in his *Lives of the Uneducated Poets*[27] and by other writers.

In addition to Duck's characterization of the whole account as "very false" we have some interesting comments in letters from Dr. Alured Clarke, Prebendary of Winchester Cathedral and an early patron of Duck, to Mrs. Charlotte Clayton, Lady Sundon, lady of the bedchamber to Queen Caroline, who interested herself in Duck's behalf with her royal mistress. In a letter dated August 18, 1730 he writes: "My Lord Tankerville having carried some of the Thresher's poetry from this country to Windsor, I fancy you will not dislike the account you'll find of him in another cover. . . . I am told the Curate's letter was written about two years ago."[28] On September 19, he has more to say on the subject: "I find, upon examination, there are some mistakes in the written accounts of him, which I sent before I had seen him, as there are in the verses, which he will correct when you give him leave. He speaks so well of his wife, that I believe it would give him pain to see so indifferent a character of her in writing."[29] Mrs. Thomson in the introduction to these letters states that the Curate referred to is Mr. Stanley. Spence in the *Full Account of Duck* refers in a footnote to an account by the Reverend Mr. Stanley, one of Duck's early patrons. The passage quoted from Dr. Clarke above makes it seem likely that this account was the source used by the unauthorized biographer; and apparently neither is to be accepted as authoritative and dependable.

Duck is represented as discussing his domestic life of this period in a poem called **"On Providence,"** appended to the one called **"Royal Benevolence,"** which was published under his name in 1730. It was probably a pirated publication, and there is some doubt even as to whether it was written by Duck.[30] The passage referred to, bears a close resemblance to the statements of the spurious biography:

> The Wife would say, How can you be content?
> I know not how to pay your Quarter's Rent.

> I bid her look on Birds in Bushes there,
> And see the little silly Insect here;
> Behold the Order of the Universe,
> And ask the Hen and Chickens for a Purse.
> She talked, like Woman, guided by a Will,
> Who nothing knew of real Good or Ill:
> But when she had the Course of Things survey'd,
> She own'd, what all must own, Heav'n sends its Aid
> To all its Creatures, Reason and Instinct join,
> And both, with Care, compleat our God's Design.

However good a comrade in adversity Ann Duck may have been, she did not live to share Stephen's good fortune. The poet left his native village to be presented to the Queen some time about October 4, 1730,[31] and on October 15, Dr. Clarke wrote to Mrs. Clayton from Winchester: "I received the inclosed account of the death of Stephen's wife this morning, and I supposed (by the name) it comes from the young farmer with whom she used to read." He had answered this communication by a countryman "who promised to deliver it into Mr. Lavinton's own hand. I told him I could not say with any certainty where Stephen was at present and that I believed he could hardly get to Charlton[32] again this fortnight; and did not doubt of his care in doing everything proper to the children till Stephen came." He questions the advisability of letting Stephen know of his misfortune until after his first interview with the Queen. ". . . I could not be sure you would think it proper to deject him with such ill news before her Majesty had seen him, for which, in my letter to Mr. Lavinton, I thought it best to set his return home at some little distance of time. I suppose this alteration in his family will incline him to send his children to some friend in the country where they are, till they are grown up, rather than bring them into a more expensive place."[33] He writes further on October 25: "By some expressions that fell from him here, I was apprehensive he would be very much affected by the death of his wife, for he was very solicitous about the long journey she was to take, and had resolved to ask her Majesty's leave to return home in order to bear her company to Kew, that she might be under no fears on the road. I hope he has by this time recovered his temper. I do not know but we may promise ourselves one of his best strains of poetry on this occasion, from the natural and constant correspondence there is between the mind and the affections."[34]

Duck, with his usual desire to be obliging, tried to rise to Dr. Clarke's expectations on this occasion by writing *A Pastoral Elegy.*

> As thus I spake, around I cast my Eye,
> And saw celestial Celia drawing nigh:[35]
> I saw; but wonder'd why her heav'nly Mein
> Was clouded o'er, that us'd to be serene.
> Celia's the Mistress of the flow'ry Plain
> Whose Bounty's known to ev'ry worthy Swain: . . . .

> "Thy pleasing Hopes are blasted all at home;
> Thy Sylvia, O!"—She said, and dropt the rest;
> But my presaging Heart too rightly guess'd:
> I silent stood, and spoke my Grief with Tears;
> You know, my Heart was firmly link'd to her's.[36]

This forced lamentation is only too typical of the way in which Duck maltreated his poetic talent for the sake of meeting the expectations of patrons.

The Thresher's Labour,[37] in addition to being the best poem Duck ever wrote, is valuable as autobiographical material, giving us a bird's-eye-view of a typical year of his life as an agricultural laborer. He begins his account at the end of the harvest season when the master calls his laborers together and assigns them their posts for the threshing:

> Divested of our Cloaths, with Flail in Hand,
> At proper Distance, Front to Front we stand:
> And first the Threshal's gently swung, to prove,
> Whether with just Exactness it will move:
> That once secure, we swiftly whirl them round;
> From the strong Planks our Crab-tree Staves rebound,
> And echoing Barns return the rattling Sound.
> Now in the Air our knotty Weapons fly,
> And now with equal Force descend from high; . . . .
> In briny Streams our Sweat descends apace,
> Droops from our Locks, or trickles down our Face.
> No Intermission in our Work we know;
> The noisy Threshal must for ever go.
> Their Master absent, others safely play;
> The sleeping Threshal does itself betray.
> And yet, the tedious Labour to beguile,
> And make the passing Minutes sweetly smile,
> Can we, like Shepherds, tell a merry Tale;
> The Voice is lost, drown'd by the louder Flail.

But when the work is completed, the Master is far from satisfied:

> "Why, look ye, Rogues, d'ye think that this will do?
> Your Neighbours thresh as much again as you."

Winter passes, and the changing seasons bring their own peculiar labours:

> But soon as Winter hides his hoary Head.
> And Nature's Face is with new Beauty spread:
> The lovely Spring appears, refreshing Show'rs
> New cloath the Field with Grass, and blooming
>   Flow'rs.
> Next her the rip'ning Summer presses on,
> And Sol begins his longest Race to run.
> Before the Door our welcome Master stands;
> Tells us the ripen'd Grass requires our Hands.
> The grateful Tiding presently imparts
> Life to our Looks, and Spirits to our Hearts.
> We wish the happy Season may be fair;
> And joyful, long to breathe in op'ner Air.
> This Change of Labour seems to give such Ease,
> With Thoughts of Happiness ourselves we please. . . .

This happiness, however, is short-lived:

> But when the scorching Sun is mounted high,
> And no kind Barns with friendly Shade are nigh;
> Our weary Scythes entangle in the Grass,
> While Streams of Sweat run trickling down apace.
> Our sportive Labour we too late lament;
> And wish that Strength again, we vainly spent.

Noon-time affords but little relief, for their weariness is so great that they can scarcely swallow their food, nor is the beer a more efficient source of satisfaction. Evening finds them almost too fatigued to find their way home:

> Homewards we move, but spent so much with Toil,
> We slowly walk, and rest at ev'ry Stile.
> Our good expecting Wives, who think we Stay,
> Go to the Door, soon eye us in the Way.
> Then from the Pot the Dumplin's catch'd in Haste,
> And homely by its Side the Bacon plac'd.[38]

Women are employed in preparing the hay, and about their usefulness Duck is not very optimistic:

> Our Master comes, and at his Heels a Throng
> Of prattling Females, arm'd with Rake and Prong;
> Prepar'd, whilst he is here, to make his Hay;
> Or, if he turns his Back, prepar'd to play;
> But here, or gone, sure of this Comfort still;
> Here's Company, so they may chat their Fill.
> Ah! were their Hands so active as their Tongues,
> How nimbly then would move the Rakes and Prongs!

The haying over, they work in the barns for a short time, and welcome the respite from the parching sun. The harvest is soon ready for reaping, and the laborers are awakened early:

> His hasty Summons we obey; and rise,
> While yet the Stars are glimm'ring in the Skies.
> With him our Guide we to the Wheat-field go,
> He to appoint, and we the Work to do.

Stephen is not blind to the beauties of Nature among which he toils:

> Ye Reapers, cast your Eyes around the Field;
> And view the various Scenes its Beauties yield.
> They look again, with a more tender Eye,
> To think how soon it must in Ruin lie!

but they in no way lessen the dreariness and hardship of his labors:

> Think what a painful Life we daily lead;
> Each Morning early rise, go late to Bed:
> Nor, when asleep, are we secure from Pain;
> We then perform our Labours o'er again:
> Our mimic Fancy ever restless seems;
> And what we act awake, she acts in Dreams.
> Hard Fate! our Labours ev'n in Sleep don't cease;
> Scarce Hercules e'er felt such Toils as these!

The harvest done, there is the brief enjoyment of the feast given by the master before the annual round of toil begins again:

A Table plentifully spread we find,
And Jugs of humming Ale, to chear the Mind;
Which he, too gen'rous, pushes round so fast,
We think no Toils to come, nor mind the past.
But the next Morning soon reveals the Cheat,
When the same Toils we must again repeat;
To the same Barns must back again return,
To labour there for Room for next Year's Corn.

It was in dealing with this familiar material that Duck approached the status of a genuine poet, but he had not the wisdom to continue dealing with such subject-matter; and references to agricultural life and labor are very rare in the works of his maturer years. Crabbe, some fifty years later, realized the difficulty of utilizing actual experience in agricultural occupations for the purposes of poetry, and in this connection, bore Duck in mind:

Yes, thus the Muses sing of happy swains,
Because the Muses never knew their pains:
They boast their peasants' pipes; but peasants now
Resign their pipes and plod behind the plough;
And few, amid the rural tribe, have time
To number syllables, and play with rhyme;
Save honest Duck, what son of verse could share
The poet's rapture, and the peasant's care?
Or the great labours of the field degrade,
With the new peril of a poorer trade?[39]

The most interesting portions of Spence's account have to do with Duck's efforts at self-education, resumed several years after his schooling had ended:[40]

These constant Employments had taken up so much of his Time and Thoughts, that he had forgot almost all the Arithmetick he had learn'd at School. However he read sometimes a little by chance, and thought oft'ner. He had a longing after Knowledge; and when he reflected within himself on his want of Education, he begun to be particularly uneasy, that he shou'd have forgot even something of what he had learnt, at the little School he was at. He thought of this so often, that at last he resolv'd to try his own Strength, and if possible to recover his Arithmetick again.

His first Attempt of this Kind I take to have been almost Six Years ago [probably in 1724]. Considering the Difficulties the poor Fellow lay under, this Inclination for Knowledge must have been very strong in him. He was then Married, and at Service: he had little Time to spare; he had no Books, and no Money to get any. But he was resolv'd to go through with it; and accordingly us'd to work more than other Day-Labourers, and by that means got some little matter added to his Pay.

This he invested in three volumes: a Book of Vulgar Arithmetic, one of Decimals, and one of Measuring of Land. And these he mastered by studying at night.

He was fortunate in having the friendship of at least one kindred spirit. "I have asked him," his biographer continues, "whom he had that he cou'd Talk and Converse with in the Country; and was Pleased to find him, in this Particular, happier than I expected. He said, He had one Dear Friend, that he mention'd with uncommon Affection. They used to Talk and Read together, when they cou'd steal a little Time for it. I think too, they sometimes studied their Arithmetick together." This friend had during some two or three years of service in London acquired some standards of literary taste and a small library, "which by this time possibly may be encreas'd to two or three Dozen of Books." Stephen in his simplicity confided to Spence: "That his Friend can Talk better than him, as having been more used to Company; but that he himself has been more used to Poetry, and in that can do better than his Friend." This naïve remark makes it appear as if the friend were one of Duck's fellow-laborers, but there seems to be some reason for identifying him with the Menalcas of Duck's pastorals. Menalcas reappears in Duck's works as having entertained the poet on his return visit to Wiltshire in 1735, and Duck in this connection refers to him as "kind Menalcas, partner of my Soul."[41] In a footnote to the same poem, he identifies him as "a Farmer, once the Author's Master, and still his Friend."

Without such encouragement, Spence considers that Stephen's improvement would agree better with a Romance than with reality, particularly with the account of Hai Ebn Yokdhan and the young Hermes in Mr. Ramsay's *Cyrus*.[42] The reading and discussion with this friend seem to have been, during this period, the principal sources of happiness in Stephen's life. "We may imagine 'em both to have had very good natural Sense, and a few good Books in common between them: Their Minds were their own; neither improv'd, nor spoil'd, by laying in a Stock of Learning: . . . ." Spence furnishes us with a rather lengthy list of the books familiar to Duck up to this period:

I need not mention those of Arithmetick again; nor his Bible. *Milton,* the *Spectators,* and *Seneca* were his first Favourites: *Telemachus,* and another Piece by the same Hand,[43] and *Addison's* Defence of Christianity, his next. They had an *English* Dictionary[44], a sort of an *English* Grammar; an *Ovid* of long standing with them, and a *Bysshe's* Art of Poetry of later acquisition. *Seneca's* Morals had made the Name of *L'Estrange* dear to them; and as I imagine might occasion their getting his *Josephus* in Folio, which was the largest Purchase in their Collection. They had one Volume of *Shakespear,* with Seven of his Plays in it. *Stephen* had read Three or Four other Plays; some of *Epictetus, Waller, Dryden's Virgil; Pryor, Hudibras; Tom Brown,*[45] and the *London Spy.*[46]

It was probably with this list in Mind that Dr. Clarke, writing of Duck to Mrs. Clayton, remarks: ". . . he has, accidentally, had much greater advantages from his want of education, than he could possibly have had otherwise: for it seems he has only read the best books, and has contracted no false turn of mind by such writings as cost other people . . . more pains to forget than they can prevail with themselves to take. . . ."⁴⁷

Of the works enumerated *Paradise Lost* seems to have had the most important influence on Duck's mental development and later work. Spence tells us that he was obliged to read it "twice or thrice with a Dictionary":

> Indeed it seems plain to me, that he has got English just as we get Latin. Most of his Language in Conversation, as well as in his Poems, is acquir'd by reading. The Talk he generally met with has been so far from helping him to the manner in which he speaks that it must have put him even to the difficulty of forgetting his Premier-Language. . . . His common Talk is made up of the good Stile, with a mixture of the Rustick: tho' the latter is but very small in proportion to the former.

> He studied *Paradise Lost,* as we study the Classicks. The new Beauties in that Poem, that were continually opening upon his Mind, made all his Labour easy to him. He work'd all Day for his Master; and, after the Labour of the Day, set to his Books at Night. The Pains he has taken for the Pleasure of Improving himself are incredible; but it has answer'd too beyond what one cou'd imagine: for he seems to understand even the great and deeper Beauties of that Poem tolerably well; and points out several particular Beauties, which it requires a nice and just Eye to discover.

After some discussion of Duck's methods of working, Spence returns to the subject of Milton's influence:⁴⁸ "'Tis not yet three Year ago that he first met with *Milton*; and I believe that was the first Poet of real value that he ever studied in earnest." Stephen assured him "that when he came afterwards to read *Addison's* Criticisms on *Milton* in the *Spectators,* 'Twas a high Pleasure to him, to find many things mention'd there, in the Praise of *Milton,* exactly as he had before thought in reading him. . . . Upon his being ask'd, Which Part he lik'd best in the *Paradise Lost,* he nam'd the Angel's account of the Creation, in the Seventh Book;". . . . The great admiration he had for Milton, however, could not, apparently, bring him to a liking for *Paradise Regained*: "He wonder'd how Milton cou'd write so incomparably well, where he had so little to lead him; and so very poorly, where he had more." In regard to the rumor that Stephen could repeat most of *Paradise Lost* by heart, Spence says: "I am sure, he can repeat a great deal of it; and he says, that (before these late Hurries) he could repeat a great deal more." He considered that in repeating Duck sometimes improved on the original by mistake, as in the following lines:

> His words here ended; but his *meek Aspect*
> *Silent* yet *spake,* and breath'd *immortal* Love
> To *mortal* Man. . . .

(Book III, lines 266ff)

Stephen in attempting to repeat this passage could not remember it exactly, but thought it ran something like this:

> . . . His Aspect meek
> Breath'd Love immortal to Mankind.

After Milton, the author exercising most influence on Duck was Addison in the *Spectator,* which the thresher acquired from his friend. "*Stephen* tells me that he has frequently carried them with him to his Work. When he did so, his method was to labour harder than any Body else, that he might get Half an Hour to read a *Spectator* without injuring his Master. By this means he used to sit down all over Sweat and Heat; and has several times caught Colds by it."⁴⁹

When Spence accidentally referred to the *Spectator* as prose, Stephen was ready with a comment: "'Twas true, they were *Prose*; but there was something in 'em that pleas'd almost like Verse." he mentioned particularly the "Critical Papers on Wit, those on *Milton*; the *Justum & Tenacem* from *Horace,* Mr. *Pope's Messiah*; and the several scatter'd ones, written in the Cause of Virtue and Religion." The more Romantic Spence wondered "how he came to miss those on the Pleasures of the Imagination."⁵⁰

Duck has a tribute to Addison in his poem *Description of a Journey, etc.* probably written in 1735, that runs as follows:

> If Pride, or Passion check my doubtful Sail,
> Let thy Instructions lend a friendly Gale,
> To waft me to the peaceful, happy Shore,
> Where thou, immortal Bard! art gone before:
> Then those who grant me not a Poet's Name,
> Shall own I left behind a better Fame.⁵¹

Familiarity with Milton and Addison had given the thresher standards by which he was enabled to judge other literary productions:

> He had formerly met with *Tom Brown's Letters from the Dead,* and the *London Spy,* and read 'em, not without some Pleasure: but after he had been some time conversant with the *Spectators,* he said, 'He did not care much to look into them. He spoke of *Hudibras* in another manner: he saw a great deal of Wit in it, and was particularly pleas'd with the Conjuror's Part in that Burlesque; but after all, 'tis not a Manner of writing that he can so sincerely delight in, as in the Moral, the Passionate, or the Sublime.

> Telemachus he admires much; and has taken some fine Strokes from it. Upon asking him what Plays he had read, He nam'd particularly *Julius Caesar, Hamlet, Cato, Venice Preserv'd,* and the *Orphan. Venice Preserv'd* he said gave him the most *horror*; a word which I took notice he used sometimes for Concern, and sometimes in its proper Sense. He cou'd not bear the Comick Parts in it. *Hamlet* he lik'd better than *Ju-*

lius: and in *Hamlet* pointed out that celebrated Speech, *To be, or not to be,* &c., as his favourite Part merely of his own Taste. He did not admire Shakespear's Comedy, said he was too high, and too low: yet he lik'd the *Grave-Diggers* well enough; that was pretty, and had Humour in it.

Spence read him some of *Hamlet* and the speeches of Antony to the people in *Julius Caesar,* and noted his emotions on hearing: "He trembled as I read the Ghost's Speech; . . . . As I was reading to him, I observ'd that his Countenance chang'd often in the most moving Parts: His Eye was quick, and busy all the time: I never saw Applause, or the shifting of proper Passions, so strong in any Face as in his."[52] Southey quotes this passage as illustrative of possible mental instability which finally culminated in the poet's suicide during what seems to have been a condition of mental aberration.[53] Duck's native simplicity was certainly not unimpressionable; but one feels that Southey was playing somewhat fast and loose in the rôle of amateur abnormal psychologist.

Cato Duck indicated as his favorite play, but he disapproved of the death of the hero by his own hand: "he thought very justly, that *Cato* ought to have liv'd, and to have suffer'd; and that a Christian Poet should not paint a Man so great who is to Kill himself."

Spence finds particular cause for admiration in the "excellent Moral Turn" of the thresher's thoughts: "He has read and speaks highly of the Arch-Bishop of *Cambray's* Demonstration of the Being of a God, and Mr. *Addison's* Defence of the Christian Religion. . . . He had lik'd the little he had read of *Epictetus*; but 'twas *Seneca* that had made him Happy in his own Mind."[54]

Stephen's inclination towards poetry seems to have been mingled with a particular susceptibility to another related art, music, and also to balladry, although it is significant to note that, unlike Burns, he avoided in his own writings the forms of the ballad and the folk-song. Spence says:

> I find by him, that from his Infancy, he has had a Cast in his Mind toward Poetry. He has delighted as far back as he can remember in Ballads, and in Singing. He speaks of strange Emotions that he has felt on the top Performances of the little Choir of Songsters in a Country Chancel: and mentions his first hearing of an Organ, as a remarkable Epoch of his Life. I find that Musick sometimes makes him melancholy: which I ask'd him, upon remembering that 'twas *Shakespeare's* Case before him; and he told me that upon hearing an Anthem, he has been forc'd to turn away, and has found his Eyes on a suddain full of Tears. This, no doubt, was a Melancholy of the pleasing kind. He seems to be a pretty good judge too of a Musical Line; but I imagine that he does not hear Verses in his own Mind, as he repeats them. . . . I mean that his Ideas of the Notes in a Verse, and his manner of repeating the same Verse,

are often different: For he points out an harmonious Line well enough, and yet he sometimes spoils its harmony by his way of speaking it.[55]

The following lines by Duck himself corroborate these statements:

> Thus, in a grateful Concert, may we hear
> The Sounds at once surprize, and charm our Ear;
> The trembling Notes, in hasty Fugues, arise;
> And this advances, e're the former flies;
> All seem to be confus'd, yet all agree,
> To perfect the melodious Harmony.[56]

The opening stanza, moreover, of a poem entitled **"On Music"** suggests some real appreciation:

> Music the coldest Heart can warm,
> The hardest melt, the fiercest charm;
> Disarm the Savage of his Rage,
> Dispel our Cares, and Pains assuage;
> With Joy it can our Souls inspire,
> And tune our Tempers to the Lyre;
> Our Passions, like the Notes, agree,
> And stand subdu'd by Harmony.[57]

According to Spence, Duck credited his first creative impulses to the *Spectators*. He told that clergyman that they "improv'd his Understanding more than any thing. The Copies of Verses scatter'd in those Pieces, help'd on his natural Taste: he was willing to try whether he cou'd not do something like 'em. He sometimes turn'd his own Thoughts into Verse while he was at work; and at last begun to venture those Thoughts a little to Paper. What he did of this kind was very inconsiderable: only scatter'd Thoughts, and generally not above four or five Lines on the same Subject: which, as there was no body thereabouts that car'd for Verses, nor any body that cou'd tell him whether they were Good or Bad, he generally flung into the Fire as soon as he had pleas'd himself enough in reading them."[58] These precautions, however, did not prevent the matter from being rumored about with the following significant results:

> *Stephen*, who had before the Name of a Scholar among the Country People, was said now to be able to write Verses too. This was mention'd accidentally, about a Year ago, before a young Gentleman of *Oxford,* who sent for *Stephen,* and after some Talk with him, desired him to write him a Letter in Verse. That Letter is the Epistle which stands the Last in his Poems, but was really the First whole Copy of Verses that ever he wrote.[59] The Gentleman who employ'd him, upon reading those Lines, thought 'em too Good to be his own; and gave him so little Encouragement, that here all was like to be lost. *Stephen* might never have wrote any more, had not the Copy of this Epistle been left by chance at a Place, where it fell into the Hands of some Clergymen in the Neighborhood. They were very well Pleased with it; and upon examining into the thing more closely, found the Man had a good deal of Merit. They gave him some Presents, which as things stood then, were a great Help to him; and encourag'd him to go on, as much as they cou'd.

This reviv'd his Spirits again: And, as he had wrote some Verses on *Poverty* before the Epistle, after this he carried those Thoughts farther, and finish'd the Copy on that Subject, as it stands in the printed Collection I send you: so that this is his Second Copy. You see I am very careful in settling the Chronology of his Poems: Such a Genius is a Curiosity; and one wou'd willingly know which are his first Productions.

The Composition which was next in order is that on his own *Labours*: That Subject was given him by one of those [Mr. Stanley, according to Spence's footnote] who first encourag'd his Taste for Poetry. . . .[60]

The identity of the young Oxford scholar already referred to is a vexing problem with a mass of more or less conflicting evidence. Southey assumes that the "young Oxonian" and Mr. Stanley were one and the same,[61] but the passage from Spence quoted above would seem to imply the contrary. It is worthy of note that in the revised account prefixed to Duck's poems, Spence omits the passage about the suspicions of the young scholar and his failure to encourage Duck.[62]

In the **"Description of a Journey"** probably written in 1735, Duck refers in a footnote to "Rev. Mr. Stanley, Rector of Pewsey, who first encouraged the Author," and in the poem itself speaks of his disappointment at not finding his friend at Pewsey.[63] Later in the same poem, the following tribute declares that he visited Paultons:

> To see the Friend, who first my Lays approv'd,
> Who loves the Muse, and by her is belov'd;
> Who taught her tender Pinions how to fly,
> Told when she crept too low, or soar'd too high.
> O Stanley! if, forgetful of thy Love,
> I e'er to Gratitude rebellious prove;
> Still may I want a Friend, but never find;
> May Fortune, Phoebus, Stanley, prove unkind.[64]

The account used in the pirated edition, of course, does not fail to give a picturesque version of Duck's experience with his first patron. It tells us that at the christening of Duck's last child one of the women present "happen'd to blab it out" to the clergyman *That Mr. Duck was a Man of great Learning, and had Wit enough to be a Parson, for that he could make Verses like any mad* [sic] *and as good as ever she had heard in her Life."* The Doctor "who is a dignify'd Person in the University of *Oxford* had some Discourse with Mr. Duck, and gave him a Theme, with some Directions for the Improvement of his Genius: . . . ." But when Stephen presented him with the verses requested, the Doctor advised him to burn them. This was a "most cruel Discouragement," and the poor poet "was almost out of Conceit with himself." However, in spite of this setback and the continual nagging of his wife, Stephen "went on writing and burning . . ." until "his Fame at length began to rouze the Wits of *Wiltshire,* and he was admitted to the Tables of a great many worthy Gentlemen."[65]

Another reasonably plausible hypothesis as to the identity of the Oxford scholar is that he may have been a Mr. Winder, to whom Duck addresses some verses: To Mr. WINDER, (now Fellow) of CORPUS-CHRISTI, OXFORD; in Answer to a LATIN Epistle, which he sent me.[66] Returning from a journey to Wiltshire and other parts in 1735, the poet visited Oxford, and according to the following lines was entertained at Corpus Christi College through the kindness of the same Winder:

> Nor less should Foxe's[67] Fame adorn my Lays,
> Whose pious Care the decent Fabric rear'd,
> Which kindly shelter'd the unworthy Bard;
> Nor the unworthy Bard should leave unpaid
> The grateful Debt, contracted while he stay'd:
> Thy Favour, chiefly, Winder, should be known
> In lasting Numbers, tuneful as thy own.[68]

These are the only references to persons connected with Oxford found in any of Duck's works; and on the whole the evidence seems insufficient for identifying the young Oxford scholar with Mr. Stanley.

The Thresher's Labour was dedicated to the Reverend Mr. Stanley, and the opening lines are a tribute to him:

> The grateful Tribute of these rural Lays,
> Which to her Patron's Hand the Muse conveys,
> Deign to accept: 'Tis just the Tribute bring
> To him, whose Bounty gives her Life to sing;
> To him whose gen'rous Favours tune her Voice;
> And bid her, 'midst her Poverty rejoice.

Duck's particular debt of gratitude to Stanley seems to have been occasioned by much-needed financial assistance. In the preface to his collected poems, he tells us that he would gladly make known his obligations to the persons who first took notice of him, but fears to give them offence. He cannot refrain, however, from returning thanks *"to a Reverend Gentleman of WILT-SHIRE, and to another of WINCHESTER: The former made my Life more comfortable, as soon as he knew me; the latter, after giving me several Testimonies of his Bounty and Goodness, presented my first Essays to a lady of Quality attending on the Queen, who made my low Circumstances known to Her MAJESTY."*[69] The Reverend Gentleman of Wiltshire is probably Stanley, and the other of Winchester is undoubtedly Dr. Alured Clarke, whose relations to Duck will later be discussed.

Besides these feeling tributes to Stanley, Duck dedicated to him **"An Imitation of the Sixteenth Ode of the Third Book of Horace,"** an essay in verse on the power of gold. He discusses his own contented state in his modest circumstances (one of his favorite themes), and addressing Stanley continues:

> What tho' no Flocks, on *Richmond* Plain
>   With Fleeces deck my Pride?
> What tho' I seldom drink *Champagne,*

Or quaff the purple Tide?
If these I wanted, were your Bard to ask,
I know, your gen'rous Soul would send a *Cask*.[70]

Spence tells us that after the completion of *The Thresher's Labour* the poet was "employ'd from the same quarter in his **'Shunammite.'**"[71] The poem is dedicated to Mrs. Stanley, and in his **"Description of a Journey"** Duck refers to Musidora as "The Dame who bad me sing Jehovah's Praise," and mentions in a footnote that the reference is to Mrs. Stanley, "who desired the Author to write the **'Shunammite.'**"[72]

This poem seems to have marked a turning point in Duck's career. According to Spence's record, we are told: "as this far exceeded any of the rest, I think from hence we may date the Aera of his rising in his Character and Circumstances. Upon this it was that Persons of Distinction began to send for him different ways. In short, it got him Fame enough to be pretty troublesome to him at first; tho' it is likely to end in a much happier Settlement of Him and his Affairs, than cou'd ever have been dreamt of by him at his first setting out."[73]

The example set by the Stanleys of supplying subjects for the thresher, with a request that he try his hand at them, seems to have been taken up by others. Duck tells us in his preface that a number of the pieces in the collection were written to order, and Dr. Clarke in writing to Mrs. Clayton lamented the too common practice of curious and interested persons who frequently set the thresher to work on subjects of their own choosing.[74]

The list of distinguished persons who at about this period interested themselves in Duck's behalf is a long one, including besides the unidentified Oxford patron, Rev. Mr. Stanley, Dr. Alured Clarke, and Joseph Spence, such figures as the Honourable Mr. Bathurst; Lady Hartford; the Lord Viscount Palmerston; Lord Tankerville; the Earl of Macclesfield; Mrs. Charlotte Clayton, Lady Sundon; and finally Caroline of Anspach, Queen of the ruling sovereign, George II.

The Reverend Joseph Spence, Professor of Poetry at Oxford, who remained on terms of friendship with Duck until the end of the latter's life, was notable for his kindness to talented persons in indigent circumstances. Besides Duck, he patronized Thomson[75] and the blind Scotch poet, Thomas Blacklock, Robert Dodsley, and Samuel Richardson.[76] In the *Introduction* to his *Account of the Life, Character, and Poems of Mr. Blacklock, Student of Philosophy in the University of Edinburgh* (1754), he says: "I know not how it is but I always feel myself of such a make, that I can never see a Man of Merit in Distress without Compassion; and sometimes, even not without Indignation."[77]

The title page of Spence's account of Duck reads as follows:

A | Full and Authentick | Account | of | Stephen Duck. | The | Wiltshire Poet. | Of his Education; his Methods | of Improving himself; how | he first engag'd in Poetry; and | his great Care in writing. | Of each of his particular Poems; of the | first Encouragements he met with; and | his original Sentiments on several Books, | Things, *&c.* | In a Letter to a *Member* of | Parliament. | By J———S———Esq; Poetry Professor for the | University of Oxford.

John Underhill, in his edition of Spence's *Anecdotes,* thinks the member of Parliament may have been Henry Rolle of Stevenstone, North Devon.[78] This was probably Henry Rolle, mentioned in the *Dictionary of National Biography* as the uncle of John, Baron Rolle of Stevenstone, (1750-1842), himself created Baron Rolle of Stevenstone, in January 1747-8.[79]

The notice in the *Gentleman's Magazine* under "Books published in March 1731" of *Memoirs of the Life of that celebrated Wiltshire Poet, Mr. Steph. Duck* refers in all probability to Spence's account and enables us to date its publication exactly.[80] The same account, considerably altered, chiefly in the way of omissions, was later prefixed to the various editions of *Poems on Several Occasions.* Duck in his *Preface* apologizes for allowing the inclusion of this material:

> I am afraid the Letter relating to myself, wrote by a worthy and learned Gentleman, will be thought an improper Thing in a Publication made by myself. But, as I was desir'd to prefix it, by Persons whom I think it an Honour to obey, I hope it will be pardon'd; and the rather, because a very false Account had been publish'd before, by a Person who seems to have as little Regard for Truth, as he had for Honesty, when he stole my Poems.[81]

The various other persons who interested themselves in Duck are rather difficult to arrange chronologically in his biography. Spence suggests in a passage quoted above that there may have been several of whom we have no record, and in addition he suggests: "'Twould be tiresome to enumerate all the little Particulars of his Good Fortune."[82] The next patron referred to after the Oxford scholar and Stanley is undoubtedly Bathurst: "Among the first who had a Curiosity for seeing a Man of so particular a Character, was the Honourable Mr. *B . . . t*: and I believe *Stephen* had never, 'till that Visit, seen three or four Pieces of Gold together, that were his own to do what he wou'd with."[83] The identity of B . . . t would seem to be established by a passage in Duck's **"Description of a Journey"**:

> I next to BATHURST's rural Seat ascend
> BATHURST, my infant Muse's gen'rous Friend![84]

We are told in a footnote that the "rural seat" is Clarendon Park. This is interesting in the light of the statement in the discredited biography that Duck was born "near the seat of Peter Bathurst, Esq., at Clarendon Park in the County of Wilts."[85]

Spence indicates chronology to some extent. After his account of Mr. Bathurst's visit he continues:

> The next great Step was the Earl of M———d's send-
> ing for him into *Hamshire,* where his Lordship was
> then on a Visit. That great Critick in Men, as well as in
> all sorts of Learning, very much approv'd of his
> Compositions; and yet was more surpriz'd with what
> he found to be in the Man, than he had been with
> anything in his Writings. His Lordship, and another of
> the most Penetrating Men in *England,* examin'd him
> very minutely. His Answers were plain, and yet sur-
> prizing. After seeing him several times, and always
> Rewarding him, his Lordship form'd that Opinion of
> him, which ('tis generally thought) occasion'd an open-
> ing to his last & highest Good-Fortune.[86]

The credit for bringing Duck and his works to the attention of royalty seems to be divided between Lord
Macclesfield or Lord Tankerville and Mrs. Clayton,
coöperating with Dr. Alured Clarke. The title-page of
Poems reads as follows:

> *Poems on Several Subjects* Written by | Stephen Duck,
> | Lately a poor *Thrasher* in a Barn in the | County of
> *Wilts,* at the Wages of Four | Shillings and Six-Pence
> per Week: | Which were publickly read by the Right
> Honourable the Earl of *Macclesfield,* | in the Drawing-
> Room at *Windsor* Castle, on | *Friday* the 11th of
> *September,* 1730, to Her | Majesty. | Who was thereupon
> most graciously pleased to take | the Author into her
> Royal Protection, by allowing | him a salary of Thirty
> Pounds *per Annum,* and | a Small House at *Richmond*
> in *Surrey,* to live in, | for the better support of Himself
> and Family.[87]

Here the credit seems to be given to Macclesfield for
the reading only; whereas in the spurious account of
Duck prefixed to this edition, we are told merely that a
copy of his poems was sent to the Earl of Tankerville at
Windsor where "the Honourable Mrs. Clayton of her
Majesty's Bedchamber saw it and presented it to the
Queen."[88] Dr. Clarke, in a passage already quoted from
his first recorded letter to Mrs. Clayton about Duck,
refers to Lord Tankerville, as having "carried some of
the Thresher's poetry from this country to Windsor."[89]

The letters which passed between Dr. Alured Clarke
and Lady Sundon, however, indicate that she acted as a
go-between for Duck and the Queen to a considerable
extent. Andrew Kippis in the 1793 edition of *Biographia
Brittanica* says that a clergyman of Winchester
(probably Dr. Clarke) presented Duck's first poetical efforts to a lady in waiting on the Queen, and implies that
it was by this means that Duck's good fortune was
made possible.[90]

Spence regrets that he has not made a more exact
catalogue of the works read by Duck, in view of the
interest aroused by the thresher, but adds: "I hear Lady
H———d, who call'd upon *Stephen* in the Country since

I saw him, had the Curiosity to take an exact Catalogue
of them all."[91] The lady in question is probably Frances
Thynn, Countess of Hertford, afterwards (1748) Duchess of Somerset, and at this earlier period a lady of the
bedchamber to the Queen.[92] Dr. Alured Clarke helps to
establish her identity in one of his letters to Mrs. Clayton: "I leave him [Duck] to acquaint you with what has
passed between him and Lady Hertford."[93] Duck may
be referring to this lady in the **"Description of a
Journey"**:

> Within the Basis of the verdant Hill,
> A beauteous Grot confesses HERTFORD's Skill.[94]

Others, besides Stanley and Bathurst, rendered material
assistance to the poet. Spence quotes Duck as saying: "I
have got my Wish, . . . I desir'd to please the Gentlemen who set me about any thing: and have got about
Twenty Pound beside; and indeed it was bad with us
before."[95] Dr. Clarke asks Mrs. Clayton's coöperation in
caring for money that has been gathered for Duck: "He
has promised not to meddle with any of the money, that
has been gathered for him; and if you approve of it, I
should be glad to lay it in your hands till I come to
town, when I shall have some to add to it, which may
be put out upon security for the benefit of his family, or
for his own use, if misconduct or any other accident
should make it expedient for him to return into Wiltshire."[96] In a later communication he mentions that he
has collected between twenty and thirty guineas for
Stephen at Winchester[97] and further on he writes: "I
have inclosed a bill for the money I have received for
Stephen here, which you will please to send, if you
should intend to make any use of his money before I
have the honour of waiting on you."[98]

Dr. Alured Clarke (1696-1742), dean of Exeter, was a
brother of Charles Clarke, baron of the exchequer. In
1723 he received the living of Chilbolton in Hampshire
and a prebendal stall in Winchester Cathedral. He
became Prebendary of Westminster in 1731, and dean
of Exeter in 1741. Mrs. Thomson says he was a Fellow
of Corpus Christi College, Cambridge, and Chaplain to
George I, and in 1731 to George II. He was particularly
noted for his benevolence, and is reported as having
devoted all his surplus income to works of charity. He
was apparently very loyal to the Queen, and his
principal literary work is *An Essay towards the
Character of her late Majesty, Caroline,* 1738.[99]

Dr. Clarke's extant letters to Mrs. Clayton concerning
Duck bear the following dates: August 18, September
19, October 4, October 8, October 15, and October 25,
1730.[100] The first of these, written before he had seen
the thresher, opens with the passage quoted above, in
which he refers to Lord Tankerville and the account
written by the Curate; he goes on to remark that he will
be able to judge of the man when he has seen him.[101] In
the next letter, he describes his first impressions:

I have had the Thresher with me all this week, and have prepared him as well as I could for her Majesty's bounty. It was with a good deal of caution, and very gradually, that I informed him what had been done for him, and I thought it best not to let him return to his family till he had taken some time to compose his thoughts. But I had the pleasure of finding my hopes more than answered in the trial; for though he expressed the utmost gratitude, he did not show the least exultation of spirit by any part of his conduct, and has made as many just reflections on the change of his condition as could have been done by the most experienced sage of them all; and, in truth, I have had so much entertainment in observing the quick relish he has of any sort of useful knowledge, that as little as I love teaching, I should think it the highest employment of my time to spend it in communicating all I could to a mind so well disposed to receive it.

He left me this morning, and, if her Majesty pleases, will be at Windsor in a fortnight, and leave his family to come afterwards, when he is settled and ready to receive them; and I have promised to send to him as soon as I have the honour of your commands on this head.[102]

The following in Dr. Clarke's letter of October 4, 1730, would seem to date Stephen's departure for Windsor:[103]

> I hope the bearer, Stephen Duck, will come safe to you on Wednesday, and I beg leave to assure you, that it is a great concern to me not to be able to deliver him into your hands myself. . . . I think myself very happy in the approbation of my thoughts in relation to poor Stephen, who will bring you a specimen of his gratitude in the way of pastoral, which he never tried before, and are, I think, very well for the first attempt.[104] I have received three letters from Dr. Lockyer, who is at Sherburn, to send him to my Lord Macclesfield, who (the Dean said in his second letter) had *her Majesty's leave to take care of him for some time*; . . . .[105]

In the letter of October 15, in which the death of Stephen's wife is announced, he says: "I suppose, by his letter, it will not be long before he is fixed at Kew, if he be not there by this time."[106]

The next letter is in reply to one from Mrs. Clayton, in which apparently she describes her impressions of the thresher on his arrival at Windsor: "You have made me very happy by your obliging letter, and the satisfaction I have in not having raised any expectations of Stephen but what he has hitherto answered."[107]

Dr. Clarke took the task of completing Stephen's education very seriously, and in his letters prescribes to Mrs. Clayton the course of reading and study that the poet should follow. He recommends first of all Chambers's *Dictionary,* Danet's *Dictionary of Antiquities,* and Bailey's *Etymological Dictionary,* and suggests that they be bought out of the money collected for him. "He has at present," the doctor continues, "'so great an aversion to drollery, ridicule, or jingle [did he include

popular ballads under this opprobious term?], and is like to succeed so well in the more manly way, that I hope neither Swift, nor Montaigne, nor South, nor the writers in the Dunciad Controversy, nor even Cowley, will fall into his hands." Much of Duck's later poetry would seem to indicate that the Doctor's hope was not realized, and his apprehensions only too well founded. *Hudibras,* he learns from Duck, did not please the latter, for "I think he told me he seemed to play the fool too much." The Doctor volunteered, with Her Majesty's consent, to spend some time in her library at Richmond selecting suitable literature for the consumption of the thresher.[108] In the meantime he had some further suggestions to make: ". . . I would propose it to your consideration whether anything, better could be put into his hands than Burnet's Theory of the Earth and Ray's Wisdom of God in the Creation. The one would let him into new worlds that are yet unknown to him, and so enlarge the number of his ideas; and the other is one of the noblest philosophical romances that ever was wrote, and consequently the properest food to feast a poetic genius with; and they will be very good preparations for such a book as Dr. Clark's Rohault, which will give him at one view a complete notion of Descartes' System, as well as the principles upon which the present philosophy is established; for, without some general comprehension of these things he will soon find himself at a great loss for materials, which he will continually be supplying himself with when once such a field is opened to him." These recommendations seem to make it clear that the Doctor was no primitivist in his attitude toward Duck and his work; his further recommendation that the thresher get Pope's *Essay on Criticism* by heart serves to bear out the impression that his aim was to Neo-classicize the new poet. Of course his efforts were, from a literary point of view, ill-advised; for whatever charm Duck's poetry possessed, came to him from his sincere artistic expression of the realities he knew and not from any extrinsic veneer that a man of his age and circumstances could acquire.

The good Doctor enclosed a collection of plays for Duck, from which Mrs. Clayton was to make a selection, quoting Spence to the effect that the plays are bound up in volumes, "as they are figured in his paper. . . ." This makes it appear as if Spence and Clarke coöperated in the effort to complete Duck's education, and as if Spence were responsible for the dramatic selections. Dr. Clarke has a few recommendations to make on this subject: "I should be afraid of his meddling with anything of Lee's, and have therefore crossed the ninth volume; . . . ." Later he suggested that Steele's plays were perhaps enough, and thought that Duck might read all of Shakespeare; for surely "Stephen will suck the flowers, and leave all the puns and low conceits behind him." The Doctor is unable to get a satisfactory translation of Homer, and decides that Stephen must read Pope's.[109] One wonders whether he did not unconsciously consider his strange pupil as a sort of docile Frankenstein to be educated into civilization rather than really encouraged to produce art: but art and civilization were synonomous not only to the Queen Anne wit, but even to the incipient Sentimentalist of Dr. Clarke's generation.

Charlotte Clayton, Lady Sundon, lady of the bedchamber to Queen Caroline, was the wife of William Clayton of Sundon Hall, afterwards Baron Sundon of Ardagh in the Irish peerage.[110] She had wielded considerable influence over Queen Caroline since 1714, and showed attention to various literary men, including besides Duck, Steele, Richard Savage, and, during his stay in England, Voltaire.[111] She had seemingly interested herself in Stephen's progress some months earlier than the date of Dr. Clarke's communications; for a letter dated February 19, 1730, and signed F. Lewis reads to the following effect: "My dutiful thanks for your most obliging message by Stephen Duck to me should have been personally acknowledged much sooner. . . . I even rejoice at the progress we have made and that your Ladyship will have the pleasure of seeing poor Stephen a considerable proficient in the Latin tongue sooner than can well be imagined."[112] Stephen was indeed undergoing a severe course in Georgian civilizing instruction.

The amount of responsibility that she assumed toward the thresher on his arrival at Windsor is indicated by several passages from Dr. Clarke's letters: in that of October 4, "I have told him he is to be wholly under your direction, as you will observe in the conclusion of his pastoral,[113] and am more strongly convinced of the necessity of his being under your care, that her Majesty may be freed from any troublesome solicitations about him, and be out of the way of the epigrammatic Maecenas's of the age; and therefore I think it the highest instance of her Majesty's goodness and regard to him not to permit him to Court."[114] On October 15, he wrote: "Whenever you think proper to send him, I believe it will be a great ease to him to receive orders from you not to go to any place he shall be invited to during the time he has leave to be absent from Kew." In the same letter he spoke of receiving two communications from Stephen which are full of Mrs. Clayton's goodness to him and from which he quotes: "I have no reason to believe that the good lady will cease to be my friend, till I cease to be an honest man."[115]

Spence gives us a rather vague account of the Queen's patronage of Duck:

> I need not tell you that the Queen, who is always fond of Merit wherever She finds it, upon seeing his Pieces, and the Genius that appear'd throughout them, express'd a particular Satisfaction in such an Opportunity of doing Good. Her Majesty resolv'd im-

mediately to take him out of his Obscurity, and the Difficulties he had labour'd under. A Poetical Retirement was thought of: every thing was consider'd with the greatest Judgment: There was now more danger of his having too much than of his continuing to have too little: the great Goodness of Her Majesty condescended to proportion it self to the Poor Man's Condition; and everything was settled in such a manner, as might render it most effectually a Reward and Blessing to him.

> Were one to write a counterpart to *Pierius Valerianus*, I mean a Piece on the *Felicity of Poets*; it would scarce afford a single Instance that cou'd come up to this in all its Parts: and yet, I must say, I think the Man thoroughly deserves his good Fortune."[116]

Some difference of opinion exists among authorities as to the amount of the pension settled on Duck by the Queen. The two sources for information on this matter are the statement on the title-page of **Poems on Several Subjects** to the effect that the Queen allowed the thresher "a salary of Thirty Pounds per Annum, and a Small House at Richmond in Surrey . . ."; and a footnote in a current number of the *Grub-Street Journal*, stating that when Duck appeared before the Queen at Windsor for the first time with a poem "on her late benevolence to him," she "was graciously pleased to order him a further yearly gratuity; which with the house he lives in amounts to 80£ per annum."[117] Kippis, although admitting that some reports give the sum as thirty pounds a year states that he had "always understood it to be fifty."[118] Possibly this "fifty" included the value of the house-rent, and thus Kippis and the title-page of the **Poems** may agree. Knowing the fondness of the *Grub-Street Journal* to exaggerate when it intended to cast a slur, one is inclined to look upon the smaller sum as more probable.

Duck later described his first meeting with his royal patroness in Richmond Park:

> Here first the Muse (auspicious was the Place!)
> Rejoic'd to see her Royal Guardian's Face:
> How mild, yet how majestic, was her Look!
> How sweetly condescending all she spoke![119]

His gratitude to her seems always to have been heartfelt and sincere. In his poetry he pays frequent tributes both to her and to other members of the royal family, not only during her life-time, and on the occasion of her death, but even in his last poem published some eighteen years later.[120]

The steps by which Duck ascended the social scale from wretched obscurity constitute perhaps the most melodramatic chapter in his biography, especially in an age when social position depended almost exclusively on birth; but the later chapters which tell the results, intellectual, spiritual and artistic, in his fortunes, as far as the meagre records allow, suggest various psychological and sociological questions. The merits of the thresher's poetry seem hardly to account for his spectacular success; neither does it seem plausible that the large group of distinguished patrons and patronesses who competed with one another in his behalf had become suddenly engulfed in a wave of sentimental primitivism. An explanation must be sought in the man himself; in the hunger for intellectual expansion that the monotonous labours of the threshing-floor could not deaden; in the appeal of his personality; and in the simple uprightness of his character. Quite clearly the thresher deserved a better fate than to labor all his life in the barn and in the fields; but whether this deserved good fortune came in his transfer to the aristocratic society of Richmond, it is difficult to determine. In short one wonders whether his life as protégé of royalty brought out the best that was in him any more than his life as a farm-laborer had done.

Notes

1. Havens, *Influence of Milton,* 359.

2. Tinker, *Nature's Simple Plan,* 92.

3. *Introduction* to the *Account of the Life, Character, and Poems of Mr. Blacklock,* 1754, 3-4. Spence explains in a footnote that the three referred to are Mr. Duck, Mr. Dodsley, and Mr. Richardson.

4. *Epistles to Mr. Pope. Epistle I.* Young, however, seems affected with primitivism when in his *Conjectures on Original Composition* (p. 17), he says: "Many a genius, probably, there has been, which could neither write, nor read. So that genius, that supreme lustre of literature, is less rare than you conceive."

5. *Gent. Mag.,* I, 1731, 11; *Memoirs of Society of Grub-street,* I, Jan. 21, No. 55, 268.

6. Walpole, *Letters,* ed. Cunningham, I, 11-12; *Gray and his Friends,* ed. Tovey, 89.

7. *The Adventurer,* IV, No. 115, 76-83. That this tendency was still alive in 1778, twenty-two years after Duck's death is indicated by a passage in *Monthly Review,* LVIII, 162, to the effect that "certain journeymen taylors, shoemakers, barbers, Spitalfield-weavers, and other handicraftsmen, and that certain apprentices, shopmen, etc. . . . , have presumed to make rhymes and discharge them on the Public. . . ." This was the *Review's* acid comment on the appearance of *The Auction; a Town Eclogue.* By the Honorable Mr.—.

8. *Nature's Simple Plan,* 90-91.

9. Southey (*Uneducated Poets,* 163, ed. Childers) quotes from Sheridan the elder to the effect that "Wonder, usually accompanied by bad taste, looks only for what is uncommon and if a work comes out under the name of a thresher, a bricklayer, a milkwoman, or—a lord, it is sure to be eagerly sought after by the million." "Bricklayer" is probably a reference to Henry Jones (1721-1770), and "milkwoman" to Ann Yearsley (1756-1806).

10. Southey (*ibid.,* 165) says: "The benevolent persons who patronized Stephen Duck, did it, not with the hope of rearing a great poet, but for the sake of placing a worthy man in a station more suited to his intellectual endowments than that in which he was born."

11. This obscurity as to Duck's birth and parentage, Spence's rather significant silence on the subject, the reference to him in *A Curatical Battle for Q Chappel* (see Ch. III below) as "half strain" and "half bred Duck" and his remarkable rise to favor in later life, suggest the hypothesis that Duck may have been an illegitimate child, possibly of good paternal family, who was bound out to a farmer in infancy. I have been unable, however, to find any definite confirmation of this supposition.

12. *Biog. Brit.,* V, 414ff.

13. The Avon is mentioned in *A Handbook for Residents and Travellers in Wilts and Dorset,* 171; and in *N. and Q.* 8th Ser., II, 1892, 466.

14. *Poems on Several Occasions,* 1738, *Preface,* xv.

15. *Poems on Several Subjects,* seventh edition, 1730: *Some Account of the Author's Life,* iii.

16. *Ibid.,* third edition, 1730, 32; fifth edition, *ibid.*

17. Most biographical dictionaries are silent on the question of the date of Duck's birth. M. Hennet, *Poétique Anglais* (1806), Tome Second, 73, and the *Chambers' Biographical Dictionary,* ed. Patrick and Groome, (1897) 315, follow the spurious account in giving the date 1705. J. Lemprière in *Universal Biography,* I, says that "Duck began to apply himself to study at the age of 24." It can be established by a statement in the account of Duck by Joseph Spence that it was in 1724 that this event took place. Spence, writing, probably in 1730 and certainly not later than 1731, tells us that Duck's efforts to recover his arithmetic took place about six years before (*Full Account of Duck,* 7).

18. Spence, *Anecdotes,* etc., ed. John Underhill, *Introduction,* xxiii.

19. *Biog. Brit.,* VI, Part II, *Supplement,* 42-43. The 1793 edition of this facile compilation dates the event as "in the beginning of the present century." *A Brief Biographical Dictionary,* by the Rev. Charles Hole and William A. Wheeler, (1866), 137, says he was born in 1700. Both of these

articles refer to Spence's account as a source, the latter specifically to the 1764 edition; but in no version of Spence's account is there any mention of Duck's birth. There is in the original pamphlet (1731 edition, 5) a reference to "a former Letter" in which such information may have been included. Edward Walford in *Greater London,* II, 348, states that Duck was born about 1700 and that at the age of thirty he made the acquaintance of the Reverend Joseph Spence. W. H. Wilkins in *Caroline the Illustrious,* II, 180, states that Duck's poems were unpublished until he reached the age of thirty. The first pirated edition of his works appeared in 1730. "E. W." in *N. and Q.,* 4 Ser., IV, 549, assumes that Duck was twenty-four at the time of his marriage in 1724.

20. *Poems on Several Occasions,* 1738, 35.

21. Queen Anne recommended the design of the charity schools in a letter to the Archbishops of Canterbury and York, dated August 20, 1711. This fact may shed some light on the date of Duck's birth (Ashton, *Social Life in the Reign of Queen Anne,* 16), and clearly points to the probability of the later date, 1705.

22. *Full Account of Duck,* 1731, 6.

23. *Poems on Several Subjects,* seventh ed., 1730: *Some Account of the Author's Life,* pp. iii-iv.

24. For a variant of this date, found in the record of the boy's admission to Eton College, see Ch. III below.

25. *N. and Q.* 4 Ser., IV, 549. The Reverend H. B. M. Smith informs me as follows: "I should think that your extracts from the Charlton register taken from *Notes and Queries* are correct copies, although I am not in a position to verify them."

26. *Poems on Several Subjects,* third ed., pp. iv-v.

27. Ed. J. S. Childers, 93. John Britton in *The Beauties of Wiltshire* (1801), I, 126ff, and a correspondent in *N. and Q.,* 4th Ser., IV, 1869, 347, signing himself "H. H.", also make use of this story.

28. Thomson, Mrs. Katharine Byerley, *Memoirs of the Court and Times of King George the Second, and His Consort Queen Caroline, including Numerous Private Letters of the Most Celebrated Persons of the Time Addressed to the Viscountess Sundon, Mistress of the Robes to the Queen, and her Confidential Adviser, exhibiting much of the Secret, Political, Religious, and Literary History and a Variety of Particulars not Mentioned by our Historians.* I, p. 187. G. A. Aitken in an account of Lady Sundon in *D. N. B.* [*The Dictionary of National Biography*] says that the work is gener-

ally inaccurate. The following statements, when compared with known facts of Duck's biography, serve to confirm this opinion: "He studied for the Church, at which of the Universities, if, indeed, at either, we know not. Certain it is, however, that either in the year 1746 or 1749, he was ordained; and, was afterwards appointed keeper of the Queen's select library at Richmond." (I, 205). The letters from Dr. Clarke in this volume are quoted from extensively below, but always with the possibility of their inaccuracy in view.

29. *Ibid.,* 192.

30. See Ch. II below.

31. Thomson, *Memoirs,* etc., I, p. 194.

32. Frederic Turner in *N. and Q.* 11 Ser., VIII, 1913, 102, says that Duck's first wife died at Calne a few weeks after her husband's poems were read at Windsor.

33. Thomson, *Memoirs,* etc., I, 200.

34. *Ibid.,* I, 203.

35. Celia, probably Mrs. Clayton.

36. *Poems on Several Occasions,* 1738, 39-47.

37. *Ibid.,* 7-20.

38. H. E. Malden, *The Victoria History of the County of Surrey,* IV, 438, quotes this passage, and mentions that the same fare was offered to Cobbett as a Sunday dinner by a cottager between Chiddingfold and Thursley.

39. Crabbe, *The Village,* lines 21-30.

40. *Full Account of Duck,* 1731, 6-11.

41. *Description of a Journey,* etc. (*Poems on Several Occasions,* 142).

42. Probably *The Travels of Cyrus,* by Sir Andrew Ramsay (1686-1743).

43. On page 25 of the *Full Account of Duck,* Spence says that Duck has read the Archbishop of Cambray's *Demonstration of the Being of a God.*

44. The biography prefixed to *Poems on Several Subjects,* p. iv, says that Duck owned Bailey's *English Dictionary.*

45. *Letters from the Dead to the Living,* By Mr. Tho. Brown, Capt. Ayloff, Mr. Hen. Barker, London, 1702.

46. *The London Spy.* [by Ned Ward]. Compleat In Eighteen Parts. The First Volume of the Author's Writings. The Third Edition, London, 1706.

47. Thomson, *Memoirs,* etc., I, 188.

48. *Full Account of Duck,* 22-23.

49. *Ibid.,* 11.

50. *Ibid.,* 23.

51. *Poems on Several Occasions,* 1738, 165.

52. *Full Account of Duck,* 23-24.

53. *Uneducated Poets,* ed. Childers, 112.

54. *Full Account of Duck,* 24-25.

55. *Ibid.,* 9-10.

56. *On Richmond Park and Royal Gardens* (*Poems on Several Occasions,* 1738, 53.)

57. *Poems on Several Occasions,* 1738, 49-51.

58. *Full Account of Duck,* 11-12. It is this late statement which Spence in a footnote credits to Mr. Stanley's account.

59. *To a Gentleman who requested a Copy of Verses from the Author* (*Poems on Several Occasions,* 1738, 1). These verses stand last in the third and fifth pirated editions of 1730. This fact would seem to indicate that the poems were in print when Spence's account was written. The account in *D. N. B.* places the writing of these verses in 1729. This assumption may be founded on the statement in the preface to *Poems on Several Occasions* (1736, p. xii) that the oldest poem in the collection was "little more than six Years of Age. . . .

60. *Full Account of Duck,* 12-13.

61. *Uneducated Poets,* 93. Southey omits any reference to the former's non-committal policy, and later explains that "Mr. Stanley, who was now in holy orders, gave him for a subject of his next poem, his own way of life. . . ." (*Ibid.,* 95-96).

62. *Poems on Several Occasions,* 1738, xxvii. Kippis (*Biog. Brit.,* V, 413) and John Britton (*Beauties of England and Wales,* XV, 409) seem to follow Spence in implying that the Oxford student and Mr. Stanley were two different persons. *Alumni Oxoniensis, 1715-1886,* by Joseph Foster, Oxford, London, 1888, IV, 1343, contains the following entry: "Stanley, Hoby, s. William of Eling, Hants, arm. Merton College, matric. 30 April, 1716, aged 17: B. A. 1 Feb. 1719-20, M. A. 1723."

63. *Poems on Several Occasions,* 1738, 146.

64. *Ibid.,* 155.

65. *Poems on Several Subjects,* seventh ed., iv-v.

66. *Poems on Several Occasions,* 138.

67. Founder of Corpus Christi College.

68. *Poems on Several Occasions,* 163. *Alumni Oxoniensis,* IV, 1587, contains the following entry: "Winder, Thomas s. Thomas, cler. Corpus Christi

Coll. matric. 27 May, 1727, aged 13; B. A. 1731, M. A. 26 Feb. 1734-5." If we are to identify this person with Duck's patron, he was extremely youthful at the time he first took notice of Duck.

69. *Ibid.,* xv-xvi.

70. *Ibid.,* 219. *Gent. Mag.* VII, 25, contains under list of deaths for 1737—"Feb. 16—Rev. Mr. Stanley, Rector of Pewsey, Wilts., worth 4001 per Ann."

71. *Full Account of Duck,* 13.

72. Elsewhere, Duck gives us the following sketch of her character (*Poems on Several Occasions,* 1738, 149):

> Uncharm'd with all the flutt'ring Pomp of Pride,
> Heav'n, and domestic Care her Time divide:
> In her own Breast she seeks a calm Repose,
> And shuns the crouded Rooms of *Belles* and *Beaux.*

73. *Full Account of Duck,* 13. Britton (*Beauties of England and Wales,* XV, *Wiltshire,* 409) says that the *Shunammite* was the means of procuring the patronage of Queen Caroline. A lampoon on Duck which the *Gentleman's Magazine* (I, 1731, 150) purports to quote from the *Grubstreet Journal* (Apr. 8, No. 66) attributes Duck's success with the pious Queen to his choice of subject:

> *"Things done by men of God for Shunammite."*

74. Thomson, *Memoirs,* etc., I, 190-191. See Chapter IV below. The spurious biography has a story to the effect that Duck was asked by a noble Earl to write on the Sun, a request to which he replied: *"That as he had no true knowledge,* nor had read anything of the Nature of that great Luminary, he was at present incapable of such a Task." It is significant that the peasant poet felt the need of documenting himself before composition.

75. Austin Dobson, *Eighteenth-Century Vignettes,* 32.

76. Spence, *Account of the Life, Character, and Poems of Mr. Blacklock,* 4n.

77. Blacklock, ed. Spence, 3. Spence was also the author of an account of the learned tailor, Robert Hill, in the form of *A Parallel; in the Manner of Plutarch, between a most celebrated Man of Florence; and One, scarce ever heard of in England* (In Dodsley's *Fugitive Pieces on Various Subjects by several Authors,* II).

78. Introduction, xxiii.

79. J. M. Rigg in *D. N. B.* under John Rolle. In Nichols' *Literary Anecdotes of the Eighteenth Century* we are told that Spence "left the pamphlet in the hands of a friend [Robert Lowth, afterward Bishop of London], to be published as soon as he

had left England with that Grub-street title, which he had drawn up merely for a disguise, not chusing to have it thought that he had published it himself." (I, No. IX, 643n; and II, 373n). The following preface to the published account makes it clear that the work appeared without Spence's consent: "Tis not material to tell you very minutely how the following Letter came into my Hands: As to what is necessary, I can take upon me to say, that it was really written by Mr. *Spence,* and that this is a true Copy of it. The Author, who is now Abroad, I hope will pardon me, for Endeavoring to make us able still to enjoy thus much of his Conversation here at Home . . ." He concludes with remarks to the effect that while it may look unfair to publish without the author's consent, he has confidence that the letter cannot injure Mr. Spence's character and will be of much interest to the public. (*Full Account of Duck,* 3-4). The author himself writing to his mother from Lyons in June, 1731, says: "Any bookseller is certainly a rascal that pretends to fling out things of any kind about my old friend, Stephen Duck, in my name. I don't know what those people that deal in spoiling paper are doing in England, but whatever 'tis I wash my hands of it. Whoever did it, if it can be of any service to honest Stephen any way, I shou'd not be sorry for the scandal that I may undergo for it." (*Anecdotes,* ed. John Underhill, Introduction, xxiiin). Frederic Turner (see *N. and Q.,* 11th Ser., VIII, 102) quotes from some manuscript notes by Isaac Reed which he found bound up in a copy of Duck's poems in his possession, as follows: "Bishop Lowth told Mr. Nichols that this pamphlet was published by Mr. Spence himself, and that his name was printed with the addn. of Esq. to it merely as a Blind to mislead the Publick into the idea that it appeared without his consent." Spence was ordained in 1724.

80. *Gent. Mag.,* I, 1731, 136.

81. *Preface,* xiv-xv. The account was printed in an abridged form in *Gent. Mag.* (VI, 317) for 1736 (the year of the first edition of *Poems on Several Occasions*) together with Duck's dedication of this collection *To the Queen.*

82. *Full Account of Duck,* 14.

83. *Ibid.,* 13-14.

84. *Poems on Several Occasions,* 153.

85. Walpole tells an incident of Peter Bathurst's helping to carry one of his own servants who had attempted to shoot him before Henry Fielding, then Middlesex justice. Fielding would not see them, and on forcing their way in they found him banqueting in disreputable company. (See *Letters,*

ed. Cunningham, II, 162). Walpole also establishes his identity as the brother of Allen Bathurst (1684-1775) first Earl Bathurst, who represented Circencester in Parliament from 1705 to 1712, when he was created Baron Bathurst. He was a friend of Pope, Swift, and other wits of the day. (See account by W. P. Courtney in *D. N. B.* under Allen Bathurst).

86. *Full Account of Duck,* 14.

87. 1730 edition.

88. *Poems on Several Subjects,* seventh ed., p. v. According to Turner (*N. and Q.,* 11th Ser., VIII, 102), Reed gives the credit to the Earl of Macclesfield, rather than to Lady Sundon, as do M. Hennet in *Poétique Anglais* (Tome Second) and J. M. Attenborough in an article on Duck in the *Cornhill Magazine* (June, 1903, 798ff).

89. Probably Charles Bennet, second Lord Ossulston, who in 1695 married Mary, only daughter of Forde Grey, Earl of Tankerville, and at the latter's death in 1701 was created Earl of Tankerville. (See Goodwin Gordon in *D. N. B.* under Forde Grey). (See also *Caroline the Illustrious,* by W. H. Wilkins, II, 181).

90. *Biog. Brit.,* V, 16. Molloy in *Court Life Below Stairs,* II, 214, says that Duck was brought to the notice of the Queen by Dr. Clarke "Through Mrs. Clayton's representations to the Queen . . ." Leslie Stephen in *D. N. B.* credits Lady Sundon with recommending the poet to the Queen and, like Jones, credits Macclesfield, merely with reading the poet's works aloud to her.

91. *Full Account of Duck,* 9.

92. See Johnson's *Lives of the Poets,* ed. Cunningham, II, 144 and n. Johnson credits her with having befriended Savage. The editor in a footnote tells us that Thomson dedicated his poem on *Spring* and Shenstone his *Ode on Rural Elegance* to this lady. She is mentioned in Walpole's *Letters* (II, 395n.) as the friend of Thomson, Savage, Shenstone, and Isaac Watts. On the death of the Queen in 1737 she retired from Court with her cousin, Henrietta Louisa Fermor, Countess of Pomfret, (See Goodwin Gordon in *D. N. B.* under Fermor, Henrietta Louisa) to whom Duck dedicated his poem *Felix and Constance* (*Poems on Several Occasions,* 177).

93. Thomson, *Memoirs,* I, 196.

94. *Poems on Several Occasions,* 1738, 148.

95. *Full Account of Duck,* 25-26.

96. Thomson, *Memoirs,* I, 190; see also Wilkins, *Caroline the Illustrious,* II, 181.

97. Thomson, *Memoirs,* I, 196.

98. *Ibid.,* I, 202.

99. Thomson, *Memoirs,* I, 182. See also W. P. Courtney in *D. N. B.* under Alured Clarke.

100. Thomson, *Memoirs,* I, 187ff.

101. *Ibid.,* 187.

102. *Ibid.,* 189-190.

103. Windsor mentioned in Wilkins, *Caroline the Illustrious,* II, 181.

104. Probably *Gratitude. A Pastoral (Poems on Several Occasions,* 1738, 34-39).

105. Thomson, *Memoirs,* I, 194-195. This date does not agree with that given in a footnote to some satirical verses on Duck found in the *Memoirs of the Society of Grub-Street* (I, 195) under date of Thursday, October 8, 1730, and quoted from the *Post-boy* for October 7, in which Duck is represented as having waited on the Queen at Windsor "last friday night [October 2]" and having presented her with a poem "on her late benevolence to him" (probably *Royal Benevolence* discussed in Chapter II below).

106. Thomson, *Memoirs,* I, 202.

107. *Ibid.,* 202-3.

108. Thomson, *Memoirs,* I, 191-192.

109. *Ibid.,* I, 198.

110. Duck addressed some complimentary verses *To the Right Hon. William Clayton, Esq.; (now Lord Sundon) on his being elected Representative in Parliament for Westminster without Opposition (Poems on Several Occasions,* 1738, 136.)

111. See G. A. Aitken in *D. N. B.* under Lady Sundon. Walpole (*Letters,* ed. Cunningham, I, cxxx) refers to the Queen's "confidante, Lady Sundon, an absurd and pompous simpleton. . . ." He says later that her hold upon the Queen depended upon her accidental knowledge of the Queen's secret, the fact that she was afflicted with a rupture (*Ibid.,* I, 114). Walpole seems inclined to speak slightingly of her; on the other hand, Hervey is quoted (*D. N. B.*) as saying that she despised "the dirty company surrounding her," and took pleasure in doing good "often for persons who could not repay her."

112. Thomson, *Memoirs,* I, 420. A certain Lewis is quoted in *Lines to Lord Bathurst,* included in Pope *Works* (Cambridge ed., 102).

113. The end of *Gratitude* is a tribute to the Queen. It was probably revised.

114. Thomson, *Memoirs,* I, 195-196.

115. *Ibid.,* I, 200-201.

116. *Full Account of Duck,* 14-15.

117. *Memoirs of the Society of Grub-Street,* I, 195, quoted from the *Postboy,* October 7.

118. *Biog. Brit.,* V, 416. John Underhill in the *Introduction* to Spence's *Anecdotes* (xxiii) sets the amount at thirty pounds, and Stephen in *D. N. B.* says that it was either thirty or fifty pounds.

119. *On Richmond Park and Royal Gardens, (Poems on Several Occasions,* 1738, 59-60).

120. *Caesar's Camp; or St. George's Hill,* 1755, 12 (in *Miscellaneous Tracts,* 1740-1755).

Bibliography B

<small>Works Containing Material on Duck and on His Background</small>

Ashton, John: *Social Life in the Reign of Queen Anne,* London, 1897.

Attenborough, J. M.: In *Cornhill Magazine,* June 1903.

Brayley, Edward Wedlake: *History of Surrey,* London, 1841 (Vols. II and III).

Brief Biographical Dictionary, by the Rev. Charles Hole and Wm. A. Wheeler, New York, 1883.

Britton, John: *The Beauties of Wiltshire,* London. 1801.

Chambers' *Biographical Dictionary,* ed. David Patrick and F. H. Groome, London, 1897.

Crabbe, George: *Poetical Works,* ed. A. J. Carlyle and R. M. Carlyle, London, 1908 (*The Village*).

Dobson, Austin: *Eighteenth Century Vignettes,* Oxford, 1923 (Vol. I). Second series, London, 1894.

Handbook for Residents and Travellers in Wilts and Dorset, London, 1899.

Havens, Raymond Dexter: *The Influence of Milton in English Poetry,* Cambridge, Mass., 1922.

Hennet, M., *Poétique Anglais,* Paris, 1806. (Tome Second).

Hole, the Rev. Charles (see *Brief Biographical Dictionary*).

Malden, H. E.: *The Victoria History of the County of Surrey,* London, 1911 (Vols. III and IV).

Molloy, J. Fitzgerald, *Court Life Below Stairs,* London, 1882. (Vol. II).

Nichols, John; *Literary Anecdotes of the Eighteenth Century,* London, 1812 (Vols. I, II, III, V).

Notes and Queries: 4 Ser., IV, 1869, 117, 347, 423, 549.

Southey, Robert: *The Lives and Works of the Uneducated Poets,* ed. J. S. Childers, London, 1925.

Spence, Joseph: *An Account of the Life, Character, and Poems of Mr. Blacklock, Student of Philosophy in the University of Edinburgh,* London, 1754.

Spence, Joseph: *A Full and Authentick Account of Stephen Duck, the Wiltshire Poet,* London, Printed for J. Roberts in Warwick-Lane . . . 1731. (Revised and published with *Poems on Several Occasions,* 1736, 1737, 1738, 1753, 1764. Abstract published in *The Gentleman's Magazine,* VI, 1736, 317).

Spence, Joseph, *Anecdotes,* ed. John Underhill, London, 1890.

Thomson, Mrs. Katharine Byerley: *Memoirs of the Court and Times of King George the Second, and His Consort Queen Caroline, including Numberous Private Letters of the Most Celebrated Persons of the Time Addressed to the Viscountess Sundon, Mistress of the Robes to the Queen, and her Confidential Adviser,* London, 1850.

Tinker, Chauncey B.: *Nature's Simple Plan,* Princeton, 1922.

Walford, Edward: *Greater London,* London [1884] (Vol. II).

Walpole, Horace: *Letters,* ed. Cunningham, London, 1857 (Vol. I); 1886 (Vol. VIII).

Wilkins, W. H.: *Caroline the Illustrious,* London, 1901 (Vol. II).

Young, Edward: *Letters* (In *Calendar of the MSS. of the Marquis of Bath,* London, 1904, Vol. I).

Moira Ferguson (essay date 1985)

SOURCE: Ferguson, Moira. Introduction to The Thresher's Labour *by Stephen Duck and* The Woman's Labour *by Mary Collier,* pp. iii-xii. Los Angeles: The Augustan Reprint Society, William Andrews Clark Memorial Library, University of California, 1985.

[*In the following essay, Ferguson discusses* The Woman's Labour *by Mary Collier, a washerwoman and contemporary of Duck, as the angry response to what Collier perceived as a denigration of women workers in* The Thresher's Labour.]

Posterity has been somewhat kinder to Stephen Duck, who wrote *The Thresher's Labour* (1730, 1736), than to Mary Collier, who in 1739 angrily responded to his poem with *The Woman's Labour.*[1] Mary Collier's poem, along with some other of her writings, appeared in several scattered editions and reprints between 1739 and 1780, but public notice was slight. She lived as a washerwoman while Duck was given a small house and various minor court appointments by Queen Caroline.[2]

Yet for all his relative success, the phrase "torments of the soul" might well be applied to the later life and career of Stephen Duck, the thresher, whose poems were brought to royal attention by Lord Macclesfield in 1730; in 1756 Duck drowned himself after his meteoric rise to fame was followed by a protracted leveling-off period. "Discomforts of poverty," by contrast, better describes the situation of Mary Collier, the Petersfield washerwoman, who engaged in a one-sided "flyting" with Duck because of his derisive attitude toward women who toiled alongside men in the fields.

The fundamental disruption of the English countryside caused by the enclosure of land partly explains Duck's grueling account of physical and psychological endurance in *The Thresher's Labour.*[3] In this unjust situation the villain was the greedy, callous farmer, the victims were the workers. Rural English society was dividing into landlords, leaseholding farmers, and landless laborers. "The result was the transfer from the village community to the individual farmer of a whole range of economic decisions which had hitherto been decided collectively."[4] The destruction of the traditionally collective decision-making processes in their communities was an unstated lament. Small wonder that they decried their lot in tandem in the face of encroachment.

Unfortunately, rural laborers had scant opportunity to alert the public to their situation, since they neither could afford to publish nor were encouraged to protest their displacement. If they ignored cultural bias and wrote nonetheless, they still stood in desperate need of a patron.

Aside from Queen Caroline, several others encouraged Duck, among them the Reverend Mr. Stanley; Dr. Alured Clarke (an early patron); the Reverend Joseph Spence, Professor of Poetry at Oxford; Lady Hartford; and the Earl of Macclesfield, who read Duck's poems in 1730 to Her Majesty.[5] The queen awarded Duck a £30 annuity and a modest house in Surrey. In 1733 she appointed him yeoman of the guard. In the same year he married the queen's housekeeper, Sarah Big (his first wife having died in 1730). Two years later Caroline appointed him keeper of her private library. At the queen's death in 1737 a grief-stricken Duck wrote a moving elegy. He took holy orders in 1746 and became chaplain to a regiment of Dragon Guards in 1750. A preacher at Kew Chapel in 1751, he retired to the living of Byfleet in Surrey the next year.

Duck's creative life, however, was anything but smooth. Within three and a half months after his poems were read to the queen, seven pirated editions appeared. In

1736 the first authorized collected quarto edition was "printed for the author." As testimonies to Duck's growing fame, this edition contained an account of the author by Joseph Spence and a list of over six hundred subscribers, headed by the Prince of Wales and five other royal personages. Another collected edition, in octavo, was printed that year for W. Bickerton, and this edition was reprinted in 1737 with an additional title page and an engraving of the author.

In his account of the author, Spence narrates the still-cloudy circumstances that brought the poems of a thresher to the queen's attention. Apparently Duck had written poems for a long time, frequently burning his work, until rumors about him reached the ears of "a young Gentleman of *Oxford,* who sent for *Stephen.*" For him Duck wrote an epistle, then "some scatter'd Verses on *Poverty,*" and then "the Composition . . . on his own *Labours.*"[6]

Spence explains that he had himself spent "a Week's Conversation with him in all his Simplicity," obtaining Duck's "Circumstances," how he acquired a little arithmetic, learned to read, and "successively engag'd in the several lowest Employments of a Country Life." Spence admires the fact that Duck nurtured such a "Longing after Knowledge" that he worked harder than other day laborers to pay for books. He also "work'd all Day for his Master; and, after the Labour of the Day, set to his Books at Night."

Spence's own view sustained the popular eighteenth-century view of Duck as a natural creative talent. Spence's description—"he us'd to sit down all over Sweat and Heat [when he could snatch a half hour from threshing], without regarding his own Health, and often to the Prejudice of it"—matches Duck's self-portrait in *The Thresher's Labour.*

An oddly blended but strong amalgam of the dire reality of Duck's laboring life and inner turmoil, *The Thresher's Labour* is more than an encomium to industry and a condemnation of tyranny. It uncovers the reality of living in the country in contrast to the mythological unreality of the pastoral, in which swans glide through an Elysian paradise.[7] Spence tips his hat to Duck's formality of classical allusions, epic devices, conventional phraseology, and the verse couplet with dialogue and meter equally conventional, yet supple and expressive of mood, into all of which he injects—despite the fiat of decorum to which he feels the need to adhere—a sense of the hard-edged quality and rhythm of quotidian rural laboring life. Self-reflection, a sensitivity to nature's harmonies, energetic immersion in the job well done, and an absence of complaint further enhance the work. At the heart of the poem is the mental struggle to cope with physical rigor. In keeping with a growing eighteenth-century tendency to admire the underprivileged, readers sympathized with the laborers' diurnal, Sisyphean task, commending Duck's endurance and critical of his subjugation.

In *The Country and the City* Raymond Williams sensitively discusses the cost to Duck of public acceptance: "It is easy to feel the strain of this labourer's voice as it adapts, slowly, to the available models in verse: the formal explanation, the anxious classical reference, the arranged subordinate clauses of that self-possessed literary manner."[8] Despite Duck's class-conscious oversolicitousness, his self-assurance that his life is worthy, his unmediated, uncompromising laborer's posture, and the raw feelings that his work exudes ultimately reverberate to haunt the reader.

Nevertheless, Duck's just iconoclasm and his political and personal frustrations neither cajoled nor placed Mary Collier, who rejected the poem out of hand, talking from experiences not dissimilar to his. She was not, though, out to lampoon him. Other poets, jealous of his intrusion on their class-locked poetic territory, undertook that task with relish.[9]

In the autobiographical preface to the expanded 1762 edition of *The Woman's Labour,* Mary Collier explains why Stephen Duck's poem so infuriated her in its relegation of women to the status of dilatory, feckless characters and elucidates the circumstances and consequences of her decision to respond:

> After several Years thus Spent [(in Petersfield) "Washing, Brewing and such labour"], Duck's Poems came abroad, which I soon got by heart, fancying he had been too Severe on the Female Sex in his *Thresher's Labour* brought me to a Strong propensity to call an Army of Amazons to vindicate the injured Sex: Therefore I answer'd him to please my own humour, little thinking to make it Public it lay by me several Years and by now and then repeating a few lines to amuse myself and entertain my Company, it got Air.

> I happen'd to attend a Gentlewoman in a fit of Illness, and she and her Friends persuaded me to make Verses on the Wise Sentences, which I did on such Nights as I waited on her. I had learn'd to write to assist my memory, and her Spouse transcrib'd it with a promise to keep it private, but he exposed it to so many, that it soon Became a Town Talk, which made many advise me to have it printed and at length I comply'd to have it done at my own charge, I lost nothing, neither did I gain much, others run away with the profit.[10]

Without this kind of patronage and encouragement, however slight, Collier's poems had barely a chance of publication. Lacking Duck's fortuitous access to the queen, Collier had to be content with high-powered local men who treated her as a curiosity,[11] a Petersfield version of Duck but perhaps even more eye-catching, as a woman and a laundress. Indeed, Collier seems to be the first known rural laboring woman in England to publish creative work.

In the preface to the 1739 first edition, one "M. B." had condescendingly introduced Collier to the public, and Collier spoke only through her poems.[12] But in the 1762 edition Collier, no longer a humble neophyte unable to speak for herself, sketches her own life. She was born, she states, "near Midhurst in Sussex of poor, but honest Parents, by whom I was taught to read when very Young." Sent out "to such labour as the Country afforded" when her mother died, she "lost" her education, but kept up her "Recreation" in reading, living with her father till he died. At this juncture she went to Petersfield, where she worked as a washerwoman till she was sixty-three, then took over the management of a farmhouse in nearby Alton till she was seventy years old and incapacitated. By 1762 she had "retired to a Garret (The Poor Poets Fate) in Alton where I am endeavouring," she concludes, "to pass the Relict of my days in Piety, Purity, Peace, and an Old Maid."[13]

Opening her polemic with an ironic apostrophe to Duck, Collier acknowledges her own inferior treatment and condition: "No Learning ever was bestow'd on me; / My Life was always spent in Drudgery" (6). She then expands her topic boldly to include all women, or at least all poor women. Like her, they live under conditions of slavery and drudgery, "the Portion of poor Woman-kind" (6). "Time and Custom by degrees" have eroded the natural "Homage" (6) that men owe to women. Because of grinding mistreatment, "All the Perfections Woman once could boast, / Are quite obscur'd, and altogether lost" (16).

Again and again, Collier returns to the endless double shift worked by women who labor at home and in the fields or in the homes of others, and to their consequent and inevitable lack of rest and time for reflection: "Our Toil and Labour's daily so extreme, / That we have hardly ever *Time to dream*" (11).

To ridicule the idea that men work harder than women, she tells of washing the mistress's clothes until "Not only Sweat, but Blood runs trickling down / Our Wrists and Fingers" (14) and of polishing brass and iron until "Our tender Hands and Fingers [we] scratch and tear" (15-16). She compares the women laborers' grueling housework to the agricultural labor of men whom Duck described as sootied with peas: "Colour'd with Dirt and Filth we now appear; / Your threshing *sooty Peas* will not come near" (16).

At least the honest farmer who employs women haymakers appreciates the value of female industry, while husbands—and poets—remain insensitive to female "toil and sweat" (7-8). Thus Collier nullifies Duck's contempt for the bullying farmer who employs "foolish" women. And unlike Duck, she uses the language of actual labor to bring the strenuous struggle of rural women to life: scenarios of gleaning, reaping, sewing,

child tending, charring, brewing, scrubbing, rescrubbing, flash past her readers. Thus her middle-class readers are brought face to face with the work from which their profit and leisure ultimately derive.

Refuting Duck's objections to women's social conversation during work, she reminds him of the "domestic Toils incessant" (9) that women must endure. They rise early to dress and feed children; they mend clothes and toil at field work, often holding their children in their arms. They return to set the home in order; they prepare meals, set the table, make beds, feed swine and other animals, and welcome back the husband whose needs they cater to. Women do not enjoy the patriarchal privilege of a prepared meal and instant rest, being obliged instead to sit up all night at times with fractious infants. Contrary to conventional wisdom, women are men's protectors. And for unmarried women like Collier, "*Old Age* and *Poverty*" are all the future offers. Her message is as brief and her tone as grim as the joy she anticipates: "For all our Pains, no Prospect can we see / Attend us, but *Old Age* and *Poverty*" (15).

The last half of Collier's poem is principally concerned with the audacious exploitation of hired female domestic labor in country houses. A modern historian acknowledges that "among the longest hours of outworkers were those of the wretched women who went out to wash by the day."[14] Often they began at one in the morning and worked a day and a half for a day's wages. A pioneer in charting laboring women on the new feminist map, Collier refuses to countenance any suggestion of their insignificance. She evokes this gruelingly long day of servitude: it begins "several Hours . . . / Before we can one Glimpse of Day-light have" (13) and "we know not when 'twill end" (14). Again she draws a distinction between male and female work: "When Ev'ning's come, you Homeward take your Way, / We, till our Work is done, are forc'd to stay" (15).

Collier's ending also reinforces the interrupted nature of women's working lives, particularly for those who labor seasonally and for those who are hired by the hour—for all of them no security exists. The poem's abrupt ending suggests not simply artistic awkwardness but a sense of "that's enough," and perhaps, in its quick flourish, the poetic feeling of pride in herself as a poet and as a worker.

Despite the overriding similarities between Duck and Collier, their gender inscribes their texts with significant differences. Collier paints a bleak picture of the eighteenth-century double shift in her simple narrative about a superwoman, most likely a composite portrait. As she describes it in her 1762 autobiographical preface, her life differs somewhat from that of the farm laborer-wife in her poem, who awaits a thresher husband with bacon and dumplings, ready for a night of housekeeping and child tending. So especially downtrodden an existence appears to exasperate Collier and possibly explains her choice in remaining single.

For Collier, however, Duck was no class enemy. True, he cherished, it seems, patriarchal values, but perhaps her twenty years of scrubbing, which paralleled his uneven career, caused her to view him in a different light, for his suicide prompted her to write a poignant elegy that expressed the sense of class solidarity implied at the end of *The Woman's Labour.* She praised Duck for his spectacular rise but noted sadly how adversely his life was affected.

We sense in the elegy a Collier who in her own life encountered something of Duck's dark nights of the soul, but the complexities of life with which he ultimately failed to cope affirm her endurance. In the last edition of Collier's poems (1762), the polemic and the elegy lie within the same pages, displaying the contrasting reactions of this remarkable pair of eighteenth-century worker-poets to life and the consequences of literary recognition.

Notes

1. Confusion exists over Stephen Duck's early editions because his work was pirated almost immediately after he read his poems at court. An unauthorized edition, *Poems on Several Subjects,* appeared in 1730 and went into seven editions within months of the royal reading. The eighth and ninth pirated editions (like the others, in octavo) appeared in 1731 and 1733 respectively. In the preface to an allegorical poem published in 1734, *Truth and Falsehood,* Duck informs the reader that "this is the first Contract I ever made with a Printer, and consequently the *Thresher's Labour,* the *Shunamite,* etc. were never publish'd with my Approbation."

Mary Collier's *The Woman's Labour* was first published (in octavo) in 1739, and that edition is reproduced here. A second edition (also in octavo) was published in the same year. The third edition (octavo, 1740) contains a statement, dated 21 September 1739 and signed by nine Petersfield residents, including the prominent Thomas Swanneck, testifying to the "authenticity" of Mary Collier. In so testifying they also attest to biased social attitudes toward laboring class creativity. The British Library has two versions of the 1762 collection (with additions) entitled *Poems, on Several Occasions.* The first (shelf mark 11632. f. 12, no title page) is prefaced by "Some Remarks of the Author's Life drawn by herself." The second (shelf mark 11658. de. 53, no date, and printed in Petersfield) is described as "A New Edition." The "Advertisement" states: "In offering to the public

a new edition of those poems, the principal object is, to snatch from oblivion the works of a woman in the most humble sphere in life, and without education; at the same time it must be a convincing proof to every reader, that had her genius been cultivated, she would have ranked with the greatest poets of the kingdom." This edition includes "The Advertisement to the first edition," without the initials M. B. but with an added paragraph containing the third edition's authenticating statement.

2. For biographical and related information about Duck, see Rose Mary Davis, *Stephen Duck, the Thresher-Poet,* University of Maine Studies, 2d ser., no. 8 (Orono, Maine: University Press, 1926); C. Lennart Carlson, *The First Magazine: A History of the Gentleman's Magazine* (Providence, R.I.: Brown University Press, 1938), 209-10; and Robert Southey, *The Lives and Works of the Uneducated Poets,* ed. J. S. Childers (London: Humphrey Milford, 1925).

3. For the phenomenon of enclosure and its effect on the life of the rural proletariat, see Roy Porter, *English Society in the Eighteenth Century* (London: Allen Lane, 1982); T. S. Ashton, *An Economic History of England: The Eighteenth Century* (London: Methuen and Co., 1955); Christopher Hill (who disagrees that enclosures happened without detriment to country people), *Reformation to Industrial Revolution* (London: Weidenfeld & Nicolson, 1967); E. J. Hobsbawm, *Industry and Empire* (London: Weidenfeld & Nicolson, 1968); and Raymond Williams, *The Country and the City* (New York: Oxford University Press, 1973).

4. Lawrence Stone, "The Rise of the Nuclear Family in Early Modern England: The Patriarchal Stage," in *The Family in History,* ed. Charles E. Rosenberg (Philadelphia: University of Pennsylvania Press, 1975), 32.

5. For patrons and advocates of Duck, see Davis, 9, 26, and passim.

6. The quotations from Spence in this and the two subsequent paragraphs are from "An Account of the Author, In a Letter to a Friend. Written in the Year 1730," in Stephen Duck, *Poems on Several Occasions* (London: Printed for the Author, 1736), xi-xx. *The Thresher's Labour* is reproduced here from this 1736 quarto edition.

7. Martin S. Day, *History of English Literature,* vol. 2, *1660-1837* (Garden City, N.Y.: Doubleday, 1963), 92.

8. Williams, 88.

9. See Davis, chap. 2, for attacks on Duck.

10. "Some Remarks," iii-iv.

11. The sizable subscribers' list to the 1762 edition of Collier's poems suggests that her employers were well known, since the names include several local titled and professional persons. Interestingly, the affluent Joliffe family to whom Petersfield "passed by purchase" in 1739 were not subscribers. See B. B. Woodward, Theodore C. Wilks, and Charles Lockhart, *A General History of Hampshire, or The County of Southampton, Including the Isle of Wight,* 3 vols. (London: Virtue and Co., n.d.), 3:320.

12. M. B., "Advertisement," *The Woman's Labour*: ". . . she is ready to own that her Performance could by no Means stand a critical Examination, yet she flatters herself that, with all its Faults and Imperfections, the candid Reader will judge it to be Something considerably beyond the common Capacity of those of her own Rank and Occupation" (sig. A2v).

13. "Some Remarks," iii, v. The West Sussex Record office shows a baptism record for Mary Collier at Heyshott, Sussex, in 1679, copied from the Bishops' Transcripts of the registers for the parish (the original registers have not survived). The parents are Robert and Mary Collier (Collyer). There are also documents in the Cobden Archives about a Robert Collyer of Heyshott, Yeoman, which include a post-nuptial settlement made in 1678 by Robert and Mary Collier. I thank Patricia Gill, County Archivist of the Archive Repository of the West Sussex County Council and of the Diocese of Chichester, for information, generously extended.

14. Dorothy M. George, *London Life in the Eighteenth Century* (New York: Capricorn, 1965), 207-8 and passim. See also Ivy Pinchbeck, *Women Workers and the Industrial Revolution, 1750-1850* (New York: F. S. Croft, 1930), 55 and passim, for the earnings of women as day laborers.

Linda Zionkowski (essay date November 1989)

SOURCE: Zionkowski, Linda. "Strategies of Containment: Stephen Duck, Ann Yearsley, and the Problem of Polite Culture." *Eighteenth Century Life* 13, n.s. no. 3 (November 1989): 91-108.

[*In the essay below, Zionkowski explores the ramifications of the expanding book trade in the eighteenth century on the careers of Duck and milkwoman/poet Ann Yearsley, noting that their literary success also encouraged conformity in their writings.*]

For nearly a century, studies of eighteenth-century print culture have celebrated the liberating effects of the commerce of letters. According to the accepted version of events, the expansion of the book trade gave writers independence from patrons and, theoretically, made it possible for authors of all classes and backgrounds to bring their work to press. Alvin Kernan, for instance, has documented the replacement of an "authoritarian, court-centered" system of letters by a "democratic literary system," noting that the latter released writers' creative energies by "challenging and reducing established authority's control of writing."[1] Alexandre Beljame, A. S. Collins, and J. W. Saunders likewise applaud the opportunities for expression that writers enjoyed when the court no longer functioned as the source and judge of literature, and Raymond Williams sees the development of new literary forms and the increase in writers from nonaristocratic backgrounds as steps toward a more inclusive, diverse culture.[2]

The experience of uneducated, or working-class, writers initially seems to validate this view of the book trade's progressive nature. Beginning with the circulation of poems by the thresher Stephen Duck in 1730, several laboring poets brought their work to press, including washerwoman Mary Collier, weaver John Banks, bricklayer Robert Tatersal, and milkwoman Ann Yearsley. Patrons assisted these writers in publishing their works, but the commercial press further enabled them to reach an audience outside of their patrons' circles. Their popularity is revealed in the length of their subscription lists and the multiple editions of their works. Yet such success, together with the novelty of their appearance in print, proved disturbing to more polite authors. In 1731, an essay in the *Grub-street Journal* (probably written by Pope) deplored the publication of poems by Duck and Banks on the grounds that their dabbling in literature disrupted society; "To have the fields neglected, and the loom forsaken, is a melancholy prospect; and looks as if we should in time have neither bread to eat, nor cloaths to put on" (21 January). The essay goes on to advise that "the best way to encourage the Weaver, would be constantly to wear the manufacture of Great Britain; and the most suitable encouragement to the Thresher, would be to give him a small farm in the country; [laying] both under an absolute restraint, never more to write a line in rhyme or measure." Samuel Johnson makes a similar complaint several years later. After arguing that the "itch of literary praise" has seduced laborers from their "proper occupations," he sets up qualifications for authorship, the institution of which would "replace the tradesman behind his counter, and send back the farmer to the mattock and the flail."[3]

Johnson, Pope, and Swift (who wrote a satiric epigram on Duck) view working-class poetry as subversive. By writing, the laboring poets appropriate a privilege belonging to their superiors and neglect the work suited to their station; only silencing them will preserve the social structure and economy of England. Moreover, the rush to the press encouraged by the book trade enabled the likes of artificers and laborers to undermine traditional aesthetic values and standards for literary work. According to the editors of the *Grub-Street Journal*, poems by laboring writers disturb polite readers by "stunning our ears, and tiring our patience" (21 January 1731). Johnson agrees, noting that writers ignorant of the proper modes of expression waste readers' time, corrupt their taste, and destroy the language with "barbarisms" (*Adventurer,* no. 115, *Works,* 2:461).

These criticisms suggest that the idea of a "democratic" commerce in letters was a source of controversy rather than of comfort for authors. The threshers and bricklayers who ventured to publish their work apparently threatened the domain of genteel writers and made literary culture less exclusive than it had been in the past. But despite the rhetoric of Johnson, Pope, and Swift, working-class writers exerted little influence over literary practice. I argue that the careers of Stephen Duck and Ann Yearsley refute the idea of an egalitarian commerce in letters because the system of commercial print under which they wrote diffused whatever challenges they offered to elite culture. Rather than disrupting the norms of polite literary practice, Duck's and Yearsley's incursion into print reaffirmed and validated these norms; and their poetry never presented an audience with anything unfamiliar or strange. Indeed, their knowledge of verse and aesthetic "taste" mirrored that of their refined readers who derived a concept of literature from the classic texts of Shakespeare, Milton, and Dryden, which were among the staples of the book trade. Moreover, patrons used the medium of print to construct an appropriate professional identity for Duck and Yearsley; their management of the poets' education and the narratives they prefixed to the poets' verse rendered Duck and Yearsley unobjectionable to polite readers. Finally, works by Duck and Yearsley reveal the value and power of traditional literary forms—forms made even more powerful by being popularized through the trade in letters. Although the conventions of elite poetry may be foreign to the experience about which they wrote, Duck and Yearsley had to acknowledge these conventions in order to develop a poetic voice that their audience would recognize and approve. The following pages will examine how Duck's and Yearsley's work was brought into conformity with the culture of their superiors, and will determine the extent to which these poets, writing nearly fifty years apart, accepted or rejected that culture.

* * *

In a letter to Pope dated 11 September 1730, Joseph Spence announced the discovery of Stephen Duck, a "common Thresher" found to have literary talent: "All our conversation turns on it; & every body is surpriz'd that hears it. Tis a Man without anything of what is

cald Education, grown up into an Excellent Poet all at once."[4] Many seem to have shared Spence's enthusiasm; within a few short months of his removal from Wiltshire to London, Duck had indeed become the "favorite Poet of the Court."[5] Several patrons helped him gain preferment: upon hearing of Duck's attempts at writing, the neighboring clergy encouraged him, especially Mr. Stanley who commissioned poems from him that reached the attention of Dr. Alured Clarke, the king's chaplain. Through the offices of Charlotte Clayton, an acquaintance of Clarke and lady of the bedchamber to Queen Caroline, Duck was introduced to the court. Lord Macclesfield read Duck's poems to the queen in September 1730. Later that year, the poet received a pension of £30 per annum and a small house at Richmond in Surrey. Preferment continued throughout Duck's life, and included posts as one of the yeomen of the Guards, keeper of the queen's library at Richmond, and, finally, rector of Byfleet, Surrey. Duck died in the spring of 1756, apparently by suicide.[6]

As Spence's remarks show, the display of talent unexpected in a thresher aroused patrons' generosity toward Duck. Yet he may have owed his recognition as an "Excellent Poet" not to the essential greatness of his poems, but to his skill in adopting a style that sophisticated readers considered "poetic." Despite class boundaries, Duck and his patrons shared the same canon and held common beliefs about what constitutes poetry—a coincidence that the commerce in letters had only recently made possible. In a letter prefaced to the first authorized edition of Duck's poems, Spence relates how the poet and an unidentified friend together studied classics of elite culture: their library included Seneca, Ovid, Epictetus, Shakespeare, Milton, Waller, Dryden, Addison, and Prior, among others. Spence notes approvingly the method by which Duck moved beyond his provincial, class-bound vocabulary and modes of expression to familiarize himself with the language of learned gentlemen. With a dictionary, Duck poured over Milton: "He has got *English* just as we get *Latin.* He study'd *Paradise Lost,* as others study the Classics."[7] Products of print culture also influenced Duck's first efforts at poetry. Instead of adopting as models for his verse the ballads or hymns that he would have heard, Duck turned to the *Spectator*: "The *Spectators* improv'd his Understanding, he says, more than anything. The Copies of Verses scatter'd in those Pieces, help'd on his natural Bent [toward poetry]; and made him willing to try, whether he could not do something like 'em" ("Account," pp. xx-xxi). Even after Duck became recognized as a poet, he still referred to the authority of the printed canon to justify his use of certain words or techniques: as Spence notes, he "had Authorities [like Pope and Milton] to produce in several little Particulars, where one would not expect it" ("Account," p. xxvi).

Despite its detail, Spence's description of Duck's beginnings does not explain the novelty of the poet's decision to write; he suggests only that an innate or "natural Bent" for verse inspired Duck's work. Yet if his motive for writing remains obscure, we see that the discourse of polite culture, disseminated to the laboring classes by commodified print, helped determine the form that this writing would take. Patrons, too, brought Duck's verse into line with the standards of elite literature, and accomplished this by making suitable texts available to him. Before Duck took his place at court, and before he arranged his poems for publication, Alured Clarke and Charlotte Clayton supervised his continued education. While Clarke admits that "it would be very impertinent . . . to pretend to lay down rules for forming a poet," he constructs a reading list for Duck, proscribing works by Swift, Montaigne, Cowley, and Lee as too licentious and trivial and recommending those by Homer, Shakespeare, Steele, and Pope.[8] Clarke likewise acquaints him with the dominant system of aesthetics, advising him "to get . . . Pope's Essay on Criticism by heart" ("Alured Clarke to Mrs. Clayton," 19 September 1730, *Memoirs,* 1:194). Clarke and Clayton, then, had every right to call Duck "our poet"; by controlling his knowledge of literary culture, they tried to determine the character of his writing.

Management of Duck's career, however, did not end with censorship of his reading. Recognizing the possibilities for self-creation that print affords, Clarke, Clayton, and Spence worked to mediate the relation between Duck and his audience so as to mold Duck's professional identity to their own specifications. "To give the public a favourable opinion of the author," Clarke and Clayton prosecuted the printer of a pirated copy of Duck's verse; they feared that its incorrectness would prejudice Duck's readers ("Alured Clarke to Mrs. Clayton," 25 October 1730, *Memoirs,* 1:203). By the time Duck went to press with his *Poems on Several Occasions* (1736), they had brought him to the notice of several titled benefactors, whose names grace the volume's subscription list and add prestige to the poet's work ("Alured Clarke to Mrs. Clayton," 19 September & 4 October 1730, *Memoirs,* 1:190, 196). Spence's letter of recommendation for Duck—prefixed to all editions of his *Poems*—most clearly shows the construction of an image of Duck that would please elite audiences. Spence obscures the specific circumstances of Duck's life and work, and makes him a character in a "true History." For instance, Spence's account of Duck ("Our retired Philosopher") at study with his friend suggests that his actions have value solely as entertainment for genteel readers. To his patron Duck seems an object of amusement: "I have sometimes thought, how agreeable a thing it would have been, to have been conceal'd within hearing of them, when they were in the midst of some of their most knotty Debates" ("Account," p. xviii). Spence also fabricates the character of untutored

genius for Duck by certifying the authenticity of his verses and by demonstrating the depth of his sensibility to literature: "As I was reading to him, I observ'd that his Countenance chang'd often in the most moving Parts: His Eye was quick and busy all the Time; and, to say the Truth, I never saw Applause, or the shifting of proper Passions, appear so strongly in any Face as in his" (p. xxviii). Spence ends his narrative with a guarantee of Duck's humility, his abdication of authority as a poet, and his subjection to the judgment of his social superiors:

> He was told . . . That he should never speak too highly in Praise of the Poems he had written. He said, "If that was all, he was safe; that was a Thing he could never do, for he could not think highly of them: Gentlemen indeed, he said, might like 'em, because they were made by a poor Fellow in a Barn; but that he knew, as well as any body, that they were not really good in themselves."
>
> (p. xxx)

The value of Duck's poems, then, resides wholly in their appeal as curiosities to an audience of gentlemen. As Spence hints, these supporters would accept and patronize Duck as long as he does not demand recognition and respect as a poet, or as long as he retains the identity that his patrons bestow upon him. Appropriating several pages of Duck's *Poems,* Spence objectifies the poet, declaring him and his works commodities for the entertainment of the polite, and thus qualifies the self-assertion that publishing his work entails. This introduction to Duck's verse undermines the democratic system of letters supposedly created by the book trade; by questioning Duck's capability and authority as a writer, it relegates him to an insignificant position on the margins of English literary culture.

In his own prefatory material to the *Poems,* Duck seems to have adopted completely the prejudices of elite readers. Comparing Caroline to "the Supreme Being, who continually supports the meanest Creature, which his Goodness has produced" (**"To the Queen,"** *Poems,* pp. iii-iv), Duck displaces his creativity onto his patron and obscures himself as the origin of his poems. In his preface, he also denies any impulse toward self-expression, almost as if acknowledging that the act of writing is presumptuous for one of his class: "I have not been so fond of writing, as might be imagin'd from seeing so many Things of mine as are got together in this Book. Several of them are on Subjects that were given me by Persons, to whom I have such great Obligations, that I always thought their Desires Commands" (pp. xi-xii). Duck's self-abnegation shows his awareness of his marginal position in the Augustan literary milieu. While print culture allowed him access to the press, laborers were believed unfit to write, and this contradiction results in Duck's simultaneous presentation and denial of his work. As the poet himself describes it in his address "To a Gentleman, Who Requested a Copy of Verses from the Author": "Ill suit such Tasks with one who holds the Plough, / Such lofty Subjects with a Fate so low" (ll. 9-10).

These lines suggest the extent to which Duck's verse ratifies elite literary conventions. In fact, Duck adds to the authority of such conventions and practices by ultimately adopting them and by proposing few alternatives derived from his native culture. His poems, mostly occasional and mostly written in heroic couplets, take as their subjects the themes of gratitude, contented poverty ("Free from the Cares unwieldy Riches bring"), and Duck's own unworthiness of his benefactors' bounty.[9] Throughout his verses, Duck invokes the standard figures of the English canon; Milton, Pope, Thomson, and Addison are his models for imitation, Addison being singled out as a mentor of morality ("O! may thy Labours be a Star to guide / My Thoughts and Actions o'er Life's devious Tide"),[10] and Milton being reserved the honor of an epigram celebrating his genius ("Ad Joannem Miltonum").

According to scholars and critics, Duck's failure as a poet arises from his over-attention to what he considered the proper themes and forms of literature. From its initial reception to the present, Duck's work has been called derivative. Maynard Mack, for one, states that Pope's estimate of the poet—"no imagination, all imitation"—"say[s] all that is necessary about Duck's poetry," and Duck's most recent biographer admits that his work "exhibits practically no development or evolution."[11] But if Duck's verse seems pedestrian and ordinary, the reasons may not wholly lie in his lack of genius or his exaggerated eagerness to please his patrons.[12] Rather, the poetic forms available to Duck—those modes of articulation that hinder or enable poetic expression at different times—could not be adapted to record the experience of a poet from a class outside the boundaries of polite culture. Form, Raymond Williams argues, is a function of real, historically variable social relationships between people, and between people and things. Arising from these relationships (which are in part based on class), literary form can enforce the cultural hegemony of one group over another by excluding certain articulations and promoting others.[13] And the logic of print solidifies this hegemony by replicating and disseminating examples of such dominant forms as the available, reigning mode of poetic speech.

Duck's career displays how prevailing literary modes urge writers into conformity with the values, beliefs, and tastes of the ruling elite. *The Thresher's Labour,* one of Duck's earliest poems, has the reputation of being his best; critics praise its novelty and authenticity, for it recounts in detail the tasks Duck performed as a farm laborer.[14] Duck's achievement in this work is significant. With its description of the threshers' soul-

draining work, and the "Sweat, the Dust, and suffocating Smoak" that accompany it, the poem breaks new ground: it represents subject matter long ignored by writers and introduces realism into the tradition of stylized poetry on country life. Duck's authoritative comments on rural workers' boredom, fatigue, and mistreatment by their masters ("He counts the Bushels, counts how much a Day; / Then swears we've idled half our Time away" [ll. 72-73]) pose a challenge to the conventions of pastoral verse—a genre often employed by polite poets like Pope and Ambrose Philips. In one passage, for instance, Duck illustrates the difficulty in making verses under the conditions of his work. Unlike the tuneful swains who inhabit the lines of pastorals, the threshers have no mental entertainment to ease the monotony of their tasks:

> But we may think—Alas! what pleasing thing,
> Here, to the Mind, can the dull Fancy bring?
> Our Eye beholds no pleasing Object here,
> No chearful Sound diverts our list'ning Ear.
> The Shepherd well may tune his Voice to sing,
> Inspir'd with all the Beauties of the Spring.
> No Fountains murmur here, no Lambkins play,
> No Linnets warble, and no Fields look gay;
> 'Tis all a gloomy, melancholy Scene,
> Fit only to provoke the Muse's Spleen.
>
> (ll. 52-61)

Threshers, Duck complains, are denied access to the accepted materials of pastoral poetry—fountains, lambs, linnets, and gay fields—and their subjective experience is matter unfit for verse. Realizing that he cannot follow the conventions expected of poems describing rural life, Duck implies that these conventions frustrate his creativity. But while *The Thresher's Labour* appears to criticize the artificiality of pastoral verse, it still adheres to the modes of expression that characterize elite literary forms. In places, the poem betrays signs of the strain involved in accommodating its subject to a polite audience of patrons and educated readers. Duck seems determined to prove himself a cultivated, and therefore acceptable, writer. Labored syntax, periphrasis to achieve a "high" tone ("knotty Weapons" for Crabtree staves), and multiple references to classical mythology surface throughout the poem, as in a passage describing the threshing of the corn:

> Down one, one up, so well they keep the Time,
> The *Cyclops'* Hammers could not truer chime;
> Nor with more heavy Strokes could *Aetna* groan,
> When *Vulcan* forg'd the Arms for *Thetis'* Son.
>
> (ll. 38-41)

Duck's ready imitation of neoclassical forms in later verses may not entirely arise from his weak creativity and strong desire to please his benefactors. Rather, in order to articulate at all, Duck had to write in the forms and styles available to him. And in the 1730s, few or no modes existed for the expression of laboring-class concerns; the vogue for primitivism had not yet begun, and Duck was certainly too intimidated by the custodians of polite culture to initiate new forms of his own. After **The Thresher's Labour,** then, appear poems like **"On Richmond Park,"** a pastoral celebrating "blissful Groves," "flow'ry Plains," and (in a startling turnabout from his original view of farm life) the liberty and happiness of Britain's country "Swains." The representation of rural laborers likewise changes in Duck's **"Description of a Journey to Marlborough."** Passing through the countryside, the poet challenges some threshers to a competition at the "laborious Sport" of mowing and later depicts their feast in his honor: labor which had once been described as "endless Toils" becomes a game, and instead of seeing the feast as the "Cheat" he had called it earlier, he now praises Lord Palmerston for the "gen'rous Treat" given to the mowers (ll. 61-66). It seems that with Duck's adoption of forms like the pastoral and the prospect poem, his literary identity changes. The poet who had portrayed himself as a thresher barred from poetic expression now aligns himself with the owners of the property whose beauty he celebrates in his verse. Significantly, after **The Thresher's Labour,** Duck wrote no more poems about his work on the farm; his success in adapting to the forms of elite culture gave him a poetic voice, but also prevented him from speaking to the concerns of his own class.

Despite the fears of contemporaries like Swift and Pope, Stephen Duck exercised little influence over English literary culture. Not even his popularity with readers could ensure his place in the canon. While booksellers reprinted numerous editions of his poems, and while his works continued to appear in periodicals and collections of verse as late as 1830, Johnson excluded him from the *Lives of the Poets,* and most later anthologists ignore his place in the literary milieu of his day (Davis, pp. 172-73). Rather than attesting to the democratic nature of print culture, Duck's experience reveals how class hegemony over literary expression is preserved even as modes of literary production change. Later in the century, however, the hegemony of polite culture seemed to weaken as more untutored writers brought their works to press. Whereas Duck's success in the 1730s encouraged a few other laborers to seek patronage ("Since Rustick Threshers entertain the Muse / Why may not Bricklayers too their Subjects chuse?"),[15] after 1770 several such writers began to publish independently of a role model. Although these authors still found it difficult to earn a living from their work, the market for copy apparently sustained them for some time: instead of publishing one or two volumes (like Duck), writers such as Ann Yearsley, Robert Bloomfield, and James Woodhouse enjoyed longer careers, often producing many different kinds of literary work.[16] With the growth of the book trade, the opportunities for laboring writers to get their texts printed and distributed to readers apparently increased, and from this change in literary production would seem to follow a more heterogeneous literary culture.

Ann Yearsley's career reveals at once the possibilities for this heterogeneity and the limitations set upon it. Like Duck, Yearsley first grew acquainted with poetry from editions of classic texts; as a young woman in Bristol, she read some Shakespeare, *Paradise Lost,* "Eloisa to Abelard," Young's *Night Thoughts,* and a translation of the *Georgics*—books which her mother, a milkwoman, supposedly borrowed from her employers. The book trade also aided her education by circulating cheap prints: gazing at these pictures displayed in shop windows made Yearsley familiar with mythology.[17] Fragmented as her reading was, it apparently enabled Yearsley to express herself in the poetic language and style common to the time. After reading a manuscript of her verse given to him by Hannah More, Horace Walpole declared himself surprised at the "dignity of her thoughts and the chastity of her style": "Her ear . . . is perfect—but *that* being a gift of nature, amazes me less. Her expressions are more exalted than poetic; and discover taste . . . rather than discover flights of fancy, and wild ideas, as one should expect."[18] More was likewise amazed that "without having ever conversed with any body above her own level, [Yearsley] seems to possess the general principles of sound taste and just thinking."[19] Walpole and More, of course, expected a provincial, unlettered poet to display a primitive manner of writing and an unorthodox, undisciplined aesthetic sense. But the trade's dissemination of print into all regions of England made this exceptional milkwoman familiar with the materials and aesthetics of polite culture. She took to her books and imitated them, perhaps because she sympathized with their largely melancholy themes.[20] And, as Yearsley's sophisticated verse and taste suggest, the trade's circulation of texts, by giving the poet a mode of expression, ensured that she would reproduce the dominant literary forms.

Yearsley's education, however, was not wholly a function of print. Her first patron, Hannah More, also introduced her to the norms of elite culture. More met the poet in September 1784, after seeing a copy of Yearsley's verses. Impressed with the talent evident in "a milker of Cows, and a feeder of Hogs, who has never even *seen* a Dictionary," More took it upon herself to give Yearsley a small allowance that would relieve her poverty and sustain her while she prepared a volume of verse.[21] She also supervised her reading and writing. While commending Yearsley for developing a "professional" interest in literature, she decided to acquaint the poet with Dryden, Ossian, and "the most decent of the Metamorphoses" ("To Elizabeth Robinson Montagu,"

27 September 1784, *Female Spectator,* p. 279); Horace Walpole, More's long-time correspondent, likewise provided a reading list for Yearsley:

> Give her Dryden's *Cock and Fox,* the standard of good sense, poetry, nature and ease. I would recommend others of his tales, but her imagination is already too gloomy, and should be enlivened; for which reason I do not name Mr Gray's *Eton Ode* and *Churchyard.* Prior's *Solomon* (for I doubt his *Alma* . . . is too learned for her limited reading) would be very proper. . . . Read and explain to her a charming poetic familiarity called, *The Blue-Stocking Club* [More's own "Bas Bleu"].
>
> (13 November 1784, *Walpole's Correspondence,* 31:221-22)

Walpole's and More's selection of texts shows both patrons anxious to train Yearsley in accepted poetic forms and subjects. Representing "the standard of good sense, poetry, nature and ease," works by educated writers are offered as models to curb the excesses or faults that distinguish Yearsley's verse from the classics of polite culture.

Despite their professed delight over Yearsley's untutored genius, More and Walpole sought to channel this talent into suitable modes of writing; like Duck's patrons, they felt impelled to cultivate untrained ability rather than leave it to flourish on its own. Their interest in propriety even extends beyond Yearsley's poetry. Keeping the example of Stephen Duck in mind ("an excellent Bard as a *Thrasher,* but as the Court Poet, and rival of Pope, detestable" ["To Elizabeth Robinson Montagu," 27 September 1784, *Female Spectator,* p. 279]), they agree on the necessity of Yearsley's remaining in her station. Since contemporaries defined poetry as something beyond the domain of laborers, More and Walpole insist that Yearsley not take her talent or her writing too seriously. More worries that freeing her from domestic chores would make her "*idle* or *useless*"; Walpole fears that encouraging her poetry would "divert her from the care of her family, and after the novelty is over, leave her worse than she was."[22] Lest Yearsley begin to desire the cultural prestige and authority that polite writers enjoy, Walpole urges More to make her conform to her class: "I am sure you will not only give her counsel for her works, but for her conduct; and your gentleness will blend them so judiciously, that she will mind the friend as well as the mistress. She must remember that she is a Lactilla, not a Pastora, and is to tend real cows, not Arcadian sheep" (13 November 1784, *Walpole's Correspondence,* 31:220-21).

In order to construct Yearsley's identity as "Lactilla"— and to prevent the ambition that her talent might arouse in her—More mediates Yearsley's relation to her audience in a printed introduction to her poetry. *Poems on Several Occasions* appeared in 1785; More had helped prepare the collection by copying the manuscripts and correcting their punctuation and grammar, canvassing for subscribers, and securing her own publisher for the project. As a preface to the poems was included a letter from More to Elizabeth Montagu, dated 20 October 1784. The letter's description of Yearsley in effect fictionalizes her, making her a character in a narrative controlled by More. More's opening paragraphs depict Yearsley's distress and near-starvation as "a scene which will not bear a detail"; she quotes Gray's "Elegy" ("Chill Penury repress'd her noble rage, / And froze the genial current of her soul") by way of apology for Yearsley's unrefined verses, and invokes a genealogy of unlettered geniuses, comparing "our poor Enthusiast" to Shakespeare (pp. v, viii-ix). While More tells readers of the specific hardships under which Yearsley wrote, she at the same time turns to fictions—Gray's impoverished villagers, the image of Shakespeare holding horses at the playhouse door—to describe Yearsley and her career. Other devices also serve to make the poet acceptable to her audience. Aware that readers might censure Yearsley for neglecting her housework for writing, or suspect her of trying to rise above her station, More depicts her as a good wife and mother and a grateful recipient of patrons' attentions—a stock image of women and the poor that the public would find pleasing:

> Pressing, as her distresses are, if I did not think her heart was rightly turned, I should be afraid of proposing such a measure, lest it should unsettle the sobriety of her mind, and, by exciting her vanity, indispose her for the laborious employments of her humble condition; but it would be cruel to imagine that we cannot mend her fortune without impairing her virtue.
>
> (p. xi)

By sentimentalizing Yearsley as a struggling Shakespeare or as Gray's unlettered muse, and by assuring subscribers of the poet's docility as one of the deserving poor, More tries to evoke readers' sympathy and deflect their criticism. But the character that she constructs in the preface also undermines whatever subjectivity that Yearsley's poems might express. Yearsley's access to print hardly allowed her the self-expression that publication seemed to encourage; her patron, who helped bring her work to press, also used print to create "Lactilla." Adopting the same strategy that Spence used—the prefatory narrative or letter of introduction—More, like Spence, attempts to shape the image of the poet that the volume conveys. In her poems, however, Yearsley herself accepts More's and Montagu's transformation of her. "On Mrs. Montagu," for instance, describes the change in Yearsley effected by her patrons' tutelage. "To Misery resign'd" and jealous of the privileges that her benefactors enjoy, Yearsley at first resists their efforts to educate her in the culture and religion of their class: "Unwelcome is the first bright dawn of light / To the dark soul" (ll. 38-39). But later in the poem, she credits them with her enlightenment and release from the antagonism that her class position had aroused in her:

> The effort rude to quench the cheering flame
> Was mine, and e'en on *Stella* [More] could I gaze
> With sullen envy, and admiring pride,
> Till, doubly rous'd by *Montagu,* the pair
> Conspire to clear my dull, imprison'd sense,
> And chase the mists which dimm'd my visual beam.
>
> (ll. 45-50)

"Night" continues the theme of the poet's altered perspective. Despairing of relief for her troubles, Yearsley became "More savage than the nightly-prowling wolf"; an "agony of change" overcomes her, though, when her patrons introduce her to polite life, sentiments, and behavior: "Ah, *Stella!* I'm a convert; thou hast tun'd / My rusting powers to the bright strain of joy" (ll. 209-10).

With few exceptions, Yearsley's *Poems on Several Occasions* validate her patrons' attempts to mold her into their ideal of "Lactilla." While the poet occasionally asserts herself as independent of More's control ("Mine's a stubborn and a savage will; / No customs, manners, or soft arts I boast, / On my rough soul your nicest rules are lost" ["To (Stella); on Her Accusing the Author of Flattery," ll. 8-10]), the poems in this collection, with their repeated themes of gratitude and awakened sensibility, assert that Yearsley welcomed More's influence over her work. Like Duck's **Poems on Several Occasions,** Yearsley's volume sustains rather than subverts ruling-class authority over literature, for it upholds the belief in a homogeneous culture to which outsiders must aspire.

Given the exclusivity of this culture, More's connection with Yearsley's project was essential for its success; her patronage legitimized the work in the eyes of the subscribers she solicited. These subscribers included such luminaries of English arts as William Cowper, Frances Burney, Mrs. Garrick, Sir Joshua Reynolds, Anna Seward, and Horace Walpole. Besides bringing recognition to Yearsley, the edition also brought her a small fortune. A deed signed by Yearsley and her husband gave More the power to invest the profits from the sale—about £350—in the names of More and Montagu; More was to distribute the interest from that sum to Yearsley "to cloathe her family and furnish her House."[23]

Acting in the manner conventional to patrons (and consistent with their suspicion of the poor), More took responsibility for the Yearsley's finances. But in contrast to Stephen Duck, who quietly accepted his patrons' guardianship, Yearsley rebelled against this control. In a letter to More she accused her patron of showing more vanity than generosity, and demanded the right to man-age her earnings from the poems: "You have led me to sign a settlement which defrauds me of my right, and makes it ever received your peculiar gift" (16 September 1785, *Female Spectator,* p. 285). Taken aback by Yearsley's resentment, More charged "our milkwoman" with "open and notorious ingratitude," and criticized herself for encouraging Yearsley's self-assertion ("Is not this great Babylon that *I* have built?").[24] Her friend Walpole vented his outrage in similar terms: "How strange that vanity should expel gratitude—does not the wretched woman owe her fame to you as well as her affluence!" ("To Hannah More," 14 October 1787, *Walpole's Correspondence,* 31:254-55).

Although scholars often attribute the cause of this quarrel to Yearsley's defensive pride, the dispute between patron and client also has its roots in the dynamics of commodified print. This system of literary production made the author rather than the patron the source of a text's monetary and aesthetic value; patronage, by contrast, required that writers present their works to an educated elite whose gifts supported them and whose approval guaranteed their success. For instance, Duck, in his dedication of the **Poems,** states that his work belongs to his benefactor: "Your Majesty has indeed the same Right to them, as You have to the Fruits of a Tree, which You have transplanted out of a barren Soil into a fertile and beautiful Garden" (**Poems,** pp. iii-iv). The sale of texts for money, however, disrupts this relation between patrons and authors; when print is commodified, authors are presumed to have a property in their works which they sell to booksellers for a price—a sum determined by the "worth," or the reputation and abilities, of the author. In the fifty years separating Duck and Yearsley, the increased commercial trade in literature strengthened this idea of authorial ownership, which the House of Lords in 1774 finally codified into law.[25] Yearsley invokes the concept of authors' exclusive property in their texts when she announces her "right" to the profits of her poems. More and Walpole, by contrast, insist on the privileges and respect due to patrons, whose social prestige and financial support bolster the value of a work.[26]

Yearsley's refusal to accept More's management of her career (and More's surprise at Yearsley's "ingratitude") reveals the threat that commodified print posed to the cultural dominance of a learned elite. In a "Narrative" that she prefixed to the fourth edition of *Poems on Several Occasions* (and to her subsequent *Poems on Various Subjects*), Yearsley used her access to print to further subvert More's authority: this narrative, addressed to her subscribers, justifies the poet's part in the quarrel over control of her earnings while condemning More's role in it. Through dramatizing her confrontation with More and reflecting on More's conduct, Yearsley creates fictions of herself and of her patron much as More had created the fiction of Yearsley in her prefatory letter to Montagu. Yearsley's narrative, in fact, seems to mimic More's letter and suggests the poet's appropriation of a literary form previously restricted to patrons; More, who had used her preface to simplify and diminish Yearsley's identity, finds this strategy turned upon herself. The narrative opposes Yearsley's version of events to More's "varnished tale," and uses the clichés that More had earlier employed to characterize Yearsley—the humble peasant, the good mother—as a shield to protect the poet against More's attacks. It represents More as proud, capricious, and disposed toward "low scurrility" when contradicted. Yearsley, however, appears submissive, complaisant ("I relinquished all, even the rights of a mother, at Miss H. More's request"),[27] and oppressed by obligations. Her request for a copy of the deed that made More and Montagu her trustees arises from "the most powerful and natural [motives] that can posses the female breast"—concern for her children's future (*Poems on Various Subjects,* p. xxi); by implication, the offense More took at this request results from the egotism common to spinsters. Yearsley also portrays her patron as unforgiving. Communicating with More through their bookseller—an act that suggests their equality as professional writers—Yearsley offers to end the dispute if More would print a paragraph exonerating her character in the Bristol *Public Advertiser* (More refused). Finally, Yearsley closes the narrative by denying that her poems owe any of their merit to More's corrections and by proposing a new volume of work to prove her literary talent. Although a laborer and a stranger to polite culture, Yearsley (and not her patron) gives her poetry its value.

In her narrative, Yearsley adopts a form of discourse that had been limited to the educated elite: she defines More's character as More had defined hers, and Spence had defined Duck's. And usurping the privilege of the elite did not ruin her career: for her second work—*Poems on Various Subjects* (1787)—she secured a good number of subscribers, found a bookseller willing to publish the volume, and discovered a nonintrusive "protector" in the earl of Bristol. Yearsley's consciousness of her exclusive control over her writing, and over the public presentation of herself that writing allows, appears throughout the poems in this collection. In "To Those Who Accuse the Author of Ingratitude," Yearsley refutes the reputation that her detractors bestow upon her by rumor or in print; she claims that critics are too ignorant to fathom her:

> Ask the World's great Sire,
> Why, in Creation's system, *He* dare fix
> More orbs than your weak sense shall e'er discern?
> Then scan the feelings of Lactilla's soul.

> (ll. 45-48)

By insisting on her depth of character, Yearsley exposes the presumption of those like More who affect to understand her motives and thus reduce her to the common stereotypes of the simple, worthy peasant or the rude, ungrateful pauper. But Yearsley not only rejects these attempts to label and contain her subjectivity; she also rejects the ruling-class culture that allows this containment to occur. In a poem "Addressed to Ignorance," Yearsley reasons that knowledge of the ancients, although considered essential for writers at the time, would only restrain her creativity. Invoking Ignorance as a deity, Yearsley prefers inspired, if unpolished, composition to feeding on "scraps of the Sage":

> Then come, gentle Goddess, sit full in my looks;
> Let my accents be sounded by thee:
> While Crito in pomp, bears his burden of books,
> On the plains of wild Nature I'm free.

> (ll. 9-12)

Her poem to an "Unlettered Poet, on Genius Unimproved" reveals the same disregard for the canon of elite literature. Reassuring her colleague about his abilities, Yearsley states that her alienation from this literary culture empowered rather than inhibited her writing:

> Like thee, estrang'd
> From Science, and old Wisdom's classic lore,
> I've patient trod the wild entangled path
> Of unimprov'd Idea. Dauntless Thought
> I eager seiz'd, no formal Rule e'er aw'd;
> No Precedent controul'd; no Custom fix'd
> My independent spirit.

> (ll. 34-40)

Here Yearsley echoes theorists like Edward Young ("Conjectures on Original Composition") and William Duff (*An Essay on Original Genius*) on the superiority of innate genius as the source of poetic invention ("Deep in the soul live ever tuneful springs, / Waiting the touch of Ecstasy, which strikes / Most pow'rful on defenceless, untaught Minds" [ll. 49-51]). Yet Yearsley is not merely justifying her work by repeating commonplaces of contemporary literary criticism. Instead, her disregard for conventional, time-honored rules and customs guiding literary production has an explicit political focus. Young and Duff, for instance, offer Homer and Shakespeare as examples of innate poetic talent; their idealization of these writers coincides with critical judgments made on them since the late seventeenth century, and both unlettered geniuses already enjoyed distinction in contemporary culture. Yearsley, however, selects Chatterton for her model and makes this selection at least partly because of their common social class. In her "Elegy" on the poet, Chatterton appears a "hapless Genius . . . by Pride opprest"; although "wrapt in [Apollo's] glories," he is neglected by patrons until "latent Anguish" eventually kills him. The poet's ghost, though, remains to inspire "some rustic Muse" who may remember him, and Yearsley ends the poem by invoking his influence: "Yet shalt thou live! nor shall my song be vain / That dares not thine, but dares to imitate" (ll. 55-56). Yearsley's affinities with Chatterton extend beyond their possession of untrained talent: she identifies with his abuse by the polite world and sees upper-class control of literary production as the cause of his misery: "Scorning to fawn at laughing Insult's knee" (l. 8), Chatterton is left to die. By declaring Chatterton her predecessor, Yearsley attempts to remove herself from the literary tradition and system of cultural production that patrons like More uphold.

In her "Elegy" and throughout *Poems on Various Subjects,* Yearsley displays an acute political consciousness of the hegemony exercised by the guardians of culture: their financial support (or the lack thereof) makes laboring writers dependent on their approval; their social power enables them to determine authoritatively writers' characters in print; and their aesthetic system, grounded upon a knowledge of ancient and modern literary classics, devalues the work of uneducated writers. Of course, the publication of Yearsley's verse challenges this control; its appearance suggests that commodified print reduced the cultural dominance of the ruling elite. Moreover, booksellers, readers (especially in Bristol), and critics endorsed her work. Despite her break with More, Yearsley's poems continued to appear in the Bristol newspapers, the *Monthly* and *Critical Review* generously praised her writings, and her profits from booksellers enabled her to establish a circulating library at Bristol Hot Wells.[28] But after Yearsley's final collection of poems, *The Rural Lyre,* appeared in 1796, printed evaluations of her work changed and her reputation fell. Twenty-five years after her death, Southey included her in his *Lives and Works of Uneducated Poets*; by categorizing her in this fashion, he separates her from mainstream literary culture and ranks her with other writers valuable as curiosities. Southey justifies her exclusion from the canon because of her ignorance and her failure to master the proper forms of expression: "Very few passages can be extracted from her writings which would have any other value than as indicating powers which the possessor knew not how to employ" (pp. 132-33). Writing more than a century later, Joyce Tompkins agrees with Southey's opinion of the poet's work. According to her account, Yearsley could not meet the requirements of eighteenth-century poetic style, since "the highly formalized couplet and blank verse required a more firm and delicate touch than she could give" (p. 96). Tompkins therefore recommends leaving her work in deserved obscurity: "It is certainly unlikely that her poems will ever be republished, and indeed the reading public has no need of them" (p. 96). Finally, More's biographers denigrate Yearsley for her conduct as well as her writing. From 1834 to as late as 1952, biographies of More commend More's condescension and deplore Yearsley's self-assertion and unseemly confidence in her talent.[29]

Although Yearsley succeeds in exposing the political suppression underlying elite literary practice, subsequent writers judge her according to the norms of that practice. Yearsley's access to print allowed her to challenge publicly the systems of patronage and aesthetics that molded her subjectivity and verse into conformity with the models preferred by the polite. Yet at the same time, print encouraged the replication of dominant cultural values, and secured their influence for years after the poet's death. The result has been scholars' disregard for Yearsley's critique of contemporary letters. Until very recently, the reification of literary form and the apolitical account of patronage set forth in discussions of Yearsley silenced the poet's dissent from elite culture by discouraging us from reading her work.[30]

*   *   *

As the careers of Duck and Yearsley show, commodified print by no means democratized eighteenth-century writing. Rather, the conventions of polite literary culture—conventions promoted by upper-class benefactors—nearly overdetermine Duck's works and devalue Yearsley's poetry of resistance. While the book trade might have provided many writers with an alternative to patronage, eminent people like Clarke, Spence, and More could still exert control over literary production. Besides bestowing the traditional gift of money, Duck's and Yearsley's patrons exercised their authority by educating writers with "model" texts, preparing and correcting their volumes for the press, and creating a new literary form—the prefatory narrative—designed to influence writers' reception by the public. The system of commercial print, it seems, often increased the cultural hegemony of the elite instead of eroding it. But the experience of Duck and Yearsley not only suggests the shortcomings apparent in histories of writers' relation to print; it also reveals that the focus of such histories is limited to the point of distortion. Most of these studies center their analyses on canonical figures such as Congreve, Hume, or Johnson, while the roles that lesser-known writers played in the literary milieu are minimized or overlooked. This concentration on major figures in literature, and the assumptions about the egalitarian or authoritarian state of letters that are derived from their careers, serve to collapse important distinctions between writers and obscure the anxieties and conflicts that characterized the market in texts. Reconstructing the issues that arose around publications by laborers will not entirely revise literary history. But it will illustrate that the book trade, rather than giving a forum to writers of various cultural backgrounds, actually promoted a homogeneous literature by encouraging the repression of class diversity among authors.

Notes

1. *Printing Technology, Letters and Samuel Johnson* (Princeton: Princeton Univ., 1987), pp. 4-5. I am grateful to the Ohio University Research Committee for its financial support of this article, and to Frank Donoghue for his careful reading of the manuscript.

2. See Beljame, *Men of Letters and the English Public in the Eighteenth Century,* ed. Bonamy Dobrée, trans. E. O. Lorimer (1897; London: Kegan Paul, Trench, Trubner, 1948), pp. 317, 385; Collins, *Authorship in the Days of Johnson: Being a Study of the Relation between Author, Patron, Publisher and Public, 1726-1780* (London: Robert Holden, 1927), p. 196; Saunders, *The Profession of English Letters* (London: Routledge & Kegan Paul, 1964), pp. 123-24; Williams, *The Long Revolution* (N.Y.: Columbia Univ., 1961), pp. 230-45.

3. *The Adventurer,* no. 115, *The Yale Edition of The Works of Samuel Johnson,* 15 vols. (New Haven: Yale Univ., 1958-), 2:459.

4. *The Correspondence of Alexander Pope,* ed. George Sherburn, 5 vols. (Oxford: Clarendon, 1956), 3:132.

5. "Gay and The Duchess of Queensbury to Swift," 8 Nov. 1730, *Correspondence of Alexander Pope,* 3:146. In his response to Gay, Swift reports the rumor that Duck was a candidate for the post of Poet Laureate: "The vogue of our few honest folks here is that Duck is absolutely to Succeed Eusden in the Lawrell, the contention being between Concannan or Theobald, or some other Hero of the Dunciad" ("To Gay and The Duchess of Queensbury," 19 Nov. 1730, *Correspondence of Alexander Pope,* 3:151).

6. I owe all biographical information regarding Duck to Rose Mary Davis, *Stephen Duck, the Thresher Poet,* University of Maine Studies, 2nd ser., no. 8 (Orono: Univ. Press, 1926).

7. "An Account of the Author," in *Poems on Several Occasions,* by Stephen Duck, 2nd edn. (London, 1737), p. xx. Hereafter "Account" in text. Duck's poor pronunciation of verses reveals the extent to which he gleaned his knowledge of poetry from texts. As Spence observes, "his Ideas of the Notes in a Verse, and his Manner of repeating the same Verse, are often different: For he points out an harmonious Line well enough; and yet he generally spoils its Harmony by his way of speaking it" (p. xix).

8. "Alured Clarke to Mrs. Clayton," 19 Sept. 1730, *Memoirs of Viscountess Sundon,* ed. Katharine Thomson, 2 vols. (London, 1847), 1:193, 191; "Alured Clarke to Mrs. Clayton," 8 Oct. 1730, 1:198.

9. These poems include "On Poverty" and "Gratitude: A Pastoral."

10. Duck praises Addison in "A Description of a Journey to Marlborough" (ll. 461-82).

11. Mack, *Alexander Pope: A Life* (N.Y.: Norton; New Haven: Yale Univ., 1985), p. 905n; Davis, p. 165. Michael Paffard declares Duck's poems "empty and unoriginal, apart from a few neatly turned epigrams" ("Stephen Duck, the Thresher Poet," *History Today* 27 [1977]: 472) and Robert Southey maintains that although Duck's "talents for poetry were imitative rather than inventive," he was "incapable of imitating what he clearly saw was best" (*The Lives and Works of the Uneducated Poets,* ed. J. S. Childers [London: Humphrey Milford, 1925], p. 113).

12. Southey (pp. 118-19) and Paffard (p. 472) offer the desire to please as the reason for Duck's mediocrity; H. Gustav Klaus, however, provides a more complex explanation: "The pressure toward aesthetic integration (particularly during the Augustan Age) was too strong for the poetic and intellectual capacity of the plebian poets to be able to escape its effects" (*The Literature of Labour: Two Hundred Years of Working-Class Writing* [N.Y.: St. Martin's, 1985], p. 19).

13. *Marxism and Literature* (N.Y.: Oxford Univ., 1977), pp. 186-91. Fredric Jameson elaborates on the relation between literary form and ways of life: "The adequation of object to subject or of form to content can exist as an imaginative possibility only where in some way or other it has been concretely realized in social life itself, so that formal realizations, as well as formal defects, are taken as the signs of some deeper corresponding social and historical configuration which it is the task of criticism to explore" (*Marxism and Form: Twentieth-Century Dialectical Theories of Literature* [Princeton: Princeton Univ., 1971], p. 331).

14. Raymond Williams, for instance, praises the "simple power" of "The Thresher's Labour" in *The Country and the City* (N.Y.: Oxford Univ., 1973), p. 88.

15. This couplet introduces Robert Tatersal's vol. of verse, *The Bricklayer's Miscellany* (1734).

16. Klaus notes how uneducated writers in the century's later decades differ from their predecessors (*The Literature of Labour,* pp. 6-7).

17. Since no biography of Yearsley exists, I have taken my information about her early years from Hannah More's intro. to Yearsley's 1st vol. of verse, *Poems on Several Occasions* (London, 1785).

18. "To Hannah More," 13 Nov. 1784, *Horace Walpole's Correspondence,* ed. W. S. Lewis, 48 vols. (New Haven: Yale Univ., 1937-83), 31:219.

19. More, "A Prefatory Letter to Mrs. Montagu," *Poems on Several Occasions,* p. xvi.

20. As More notes, the Yearsley family's near-starvation, and the death of Yearsley's mother from malnutrition, "left a settled impression of sorrow on her mind" ("To Mrs. Montagu," *Poems,* p. v).

21. "To Elizabeth Robinson Montagu," 22 Oct. 1784, *The Female Spectator: English Women and Writers Before 1800,* ed. Mary R. Mahl & Helene Koon (Bloomington: Indiana Univ.; Old Westbury: Feminist Press, 1977), p. 280.

22. "To Elizabeth Robinson Montagu," 22 Oct. 1784, *Female Spectator,* p. 280; "To Hannah More," 13 Nov. 1784, *Walpole's Correspondence,* 31:220.

23. "To Elizabeth Robinson Montagu," June 1785, *Female Spectator,* p. 282. More set forth the terms of the deed (signed on 10 June 1785) for Montagu's approval: "I have laid out the money in your name, madam, and mine, having first had an instrument drawn up by the Lawyer signed by Yearsley and his wife, allowing us the controul of the money, and putting it out of the Husband's power to touch it."

24. "To Elizabeth Carter," 1785, *Memoirs of the Life and Correspondence of Mrs. Hannah More,* ed. William Roberts, 3rd edn., 4 vols. (London, 1835), 1:390-91.

25. For an account of how the concept of literary property affected writers and their work, see Mark Rose, "The Author as Proprietor: *Donaldson v. Becket* and the Genealogy of Modern Authorship," *Representations* 23 (Summer 1988): 51-85.

26. Donna Landry argues that More's concept of patronage conflicts with her appreciation for Yearsley's unusual talents. While admiring the poet for persisting in her craft despite her hardships, "More cannot countenance the move towards fracturing the 'natural' connection between literature and middle-class privilege that Yearsley's independent pursuit of a literary career might bring about" ("The Resignation of Mary Collier: Some Problems in a Feminist Literary History," in *The New Eighteenth Century,* ed. Felicity Nussbaum & Laura Brown [N.Y.: Methuen, 1987], pp. 100-01).

27. "Mrs. Yearsley's Narrative," *Poems on Various Subjects* (London, 1787), pp. xvi-xvii.

28. *The Monthly Review,* for instance, praised *Poems on Various Subjects* for its "originality of thought and expression" and its "boldness and grandeur of imagery": "The justness of the observation, *Poeta nascitur, non fit,* was never more powerfully exemplified than by herself" (November 1787). *The Critical Review* expressed the same opinion of Yearsley's work: "In regard to modulation of numbers, particularly in blank verse, we know few authors superior to the Bristol milk-woman. Her sentiments are often equally just and original, her diction strong and animated, and her pauses judiciously varied" (November 1787). Both reviews also took Yearsley's side in her conflict with More, and commended her "Narrative" for its "proper spirit." Regard for Yearsley's work remained high into the next decade; as late as 1795, the booksellers G. G. and J. Robinson paid her £200 for her novel, *The Royal Captives.* For an account of Yearsley's career after More, see J. M. S. Tompkins, "The Bristol Milkwoman," in *The Polite Marriage: Eighteenth-Century Essays* (Cambridge: Cambridge Univ., 1938), pp. 58-102.

29. These biographies range from Roberts's *Memoirs* (1834) to M. G. Jones's *Hannah More* (Cambridge: Cambridge Univ., 1952).

30. Moira Ferguson's recent article is invaluable in resurrecting interest in Yearsley and in guiding readers to sources of information about the poet. See "Resistance and Power in the Life and Writings of Ann Yearsley," *The Eighteenth Century: Theory and Interpretation* 27 (Fall 1986): 247-68.

E. P. Thompson (essay date 1989)

SOURCE: Thompson, E. P. Introduction to The Thresher's Labour *by Stephen Duck and* The Woman's Labour *by Mary Collier,* edited by E. P. Thompson & Marian Sugden, pp. i-xiii. London: The Merlin Press, 1989.

[*In the following essay, Thompson contrasts Duck's* The Thresher's Labour *with Collier's response to it, concluding that the latter is sharper in its depiction of the life of farm laborers, as well as more attuned to nuances of gender and class.*]

[**The Thresher's Labour** and *The Woman's Labour*] should be more widely known and enjoyed than they are. Stephen Duck's is still remembered, but Mary Collier's is known only to a few specialists. Both are vigorous poems in which a way of livelihood is imaginatively realised. Both betray cultural insecurities when they attempt to follow the polite models of the time, and then recover authenticity when the details of habitual labour take us into places for which the polite culture provides little precedent.

Both poems are about daily labour. It is interesting that, in each case, this is the best poem that the poet wrote. Duck wrote and published a good deal, but the rest of his output is deservedly forgotten, and much the same is true of the small published output of Collier. This is not just a judgement from the standpoint of social history—although, obviously, authentic accounts of labour by labourers have a particular interest. It is also the case that the poets' feelings were far more directly engaged when they reflected on threshing or on laundering than when they turned to approved 'poetic' themes, and in the case of *The Woman's Labour,* the gender polemic gives an additional lift and wit to the lines.

Stephen Duck was born in 1705 in Great Charlton in Wiltshire. His family was, perhaps, of 'husbandman' or upper labouring status, aspiring to be yeomen. Stephen was sent to a local charity school. By one account he was learning so fast that his 'prudent Parent . . . removed her Son from School to the Plow, lest he might become too fine a Gentleman for the Family that produced him.' By another (and more reliable) account he attended until he was 14—a late school-age for a labourer's child. He worked for a while with his father, who for a short time was able to rent a small farm. Then he went into service, living-in with one farmer or another. When he married in 1724 he presumably took a cottage of his own, where two sons and a daughter were born to his wife Ann. Early editions of his poems describe him as 'lately a poor thresher', with a weekly wage of 4s 6d.

At about the time of his marriage he set about his self-education, in such time as he could snatch from work, sometimes setting to his books late at night, sometimes sitting down 'all over Sweat and Heat' to read in an interval of labour. From arithmetic he graduated to poetry. He had a friend who had been in service in London, and who had a library of two or three dozen books, which included some volumes of the *Spectator,* a translation of 'Seneca's Morals', and *Paradise Lost.* He also bought and borrowed other books, including an odd volume of Shakespeare (with seven plays), Dryden's 'Virgil', Bysshe's *Art of Poetry,* Butler's 'Hudibras', and some Addison. There was also some Ovid in translation and the *London Spy.*

We owe knowledge of this reading to the Reverend Joseph Spence, Professor of Poetry at Oxford University, who spent the better part of a week talking with Duck in 1730. Duck had delighted in ballads and in singing from his childhood, but the acquisition of polite literature required an essay in translation. He pored over the works with Bailey's dictionary and an English grammar beside him, and, in Spence's words,

> He has got English just as we get Latin. Most of his Language in Conversation, as well as in his Poems, is acquir'd by reading . . . His common Talk is made up of the good Stile, with a mixture of the Rustick.

He was soon writing verses, and burning them, and by 1729 (when he was twenty-four) he was being talked about as a local wonder. When his third child was

christened one of the women attending boasted to the officiating clergyman that 'Mr Duck was a Man of great Learning, and had Wit enough to be a Parson.' Several clergy and local gentry became interested, suggested themes to him, and his verses 'were handed about the Country with great Applause in Manuscript'. He was even 'admitted to the Tables of a great many worthy Gentlemen'. His reputation rested less upon *The Thresher's Labour* than upon 'The Shunammite'; a formal literary production based on the Book of Kings, 2, IV which earned high praise from Joseph Spence for its epic machinery and observance of proprieties.

The genius in the threshing barn became a theme of genteel conversation and a target for competitive patronage. When the Earl of Macclesfield visited Hampshire in the summer of 1730 he 'sent for' Duck. Dr Alured Clarke, Prebendary of Winchester Cathedral, took a particular and possessive interest in the thresher poet. He had highly-placed friends, including Mrs Clayton (subsequently Lady Sundon), an influential lady-in-waiting to Queen Caroline. Dr Clarke sent Duck's poems to Mrs Clayton, who told the queen about the rustic genius and (on September 11th) the Earl of Macclesfield read some of the verses to Caroline. 'Her Majesty resolv'd immediately to take him out of his obscurity,' and he was summoned to her presence.

Dr Clarke's letters to Mrs Clayton survive, and they show how the two of them were managing this interesting affair. The queen had already indicated that she would settle an income on Stephen Duck, who would at first be employed in some gardening at Kew and in repairing his deficient education. On September 19, Dr Clarke wrote from Winchester that he had had 'the Thresher' with him all week, preparing him for Her Majesty's bounty. He would send Duck to Windsor in a fortnight, but his family would follow afterwards 'when he is settled and ready to receive them'. An additional sum had been gathered for him, but Duck had 'promised not to meddle with any of the money'. Clarke advised that the money (which he was sending on to Mrs Clayton) 'should be put out upon security for the benefit of his family, or for his own use, if misconduct or any other accident should make it expedient for him to return into Wiltshire'. It seems that the elevation of 'poor Stephen' (as these correspondents sometimes referred to him) was probationary and conditional upon his good conduct. Clarke further advised that Duck should read in the theory of horticulture, for 'then he will be sure of a provision for his family if his muse should forsake him'.

On October 4th Stephen Duck was at length despatched—not (as it seemed best on second thoughts) to the Court at Windsor but to Kew. He seems to have been concerned about his wife (of whom 'he speaks so well') and he planned to return soon and fetch his family with him. He was accompanied and followed by letters to Mrs Clayton in which Clarke advised as to his reading. He must be given Burnet's *Theory of the Earth,* Ray's *Wisdom of God in the Creation,* and Dr Clark's *Rohault,* which would introduce him to 'Descartes' System'. He must also get Pope's *Essay on Criticism* by heart, and Clarke even sent on a note of introduction to Pope—not because he approved of such a disloyal fellow but because 'it would be prudent not to expose [Duck] to the malice of the Dunciad Club'. Clarke's next letter gave further advice on reading, and his next (October 15) enclosed an account, from a farmer in Duck's village, of the death of Stephen's wife, Ann. In response the Prebendary lied to the farmer, saying he was not certain where Stephen Duck was; and, in a letter to Duck, he made no mention of the small matter that his wife had died, since (he explained to Mrs Clayton) 'I could not be sure you would think it proper to deject him with such ill news before Her Majesty had seen him . . .' Clarke had placed Duck completely in Mrs Clayton's charge, and no doubt he would be returned to his bereaved family 'whenever you think proper to send him'. Clarke supposed that Duck would board his children out somewhere in the country. (At least one of his two sons was to be schooled at Eton). Ten days later (October 25th) Dr Clarke's spirits had risen once more. Ann's death might stimulate Stephen to produce verses worthy of the queen's patronage; 'I do not know but what we may promise ourselves one of his best strains of poetry on this occasion, from the natural and constant correspondence there is between the mind and the affections'. Patronage of this order is simply a form taken by the conspiracy of the polite against the poor.

Queen Caroline granted to Duck £30 (and perhaps more) per annum and a small house in Richmond, close to her own favourite residence at Richmond Lodge. A tutor was found to help 'poor Stephen' in the Latin tongue. But Dr Clarke advised—despite the pirated editions of Duck's poems—that there should be a delay in any authorised edition, since this 'may give him time to make considerable alterations in what he has done . . .' Duck had been extracted in one moment from his home, his occupation, his community, and also his family; and his patrons were doing their best to tame and make polite his muse.

Some social drama was going on which it is difficult now to interpret. In one sense Stephen Duck's story dramatises the almost unbridgeable gap which had developed in the early eighteenth century between polite and plebeian cultures. The early editions of Duck's poems (1730, 1731 and 1733) were all pirated, and they include an unauthorised biographical note in which someone who pretended to Duck's acquaintance described how his wife, Ann, was always scolding him for neglecting his labour, 'and when he was Scanning

his Lines, she would oftentimes run out and raise the whole Neighbourhood, telling them "that her Husband dealt with the Devil, and was going mad because he did nothing all day but talk to himself, and tell his Fingers".' True or false (it was probably false) the story is symptomatic of the times; it stereotypes what the gulf between the 'good Stile' and 'the Rustick' was supposed to be. On the other hand, this gulf was not quite unbridgeable. Genius could take wing and fly across. A sardonic critic (possibly Pope) noted of Stephen Duck's first appearances at Queen Caroline's court—

> All the Wits and Criticks of the Court flock'd about him, delighted to see a *Clown* with a ruddy hale Complexion and in his own long Hair, so top-full of Poetry; and at the first sight of him all agreed he was born to be *Poet Laureate.*

Contradictory impulses were at work. The genteel were wary of enthusiasm and the strategies of the polite culture were intended to discourage the uncultivated and the rude. In the 1730s there was little Romantic yearning for the primitive. Yet at a time when nearly every genteel accomplishment went about in wigs, there was at least novelty in encountering a poet in his own hair and speaking in an unclassical tongue. And since Duck had made painstaking efforts to cultivate himself, he was an estimable object of patronage. Joseph Spence wrote to Pope that "Tis a Man without anything of what is cald Education, grown up into an Excellent Poet all at once . . . One sees the Strugles of a great Soul in him . . . his Ignorance as he manages it has something even agreeable in it.' (Pope thought little of Duck's verse, but he told Gay that the man was 'harmless', and they seem to have co-existed at Richmond agreeably as neighbours).

The discovery and patronage of merit reflected honour also on the patron. Queen Caroline was no judge of English poetry; she was German by birth, she conversed with her family in French, and her command of English was always imperfect. But she was a good judge of the gestures of patronage, at a time when ostentatious liberality was part of the necessary public image of the great.

The list of subscribers at the front of the 1736 edition of Duck's *Poems on Several Occasions* is headed by His Royal Highness the Prince of Wales, and includes four princesses, seventeen dukes and duchesses, forty-three countesses, earls, marquises and viscounts, the archbishops of Canterbury and of York and eight other bishops, three Lord Chief Justices, the Master of the Rolls, Sir Robert Walpole, the Speaker of the House of Commons, the Recorder of the City of London, thirty-nine Ladies, thirty-seven Lords, a multitude of baronets, gentry and clergy, and even a few humble mortals who included Alexander Pope and Jonathan Swift. It is a remarkable subscription, and it suggests that the modest and mild-mannered Duck had made few personal enemies. It also suggests that the subscribers thought it politic to stand well with Duck's patron, Queen Caroline. Lord Palmerston extended the gesture of patronage from the individual to the class, by appropriating the rent of an acre of land to provide an annual dinner and strong beer to the threshers of Charlton in honour of their former comrade—a dinner which Duck himself once attended.

What Stephen Duck thought about all this it is not possible to know. He did say that gentlemen might like his poems 'because they were made by a poor Fellow in a Barn'. But before his sudden translation to the court, the poet he most 'admired and doted on' was Milton, a poet who did not write in a wig. (It is said that Duck had committed most of *Paradise Lost* to memory.) From the time of his elevation, notions of propriety elbowed aside the Miltonic impulse. Duck was prompted, advised on his reading, educated in the classics, and made a yeoman of the guard. He married Sarah Big, Queen Caroline's housekeeper at Kew Green. The queen constructed an ornate grotto called 'Merlin's Cave', supplied with a collection of books, and Duck was appointed librarian and caretaker. He became an object of envy to the unpatronised, and of more general ridicule. Swift wrote:

> The thresher, Duck, could o'er the Queen prevail:
> The proverb says, no fence against a flail.
> From *threshing* corn, he turns to *thresh* his brains,
> For which her Majesty allows him *grains*:
> Tho' 'tis confest, that those who ever saw
> His poems, think them all not worth *a straw.*

From the moment that he left the thresher's barn it was downhill all the way. Of his subsequent verse Raymond Williams has written (in *The Country and the City*) that 'it is easy to feel the strain of this labourer's voice as it adapts, slowly, to the available models in verse: the formal explanation, the anxious classical reference, the arranged subordinate clauses of that self-possessed literary manner'. This is well said, but I cannot agree that the adaptation is slow. Duck capitulated at once to whatever his patrons expected or advised, presenting them with self-deprecating, mannered, and sometimes abjectly deferential poems. He also wrote occasional pieces (*To His Royal Highness, the Duke of Cumberland, on His [Twelfth] Birth-Day*) as the Queen's unofficial laureate. It is not (John Lucas has written) that Duck's poems are incompetent. He works hard at mastering the modes and proprieties of the time, and his poems read like accomplished exercises or studied imitations of approved forms—Pindarics, Horatian Odes, epistles and the rest; but 'poem after poem

contains its unsurprisingly apt classical allusion, its stock simile, its tamely generalised diction'. In one of his better exercises (**'To Death—An Irregular Ode'**) he confessed:

> I, like the rest, advance my Lays;
> With uncouth Numbers, rumble forth a Song,
> Sedately dull, to celebrate thy Praise;
> And lash, and spur the heavy lab'ring Muse along.

The best of his later poems may be **'A Description of a Journey to Marlborough, Bath, Portsmouth, &c'**, in which, amidst ingratiating passages to patrons, there is a humdrum authenticity of a travel journal, and, as when he tries his hand at mowing once more, a stirring of regret at his life's translation. In 1746 he was ordained in the Church of England; he drew large congregations as a preacher at Kew Chapel, and he became Rector of Byfleet in Surrey in 1752. In 1756 he drowned himself in some water behind 'The Black Lion' in Reading.

The Thresher's Labour commences firmly in a capitalist countryside. The substantial tenant farmer is counting 'the Profits of the Year', but is anxious about paying 'threat'ning Landlord's Rent'. The farmer 'calls his Threshers forth', and the labourers are clearly tied by bonds of obligation as well as need to the farmer. The labour appears to be at day or week rates, and discipline is maintained by the direct surveillance of the employer. Duck's description of threshing disabuses us of any notion that 'mechanical' and repetitive labour must await the coming of industrialism and the production-line.

The hay harvest commences light-heartedly and competitively, but soon it also assumes its own monotony. In the brief interval between the hay and cereal harvest, those labourers who are also threshers (and therefore have some permanence on the farm's labour force) return to their work in the barns. At cereal harvest, once again vigour and enthusiasm give way to exhaustion:

> Before us we perplexing Thistles find,
> And Corn blown adverse with the ruffling Wind:
> Behind our Backs the Female Gleaners wait,
> Who sometimes stoop, and sometimes hold a Chat. . . .

We end with the obligatory set-piece of the carrying-in of the harvest, followed by the harvest-home supper with the ritual inversion of social orders as the master serves his own labourers. 'But the next morning soon reveals the Cheat.'

Duck's poem reveals that the women perform only light, marginal contributions in this epic of arduous male labour. The women may remain in their cottages, to be scared by the sooty appearance of the labourers when they return from threshing peas. Or, when the women come into the farmer's hayfield, they are 'prattling Females' who are—

Prepar'd, whilst he is here, to make his Hay;
Or, if he turns his Back, prepar'd to play. . . .

They gossip like sparrows, waste time, and when they run for shelter in the rain-storm this provides light relief in Duck's sombre poem. Even when they are gleaning, they stop to chat. Men had long known about the deficiencies of female labour, and Duck's poem confirmed this knowledge. Who, after all, would know better than a Wiltshire thresher?

Well, perhaps a woman labourer might? Duck's poem annoyed Mary Collier, a Hampshire washer-woman, enough to inspire her to a reply, which was first published in 1739. Predictably, when *The Woman's Labour* was first published there was speculation that the poem had been written by a man—perhaps even by Stephen Duck. But Mary Collier did exist. She was born in the late 17th century, so that when her poem was published she was over fifty. She started life near Midhurst, in Sussex; never went to school; but was taught to read when very young by her mother, upon whose early death she 'lost her education'. She continued to read as 'recreation', and the little account that we have of her reading suggests that its staple was the works of pious Protestantism—Fox's *Book of Martyrs* and his *Acts and Monuments*, Speed and Baker's *Chronicles* and Flavius Josephus's *Works*—variants on Old Testament history and the early records of the Jews. But she probably also had access to those other staples of the commoners' reading—almanacs, chapbooks and the like, for she confessed that when young 'any foolish History highly delighted me'.

Mary Collier spent the years of her first vigour in looking after her ailing father, alongside such occasional employment 'as the Country afforded'. She did not marry, and on her father's death she moved to Petersfield in Hampshire where she worked as a washer-woman and itinerant household brewer until the age of sixty-three. Then she went for a few more years to be housekeeper at a farm near Alton. She is last heard of, in her seventy-second year, writing a bad poem in honour of the marriage of George III. She had then retired to a 'garret' in Alton, where she was 'endeavouring to pass the Relict of my days in Piety, Purity, Peace, and an Old Maid'.

There was no dramatic life-translation for Mary Collier. A few local gentlewomen and gentry gave her a little support, and an edition of her poems, published in Winchester in 1762, was endorsed by a substantial list of subscribers. But *The Woman's Labour* earned her no further preferment. As she had predicted—

For all our Pains, no Prospect can we see
Attend us, but Old Age and Poverty.

Collier's poem is a telling critique, in the old folk-mode of the 'argument of the sexes', of Duck's male prejudice:

Those mighty Troubles which perplex your Mind,
(*Thistles* before, and *Females* come behind) . . .

But her rejoinder to Duck is witty rather than hostile. Indeed, when *The Thresher's Labour* first appeared she got the poem by heart, until 'fancying he had been too Severe on the Female Sex . . . brought me to a Strong propensity to call an Army of Amazons to vindicate the injured Sex'. She answered *The Thresher's Labour* 'to please my own humour, little thinking to make it Public'. 'It lay by me several Years and by now and then repeating a few lines to amuse myself and entertain my Company, it got Air.' A gentlewoman whom she nursed through an illness, and her friends, encouraged Collier further until her verses 'became a Town Talk'. Perhaps (as with Duck) these patrons did a little to polish the poems for publication, but there is no evidence of serious interference.

Although Collier herself was single, her poem is a forceful statement of the married woman's dual roles. After a day's haymaking, she returns to prepare dinner for her labouring husband, to feeding the pigs and attending to the children. In cereal harvest, she reaps, gathers or gleans. The infants are carried to the fields and tended in between spells of labour. The second part of the poem describes Collier's own occupation of 'charing' (washing, cleaning, brewing) at the houses of the wealthy. The accounts here are much less familiar and (for their time) they may be unique.

Both Duck and Collier are concerned with the relation of labour to sociability. Duck professes to scorn the 'prattling females' who combine gossip with their work, and this is satirised as a feminine weakness. But Duck is not consistent here, for he has earlier lamented that the noisy work of threshing prevents the labourers from 'beguiling' the time by telling tales like shepherds. In the hay and harvest field, however, the emphasis is (with Duck) upon male competitiveness in labour—

As the best Man, each claims the foremost Place,
And our first Work seems but a sportive Race . . .

At noon the male labourers retire, too exhausted (it seems) to do more than drink and 'faintly eat'. Whereas the women are always able to 'chat'. Collier, by contrast, will not apologise for the intermingling of work and sociability. She perhaps gives a little ground to the male stereotype of feminine gossip ('The only Privilege our Sex enjoy'), but then she goes over to a spirited defence:

For none but *Turks,* that I could ever find,
Have Mutes to serve them, or did e'er deny
Their Slaves, at Work, to chat it merrily.

What emerges from Duck's poem is a greater sense of the imposition of work-discipline and a greater sensitivity to the employer's disapproval. The threshers submit to their master's curses 'just like School-boys'. The male labourers, possibly, were more aware of their vulnerability to dismissal if they offended the master; whereas the women, whose labour was more occasional or seasonal but whose labour was indispensable during the hay and cereal harvests, were, in a sense, in a stronger position. This might suggest that the male labourer, in selling his labour, must sell at the same time his right to express himself in other ways; he must curb his sociability, and this discipline made him resent the 'prattling Females' who had sold only their labour for a few weeks, and who maintained what was now seen as a 'female privilege'.

A related question is the degree of deference expressed in the two poems. Of course, neither poet questions the necessity of wage-labour. But, contrary to one stereotype, the woman's poem is less deferential than the man's. And yet this is because—and here we do return to an old stereotype—the woman views her situation less impersonally, more 'subjectively', than the man.

In Duck's poem the 'Master' appears—whether cheerful or cursing—as a scarcely-personal element in the labourers' situation, like the weather. He is defined by his role, and while there is an undercurrent of resentment (the Master's curses are unfair, the inversion of the harvest-home is a Cheat') this resentment is not personalised nor is it even generalised into a class complaint, except at the 'painful' lot of Labour. The gentry do not appear in Duck's poem at all, except in the deferential invocation to a patron (the Reverend Stanley) with which the poem starts. And a little resentment expressed against a farmer-employer would cause no offence to a genteel reader, since in paternalism's self-image it was the duty of the rich to protect the poor from the grasping middling ranks.

Collier's poem is sharper. She shows no resentment at the farmer; one suspects that she rather enjoys the sociable weeks of harvest, despite the heavy work. But with 'charing' at the great house we enter another world, and a world in which we are situated within the perceptions of an underpaid and overworked labouring woman who is confronting an overprivileged Mistress and who sees her not only in her role as an employer but also as another woman. She has already laboured 'with the utmost Skill and Care' at the difficult and luxurious laundry (cambricks, muslins 'which our Ladies wear', 'Fashions which our Forefathers never knew')—she has already laboured for some hours before her Mistress (a 'drowsy Mortal') gets up and appears with '*perhaps* a Mug of Ale', and with, certainly, a string of superfluous commands. When she is cleaning the pans and pewter, 'Trumpery' is brought in 'to make complete our Slavery'. The language implies questions as to the humanity of class divisions, and as to the rationality of luxuries which depend upon the degrading labour of

others. What make for the feminine 'Perfections' of the Mistress obscure the feminine nature of the labourer. The great house is seen as self-centred and insensitive, summoning labour at any hour of the night to meet its occasions. The final quatrain of Collier's poem takes this personal confrontation between two women to the point of explicit generalisation:

> So the industrious Bees do hourly strive
> To bring their Loads of Honey to the Hive;
> Their sordid Owners always reap the Gains,
> And poorly recompense their Toil and Pains.

Mary Collier was not only writing searchingly about gender roles but she was writing irreverently about the oppressions and the sensibility of class as well. These closing couplets may have been suggested to her directly by her countrywoman's experience. Yet they could also be read as an allusion to Bernard Mandeville's 'The Fable of the Bees', whose provocations became the subject of debate and of scandal in the decade after 1723. Could she have read this, or listened in on the debate about the relation between private vices ('Millions endeavouring to supply / Each other's Lust and Vanity') and public benefits? Mandeville argued that luxury (fueled by avarice, pride, prodigality, &c) created employment and national wealth. Collier shows us the underside of luxury, in the laundry and the kitchens, and also the humbug about 'national' wealth. Mandeville's hive has no owner (or it is owned by the bees) whereas Collier's does, and they are 'sordid'. Whether Collier was alluding to this debate at the origin of capitalist political economy or not, the lack of deference in her poem may explain why the little patronage which she received fell far short of the translation of the Reverend Stephen Duck.

Bridget Keegan (essay date summer 2001)

SOURCE: Keegan, Bridget. "Georgic Transformations and Stephen Duck's *The Thresher's Labour.*" *Studies in English Literature, 1500-1900* 41, no. 3 (summer 2001): 545-62.

[*In the essay below, Keegan argues that in* The Thresher's Labour *Duck made a significant artistic contribution to the eighteenth-century debate regarding the use of the georgic style of poetry.*]

> Who casts to write a living line, must sweat
>
> Ben Jonson

No early-eighteenth-century poet sweated more, both in and about his poetry, than Stephen Duck.[1] A glance at **The Thresher's Labour** reveals five descriptions of sweating in this 283-line poem. This perspiration was a necessary by-product of the arduous manual labor that forms the text's central subject. Moreover, such sweat has typically been read as a sign of authenticity of experience, a category which has allowed critics to classify Duck as a minor poet and the poem as a paraliterary phenomenon. Although even Raymond Williams has tried to rescue Duck's name from its "'limiting' associations," Williams's strategy is ultimately similar to those who have been responsible for the initial limiting of Duck's relevance.[2] Williams argues for the poem's "simple power" heard behind "the strain of this labourer's voice."[3] As such, Williams marshals the same standard of documentary accuracy that has impeded sustained analyses of the poem's literary (and not just historical) attributes and achievements. Because he was involved in manual labor, critics for nearly three centuries have found themselves profoundly uneasy in approaching seriously Duck's poetic labors.

Although *The Thresher's Labour* is typically mentioned in most standard literary histories of the period, when it is discussed in any detail, it is assessed and occasionally praised for its historical veracity. How might an understanding of the poem's relevance be altered if it were read as more than the "realistic" representation of sweating agricultural laborers? What if it was to be interpreted as the product of an intellectual effort, the invention of a self-conscious creative agent—a poet who worked as a thresher and not a thresher who also happened to be a poet? My purpose in this essay is to move beyond the conventional justifications for Duck's marginal importance, as merely an interesting literary anecdote (primarily owing to his having been the target of ample Scriblerian scorn) or as evidence for a nascent "working-class" consciousness. Instead, Duck should be seen as a key contributor to the significant experimentations with the form of the georgic underway in the first half of the eighteenth century. To date, only John Goodridge has examined in detail the specifically literary dimensions of Duck's poem, such as its use of voice, imagery, or the meeting or innovating of generic conventions.[4] Goodridge's reading is exemplary; however, Duck's poem is complex enough to sustain more than one such analysis.[5]

My contention is that in the poem Duck is just as concerned with engaging the debate about the formal nature and purpose of the georgic (particularly as it was articulated by Joseph Addison in his preface to John Dryden's Virgil), as he was in describing the act of threshing. After reviewing some of the poem's critical reception, I wish to test the limits of the "'limiting' associations" surrounding Duck's status as a poet in order to demonstrate that he is deliberately responding to, and often challenging, early-eighteenth-century theories of georgic. in *The Thresher's Labour,* Duck speaks to the debate primarily through careful stylistic innovations at the level of voice. The layering of voices within *The Thresher's Labour* reveals Duck's poetic craftsmanship

and the complexity and importance of his contribution to the development of the georgic form.

Gustav Klaus is one of the first twentieth-century critics to initiate more ambitious claims for *The Thresher's Labour.* Klaus asserts that Duck's "greatest merit is his intuitive recognition that work is a theme worthy of literary treatment."[6] Klaus locates the poem's value in its accuracy: "Never before had there been such a truthful description of workaday routine in verse."[7] Klaus does claim that there is some importance to Duck's use of voice, in particular to his unique use of the collective pronoun "we." Yet this innovation is explained in terms of that voice's relationship to what Klaus sees as the poem's political agenda. For Klaus, it suggests Duck's (largely unsubstantiated) status as spokesperson for the oppressed. Such a position is less easy to defend upon close reading. Klaus is correct to point out Duck's influence on subsequent laboring-class and artisan poets, but he unnecessarily politicizes the inspiration Duck provides. Thus, Klaus downplays the poem's stylistic nuances in favor of locating larger political implications; Klaus overreaches in his effort to ascertain proletarian solidarity in the text without fully developing his provocative claims about the poem's language. By anachronistically putting Duck's experiments with voice in the service of a Marxist agenda, and not of a generic one, Klaus ignores crucial dimensions of the poem.

Other critics tend toward similar elisions. Morag Shiach accounts for the work of Duck and his successors as mediated by factors representative of the hegemonic culture, including patronage trends and shifting ideologies of the nature and value of rural life. Shiach does discuss the odd generic status of *The Thresher's Labour*: "The form of this poem is difficult to specify." Shiach labels it "anti-georgic" because of the layering of voice: "Its use of the collective pronoun, 'we' also signals its problematic relation to lyric traditions of poetic writing."[8] Regrettably, this observation goes undeveloped. Richard Greene confronts the question of genre more explicitly and originally. Greene classifies *The Thresher's Labour* as "counter-pastoral"[9] and suggestively sees its similarities to John Gay's Shepherd's Week. Nevertheless, although he settles upon a generic category, he is quick to remind us of James Sambrook's assertion of Duck's inventiveness in matters of form. Sambrook writes: *"The Thresher's Labour* is 'one of the earliest eighteenth-century poems to belong to no recognized literary kind.'"[10] Pastoral, anti-pastoral, counter-pastoral, georgic, anti-georgic, or plebeian georgic, *The Thresher's Labour* has been called all of these, but still there remains no critical consensus.[11] Yet, making a generic classification is essential to understanding the formal accomplishments of Duck's poem. According to Greene, Duck "altered by degree the conditions of public discourse."[12] *The Thresher's Labour* not only invited laboring-class speakers to enter into public discourse; it also, as Goodridge has revealed, affected one of the most important georgic poems of the century, James Thomson's *The Seasons.*[13]

Arguing contrary to Greene is Linda Zionkowski, who states unequivocally that Duck had little impact on the English canon.[14] She claims that Duck, and other laborer poets after him, were not proof of a political "democratization" of print culture: "Rather than disrupting the norms of polite literary practice, Duck's and [Ann] Yearsley's incursion into print reaffirmed and validated those norms; and their poetry never presented an audience with anything unfamiliar or strange. Indeed, their knowledge of verse and aesthetic 'taste' mirrored that of their refined readers who derived a concept of literature from the classic texts of Shakespeare, Milton, and Dryden, which were among the staples of the book trade."[15] What is unique about Zionkowski's position is that where other critics argue for Duck's work in so far as it deviates from literary conventions (and hence is somehow "revolutionary," a stance which unfortunately seems to be one of the only critical justifications for studying poetry written by those of the lower ranks of society), she reminds us of Duck's mastery of poetic convention: "He [Duck] may have owed his recognition as an 'Excellent Poet' not to the essential greatness of his poems, but to his skill in adopting a style that sophisticated readers considered 'poetic.' Despite class boundaries, Duck and his patrons shared the same canon and held common beliefs about what constitutes poetry—a coincidence that the commerce in letters had only recently made possible."[16] The generic ambiguities of Duck's poem are not due to the fact that he was a confused poet; rather they are entirely self-conscious, in so far as Duck also revealed himself to be entirely aware of the laws of the genre within and against which he worked. Zionkowski considers Duck's poem as purely pastoral, which leads her to aver that the form of pastoral is not accommodating to Duck's experience and hence produces a "strain"[17] as Duck essays a form that does not relate to his experience. However, in his poem, Duck himself admits that the pastoral is not his chosen form. Zionkowski ignores that Duck adopts the georgic rather than pastoral mode. If the poem is read as attempting idealized pastoral norms, even as it critiques them, then it is simple to read it as a failure. But if it is "straining" to be something else, as well as working within norms and forms recognizable to readers, it demands another standard of judgment. Although Duck's work should be seen in dialogue with contemporary pastoral as well as anti-pastoral satires, such as Gay's Shepherd's Week (as all georgics of the period should), it should be analyzed primarily in its relations to the georgic.

Reading Duck's poem in terms of the generic development of the georgic in the early eighteenth century and examining how he experiments with poetic voice within the genre demonstrate that, although its appearance was influenced by extraliterary forces, *The Thresher's Labour* is produced by an artist who was entirely in control of his craft. It was written by an individual who thought about, and responded to, his experience and that of his potential audience. Though Duck's work may have been affected by meddling patrons or lack of access to a complete classical library, within his poem he nonetheless envisioned himself speaking directly to theories of genre circulating at the time of the poem's composition. In particular, Duck addresses one of his central literary role models: Addison. Duck's poem must be read alongside and against Addison's essay on georgic and Dryden's translation of Virgil, both of which (if we are to believe Joseph Spence) Duck had read carefully before starting to write.[18] We know from Spence, in his detailed 1730 account of Duck's life and studies, that Duck made thoughtful choices in composing his poems. In his biographical letter prefatory to the poems, Spence assures the reader of Duck's attentiveness in composition: "When you have read his *Poems,* and consider the Manner he has been bred up in, I doubt not you will think they have Merit: But I assure you, they give an imperfect Idea of the Man; and, to know how much he deserves, one should converse with him, and hear on what Reasons he omitted such a Part, and introduc'd another, why he shortens his Style in this Place, and enlarges in that; whence he has such Word, and whence such an Idea."[19] We know too from Spence that Duck had collected a good-sized library, and owned and had read Dryden's Virgil, to which the preface by Addison is attached. Addison's essay is a central document in the history of the georgic, and one whose influence on Duck has not been sufficiently examined.

The georgic is, as Kurt Heinzelman has aptly observed, a "weird" genre, one that though it was central to eighteenth-century poetics, has become, after Romanticism, even weirder to twentieth-century critics. It is weird because (like Duck himself) it has, according to Heinzelman, "been defined by exclusion." The georgic, the middle term of the classical Virgilian rota, is perilously formally "in between," frequently understood "as a subset of pastoral, now as a proleptic epic, even at times as a species of satire (mock-pastoral or mock-heroic)."[20] Calling the georgic a "low-wattage genre" and emphasizing Virgil's diminution of his poetic labors on the topic of labor, Heinzelman argues that the reasons for the georgic's marginalization are similar to the reasons for the marginalization of authors who wrote in the mode: namely the prescription that their function be limited to conveying largely factual information.[21] Heinzelman asserts that "the inherent referentiality of the georgic, its very historicity, tends to be a literary liability."[22] For readers today, studying eighteenth-century georgics can be a tedious endeavor. It is difficult to see the literary value of poems about cider production, or to be moved by a poet's skill in describing hoof rot prevention in sheep. Such topics seem better suited to the cultural historian or the anthropologist. Their worth becomes even more dubious when they are written by authors whose social and educational pedigrees are suspect.

If Duck had the Addisonian model in mind while writing *The Thresher's Labour,* then he was most certainly confronted with the potentially incommensurable discursive dilemma that Addison's essay highlights. While the georgic might seem the "natural" mode for Duck to adopt, paradoxically, the very lineaments of the form, as they were set forth by Addison and subsequently came to be understood in the Augustan era, actively excluded those speakers perhaps most capable of fulfilling its instructional function. As Addison famously remarks: "the precepts of husbandry are not to be delivered with the simplicity of a plowman, but with the address of a poet."[23] Addison further exhorts that "the low phrases and turns of art, that are adapted to husbandry," should not "have any place in such a work as the Georgic, which is not to appear in the natural simplicity and nakedness of its subject, but in the pleasantest dress that poetry can bestow on it."[24] The Addisonian georgic is a genre that is, professionally speaking, at odds with itself, setting the farmer/laborer and the poet in discursive opposition to each other, even while thematically identifying rural labor with the labor of poetry. Comparing Hesiod to Virgil, Addison writes: "We see in one [Hesiod] the plainness of a downright countryman, and in the other, something of a rustic majesty, like that of a Roman dictator at the plough-tail."[25] Duck's work, and the source of a great deal of creative sweat for him, was in making his experiments with voice work both within and around the Addisonian vision of georgic.

In order to speak properly as a poet, Duck had to linguistically distance and control the signs of his other vocational identity, the very one which may have granted him empirical authority to compensate for his lack of a formal education. Duck's efforts to mediate the conflict between what George Crabbe memorialized as "The poet's rapture and the peasant's care" are legible at the level of voice and specifically in the use of pronouns in the poem.[26] Moreover, by comparing the subtle but important stylistic shifts between the two main variant editions of the poem, the first from 1730 and the second from 1736 (by which time Duck was comfortably settled with his royal sinecure), we see that it is voice and significant pronouns that Duck revises.[27] Duck solves the problem of the proper voice for georgic through creating a society of voices, representing at least four (although arguably five) separate vocal layers speaking to and with each other in the poem. Far from

being a sign of Duck's "confusion," this multiplication of speaking voices in the poem argues a sophistication that most critics have been unwilling to acknowledge.

Addison's central prescriptions for proper georgic writing and for identifying Virgil's particular success in the poem focus on the issue of voice. Addison appears to be more concerned with who is speaking in the poem and how he speaks over and above what the speaker says. The georgic thus, while devoted to instructions about work, also requires the author to make specific choices in language and style. Addison's well-known advice on the latter point is worth quoting in full: "He ought in particular to be careful of not letting his subject debase his style, and betray him into a meanness of expression, but every where to keep up his verse in all the pomp of numbers, and dignity of words. I think nothing which is a phrase or saying in common talk, should be admitted into a serious poem; because it takes off from the solemnity of the expression, and gives it too great a turn of familiarity."[28] Language is important because of the overall effect the poem is to create for its reader, allowing him or her to be elevated above the "low" subject matter. In one of the most often cited lines of the essay, Addison ascertains that Virgil's accomplishment is that "He delivers the meanest of his precepts with a kind of Grandeur, he breaks the clods and tosses the dung about with an air of gracefulness."[29]

It is difficult to locate anything explicitly crude in Duck's language—at least anything that would offend the letter of Addison's laws. Even his use of the laborers' sweat has a precedent in *Paradise Lost* (another work Duck knew well). Indeed, most of the earliest criticism of Duck's poem witnesses an anxiety that this "poor thresher" imitates poetic diction perhaps too well for a person of his station. As Zionkowski argues, Duck's poetry is fluent in the poetic convention and idiom of its day. Reading contemporary eighteenth-century appraisals of *The Thresher's Labour,* one begins to suspect that it was not the speech but the speaker who was considered antipathetic to Addison's rules of decorum. In the editions of 1730 and 1736, extensive biographical information precedes the text of the poem. The details provided therein would preclude the poem's ever being fully capable of fitting into the Addisonian model. According to such standards, because the voice in the poem ultimately originated with a real laborer, it must fail as georgic before the verse even begins, regardless of the personae depicted as speaking in the poem.

However, by listening attentively to the layering of voices in Duck's work, it is possible to move beyond the presupposition that the poem is a failure simply because of who wrote it. Instead of regarding the modulations of voice in the poem as a congenital imperfection produced by a rural clown, we should view the poet's stylistic decisions as indicative of his insight into the tradition he was writing against and within. By doing so, it may be demonstrated that in the language of *The Thresher's Labour,* Duck transforms the georgic to provide the blueprint for much of the poetry produced by subsequent laboring-class and genteel georgic writers.[30] For Duck and others after him, the georgic became the privileged but contested generic space within which they worked to claim and explore new vocational identities. Like the Virgilian prototype, these poems teach the worth of work. But instead of categorically celebrating such endeavors, they openly address the ambiguous value of labor as a source of joy and pain. A sustained reading of *The Thresher's Labour* illustrates a sophistication in the registers of voice that anticipate the limits and possibilities of georgic expression that later poets, both refined and rustic, confront.

There are four separate central voices in *The Thresher's Labour* (with a fifth voice implied in the 1730 edition). The first voice to speak in the poem is clearly not that of a farm laborer; it is a voice that identifies itself in line 10 as speaking about rather than as the "poor Thresher."[31] Described in the opening stanza as the voice of the Muse, it prefigures the voice of the poet that appears later in the poem. At the outset, the Muse, the conventional source of poetic voice, does not speak for herself and does not use a proper pronoun. Although the speaker in the first stanza follows the Virgilian model astutely, providing a precis of what will follow and indicating the conditions of the poem's production for a particular patron, the one difference between the opening of Duck's and Virgil's first georgic is the absence of the assertive first person pronoun of the speaker. Compare the opening of Dryden's translation:

> What makes a plenteous Harvest, when to turn
> The fruitful Soil, and when to sowe the Corn;
> The care of Sheep, of Oxen, and of Kine;
> And how to raise on Elms the teeming Vine:
> The Birth and Genius of the frugal Bee,
> I sing, Mecaenas, and I sing to thee.
>
> (lines 1-6)[32]

with Duck's first stanza (the alterations made to the 1736 edition are included in square brackets):

> The grateful Tribute of these rural Lays,
> Which to her Patron's Hand the Muse conveys,
> Deign to accept; 'tis just She [the] Tribute bring
> To Him whose Bounty gives her Life to sing:
> To him whose generous Favours tune her Voice,
> And bid her 'midst her Poverty rejoice.
> Inspir'd by These, she dares her self prepare,
> To sing the Toils of each revolving Year:
> Those endless Toils, which always grow anew,
> And the poor Thresher's destin'd to pursue;
> Ev'n these with pleasure can the Muse rehearse,

> When you, and Gratitude, command [demand] the Verse.
>
> (lines 1-12)

Whereas Dryden's Virgilian poet speaks self-confidently in the first person, the voice in Duck's song is displaced onto the Muse. Moreover, while both sing for a patron, in Duck's poem, the Muse is compelled to speak in response to the reported command (or in 1736, the demand) of the powerful but unrepresented voice of the patron. The poem then, as Duck creates it, is explicitly not originally the product of the laborer, a fact which all readers but Goodridge have failed to discover. As such, at the outset, it conforms to Addisonian parameters. This verbal exchange of the literary work between Muse and patron frames the ensuing account of the exchange of labor—agricultural work—between farmer and thresher. The laboring voices represented in the body of the poem are not given precedence, but are mediated through the words of more traditional and respectable literary figures: the Muse and the patron.

The next voice that appears in the poem is again not the voice of the laborer, but the voice of the farmer or master, who calls upon his threshers to work for him just as the patron had called upon the Muse to perform her labor. Tellingly, the verb "command" is used in both instances. In the 1730 edition, the second stanza also introduces another voice into the labor relations depicted in the inner frame of the poem—that of the landlord, a voice that is silenced in 1736, when Duck was well ensconced in royal preferment and when, perhaps, he was less inclined to suggest any tensions in rural labor relations. These lines begin the second stanza (the lines deleted in 1736 are included in square brackets):

> Soon as the Harvest hath laid bare the Plains,
> And Barns well fill'd reward the Farmer's Pains;
> What Corn each Sheaf will yield, intent to hear,
> And guess from thence the Profits of the Year:
> [Or else impending Ruin to prevent,
> By paying, timely, threat'ning Landlord's Rent,]
> He calls his Threshers forth: Around we stand,
> With deep Attention waiting his Command.
>
> (lines 13-20)

Just as the Muse was subject to the "command" of the patron, here the farmer/master who commands the laborers is shown (in the 1730 edition) to be subject to the "threat" of the otherwise silent landlord. Both Muse and farmer speak in response to the voices of those to whom they are subject. Yet it is noteworthy that although a parallel exists between farmer and Muse, they are never precisely identified. Indeed, Duck (or perhaps an editor) is careful, in the editions after 1736, to put the farmer's remarks in quotation marks, more clearly separating them and guarding against any mistaken conflation. With the farmer's speech reported in quotation marks, it becomes even more explicit that the poem is not spoken by a farmer but by a poet, speaking through or as the Muse, who quotes the farmer's speech.

The lines introducing the farmer's voice, however, also introduce the collective voice, the "we" of the farm laborers. Duck's use of this we is distinctive and has already yielded ample critical commentary. Most notably, it has been read as articulating a nascent collective proletarian voice in poetry. However, this use of a first-person plural pronoun throughout a good portion of the poem's description of agricultural labor has a generic as well as a potentially political aim. By this device of the modulation of voice, Duck solves the problem of how a real "Plow-man" like himself could exchange that vocation for that of poet, and, in keeping with the Addisonian precepts, write in the georgic mode. The "we," though it may at times include the "I" of the poet, offers a separate perspective from that "I." The "I" and the "we" perform different kinds of work within the poem. While the "we" reports on the manual labor, the "I" distinguishes itself by translating that labor into more figurative discourse, making the work stylistically fit for verse.

Not only is the collective voice clearly separated from the voice of the poet, the very nature of the labor that the collective voice undertakes prevents its poetic expression—indeed the first time the "we" speaks, it speaks of being silenced. This is evident early in the poem, in a description of the work that commingles a realistic rendering with dense classical allusions (implicitly inserted by the muted poetic "I" to properly elevate the "low subject"):

> Now in the Air our knotty Weapons fly;
> And now with equal Force descend from high:
> Down one, one up, so well they keep the Time,
> The Cyclops Hammers could not truer chime;
> Nor with more heavy Strokes could Aetna groan,
> When Vulcan forg'd the Arms for Thetis' Son.
> In briny Streams our Sweat descends apace,
> Drops from our Locks, or trickles down our Face.
> No intermission in our Works we know;
> The noisy Threshall must for ever go.
> Their Master absent, others safely play:
> The sleeping Threshall does itself betray.
>
> (lines 38-49)

The clamor of the work prevents communication. The workers, the "we," cannot speak above the noise of their activities. In order to do so, they would have to stop working. Quite literally, the labor of threshing is antithetical to the labor of creating poetry. The laborers speak in the poem only to underscore their inability to speak as a consequence of that labor. Duck acknowledges that threshers cannot be poets, but cleverly, in so doing, contradicts himself and contests the initial

premise. In a barbed anti-pastoral critique, the collective voice comments: "Can we, like Shepherds, tell a merry Tale? / The Voice is lost, drown'd by the noisy Flail" (lines 52-3). The "Voice" is presented in the process of disappearance, yet it speaks nonetheless.

The activity of work does not merely prevent lyrical effusions, the scene and subject of the work are decidedly uninspiring. Even if the "we" wished to think poetic thoughts,

> —Alas! what pleasing thing
> Here to the Mind can the dull Fancy bring?
> The Eye beholds no pleasant Object here:
> No chearful Sound diverts the list'ning Ear.
>
> (lines 54-7)

The laborers' voice is doubly silenced, for their very subject provides scant matter for song: "Tis all a dull and melancholy Scene, / Fit only to provoke the Muses Spleen" (lines 62-3). Duck allows the laboring voices to enter into poetic discourse negatively. They speak in the poem only to announce the unsuitability of their labor to literature, even as the implicit "I" who has initiated the poem (masquerading as the Muse) proves otherwise with the insertion of extensive classical allusions. This strategy enables Duck to resolve the inherent paradox of the georgic, the challenge faced by all poets who attempt to put hard labor into poetry, or again, in the infamous words of Addison: "he breaks the clods and tosses the dung about with an air of gracefulness."

Although he must negotiate how to include his own voice as a laborer, Duck continues to fulfill many of the Addisonian expectations of the georgic. It is precisely those more conventional moments that are explicitly recorded by a singular poetic "I," a speaking subject distinct from the threshing "we." While the voice remains implicit at several junctures in the poem, this "I" emerges strongly at significant moments. Duck uses the "I" to announce a shift to a more elevated (and literary) perspective. The singular poetic voice emerges clearly in the seventh stanza, actively separating the persona of the poet from that of the thresher. After lines that describe how the laborers' initial enthusiasm for work flags with the day's increasing heat, the lines recount:

> Thus in the Morn a Courser I have seen,
> With headlong Fury scour the level Green,
> Or mount the Hills, if Hills are in his way,
> As if no Labour could his Fire allay,
> Till the meridian Sun with sultry Heat,
> And piercing Beams hath bath'd his Sides in Sweat;
> The lengthen'd Chace scarce able to sustain,
> He measures back the Hills and Dales with pain.
>
> (lines 127-34)

The content of this analogy indicates that the speaker may not be a member of the laboring ranks, as it uses images from the hunt, an activity reserved for the gentry. The analogy further likens the laborers' activities to those of animals, naturalizing labor and potentially dehumanizing the worker. This is a strategy that will be repeated in the subsequent simile (one that has gained Duck the opprobrium of many feminist readers) wherein he likens talking women to a flock of chattering birds. While there is much to object to in this latter image, it is worth noting that both male and female laborers suffer a similar naturalization through figurative language. The speaker in these lines appears as a spectator rather than as a participant in the labor performed. The labor is naturalized as the language of the poem becomes more figurative. This "I" adopts a distinctly distant, almost epic tone, and does not sweat himself but observes others sweat. Although the more prosaic "we" returns in line 135, the "I" reappears in line 190. Once more, it adopts the position of spectator and completes an epic simile describing the garrulous women workers, in a passage that would be Mary Collier's main point of contention. As Collier in the eighteenth century and Donna Landry, Moira Ferguson, and others in the late twentieth century have rightly noted, it is precisely the female laborers' speech that inspires the collective scorn of the male laborers.[33] While the misogyny of this passage should not go unremarked, a jealousy resounds through these lines. As noted above, the first words spoken by the "we" are a complaint about the inability to speak. Thus, the resentment toward the women, who have some liberty to talk, might be interpreted as an envy of their greater freedom. Nevertheless, the women's freedom, too, is limited, for they must await the master's absence to express themselves fully and playfully:

> Our Master comes, and at his Heels a Throng
> Of prattling Females, arm'd with Rake and Prong:
> Prepar'd, whils't he is here, to make his Hay;
> Or, if he turns his Back, prepar'd to play.
> But here, or gone, sure of this Comfort still,
> Here's Company, so that they may chat their fill:
> And were their Hands as active as their Tongues,
> How nimbly then would move their Rakes and
>   Prongs?
>
> (lines 163-70)

There is a resentment of the women for the pleasures they can take in their labor through the opportunity it provides for conviviality, an opportunity that was denied the male workers. Although their speech is increasingly represented as a kind of cacophony, its vigor and enthusiasm are not entirely negative:

> All talk at once, but seeming all to fear,
> That all they speak so well, the rest won't hear;
> By quick degrees so high their Notes they strain,
> That Standers-by can nought distinguish plain:
> So loud their Speech and so confus'd their Noise,
> Scarce puzzled Echo can return a Voice;

> Yet spite of this, they bravely all go on,
> Each scorns to be, or seem to be, outdone.
>
> (lines 177-84)

Much as their male counterparts heroically engaged in a competitive effort to "try their Strength" upon the uncut fields on the first day of the harvest, the women too engage in their own "sportive labor," which is noted to be with its own bravery. As with the competitive labor of the men, the interruption of the "competition" among the women by a cloudburst is naturalized by the intrusion, once again, of the first person voice:

> Thus have I seen on a bright Summer's Day,
> On some green Brake a Flock of Sparrows play;
> From Twig to Twig, from Bush to Bush they fly,
> And with continu'd Chirping fill the Sky;
> But on a sudden, if a Storm appears,
> Their chirping Noise no longer dins your Ears.
>
> (lines 191-6)

The "I" of this stanza once again separates itself to perform the poetic work of naturalizing rural labor.

This is not the last time the "I" will identify itself to render manual labor fit for verse. The "I" appears a final time and further underscores its difference from the collective voice of the workers by engaging in a direct address, an apostrophe to the laborers about to begin the harvest:

> Ye Reapers, cast your Eyes around the Field,
> And view the Scene its different Beauties yield:
> Then look again with a more tender Eye,
> To think how soon it must in Ruin lie.
>
> (lines 223-6)

However, at the very moment that the "I" announces its separation from the laborers through the apostrophe, and through calling upon them to notice the beauties of an uncut field, the voice appears simultaneously to be subsumed in the "we":

> For once set in, where-e'er our Blows we deal,
> There's no resisting of the well-whet Steel:
> But here or there, where-e'er our Course we bend,
> Sure Desolation does our Steps attend.
>
> (lines 227-30)

These crucial lines, describing the climax of the agricultural year, the harvest, and announcing the climax of the poem with the final epic simile, make it unclear as to whether the lines are the product of the "I" of the poet or the "we" of the laborers. These lines are devoid of any pronouns:

> Thus, when Arabia's Sons, in hopes of Prey,
> To some more fertile Country take their way;
> How beauteous all things in the Morn appear,
> There Villages, and pleasing Cots are here;
> So many pleasing Objects meet the Sight,

The ravish'd Eye could willing gaze 'till Night:
But long e'er then, where-e'er their Troops have past,
Those pleasant Prospects lie a gloomy Waste.

(lines 231-8)

These lines accomplish several goals even as they obscure the distinction between the two voices. They seem to work at cross-purposes thematically as well as vocally, likening the work of harvesting to a heroic martial task. However, they also compare it to the act of destroying "pleasant Prospects." Quite literally, the act of reaping, however valiant, ruins the prospects of and for poetry.

It is no surprise then that while the arduous nature of the collective "we's" labor continues to the poem's conclusion, the "I" does not reappear. In describing the thresher's labor, Duck is describing the silencing of the poet who would sing of that labor. This may account for why Duck never returned to the theme of his previous employment and devoted the rest of his subsequent career to more conventional occasional and religious verse. *The Thresher's Labour* is a georgic that attempts to fulfill, and largely succeeds in fulfilling, the spirit, if not the letter, of Addison's rules. Yet as it does, it enacts at the level of voice the limitations of those rules to accomplish their aim. It is thus all the more compelling that in the 1736 edition, when Duck had been safely distanced from engaging in rural labor, his emendations to the poem include primarily the insertion of more classical allusions. More notably, however, he does not erase the collective voice, the "we," but in a few instances, he inserts additional direct notations of the first person plural.

While some of the alterations may have originated with friends and patrons, that Duck would continue to work with the poem at the level of its representations of voice strongly indicates that his use of this range of voices— the powerful yet infrequently heard voice of the patron and the landlord, the first person speakers of the farmer/ master and of the poet, the collective voice or the "we" of the workers, and the voices of the women laborers— was thoroughly intentioned. It is regrettable that these generic innovations did not extend beyond this single, but important instance. And although it is a single instance, it is interesting enough to merit recognition for Duck not merely as a thresher who wrote poetry but as a poet who contributed to the development of the georgic. That contribution, much as we might fail to acclaim it today, was not unnoticed by his contemporaries. As Goodridge has convincingly argued, it is highly probable that Duck's poem influenced Thomson in his revisions of *The Seasons*.[34] Moreover, Duck's poem further inspired numerous georgics by those of laboring and artisanal ranks, who found their voices from reading Duck's experiments with the layering of voice. Not only did Collier respond eloquently to Duck's represen-

tation of female voices, but so did Robert Dodsley, whose later work as a publisher gave many of the eighteenth century's more celebrated voices a place in print. Dodsley's *A Muse in Livery, or the Footman's Miscellany* (1732) was one of the many laboring georgics that were explicitly written in response to Duck, and such responses continued into the nineteenth century.[35] This is all the more reason why Duck's place in the history of the georgic ought to continue to be examined.

Notes

1. The epigraph comes from Ben Jonson, "To the Memory of My Beloved, the Author. Mr. William Shakespeare, and What He Hath Left Us," in *Ben Jonson and the Cavalier Poets,* ed. Hugh Maclean (New York: W. W. Norton, 1974), p. 87, line 59.

2. Raymond Williams. *The Country and the City* (New York: Oxford Univ. Press. 1975], p. 88.

3. Ibid.

4. John Goodridge, *Rural Life in Eighteenth-Century English Poetry* (Cambridge: Cambridge Univ. Press, 1995).

5. While the Justificatory terms may have changed, the tendency to continue to resist granting Stephen Duck (and the many laboring-class poets after him) an active role in creating their art persists today. While it is no longer theories of "natural genius" called in to explain (or explain away) the poet's accomplishments, modern critics continue to rely upon extraliterary occurrences (such as the shift away from aristocratic patronage or the rising literacy rates) to account for the appearance of the poetry. A glimpse at nearly three centuries of criticism of laboring-class poets from Duck forward shows a consistent pattern of evaluating context over and above (and even instead of) the text, and regarding the poem as artifact rather than art.

6. H. Gustav Klaus, *The Literature of Labour: Two Hundred Years of Working-Class Writing* (Brighton UK: Harvester, 1985), p. 11.

7. Klaus, p. 12.

8. Morag Shiach, *Discourse on Popular Culture: Class, Gender, and History in Cultural Analysis, 1730 to the Present* (Oxford: Polity Press, 1989). p. 48.

9. Richard Greene, *Mary Leapor: A Study in Eighteenth-Century Women's Poetry* (Oxford: Clarendon Press, 1993). p. 105.

10. Quoted in Greene, p. 108.

11. Goodridge provides a thorough and compelling discussion of the poem's generic status in the introductory chapter to his *Rural Life in Eighteenth*

Century English Poetry. Goodridge makes valid and interesting claims for classifying the poem as "proletarian anti-pastoral" largely because the georgic "presents a positive, and even a heroic view of labour, as a pleasurable and a socially progressive activity" (p. 6). However, given Duck's intimate familiarity with Virgil's *Georgics,* and given the fact that Virgil himself is often ambivalent about the "joys" of work, Duck may in fact be closer to the classical (rather than the neoclassical) prototype of the genre.

12. Greene, p. 109.

13. Goodridge, pp. 79-80.

14. Linda Zionkowski, "Strategies of Containment: Stephen Duck, Ann Yearsley, and the Problems of Polite Culture." *ECLife* [*Eighteenth Century Life*] 13, 3 (Autumn 1989): 91-108, 98.

15. Zionkowski, p. 92.

16. Zionkowski. p. 93.

17. Zionkowski, p. 97.

18. Joseph Addison, "Essay on Virgil's Georgics," in *The Works of Joseph Addison,* ed. George Washington Greene, 6 vols. (Philadelphia: J. B. Lippincott, 1888), 2:379-88.

19. Joseph Spence, "Preface" in *Poems on Several Subjects* (London, 1730), pp. Xv-xvi.

20. Kurt Heinzelman, "Roman Georgic in the *Georgian Age: A Theory of Romantic Genre,*" *TSLL* [*Texas Studies in Literature and Language*] 33, 2 (Summer 1991): 182-214, 185.

21. Ibid.

22. Heinzelman, p. 192.

23. Addison, 2:380.

24. Addison, 2:384.

25. Addison, 2:386.

26. George Crabbe. *The Village,* book 1, line 28, in *Eighteenth-Century Verse,* ed. Roger Lonsdale (Oxford: Oxford Univ. Press, 1984), p. 670.

27. Duck's poems went through at least six editions (some of which were actually simple reprints labeled as separated editions) in 1730. These editions, Duck later claimed, were "pirated," and he asserted that the edition brought out in 1736 represented his poems as he wished them to appear. The history and implications of this "piracy" are difficult to unravel. The earliest editions of 1730 were produced by James Roberts, a thoroughly reputable printer who published both John Gay and Alexander Pope. David Fairer, in a personal email communication of 14 October 1999, speculates that Duck's complaints in 1736 were meant to assuage his patrons that the edition he produced for them was the authentic one. Because there is no record of an overt controversy or lawsuit, there is little reason to doubt Duck's partial involvement in bringing forth the 1730 text, upon which most of the discussion in this essay is based. As it was the first 1730 edition ("pirated" or not) that brought Duck to public attention, I have chosen to use it as the text for my argument, noting the later revisions as they occur.

28. Addison 2:384.

29. Addison 2:386.

30. The list of poets and poems directly influenced by Duck includes, among others, John Bancks's *The Weaver's Miscellany* (London, 1730), Mary Collier's *The Woman's Labour* (London, 1739), and Robert Tatersal's *The Bricklayer's Miscellany* (London, 1734-35]. Duck's indirect influence can be felt into the Romantic age in the works of poets such as Robert Bloomfield and John Clare.

31. Duck, *The Thresher's Labour,* in *Poems on Several Subjects,* pp. 15-25. All subsequent citations of the poem will be from this edition and will appear parenthetically within the text.

32. John Dryden, *The Poems of John Dryden,* ed. James Kinsley, vol. 2 (Oxford: Clarendon Press, 1958), p. 918.

33. See Donna Landry, *The Muses of Resistance: Laboring-Class Women's Poetry in Britain, 1739-1796* (Cambridge: Cambridge Univ. Press, 1990), pp. 56-77. See also Moira Ferguson, *Eighteenth-Century Women Poets: Nation, Class and Gender* (Albany: State Univ. of New York Press, 1995), pp. 7-25.

34. Goodridge, p. 63.

35. For the most significant overview of Duck's influence on subsequent laboring-class authors, see Goodridge's two essays: "Some Predecessors of Clare: 'Honest Duck'" (*JCSJ* 8 [*John Clare Society Journal*] [19891: 5-10) and "Some Predecessors of Clare: 2. Responses to Duck" (*JCSJ*9 [1990]: 17-26).

Peggy Thompson (essay date summer 2004)

SOURCE: Thompson, Peggy. "Duck, Collier, and the Ideology of Verse Forms." *Studies in English Literature, 1500-1900* 44, no. 3 (summer 2004): 505-23.

[*In the following essay, Thompson explores how Duck's and Collier's use of the heroic couplet verse form influenced* The Thresher's Labour *and* The Woman's Labour.]

"Can we plausibly think of verse forms as having ideologies? Are patterns of rhetoric, thought, and value so fully built into structure that one can speak usefully in an absolute sense of what a particular form represents culturally or what kinds of work it can do?"[1] So asks J. Paul Hunter in an important article on the heroic couplet, a verse form that has frequently been discussed in terms that imply affirmative answers to his questions. For example, a frequently cited essay on the late seventeenth-century couplet quotes a passage from John Dryden's *Fables* and then claims: "It is impossible not to conclude that the neo-classical cast of verse carried a pattern of wit which was too strong even for Dryden's compunctions. Nothing can be plainer than that this verse is neither Chaucer nor yet what Dryden set himself to write."[2] In other words, despite his intentions, the verse form made Dryden write as he did. These remarks are based on a careful definition of the couplet as it appeared at a particular time and place. In its attention to the specific features of the form as it was handed to Dryden, the essay, published in 1935, anticipates Hunter, who insists that if we are to think about the ideology of form, it must be "in particular historic moments and for particular groups of authors and readers."[3] But in its conclusions about Dryden particularly, the essay goes much farther than Hunter does in characterizing the determining strength of those forces, as does another landmark study of the couplet published in 1969, which begins with a chapter on "The Nature of the Closed Heroic Couplet." The word "nature" suggests a formalism more essential than does the introductory paragraph, where one reads only of "several points of general similarity."[4] But elsewhere, a determining force is clearly attributed to the couplet: although "the second line of a closed couplet is *essentially* climactic . . . we can recognize its *built-in* qualities of flexibility and variety."[5] When analyzing particular poets' use of the couplet, the author does not escape this essentialism, but instead is trapped by it. For example, after arguing that Alexander Pope's couplet practice "presents us with one great style and one great vision . . . that of unity in diversity," he must characterize unresolved tensions between the poet and his society as "beyond the implicit bounds of his form . . . beyond the limits of its efficacy."[6] Thus, the critical language of even this comprehensive study reveals a reluctance or inability to alter one's understanding of the limits and bounds of Pope's couplet, even in the face of Pope's actual practice.

Hunter's concern is with a more recent group of critics who have similarly let their assumptions about the couplet blind them to what poets such as Pope actually do with this form. Significantly, these critics share Hunter's historicist perspective and argue that formalist criticism has regularly been used to advance elitist interests under the guise of "neutral" and "universal" aesthetic standards.[7] But in their efforts to correct disingenuous claims of neutrality for formalist criticism, they have veered to a kind of formal determinism that keeps them from recognizing the multiple meanings that literary forms can and do convey. More specifically, Hunter notes that "those who wish to distance themselves politically from what they take to be the rigid social propositions Pope uses couplets to make . . . tend to talk about the couplet's central features in broad theoretical terms, emphasizing balance, symmetry, and closure as essential features, as if the terms themselves coded an authoritative and fixed universe."[8] These assumptions about the couplet in turn allow the same critics to reinforce their assumption that Pope was a rigid, self-righteous poet who lacked awareness of his self-contradictions. By examining carefully how Pope actually uses the couplet, Hunter identifies a much more complexly aware and hesitant poet, in his early career especially. Hunter argues that when thus historicized, formal criticism will provide such insight, but when based on a priori generalizations or essentialist assumptions, it will construct poets and poetry that do not exist.[9]

My purpose in this essay is to look carefully at the work of two of Pope's contemporaries in order to address further the central questions posed in Hunter's article as well as in the more general, current conversation about formalism.[10] Can a poet use the heroic couplet without being confined to an essential or inherent meaning in that form? And can readers of poetry talk usefully about the couplet without invoking essential meanings for it? I have chosen to focus on the careers and work of two laboring-class poets, Stephen Duck (1705-56) and Mary Collier (1690-1762), especially **The Thresher's Labour** (1730, 1736) by Duck and *The Woman's Labour* (1739) by Collier. These are not only the most well-known and highly praised poems by these authors; they are also the poems in which Duck and Collier are most intent on escaping the subjects and attitudes of their patrons, where they most explicitly voice complaint on behalf of their class and gender. If scholars of the couplet can find tension between Dryden's intentions and his poetic form, and between Pope's state of mind and his form, what kind of conflict will we discern between two laborers' most subversive poems and a verse form overwhelmingly favored by the educated elite and allegedly inseparable from "an authoritative and fixed universe"? What evidence can we find, in short, for or against an ideology of the heroic couplet?[11]

As James Sutherland pointed out over fifty years ago, of the forty-three eighteenth-century poets included in Samuel Johnson's *Lives,* thirty-three received university training at Oxford, Cambridge, Trinity, or Edinburgh. Of the remaining ten, four had a thorough grounding in the classics at Westminster, and two were educated as noblemen at home. In addition to the classical education of these poets (as well as of their readers), Sutherland cites the poets' wide general reading and extensive travel, their close relationships with aristocratic patrons, the relatively high cost of published poetry, and the dominance of classical models, neoclassical rules, and polite taste to support his characterization of eighteenth-century poets and poetry as "fundamentally aristocratic." Sutherland quotes a damning critical judgment by John Dennis—"What ploughman, what tinker, what trull is not capable of saying the like?"—to illustrate the widespread assumption that poetry is by definition beyond the grasp of the laboring class.[12] It is little wonder then that the literary work of laborers Duck and Collier, the former of whom allegedly "got English" as others acquired Latin or Greek, was greeted with various blends of astonishment, curiosity, skepticism, and condescension, for their lives, especially their educations, could hardly differ more from those summarized by Sutherland.[13]

Duck's formal education was limited to a few years at a rural charity school. From the ages of fourteen to twenty-five he worked as a day laborer, doggedly studying three arithmetic books he had purchased with overtime wages and then greedily devouring and discussing the small library of a friend who had worked in London. Against all odds, his poetry came to the attention of a series of influential friends and patrons, culminating in Queen Caroline, who gave the thresher-poet an annuity, a small house, and successive positions at court. The first authorized collection of his poetry, published in 1736, attracted a distinguished list of over six hundred subscribers. In 1746, Duck took Holy Orders and eventually retired to the living at Byfleet, Surrey. He drowned, apparently a suicide, ten years later. Though less bizarre, Collier's life and career are even less consistent with Sutherland's characterization of the poet who regularly employed the neoclassical couplet. Collier had no formal education; she learned to read at home and claims to have begun writing verses primarily to aid her memory. She eventually published two collections: *The Woman's Labour . . . To which are added The Three Wise Sentences,* at her own expense in 1739, and *Poems, on Several Occasions,* by subscription in 1762. But she never escaped a life of hard labor, working as a laundress, brewer, domestic servant, field hand, and housekeeper until ill health forced her to retire to a garret at age seventy.

Although their lives took very different directions once their poetry was noticed, both thresher and woman were subject to constant reminders of how anomalous their identities as poets were. Most obviously, both were formally interrogated regarding the authenticity of their work; Duck was subjected to a strict examination by Lord Macclesfield, who then became a chief patron, and Collier was quizzed by nine Petersfield residents, who testified to her authenticity in the third edition of *The Woman's Labour.* Hardly less subtle were the

indignities accompanying the most condescending sort of patronage. Duck was moved from one contrived position to another. As keeper of the queen's library at Merlin's Cave, one of Caroline's improvements at Richmond Gardens, Duck was set up—in biographer Paul Jacob's telling description—as "a living monument to the queen's bounty . . . representing progress as a raw natural resource raised to the level of its natural merit."[14] Even worse, as master of Duck Island in St. James's Park, he became, in Jacob's words, "a glorified garden ornament." More generally, Betty Rizzo claims that humble and dependent poets such as Duck "made splendid household pets who could fawn in words."[15] And indeed, in response to such awkward generosity, Duck is notoriously disconcerting in his relentless, groveling expressions of gratitude and unworthiness. For example, on visiting Oxford, training ground of so many of the poets Johnson would later deem worthy of inclusion in his *Lives,* Duck writes, "Forgive me, God of Verse, who daring greet / Thy Sacred Temples with unhallow'd Feet."[16] Duck's continual confessions that he was not worthy to be a poet were apparently not enough for his many detractors, great and small. Swift's "quibbling epigraph" is one of several attacks on Duck as poet that invoke Duck's identity as agricultural laborer:

> The Thresher, Duck, could o'er the Queen prevail;
> The proverb says, *no fence against a flail.*
> From *threshing* corn, he turns to *thresh* his brains,
> For which her Majesty allows him grains.[17]

Once Duck took Holy Orders, the humiliation continued; crowds initially flocked to hear him preach, not out of piety, but out of curiosity. One is reminded of Johnson's infamous remark about a woman's preaching: the wonder is that it is done at all. Johnson's famous epigram is a truncated precursor of the current theoretical position that insists on distinguishing allegedly universal and ideologically neutral aesthetic standards, by which the preaching of women and Duck was considered negligible, from allegedly nonliterary considerations, such as curiosity, sympathy, and politics, which drew attention to their preaching nonetheless. It is thus an early example of the kind of ahistorical criticism that has recently prompted others, in what Hunter sees as a reductive overreaction, to identify essential political meaning in dominant literary forms.

Johnson's epigram is also a pointed reminder of the additional difficulties Collier faced in identifying herself as a poet; she was not only an uneducated laborer; she was also a woman. For further evidence that Collier's voice would not be taken seriously, one need look no farther than Duck's characterization of female "Prattle" in **The Thresher's Labour**: "So loud's their Speech, and so confus'd their Noise, / Scarce puzzled Echo can return the Voice."[18] As Donna Landry has pointed out,

Duck here "represents women as, metaphorically and temporarily at least, outside the symbolic order of language altogether."[19] Although these and similar passages spurred Collier to respond directly and strongly in *The Woman's Labour,* she never challenges the institutional bases of sexism in education, government, or religion. Citing the "rhetorically 'male-identified'" perspective from which Collier usually writes, Landry speculates, "It is as if . . . Collier [were permitted] access to the public on the condition that radically different female desires and recommendations not be featured too prominently in her work."[20] There is much evidence to claim the same about Duck and any "radically different [laboring-class] desires and recommendations" he might have wanted to express. Hence, the overwhelmingly safe nature of the subjects about which both laborers wrote: biblical stories, topics suggested by their patrons, and, most significantly, contentment in poverty and humble acceptance of God's will.[21]

The interrogation, condescension, and ridicule of others and the apologies and accommodation of Duck and Collier all evidence a powerful dissonance between Duck's and Collier's identities as poets and their identities as laborers and, in Collier's case, as a woman.[22] When, atypically, Duck and Collier write angrily about thresher's and woman's labor as inadequately recognized and unfairly compensated, they foreground rather than suppress the differences that so clearly distinguish them from other poets. But they do so in the dominant verse form of those other poets, the heroic couplet.[23] If the couplet has an essential ideology, then, surely it would appear here, in resistance to Duck's and Collier's subversive content. In a well-known remark, Raymond Williams has claimed about Duck, "It is easy to feel the strain of this labourer's voice as it adapts, slowly, to the available models in verse."[24] But others have praised both poets for their adaptation of the couplet to their rhetorical ends. Moira Ferguson, for example, characterizes Duck's couplet in *The Thresher's Labour* as "supple and expressive of mood." Similarly, Landry claims that in *The Woman's Labour,* "Collier makes the couplet form seem flexible and accommodating, not constraining."[25] My own analysis of the couplet in these two georgics argues that Collier is more consistently successful than Duck in maintaining control of the couplet and that she thus refutes the implication of Duck's struggles, that the heroic couplet is ideologically limited in the kinds of values and ideas it can convey.

Like so many of Duck's poems, *The Thresher's Labour* originated in the suggestion of one of his patrons. In this case, the Reverend Mr. Stanley suggested Duck write about his own life, probably without any comprehension of the harshness of that life or of the discomfort Duck might feel focusing on his former existence while struggling to solidify his new identity as a man of let-

ters moving in aristocratic circles. This tension is immediately apparent in the opening lines, where Duck introduces his class-based lament only after imitating Pope and other neoclassical authors by using the couplet to affirm and mirror the order of a just exchange, praise for patronage:

> The grateful Tribute of these rural Lays,
> Which to her Patron's Hand the Muse conveys,
> Deign to accept: 'Tis just she Tribute bring
> To him, whose Bounty gives her Life to sing;
> To him, whose gen'rous Favours tune her Voice;
> And bid her, 'midst her Poverty, rejoice.
>
> (p. 10, lines 1-6)

In an analogous passage at the beginning of "Windsor Forest," Pope honors his patron, Sir George Granville, as a source of order in the rich profusion of Windsor Forest, "Where Order in Variety we see, / And where, tho' all things differ, all agree."[26] In form as well as content, Pope's interrupting clause, "tho' all things differ," only reinforces the notion that contrast and differences are contained by the order Granville helps make possible.[27] However, the cumulative power of the parallel passages describing Duck's bountiful patron is interrupted by a reference, not to apparent disorder, but to real "Poverty," which, as the condition and result of the thresher's labor, is the theme of Duck's song. After this furtive introduction to his disturbing subject, Duck dwells for the next four lines on the "endless Toils" of the "poor *Thresher,*" only to conclude his verse paragraph with a return to grateful praise of his patron, "Ev'n these [the toils], with Pleasure, can the Muse rehearse, / When you and Gratitude demand her Verse" (p. 10, lines 9, 10, 11-2). It is an uneasy containment; Duck will bemoan one patronizing relationship, that with his agricultural master, within a frame of gratitude for another, that with his literary patron. These lines thus exhibit the sort of hesitancy or unresolved tension Hunter claims we will find in Pope if we look beyond the apparent closure of the couplet, or rhyming unit, and examine the larger unit of meaning, the verse paragraph. His form thus serves Duck well here to convey the anomalies of his strange existence. As he proceeds, however, his couplets repress his resentment of the farmer and thereby convey not tension and qualification of ideas, but an unintentional inversion of values and reversal of meaning:

> Soon as the golden Harvest quits the Plain,
> And CERES' Gifts reward the Farmer's Pain;
> What Corn each Sheaf will yield, intent to hear,
> And guess from thence the Profits of the Year,
> He calls his Reapers forth: Around we stand,
> With deep Attention, waiting his Command.
>
> (p. 11, lines 13-8)

The passage shows no hint of discontent with the farmer-laborer relationship. Indeed, "pain" is attributed, not to the worker, but to the farmer, whose "Profits" are characterized as an unproblematic, if not natural, reward for his undefined hardship. Moreover, the crucial distinction between good and bad masters we saw in the opening lines threatens to collapse, for this same farmer is given the imperative powers that Pope attributes to his patron Granville in "Windsor Forest" as part of a right and natural order. Conversely, the laboring threshers of the title, whose toils we have just been told, "always grow anew" (p. 10, line 9), are introduced with unintentional irony as motionless; they stand to attend the farmer, whose power to "[c]ommand" is punctuated by the final position of that word in the sentence and the rhyming couplet.

Duck's couplets continue to work against his purpose as they continue to reinforce the economic order he means to rail against:

> To each our Task he readily divides,
> And pointing, to our diffrent Stations guides.
> As he directs, to distant Barns we go;
> Here two for Wheat, and there for Barley two.

> (p. 11, lines 19-22)

The division, the pointing, and the guiding all issue from the Farmer; this is his order and it appropriates the order of Duck's couplets in the two half lines that specify the content of his directions—"Here two for Wheat, and there for Barley two."[28] Something similar happens when Duck has the oppressive Farmer speak, "'So dry the Corn was carry'd from the Field, / So easily 'twill thresh, so well 'twill yield'" (p. 11, lines 25-6). The three-part parallelism—so dry, so easily, so well—again recast the thresher's labor, not as the source of the thresher's misery, but as part of an unquestioned order that culminates in the Farmer's "yield."

Elsewhere, Duck is more successful in controlling the power of the couplet, in making it serve his rhetorical ends. This is especially true once he leaves the Farmer behind and begins to describe the actual work of the threshers, thus resisting the effacement of his labor and insisting on its representation:

> With rapid Force our sharpen'd Blades we drive,
> Strain ev'ry Nerve, and Blow for Blow we give.
> All strive to vanquish, tho' the Victor gains
> No other Glory, but the greatest Pains.

> (lines 116-9)

Duck's emphasis here and in the several lines preceding is on the almost epic energy of the formerly "motionless" threshers as they "strive," "strain," and "drive." The last two lines move rapidly from heroic effort—"all strive to vanquish"—to its unjust reward: great suffering. Now the couplet, particularly the ironic rhyme between "Victor gains" and the final, emphatic "greatest Pains," calls attention to the injustice and futility of the

thresher's life.[29] In another passage describing the threshers' perspective, Duck again employs his verse form effectively:

> Before us we perplexing Thistles find,
> And Corn blown adverse with the ruffling Wind.
> Behind our Master waits; and if he spies
> One charitable Ear, he grudging cries,
> "Ye scatter half your Wages o'er the Land."
> Then scrapes the Stubble with his greedy Hand.

> (pp. 24-5, lines 240-5)

Duck stresses the threshers' entrapment by placing them between two parallel couplets: "Before" stretches the scene of their thankless labor among "perplexing" and "adverse" elements; "Behind" is the relentless master, reduced to a spying eye, a grudging voice, and a greedy hand.

Despite these successes, Duck again appears to be overpowered by the couplet as he describes the final stages of the harvest:

> Pleas'd with the Scene, our Master glows with Joy;
> Bids us for Carrying all our Force employ;
> When strait Confusion o'er the Field appears,
> And stunning Clamours fill the Workmens Ears;
> The Bells and clashing Whips alternate sound,
> And rattling Waggons thunder o'er the Ground.
> The Wheat, when carry'd, Pease, and other Grain
> We soon secure, and leave a fruitless Plain;
> In noisy Triumph the last Load moves on,
> And loud Huzza's proclaim the Harvest done.

> (p. 26, lines 261-70)

Like the opening passage of "Windsor Forest," Duck's enjambed lines here convey a scene of apparent chaos and confusion transformed into a pleasing conclusion. But it is so only to the oppressive master. This seems then to be another instance in which Duck inadvertently affirms as "Triumph" the very system he intends to attack. Moreover, the next passage transforms the hated master into a generous host of a celebratory feast. But in subsequently characterizing the feast, especially the "too gen'rous" ale, as a "Cheat" (p. 27, lines 275, 277), Duck by extension implies that the harvest as triumphant conclusion is also an illusion. From the laborer's corrective point of view, his work is not the prelude to a happy ending; it is simply endless:

> But the next Morning soon reveals the Cheat,
> When the same Toils we must again repeat;
> To the same Barns must back again return,
> To labour there for Room for next Year's Corn.

> (p. 27, lines 277-80)

The parallelism is heaviest here between the last line of the first couplet and the first line of the second; the couplets are thus linked as are the thresher's years with a torturously iterative process, which Duck's final allusion to Sisyphus reinforces:

Like Sɪsʏᴘʜᴜs, our Work is never done;
Continually rolls back the restless Stone.
New-growing Labours still succeed the past;
And growing always new, must always last.

(p. 27, lines 283-6)

The words "New-growing" and "growing" are absorbed into the dense diction of ceaseless, inescapable labor: "never done," "Continually rolls back," "restless," "still," "always," "must always." Thus, in Duck's unique georgic, agricultural success, or growth, is to be lamented, not celebrated, because it perpetuates an economic system in which labor and reward are unjustly separated. At times, the power of Duck's couplets to distinguish, order, and assert seems ironically to affirm this system, but elsewhere, Duck uses the same form to reveal and condemn its injustice.

The Thresher's Labour exposes and corrects, not only the callous and incomplete perspective of the master-farmer, but also the frustrating inaccuracy of literary pastorals: "No Fountains murmur here, no Lambkins play, / No Linnets warble, and no Fields look gay" (p. 13, lines 58-9). Ironically Duck's own poem assumes the role of falsifying poetic construction in its portrayal of the female hay-makers as "a Throng / Of prattling Females" (p. 19, lines 162-3), who stop work the moment the master's back is turned and whose tongues move more nimbly than their rakes and prongs, but produce no more sense than a flock of "chirping" sparrows. Nothing that female agricultural laborers of early modern England customarily worked and talked in groups of seven to fifteen, Anthony Fletcher concludes that "[m]en needed their contribution to a basic standard of living far too earnestly for them to question this degree of independence from their eye and control."[30] Duck's characterization of the throngs of women segregated by a division of labor, however, betrays the anxiety men may have felt about their unsupervised congregation. A further summary of Duck's poem reads like a litany of sexist representations to be found in men's labor historiography. The category of worker is constructed as male (their sweaty, muscular arms compared to those Vulcan forged for Aetna), homes are havens from the men's work (not the scene of women's work), and the products of women's labor (the "Cocks appear[ing] in equal Rows" and the "Dumplin" the exhausted men eat in haste [p. 22, line 202; p. 19, line 154]) displace both the female worker and the work itself.[31] Though Collier had admired and even memorized Duck's works, she was so infuriated by **The Thresher's Labour** that she responded vehemently with *The Woman's Labour.*

If Duck's couplets sometimes seem to affirm the false perspective he sets out to correct, Collier avoids the parallel trap of reinforcing the sexism her poem laments. Rather, she begins by deftly using the couplet to argue from an imagined Golden Age during which women received respect and obedience:

When Men had us'd their utmost Care and Toil,
Their Recompence was but a Female Smile;
When they by Arts or Arms were render'd Great,
They laid their Trophies at a Woman's Feet.[32]

The parallel phrases beginning with "When" reinforce the order of female authority and superiority described in the passage. Similarly, the conclusion of each couplet—"a Female Smile" and "a Woman's Feet"—reiterate the idea that women's approval, homage, and pleasure were the end, or purpose, of all male activity. As Landry notes, quoting Christopher Middleton, Collier's vision here thus reverses gender relations in feudal England: "direct, personal servicing of men by women . . . both in and out of marriage."[33] Women's biological capacity to reproduce apparently did nothing to qualify their subordinate role, but on this subject, too, Collier's poem leaps over history to a prehistory in which child-bearing justifies the homage men gave to women:

They, in those Days, unto our Sex did bring
Their Hearts, their All, a Free-will Offering;
And as from us their Being they derive,
They back again should all due Homage give.

(p. 6, lines 21-4)

The symmetry of the couplet repeats the just, if unhistorical, exchange it describes: life flowing from the woman, homage flowing back to her.

When Collier shifts her focus back to the current order, that of male oppression, she does not let her poetic form seem to affirm that order. Rather, she uses the couplet to expose the system's abuses. For example, she draws power from the expectation of the end-stop by violating it as she gives vent to her anger at Duck in a twelve-line accusatory sentence addressed directly to "you, great Duck." The conclusion to which she thus builds is powerful and harsh, "But on our abject State you throw your Scorn, / And Women wrong, your Verses to adorn" (p. 7, lines 41-2). The two parts of the second line allude to the same two identities that Duck's opening lines uneasily acknowledge: his identity as oppressed laborer, which he betrays by wronging women of his class, and his identity as patronized poet, which he aggrandizes by adorning his verses with scorn of women. Collier, in other words, uses the structure of the couplet to compress and emphasize her complaint about how Duck has attempted to resolve the tension conveyed in his dedication; he has demeaned female members of his class to win favor with his patrons and readers. The force of the accusation is underlined by the rhyme—scorn / adorn—and, of course, the long-awaited end-stop. Collier also effectively plays against the expected end-stop when she describes the endlessness of women's labor.[34] Referring to the heaps of fine linen that greet the washerwomen in the cold predawn hours, for example, Collier "heaps" an extra line onto the couplet:

> Cambricks and Muslins, which our Ladies wear,
> Laces and Edgings, costly, fine, and rare,
> Which must be wash'd with utmost Skill and Care
>
> (p. 13, lines 159-61)

Here the violated couplet reflects a violated order of day and night, work and rest. The triplet, which itself calls attention to the woman's extended labor, is part of a sentence that is fifteen lines long and thus further mimics the apparent endlessness of her toil.

Collier has many such multiline sentences in her poem, but she also is able to exploit the concision of the tiny stanza form to make her point. Still stressing the nighttime labor of women, for example, she writes, "When Night comes on, unto our Home we go, / Our Corn we carry, and our Infant too" (p. 10, lines 101-2). The two parts of the first line introduce the ordered relationship of "Night" and "Home," which for men means sanctuary from their labor.[35] But the second line of the couplet, with its powerful zeugma "carry," reminds us of women's double burden, which will not allow them to rest either at night or at home. Collier goes on to describe the multiple responsibilities of women in another enjambed passage that concludes with reference to many more burdens than two: "So many Things for our Attendance call, / Had we ten Hands, we could employ them all" (p. 10, lines 107-8). Frequently, Collier uses the divisions of the couplet to clearly contrast this multifaceted labor to the work of Duck (whom she continues to address directly):

> Now night comes on, from whence you have Relief,
> But that, alas! does but increase our Grief;
>
> . . . . .
>
> When Ev'ning's come, you Homeward take your Way,
> We, till our Work is done, are forc'd to stay.
>
> (pp. 14-5, lines 188-97)

The divisions between the lines of each couplet reinforce the division of labor to which the couplets refer, but the passages do not imply, as Duck's occasionally do, that this division is somehow a right order, for Collier's diction ("alas," for example, and "forc'd") and especially her rhymes ("Relief . . . Grief," "your Way . . . forc'd to stay") clarify and reinforce the injustice of the division. Despite the gendered inequities to which her couplets thus call attention, Collier concludes her poem by returning to the classist oppression that should unite male and female laborers:

> So the industrious Bees do hourly strive
> To bring their Loads of Honey to the Hive;
> Their sordid Owners always reap the Gains,
> And poorly recompense their Toil and Pains.
>
> (p. 17, lines 243-6)

The lines contain and contrast the disparate fates of owner and worker: gains, on the one hand, toil and pains, on the other. "Their owners"—and the pronoun is ominously ambiguous—"reap" only financially while those who physically reap, who "strive / To bring their Loads," expend their days, nights, years, and lives in endless, thankless effort.[36] Collier's simple diction and direct rhyme state her case plaintively and powerfully within and, indeed, through the characteristic parts of the couplet.

At times, Duck's struggles in *The Thresher's Labour* seem to support the hypothesis that form can control or determine meaning, that "patterns of rhetoric, thought, and value [are] so fully built into structure that one can speak usefully in an absolute sense of what a particular form represents culturally or what kinds of work it can do." More specifically, whenever the poem reaffirms the current socio-economic order despite Duck's clear unhappiness with it, the example of *The Thresher's Labour* suggests that the couplet does indeed have a necessary connection to a hierarchical and authoritative universe. But at his better moments, Duck uses the couplet to convey rather than betray his class-based anguish, to unmask the master's order as a cheat, and to contrast it to the endless sameness of his own life. These moments of control suggest what Collier's more consistent success in *The Woman's Labour* more powerfully supports: however "fundamentally aristocratic" poetry of the 1730s may be, for however many reasons, even its most dominant verse form does not have an essential ideology. In representing a prehistorical matriarchy, in conveying the nightmarish demands placed on women laborers and contrasting them to Duck's own male labor, and in expressing her angry disappointment in Duck, Collier makes the form of classically educated men work for her. Thus, this brief foray into the poetic labor of thresher and woman reinforces Hunter's arguments in many ways: it denies an essential meaning or ideology of form, but acknowledges that forms can support powerful tendencies and patterns; it provides further evidence that the meanings of a verse form must be derived from actual practice—Duck's and Collier's similar circumstances and purposes certainly did not extend to similar uses of the couplet; and most importantly, it supports Hunter's plea that in our reaction to the ahistorical formalism of the past, we do not deny the role formal analysis can play in fruitful literary inquiry.

Notes

1. J. Paul Hunter, "Form as Meaning: Pope and the Ideology of the Couplet," *ECent* [*Eighteenth Century*] 37, 3 (Fall 1996): 257-70, 258.

2. George Williamson, "The Rhetorical Pattern of Neo-Classical Wit," *MP* [*Modern Philology*] 33, 1 (August 1935): 55-81, 80.

3. Hunter, p. 258.

4. William Bowman Piper, *The Heroic Couplet* (Cleveland and London: Press of Case Western Reserve Univ., 1969), p. 6.

5. Piper, p. 8; my emphasis.

6. Piper, pp. 145, 149-50.

7. See for example Felicity Nussbaum and Laura Brown, "Revising Critical Practices: An Introductory Essay," in *The New Eighteenth Century: Theory, Politics, English Literature,* ed. Nussbaum and Brown (New York and London: Methuen, 1987), pp. 1-22.

8. Hunter, p. 260. Hunter cites Brown as an example of a perceptive critic who weakens her analysis of Alexander Pope by imposing a meaning on his poetic form (pp. 260-2).

9. In a very similar argument, Anne Janowitz also rejects the notion that form determines meaning while urging us, nonetheless, to pay careful attention to the meanings of form in particular instantiations ("Class and Literature: The Case of Romantic Chartism," in *Rethinking Class: Literary Studies and Social Formations,* ed. Wai Chee Dimock and Michael T. Gilmore, Social Foundations of Aesthetic Forms [New York: Columbia Univ. Press, 1994], pp. 239-66). Just as Hunter warns us of the misreadings that result when we assume the heroic couplet is ideologically wedded to "an authoritative and fixed universe," Janowitz argues against the assumption that the flourishing of the lyric form was inseparable from the affirmation of a unified bourgeois subjectivity (p. 241).

10. Evidence of increased interest in formalism within eighteenth-century studies can be found in two panels at two recent meetings of the American Society for Eighteenth-Century Studies: "Formalist Criticism in an Age of Historicism: Can There Be a Non-Essentialist Formalism?" chaired by Hunter, 4 April 1998, South Bend IN; and "Formalism and Eighteenth-Century Studies," chaired by Howard Weinbrot, 25 March 1999, Milwaukee WI. In addition, David H. Richter has recently edited a collection of essays, *Ideology and Form in Eighteenth-Century Literature* (Lubbock TX: Texas Tech Univ. Press, 1999). Coincidentally, there has been an upsurge of interest in laboring-class poetry of the eighteenth century as evidenced by the publication in-progress of the six-volume *English Labouring-Class Poets, 1700-1900,* ed. John Goodring (London: Pickering and Chatto, 2003-) and by a special issue of *ECent* on the laboring-class tradition (42, 3 [Fall 2001]).

11. To pose these questions, of course, risks essentializing class and gender at the moment I am trying to test whether one can avoid essentializing literary form within formal analysis. As Peter Hitchcock reminds us in a recent article, "They Must Be Represented? Problems in Theories of Working-Class Representation," *PMLA* 115, 1 (January 2000): 20-32, 29, people "come to think and feel in class ways through their relations to capital, but they do not represent these relations in unified or pure forms." One of the chief agents in splintering the illusion of a unified working-class subjectivity has been the study of gender, theorists of which have responded variously to the accusation of essentialism. For examples of feminist deconstruction of masculine constructions of the laboring class, see Ava Baron, ed., *Work Engendered: Toward a New History of American Labor* (Ithaca and London: Cornell Univ. Press, 1991), and Barbara Foley, *Radical Representations: Politics and Form in U.S. Proletarian Fiction, 1929-1941,* Post-Contemporary Interventions (Durham and London: Duke Univ. Press, 1993). In referring to both Stephen Duck and Mary Collier as laboring-class poets and to Collier as an advocate for women within that class, I am not assuming an essential or unified subjectivity for either, but instead am employing the categories of class and gender as relational, i.e., as they are used by these poets to differentiate themselves from the vast majority of preceding and contemporary poets using heroic couplets.

I am also aware of issues raised by using the term "class" as opposed to "rank" or "order" when discussing literature of preindustrial England and by applying scholarship on the "working class" to that literature. For an excellent summary of these issues, see William J. Christmas, *The Lab'ring Muses: Work, Writing, and the Social Order in English Plebeian Poetry, 1730-1830* (Newark: Univ. of Delaware Press, 2001), pp. 42-5. Though Christmas does not focus on the couplet form and though he assumes rather than concludes that textural forms did not limit or determine meaning, he poses questions similar to those I pose here: "what ideological representations were produced and reproduced in textual forms in the eighteenth century that were intended to keep men and women of the laboring classes in their appointed places in the social order? . . . in what ways did plebeian poets contest or counter these representations in their own published texts?" (pp. 48-9).

12. James Sutherland, *A Preface to Eighteenth Century Poetry* (Oxford: Clarendon Press, 1948), pp. 44-63, 50; John Dennis, *The Critical Works of John Dennis,* ed. Edward Niles Hooker, 2 vols. (Baltimore: Johns Hopkins Press, 1943), 2:37, qtd. in Sutherland, p. 60. This is not to deny a concurrent growing interest in the original genius of the

natural poet, but, as Betty Rizzo points out, "though these poets [and Duck was prominent among them] had a potentially revolutionary function—intended to demonstrate the superiority of nature and Homer over neo-Augustan tradition, they usually produced instead an assurance, comforting to the establishment at least, of the superiority of art, Dryden, and Pope" ("The Patron as Poet-Maker: The Politics of Benefaction," *SECC* [*Studies in Eighteenth-Century Culture*] 20 [1990]: 241-66, 241-2). See also James M. Osborn, "Spence, Natural Genius, and Pope," *PQ* [*Philosophical Quarterly*] 45, 1 (January 1966): 123-44.

13. The phrase "got English" comes from Joseph Spence, *A Full and Authentick Account of Stephen Duck, the Wiltshire Poet* (London, 1731), p. 10; qtd. in Sutherland, p. 52. The biographical information that follows comes from Rose Mary Davis, *Stephen Duck, The Thresher-Poet,* Univ. of Maine Studies, 2d ser., 8 (Orono ME: Univ. Press, 1926); and Paul Jacob, "Stephen Duck," in *Eighteenth-Century British Poets, First Series,* vol. 95 of *The Dictionary of Literary Biography* (Detroit, New York, and London: Gale Research, 1990), pp. 47-56. Biographical information on Collier comes from Donna Landry, "The Resignation of Mary Collier: Some Problems in Feminist Literary History," in Brown and Nussbaum, eds., pp. 99-120.

14. Jacob, p. 54. Rizzo, pp. 244-8, argues that Caroline thus uses Duck to rebuff the classically trained Pope for his haughty independence.

15. Jacob, p. 54; Rizzo, p. 242.

16. Duck, "A Description of a Journey to Marlborough, Bath, Portsmouth etc."; qtd. in Davis, pp. 83-4.

17. Jonathan Swift, "On Stephen Duck. The Thresher and Favourite Poet. A Quibbling Epigram" (1730); qtd. in Davis, p. 53. See pp. 53-60 for a survey of attacks on Duck.

18. Duck, "The Thresher's Labour," in *The Thresher's Labour (Stephen Duck) and The Woman's Labour (Mary Collier),* intro. Moira Ferguson (London, 1736; facsimile rprt. Los Angeles: Clark Memorial Library, 1985), p. 21, lines 188, 180-1. Hereafter Ferguson; subsequent references will appear parenthetically in the text by page and line number.

19. Landry, "Resignation," p. 108.

20. Landry, "Resignation," p. 117. However, in *The Muses of Resistance: Laboring-Class Women's Poetry in Britain, 1739-1796* (Cambridge: Cam-

bridge Univ. Press, 1990), p. 56, Landry allows that Collier challenges sexual, social, and political assumptions, and she identifies in Collier's work a feminist critique of the misogyny embedded in emergent working-class consciousness. Christmas, p. 117, points out this same shift.

21. Christmas, p. 65, argues that Duck established a model of honesty, industry, and piety for plebian poets that was ideologically useful to polite society, though he also argues that social critique was possible and did occur within this model. He contends, p. 50, that laboring-class authors were capable of borrowing high culture forms without total complicity. Again, his argument converges with my conclusions, though he does not focus on the couplet as I do.

22. Christmas, pp. 89-90, explains how the title page and verse epistle appended to the pirated 1730 edition of Duck's poems attempt to capitalize on his dual identities by stressing the tension between Duck's rural background and his current position as court poet. Similarly, the copperplate illustration of Duck positions him between a writing table and a barn, holding a copy of Milton in one hand and a threshing flail in the other.

23. Both Duck and Collier wrote in other forms, but primarily in heroic couplets. For a lucid summary of forces leading Duck to elite literary conventions, see Linda Zionkowski, "Strategies of Containment: Stephen Duck, Ann Yearsley, and the Problem of Polite Culture," *ECLife* [*Eighteenth Century Life*], n.s., 13, 3 (November 1989): 91-108, 95-7.

24. Raymond Williams, *The Country and the City* (London: Chatto and Windus, 1973), p. 88.

25. Ferguson, "Introduction," in Ferguson, p. v; Landry, "Resignation," p. 109.

26. Alexander Pope, "Windsor-Forest," in *Pastoral Poetry and "An Essay on Criticism,"* ed. E. Audra and Aubrey Williams (London and New Haven: Methuen, 1961), pp. 149-50, lines 15-6. This is vol. 1 of The Twickenham Edition of the Poems of Alexander Pope, 6 vols., gen. ed. John Butt.

27. Hunter, pp. 263-4, cites "Windsor Forest" as an example of Pope's early work that complexly questions rather than simply asserts, in this case, England's prosperity under Queen Anne. He does not and would not, I believe, quarrel with my brief comments on Pope's opening lines.

28. John Goodridge does point out that the workers here are no more than "numbers to divide up arbitrarily" (*Rural Life in Eighteenth-Century English Poetry,* Cambridge Studies in Eighteenth-

Century English Literature and Thought 27 [Cambridge: Cambridge Univ. Press, 1995], p. 25).

29. Goodridge, who prefers the pirated 1730 edition as uninfluenced by efforts to classicize Duck's poem, concedes that the earlier version, quoted below, lacks the sharp irony of the 1736 edition:

> With rapid force our well-whet Blades we drive,
> Strain every nerve, and blow for blow we give:
> Tho' but this Eminence the foremost gains,
> Only t'excel the rest in Toil and Pains.

(p. 31)

30. Anthony Fletcher, *Gender, Sex, and Subordination in England, 1500-1800* (New Haven: Yale Univ. Press, 1995), p. 253.

31. On constructing the worker as male, see Foley, p. 221, and Fletcher, pp. 253-4; on the home as a haven for men, see Baron, p. 6; on laborers being displaced by the products of their labor, see Hitchcock, p. 24.

32. Collier, *The Woman's Labour,* in Ferguson, p. 6, lines 17-20; subsequent references will appear parenthetically in the text by page and line number.

33. Christopher Middleton, "The Sexual Division of Labour in Feudal England," *New Left Review* 113-4 (Jan/April 1979): 147-68, 164, qtd. in Landry, "Resignation," p. 289 n16.

34. The degree to which women work more than men according to these two poems has become an issue of contention. It seems clear that Collier provides more evidence of night work for women than Duck does for men. It is not clear that women work more in the winter despite Landry's claim that Duck glosses over seasonal respite for men ("Resignation," p. 113). Collier describes at length the charring women do during the winter, but Duck similarly describes the threshing that men do in barns, as Goodridge, pp. 44-5, has pointed out.

35. See Goodridge, pp. 71-8, for a more detailed analysis of how Duck and Collier represent the homecoming scene, "a universal western ideal" (p. 71).

36. Christmas, p. 127, points out that in the 1730s, bees were still being destroyed by fumigation in order to harvest the honey. Such information gives Collier's reference to the workers' "poor recompense" a grim and powerful irony. For more on the bee image, see Goodridge, pp. 51-2, and Christmas, pp. 126-7.

James Mulholland (essay date 2004)

SOURCE: Mulholland, James. "'To Sing the Toils of Each Revolving Year': Song and Poetic Authority in Stephen Duck's *The Thresher's Labour*." *Studies in Eighteenth-Century Culture* 33 (2004): 153-74.

[*In the essay below, Mulholland examines Duck's contribution to eighteenth-century pastoral poetry, pointing out that "Duck's verse creates a model for a new type of pastoral song indebted to a more accurate depiction of rural labor."*]

The eighteenth century marks a peculiar and difficult moment for the English pastoral tradition. For some scholars, exemplified perhaps by Frank Kermode, the pastoral, properly defined, does not survive into the eighteenth century.[1] Others argue that the changing conditions of the English countryside require unique generic transformations of eighteenth-century pastoral.[2] Responding to changes in the English countryside, particularly in agrarian labor, pastoral undergoes a redefinition throughout the century whose instability arises from both the adaptation and the persistence of its classical conceits.[3] One author who exemplifies this dual process of generic innovation and conservation is Stephen Duck. Duck, who worked as a thresher in England, composed and circulated *The Thresher's Labour* in 1730. He has received renewed critical treatment in the last decade, in part because the poem presents a detailed account of his rural labor, and also because its rapid success in the literary culture of England secured for him the patronage of Queen Caroline, which initiated his personal transformation from agrarian laborer to poet.[4]

Recent criticism considers *The Thresher's Labour* an important starting point for a poetry that describes rural labor and the English countryside more accurately, rather than portrays an idealized golden age. The meticulous description of the thresher's physical labor often is interpreted as a reflection of the larger social and economic changes precipitated by agrarian capitalism and by the continued enclosure of common land.[5] In addition, Duck represents one of the most visible origins of "plebeian" authorship during the eighteenth century. His dual identity as an agrarian laborer and a poet makes his career a fertile context in which to investigate changes in eighteenth-century authorship and its relationship to mass print.[6] In connection with all of these themes, this article examines *The Thresher's Labour* in relation to orality, one aspect of the poem that has been overlooked in recent studies. It argues that with *The Thresher's Labour* Duck modifies the convention that the pastoral poem is a song, and, in the process, engages with a broader type of pastoralism that encompasses what are typically seen as separate pastoral and georgic modes. Duck's reinvented pastoral song uniquely registers the conditions of his labor, and, therefore, reflects wider social and economic changes of the English countryside.

Singing also permits Duck to reconcile his dual status as an agrarian laborer and as a poet. The use of singing in *The Thresher's Labour* suggests, moreover, the roles that manuscript and print play in publicizing the conditions of the English countryside to a primarily urban and upper-class readership. The subtle acknowledgement of manuscript and print circulation isolates the relationship between orality and literary in the poem, and reveals the ways that Duck differentiates singing from other types of orality—such as the speech of women laborers—that remain largely unrecognized by literate technologies. Finally, this article considers *The Thresher's Labour* within the larger context of Duck's poetic career, and demonstrates the significance of the metaphor of singing for contemporary responses to Duck's poetry by authors such as Jonathan Swift, Robert Dodsley, and George Crabbe.

The perception that pastoral originates with the song of shepherds makes singing fundamental to the artistry of the pastoral poem. In the early-eighteenth century, singing reflects pastoral's supposed origin in an ideal golden age. In *The Guardian* 22, the critic and author Thomas Tickell is explicit about the correlation between the abundance of nature and the presence of song in pastoral poetry. He claims, for example, that pastoral begins in "a state of ease, innocence and contentment; where plenty begot pleasure, and pleasure begot singing, and singing begot poetry, and poetry begot pleasure again."[7] The abundance of nature generates the conditions that make singing, and therefore poetry, possible. For Tickell, it is natural that pastoral poetry should "transport us to a kind of *Fairy Land*, where our ears are soothed by the Melody of Birds, bleating Flocks, and purling Streams; our Eyes enchanced with flowery Meadows and springing Greens; we are laid under cool Shades, and entertained with all the Sweets and Freshness of Nature" (105). In Tickell's pastoral, the presence of singing signifies the ease, pleasure, and contentment of the golden age.

In "A Discourse on Pastoral Poetry" (1709) Alexander Pope also emphasizes pastoral's origin in song and in a pre-modern golden age. He declares that pastoral begins with the leisure of shepherds and that no diversion was more proper "to that solitary and sedentary life as singing, and that in their songs they took the occasion to celebrate their own felicity."[8] Singing emphasizes the felicity of shepherds and the leisure of their occupation so that pastoral poetry "consists in exposing the best side only of the shepherd's life, and in concealing its miseries" (120). Yet Pope's "Discourse" also suggests some of the latent possibilities for transforming the pastoral eventually taken up by authors such as Duck.

The emphasis upon the leisure of rural laborers in "Discourse" encourages speculation about its opposite, and admits the possibility of investigating the conditions of rural labor. To depict the conditions of rural labor and the English countryside, Duck modifies the pastoral by exposing its antecedent preoccupation with the difference between leisure and labor.

That song serves as a means of political or social commentary is not new to the pastoral tradition or unique to the eighteenth century. Toward the end of the first of Virgil's *Eclogues,* Meliboeus, removed from his property and divested of his flock by civil unrest in Rome, abruptly states: "I'll sing no songs."[9] Meliboeus's forthright assertion that he'll no longer sing possesses both an aesthetic and a political purpose: his decision not to sing indicates both the conclusion of Virgil's first eclogue and the end of the stable political and prosperous economic conditions that make singing possible. To place it within Tickell's terminology from *The Guardian,* if plenty begets pleasure and pleasure begets singing, then Meliboeus demonstrates that the lack of leisure and plenty culminates with the cessation of singing. Even in the classical pastoral, therefore, singing acts as an interchange between the aesthetic realm and the social and political realm, and serves as a measure of social, political, and economic change.

In *The Thresher's Labour,* Duck identifies the changing conditions of the English countryside and of the pastoral tradition in a way similar to Meliboeus at the conclusion of Virgil's first eclogue.[10] Though *The Thresher's Labour* does not describe the outright cessation of singing, early in the poem the speaker creates a vivid portrait of the thresher at work:

> Nor yet, the tedious Labour to beguile,
> And make the passing Minutes sweetly smile,
> Can we, like Shepherds, tell a merry Tale;
> The Voice is lost, drown'd by the louder Flail.
> But we may think—Alas! What pleasing thing,
> Here, to the mind, can the dull Fancy bring?
> Our eye beholds no pleasing Object here,
> No chearful Sound diverts our list'ning Ear.
> The shepherd well may tune his Voice to sing,
> Inspir'd with all the Beauties of the Spring.
> No Fountains murmur here, no Lambkins play,
> No linnets warble, and no Fields look gay.[11]

What's noticeable about this passage is the conscious contrast between the thresher and the shepherd. The description of the thresher differs remarkably from that of the shepherd, and this contrast extends to their experience of voice. Whereas the shepherd "well may tune his voice to sing / Inspir'd by all the beauties of the Spring," the thresher's "Voice is lost, drown'd by the louder flail" so that "no cheerful sound diverts [his] list'ning Ear" (13). In this instance, it is the relationship to *singing* voice that announces the difficulties of the thresher's labor, and the difference of his labor from that of the shepherd. The shepherd, surrounded by playful lambkins and murmuring fountains, finds ample means and subject matter for song, and through his song he cheerfully diverts himself from his labor. The thresher, by contrast, does not work in an environment conducive to song. Laboring when the outdoor work of harvest is complete, the thresher toils while closely confined within the barn.[12] But the techniques involved in threshing are even more important than the location of his work. The thresher's "louder flail" drowns out his voice; his song is overwhelmed by the tools involved in his labor, making it impossible for that song to be heard. The thresher, Duck laments, cannot "beguile" his labor and make the "passing Minutes sweetly smile" by hearing a "merry tale" (13).

The differentiation of the thresher and the shepherd signals Duck's revision of the artistic conventions of pastoral. In "The Pastoral Revolution," Michael McKeon organizes the value-laden oppositions of leisure and labor and of the bucolic and the georgic within the larger category of pastoralism. The "pastoral" and the "georgic," McKeon contends, "occupy alternative and partial positions on the pastoral continuum that is defined not by the dichotomous opposition of nature to art but by the fluidity with which the differential may be variously enacted."[13] He continues that pastoral "works both to affirm and to suspend such oppositions—to conceive of them, that is, not dichotomously but dialectically" (271). One of the most powerful and important separations occurs with Virgil's *Eclogues* and his *Georgics,* where the *Eclogues* come to represent the bucolic impulse and the *Georgics* originate the georgic impulse. Yet the last line of Virgil's *Georgics* is the first line of his *Eclogues,* demonstrating a circularity that implies that pastoral and georgic are more continuous than separate (269). One might argue that the availability or unavailability of singing designates two different positions on this pastoral continuum. Duck's contrast of the thresher from the shepherd benefits from his sophisticated attention to the imbricated relationship between leisure and labor in pastoral. His representation of the thresher rather than the more traditional shepherd designates the difference between his own pastoral and the neoclassical pastoral of Tickell and Pope. In this way, the social and political potential of *The Thresher's Labour* relies not so much upon the difference between pastoral and georgic, but upon Duck's ability to transform pastoral by contrasting the shepherd's ability to sing with the thresher's inability to be heard while singing.[14]

The availability or unavailability of singing in *The Thresher's Labour* provides immediate access not only to formal issues of eighteenth-century pastoral, but also to social and economic changes in the English countryside. *The Thresher's Labour* presents a detailed depiction of one aspect of modern agrarian labor.[15] These working conditions differ substantially from those experienced by the shepherds of Tickell's and Pope's pastorals. Yet it is notable that Duck never specifies the historical moment of the thresher or the shepherd in the poem. Despite Pope's insistence that shepherds' song originates in the golden age, Duck does not explicitly associate threshers with the modern English countryside and shepherds with a pre-modern golden age.[16] Instead, it is the different rhythm of their labor rather than different historical periods that further distinguishes threshers from shepherds. At one point in *The Thresher's Labour,* while addressing the peculiar rhythm of his work, the thresher states matter-of-factly that "No intermission in our Work we know; / The noisy threshal must for ever go" (12). It is the noise of the flail that marks out the thresher's time so that "in the Air our knotty Weapons fly, / And now with equal Force descend from high; / Down one, one up, so well they keep the Time" (12). By the end of the poem the thresher is even more explicit:

> Thus, as the Year's revolving Course goes round,
> No Respite from our Labour can be found:
> Like Sɪsʏᴘʜᴜs, our work is never done;
> Continually rolls back the restless Stone.
> New-growing Labours still succeed the past;
> And growing always new, must always last.
>
> (27)

The final image of Sisyphus reinforces the unique rhythm of the thresher's labor. Whereas the shepherds of Pope's "Discourse" possess time for leisure, for the thresher "the threshal must forever go" so that "No Respite from our Labour can be found" (13, 27). The sound of the flail manifests materially the uniform temporality of threshing that "grow[s] always new" and therefore "must always last" (27). In this way, *The Thresher's Labour* does not differentiate the shepherd from the thresher through the temporal markers of premodern golden age and modern British agriculture— that is, through the past and the present—though these markers may be accurate. It is the thresher's mode of labor—noisy, mechanical, and repetitive yet "always new"—that differs so greatly from that of the shepherd. The noise of the thresher's flail and the thresher's song, moreover, represent two types of competing oralities and competing temporalities. The physical intensity of threshing, resulting from the noise of the thresher's tools and the uniform organization of his time, overwhelms both leisure and song. The way that the noise of the flail drowns out the thresher's song and efficiently organizes his time, therefore, demonstrates the evident difference between Duck's pastoral, grounded in the depiction of rural labor, and the idealized pastoral of Tickell and Pope.[17]

Yet one might ask who would hear the thresher's song if it could be heard over the noise of the flail? Considering Duck's meticulous attention to singing, it is unsurprising that he uses the metaphor of singing to answer this question. One of the most important features of the poem is its prominent dedication: "To the Reverend Mr. Stanley." Stanley was a local clergyman who noticed Duck while he was employed as a thresher, and the opening stanza of *The Thresher's Labour* figures Stanley's patronage as essential to the creation of the poem:

> The grateful tribute of these rural Lays,
> Which to her Patron's Hand the Muse conveys,
> Deign to accept: 'Tis just she Tribute bring
> To him, whose Bounty gives her Life to sing;
> To him, whose gen'rous Favours tune her Voice;
> And bid her, 'midst her Poverty, rejoice.
> Inspir'd by these, she dares herself prepare,
> To sing the Toils of each revolving Year;
> Those endless Toils, which always grow anew
> And the poor *Thresher's* destin'd to pursue:
> Ev'n these, with Pleasure, can the Muse rehearse
> When you and Gratitude demand her verse.
>
> 　　　　　　　　　　　　　　　　　　(10)

The opening stanza introduces Stanley as an important facilitator of the poem. It is significant, though, that Duck uses singing to relate Stanley's patronage to the overall operation of the poem. It is Stanley's "bounty" which permits the Muse to sing and his "generous favours" that "tune her voice." The metaphor of "tuning" the Muse's voice is particularly noteworthy. It suggests that the Muse possesses a wide vocal register, and that the attention of individuals such as Stanley allows the Muse to discover the appropriate tone and articulation with which to depict the specific labors of the thresher.

Yet if the addressee of the opening stanza is fairly clear, its speaker is not. Whereas the majority of *The Thresher's Labour* appears in the voice of a male thresher, the opening stanza involves the voice of a female Muse and creates a significant ambiguity about the relationship between the singing Muse and the thresher. One could interpret this as a typical image of inspiration by a Muse. Yet the opening stanza of the poem troubles the possibility of identifying an anonymous thresher, or even Duck, as the speaker of these lines. It is her voice that sings "the toils of each revolving year; / Those endless Toils, which always grow anew / And the poor Thresher's destined to pursue" (10). The stanza ends by arguing that Stanley and gratitude demand "her verse." About the multiple speakers of *The Thresher's Labour,* Bridget Keegan claims that "the poem, as Duck creates it, is explicitly not originally the product of the laborer."[18] She continues that the "verbal exchange of the literary work between the Muse and patron frames the ensuing account of the exchange of labor—agricultural work—between the farmer and thresher" (553). The displacement of the thresher's poetic authority onto the Muse reinforces the

thresher's alienation from the products of his own labor—both of his agricultural labor and of his "voice." The exploitation of the thresher's labor repeats itself in the framework of the poem, where the thresher cannot speak of his own labors without the mediation of a patron and a conventional Muse. Duck responds to this required mediation through his complicated use of pronouns; as Keegan states, throughout the poem Duck creates a "singular poetic 'I,' a speaking subject distinct from the threshing 'we'" (556). The "we" records the manual labor of the thresher and the "I" translates that labor into a more suitable figurative discourse (555).

While Keegan rightly points out the necessary mediation of the poem, one might add that Duck formulates the poem as the song of a female Muse and, in the process, partly replaces his own authorship of the poem with the image of a creative circuit between a generous patron and a singing female Muse. Yet one need not interpret Duck's separation of poetic authority in the opening stanza between a patron and a singing female Muse solely as a devaluation of the thresher's voice and of Duck's poetic authority. If one of the explicit questions of *The Thresher's Labour* concerns the possibility of the thresher singing, then Duck's separation of poetic authority between his patron and a singing female Muse demonstrates, at the level of the overall poem, one solution to Duck's anxiety about poetic authority. McKeon declares about pastoral in the eighteenth century that "when the customary objects of pastoral representation become also its authorial subjects, the contemporary revolution in status and gender categorization becomes quite explicit."[19] Duck's identification with both the unheard male thresher and the singing female Muse allows him to partly inhabit both the subject and the object of pastoral within the same poetic exercise, and the convention that the pastoral poem is a song creates one opportunity for Duck to negotiate his own ambiguous status both as subject and object. Singing supplies a solution to the problem of representing the conditions of modern agrarian labor both as a participant in those conditions and as an observer of those conditions—that is, as a thresher and as a singer. In effect, the separation of poetic authority in *The Thresher's Labour* recapitulates the entire occasion of the poem: the Muse sings of how the thresher's song cannot be heard over the noise of his own labor.

Duck's description of the entire poem as the song of a Muse suggests that the scribal or the printed poem succeeds in making the thresher "heard" when the thresher's song could not. The speaker, for example, asserts that the Muse's "rural lays" are conveyed to the patron's *hand,* which presumes a tangible, material form for the poem.[20] The seemingly contradictory image of the Muse's song being conveyed to the patron's hand subtly acknowledges the scribal and printed forms of the poem, and imagines the creation and circulation of *The*

Thresher's Labour as a successful translation from song into manuscript and print. If the thresher's song represents an aesthetic form that cannot be recognized over the noise of his own labor, then the manuscript and printed versions of *The Thresher's Labour* preserve one account of that lack of recognition. William Christmas argues that Duck's poem "gives public, plebeian voice to rural laboring life."[21] One could further argue that the wide circulation of the poem in manuscript and print is the most tangible evidence of the degree to which the poem succeeds in publicizing the conditions of rural labor. The poem's ability to "give voice" is predicated upon the circulation, in script and print, of the thresher's inability to be heard while singing. Therefore, song contributes the essential metaphor that describes the poem's existence both as manuscript and print, and its potential to publicize the conditions of rural labor. In effect, the literate circulation makes the thresher's song "heard." In *The Thresher's Labour,* however, singing is not simply a synonym for literacy, or for writing. As the opening stanza demonstrates, the poem conceives of its own creation as a translation from singing into manuscript and type—that is, from orality to literacy.

The Thresher's Labour did circulate quite successfully in the literary culture of England during the 1730s, and the popularity of the poem provoked a number of satires that raise additional questions about Duck's figuration of poetic authority.[22] Many of these satires scrutinize Duck's suitability as a poet by emphasizing his history as a thresher. One of the most acidic examples of this type of response is Jonathan Swift's "On Stephen Duck, the Thresher, and Favourite Poet" (1730). In his poem, Swift dismisses Duck's poetry by insisting upon its fundamental similarity to agrarian labor. Swift begins his poem:

> The Thresher Duck could o'er the Queen prevail.
> The proverb says, 'No fence against a flail.'
> From *threshing* corn, he turns to *thresh* his brains;
> For which Her Majesty allows him grains.[23]

Swift's image of Duck prevailing over the Queen refers to Duck's acquisition of a royal sinecure from Queen Caroline, largely due to the popularity of *The Thresher's Labour.* But it is also significant that Swift claims Duck composes his poems by "thresh[ing] his brains." In Swift's image, the "rural lays" of *The Thresher's Labour* are more like an agricultural harvest than a song, and Duck merely threshes his brain in the same way that he once threshed corn. Swift's association of Duck's brain with nature's bounty—both of which can be threshed—realigns him with the object, rather than the subject, of the traditional pastoral.[24] While in *The Thresher's Labour* the unheard thresher and the singing Muse contribute to an image of Duck's ambiguous authorial identity, Swift attempts to conflate these two

positions and to associate Duck with the bounty of nature rather than the artfulness of the singer. Swift's basic assertion is that Duck remains a thresher whether the final product is a harvest or a poem.

Yet the metaphor of singing suggests another possible interpretation of Duck's transformation from threshing corn to "threshing his brains." If one allows that he represents his ambiguous position as both subject and object of pastoral through the singing Muse and the unheard thresher, then these two positions may help describe his own transformation from agrarian laborer to working poet. In his "Epistle to Stephen Duck" (1732), the laboring poet Robert Dodsley addresses the issue of laboring-class authorship through the metaphor of singing. Dodsley is a footman (who would eventually become a renowned bookseller), and his position demonstrates some clear affinities to that of Duck:

> So you and I, just naked from the shell,
> In chirping notes, our future singing tell;
> Unfeather'd yet, in judgement, though, or skill,
> Hop round the basis of Parnassus' hill:
> Our flights are low, and want of art and strength
> Forbids to carry us to the wish'd for length.
> But fledg'd and cherish'd with a kindly spring,
> We'll mount the summit, and melodious sing.[25]

The optimism of Dodsley's figuration of himself and Duck as newborn birds—or even as "ducklings"—ready to ascend Parnassus derives from singing. While Duck and Dodsley remain "unfeather'd" in poetic judgment or skill, their "chirping notes" promise more able "future singing," and their ascent up Parnassus results from their "flights" of song. For Dodsley, occupying the position of singer indicates the success of their ascent. The ascent up Parnassus, moreover, denotes two material transformations: it signifies entry into the exclusive realm of polite literary culture and a corresponding elevation in social status.

Duck himself relies upon the identity of singer to evaluate his ambiguous status as a poet. A few years after the composition of *The Thresher's Labour,* he again uses singing to detail his peculiar position as a poet who began as an agrarian laborer. In his lengthy **"A Description of a Journey,"** Duck self-consciously considers his new identity as a poet and his increasingly distant identity as a thresher. At one point in the poem, he describes a feast held once a year in his honor in Wiltshire, the county in which he was born and where he worked as a thresher.[26] In the process of portraying the holiday, he employs song, and the concept of an oral tradition in general, to envision his newer status as a poet:

> Hence, when their children's children shall admire
> This Holiday, and, whence deriv'd, inquire;
> Some grateful Father, partial to my Fame,
> Shall thus describe from whence, and how it came.

"Here, Child, a *Thresher* liv'd in ancient Days;
Quaint Songs he sang, and pleasing Roundelays,
A gracious QUEEN his Sonnets did commend;
And some *great Lord,* one TEMPLE, was his *Friend*:
And feast *the Threshers,* for *that Thresher's sake.*"

Thus shall Tradition keep my Fame alive;
The *Bard* may die, the *Thresher* still survive.[27]

Written a few years after the enormous success of *The Thresher's Labour,* in this passage Duck imagines himself as the thresher whose singing finally has been heard. The lines themselves shift between Duck speaking in his own voice about the holiday, and the voice of a thresher ("Some grateful Father") who recounts its origin. **"A Description of a Journey"** contains some ambitious self-figuration: the now singing thresher is an "ancient" whose song secures his own reputation for posterity through the reproduction of oral tales by other threshers such as the "grateful Father." Much like Dodsley's "Epistle," Duck's **"A Description of a Journey"** formulates his literary success as an ascent to the position of the singer, and the references to "Bard" and "Thresher" suggest his earlier separation of Muse and thresher. Even at this early point in his career as a poet, Duck represents himself as someone who has occupied the position of the singer which, paradoxically, preserves for posterity his fame as a thresher. That it is the oral tradition, rather than literate circulation, that perpetuates Duck's fame further accentuates the paradox, and reverses the idea from *The Thresher's Labour* that literate circulation makes the thresher's song "heard."

"A Description of a Journey" creates a sophisticated continuity between the artist and the laborer, though in a much different manner than the one that Swift proposes in his satire. It is telling that Duck declares that his *singing* secures for future threshers some momentary respite from their labors. He associates his role as a singer, and his labor as a poet more generally, with the alleviation of the threshers' conditions. Yet he also elevates himself to the position of singer by acting as a benevolent patron to the nameless threshers in the same way that Stanley acts as a patron to the Muse in *The Thresher's Labour.* Thus, **"A Description of a Journey"** reveals some of the implicit goals and contradictions of Duck's poetic career. If, as Christmas argues, Duck's verse publicizes the conditions of rural labor, then his success as a singer is an essential part of that publicity; in Duck's representation, the ability to "give voice" to rural laborers rests upon his skill as a singer rather than his authenticity as a thresher.

While Duck's self-characterization as a poet relies upon presenting himself as like the singing female Muse of *The Thresher's Labour,* it is also important to distin-guish the singing female Muse from Duck's fellow women laborers. At one point in *The Thresher's Labour,* the thresher describes a group of women laborers at work:

Our Master comes, and at his Heels a Throng
Of prattling Females, arm'd with Rake and Prong;
Prepar'd, whilst he is here, to make his Hay;
Or, if he turns his Back, prepar'd to play:
But here, or gone, sure of this Comfort still;
Here's Company, so they may chat their Fill.
Ah! were their Hands so active as their Tongues,
How nimbly then would move the Rakes and Prongs.

(19-20)

The description of the women's speech is even more severe. The thresher states that

what they speak, the rest will hardly hear:
Till by degrees so high their notes they strain,
A Stander by can nought distinguish plain.
So loud's their Speech, and so confus'd their Noise,
Scarce puzzled ECHO can return the Voice.

(20-21)

About this moment McKeon writes: "within the context of Duck's radicalized pastoralism, the speaking thresher should find a class ally in the women, who enforce custom and resist the regimentation of the work week by setting their 'tongues' against their 'hands,' their 'play,' against their work. . . ."[28] It is the thresher's posture as a poet, McKeon claims, that leads him momentarily to identify with the master and not acknowledge the possible identification with women laborers, and to make their speech unintelligible. Donna Landry suggests that the concept of the oral tradition is one way to understand Duck's depiction of the women's speech as unintelligible. Duck objects to women's speech because "such gatherings for gossip and other forms of exchange are an expression of community among these rural women, for whom there are so few opportunities for recreation and amusement. In a sense, these women have become custodians of the oral tradition to which their relative exclusion from print culture has increasingly relegated them."[29] In Landry's account, the oral tradition and print reinforces the sexual difference between women and men, and corresponds with the wide exclusion of women, especially laboring women, from access to print at this particular historical moment. Moreover, women's access to a community organized through orality provides one of the most effective means for them to resist the exploitation of their labor; that is, to set their "tongues" against their "hands."

Both McKeon's and Landry's accounts permit a further specification of Duck's reaction to the "prattling females." One of the reasons that the thresher identifies so readily with the master results from Duck's objection to the particular type of orality that women laborers come to represent in *The Thresher's Labour.* Duck expresses his disinterest in female community by characterizing their speech in terms similar to that of the flail; for example, the thresher's claim about women laborers—that "so loud's their Speech, and so confus'd their Noise / Scarce puzzled ECHO can return the Voice" (21)—recalls the earlier description of the "noisy threshal" that "must forever go" and how the thresher's voice is "drown'd out by the louder flail." Duck's objection to the noise of women's speech indicates that his identification with the song of the female Muse does not extend to an equal identification with another readily available version of orality: that of women laborers. The thresher's criticism of the women's speech results, in part, from Duck's association of the unheard song of the thresher with the Muse's song, and the separation of each from the speech of women laborers. In this way, Duck's identification with the singing female Muse paradoxically reinforces sexual difference through the differentiation of orality. Much as he positions himself as a singer in **"A Description of a Journey"** by elevating himself to the role of beneficent patron, in *The Thresher's Labour* he elevates himself to the status of singer by separating song from the supposedly unintelligible speech of women laborers. And women's orality is not only unintelligible to the thresher but, as Landry suggests, it is also unintelligible to the literate techniques of the poem and print culture in general. Therefore, while singing in *The Thresher's Labour* provides access to important historical changes in the English countryside, Duck's deliberate valuation of a particular type of orality—one that can be reproduced in manuscript and print—obscures the existence of other types of orality that also substantiate, but resist, those historical changes.[30]

In *The Thresher's Labour,* and throughout Duck's career, the trope of singing provides access to the conditions of the English countryside and describes his difficult negotiation of his status as a poet. George Crabbe's *The Village* (1783) is another eighteenth-century pastoral that uses singing, and Duck's ambiguous identity as an author and an agrarian laborer, to comment upon pastoral. Early in *The Village,* Crabbe characterizes his poetic endeavor as a song:

> On Mincio's banks, in Caesar's bounteous reign,
> If Tityrus found the golden age again,
> Must sleepy bards the flattering dream prolong,
> Mechanic echoes of the Mantuan song?
> From truth and nature shall we widely stray,
> Where Virgil, not where Fancy led the way?
>
> Yes, thus the Muses sing of happy swains
> Because the Muses never knew their pains[31]

The most striking feature of these lines is Crabbe's unabashed reconsideration of the classical pastoral. The references to "Tityrus" and Caesar demonstrate that the

target of his reconsideration is Virgil's *Eclogues* and its imitators. Crabbe's question—"shall we widely stray / Where Virgil, not where Fancy led the way?"—imagines the imitation of Virgil, and perhaps the classical pastoral in general, as the mystification rather than the revelation of truth and nature. It is meaningful that Crabbe characterizes the imitation of the Virgilian pastoral as "mechanic echoes of the Mantuan song." His emphasis upon the capacity of mechanical echoes to obscure the truth and nature of pastoral suggests both that imitation of the classical pastoral is artificial and mechanistic, and that the nature of the English countryside requires a significantly transformed pastoral song rather than an echo of the classical.

Crabbe's reexamination of the Virgilian pastoral results in an unexpected alternative. Moments after describing the "mechanic echoes" of Virgil's modern imitators, Crabbe offers Stephen Duck as an example of an alternate pastoral. He asks "Save honest Duck, what son of verse could share / The poet's rapture and the peasant's care?" (27-28). It is significant that Crabbe establishes Duck as someone who participates both in the "poet's rapture" and in the "peasant's care"—that is, participates both as the subject and the object of pastoral. Duck's own negotiation of subject and object indicates the profoundly new demands of eighteenth-century pastoral, and his ability to feel the "poet's rapture" and the "peasant's care" makes him a unique origin for a pastoral tradition able to depict the English countryside more accurately. His simultaneous identification with "poet" and "peasant" constitutes the innovation of his verse, and it is instructive that the ambiguity of voice in *The Thresher's Labour* later becomes one criterion for truthfulness in *The Village.*

Yet it is the first stanza of *The Village* that most prominently reveals the characteristics of the new pastoral song that originates with Duck. Crabbe opens the poem by stating:

> The Village life, and every care that reigns
> O'er youthful peasants and declining swains;
> What labour yields, and what, that labour past,
> Age, in its hour of languor, finds at last;
> What forms the real picture of the poor
> Demands a song—The Muse can give no more.
>
> (1-6)

The reference to song recalls Duck's own use of singing to gain access to the social and economic history of the English countryside, and the first stanza of *The Village* continues to make explicit many of the concerns of *The Thresher's Labour.* Much like Duck, Crabbe describes his own poetic project as an adaptation of pastoral song, which he imagines as the continuation of Duck's career. One of the most explicit political statements of *The Village* is that the empirical impulse of later eighteenth-century pastoral demands a particular type of song from the Muse, reflected not by imitations of Virgil but by Duck's ability to feel both the "poet's rapture" and the "peasant's care." Later in *The Village* Crabbe asks:

> Nor you, ye poor, of lettered scorn complain,
> To you the smoothest song is smooth in vain,
> O'ercome by labour and bowed down by time
> Feel you the barren flattery of a rhyme?
>
> Can poets soothe you, when you pine for bread,
> By winding myrtles round your ruined shed?
> Can their light tales your weighty griefs o'erpower,
> Or glad with airy mirth the toilsome hour?
>
> (55-62)

Much like the differentiation of orality in *The Thresher's Labour,* Crabbe distinguishes between two types of song: between the "smoothest songs" of Virgil's imitators and a new type of song that originates with the "real picture of the rural poor." Crabbe's questions about the "smoothest song" of Virgil's imitators reveal equally profound questions about a song that originates in the "real picture of the rural poor": does his reinvented pastoral song succeed in soothing the rural poor in a way that the "smooth songs" of Virgil's imitators do not? The question is not rhetorical and Crabbe's answer is not obvious. Still, the opening stanza indicates a substantial transformation of the pastoral tradition because the emphasis upon a more empirical description of the English countryside requires fundamental changes to the Muse's song. Rather than "winding the myrtles round the ruined shed" the speaker claims to "paint the cot / As truth will paint it, and bards will not" (60, 53-54). Furthermore, the opening stanza establishes that the rural poor play a significant role in the Muse's song. While in *The Thresher's Labour,* the patron serves as an important facilitator of the Muse's song, in *The Village* it is the real conditions of the rural poor that demand a new type of pastoral song from the Muse.

Yet, in many ways, *The Village* reconsiders the relationship between pastoral song and the alleviation of the conditions of rural laborers that Duck takes up years earlier in his **"A Description of a Journey."** In the latter poem, Duck imagines that the publication of his "quaint songs" momentarily alleviates the working conditions of rural laborers. *The Village,* by contrast, is less optimistic about the possibility that singing, or even literate publication, can alleviate the conditions of the poor. Though the speaker of *The Village* claims to create a pastoral grounded in the accurate description of the countryside, the poem also states that the Muse can give no more than a song, which suggests that a song, even one derived from the "real picture of the poor," has a limited effect. *The Village* does not represent the Muse's song as an artistic endeavor that ultimately compensates the rural poor. Rather, the speaker suggests, that song may only describe, rather than not alleviate, those conditions.

That Crabbe offers Duck as a representative figure of his rejuvenated pastoral song signifies Duck's continued importance within eighteenth-century pastoral, an importance that often remains unacknowledged. In many ways, Duck's verse creates a model for a new type of pastoral song indebted to a more accurate depiction of rural labor, and *The Village* exists in a much transformed pastoral tradition that begins with **The Thresher's Labour.** Duck uses the idea that pastoral is a song to distinguish his representation of the thresher from the early eighteenth-century pastoral's representations of shepherds and of an idealized golden age. He adapts the pastoral convention of singing to comment directly upon the changing social and economic conditions of the English countryside, much as Virgil subtly commented upon the civil unrest in Rome in his first eclogue. The metaphor of singing, moreover, introduces one effective way for Duck to consider his ambiguous status both as the subject and the object of pastoral, and to explain his transformation from an agrarian laborer to a poet. It is his complicated negotiation of subject and object that makes him significant for *The Village,* and attracts the scrutiny of his contemporaries.

Duck also figures the creation of **The Thresher's Labour** as the translation from song into manuscript and type. The ways that he employs singing to elucidate the creation and circulation of his poem raises larger questions about the relationship between orality and the representation of poetic authority during the eighteenth century. His careful differentiation of the thresher's song from other types of orality, particularly from the speech of fellow women laborers, calls for further consideration of the ways that orality reinforces sexual difference, and of the ways that women authors utilize orality to construct their own poetic authority. The affinity between Duck's song and scribal and print circulation, and the more common exclusion of women's speech from literate reproduction, demonstrates the need for a more precise sense of the differences that exist in orality, and to what degree orality impacts upon poetic discourse of the eighteenth century. In a century often highlighted for the importance of print culture, Duck's complicated use of the metaphor of singing suggests the ways that orality remains an essential though still unacknowledged resource for authors.

Notes

A shorter version of this paper was presented at the thirty-third annual meeting of the American Society for Eighteenth-Century Studies in Colorado Springs, Colorado. I would like to thank the panel chair, Mark Pedreira, and the participants: J. Douglas Canfield,

Hueikeng Chang, and Michael Schwartz. I would also like to thank Michael McKeon and Paula McDowell for reading early versions of this essay, and the anonymous readers for *Studies in Eighteenth-Century Culture.*

1. *English Pastoral Poetry: From the Beginnings to Marvell,* ed. with an introduction Frank Kermode (New York: Barnes and Noble, 1952). In his introduction, Kermode argues that after the seventeenth century the pastoral "live[s] in a quite different atmosphere, and in a quite different relationship to its readers" (42). The relationship and atmosphere are so different that Kermode ends his collection with the poetry of Andrew Marvell.

2. For broad surveys of pastoral in the eighteenth century, see J. E. Congleton, *Theories of Pastoral in England, 1684-1798* (Gainesville, Florida: University of Florida Press, 1952); A. J. Sambrook, "An Essay on Eighteenth-Century Pastoral, Pope to Wordsworth (I)," *Trivium* 5 (1970): 21-35, and "An Essay on Eighteenth-Century Pastoral, Pope to Wordsworth (II)," *Trivium* 6 (1971): 103-15. Raymond Williams associates the eighteenth century with a counter-pastoral tradition in opposition to the aristocratic ideals of seventeenth-century pastoral; see, *The Country and the City* (New York: Oxford University Press, 1973), 13-35, 68-96. For an argument about how pastoral continues to enact aristocratic modes in the eighteenth century and the early nineteenth century, see Roger Sales, *English Literature in History, 1780-1830: Pastoral and Politics* (New York: St. Martin's Press, 1983), especially 13-18. For criticism that evaluates Duck within the pastoral tradition, see John Goodridge, *Rural Life in Eighteenth-Century English Poetry* (Cambridge: Cambridge University Press, 1995): 6-7, 12-15. John Barrell considers Duck's representation of farmworkers in the eighteenth century. See his "Sportive Labour: The Farmworker in Eighteenth-Century Poetry and Painting," in *The English Rural Community: Image and Analysis,* ed. Brian Short (Cambridge: Cambridge University Press, 1992), 118-20; and also his argument about the changing relationship to pastoral in the visual arts in *The Dark Side of the Landscape: The Rural Poor in English Painting, 1730-1840* (Cambridge: Cambridge University Press, 1980). For a helpful discussion of women authors and pastoral, consider Ann Messenger, *Pastoral Tradition and the Female Talent: Studies in Augustan Poetry* (New York: AMS Press, 2001), especially 1-15.

3. See Michael McKeon, "Surveying the Frontier of Culture: Pastoralism in Eighteenth-Century England," *Studies in Eighteenth-Century Culture,* ed. Syndy M. Conger and Julie C. Hayes (Baltimore: Johns Hopkins University Press, 1998): 7-28.

McKeon argues that the instability of the pastoral is not accidental, but rather "congenital and constitutive of the genre" so that pastoral "takes as its subject the problem of conventionality itself" (9).

4. Rose Mary Davis, *Stephen Duck, The Thresher-Poet* (Orono: University of Maine Studies, 1926). Davis's work, though dated, remains the most complete account of Duck's life. See also Joseph Spence, "An Account of the Author, in a Letter to a Friend." Written in 1730, Spence's account was published in 1731, with slight changes, as *A Full and Authentick Account of Stephen Duck, the Wiltshire Poet* (London, 1731) and as a preface to Duck's *Poems on Several Occasions* (London, 1736).

5. For different discussions of the radicalism of Duck's attention to the detail of rural labor, see Williams, 87-90; H. Gustav Klaus, *The Literature of Labour: Two Hundred Years of Working-Class Writing* (New York: St. Martin's Press, 1985), 11-14; McKeon, "Surveying the Frontier of Culture," 21-23. On the "rural realism" of Duck's poetry and its relationship to the actual practices of agrarian labor, see Goodridge, 15-17, 18-22, 30-32, 37-39, 44-49. For a good summary of the changing practices of eighteenth-century agriculture, see E. L. Jones, "Agriculture: 1700-1800" in *The Economic History of Britain Since 1700. Vol. 1: 1700-1860.* ed. Roderick Floud and Donald McCloskey (Cambridge: Cambridge University Press, 1981), especially 70-82.

6. On Duck's place in plebeian authorship of the eighteenth century, see William Christmas, *The Labr'ing Muses: Work, Writing, and the Social Order in English Plebeian Poetry, 1730-1830* (Newark: University of Delaware Press, 2001), 20, 64-66, 75-76, 79, 84, 107-08. Also consider Bridget Keegan, "Georgic Transformations and Stephen Duck's *The Thresher's Labour,*" *Studies in English Literature* 41, 3 (Summer 2001): 546, 548-52. Keegan focuses upon how Duck transforms the georgic tradition to accommodate his position as an agrarian laborer producing georgic poetry.

7. *The Guardian,* ed. with an introduction John Calhoun Stephens, (Lexington: University of Kentucky Press, 1982), 105.

8. Alexander Pope, "A Discourse on Pastoral Poetry," *The Poems of Alexander Pope,* ed. John Butt (New Haven: Yale University Press, 1963), 119. Pope's "Discourse" was first published in Tonson's *Miscellanies* in 1709, though Pope insists in a headnote that it was composed in 1704.

9. Paul Alpers, *The Singer of the Eclogues: A Study of Virgilian Pastoral* (Berkeley: University of

California Press, 1979), 15. Virgil's *Eclogues* were written around 40 B.C. The civil unrest in Rome at that time serves as an important context for the representation of song in the first eclogue, and for the *Eclogues* as a whole. Alpers claims, for example, that "it is essential to keep in mind that the *Eclogues* were written under the first triumvirate, when Octavian was young, Italy was torn by civil wars, and the political situation was at best uncertain" (3).

10. Duck was familiar with both Virgil's *Eclogues* and *Georgics.* Spence claims that Duck owned John Dryden's 1697 translation of Virgil, which contained both these works ("Account," xiii).

11. *The Thresher's Labour and The Woman's Labour,* ed. with an introduction Moira Ferguson, Augustan Reprint Society 230 (Los Angeles: William Andrews Clark Memorial Library, 1985), 13. Unless otherwise stated, all the selections from Duck's poetry refer to this edition and subsequent references appear parenthetically in the text. Ferguson's edition of *The Thresher's Labour* is based upon Duck's *Poems on Several Occasions,* published in London in 1736. Though this is the first authorized edition of Duck's poetry, *The Thresher's Labour* was published numerous times between 1730 and 1736, and those printings contain variations. For a discussion of these differences, and the merits of using the 1730 edition of *The Thresher's Labour,* see the introduction to *The Thresher's Labour by Stephen Duck and The Woman's Labour by Mary Collier,* ed. E. P. Thompson and Marian Sugden (London: The Merlin Press, 1989); and Peter J. McGonigle, "Stephen Duck and the Text of *The Thresher's Labour,*" *The Library* 4, Sixth Series (1982): 288-96. McGonigle observes that Duck's patrons, such as Spence, were involved in the revision of the poem—though the evidence about exactly how is scant—and that the 1736 version reveals a "movement towards the polite Augustan literary mode" (291, 288). He argues (without judging its value) that the 1736 version provides a less authentic vision of the thresher (289). It is notable that the passages that deal explicitly with song remain largely unchanged between the 1730 and 1736 versions of the poem. I have selected from the 1736 version because it demonstrates the full extent of Duck's "literate" translation of song. Furthermore, it represents his final, authorized text, and since I argue that from the inauguration of the poem he self-consciously considers the role of the patron in the figuration of its creation, his patrons' involvement in the 1736 version does not necessarily represent an abdication of authority.

12. Goodridge points out that threshing occurs indoors, often during the winter when the summer work of harvesting has been completed (32, 44).

13. McKeon, "The Pastoral Revolution" in *Refiguring Revolutions: Aesthetics and Politics from the English Revolution to the Romantic Revolution,* ed. Kevin Sharpe and Stephen N. Zwicker (Berkeley: University of California Press, 1998): 271.

14. A number of recent critics argue that Duck is not a proper "pastoral" poet, but rather uses the georgic tradition. See, for example, Keegan's "Georgic Transformations," where she states that though "Duck's work should be seen in dialogue with contemporary pastoral as well as anti-pastoral satires . . . it should be analyzed primarily in its relations to the georgic" (548). Christmas articulates a similar position in *The Labr'ing Muses* when he states that Duck "counters the pastoral with a thoroughly modern rendering of the thresher's experience" that aligns Duck more closely with the georgic (82). Building from McKeon's insight, a pastoral continuum more adequately expresses Duck's contrast between shepherds and threshers, a contrast that suggests elements of what might be understood as both pastoral and georgic.

15. There are other types of agrarian labor present in the poem, particularly harvesting and haymaking. But, as Goodridge observes, the recurrence of threshing in the poem indicates that Duck saw threshing as his primary activity (44).

16. In his "Discourse," Pope claims that the shepherds' song originates from "that age which succeeded the creation of the world" (119).

17. For a description of the noisiness and physical intensity of threshing, see Goodridge, 44-46. The way that threshing, with its uninterrupted intensity, overwhelms song may not represent a general case for all manual labor, or even for all agrarian labor. See Bruce R. Smith, *The Acoustic World of Early Modern England: Attending to the O-Factor* (Chicago and London: University of Chicago Press, 1999). Examining primarily the acoustic "soundscape" of sixteenth-century and seventeenth-century England, Smith argues that "the sonic consequences of open-field farming were conversation, shouts, and song" that helped to create "a strong sense of community" (79). This differs from the type of enclosed field farming more prevalent in the eighteenth century and most likely practiced by Duck, where, due to the dispersal of labor, it is not clear if "acoustic community" was as easy to create (79). For another case that relates the conditions of labor with the

composition of poetry, see Keegan, "Cobbling Verse: Shoemaker Poets of the Long Eighteenth Century" *The Eighteenth Century: Theory and Interpretation* 42, 3 (Fall 2001): 195-217. Keegan specifically contrasts shoemaking and threshing (200-01), and focuses throughout upon the written composition of verse and its similarity to oral poetry.

18. Keegan, "Georgic Transformations," 553.

19. McKeon, "Surveying the Frontier of Culture," 21.

20. The two opening lines of the poem are as follows: "The grateful tribute of these rural Lays, / Which to her Patron's Hand the Muse conveys . . ." (13). It is also important to note that during this period the term "lay" can refer specifically to a song. One definition of "lay" in the *OED* is "a short lyric or narrative poem intended to be sung."

21. Christmas, 84.

22. For a detailed account of the circulation of Duck's "The Thresher's Labour" see Davis, 30-31. For an account of the reaction of his contemporaries, particularly satirical responses, see Davis, 45-52, 55-6, 59-60.

23. *The Complete Poems,* ed. Pat Rogers (New Haven: Yale University Press, 1983), 447, lines 1-4.

24. Swift's realignment of Duck with the object rather than the subject of pastoral is even more pronounced if one considers that "allow[ing] him grains" presents Duck as an animal of the same name, plucking stray grains from the ground. Puns on Duck's name are common in satires of him and his verse, and perhaps demonstrate the furthest extent of pastoral objectification.

25. Robert Dodsley, *A Muse in Livery: or The Footman's Miscellany* (London, 1732), 19. For a broader discussion of Dodsley's epistle to Duck, see Christmas, 107-108. On Dodsley's relationship to Duck, see Harry M. Solomon, *The Rise of Robert Dodsley: Creating the New Age of Print* (Carbondale and Edwardsville: Southern Illinois University Press, 1996), 19-28. Dodsley's identification with Duck's position is not representative of all responses from laboring authors, and not all laboring authors can be seen as allied along class lines. For an interesting example, see Robert Tatersal, *The Bricklayer's Miscellany: or, Poems on Several Subjects* (London, 1734), 23-5. Though Tatersal's consideration of Duck's value is more positive than that of Swift's satire, Tatersal imagines his own bricklaying trowel engaged in combat with Duck's flail, suggesting spirited competition among laboring authors.

26. See R. G. Furnival, "Stephen Duck: The Wiltshire Phenomenon, 1705-1756," *The Cambridge Journal* 6 (1953): 486-96. Furnival reports that land was set aside in Wiltshire, the county of Duck's birth, and the rent from that land was used to entertain local laborers each year (496). "Temple" is Henry Temple, first Viscount Palmerston, the benefactor of the feast, to whom Duck's "A Description of a Journey" is dedicated. For more information about Temple's role in the creation of Duck's feast, see *Dictionary of National Biography,* s.v. "Temple, Henry, first Viscount Palmerston."

27. Duck, *Poems on Several Occasions* (London, 1736), 211-12. Davis suggests that the poem was composed in 1735, though this date cannot be verified (24).

28. McKeon, "Surveying the Frontier of Culture," 23.

29. Donna Landry, *The Muses of Resistance: Laboring-Class Women's Poetry in Britain, 1739-1796* (Cambridge: Cambridge University Press, 1990), 67.

30. One of the most eloquent and deliberate responses to *The Thresher's Labour* is Mary Collier's *The Woman's Labour* (London, 1739). In her poem, she both rebuts Duck's claims about women agrarian laborers, and depicts the conditions of women's rural work. For a discussion of the representation of women's labor in eighteenth-century pastoral and georgic, see Landry, 22-29. On the sexual division of agrarian labor, see Robert Shoemaker, *Gender in English Society, 1650-1850: The Emergence of Separate Spheres?* (London and New York: Longman, 1998), 150-59.

31. George Crabbe, *Selected Poems,* ed. with an introduction and notes Gavin Edwards (New York: Penguin, 1991), 3, lines 15-22. All selections from Crabbe's poetry refer to this edition and subsequent references appear parenthetically in the text.

Steve Van-Hagen (essay date fall 2005)

SOURCE: Van-Hagen, Steve. "Literary Technique, The Aestheticization of Laboring Experience, and Generic Experimentation in Stephen Duck's *The Thresher's Labour.*" *Criticism* 47, no. 4 (fall 2005): 421-50.

[*In this essay, Van-Hagen suggests that Duck's themes transformed his poetic style so that his verse became "generically distinct," characterized by evocative descriptions of labor and respectful treatment of laborers.*]

The year 2005 was the tri-centennial of the birth of Stephen Duck, the "thresher poet" of Wiltshire accorded patronage by Queen Caroline after the success of poems including **The Thresher's Labour** and **"The**

Shunamite" (both 1730). The year 2006, meanwhile, is the 250th anniversary of his (probable) suicide in a river behind a Reading tavern. These anniversaries, coupled with the recent surge of interest in Duck and other laboring-class poets make this an appropriate moment to reexamine his most celebrated and discussed individual work.[1]

The Thresher's Labour is believed to have been composed third of Duck's extant poems[2] (after **"To a Gentleman, who requested a Copy of Verses from the Author"** and **"On Poverty,"** and immediately before the biblical-historical **"The Shunamite"**).[3] Even now, these, as well as other significant poems, such as **"On Richmond Park, and Royal Gardens," "A Description of a Journey to Marlborough, Bath, Portsmouth, &c."** (both 1736).[4] *Every Man in his own Way: An Epistle to a Friend* (1741), and the prospect poem *Caesar's Camp* (1755), are often read (if at all) for the light they shed on *The Thresher's Labour* and its author. Despite Joseph Spence's view that **"The Shunamite"** was his finest poem,[5] Duck's biographer Rose Mary Davis calls *The Thresher's Labour* "the best poem" he wrote,[6] adding, "critics are almost unanimous in placing this poem, from the point of view of merit, at the head of Duck's works."[7] Commentators in the eighty years since her assessment have tended to agree, or if they have not always been concerned with aesthetics, nonetheless often concur that *The Thresher's Labour* is Duck's most noteworthy work. As John Goodridge has written with reference to laboring-class poets in general, "one thing these writers have rarely been allowed to be is poets . . . Historically, the considerable interest there has been in labouring-class poetry has not always extended to a recognition of literary merit."[8] Yet a number of recent treatments of the poem have focused anew on its "literary" and formal achievements.[9] In the wake of these readings, some of which concentrate on the relationship of *The Thresher's Labour* to existing genres such as georgic and pastoral,[10] the aim of the present essay is to plot the poem's attempts to reconcile laboring-class experiences with verse, with reference to poetic mediums, techniques, and genres.

The Thresher's Labour was composed when one of Duck's patrons, Rev. Stanley, suggested that he write about the life he knew.[11] As a necessary part of doing so, a laboring-class poetic voice and a mode of writing about labor that dominates the poem emerged. In enabling the representation of experiences, this mode fosters an informal, confidential tone of friend to friend rather than of poet to public.[12] It tends to produce narrative, descriptive verse, describing the vigorous performance of physical labor and depicting labor and laborer with respect and dignity. It does not just describe everyday objects or processes, however, but mimetically *evokes* the sights and sounds of physical labor. This mode is interested in physical objects as they are rooted in a world of sights, sounds, and smells, yet is suspended within the amber of neoclassical versification (the heroic couplet), and mingles specific everyday and colloquial terms with a familiar neoclassical poetic medium. In advancing these arguments through a detailed close reading, I will also be concerned to suggest that whereas *The Thresher's Labour* has long been defined in terms of being either pastoral or georgic, there are good grounds for arguing that it should be considered generically distinct.

II

The heroic couplets in which *The Thresher's Labour* is written were, as critics including J. Paul Hunter and Margaret Anne Doody have observed, the dominant medium of their time.[13] As Bridget Keegan has argued, laboring-class poets were particularly influenced by the couplet's greatest practitioner, Alexander Pope (and other canonical figures who regularly used the couplet, such as Jonathan Swift).[14] The extent to which Duck was familiar with Pope's work when he wrote the first version of *The Thresher's Labour* (in or before 1730) is unclear, although he was certainly familiar with (at least some of) it when he wrote his next work, **"The Shunamite."** He was also familiar before this with the work of other purveyors of the couplet who either influenced or were themselves influenced by Pope, as well as with at least some journals in which allusions to the Pope-Philips "pastoral wars" (discussed below) could be found.[15] Davis for one suggests that lines 52 to 63 of *The Thresher's Labour* are a direct response to Pope's *Pastorals*.[16] Even if she is wrong, it is clear that through a process of either direct or indirect influence, Duck writes in couplets that are stylistically comparable with Pope's (for reasons discussed subsequently), and that Pope, as the neoclassical couplet's acknowledged master, makes for an obvious comparison. This Popean medium was at least partly enabling for a poet such as Duck. It offered, for instance, a fixed and simple pattern of rhyme and meter that was (potentially) easy to at least mimic. It set standards of mellifluousness and taut concision, and could encourage the learner to proceed securely, one couplet at a time. If much of the pastoral vocabulary Pope used to describe (supposed) rural life did not fit rustic actuality, it contained further vocabulary—for example, "woods," "shepherd," "trees," "fields"—that was far less objectionable. Potentially formless day-to-day experience could be ordered into manageable units at the level of both couplet and verse paragraph. There was a "manner" that a sensitive reader, even of limited education, could readily acquire; "matter" was to hand, part of the time at least, in the shape of the worker poet's experiences.

For poets wanting to represent their laboring experiences mimetically, however, Pope's medium could offer at least some constraints. A simple survey of its incontrovertible characteristics would demonstrate, in purely empirical terms, that the Popean/neoclassical heroic couplet militates against "natural" word order because of the need to produce end rhymes; it is copiously end-stopped, with the unintentional effect of breaking any narrative into fragments; and it frequently contains archaism, "poeticized" language or euphemism, Latinate constructions and word order, abstract (often personified) nouns, parallelism and antithesis, and recurrent exclamations, apostrophes, and rhetorical questions. These practices arguably impede the direct expression of personal experience. They imply that poetry can be written only with specialized diction, derived from extensive reading and knowledge of the classics, differing (sometimes considerably) from everyday speech. Such practices suggest that personal (particularized) experiences can be of interest only if they are subsumed into generalization, usually of an aphoristic kind. They implicitly propose that the poet must be distanced from personal experience and even from the familiar external world, translating these phenomena into a heightened "artificialized" medium. Hence the degree of translation apparently required is likely to denature the experiences and observations of any working man or woman.

Pope's medium had a variety of strengths that made it well suited to his usual aims,[17] but as his use of the end-stopped, self-contained couplet implies, writing narrative was only rarely one of them.[18] Even *The Rape of the Lock*—which may seem to consist of narrative— repeatedly forsakes story for set piece.[19] One need only consult Pope's verse translations of *The Odyssey* or *The Iliad*—where he could scarcely avoid the necessity to write narrative—to confirm that his medium did not readily lend itself to this purpose.[20] Hence, in some respects, Pope emerges as a questionable (direct or indirect) stylistic model for Duck, who *does* write narrative and clearly, in **The Thresher's Labour,** wants to convey the sequential flow of experienced events. As a result, Duck would have to find compensating strategies.

Such a reading might beg the question of why Duck chose to utilize the couplet at all. A number of suggestions have been made.[21] Duck was not simply inhibited by the formal models of the age: he *wanted to write verse*. The essence of the challenge is not simply any recalcitrance of the dominant medium, but the general difficulty of transposing diurnal life, the ordinary, into art—which must, by definition, be in some sense extraordinary, as explored at length by Ellen Dissanayake, whose "recent cross-cultural study of artistic behavior, *Homo Aestheticus: Where Art Comes from and Why,* mounts an impressive argument for the category of 'making special' as a universal in cultural life."[22] Duck did not have to feel frustrated at any limitations of the available medium; presumably he would have relished seeing fragments of everyday life

suspended within neoclassical versification. Indeed, this was the nature of the exercise: to translate aspects of his life into poetry, to "make special" (with the accompanying status bestowed upon both subject matter and author). Hence one need not concur with Linda Zionkowski that Duck was defeated by the medium in which he wrote, because it forced him to work with a vocabulary that was foreign to his experience.[23] Attempting to *mingle* vernacular/idiom with other verse ingredients, to produce poetry rather than a diary entry or documentary sketch, was exactly the challenge he embraced. Ann Messenger argues similarly in writing about Mary Leapor, who, she asserts, "wanted to express her truth in the high art she so much admired. Her truth meant the perceptions and feelings of a workingclass woman, intimately acquainted with the realities of village, farm, and kitchen, yet speaking for herself as an individual, not simply as a representative of a category of people. The high literary art she aspired to is an art of conventions, forms, and 'numbers' fine-tuned by her admired Pope. To bring the two together was her problem."[24] If Duck could demonstrate that his subject was fit for verse, it would be to the credit of both the subject matter and the medium that could accommodate it. Hence, as Keegan summarizes, "labouring-class poets of the mid-eighteenth century write both *in response to and in reaction against*" the canonical verse of the age (my italics).[25]

As Keegan's summary implies, Duck's enterprise was informed by the two literary modes that offered some point of entry into writing of labor in verse: the pastoral and georgic. Neither offered a truly suitable model for doing this, even though aspects of the rest of this section touch on issues that cannot be fully examined here.

Duck's critical engagement with the bucolic begins early in **The Thresher's Labour.** He stresses both the beauty of nature and the affinity with the natural world felt by men like himself who work on the land, while also wishing to disabuse his readers of any notion that the lives of the former are easy or comfortable. Threshing itself was a mostly indoor occupation, and when describing it Duck emphasizes that working conditions were poorer than the pastoral would lead readers to believe:

> Can we, like Shepherds, tell a merry Tale?
> The Voice is lost, drown'd by the noisy Flail.
> But we may think—Alas! what pleasing thing
> Here to the Mind can the dull Fancy bring?
> The Eye beholds no pleasant Object here:
> No chearful Sound diverts the list'ning Ear.
> The Shepherd may well tune his Voice to sing,
> Inspir'd by all the Beauties of the Spring:
> No Fountains murmur here, no Lambkins play,
> No Linets warble, and no Fields look gay;
> 'Tis all a dull and melancholy Scene,
> Fit only to provoke the Muses' Spleen.[26]

Nor is this the only passage in Duck's work to enter into debate with the pastoral and aim at what James Mulholland calls "a poetry that describes rural labor and the English countryside more accurately."[27] In the preceding two decades, the nature of pastoral had become hotly contested with the outbreak of hostilities between Pope and Ambrose Philips. In 1709 the sixth volume of Jacob Tonson's miscellanies included a set of pastorals by each poet. Pope's (predominantly) Rapin-influenced neoclassical versions were ostensibly set in an appropriately timeless Golden Age, despite references to Windsor and Thames, whereas Philips's rationalist alternatives were set in the English countryside. Naturally, critics compared rival philosophies, but when Thomas Tickell's (anonymous) essays appeared praising Bernard de Fontenelle's rationalist prescriptions and illustrating the argument with examples from Philips,[28] the slighted Pope was stung into a retort. This manifested itself in a now-notorious mock essay (published in the *Guardian*, no. 40, after the editor, Sir Richard Steele, was tricked into publishing it) praising Philips yet evidencing these mock claims with some of Philips's most inelegant verses. For good measure, these examples were then contrasted with some of Pope's (clearly superior) work.[29]

Despite the controversy, as David Fairer observes, "the neo-classicist and the rationalist did agree on several points—that pastoral must be simple and dignified, avoiding courtly wit on one side and rustic clownishness on the other; *and that hard work of any kind was banned*" (my italics).[30] Irrespective of whether set in the English countryside or not, pastoral by definition excludes the labor that constituted Duck's primary theme. As Jonathan N. Lawson, who identifies poets such as Duck and Robert Bloomfield with Hesiod, summarizes, "the rural poet differs from the pastoralist (and, I might add, the romanticist) because his first concern is the things, folk, and events of the countryside which are important in themselves."[31] These, then, are the contemporary contexts in which it is tempting to read Duck's lines, which function as an effective, ironic comment on the gap between the pastoral myth and Duck's working life. He and his comrades do not always work outdoors, and the weather outside in winter is less palatable than in the pastoral ideal. The chasm is emphasized with the use of conventional pastoral language of the kind regularly employed in Pope's *Pastorals*: "No Fountains murmur here, no Lambkins play, / No Linets warble, and no Fields look gay" (ll. 60-61).[32] He is no idle piping shepherd, his verse not theirs: for him, "No chearful Sound diverts the list'ning Ear" (57). The passage is additionally noteworthy because it provides an overt instance of a recurring tactic: *The Thresher's Labour* is influential within laboring verse not just because it provides a model for laying claim to desired laboring-class identities, but also because it provides a series of *rejections* of unwanted definitions imposed by others.[33]

Yet while Duck responds to the pastoral with irony, this does not extend to any great resentment; being able to define himself against it is a useful way in to his project. A chimney sweep, for instance, would have lacked even this means of poeticizing his labors.

Ostensibly, the georgic offered a more promising model with its specificity and plentiful accounts of actual labor. There are considerable differences, however, between what John Chalker terms "Formal English Georgics" and Duck's project. Such georgics—John Dyer's *The Fleece*, Robert Dodsley's *Agriculture*, Christopher Smart's *The Hop Garden*, James Thomson's *The Seasons*, John Philips's *Cyder*, and James Grainger's *Sugar Cane*—were "seriously didactic: the advice that they give derives from contemporary farming manuals and the authors are clearly interested in practical agricultural matters. But they also have a strong literary motive, and emphasize frequently the 'imitative' aspect of their work."[34] Both these formal georgics and *The Thresher's Labour* depict labor with respect and dignity, and both are avowedly "literary," intertextual productions. However, for a variety of reasons the georgic, like pastoral, leaves vacant the space that Duck's poem would occupy.[35] For instance, Duck attempts—and often achieves—genuine informality, both of tone and vocabulary. By contrast, the formal georgic was often characterized by periphrasis, resulting in a gap between matter and manner. One *could* write about farming/ agriculture/labor in the georgic, but only by abstracting the subject matter to the extent that much of the necessary vocabulary was removed. As Joseph Addison wrote: "I think nothing which is a Phrase or Saying in common talk, should be admitted into a serious Poem; because it takes off from the solemnity of the expression, and gives it too great a turn of familiarity: Much less ought the low phrases and terms of art, that are adapted to Husbandry, have any place in such a work as the Georgic, which is not to appear in the natural simplicity and nakedness of its subject, but in the pleasantest dress that Poetry can bestow on it." Virgil, Addison asserts, gives "his verse the greater pomp," in order to "preserve it from sinking into a Plebeian stile."[36] Accordingly, Keegan devotes a whole article to arguing that *The Thresher's Labour* was Duck's attempt to dispute Addison's views,[37] by no means confined to Addison alone.[38] Dryden's concern with elegance rather than accuracy when translating *The Georgics*—which Duck studied—meant that a long passage describing agricultural implements ended with the observation, "I could be long in precepts, but I fear / So mean a subject might offend your ear."[39]

It is the desire to reconcile two irreconcilables by writing a poem glorifying everyday subject matter in a neoclassical style that prompts Chalker to record that for generations of critics such georgics were "faintly absurd and sterile offshoots of Augustan orthodoxy."[40]

Tim Fulford makes a not dissimilar point arguing that Dyer's *The Fleece* risked "bathos as a gap opened between his mundane subject matter and his epic diction."[41] This can be seen in the poem's proliferation of Latinate, polysyllabic words (and in, for instance, Dodsley's *Agriculture*) ending in suffixes like "ious" or "eous."[42] They come about because the georgics were written for fundamentally different purposes than Duck's poem, with at least some different aims.[43] Instead of the formal georgic's didactic purpose to convey factual knowledge, Duck aimed at communicating an *understanding* of particular human experiences. The formal georgics are undeniably often experiential, and there is factual knowledge to be gleaned from Duck's poem. The priorities in the formal georgics and in Duck's poem are arguably reversed, however. Duck is concerned with establishing both an individual and, to some extent, a collective laboring-class poetic voice.[44] The formal georgics offer little precedent for this, so much so that their writers—particularly Dyer and Grainger—drew criticism in later years for their laudatory tone that celebrates nationalism, imperialism, and the exploitation of workers.[45] Another significant difference between the formal georgic and Duck's poem is the question of scale. Whereas Duck points predominantly to local places and landmarks, Dyer, because of his different purpose, often refers to bigger and more exotic locations, both contemporary and classical.[46]

There is little precedent even for Duck's intimate first-person voice (either singular or plural) in the formal georgic. An exception is *The Seasons,* but here the narrator is a distanced observer, not a participant in labor. This is not to doubt the "authenticity" of the labor Thomson describes, but the poem offers no precedent for presenting the laborer's viewpoint. Analyzing labor in the poem—such as the passage depicting field labor in "Spring," lines 32 to 47—one finds a reasonably specific vocabulary that is largely devoid of the classical constructions present in *The Fleece* and *Agriculture,* a "Plow," a "Furrow," a "Sower," "Grain," and "The Harrow."[47] However, Thomson neither aims at nor achieves the intimate, confidential mode that Duck would shortly attempt. Laboring processes are summed up quickly, receiving just sixteen lines in a book of the poem that runs to nearly twelve hundred. Since Thomson's focus lies elsewhere, there is no scope for individualizing the laborers; one simply finds "th'impatient Husbandman" and "the Sower." It highlights the gap between Duck's and Thomson's respective approaches to labor that by line 67 the view of the latter "expands, the plough turns from a thing into a symbol . . . and the sharp particularity of the ploughman bending over and scraping his ploughshare yields to generalizations about Autumn's treasures and the better blessings of England's export trade."[48] It has often been observed that pastoral tends to see the rustic in metaphorical terms. Here, Thomson *does* see particularity, but shifts his gaze to the larger, generalized picture that the plowman can be made to represent, which is the patriotic theme of (inter)national mercantile success. Duck seeks to occupy a different space, by looking at the laborer with the same "sharp particularity," but making it the predominant focus of his verse. Doing this would result in the creation of a new "kind" of poem.

III

I will undertake to display and describe the characteristics in *The Thresher's Labour* that fuse into what is describable as the emergence of a "Duckian mode" of poeticizing manual work before describing the poem's generic characteristics. Despite its title, the poem tells the story in 284 lines of Duck's working life over the period of a year. Threshing is only one task that he performs. Others include winnowing (separating grain from chaff by tossing the threshed corn), haymaking, and reaping/harvesting. Recurring themes include the repetitive, cyclical nature of tasks undertaken, as well as the conditions and hardships of labor, the consolations that provide brief respite, and the tyranny of time, governing their lives and labor. A key point to stress is the wide *range* of lived experience present: not just the labor undertaken, but its physical and psychological consequences, the ways in which these repercussions dominate laborers' home lives (and even their dreams), coping strategies, and the comradeship and friendly rivalry between coworkers.

The poem's tone is particularly significant. Duck enlightens but never lectures, addressing his reader with amiable friendliness, partly because he addresses a predominantly polite readership,[49] and partly out of genuine civility and humility. Despite Rev. Stanley's suggestion of the topic, what became *The Thresher's Labour* is written on behalf of the laboring community on the farm where Duck works; yet he also asserts the importance and relevance of his own experience, not least of trying to combine his role of poet with that of worker. It is intrinsic to my argument that the poem's subject matter continually generates a vocabulary, a narrative energy, and a pressure toward onomatopoeia and other kinds of mimicry that impact directly on the versification; accordingly, my analyses will recurrently move between the former (subject matter) and the latter (versification).

Having fulfilled his dedicatory duties to patrons and established his poem's purpose (ll. 1-12), Duck begins his account of the annual cycle of work by relating how the farmer gathers his laborers around him, allocating threshing duties:

> He calls his Thresher's forth: Around we stand,
> With deep Attention waiting his Command.
> To each our Tasks he readily divides,

And pointing, to our different Stations guides.
As he directs, to different Barns we go;
Here two for Wheat, and there for Barley two.
But first, to shew what he expects to find,
These Words, or Words like these, disclose his Mind:
So dry the Corn was carried from the Field,
So easily 'twill Thresh, so well 'twill Yield;
Sure large Day's Work I well may hope for now;
Come, strip, and try, let's see what you can do.

(ll. 19-30)

Duck presents the men standing around together, contemplating the hard physical slog ahead. Like Mary Collier's later *The Woman's Labour*, Duck's poem draws the reader into a circle of workers to hear the employer's instructions; we become one of them, hearing what, and as, they do. In lines 27 to 30 Duck reproduces everyday dialogue almost verbatim. As Hunter argues, the "public" couplets of argument and conversation written by the period's canonical poets "don't try to emulate talk *exactly*" (my italics).[50] Duck, by contrast, *does* aim to reproduce speech as nearly as he can. They are "These words, or words like these:" the closest he can get using couplets. Duck manages similarly well when the Master later admonishes them for—allegedly—not being productive enough: "Why look ye, Rogues! D'ye think that this will do? / Your Neighbours thresh as much again as you" (ll. 76-77). For serious, formal, non-satirical, narrative/descriptive verse—as opposed to the informality of the dialogue or epistle form—this is unusually specific.

Duck continues by introducing the labor that is so central to his enterprise:

Divested of our Cloaths, with Flail in Hand,
At a just Distance, Front to Front we stand;
And first the Threshall's gently swung, to prove,
Whether with just Exactness it will move:
That once secure, more quick we whirl them round,
From the strong Planks our Crab-Tree Staves rebound,
And echoing Barns return the rattling Sound.
Now in the Air our knotty Weapons fly;
And now with equal Force descend from high:
Down one, one up, so well they keep the Time,
The *Cyclops* Hammers could not truer chime;
Nor with more heavy Strokes could *AEtna* groan,
When *Vulcan* forg'd the Arms for *Thetis'* Son.
In briny Streams our Sweat descends apace,
Drops from the Locks, or trickles down our Face.

(ll. 31-45)

Physical details—the Flail, Threshall, Planks, Staves, and Barns—mingle or combine with wordplay and classical allusion. There is an experiential account of what is actually done, providing authentic detail in abundance. First we have the account of the testing of the threshall before it is swung: the threshers appear to stand face-to-face ("Front to Front"), presumably in two lines. They establish that the distance between them is "just" to prevent possible accident. Then there is the alternate striking—"Down one, one up"—presumably as between the two lines of men, while the reversal of stress in the first foot of "Down one, one up" conduces neatly to an imitation of the alternating blows of the flails. The inference is that they can neither break time nor pause, and hence the sweat. The alliterative, onomatopoetic "we whirl" conveys the impending giddy, light-headed sensation of being drunk with exhaustion, lactic acid surging through the body. In line 36 the six strongly (and equally) stressed syllables (strong/Planks/Crab/Tree/Staves/(re)bound) convey the sense (and sound) of powerful, strenuous, equal whacks. The description would seem certain to close with a full stop after "rebound" at the end of a couplet, but the effect of the echo, mimicking the "echoing Barns," is achieved by line 37, completing an unexpected triplet that is not in any sense random or accidental, but absolutely interdependent with the sense of the poem. The onomatopoeic "rattling" continues the preoccupation with sights and sounds. The classical allusions (ll. 41-45) provide a deliberate contrast with the physical/experiential nature of the preceding lines, another instance of Duck's tendency to mingle or juxtapose seemingly contrary elements within his descriptions of labor. The reference to the chiming of Cyclops' hammers functions doubly, indicating how deafening the noise is, but also signifying that whereas laborers might be little regarded by their social betters, arduous labor was *once* the stuff of heroic legend (also seen in the reference to Vulcan). Lines 41 to 43 are heavily influenced by Dryden's translation of Virgil's *Georgics*.[51] Not only was such labor mythical, but it was also deemed worthy of praise within elevated verse and translated by as recent and celebrated a figure as Dryden. The concluding lines— "In briny Streams our Sweat descends apace, / Drops from our Locks, or trickles down our Face"—could arguably exist nowhere else in (non-satirical) verse at this time.[52] Duck's return after the Vulcan interlude to the sweat, the material consequence of hard physical exertion, seems deliberately—and successfully— bathetic in this context: after the brief classical sojourn, we are suddenly back in everyday working life. Above all, there is a great—and for the time, unusual— sequential narrative energy; here ten lines are devoted to the single process of threshing, and because they amount to an extended description of a single, continuous experience, Duck's couplets are not self-contained in the Popean manner.

The verbal texture of the vocabulary, seen in, for example, lines 35 to 36, is another important aspect of the passage. These lines are awkward to pronounce, rugged, or, to use a word favored by Duck himself, "knotty." The conventional usage of many words within neoclassical verse, in relation to both rural and other affairs, was generic: a "swain" stood for an all-purpose country laborer; a "flood" for an all-purpose water feature. However, once a "swain" becomes a "thresher," the reader is invited into a different and less artificial or literary landscape; the focal length has *changed.* We are in neither the pastoral world nor (for the most part) that of formal georgic with its technical, scientific vocabulary. Many such generic words—"breeze," "trees," "groves," "nymphs" (for instance), all repeatedly used in Pope's *Pastorals*—were readily subsumed into familiar patterns of mellifluousness.[53] Even the word "thresher," however, has a vigor that makes it more jagged than "swain," and promotes new sound patterns. The same is true of vocabulary such as "strong planks," "Crab-Tree staves," and much else throughout *The Thresher's Labour.*

Duck's complex treatment of labor itself is clearly crucial to a proper consideration of the poem. Albert Camus says of Sisyphus (with whom Duck later draws a comparison), "The struggle itself towards the heights is enough to fill a man's heart. One must imagine Sisyphus happy."[54] If we might not say the same of the poem's speaker (although one recalls the influence upon Duck of the stoic Seneca), work is at least "transformed" and "justified by a wider context" for him.[55] While he deplores the conditions in which he and his workmates sometimes work, and loathes and dreads the constant round of toil to which they are subject, there is healthy respect, if not for work itself, for the Herculean *challenge* of unremitting toil. There is pride not only in doing a good job, but also in the exertions undertaken to provide honestly for his family. He also relishes the comradeship between himself and his coworkers, the bonds forged between men who are dependent on one another. Duck is in full flow describing the nobility of hard work. This work is often tedious, but not always. It is a real joy, for instance, when the threshing is over and it is time to begin the haymaking:

> Before the Door our welcome Master stands,
> And tells us the ripe Grass requires our Hands.
>   . . . . .
> This Change of Labour seems to give much Ease;
> And does, at least, Imagination please.
> With Thoughts of Happiness our Joy's complete,
> There's always Bitter mingled with the Sweet.
> When Morn does thro' the Eastern Windows peep,
> Strait from our beds we start, and shake off Sleep;
> This new Employ with eager haste to prove,
> This new Employ becomes so much our Love:
> Alas! That human Joys shou'd change so soon,
> Even this may bear another Face at Noon!
>
> (ll. 90-91, 96-105)

Admittedly much of this joy is at the end of the threshing, and at the end of winter and start of spring. Haymaking is not in itself unappealing, though, and it is almost a privilege to work outside after the indoor threshing. The more enjoyable aspects are enough to elevate these jobs to the status of being "Bitter Sweet,"

as opposed, by implication, to the threshing that produces much of the former sensation and little of the latter. This passage is the beginning of a long portrayal of the renewed optimism and vigor at the start of spring that eventually gives way to exhaustion and fatigue.

Immediately afterward, we encounter a further passage on labor:

> A-cross one's Shoulder hangs a Scythe well steel'd,
> The Weapon destin'd to unclothe the Field:
> T'other supports the Whetstone, Scrip, and Beer;
> That for our Scythes, and These ourselves to chear.
>
> (ll. 108-11)

This is a particularly good illustration of the "mingling" of the Duckian mode of aestheticizing labor. The first two lines exhibit the balance and contrast associated with the neoclassical couplet: in the first line we have the actual name of the implement, a "Scythe well steel'd," slung across a shoulder; in the second we find a neoclassical synonym, "The Weapon destin'd to unclothe the Field." The specific and everyday come together with the general and neoclassical in a perfect microcosm of the Duckian mode and technique. Balance is further reinforced by the fact that this is a description of the—equally essential—objects resting on either shoulder: on one food and drink, and on the other the implement necessary to perform one's labor. There follows a passage about the men using the idea of a contest as a motivational tool, before the couplet "Our weary Scythes entangle in the Grass, / And Streams of Sweat run trickling down a-pace." (ll. 124-25). These lines recall lines 44 and 45, quoted earlier, and the circular, Sisyphean nature of their experiences becomes explicit in the poem's final lines.[56] Far from needless or dull repetition, this is deliberate self-reflexivity, in a poem constructed throughout in a more meticulous manner than has often been acknowledged.

Then comes the invigoration that results from being a part of the whirlwind of activity that is the harvest:

> Our well-pleas'd Master views the Sight with joy,
> And we for carrying all our Force employ.
> Confusion soon o'er all the Field appears,
> And stunning Clamours fill the Workmens Ears;
> The Bells, and clashing Whips, alternate sound,
> And rattling Waggons thunder o'er the Ground.
> The Wheat got in, the Pease, and other Grain,
> Share the same Fate, and soon leave bare the Plain:
> In noisy Triumph the last Load moves on,
> And loud Huzza's proclaim the Harvest done.
>
> (ll. 259-68)

A number of the common features of neoclassical versification are present. All ten lines are end-stopped. Duck is compelled, as practitioners of the heroic couplet often are, to tamper with "natural" word order so as to make the rhyme, as in line 260. Line 264 contains a conventionally poetic contraction, "o'er," and primacy is given to the abstract nouns "Confusion" and "Clamours." As is common in pastoral verse, Duck alludes to "the Plain," even though there are actually rather few in England. The sights and sounds of vigorous field labor are simultaneously evoked, however, and more than this, there is an excitement at just being involved, a sense of triumph at having completed a long, arduous, honest job. There is an adrenaline rush in this frenzy of activity, as if Duck is swept along by this tide of people all working toward the same goal. There is everyday vocabulary—"Bells," "Whips," "Waggons," "Wheat," "Pease," "Grain"—and concentration on the onomatopoeic "clashing Whips," "rattling Waggons," and "Huzza's." These "Huzza's" signal a kind of respite, not just from the labor, but also from this visual and aural overload. There is a momentum that the resources of verse are positively *required* to convey. A comparable passage in Duck's work dealing with his absorption in the sights and sounds of physical labor is provided by the account of industry in **"A Description of a Journey to Marlborough, Bath, Portsmouth, &c."** (ll. 367-96).[57]

Duck always takes pride in work and is disturbed that an employer (or reader) may think he has done less than his best. When the farmer admonishes the gang of laborers for (allegedly) making a bad job of the threshing, Duck tells us:

> Now in our Hands we wish our noisy Tools,
> To drown the hated Names of Rogues and Fools,
> But wanting those, we just like School-boys look,
> When th'angry Master views the blotted Book:
> They cry their ink was faulty, and their Pen;
> We, The Corn threshes bad, 'twas cut too green.

> (ll. 78-83)

Duck presents himself and his coworkers as ashamed and embarrassed at being told they have done a bad job, leading them to make what they are worried seem to be excuses. Yet the pride they take in their industry suggests that they are not the rogues or fools the Master calls them, and that "The Corn threshes bad, 'twas cut too green" is not mere idle excuse.

Attempting to sum up Duck's complex approach to labor itself, Goodridge writes of the threshing scenes, "It would be quite wrong to overemphasise the pride and pleasure in Duck's work: it is an undercurrent, not the main text, which shows a debilitating and backbreaking routine. Nevertheless an awareness of Duck's feelings of pride and pleasure, here and in the mowing scene, allows us a fuller picture of his ideas about work."[58] That *The Thresher's Labour* is the product of a man who wants to educate his so-called betters about the hardship laborers bear is again important. To go

further than Goodridge: Duck does not deny the satisfaction he derives from the struggle for the survival of himself and his family, or the solace found in labor's redemptive nobility. He would never want his words to be mistaken for laziness or sloth, or for a denial of the virtues of hard, honest labor.

He is, however, frank about the physical, mental, and emotional stress resulting from a life of toil. This stress emanates from a number of factors: working hours, conditions, and their consequences, such as fatigue and illness:

> When sooty Pease we thresh, you scarce can know
> Our native Colour, as from Work we go;
> The Sweat, and Dust, and Suffocating Smoke,
> Make us so much like *Ethiopians* look:
> We scare our Wives, when Evening brings us home;
> And frighted Infants think the Bug-bear come.
> Week after Week we this dull Task pursue,
> Unless when winnowing Days produce a new;

> (ll. 64-71)

The allusion is to the threshing of pea plants, to release the dried peas.[59] The repeated "s" and "t" sounds in "The Sweat, and Dust, and Suffocating Smoke," seem to suggest the laborers' need to spit, and the commas seem positioned to convey the impression of one imposition and hardship piled on another. Again, one notes the informal mode of address: "When sooty Pease we thresh, *you* scarce can know" (my italics).

Sweat, dust and "Smoke" are not the only factors that make life unpleasant. The laborers have only the shelter of the barns to protect them from the winter weather, and Duck also, more than once, describes how difficult laboring under a fierce summer sun can be:

> But when the scorching Sun is mounted high,
> And no kind Barns with friendly Shades are nigh,
> Our weary Scythes entangle in the Grass;
> And Streams of Sweat run trickling down-a-pace;

> (ll. 122-25)

Finally there is the recurrent weariness and near-exhaustion:

> Our time slides on, we move from off the Grass,
> And each again betakes him to his Place.
> Not eager now, as late, our Strength to prove,
> But all contented regular to move:
> [. . .]
> Homewards we move, but so much spent with Toil,
> We walk but slow, and rest at every Stile.
> Our good expecting Wives, who think we stay,
> Got to the Door, soon eye us in the way;
> Then from the Pot the Dumpling's catch'd in haste,
> And homely by its side the Bacon's plac'd.
> Supper and Sleep by Morn new Strength supply,
> And out we set again our Works to try:

But not so early quite, nor quite so fast,
As to our Cost we did the Morning past.

(ll. 144-47, 152-61)

Here the workers' diminishing strength is (however temporarily) restored. This is also a good example of the poem veering into areas of laboring experience uncharted by either pastoral or georgic, providing a precedent for other laboring poets wishing to transgress generic boundaries. Domestic laboring life is illuminated, strong medial pauses clearly intended to mimic the real-life slowing down described. Food is highlighted with specific references to "homely" everyday foods such as "Dumplings" and "Bacon." Elsewhere, in (yet) another passage bemoaning how far pastoral convention has strayed from the reality of rural labor, things are differently described. The workers sit down underneath a "shady Tree," tired "with Heat and Labour," and

> From Scrip and Bottle hope new Strength to gain;
> But Scrip and Bottle too are try'd in vain.
> Down our parch'd Throats we scarce the Bread can
>   get,
> And quite o'er-spent with Toil, but faintly eat;
> Nor can the Bottle only answer all,
> Alas! the Bottle and the Beer's too small.
>
> (ll. 138-43)

A passage such as this, ending with the pun lamenting the (too) weak beer, is a precursor of later desperate musings on the inadequacy of a laborer's provisions (see, for instance, Robert Tatersal's "The Bricklayer's Labours").[60] Just as food sometimes fails to give hoped-for respite, even sleep can fail—hence lines 251 to 54, complaining that labor even dominates their dreams.

A final dimension of Duck's treatment of labor is his description of the various methods that the laborers use to motivate themselves, faced with lengthy spells of repetitive exhausting work. They see the work as a trial of strength:

> The Grass and Ground each chearfully surveys,
> Willing to see which way th'Advantage lays.
> As the best man, each claims the foremost Place,
> And our first Work seems but a sportive Race:
> With rapid Force our well-whet Blades we drive,
> Strain every nerve, and Blow for Blow we give:
> Tho' but this Eminence the Foremost gains,
> Only t'excel the rest in Toil and Pains.
> But when the scorching Sun is mounted high,
>   . . . . .
> Our sportive Labour we too late lament,
> And wish that Strength again, we vainly spent.
>
> (ll. 114-22, 126-27)

It is important to stress that what Duck describes seems not competition in any hostile sense, but an attempt to try to out-do one another in a friendly spirit of rivalry.

The laborers survey the "Grass and Ground . . . chearfully." Trying to seek out advantage for themselves is a precious diversion from the monotony of work, which turns into a "sportive Race" ("sportive" is the key word). In a similar passage in **"A Description of a Journey,"** Duck, back in his native Wiltshire to attend the inaugural Duck Feast, cannot wait to wield again the trusty flail, scythe, and threshall, again entering into a competition with his former fellows (cf. ll. 41-50). The equivalent vignette in *The Thresher's Labour* is a microcosm, however, of how the harvest culminates in the cheat of the harvest-home supper before the cycle resumes. The "sportive Race" likewise turns out to be a deception and ends in lament. The very coping strategy used to deal with monotony *itself* compounds the laborers' disillusionment when it comes to an end.

There are additional observations that will develop points already raised. These relate to the poem's structure and intricate patterning; the consequences of attempting continuous narrative in the couplet form that tended to produce compact epigrams; and the question of an apt description of the function of the poem. The controversial gleaning passage (ll. 164-205) has been of great interest to feminist critics who are concerned with a gender-based dialogue between Duck and Collier. It is equally relevant to the poem's overall structure, as is the closing comparison with the labors of Sisyphus:

> Like *Sisyphus,* our Work is never done,
> Continually rolls back the restless Stone:
> Now growing Labours still succeed the past,
> And growing always new, must always last.
>
> (ll. 281-84)

While this is the only time that Duck explicitly alludes to Sisyphus, these lines function as an apt conclusion, because they provide a definitive image of the circular nature of the laborers' lives that is to the fore throughout. The pattern is defined by repeated respites, followed by inevitable disappointments. The interlude—for this is what it is—that the controversial gleaning passage provides also takes its place within a scheme of transitory diversions.

After eighty-three lines of introduction describing various occupations undertaken during autumn and winter, a lengthy passage proceeds until line 163 showing how, from a position of renewed vigor and optimism at the onset of spring, exhaustion sets in. The gleaning interlude then begins, in which the pressure of this relentless, frenetic activity is released; it is succeeded by the gathering of the harvest, another frantic period of work culminating in line 268 before the "Cheat" passage and the (Sisyphean) conclusion (ll. 269-84). In this way, the poem is divided into a clearly symmetrical pattern: introduction; frenzied activity; diversion/interlude; frenzied activity; conclusion. Duck creates tension, releases it with the gleaning passage, and then increases it again with the description of the harvest before concluding with exhaustion and disillusionment.

The poem's patterning is more intricate yet. As part of the Sisyphean cycle, even the periods of frenetic activity contain mini-digressions in the shape of epic similes. The first occurs from lines 128 to 135 (beginning "Thus in the Morn a Courser I have seen,") in the middle of the extended passage of exhausting activity from lines 84 to 163. In this instance, a sporting element is introduced, as if recapturing in a different poetic register the workers' own sportive hopes. The horse that began the hare course with exuberance returns home across country with sweaty sides and painful limbs. In the middle of the second passage of such activity, another mini-digression occurs, from lines 232 to 239 (beginning "Thus when Arabia's Sons, in hopes of Prey"). Here, the Arabs are also going hunting, but their prey consists of prosperous villages in a fertile country laid waste by the raiding party; the introduction of Bedouin raiders lends an elevatedly global perspective to Duck's portrayal of the harvest field.[61] The informal voice of the worker poet is not the poem's only voice, as Keegan (and Goodridge before her) has noted.[62] Keegan makes a differentiation between the "we," which she argues is the voice of the laborer, and the voice of the (Addisonian) poet. The latter, she claims, is evident in two passages featuring the pronoun "I" and in one without a personal pronoun that nonetheless corresponds to the voice of the passages elsewhere narrated by the "I." The two extracts I have identified, in the middle of passages of frenzied activity, are two of these three passages. The other, from lines 192 to 204 (beginning "Thus I have seen on a bright Summer's Day"), occurs at the end of the digressionary gleaning passage, a diversion within a digression, as it were.

Keegan argues that lines 232 to 239 "obscure the distinction between the two voices . . . It is no surprise then that while the arduous nature of the collective 'we's' labor continues to the poem's conclusion, the 'I' does not reappear. In describing the thresher's labor, Duck is describing the silencing of the poet who would sing of that labor."[63] She contends, then, that Duck suggests he cannot be a(n Addisonian) poet and simultaneously a poet of labor. This is not necessarily the case. As the "I" demonstrates, the poem simultaneously aestheticizes the experiences both of a group of threshers *and* of one particular thresher, who is also a poet. The "I" passages emphasize Duck's "otherness," that his status as a poet divides him from his fellows. This is Duck's articulation of the paradox later alluded to and examined by a variety of laborer-bards, of what it is to be a "laboring poet." As soon as a laborer attains "poethood," he or she is by definition separated from his or her workmates. As Duck experiences the same laboring activities as his coworkers, he relates them to classical precedent and experiments with the means of poeticiz-

ing them. We find ourselves in the midst, then, of a self-reflexive work, as Duck poeticizes the very processes through which he arrives at the poem we are reading. Just as he earlier describes testing the threshall, he tests his ability to poeticize these experiences. These experiments include speaking through the "worker" mode and the "poet" mode and devising a means of moving between them.

That the three "poet" passages are epic similes accounts for their more formal, detached register (despite use of the first person in two). Not only do the identities of "(Addisonian) poet" and "thresher" not coexist easily (as Duck recorded in another poem, **"To a Gentleman who requested a Copy of Verses from the Author,"** ll. 5-10),[64] but they also, in fact, jar conspicuously. In conventional epic the transition is between the elevated and the mundane. For instance, in Book I of *Paradise Lost,* John Milton describes the fallen angels converging upon the newly constructed palace of Pandemonium, his major subject, by means of a contrast with a swarm of bees:

> As bees
> In springtime, when the sun with Taurus rides,
> Pour forth their populous youth about the hive
> In clusters; they among fresh dews and flowers
> Fly to and fro, or on the smoothed plank,
> The suburb of their straw-built citadel,
> New rubbed with balm, expatiate and confer
> Their state affairs[65]

The movement is away from the grandiose and toward the humble or everyday. In order to emphasize this, and despite the fact that "Bee similes were commonplace in the epic tradition from Homer through the Renaissance," as Scott Elledge notes, "Milton characteristically enriched the significance of his version with meaningful detail. Instead of wild bees (as in Homer and others) Milton refers to a domestic swarm."[66] The simile has a number of purposes. By recalling Homer, as Elledge implies, Milton locates his enterprise in the epic tradition. The homely comparison helps readers to imaginatively assimilate a scene beyond normal human imagination; and it widens the range of human experience spanned in the poem as a whole, thereby contributing to the traditional epic aim of being (as far as possible) comprehensive, universal, and encyclopedic. Additionally, such similes can manipulate the dramatic tension of the poem, and therefore heighten the reader's dramatic experience, by means of a variation of mood, pace, and tone.

Whereas, to broaden the scope of a supernatural narrative, Milton uses such similes to incorporate the everyday, Duck, by contrast, broadens the scope of an everyday narrative by using simile to incorporate classical, oriental, and sporting allusions. In doing so, he highlights his poetic otherness even as he seeks to illustrate the epic potential of his laboring theme. As he proves, intentionally or otherwise, a thresher *can* write poetry about his working life, but however he seeks influence by imitating those who inspire him, the end result will necessarily be *different* (though not in any pejorative sense). Each epic simile in Duck's poem is brought abruptly to an end by the labor to which the poet-narrator is returned, as the register becomes less formal. The first of the three simile-digressions (ll. 128-35, the comparison of the swift courser with the workers) is followed by "With Heat and Labour tir'd, our Scythes we quit, / Search out a shady Tree, and down we sit," as the effects of his own labor suddenly bring his private, poetic musings to a halt (ll. 136-37). Similarly, the second such digression (ll. 192-99, on a flock of sparrows playing, embedded within the wider digression on gleaners) is succeeded by "But now the Field we must no longer range, / And yet, hard Fate! still Work for work we change" (ll. 206-07). Finally, the third digression in the voice of the would-be Addisonian poet (ll. 232-39) is succeeded by "The Morning past, we sweat beneath the Sun, / And but uneasily our Work goes on."

What Duck seeks is the *intersection* between laboring experience and literary convention, a means of subduing raw experience to existing literary form. Within these terms, what he produces is far from unsuccessful: if it is impossible to tell, from human experience, whether a swarm of bees resembles the gathering of the gods (since no one has ever seen the latter), tired laborers at the day's end can be appropriately contrasted with a wearied courser, a simile that is none the less epic because human experience confirms its veracity. Duck's experiments in providing "epic" similes in the inverse of the direction seen in conventional epic ("lower" to "higher" instead of the opposite) demonstrate his appreciation of the epic potential of his theme of the struggle of honest individuals to survive despite working long hours that are mentally and physically exhausting. This potential is admittedly not developed to its logical conclusion within laboring verse until James Woodhouse's *The Life and Lucubrations of Crispinus Scriblerus.*[67] Writing in the 1790s, Woodhouse, one of a number of subsequent figures who attempt to fill a space opened up by Duck, consciously constructs himself as a Duckian literary descendant and poeticizes the epic scale of both the emergence of the proletariat and his own struggles.[68] In *The Thresher's Labour* there is a strong sense of the *possibly* epic status of the struggle of the laborer.

There is also a sustained sequential energy in Duck's poem, because instead of using the couplet to produce the compact epigram (for the reasons explained by Hunter), he narrates continuous events (as discussed in the analysis of the threshing passage). It was this concentration on creating a series of near-epigrams that

usually made narrative energy an irrelevance in much contemporary verse, since there was rarely a sustained attempt to describe or a sustained story to tell.[69] The primary experiences Duck represents cannot easily be subdivided or miniaturized in self-contained couplets—as seen in a number of vignettes quoted. The high number of lines beginning with "And" seems relevant here—no fewer than forty-five in all. Pope also often begins lines with "And"—particularly in his minor verse—but at his most formal does so more rarely. If he does so begin a line, it is invariably in the second line of a couplet; Duck is driven on numerous occasions to begin a couplet's first line with "And" (e.g., *TTL* [*The Thresher's Labour*] ll. 33, 112, 170, 174). It is noteworthy that of the ten lines describing the end of the harvest (ll. 259-68), four begin with "And"—Duck's natural urge is to attempt to continue narrating ongoing experiences. A comparison with Clare's "Mouse's Nest" is instructive; five of the fourteen lines begin with "And," because what Clare describes is *a single experience.*[70] Duck writes in a similar spirit: sustained experiences, such as those of several hours' manual labor at the same task, are likely to be falsified beyond even poetic license if subdivided into a sequence of (near) autonomous couplets. A related point concerns the various lines in the poem (e.g., ll. 3, 54, 64, 86, 92, 112, and 164) where the sense decrees that the lines run strongly on—a natural overcoming of repetitive end-stopping.[71]

Overall, Duck's strengths lie in his stamina, weight of subject matter, and accumulation of effect. For all its variations, his verse is clearly not as nimble or agile as that of at least some other laboring poets (Leapor's *Crumble-Hall,* mentioned briefly below, and in which the amiable speaker takes the reader on a tour of the house and grounds, springs to mind). By the end, however, we have a sustained sense of the sights and sounds of Duck's everyday working life—and of the gamut of emotions that the workers run. This accumulation of effect is such that, by definition, lengthy passages have to be read in order to appreciate it—Duck's poem repays brief, isolated quotation less than, for instance (and to generalize), Pope. At the least, isolated quotation makes it hard to praise Duck in the same way, because Duck does not aim at producing as much meaning/suggestion in a short space. By the standards Duck's poem demands to be judged, it is a not-insignificant success.

IV

I am interested, finally, in attempting a definition of a particular "kind" of poem inaugurated by *The Thresher's Labour,* distinct from, though interrelated with, my earlier definition of the general mode of poeticizing labor seen in the poem. According to Richard Greene: "*The Thresher's Labour* demonstrated that the experiences of labour itself could be the basis of poetry . . . As a model for labouring poets, this composition is especially important. James Sambrook observes that *The Thresher's Labour* is 'one of the earliest eighteenth-century poems to belong to no recognized literary "kind."' That Duck had opened a new avenue of literary expression is evident from the number of poems published in the 1730s, often addressed to him, in which poets assert the literary possibilities of their own labour."[72] Far from being the "kind" of poem that laboring-class and female poets regularly produce, poems such as *The Thresher's Labour* and later attempts in this vein that it influenced—such as Collier's *The Woman's Labour,* Robert Tatersal's "The Bricklayer's Labours," and, to some extent, Leapor's *Crumble-Hall*—occupy a position of prominence within the oeuvres of their writers. Elsewhere these poets attempt more traditional "kinds," such as pastoral, epistle, elegy (as well as, in some cases, other poems featuring a Duckian medium of writing about labor—or at least about the everyday). There is normally only room for one such central poem in each poet's oeuvre. The poems are predominantly experiential and employ everyday language, sometimes even incorporating dialect or vernacular, and an informal tone of friend addressing friend (replicated in other poems by these figures), mingled with the more formal commonplaces of neoclassical versification.

It might be misleading to describe these poems as a "genre," since there *are* differences between them, but all feature the Duckian mode and appear to fulfill the same, or a very similar, function. They represent an attempt to describe their authors' specific occupational labor and to assert that their experiences are of sufficient significance to merit individual recognition. They also appear to point forward politically and sociologically in that they are written on behalf of an occupational community that is unable to express its own views in literary form. Duck, while notionally writing on behalf of threshers, represents a wider occupational group of laborers on the farm on which he works; Collier attempts to represent the views and experiences of laboring women; Leapor writes of domestic servants; and Tatersal of bricklayers. The poems all seek to educate readers about the realities of working life and experience, at the same time establishing that their authors merit the title of poet.

To arrive at a descriptor for such poems, some reference to the idea of "self-assertion" would seem desirable. The poets are all individuals who are theoretically excluded from writing poetry by virtue of their occupations, and hence find it necessary to write a major autobiographical poem asserting their right to compose verse, while also affirming the existence of a wider laboring community. This also accounts for the fact that women poets (including those of other social classes) in this period, equally excluded from a literary form produced by and for men of the middle and upper social orders, write poems asserting something similar.[73] Ideally, any descriptive term would also involve reference to the experiential nature of these verses, and to the fact that their writers reject definitions imposed on them by others in favor of a right to self-definition. To describe these poems as "assertive of the value of individual experience and identity, and of the right to self-definition, on behalf of the writers themselves and of their fellow laborers" may not win commendations for brevity, but it does encompass these various elements. That this description extends beyond merely two or three words is not necessarily a bad thing; too restrictive a description would only risk imprisoning Duck's poem within another tight definition one imagines he would have been keen to escape.

As argued, for Duck, poeticizing his experiences did not just endow his subject matter with dignity by "making special," but it also implied a claim for the status of *poet,* rather than mere (anonymous) folk songster or diarist. Duck's affinity with the working people of his home county of Wiltshire, and his fame,[74] were sealed in 1735 with the inauguration of the Thresher's Feast, which endures today, an event of a nature seldom accorded to songster or diarist.[75] The following passage from **"A Description of a Journey,"** describing Duck's experience of attending the inaugural feast, is unusual within Duck's (largely) self-effacing works and forms an apt conclusion. Just as the following predicts, it was as "the Thresher," partly on account of the lasting achievement of his most sustained and influential composition, that he attained a lasting renown that has endured for nearly three centuries:

> Oft as this *Day* returns, shall *Threshers* claim
> Some Hours of Rest sacred to TEMPLE's Name;
> Oft as this *Day* returns, shall TEMPLE chear
> The *Threshers* Hearts with Mutton, Beef and Beer:
> Hence, when their Childrens Children shall admire
> This Holiday, and, whence deriv'd, inquire;
> Some grateful Father, partial to my Fame,
> Shall thus describe from whence, and how it came.
>
> 'Here, Child, a *Thresher* liv'd in ancient Days;
> Quaint Songs he sung, and pleasing Roundelays;
> A gracious QUEEN his Sonnets did commend;
> And some *great Lord,* one TEMPLE, was his *Friend*:
> That Lord was pleas'd this Holiday to make,
> And feast the *Threshers,* for *that Thresher*'s sake.'
>
> Thus shall Tradition keep my Fame alive;
> The *Bard* may die, the *Thresher* still survive.
>
> (ll. 91-106)[76]

Notes

I am grateful to the editors for their helpful comments on this article, and to Michael Irwin, who read and commented on earlier versions of the essay.

1. The issue of the most appropriate descriptors for such poets has been much discussed because of the dangers of anachronism attached to terms like "working-class," "proletarian," and even "laboring-class" within an eighteenth-century context. For a thorough discussion of these issues, and of why "plebeian" and "laboring-class" are less objectionable than available alternatives, see William J. Christmas, *The Lab'ring Muses: Work, Writing, and the Social Order in English Plebeian Poetry, 1730-1830* (Newark: University of Delaware Press, 2001), 41-43.

2. See Joseph Spence, *Full and Authentick Account of Stephen Duck, the Wiltshire Poet* (London, 1731), 12-13, cited by Rose Mary Davis, *Stephen Duck, the Thresher-Poet* (Orono: University of Maine Press, 1926), 21-22. An (unauthorized) account of Duck's life (later widely reprinted and cited elsewhere) prefixed to the seventh edition of *Poems on Several Subjects* (1730) suggests Duck burned early poems in dissatisfaction, and that he "went on writing and burning, and his Wife continually scolding, because he neglected his Labour" (iv).

3. All were initially published in the pirated *Poems on Several Subjects* (London, 1730, hereafter *PoSS*), and then in the authorized *Poems on Several Occasions* (London, 1736, hereafter *PoSO*).

4. Both were published in *PoSO*. They can be found, like *Every Man in his own Way,* in William Christmas, ed., *Eighteenth-Century English Labouring-Class Poets, 1700-1740,* vol. 1 of *Eighteenth-Century English Labouring-Class Poets, 1700-1800,* 3 vols., gen. ed. John Goodridge (London: Pickering and Chatto, 2003), 1:127-80.

5. Davis, *Stephen Duck,* 135.

6. Ibid., 11.

7. Ibid., 134.

8. John Goodridge, "General Editor's Introduction," in Christmas, ed., *Labouring-Class Poets,* 1:xiii-xv.

9. See, for instance, John Goodridge, *Rural Life in Eighteenth-Century English Poetry* (Cambridge: Cambridge University Press, 1995), 1-88; Bridget Keegan, "Georgic Transformations and Stephen Duck's *The Thresher's Labour,*" *Studies in English Literature* 41 (2001): 545-62; James Mulholland, "'To Sing the Toils of Each Revolving Year': Song and Poetic Authority in Stephen Duck's *The Thresher's Labour,*" *Studies in Eighteenth-Century Culture* 33 (2004): 153-74. I am grateful to Wil-

liam Christmas for bringing Mulholland's essay to my attention and for providing me with a copy. Although her article is primarily focused on Christian Tousey and Mary Leapor—mentioning Duck only twice in passing—Carolyn Steedman's "Poetical Maids and Cooks who Wrote," *Eighteenth-Century Studies* 39, no. 1 (2005): 1-27, also reflects a recent turn toward aesthetics in the study of eighteenth-century laboring-class verse. See pp. 14-18, where Steedman uses eighteenth-century (and more recent) linguistic theory to consider why so many laboring-class writers wrote poetry (rather than other literary forms).

10. For example, Keegan, "Georgic Transformations;" and Mulholland, "Song and Poetic Authority."

11. All sources for this claim can be traced back originally to Spence's *Full and Authentick Account,* 21. *The Thresher's Labour* (hereafter *TTL*) was originally dedicated to Stanley's wife. Many if not all of the topics for Duck's early poems appear to have been initially suggested by patrons.

12. A thorough discussion of the public nature of much early eighteenth-century verse is provided by J. Paul Hunter in "Couplets and Conversation," in *The Cambridge Companion to Eighteenth-Century Poetry,* ed. John Sitter (Cambridge: Cambridge University Press, 2001), 11-35 (esp. 14-18).

13. See ibid., 13. See also Margaret Anne Doody, *The Daring Muse: Augustan Poetry Reconsidered* (Cambridge: Cambridge University Press, 1985), 232. For Samuel Johnson's preference for rhyming couplets, see *"from Milton": The Lives of the Most Eminent English Poets* (rev. ed. London, 1783), in John Milton, *Paradise Lost,* ed. Scott Elledge (New York: W. W. Norton, 1975), 533. Subsequent references to Milton's *Paradise Lost* are to this edition.

14. Bridget Keegan, ed., *Eighteenth-Century English Labouring-Class Poets, 1740-1780,* vol. 2 of *Eighteenth-Century English Labouring-Class Poets, 1700-1800,* 3 vols., gen. ed. John Goodridge (London: Pickering and Chatto, 2003), 2:xvi.

15. On Duck's known early influences—the Bible, Milton, the *Spectator,* Seneca, Addison, Ovid, Bysshe, Shakespeare, Epictetus, Waller, Dryden, Virgil, Prior, and Ned Ward—see Davis, *Stephen Duck,* 16-22, 137-41. All information on this subject ultimately derives from Spence, *Full and Authentick Account,* 22-23. On the influence of Denham, see Davis, *Stephen Duck,* 134. On the influence of Latin authors on Duck, see ibid., 161-64. Goodridge suggests that William Diaper's

"Brent" (1726) may have been a (partial) model for *TTL,* and also argues for Duck's and Thomson's mutual influence upon one another (*Rural Life,* 112-15, 79-80). On Duck and Pope, see Davis, *Stephen Duck,* 35, 45-53, 127, 132, 149-50, 152, 154, 159. Spence records that Duck's allusion to "flow'ry Carmel" in "The Shunamite" was a quotation from Pope (*Full and Authentick Account,* 20). Davis establishes that Duck alludes to the poem concerned—*Messiah*—on a number of further occasions (*Stephen Duck,* 140).

16. See Davis, *Stephen Duck,* 132.

17. Hunter demonstrates most effectively that the couplet was ideally suited to engaging the reader in debate in "public" poems such as Pope's *Moral Essays* ("Couplets and Conversation," esp. 14-15, 26-29).

18. Sitter has even suggested that this was characteristic of verse throughout the century. See John Sitter, "Questions in Poetics: Why and How Poetry Matters," in Sitter, ed., *Cambridge Companion,* 133-56 (esp. 137).

19. Canto 1 opens with a (mock) epic invocation. Ariel's speech (beginning in 1.27 ff.) is another set piece—a stylized self-contained sequence, often determined by convention—in that it explains the "machinery" and offers a mock divine warning (as from an oracle) in lines 107-14. (See *The Rape of the Lock,* in *The Poems of Alexander Pope,* ed. John Butt [London: Routledge, 1963], 219, 221-22. Subsequent references to Pope's poems are to this edition and will be given appropriately in the text.) The absence of narrative is illustrated by the fact that Belinda does not even wake until line 115. What follows is again a set piece of epic parody, incorporating the worship of a god (Belinda herself) and the arming of a heroic warrior for battle. The narrative, such as it is—Belinda getting dressed—could be delivered in a single line; the rest is all set piece. So the poem continues through the succeeding four cantos, additional well-known lengthy set pieces including: Ariel's speech to the other spirits (2.73 ff.); the "Coffee/Ombre" scene (3.105 ff.); and the "Cave of Spleen" (4.19 ff.). Amid the 178 lines of canto 3, the essential narrative "action" takes place in just one couplet—"The meeting Points the sacred Hair dissever / From the fair Head, for ever and for ever!" (ll. 153-54). The "story" deducible from the poem is for Pope a means to a series of brilliant parodic ends. His allusiveness is a way of infusing every line with extra significance; what he chooses to forego in terms of narrative energy he more than gains in allusive density.

20. Davis states that Dr. Alured Clarke, entrusted with the task of Duck's education, was "unable to get a satisfactory translation of Homer" and so decided "that Stephen must read Pope's" (*Stephen Duck,* 35). Davis's source is Katherine Byerley Thomson, *Memoirs of the Court and Times of King George the Second, and his Consort Queen Caroline,* 2 vols. (London: H. Colburn, 1850), 1:198. Comparison of a representative passage of Pope's translation of *The Iliad* with Chapman's makes the point clearer. If one compares 5.91-109 of Pope's version (*The Iliad of Homer, Books I-IX,* ed. Maynard Mack [London: Methuen, 1967], 270-72) with its equivalent (George Chapman, trans., *Homer's Iliad and Odyssey,* ed. Richard Herne Shepherd [London: Chatto and Windus, 1924], *Iliad* 5.66), one finds very different kinds of couplets. Pope's neoclassical variety (although he risks one triplet in the passage), which facilitates brilliantly compact epigrams, are composed of pentameter and regularly end-stopped. They feature, certainly in this passage, little enjambment and no punctuation beyond the end-stopping. By contrast, Chapman's (heptameter) couplets feature both regular enjambment and punctuation: five of the sixteen lines in his equivalent extract are punctuated with medial stops. Pope's shorter, end-stopped couplets tend to fragment into tight, self-contained units, whereas Chapman can better capture the narrative flow of events. Whatever happens within Pope's narrative has to do so very quickly—within no more than twenty syllables—and the subsequent occurrence has to be captured within the same space again. Each event has to be definitively separated from its predecessor and cannot run into the succeeding couplet because of repetitive end-stopping. Whereas the greatest total of successive words without either a full stop or a semicolon in Pope's passage is twenty-eight, the equivalent figure for Chapman is thirty-three, and he includes another passage of thirty words. If we compare the greatest gaps between full stops in the passages, Pope's total remains at twenty-eight words, but Chapman's, given that the final nine lines of his extract comprise one sentence, jumps to ninety-six.

21. This issue touches on numerous current debates about the laboring-class poets, many of which cannot be pursued here in the detail they merit. At least one poet, Samuel Law, did not want to write in couplets, but was compelled by patrons, an account of which can be found in "The Preface" to his *A Domestic Winter-Piece: A Poem, Exhibiting a Full View of the Author's Dwelling Place in the Winter Season* (1772). See Keegan, ed., *Labouring-Class Poets,* 2:266-67. It is obviously impossible to know whether his experience was usual, although Duck underwent a process of "classicization" at the hands of Dr. Alured Clarke

contemporaneous with a "severe course in Georgian civilizing instruction" (see Davis, *Stephen Duck,* 32, 35; quotation, 36). Davis also quotes Clarke promising to "correct" Duck's verses (9). See also Peter J. McGonigle, "Stephen Duck and the Text of *The Thresher's Labour,*" *The Library* 4, sixth series (1982): 288-96; and Christmas, *Lab'ring Muses,* 73-94. McGonigle refers to the "movement towards the polite Augustan literary mode" (288) seen in Duck's revisions of the poem between 1730 and 1736, during which time, as Davis emphasizes, he was regularly exposed to Pope's work. One modern anthologization of the poem (David Fairer and Christine Gerrard, eds., *Eighteenth-Century Poetry: An Annotated Anthology,* 2nd ed. [Oxford: Blackwell, 2003], 260-67) allows readers to make comparative judgments about the 1730 and 1736 versions by printing the former (though see note 26, below, for the line they omit) and footnoting subsequent variations in the 1736 text.

Notwithstanding coercion, a number of other theories have been advanced to account for the couplet's popularity in laboring poetry. Noting "stylistic" differences between "polite and plebeian poets," Keegan suggests that the "memorability" of the couplet was crucial to its popularity with laboring poets who composed while at work (*Labouring-Class Poets,* 2:xvi). There is a variety of anecdotal evidence for this theory. Mary Collier, for instance, never claims that she actually read *TTL,* to which she responded, but only that she *heard* and memorized it. See Collier's "Some Remarks on the Author's Life," in *Poems, on Several Occasions* (Winchester, 1762); and Fairer and Gerrard, eds., *Eighteenth-Century Poetry,* 268. See also Roger Lonsdale, ed. *Eighteenth-Century Women Poets, an Oxford Anthology* (Oxford: Oxford University Press, 1989), 171. Robert Bloomfield claimed, meanwhile, that he composed *The Farmer's Boy* in rhyme while he was at work, because it was easier to memorize than blank verse. The claim appears in a letter to his brother George, dated Sunday, 16 September 1798. The original can be found in British Library, Additional Manuscript 28, 266, 85r-85v. For a modern reprint of the letter, see Robert Bloomfield, *Selected Poems,* John Goodridge and John Lucas, eds. (Nottingham, Eng.: Trent Editions, 1998), 1.

Betty Rizzo offers another explanation for why laboring poets wrote so often in neoclassical forms: "anxiety for influence." See her "Molly Leapor: An Anxiety for Influence," *The Age of Johnson* 4 (1991): 313-43, esp. 332.

22. Sitter, "Questions in Poetics," 153. See Ellen Dissanayake, "The Core of Art: Making Special," in *Homo Aestheticus: Where Art Comes from and Why* (New York: Free Press, 1992), 39-63.

23. See Linda Zionkowski, "Strategies of Containment: Stephen Duck, Ann Yearsley, and the Problems of Polite Culture," *Eighteenth-Century Life* 13 (1989): 91-108.

24. Ann Messenger, *Pastoral Tradition and the Female Talent, Studies in Augustan Poetry* (New York: AMS Press, 2001), 174.

25. Keegan, ed., *Labouring-Class Poets,* 2:xvi.

26. *TTL,* ll. 152-63. Given the process of "classicization" Duck's work later underwent, as explored in the quotations in note 21 (above), I have elected to quote from the original 1730 version. The first three editions, pirated as they were, accidentally omitted line 97, not corrected until the third and subsequent editions of *PoSS,* and until *PoSO* in 1736. Accordingly, the edition used here is *PoSS,* 4th ed. (billed on the title page as "The Fourth Edition, Corrected"), 15-25. Further references to *TTL* are to this edition and will be given by line numbers only in the text. These line numbers are as found in Christmas, ed., *Labouring-Class Poets,* 1:139-46, the only modern editor who restores the missing line. Fairer and Gerrard, for instance, anthologize the text of the first edition of *PoSS* seemingly without realizing the missing line's existence, leading them to allege that line 96 is "An unrhymed line" (*Eighteenth-Century Poetry,* 263). Hence after line 96 there is a difference in the numbering used here and in their edition. I am grateful to William Christmas for bringing this matter to my attention.

27. Mulholland, "Song and Poetic Authority," 153. For another such passage, see *A Description of a Journey to Marlborough, Bath, Portsmouth, &c.,* ll. 171-84, in Christmas, ed., *Labouring-Class Poets,* 1:160-61.

28. See the *Guardian,* no. 22 (Monday, 6 April 1713), no. 23 (Tuesday, 7 April 1713), no. 28 (Monday, 13 April 1713), no. 30 (Wednesday, 15 April 1713), and no. 32 (Friday, 17 April 1713), in John Calhoun Stephens, ed., *The Guardian* (Lexington: University Press of Kentucky, 1982), 105-07, 107-09, 122-24, 128-30, 135-37 respectively.

29. *Guardian,* no. 40 (Monday, 27 April 1713), in ibid., 160-65. Various overviews of these "pastoral wars" can be found; see Jonathan Lawson, *Robert Bloomfield* (Boston: Twayne, 1980), 133-54, and David Fairer, *English Poetry of the Eighteenth Century, 1700-1789* (Harlow: Longman, 2003), 80-86.

30. Fairer, *English Poetry,* 81.

31. See Lawson, *Robert Bloomfield,* 55, 137-48; this passage, 148.

32. See, for instance, Pope, "Spring," l. 33; "Summer," ll. 30, 72; "Autumn," l. 43.

33. Just as they are not pastoral swains, they are *not* (or do not want to be) the "Rogues and Fools" (l. 79) the Master claims; they are *not* the naughty schoolboys he makes them feel they are (ll. 80-81); and they *are not* like the female gleaners (ll. 163-204) Duck controversially represents as idle (irrespective of whether they really were). Proceeding from rejections of unwanted identities, Duck lays claim to alternatives: unlike pastoral swains, *they* toil continually in harsh conditions; despite the Master's accusations, and unlike the (apparently) idle gleaners, *they* are industrious, do *not* question the nobility of hard labor, and *do* take pride in their work.

34. John Chalker, *The English Georgic: A Study in the Development of a Form* (Baltimore: Johns Hopkins Press, 1969), 36.

35. For more about the nature of this space that opened up to be filled by Duck, see Doody, who argues that pastoral verse at the time conveyed a certain unease and sense of disequilibrium, a growing sense that there was a subject matter beyond present reach. Doody sees Gay's *The Shepherd's Week* (1714) as the ultimate realization of this, a work that was developmentally necessary so that a poem like *TTL* could subsequently emerge (*Daring Muse,* 106).

36. Joseph Addison, *The Miscellaneous Works,* ed. A. C. Guthkelch, 2 vols. (London: G. Bell and Sons, 1914), 2:7-8.

37. See Keegan, "Georgic Transformations."

38. Addison's "critical attitude became the established one for some generations" (Chalker, *English Georgic,* 17). See also Sitter, "Questions in Poetics," 142. Goodridge also acknowledges Addison's great influence upon the English georgic (*Rural Life,* 5). On later eighteenth-century criticism of the georgic, see Joseph Trapp, *Praelectiones Poeticae,* 2 vols. (London, 1711-1715), trans. W. Clarke and W. Bowyer as *The Oxford Lectures on Poetry* (London, 1742); and Joseph Warton, "A Discourse on Didactic Poetry," in *The Works of Virgil* (London, 1753).

39. See *Georgics* I, *The Works of Virgil,* trans. John Dryden, intro. James Kinsley (Oxford: Oxford University Press, 1961), vii; quotation, 51. Subsequent references to Virgil's *Georgics* are to this edition.

40. Chalker, *English Georgic,* 1. On the (until recently) adverse critical reception of Dyer's *The Fleece,* see Goodridge, *Rural Life,* 92. For specific examples of critical disapproval, see Samuel Johnson, "Life of Dyer," in *The Lives of the Poets,* ed. Arthur Waugh (London: H. Frowde, 1906), or Horace Walpole's comments in his letter to Sir David Dalrymple on 3 February 1760 (see *The Project Gutenberg E-Book of the Letters of Horace Walpole,* 4 vols., ed. Marjorie Fulton [Project Gutenberg Literary Archive Foundation, 2002], 3:40). The text is also available at http://manybooks.net/support/w/walpolehora/Walpolehoraetext03lthw310.exp.html.

41. Tim Fulford, "'Nature' Poetry," in Sitter, ed., *Cambridge Companion,* 115.

42. Such words found in the first three books of *The Fleece* alone extend to forty-five in number. Many are employed multiply, and this total excludes other polysyllabic words not ending in "ious" or "eous." An expanded list including such words that are present in *Agriculture* but not *The Fleece* would feature another twenty-one, some utilized on numerous occasions. Many are, or are derived from, scientific terms.

43. Goodridge suggests that Dyer (and, by extension, other georgic writers) were embroiled in an attempt to demonstrate through poetic means, and using Virgil as a generic model, that their subject matter was worthy of epic treatment because the nation's financial future depended on their ability to trade successfully in the world market (*Rural Life,* 96).

44. On this point, see Mulholland, "Song and Poetic Authority," esp. 164.

45. On *The Fleece,* see Richard Feingold, *Nature and Society: Later Eighteenth-Century Uses of the Pastoral and Georgic* (Sussex, Eng.: Harvester, 1978), 90-91.

46. In *The Fleece* 1.55-66 alone one finds "Shobden," "Falernum," "Vesuvius," "Herculanean," and "Pompeian"; and in the preceding twenty lines, "Banstead," "Dorcestrian," "Dover," "Normanton," "Sarum," "Stonehenge," and "Ross." A full list of all places, landmarks, nationalities, and peoples mentioned in the first book of *The Fleece* would include another thirty or forty entries, many in Latin.

47. James Thomson, *The Seasons,* ed. James Sambrook (Oxford: Clarendon, 1981), 4.

48. Ibid., xxvi.

49. Apart from the fact that the poem was initially written at the behest of patrons, subscribers to *PoSO* included six members of the royal family, eight dukes, eight duchesses, one marquis, twenty-six earls, twelve countesses, forty-three lords,

twenty-seven ladies, fifteen knights of the realm, and sixty (Right) honorables (see *PoSO*, "The Names of the Subscribers," xxi-xxxi).

50. Hunter, "Couplets and Conversation," 25.

51. *Georgics* 4.245-46, 251-53. See the note in Fairer and Gerrard, eds., *Eighteenth-Century Poetry*, 261.

52. Pope, for instance, never uses the word "briny," "trickles" appears only once, and "sweat" only four times within his oeuvre. See Edwin Abbott, *A Concordance to the Works of Alexander Pope* (1875; reprt. New York: Kraus, 1965).

53. Abbott's *Concordance* reveals that Pope never used such words as "thresher" "threshall," "planks," "Crab-Tree," "staves," "flail," "suffocating," "Bushel," "Whetstone," "Scrip," "Dumpling," "Prong," "Workmen," "Waggons," and "Huzza's." "Reaper," like "scythes," appears once. By contrast, Pope used "plain" fifty-four times; "swain" nineteen times; "groves" on thirty-five occasions; "shade(s)" seventy-three times; and "nymph" on thirty-seven different occasions.

54. Albert Camus, "The Myth of Sisyphus," in *The Myth of Sisyphus,* trans. Justin O'Brien (Harmondsworth, Eng.: Penguin, 1975), 111.

55. Fairer and Gerrard, eds., *Eighteenth-Century Poetry,* 268.

56. Ibid., 267. On the poem's conclusion, see Goodridge, *Rural Life,* 79-81. The view that Duck shows the laborer's task to be describable in "Sisyphean" terms derives from ibid., 79.

57. Christmas, ed., *Labouring-Class Poets,* 1:165-66.

58. Goodridge, *Rural Life,* 48.

59. "It was a messy business . . . With peas and beans, it is well to thresh in the open on account of the clouds of black dust which are knocked out of them" (Thomas Hennell, *Change on the Farm,* cited by Fairer and Gerrard, eds., *Eighteenth-Century Poetry,* 262).

60. For the text of this poem, see Christmas, ed., *Labouring-Class Poets,* 1:285-87.

61. I am grateful to Donna Landry for her expertise where these two similes are concerned.

62. See Keegan, "Georgic Transformations," 552ff., who acknowledges her debt to Goodridge in this regard on 553. See also Mulholland, "Song and Poetic Authority," esp. 163-64.

63. Keegan, "Georgic Transformations," 559-60.

64. The poem was only given this title upon republication in *PoSO,* having appeared earlier in *PoSS* as an untitled epistle. The young gentleman to whom it was addressed was apparently Thomas Giffard (see Christmas, ed., *Labouring-Class Poets,* 128).

65. John Milton, *Paradise Lost,* 1.768-75.

66. Ibid.

67. See *The Life and Poetical Works of James Woodhouse,* 2 vols., ed. Rev. R. I. Woodhouse (London: Leadenhall Press, 1896); for modern selections, see Keegan, ed., *Labouring-Class Poets,* 2:214-33; and James Woodhouse, *The Life and Lucubrations of Crispinus Scriblerus: A Selection,* ed. Steve Van-Hagen (Cheltenham: Cyder Press, 2005).

68. See *The Life and Lucubrations of Crispinus Scriblerus,* 4:190.

69. Prominent exceptions, of course, stand out; for example, Pope, *Epistle III. To Allen Lord Bathurst,* ll. 339-402.

70. See John Clare, *Selected Poems,* ed. J. W. Tibble and Anne Tibble (London: Everyman, 1965), 234. The word "and" occurs nine times in all in the poem.

71. See, for instance, Fairer, who maintains that in certain circumstances end-stopping needs to be "over-ridden," since otherwise the poet will be "constantly reminded of a containing metre" (*English Poetry of the Eighteenth Century,* 116; he refers to Mary Chudleigh's Pindaric, "On Solitude.")

72. Richard Greene, *Mary Leapor: A Study in Eighteenth-Century Women's Poetry* (Oxford: Clarendon, 1993), 108.

73. For a selection, see Lonsdale, ed., *Eighteenth-Century Women Poets.* Subsequent page references are to this text. Mary Barber, for instance, defended her right to write verse, claiming it was for the purposes of educating her children; see "Written for My Son . . . At his First Putting on Breeches" (120-21). For other defenses of female poets' right to acquire learning and write poetry, see Mary, Lady Chudleigh, from "The Ladies Defence" (2-3); Sarah Egerton, "The Emulation" (31-32); Elizabeth Thomas, "Epistle to Clemena. Occasioned by an Argument" (34-36) and "On Sir J—S—saying in a Sarcastic Manner, My Books would make me Mad. An Ode" (40-42); and Anonymous ("The Amorous Lady,") "On being charged with Writing Incorrectly" (146-47). For poems serving as autobiographical introductions of poets' circumstances, why they write, and so forth—a sort of "female assertion of the right to poetic self-definition"—see Martha Sansom, from "Clio's Picture. To Anthony Hammond Esq." (86-87) and Mary Jones, "An Epistle to Lady Bowyer" (156-60). This list is only selective.

74. On the poem's enduring popularity, see Davis, *Stephen Duck,* 131.

75. One is tempted to draw comparisons with one of the century's most lively rural diarists, Anne Hughes. Whereas Hughes lies undeservedly forgotten, Duck lives on because he was a *poet*: both he and his material have benefited from this accordingly higher status. Hughes's *The Diary of a Farmer's Wife, 1796-1797*, ed. Suzanne Beedell (London: Countrywise Books, 1964), includes descriptions of cooking, cleaning, baking, feeding pigs and calves, making wine, covering haystacks, corn cutting/harvesting ("fogging,") apple picking, cider making, scrubbing, butter making, cleaning the dairy, lambing, grass and hay cutting, and collecting honey from the beehives. For a direct comparison with Duck's material, see Hughes's account of the threshing (37). She conveys an endearing sense of fun and infectious enthusiasm for life, and her close relationship with her maid is clearly of interest to social historians and theorists alike.

76. "Temple" was the family name of Palmerston, the patron who funded the feast.

Jennifer Batt (essay date fall 2005)

SOURCE: Batt, Jennifer. "From the Field to the Coffeehouse: Changing Representations of Stephen Duck." *Criticism* 47, no. 4 (fall 2005): 451-70.

[*In the essay below, Batt discusses two contemporary accounts of Duck—Joseph Spence's* A Full and Authentick Account of Stephen Duck the Wiltshire Poet *and an anonymous letter published in the* Grub-street Journal—*in order to draw some conclusions about the various roles Duck played in mid-eighteenth-century literary culture.*]

The natural habitat of the poet Stephen Duck is often assumed to be the fields and barns of his native Wiltshire. Duck is frequently referred to as the "thresher poet" and is chiefly remembered for a single poem, *The Thresher's Labour,* which he wrote in 1729 or 1730 when he was employed as an agricultural laborer in Wiltshire.[1] *The Thresher's Labour* depicts the yearly cycle of "endless Toils" that an agricultural laborer must endure: threshing "Wheat," "Barley," and "Pease" through autumn and winter; mowing and haymaking in the spring and summer months; and reaping and collecting the "ripen'd Harvest" at the end of summer.[2] The first-person narrative of "the Year's revolving Course" and the repetition of the personal pronouns "we," "us," and "our" situate the speaker of *The Thresher's Labour,* often identified with Duck, within the landscape of fields and barns that he describes:

> Around we stand,
> With deep Attention waiting his [the farmer's] Command.

To each our Tasks he readily divides,
And pointing, to our different Stations guides.
As he directs, to different Barns we go;
Here two for Wheat, and there for Barley two.

(ll. 19-24)[3]

However, by the time *The Thresher's Labour* was published in 1730, Duck was in the process of leaving behind forever the landscape of fields and barns described in his poem. His poetic efforts had initially brought him local fame, interest in him had grown, and by September 1730, as was reported in the London press, Duck's "several ingenious poetical Compositions" had attracted the attention of the queen. Queen Caroline rewarded his talents with an annual pension and "a little House in Richmond Park to live in."[4] In the short term, the "Wiltshire Thresher" became a cultural phenomenon and for several months was the subject of intense interest from the press. In the longer term, Caroline's patronage meant that Duck never had to labor again, and after holding various positions attached to the royal household, he took orders as a clergyman, ultimately becoming the rector of Byfleet in Surrey.[5]

Many critics, from the late eighteenth century to the present day, have been unsettled by the abrupt change in fortunes that Duck experienced, often viewing the queen's award to the thresher not as a benevolent act of patronage but rather as a destructive act of deracination. Raymond Williams, for example, famously observed that Duck's changed circumstances represented "not only a transition from a Wiltshire field to Richmond Park and Royal Gardens" but also "a decisive literary transition, a shift from 'we' to 'the Swain.' Within a few years Duck was writing, with the worst of them, his imitations from the classics."[6] Transplanted from his native fields to an alien soil, such an argument suggests, Duck failed to flourish as a poet. Indeed, not only did this relocation impair his poetic voice, but it has also been argued that severing the poet from his roots may even have led to his death by suicide twenty-six years later.[7] While other critics may not be as blunt or explicit as Williams in attacking the royal patronage and disregarding Duck's later poetry, the almost exclusive concentration on *The Thresher's Labour* in critical accounts of the poet betrays a similar bias.[8] If Duck's importance rests entirely upon his identification as a "laboring-class poet," then his only important work is believed to be that which he wrote when he was a laborer in a field in the English countryside.

For Duck's contemporaries, however, his origins as a thresher from Wiltshire had a different resonance. When Duck was catapulted to national fame in the autumn of 1730, opinions were divided: was he a poetic genius who greatly merited the patronage he had received from the queen, or was he an unlettered yokel whose pretensions to literary fame were laughable, and the royal patronage he received simply an illustration of the debased cultural and literary standards of the Hanoverians? One way in which competing attitudes to the poet were explored was through representations of the relationship between the poet, his poetry, and his environment. People who admired Duck's poetry and who were moved by his struggle to better himself insisted on the discrepancy between the natural abilities he displayed and the constraints of his working life in order to justify elevating him from that position. Skeptical readers on the other hand, especially critics of the government and the manner in which it distributed patronage, mocked him and his patrons by focusing on the comic incongruity of a rustic thresher attempting to become a polite man of letters.

This essay will explore two accounts of Duck from the early 1730s that offer two such competing representations of the relationship between the poet and his environment. The first account, Joseph Spence's *A Full and Authentick Account of Stephen Duck the Wiltshire Poet,* was published in March 1731 but was based on conversations with the poet that had taken place in early September 1730.[9] The second, a letter submitted by an anonymous correspondent to the weekly literary periodical the *Grub-street Journal* in December 1732, relates an accidental encounter between the correspondent and Duck in a Richmond coffeehouse earlier that month. Both accounts consider the poet's engagement with contemporary print and literary culture as both a reader and a writer, focusing particularly on his relationship with the newspaper and periodical press. These accounts place Duck in two very different contexts. Spence's account, which is concerned with providing a narrative of Duck's life as a laborer, locates him firmly in the barns and fields of Wiltshire, while the *Grub-street Journal* account, written two years after the queen had granted Duck her patronage, reflects this shift in circumstances and relocates him to a startlingly new environment—a coffeehouse in the fashionable resort town of Richmond.

However, in neither account is Duck allowed to sit easily in the landscape in which he is placed. Although his account focuses on Duck's life as a laborer, Spence is extremely careful not to present Duck as an ill-educated rustic. He records Duck's literary ambitions, exemplified in the poet's close engagement with Milton's *Paradise Lost* and with the highly regarded periodical the *Spectator,* and these literary texts jar against the agricultural landscape. For Spence, who became close friends with Duck, this juxtaposition of literature and labor highlights how extraordinary Duck is, how different from his fellow laborers, and how deserving of the highest patronage. While Spence is uneasy with Duck being a laborer, the letter to the *Grub-street Journal* is uneasy at the notion of a thresher turning into a man of

letters. The *Grub-street Journal* prided itself in pillorying hack and dunce writers, among which it included Duck. The one-time agricultural laborer is depicted indulging in a thoroughly urban pastime: leisurely visiting a local coffeehouse and reading and discussing the daily papers there. Yet the scene is narrated with an unsettling tone of satiric ambiguity that implies his incompatibility with a polite or urban environment. This account suggests that despite his relocation, Duck continues to bear the marks of his agricultural origins. The contrasts and tensions between these two representations of the poet and his environment reveal not just the transformation of fortunes that Duck experienced, but also the extent to which contesting groups competed over what it was that Duck could be used to symbolize.

In *A Full and Authentick Account of Stephen Duck,* Joseph Spence describes Duck's life as a laborer in the barns and fields of Wiltshire and his earliest attempts at poetry. Spence begins by declaring that "he is really an extraordinary Man," and in his account of the relationship between the poet and his environment he particularly emphasizes how Duck's abilities far exceed the "common Conversation" of "his poor State of Life."[10] Spence was Professor of Poetry at Oxford and, as James Osborn has described, had a particular interest in people who exhibited "natural genius."[11] For Spence, Duck was not part of the collectivized "we" of the laborers of *The Thresher's Labour* but rather a talented individual. In *The Thresher's Labour,* Duck relates how in summer the laborers are sent to the fields to mow the grass. For the laborers who have spent many months threshing and confined to barns, mowing is a "long much-wished" "Change of Labour," and initially leisure and pleasure are aligned with work (ll. 92, 96). The laborers are "joyful" at this "happy Season" and head off to the fields "chearfully" and with "eager haste" (ll. 95, 94, 114, 102). Work becomes a game:

> The Grass and Ground each chearfully surveys,
> Willing to see which way th'Advantage lays.
> As the best Man, each claims the foremost Place:
> And our first Work but seems a sportive Race:
> With rapid Force our well-whet Blades we drive,
> Strain every Nerve, and Blow for Blow we give.
>
> (ll. 114-19)

The workers, the narrator included, contest heroically for renown and are united in their pursuit of glory. Yet this competition of strength is deceptive: the only "Eminence" the victor gains is "t'excel the rest in Toil and Pains" (ll. 120-21). By midday, the laborers are exhausted, lamenting their "sportive Labour" and "that Strength . . . we vainly spent" (ll. 126-27). All notions of heroism are gone, as in "pain" the laborers "Search out a shady Tree and down we sit" and try to refresh and renew themselves with food and drink (ll. 135, 137). Yet refreshment is sought "in vain," and the men are almost too tired and parched to be able to eat and to prepare for the resumption of labor in the afternoon (l. 139). In *A Full and Authentick Account*, Spence offers an interesting parallel for this scene in which Duck is portrayed racing through his own work. However, according to Spence, when Duck did so he was not motivated by competitiveness or pursuit of personal glory but rather by personal improvement: "*Stephen tells me that he has frequently carried them [volumes of the Spectator] with him to his Work. When he did so, his method was to labour harder than any Body else, that he might get Half an Hour to read a Spectator without Injuring his Master. By this means he used to set down all over Sweat and Heat; and has several times caught Colds by it.*"[12] The overexertion that in **The Thresher's Labour** had been "Strength . . . vainly spent" prompted by a rash lack of foresight and misplaced notions of heroism becomes in Spence's account an illustration of Duck's "Honesty and Industry."[13] Through his efforts, Duck gains the "Eminence" of making time to read the *Spectator* without harming the profits of his "Master" and so marks himself out as an extraordinary individual who strives for self-improvement, even at the risk of personal discomfort and illness.

At first glance the *Spectator* seems to be a very incongruous text for a Wiltshire laborer to be taking with him into the fields and barns of the agricultural landscape in which he works, yet the earliest biographical accounts of Duck attest to its importance in the poetic education of this farm laborer. "Some Account of the Author," published in October 1730, declared that Duck was "Master of a Set of the *Spectators*," and references to the *Spectator* recur throughout *A Full and Authentick Account*.[14] The *Spectator* had been a very popular newspaper, published daily between March 1711 and December 1712 and thrice weekly between June and December 1714. Each issue contained an essay, frequently on educational or moral themes, most of which were written by Joseph Addison or Richard Steele. These essays were revised and reprinted in eight volumes between 1712 and 1715, and this eight-volume set had reached an eighth edition by 1726.[15] According to Spence's notes of their conversations, Duck first encountered the *Spectator* in mid-1728, so he would have read the essays in these duodecimo volumes, not in their original format as individual folio sheets.[16] The "set of *Spectators*" of which Duck was "Master" probably did not belong to him. Spence records that Duck had a good friend with whom he frequently shared resources for self-improvement, including books. This man, named Lavington, had been to London in service and had returned with a small library, including the *Spectator*, to which Duck was given unrestricted access.[17] These borrowed volumes reflected a world very different from that experienced by the "poor *Thresher*" of **The Thresher's Labour** (l. 10). The *Spectator*, like

its predecessor the *Tatler*, had its origins in the London coffeehouses and in a vigorous urban print culture that was not only able to sustain the circulation of a daily paper claiming tens of thousands of readers, but also multiple reprints of *Spectator* essays in volume format, as well as a range of unauthorized continuations and spin-offs.[18] The primary concern of the *Spectator* was to foster an urbane and sociable politeness in society, a concern that might seem irrelevant for a laborer who was exhausted after a long day of threshing, mowing, or harvesting.[19]

Although Spence's depiction of a tired, sweaty, and grimy laborer sitting in a field or in a barn reading his borrowed duodecimo reprints seems thoroughly alienated from both the vibrant metropolitan print culture and the ethos of urbane politeness that the *Spectator* represented, in *A Full and Authentick Account* Spence actually implies that Duck is the *Spectator*'s ideal reader. In the first issue, in the guise of Mr. Spectator, Addison hopes his daily paper will "contribute to the Diversion or Improvement of the Country in which I live."[20] In describing Duck's engagement with the *Spectator*, Spence revisits these notions of "Diversion" and "Improvement:" "The *Spectators*, you know, he has read with great Pleasure, and great Improvement."[21] The *Spectator* was concerned with not just *reflecting* a polite society, but with *creating* that polite society. The *Spectator* set no restrictions on readership or participation in the creation of this polite society. Addison actively courted a range of readers, from "well regulated Families" to idle "Gentlemen" to women, and both in newspaper and volume format the *Spectator* had a socially and geographically diverse readership.[22] And though it was never explicitly stated, participation in this polite society was presumably also open to literate Wiltshire farm laborers. Spence presents Duck as an exemplary student of the *Spectator*: indeed, his trajectory from the fields to the court might be seen as the ultimate illustration of the transcendent social values and morality that the *Spectator* aimed to teach. Describing Duck through his relationship with the *Spectator* legitimates the laborer's social progression and allows Spence to demonstrate that his new friend is a worthy recipient of the highest patronage.

The *Spectator* may have improved Duck's manners and his understanding of the world, and perhaps assisted him in the transition from rustic to courtier, but most important was the influence it had on his thinking about literature and literary texts.[23] Duck was very receptive to the recommendations of the *Spectator*. His views on Samuel Butler's *Hudibras*, for example, closely echo those expressed by Addison.[24] But the *Spectator* did more than tell him what to think. It also provided an authoritative standard against which he could measure his own critical judgments: "He has assur'd me, with all his usual Innocence and Simplicity, That when he came afterwards to read *Addison*'s Criticisms on *Milton* in the *Spectators*, 'Twas a high Pleasure to him, to find many things mention'd there, in the Praise of *Milton*, exactly as he had before thought in reading him. Here we must depend on his Credit; which I need not tell you with me is very good."[25] Spence insists upon Duck's critical acuity by asserting that he arrived independently at the same conclusions as Addison in his highly regarded Milton papers.[26] In addition to his inherent critical astuteness, Spence associates Duck once more with another praiseworthy characteristic: honesty. Duck's keen and discriminating mind is complemented by his natural "Innocence and Simplicity."

Spence presents Duck as more than an empty vessel for receiving the opinions of Addison and Steele. He is a critical and engaged reader, as his analytical responses to the *Spectator* itself further demonstrate. In *Spectator* no. 58, Addison declares he wanted "to establish among us a Taste of polite Writing,"[27] and according to Spence, the *Spectator* did "establish" such a "Taste" in Duck, leading him to reform his reading habits and turn away from less "polite" kinds of writing: "He had formerly met with *Tom Brown's Letters from the Dead,* and the *London Spy,* and read 'em, not without some Pleasure: but after he had been some time conversant with the *Spectators*, he said, 'He did not care much to look into them.'"[28] The *Spectator* contains no proscriptions against either *Letters from the Dead to the Living* by Thomas Brown or Edward Ward's *London Spy.* Duck rejects these not because he has been told to but because in comparison with reading the *Spectator* they no longer bring him "Pleasure." Like the *Spectator*, the *London Spy* began as a periodical and was collected and revised into volumes many years before Duck came to read it. Both periodicals feature fragments of verses scattered in with the prose, and both take metropolitan London as their theme and backdrop, but there are several differences between them in terms of content and style.[29] Although the preface to the *London Spy* declares that it intends to "to scourge vice and villainy,"[30] its attempts at moralizing are sporadic and unsustained and are frequently undercut, especially in the earlier chapters, by bawdy sexual innuendo and the gleeful depiction of whores, pimps, thieves, con men, and other low-life characters. In contrast, the *Spectator* was far less licentious. According to Spence, Duck "seems to have an excellent Moral Turn in his Thoughts" and was particularly attracted to the "scatter'd [papers in the *Spectator*], written in the Cause of Virtue and Religion."[31] Stylistically, the *Spectator* was also more appealing to Duck. The prose of the *London Spy* is at times bewilderingly verbose and dense with incessant and often lewd similes, as well as being littered with "arses," "farts," and besmeared with "sir-reverence" (human excrement). In contrast, the prose of the *Spectator* drew high praise from Duck: "I remember particularly, That on my happening to call 'em *Prose*; he said,

''Twas true, they were *Prose*; but there was something in 'em that pleas'd almost like Verse.'"[32] By 1730 the prose style of the *Spectator* was greatly lauded, and Duck's enthusiastic praise would be echoed several years later by Joseph Warton, in his *Essay on the Writings and Genius of Pope,* where he declared that "in various parts of [Addison's] prose-essays, are to be found many strokes of genuine and sublime poetry."[33] Spence offers the opposition between the polite and the impolite text as further evidence of Duck's genteel literary discrimination.

Spence also records that the *Spectator* was fundamental to Duck's poetic development. It prompted him to write poetry: "The *Spectators* improv'd his Understanding more than any thing. The Copies of Verses scatter'd in those Pieces, help'd on his natural Taste: he was willing to try whether he cou'd not do something like 'em. He sometimes turn'd his own Thoughts into Verse while he was at work; and at last begun to venture those Thoughts a little to Paper."[34] Some modern critics have believed that Duck's natural abilities should have been inspired by popular oral traditions, such as "the ballads or hymns that he would have heard," but according to Spence, it was the *Spectator* that "help'd on his natural Taste" and led him to attempt poetry.[35] For Spence, indeed, the question was not "why not ballads?" but "why not Milton?" Duck held Milton in great esteem, but his first poetic efforts were inspired by the short occasional verses in the *Spectator* rather than the epics of Milton. Spence records that he asked Duck why "as *Milton* had been his Favourite Poet . . . none of his Pieces are in *Miltonick* Verse." Duck replied (demonstrating his renowned humility) that he wrote the whole of his biblical poem, **"The Shunamite,"** in "Blank Verse: [but] that upon reading it over, he found his Language was not Sublime enough for it," and so "he was forc'd to write it all over again, and turn it into Rhime."[36] The poems in the *Spectator*, in contrast with Milton's epic achievements in *Paradise Lost, Paradise Regained,* and *Samson Agonistes,* provided an accessible model for an uncertain but aspirant poet.[37] The *Spectator* also provided him with material for his poems. Spence questioned Duck closely about the composition of **"The Shunamite,"** and Duck offered him sources for some of his diction. The phrase "*Flow'ry* Carmel" (l. 5), he explains, "quotes Mr. *Pope*."[38] "Carmel's *flow'ry Top*" is found in Pope's *Messiah,* which had been first printed in the *Spectator* in 1712.[39] The *Spectator* was also the source for one of his longest poems, *Avaro and Amanda,* which was begun by September 1730 but not published until 1736.[40] *Avaro and Amanda* was based on "The History of Inkle and Yarico," a narrative about an "Indian Maid" (Yarico) and her treacherous English lover (Inkle), which had featured in *Spectator* no. 11.[41]

The *Spectator* may also have provided inspiration for another of Duck's poems, **"On the Queen's Grotto,"** which was written in 1732. The "Grotto" celebrated in the poem was a recently completed structure built in Richmond Gardens at the instigation of Queen Caroline. In late 1732 the grotto was a very popular subject for poetry published in newspapers, magazines, and pamphlets.[42] Despite its great topicality, however, Duck's poem has several parallels with a poem about a different grotto that had been first published in the *Spectator* in 1714.[43] Duck's poem begins with an address to Calypso, the grotto-dwelling sea nymph from Homer's *Odyssey*: "Now blush, Calypso; 'tis but just to yield, / That all your mossy Caves are here excell'd."[44] While Duck may have sourced this allusion from an array of locations, including Pope's translation of the *Odyssey,* or the Archbishop of Cambray's *The Adventures of Telemachus,* both of which he had read by 1732,[45] these lines may also echo *"To Mrs.* M. L. *on her* GROTTO," an anonymous poem from *Spectator* no. 632. This also begins with an address to Calypso: "A Grotto so compleat, with such Design, / What Hands, *Calypso,* cou'd have form'd but Thine!" (ll. 1-2). There are several other echoes between the two poems. Duck's "mossy Caves . . . here ex*cell*'d" (l. 2) recalls the *Spectator* poem's reference to "Mossie Cells" (l. 15), while the address to "Mrs. M. L." as the "Founder" of the grotto (l. 40) might be reflected in Duck's reference to Caroline as "Imperial Foundress" (l. 29). Several rhymes are also echoed from one poem to the other, and the cumulative effect of these echoes suggests that Duck may have had *"To Mrs.* M. L. *on her* GROTTO" in mind when he wrote his own poem.[46]

Although Duck may have been as greatly influenced by the *Spectator* when he wrote **"On the Queen's Grotto"** in 1732 as Spence records he had been in 1730, this poem reflects a very different relationship between the poet and the environment from the one Spence had described. Duck places his poetic self in the garden at Richmond, in contemplation of the grotto, as he implores Calypso to "see" "here" "this *Building*'s Beauty" (ll. 3, 2, 8). The poem signals that Duck is no longer part of an agricultural landscape: he has been relocated to the polite and fashionable environs of Richmond. In addition to Richmond Gardens, the area was also host to several royal palaces and the royal hunting ground at Richmond Park. Both Richmond and nearby Kew were fashionable resorts, located a pleasantly convenient distance from London.[47] Ever since Duck had been catapulted to national fame in 1730, he had been closely associated with this landscape. Reports of the queen's patronage had declared that he had been given "a little House in Richmond Park to live in," and there was even speculation that he was to be given the grotto itself for his "ordinary residence."[48] In fact, Duck seems to have been given a house in the village of Kew, adjacent to Richmond

Gardens.[49] Several poems celebrating the grotto allude to Caroline's patronage of Duck and situate him in the bucolic landscape surrounding the edifice. Catharine Cockburn, for example, praises Caroline for having removed Duck from the oppressive hardships of toil, and "seat[ing] him at ease near her lov'd Hermitage."[50] As the queen's favored poet, and living so close to Richmond Gardens, Duck was in an ideal position to function as a "court poet" and produce a panegyric on the grotto.

The publication of **"On the Queen's Grotto"** caused a controversy that adds a further dimension to this vision of Duck at Richmond. *"On the* QUEEN'S *Grotto.* By STEVEN DUCK" was published in the *Daily Post-Boy* on Monday, 11 December 1732.[51] In the next month the poem was reprinted in at least five other London newspapers, as well as in the December issues of the *London Magazine* and the *Gentleman's Magazine.*[52] It also attracted a short critical essay in the *Whitehall Evening Post* and was reprinted in at least one provincial paper.[53] However, according to a letter printed in the *Grub-street Journal* on 28 December 1732, the publication of the poem was against the wishes of the author. The letter begins with a complaint about some of the unscrupulous practices of the world of newspaper journalism. In particular, the anonymous correspondent is concerned with what he claims to be a recent development: the news gatherers, formerly interested in collecting news and gossip to print in their papers, have now turned their attentions to poetry. And not only do they steal poetry, but they reprint it in an unrecognizable manner. He writes: "They now collect scraps of poetry; some entire manuscripts; rase out ends of verses; tag on others; and so hack and maul, and piece, and plaister the most minute production, that when an author sees it in a publick paper, he is ashamed to acknowledge the legitimate issue of his own brain."[54] This, it seems, is what had happened to Duck's poem. As evidence for his accusation, the correspondent cites the recent publication of "a Copy of Verses on the HERMITAGE, written by Steven Duck." He offers a *Spectator*-esque description of the scene when Duck discovered that his work had been stolen, mutilated, and published without his consent:

> I happen'd to see him at a coffee-house, not far from the subject of his poem [presumably at Richmond]; and while he was very diligently reading the *Daily Post-boy,* (if I mistake not,) I observ'd him to change colour, knit his brows, and sometimes give a disagreeable pish. Seeing these conunctions and agitations in his countenance, I took the freedom to ask him what he discover'd in the paper that was able thus to—*distort his visage into frowns?*—What do I discover, said he? I discover a knave and a fool within two letters of one another—I was surpriz'd to observe a man who (as I have heard) is naturally sedate, and not easily provok'd, so suddenly break forth into a passion; and not without some resentment, demanded what he meant by knave and

fool?—Sir, say'd he, (giving me the paper) you shall see. Here is a short copy of verses in my name: true, I writ them, and, doubtless, with some faults; but not so many as they have now. That thief J[one]s, (you know who I mean, say'd he, the r[ogu]e that stole my first poems) is worse than Cacus; for tho' he stole the cows, he did not cut their tongues out; by which their master knew them, and detected the thief: but this J[one]s, said he, so murders a thing when he has stolen it, that there is no knowing it again, tho' we meet it in the market.—Hearing him speak thus I begg'd him to give me a genuine copy, which he did very willingly. And having read it, I own his resentment seems in some measure reasonable: I therefore, Mr. Bavius, communicate his performance to you, (according to the author's own desire,) which, if you will honour with a place in your paper, you will do justice to an honest man, and oblige your constant reader.[55]

This extraordinary scene places Stephen Duck, the "thresher poet," in a Richmond coffeehouse. No longer is Duck depicted as a laborer, reading secondhand *Spectator* essays in the fields: now in the coffeehouse in Richmond he has access to the daily London papers.[56] He has become part of the coffeehouse landscape, a celebrity who is recognizable to onlookers such as the anonymous correspondent who provides this account. In collaborating with the correspondent to provide the *Grub-street Journal* with the correct text of his poem, Duck is more than a consumer of print culture. He is an active participant, even if that participation has to be mediated through the authority of someone else. This scene is an interesting counterpoint to Spence's depiction of Duck in the fields of Wiltshire, but it also complicates Cockburn's vision of Duck sitting "at ease" near the "Hermitage." It presents Duck sitting "at ease" not in the royal Richmond Gardens but in a busy Richmond coffeehouse.

Although this scene has not been recorded by any of Duck's biographers, it is probable that the events narrated did take place.[57] Several details tally with various aspects of the Duck legend. For example, according to Spence, Duck was very modest about the extent of his poetic achievement, telling him that "he could not think highly of" his early poetry, and "he knew as well as any Body, that [the poems] were not really good in themselves."[58] The remark in the *Grub-street Journal* letter that "I writ them, and doubtless, with some faults" demonstrates a similar kind of modesty. Duck's complaints about the theft of his "first poems" seem particularly plausible, because this was an abuse that continued to preoccupy him until at least 1736. When Caroline's patronage of Duck was announced in September 1730, his poetry became extremely saleable. A publisher acquired a manuscript copy of Duck's poems and proceeded to publish "*Poems on Several Subjects* by Stephen Duck." This pamphlet went through seven editions in eleven days.[59] The publication of these poems was apparently without the knowledge

or agreement of the author. His patrons, including George II's Chaplain in Ordinary, Alured Clarke, and Queen Caroline's Lady of the Bedchamber, Charlotte Clayton, were keen to protect the interests and reputation of their new charge and took measures to prevent the further publication of the poems. Erasmus Jones, a news gatherer for one of the London papers, who is described in the *Grub-street Journal* account as a "thief" and a "r[ogu]e," was blamed—or perhaps made into a scapegoat—for the "theft" of the poems.[60] The battle that ensued between the patrons and the publishers had a public dimension, as each party used the press to issue denunciations and counter-denunciations of the other. On 14 October 1730 the *Daily Post* carried a notice, signed by Duck but probably instigated by his patrons, asserting that *Poems on Several Subjects* was both "spurious" and erroneous. The publishers of *Poems on Several Subjects* responded by placing an advertisement for their pamphlet in the same paper, directly below this notice, that denounced Duck's statement as a "sham Advertisement." Duck and his patrons then responded by forcing "J. Jones" (who may or may not be the same person as Erasmus Jones) to apologize and confess, in an advertisement in the *Evening Post* on 15 October, that *Poems on Several Subjects* was indeed "spurious."[61] The "theft" still rankled in 1734, when Duck's poem *Truth and Falshood* was both advertised with, and prefaced by, the statement that "the *Thresher's Labour*, "The Shunamite," &c, were never published with my Approbation," and Duck returned to the theme in the prefatory material of *Poems on Several Occasions* in 1736, where he again fulminates against Jones, the man who "stole my poems."[62] The representation of Duck in the coffeehouse is, then, either a narrative of actual events or a well-researched and carefully executed fabrication.

However factually accurate the scene may be, the *Grub-street Journal* is an odd choice of newspaper in which to mount such a defense of Duck's rights. Edited by Richard Russel ("Mr. BAVIUS"), the paper had been inspired by Pope's *Dunciad* and attempted to carry on, on a weekly basis, the war against the hacks and the dunces that Pope had initiated.[63] When Caroline's patronage of Duck had been announced in the autumn of 1730, the *Grub-street Journal* had been one of the main forums for satiric attacks directed against both the poet and his patrons. Caroline's patronage of the thresher was regarded as symptomatic of the debased cultural and literary standards of the Hanoverian government.[64] Duck's agricultural origins had been one major theme of the *Grub-street Journal* attacks. It featured numerous poems that alluded to "fields" and "barns" and derided his labored poetical efforts, and its most recent reference to Duck had been in August 1732, when it had ridiculed him by comparing him to another (imaginary) aspirant rustic poet, "Hobbinol Lubbin."[65] Another significant theme of the *Grub-street Journal*'s response to Duck was to highlight the contested issue of authority surrounding the publication of *Poems on Several Subjects.* In 1730, when the patrons and the publishers had battled so publicly about *Poems on Several Subjects,* the *Grub-street Journal* gleefully provided an arena to host the debates, printing a series of letters from both supporters and detractors that explored issues of authorship and authenticity and mocked the publishing phenomenon that Duck's poems had become. On 31 December it reprinted the series of advertisements and counter-advertisements that had appeared in the *Daily Post* and the *Evening Post* on 14-15 October, drawing attention once more to the public quarrel and making it available for any readers who had originally missed it.[66] The letter concerning **"On the Queen's Grotto"** recalls the *Grub-street Journal's* ambiguous attitude toward these debates about authority of two years earlier. The unstable tone of the narration of the scene in the coffeehouse suggests a possible satiric undercurrent to this representation of Duck. The comic dramatization of Duck, for example, as he "change[s] colour, knit[s] his brows, and sometimes give[s] a disagreeable pish," suggests an amused and entertained, not genuinely sincere, sympathy with his plight as an abused author.

Several aspects of the narrative suggest that the former agricultural laborer is as uncomfortable in a coffeehouse in Richmond as Spence suggested he had been as an aspiring poet in the fields of Wiltshire. Without making any explicit reference to Duck's former career as a laborer, there are several hints that suggest Duck does not blend well into the coffeehouse landscape. Duck is presented as "very diligently reading" the *Daily Post-Boy.* The care and attention that Duck had once applied to reading the improving essays of the *Spectator* has been redeployed to an examination of current affairs in the daily papers, signaling Duck's movement from the rustic periphery toward the urban center. The adverb "diligently," however, contains a suggestion of strain and exertion; it may also carry connotations of learned or studied behavior, implying that Duck finds reading these papers neither easy nor natural. Duck's conspicuous classicism in his reference to "Cacus" may also hint at a discomfort in this environment. Cacus was the son of Vulcan, who, as is related in Book VIII of the *Aeneid,* stole cattle from Hercules but was discovered because of the noise made by the animals. Duck's tendency to wrench situations to fit classical or mythological precedents previously had been demonstrated in his poem *The Thresher's Labour,* with its references to Vulcan and Hercules, as well as to Cyclops, Thetis, and Sisyphus.[67] Duck displays a gauche eagerness to show off his scraps of classical knowledge and to fit into a learned and witty society. Unwittingly, perhaps, this bovine allusion also recalls his agricultural

origins (although Spence doesn't record whether Duck himself ever worked with cattle). In addition, although Duck complains about the theft of his poem, he is depicted as helpless, unable to act alone to remedy the situation. Lacking authority himself, he needs to co-opt the authority of the anonymous correspondent to challenge the unscrupulous publishers. These ambiguities of tone unsettle the letter's presentation of Duck as a leisured poet and coffeehouse patron. Combined with the *Grub-street Journal's* reputation for satirizing dunce poets, it is very possible that Duck, and by association, his royal patrons, are being derided here for their attempts to turn an agricultural laborer into a man of letters.

Yet whether or not this scene has satiric intent—indeed, whether or not it is factually accurate—what is most significant is the context in which it places Duck. Taking the "thresher poet" from the fields and placing him in an urban coffeehouse, it marks a conceptual shift in how the poet could be represented. It is true that the *Grub-street Journal* letter depicts him being used and abused by the vagaries of print culture and by publishers who print his poems without his consent, that he is shown as lacking the agency himself to combat such abuses, and that this situation is narrated in an ambiguous and possibly unsympathetic voice. However, it is also true that the letter depicts Duck attempting to participate in that print culture, visiting a coffeehouse in Richmond or Kew, reading and discussing the daily papers there, and collaborating with another coffeehouse patron to intervene in print culture by submitting a letter to a newspaper.

According to Spence, Duck told him that he believed his poems attracted the attention they did only because they were written "by a poor Fellow in a Barn," and as Bridget Keegan has argued, the novelty of the poet's social origin continues to draw "investigators to study Duck."[68] However, despite Duck's declaration, for his contemporaries his social origins were only part of the appeal. Much of the attention Duck attracted was not just because he was a "poor Fellow in a Barn" but also because he had received the queen's patronage. These factors combined to turn Duck into an iconic figure with great symbolic potential. As Spence showed, he could represent theories of natural genius or demonstrate the benevolence of the queen, or conversely, as the *Grub-street Journal* letter implied, he could illustrate the debased cultural and literary standards of the ruling elite. But Duck was more than just a symbolic figure. He was a laborer who strove to educate himself and who revealed great natural talent, and he became a poet attached to the Hanoverian court, a celebrity in literary life, and a participant in print culture, as well as a frequenter of coffeehouses. This essay has begun to explore some of the roles Duck played in mid-eighteenth-century print and literary culture, but in focusing on representations of Duck from the early 1730s it is necessarily limited in scope. Duck continued to write, to publish, and to participate in literary culture until his death in 1756, and an examination of his activities through this later period would undoubtedly enhance our understanding of him as more than "a poor Fellow in a Barn."

Notes

1. The only modern biography of Duck, by Rose Mary Davis, is titled *Stephen Duck: The Thresher Poet* (Orono: University of Maine Press, 1926). Duck has been the focus of a number of studies that highlight his social and economic background, from Robert Southey's *Lives and Works of the Uneducated Poets* (ed. J. S. Childers [1831; London: Humphrey Milford, 1925], 88-113) to William Christmas's 2001 work *The Lab'ring Muses: Work, Writing and the Social Order in English Plebeian Poetry, 1730-1830* (Newark: University of Delaware Press, 2001). *The Thresher's Labour* has been the subject of several recent essays: see John Goodridge, *Rural Life in Eighteenth-Century English Poetry* (Cambridge: Cambridge University Press, 1995), 11-88; Bridget Keegan, "Georgic Transformations and Stephen Duck's *The Thresher's Labour*," *Studies in English Literature* 41, no. 3 (Summer 2001): 545-62; Peggy Thompson, "Duck, Collier, and the Ideology of Verse Forms," *Studies in English Literature* 44, no. 3 (Summer 2004): 505-23; James Mulholland, "'To Sing the Toils of Each Revolving Year': Song and Poetic Authority in Stephen Duck's *The Thresher's Labour*," *Studies in Eighteenth-Century Culture* 33 (2004): 153-74. *The Thresher's Labour* also has been reprinted recently in several major anthologies of eighteenth-century poetry: see Roger Lonsdale, ed., *The New Oxford Book of Eighteenth Century Verse* (Oxford: Oxford University Press, 1984), 224-25, and David Fairer and Christine Gerrard, eds., *Eighteenth-Century Poetry: An Annotated Anthology* (Oxford: Blackwell, 1999), 249-56.

2. Stephen Duck, *The Thresher's Labour,* ll. 9, 24, 64, 215. Unless otherwise stated, all references to Duck's poems are taken from William J. Christmas, ed., *Eighteenth-Century English Labouring-Class Poets, 1700-1740,* vol. 1 of *Eighteenth-Century English Labouring-Class Poets, 1700-1800,* 3 vols., gen. ed. John Goodridge (London: Pickering and Chatto, 2003), and will be included by line number only in the text.

3. Bridget Keegan astutely examines Duck's use of pronouns in "Georgic Transformations and Stephen Duck's *The Thresher's Labour*," 552-60.

4. *Daily Post* (no. 3436) Wednesday, 23 September 1730. *Poems on Several Subjects* was first offered for sale on Monday, 28 September (see *London Evening Post,* [no. 438], 26 September 1730).

5. For biographical details of Duck, see Davis, *Stephen Duck,* and Leslie Stephen, "Stephen Duck," rev. William R. Jones, *Oxford Dictionary of National Biography* (2004).

6. Raymond Williams, *The Country and the City* (London: Chatto and Windus, 1973), 90.

7. Duck drowned in 1756, possibly as a result of suicide. Davis summarizes the debates over his death in *Stephen Duck,* 107-16. As Davis describes, several eighteenth-century critics made explicit links between the patronage and the suicide, but most of Duck's modern biographers have been careful to refrain from emotive judgments. See, for example, Christmas, ed., *Labouring-Class Poets,* 1:129; Stephen, "Stephen Duck," rev. Jones, *Oxford Dictionary.*

8. For a summary of critical attitudes to Duck, see Bridget Keegan, "Stephen Duck, *Poems on Several Occasions,*" in David Womersley, ed., *A Companion to Literature from Milton to Blake* (Oxford: Blackwell, 2000), 301-07. Notable exceptions to this concentration on *The Thresher's Labour* include the discussion of "On Mites. To a Lady" in Margaret Anne Doody, *The Daring Muse: Augustan Poetry Reconsidered* (Cambridge: Cambridge University Press, 1986), 129, and the discussion of "On the Marriage of his Serene Highness the Prince of Orange" and Duck's elegy for Caroline, *The Vision, A Poem,* in Tone Sundt Urstad, *Sir Robert Walpole's Poets: The Use of Literature as Pro-Government Propaganda, 1721-1742* (Newark: University of Delaware Press, 1999), 160-61, 168-69.

9. In September 1730 Spence first met Duck, and they conversed over several days; Spence made notes about their conversations, and these formed the basis for *A Full and Authentick Account of Stephen Duck the Wiltshire Poet,* which was first published in March 1731. Spence's notes of the conversations have been transcribed and published by James M. Osborn in "Spence, Natural Genius and Pope," *Philological Quarterly* 45, no. 1 (January 1966): 123-44. For an account of the probable circumstances of the publication of the pamphlet, which may have happened without the knowledge of Spence, see Austin Wright, *Joseph Spence: A Critical Biography* (Chicago: University of Chicago Press, 1950), 45-47. In 1736 *A Full and Authentick Account* was revised slightly, and as "An Account of the Author in a Letter to a friend, written in the year 1730" was incorporated

into the prefatory material of Duck's *Poems on Several Occasions*. It was reproduced in all subsequent reprints of *Poems on Several Occasions* (1738, 1753, 1764) and in the apparently pirated *The Beautiful Works of the Reverend Mr. Stephen Duck* (London, 1753). It has proved the major source for most biographical accounts of Duck, from Southey's *Lives of the Uneducated Poets* (1831) to the *Oxford Dictionary of National Biography* (2004).

10. Spence, *Full and Authentick Account*, 7.

11. See Osborn, "Spence, Natural Genius and Pope."

12. Spence, *Full and Authentick Account*, 11.

13. Ibid.

14. Stephen Duck, *Poems on Several Subjects*, 7th ed. (London, 1730), "Some account of the Author," iv.

15. For details of the authorship and publication history of the *Spectator*, see Donald F. Bond's introduction to *The Spectator*, 5 vols. (Oxford: Clarendon Press, 1965), 1:xliii-lxxxiii.

16. Osborn, "Spence, Natural Genius and Pope," 127. The success of the *Spectator* led to several attempts at continuations, including a spurious *Spectator* that ran from January to August 1715; the essays in this twice-weekly paper were collected into a "Vol. Ninth and Last," which was published as a duodecimo volume in 1715. Duck told Spence that "Lav[ingto]n has all ye Spect[ato]rs" ("Spence, Natural Genius and Pope," 127), and it is likely that as well as the eight-volume set of "official" *Spectators,* this included the spurious "Vol. Ninth and Last." Among the papers that Spence records Duck "mention'd, with more regard than usual" is "the *Justum & Tenacem* from Horace" (*Full and Authentick Account*, 23). "Justum & Tenacem" is the first line of Horace's Ode 3, Book 3. There is no essay on this poem in the eight-volume *Spectator,* nor do any of the essays have "Justum & Tenacem" as their epigraph. However, it is the epigraph of an essay dated 12 February 1715 (no. 12) in the "Vol. Ninth and Last," 51-54.

17. Spence, *Full and Authentick Account*, 7-9, 11; Osborn, "Spence, Natural Genius and Pope," 127.

18. Markman Ellis has recently discussed the links between the coffeehouses and these periodicals. See "The Philosopher in the Coffee-House," in *The Coffee House: A Cultural History* (London: Weidenfeld and Nicolson, 2004), 185-206. See also Brian Cowan, *The Social Life of Coffee: The Emergence of the British Coffeehouse* (New Haven, CT: Yale University Press, 2005), esp. 225-56, and Lawrence E. Klein, "Coffeehouse Civility, 1660-1714: An Aspect of Post-courtly Culture in England," *Huntington Library Quarterly* 59, no. 1 (1996): 31-51. In *Spectator* no. 10 (12 March 1711), Addison claims that "there are already Three Thousand" copies of the *Spectator* "distributed every Day;" he makes the "modest" suggestion that each of these may be read by "Twenty Readers," resulting therefore in "about Three-score thousand Disciples in *London* and *Westminster.*" *Spectator* 1:44. See also 1:xx-xxix, lxix-lxxvi.

19. On the idea of politeness in the eighteenth century, see Lawrence E. Klein, *Shaftesbury and the Culture of Politeness: Moral Discourse and Cultural Politics in Early Eighteenth-Century England* (Cambridge: Cambridge University Press, 1994).

20. *Spectator* 1:5 (no. 1), 1 March 1711.

21. Spence, *Full and Authentick Account*, 23.

22. *Spectator* 1:44-46 (no. 10), 12 March 1711. Bond discusses the *Spectator*'s wide-ranging readership, *Spectator* 1:lxxxviii-xcvi. One critic has described Addison's task thus: "he fixed his eyes not on the Court alone, but on society as a whole, and he sought to open Everyman's eyes to literature; better still, to open his mind, form his judgment, teach him to think and provide him with general ideas on art and life. He made it his business to conduct a course on literature and aesthetics." See Alexandre Beljame, *Men of Letters and the English Public in the Eighteenth Century, 1660-1744: Dryden, Addison and Pope* (London: Kegan Paul, Trench, Trubner, 1948), 293.

23. Fiona Stafford discusses the effect that reading the *Spectator* may also have had on "Duck's accent and provincial dialect" in "Scottish poetry and regional literary expression" in John Richetti, ed., *The Cambridge History of English Literature, 1660-1780* (Cambridge: Cambridge University Press, 2005), 340-62; this passage, 346-47.

24. Compare Duck's comments that "he saw a great deal of Wit in it . . . but after all, 'tis not a Manner of writing that he can so sincerely delight in, as the Moral, the Passionate, or the Sublime" (Spence, *Full and Authentick Account*, 23-24) to Addison's declaration that "If *Hudibras* had been set out with as much Wit and Humour in Heroic Verse as he is in Doggerel, he would have made a much more agreeable Figure than he does; though the generality of his Readers are so wonderfully pleased with the double Rhimes, that I do not

expect many will be of my Opinion in this Particular" (*Spectator* 2:468 [no. 249], 15 Dec 1711).

25. Spence, *Full and Authentick Account,* 22.

26. Addison's essays on *Paradise Lost* were published every Saturday between 5 January 1712 (no. 267) and 3 May 1712 (no. 369). Bond argues that they were instrumental in furthering Milton's reputation in the eighteenth century, *Spectator* 2:537-38, n. 3.

27. *Spectator* 1:245 (no. 58), 7 May 1711.

28. Spence, *Full and Authentick Account,* 23.

29. Indeed, the overlap between the two periodicals is such that several times in Bond's notes to the *Spectator* he uses the *London Spy* to verify or provide further contextual detail for events described in the *Spectator.* See, for example *Spectator* 1:36, 61, 90, 131, and others.

30. Edward Ward, "To the Reader" in *The London-spy compleat* (London, 1703), n.p.

31. Spence, *Full and Authentick Account,* 25, 23.

32. Ibid, 23.

33. Joseph Warton, *An Essay on the Writings and Genius of Pope* (London, 1756), 270. Bond discusses the praise that the *Spectator*'s prose attracted in the eighteenth century in his introduction, *Spectator* 1:xcviii-cii.

34. Spence, *Full and Authentick Account,* 11-12.

35. See Linda Zionkowski, "Strategies of Containment: Stephen Duck, Ann Yearsley, and the Problem of Polite Culture," *Eighteenth-Century Life* 13, no. 3 (November 1989): 91-108; this passage, 93. James Mulholland has discussed the relationship of *The Thresher's Labour* to oral (and pastoral) traditions of song in "Song and Poetic Authority in Stephen Duck's *The Thresher's Labour.*"

36. Spence, *Full and Authentick Account,* 17.

37. According to Spence's notes, Duck had read all three of these poems. Osborn, "Spence, Natural Genius and Pope," 128.

38. Spence, *Full and Authentick Account,* 20.

39. *Spectator* 3:419-22 (no. 378), 14 May 1712.

40. In his notes from his conversations with Duck, Spence recorded that "He is now turning Inkle and Yarico into Verse" (Osborn, "Spence, Natural

Genius and Pope," 128). "Avaro and Amanda, a poem in four cantos. Taken from the Spectator Vol. 1 No. xi," *Poems on Several Occasions* (London, 1736), 85-128.

41. *Spectator* 1:49-51 (no. 11), 13 March 1711. Duck was not alone in versifying Steele's narrative: it was a very popular story throughout the eighteenth century. For other examples, see Lawrence Marsden Price, *Inkle and Yarico Album* (Berkeley: University of California Press, 1937) and Frank Felsenstein, ed., *English Trader, Indian Maid: Representing Gender, Race, and Slavery in the New World—An Inkle and Yarico Reader* (Baltimore: Johns Hopkins University Press, 1999). Duck added a delightfully dramatic touch of poetic justice with the brutal killing of the "Wretch" Avaro (Inkle): stranded on a deserted island after selling his lover and their unborn child to a slave trader, he is attacked by a wolf who "Tore out his Heart, and lick'd the purple Flood; / For Earth refus'd to drink the *Villain's* Blood" (*Poems on Several Occasions,* 128).

42. For an account of the grotto and some of the poetry that was written about it, see Judith Colton, "Kent's Hermitage for Queen Caroline at Richmond," *Architectura* 4 (1974): 181-91; and Emma Jay, *Caroline, Queen Consort of George II, and British Literary Culture* (PhD diss., Oxford University, 2004), 236-49.

43. *Spectator* 5:161-62 (no. 632), 13 December 1714. Published anonymously, the poem was by the Rev. James Ward. It had been reprinted several times, most recently in a shortened form in the *Gentleman's Magazine* (July 1732), 870.

44. Duck, "On the Queen's Grotto, in Richmond Gardens," in *Poems on Several Occasions,* 166.

45. Among the books Spence lists Duck having read by September 1730 was a translation of the Archbishop of Cambray's *The Adventures of Telemachus,* a text that begins with a description of Telemachus's sojourn in Calypso's grotto (*Full and Authentick Account,* 9). It is very likely that Duck had also read Pope's version of Homer by 1732. In a letter written in October 1730 discussing the books Duck should read, his patron Alured Clarke declared, "I believe he must read Mr. Pope's [translation of Homer] at his most leisure times" (Dr. Alured Clarke to Mrs. Clayton, 8 October 1730 in [Mrs.] Thomson, *Memoirs of the Viscountess Sundon,* 2 vols. (London, 1847) 1:198). Spence, who was the author of an essay on Pope's *Odyssey* (published in 1727), may also have recommended it to him.

46. Trace/Place ("*To Mrs. M. L.,*" ll. 26-27; "On the Queen's Grotto," ll. 15-16); Lays/Praise ("*To Mrs. M. L.,*" ll. 39-40; "On the Queen's Grotto," ll. 31-32).

47. For an account of Richmond and Kew in the 1730s, see John Cloake, *Richmond Past: A Visual History of Richmond, Kew, Petersham, and Ham* (London: Historical Publications, 1991), esp. 22-36, and Michael Baxter Brown, *Richmond Park: The History of a Royal Deer Park* (London: Robert Hale, 1985), 71-81. See also James Sambrook, *James Thomson: A Life* (Oxford: Clarendon Press, 1991), 157-59, and Maynard Mack, *The Garden and the City* (Toronto: University of Toronto Press, 1969), 11-21.

48. See *Daily Post* (no. 3464), 26 October 1730. This report was repeated in a range of other papers, including the *St. James Evening Post* (no. 2412), 27 October 1730; *Applebee's Original Weekly Journal*; the *British Journal* (no. 148); the *Craftsman* (no. 226); and the *Weekly Register* (no. 29) (all 31 October 1730).

49. Jay, *Caroline and British Literary Culture*, 69; J. L. Nevinson, "Stephen Duck at Kew," *Surrey Archaeological Collections* 58 (1961): 104-07.

50. "Verses, occasion'd by the Busts in the Queen's Hermitage, and Mr. Duck being appointed Keeper of the Library in Merlin's Cave," *Gentleman's Magazine* (May 1737), 308. The poem was reprinted in the posthumous *The Works of Mrs. Catharine Cockburn*, 2 vols. (London, 1751), 2:572-75. In both printed versions of the poem, it is dated 12 August 1732; however, the poem carries an allusion to Caroline's later Richmond Gardens feature, "Merlin's Cave," which dates at least part of the poem to c. 1735. See the essay "The Life of Mrs. Cockburn" for a brief account of the composition and publication of the poem (*Works of Mrs. Catharine Cockburn*, 1:xxxvii). Duck is also linked to the grotto in Edward Cobden's poem "On the Queen's Grotto" ("This indigested Pile appears"), published in the *Weekly Miscellany* on 27 January 1733 (no. 7) and reprinted in that month's issues of the *London Magazine* and the *Gentleman's Magazine*. The poem was reprinted in Cobden's *Poems on Several Occasions* (London, 1748), 18-19. See also Matthew Green's *The Grotto, A Poem, Written by Peter Drake, Fisherman of Brentford* (London, 1733).

51. *Daily Post-Boy* (no. 7102), 11 December 1732.

52. *Whitehall Evening Post* (no. 2281), *London Evening Post* (no. 785), both 12 December 1732; *Read's Weekly Journal* (no. 404), the *Weekly Reg-*

ister (no. 140), both 16 December 1732; *Grub-street Journal* (no. 157), 28 December 1732; *London Magazine, Gentleman's Magazine,* December issues (c. 2 January 1733).

53. *Whitehall Evening Post* (no. 2285), 21 December 1732; *Northampton Mercury* (vol. 8, no. 35), 18 December 1732.

54. *Grub-street Journal* (no. 157), 28 December 1732.

55. Ibid.

56. One contemporary account of the coffeehouse at Richmond declared it was a place where one could "take a Game at Billiards, read fresh News, or improve your Politicks." *A Description of the Royal Gardens at Richmond in Surry* (London, 1736?), 27.

57. In 1736 "On the Queen's Grotto, in Richmond Gardens" was published in Duck's *Poems on Several Occasions*. A comparison of the texts of the poem as printed in the *Daily Post-Boy* and the *Grub-street Journal* with this text adds credence to the likely accuracy of this story: the *Grub-street Journal* version of the poem is closer to the authorized version than is the *Daily Post-Boy* version. However, the differences between the "authorized" (i.e., *Grub-street Journal* and *Poems on Several Occasions*) versions of the poem, and the "unauthorized" text (the *Daily Post-Boy* version) are actually rather minimal. Most of the differences are incidentals—punctuation, spelling ("blest" or "bless'd"), italics, and capitals. There are a few slightly more significant textual changes: "you Learned" becomes "ye learned" (l. 25), and "Off'rings" becomes "off'ring" (l. 31). While these alterations make no real impact on the sense of the poem, the alteration of "honour'd by the GOD" to "honour'd with the Gods" (l. 14) affects the meaning, shifting the sense from a Christian singular God to plural pagan gods. The correction of "But cease, my Muse and cast thy Wand'ring Eyes" to "wond'ring eyes" (l. 21) makes the speaker into a more awed spectator of the scene he is beholding. The lines "cast thy Wand'ring Eyes / Where *Phoebus'* lofty Domes Majestick rise; / Where tuneful Strains have sung the Grotto's Praise / Contending each, till each deserves the Bays" (ll. 21-24) had received criticism in a short critical essay about the poem printed in the *Whitehall Evening Post* ([no. 2285], 21 December 1732), where it was objected that "The *Strains of the Domes* seems to be an Expression too harsh, and unnatural; nor is it a proper Metaphor to say, the *Strains deserve the Bays.*" The version of the poem sent to the *Grub-street Journal* records "tuneful Strains" as a misprint: it becomes "tune-

ful Train," and refers to the students of "Westminster and Eton Schools" ("*Phoebus'* lofty Domes") rather than to the "Domes" themselves.

58. Spence, *Full and Authentick Account,* 26.

59. The first edition of *Poems on Several Subjects* was advertised as being for sale from Monday, 28 September (*London Evening Post,* [no. 438], 26 September 1730). The seventh edition was advertised on 9 October 1730 in the *Daily Post* (no. 3450). Several of these "editions" are clearly *new* editions, being rearrangements of type, ornaments, and so forth: the third edition offers a "corrected" text, supplementing three lines of verse that had been omitted from the previous editions; the fifth edition has different ornaments; the seventh edition represents a thorough remodeling of the pamphlet to include an engraved representation of Duck, a biographical account of him (of possibly suspect authenticity), and two ambiguously commendatory/satirical poems. The bibliographical history of the seventh edition of *Poems on Several Subjects* is rather difficult to untangle: see D. F. Foxon, *English Verse 1701-1750: A Catalogue of Separately Printed Poems with Notes on Contemporary Editions,* 2 vols. (Cambridge: Cambridge University Press, 1975), 1:200. The second, fourth, and sixth "editions" of *Poems on Several Subjects* appear actually to be re-impressions of the preceding editions.

60. Thomson, *Memoirs of Viscountess Sundon,* 1:198-204; Christmas, introduction to *Labouring-Class Poets,* 1:xxi-xxii.

61. *Daily Post* (no. 3454), 14 October 1730; *Evening Post,* 15 October 1730; see also *Grub-street Journal* (no. 52), 31 December 1730. For Clarke's involvement in organizing the advertisement on Duck's behalf, see Thomson, *Memoirs of Viscountess Sundon,* 1:196. This public battle was mocked in the advertisements for, and prefatory material of, *The Thresher's Miscellany,* a spin-off pamphlet that tried to capitalize on the interest in the "Thresher" poet. Arthur Duck, *The Thresher's Miscellany* (London, 1730); see advertisements in *The Daily Journal* (nos. 3055, 3057, 3071, 3072, 3079), 21 and 23 October 1730; 9, 10, and 18 November 1730.

62. *Truth and Falshood* was advertised with this declaration in, for example, the *Whitehall Evening Post* (no. 2447), 5 January 1734; the *General Evening Post* (nos. 42, 44), 5 and 10 January 1734; and the *St. James Evening Post* (no. 2841), 10 January 1734. It also formed part of the preface of

the pamphlet. Duck, *Truth and Falshood, A Fable* (London, 1734) (sig. Br). Duck, preface to *Poems on Several Occasions,* ix.

63. See James T. Hillhouse, *The Grub-street Journal* (Durham, NC: Duke University Press, 1928), and Bertrand A. Goldgar, introduction to *The Grub-street Journal, 1730-1733,* 4 vols. (London: Pickering and Chatto, 2002), 1:vii-xv.

64. The conflict between the Hanoverian government and men of letters such as Pope and Swift is explored in Bertrand Goldgar, *Walpole and the Wits: The Relation of Politics to Literature, 1722-1742* (Lincoln: University of Nebraska Press, 1976).

65. See, for example, *Grub-street Journal* (no. 40), 8 October 1730; (no. 46), 19 November 1730; and (no. 138), 24 August 1732.

66. *Grub-street Journal* (nos. 49, 50, 52), 10, 17, and 31 December 1730.

67. Duck probably acquired this knowledge about Cacus from Dryden's Virgil (*Aeneid,* Book VIII, l. 256ff), which, according to Spence, Duck had read by September 1730 (Spence, *Full and Authentick Account,* 9). See Duck, *The Thresher's Labour,* ll. 41-43, 256, 281-82.

68. Spence, *Full and Authentick Account,* 26. Keegan has called for a "re-examination" of Duck's poetry beyond *The Thresher's Labour* in an attempt to "expand our appreciation of Duck as more than just 'a poor Fellow in a Barn'" ("Stephen Duck, *Poems on Several Occasions,*" 302, 307).

FURTHER READING

Criticism

Clymer, Lorna. "The Work of Poetry." *Eighteenth-Century Studies* 40, no. 4 (summer 2007): 659-64.
    Brief commentary on Duck's success as a "cautionary tale" in the context of reviewing *Eighteenth-Century English Labouring-Class Poets* (2003, edited by John Goodridge).

Ennis, Daniel J. "The Making of the Poet Laureate, 1730." *The Age of Johnson* 11 (2000): 217-35.
    Discusses the process of choosing England's Poet Laureate in 1730, when Duck and Colley Cibber were the main contenders for the post.

Peel, J. H. B. "From Farm Labourer to Court Poet." *The Listener* 68 (18 October 1962): 616-19.

Surveys Duck's life and career, concluding that a desire to remain a fashionable poet, composing "thoroughly bogus pictures of rural life," inevitably led to his unhappiness.

Additional coverage of Duck's life and career is contained in the following sources published by Gale: *Dictionary of Literary Biography,* **Vol. 95;** *Literature Resource Center***; and** *Reference Guide to English Literature,* **Ed. 2.**

Ted Hughes
1930-1998

(Full name Edward James Hughes) English poet, playwright, short story writer, children's author, critic, essayist, and translator.

For further information on Hughes's life and career, see *PC,* Volume 7.

INTRODUCTION

England's Poet Laureate from 1984 until his death in 1998, Hughes was a prolific writer in a variety of genres, but was best known for his dark poetry filled with images of aggression and violence bordering on the nihilistic. His literary reputation suffered greatly after the 1963 suicide of his wife, the writer Sylvia Plath, as many prominent feminist critics blamed Hughes for her death and criticized his role as her literary executor.

BIOGRAPHICAL INFORMATION

Born on August 17, 1930, in Mytholmroyd in Yorkshire, Hughes was the youngest of three children; his parents were Edith Farrar Hughes and William Henry Hughes, a carpenter. The family moved to Mexborough in South Yorkshire when Hughes was seven years old, and he began attending school there. He was encouraged by his teachers and was producing poetry by his adolescent years. In 1948, Hughes was awarded a scholarship to Cambridge University, but deferred his education temporarily in order to serve in the Royal Air Force for two years as a wireless mechanic. He entered Pembroke College, Cambridge in 1951, initially to study literature; however, he later changed to archeology and anthropology, focusing in particular on the study of myth. Hughes graduated from Cambridge in 1954, and two years later, on June 16, 1956, married the American writer Sylvia Plath, who was at Cambridge on a Fulbright fellowship. The two settled initially in Massachusetts, where Hughes taught at the University of Massachusetts, Amherst. In 1959, the couple returned to England where their two children were born, Frieda in 1960 and Nicholas two years later. In 1962, Hughes left Plath for Assia Gutmann Wevill, with whom he had been having an affair; less than a year later Plath committed suicide. Wevill and Hughes had one daughter, Shura, born in 1965; four years later Wevill killed both

herself and the child. A year after that Hughes wed Carol Orchard to whom he was married for the remainder of his life.

Following Plath's suicide, Hughes gave up writing poetry for a number of years, concentrating instead on the handling of Plath's literary estate. He was reviled by readers and critics, particularly American feminists, for what they believed to be his role in Plath's death, and for what they considered his self-serving editorial choices regarding the posthumous publication of her writings and the destruction of the diaries she kept just before her death. The controversies surrounding his personal life almost completely overshadowed Hughes's literary reputation, and over the years Plath's work became far more famous than his own. Although he was haunted by poverty throughout his professional career—he often supplemented his income by selling off his manuscripts—Hughes became one of the richest poets in England as a result of the royalties from Plath's writings. He died October 28, 1998, from cancer in Devonshire, England; one obituary identified the once-famous poet as Sylvia Plath's husband in its headline.

MAJOR WORKS

Hughes began publishing his poetry in various Cambridge literary magazines after his graduation in 1954. His first book of poetry, *The Hawk in the Rain,* appeared in 1957 and included "The Thought-Fox," which has been included in a number of anthologies. Hughes's next book, *Lupercal,* followed in 1960; both volumes feature images from the animal world, and a number of poems are written from the perspective of various animals whose instinctive behavior is privileged over the rational actions of humans. In 1967, Hughes produced *Wodwo,* described by Leonard M. Scigaj as "a very complex, forbidding book." It was followed three years later by *Crow: From the Life and Songs of the Crow,* considered Hughes's masterpiece by many critics. These two volumes constitute Hughes's extended critique of Western culture.

His next major efforts, *Cave Birds* (1975), (which was enlarged and reissued three years later as *Cave Birds: An Alchemical Drama*) and *Gaudete* (1977), both contain elements of mythology and surrealism. In 1979 Hughes turned to ecological matters with *Remains of Elmet,* apparently inspired by a collection of black and white photographs of the dying factory towns of West Yorkshire where Hughes grew up. The collection is organized around imagery of decay and decomposition, but where his earlier poetry railed against the Industrial Revolution, the poems of *Remains of Elmet* signal a certain calm acceptance of natural cycles. In "Tree," one of the poems of the collection, "Hughes feels the rhythm of nature only when he ceases his declamatory rhetoric," according to Scigaj. Also in 1979, Hughes published *Moortown,* consisting of poems that had earlier been published either in magazines or in limited editions. Many of them deal with farming and animal husbandry and are based on Hughes's experiences working on Moortown, his farm in Devon. The emphasis on nature and the environment continued to inform the poetry of *River,* published in 1983, featuring a fisherman as the poetic persona.

In 1998, Hughes broke his long silence on the subject of his marriage to Plath with the publication of *Birthday Letters,* consisting of poetry he claimed he had written over a period of twenty-five years, although some scholars question that assertion. It was his final publication before his death that same year. In 2003 *Collected Poems* was published, a volume that runs to more than thirteen hundred pages and includes uncollected poems and those that appeared in privately-printed limited editions.

CRITICAL RECEPTION

Hughes's poetry has often been criticized for its aggressive tone and violent imagery and for some critics, particularly feminists, it reflects the scandalous elements of Hughes's life and relationships with women. Feminist critics have long objected to Hughes's images of violence against women as well as his representations of women as duplicitous or themselves violent. Harriet Zinnes believes, though, that the "omnipresent" violence in Hughes's work should not be considered merely an extension of his treatment of women in life. Zinnes contends that "Hughes's use of violence is unrelated to any kind of irrelevant sensationalist publicity. It is a consequence of his whole vision of life." Nathalie Anderson also considers that his often dismissive or reductive approach to women in his poetry is more complicated than it would first appear. "Hughes's disquieting presentation of women is part of a larger indictment—ultimately of a society which represses not only what Hughes perceives as a female principle within the psyche, but actual women as well," according to Anderson.

Graham Bradshaw (see Further Reading) has examined parallels between Hughes's critical essay on Shakespeare and his own poetry, contending that Hughes is preoccupied with the split between generally-accepted human values versus "the nature of nature." According to Bradshaw, "Hughes is exceptionally alive to the terrifying Shakespearean evocation of an unaccommodated universe." Dwight Eddins, who finds parallels between the philosophy of Schopenhauer and the poetry of Hughes—particularly in "the stark, unsettling nature poems" of *Wodwo*—comments on "the affinity between the poet's fleeting visions of animal savagery and the philosopher's sustained ruminations on it." Scigaj, in his discussion of *Wodwo,* sees the collection as "a departure from Hughes's early faith in human potential in historical time" and as evidence of the poet's "surrealistic disenchantment with Western culture." Paul Bentley (see Further Reading) reports that the poetry of *Wodwo* and *Crow* was "born out of the experience of the second world war, the concentration camps and post-war totalitarianism." Scigaj notes another shift later in the poet's career with the publication of *Remains of Elmet, Moortown,* and *River,* all of which exhibit "a new humility and compassion for the role of all living creatures in the drama of life and death, and a deep reverence for the wonders of natural events."

Most recently, critics have debated the merits of *Birthday Letters,* the 1998 volume of verse-letters addressed to Plath in an apparent attempt to set the record straight regarding their relationship and her suicide. Lynda K. Bundtzen surveys the critical response to the volume, noting that many critics found it "boringly repetitious" and filled with blame for Plath and justification for Hughes's own actions. Leslie Cahoon explores similarities between Ovid's Orpheus and Hughes's poetic persona in *Birthday Letters.* According to Cahoon, both use their texts "to re-envision the beloved wife's death as justly deserved punishment combined with a cruel fate, but with no recognition of any responsibility or complicity on the husband's part." Sarah Churchwell, who has studied Hughes's appropriation and reworking of many of Plath's poems, points out that "*Birthday Letters,* purportedly 'Hughes's version,' his side of the story, repeats her side of the story in order to revise it." Bundtzen, however, believes that the focus on the biographical elements of *Birthday Letters* has prevented critics from interpreting the poetry based on its literary merits.

The publication of *Collected Poems* in 2003 has prompted a number of critics to return to a discussion of the value of the poems themselves. Ryan Hibbett reports that the volume "is, for many, a welcome counterthrust to what is perceived as a threatening and invasive interest in Hughes's personal life." Hibbett expresses the hope that "distractions aside . . . we can get back to the proper business of appraising Hughes's talents and evaluating his place in the British literary tradition." Such is the approach of Michael Hofmann, who praises *Collected Poems* and contends that Hughes "is at least arguably the greatest English poet since Shakespeare." Jeffrey Meyers, too, reports that "his poems transcend the deeply flawed man who wrote them," and contends that "Hughes now stands—with Seamus Heaney, Philip Larkin, and Geoffrey Hill— among the outstanding English poets since the war."

PRINCIPAL WORKS

Poetry

The Hawk in the Rain 1957
Lupercal 1960
Recklings 1966
Wodwo 1967
Crow: From the Life and Songs of the Crow 1970
Selected Poems 1957-1967 1972
Prometheus on His Crag: 21 Poems 1973
Cave Birds 1975; also published as Cave Birds: An Alchemical Drama [enlarged edition], 1978
Gaudete 1977
Orts 1978
Moortown 1979
Remains of Elmet: A Pennine Sequence 1979
Selected Poems 1957-1981 1982
River 1983
Flowers and Insects: Some Birds and a Pair of Spiders 1986
Wolfwatching 1989
Rain-Charm for the Duchy & Other Laureate Poems 1992
Tales from Ovid [translator] 1997
Birthday Letters: Poems 1998
Howls and Whispers 1998
Collected Poems 2003

Other Major Works

The Wound (play) 1962; revised version produced 1972
The Price of a Bride (juvenile drama) 1966
The Iron Giant: A Story in Five Nights (juvenilia) 1968
Eat Crow (play) 1971
Shakespeare and the Goddess of Complete Being (criticism) 1992
Winter Pollen: Occasional Prose (essays) 1995

CRITICISM

Leonard M. Scigaj (essay date 1986)

SOURCE: Scigaj, Leonard M. "Goodbye to the Cenotaphs: Wodwo 1967." In The Poetry of Ted Hughes: Form and Imagination, pp. 85-121. Iowa City, Iowa: University of Iowa Press, 1986.

[In the following excerpt, Scigaj discusses the 1967 volume Wodwo, which the critic believes represents a departure from Hughes's earlier devotion to formalism and a turn to poetry that is more private and emotional.]

> Everything we associate with a poem is its shadowy tenant and part of its meaning, no matter how New Critical purist we try to be. . . . [Dylan] Thomas's life, letters, and legends belong to his poetry, in that they make it mean more. . . . Then suddenly we hear the voice that polished the voices, the demon stylist, a cold, severe, even ruthless sort of person. . . . Clearly enough, an abandoned surrealistic or therapeutic torrent was the last thing Thomas allowed his reservoirs to become. . . . In his life, the reflex of this vision was a complete openness toward both inner and outer worlds, denying nothing, refusing nothing, suppressing nothing. . . . What he was really waiting for, and coaxing with alcohol, was the delicate cerebral disaster that demolishes the old self for good, with all its crushing fortifications, and leaves the atman a clear field.
>
> —Hughes, 1966[1]

Wodwo (1967) is a very complex, forbidding book, possibly the most elusive and difficult book of poetry Hughes has written to date. Its unique combination of surrealism, mythic psychodrama, and Oriental psychology distills a period of great productivity and intellectual gain in Hughes's literary life and chronicles many complications in his private life. In the sixties Hughes's poetic psyche is thrown back upon itself, to depend upon its own subconscious resources; initially a divorce ensues between the inner and outer worlds of his art. The result of the anguished withdrawal is no less than a loss of faith in the enterprises of Western culture and human involvement in goal-seeking activity in historical time—a complete reversal from the formalism of the fifties. The central persona of Wodwo recoils in surrealistic flight, like the Spectre of Tharmas in Night VI of Blake's Four Zoas, from a Urizen-like destructive universe of all-conquering science and webs of religious mystery that stunt the development of emotional and imaginative life. But the poetic psyche is not left helpless: through the agony of the ordeal, Hughes is able to locate new powers within the self, powers deriving in part from surrealism itself, from primitive folklore and the shaman's art, and from Oriental psychology. These new powers offer important survival strategies for moderns.

Between 1960 and 1967 Hughes published no less than thirty-seven book reviews, four introductions, four essays, and seven short stories. He also completed dozens of BBC scripts and broadcasts and thirteen dramatic works (some for children) and published four volumes of children's verse and stories. When one adds the thirty-two minor poems of Recklings (1966), the forty-one major poems of **Wodwo,** and the dozens of uncollected pieces published during these seven years, the total output becomes prodigious. The elliptical poems and the enigmatical tripartite structure of **Wodwo** reflect the enormous gains in knowledge and imaginative reach that the contents of Hughes's essays, broadcasts, and reviews of this period convey, gains that often caused reviewers to gloss lightly over the volume, or to admit that this "baffling" collection contained "impenetrable" poetry and a structure that appeared "hastily considered and arbitrary."[2]

As Hughes abandons formalism, the emotional content of his private experience surfaces more directly in his poetry. **Wodwo** expresses the many moods that a prolific writer trying to establish himself experiences under the joys, strains, and tragedies of a private life that included the birth of Frieda Rebecca Hughes (1 April 1960) to a pair of immensely talented but impecunious poets, the sharing of childrearing duties in a cramped London flat, the onerous difficulties of writing while refurbishing the rural Devon home that the family occupied late in 1961, the birth of Nicholas Farrar Hughes (17 January 1962), and finally the broken marriage and the trauma and aftershocks of Sylvia Plath's tragic suicide (11 February 1963). Hughes's private life seldom intrudes directly into his creative work—poems like **"Full Moon and Little Frieda"** and **"Out"** are exceptions—but one can locate oblique references and analogous moods in the torment of **"Song of a Rat"** and the painful self-examination of *Eat Crow* (originally composed in 1964) and identify in **"Snow"** an elaborate prose allegory of the desk poet struggling to concentrate his energies on his art amid emotional fluctuations and snowdrifts of domestic duties, deadlines, appointments, and piles of incoming mail.[3]

Under such pressures, the choice of surrealism as Hughes's major poetic mode in the sixties seems natural, a fitting outgrowth of his public and private circumstances. One may be tempted, given the above factors, to dwell on the biographical overtones of the definition of surrealism that Hughes supplied near the time he arranged the poems of **Wodwo.** In the "Vasco Popa" essay (1967), Hughes praises the Yugoslav poet's refusal to "surrender to the dream flow for its own sake" or to provide a "relaxation from the outer battle." Hughes considers Popa's form of surrealism to be similar to the surrealism of folklore, which is "always urgently connected with the business of trying to manage practical difficulties so great that they have forced the sufferer temporarily out of the dimension of coherent reality into that depth of imagination where understanding has its roots and stores its X-rays." He distinguishes this from literary surrealism, which he argues "is always connected with an extreme remove from the business of living under practical difficulties and successfully managing them."[4]

The vast majority of the poems of **Wodwo,** however, offer no direct biographical referents for these "practical difficulties." The poems, prose, and drama of parts I and II are filled with imagery and mythic allusions that adumbrate states of psychological withdrawal, and part III contains ecstatic moments of participation in nature. Personal biography in the surrealist works of the sixties exists only as an analogue, at a high level of generalization, that influences and parallels, but does not determine, the thought and content of the poems. Plath's suicide may have thrown the surrealistic mode into overdrive, after a two-year poetic silence, but **"Snow,"** the most surrealistic story in **Wodwo,** was published before the move to Devon; **"The Rescue,"** one of the most surrealistic poems in the volume, appeared in print before the marital breakdown; and *The Wound,* **"Bowled Over,"** and **"The Green Wolf"** all antedate Plath's suicide.[5] Hughes's poetic intuition may have seen disaster coming in his private life, and he may well have opened the floodgates a few notches to allow his art access to feelings generated in his domestic life, but the sixties surrealism is more the direct, natural, and even inevitable outgrowth of the poet's obsession with the genetic inheritance of aggression in the individual and society and the testimony of his story of a soul, his imagination's relationship to the inner and outer worlds of his art.

Hughes's assessment of literary surrealism as being removed from the "outer battle" actually suits the cloudy reveries of symbolist poets such as Mallarmé and Verlaine, or the early Dadaist nihilism that spent itself by the time André Breton published his first surrealist manifesto in 1924. The original French surrealists were for the most part passionately concerned with embracing the outer world, *after recreating it*—after making it superreal by stripping it of the conventional descriptions of realism and people's naturalistic enchainment to their physical and social situation, and then *adding* the imaginative and psychological truths that free association, dreams, linguistic play, and automatic writing unlocked. Surrealism is one branch of modernist formal experiment; it recreates reality by adding the subjective dimension.

In their work the French surrealists principally responded to the social upheaval of the early twentieth century. Breton coupled Freudian therapy with his ministrations to the wounded as a neurological intern in Nantes during World War I to germinate many of the central tenets of surrealism that later found their way into his prose and poetry. Apollinaire's embrace of the concrete object as a celebration of the newness of life in *Calligrammes* (1918) was very much a survival tactic, a hopeful optimism in the wake of war. Paul Eluard, recognizing the necessity for social as well as artistic change, flirted with communism in the thirties, and Louis Aragon's early metaphysical anguish remained unchanged after three decorations in World War II. Save for a few short years of Dadaist revolt against logic and a dead culture, the original surrealists did not abandon the "outer battle." Pierre Reverdy, a cardiac patient most of his life, presents in "Sound of Bell" a striking image of depopulated Paris during World War I, as the world and his heartbeat stop at once. The alienation of feeling is very much like what one finds in poems such as **"A Wind Flashes the Grass"** in part I of **Wodwo.**[6]

Breton used Freudian therapy to awaken the subjective psyche; he obtained monologues from the wounded soldiers that were "unencumbered by the slightest inhibition" and "as closely as possible, akin to *spoken thought.*"[7] This is very similar to the form Hughes's imagination takes in **Wodwo.** Hughes undergoes an "abandoned surrealistic or therapeutic torrent" that engages the imagination more immediately by circumventing the "demon of artistic or rather verbal self-consciousness, [the] super-ego stylist"—exactly what he believes Dylan Thomas failed to achieve late in his life, as quoted in part in the epigraph to this chapter.[8] By submitting to a surrealistic torrent, Hughes hopes to make his emotional life more directly and immediately accessible to his art and to uncover a more essential self than could be realized under the conscious control of his earlier formalism. This essential self appears in part III of **Wodwo**; it derives, as we shall see later, primarily from Oriental psychology, but only after a necessary surrealistic liberation of the subjective psyche.

Through alienated feeling and metaphysical thirst; suggestive miracles of language and macabre, absurdist humor; hallucination and contradiction; unusual juxtapositions of the concrete and the abstract, the human and the nonhuman; and farfetched similes and metaphors, the surrealists dislocated the outer world from its normal referential or realistic context, only to recover it transformed and enriched by the infinite perceptivity of the awakened imagination, augmented by subconscious resources.[9] One can see Hughes experimenting with surrealist techniques—especially the use of contradiction, the odd mixing of the human and the nonhuman, and the macabre humor—in **"After Lorca,"** an uncollected 1963 poem that ends in a final terrifying release of godly song:

> The clock says "When will it be morning?"
> The sun says "Noon hurt me."
> The river cries with its mouthful of mud
> And the sea moves every way without moving.
>
> Out of my ear grew a reed
> Never touched by mouth.
> Paper yellows, even without flame,
> But in words carbon has already become diamond.
>
> A supple river of mirrors I run on
> Where great shadows rise to the glance,

> Flowing all forward and bringing
> The world through my reflection.
>
> A voice like a ghost that is not
> Rustle the dead in passage
> Leaving the living chilled,
> Wipe clear the pure glass of stone.
>
> Wipe clear the pure stone of flesh.
>
> A song tickling God's ear
> Till he laughs and catches it with his hand.
> A song with a man's face
> That God holds up in his fingers.[10]

Hughes uses some of these surrealist techniques in **Wodwo,** but most of the poems gravitate toward feelings of pained libidinal withdrawal from the landscape depicted, laced with oblique mythic allusions that delineate states of alienation and psychological dysfunction.

Though he certainly read Lorca and Kafka during this period, folklore and related primitive methods of solving "practical difficulties" provide the major sources for Hughes's surrealism in the sixties. Three influences converge here: his reviews of primitive folklore in the early sixties; his development of the concept of the poet as shaman, after a 1964 review of Eliade's *Shamanism*; and an unpublished libretto he wrote in 1960 on the *Bardo Thödol,* the *Tibetan Book of the Dead.* In reviewing C. M. Bowra's *Primitive Song,* Hughes admires the primitive poets' total absorption in the moment, with the complete attentiveness of the whole psyche, not just the abstracting intellect. Bowra observes that this is a reflex of the close proximity of art and necessity in primitive living.[11] Hughes agrees: primitive poems function as "power-charms, tools and practical agents in the business of gaining desired ends, or deflecting the spirits of misfortune from planting their larvae in the psyche."[12] He refers his readers to Paul Radin's *African Folk Tales and Sculptures* in another review, and to B. H. Chamberlain's collection of Ainu tales, for weirdly engrossing stories that are as "inspired and astonishing" as Kafka's.[13]

The function of the shaman is central to Hughes's sixties surrealism. The shaman is a religious expert in the art of psychic healing—both for individual primitives and for society—who undergoes ecstatic psychic ascents to heaven and descents to hell, with all manner of related physiological pain, for the purpose of acquiring an elixir or healing power for patients. Eliade emphasizes several times in *Shamanism* that what is really central to the shamanic experience is undergoing the concrete psychological *process* of death, dismemberment, and resurrection. The process is similar to that of an initiation rite, except that the shaman experiences it repeatedly, whenever the psychic health of the individual or the society demands.[14] The first two stages are always replete with surrealistic experiences of alienation, maiming, and death—where the body is torn open and devoured by a ravenous animal, after the eyes, heart, bowels, and intestines are plucked out. This surrealistic process of deathly withdrawal, with the addition of mythic and Oriental elements, will become the formal paradigm for *Wodwo* and *Gaudete,* and Crow's inability to undergo this process will account for much of the satiric humor of *Crow.* Hughes describes the process and its purpose very clearly in his 1964 review of *Shamanism:*

> Shamanism is not a religion, but a technique for moving in a state of ecstasy among the various spiritual realms, and for generally dealing with souls and spirits, in a practical way, in some practical crisis. It flourishes alongside and within the prevailing religion. . . . the most common form of election comes from the spirits themselves: they approach the man in a dream. . . . The central episode in this full-scale dream, just like the central episode in the rites where the transformation is effected forcibly by the tribe, is a magical death, then dismemberment, by a demon or equivalent powers, with all possible variants of boiling, devouring, burning, stripping to the bones. From this nadir, the shaman is resurrected, with new insides, a new body created for him by the spirits. . . . His business is usually to guide some soul to the underworld, or bring back a sick man's lost soul, or deliver sacrifices to the dead, or ask the spirits the reason for an epidemic, or the whereabouts of game or a man lost. . . . The results, when the shaman returns to the living, are some display of healing power, or a clairvoyant piece of information. The cathartic effect on the audience, and the refreshing of their religious feeling, must be profound.[15]

Lévi-Strauss explains the therapeutic process involved by adopting the psychoanalytic term "abreaction," the patient's intense reliving of the initial trauma until it is overcome. In primitive cultures the shaman abreacts *for* the patient, who empathizes with the intense, trancelike experience that the shaman undergoes. Healing wisdom or a mythic kernel of knowledge, imparted in the final resurrection stage, reorients the patient toward a more useful and purposive relationship with society.[16]

Hughes broadens the scope of this shamanic process to encompass a great deal of literature, in the process offering his readers a significant insight into the formal organization of *Wodwo.* In his *Shamanism* review, Hughes conflates the shaman's psychic journey with "the basic experience of the poetic temperament we call 'romantic'" and then asserts that this journey is also "the outline, in fact, of the Heroic Quest." Joseph Campbell, after detailed examination of the central myths of many primitive cultures, also speaks of a "formula" for the "adventure of the hero," and in similar terms: "a separation from the world, a penetration to some source of power, and a life-enhancing return," or

a "dying to the world" and a rebirth "filled with creative power."[17] A three-stage surrealistic, heroic adventure, toward a visionary achievement of a healing power, is the central formal pattern underlying the structure of *Wodwo.* This pattern explains the enigmatical "Author's Note" that prefaces the volume: "The stories and the play in this book may be read as notes, appendix, and unversified episodes of the events behind the poems, or as chapters of a single adventure to which the poems are commentary and amplification. Either way, the verse and the prose are intended to be read together, as parts of a single work."[18]

Unlike the Coleridgean fusion of a vitalistic metaphysic with concrete nature in *Hawk,* or the Yeatsian meditations upon concrete instances of love and aggression in *Lupercal, Wodwo* begins with a complete divorce between the inner and outer worlds, the result of an anguished revulsion from the landscape depicted. In parts I and II a single recurrent persona undergoes states of neurotic and then psychotic withdrawal from the outer world and finally experiences an imaginative death and dismemberment in *The Wound.* The *Bardo Thödol,* originally a shamanistic text, provides the Oriental psychology that informs many of the ecstatic moments of union with nature in part III. But rather than further postpone discussion of individual part I poems, we shall save consideration of the *Bardo Thödol* for a more appropriate moment, when elucidating part III.

Both the surrealism and the shamanism deepen Hughes's understanding of his inner world in *Wodwo.* The aggression that Hughes reconciled through New Critical formalism in *Lupercal* leaks its "Cordite oozings of Gallipoli" once again, but through surrealistic torrents that resolve themselves only in the shamanistic structural progression of the volume. The outer world causes of this aggression are specified in *Wodwo,* but left relatively undeveloped. **"Boom"** and **"Public Bar TV"** extend Hughes's meditations on the sterile materialism and scientific rationalism of modern Western culture that began in **"Fourth of July"** and the uncollected **"A Fable."** **"Logos"** (British *Wodwo* only) and part I of **"Gog"** deepen meditations on the denial of the instincts in Christianity that began in **"The Perfect Forms."**[19] Comprehending the causes of aggression is secondary to experiencing the inner suffering in *Wodwo.* Hughes will reverse this hierarchy in *Crow.*

Before *Wodwo* Hughes seems eager to applaud participation in temporal experience and cultural advancement. *The Hawk in the Rain* ends with a qualified approval of Bishop Farrar's martyrdom; *Lupercal* concludes with an expression of faith in the Luperci's ritual efforts to reempower man "age to age while the body hold." The personae of *Hawk* poems either wrestle with experience and their libidinal energies or are satirized for failing to do so. Hughes salutes Nicholas

Farrar, Thomas Browne, and the Retired Colonel in *Lupercal* for articulating the best cultural values of their respective ages. In the early war poetry Hughes typically reconciles human aggressiveness in the tensions and artifice of New Critical or wolf mask formalism, while affirming the worth of the individual soldier's survival struggle. But in *Wodwo* this confidence in historical enterprises in Western culture vanishes completely. The personae (really one central persona) disdain cultural roots, for nightmarish obsessions with human destructiveness obtrude. In part I especially, imagery of fear, turmoil, blood, and death oscillates with imagery of emptiness, silence, sleep, and surrealistic fright at nature's cycles of birth, destruction, and renewal.

Oblique mythic allusions frequently compound the inner agony of part I of *Wodwo,* often to articulate a disaffection with modern Western culture. Joseph Campbell in *Creative Mythology* adopts the Old Germanic term *wyrd* to characterize the Western hero's central mythic adventure since the breakdown of medieval Catholicism. *Wyrd* signifies the process of winning a consciousness-enlarging transformation of eros within the self, after psychological rounds of love and death in time and historical experience.[20] Both Campbell in *Creative Mythology* and Graves in *The White Goddess* allude to the proliferation of animals as fertility symbols in primitive societies—pigs, boars, bulls—to underscore the pervasiveness of belief in this transformational round. The central persona of part I of *Wodwo,* however, openly fears this process. The persona of **"A Vegetarian,"** as the title implies, refuses to partake of this carnal round; he sees only the destructive portion—the "snaring and rending"—and expects only death from his frightened stasis.

The central reason for the surrealistic disenchantment with Western culture in **Wodwo** is a more deeply and directly experienced consciousness of the effects of world war upon moderns. A bullet's "kiss of death" sends the persona reeling in **"Bowled Over."** Churches and farmland ("patched fields"), the products of human culture, spin in a disoriented loss of meaning and purpose, a convulsed "Desertion in the face of a bullet." **"Unknown Soldier"** and **"Flanders,"** poems published early in the sixties and collected in *Recklings,* also attest to Hughes's preoccupation with war, as do reviews of the war poetry of Keith Douglas, Wilfred Owen, and others during this period,[21] and the *Wodwo* poems **"Scapegoats and Rabies"** (American edition of *Wodwo* only) and **"Karma."**

As Hughes's poetic consciousness is thrown back upon its own inner resources, childhood memories of World War I stories shared by his family surface. World War I affected him deeply because, in Hughes's own words, "my father fought in it, and brought home his share of scars and medals, and at the family gatherings everybody seemed to talk about nothing else but the war, who had been killed and how and so on."[22] World War I became a "fairy-story world" to him, because at an impressionable age his generation "got the experience secondhand but fairly whole. And as it occurred to the actual participants."[23] But in the surreal mood of *Wodwo,* this "fairy-story world" sours into a nightmarish indictment of Western civilization. Though placed in part III of *Wodwo,* **"Out"** provides a necessary thematic framework for the nightmarish visions of aggression in many part I poems. Here, in a tone of rueful indignation, Hughes considers his father's victimization and near death by Gallipoli shrapnel (section I), with an eye to the genetic consequences for himself as a more impoverished "luckless double" of the next generation, the product of an automatic regenerative power in nature (section II) that simply will not surrender.

Section III of **"Out,"** however, presents a new insight into the mass warfare of the twentieth century. Here Hughes reasons that the stark anonymity of amassed millions, insulated from the enemy by machines, militates against even the ability of the psyche to place such slaughter within a larger humanistic retributive scheme. The function of the poppy, emblematic of a remembrance of the sleeping dead from antiquity to John McCrae's "In Flanders Fields" and contemporary Memorial Day customs, is rendered worthless; lost forever are the old ritual intuitions of the potential of the next generation to outlive historical animosities and to repay the debt owed the dead by following their ideals and conquering the foe. Hughes seems to ask McCrae how can we take up our countrymen's "quarrel with the foe" when the individual soldier's humane responses collapse as he stands in a no-man's land between astronomical body counts and inhuman but terribly efficient machine gun barrels. In a review of I. M. Parsons's anthology of World War I poets (*Listener,* 5 August 1965), Hughes writes that the four years of World War I were not enough to digest "the shock of machine guns, armies of millions, and the plunge into the new dimension, where suddenly and for the first time Adam's descendants found themselves meaningless."

This new dimension of meaninglessness in section III of **"Out"** replaces the persona's former faith in nature's cyclic ability (the "refreshing of ploughs / In the woe-dark under my mother's eye—") to imbue wartime death with value. The carnage of Gallipoli transforms the poppy, emblematic of the ideals and courage of the slain, into a "canvas-beauty puppet on a wire"—a worthless, "bloody-minded" flower. **"Out"** ends with the firm resolve to bid "Goodbye to the cenotaphs on my mother's breasts" and "Goodbye to the remaindered charms of my father's survival." Instead of the affirmation of the "old spark of the blood heat" in **"Luperca-**

lia," Hughes now affirms that he will no longer be constrained by genetic habit to participate unconsciously in repeat performances of the errors of Western cultural history. There is no stronger statement in *Wodwo* of a departure from Hughes's early faith in human potential in historical time.

On the subject of the involuntary transmission of aggressive tendencies Hughes writes, in a *Wodwo* period review (*New Statesman,* 2 October 1964), that "The possibilities of what a child might absorb from its lineage . . . are awful, which is what alarmed Freud." Freud treated violence in his late work as part of thanatos, the death instinct, which is usually fused with eros or libidinal energy in the ego, but can be directed outward in aggressive acts. More specifically, when Freud tried to explain the slaughter of World War I, one answer he developed was that of a repetition-compulsion biological urge, like cellular replacement, to regress to an earlier level of evolution. The other concept Freud developed was that of "archaic heritage" or "phylogenetic inheritance": inherited memory traces in the genes, innately present at birth, of the primordial crime—parricide, the son's first rebellious act against the cruel despotism and sexual covetousness of the patriarch in the primal horde.[24] In parts I and II of *Wodwo* Hughes treats aggression in ways similar to both Freudian theories—the compulsive repetitiousness that breeds hostility and the inherited phylogenetic predisposition toward violent behavior.

One can infer that the domestic antagonisms and their "blood weight of money" in **"Her Husband"** surface daily in that couple's life, and in the lives of millions of working-class families; the jaguar in **"Second Glance at a Jaguar"** exhibits a compulsive, inexhaustible power to "keep his rage brightening"; and in **"Thistles"** the warriors return to fight "over the same ground." The surreal **"Ghost Crabs"** symbolize both the aggressive traits and the repetition-compulsion urge present in the dissolution of the human personality during sleep:

> All night, around us or through us,
> They stalk each other, they fasten on to each other,
> They mount each other, they tear each other to pieces,
> They utterly exhaust each other.
> They are the powers of this world.
> We are their bacteria,
> Dying their lives and living their deaths.
> At dawn, they sidle back under the sea's edge.
> They are the turmoil of history, the convulsion
> In the roots of blood, in the cycles of concurrence.

In both **"Ghost Crabs"** and **"Second Glance at a Jaguar"** Hughes, like the shaman, *becomes* the animal; he experiences the animal's destructive power in a "surrealistic or therapeutic torrent" of intense, sustained, nightmarish energy.

Often in part I the mood of surrealistic revulsion is so great as to occasion a general libidinal withdrawal from the landscape depicted. The alternate shuddering and silence of the wind-blown trees and the vision of the shadow of the ploughman's bones in **"A Wind Flashes the Grass"** mirror the persona's own state of anxiety and fear at the prospect of mortality in the time-bound world of woe. In the last two lines of the poem, the conscious use of the pathetic fallacy reveals the persona's fear at the momentary nature of both humans and landscape. Similarly, the persona of **"Sugar Loaf,"** in noticing the hill's time-bound vulnerability to erosion, becomes disconcerted by the hill's ignorance of the process. Unsettling images of naked susceptibility to pain mirror a torment within the psyche of the persona. Water becomes "wild as alcohol," and "nude and tufted" reeds shiver, mirroring the persona's vulnerability.

In certain part I poems the psychological torment occasioned by the private and the larger cultural tragedy is so great as to cause a complete displacement into the realm of surrealistic nightmare. In **"Cadenza," "The Rescue,"** and **"Stations"** the central persona experiences more psychotic states of personality breakdown and libidinal withdrawal. In **"Cadenza"** and **"The Rescue"** the dissolution of the ego and the abandonment of a normal relationship with daily living is feared, but is taking place nevertheless. Noise is preferred in both cases as supportive reinforcement to the security needs of the ego. But in **"Cadenza"** the soloist's egocentric refusal to relinquish his dominance leads to an aggressive combat with the orchestra. Metaphors become mixed and metaphoric vehicles become purposely confused to present surreal images of disorientation. The soloist perceives himself as a "coffin attended by swallows," one that "will not be silent." But the attempt at an Osiris-like rebirth runs amuck. The sea "lifts swallow wings" and parts clouds that are "full of surgery and collisions." Then the sea-swallow becomes a sky that "dives shut like a burned land back to its spark—." Finally the soloist's frenetic playing takes its grim toll: "Blue with sweat, the violinist / Crashes into the orchestra, which explodes." Instead of the surreal humor that closes **"Logos"** and **"Ghost Crabs,"** the psychotic frenzy of **"Cadenza"** leads to a complete annihilation of ego and will. The soloist's refusal to accept the dissolution of his former self-image (the coffin) causes a rather complete disintegration of the psyche.

In **"The Rescue"** the persona learns that the reality of his psychological state is one of silence, a dying away from the temporal world. The "five," perhaps the five senses, are too fragile for noises from the world of the living. What the psyche wants to see—"The flash of wet oars slashing their eyes back alive" and the rescue by "the long white liner anchoring the world"—is "wrong." In reality the five "just stood sucked empty / As grasses by this island's silence." Hughes conveys a mood of deathly surrealistic estrangement from normality through nightmare images of "sailors white / As maggots" and "mummies with their bandages lifted off," followed by the soundless "pouring faces" from the ship's "dazzling side."

The meditations of **"Stations"** present a more complete abandonment of the conscious analytic ego, prized by our empirical culture as the prime locus of thinking and experiencing. In section III the persona is "complacent" in his inability to ratiocinate, to make even "one comparison," and feels completely estranged even from his former artistic labor. Only an **"Absence"** remains to weep "its respite through [his] accomplished music." In section IV the abandonment of language is presented surrealistically as a severing of the head by the train-wheels of time, in an unfamiliar landscape, a dream image of alienation:

> Whether you say it, think it, know it
> Or not, it happens, it happens, as
> Over rails over
> The neck the wheels leave
> The head with its vocabulary useless,
> Among the flogged plantains.

The mythic psychodrama in part I of **Wodwo** leads toward a total dissolution of the ego-oriented personality. The "abandoned surrealistic or therapeutic torrent" is therapeutic to the extent that the central persona gradually acknowledges his suffering and his preference for emptiness, withdrawal, and absence, over participation in goal-directed activity in Western culture. The persona learns to submit, to suffer his fate or *"dree his weird,"* as the Scots say, and repudiate the Western *wyrd* of Campbell's monomyth.

"Scapegoats and Rabies" is perhaps the quintessential part I **Wodwo** poem. Though it appeared only in the American edition, its first publication in early 1967 (*New Statesman,* 13 January 1967) indicates that it was probably written in mid or late 1966, at the time Hughes was organizing **Wodwo**. In **"Scapegoats and Rabies"** one recognizes a complete surrealistic dislocation into nightmare, the most straightforward analysis of war in terms similar to the Freudian repetition-compulsion biological urge, the extreme moral anguish and sensitivity of the poet to human suffering, and a clear expression of an Oriental way out of this impasse.

Nightmarish images of anonymous dead soldiers obtrude in a garish montage in the first section of **"Scapegoats and Rabies."** Both heredity and the nurture provided by Western culture combine as causes: stares from old women, trembling chins from old men, bow-legs from toddlers, facelessness from "the mouldering / Of letters and citations / On rubbish dumps." The funeral parade is endless, for the repetition-compulsion "drumming / Of their boots" is "concentrating / Toward a repeat performance" in future genera-

tions. The sardonic, almost misanthropic mood of the poem leads to surrealistic images of loathing, disgust, and putrefaction, as the persona perceives the soldiers getting

> their hopelessness
> From the millions of the future
> Marching in their boots, blindfold and riddled,
> Rotten heads on their singing shoulders,
> The blown-off right hand swinging to the stride
> Of the stump-scorched and blown-off legs
> Helpless in the terrible engine of the boots.

Sections II and III present the poet as General undergoing the psychic shock of having his head torn apart by each memory-trade of the events of war, by a searing, agonized consciousness of human aggression through the ages, presented as a paranoid sensitivity to every bullet, every shellburst. The General's face is a lantern of light in the darkness of war, its flame blown out and relit in response to the explosive staccato outside.

Sections IV and V continue the sardonic mood with an allegory of a soldier's outfitting for battle, his near-death and resuscitation in the mud of historical time. Since the poet-General, like Diogenes searching with his lantern for an honest man, cannot locate a receptive culture, the only alternative is to exorcise that culture's aggressiveness for the self's sanity. As Christ once exorcised a demon into the Gaderene swine (Mark, 5), so Hughes creates a faceless stereotype as collective cultural scapegoat. This soldier's battledress is woven by some of the most reprehensible elements of contemporary civilization—its materiality and smug conspicuous consumption, niggard of self-comprehension (IV: stanza I), its petty smallmindedness and selfishness (IV: stanza II), and the poverty and scurrility of its cultural, political, and economic products (IV: stanzas IIIff.). After being shot while traversing no man's land "In a shouting flight / From his own stink," the soldier in section V embraces London and the mud of time and human history in a state too hopelessly maimed to muster any resistance. More so than any other passage in **Wodwo,** sections IV and V of **"Scapegoats and Rabies"** present an indictment of the enterprises of contemporary Western civilization, though the specific images are geographically British in reference.

The way out of the impasse presented in **"Scapegoats and Rabies"** is through the abandonment of the Western analytic ego—a machine that passively ingests information from the outside and functions as a security-seeking defense mechanism against the outside world—and a retrenchment to a sense of self as the generator of one's own perceptions of reality, in a way that *unifies* the perceiving consciousness with external reality. Hughes's imagination, initially employed in **Wodwo** in coaxing to consciousness a torrent of surreal images from the depths of his inner world and identifying with shamanic animal energy, once again is able to unify the inner and outer worlds of his art—from the locus of an Oriental subjective monism.

The poet as General in section II of **"Scapegoats and Rabies"** transcends the subject/object dualism of his Western culture by opting for an excarnation of the fleshy body and its automatic responses to the environment and adopting an Oriental subjective monism, a realization of the self as the creator of reality-for-the-self, of its own unitive relationship with nature:

> Knives, forks, spoons divide his brains.
> The supporting earth, and the night around him,
>
> Smoulder like the slow, curing fire
> Of a Javanese head-shrinker.
>
> Nothing remains of the *tête d'armée* but the skin—
> A dangling parchment lantern
>
> Slowly revolving to right, revolving to left,
>
> Trembling a little with the
>
>   incessant pounding,
>
> Over the map, empty in the ring of light.

III

Wit's End

The General commits his emptiness to God.

To leave the fleshy body's instinctual and emotional dependencies upon a comforting external environment, and to abandon the analytic ego and dualistic thinking, is to experience the Buddhist state of *śūnyatā,* a state of complete personality dissolution and a realization of emptiness, of the fullness of nothingness, where "nothing" is understood as a nondualistic involvement in the plenitude of *all* of reality (i.e., no one thing).[25] What is accomplished in the process is a fresh, direct, precognitive perception of reality in its suchness, before the conscious mind labels with Aristotelian classes and categories, semantic descriptions, and their underlying cultural assumptions. After achieving the *śūnyatā* state, the initiate can progress to a state of perception where the self-as-creator fuses with the activities of nature, in any of a number of ways: a recognition of the *ātman* or self-soul of the Upanishads as the generator of all that is perceived;[26] or the yogic *īshwara pranidhāna,* the God within the self as the creator and ground of all being;[27] or the *satori* sense of ecstatic participatory involvement in the isness of all reality, in Zen.[28] Section III of **"Scapegoats and Rabies"** begins with a resurrection of the self as creator of reality; the line "The General commits his emptiness to God" indicates a movement from *śūnyatā* to yogic *īshwara pranidhāna.* By the end of the section the General has realized a

new sense of power as the generator of reality-for-the-self, as his hand sweeps the battlefield "flat as a sheet of foolscap" and he affirms a sympathetic commitment to his brethren:

> I AM A LANTERN
>   IN THE HAND
>   OF A BLIND PEOPLE

In sections II and III of **"Scapegoats and Rabies"** Hughes may also have been meditating upon passages in the Śvetāśvatara Upanishad (1: 14; 2: 11-16), wherein the macrocosmic all-space fuses with the soul within the subjective self to create the *ātman* of Oriental monism. In this passage the two concepts fuse into the *ātman* through imagery of fire, God, crystal, and inwardly illuminated lantern, similar to that of sections II and III of **"Scapegoats and Rabies."** Both the fire of yogic meditation and the purgative fire at the end of section II of **"Scapegoats and Rabies,"** the "slow, curing fire / Of a Javanese head-shrinker," lead to a death of the old conscious ego and the attainment of an inner personal godliness. The motif of the willed, self-devouring of the carnal self leading to an excarnation of the flesh, and of the presence of God in all fiery, world-destroying cataclysms, leaving only the "Face of Glory" mask, is a prominent motif of Vedic Śivaite mythology. This fiery, self-destructive aspect of Śiva particularly delighted the aboriginal Javanese long after their conversion to Hinduism.[29]

One must be careful to realize that Hughes does not subscribe to a simplistic either/or, Western versus Eastern, position; nor is he an ardent devotee of a particular branch of Oriental orthodoxy. Hughes is entirely eclectic, mainly interested in the survival of the spirit and the integrated psyche, and will use, as he has told Ekbert Faas, whatever serves: "You choose a subject because it serves, because you need it."[30] Like Jung, Campbell, and Lévi-Strauss, Hughes is particularly interested in conflating the folklore, myth, and ritual patterns of primitive and non-Western cultures in order to comprehend the psychological and spiritual common denominators operative, and to discover what survival potential these kernels may hold for contemporary people.

One who is capable of the perceptual and psychological revolution of recognizing the *ātman* as generator of all that the self perceives is freed from bondage to instinctual cravings and attachments, from dualistic thinking and preoccupation with temporality, and becomes the world-all, as in the Bṛihad-Āranyaka Upanishad (4.4.12-13):

> If a person knew the Soul [Atman],
> With the thought "I am he!"
> With what desire, for love of what
> Would he cling unto the body?

He who has found and has awakened to the Soul
That has entered this conglomerate abode—
He is the maker of everything, for he is the creator of
all;
The world is his: indeed he is the world itself.[31]

The *ātman* of the Upanishads was very much on Hughes's mind as he organized the poems of *Wodwo*; one need only repeat the last epigraph quote to this chapter, from Hughes's review of Dylan Thomas's *Selected Letters* (*New Statesman,* 25 November 1966): "What he [Thomas] was really waiting for, and coaxing with alcohol, was the delicate cerebral disaster that demolishes the old self for good, with all its crushing fortifications, and leaves the *atman* a clear field."

The *ātman* union of inner and outer worlds exemplifies the "that art thou" doctrine of the Chāndogya Upanishad (6:8-16), where the "that" is the totality of the perceived environment as it exists for the perceiving consciousness, and the "thou" is the God, the creator-originator of all that is perceived. In yogic meditation the adept can achieve a state of *samādhi,* of agreement or unity with the whole of reality; this union can be achieved either by focusing upon an object of consciousness ("with seed"; *samprajñāta*) or without consciousness of an object ("without seed"; *asamprajñāta*).[32] In Chinese and Japanese Zen the experience of *satori* or totalistic unity with the infinite is also cognate, though it dawns upon the initiate in an instantaneous and ecstatic epiphanic moment.[33] Through such meditative practices one can obliterate the mental baggage acquired from an overly rational and overly aggressive culture and experience reality afresh, direct, without labeling.

Certain poems in part I of *Wodwo* assist in liberating the *ātman* by achieving the *śūnyatā* state of emptiness, of death to the analytic ego, in order to experience the fullness of nothingness, the fullness of *all* creation. In section III of **"Root, Stem, Leaf"** (American edition only) the persona imagines himself to be utterly anonymous, as forgotten as a discarded heirloom spoon "blackening / Among roots in a thorn-hedge." This leads to a knowledge of the plenitude of all existence at the end of the section, wherein "Everything is inheriting everything." Of the part I poems in *Wodwo*, section III of **"Stations"** relates the most completely realized state of *śūnyatā* emptiness; here the persona experiences a queer state of complete dissolution and absence, of estrangement even from his own act of writing:

> You are a wild look—out of an egg
> Laid by your absence.
>
> In the great Emptiness you sit complacent,
> Blackbird in wet snow.
>
> If you could make only one comparison—
> Your condition is miserable, you would give up.

But you, from the start, surrender to total Emptiness,
Then leave everything to it.

> Absence. It is your own
> Absence

> Weeps its respite through your accomplished music,
> Wraps its cloak dark about your feeding.

"The Green Wolf" and **"The Bear,"** the concluding poems (except for **"Scapegoats and Rabies"** in the American edition) of part I of *Wodwo,* further assist in demolishing the old egocentric self, as prelude to recognizing the sleeping *ātman* within. In **"The Green Wolf"** the title allusion to the scapegoat victim of the purgatorial Beltane Fires of Normandy combines with imagery of a cerebral hemorrhage or stroke (the "dark bloodclot" of line 9) to reinforce a state of deathly neurotic withdrawal.[34] In this state of self-negating passivity, forces in the external environment assist in a destructive process: hawthorn blossom and beanflower symbolize, respectively, powers of erotic seduction and destruction.[35] The "deathly perfume" of the hawthorn blossom, and the tiger stripes of the beanflower, "unmake and remake" the persona in a surrealistic vision of death:

> One smouldering annihilation
> Of old brains, old bowels, old bodies
> In the scarves of dew, the wet hair of nightfall.

"The Green Wolf" was originally published as **"Dark Women"** (*Observer,* 6 January 1963), with only minor differences from the *Wodwo* version. The original poem title contains a cryptic allusion concerning the sundering of the old conscious ego. In cabbalistic lore Ama is the destructive aspect of Binah or Understanding, the third Sephirah in the cabbalistic Tree of Life. Ama attests to the arduous labor needed to achieve any goal and the necessity of disrupting and destroying the old self-image to create fertile ground for personality growth. She is usually known as the "Dark Mother," carries a disciplinary bar of wood in her left hand, and is depicted as a gigantic Mother Superior completely shrouded in black.[36]

In **"The Bear,"** the final poem in the part I psychodrama of withdrawal and personality dissolution, the bear represents the "gleam in the pupil" of a transcendent self, which can be revealed through opening the *prajñā-cakṣu,* the Buddhist third eye of transphenomenal wisdom.[37] The bear's "price is everything"—a resignation to the death of the conscious ego. In return he grants a largesse of comprehension of self-and-world, gluing beginning and end, offering knowledge deeper than a well, wider than the universe. He is a "ferryman / To dead land," but not as a functionary like Charon, for in primitive cultures he symbolizes a godly regeneration-through-death. In shamanic initiations the bear is often a theriomorphic vehicle of dismemberment toward the attaining of new life and mystical powers.[38] The bear's abode is "In the huge, wide-open sleeping eye of the mountain," the principal residence of the gods to primitives.[39] The Ainus of northern Japan practiced the earliest form of the "animal master" ritual known, with a bear as its focus; its purpose was to affirm that the process of destruction was only a stage in a recurring cosmic drama of rebirth and regeneration. Hence the young bear, sacrificed with elaborate ritual, was *joyously* sent home to its cosmic abode.[40]

The stories of part II repeat the mythic psychodrama of surrealistic withdrawal and dissolution of the personality. The central characters exhibit varying stages of neurotic and psychotic behavior caused by the repression of instinct and withdrawal from other-directed libido. Grooby's inability to withstand three hours of harvest heat in **"The Harvesting"** leads to an anguished preoccupation with mortality. As aging victim of the temporal round of birth/death, but without the capacity to transcend his situation, he himself becomes the hare hunted by the "big, white bony greyhound," as in the epigraph chant from the seventeenth-century Allansford witch coven.[41] In **"Sunday"** what at first appears to be a sexual initiation for Michael results in neurotic flight. The girl is inaccessible, presided over by an "expert" male companion, and instead of a knowing lure to sexual initiation she offers only "mesmerized incredulity." The girl is too much a product of the "harmless, church-going slopes" to be of aid in Michael's sexual quandary. The only initiation into the birth/death sexual round offered in the story is the sham, degraded showmanship of Billy Red's rat catching. Neither the girl nor Billy Red's grotesquery appeals to Michael, who flees in speechless revulsion at the entire ordeal.

The more severe estrangement from object-directed libido in **"The Suitor"** and **"The Rain Horse"** leads to more pronounced neurotic behavior. In **"The Suitor"** the estrangement from eros is presented symbolically and in a surrealistic landscape—in the continuing darkness and blocked bedroom window of the girl's house, the pummeling received by the man in the trilby (the repressed instinctual component of the suitor's ego), and the final surrealistic tableau of alienated instinct when the suitor faces away from the flute-playing man in the trilby. Here the flute notes of Pan work their way up the house wall in complete dissociation from the suitor, though he has walked five miles in never-used dancing shoes in the hope of an encounter based entirely upon the girl's chance smile in the school corridors. In **"The Rain Horse"** the alienation of instinctual life is so total that an eruption of demonized eros ensues when the young adult businessman returns home after a twelve-year absence. The environment of his nurture elicits only boredom and impatience, and the impatience

soon turns to anger at the discomforts of mud and rain. The horse appears exactly at this point and becomes malevolent *only* when the man resolves not to deal with the animal's watchful presence—when he decides to repress his emotions and banish the horse from consciousness. Thus the horse symbolizes the repressed libidinal energies in the man's own psyche, a favorite technique of German expressionist drama.[42] Of course whatever is banished from consciousness will return to confront the agent of the repression as a demonized force that appears to be outside the agent. So the horse that originally "was watching him intently" soon returns as a destructive agent in a surrealistic guise:

> He took control of himself and turned back deliberately, determined not to give the horse one more thought. If it wanted to stare at him, let it. He was nestling firmly into these resolutions when the ground shook and he heard the crash of a heavy body coming down the wood. Like lightning his legs bounded him upright and about face. The horse was almost on top of him, its head stretching forwards, ears flattened and lips lifted back from the long yellow teeth. He got one snapshot glimpse of the red-veined eyeball as he flung himself backwards around the tree. Then he was away up the slope, whipped by oak twigs as he leapt the brambles and brushwood, twisting between the close trees till he tripped and sprawled.

After a final truce the persona feels lobotomized, but fails to recognize that the cause of this feeling is his having shirked the burden of the experience, of having refused the chance for psychological reclamation.

"Snow" is at once the most psychotic of the short stories and the one that most foreshadows the Oriental conclusion of part III. Here the normal rational thinking process is equated with the blinding, lifeless snow, the strangling snowdrifts of conscious rationality. In **"Snow"** a partly amnesiac survivor of a plane crash in the Arctic wilderness must concentrate and discipline his survival energies and distrust his tendency to lapse into a muddleheaded optimism. The key to successful endurance provided by the story is to withdraw one's awe, fears, and attachments to the temporal world and learn to awaken a deeper, more essential self at the root of one's inner being. The survivor learns that "My mind is not my friend" and that "It's my mind that has this contemptible awe for the probably true, and my mind, I know . . . is not me and is by no means sworn to help me." The central character of **"Snow"** appears to heed the warning of Patanjali, at the outset of his *Yoga Sutras* (no. 2), that one must control the mind's habitual flow of ideas and conventional choice making, through concentration and meditation.[43] The Hindu chant invoked by the survivor, "O Jewel of the Lotus," is the mantra of Chenrazee, *Om Mani Padme Hum,* used like all mantras as a power charm to focus one's willpower and meditative energies and to invoke supernormal powers for practical or religious reasons. The survivor remains alive at the conclusion of the story because he trusts his inner powers and disciplines his need for reassurances from conventional rationalizations, or even from his chair, his one anchor to the phenomenal world. As he develops this meditative control he is even tempted to "go deep into the blizzard" and leave the chair altogether.

The radio play *The Wound* presents the second stage of the shamanic/heroic "single adventure" of **Wodwo,** the shaman's experience of dismemberment, or the hero's visit to the underworld. In an interview with Anthony Thwaite, broadcast on BBC radio ("New Comment": 29 January 1963), Hughes states that the action of *The Wound* occurs entirely inside Ripley's wounded head in the space of two seconds after he is shot in battle. The play illustrates certain psycho-physiological realities that Ripley must confront as he decides whether to live or to die. "The hero," Hughes remarks to Thwaite, "is just the personality absolutely collapsed back into a world which is the body—this body of mud and decomposing things." Like the Eskimo shaman who must confront a mystical vision of his own skeleton during his initiation,[44] Ripley must confront the reality of his dying self—take an instantaneous psycho-biological inventory, recognize his potential collapse into the decomposition of animal instinct and death, and decide whether to submit to the blood-drinking ogresses (Persephone's minions) at the white chateau. If he cannot muster the necessary vital forces to survive, then he should exchange his soldier's uniform for the more rigorous formal attire of the dead and dance with them at their ball later in the play.

Ripley actually confronts his skeleton twice in *The Wound.* Early on he gazes incredulously at his prone body, cataloguing each part serially, as if dismembered, but not recognizing it as his own. The vital signs are weak; only a single finger flicks at the stars. The central confrontation with his wounded self occurs later, when he gazes at Massey's dead body in the adjacent armory-museum. Hughes has told Thwaite that at this point "Massey is the projection of the thing that's wrong with Ripley." Here Ripley comprehends the import of his projection and resolves to live, to terminate what Hughes characterizes as the "traditional visit to the House of the Dead." As he gathers his energies in his inner world, Ripley survives a nine-mile walk for help in the "real" world in a state of unconscious automatism.

Ripley survives because he is able to reunite with his anima, the feminine principle that Jung perceived as the "leaping and twinkling of the soul" that brings man out of his idleness and ensnares him into life.[45] To Thwaite, Hughes characterizes the Girl of the drama as "the gift itself," the "little bit of life that brings him through all this ordeal and enables him to come back into life and the real world." The reclamation process is not easy, for

Ripley has very definite inhibitions and fears, a "bitch-proof" misogyny exacerbated by battle stress. The Girl gives Ripley his first conscious inkling that he is indeed shot in the head, in her second visit. She accentuates with romantic irony the ambivalence of life and death in our aggressive Western culture in her third visit: she tells Ripley that the noise he hears is both "your life, working at the hole in your head," and "the war, working at all the undead." In her fourth and last visit she supplies needed support to return Ripley to the world of the living. The Girl is a power mobilized from Ripley's unconscious, as was the insight that Massey is his potentially dead self: the armory-museum is illuminated by a rotten phosphorescent fish, a surrealistic version of the archetypal Christian symbol of sustenance won from the unconscious.[46]

Much textual evidence exists in *The Wound* to indicate that Hughes attaches a great deal of ambivalence to Ripley's survival. The action takes place on midsummer's eve, "when all the disasters occur"—when, according to Frazer, scapegoat victims were traditionally immolated in fires in primitive Western societies.[47] Surrealistic images of horror, devouring, even of cannibalism, abound in *The Wound,* and there is deep irony in Ripley's muttered offer of marriage to his vision of femininity when he is finally rescued. The two soldiers who rescue his bleeding body, encased in the mud of war, accentuate the irony: "what's he smiling at? Look at this, grinning away as if he'd been crowned."

The mythic superstructure of *The Wound* is entirely Western, but the fruit of the quest is not spiritual enlargement. The dominant images of this radio play are entirely negative, and Ripley's mantra is the unreflective "Keep going!" Massey hammers this inane command into Ripley at the outset of the play. If Massey is, in Hughes's own words, a "projection of the thing that's wrong with Ripley," then his problem is the malaise of modern Western culture. For what *The Wound* reveals of this culture is its hyperkinetic adventure urge, an obsession so poisoned by its repetition-compulsion aggressiveness that it is incapable of striving for any humanistic goals. Like the soldiers "helpless in the terrible engine of the boots" in **"Scapegoats and Rabies,"** Ripley is more the victim of destructive energies than a successful quest hero. Ripley barely survives this initiation into the destructive horrors at the bottom of the self and contemporary Western civilization; he returns to the wartime world of "Bleeding mud" in a state of utter helplessness. As soldiers carry Ripley's limp body to camp, the voyage to the underworld ends. The **Wodwo** leitmotif of the dissolution of the conscious Western ego also ends here, allowing the leitmotif of the development of the *ātman* within the self to flower in part III.

Though Hughes became acquainted with Oriental mythology during his undergraduate work in anthropology at Cambridge, his work on the *Bardo Thödol* libretto immediately after **Lupercal** was crucial in deepening this interest. While at Yaddo in September 1959, Hughes met the Chinese composer Chou Wen-chung, who persuaded him to write the libretto for a large orchestral composition based upon the *Tibetan Book of the Dead.* According to Hughes, the work involved a "Gigantic orchestra, massed choirs, projected illuminated mandalas, soul-dancers and the rest." Though the project ultimately died for lack of expected funding, Hughes worked and reworked the libretto a great deal after his return to England that autumn, at least through November 1960, later admitting that he "got to know the *Bardo Thödol* pretty well" during that period.[48] More than deathbed prayers and instructions to the dying, the *Bardo Thödol* is to be used throughout adult life as a meditative guide to the Buddhist art of dying to the phenomenal world.[49] As Carl Jung writes in his "Psychological Commentary" to the *Bardo,* the purpose of the meditation is deliberately to induce a psychological state "transcendent over all assertion and predication," where the initiate realizes that "the 'giver' of all 'given' things dwells within us" and that "even the gods are the radiance and reflection of our own souls."[50]

As the deceased passes from the *Chikkai Bardo* state of the first four days after death into the *Chönyid Bardo* state of the fifth to fourteenth days, the possibility of experiencing the liberating *nirvana* of the Void, the *Dharma-Kāya* of Clear Light, lessens markedly, for karmic illusions appear, urging the soul back to participation in the phenomenal world. Here the text constantly exhorts the deceased not to fear or desire such illusions, to abandon egotism and recognize that all thought-forms are "the radiance of thine own intellectual faculties come to shine. They have not come from any other place. Be not attracted towards them; be not weak; be not terrified; but abide in the mood of non-thought formation. In that state all forms and radiances will merge into thyself, and Buddhahood will be obtained."[51] For those unable to abandon egotism, the devices of intellect, and fears or attachments to objects in the phenomenal world, the final *Sidpa Bardo* state of involvement with animal instinct dawns on the fifteenth day after death; here the deceased are whirled about by karmic winds and the play of instinct until reincarnation at the womb door results forty-nine days after death.

The central persona of part I fails to recognize that fears of participation in temporal experience in Western culture are self-created. The persona of **"A Vegetarian,"** for instance, is tripped on "Eternity's stone threshold," by his fear of sundering his automatic instinctual dependency upon the environment. Both **"A Wind Flashes the Grass"** and **"Sugar Loaf"** contain imagery of wind-driven environments similar to that of the *Sidpa Bardo,* and for similar reasons: in each case

the persona fails to recognize that his own winds of instinctual dependency cause the macabre, fearful gusts. The *Bardo,* originally an animistic, shamanistic text of the pre-Buddhist Bönpos, contains numerous surrealistic passages with constant reminders that the causes of the surreal visions are entirely within the self, in cravings and instinctual attachments to the environment that manifest themselves in what we in the West know as the Seven Deadly Sins. The *Bardo* counsels the need for a higher level of self-possession that can free one from such automatic emotional responses. The real beauty of the *Bardo,* however, is that it also reveals how one's emotional state influences one's perceptions, or how a surrealistic vision is a self-caused refusal to achieve the lucidity of the *Dharma-Kāya.* Consider the following passages from the *Sidpa Bardo:*

> O nobly-born, at about that time, the fierce wind of *karma,* terrific and hard to endure, will drive thee [onwards], from behind, in dreadful gusts. Fear it not. That is thine own illusion. . . . Apparitional illusions, too, of being pursued by various terrible beasts of prey will dawn. Snow, rain, darkness, fierce blasts [of wind], and hallucinations of being pursued by many people likewise will come; [and] sounds as of mountains crumbling down, and of angry overflowing seas, and of the roaring of fire, and of fierce winds springing up.

> When these sounds come one, being terrified by them, will flee before them in every direction, not caring whither one fleeth. But the way will be obstructed by three awful precipices—white, and black, and red. They will be terror-inspiring and deep, and one will feel as if one were about to fall down them. O nobly-born, they are not really precipices; they are Anger, Lust, and Stupidity. . . .

> Then [one of the Executive Furies of] the Lord of Death . . . will cut off thy head, extract thy heart, pull out thy intestines, lick up thy brain, drink thy blood, eat thy flesh, and gnaw thy bones; but thou wilt be incapable of dying. Although thy body be hacked to pieces, it will revive again. . . .

> Thy body being a mental body is incapable of dying even though beheaded and quartered. In reality, thy body is of the nature of voidness; thou needst not be afraid. The Lords of Death are thine own hallucinations.[52]

Imagery of the demonic and disorienting in nature and animals always precedes a counsel directed toward achieving a knowledge of the self as generator of values, a counsel similar in some respects to the *ātman* of the Upanishads. The last two passages present a Bön-po version of the shamanistic stages in the heroic adventure, especially the surrealism of the first stage.

The goal of Hughes's use of Oriental psychology is not, however, to attain the self-absorbed, world-annihilating state of yogic *samādhi* or the *nirvana* of the Clear Light in *Bardo* thought, but to return to the world cleansed of overdependence upon a rational analytic ego that leads to aggression, fortified with the awakened *ātman* within the self as the generative center of experience and capable of merging with a nature newly perceived as benign. This is closest to the practices of modern Zen. The psychic process in Zen begins with the *Mahāyāna* principle of emptiness, *śūnyatā*, when all impediments of consciousness are annihilated, and the mind rests in a passive state of personality dissolution, devoid of thoughts, experiencing the fullness of nothingness. The process ends in *satori* as a psychological upheaval occurs wherein the intellect as the primary seat of knowledge is displaced by an intuitive grasp of the totality of Being, a grasp that is periodically realized *within* the world of mundane tasks.[53]

The personae of part III of **Wodwo** look upon life from a newly won position of self-assurance and self-control, with a calm exercise of judgment. Moods of Oriental serenity (*śānti*) and a Buddha-like compassion and pity for those who cannot transcend the temporal world predominate in part III. The personae are often able, especially in the final poems of the volume, to fuse with the landscape, to view nature with a new beatitude of spirit, and thus to envision a universe of plenitude, of "benign holy powers." Poems such as **"Mountains,"** **"Gnat-Psalm," "Skylarks," "Full Moon and Little Frieda,"** and **"Wodwo"** present nature as benevolent, transfigured by a newly won sense of freedom wherein the psyche of the persona is not subject to an emotional dependency or ego dependency upon either the environment or cultural givens, but is rather a bemused spectator who can view nature as a soothing companion because of an already achieved calmness of mind. The persona of part III, like the adept of Japanese Zen, views nature "as a friendly, well-meaning agent whose inner being is thoroughly like our own, always ready to work in accord with our legitimate aspirations," in the words of D. T. Suzuki.[54] This is the result of what Thomas Merton has called Zen's "ontological awareness of pure being beyond subject and object, [its] immediate grasp of being in its 'suchness' and 'thusness.'"[55] In **Wodwo** Hughes finds the serenity of Zen preferable to a culture where repressed libido periodically erupts into mass violence, and a necessary healing balm for a distressed psyche.

"Skylarks" and **"Gnat-Psalm"** in part III of **Wodwo** are similar in the ability of the central persona to revel in a sense of identity with the animal or insect viewed. In a totally absorbed state of mind, the persona participates in the activities of the perceived object. In Zen this is the contemplation of the object in its *sono-mama* state, in the broadest and deepest aspects of the "situation as it finds itself," in the words of Suzuki; it is an experience of an "underlying sense of identity" with the perceived object most often found in haiku artists such as the eighteenth-century Zen poet Bashō.[56] In section IV of **"Skylarks,"** for instance, the persona's

visionary gaze parallels the upward flight of the lark and its downward exhaustion in a sense of communality with the lark's energetic aspirations:

> Dithering in ether
> Its song whirls faster and faster
> And the sun whirls
> The lark is evaporating
> Till my eye's gossamer snaps
>   and my hearing floats back widely to earth
>
> After which the sky lies blank open
> Without wings, and the earth is a folded clod.

At the conclusion of the poem the persona attains such a state of sympathy and harmony with the larks' escapades that he recognizes in the arc of their efforts a metaphor for the entire joyous agony of life, a paying back with their labor the life-principle that gave them the breath of existence.

Similarly, in **"Gnat-Psalm,"** the persona's absorption in the frenetic, untiring activities of the gnats inspires him to create a metaphor for the totality of life as an unceasing expenditure of energy:

> O little Hasids
> Ridden to death by your own bodies
> Riding your bodies to death
> You are the angels of the only heaven!
> And God is an Almighty Gnat!
> You are the greatest of all the galaxies!
> My hands fly in the air, they are follies
> My tongue hangs up in the leaves
> My thoughts have crept into crannies

When one's thoughts have "crept into crannies" one experiences a fusion of psyche and landscape, a sense of *ātman* self-identity with the environment. Hughes may have been meditating upon an often repeated passage of Suzuki's where he contrasts Bashō's ability to make his ecstatically absorbed contemplation of a flower a *sono-mama* unitive experience of the entirety of the situation in which the flower is found with the analytic Tennyson ("Flower in the Crannied Wall"), who must pluck his flower from its cranny and surround it with abstractions.[57]

In **"Gnat-Psalm"** the gnats, environment, and persona also fuse with the poet's moment-to-moment activity of writing the poem. All are at work "Scrambling their crazy lexicon" in an expenditure of joyous suffering; insistent relative clause repetitions reinforce a frenetic tone wherein everybody is "everybody else's yoyo." The persona discovers that the gnats "are their own sun / Their own brimming over / At large in the nothing." The solar fire motif heightens the import of the self-consuming energy of the gnats by fusing it with the self-consuming energy of nature in the poem. The gnats in their sacrificial energy are "giving their bodies to be burned"; their wings are "blurring the blaze" even as the fiery energy of the sun "blasts their song." This is similar to the vision of the world as a sacrificial fire of energy in the Chāndogya Upanishad (5:4-8); Hughes himself once alluded to the "Heraclitean/Buddhist notion that the entire Universe is basically made of fire."[58]

"Gnat-Psalm" is an apt illustration of what the ninth-century Chinese Zen master Rinzai called "sincerity," a placing of one's whole being into action in the moment, holding nothing in reserve. The final image of the gnat's dizzying fury as rolling the persona's skull into outer space approximates Rinzai's "true man of no-title" who pervades the entire world of time and space.[59] In utter sympathy with the tarantellalike joyous suffering of the gnats, the persona achieves an *ātman* identity with the created universe, a perception so fully and ecstatically experienced as to indicate a state of *satori*.

Both "Skylarks" and "Gnat-Psalm" employ the casuistical tendency of Zen to express the transcendence of dualistic thinking through expressions of negations. In section IV of "Skylarks" the persona views the upward flight of the lark as "Scrambling / In a nightmare difficulty / Up through the nothing." The psalmody in "Gnat-Psalm" is "of all the suns," of a unitive experience possible because initially the gnats are "their own sun / Their own brimming over / At large in the nothing." Their bearded faces weave and bob "on the nothing." The monism behind this overspill of the subjective onto the objective is what negates the objective universe into "no matter" and creates a sea of "nothing." The casuistical reasoning employed in these uses of negations parallels that used by Nāgārjuna in his doctrine of the "Eight No's," which Suzuki compares to seeing things in their *sono-mama* "suchness" or "allness."[60] According to Suzuki, what is accomplished by such negating is a transcendent, godly affirmation of life, for whereas temporality is always becoming, changing or negating itself moment by moment, "The eternal must be an absolute affirmation which our limited understanding defines in negative terms."[61] The complete negation is thus "no one time" or "no one thing"—an unchanging, all-encompassing fullness, an allness of benign nature in an absolute present. Through the use of Zen casuistry, the exuberant tone, and the fusion of persona and landscape with the activities of the gnats, Hughes successfully conveys the most fully realized experience of *satori* in *Wodwo.*

Unlike the worried persona of "Sugar Loaf" in part I, the persona of "Mountains" admires the mountains' detachment from the world of human emotions and nature's cycle of birth and death and responds warmly to their peace and contentment. Both mountains and persona are oblivious to all striving or anxious yearning for temporal rewards; they are at home in an essential selfhood that cannot be disturbed by the flux of the phenomenal world. Mountains, often in the history of literature a symbol for the integrated self, here represent an integration of self and cosmos. A fresh ambiguity in the first lines of the poem reinforces this integration. It is impossible for the reader to tell if the configuration of stones, which becomes a pointing finger, leads the persona's gaze up the mountain's shoulder to the sleeping divinity believed by primitives to be residing in the center or up the persona's shoulder to his own eye. A both/and congruence of perceiver and object is intended.

Both "Full Moon and Little Frieda" and "Wodwo," the closing poems of *Wodwo,* present affirmative experiences of congruence with a benign nature. The persona of "Full Moon and Little Frieda" views the child as a "mirror," a brimming pail of offering, who gazes at the moon, the largest reflecting object in the cosmos available to the naked eye. The resulting astonishment at the recognition of an identity of mirroring artworks is very striking and describes another experience of *satori,* of the undifferentiated original essence of the cosmos, at times called by Buddhist poets the "full moon of suchness."[62] When little Frieda speaks the word "moon," one of the first words she ever articulated as a toddler, subject and object, self and environment merge in ecstatic recognition of self-in-other, in the clarity of spotless, mutually reflecting mirrors. The cows that loop the hedges "with their warm wreaths of breath" earlier in the poem convey an almost nativity-scene sense of the purity and supportiveness of a benign nature in attendance. The cows, sacred in Oriental symbology as representations of the plenitude of creation, are an apt background for Frieda's offering of self as a brimming pail of youthful purity to an equally pure moonlight.

Hughes has stated that his objective in writing "Wodwo," the final and title poem of the volume, was to catch this "half-man half-animal spirit of the forests," originally from *Sir Gawain and the Green Knight,* in a moment of self-discovery, and with a sense of bewilderment as to just what *is* to be its relationship to the world it is in the process of discovering.[63] In the poem the Wodwo discovers itself *as* it discovers the world; both experiences, identical when the *ātman* is awakened in the "exact centre" of existence, lead to the Wodwo's discovery that it "can go anywhere" and that it seems "to have been given the freedom of this place." As "exact centre" of existence-for-the-self, the Wodwo is the generator, the creator of its own universe, moment by moment. This frees it to inspect, rather than accept unthinkingly, the assumptions and beliefs of different cultures—and frees it especially from acquiescing to a Western goal-oriented adventure mythos tainted by aggression. With such freedom the Wodwo becomes, like Hughes himself, the peripatetic, eclectic anthropologist.

Though poems placed earlier in the ordering of part III of *Wodwo* do not relate instances of *satori* fusion with the landscape, they usually articulate positions of self-assurance and self-control from personae exercising calm judgment. Only in **"Gog," "New Moon in January,"** and **"Karma"** do personae express moods of agitation, and in each case the disquiet is resolved, unlike part I, in the individual poems themselves. Many of the more baffling poems are influenced by Oriental concepts.

In **"Karma"** the poet's meditation upon the sufferings and carnage created in a "hundred and fifty million years" of human civilization is the Buddhist retracing of time and karmic bondage to suffering (*pratiloman*) in order to absorb it and arrive at the timeless, the point before temporal duration where liberation is possible.[64] Then, by wiping away the dust of all earthly objects from the karmic mirror, as in the *Sidpa Bardo*,[65] one attains the objectless state. In **"Karma"** the persona experiences acutely the legacy of war; his suffering is so intense as to dislocate time and causality onto the plane of surrealistic nightmare, as in part I. But unlike part I, in **"Karma"** the persona solves his own problem in the poem itself. Unable to find a rationale or augury (the "poulterer's hare" knows nothing) to make this legacy of pain comprehensible, the persona finally achieves a quietude of spirit in a "seamless" state transcendent of the stitchings of time and causality. By absorbing the pain, instead of refusing the blame, the persona is finally able to stand firm in an assertion that the answer is "Not here," not available to analytic reasoning. At this point the persona's consciousness has achieved the objectless state of "the mirror's seamless sand." Wiping clean the dust of phenomenality from the karmic mirror is a favorite Zen simile for the process of attaining the objectless state of transcendence, as in the following verse by the Zen poet Yoka:

> The mind is an organ of thought and objects are set
> against it:
> The two are like marks on the surface of the mirror;
>   When the dirt is removed, the light begins to shine.
> Both mind and objects being forgotten, Ultimate
> Nature reveals itself true.[66]

Section I of **"Gog"** is a meditation on the dragon of Revelations 12:4 who has been awakened by the Christian Logos-God's assumption of total power ("I am Alpha and Omega": Rev. 1:11; 21:6; 22:13) and his expulsion of the world and the flesh to the sphere of the devil. The world of created matter becomes a world of "motherly weeping" and uncontrolled action, for which the dragon suffers in the form of a consciousness of guilt and fear: "I do not look at the rocks and stones, I am frightened of what they see." But the persona of section II (British edition only) no longer suffers from this aversion to the phenomenal world: "The stones are as they were. And the creatures of earth / Are mere rainfall rivulets, in flood or empty paths." At this point the persona experiences a *śūnyatā* state of personality

dissolution and a recognition of the fullness of all creation: "The atoms of saints' brains are swollen with the vast bubble of nothing." Apocalyptic writings of individual converts can no longer harm. In this state of dissolution the persona also recognizes that the dust of eros in the phenomenal world darkens the karmic mirror with "Death and death and death—." The "bright particles" of the dust that is "in power" produce the alluring "eyes and / Dance of wants" that ultimately lead to the dissolution of the grave.

Section III of **"Gog"** (also British edition only) is a prayer to the unborn child of Revelations 12:1-5, who is to "rule all nations with a rod of iron" and cast the dragon Gog from heaven. But the persona hopes that this quester will accomplish more than the Revelations prophecy of an aggressive conqueror; here he hopes that the child will be strong enough to penetrate beyond the illusory phenomenal world of love/death and its ultimately destructive energy. Because Christianity represses instinctual life, questing in a Western goal-oriented fashion in the temporal world will cause destructive outbursts of repressed libido: the quester's horse is "shod with vaginas of iron," the grail is "fanged," and it resides in an environment dominated by the "salt milk drug of the mothers." A better path would be to follow the *Bardo* exhortation to regard the phenomenal world as *māyā* or illusion and avoid entering the womb door into that world. By avoiding the womb door the initiate attains a supernormal birth into the world of the Clear Light, the *nirvana* release from rebirth.[67] In section III of **"Gog"** the persona advises the child to pierce the veil of phenomenality. Whereas Coriolanus relented from conquering Rome at his mother Volumnia's request, the child quester should be even more nonviolent; he should pierce with his awakened understanding through the temporal world of *māyā* and refrain from acting. He is exhorted rather to "follow his weapons toward the light," which in context is an alternative to octopus maw, cradle, and womb wall of *māyā*—perhaps the "*Dharma-Kāya* of Clear Light," the state of nirvanic illumination in the *Chikkai Bardo*. The ending of section III, however, indicates that the child is too blinded by his cultural givens to attain any liberation: his compass is his "lance-blade, the gunsight" and will only result in endlessly recurring cycles of destruction. The only "light" he follows is the one-sided rationalism of his religion and his Western culture. A soured attitude toward Christianity's banishment of the instincts predominates in the tone of **"Gog,"** especially in section III, but in sections II and III the persona is in control of his subject matter, exercising firm judgment.

As with the three sections of **"Gog,"** the progression of the three sections of **"Song of a Rat"** constitutes a penetration to a higher comprehension of reality based upon an Eastern model. The situation presented in section I is that of the trapped rats of the short story **"Sunday."** Yet the persona of section I, in contrast to the callow Michael, has compassion and pity for an animal too dependent upon its relationship with the physical environment to acquire an Oriental consciousness. "'This has no face, it must be God'" and "'No answer is also an answer'" are modernizations of ancient Zen *kōan* designed to destroy human dependence upon logic and objectivity en route to *satori,* as in Eno's *kōan* "Show me your original face before you were born," in response to Ming's request for instruction, or Shên-kuang's perfect silence in response to Bodhidharma's request to his pupils to exhibit their greatest insights, or the silent nonlectures on *satori* delivered by Yakusan and Hayakujo.[68] *Kōan* are unanswerable, designed to reveal the limited contexts in which human reason operates, and to promote the realization that all authority, truth, and motivation must come entirely from within the self, not from external authority. By trying to escape its predicament the rat is merely pitiable, until it achieves a sudden moment of understanding, presented in section II, which differs markedly from the rat's resignation in **"Sunday."**

In **"The Rat's Vision,"** section II of **"Song of a Rat,"** a moment of insight into the meaninglessness of what is now perceived as a desolate, alienating landscape causes a withdrawal into a subjectively realized personal godliness or *ātman,* a "Forcing" of "the rat's head down into godhead." Paralleling this is a loss of the rat's sense of dependency upon the farmyard environment, due to a new perception of the futility of remaining in a futureless and fatalistic pastoral scene, now an illusory "wobbling like reflection on water."

The imagery and symbolism of section III, **"The Rat's Flight,"** indicate that the rat has fled the temporal world. The rat supplants hell by casting its material body to the dogs while achieving a state "Never to be buried" as "the Shadow of the Rat / Cross[es] into power." This psychological process is attended by thunder and lightning imagery, standard procedure for instances of *ātman* illumination in the Upanishads and of *satori* in Zen.[69] The rat no longer screeches in his trap; he has attained a spiritual body and has freed himself by trusting to inner powers and self-reliance. In Hindu mythology the rat, because of its uncanny ability to overcome obstacles and find a route into the bolted granary, is the theriomorphic counterpart of Ganeśa, "The Lord and Master of Obstacles," son of Śiva and his consort.[70] If Hughes deliberately intends a reference to the Jungian archetype of the Shadow in section III, the reference is appropriate, for when the Shadow crosses into conscious life in Jungian psychology, the formerly unconscious abilities and energies become integrated into a higher state of consciousness, and with a new feeling of power.[71] The three parts of **"Song of a Rat,"** one of the very few poems Hughes wrote soon after Plath's suicide,[72] recapitulate the structural organization of **Wodwo.**

As in sections II and III of **"Song of a Rat,"** the persona of **"You Drive in a Circle"** recognizes the barrenness of temporality. As he careers through sheets of rain in a rural landscape, he realizes that roads offer a change of place not worth the taking, that the resistance of the elements is not worth the expense of energy, and that the scenery of sheep-filled moors contains for him only the futility of an unconscious obeisance to animal and vegetable function. This persona no longer fears landscape or animals, as in part I of **Wodwo;** with Buddha-like compassion and pity he addresses the sheep's enchainment to instinctual processes that go nowhere. A recognition of the yogic *īshwara pranidhāna,* the God within the self as the transphenomenal ground of all being, is the destination abandoned by the persona when he opened his automobile door. The fact that he does realize this during his journey indicates that he is beginning to acknowledge that inner self as the source of wisdom. The last line of the poem, "Your destination waits where you left it," echoes a line from *The Zenrin* on the inner location of wisdom: "If you do not get it from yourself, / Where will you go for it?"[73]

The persona of **"You Drive in a Circle"** also recognizes the necessity of merging subject and object within the self as he characterizes the low rainclouds as "the mist-gulfs of no-thinking." The word "no-thinking" is a precise term in Buddhist thought: both *munen* and *acintyā* mean literally "no-thinking" or "beyond thinking" and are aspects of the experience of Oriental Enlightenment dealing with the merging of rationality and irrationality, subject and object, when the spiritual self penetrates through the analytic thinking of consciousness and one achieves an intuitional state of self-identity with the universe.[74] The persona at the conclusion of **"You Drive in a Circle"** realizes that "Everything is already here"—within the subjective self's intuitional powers, which have no necessary "anchor" in the temporal world.

One final poem influenced by Oriental concepts is **"Theology,"** the opening poem of part III of **Wodwo.** Unlike the serpent of **"Reveille"** in part I, the serpent of **"Theology"** ends rather than initiates a temporal process by digesting the Christian myth of the Fall and sloping off to another realm, a private "Paradise" unencumbered by the complaints of a peevish God. The serpent's power to isolate himself from the historical process and the collocation of his smiling with his private paradise suggest that the paradise alluded to is the Western Paradise of Amitabha, the realm away from historical time in the Pure Land School of Chinese Buddhism. In the **"White Lotus Ode,"** a poem typical of the Pure Land School, whose title Hughes alluded to in an early poem,[75] the compassionate smile and transcendent abode of Amitabha is available to all those wandering in the depths of temporality who invoke his name. To those confined by "the body's oppressive sorrows" Amitabha offers "a spiritual body" in a paradise "brightened with gladness"; he "sends his smile out to the dwellings of the suffering" and "draws every burdened soul up from the depths / And lifts them into his peaceful abode."[76] The snake of **"Theology,"** able to slough the skin of temporality, the "dark intestine" of Western cyclic renewal through temporal birth/death, is closest to Ananta or Śeśa, the Hindu cosmic snake, who resides in the supratemporal realm. Viṣṇu dreams the lotus dream of the universe while reposing on Ananta. As Balarama, half brother of Kriśna, rests lost in thought beneath a tree on the ocean shore, the immortal serpent essence of Śeśa crawls out of his mouth and returns to the paradisal Abyss.[77]

The remaining part III poems, though not influenced by Oriental concepts, are similar in their recognition that goal-oriented striving in the temporal world of Western *wyrd* is folly. **"Heptonstall,"** the town whose graveyard houses the remains of Sylvia Plath, is a "black village of gravestones" in which the only comfort and surety is the meaningless rain of mutability. Viking invaders in **"The Warriors of the North"** have tainted Western culture with the anal obstinacy, covetousness, and rapacity behind their urge for conquest. This taint affects the future: following Weber and Tawney, Hughes intimates that the intense worldly industriousness required by Calvinism and other Protestant sects as proof of Election differs very little from the avarice that attends the heroic urge for conquest. The wolves of **"The Howling of Wolves"** are pitiable; unlike the feared carriers of ancestral evil or reempowering wolf mask divinities of **"February"** in *Lupercal,* these wolves are uncomprehending creatures living by blind instinct. The landscape of **"Pibroch"** is destitute, worthwhile only as a veil of materiality to be pierced by the "staring angels" of one's visionary thoughts. Hughes finds the mind/spirit dichotomy of **"Kreutzer Sonata"** to be a laughable, self-castrating process of mutual cancellation, the product of the delusions of unenlightened, analytic reason. The three sections of **"Wings"** argue that the advancements of twentieth-century philosophy, literature, and science in the West attest to contemporary alienation from any form of ancestral wisdom, for each individual is now hopelessly isolated in existential agony (Sartre in section I) in a universe the teleology of which humans are incapable of understanding (Kafka in section II), but whose scientific advancements have blasted humans to star vapor (Einstein in section III).[78] The persona of **"New Moon in January"** utters the faint shriek of Shelley's "Epipsychidion" in the hope of transcending the temporal world of blood and death through inner powers. With the single exception of

"New Moon in January," the personae of these part III poems articulate the folly of goal-oriented involvement in Western culture with self-control and calm judgment.

In *Wodwo* the central persona bids "Goodbye to the cenotaphs" as he disencumbers himself of failed cultural beliefs in the wake of world wars and relocates final authority within the strength of an awakened inner self. Like the French surrealists, Hughes reverts to the dream world and subconscious energies to find a more direct, emotionally true mode of expressing the psyche's participation in external reality than could be had through the conventions of realism and naturalism. He supersedes the surrealists in constructing a complex formal design where shamanic journey and heroic quest meet in psychodrama, in the story of the soul's salvation. At the core of *Wodwo* resides a unique psychological and epistemologic movement from Western dualism to an Eastern subjective monism, as an antidote for an overly aggressive Western culture that has lost contact with the psyche's needs for wholeness and inward development. We comprehend this movement through the esthetics of the formal design, in recognizing how Hughes employs his imaginative resources in developing the changing relationship of persona to landscape. *Wodwo* contains no mimesis of "normal" reality, nor an imitation of life that incorporates any evaluation of conduct according to Western social mores. The more Hughes becomes the eclectic anthropologist, the more modernist form underlines and conveys meaning.

Hughes was not able in the sixties to sustain the serene vision of a benign nature that he achieved in part III of *Wodwo.* He completed an adaptation of the bloody psychodrama Seneca's "Oedipus" for Peter Brook in 1968, and then the deaths of his companion Assia and her child Shura in March of 1969 caused him to abandon the more positive ending that he had planned for his Crow sequence.[79] The *ātman,* the active organizer of perception within the self, is what Crow, imprisoned in his empirical eye, cannot attain. Hughes will once again use folklore surrealism, but in an entirely different way—to reveal Crow's inability to transcend his instinctual cravings and rational, dualistic thinking, and to specify the scientific and religious causes of aggression in Western culture. An extreme, almost Jain-like loathing of Western cultural enterprises will continue in *Crow* and in the main action of *Gaudete,* until *Orpheus* (1973) and the *Gaudete* **"Epilogue"** (written in 1975) revise this position. Achieving a state of serenity will be the goal of the highly syncretic poetry of the mid- and late seventies.

In *Wodwo* Hughes is not asking us to exchange our Bibles and pocket calculators for the loincloths of Oriental asceticism; he is clearing a fresh path for an important revolution in perception that can free the individual from unconscious habituation to failed values. He is also suggesting that we can acquire a self-control that can lead to a mastery of our instincts, emotions, and destinies. The Wodwo may be a pacifist given to reflection and meditation, but there is much quiet strength in the resolve to live through involved, moment-by-moment cognition rather than according to the usual unreflective acceptance of cultural givens. The Wodwo's opposite is Crow, who expects to achieve wonders through an uncritical, conventional involvement in the myths of his culture.

The poems of Wodwo indicate that the *Bardo Thödol* and the *ātman* of the Upanishads taught Hughes a wisdom similar to that of Blake's Los, who will not "Reason & Compare," for his "business is to create" (*Jerusalem*: plate 10). Perception in part III of **Wodwo**, as in late Blake, is an *active* process of seeing reality as an extension of the imagination's power to unify and transform, not a passive ingesting of empirical facts and concepts. This transformation of the outer world through an awakened imagination in part III of **Wodwo** prefigures the third phase of Hughes's story of a soul. But Hughes is not able to attain this enlightened mode of perception again until the mid-seventies, in the **"Epilogue"** of **Gaudete.** Before foregoing the surreal, kinetic energies of the sixties, Hughes delineates the outward scientific and religious causes of Western aggression in the mythic satire of **Crow** and in the sexual escapades of the changeling Reverend Lumb in **Gaudete.**

Notes

1. Hughes, "Dylan Thomas's Letters," review of *The Selected Letters of Dylan Thomas,* ed. Constantine Fitzgibbon, *New Statesman,* 25 November 1966, p. 733.

2. See Louise Bogan, "Verse," *New Yorker,* 30 March 1968, p. 137; J. M. Newton, "Ted Hughes's Metaphysical Poems," *Cambridge Quarterly,* 2 (Autumn 1967), 401; John Ferns, "Over the Same Ground," *Far Point,* 1 (Fall/Winter 1968), 69; Anthony Hecht, "Writers' Rights and Readers' Rights," *Hudson Review,* 21 (Spring 1968), 211-13.

3. Hughes married Sylvia Plath on Bloomsday, 16 June 1956; they moved to Devon in early September 1961. Sylvia's letters to her mother in September and October of 1961 indicate that they enjoyed the change immensely, although much work was necessary both inside and in the garden. Hughes, the son of an expert carpenter, made some of their furniture. Plath wrote to her mother that "Snow" presents "the *feeling* of being lost and struggling against terrific unknowns and odds, something most people feel at one time or another. I find it the most compelling of Ted's stories because it *fits* one's own experience so beautifully" (Plath, *Letters Home,* pp. 427-32).

The narrator of "Snow" does his dreaming (writing?) on a "farmhouse sort of chair," but hasn't dreamt much about his twenty-third and twenty-fourth years, and nothing at all from his twenty-sixth onward. Hughes, born 17 August 1930, was twenty-six when he married Plath. The narrator's discrepancy between his present age and his age when appearing in dreams may simply indicate that he hasn't yet achieved enough distance from recent events to make them available to his dreaming. But he also has the "working hypothesis" that he is a partly amnesiac survivor of a plane crash. Whether the crash that numbs recent memory has any clear reference to Hughes's marriage or his private life is uncertain, but at one point the narrator considers that his chair may be a "harness," "invented" between his twenty-sixth birthday and the crash. The clarity of the surreal dislocation invites biographical speculation.

4. Hughes, "Vasco Popa," *Tri-Quarterly,* 9 (Spring 1967), 204-5.

5. "Snow" was first published in *Introduction* (London: Faber and Faber, 1960); "The Rescue," *Observer,* 29 October 1961; *The Wound,* broadcast 1 February 1962; "Bowled Over," recorded 29 August 1962 for Argo Records' *The Poet Speaks*; "The Green Wolf," *Observer,* 6 January 1963 (as "Dark Women").

6. Translated by Anna Balakian in her *Surrealism: The Road to the Absolute,* p. 111.

7. Breton, "Manifesto of Surrealism" (1924), in André Breton, *Manifestos of Surrealism,* trans. Richard Seaver and Helen R. Lane, pp. 22-23.

8. See note 1.

9. Balakian, *Surrealism,* pp. 152ff.; Balakian, *Literary Origins of Surrealism,* pp. 14-37.

10. Hughes, "After Lorca," *Poetry,* 103 (December 1963), 154-55.

11. C. M. Bowra, *Primitive Song,* pp. 88, 92.

12. *Listener,* 3 May 1962, p. 781.

13. Hughes, "Tricksters and Tarbabies," p. 35.

14. Eliade, *Shamanism,* pp. 33-34, 64-65, 76, 95.

15. *Listener,* 29 October 1964, pp. 677-78.

16. Claude Lévi-Strauss, *Structural Anthropology,* trans. Claire Jacobson and B. G. Schoepf, pp. 181-83.

17. Campbell, *Hero,* pp. 30, 35-36; *Masks: Creative,* p. 362.

18. Hughes, *Wodwo* (New York: Harper and Row, 1967), p. 7. Subsequent citations derive from this edition.

19. Hughes, "A Fable," *Times Literary Supplement,* 9 September 1960, p. 70. The American and British editions of *Wodwo* contain slightly different poem selections. The Harper and Row edition contains "Root, Stem, Leaf" and "Scapegoats and Rabies," both of which are omitted in the Faber and Faber edition; the British edition contains "Logos," not printed in the American edition, and adds sections II and III of "Gog." Otherwise the two editions follow the same sequence of poems, stories, play, and poems, with no line variations. Pagination differs.

20. Campbell, *Masks: Creative,* pp. 121, 553, 636, 647.

21. Hughes, "The Poetry of Keith Douglas," *Listener,* 21 June 1962, pp. 1069-70; "The Crime of Fools Exposed," pp. 4, 18; untitled review of *Men Who March Away,* p. 208.

22. Hughes, "Modern Poetry," *BBC Talks for Sixth Forms,* prod. Tom Butcher, recorded 24 May 1963.

23. Hughes, "On Writing for Radio," an unscripted interview with Anthony Thwaite, recorded 16 January 1963 by the BBC, transcribed from a teledictaphone recording.

24. For well-documented summary discussions of Freud's thoughts on aggression and the thanatos death instinct, see Liliane Frey-Rohn, *From Freud to Jung,* trans. F. E. Engreen and E. K. Engreen, pp. 126-32; Richard Wollheim, *Sigmund Freud* (New York: Viking Press, 1971), pp. 206-13. The principal source for Freud's comments on the repetition-compulsion organic drive is the *New Introductory Lectures on Psycho-analysis,* trans. W. J. H. Sprott, pp. 133-39.

25. D. T. Suzuki, *Mysticism: Christian and Buddhist,* p. 28.

26. Hume, *Thirteen Principal Upanishads,* pp. 42ff.

27. Patanjali, *The Authentic Yoga,* trans. P. Y. Despande, pp. 41 ff.; Ernest Wood, *Yoga,* pp. 43-44, 72.

28. Suzuki, *Living by Zen,* pp. 46-88; Suzuki, "The Oriental Way of Thinking," *Japan Quarterly,* 11 (1955), 51-58.

29. Heinrich Zimmer, *Myths and Symbols in Indian Art and Civilization,* ed. Joseph Campbell, pp. 175-84.

30. Faas, "Ted Hughes and Crow," p. 15; rpt. Faas I, p. 204.

31. Reprinted in Hume, *Thirteen Principal Upanishads,* p. 142. The brackets are Hume's. See also Chāndogya Upanishad (2.21.4), in ibid., p. 199.

32. Wood, *Yoga,* pp. 60-61, 68ff.

33. Suzuki, *Essays in Zen Buddhism, Second Series,* ed. Christmas Humphreys, pp. 30-36; Suzuki, Erich Fromm, and Richard De Martino, *Zen Buddhism and Psychoanalysis,* pp. 17-18, 49-56.

34. Frazer, *Golden Bough,* abridged ed., pp. 628-29, 664.

35. Robert Graves, *The White Goddess,* pp. 169, 176.

36. Knight, *Practical Guide to Qabalistic Symbolism,* I, 90-94; Dion Fortune, *The Mystical Qabalah,* pp. 139, 156-57.

37. Suzuki, *The Essentials of Zen Buddhism,* ed. Bernard Phillips, pp. 327, 396, 400.

38. Eliade, *Shamanism,* pp. 58-64, 434-36; Campbell, *Masks: Primitive,* pp. 334ff.

39. Eliade, *The Myth of the Eternal Return,* trans. Willard R. Trask, pp. 6, 9, 12-17.

40. Campbell, *Masks: Primitive,* pp. 334-49.

41. Graves, *White Goddess,* pp. 401-2. The response portion of the first stanza of the chant, not reprinted in the epigraph to "The Harvesting," specifies the greyhound as pursuer. Graves interprets this as evidence of the White Goddess as hagdestroyer of the male—nature in its predatory aspect. In "The Harvesting" a white greyhound is mentioned early in the story; it is doubtless the same dog that in the last paragraph opens its enormous white head to attack Grooby.

42. Walter H. Sokel, *The Writer in Extremis,* pp. 33-35.

43. Patanjali, *The Authentic Yoga,* pp. 19-24; Wood, *Yoga,* p. 15.

44. Eliade, *Shamanism,* pp. 62-63.

45. Jung, *Archetypes, Part I,* pp. 26-27.

46. Jung, *Aion,* trans. R. F. C. Hull, pp. 36-183, esp. pp. 182-83.

47. Frazer, *Golden Bough,* abridged ed., pp. 709-17.

48. Faas, "Ted Hughes and Crow," pp. 16-17; rpt. Faas I, p. 205. See also Plath, *Letters Home,* pp. 354, 371, 399. Hughes's libretto has unfortunately not been published to date.

49. Lama Anagarika Govinda, "Introductory Foreword" to *Bardo,* pp. lx-lxi. In the *Bardo* itself, see also p. 151.

50. *Bardo,* pp. xxxix, xl, xlvi.

51. Ibid., p. 123.

52. Ibid., pp. 161-62, 166-67.

53. Suzuki, *Essays in Zen Buddhism, First Series,* ed. Christmas Humphreys, pp. 214-66; Suzuki, *The Essentials of Zen Buddhism,* p. 359.

54. Suzuki, *Zen and Japanese Culture,* p. 350.

55. Merton, *Mystics and Zen Masters,* p. 14.

56. Suzuki, *The Essentials of Zen Buddhism,* pp. 362-63.

57. Suzuki, *Mysticism: Christian and Buddhist,* pp. 100-102; *Zen Buddhism and Psychoanalysis,* p. 12; *The Essentials of Zen Buddhism,* pp. 360-61.

58. Hughes, "Superstitions," p. 500.

59. Suzuki, "Zen and the Modern World," *Japan Quarterly,* 5, 4 (October/December 1958), 458.

60. Suzuki, *The Essentials of Zen Buddhism,* p. 358. Similar poems using negations, written by other Zen masters, are reprinted in Lucien Stryk, ed., *World of the Buddha: A Reader,* pp. 311, 353.

61. Suzuki, *The Essentials of Zen Buddhism,* p. 357.

62. Suzuki, *Living by Zen,* p. 76.

63. Hughes, *Poetry in the Making,* pp. 62-63.

64. Eliade, *Myth and Reality,* trans. Willard R. Trask, pp. 85-86.

65. *Bardo,* pp. 171, 177, 186; see also Eliade, *The Myth of the Eternal Return,* pp. 98-99.

66. Trans. and rpt. Suzuki, *The Essentials of Zen Buddhism,* p. 236. The image of wiping clean the karmic mirror is one of the most common in all of Oriental literature. See, for instance, Śvetāśvatara Upanishad, 2:14, in Hume, *Thirteen Principal Upanishads,* p. 399; Yoka Daishi's "Song of Enlightenment" in Suzuki, *Manual of Zen Buddhism,* p. 107.

67. *Bardo,* p. 188.

68. Suzuki, *Essays in Zen Buddhism, First Series,* pp. 225-26, 191, 263.

69. See Kena Upanishad, 4:29, in Hume, *Thirteen Principal Upanishads,* p. 339; Suzuki, *Essays in Zen Buddhism, First Series,* pp. 261, 245.

70. Zimmer, *Myths and Symbols,* pp. 70, 183, and plate 53.

71. Jung, "On the Psychology of the Trickster Figure," in Radin, *The Trickster,* pp. 202-9.

72. Sagar, *Art of Ted Hughes,* p. 61.

73. Reprinted in Robert Sohl and Audrey Carr, eds., *The Gospel According to Zen,* p. 28.

74. Suzuki, *The Essence of Zen Buddhism,* pp. 13-14.

75. "O White Elite Lotus," *Critical Quarterly,* 4 (Winter 1964), 319; rpt. *Achievement,* p. 318.

76. Reprinted in E. A. Burtt, ed., *The Teachings of the Compassionate Buddha,* pp. 211-12.

77. Zimmer, *Myths and Symbols,* pp. 37-38, 89.

78. See chapter 1, note 47.

79. Faas I, pp. 18, 116-17.

Bibliography

Balakian, Anna. *Literary Origins of Surrealism: A New Mysticism in French Poetry.* 2nd ed. New York: New York Univ. Press, 1966.

————. *Surrealism: The Road to the Absolute.* 2nd ed. New York: E. P. Dutton, 1970.

Bogan, Louise. "Verse." Rev. of *Wodwo,* et al. *New Yorker,* 30 March 1968, pp. 133-38.

Bowra, C. M. *Primitive Song.* New York: World Publishing, 1962.

Breton, André. *Manifestos of Surrealism.* Trans. Richard Seaver and Helen R. Lane. Ann Arbor: Univ. of Michigan Press, 1969.

Burtt, E. A., ed. *The Teachings of the Compassionate Buddha.* New York: New American Library, 1955.

Campbell, Joseph. *The Hero with a Thousand Faces.* 2nd ed. 1968; rpt. Princeton: Princeton Univ. Press, 1973.

————. *The Masks of God: Creative Mythology.* New York: Viking, 1968.

————. *The Masks of God: Primitive Mythology.* New York: Viking, 1960.

Eliade, Mircea. *Myth and Reality.* Trans. Willard R. Trask. New York: Harper and Row, 1963.

————. *The Myth of the Eternal Return.* Trans. Willard R. Trask. New York: Pantheon, 1954.

————. *Shamanism: Archaic Techniques of Ecstasy.* Trans. Willard R. Trask. Princeton: Princeton Univ. Press, 1964.

Evans-Wentz, W. Y., ed. *The Tibetan Book of the Dead.* Trans. Lama Kazi Dawa-Samdup. 3rd ed. 1957; rpt. London: Oxford Univ. Press, 1974.

Faas, Ekbert. "Ted Hughes and Crow." *London Magazine,* 10 (January 1971), 5-20.

————. *Ted Hughes: The Unaccommodated Universe.* Santa Barbara: Black Sparrow, 1980 (Faas I).

Ferns, John. "Over the Same Ground." Rev. of *Wodwo. Far Point,* 1 (Fall-Winter 1968), 66-70.

Frazer, Sir James G. *The Golden Bough: A Study in Magic and Religion.* Abridged ed. 1922; rpt. New York: Macmillan, 1951.

Freud, Sigmund. *New Introductory Lectures on Psycho-Analysis.* Trans. W. J. H. Sprott. 1933; rpt. London: Hogarth Press, 1962.

Frey-Rohn, Liliane. *From Freud to Jung: A Comparative Study of the Psychology of the Unconscious.* Trans. F. E. Engreen and E. K. Engreen. New York: G. P. Putnam's Sons, 1974.

Graves, Robert. *The White Goddess: A Historical Grammar of Poetic Myth.* 2nd ed. New York: Farrar, Straus, and Giroux, 1966.

Hecht, Anthony. "Writers' Rights and Readers' Rights." Rev. of *Wodwo,* et al. *Hudson Review,* 21 (Spring 1968), 207-17.

Hughes, Ted. "A Fable." *Times Literary Supplement,* 9 September 1960, p. 70.

————. "After Lorca." *Poetry,* 103 (December 1963), 154-55.

————. "The Crime of Fools Exposed." Rev. of *The Collected Poems of Wilfred Owen,* ed. C. Day Lewis. *New York Times Book Review,* 12 April 1964, pp. 12, 18.

————. "Dylan Thomas's Letters." Rev. of *The Selected Letters of Dylan Thomas,* ed. Constantine Fitzgibbon. *New Statesman,* 25 November 1966, p. 733.

————. "Modern Poetry." *BBC Talks for Sixth Forms.* Prod. Tom Butcher. Recorded 24 May 1963.

————. "On Writing for Radio." Unscripted interview with Anthony Thwaite. *BBC Third Programme.* Recorded 16 January 1963.

————. *Poetry in the Making.* London: Faber and Faber, 1967. Published in America as *Poetry Is.* Garden City: Doubleday, 1970.

————. "The Poetry of Keith Douglas." *Listener,* 21 June 1962, pp. 1069-70.

————. "Superstitions." Rev. of *Astrology,* by Aldus, and *Ghost and Divining-rod,* by T. C. Lethbridge. *New Statesman,* 2 October 1964, p. 500.

————. "Tricksters and Tarbabies." Rev. of *Literature among the Primitives,* and *The Primitive Reader,* by John Greenway. *New York Review of Books,* 9 December 1965, pp. 33-35.

————. "Vasco Popa." *Tri-Quarterly,* 9 (Spring 1967), 201-5.

————. *Wodwo.* London: Faber and Faber; New York: Harper and Row, 1967.

Hume, Robert E., ed. and trans. *The Thirteen Principal Upanishads.* 2nd ed. 1931; rpt. New York: Oxford Univ. Press, 1971.

Jung, Carl Gustav. *Aion: Researches into the Phenomenology of the Self.* Trans. R. F. C. Hull. Ed. Sir Herbert Read, et al. Bollingen Series XX, Vol. IX, Part II. New York: Pantheon, 1959.

————. *Archetypes and the Collective Unconscious.* Trans. R. F. C. Hull. Ed. Sir Herbert Read, et al. Bollingen Series XX, Vol. IX, Part I. New York: Pantheon, 1959.

Knight, Gareth. *A Practical Guide to Qabalistic Symbolism.* 2 vols. New York: Samuel Weiser, 1978.

Lévi-Strauss, Claude. *Structural Anthropology.* Trans. Claire Jacobson and B. G. Schoepf. New York: Basic Books, 1963.

Merton, Thomas. *Mystics and Zen Masters.* New York: Delta, 1967.

Newton, J. M. "Ted Hughes's Metaphysical Poems." *Cambridge Quarterly,* 2 (Autumn 1967), 395-402.

Patanjali. *The Authentic Yoga.* Trans. P. Y. Deshpande. London: Rider, 1978.

Plath, Sylvia. *Letters Home: Correspondence 1950-1963.* Ed. Aurelia Schober Plath. New York: Harper and Row, 1975.

Radin, Paul. *The Trickster: A Study in American Indian Mythology.* 1956; rpt. New York: Greenwood Press, 1969.

Sagar, Keith. *The Art of Ted Hughes.* 2nd ed. London: Cambridge Univ. Press, 1978.

————, ed. *The Achievement of Ted Hughes.* Athens: Univ. of Georgia Press; Manchester: Manchester Univ. Press, 1983.

————, and Stephen Tabor. *Ted Hughes, A Bibliography: 1946-1980.* London: Mansell, 1983.

Sohl, Robert, and Audrey Carr, eds. *The Gospel According to Zen.* New York: New American Library, 1970.

Sokel, Walter H. *The Writer in Extremis: Expressionism in Twentieth Century German Literature.* 1959; rpt. Stanford: Stanford Univ. Press, 1968.

Stryk, Lucien, ed. *World of the Buddha: A Reader.* Garden City: Doubleday, 1968.

Suzuki, Daisetz T. *Essays in Zen Buddhism, Second Series.* Ed. Christmas Humphreys. 1950; rpt. London: Rider, 1958.

————. *The Essence of Zen Buddhism.* London: Buddhist Society, 1947.

———. *The Essentials of Zen Buddhism.* Ed. Bernard Phillips. New York: E. P. Dutton, 1962.

———. *Living by Zen.* London: Rider, 1950.

———. *Mysticism: Christian and Buddhist.* New York: Harper and Brothers, 1957.

———. "The Oriental Way of Thinking." *Japan Quarterly,* 11 (1955), 51-58.

———. *Zen and Japanese Culture.* 1938; rpt. New York: Pantheon, 1959.

———. "Zen and the Modern World." *Japan Quarterly,* 5, 4 (October-December 1958), 452-61.

Wollheim, Richard. *Sigmund Freud.* New York: Viking, 1971.

Wood, Ernest. *Yoga.* Rev. ed. 1962; rpt. Baltimore: Penguin, 1972.

Zimmer, Heinrich. *Myths and Symbols in Indian Art and Civilization.* Ed. Joseph Campbell. New York: Pantheon, 1946.

Leonard M. Scigaj (essay date 1991)

SOURCE: Scigaj, Leonard M. "Language and Ecology: *Remains of Elmet, Moortown,* and *River.*" In *Ted Hughes,* pp. 109-44. Boston: Twayne, 1991.

[*In the following excerpt, Scigaj examines Hughes's poetry collections of the late 1970s and early 1980s, finding that the poems from this period are imbued with humility and reverence for nature.*]

DISMANTLING THE SCAFFOLDS: *REMAINS OF ELMET*

Having taken his structuralist critique of contemporary Western culture to the limit in *Wodwo* and *Crow,* and his Jungian paradigm for psychological renewal to the limits of mythic surrealism in *Gaudete* and *Cave Birds,* Hughes in the late seventies began to disassemble his superstructure and pare down his style to concentrate on his immediate responses to nature. A second marriage and work at the Moortown farm doubtless influenced this transformation, as did Hughes's well-known desire to explore the hinterlands of the psyche that makes him impatient with any achieved style. The result in his more recent poetry is a new humility and compassion for the role of all living creatures in the drama of life and death, and a deep reverence for the wonders of natural events. Instead of distanced jeremiads against rational empiricism, Hughes offers exempla of how to get in touch with our ecological second skin in *Remains of Elmet* (1979), *Moortown* (1979), and *River* (1983).

THE DECOMPOSITION PROCESS

Basic ecology within the energy transfer of trophic or feeding organisms dictates that to restore nutrients to the soil for further growth, decomposers such as bacteria and fungi must comprise the largest biomass in the food chain after producers or plant life.[1] The main storage place for the nutrients, the capacitor for the energy transfer, is of course the earth. In an early BBC broadcast (1961), Hughes characterized the earth as the strongest of the elements, and also the most passive and silent.[2] Arranged as a dialogue among the four elements, *Remains of Elmet* contains a central analogy between this ecological process of decomposition and the dismantling of Hughes's great sixties monomyth: his indictment of the empiricism and religious repression of post-Industrial Revolution Western culture. Rather than continue to ascend the rungs of his monomyth ladder, Hughes dismantles it to arrive at the rag-and-bone-shop of his heart's immediate responses to nature.

Hughes began writing the poems of *Remains of Elmet* after Fay Godwin sent him the black and white photographs of West Yorkshire that appeared in the Faber and Harper and Row trade editions. Many of the photographs reminded Hughes of his youthful haunts at Mytholmroyd, his birthplace, and nearby Heptonstall. The innocence that seemed lost through adult sophistication was recoverable in part through memory, that Proustian *recherche du temps perdu* that Hughes hints at in the dedicatory poem. In *Elmet* Hughes seemed to agree with Wordsworth's dictum that the child is father of the man, for central experiences in his youth did form his character. Conflict with the dying Industrial Revolution textile culture of the Calder Valley, childhood meditations while fishing, family experiences that included memories of the Great War, and conflicts with the very landscape of the region—the high moors and Scout Rock—divided his soul and either nurtured or impeded his spiritual growth. From these elements, discussed in part in chapter 1 of this study, Hughes developed his worldview.

Yet a curious double movement exists in *Remains of Elmet,* for while the photographs revive memories of the dying Industrial Revolution factory system of his youth, Hughes at the same time deconstructs his interest in it through the decomposition process, a central organizational motif. The culture of his youth did form his character, but it no longer manifests such a tenacious hold upon his thinking and the photographs remind him of nearly forgotten experiences that no longer motivate. While the factories are abandoned and the stone walls of the Enclosure Acts sag and fall, the creative energy awakened by Hughes's responses to that culture is enfolded back into the poet's psyche for further growth. The birds (air or spirit), rain (water), and the peculiar purplish light of the region (fire—the sun's transformational energy) comprise elements of an ecological system that assists in the process of decomposition, with Hughes identifying most with the passive receptivity of the earth.

Acceptance of the past is the main posture of *Elmet,* with the silent earth reclaiming a spent personal and cultural adventure: "Cenotaphs and the moor-silence! / Rhododendrons and rain! / It is all one. It is over" (87). "Time sweetens" (43) a process of decomposition that includes even the stone walls and the phallic factory chimneys, the most conspicuous remains of the Calder Valley:

> Brave dreams and their mortgaged walls are let rot
> in the rain.
>
> The dear flesh is finally too much.
> Heirloom bones are dumped into wet holes.
> And spirit does what it can to save itself alone.
>
> Nothing really cares. But soil deepens
> . . . . .
>
> Before these chimneys can flower again
> They must fall into the only future, into earth.

(14)

LIBERATION FROM MECHANISTIC CULTURE

The titles and content of individual *Elmet* poems are very difficult to remember, for most are variations on a few central themes repeated in almost every poem throughout the volume. One important theme concerns the liberation of the land after enslavement by the rigid machine culture of the Industrial Revolution. Within a 25-year period beginning in 1765, all the essential inventions needed to spawn the Manchester factory system, England's first, occurred: Arkwright invented his waterframe for spinning thread, Hargreaves his spinning jenny, and Cartwright his power loom. Watt was perfecting his steam engine throughout this period, adding by 1790 his final important modifications: a pressure gauge and a governor for automatic speed control. In the next decade Manchester doubled in size to 100,000 in a country of small villages.[3] These events set the stage for the nineteenth-century textile trade in the Calder Valley.

In *Elmet* Hughes evaluates the remnants of Industrial Revolution culture. The walls of the Enclosure Acts are "Endless memorials to the labour / Buried in them"; as they enchained the land both "wore to a bowed / Enslavement," with the lives of spent humans becoming a compost dropped "into the enclosures / Like manure," leaving a "harvest of long cemeteries" (33). Rock, like the land, allowed itself to be "conscripted" into "four-cornered" factory and church walls, enduring patiently the "drum-song of the looms" that mesmerized humans into replaceable machine cogs:

> And inside the mills mankind
> With bodies that came and went
> Stayed in position, fixed like the stones
> Trembling in the song of the looms.

(37)

This aggressive obstinacy and rigidity Hughes attributes in part, as he did in *Wodwo,* to continental invaders, especially the ninth-century Vikings. Hughes considers their legacy in **"For Billy Holt,"** a poem about a famous resident of nearby Todmorden (1879-1977) who epitomized the Yorkshireman's love-hate relationship with the mills. As a youth Holt worked as a weaver; as an adult he served in World War II, sailed around the world, and toured Italy on a 10-year-old horse. He wrote novels and travelogues, painted, and broadcast BBC programs. Though he received a patent for an improved shuttle for automatic weaving, he also championed workers' rights tirelessly as a socialist between the wars.

When Hughes introduced **"For Billy Holt"** in a BBC radio reading, he repeated the part of his *Elmet* introductory note about West Yorkshire having long been a hideout for criminals and nonconformists. Billy Holt took a "special pride" in the area's "laconic perversity of character," and Hughes in the poem responded by identifying some of the "Elmet" inheritance that formed the "rudiments" of that character. In a fine interweaving of ecological and anthropological insights, Hughes stated in a BBC radio reading that he used the word "Elmet" as a "naturally evolved local organism, like a giant protozoa, which is made up of all the earlier deposits and histories, animated in a single glance." The "remains" are "distortions peculiar to the ingredients," caught in the lens of the poet's eye ("Elmet").

In the poem Hughes reminds Holt that the badlands environment that he frolics in is depraved. Norse invaders reduced the land to private property and wealth, a "far, veiled gaze of quietly / Homicidal appraisal," one of the most chilling phrases in all of Hughes's poetry. Holt's exuberance is insufficient to escape a Viking inheritance that remains genetically anchored in his facial features and the limitations of his North Country culture.

The Industrial Revolution brought "the bottomless wound of the railway station / That bled this valley to death." Taking the long anthropological view, Hughes asserts that mills and railroads brought a machine rigidity that permeated the entire culture, repressed instinctual life, and ultimately led to anonymity and death— the cenotaph beneath a sky like an "empty helmet / With a hole in it" (34). The silence of earth and forests can "Muffle much cordite"; the "leaf-loam silence" can quiet the throb of the mills and the earth can accept the detritus of machine culture, the "old siftings of sewing machines and shuttles" (13).

Taoist Receptivity

Hughes's interpretation of the consequences of post-Industrial Revolution science and technology is not new; we have seen it before in **Wodwo, Crow,** and **Gaudete.** What is new is his posture of humble acceptance, the recognition that this cultural idea has lost its compulsive force as a theme in his poetry. As Lumb in **Gaudete** was compared to an oak tree, so the central persona of **Elmet** is compared to a tree that has learned the folly of fulminating and the wisdom of acceptance. In **"Tree"** Hughes feels the rhythm of nature only when he ceases his declamatory rhetoric. The persona of **"A Tree,"** pummelled by natural forces like Lear in the storm, learns to divest himself of all self-serving uses of language. His ecological second skin tells him to accept the cycles of nature, to learn how to shed the old and let it decompose in silence. So he resigns himself "To be dumb" and receptive, to let his psyche be buffeted and renewed without goal-oriented volition. His body "Lets what happens to it happen."

This earth-oriented silence and receptivity in **Elmet** derives in part from the laconic, taciturn attitude toward nature of Hughes's Yorkshire nurture, and in part from an interest in Taoism that first appears in his work in **Elmet** (see my comments on Taoism in chapter 1). Chuang Tzu, for instance, writes that when the Great Clod bellows, the wind cries wildly among all the objects of creation. One should rather plant Hui Tzu's tree, a tree too gnarled to be useful, in the field of the Broad-and-Boundless, and relax, doing nothing, wandering freely. Taoist *yu,* free and easy wandering, activates the intuition and reminds us to delight in natural processes without becoming attached or possessive. One should blend or merge with the vastness of nature, in a single flow.[4] In America, however, the Taoist maxim "go with the flow" is too often torn from its ecological roots and twisted into "follow the crowd" or "conform"—to the urgings of mass media, mass merchandizing, or situational ethics.

The Taoist tenet of merging or becoming one with the changes or flow of natural events contains an important ecological application. For the ecologists Frank Darling and Paul Sears, for instance, ecological responsibility begins when one recognizes that the individual "is not just an observer and irresponsible exploiter but an integral part" of the ecosystem.[5] Feeling integrated with our ecological second skin does not promote the utilitarian abuse of the environment that one becomes acculturated to when rational empiricism is the model for dealing with nature. Crow can only "peer" at nature because his analytic ego divorces him from it; hence nature becomes one giant laboratory to be manipulated for possession and profit.

Elmet contains other important Taoist principles. "'Think often of the silent valley, for the god lives there'" (13), the only quoted passage in **Elmet,** is a Taoist proverb that emphasizes the receptivity, acceptance, and womblike mystery characteristic of the feminine yin principle of Taoism, Lao Tzu's Valley Spirit.[6] Water emphasizes the virtues of patience and receptivity, as it follows the given contours of the land. Water at rest symbolizes clarity and perfect harmony.[7] In **Elmet** the rock, cut into a "four-cornered" sameness (37) that reflects the Protestant "hard, foursquare scriptures" (56), is no match for "the guerilla patience / Of the soft hill-water" (37).

Birds, messengers of the spirit world of air in **Elmet,** are most like Taoist sages in their capacity for free and easy wandering. In **"Curlews Lift"** the emphasis upon the birds' ability to strip away all but their cry parallels Hughes's new imperative to pare down his language to essentials. Roaming the spiritual vastness without the need to possess or analyze, the curlews merge into the allness of being. As the man observes the curlews "Drinking the nameless and naked / Through trembling bills," he appears to grasp Lao Tzu's characterization of ultimate Tao as The Nameless.[8]

In **"Widdop"** Hughes appears to assert that the world was created from nothing and that all created being returns to nothing by pointing to the flight of a gull gliding "Out of nothingness into nothingness." Nothingness in Zen and Taoism also conveys a grasp of the nondifferentiated allness of being and the merging of opposites into unity, what Chang Chung-yuan considers the goal of Taoism.[9] The flight of Hughes's gull is most reminiscent of Chuang Tzu's parable of the white colt, where the life of all differentiated being, including the lives of humans, is likened to the passing of a white colt glimpsed through a crack in the wall.[10] Birds in **"Dead Farms, Dead Leaves"** similarly appear to "Visit / And vanish." Preoccupation with selfhood ceases when one grasps the allness of being.

Light on the moors is entrancing, elevating, and gradually in **Elmet** comes to symbolize a grasp of the spiritual dimensions of the environment, illuminated by the poet's visionary presence of mind. Hughes in his BBC essay about Scout Rock identified the light on the moors as "at once both gloomily purplish and incredibly clear, unnaturally clear," helping to create an "exultant" mood ("The Rock"). Bound to the wheel of pain in a world of opposites, light scalds trees (63), is ground by the millstone of sky (66), and alternately glares and throws glooms about the moors (68). Light is the testament of the sun's energy at dawn, "Bubbling deep in the valley cauldron," (121); after rain, light appears in a "golden holocaust" of sunshine at the cloud's edge (68). In other poems light imagery carries heavier philosophical freight. Beams of light become points of entry into the visionary world beyond phenomenality in **"Heptonstall Cemetery,"** as in the Fay Godwin photo on the facing page. In **"Open to Huge Light,"** Hughes creates a mood of meditative trance where the light bears the mystic wind-shepherds "From emptiness to brighter emptiness / With music and with silence."

THE NURTURING CADDIS

When Hughes unites all the elements in his fugue—light, stones, water, and wind—he creates the most astonishing image in *Elmet,* a memorable stanza attesting to just how much we depend upon our environment as our ecological second skin. Here the four elements are the infinitely fragile and infinitely necessary "armour of bric-a-brac / To which your soul's caddis / Clings with all its courage" (16). Hughes's reference to the caddis or larval case of the caddis fly signifies a faith in the real world as the point of origin for moltings into mystic visions.

Many of the poems in *Elmet* are meditations upon the poet's own caddiscase nurture, his days as a Yorkshire youth. Hughes's memories of his childhood are mostly positive, though some of the poems contain moments of regret, sadness, a disturbing sense of menace, or even a sense of outrage. Within the ecological design of the volume, Hughes reveals in these poems a sense of nature imparting a special gift that the poet responds to with a sense of stewardship. Hughes not only accepts the gift, but does so with the conviction that his Yorkshire environs provided a very adequate, even unique training ground for his spiritual development.

From his bedroom window Hughes as a child could see a football field on a ridge above and often watched soccer games from this distance. **"Football at Slack"** pays tribute to the indomitable spirit of sportsmen who braved the rain until the sun acknowledged their persistence, while **"Sunstruck"** probes deeper into the human desire for freedom and exhilaration that surfaces in our workaday world only on weekends, with the specter of Monday labor lurking in the shadows.

Other poems present a child's first consciousness of ecological issues through allusions to Eliade's *illud tempus* moment of original Edenic purity believed by tribal cultures around the world to have existed before cultural and social divisions.[11] **"The Long Tunnel Ceiling"** records the child's first encounter with a trout, a fish believed by the young Hughes to have magical properties because of its heritage in unspoiled nature. Hughes called the trout "the authentic aboriginal in that polluted valley, the holiest creature out there in its free, unspoiled, sacred world" (**"Elmet"**). In **"The Canal's Drowning Black"** Hughes records how basic ecology teaches moral values when a childhood expedition to capture loach places him in league with his confining culture. He rests the jam jar crammed with these small fish, pilgrims from the Oligocene, "On a windowsill / Blackened with acid rain fall-out / From Manchester's rotten lung," and soon feels guilty enough to liberate the expired loach by flinging them "Back into their Paradise and mine."

Another Eliadian moment of paradisial unity with nature occurs in **"Cock-Crows."** Here the young Hughes and his older brother Gerald had climbed up a high ridge before dawn and listened to the cocks crowing in Thornber's chicken farm below at first light (**"Elmet"**). The entire poem is an epiphany of unspoiled nature rising at dawn to greet them, with the "fire-crests" and "sickle shouts" of the cocks glazed in the molten metals of the sun's rays. **"Cock-Crows"** has a sustained strength of vision that is unmistakably Hughes's donnée, a quality in his work we too often take for granted.

From this moment of Edenic beauty and purity Hughes presents the postlapsarian departure of his brother Gerald in **"Two."** After Gerald moved permanently to Australia following World War II, the brothers seldom saw each other. Though Hughes was too young to fight, World War II has always reminded him of this great sadness in his family life. From the paradisal "morning star" the pair descend to the hills to find the violence of war. Hughes communicates an irreparable rift in his family bonding by suggesting a corresponding psychic shock in his art—the shaman's loss of his talismans for Edenic contact with nature: "The feather fell from his head. / The drum stopped in his hand. / The song died in his mouth."

Hughes celebrates medieval Christianity in **"Heptonstall Old Church"** by responding imaginatively to Fay Godwin's photograph on the facing page (119). Erected in 1260, St. Thomas à Becket Church has been a ruin since a storm badly damaged its roof in 1847. Hughes sees the remaining walls as the carcass of a "great bird" that once landed with an uplifting, civilizing idea. But the energy of that civilizing idea spent itself and the remnants, a comotose Methodism, became in Hughes's childhood a force that further separated him from paradisal union with family and the natural world.

In **"Mount Zion"** Hughes recounts his "waking nightmare" of being inducted into religious conformity at the age of five (**"Elmet"**). The Heptonstall area, just a few miles from Hughes's Mytholmroyd birthplace, was one of the cradles of West Yorkshire Methodism in the eighteenth century. A church there boasts a foundation stone set when John Wesley himself preached in the area, and Heptonstall's octagonal chapel constructed in 1764 is said to be the oldest Wesleyan chapel in continuous use. Hughes's induction into Methodism is macabre, ghastly; like a calf led to the slaughterhouse Hughes in **"Mount Zion"** is marched in, scrutinized by "convicting holy eyes," imprisoned with elderly women "crumpling to puff-pastry, and cobwebbed with deaths."

Hughes controls the energy of this indictment with sardonic satire: the poem ends with the "mesmerized commissariat" engaged in "Riving at the religious stonework" to crucify a heretical cricket that dared to buck the rigid, foursquare catechism. Luckily Hughes, like Michael in the *Wodwo* story "Sunday," managed to escape regular church attendance and has never subscribed to any orthodox religion.

Nevertheless, the gloomy shadows of Scout Rock described by Hughes in his BBC radio essay derived in large part from a nexus of patriarchal menace that included foursquare scriptures, machine monotony and pollution, and wartime deprivation. All left their accents upon the ecology and environment of the area. In **"Under the World's Wild Rims,"** Hughes intimates that walking to school amid predawn darkness, factory soot, and watchful skylights became a horrific experience, like chancing upon a guarded excavation of a cultural disaster.

The geological and ecological environment of West Yorkshire affects the psychological and spiritual climate of all its inhabitants. As he introduced **"Wild Rock"** in his BBC radio presentation of *Elmet* poems, Hughes even contended that the textile trade grew up as an indigenous response to the geological and climatic environment, with Bradford worsteds a natural reply to the cold, frequent rain, and the pneumonia and rheumatism endemic to the area (**"Elmet"**). The wild energy, roughness, and penury of the West Yorkshire environment certainly affected Emily Brontë's spirit, as reflected principally in the stormy passion of Heathcliff in *Wuthering Heights*. Hughes comments upon the fatal attraction of the moors and Pennine cliffs to the Brontë family in **"Emily Bronte"** and **"Haworth Parsonage."**

Having become reconciled to the effects of his childhood environment upon his character, Hughes's visionary eye opens the Yorkshire landscape to offer a benediction for departed relatives in the penultimate poem of *Elmet*. Wind and spray impel the mind to spiritual flight in **"Heptonstall Cemetery,"** the location of the Hughes family burial ground. Here the spirits of Hughes's mother Edith, uncles Thomas and Walter, and first wife Sylvia Plath become feathers on the wings of a giant swan flying westward. The swan vision leads to a dream recounted in **"The Angel,"** the final poem of *Elmet*.

"The Angel," like the earlier **"Ballad from a Fairy Tale"** in *Wodwo*, concerns a dream premonition of Sylvia Plath's death some two years before her actual suicide (Scigaj, 253-54). The *Elmet* poem, a much less ominous recension, ends with the poet's Yorkshire roots allaying his grief. Angels are embodiments of poetic intuition and spiritual revelation in the work of both Hughes and Plath. The macabre angel, made of "smok-ing snow" and "cast in burning metal," delivers a purely visual message in the dreamscape of the poem. Part of the Angel's message concerns the enigmatic white square of satin worn where the halo ought to be. Ted and Olwyn Hughes in conversation identified this satin square as the cloth covering Plath's face when Hughes first viewed the body.

Remains of Elmet may appear a slight volume upon first reading, for the relaxed rhythms and condensed thematic interweavings might imply that Hughes was content simply to ruminate upon photographs of his past without much direction or sustained pressure. But the more one reads the volume the more its subtle austerity and delicate moods become visible, and the more one discovers that its landscapes are imaginatively arranged to suggest how the confluence of regional geology and environmental powers do color our moods and mold our character. Original images and apt cadences in *Elmet* offer the reader a glimpse of West Yorkshire that is as revealing and insightful as anything James Herriot has written. Consider the rough, tumbling cloudscapes of the region as "The witch-brew boiling in the sky-vat" (19), the soft "wobbling water-call" of the curlews invading the moor silence (28), and the wind like an anesthetic in the trees sending "swift glooms of purple" and "swabbing the human shape from the freed stones" (103).

Also consider the trancelike mesmerizing state of **"Widdop"** or **"Bridestones,"** where Hughes's intense concentration produces poems that are deeply moving, activating obscure psychic energies for absorbed communion with the land. Consider the abundance of refreshing images in cleanly articulated, uncluttered lines, as when "The light, opening younger, fresher wings / Holds this land up again like an offering / Heavy with the dream of a people" (20). Consider the delicious play of assonance throughout the volume, with Hughes moving deftly up and down the register to reveal the moody bleakness of West Yorkshire, as in "The glare light / Mixed its mad oils and threw glooms" (68). Most of all, consider the new mood of serene acceptance in Hughes, which extends to include a sympathy with the dead and with aged pensioners "Attuned to each other, like the strings of a harp" (89).

Hughes is most sympathetic throughout the volume to the vast labor of generations, the human dreams and the human suffering seen in the ruins of the culture. Words in *Elmet* mean little to Hughes without experience—the hand of Lear smelling of pain and mortality. We see this especially in **"Churn-Milk Joan,"** where linguistic deformation over time turned the *jamb* of a simple dairy farmer's payment stone into a *Joan*. A trite story developed to explain the use of Joan, a story that was an indigenous folktale product consonant with the peculiar desolate character of the moors. But for Hughes the story merits censure because "Her legendary terror was not suffered." The tale is pure fantasy, the product of weak imagining not grounded in actual experience.

Remains of Elmet is a rich glacial deposit of 50 years of Hughes's deep experience. Freed of his sixties monomyth, Hughes continued to follow the immediate responses of his spirit to compose some of his most riveting poems in the opening farm elegies of *Moortown* and the delicate riverscapes of *River*.

WORDS AND RESPONSIBILITY: *MOORTOWN*

Having developed a richly complex mythic and surrealistic interpretation of contemporary Western culture in his sixties volumes, Hughes could have continued to fashion ever more intricate, esoteric works, as Blake did in his late prophetic visions. Instead he pared his verse to a compelling meditative stringency in the taut, spare lines of the *Gaudete* **"Epilogue"** and *Remains of Elmet.* Deeper states of consciousness became accessible to his probing as he also strove to achieve a greater fidelity of words to actual human experience.

Hughes was forging his own unique response to the great postwar devaluation of language. Language has lost its vitality, has become corrupted and exhausted by advertising and mass culture. In his essay "The Retreat from the Word," George Steiner wrote that the inflated rhetoric of oratory and propaganda has similarly devalued language in the postwar world, while the triumphs of science in harnessing the natural world appear to indicate that "reality" in the West lies outside verbal language—in the forbidding and specialized languages of mathematical symbols, equations, and scientific formulae. Steiner asserted that poets should resist, as did the French symbolists, confinement to fact and objective analysis, and prove again that language contains a magical "Power of incantation." Poets should be magical enchanters who liberate subconscious energies and "pass from the real to the more real" in language that is both clear and precise.

Had Steiner written his prophetic essay in 1981 instead of 1961, he certainly would have added Hughes to this privileged list of magical enchanters and liberators. In *Moortown* (1979) language attains a depth commensurate with subjective and objective experience richly lived and powerfully felt. Hughes's considerable linguistic and observational powers work at full tilt, often restoring to language the "measure of clarity and stringency of meaning" that Steiner feels is an absolutely necessary bulwark against cultural chaos.[12]

Hughes's response to the contemporary devaluation of language is a central concern of his most recent work. True to his English sense of culture as something rooted in the character of a geographic region and the actual lived experience of its inhabitants, Hughes in both *Moortown* and *River* strove to communicate honest actual experience and deep states of consciousness in words that are neither flattened nor inflated. Three years before publishing *Elmet* and *Moortown* Hughes wrote that he prized a language created by an imagination that is "both accurate and strong," that could envision blueprints of our deepest psychic life while integrating innerworld forces with the unvarnished actual conditions for living in the outer world. Hughes endeavored to create a clean, direct poetic line that could grasp inner and outer worlds simultaneously and flexibly, and a spare, precise language that "keeps faith, as Goethe says, with the world of things and the world of spirits equally" ("Myth 2," 92).

THE FRESH SIMPLE PRESENCE

After the powerful and very unified *Crow, Gaudete, Cave Birds* and *Remains of Elmet, Moortown* at first appears a lesser work, an amalgam of previously published limited edition poems and uncollected magazine poems, some of which first appeared in the sixties. It possesses neither the epic and psychological grandeur nor the unity of subject of its predecessors. The first, second, and fourth sections of *Moortown* originally appeared as Rainbow Press limited editions— *Moortown Elegies* (1978), *Prometheus on His Crag* (1973), and *Adam and the Sacred Nine* (1979), respectively—while the third section, "Earth-Numb," reprints poems from the Rainbow Press *Orts* (1978) and from uncollected verse publications from as far back as 1963.

Yet Hughes has a purpose in combining these works, even though some of the poems in the "Earth-Numb" section remain esoteric, with their themes not fully realized. Elsewhere I wrote of the Blakean serpent alchemy in *Moortown* as a unifying principle: from the limited Beulah world of nature the poems progress through the worlds of Generation and Ulro finally to achieve the Edenic creativity of Los, with these four stages corresponding to the above four sections (Scigaj, 257-86). Hughes's struggle to find an adequate language to convey the inner and outer worlds of experience accurately and responsibly comprises another and equally significant unifying principle that functions as a reliable guide for interpreting *Moortown.*

When Hughes regularly worked in the early seventies as a farmhand on his Devon farm Moortown, managed by his father-in-law Jack Orchard, he carried a pocket journal in which he jotted down the fresh details of farm life for later use. Hughes soon switched from prose to verse jottings because he learned he was able to relive the experience more deeply in rough verse. When he tried to rework a farming experience into a poem weeks later, he found he lost much of the original freshness: his concentration gave way to inner-world considerations such as conscience while his nimble stylistic versatility began to rob the experience of its uniqueness and "assault it with technical skills." He found that his technical mastery "destroyed the thing [he] most valued—the fresh, simple presence of the experience," so he decided to discipline himself to catch the event honestly, near the moment he experienced it, and leave it in its unique freshness.[13]

The result was *Moortown Elegies,* a series of farming poems that are fine examples of Steiner's "clarity and stringency of meaning." Fidelity to the actual experience, rendered honestly but vividly, with a minimum of stylistic distortion, was a high priority for Hughes in every poem. Hughes had already written farming poems in his children's volume *Season Songs* (1974). Here vibrant description alternated with a touching sympathy that often aggrandized simple events in the natural world by adding mythic adornments or personification, or by using the pathetic fallacy or sentiment to capture the imagination of the younger reader and convey a sense of wonder and delight at nature's vitality and variety. Spring became a "tremendous skater" leaning into the curve of a new year in **"Spring Nature Notes"** or a young girl weeping rain at her coming-out party in **"Deceptions."** Hughes reworked the John Barleycorn myth in **"The Golden Boy,"** developed the quest motif in **"Autumn Nature Notes,"** rehearsed the myth of the dying vegetation god of the waning year in the stag hunt of **"The Stag,"** and personified elements of the natural world in nursery-rhyme dialogues such as **"Leaves"** and **"There Came a Day."** The poems carried the fresh clean scent of a spring shower. A light touch modulated the sentiment of poems such as **"A March Calf,"** but one saw on every page the gleaming technical mastery of the poet enriching and arranging the context.

As Hughes "keeps faith . . . with the world of things" in the opening "Moortown" section, adornments such as personification or use of the pathetic fallacy are rare. The image of the earth as an invalid surviving winter's operation derives from one of two poems (**"March Morning unlike Others"**) reprinted from *Season Songs.* Rendering in human logic the bull's dissatisfaction in **"While She Chews Sideways"** or the calf's contentment in **"A Happy Calf"** is a very slight extension of a great wealth of descriptive detail from a sequence of real-world actions sustained throughout the poem. Here the focus remains firmly fixed on the individual animal. The depiction of the cattle standing in a "new emptiness," and the uprooted farmland left with "a great blank in its memory" after the death of Jack Orchard is sober and unsentimental, earned by the entirety of the sequence.

In the opening section of *Moortown* Hughes restricted himself to recording farming events as they actually happened. By writing very near the actual event he achieved a startling accuracy of observation with a minimum of adornment. Fidelity to the actual event liberated his style and allowed him to concentrate upon the simultaneous fusion of outer and inner experience in the honest passing of the lived moment. Intense absorption in small details in the outer world individualized farm animals and revealed character in situations where most readers would lump animal behavior into rude stereotypes and abstract categories. The net effect is to cleanse and refresh the reader's perceptions, to enable the reader to live more deeply and intensely. At the same time the reader witnesses the farmhand's inner-world engagement as a steady, willing submission to the requirements of managing the farm.

"Rain," the very first poem of "Moortown," not only introduces Jack Orchard's tenacious struggle with the elements, but erects the boundary of the actual around the entirety of the section as the men erect fence posts. Hughes recollects the same event in **"A Monument,"** near the end of the opening section, as if to emphasize by formal means the boundary of the actual enclosing "Moortown." Orchard is the master farmer who shows his observant disciple how to manage nature—by plunging his bruised, soiled hands into it. Hands are levers with which to maintain the farm's ecological balance, but more importantly hands-on experience is a much surer way of immersing oneself in nature than relying upon words. Rain and mud test the mettle of the laborers while the stoic endurance of the sniffing animals nearby counsels patience. In **"Dehorning,"** the next poem, the language renders the experience faithfully and vividly because Hughes limits his writing to the simple actual occurrences. Men "Grimace like faces in the dentist's chair" as they weather the shock and commotion of cows in pain. A severed artery squirts "a needle jet / From the white-rasped and bloody skull crater" as the men remain totally absorbed in their exacting work.

The opening section instructs the reader about the limits of the actual as it engages him or her in firsthand experience. Ultimately, managing the actual works farmers to death, a fact indicated by the concluding elegies, but death is here presented as the fulfillment of a deep commitment to living. In **"A Monument"** Hughes remembers the master farmer stubbornly "using [his] life up" erecting wire fence "through impassable thicket, / A rusting limit" or "boundary deterrent." Crucified to the world, his head is "Skull-raked with thorns" while his hands, like "old iron tools" completing necessary projects, weathered to "creased, glossed, crocodile leather" striated with the scars of painful accidents, as when snapped barbed wire ripped a half-inch furrow through them (63). But his stoic endurance of pain and his commitment to managing nature earns the farmer the blessing of the White Goddess. After his death the

Goddess transforms his "'bloody great hands'" into "a final strangeness of elegance" in the concluding line of the opening section (64), an apotheosis signifying union with the feminine principle of creation.

Unlike traditional elegies such as Milton's "Lycidas" or even Lowell's "The Quaker Graveyard in Nantucket," the concluding elegies of "Moortown" restrict their focus to the actual. Hughes avoids all conventions that emphasize technical mastery over actual observation: here are no invocations to the muse, personifications of natural forces, processions of mourners, digressions on the church, or enlargements of context to include pathetic fallacy invectives against death or consoling hopes for immortality. The boundary of the poet's penetration is the actual event. Yet the restricted gaze produces poetry that steeps the reader in the lush redolence of the actual, with images plump and clean as freshly washed grapes. The poetic line is simple, effective, and satisfying because the images are neither crammed into the line nor insisted upon.

Simple natural images alternate the feel of enduring the rough weather and crises of farm management with the quiet peace and contentment of uneventful days. Cows plant themselves against the wind at the Moortown farm "like nails in a tin roof" about to blow off (11), and sheep weather a snowstorm in a shed surrounded by "clapping wings of corrugated iron" while the snow nearly succeeds in "erasing" the blind oaks (24). The anxious hurry of rapid hay bailing under threat of a storm yields to the elation of accomplishment crowned by the rain's falling "Softly and vertically silver," creating a sudden "tobacco reek" as the last load nears the barn (50). Hughes accents a contented calf's meditations on the young "pulse of his life" by observing a buttercup that "leans on his velvet hip" (41), while "Sundown polishes the hay" and "The warmed spices of earth / In the safe casket of stars" nurse a sick calf (46). When a lamb born without the will to live dies in a day, "The wind is oceanic in the elms" (55). But when a dumb calf learns to suck, the mother stills her refractory behavior as "the happy warm peace gathered them / Into its ancient statue" (48).

Instead of a selfish utilitarian appropriation of nature, the master farmer and his assistant fulfill in their husbandry the laudable ecological goal of stewardship, assisting nature with hands that function equally well in heavy labor and in the delicate midwifery of reaching into animal wombs to assist lambings. The stewards save a calf striken by scour and trapped in a disk harrow (44-46), teach a dumb calf how to suck (47-48), and save the mother of a strangled lamb trapped in the womb at birth (32-33). Often nature can manage without aid, or the weather limits midwifery to a dab of antiseptic and a run for cover in a hailstorm (37-38). Herding new lambs into a shed to save them from almost certain death in a late winter snowstorm merits a moment of satisfied prediction, for in a day or so the lambs "Will toss out into the snow, imperishable / Like trawlers, bobbing in gangs" (25).

Animal husbandry educates one to the limits of the purely natural, for Hughes becomes extremely aware of the animals' dependence upon instinct and habit, and their total lack of understanding. Lost in their cud-munching stolidity, they are indifferent to management by sympathetic human hands, and comprehend little. Their hooves are "knee-deep in porage of earth" (11). Lambs and their mothers are distrustful, anxious, and entirely unappreciative of being brought to the cover of a shed during snowstorms (17-18, 24). Lambs freed for pasture in the spring fear it; they long to return to the shed stalls of their birth (35). The lambs bleat woe as they try to identify their newly shorn mothers; lacking any real freedom or initiative, they simply "fit themselves to what has happened" (56). Rams and bulls cannot understand their balked sexuality (28-29, 52-53). Meditations upon the animal world have limits; in their shit-patched unconsciousness animals do not coax the artistic imagination to flower or soar, for they are not "the soul's timely masterpiece" (36).

Tearing consciousness away from absorption in the actual creates problems. Conscience, introspection, and memory can obstruct action and stymie participation in natural events. The assistant farmer worries himself with instances where his tardiness or physical limits result in unsuccessful calvings (8-10) or lambings (30-33, 54-55). When he meditates upon the necessary technological extensions of his hands, he finds himself caught in "a trap of iron stupidity" on his tractor (20). Simple natural events can create a wild whir of "Crazily far thoughts" but no penetration into the right cause for the surprising presence of the blue-black birth sac half-dropped from a cow's tail (26). The potentially transcendent events of **"Roe Deer"** and **"Coming Down through Somerset"** only confirm that the limits of absorption in the actual are severe; the actual sustains a "dimension" that is very ordinary (22-23) and restricted to the temporal flow (42-43). Hughes sees the physical labor and its pain etched in the folds of the master farmer's hands, but can a farmer ever extricate his mind from passive submission to the actual?

WORDS ARE THE BIRDS OF EVERYTHING

This is precisely Prometheus's problem in "Prometheus on His Crag," the second section of **Moortown.** An offshoot of his 1971 *Orghast* meditations upon the roots of Western and Near Eastern myths, the 21 short poems of "Prometheus" contain Hughes's attempt to resolve the problems of the relationship of consciousness and its wordy products to the pain, infirmities, and restrictions of actual living. Humans aspire to godlike freedoms and immortality, but live inside mortal, decaying bodies adrift in a world of pain. Perhaps the "numbness" Hughes spoke of as the motive for creating this sequence (Sagar, 147) was the numbness of living life restricted to the animal level of unawareness. Does the stewardship of nature allow life to be lived at levels above the numbingly passive submission to circumstances? Does a richer mode of consciousness exist beneath the surface preoccupation with objective analysis that Western culture valorizes? The lean language strips the poems to a stark majesty and a craggy intensity that is at once hypnotic and beguiling.

G. S. Kirk, in his Lévi-Straussian analysis of the Prometheus myth as contained in Hesiod, the oldest extant source, concludes that humans in this Greek myth lived in Edenic unity with the gods until Prometheus's cunning caused Zeus to withdraw fire from mortals and expel them. Both Zeus's withdrawal of fire from humans (after Prometheus tries to trick him with inadequate ritual food offerings), and the arrival of pain and disease (as Zeus retaliates with the vulture and Pandora), relate to the attempts of early Greeks to mediate human aspirations for divine freedoms and our actual enchainment to a world of pain. Prometheus's final return of fire to humans and his willingness to endure his daily pain mediates the opposites.[14]

Hughes dovetails the final fire theft, the pain inflicted by the vulture, and the arrival of disease and infirmity from Pandora's box by having Prometheus place the stolen fire in the wombs of females (#13) and in the potentialities of consciousness (#7).[15] Prometheus's liberation depends upon understanding the significance of what he has done and learning to mediate the opposites of aspiration and pain by developing his imaginative life. How can his salvation lie in his submission to the world of pain he has created? To some extent Hughes is utilizing the well-worked romantic myth, summarized by Northrop Frye, Harold Bloom, and countless others, of how consciousness sunders the naive unity of the mind with nature, making us aware of our separateness. The task is to transform self-consciousness into redemptive vision in the mediatory realm of the imagination.

Words, because they name discrete objects and are the tool of the reasoning mind, may reinforce a consciousness of separation and fragmentation, especially when in the service of empirical analysis, the world of Blake's Urizen. In Hughes as in Blake, this only exacerbates the loss, creating the cold equations of matter and space. Awakening to this fallen condition, Prometheus feels both fright (#1) and the strength of an individuality that paradoxically comes from sundering the Edenic unity of self and nature (#2).

Prometheus's first shout—interesting self-consciousness, voice, and language—sunders the Eden of "holy, happy notions"; in its place he develops a consciousness of the daily pain that attends existence—the vulture (#3). The shout represents the awakening of language as an instrument that can either reinforce through objective analysis a sense of separation from the world, or function as a probe toward an awareness of deeper states of being that can possibly reestablish moments of unity. For Hughes "words are the birds of everything" (#19), and Prometheus must learn to use them to become aware of deeper levels of being, not simply to scatter his thoughts into identifications of separate categories through ordinary analytic thinking—the "space-fright" of poem #19.

From Prometheus's first consciousness of language, his first "world's end shout" that awakened the vulture, the birds of words have become "what birds have ever since been, / Scratching, probing, peering for a lost world" (#3). The vulture is created by the sun's fiery energy, and as it daily splays Prometheus it creates the "headline letters" (#4) of words, the vehicle for recording either the fragmentary ordinary world, as in the endings of poems #7 and #11, or for articulating the struggle to reintegrate the self and the world of pain into the visionary unity hinted at in poem #17.

To regain his freedom Prometheus must return authority to within himself. He had recently divested himself of authority by investing it in man and God, beings in the space outside the self (#9), and this has pinned him to the rock of space, leaving freedom possible only in his "soul's sleepwalking" (#15) after enduring the daily pain of having his liver torn out. As with Sogis in *Orghast,* Prometheus must transform the pain of existence into spiritual illumination. To be human is to exist between the godly and the animal, as Sogis exists between Pramanath and Agoluz in Hughes's *Orghast* mythology (Smith, 96-97). The lizard, an animal of divination for Castaneda's Yaqui shaman Don Juan,[16] gives Prometheus an intuition of how lucky he is to be human: to be between the extremes makes possible both the expression in words of the conflict between aspiration and pain, and the possible mediation of the conflict in the realm of the imagination.

Once Prometheus receives the lizard's hint in poem #18, he is ready for his crucial moment of understanding: the recognition that the daily pain of existence, the vulture, is a "Helper" toward extending his awareness of deeper levels of being that can reunite self and world (#20). Words, though they can only articulate circling images of these altered states of consciousness (#20), are nevertheless crucial for probing the self's unacknowledged legislator within and reempowering the self to overcome obstacles.

With volcanic force Prometheus's new understanding frees him of bondage to the fragmentary actual world in the final poem. Twenty-one bulletins of "Puddled, blotched newsprint" have recorded a genuine struggle, articulated in words, toward becoming aware of deeper levels of being where self and world do not stand isolated, separate, chained in objective analysis. In the concluding lines Prometheus "balances" self and world in a floating state of unison on "peacock film," a bird whose rainbow feathers Jung identified with the reintegrated self in alchemy and Gnosticism (Jung 9a: 375).

Words Magical and Unmagical

The confrontation between the poetry of incantation and poetry occasioned by the recording of events where limited consciousness constricts vision occurs especially in "Earth-Numb," the third section of **Moortown.** Hughes introduced his BBC reading of "Earth-Numb" poems by stating that he consciously strove to develop the boundary theme: "The boundary . . . runs between awareness, and unawareness, between the life of the one and the mere circumstances of the other, and the baffled sort of collision between them."[17]

From his introductory comments in both the BBC "Earth-Numb" reading and a different, taped recording of **Moortown** poems, it is clear that what Hughes means by "awareness" and "the life of the one" concerns the ability of words to produce magical, incantatory effects that liberate repressed energies while strengthening and deepening our sense of self, our grasp of deeper powers and levels of awareness. For Hughes, poetry is "a biological healing process" that is "energizing": it creates a "final mood of release and elation," an "upbeat" psychological state that promotes well-being and success. Hughes compares poetry by analogy to the magical chants that tribal hunters recited before the hunt to hypnotize themselves into a "state of alertness and concentration of perfect confidence" that would promote success.[18]

The poem **"Earth-Numb"** receives pride of place because Hughes believed its incantatory language actually ended a period of poor success at catching salmon. The poem begins with a stillness that is electric with tension. Hughes's concentrated "searching / Like the slow sun," is about to galvanize nature into an explosive response. The language packs great power into simple, concise description. Dawn is "a smoldering fume," with birds "simmering" and sycamore buds "unsticking." All await the sun's concentrated energy, which the poet mimes with his hypnotically steady, incremental imagery. The images of a flower opening and a surgeon conducting open-heart surgery create just the right mood of delicacy and hold-your-breath tension.

Suddenly the reader is jolted by the force of Hughes's language into an essential contact with the real event, as the fish grabs the hook with a bang and "the river

stiffens alive" while a "piling voltage hums, jamming me stiff." Hughes vividly recreates the process of catching the fish with "terrifying / Gleam-surges" and "Cartwheels," as if he "were the current." The energy released in the descriptive language unites poet, fish, and reader in the moment of struggle. The mood finally relaxes as the trapped fish gags his last and his eyes absorb their final glimpse of reality.

Many poems in "Earth-Numb" reside on the other side of the boundary, where tourists, tramps, secretaries, and retirees are treated satirically for their inability to develop strong individual selves. They have negated their potential for becoming free, authentic beings and have become prisoners of cravings for food and drink (131) or the thrill of possessions (93, 102-3). Others wrap themselves in egotism (97-98), rigid religious orthodoxy (94-96), sexual conquest (101), or are left with the dregs of a life that has never cohered into a self-reliant strength of personality (99-100). Some poems remain obscure, their themes insufficiently realized (160-63), or their symbolism puzzling and inaccessible until one finds the proper referential key (111, 159, 164).

Heideggerian Language

Other poems appear to be Heideggerian extensions of Blake's critique of scientific space-time—Heideggerian because intimately concerned with the nature of language and being. For Martin Heidegger the uniform measuring of time and space into numerical units creates a "desert" of self-enclosed units, uniformly equal and indifferent, which become aggressive technological tools for the dominance of the earth.[19] Macbeth's four nightmares in **"Four Tales Told by an Idiot"** end in a fear of the scientific space he has divorced from himself—the Urizenic vacuum of Crow's "Black Beast." Technological conquest becomes a frantic digging at a black hole in space.

For Heidegger, it is the customary nature of language to bring the fourfold elements of the earth together in their nearness to the speaking subject through the "saying" of language. Though language itself has no *thinghood,* no essential being, it is at the essential core of humans' experience of the world. Words bring the elements together to constitute a simultaneous grasp of self and environment in the moment of their encounter, where past and present coalesce as one moves toward the future. Only through language can humans express their relatedness to the elements of the earth; the essence of language is relatedness, a bringing together, the expression of a potential coherence of self and the elements to constitute "world."[20]

In the last of the "Seven Dungeon Songs" the persona struggles to make the elements of the earth fuse into an essential wholeness of world that would "speak"

(Heidegger would use the word "say" or "make appear") the self's sense of relatedness in the felt moment of experience. The opening songs suggest how difficult a struggle this is, for our Western understanding of experience is otherwise. In the first song the Western babe mortally wounds the cosmic wolf "in the jaw"; here the first consciousness of language (the babe's laugh and cry) is concurrent with a sense of injury and, in the second song, the desire to dominate the wolf's "offspring," the "space-earth" of the poem's first line. The elements that should cohere into a Blakean or Heideggerian "world" lie in their separateness, in "bits and pieces," while the creative principle mourns the division in the third song and the "Tree of light" weeps in the fourth. A Macbeth-like neurotic frenzy occurs in the fifth song, with the persona desiring to "rush to and fro" to attach broken parts.

The last two of the "Seven Dungeon Songs" suggest the possibility of wholeness should the persona recognize the self as the originator of one's experience of the world. The sixth song suggests that all beyond the individual is silent until called to "world" by the self's saying, for no oracle, witnesses, rocks, birds, dust, or light cohere of themselves. They await the human call to world in the act of speech, suggested in the final song's faith that cliff, water, and all the elements could fuse with a reconstituted body to articulate the truth of actual experience. The seventh song especially conveys Heidegger's sense of the "pure simplicity" that a mature poet can experience in his awareness of language's power to speak an originative event in a poem, a simultaneous constitution of self and the elements to produce "world."[21] The "Earth-Numb" poems **"A Citrine Glimpse," "Life Is Trying to Be Life,"** and **"Song of Longsight"** are all concerned with failures to constitute the "world" of the moment; an alienation of all outside the self produces the deathly inertia of scientific measurement in the coldness of space.

"Acteon," possibly the most spellbinding individual poem in **Moortown,** presents the consequences of acculturation to a divorced, mechanistic space. Acteon's perception will never be a synergetic grasp of the other through the speech of a unified self, as it might be were Hughes to write an eighth dungeon song. The face or nodal point of coherence of the other (the finished puzzle) cannot be grasped when the self is speaking "hooverdust." Instead of uniting into a grasp of world, the puzzle pieces zigzag out of control when language speaks the speech of technological gadgetry. The elements, lacking relatedness, become devouring hounds, minions of dominance, while the technocrat speaker remains distant, unmoved, anesthetized. The children of **"Deaf School,"** because they lack the ability to hear speech and to experience hearing their own speech, are

likewise left to perform mechanistic gestures in space that will always remain separate and never cohere to a Heideggerian "world."

The predatory fish in section 1 of **"Photostomias"** (originally **"Chiasmadon"**) is depicted as a mathematical calculus, a "final solution" intent only upon his prey. The second section, however, locates a corresponding fiery agent of transformation within the unconscious of humans, a "Buddha-faced" tiger that fuses self and the elements into a coherent world where "Earth is gulping the same / Opium as the heart." The third and last section indicates that this transformative agent can empower language to evoke something akin to Heidegger's nearness, that relatedness where self and earthly elements cohere in the moment of their saying. The tiger in **"Tiger-psalm"** is a "Beast in Blossom" because, one with its environment, it pounces upon its prey with an economical, instantaneous directness. The tiger for Hughes represents an analogous human power—the seizure accomplished in the act of perception itself. More exactly, it is the Oriental act of perception that annihilates discrete objects by transforming them into a unitive vision of allness. Conceived as a dialogue between the Buddha (the tiger) and Socrates (machine-gun dialectical logic),[22] **"Tiger-psalm"** contains a tiger that "Kills like the fall of a cliff, one-sinewed with the earth, / Himalayas under eyelid, Ganges under fur."

Many of the 25 sections of **"Orts"** (the word means "table leavings") are leavings from **"Lumb's Remains,"** an early version of the *Gaudete* **"Epilogue."** Both sequences share the theme of grappling with the problems of consciousness, the erotic and aggressive components of the id, the world of pain and the inevitability of death in the quest to envision the White Goddess. In **"Orts"** the struggle to attain a clear vision of a feminine principle is still in process, and the only vision of the Goddess that the persona is capable of realizing is the dim Persephone-like figure who walks the lawn in the last section. Yet even more so than the *Gaudete* **"Epilogue,"** the poems of **"Orts"** concern attaining the power to use language accurately and faithfully to record the struggle. The eyes are always open to achieve "being" as an astonished vision of a welcoming host or Yeatsian "swan launching / Into misty sunrise" (**#1**), but brain and emotions are seldom alert enough and sufficiently in concord to seize the moment fully and articulate it exactly.

Words in **"Orts"** scatter from humans like seeds from a tree, but are these seeds living—do they articulate the real originative event—or are they senile (**#2**)? Are words granite gravestones reminding the writer of what is missing (**#3**)? Do words function as they do for many poets: as glib illusions that cause the clear "simple light" to flee as it did when the first words of aboriginal humans fragmented experience into abstractions (#**6**)? Do "the airiest words" codify into rigid orthodoxy (#**9**)? Are words shadowy masks that obscure an ulterior purpose (#**11**)?

The instincts arrive with man-eating music, a *"Grosse Fuge"* (#**7**) or a powerful express train (#**19**), but the human capacity to turn erotic charge into spiritual vision is too often lacking. Our perceptions are narrowed and our transformative powers atrophied by a culture that prizes rational consciousness—the symbolic food fed to empty coats in insipid, unvarying highway restaurants (#**5**). Though children have the bravura to believe that the words they utter will be tools for the seizure of reality, an "occupying army" of vocables, their weakly articulated visions will wear them out, will function as decomposers, not as revitalizing inspiration. Their words are infected larvae that will devolve into bacteria (#**23**).

ADAM'S WORDS: THE BIRDS OF EVERYTHING

Some of the most dazzling poetry Hughes has written appears in "Adam and the Sacred Nine," the concluding section of *Moortown*. It testifies to the power of human speech to transform the self and to ascend beyond the mundane. Here Hughes adapts the shaman's ecstatic flight to enlist supernatural aid for the purpose of creating one's "world" anew and healing self and community.

Hughes introduced selections from *Adam and the Sacred Nine* in a BBC radio reading by stating that God, who has lost patience with Adam's torpor, sends down "nine divine birds to become his guardian exemplary spirit" after all the creatures of the world have failed to convince Adam to "pull himself together and get moving."[23] The phrase "guardian exemplary spirit" specifically refers to the shaman's practice of enlisting helping spirits at the outset of his spiritual journey. Adam will revive himself through a shamanic flight that is coextensive with a revitalization of the power of language within himself.

In *Shamanism* Eliade wrote that very often American Indian or Eskimo shamans mimic the calls of birds to enlist them as guides to the world of the dead, and as vehicles to impel the upward ascent to vision. The shaman's use of such animals signifies a desire to abolish profane historical time and return to the reempowering prelapsarian moment of unity with all creatures. The birds grant the shaman the power to travel freely through earth, underworld, and sky in order to ensure the success of the flight (Eliade, 96-109).

As with Sogis in *Orghast* and Prometheus in *Moortown,* Adam will revive himself by recognizing that within his inner world he has the capacity to transform,

with the aid of language and the imagination, his "fallen" state into one of spiritual ecstasy and visionary fulfillment. Language and the imagination will enable him to mediate the contradictions of his situation and revive his prophetic "voice" when the Phoenix arrives (#**11**). Prior to this the magic of the sparkling, highly evocative language of the other birds enables Adam to integrate his faculties and reunite with the four elements to utter a Heideggerian world.

The fresh, vivid images combine with a clean poetic line that contains a wonderful combination of vitality and compression. Individualizing traits of bird species quickly and effortlessly develop symbolic dimensions, suggesting scarcely definable psychic powers in humans. The Falcon's powerful, direct flight suggests a kindred power within humans for grasping situations completely and instantaneously (think of the Mozart reference in the *Lupercal* poem **"Thrushes"**); the Skylark's long, liquid warble in flight becomes a continual labor of joyous energy to adorn the sun with its crest; the daylong flight of the Swift "Shears" its way with "Whipcrack" movements of its long, slender wings, expanding beyond its bodily limits to satisfy spiritual burnings; the restless Wren's loud, rasping succession of notes becomes "A blur of throbbings" where "His song sings him"; the earless Barn Owl's nonrotating eyes become a stare "fixed in the heart of heaven" while its screams lead to a chiasmic eating of heaven and earth by each other as if participating in an Indian Yab Yum ritual.

Then the Dove comes with its rainbow breast, suggesting peace, promise, and a great capacity to absorb pain. Possibly the first bird to be domesticated by humans, the dove sacrifices herself to the mutable world. The pain of Jack Orchard, Prometheus, the persona of **"Orts"**—the pain of the entire volume—becomes transfigured into vision as the Crow whispers survival and the Phoenix "voice" of prophetic utterance follows. In each poem the bird's perceptive powers and song (speech) combine to unite self and environment, reviving the fallen Adam by awakening his imaginative life, the mediating realm where words can flower into visions that know no boundaries. The sequence and the volume end with Adam's thoroughly refreshed vision and his first words. Words convey Adam's fresh grasp of his world as if he were "the first host, greeting it, gladdened."

THE CEASELESS GIFT: RIVER

Though much of his seventies work criticized Western science and religion, Hughes also offered guides to heal and transform the inner self through developing one's imaginative life in the *Gaudete* **"Epilogue,"** the Jungian alchemy of *Cave Birds,* and the "Prometheus on His Crag" and "Adam and the Sacred Nine" sequences of *Moortown*. *River* extends Hughes's meditations upon how to perceive the outer world, a project initiated with the Taoist vistas of *Remains of Elmet* and continued in the farming poems of *Moortown*.

As *Crow* is Hughes's *Iliad,* an account of a destructive battle with the environment caused by scientific objectivity and alienated instinct, so *River* (1983) is his *Odyssey,* an absolutely stunning poetic voyage that teaches us how to refresh our senses and, more importantly, save our planet. In *River* Hughes offers his readers a complete guide to a life-enhancing mode of perceiving that is consonant with the current thinking of ecologists, historians, ethicians, and theologians about how to live holistically and ensure the survival of our fragile planet. *River* will one day be recognized as one of the central literary masterpieces of the world; it should be required reading for all humans on our planet to help them attain responsible adulthood.

ECOLOGICAL ANIMISM

The historian Lynn White, Jr., in an essay often quoted by ecologists, argued that Christianity paved the way for the ecological ravages of modern science by condemning the animism of tribal cultures as an idolatrous belief in a spirit world inhabiting nature. Once Christianity drained the spirit out of nature, humans could exploit it without regard to the needs of animals and plants or the preservation of minerals. In the West the Medieval Church supported the biblically approved domination of humans over nature (Gen. 1:28) by sanctioning a spirit of inquiry into nature's operations and by considering Saint Francis—the sole environmentalist of the Medieval church—a near-heretic.[24]

White's bold assertions do have some validity, though they oversimplify. Civilizations based on other religious traditions certainly contributed to erosion, deforestation, and other forms of natural resource depletion. And the context surrounding Genesis 1:28 can lead to another interpretation: that humans are stewards entrusted with the care and preservation of all entities in nature's hierarchy. Human freedom and the weak will's tendency toward pride are the real culprits, and these are present at all times and in every civilization and religious denomination.[25]

Nevertheless, major ethicians such as Eugene C. Hargrove, K. S. Shrader-Frechette, Holmes Rolston III, Paul W. Taylor, and others speak in accord with Christian theologians and cultural historians such as John B. Cobb, Jr., Thomas Berry, and Ian Barbour in advocating a new vision of Christian stewardship that would be ecologically sound and promote equality among nations. Some feminist theologians venture further, breaking with Catholicism (Mary Daly), Protestantism (Carol P. Christ), and Judaism (Judith Plaskow) by calling for a new, nonpatriarchal religion with an ecologically grounded creation story. Apparently what is needed is a vision that combines the sense of the sacred in nature found in the animism of tribal cultures with the humility of Saint Francis.

Most would at least agree with the position of the intellectual historian Roderick Nash, who wrote in his *The Rights of Nature* that nature, like humans, has rights. Bedrock would be the ecologist Aldo Leopold's position, first stated in his 1949 essay "The Land Ethic," that what is ethical is what preserves "the integrity, stability, and beauty of the biotic community."[26] Hence endangered species have the right to survive, rocks have the right not to be polluted with oil spills, and the ozone layer has the right not to be depleted. The perspective articulated by the Catholic cultural historian Thomas Berry in *The Dream of the Earth* summarizes the new ecological awareness: "What we need . . . is the sensitivity required to understand and respond to the psychic energies deep in the very structure of reality itself . . . [in a spirit of] cooperative understanding . . . [akin to] the ultimate wisdom of tribal peoples and the fundamental teaching of the great civilizations."[27]

Hughes's essays and poetry place him in the vanguard of this burgeoning ecological awareness. White's observations are almost indistinguishable from many 1970 essay statements made by Hughes concerning the failure of Christianity, and Berry's remarks are very similar to many statements Hughes has made in essays concerning what nature and tribal cultures can teach humans about survival. The gorgeous poetry of *River* is distillation of Hughes's grasp of ecology. Far from being merely a group of lovely poems and photographs about fishing (unfortunately, the American Harper and Row edition does not include the vibrant Peter Keen color photographs of the Faber edition), *River* is an ecological primer about learning to perceive the animistic energies that the fisherman persona experiences in nature. Often the poems are rendered with a wonderful Heideggerian simplicity and nearness of language. The sacredness of nature appears on every page in the recurrent light and water imagery, and the persona achieves a sense of delighted participation in nature after first exercising a humble reverence for its processes.

In the second half of *River* Hughes confronts the original mythopoeic moment identified and discussed by Joseph Campbell: a consciousness of death as the loss of the inhabiting spirit, which prompts meditations about where that spirit came from and where it returns to.[28] Just as early hunters postulated Animal Masters, spiritual beings who provided the tribe's main sustenance, Hughes seems to posit in his exaltation of solar light and the water cycle a Spiritual Master who sustains a cyclic round consonant with the speculations of Tao-ists, Greeks, and many ancient and tribal cultures.

After the ecstasies of late summer leaping and midwinter mating, the salmon, who typify the survival struggles of all animate beings in *River,* await death patiently, ready to drop a body that is "simply the armature of energy" (73). Their spiritual essence will then return to a su-pratemporal Source, for throughout *River* a Spiritual Master illuminates and invigorates all with its animistic energy. Water is chrism for survival and light is revela-tion of the Source. In the title poem of *River* "water will go on / Issuing from heaven / In dumbness uttering spirit brightness," and in "Salmon Eggs," the conclud-ing poem of the volume, the river's "piled flow" reveals a "ponderous light of everlasting."

Leopold once wrote that "The most important character-istic of an organism is that capacity for internal self-renewal known as health."[29] This health is dependent upon the dynamic interaction of healthy organisms in the ecosystem. Through the mana power of his language, Hughes in *River* attempts to convey a sense of intimacy and holistic interaction with the environment that promotes psychological renewal and a reverence for nature. This can lead to such intelligent conservation practices as fish hatcheries—the restocking of the salmon supply described so reverently in **"The Morn-ing before Christmas."** Primarily, however, the poems in *River* indicate that Hughes is most often concerned with evoking a sense of astonishment and aesthetic delight in the powers and vitality of nature—something akin to the animism of tribal cultures—in order to promote self-renewal in humans and a reverence for nature.

"Animism," a term coined by Sir Edward Burnett Tylor in his 1871 study *Primitive Culture,* has come to be understood as a polytheistic system in which animals and the elements of nature are believed to be endowed with vitalistic spirits. Shamans on their ecstatic journeys could tap the energies of these spirits, and the psycho-logical and spiritual health of individual and community depended upon enlisting the aid of these energies and avoiding offenses such as transgressing sacred groves, using resources wastefully, or offending through improperly executed rituals, food offerings, etc. Though many anthropologists still consider animism as a child-ish view of nature, ecologists have for decades been pointing out the environmental soundness of this so-called primitive system, for it promotes resource conservation and reverence for the natural world.

It would be wrong to ascribe to Hughes a deliberate intent to reintroduce the animism of tribal cultures, but his reading is steeped in cultural anthropology, and his belief in nature's vitality has only deepened since *The Hawk in the Rain. River* celebrates nature's powers to

refresh one's perceptions and promote psychological renewal. The river, the central symbol in the volume, is the "Primitive, radical / Engine of earth's renewal" that "Tries and tries to wash and revive / A bedraggle of dirty bones" (17). Because the hydrological cycle of the river will "return stainless / For the delivery of this world," it is "a god, and inviolable. / Immortal. And will wash itself of all deaths" (51).

Brilliant sequences of imagery occur in *River* to convey a vitalistic energy that leaves one with a sense of astonishment and awe at the power and beauty of nature. The mana power of Hughes's language gener-ates energies kindred to those felt within the animistic beliefs of tribal cultures. Most often the river's sustenance is linked to an overspill of the sun's energy, as if the river's true source were the sun's tipped bucket of molten metal or an electric current sparked from the sun's generator (7). Salmon leap in it (66) and live in its "surge-ride of energy" (73). When the folktale Trickster Mink leaves his Northern Night and enters the river, he becomes animated, "Aboil with lightnings / He can't get rid of" (21). Even a small salmon nibbling the fisherman's hook has an electric shock "flash of arm for leverage" to wrench the pole away (32). An ewe enter-ing the river is "lowering herself / To the power-coils / Of the river's bulge, to replenish her udder." Here the river "Embellishes afresh and afresh / Each detail" as Hughes's language bathes the reader in a vitalistic energy that seems omnipresent and emotionally cleans-ing (18).

At other times Hughes conveys the animistic energy of the river through moments of sexual or religious ecstasy. During the low water of August, the river teases with the slow allurements of an idle woman, offering sensual delights where "Thrills spasm and dissolve" (60). Hughes captures the animated energy of even the lowly stump pool in spring, when it boils up with oxygen as if to burst its bonds and remove the hill-wood's bridal veil (27). When the river is perfectly calm, rivergazing can suddenly pitch a fisherman or birdwatcher into mo-ments of ecstasy akin to the "epileptic's strobe," Muez-zin's "Bismillah," or dervish's frenzy (71).

Most often Hughes portrays the spiritual component of the river's animistic energy through light imagery. Light imagery coalesces with river water regularly to imbue riverscapes with a numinous aura, a sense of the sacred-ness of the hydrological cycle. Cock minnows gathering in a pool at Easter work together solemnly in the "lit water," an image Hughes expands at the poem's conclu-sion to convey brightness from the Source blessing their labor "In the wheel of light— / Ghostly rinsings / A struggle of spirits" (23). On the island of Skye an encounter with a salmon leaves the fisherman with a sense of being momentarily absorbed into the spirit world after miles of hiking toward the river's source while staring at the pool tail's "superabundance of spirit" (31). Under water, the mystical sea-trout "Hang in a near emptiness of light" (40); the West Dart River "spills from the Milky Way, pronged with light" (39); and the river's "Unending" sustenance, a wine distilled from the harvest it helped to fertilize, is squeezed from hills packed "Tight with golden light" (45). An abundance of visual and auditory similes and metaphors revive in the reader a sense of participation in an ecosystem that fulfills much more than one's craving for facts and analysis.

A 1980 fishing trip to southeastern Alaska produced the epiphanic **"That Morning,"** where Hughes and his son Nicholas stand waist-deep in a river so filled with golden salmon that they experience a momentary transfiguration during which the body drops its "doubting thought." The poem's title echoes Eliade's *illud tempus* moment of paradisal unity with nature that so frequently appeared at the core of tribal myth making. In a "dazzle of blessing" the freed body becomes a vehicle for the spirit, a "spirit-beacon / Lit by the power of the salmon." When two golden bears wade in to prong salmon beside the fishermen, as if no separation existed between the orders of humans and animals, light and water imagery once again coalesce: the poem ends with all "alive in the river of light / Among the creatures of light, creatures of light."

As in tribal animism, animals in *River* possess an energy, a power of concentration, and a singleness of purpose that at times makes them superior to humans. The sea-trout concentrate in yogic trance, oblivious to the ordinary (40-41), while the eel, alive in a body ill-suited for grasping the outer world, appears so patient and self-absorbed as to be otherworldly (69). The mink lives in such a frenetic expenditure of energy that he can make love "Eight hours at a go" (21), while the damselflies of **"Last Act"** rehearse the whole span of copulation and death within minutes, for the female's fierce embrace often kills the male and the oviposition of eggs near the water line soon after leaves her vulnerable to predators.

Kingfisher and cormorant have the ability to dive and grasp their prey with an instantaneous crackle of energy. The kingfisher dives with a sudden "blue flare," like a taut electric wire suddenly snapped. He exits with a diamond-cutter's precision, leaving a "rainbow splinter" of blurred energy. In his swift and precise movements he appears superior to humans, closer to god: "Through him, God, whizzing in the sun, / Glimpses the angler" (47). In **"A Cormorant"** the bird, unlike the preoccupied fisherman, achieves his purpose by concentrating so single-mindedly that he becomes one with his prey, like an aborigine still absorbed in his prehunt trance. A second, more incisive look at the cormorant in **"A Rival"** reveals a ruthlessness beneath the single-

mindedness. Technological and predatory imagery characterize the cormorant as one whose self-interest and dictatorial iron will leads to ecological disaster.

EVERYTHING IS CONNECTED

Unlike the cormorant, the river sustains an ecosystem that interrelates humans with animals, vegetation, the land and its minerals. **"River Barrow"** is one of many poems in which Hughes suggests that the best way for humans to refresh their perceptions and experience psychological renewal is to achieve a consciousness of this relatedness. Here language conveys a Heideggerian presence; Hughes refreshes our capacity for experiencing the nearness and relatedness of the environment by interweaving past and present while the river pulses with its "living vein" toward the future. Humans integrate peacefully with animals, insects, vegetation, and river water while appreciating a dynamic yet balanced ecosystem:

> We sprawl
> Rods out, giant grasshopper antennae, listening
> For the bream-shoal to engage us.
>
> The current
> Hauls its foam-line feed-lane
> Along under the far bank—a furrow
> Driving through heavy wealth,
> Dragging a syrupy strength, a down-roping
> Of the living honey.
>
> It's an ancient thirst
> Savouring all this, at the day's end,
> Soaking it all up, through every membrane
> As if the whole body were a craving mouth,
> As if a hunted ghost were drinking—sud-flecks
> Grass-bits and omens
> Fixed in the glass.
>
> Trees inverted
> Even in this sliding place are perfect.
>
> All evil suspended. Flies
> Teem over my hands, twanging their codes
> In and out of my ear's beam. Future, past,
> Reading each other in the water mirror
> Barely tremble the thick nerve.
>
> Heavy belly
> Of river, solid mystery
> With a living vein.

Experiencing the ecological relatedness of nature can cleanse the self of the surface clutter of schedules and objectives that complicate one's life. Appreciating the beauty of nature at first-hand can relieve one of the stress of ordinary analytic thinking and egocentric decision making. **"Go Fishing"** is a triumph of sound ecological thinking that also synthesizes the advice of Patanjali's *Yoga Sutras* and most Zen and Taoist masters. The lambent mood and wonderfully tactile imagery point the reader toward desiring to bathe once again in the elements of nature and know them at first hand, in their honest, precognitive *suchness,* without labeling and distancing. This simplicity conveys the real relation of self to experience that Heidegger considers the fundamental purpose of language. To "Lose words" in the sense of losing the commonplace tags for objects, to "Let brain mist into moist earth" in the sense of divesting oneself of analytic thinking, and to be "Dismembered" by the "sun-melt" of river and the elements, is to experience anew the tactile relational presence of nature, the *whatness* that words refer to. Only at this moment can one "Try to speak and nearly succeed"—a further stage of progress than the subjunctive mode at the end of "Seven Dungeon Songs" in *Moortown.*

THE HUMBLE FISHERMAN

The fisherman persona whose adventures the reader follows throughout *River* is a hunter, a sport fisherman on a quest for the salmon. But his interest does not end with the challenge and finesse of catching a few salmon to eat. He has a deep curiosity about this marine survivor from the Paleolithic; he wants to locate its spawning grounds in the stump and source pools of rivers, learn its ways, and discover what the salmon have to teach him—what wisdom from prehistory they can impart (31, 55). He is responsive to the ecology of each area because he possesses a certain humility about the intervention of humans in nature, and respects the interrelatedness of things. He knows that, when humans disturb the meditations of sea-trout, the fish will "scram" (41) and he knows that he is an interloper (54-55) whose species has polluted the river with "bicycle wheels, car-tyres, bottles / And sunk sheets of corrugated iron" (74).

The fisherman's gentle, self-deprecating irony in many early *River* poems indicates that he is aware of the limitations of his ordinary rational mind and is willing to learn from nature. As he peers down at the salmon in the March river water, he experiences the sadness of separation: he views salmon **"Trapped"** in a "sandstorm boil of silt" while his consciousness, equally trapped in the element of air, is "a guttering lamp" (19). A cormorant can spear its prey with no aid save his naked eyes, wings, and claws, but the fisherman flounders in seven-pound waders, a heavy jacket, a sagging bagful of lures, a hat that embarrasses him, and a six-foot-long net that snags on every twig and fence-barb (25-26). For only a nibble from a small salmon he must walk for miles through suck-holes and clatter-brooks while repeatedly glancing at his watch so he will not miss the boat home (30-33). Always the self-deprecating irony is soft and ingratiating, for the fisherman (and the reader) soon become sensitized to how quickly toil can lead to astonished revelation in the unforgettable contact with a salmon.

ANIMAL AND SPIRITUAL MASTER

"After Moonless Midnight" is a pivotal poem in *River,* for here the fisherman persona loses his ironic distance and becomes trapped in the river-fetch. From here on he begins to commune more directly with the river and to empathize much more deeply with the survival struggle of the salmon. The fish, with their "magical skins," initiate him into a mythopoeic drama of mortality and transcendence. The hunter becomes the hunted when the river whispers "'We've got him.'" As the fisherman begins to understand the larger dimensions of the hunt ritual, a spiritual realm opens, revealing the origins of the idea of the sacred.

The salmon are magical creatures for the Indians of the Northwest Coast of North America, and it is no wonder that many of their great festivals coincide with the salmon runs. The salmon are their main source of food, and the salmon as provider reaffirm a religious dimension and inculcate an ecologically sound reverence for life. The salmon for these Indians are the gift of Salmon Woman or Bright-Cloud Woman, who ensures a plentiful supply of the fish as long as Trickster reveres her.[30] This is a type of myth that Joseph Campbell calls the Animal Master, a way Paleolithic hunting tribes resolved the problems of guilt arising from the necessary eating of an animal they otherwise admired. They postulated a spiritual realm that received the departing spirit of the animal who has lost a moral body of little importance. Belief in a spiritual abode for humans appears to have first occurred at the same time among hunting tribes, for the earliest anthropological evidence of belief in an afterlife occurs with the cave paintings of the hunt and the deposit of tools, weapons, and treasures in the burials of hunting tribes. The cave was the cathedral of the spirit, a supratemporal dimension that tribal hunters actually believed to exist. Burial gifts were deposited in the belief that the spirit of the departed still lives in a transcendent realm.[31]

Though Hughes does not directly allude to Animal Master myths in *River,* his reverential language supplies the spiritual equivalent of the cave cathedrals of Paleolithic hunters, and we know from his *Crow* poems that he developed a very masterful and intimate knowledge of the Northwest Coast Indian Trickster myths. **"The Morning Before Christmas,"** an early poem in *River,* conveys a sympathy with the survival struggle of the salmon, but without application to the spiritual needs of humans. Gradually the fisherman hunter does become aware of how the salmon's struggle reveals the mysteries of life and death and typifies the survival struggle of all beings. This awareness promotes a deeper, more sympathetic bond between hunter and hunted.

Hughes supplies some necessary factual information about the life cycle of the salmon in two *River* poems and a note. **"The Morning before Christmas"** mentions that the salmon's chances are "five thousand to one against survival." Though only Pacific salmon always die after mating, the survival chances of Atlantic salmon are also very poor. A note to a photograph on page 126 of the Faber edition states that very few survive the spawning run. At the river's mouth commercial nets and natural predators such as seals, sea lions, and otters await the salmon runs. Sport fishermen, winter cold, low river water, summer pollution, and the harvesting of sand-eel also reduce the Atlantic salmon population.

In **"October Salmon"** one learns that the Atlantic salmon return to spawn and probably die at an average of six pounds weight and four years of life. This prompts a cri de coeur in stanza 9, a very direct expression of grief over the shortness of life. Since Hughes has been an avid fisherman since age three and completed *River* past the age of 50, a biographical dimension appears obvious. To mediate and resolve the contradictions of mortality for humans as well as the salmon, Hughes adapts the Animal Master myth. The concluding salmon poems of *River* open a cathedral for the spirit and reveal the presence of the eternal in the temporal.

More than half of the poems following **"After Moonless Midnight"** are concerned with mortality and death. The meditative and often ironic "I" gradually disappears as the fisherman becomes absorbed in the drama of the salmon. Implicitly the salmon's deathward journey relates to the fisherman's own, and he slowly reconciles himself to his intuition that this journey is in harmony with the natural order of the ecosystem. As fall arrives the sense of the deathly in the river's flow becomes more intense and so does the fisherman's identification with the salmon. The poignant irony of the salmon's end—to die so soon after mating—is mediated by the hope for the continuance of the inhabiting spirit in a transcendent realm, the abode of a Spiritual Master.

Immersing oneself in first-hand experience does have its dark side, as does the river. The river in **"Last Night"** smells of sickbeds and slimes at night, leaving the fisherman feeling as if he "stood in a grave" when he stands "In the dying river." **"In the Dark Violin of the Valley"** conveys a similar feeling of temporality and death as the fisherman senses the gradual, unrelenting erosion of the river "Cutting the bed-rock deeper" with its dark violin music at night. These poems develop earlier reflections on the mortality of all who depend upon the river. The river may be an immortal god, but the "river's cargo" in **"Four March Watercolours"** is "A solution / Of all dead ends—an all-out evacuation / To the sea." A leaping trout must return immediately to water, a "peculiar engine" that "works it to death" in **"Ophelia."**

As August ends, the salmon and sea-trout move up the river to mate and spawn in hollowed-out riverbed grottos. In low water **"An August Salmon"** is a bridegroom "rapt" in visions and patient in his wedding cell. He has "the clock of love and death in his body" and like a monk kneels and "bows / Into the ceaseless gift / That unwinds the spool of his strength." Moved by the salmon's martyrlike resignation to the natural order, the fisherman becomes aware of a cosmic dimension, an instance of White Goddess drama with her male consort, as he observes the salmon awaiting "execution and death / In the skirts of his bride." When the river begins to cool toward winter, the fisherman senses in **"August Evening"** a sacred drama in the "religious purpose" of the sea-trout processions: "Robed in the stilled flow of their Creator / They inhale unending. I share it a little." The sense of mutuality in a sacred drama becomes more acute.

Hughes revised **"The Gulkana,"** another poem written about his 1980 Alaskan fishing trip, for the American Harper and Row edition, adding about 42 lines. Thirty of these added lines occur at the point where the fisherman lands a huge Chinook salmon and gazes into its eye. The added lines speak of a resignation to the cycle of love and death as ordained by nature. This is expressed through an imagined ritual on a tribal "platform of water" where the river tears the flesh from the fish in a "dance-orgy of being reborn." Also added are lines suggesting a premonition of the fisherman's own death as he writes the poem "Word by word" on the return flight. Here he admits that the "burden of the river" caused "a secret bleeding of mourning / In my cave of body" as he inspected the huge salmon's eye. Once again Campbell's original mythopoeic moment occurs: knowledge of eventual death directly precedes the hope for the continued existence of an essential spiritual core.[32]

The final three salmon poems in *River* contain an apotheosis of the plight of the salmon with emphasis upon the sacredness of a drama preordained by nature and in accord with her ecological cycle. The intense identification of fisherman with his prey is reinforced with sacramental and light imagery to arrive at a mystical participation in the salmon's death, as in Animal Master rituals. Consent to the cycle as ecologically providential transforms death into resplendent rebirth, with a majestic assertion at the conclusion of **"Salmon Eggs,"** the last poem, that *"only birth matters."*

A patient, humble acceptance of his role adds dignity to the salmon of **"September Salmon."** Oblivious to weir and insects, he wears his scars of age. Buoyant in sacramental imagery, he appears "sacred with lichens" for an autumn benediction. In the final stanza he "adds his daub" as he leaps into the September sun. **"October Salmon"** is a more rhetorical testimonial to the salmon's toil and a sympathetic outcry against death. Having served nature loyally, the salmon returns home, his skin leprous with sores for badges. A steady veteran, he finds the pool of his birth an appropriate home for his death. He expects no favors; indeed the river's "flow will not let up for a minute."

As the fisherman cries out against the salmon's subjugation in **"October Salmon,"** a bonding occurs: through an intense sharing in the salmon's suffering, the fisherman becomes the salmon, the salmon is the fisherman. The eternal aspect of the life and death cycle dawns upon the fisherman, and the full message of death breaks in upon him: "And that is how it is, / That is what is going on there." The body is just the "armature of energy," a vehicle to be dropped to free the spirit for a return to "that covenant of Polar Light." Yet here the fisherman communes so intensely with the physical agony of the salmon and the indignity of its plight that he fails to take any consolation in the heavenward return of the spirit.

Only by losing his ego in **"Salmon Eggs,"** the concluding poem of **River,** is the fisherman prepared for the final spiritual revelation. When "my eyes forget me" (the "me" of egocentric selfhood), the fisherman becomes one with the "piled flow" and the "ponderous light of everlasting." He consents to the holiness of the process, the "Perpetual mass / Of the waters," for he recognizes the eternal within the temporal, the presence of a Spiritual Master who has ordained this process. All issues from "the swollen vent / Of the nameless," the Tao or supratemporal first principle. The poem is superbly crafted, with short stanzas that mark deepening stages of insight. Subtly evocative rhythms buffet a language that whispers softly a sense of spiritual beatitude, as if spoken in Chartres. The fisherman disappears into the river's great silence, swathed like a Zen adept in the allness of nature.

"Where there is no vision, the people perish," states Proverbs 29:18. All of **River,** but especially **"Salmon Eggs,"** offers a wonderfully positive and life-enhancing alternative to Crow's myopic vision. Hughes has constructed a cathedral of ecological vision to show his readers how to enliven their imaginations and save our planet.

Notes

1. R. J. Putman and S. D. Wratten, *Principles of Ecology* (Berkeley and Los Angeles: University of California Press, 1984), 84.

2. "Earth," *BBC Light Programme,* recorded 28 September 1961.

3. Donard Worster, *Nature's Economy: The Roots of Ecology* (1977; reprint, Garden City, N.Y.: Doubleday Anchor, 1979), 12-13.

4. Chuang Tzu, *The Complete Works of Chuang Tzu,* trans. Burton Watson (New York: Columbia University Press, 1968), 36, 47, 94, 168.

5. Paul Sears, "Ecology—a Subversive Subject," *Bioscience* 14, no. 7 (July 1964): 12.

6. Waley [, Arthur, ed. and trans.] *The Way and Its Power,* [*A Study of the "Tao Te Ching" and Its Place in Chinese Thought* (New York: Grove Press, 1958),] 149, 174, 178, 206, 217.

7. Chuang Tzu, *Complete Works,* 74.

8. In Waley, *The Way and Its Power,* 141.

9. Chang Chung-yuan, *Creativity and Taoism* (New York: Harper & Row, 1970), 5, 7, 36; [D. T.] Suzuki, *Essays in Zen Buddhism, First Series,* ed. Christmas Humphreys (1949; reprint, New York: Grove Press, 1961), 214-66.

10. Chuang Tzu, *Complete Works,* 240.

11. Mircea Eliade, *Myth and Reality,* trans. Willard R. Trask (New York: Harper & Row, 1963), 139-40; *Myths, Dreams, and Mysteries,* trans. Philip Mairet (New York: Harper & Brothers, 1960), 15.

12. George Steiner, *Language and Silence* (New York: Atheneum, 1970), 12-35.

13. "Moortown," *BBC Radio 3,* prod. Fraser Steel, recorded 6 February 1980, 1-2.

14. Kirk, *Myth* [Kirk, G. S. *Myth: Its Function and Meaning in Ancient and Other Cultures* (Berkeley and Los Angeles: University of California Press, 1970)], 196-97, 226-30; *The Nature of Greek Myths* (Baltimore: Penguin, 1974), 136-43.

15. Discussion and poem numberings refer to the "Prometheus on His Crag" section of the 1979 Harper & Row *Moortown.* The original 1973 Rainbow Press *Prometheus on His Crag* contained encounters with Pandora (#5) and Io (#12), and a poem discussing Prometheus's understanding of his fire theft (#17). For the *Moortown* version Hughes deleted these three poems. The *Moortown* "Prometheus" poems numbered 5, 7, and 17 are new. See Scigaj [, Leonard M. *The Poetry of Ted Hughes: Form and Imagination* (Iowa City: University of Iowa Press, 1986)], 269-72 for an analysis of these changes.

16. Carlos Castaneda, *The Teachings of Don Juan* (New York: Pocket Books, 1974), 109-19. This is the first of Castaneda's *Don Juan* books; Hughes reviewed the fourth, *Tales of Power,* very enthusiastically for the London *Observer,* 5 March 1972, 32.

17. "Earth-Numb," *BBC Radio 3,* prod. Fraser Steel, recorded 6 February 1980, 1.

18. In *Ted Hughes and R. S. Thomas Read and Discuss Selections of Their Own Poems. The Critical Forum* (Battle, Sussex, England: Norwich Tapes, 1978).

19. Martin Heidegger, "The Nature of Language," in his *On the Way to Language,* trans. Peter D. Hertz (New York: Harper & Row, 1971), 105.

20. Ibid., 57-108.

21. Ibid., 69, 92.

22. Sagar, "Fourfold Vision in Hughes," in *Achievement* [*The Achievement of Ted Hughes* (Manchester: Manchester University Press; Athens: University of Georgia Press, 1983)], 307.

23. Hughes, "Earth-Numb," *BBC Radio 3,* 11.

24. Lynn White, Jr., "The Historical Roots of Our Ecologic Crisis," *Science* 155 (1967): 1203-7.

25. See Robert H. Ayers, "Christian Realism and Environmental Ethics," reprinted in *Religion and Environmental Crisis,* ed. Eugene C. Hargrove (Athens: University of Georgia Press, 1986), 154-71, for a solid response to White's argument.

26. Aldo Leopold, *A Sand County Almanac* (New York: Oxford University Press 1949), 224-25. See the discussion of Leopold's integrity concept in Roderick Nash, *The Rights of Nature* (Madison: University of Wisconsin Press, 1989), 63-74.

27. Thomas Berry, *The Dream of the Earth* (San Francisco: Sierra Club Books, 1988), 48-49.

28. Joseph Campbell, with Bill Moyers, *The Power of Myth,* ed. Betty Sue Flowers (New York: Doubleday, 1988), 71.

29. Leopold, *Sand County,* 194.

30. Franz Boas, *Tsimshian Mythology* (Washington, D.C.: U.S. Government Printing Office, 1916), 76-79, 668-70.

31. Campbell, *Power of Myth,* 69-89.

32. Except for single word alterations, Hughes lengthened the revised "The Gulkana" in three places for the American Harper and Row edition. At the beginning of the poem he suggests a mythic scenario with the addition of nine and a half lines. Only the lines from "Strange word" through "crumpled map" occurred in the original Faber version. The most major revision is an expansion of 30 new lines beginning with "And its accompaniment" through "Into that amethyst." The final major revision is the addition of three and one-half lines beginning with "The burden of the river moved in me" through "In my cave of body."

Nathalie Anderson (essay date 1994)

SOURCE: Anderson, Nathalie. "Ted Hughes and the Challenge of Gender." In *The Challenge of Ted Hughes,* edited by Keith Sagar, pp. 91-115. New York: St. Martin's Press, 1994.

[*In the following essay, Anderson examines Hughes's treatment of women in his poetry, particularly in 1970's* Crow *and the 1990 collection* Wolfwatching.]

That a chill exists separating Ted Hughes from the feminist community (if we can speak of so great a multiplicity as if it were a single entity) scarcely needs documenting, nor is its origin difficult to locate. Bestselling biographies, accusations volleyed back and forth on the pages of daily newspapers, lawsuits, even graveyard disturbances have—astoundingly, twenty-seven years on—kept alive the controversy surrounding Hughes's relationship with Sylvia Plath; mere school-girls can recognise that 'man in black with a Meinkampf look'.[1] From Robin Morgan's sweeping indictment of Hughes as philanderer, rapist, purveyor of his wife's image, and 'one-man gynocidal movement' in her 1972 poem 'Arraignment', to Marjorie Perloff's now famous analysis in the *American Poetry Review* of his apparently self-defensive editing of *Ariel,*[2] feminists have accused, pursued, assigned blame. And not feminists alone: the influence of this particular view is startlingly widespread. I particularly remember the staid, even patriarchal Chair of a conservative Deep South English department who asked me in a job interview how I could write about Ted Hughes, since he'd killed Sylvia Plath. This, for many quite ordinary, unimaginative, non-vindictive people, is the accepted wisdom: Hughes kills. Hughes is inimical—no, downright dangerous to women.

I mention these perilous assumptions in part to demonstrate the dangers of hyperbole—Plath's death, though tragedy, was clearly no murder—and in part to draw attention to the undeniable fact that many readers (and non-readers) of Hughes's work seem unable to extricate his poetry from his private life. I write here not biographically but literarily: I wish to examine the appearance of women as double-edged emblems in Hughes's work, particularly in *Crow.* But the actual relations that lie behind the poems make these scholarly conclusions rather more personal than is usual, and offer the potential—a rather perilous one—for insight into the man as well as his work.

Double-edged emblems: for many women readers, who have looked for some vision of themselves in his poems, Hughes's female figures scarcely seem ambiguous at all. Such readers will recall poems that dismiss or reject women ('**Secretary**' in *The Hawk in the Rain,* for example), that satirise their duplicity or their insatiability ('**Witches**' in *Lupercal,* for example, or the *Gaudete* narrative), that reduce them to wombs or vaginas ('**Gog**' in *Wodwo,* or '**The Battle of Osfrontalis**' in *Crow*), that enact violence against them ('**Song for a**

Phallus' in *Crow,* for a start), that perceive them as violent themselves (the *Gaudete* lyrics). Yet in each case, and with increasing purpose, Hughes's disquieting presentation of women is part of a larger indictment—ultimately of a society which represses not only what Hughes perceives as a female principle within the psyche, but actual women as well. If we cannot define Hughes himself as feminist—and I certainly do not propose to do so—we can nevertheless acknowledge that feminists too endorse this position. Indeed, it is instructive to compare Hughes's stance towards scientific empiricism in *Crow* with that of Adrienne Rich in her first explicitly feminist volume, *Diving into the Wreck,* which was published two years later.[3] If, as we might plausibly argue, Hughes betrays his own ambivalence towards women in his work, he also amply demonstrates his awareness that such ambivalence is symptomatic of a societal neurosis crying out for cure.

I begin my analysis from two premises, or rather observations, about Hughes's characteristic approaches: the first is that he tends to speak in terms of dichotomies, the second that these dichotomies often blur on examination. These tendencies are particularly clear in Hughes's essay 'The Rock', his contribution to the BBC series on 'The Writer and His Background', broadcast in 1963 after the publication of *Lupercal*.[4] In this piece, written to explain 'where the division of body and soul began', Hughes delineates two geological entities or conceptual principles that moulded his childhood—the rock, 'a dark cliff . . . to the south', 'both the curtain and backdrop to existence', and the moors, 'a gentle female watery line' to the north:

> The rock asserted itself, tried to pin you down, policed and gloomed. But you *could* escape it, climb past it and above it, with some effort. You could not escape the moors. They did not impose themselves. They simply surrounded and waited.

Hughes's developing dichotomy here—rock against moor; the trap of the body against the unfettered soul—falters as he describes each in similar terms. The rock's policing and the moor's ambush each suggest a sinister inevitability, a confrontation to be escaped or delayed. While a trick of light 'or some overnight strengthening of the earth' might magnify the intensity of the rock, might '[rear] it right over you', the moors 'hung over you at all times'. While the shadow of the rock produces 'A slightly disastrous, crumbly, grey light, sunless and yet too clear', light on the moors is 'at once gloomily purplish and incredibly clear, unnaturally clear'. A climber on the rock 'felt infinitely exposed', felt 'an alarming exhilaration'; on the moors, objects seemed 'more exposed to the radio-active dangers of space, more startled by their own existence', 'exultant'. And finally, while from above or below 'you cannot look at a precipice without thinking instantly what it would be like to fall down it, or jump down it', while the stories

Hughes remembers of the rock involve death and falling—'. . . my brother told of a wood-pigeon shot in one of those little oaks, and how the bird set its wings and sailed out without a wing-beat stone dead into space to crash two miles away on the other side of the valley'—the effects of the moor are disturbingly similar: 'you began to feel bird-like, with sudden temptings to launch out in the valley air'. Clearly, Hughes experiences rock and moor as distinct entities or states—the rock masculine, puritanical, repressive, deadening; the moors feminine, atavistic, liberating, vital. Equally clearly, he finds it difficult to differentiate precisely between these entities: each looms; each exposes the vulnerable to a disquieting clarity; each fosters desolation and exultation; each prompts the sensitive to flight—a dead fall, an illusion of soaring. Each, we might say, both embodies enormity and exemplifies a possible stance for coping with it. Thus as the rock oppresses, it suggests regulation—policing—as an appropriate response to existence; the result is a deadening, a numbness—the flight of a dead bird on set wings across a valley. One implication here is that escape from the rock's oppression requires numbness. But 'you could not escape the moors', and this inescapable quality suggests that, however far one might fly, some disturbing essence lies in wait within the numbness, and essence that might as well be embraced as held temporarily at bay.

This pattern of asserted but questionable dichotomy pervades Hughes's work. Like Alex Davis, I trace in his poetry an anxiety towards enormity, infinite darkness, personal insignificance—death—which culminates and finds transcendence in the controlled disasters of *Crow.* We might recall here his 1957 *Poetry Book Society Bulletin* statement: 'What excites my imagination is the war between vitality and death'.[5] But so strong is the anxiety that vitality often seems merely another form of death. From the beginning, Hughes associates this anxiety with female figures. Thus in **'Billet-Doux'** from *The Hawk in the Rain,* the speaker maintains, 'I am driven to your bed and four walls / From bottomlessly breaking night', 'By the constellations staring me to less / Than what cold, rain and wind neglect'; thus the lovers of **'Incompatibilities'**, also from that volume, enter 'black-outs of impassables', 'The maelstrom dark', 'the endless / Without-world of the other'. Sexuality, seemingly a refuge from nothingness, thrusts its refugees into negation.

And while 'refugees' may imply that male and female are equally menaced, Hughes's sympathies are clearly with the male, with—for example—the jaded lover of **'Two Phases'** who

> Sweats his stint out,
> No better than a blind mole
> That burrows for its lot

Of the flaming moon and sun
Down some black hole.

'The endless / Without-world of the other' is here more vaginal than existential, the motive force more binding than driving, the blindness more deluded than instinctual. Where the lover of **'Billet-Doux'** is impelled to sex by existential dread—'I come to you enforcedly'—the mole as sexual labourer is exploited, trapped in relation. In either situation, the woman is almost incidental to the man's dilemma.

Indeed, for the most part, women in these early poems are satirised, condemned outright, or curiously anonymous—'some black hole'. 'Any woman born', asserts Fallgrief of **'Fallgrief's Girl-Friends'**, 'having / What any woman born cannot but have, / Has as much of the world as is worth more / Than wit or lucky looks can make worth more'. Fallgrief's assumption that value derives from sexuality—'What any woman born cannot but have'—works in context to deny the force of mere appearance, the seductions of 'admiration's giddy mannequin', and even to glorify female essence, but it simultaneously erases female individuality, 'wit' as well as 'looks'.

Fallgrief 'meant to stand naked / Awake in the pitch dark where the animal runs, / Where the insects couple as they murder each other'. He assumes that his denial of appearances will reveal the predatory reality of sexual relation, or—to put this less abstractly—that reducing his partner to 'What any woman born cannot but have' will strip the falsifying glamour from a terrifying animalistic function. Fallgrief here is not himself animal, insect, or murderer; rather, he is a witness, a hero. 'Naked', he is vulnerable to attack; 'awake', he is vulnerable to the enormity he perceives. Having discarded both physical and mental protection, Fallgrief intends consciously to observe the running animal of his own unconscious. This heroic act may require woman as the locus of enormity, but what drives the man has little otherwise to do with his girl-friend. 'He meant to stand naked / Awake' implies also 'alone'.

By the poem's conclusion, however, Fallgrief 'has found a woman with such wit and looks / He can brag of her in every company'. Though attributed to 'chance'—mere accident—this culminating change seems both a consequence of heroic risk and a distraction from it, both reward and punishment. 'The chance changed him'—changed his refusal of intellect and beauty, changed his heroic intention. The woman's anonymity underscores Hughes's ambivalence: does the poem chart Fallgrief's luck in finding a package with 'such wit and looks', or his fall from grace in bragging about his distracting find?

Despite such ambivalence, this admired woman nevertheless highlights a more significant admiration for

women elsewhere. In **'Billet-Doux'**, for example, girls who 'Sweeten smiles, peep, cough' are contrasted with an approved woman

Who sees straight through bogeyman,
The crammed cafes, the ten thousand
Books placed end to end, even my gross bulk,
To the fiery star coming for the eye itself,
And while she can grabs of them what she can.

Cut from the same heroic mould as Fallgrief's idealised self, this woman is still more capable than he: where he 'meant to stand', she 'sees straight through' appearances, she 'grabs of' essence. Margaret Dickie Uroff has argued persuasively that such capable partners reflect Hughes's relationship with Plath: 'her presence is everywhere felt in Hughes' elevation of women to predatory status equal with men'.[6] Yet even here the woman is more paradigm than individual. Love—which the speaker of **'Billet-Doux'** dismisses as 'a spoiled appetite for some delicacy'—is a state that occurs rather than a relationship which develops. Lovers are 'found', stumbled over, encountered. Sex is the locus of enormity, a concentration which makes more perilous the 'Without-world' of existence. Heroes—male or female—may pluck the 'fiery star' from the void, but embrace annihilation in their very heroism. The woman who 'sees straight through' and 'grabs . . . what she can' is preferable to the affected and repressed, but is herself faceless, reduced to function, and—like the male persona of these poems—doomed.

It is interesting in this context to recall the conclusion to **'Bawdry Embraced'**, a poem from *Recklings* explicitly dedicated to Plath, where '. . . every ogling eye / Is a cold star to measure / Their solitude by'. The marriage of equals here is by implication hot rather than cold, a star of greater magnitude; 'Their solitude' emphasises their uniqueness, the distance that separates them from merely 'ogling eye[s]'. Yet even here, the figuring of mutuality in terms of solitude raises the spectre of isolation, and the 'cold star' as standard paradoxically lowers the poem's temperature even as it gestures towards warmth.

Hughes's second volume, *Lupercal,* offers as a stance towards enormity the figure of a dreaming tramp, dead to outer reality, open to inner 'blackouts of impassables'. In his debilitation, his self-negation, and his connection with the animalistic underworld, the tramp serves as a corrective to the posturing hero of *The Hawk in the Rain*. Most particularly, he is—despite 'Dick Straightup'—no lover: women are virtually missing from the volume, serving when they do appear mainly as props—the mother in **'Everyman's Odyssey'**, the barren women in **'Lupercalia'**. Only **'To Paint a Water Lily'** and **'The Voyage'** may be construed as love poems. It is as if Hughes is insisting that his proper arena—despite the earlier failed attempts to ground existential nausea in sexuality—has nothing to do with sex. His new hero exists in blank potentiality.

This passive figure thus provides an intriguing parallel for the anonymous 'one, numb beyond her last of sense', whose death is posed against nuclear annihilation in **'A Woman Unconscious'**. Is hers 'a lesser death' than global world-cancelling black', Hughes asks, conflating private loss with that ultimate cancellation as the woman 'Close[s] her eyes on the world's evidence', cancelling it. Where the tramp survives enormity, even in death, to find deity 'In an animal's dreamed head' (**'Crag Jack's Apostasy'**), the woman's parallel submersion negates the promise of transcendence implicit in this stance. Valued because sunk beyond consciousness, yet debilitated beyond human aid, she dissipates admiration for the tramp's endurance in poignancy, as a stony emblem of loss.

Moreover, although the woman remains firmly anonymous and firmly real, the description of holocaust as 'A melting of the mould in the mother' gestures towards an identity of mother and world, so that a cancellation of one literally cancels the other. Interestingly, Hughes's most conventional love poems—**'The Voyage'** here, and **'Song'** in *The Hawk in the Rain*—ratify this cancellation in romantic tropes. Each assumes loss: 'Without hope move my words and looks / Towards you'; 'when I shall have lost you'. Each affiliates the beloved with the elemental: 'a marble of foam' caressed by the tide, 'a shaped shell' through which the wind harmonises, a cloudy 'fire' lit by the moon in **'Song'**; as unfixable in **'The Voyage'** as the sea. Each ends in disaster: 'my hands full of dust'; 'The sea's . . . / Other than men taste who drown out there'. To lose the beloved is to lose the world; devotion to her involves the risk of elemental annihilation.

The unconscious woman of *Lupercal,* vulnerable on 'the white hospital bed', becomes in Hughes's radio play 'The Wound' a composite figure whose 'mundiform belly' is 'sliced . . . / With joy. / To numbers' by such authorities as 'The Coroner', 'medical specialists', 'Experimental psychologists', 'Zoologists', 'Bacteriologists', 'Anthropologists'. The hospital, implicitly incapable of saving its patient in **'A Woman Unconscious'**, becomes in 'The Wound' the site of active dismemberment, of purposeless vivisection, of rape: the researchers do not find what they 'hoped for. / Lusted for'. As in the earlier volumes, this vulnerable female figure both embodies and distances enormity; the 'mundiform belly' again equates woman and world, enlarging a single atrocity into global catastrophe. The significance of the woman's vulnerability has shifted, however: tragically silent in **'A Woman Unconscious'**, here she accuses, assigns blame.

The multiple voices of the 'mundiform belly' speak only briefly in 'The Wound': this scene—part of a soldier's nightmarish visit to the underworld—comprises perhaps three pages of the play's forty-two. While neither 'The Wound' nor *Wodwo,* the volume in which it appears, thus centres on a paradigmatic female entity, the 'mundiform belly' reduced 'to numbers' indicates that by 1962 Hughes has consciously begun to pose against scientific empiricism a female sensibility he associates with earth itself, a spirit injured literally and metaphorically by the dominating intellect. Women represent what rationality denies.

This conclusion need scarcely surprise us, since Hughes himself repeatedly asserts it. 'The subtly apotheosised misogyny of Reformed Christianity is proportionate to the fanatic rejection of Nature, and the result has been to exile man from Mother Nature—from both inner and outer nature', he writes in 1970.[7] His 1971 experimental drama *Orghast* traces 'the crime against material nature, the Creatress, source of life and light, by the Violator, the mental tyrant Holdfast, and her revenge'.[8] Hughes's introduction to a selection of Shakespeare's verse insists:

> When the physical presence of love has been degraded to lust and forbidden lust has combined with every other forbidden thing to become a murderous devil, life itself has become a horror, the maiden has become a whore and a witch, and the miraculous source of creation has become the empty hole through into nothing.[9]

This 'empty hole' vividly recalls the ambivalences of Hughes's earliest poetry—sex as salvation, sex as deception—and thus highlights our difficulties in assessing his indictments of rationalist misogyny in *Wodwo* and later in *Crow.* If rationalism perceives the female principle as 'a horror', 'a whore and a witch', then Hughes must portray such a horror in order to present rationalism accurately. Yet to do so is to incorporate a horrific vision of woman into his own discourse—a discourse which surely reveals in some sense that which fascinates and distresses its author. 'The maiden *has become* a whore'; 'the miraculous source of creation *has become* the empty hole': Hughes's verb here pushes the association of existential meaninglessness and female sexuality beyond shortsighted misperception to identity.

In *Wodwo,* the nadir of this ambivalence occurs in **'Gog'**, where a 'horseman of iron' 'Gallops over the womb that makes no claim, that is of stone' 'on the horse shod with vaginas of iron'—one of Hughes's most controversial images. The earth here, defined through the familiar association of womb and tomb, is clearly female and clearly sinister: thus in part II, the question 'Then whose / Are these / Eyes' receives the answer, 'Death and death and death—Her mirrors'.

Even the fortuitous capitalisation of 'Eyes', 'Death', and 'Her' implies a deity at once all-powerful and intimate whose true identity—death—we can perceive mirrored in creation. The iron horseman who rides 'Out of the blood-dark womb' might thus—on the evidence of his character and origin—plausibly be her champion, an extension of her deathly will. Yet Hughes's imagery pits horseman against goddess, male against female: 'He follows his compass, the lance-blade, the gunsight, out / Against the fanged grail and tireless mouth'. In a pattern which becomes increasingly familiar in later books, the male principle—dependent on the female and bound to her symbolically—nevertheless seeks to separate himself, to destroy her. 'It's the key to the neurotic-making dynamics of Christianity', Hughes writes in his 1970 essay 'Myth and Education': 'Christianity in suppressing the devil, in fact suppresses imagination and suppresses vital natural life'.[10] And again, 'The fundamental pattern was made within Protestant Christianity that the devil, woman, nature were out of bounds'.[11] Yet in **'Gog'**, the point of view, which seems to endorse the horseman's misogyny, raises problems of interpretation. These lines, for example, with their tone of prayer or command, ironically reverse the attitude of a volume where poem after poem questions the rule of empiricism:

> Shield him from the dipped glance, flying in half light, that
> 　　　　　　　　　　　　　　　　　tangles the heels,
> The grooved kiss that swamps the eyes with darkness.
> Bring him to the ruled slab, the octaves of order,
> The law and mercy of number. Lift him
> Out of the octopus maw and the eight lunatic limbs
> Of the rocking, sinking cradle.

It is instructive to read these lines against Hughes's well-known comments on the poem from his 1971 *London Magazine* interview: **'Gog'**, he tells Ekbert Faas,

> . . . actually started as a description of the German assault through the Ardennes and it turned into the dragon in Revelations [presented as a Caliban- or Grendel-like figure in Part I]. It alarmed me so much I wrote a poem about the Red Cross Knight just to set against it with the idea of keeping it under control . . . keeping its effects under control.[12]

We can see **'Gog'** III as a conscious dramatisation of the psychological war between repression and the distended repressed, a war which—Hughes explains to Faas—transforms 'Isis, mother of the gods' into 'Hitler's familiar spirit'. Or we can see the poem as evidence that Hughes's conscious understanding masks, is a projection of, a continuing psychological war of his own.

Wodwo and ***Crow*** demonstrate that Hughes manages his ambivalence by externalising it. His dramatisation of violent men and devouring women allows him to demonstrate the power of this ambivalence without acknowledging its hold over him. He defuses it, separates it from his own sexuality, his own marriage to a psychologically demanding woman, his own upbringing. While wrestling his ambivalence into schematic form, Hughes simultaneously personifies the elemental, the inconceivable, the void, the darkness, death, meaninglessness—and what is personified can be approached, understood, sympathised with, loved, adored. Thus in **'Karma'**, 'the mother' is explicitly 'the mother / Of the God / Of the world / Made of Blood', at once embodiment of death and authority over it, to whom we cry for sustenance, for oblivion.

The various images of women to be found in *Crow* testify to the intensity of Hughes's dilemma. Female sexual organs often appear alone, disembodied and depersonalised: the 'vulva' tightening on 'man's neck' in **'Crow's First Lesson'**, the 'vaginas in a row' with which 'Words' try to tempt Crow in **'The Battle of Osfrontalis'**, 'The horrible over of fangs' in **'Crow's Account of St. George'**, the 'buttocks' under which Crow is caught in **'Crow and Mama'**. Sex is repellent or mechanical: the apparent cannibalism of post-nuclear horrors in **'Notes for a Little Play'**, the regenerative efforts of two halves of a cut worm in **'A Childish Prank'**, the waving legs and open 'maw' of the Sphinx in **'Song for a Phallus'** where Oedipus 'stood stiff and wept / At the dreadful thing he saw'. 'Knife', 'fangs', and reflexive strangulation assert the danger of engaging the female: even 'the soft and warm that is long remembered' culminates in 'a volcano' (**'Magical Dangers'**).

With such excuses, it is not surprising that the female is often the object of violence: confronted with vaginas, Crow 'called in his friends'; confronted with the 'oven of fangs', the obsessed scientist 'bifurcates' it with a Japanese sword; confronted with the 'dreadful' 'maw', Oedipus 'split[s] / The Sphinx' with 'an axe' as he eventually 'split[s] his Mammy like a melon'; Crow's every action deforms the mother he cannot escape. Most of this violence is clearly phallic, suggesting a doubleness to each action—a murder, a rape, a feminist's nightmare.

Yet, while few readers can perceive this pattern of aversion and reactive violence undisturbed, it is also clear that a depiction of such pathology is part of Hughes's criticism of a pathologically unbalanced culture. Neither Oedipus nor the scientist is presented heroically; their fatal limitations, evidenced in their cataclysmically disproportionate violence to those they ostensibly love, form the thematic focus of their respective poems. **'Crow and Mama'** begins with *inadvertent* violence manifesting implicit reciprocity: 'When Crow cried his mother's ear / Scorched to a stump'. Only at the fifth couplet, nearly half-way through the poem, does the reciprocity become explicit and the violence reactive:

'When he stopped she closed on him like a book / On a bookmark, he had to get going'. From this point on, Crow's attempts to achieve independence, increasingly drastic, repeatedly entangle his mother, his eventual rocket flight to the moon lets him out 'Under his mother's buttocks', a circumstance analogous to 'a book / On a bookmark' or to a disturbing rebirth—that is, to a pre-existent rightness, a reassertion of relationship. Crow's relationship with his mother is thus by implication that which cannot be escaped, wholeness; its violent aspect signifies imbalance and fragmentation. In a similar image, once Oedipus splits his mother to discover 'What's on the other side' of 'The World' he perceives as 'dark', 'He found himself curled up inside / As if he had never been bore . . .'. Interrelatedness reasserts itself; the pattern, denied, begins again.

Against fragmentation and denial, *Crow* poses a grim transcendence. 'Man' in **'Fleeing from Eternity'** is 'faceless . . . / Eyeless and mouthless bald face' until 'He got a sharp rock he gashed holes in his face / Through the blood and pain he looked at the earth'. 'Blood and pain' serve as his sense organs; only through suffering can he perceive the 'woman singing out of her belly', reminiscent of the 'mundiform belly' in *Wodwo,* and 'exchange' 'eyes and a mouth'—'life'—for her song. Even in this void, even through disaster, transcendence can find a way: 'The song was worth it'. 'The mind is its own place', says Milton, 'and in itself / Can make a Heaven of Hell, a Hell of Heaven'. Hughes might say that 'the mind' has already made 'a Hell of Heaven'; when we admit our complicity in hellishness, abandon our resistance to what we have defined as hell, we may find ourselves among the 'staring angels' (**'Pibroch'**), able to sing.

Yet **'Fleeing From Eternity'** admits other interpretations: are the gashes, through which the man perceives, emblems of relatedness, of abandoned solipsism, of newly-achieved wholeness; or does his action only continue his flight? His 'exchange' with the singing woman deepens this ambiguity: 'He gave her eyes and a mouth' means that he gashed her face; 'in exchange' does not necessarily imply that he has given up anything himself; 'exchange' can thus be read as a rationalisation of theft, of rape; indeed, despite the gift of 'life', 'The woman felt cheated'. However we read the poem, its last two lines are disturbing. 'The song was worth it' implies first that the man has given his life for it, but his laughter indicates that he has not lost his newly-gashed mouth. If both he and the woman are now alive, 'The song was worth it' suggests that, having heard the song—whether he has stolen it or has simply reimbursed her for what she still sings—the man finds it worth giving the woman pain, or giving her a life he would have preferred to hoard. 'The woman felt cheated' suggests either that newly-acquired life, however valuable, does not make up for her loss of the song, or that her new

awarenesss, song or no, is a poor exchange for wholeness and interiority.

Perhaps, then, this poem represents a repeated crime against the earth, a renewal of fragmentation. Yet the conclusion of **'Fleeing from Eternity'** focuses less on the man's implicit crimes than on the clear value of the song, 'worth it' to both man and woman. Does Hughes control his imagery, use it to thematic advantage—does the man's behaviour toward the woman signify culpability? Or is the imagery undependable, taking to itself disgust, rage, and trepidation beyond the requirements of context—is the man's transcendence tainted?

To explore these issues of artistic control and betraying anxiety, and to assess the possibilities for healing embedded in gendered relation, as Hughes perceived them at this point in his career, it is useful to turn from *Crow* the volume to what Keith Sagar has called 'the great *Crow* project'[13]—the myth Hughes spun for himself as 'a quarry', 'a way of getting the poems'[14] during the late 1960s and early 1970s. Within that larger schema, the poems eventually identified by the volume's subtitle as 'From the Life and Songs of the Crow' were apparently conceived as literal songs occasioned by Crow's experiences within a quest narrative. Although this narrative remains almost completely invisible to us through the published work, Hughes from time to time drops tantalising hints of its details—that **'Lovesong'** from *Crow* and **'Bride and Groom Lie Hidden for Three Days'** from *Cave Birds,* for example, are answers Crow gives to the gnomic questions of an ogress he must recognise as his own bride: 'Who paid most, him or her?'[15] and 'Who gives most, him or her?' The 'alchemical wedding' that culminates this quest indicates that, in the narrative, the solution to Crow's dilemma is posited less in terms of perception—as suggested, for example, by **'Revenge Fable'** and **'Glimpse'** in *Crow* the volume—and more in terms of implicitly sexual relations between men and women. An examination of four poems from the *Crow* material which deal with such relations—**'Crow's Undersong'**, **'Crow's Song about England'**, **'Lovesong'**, and **'Bride and Groom'**—will allow us to assess the strengths and limitations of the solution Hughes offers.[16]

In *Crow* the volume, **'Crow's Undersong'** follows **'Owl's Song'**, a poem which begins with the words 'He sang'. That strategy—the poem presented as a narrative account expanding its title—prepares us to see a parallel relation between poem and title in **'Crow's Undersong'**. Yet **'Crow's Undersong'** begins 'She cannot come all the way', and that female pronoun controls the entire poem. The 'natural' way to read the poem is as the contents of Crow's song, but the parallel with **'Owl's Song'** makes the 'she' slightly peculiar, as if the poem offered not his words but an independent entity singing itself, unperceived by Crow: the undersong personified, coming about its business as in **'The**

Thought-Fox'. It's worth recalling here Uroff's sexual reading of this title: 'his view of man's place against the woman who insatiably comes and comes and comes, even while Crow attempts to fend her off by claiming she cannot manage anything but coming'.[17] Indeed, the description of the female principle offered by the poem is one which few contemporary women will appreciate—'She comes singing she cannot manage an instrument'; 'She comes sluttish she cannot keep house'; 'She comes dumb she cannot manage words'; 'She has come amorous it is all she has come for'—but it is nevertheless consistent with an incarnation of the natural, the procreative, the psychological principle opposed to rationality: 'She brings petals in their nectar fruits in their plush / She brings a cloak of feathers an animal rainbow'. We might see the title, then, as implying that this song underlies Crow's dominant persona, inarticulable but essentially significant; in a sense, it manifests the unconscious recognising itself, the devalued asserting its value. The last lines—'If there had been no hope she would not have come / And there would have been no crying in the city / (There would have been no city)'—convert apparent blame (her fault that there is crying) to necessity, agency: without her, there would be nothing. 'She cannot come all the way': what appears at first as deficiency on reflection suggests that what is missing is a 'he' to, so to speak, come with her, meet her halfway.

'Crow's Song about England'[18] brings a 'he' into play, but as the flip side of a 'she': the poem enacts the disturbing equations posited in Hughes's discussions of gender in Shakespeare's work, metamorphic equivalents reminiscent of Blake's 'The Mental Traveller'. Using *Venus and Adonis* and *The Rape of Lucrece* as paradigms through which to view the plays, Hughes perceives a persistent 'oscillation' 'from loving female to angry male';[19] here 'a girl' becomes an unspecified 'he' and then becomes 'a little girl' again. Each gender exists alone, but comes into being in reaction to the other, so the interdependence is clear; at the same time, relation is so embedded in the male's violent rejection of the female that transcendence or mutuality seems impossible. 'She trie[s] to give' herself, and then 'she trie[s] to keep' herself: neither strategy is sufficient; in each case her self is taken from her, used as evidence against her. The culminating lines of these sections—'She tried to give [or keep] her cunt / It was produced in open court she was sentenced'—indicate that female sexuality in itself constitutes a crime in this perverse society. And thus the female, 'mad with pain', underlies male violence:

> She changed sex he came back
>
> Where he saw her mouth he stabbed with a knife
> Where he saw her eyes he stabbed likewise
> Where he saw her breasts her cunt he stabbed

In its distressingly phallic violence, **'Crow's Song about England'** recalls **'Fleeing from Eternity'**, but here the societal critique works less ambiguously. 'Where he saw her mouth' turns the poem's violence simultaneously outward against other women and inward against the traces of femininity perceptible in the male self. Violence against women is thus implicitly self-destructive, implicitly a result of a society which 'frames' women in sexual roles, which defines both giving and keeping as crimes, which denies interrelation through opposition.

In **'Lovesong'** man and woman are at last coexistent, but express their love by devouring, negating the other.

> He loved her and she loved him
> His kisses sucked out her whole past and future or
>   tried to
> He had no other appetite
> She bit him she gnawed him she sucked
> She wanted him complete inside her

'In the morning', the poem concludes, 'they wore each other's face'. The poem particularises emotion through a series of correlatives as idealised love becomes 'appetite', becomes disguised spite:

> Her smiles were spider bites
> So he would lie still till she felt hungry
> His words were occupying armies
>
>   . . . . .
>
> His whispers were whips and jackboots
> Her kisses were lawyers steadily writing
>
>   . . . . .
>
> Her promises took the top off his skull
> She would get a brooch made of it
> His vows pulled out all her sinews
> He showed her how to make a love-knot

Through its contrasts, **'Lovesong'** forces us to perceive the violence implicit in possessiveness, the justifications that accompany cruelty, the societally characteristic methods of woman and man, the equivalence of overt and insidious violence, and—perhaps most intriguingly—an awareness of complicity in destruction. We might recall that, in Hughes's early 'Incompatibilities', terror transformed into desire paradoxically culminates in the solitary fall 'through the endless / Without-world of the other'. **'Lovesong'** subverts that isolation, identifies each partner's role as victim and agent, asserts the pattern of relationship which defines and contains each through that role, implies endless repetition through their interchangeability—in short, presents devouring sexuality as implicitly a manifestation of the culture's debilitating fragmentation. Crow's answer to the ogress' question—'Who paid most, him or her?'—transforms it to 'Who extorted most?'; love in this economy becomes a competition to make the other pay, to evade payment oneself. Yet to engage in this competition is to lose even one's gender: 'they wore each other's face'.

After poems in which male and female 'cannot come all the way' to each other, or supplant each other inexorably, or 'love' each other out of existence, the moving delineation of mutuality in 'Bride and groom lie hidden for three days' comes as a relief—and yet on closer examination this mutuality too becomes less equal. Though male and female share a delight in existence and in each other, 'she' characteristically *finds* the parts of his body 'She gives him his eyes, she found them / She has found his hands for him / Now she has brought his feet . . .'—while 'he' characteristically *devises* her parts:

> He has assembled her spine,
>   . . . . .
>
> And he has fashioned her new hips
>   . . . . .
>
> And now he connects her throat,
>   her breasts and the pit of her stomach
> With a single wire

Although the task facing each entity is virtually identical, Hughes emphasises the male's cleverness: where he recovers her skin, 'He just seemed to pull it down out of the air', in a masterful act of prestidigitation or sorcery; the labour of restoring her spine is explicitly 'a superhuman puzzle but he is inspired'. Her response to his gifts is emotional—'She weeps with fearfulness and astonishment'; 'She leans back . . . laughing incredulously'—while he is active, centred in his body: 'his hands . . . / . . . are amazed at themselves'; 'his whole body lights up'. Her activities are understated, mediated through the skills supposedly appropriate to femininity: she 'smooths' his skull, ties his teeth, 'stitches his body here and there / with steely purple silk'. If her final act shows an artisan's skill—'She inlays with deepcut scrolls the nape of his neck'—the paradigm of female slightness established by the rest of the poem makes the achievement something of a surprise. In 'Crow's Undersong', 'she comes singing she cannot manage an instrument', 'with eyes wincing frightened', 'she has come amorous it is all she has come for', and here too—although the incapacity is relative, the fearfulness inextricable from delight, the mutuality of desire central—she 'cannot manage' what he can, and her worth to him is ultimately, essentially sexual. When she fits his hands to his wrists 'they go feeling all over her'; his last and thus most significant act is to '[sink] into place the inside of her things', giving her her sexuality. If 'they bring each other to perfection', so that both of them can 'come all the way', that 'perfection' might nevertheless feel diminishing to a female reader.

In his *Crow* project, Hughes uses gender for purposes to which a feminist might well assent: to acknowledge and ultimately embrace devalued aspects of the self, to critique a society in which a rejection of the 'feminine' excuses self-destructive violence, to explore how such a society breeds competition and possessiveness, to offer an alternative in mutual respect and delight. Yet, even in mutuality, his female remains Other. As incarnation of Nature,[20] she is voiceless—and this voicelessness persists into more realistic portrayals: although the matched 'promises' and 'vows' of **'Lovesong'** implicitly put words in both mouths, 'his words' are explicitly paired with 'her laughs', 'his whispers' with 'her kisses'. Although each poem apparently seeks to revalue the female, in each case her insufficiency comprises part of the poem's logic—even to the point of explaining violence towards women through outraged femininity in **'Crow's Song about England'**. And in each case the female is essentially sexualised, defined by her sexuality. If part of Hughes's point is that the Western (male) intellect must recognise and embrace its intuitions, its emotions, its connectedness, its sexuality, that laudable precept nevertheless rests on an identification of the female as intuitive, emotional, connected, and sexual—an object available to be embraced, rather than a fully realised partner, a complex subjectivity. While **'Lovesong'** and **'Bride and groom'** grapple intriguingly with this dilemma, the closed sexual arena—whether claustrophobic, or more appealingly intimate—ratifies the limited definition of the female and thus implicitly assents to objectification.

In the twenty years since the publication of *Crow,* Hughes has continued to experiment with the configurations that dominate the early books: repressive piety, debilitating rationalism, reciprocal violence, unperceived culpability, grim transcendence. Women still punctuate these experiments, as active agents and as passive victims.

Thus the baboon-woman who joins with the priest in the mutual rebirth of the *Gaudete* narrative, and the biting goddess of its lyrics, are matched in *Cave Birds* by the woman whose 'heart stopped beating' 'While I strolled' ('Something was happening'), and by the 'earth / . . . [that] turned in its bed / To the wall' ('In these fading moments I wanted to say'): thus the vampiric snow woman of *River,* whose 'kiss / Grips through the full throat and locks on the dislodged vertebrae' (**'Japanese River Tales'**) of the now-freezing stream, is matched by the 'earth invalid' of *Moortown,* who 'Leans back, eyes closed, exhausted, smiling / Into the sun' 'While we sit, and smile, and wait, and know / She is not going to die' ('March morning unlike others'). Even the 'empty hole through into nothing' appears with striking corporeality in the Sheela-na-gig which serves *Gaudete*'s Lumb as an object of contemplation:

> The simply hacked-out face of a woman
> Gazes back at Lumb

Between her raised, wide-splayed, artless knees
With a stricken expression.
Her square-cut, primitive fingers, beneath her buttocks
Are pulling herself wide open—

(*Gaudete*, p. 110)

The conclusion of this section—'Heavens opening higher beyond heavens / As the afternoon widens'— transforms the violence implicit in 'hacked-out' and 'stricken' into a redeeming vision of the universe giving birth to itself. Indeed, these volumes generally point towards healing: the convalescent earth is still a **'Woman Unconscious',** but we 'know / She is not going to die'.

Whatever the successes of these more recent volumes, however, *Crow* remains a point of strength in Hughes's career, with a continuing power to fascinate, to influence, and—emphatically—to disturb. This disturbing quality explains in part the notoriety that has dogged its author. Myth—Hughes's method in *Crow*—involves a therapeutic representation of personal anxieties. The encounter with the shadow requires that we face what we most fear, a fear compounded by the societal assumptions that formed us and by our uneasy suspicion that what we despise in others is present in ourselves. For readers who share the assumptions and anxieties of the author the myth may offer a healing insight—or it may represent unbearable threat. For readers who do not share these assumptions—or no longer share them— the myth may appear not as an exploration encouraging insight and redefinition, but as evidence of an indictable society—as in fact it is. And to the extent that diagnosis and neurosis overlap, the reader may be led to equate the physician with the illness he describes. Rather than commend the myth for the accuracy of its aim, the reader will then reject it as a symptom of this ill. Can bigotry seek to eradicate itself? Can neurosis hazard a cure?

In *Crow,* Hughes's probing to the split between consciousness and instinct leads him to a sexual correlative, a figuration which is convincing as an analogue for unacknowledged interdependency in the psyche, and which allows Hughes to submerge sexual anxiety in an indictment of the society that, at some level, produced and ratified it. By displacing his anxieties to what David Holbrook terms a 'split-off indestructible self'[21]— Crow—he both obscures his own guilt—including his guilt as a survivor—and triumphs over death and nothingness. Sexual anxiety and mortal anxiety intertwine: rejection of the female, all too natural in the context of the 'horrible oven of fangs' and the 'octopus maw', is nevertheless a form of suicide.

For a man who came to age in the early 1950s, the assumptions at the heart of this figuration can be surprising only in their intensity—indeed, they are the familiar assumptions of Romanticism, stripped bare. Given

Hughes's indictment of rational materialism and his recognition of the female principle as essential to wholeness, he must be stunned by feminist rejection of his work. In order to write, we might posit, Hughes cannot accept such criticism; his philosophy is a product of personal development, a means of externalising and thus controlling personal anxiety. Is it possible for a reader to sympathise with Hughes's artistic and personal dilemmas, to assent to his mythic paradigms, to deplore with him societal objectifications, to keep message and messenger separate?

Rather than attempt to address such questions—which must in any case remain rhetorical—we may find it intriguing to shift focus to Hughes's most recent work. Does Hughes continue to deploy female figures emblematically and ambivalently? How might a feminist reader respond to *Wolfwatching*?

At first glance, the volume may seem more a compendium than a unity: it contains naturalistic animal poems, densely mythic poems, seemingly autobiographical poems, poems about war, poems of place—a virtual catalogue of the many distinct styles and themes with which Hughes has experimented during his career. But closer examination reveals coherence and design, founded once more in gender.

Wolfwatching begins with a hawk (a sparrow-hawk)— 'The warrior / Blue shoulder-cloak wrapped about him'—and ends with doves—'Nearly uncontrollable love-weights. / Or now / Temple-dancers'. The volume is thus framed by slightly disguised or displaced emblems of war and peace, the masculine and the feminine. The volume's two mythic poems create a second, interior frame, as both **'Two Astrological Conundrums'** (the second poem in the volume) and 'Take what you want but pay for it' (the fourth from the end) explore gendered emblems of relation. The first 'Conundrum' offers the fable of the tigress who

. . . promised to show me her cave
which was the escape route from death
And which came out into a timeless land.

To find this cave, she said, we lie down
And you hold me, so, and we fly.

In its vaginal 'cave', the 'escape route from death', this poem recalls the sexual solutions of *The Hawk in the Rain,* but removed from literal interaction to a more mythic, shamanistic relation with the goddess. 'Folded / In the fur', 'dissolved / in the internal powers of tiger', the protagonist has the opportunity to become 'The neverdying god who gives everything', but somehow fails:

> I heard
> A sudden cry of terror, an infant's cry—
> Close, as if my own ear had cried it.
>
> . . . . .
>
> A bright spirit went away weeping.

'Take what you want but pay for it' offers a similarly mythic use of the female. Here Adam's wounded body, tortured by God so that it 'Shall destroy [the soul's] peace no more', 'exhal[es] . . . from the blackest pit of all'

> A misty enfoldment which materialized
> As a musing woman, who lifted the body
> As a child's effortless, and walked
> Out of the prison with it, singing gently

In the first poem, 'terror' brings the protagonist back to earth, perhaps as an infant reborn in the chain of existence, driving away the 'bright spirit' who might have delivered him as an equal into godhead. In the second, 'despair' draws out the female emanation who frees the body, nurtures it, mothers it. In the first case, mothering represents the protagonist's failure; in the second, the body's victory—but in each case the duality of female and male, mother and child signals a deeper unity, misperceived as separation in the first poem, valued as relation in the second.

These poems exploring a quasi-Blakean mothering principle alert us to other references to mothers peppering the volume. In **'Slump Sundays'**, the 'seed-corn' of experience 'Lugged back from the Somme . . . served for a mother-tongue'; in 'Dust as we are', the 'knowledge' brought back by 'My post-war father' fills the speaker: 'After mother's milk / This was the soul's food'. Women structure the postwar world as representatives of society, of relation at once intimate and judgemental. In the father's memory, 'naked men / Slithered staring where their mothers and sisters / Would never have to meet their eyes'; when the man in **'Sacrifice'** belatedly determines to join his brothers' business, 'The duumvirate of wives turned down their thumbs'. Hughes's familiar trope of reciprocity—'When Crow cried his mother's ear / Scorched to a stump'—appears here through the identity of men with their families: when the man in **'Sacrifice'** hangs himself,

> his sister, forty miles off,
>
> Cried out at the hammer blow on her nape.
> And his daughter
> Who'd climbed up to singsong: 'Supper, Daddy'
> Fell back down the stairs to the bottom.

In **'Walt'**, the German's wartime bullet 'brought him and his wife down together / With all his children one after the other'. Again and again, the aftermath of war is triangulated through women: sisters, daughters, wives, mothers of the next generation, where the repercussions echo.

The two poems in the volume which might be portraits of Hughes's own mother play intriguingly with the motifs of mothering suggested in the mythic poems. In **'Source'**, the mother weeps without apparent cause, as if she 'could dissolve yourself, me, everything / Into this relief of your strange music'; in **'Leaf Mould'**, the mother carries 'your spectre-double, still in her womb', and the poem ends with the memory of how it felt 'as you escaped'. The repetition of dissolving and weeping from the fable of the tigress, and the anticipation of doubling, of nurturance, of modes of freedom, soon to be repeated in 'Take what you want', translate mythic unity in duality into the more literal relation of mother and uncomprehending, belatedly grateful son. The war forms a backdrop to each poem, a possible explanation of the 'mourning / That repaired you' in **'Source'**, a forest of 'cenotaphs' for 'cordite conscripts' echoed in the mother's perception of the literal forest in **'Leaf Mould'**. Where the poems about men who have survived the war delineate the impossible weight of responsibility they suffer under and pass on, these poems about mothering suggest the potential for 'relief', though in ways which at first may feel defeating or coercive.

In the paradigm of mother and child which structures the volume and raises its central questions of relation and identity, of loss of self and acceptance of pain, what happens to mutuality, to the equality of sexual relations, to the alchemical marriage?

In **'Anthem for Doomed Youth'**, the echo of Eliot's *Waste Land*—'And who's that other beside her?'—alerts us to a glimpse of the goddess, however ironic or misperceived, in the girl-friends—'portly birds'—set in the Ford's back seat by the 'doomed' brothers whose 'glances / Hawked' the countryside, searching for 'tame, fuddled coveys'.

In the far more serious poem that follows, **'The Black Rhino'**, the rhinoceros is at first explicitly male; then ambiguously 'you', 'I', 'it'; then finally, in the poem's third section, explicitly female. The shifting pronoun underscores the shift from strength to vulnerability, encompasses the entire species, and enables the sexual figuration—'an ornament for a lady's lap', 'the black hole in her head'—through which Hughes indicts both genders of the human species in the extinction of others.

'On the Reservations' too designates its section by gender, but here the first is evidently a husband, the second a wife, the third their child. In a lifetime of coal and ashes metaphorically left in his Christmas stocking, the miner of the first section recalls only one interaction with a woman, presumably his wife: 'The brochures screwed up in a tantrum / As her hair shrivelled to a cinder'. Momentary anger and lifelong disappointment equally shrivel her beauty and youth, as the couple's cramped existence reduces her to mere coal-slag, hopeless Cinderella. In her section, this diminishment speaks through the repeated phrase 'She dreams she sleepwalks', which conveys daily life as a nightmare of exhaustion, converts sleep to perpetual restlessness, and makes even the dream of walking a delusion. The surreal combinations of the horrific and the mundane culminate, however, in a lost moment of mutuality:

> Remembering how a flare of pure torrent
> sluiced the pit muck
> off his shoulder-slopes while her hands
> soapy with milk blossoms anointed
> him and in their hearth
> fingers of the original sun opened
> the black
> bright book of the stone
> he'd brought from beneath dreams
> or did she dream it

The poem's last section offers, in its portrait of this couple's 'sulky boy', the punk as alchemical child. The irony is that, like the alchemical original, he promises transcendence through transformation:

> This megawatt, berserker medium
> With his strobe-drenched battle-cry delivers
> The nineteenth century from his mother's womb:
>
> The work-house dread that brooded, through her term,
> Over the despair of salvaged sperm.
> . . . . .
> Bomblit, rainbowed, aboriginal:
> 'Start afresh, this time unconquerable.'

'Delivers' turns the berserker into postman, into midwife, into liberator: the 'nineteenth century' *is* 'the work-house dread', now loosed on the world 'afresh'; is the brood-hen, the contemplator, that brings despair to fruition; is the child himself, result of capitalism's 'dark work', who converts defeat into invulnerability by rejecting society's terms.

Finally, the volume's last poem, **'A Dove'**, never in fact specifies the dove as female, despite the opposition with the masculine hawk, despite the implications of 'love-weights' and 'temple-dancers'. Its last lines— 'Bubbling molten, wobbling top-heavy / Into one and many'—enables the evasion of difference through a refusal of gender. 'One and many': could a feminist assent to this? Maybe.

Notes

1. The 'man in black' appears in Sylvia Plath's 'Daddy', *Ariel* (Faber & Faber, London, 1965) p. 55.

2. Morgan, Robin, 'Arraignment', in *Monster* (Vintage, New York, 1972), pp. 76-7; Perloff, Mar-

jorie, 'The Two Ariels: The (Re)making of the Sylvia Plath Canon', in *American Poetry Review,* 13, No. 6 (November-December, 1984), 10-18.

3. Rich, Adrienne, *Diving into the Wreck: Poems 1971-1972* (Norton, New York and London, 1973). See, in particular, 'Meditations for a Savage Child' (pp. 53-62), or 'The Phenomenology of Anger' (pp. 25-31): 'The prince of air and darkness / computing body counts, masturbating / in the factory / of facts.'

4. 'The Rock', *The Listener,* 19 September 1963, pp. 421-3.

5. 'Ted Hughes Writes', in *Poetry Book Society Bulletin* 15 (September 1957).

6. Uroff, Margaret Dickie, *Sylvia Plath and Ted Hughes* (University of Illinois, Urbana, Chicago and London, 1979), p. 52.

7. Review of Max Nicholson, *The Environmental Revolution, Your Environment* 1, 3 (Summer 1970), pp. 81-3; rpt in Ekbert Faas, *Ted Hughes: The Unaccommodated Universe* (Black Sparrows, Santa Barbara, 1980), p. 186.

8. Smith, A. C. H. *Orghast at Persepolis* (Eyre Methuen, London, 1972), p. 47.

9. Note to *A Choice of Shakespeare's Verse* (Faber & Faber, London, 1971), p. 199.

10. 'Myth and Education', in *Children's Literature in Education,* 1 (1970), p. 66.

11. 'Myth and Education', p. 70.

12. Faas, 'Ted Hughes and *Crow* (1970): An Interview with Ekbert Faas', in *London Magazine* 10, No. 10 (January 1971), rpt in Faas, *Ted Hughes: The Unaccommodated Universe*, p. 200.

13. Sagar, Keith, *The Art of Ted Hughes* (Cambridge University Press, Cambridge 1978), p. 171.

14. Faas, p. 213.

15. Faas, p. 144.

16. It is perhaps worth noting explicitly that I have ordered these poems for the purposes of my own argument, not in an effort to replicate Hughes's intentions.

17. Uroff, p. 210.

18. First published in *Poems: Fainlight, Hughes, Sillitoe* (Rainbow Press, 1971), but more conveniently available in Keith Sagar (ed.), *The Achievement of Ted Hughes* (University of Manchester Press, Manchester, 1983).

19. *A Choice of Shakespeare's Verse,* p. 190.

20. For further considerations of the disturbing implications of this trope, see Ortner, Sherry B., 'Is Woman to Man as Nature is to Culture?' in Michelle Zimbalist Rosaldo and Louise Lamphere (eds), *Woman, Culture, and Society* (Stanford University Press, Stanford, 1974), pp. 67-87; and the collection of essays prompted by Ortner's argument, Carol MacCormack and Marilyn Strathern (eds), *Nature, Culture and Gender* (Cambridge University Press, Cambridge, 1980).

21. Holbrook, David, 'Ted Hughes's *Crow* and the Longing for Non-Being' in *The Black Rainbow: Essays on the Present Breakdown of Culture*, Peter Abbs (ed.) (Heinemann, London, 1975), p. 41.

Terry Gifford (essay date 1994)

SOURCE: Gifford, Terry. "Gods of Mud: Hughes and the Post-pastoral." In *The Challenge of Ted Hughes,* edited by Keith Sagar, pp. 129-41. New York: St. Martin's Press, 1994.

[*In the following essay, Gifford examines Hughes's late nature poetry, particularly in the collection* Moortown, *as a version of pastoral, or more properly, post-pastoral.*]

It has been clear from his earliest work that the poetry of Ted Hughes has challenged our urbanised, post-industrial, denatured society by making, first, images and, later, myths, that would reconnect our own natural energies with those at work in the external natural world. This poetry has also represented a challenge to our denatured culture which has promoted poets to key editorial positions whose work is cerebral and conspicuously disconnected from the natural world. To Craig Raine, Poetry Editor at Faber and Faber, a flood is an opportunity to make verbal conceits that are, in the end, self-referential rather than enlarging our perception of the subject-matter itself:

> Every quibble returns to the torrent,
>
> And even the slow digressions at our feet
> Are part of an overall argument.
>
> They cover all the points of grass.
> What single-minded brilliance,
>
> What logic!
> Not one of us can look away.[1]

But, of course, the reader already has 'looked away' from a flood to the surface of the language itself. The 'logic' of Nature in this poem is ignored since the mind conspicuously at work here is that of the lucid, sophisticated poet 'covering all the points' of his extended metaphor.

I have wanted to establish at the outset the bizarre incongruity between the poetry of Ted Hughes and that of his latter-day editor at Faber and Faber not only to indicate what I mean by a denatured poetic culture, but because David Moody, in an article entitled 'Telling It Like It's Not'[2] accuses Hughes of deploying the same technique as Craig Raine, with the same result. This is an argument to which I want to return in considering Hughes's most recent work.

But my main concern here is to examine Hughes's contribution to contemporary poetry by rereading his work through the perspectives of the pastoral. In choosing the term 'pastoral' as a touchstone I am aware that it is unfashionable, unreconstructed and now usually pejorative, despite Seamus Heaney's rearguard attempt to argue for its contemporary neutrality.[3] It is an indication of our denatured culture that the terms 'Nature poet' or 'Nature poetry' have also come to be used pejoratively. However, I want to make it clear that I follow Raymond Williams in *The City and The Country* and Barrell and Bull, editors of *The Penguin Book of Pastoral Verse,* in using the term 'pastoral' to represent a false construction of reality, usually idealised, often nostalgic, and distorting the historical, economic and organic tensions at work in human relationships with Nature.

Raymond Williams comments upon Pope's making explicit the deception of the pastoral tradition:

> 'We must therefore use some illusion to render a Pastoral delightful; and this consists in exposing the best side only of a shepherd's life, and in concealing its miseries.' When Pope could say that, the 'tradition' had been altered. 'No longer truth, though shown in verse.' The long critical dispute, in the seventeenth and eighteenth centuries, on the character of pastoral poetry had this much, at least, as common ground. What was at issue was mainly whether such an idyll, the delightful Pastoral, should be referred always to the Golden Age, as Rapin and the neo-classicists argued; or to the more permanent and indeed timeless idea of the tranquillity of life in the country, as Fontenelle and others maintained.[4]

Barrell and Bull anticipate a revival of comfortable, idealised nature poetry in contemporary Britain:

> Indeed, with the current concern for ecology, it is not difficult to anticipate a revival of interest in the Pastoral—Industrial Man looking away from technological Wasteland to an older and better world. . . . But now and in England, the Pastoral is a lifeless form, of service only to decorate the shelves of tasteful cottages, 'modernised to a high standard . . .'. For today, more than ever before, the pastoral vision simply will not do.[5]

Yet there is also now an evident need for poetry which engages with Nature.

Indeed, even under the metaphorical flamethrowers of the metropolitan Martians, Pan is hard to kill. Against the odds of our cultural politics, very varied Nature poetry is being written in these islands today by Sorley MacLean in Scotland, by Heaney in Ireland, by Gillian Clarke in Wales and, of course, by Hughes in England, to name but a representative few. How much of this contemporary Nature poetry, then, can be called 'pastoral'? I would want to argue that the poetry of George Mackay Brown actually sets out to achieve all of those qualities that constitute the pastoral, and given more space might suggest that he is continuously rewriting the same exemplary nostalgic, idealised pastoral poem. (Against this yardstick Craig Raine's poem would have to be termed 'a-pastoral'.) However, the Skye poet, Sorley MacLean, in 'Scrapadal',[6] asserts the historical associations of place against the seal-smooth backs of nuclear submarines in the Sound of Raasay. His poetry has clearly got beyond pastoral nostalgia, into the less comfortable tensions of what I might term the 'post-pastoral'. Gillian Clarke swims with seals,[7] but also in her latest collection, *Letting In the Rumour*,[8] describes connecting with wind power to light her house in a poem of unsentimental elemental celebration. Her recent work is clearly 'far out at sea all night' in the enlightenment of the post-pastoral! Heaney is capable of pastoral, in the first part of *Station Island*,[9] for example, as I have argued elsewhere.[10] But Heaney's poetry at its best has got beyond the pastoral. In *Field Work*[11] he uses Nature imagery as a mode of thinking about his own experiences, whether of love or of death, or of his own unease with his role as a writer. Where Heaney is a personal sounding-board for Nature, Hughes is a shamanistic maker of myths. Where Heaney's poetry cannot avoid images of Nature as its mode of expression, Hughes's poetry cannot avoid it as his subject. Both have developed a vision beyond pastoral poetry, but for both, pastoralism offers the best definition of the risk they take.

I now want to trace two strands through the work of Ted Hughes, suggesting that much of the early work is acting as militant anti-pastoral before developing into the visionary poetry that might be called 'post-pastoral'. I would like to clarify the features of Hughes's particular form of post-pastoral poetry against the background of very different contemporary Nature poets whose parallel contributions I have only been able to hint at in this Introduction. (I shall define Hughes's place within the context of other writers mentioned here in a forthcoming book, *Why Has Nature Poetry Survived?*) Finally, looking briefly at *River,* which has been regarded as Hughes's best book,[12] it is necessary to confront the possibility of pastoralism in that volume and to attempt to offer criteria for distinguishing such poetry from that which achieves the post-pastoral within the same book.

Anti-Pastoral

'Egg-Head', from Hughes's first collection,[13] has long seemed to me to be a manifesto poem, a direct challenge to the reader and an indirect challenge to pastoral poetry. It begins where Lawrence left off: in the 'otherness' of the natural world and in 'the war between vitality and death' even in the process of 'becoming'.[14] But Hughes is more ironic. The title of this poem might, for example, be considered as a play upon Lawrence's notion of 'sex in the head',[15] as the hyphen seems to be suggesting. The stance which is being ridiculed in this poem was also mocked by Blake: 'For man has closed himself up, till he sees all things through narrow chinks of his cavern.'[16] In Hughes's poem, 'So many a one has dared to be struck dead / Peeping through his fingers at the world's ends, / Or at an ant's head.' This filtering-out produces safe subjects such as a leaf's, as opposed to a tiger's, 'otherness'. It also produces beautiful distortions such as 'eagled peaks' in which the power of the eagle is defused to become the adjective describing the peak, just as 'the whaled sea-bottom' is coyly 'monstered'. These opening images are being presented as examples, taken together in this context, of inventive, seductive, pretty, pastoralism. Against such images as 'might be painted on a nursery wall' Hughes went on to celebrate the jaguar's otherness in the poem in *The Hawk in the Rain,* the enlightened destructiveness of the eagle in *Under the North Star,* and those uncomfortable mythic monsters from **'Ghost Crabs'** (*Wodwo*) to **'The Executioner'** (*Cave Birds*).

Of course the egg in **'Egg-Head'** produces a man who is also a cockerel. Thus in his first volume Hughes apparently invented the later protagonist of *Cave Birds*. The fact that this man 'trumpet[s] his own ear dead' with an overdose of Gerald Manley Hopkins should not overshadow the importance of this poem in launching a determination to '[receive] the flash / of the sun, the bolt of the earth', and to face 'the looming mouth of the earth' and 'the whelm of the sun'. Here in the verbs are the awesome forces of vitality and death: in 'whelm' and 'looming', 'flash' and 'bolt'. But here too are elements of Earth and Sun, dark and light, material and spirit, mud and god, equal in power, but only *apparently* focused upon by the 'lucid sophistries' of egg-heads like Craig Raine.

Part of the hostility towards the early anti-pastoral poetry of Hughes can be accounted for, perhaps, in the representation of his acting as a shaman bringing us images of 'wilderness'. 'Wilderness' is a concept that is more psychological than geographical. In European folklore it is what its etymology suggests, 'the place of wild beasts'.[17] As such, it's the very opposite of the pastoral. From his wilderness alternative to a 'whaled monstered sea-bottom', Hughes brought us **'The Thought-Fox'** (*The Hawk in the Rain*), **'Hawk**

Roosting' (*Lupercal*) and 'Wodwo' (*Wodwo*), all of them ultimately, of course, from the wilderness of the human psyche. What Hughes had exposed was the old fear of the dark unknown in the natural world that hovers around the Old English notion of 'wilddeer-ness'. Even walking in a safely pastoral National Park Hughes might meet a black mountain goat that could turn him under an eye 'slow and cold and ferocious as a star', as might have happened in the making of the poem 'Meeting' in *The Hawk in the Rain.* Unfortunately, Hughes's own efforts to outstare the complacently pastoral attitude to nature occasionally led to a little melodramatic distortion in the opposite direction. In what sense, for example, can a star be 'ferocious'? 'Slow and cold' perhaps, but 'ferocious' is surely a little too active compared with, say, 'fierce' in its sense of 'intense'. Just as Hughes has continued writing anti-pastoral through **'Glimpse'**, for example, in *Crow,* **'A green mother'** (*Cave Birds*), **'Lumb Chimneys'** (*Remains of Elmet*) and the correctives to the common pastoral associations with lambs in *Moortown,* so too there have been the attendant dangers of over-correction from the metallic images of **'Snowdrop'** (*Lupercal*), through the bathos of **'For Billy Holt'** (*Remains of Elmet*) to the nuclear overkill of the warrior **'Sparrow Hawk'** (*Wolfwatching*). But Hughes's greatest achievement has been in going further than any other contemporary writer beyond the 'cliché or consolation' of pastoral, as Heaney puts it.[18]

POST-PASTORAL

I want briefly to indicate five features of what I shall characterise as Hughes's post-pastoral poetry, but first I would like to focus this discussion by considering the notion of 'gods of mud'. The final stage of *Cave Birds* is that of rediscovery of the self, including the sensuality of the human body, celebrated in a poem which is the answer to the question 'Who gave most, him or her?'. The climax of a male and female 'giving each other' the exquisite discovery of the workings of the machinery of each part of their bodies is also a sexual climax:

> So, gasping with joy, with cries of wonderment
> Like two gods of mud
> Sprawling in the dirt, but with infinite care
>
> They bring each other to perfection.
>
> **('Bride and groom lie hidden for three days')**

Just as they can only achieve perfection by giving to each other, so they are both 'gods' *and* 'sprawling in the dirt'. This detail is clearly anti-pastoral in function, countering any suggestion of transcendence in 'gods' by keeping the experience animal and material. But the duality of 'gods of mud' is post-pastoral in its vision of mud and dirt as the possible context for the 'infinite care' that brings a sense of perfected fulfilment, as through that of a god. Their 'sprawling' in the mud firmly maintains the notion of 'gods' as a metaphor here.

The first feature, then, of Hughes's post-pastoral is a body of poetry that explores this tension as a dynamic process in Nature. Perhaps the earliest gods of mud were to be found in **'Crow Hill'** (*Lupercal*) where 'Pigs upon delicate feet / Hold off the sky, trample the strength / That shall level these hills at length'. The delicacy is there again, the celebration of heroic god-like lives that 'hold off the sky', and the simultaneous awareness of the presence of mud-flow levelling. But the tension between these forces is focused upon the pigs themselves within the single line that balances forces at work above and below them. Again transcendence is avoided: pigs do not fly, even on the Crow Hill of what is now 'Hughes Country'.

This dynamic duality is at work in every volume of Hughes's poetry, so that it constitutes a notion of Nature that is more wholly achieved than can be seen in the production of any other contemporary poet. The process is explicitly celebrated in **'Still Life'** (*Wodwo*) where the god in the harebell is 'the maker of the sea' and the mud is 'outcrop stone'. In **'Mosquito'** (*Under the North Star*) mud is replaced by ice, but after many deaths 'Mosquito / Flew up singing, over the broken waters— / A little haze of wings, a midget sun'. It may be midget, but its life has the light of a sun in its wings, clearly a god of 'broken waters'. In **'Salmon Eggs'** (*River*) the 'mud-blooms' of the river produce 'the nameless / Teeming inside atoms'. Such dynamics as the salmon 'emptying themselves for each other', or of a conceit such as 'The river goes on / Sliding through its place, undergoing itself / In its wheel' do not need the heavy overlay of religious functions with which this poem ultimately pleads too much.

Of course the second feature of Hughes's particular contribution to post-pastoral is his exploration of these tensions in the dramas of the myths. The female figure who makes a first appearance, perhaps, in **'Crow's Undersong'** (*Crow*) is a god of mud, an underground presence from the wilderness such as Lilith,[19] who is just as much a presence in **'How Water Began to Play'** (*Crow*) as in the poems that explicitly feature her. 'She stays / Even after life even among the bones.' Water has to meet 'maggot and rottenness' as well as 'womb' before it can achieve the vision of itself as inanimate, 'utterly worn out' but 'utterly clear'. Similarly at the conclusion of *Cave Birds* 'The dirt becomes God' in the vision of 'The risen' falcon.[20] And in the simple discovery that concludes *Adam and the Sacred Nine* (*Moortown*), 'The sole of a foot' celebrates 'with even, gentle squeeze' its fitting the surface of 'world-rock' in the ultimate down-to-earth, post-pastoral poem.

But perhaps a challenge could be made for that distinction by some of the poems in **Moortown Diary.** The recent republication[21] of the poems under that title is introduced by a political statement against 'the EEC Agricultural Policy War' which indicates just how far from the pastoral the Poet Laureate intended to take his starting-point in these poems. Here, then, is the third feature of Hughes's post-pastoral notion of Nature: that of direct responsibility for the management of it. That **'February 17th'** produces a powerfully symbolic image of a lamb's head stuck in mud, is almost incidental to the urgency of caring, practical responsibility being enacted in the poem. When that involved observation is turned upon a co-worker in **'A Monument'** the cost of a lifetime of that responsibility for Nature is seen in detail. Indeed such a detail as the 'gasping struggle / In the knee-deep mud of the copse ditch' might suggest anti-pastoral were the reader not to know that this is an elegy to an effort that is finally 'using your life up'. That tension of making and unmaking, of a 'face fixed at full effort' yet hammering the staple 'precise to the tenth of an inch' is not a long way away from the pigs of **'Crow Hill'** on their delicate feet 'hold[ing] off', while at the same time trampling a strength that is ultimately greater than themselves.

In Hughes's notion of Nature the outer processes echo the inner processes so that they are part of a whole. The organic tensions in external Nature are enacted in human nature. Processes at work in landscapes are at work in the human complex of energies. This is what 'The knight' recognises in **Cave Birds,** and Lumb in his identification with the tree from which his changeling self is made (**Gaudete**). In **Remains of Elmet** external natural processes are shown to be reflected not just in individuals but in both a farming and an industrial culture. Hence the poem title **'Dead Farms, Dead Leaves',** for example, or the poem about **'Lumb Chimneys'** 'flowering' like trees and 'falling into the future, into earth'.

This fourth feature of Hughes's post-pastoral poetry, in which outer processes reflect inner processes, is closely linked to a fifth feature concerning the way this notion of Nature is frequently expressed. If culture, human life, animal life, the workings of weather and landscape are parts of an interactive whole, then it is possible to express this relationship through an interchangeability of images. One can say that dead farms *are* the dead leaves of the culture of Elmet. Again **Remains of Elmet** provides a rich source of examples of this linguistic pattern. Perhaps the most all-inclusive is the title-poem, which sees the Calder Valley as 'the long gullet' of a creature which eats even the farms that are themselves 'stony masticators / Of generations that ate each other / To nothing inside them'.

Pastoral or Post-Pastoral?

It is this last characteristic of Hughes's achievement, which I have described as a consequence of the unity of his post-pastoral vision, that David Moody characterises as 'telling it like it's not'. For him Hughes is working a dangerous reversal: 'Hughes fairly consistently translates his birds and beasts and fishes into something man-made, and he translates anything human into the animal or the brute'.[22] The danger lies, he argues, in perceiving Nature through the *writer's* sensations and taking for granted the reality (and the rights) of the creature itself. He demonstrates this in an examination of the poem **'Earth-numb'** (**Moortown**):

> The hooked salmon is there only in the hunter's sensations; and the hunter's intelligence is so caught up in the sensations that it fails to analyse them and discover what they signify. . . . His mind is active, in throwing up a stream of associations to isolate and dramatise the sensational phase of the experience. At the same time there is a cut-off from any inward knowing and feeling what it means for the salmon. When the salmon does emerge it is only in the form of association.

Moody then quotes from the end of the poem which began with the hunter feeling himself 'hunted and haunted' by the black depths of a river which suddenly grabs him,

> Till the fright flows all one way down the line
>
> And a ghost grows solid, a hoverer,
> A lizard green slither, banner heavy—
>
> Then the wagging stone pebble head
> Trying to think on shallows—
>
> Then the steel spectre of purples
> From the forge of water
> Gagging on emptiness
>
> As the eyes of incredulity
> Fix their death-exposure of the celandine and the cloud.

David Moody writes:

> My crude response to that is 'You bastard!' The refinement of brute sensations into aesthetic effect is offensive if you have feeling for live salmon and remember that this artist has just killed one, all the while carrying on about *his* sensations.

Now I do not accept this as a wholly adequate account of what Hughes has been establishing in this poem. Against the river's apparitions which are hunting him, 'the lure is a prayer'. He is about a dangerous, delicate activity, searching with 'a prayer, like a flower opening'. When the river suddenly grabs him with 'an electrocuting malice / Like a trap' he becomes a connector between river and sky, stiff with an electrical charge that is 'something terrified and terrifying'. Thus the emergence of the ghost in the form of the salmon is a material image of both conquest and sacrifice, survival and death, gain and loss. Hughes has been re-enacting the drama of those tensions that I have suggested signify the height of his achievement. But David Moody's 'crude response' cuts through this symbolic discourse to remind us that in reality the poem is about the writer's gain at the expense of the salmon's loss. Indeed the discourse just does not ring true: a lure is not a prayer, a river is not a trap, the struggle for life of a hooked salmon cannot terrify the fisherman in any deeply-felt sense, otherwise he would not be hunting it to death. What we are confronted with in **'Earth-numb'** is the discourse of pastoral distortion.

The reason this poem is so important is not just because Hughes gives it the status of title-poem for a section of *Moortown,* but because it anticipates a whole volume of poems which has been elevated by recent Hughes scholarship to the status of a holy book. The effort to articulate the apparently transcendental insights of the 'master' has produced some remarkable critical statements. We can read that 'fish swim in a religious trance'[23] (*pace* **'Relic'** and **'Pibroch'**[24]), or that 'river-line meets horizon at the point that vanishes into the transphenomenal'.[25]

'The real task confronting critics of Ted Hughes's poetry is not one of exegesis but of discrimination', writes Edna Longley in her review of *River* for *Poetry Review*:[26] '*River* signals that the temptation of celebratory Hughes is sentimentality and abstraction, rather than verbal melodrama'. Actually, it seems clear to me that **'Earth-numb'** might qualify as evidence that 'verbal melodrama' is also a danger in the most recent writing of Hughes. Indeed if we are to accept the challenge of Edna Longley we ought to be clear about why celebration can lapse into pastoral so consistently in this one volume.

The reasons, I would suggest, are twofold. Both have already been hinted at, and they are connected. It isn't a question of images that try too hard, as Longley's own examples suggest. It is the poetry's fundamental assumption that it is now 'preaching to the converted' and that therefore the language doesn't have to justify itself. This is what I mean by the special pleading of the religious language of **'Salmon Eggs'**. What does it add to the poem to say that 'this is the liturgy / Of the earth's tidings—harrowing, crowned—a travail / Of raptures and rendings. / Sanctus Sanctus / Swathes the blessed issue'? If regeneration is a marvel to be revered, the poem's evidence should show rather than preach this to us, as indeed it has demonstrated to us brilliantly in the earlier part of this poem. Further, if this poem sanctifies the birth process in isolation it will inevitably lead to the sentimentality of 'only birth matters'. Where

is the awareness that 'the tiger blesses with a fang'? (**'Tiger-Psalm'**, *Moortown.*) It is 'inscribed in the egg' of **'October Salmon',** but its presence in 'harrowing, crowned' or 'raptures and rendings' seems glib and formulaic in the absence of the evidence here. So it is not only, firstly, that the accumulation of 'crypts', 'altar', 'liturgy', 'mass', and finally 'font' are unnecessary to the generation of awe, but secondly that the essential elemental tension is a dynamic that is not active in the poem.

'O leaves, Crow sang.' 'O river', sings Hughes through the god's head, according to Scigaj's account of Hughes's 'transfigured vision' of 'a metaphysical source' in **'Salmon Eggs'**.[27] My argument is that Hughes's post-pastoral vision regresses to pastoral when the dynamic represented by 'gods of mud' is taken for granted by the signifiers of the text. The result is a static assertion of images that remain in the realm of verbal description and hence become susceptible to David Moody's criticism of self-referential conceits such as those indulged in by Craig Raine.

'October Salmon' begins and ends in the mud of material reality. The poem begins: 'He's lying in poor water, a yard or so depth of poor safety' and returns to: 'this was the only mother he ever had, this uneasy channel of minnows / Under the mill-wall, with bicycle wheels, car-tyres, bottles / And sunk sheets of corrugated iron'. The poem evokes the tension of contradictory and complementary processes as 'after two thousand miles, he rests' dying in 'this chamber of horrors [that] is also home. / He was probably hatched in this very pool'. Thus his 'poise' can achieve the mythic, symbolic status of 'epic', for his inner process is the enacting of a larger one and his submission to it suggests an animal dignity that cannot be adequately characterised by David Moody's word 'brute': 'The epic poise / That holds him so steady in his wounds, so loyal to his doom, so patient / In the machinery of heaven'. Of course that dignity is actually the writer's reverence for this creature and the dynamic of complementary tensions that is 'the machinery of heaven'. It must remain a cause for regret, then, that this poem, which possesses all the features that I have suggested as typical of Hughes's post-pastoral poetry, should celebrate a creature which is finally failed by the poet's practical responsibility in Hughes's travelling the world to kill his kind. Finally, we may have to recognise that Hughes, as both good shepherd and fisherman, may not have escaped the contradictions of his own cultural lifestyle. It now seems more important than ever to distinguish in the poetry between the post-pastoral and the pastoral without ultimately allowing these later lapses to obscure the achievements of a body of work that, at its best, has gone more comprehensively beyond pastoral poetry than the work of any other contemporary poet.

Notes

1. *A Martian Sends a Postcard Home* (Oxford University Press, Oxford, 1979).

2. In E. J. Rawson (ed.), *The Yearbook of English Studies,* Vol. 17 (Modern Humanities Research Association, London, 1987), p. 166-78.

3. *Preoccupations* (Faber & Faber, London, 1980), p. 173-80.

4. *The City and the Country* (Chatto and Windus, London, 1973), p. 30.

5. *The Penguin Book of Pastoral Verse* (Penguin, Harmondsworth, 1974), p. 423ff.

6. *Poems 1932-82* (Iona Foundation, Philadelphia, 1987), p. 173.

7. *Swimming with Seals,* F. Steel (ed.), *Poetry Book Society Anthology* (Poetry Book Society, 1990).

8. Carcanet, Manchester, 1989, p. 9.

9. Faber & Faber, London, 1984.

10. 'Saccharine or Echo Soundings? Notions of Nature in Heaney's *Station Island*', *The New Welsh Review,* No. 10, Autumn 1990.

11. Faber & Faber, London, 1979.

12. See Scigaj, L. M., *The Poetry of Ted Hughes* (University of Iowa Press, 1986) and Robinson, Craig, *Ted Hughes as Shepherd of Being* (Macmillan, London, 1989).

13. *The Hawk in the Rain* (Faber & Faber, London, 1957).

14. I have in mind here Lawrence's sequence of six tortoise poems (published as a unit two years before the publication of *Birds, Beasts and Flowers* in 1923), but especially 'Tortoise Shout' in V. De Sola Pinto and F. Warren Roberts (eds), *The Complete Poems of D. H. Lawrence* (Heinemann, Oxford, 1964), p. 363.

15. *Phoenix* (Heinemann, Oxford, 1936), p. 657.

16. *The Marriage of Heaven and Hell,* Plate 14.

17. Nash, Roderick, *Wilderness and the American Mind* (Yale University Press, London, 1967), p. 2.

18. 'Turning Points', Radio 4, 15 November 1988.

19. See Koltuv, B. B., *The Book of Lilith* (Nicolas-Hays, 1986).

20. The lines 'We are both in a world / Where the dirt is God' appeared in the poem 'More Theology' (in *Moments of Truth,* Keepsake Press, Twickenham, 1965) which is part II of the poem 'Plum-Blossom' in *Recklings* (Turret Books, London, 1966).

21. Faber & Faber, London, 1989.

22. *The Yearbook of English Studies,* p. 175.

23. Robinson, Craig, *Ted Hughes as Shepherd of Being* (Macmillan, London, 1989), p. 205.

24. See Gifford, Terry and Roberts, Neil, *Ted Hughes: A Critical Study* (Faber & Faber, London, 1981), p. 74.

25. Scigaj, L. M., *The Poetry of Ted Hughes* (University of Iowa Press, 1986), p. 290.

26. *Poetry Review,* Vol. 73, No. 4 (January 1984), p. 59.

27. Scigaj, ibid., p. 314.

Select Bibliography

Works by Ted Hughes

Poetry

(Unless otherwise stated all titles are published by Faber and Faber, London, and Harper and Row, New York)

The Hawk in the Rain (1957)

Lupercal (1960)

Recklings (Turret Press, London) (1966)

Wodwo (1967)

Crow (1970)

Season Songs (US edn Viking, New York) (1976)

Gaudete (1977)

Cave Birds (1978)

Orts (Rainbow Press) (1978)

Remains of Elmet (1979)

Moortown (1979)

Under the North Star (US edn Viking, New York) (1981)

Selected Poems (1982)

River (1983)

What is the Truth? (1984)

Flowers and Insects (US edn Knopf, New York) (1986)

See also the thirty uncollected poems in Sagar's *The Achievement of Ted Hughes* (below).

Prose

'Context', in *London Magazine,* February 1962.

'The Rock', in *Writers on Themselves* (BBC, London, 1964).

'Secret Ecstasies' (review of Eliade's *Shamanism*), in *The Listener,* 29 October 1964.

Poetry in the Making (Faber & Faber, London, 1967).

Selected Poems of Keith Douglas (Faber & Faber, London, 1968).

A Choice of Emily Dickinson's Verse (Faber & Faber, London, 1968).

Introduction to *Vasko Popa: Selected Poems* (Penguin, Harmondsworth, 1969); extended in *Vasko Popa: Collected Poems* (Carcanet, Manchester, 1978).

'Myth and Education I' in *Children's Literature in Education* (1970).

'The Environmental Revolution' in *Your Environment* I (Summer 1970).

A Choice Of Shakespeare's Verse (Faber & Faber, London, 1971)

'Myth and Education II' in Fox, (ed.) *Writers, Critics and Children* (Heinemann, Oxford, 1976).

Selected Poems of Janos Pilinszky (Carcanet, Manchester, 1976); reprinted with minor revisions as the *The Desert of Love* (Anvil, London, 1989)

Foreword to Fairfax and Moat, *The Way To Write* (Elm Tree Books, London, 1981).

'The Hanged Man and the Dragonfly' in *The Complete Prints of Leonard Baskin* (Little, Brown and Co., London, 1984)

Introduction to *Keith Douglas: The Complete Poems* (Oxford University Press, Oxford, 1987).

See also the two interviews and excerpts from Hughes's critical writings collected in Faas (below).

BIBLIOGRAPHY

Sagar, Keith and Tabor, Stephen, *Ted Hughes: A Bibliography 1946-1980* (Mansell, London, 1983).

CRITICAL STUDIES

Bishop, Nicholas, *Re-making Poetry: Ted Hughes and a New Critical Psychology* (Harvester Wheatsheaf, Hemel Hempstead, 1991).

Faas, Ekbert, *Ted Hughes: The Unaccommodated Universe* (Black Sparrow Press, Santa Barbara, 1980).

Gifford, Terry, and Roberts, Neil, *Ted Hughes: A Critical Study* (Faber & Faber, London, 1981).

Hirschberg, Stuart, *Myth in the Poetry of Ted Hughes* (Barnes and Noble, 1981).

Robinson, *Ted Hughes as Shepherd of Being* (Macmillan, London, 1989).

Sagar, Keith, *The Art of Ted Hughes* (Cambridge University Press, Cambridge, 1975; extended edn 1978).

Sagar, Keith, (ed.), *The Achievement of Ted Hughes* (Manchester University Press, Manchester, 1983).

Scigaj, Leonard M., *The Poetry of Ted Hughes* (University of Iowa Press, Iowa, 1986).

Scigaj, Leonard M., *Ted Hughes* (Twayne, Boston, 1991).

Scigaj, Leonard M. (ed.), *Critical Essays on Ted Hughes* (G. K. Hall, New York, 1992).

West, Thomas, *Ted Hughes* (Methuen, London, 1985).

Harriet Zinnes (essay date October 1997)

SOURCE: Zinnes, Harriet. "'And He Shivered with the Horror of Creation': The Poetry of Ted Hughes." *Hollins Critic* 34, no. 4 (October 1997): 1-13.

[*In the following essay, Zinnes discusses the presence of violence in Hughes's poetry, which the critic contends has more to do with the poet's worldview than with the scandals associated with his life.*]

Sometimes the shocking details of the life of a poet increase his/her readership, make every line of the work a romantic excursion and reinforce the comforting bourgeois notion of the poet as damned or cursed or at least different from the rest of us. Of course today, when members of Parliament or our own President and candidates for that office have the scourge of scandal, the poet is less provocative. Still, Byron and Shelley, even the young Wordsworth who fathered an illegitimate child in France whom he promptly ignored, Yeats and his yearning for Maud Gonne, seem more alluring to today's scandal-seeking readers than the more subdued Tennyson. And Ted Hughes, currently crowned poet laureate of England, has all the scandalous qualifications of a large readership. Who does not know that his first wife, the American poet Sylvia Plath, committed suicide when Hughes left her in their cold London flat (and their two young children) for another woman, who later herself committed suicide. Let us hope that these readers also know that he is now happily married to a woman who enjoys farming as much as the poet does. Or have I got my own gossip wrong?

Above (or below) the scandal are the poems. Byron and Shelley, the young Wordsworth, William Butler Yeats not only have the frisson of scandal but are among the masters of English literature. And Ted Hughes? Are his works as masterly as the interest in his biography warrants? Strangely enough, many American women, loyal to Sylvia Plath, refuse to investigate the question. They become unquestioning, even arrogant feminists, with such strong sympathies for what they consider a wronged woman that they either refuse to read Ted Hughes or read him only to attack him for the violence in his work that they feel logically follows from his alleged heinous treatment of Plath. This essay, I regret to say to readers who want more scandal, is neither a defense nor an investigation of Ted Hughes and his relation to women. Since it is a study of his poetry, however, one cannot entirely disregard the influence of Sylvia Plath on the early work of Hughes. (Of course, who is to say that she is not always there, in the poems a subconscious presence.) May I simply say at this point that Hughes's work during his marriage with Plath showed at times an obvious influence.

Since violence, however, is omnipresent in the British poet's work, the use of it deserves consideration. But such a consideration has nothing to do with scandal. Hughes's use of violence is unrelated to any kind of irrelevant sensationalist publicity. It is a consequence of his whole vision of life. In the poem **"Crow Alights"** in his important book *Crow* (1971) and from which I have obtained the title of this essay, the poet describes the awakening of his "monster" Crow as a hallucination of a horror that could not be escaped because creation itself is "the virus of God." Is it any wonder that he "shivered with the horror of Creation"? This terrible negativity that dominates all of Hughes's poetry except perhaps the most recent (his prose is duplicated over and over by the nightmarish events of our times. It is not for nothing that the critic Ekbert Faas in his penetrating book on the poet entitled *Ted Hughes: The Unaccommodated Universe* (1980) names Hughes "the poet of apocalyptic doom." This "unaccommodated universe" is the world of Crow, what the poet describes as "the terrifying world of Crow" that he presents us with—a world in which Crow cannot say the word "love." It is a world of Death. Even in the earlier book, *Wodwo* (1967), Hughes approaches the notoriously bleak world of Beckett, a world that at least this reader feels is created with the same hidden compensatory satisfactions as the poet, as I shall explain later. In the poem **"Logos,"** he writes:

> And within seconds the new-born baby is lamenting
> that it ever lived. . . .

But what is even bleaker for this new creation is that the God of the Logos is overpowered by the Mother Goddess, the goddess of nature, so that even such a God is useless. With bitter humor the poet sums it all up with a withering last line: "God is a good fellow, but His Mother's against him."

It is clear that for Hughes this threatening world of *Crow* is in one way or another the human world that is even less desirable than Crow's, for unlike human be-

ings the monster bird does not know that he will die. Only occasionally does this bleak vision become entangled with sentimentality as would be easy enough for a less stringent poet. Usually the poet is firm, hard-edged, his symbolism surreal at times but somehow starkly real, as real as the knowing onslaught of Death, or like a journey that, as he noted in a review in the *New Statesman* in 1963, is a "too-easy journey toward Reality . . . toward the objectless radiance of the Self, where the world is a composition of benign Holy Powers, and toward the objective reality of the world, where man is a virtuoso bacteria." If man to Hughes is bacteria or, more frequently, beast, the visitation of Holy Powers or even its acknowledgement, one would think, must to the poet indeed be rare. But in some sense that visitation is always there, just as Hughes's almost primitive belief in the coexistence of good and evil in both man and animal (what Helen Vendler calls "his choice of the animal as human mirror") cannot ever obliterate what he also witnesses as "the elemental final beauty of the created world."

The poetic influence of Sylvia Plath is particularly noticeable in Hughes's first book *Hawk in the Rain* (1956), and as a result it is more conventional in the use of poetic forms, in its language and rhythms. Even in this book, however, Hughes's chief characteristic shudders through. The extraordinary force, the upsurging vitality of the language is always, almost frighteningly near. Whatever doom is described, therefore, whatever blindness man has in relation to the animal kingdom (a significant theme in the poet's work), however man ignores or refuses to acknowledge the evil within him and in the universe (another significant theme) is voiced with a stentorian power. In **"Hawk Roosting,"** a poem published in 1960 in the poet's second volume *Lupercal,* that was frequently anthologized and made his early reputation, the poet asserts with the energy, hyperbole, and emotion that were anathema to the Movement poets of Hughes's generation the untroubled conscience of the bird—whose very ignorance of past or future, whose lack of self-consciousness, the poet is suggesting, give him greater authority than man:

> I sit at the top of the wood, my eyes closed.
> Inaction, no falsifying dream
> Between my hooked head and hooked feet:
> Or in sleep rehearse perfect kills and eat. . . .
>
> My feet are locked upon the rough bark.
> It took the whole of Creation
> To produce my foot, my each feather:
> Now I hold Creation in my foot
>
> Or fly up, and revolve it slowly—
> kill where I please because it is all mine. . . .

And the extraordinary last line of the poem reads: "I am going to keep things like this." Here are the amazing monosyllables, the pounding resonance of a beat that defies convention, or rather is it the emphatic and powerful speech of a poet who was born in Mytholmroyd in the valley of the Yorkshire Pennines and has never lost that West Riding dialect that uses hard language to present hard facts, without evasion, with the eloquence of the concrete, of the honesty of the poet who wrote of his birthplace, "Everything in West Yorkshire is slightly unpleasant. Nothing ever quite escapes into happiness." There is also the empathic remembrance of death and murder, of the violence of war that marked his father's experience in World War I. He explains in the early book *Wodwo,* in the poem **"Out,"** that "The shrapnel that shattered my father's paycheck / Gripped me." He describes too in his poem **"TV Off"** from the volume *Earth-Numb* how when his father was wounded, he, "golden-haired," lay, unattended, with the dead, "ripened black," for two days:

Who lay a night and a day and a night and a day
Golden-haired, while his friend beside him
Attending a small hole in his brow
Ripened black.

So it is that in **"Hawk Roosting"** there is no tangled syntax as is frequently true in the poems of Hughes. Here there is all directness—the frightening energy and authority of a major voice. It is no wonder that Ted Hughes won early acclaim. And is it not perhaps true that the energy and vitality of Hughes's language and rhythms not only arise out of remembered violence and death, out of primordial and existential fears, but are in themselves expressions of defiance, of an indomitable lust for life? It is not surprising that Calvin Bedient in the chapter on Hughes in his 1974 book *Eight Contemporary Poets* describes him as "the first poet of the will to live." In one of the poet's later volumes, **The River,** in the poem entitled **"Salmon Eggs,"** Hughes notes that "Something else is going on in the river," and what is that? For Hughes, an amazing admission:

Only birth matters
Say the river's whorls.

But perhaps not so amazing. In his recent book on Shakespeare, *The Goddess of Complete Being* (1992)—he had edited a selection of Shakespeare's poetry twenty years earlier—he concludes that Shakespeare in his last plays rejects the lure of Protestantism with its embracing of reason and the individual ego and turns to the Goddess of Divine Love or as the title of his book has it, *The Goddess of Complete Being.* Shakespeare, Hughes is suggesting, is thus celebrating the ancient myth of life, death, and rebirth. And Hughes, following the master, iterates a similar celebration. In his **New Selected Poems** (1982), the last lines of the last poem published there read:

So we found the end of our journey.

So we stood, alive in the river of light
Among the creatures of light, creatures of light.

Even Hughes's first book *Hawk in the Rain* begins quietly. It opens with the poem **"The Thought-Fox,"** a poem not about animals or death but about the Muse! The first line, clearly influenced by Gerard Manley Hopkins, reads: "I imagine this midnight moment's forest," and it ends with two equally quiet lines: "The window is starless still; the clock ticks, / The page is printed." But time is remorseless, and the window holds no stars.

In the poet's 1967 volume, *Wodwo,* that strange creature, though he's fraught with a crisis of identity, finally yields to a less than passive pursuit and declares that despite a dull repetition he supposes he's "the exact center" even though

. . . there's all this what is it roots
roots roots roots and here's the water
again very queer but I'll go on looking.

One could say, therefore, if one reads closely enough that even in the early volumes where the negative seems so overpowering, a kind of hidden affirmative note pushes through. Or is it because, as Calvin Bedient stridently suggests, that in *Hawk in the Rain* especially, the violence depicted is the result of the poet's "false exploitative relation to his subject," and is therefore a "sensational extravagance," "a sniggering voyeurism" and as a consequence only surface? The fact, however, that Hughes uses such strange creatures as the Wodwo or Gog may be a reflection of his comic side or at least of his delight in caricature. And isn't caricature some form of affirmation? Margaret Dickie Uroff in her 1980 *Sylvia Plath and Ted Hughes* identifies the Wodwo as "the creature with which Sir Gawain fought . . . a wood-dweller, a troll, the wildman of the woods, either beast of monster." Hughes's Wodwo, however, may have his own disasters, but he doesn't dwell in a lilting romance. Like Crow he resides more in a comic strip. Or in a poem, and for Hughes it would be perfectly natural, for as he noted in an essay in *Poetry in the Making* (1967), "I think of poems as a sort of animal." Perhaps behind that strange statement is a deep understanding of what it is to live in a violent world. It suggests a kind of acceptance of what is as well as a helplessness. The poem emerges not only out of the will of the poet but in a certain sense out of a kind of acquiescence of being. In the created world there is the animal—without consciousness, according to the poet, but with the inevitability of pure being. He is a wodwo or a hawk or a crow. The poet with will and an extreme kind of consciousness yet creates his poem out of an equal acceptance and helplessness.

Hughes does not fight against the world. He sees it as it happens before his eyes. James Wood in his article on

England in *The Oxford Guide to Contemporary Writing* (1996) declares significantly that "Hughes's commonest vantage point is the eye, the retina, or 'the mind's eye.'" Extending that statement one could say that the British poet has no ideology really except one of a terrible hard clarity—though there is always a rather blurry Laurentian vision, a strong fascination for myths, and a belief in "a proper knowledge of the sacred wholeness of Nature." At times too he is a kind of unorthodox Manichean since he insists that both good and evil reside simultaneously in animals and man. But he is not doctrinal, not theological. As for Christianity, he would displace that religion with a "complete new Holy Ground, a new divinity," because he sees Christianity as reflecting a culture already dead. In his work there is a folkish, archaic presence, anciently religious, where somehow in the air "staring angels go through." There is an energy there. Shamanistic. Believing in the force of dreams, the holiness of them, the poet is after all rather pagan. His poem **"Gnat-Psalm"** in the early *Wodwo* illustrates that primitive energy. Here are some stanzas from that poem:

> Dancing
> Dancing
> Writing on the air, rubbing out everything they write
> Jerking their letters into knots, into tangles
> Everybody everybody else's yo-yo. . . .
>
> Riding your bodies to death
> You are the angels of the only heaven!
> And God is an Almighty Gnat!
> You are the greatest of all the galaxies!
>
> My hands fly in the air, they are follies
> My tongue hangs up in the leaves
> My thoughts have crept into crannies
>
> Your dancing
>
> Your dancing
>
> Rolls my staring skull slowly away into outer space.

So like the animal is the poem. The animal as Hughes depicts him is vicious as he has to be and calculating in order to survive in his brutal world. The poem is a depiction of that world by a very clear-eyed poet. No holds barred. Everyone of us, the poet writes, is "held in utter mock by the cats. Nine to one."

In the essay referred to above Hughes explains the relationship between the poem and the animal in an autobiographical way, and what he says about his boyhood pursuits in the fields is legendary. He writes:

> You might not think that these two interests, capturing animals and writing poems, have much in common. But the more I think back the more sure I am that with me the two interests have been one interest. My pursuit of mice at threshing time when I was a boy, snatching

them from under the sheaves as the sheaves were lifted away out of stack and popping them into my pocket till I had thirty or forty crawling around in the lining of my coat, that and my present pursuit of poems seem to me to be different stages of the same fever.

And then he adds the line I mentioned before, and more:

> In a way, I suppose, I think of poems as a sort of animal. They have their own life, like animals, by which I mean that they seem quite separate from any person, even from their author, and nothing can be added to them or taken away without maiming and perhaps even killing them. And they have a certain wisdom. They know something special . . . something perhaps we are very curious to learn.

He then makes the connection between "the special kind of excitement" in the hunting of the animal and the writing of the poem:

> The special kind of excitement, the slightly mesmerized and quite involuntary concentration with which you make out the stirrings of a new poem in your mind, then the outline, the mass and colour and clean final form of it, the unique living reality in the midst of the general, all that is too familiar to mistake. This is the hunting and the poem is a new species of creature, a new specimen of the life outside your own.

To most poets the comparison between an animal and a poem may seem astonishing though the poet's explanation of the "special kind of excitement" that arises during the "stirrings of a new poem" will certainly be familiar. But there is so little that is familiar in Hughes's handling of poems since *Crow.* And it isn't because the British poet is adhering to any easy compliance with a Modernist's desire to "make it new." If anything, if one must use labels, Hughes is a postmodernist with his comic irony, his underlying sense of a reality that is a complete joke, with an inner and outer world that is a monstrous hell. Or is this equation of poem with animal another proof of Bedient's accusation that Hughes has a "false exploitative relation to his subject"? Probably Helen Vendler would agree, who, in commenting on the poem **"February 17th"** included in the 1979 volume *Moortown,* accuses the poet of being "relentlessly subjective as he looks at the world" and of having a "powerful imaginative appetite for naming and ornamenting disaster." Let me present Vendler's argument as she uses it in connection with **"February 17th."** Explaining that Hughes has a farm in Devon and that he had found one of his ewes with a half-born lamb, as he writes, "looking out" of her "back end," Vendler quotes from the poem and defends her analysis:

> "A blood ball swollen
> Tight in its black felt, its mouth gap
> Squashed crooked, tongue stuck out,
>   black purple,
> Strangled by its mother.

"After trying in vain to pull the lamb out, Hughes fetched a razor, and

> Sliced the lamb's throat strings,
>   levered with a knife
> Between the vertebrae and brought
>   the head off
> To stare at its mother, its pipes
>   sitting in the mud
> With all earth for a body.

"Then, after decapitating the lamb, Hughes reached in to pull out the rest of it; it came (and the poem ends)

> In a smoking slither of oils and soups
>   and syrups—
> And the body lay born, beside the
>   hacked-off head."

I've used the line breaks as they appear in Vendler's article in the *New Yorker,* of December 31, 1984, but actually such a printing is unfortunate, for the poem is written in a characteristic longer line, and such a line is necessary here for the full impact of the explosion of violence and sound. Consider the different effect of the longer line as, for example, "Sliced the lamb's throat strings; levered with a knife / Between the vertebrae and brought the head off. . . ." It is interesting how here and rather frequently Hughes's verse has the marvelous ring of Old English—and notice the alliteration! Seamus Heaney too has noted how "Hughes relies on the northern deposits, the pagan Anglo-Saxon and Norse elements" in his language. Heaney remembers an interview published in the *London Magazine* of January 1971 in which Hughes noted the effect of the West Yorkshire dialect on his poetry. Hughes described it in the following way:

> I grew up in West Yorkshire. They have a very distinctive dialect there. Whatever other speech you grow into, presumably your dialect stays alive in a sort of inner freedom . . . it's your childhood
>
> self there inside the dialect and that is possibly your real self or the core of it . . . Without it, I doubt if I would have written verse,
>
> it connects you directly and in your most intimate self to Middle English poetry.

But to return to Vendler's attack on Hughes's "appetite for naming and ornamenting disaster": of course Hughes's details, emphases, and narrative line have been selective, but isn't the very function of the poet to present a vision backed up necessarily by very selective details that are prompted by that vision? The critic's function, on the other hand, is to consider the vision and weigh its validity as well as the authority of its aesthetic means.

What Helen Vendler is overlooking is the childhood of Hughes, and childhood, especially the place, the environs of the life lived as a child, is central to a poet, to his metaphors, his stories, his very plot. Consider, for example, the town with its wildlife in which the play of the boys was to catch and kill. Hughes describes his older brother in **"Capturing Animals"**:

> His one interest in life was creeping about on the hillsides with a rifle. He took me along as a retriever and I had to scramble into all kinds of places collecting magpies and owls and rabbits and weasels and rats and curlews that he shot. He could not shoot enough for me.

And then there is the strange story entitled **"Sunday"** that Hughes tells, and it is probably autobiographical because the demonic character in the story, Billy Red, was not fictional. It is about a boy whose father promises to take him to Top Wharf Pub after chapel to see Billy Red kill rats in his teeth like a terrier. The boy in "his detestable blue blazer" has to sit through the service along with the men in their "tight blue pinstripe suits." In his restlessness the boy lets his imagination wander to a favorite animal, the wolf, who here "urged itself with all its strength through a land empty of everything but trees and snow."

Yes, Hughes has a "powerful imaginative appetite for naming" but hardly "ornamenting" disaster. It is not as if he is like some of today's painters who will create an assemblage (with sensationalist aplomb, with curious grotesquerie), as the young painter Alexis Rockman does in "Route 10" that was shown in June 1997 at the Jay Gorney Gallery in New York City, containing a crushed real rat and snake on the real blacktop to preach against murder on the road. The critic Keith Sagar is right to see, on the other hand, the "authentic" in Hughes. But Vendler will hardly agree with Sagar's praise when he writes that Hughes has "the most penetrating, authentic and all-embracing poetic vision of our time." And perhaps the critic ought to remember that Hughes in an interview with Ekbert Faas confided: "Blake I connect inwardly to Beethoven, and if I could dig to the bottom of my strata maybe their names and works would be the deepest traces." It is the intensity of such earlier artists that certainly includes remembrance of disaster, sometimes shrill and exaggerated, that can be traced equally in Hughes.

Perhaps Vendler should have been warned. There is also nothing pale of polite in Hughes's language or narrative actions, especially since the British poet equates man and the animal. As he writes in *Gaudete* (1977) for example, whether it is the roar of the lions, "the cries of all wild creatures as well as people's prayers" directed at God, these must be heard as arising from the imagination so that the cries "will not chill into syntax." (Only Hughes could turn grammar into a kind of "virtual" violent act.) In the same *Gaudete,* the poet asks, pointing to "half a man / Half a face / A ripped edge," "How will you correct / The veteran of negatives / And the survivor of cease?" Perhaps his answer lies in his statement in the essay *Myth and Education* (1976) that Faas quotes:

> The inner world, separated from the outer world, is a place of demons. The outer world, separated from the inner world, is a place of meaningless objects and machines. The faculty that makes the human being out of these two worlds is called divine. That is only a way of saying that it is the faculty without which humanity cannot really exist. It can be called religious or visionary. More essentially, it is imagination which embraces both outer and inner worlds in a creative spirit.

But still there is Crow, Hughes's symbol of contemporary barbarism, who "stropped his beak and started in on the two thieves."

Alan Williamson (essay date Sept./Oct. 1998)

SOURCE: Williamson, Alan. "A Marriage Between Writers: *Birthday Letters* as Memoir and as Poetry." *The American Poetry Review* 27, no. 5 (Sept./Oct. 1998): 11-13.

[*In the following review of* Birthday Letters, *Williamson contends that the collection represents a "remarkable recovery" for Hughes as a poet.*]

Suicides are timid murderers," Cesare Pavese said. Surely one of the many strands of motive in Sylvia Plath's suicide was a wish to freeze the meaning of her estranged husband's life, to deny him any significant history beyond her. In her great poem "The Birthday Present," where the "present" is, fairly clearly, death, she wrote:

> I know why you will not give it to me,
> You are terrified
>
> The world will go up in a shriek, and your head with
> it,
> Bossed, brazen, an antique shield,
>
> A marvel to your great-grandchildren.
> Do not be afraid, it is not so.

In this strange passage, denying, but still managing to insinuate, the murderous intention, the target is not just Ted Hughes the person, but Ted Hughes the writer. The man Plath accused of "a love of the rack and the screw" will be metamorphosed into one of his own medieval North Country monstrosities. (Small wonder Hughes became a translator of Ovid, for whom "metamorphosis," Hughes says, is "the symbolic guarantee that the passion has become mythic, has achieved . . . unendurable intensity. . . .")

How near Plath's half-wish came to coming true is one of the sadder and crueler stories in contemporary literature. Her "admirers" publicly accused Hughes of murder, heckled him at readings, defaced his name on her tombstone, and argued over his exact degree of culpability through half a dozen biographies. True, Hughes brought some of the obloquy on himself by his management of Plath's literary estate. But, leaving that aside, it seems common sense that no one can be expected to (or perhaps, simply, that no one *can*) take more responsibility for another person than human beings normally do—the responsibility, say, to stick with a troubled marriage—just because that other person has suicidal tendencies. Two of the most revered women poets of our time also had partners kill themselves during periods of estrangement. Neither was ever treated with anything other than the tactful silence such tragedies deserve.

Perhaps the deepest, and least visible, damage was done to Ted Hughes the poet. The gentle-violent chronicler of the North Country—the best locally English poet since Larkin—could not come back. The despair behind books like **Crow** and **Gaudete** was perfectly real; but because its sources were so public, cheapened and (from Hughes's point of view) undiscussable, it came out as hollow existential rant. The poet-critic Paul Breslin said at the time, "If such baldly didactic work were written in praise of sweetness and light, no one would read it." Philip Larkin's parody—written when both were invited to submit poems for the Queen's Silver Jubilee, and sent in, as a practical joke, under Hughes's name—put it even more succinctly:

> The sky split apart in malice,
> The stars rattled like pans on a shelf,
> Crow shat on Buckingham Palace,
> God pissed himself.

The **Birthday Letters,** along with last year's **Tales from Ovid,** constitute as remarkable a poetic recovery as we've seen in recent memory. For the most part, Hughes has returned to the descriptive pentameter line, braced with Hopkinsian alliterative clusters of strong stresses, that characterized his best early work. Whether he's describing boaters at Cambridge ("Punt-loads of shadows flitting towards their honey / And the stopped clock"), daffodils ("Ballerinas too early for music, shiverers / In the draughty wings of the year"), or his own hypochondriac symptoms ("Soft but stunning like the kick of a camel"), he routinely strikes off lines more brilliant than we've seen since **Lupercal.** Yet the style remains relaxed, speech-based. He isn't afraid to use the commonplace word when it is the right word; or to risk locutions like "Your long, perfect, American legs / Simply went on up"—"low-energy writing," as Katha Pollitt has complained (*New York Times Book Section*, March 1, 1998), by our usual imagistic criteria, but perfectly right if the criterion is voice.

But few readers will look at *Birthday Letters,* first, for its quality as poetry. Most will come to it out of curiosity—to hear the other side of stories told and retold so often they have become legends. So we may as well start there too. Many have commented on Hughes's impact on Plath, the demigod she almost immediately made of him, "the only one . . . huge enough for me." But what of the impact of her own hyper-energetic, almost mythic, presence on him? Her eyes, for instance, "Two little brown people, hooded, Prussian" (elsewhere Hughes calls them "a crush of diamonds, / Incredibly bright, bright as a crush of tears"). But Plath appears to Hughes, from the start, as a complex, puzzling person, not just a heroine. There is her "roundy face, that your friends, being objective / Called 'rubbery' and you, crueller, 'boneless.'" There is "the mystery

> Of your lips, like nothing before in my life,
> Their aboriginal thickness. And of your nose,
> Broad and Apache, nearly a boxer's nose,
> Scorpio's obverse to the Semitic eagle
> That made every camera your enemy. . . .
> It was never a face in itself. Never the same.
> It was like the sea's face—a stage
> For weathers and currents, the sun's play and the
>   moon's.
> Never a face until that final morning
> When it became the face of a child—its scar
> Like a Maker's flaw. But now you declaimed
> A long poem about a black panther
> While I held you and kissed you and tried to keep you
> From flying about the room.

At the end of the story, too, after Plath dies, we hear a side we have not heard before, and need to. Much has been made of Plath as the emblem of all depressed, overburdened single mothers. But what of the single father, his responsibilities for parenting grown ten times graver at the very moment he feels guiltiest, most undermined by misery? And what if the occasion for guilt is not divorce, but suicide? Read **"Life After Death,"** and find out.

The story of *Birthday Letters* is, as the "black panther" scene tells us at the start, very much a story of two writers. But it is simply not true, as Diane Middlebrook has asserted, that it is the story of Hughes's "slow awakening" to his wife's genius, or that his praise of her is "a big concession." These two considered each other extraordinary from the beginning; and therefore each lived with an enlarging mirror of the panic, the stagnation, the psychic exposure that are part of any extraordinary writer's life. "Alone / Either of us might have met with a life," Hughes writes; together, "Siamese-twinned,"

> Each of us was the stake
> Impaling the other. We struggled
> Quietly through the streets, affirming each other,
> Dream-maimed and dream-blind.

Watching Plath get inexplicably angry at two children plucking azaleas, Hughes intuits the connection between her rage and her susceptibility to the "nuclear core"—

> The fountain threw off its seven veils
> As the air swayed it. Here was your stair—
> Alchemy's seven colors.
> I watched you as you climbed it all on your own
> Into the mouth of the azalea.

And he understands, too, beyond envy, fear, or admiration, that "What happens in the heart simply happens."

The worst poems in *Birthday Letters,* in their struggle to get at that "heart," summon up all the *faux*-archetypal stage-thunder of *Crow.* The best have a relaxed, light-spirited patience with the everyday and what it might reveal that reminds me, though the comparison is odd, of James Merrill. "Was that a happy day?" Hughes asks poignantly, of a day spent fishing off Cape Cod. Many dark Plathian themes had unfolded—rowing out too far, into an ebb tide, having to be rescued. But then, when the day seemed over, in "a back-channel, under beach-house gardens,"

> Six or seven feet from land, we pulled up flounders
> Big as big plates, till all our bait had gone.
> After our wind-burned, head-glitter day of emptiness,
> And the slogging row for our lives, and the rescue,
> Suddenly out of water easy as oil
> The sea piled our boat with its surplus.

And suddenly the day seems to have a shape like a life, "Curl[ing]

>   out of brilliant, arduous morning,
> Through wind-hammered perilous afternoon,
> Salt-scoured, to a storm-gold evening, a luxury
> Of rowing among the dream-yachts of the rich
> Lolling at anchor off the play-world pier.

The day, Hughes realizes, is "a small thrill-breath of what many live by"—the relaxation into the moment which insignificant work permits, and which writers miss precisely because life, for them, is always Life.

> It was a visit from the goddess, the beauty
> Who was poetry's sister—she had come
> To tell poetry she was spoiling us.
> Poetry listened, maybe, but we heard nothing
> And poetry did not tell us. And we
> Only did what poetry told us to do.

It's a moral that speaks not only to Plath's peculiar fate, but to the fate of all who live too much by words.

Near the midpoint of the book, with the extraordinary poem **"The Badlands,"** a sense of symbiotic connection between the two lovers' unconscious visions of "evil" begins to dominate. "Maybe it's the earth," Plath says, looking out on the "landscape / Staked out in the sun and left to die."

Or maybe it's ourselves.
This emptiness is sucking something out of us.
Here where there's only death, maybe our life
Is terrifying. Maybe it's the life
In us
Frightening the earth, and frightening us.

For Hughes, this terror-vision seems to take concrete shape in Plath's obsession with her dead father. There is a burst of uncharacteristic anger ("paparazzo sniper") when, reading one of her poems, he realizes that Otto has "slid into me." On their return to England, he watches with bewilderment and terror as Plath's nightmares increase along with her talent—"a sea clogged with corpses, / Death-camp atrocities, mass amputations." But he, too, begins to suffer from obsessive symptoms. After they settle in Devonshire, he has chest pains and an "unpredictable faintness . . . strengthless hands" which convince him he is dying of heart disease.

I was already posthumous.
Whatever I looked at, any cat or dog,
Saw me already dead, merely
Lurching on a few paces, perfunctory vision
Still on my retina.

My new study
Was all the ways a heart can kill its owner. . . .

He even plays Beethoven, "To reconduct that music through my aorta / So he could run me clean and unconstrained / And release me." But "[o]f all this one, / Two, three years I told you nothing."

Despite his silence, however, Hughes seems to experience his symptom as a kind of demonic possession shared with Plath, perhaps a possession by her father. That, at least, is the only way I can read the lines which conclude **"The Lodger"**:

Who was this alien joker
Who had come to evict us,
Sharing my skin, just as he shared yours,
Watching my digging, so calmly? And gazing
Over your shoulder, into the poems you polished
As into this or that or the other mirror
That tried to ignore him?

This seems, on the face of it, rather outrageously to blame Plath for Hughes's neurosis. Yet the truly uncanny connection with Otto is one the poem never mentions: Otto too misdiagnosed his own symptoms, mistaking diabetes for incurable cancer. The result was not only his early death, but the "Two, three years" of (again, unexplained) melancholia that blighted Plath's childhood. Why did Hughes need to relive these years? Was he, in any degree, conscious that he was doing so?

These are deep psychic waters. As family-systems theory tells us, married couples do become hypersensitive to, and even live out, aspects of each other's fantasies and neuroses; just as they divide up roles— one strong, one weak; one "healthy," one "sick"—that really belong to both their psyches. One can only imagine what a profounder student of marital symbioses—say, the Kundera of *The Unbearable Lightness of Being*—might have done with Hughes's material. But it is clear enough to me, from these poems, that Hughes's obsession with Plath's father-obsession was not invented after the fact, to deny his guilt; it was a vital thread in the undertexture of their marriage.

But Hughes and Plath, and indeed their whole Cambridge circle, were occultists, half-believers in Ouija, Tarot, astrology, etc. Hughes had changed his major from literature to anthropology after a fox appeared to him in a dream and said, "Why are you killing us?"; and anthropology, for him, seems to have been less a critical study than a treasure-trove of archetypes, spells, and rites. Too often, Hughes treats his and Plath's neuroses with an occultist's literalism. Otto is a Teutonic demon-king, with a retinue of priestesses, ogres, gypsy curses, characters out of Shakespeare and Bluebeard. And the style begins to sound like a dulled-down parody of Plath, mixed with *Crow*:

King Minos,
Alias Otto—his bellow
Winding into murderous music. Which play
Were we in? Too late to find you
And get to my ship. The moon, off her moorings,
Tossed in tempest. . . .

The laughter
Of Sycorax was thunder and lightning
And black downpour. She hurled
Prospero's head at me,
A bounding thunderbolt, a jumping cracker.

Et cetera. Even good poems often turn to this tone at the end, with disastrous consequences.

There are still passages that capture the texture of a deteriorating marriage with a fine realism. The savage wit of Plath's poems can be heard, unmistakeably, in a tirade against England and, implicitly, her English husband:

Was black paint cheaper? Why
Were English cars all black—to hide the filth?
Or to stay respectable, like bowlers
And umbrellas? Every vehicle a hearse.

And Hughes's bewilderment at these outbursts ("What had I done? I had / Somehow misunderstood") rings true enough. But as the story darkens, Hughes more and more falls back on his hysterical Grand Guignol style, with its two themes, Fate and the Father. When the Fate motif sounds again at the beginning of the only poem about Assia Wevill, the woman for whom Hughes left Plath, it is easy to agree with Katha Pollitt that the book has "hit the nadir of taste and the zenith of self-delusion."

Wevill is not quite the non-presence in this book that its harshest reviewers have said; but almost. Of course, Hughes was further traumatized by her own gas-oven suicide a few years later. (I have heard it rumored, but never seen it said in print, that Wevill, herself an occultist, felt Plath was urging her to this act from beyond the grave.) Be that as it may, Hughes appears by now to have made Wevill the Bad Object, as Kleineans say ("Slightly filthy with erotic mystery"), and displaced a good deal of his own guilt onto her. He has persuaded himself that Plath was his true love, and that he would have gone back to her if she had not given him such violently contradictory signals:

> He had promised her everything she asked for,
> And she had told him all she wanted
> Was for him to get out of the country, to vanish.
> I'll do whatever you want. But which do you want?
> Go together next week North
> Or for me to vanish off the earth?
> She wept, pleading for reassurance—that he have
> Faith in her, and he reeled when he should have
>   grabbed:
> "Do as you like with me. I'm your parcel.
> I have only our address on me.
> Open me or readdress me."

How complete a truth this is, no outsider will ever know.

And so we come to the question of defensiveness, of self-exculpation. Perhaps it is a question with all personal poetry. Plath did not defend, she attacked; but her uncanny ability to undermine her own attacks, to reveal the psyche's "short circuits and folding mirrors," raised her to greatness. The famous lines damning Hughes in "Daddy" are in fact prefaced with the statement "I made a model of you," acknowledging her own psychic construction of him in the image of her demon father. Because Hughes's tack is rather to present himself as reasonable, reflective, looking for Truth, his Achilles' heels are all the more evident. Again, Katha Pollitt's *New York Times* review has put the case for the prosecution best. Beyond the occult trappings and the fatalism, even,

> Incident after incident makes the same point: she was the sick one, I was the "nurse and protector." I didn't kill her—poetry, Fate, her obsession with her dead father killed her. . . . Poem after poem has the same plot: an effort at ordinary happiness, pleasure, closeness . . . turns ominous as a symbol . . . appears on the scene to foreshadow the terrible future.

And yet, and yet. It is partly, but not wholly true, as we have seen, that Hughes represents Plath as the only "sick one." And surely the repeated structure, though it

gets tiresome, owes as much to the conventions of elegy, and the nature of grief, as to the need for self-justification. Thomas Hardy's elegies, too, see the early years of his marriage, "when our day was fair," through the glass of what came later, though he was under no public attack, and freely admitted his own share of guilt.

Of course, Hughes has his own view of those who think he owes them an explanation. He is bitter at the world that treats literary celebrity as it does political; and a little bitter, even, at the melodramatic side of Plath that courted such a fate. **"Freedom of Speech"** envisages a sixtieth-birthday party, at which the guest of honor is not Plath but "Ariel," a sort of talking bird perched on Plath's knuckle eating grapes. "Only you and I do not smile"—the cost, to them, precisely that "beauty" which is "poetry's sister," but which poetry doesn't always listen to. The theme—the attack on reputation—is almost new to literature, for the simple reason that most poets as good as Hughes are mainly concerned with their *own* reputation, and far too attached to it to pay more than lip-service to its drawbacks. It is perhaps unfortunate that Hughes cannot see some, at least, of Plath's critics not as voyeurs or "hyenas," but as people who fell in love with her hyper-vivid version of experience (as earlier generations fell in love with Byron's, or Hart Crane's), and wanted to defend her against real or imagined enemies. But it will take a thick-skinned critic to read **"The Dogs Are Eating Your Mother"** without a twinge of doubt about our own enterprise.

In such a moment of humility, we might reflect that the tasks the Muse assigns writers are not always the ones we would assign. I mean, of course, the tasks that draw writers to the height of their powers. Hughes's task, in that best sense, was not to fix blame, but to reexperience his love for the woman who had set such a stamp on his entire life. Perhaps *Birthday Letters* fails, if one comes to it expecting an honest answer to every accusation Plath biographers have levelled at Hughes, over the years. But the twenty or so poems that stick to their truest task are a small masterpiece. My list would include, at a minimum, the second half of **"18 Rugby Street,"** **"Fate Playing," "The Owl," "Chaucer," "The Earthenware Head," "Wuthering Heights," "The Chipmunk," "Flounders," "Child's Park," "The Literary Life," "The Badlands," "The 59th Bear"** (except for the ending), **"Grand Canyon," "Remission"** (again, except the ending), **"Daffodils," "A Short Film," "The Rag Rug," "The Rabbit Catcher," "Robbing Myself," "Life After Death," "The Prism," "Freedom of Speech,"** and **"Red."** The alternation of white heat and relaxed everydayness in these poems makes most marriage sequences by men—even Lowell's *Dolphin*—feel emotionally cramped by comparison. Only Hardy—who was able to own up to guilt—is clearly better.

Dwight Eddins (essay date spring 1999)

SOURCE: Eddins, Dwight. "Ted Hughes and Schopenhauer: The Poetry of the Will." *Twentieth Century Literature* 45, no. 1 (spring 1999): 94-109.

[*In the following essay, Eddins probes affinities between Hughes's view of nature and Schopenhauer's philosophy, contending that the two share "a mutual obsession with animal savagery."*]

Tennyson's scarifying glimpse of nature in *In Memoriam* as a scene of primordial violence revisits a weltanschauung as old as philosophy itself—an outlook famously summed up in 1651 by Thomas Hobbes when he asserted that the "natural" condition of humanity is "warre . . . of every man, against every man" and that life in a state of nature is "solitary, poore, nasty, brutish, and short" (88-89). Ironically, Hobbes's own century would see the emergence of natural theology, with its emphasis on nature as an incarnation of the highest ethical ideal, summed up by the third Earl of Shaftesbury as "morality, justice, piety, and natural religion" (Cooper 1: 301-02). It was this view that would dominate English nature poetry well into the Romantic era, when—as the next installment of irony—the Hobbesian strain would resurface with singular vigor and trenchancy in the philosophy of Arthur Schopenhauer, Tennyson's older contemporary.

The affinity between the poet's fleeting visions of animal savagery and the philosopher's sustained ruminations on it is salient. Tennyson considers the awful possibility that mankind is linked, as an even more degenerate "monster," with "Dragons of the prime, / That tare each other in their slime" (56.22-23). And here is Schopenhauer on "the observable life of animals":

> we see only momentary gratification, fleeting pleasure conditioned by wants, much and long suffering, constant struggle, *bellum omnium,* everything a hunter and everything hunted, pressure, want, need and anxiety, shrieking and howling, and this goes on *in saecula seculorum,* or until once again the crust of the planet breaks.

> (*World* 2: 254)

Tennyson, of course, would recant in favor of a revised natural theology by poem's end, but the outlook so mercilessly articulated by Schopenhauer would become more compelling as modernist perspectives gradually impinged on the Victorian intellectual milieu. Both Thomas Hardy and D. H. Lawrence, the inheritors and elaborators—in their very different ways—of Tennyson's primordial vision, would admit to basic affinities with the German philosopher's thought.[1]

This thought finds its fullest poetic realization, however, in our own time, in the verse of Ted Hughes. His menagerie—the hawk, the jaguar, the shark, and their ilk—fits even better than Lawrence's birds, beasts, and flowers into Schopenhauer's *"bellum omnium"* of predation. A paradigm case is the cannibalistic pike, driven by appetites and killer instincts so fierce that the poet is able to find two of them, "six pounds each, over two feet long, / High and dry and dead in the willow-herb— / One jammed past its gills down the other's gullet" (**"Pike,"** *Lupercal*). The human animal figures prominently in this company of killers. In **"Mayday on Holderness,"** for instance, a "pierced helmet" and "Cordite oozings of Gallipoli" explicitly evoke "The expressionless gaze of the leopard / The coils of the sleeping anaconda / The nightlong frenzy of shrews" (*Lupercal*).

But the affinity between Schopenhauer and Hughes runs much deeper than their mutual obsession with animal savagery. From his first principle of *der Wille*—the will—which he sees as generating not only the phenomenon of hunter and hunted but all the other phenomena of existence, Schopenhauer articulates a complex ontology and epistemology that parallel in illuminating ways the poet's instinctual assumptions about what nature fundamentally is and how we perceive it.[2] When Michael Bell speaks of the language philosophy of Ernst Cassirer as providing an "explicatory parallel" or an "appropriate conceptual analogy" to the work of Lawrence, he is describing the interpretive dynamic I am assuming here—the outlining of a sort of philosophical force-field that brings out the "internal cogency and complexity" of the given author's conceptions (3-4). The aspects of Hughes's work that I wish to examine in this regard are his fabulation of a fierce feminine presence as the presiding deity of the natural order, his projection of some sort of consciousness onto the vegetable and mineral realms, his esoteric renditions of sheer dynamic process, and his stylistic evolution from explicit interpretive frameworks to implicit ones.

Hughes himself gives warrant for the Schopenhauer connection in a 1970 interview. When Ekbert Faas commented that "Schopenhauer's and Nietzsche's thought bears a striking resemblance to yours," Hughes replied:

> The only philosophy I ever really read was Schopenhauer's. He impressed me all right. You see very well where Nietzsche got his Dionysus. It was a genuine vision of something on its way back to the surface. The rough beast in Yeats' poem. Each nation sees it through different spectacles.

> (205)

The affinity with Schopenhauer that Hughes affirms here is a visceral one, the sense of a shared assumption so instinctive and elemental that it almost defies articulation: a subterranean "something" of many names, a demonic ur-force, that periodically erupts to crack the rational, harmonious "surface" of civilizations. But it is precisely because Schopenhauer so closely links the visceral with the basis of his metaphysic that Hughes's recognition here is so valuable in understanding his own poetic enterprise.

This basis is the will—the blind, compulsive, irresistible striving that is, for Schopenhauer, the ground of all being. It is not only devoid of knowledge in itself, but is unknowable in any direct way. We can experience it only through its phenomena, which include ourselves and everything else in the world. In the terms that Schopenhauer appropriates from Kant, it is the noumenon, the *Ding an sich* that transcends the phenomenal categories of space, time, and causality on which our empirical experience is totally dependent. Despite popular misconceptions, Schopenhauer is not denying the reality of the experienced world, but rather affirming the primacy and opacity of the ground that generates it and thus provides its fundamental nature and its unity.

The unity of the will is reflected in what Schopenhauer calls "the reciprocal adaptation and adjustment of . . . [its] phenomena," a primal "harmony" that makes it possible for "the *species* in the organic, and the *universal natural forces* in the inorganic, [to] continue to exist side by side and even mutually to support one another" (*World* 1: 130). But the essence of the will is also manifested in an "inner antagonism" that

> shows itself . . . in the never-ending war of extermination of the *individuals* of these species, and in the constant struggle of the *phenomena* of these natural forces with one another. . . . The scene of action and the object of this conflict is matter that they strive to wrest from one another, as well as space and time, the union of which through the form of causality is really matter.

Even though each particular conflict has its aim—the wresting of matter—no point of satisfaction and rest is ever reached, nor is there any ultimate point to the process of willing. The will itself, which comprises all that is, has no aim or limits. The ground of existence is ultimately a purposeless but perpetual dynamic—"eternal becoming, endless flux" (*World* 1: 164).

Since the volition and consciousness associated with the notion of will are absent, it is unfortunate—as Bryan Magee points out—that Schopenhauer chose a term with such strong conative implications (141-45). A much better term, in Magee's estimation, would have been *energy,* which has the imprimatur of modern physics as the underlying reality of all phenomena from the subatomic to the macrocosmic, from forces such as gravity to the matter on which these forces work. With this interpretation in mind, we can better understand how Schopenhauer is able to classify as manifestations of will not only the organic phenomena of the universe

but the inorganic. More precisely, he locates in the "dumb, insensible matter," plant life, animal life, and human life that make up the natural world "the four differentiable grades of the will's objectification" (Magee 147). The order of listing is not only the order of their evolutionary appearance but of ascent in a hierarchy based on ever-increasing individualization and ever-increasing sophistication both of structure and of response to surroundings.

Even so brief a sketch of Schopenhauer's philosophical enterprise demonstrates the purely rational grounding and the scientific respectability that he sought for it. Nonetheless, there remain stubborn traces of what we might call inspiritedness in the notion of a universal force-field that makes even inorganic nature the embodiment of a seething restlessness and of a struggle to prevail, and that has such persistently conative implications in the term—*der Wille*—that names it. We can add to this the anguished, horrified, far-from-neutral tones in which Schopenhauer again and again describes the will. As Magee points out, this particular philosopher "was possessed by the idea that there is something inherently evil, monstrous, wicked about the ultimate force that constitutes the world" (148). But even if these lingering hints of malevolent volition are contaminants in a purely philosophical sense, they provide a very useful bridge to a poetic enterprise that posits in and behind the whole of nature a devastatingly potent, amoral, and threatening presence.

It is just such a presence that utters itself in Hughes's poem **"Hawk Roosting"** (*Lupercal*), as Hughes's own description attests:

> Actually, what I had in mind was that in this hawk, Nature is thinking. . . . I intended some creator like the Jehovah in Job but more feminine. When Christianity kicked the devil out of Job what they actually kicked out was Nature . . . and Nature became the devil. He doesn't sound like Isis, mother of the Gods, which he is. He sounds like Hitler's familiar spirit. There is a line in the poem almost verbatim from Job.
>
> (Faas 199)

Hughes makes it clear that the hawk-persona here is actually the oracle for the generative process itself, the inexorable creative force that lies behind particular creatures—even "Gods"—and takes on a satanic, Hitlerian aspect for those apostles of mercy and measure who experience its pitiless, boundless functioning. As Keith Sagar points out, with respect to Hughes's biblical allusion, "In Job we find God still acknowledges as his own the most crude and savage powers of nature—behemoth and leviathan" (*Art* 49). The avatars of blind, overwhelming appearance and depredation are not incidental to the ground of being, but of its essence.

This ground, characterized as it is by a wild, irrational instinctuality, is totally antithetical to the classical notion of the Logos, the cosmic reason that orders the world and renders it intelligible. Both Schopenhauer and Hughes are fascinated by the ironies inherent in an antilogical logos. For the philosopher, consciousness was originally evolved by the will as a survival mechanism for animals that had to seek their food. It is represented by the brain, he says, "just as every other effort of the self-objectifying will is represented by an organ" (*World* 1: 150). Even at the lower levels, however, consciousness brought with it "the possibility of illusion and deception, whereby the previous infallibility of the will acting without knowledge is abolished. Thus mechanical and other instincts, as manifestations of the will-without-knowledge, have to come to its aid guided in the midst of manifestations from knowledge" (*World* 1: 151). At the highest, human, level, these problems are strikingly compounded:

> with the appearance of reason, this certainty and infallibility of the will's manifestations . . . are almost entirely lost. Instinct withdraws altogether; deliberation, now supposed to take the place of everything, begets . . . irresolution and uncertainty. Error becomes possible, and in many cases obstructs the adequate objectification of the will through actions.
>
> (*World* 1: 151-52)

This antithesis between the awful certitude of will-driven instinct and the fancy-prone irresolution of human reason provides the animating tension of **"Hawk Roosting."** The "hooked head and hooked feet" of the predator represent, like the human brain, organic "objectifications" of the rapacious will, but are free from the "falsifying dream" that debilitates the brain and causes it to send delayed or faulty commands to the extremities by which it survives. One aspect of this "dream" is the tendency to construe surroundings aesthetically rather than strategically. Phenomena that we find pleasant or exhilarating—"the high trees. . . . the air's buoyancy and the sun's ray"—are "of advantage" to the hawk in its hunt for prey. Schopenhauer finds enormous value in absorbed aesthetic contemplation precisely because it *releases* the contemplator, for the moment, from the stringent urgencies of will, enabling him or her to become "the pure subject of will-less knowing" and thus to be taken out of "the stream of time and of all other relations" (*World* 1: 197). Hughes's poem as aesthetic artifact embodies this phenomenon, but simultaneously subverts it by explicitly reinstating the ascendancy of the anticontemplative, aggressively immediate will. This is a point to which I will return later in considering Hughes's artistic development in a Schopenhauerian light.

Schopenhauer's assertion, cited above, that particular body parts represent particular objectifications of the will in its entirety is reflected in the hawk's boast that "It took the whole of Creation / To produce my foot, my each feather." The idea that the monolithic, monistic

ground of being objectifies itself in the overwhelming variety and multiplicity of natural phenomena leads to interesting corollaries for both poet and philosopher. One of these entails an essential and inescapable reciprocity between phenomenon and noumenon. In Schopenhauer's words: "If . . . all variety of forms in nature and all plurality of individuals belong not to the will, but only to its objectivity and to the form thereof, it necessarily follows that the will is indivisible and is wholly present in every phenomenon" (*World* 1: 155). The contradiction or "inner antagonism" in the will that so fascinated and appalled Schopenhauer also follows. As Bryan Magee strikingly describes it:

> In the animal world the war of all against all is a struggle in which one manifestation of the will survives by devouring, by literally eating, another. It is a hungry will, insatiable and unassuageable, and the will's phenomena have only each other to feed upon, for there is nothing else in the world. In this sense the will devours, and can devour only, itself.
>
> (155)

Since "the whole of" creation/nature/will produced the hawk's prey as well as the hawk, the voice that speaks through the latter is precisely the voice of this universal and unrelenting predation. Thus the hawk's claim that it is the devouring master of that which shaped it: "Now I hold Creation in my foot / Or fly up, and revolve it all slowly—I kill where I please because it is all mine."

This last line is, presumably, the one Hughes says he took "almost verbatim" from the Book of Job. Sagar identifies this source as Job 41:11, where God asserts that "Whatsoever is under the whole heaven is mine," and rightly emphasizes the nature of the speaker as a savage god who has not yet become "the God of Love" and "is not interested in justice or morality" (*Art* 49-50). This sorts exactly with Schopenhauer's undercutting of human reasoning processes as reflections of a logos that delineates the ultimate nature of being. These processes are, rather, the sources of the error, irresolution, and specious rationalization that the hawk contemptuously transcends: "There is no sophistry in my body: / My manners are tearing off heads," and again, "No arguments assert my right." No cosmic teleology, no eschaton, no remediation of any sort can be expected from the blind, inexorable play of creation and destruction that grounds existence, justifying Schopenhauer's gloom and the hawk's concluding claim: "Nothing has changed since I began. My eye has permitted no change. / I am going to keep things like this."

Postulating this identity, however provisional, between Hughes's nature/creation and Schopenhauer's will, leads to a more profound understanding of the rationale behind the poet's animation of vegetable and mineral existence. The monistic, universal, and dynamic nature of the will as Schopenhauer construes it lends itself well to the fiction of a quasiconsciousness, in varying modalities, that informs all the phenomena of creation and makes for a drama of constant interaction between them. This drama is played out in the poems, of course, for the benefit of a human consciousness that is all too real and acute, and that is forced into the ironic perception of just how alien and how cognitively incommensurable is the rest of the creation to which it theoretically belongs.

The title of Hughes's poem **"Still Life"** (*Wodwo*) captures vividly the irony of the will's dynamism inspiriting, as it were, even such seemingly static phenomena as an outcropping of stone and a harebell—the former the lowest grade of the will's objectification and the latter the next above it. The "boundary" between these two grades is, says Schopenhauer, "the most sharply drawn in the whole of nature." The "inorganic body" finds its "identity and integrity" in matter, while its form is "inessential and changeable." The situation of the organic body is exactly the reverse:

> its existence . . . consists simply in the constant change of the *material* with persistence of the *form*. . . . Therefore the inorganic body has its continued existence through *repose* and isolation from external influences. . . . [whereas] the *organic* body has its continuous existence precisely through incessant *movement* and the constant reception of external influences.
>
> (*World* 2: 296)

Tenaciously protecting the matter that provides its essence, Hughes's stone is a "miserly" hoarder of its constituent "nothings," smug in the belief that it can take without giving in the relentless economies of wind, sun, rain, and snow. It seeks repose and isolation by pretending to be "dead of lack," and thus to escape the exactions of Schopenhauer's "external influences." The self-deluding nature of this stratagem is revealed by the trembling, inconspicuous harebell, which—unlike the stone—vividly registers the "threats of death" inherent in nature's terrible energies. The flower depends on the "incessant movement" of these energies, but embodies and figures them at their most cataclysmic. The will in its role as "maker of the sea," as earth shaper, "sleeps" in the plant preparing the upheavals of the aeons that will see the rock relentlessly diminished and reconfigured, then submerged by the sea that uncovered it in the first place.

The notion of geological predation is more immediately dramatized in another poem from *Wodwo*, **"Sugar Loaf,"** where the antagonists are both inorganic matter and are already locked in a struggle for survival, even though the hill—like the rock of **"Still Life"**—"suspects nothing." The "trickle" of water "cutting from the hill

crown" is literally cutting away that crown by dissolution—a fitting process, since the water itself is dangerously dissolute, "wild as alcohol," whorling "to a pure pool . . . with a whisp trout like a spirit." This metaphor of inspiriting the inanimate reflects Schopenhauer's insistence that "we are compelled to recognize *volition* in every nature or tendency of a material body" ("Will" 309). The Hughesian irony is to locate in water a mode of volition analogous to that of the hawk. But here, too, Schopenhauer provides the metaphysical rationale:

> Every grade of the will's objectification fights for the matter, the space, and the time of another. Persistent matter must constantly change the form, since, under the guidance of causality, mechanical, physical, chemical, and organic phenomena, each striving to appear, snatch the matter from one another.
>
> (*World* 1: 146-47)

This observation provides a convincing background for the poet's stark prophesy, "I see the whole huge hill in the small pool's stomach," and his dark understatement, worthy of *Beowulf,* "This will be serious for the hill."

Volition as it appears in the phenomena of the will—hawk, rock, flower, hill, and water—has a purposiveness predicated not only on survival but on total dominance, since each apparent portion of will is a projection of the will as the sum of reality. But the will in itself, the will as noumenon, has no such focus and direction: "Absence of all aim, of all limits, belongs to the essential nature of the will in itself, which is an endless striving" (*World* 1: 164). As Hughes moves into the bleak sophistications of *Wodwo* and the volumes beyond, he begins to come to terms with the closely related conception of a seething, blind, indefinable energy that underlies and fuels the processes of nature in their entirety. This effort to dramatize the almost ineffable leads to an indirectness and abstruseness that yield—at least partially—to what we might call a noumenal reading of the poems involved.

"Pibroch," from *Wodwo,* is perhaps the most striking and ambitious of these works. Its title denotes a set of variations for bagpipes on a traditional dirge or martial theme. Music thus becomes an analogue of sorts for the functioning of the mysterious but fundamental dynamic that preoccupies Hughes in this poem. It is a mirroring that Schopenhauer has theorized in some depth:

> music differs from all the other arts by the fact that it is not a copy of the phenomenon, or, more exactly, of the will's adequate objectivity, but is directly a copy of the will itself, and therefore expresses the metaphysical to everything physical in the world, the thing-in-itself to every phenomenon. Accordingly, we could just as well call the world embodied music as embodied will.
>
> (*World* 1: 262-63)

Elaborating the analogy, he recognizes "in the deepest tones of harmony, in the ground-bass, the lowest grades of the will's objectification, inorganic nature, the mass of the planet," and in the higher tones above this ground "the plant and animal worlds" (*World* 1: 258).

In **"Pibroch,"** it is the steady drone of the bagpipes beneath the melody that stands in for the "mass" of "inorganic nature" so central to the poem's bleak drama. Strictly speaking, this drone is an organ point that is sustained even when the melody crosses it to produce dissonance, rather than a ground-bass varied to produce constant harmony; but this very difference serves to illustrate Schopenhauer's principle of inner antagonism, of the will turning on itself. On the phenomenal level, the notion of melodic variations acts to differentiate the sea, rock, wind, and tree of the poem as distinct antagonists and as varying modalities of quasiconsciousness. On the noumenal level, however, the whole idea of variation in a monistic forcefield is ironically undermined.

The cosmic monotony quite literally inherent in the monotone, the organ point of the inorganic, is captured by the poem's opening:

> The sea cries with its meaningless voice
> Treating alike its dead and its living,
> Probably bored with the appearance of heaven
> After so many millions of nights without sleep,
> Without purpose, without self-deception.

The principal thrust of this description, however, is not to differentiate the sea from "higher" phenomena, but to reintegrate it, symbolically, with the noumenal will of which it is a representation. The sea's very lack of distinctiveness and discrete components makes its use as a symbol of the monolithic will convincing. As Schopenhauer observes, individuality—at its peak in human beings—declines through the realms of animals and plants until "finally, in the inorganic kingdom of nature all individuality completely disappears" (*World* 1: 132). Void of rationality and meaning, aimless, mindlessly incessant, the sea as will stands in contradistinction to the "appearance of heaven," which is to say, to the *mere* appearance of a logos that betokens a moral code and a coherent teleology. Instead, the ground of being proves to be such that sleep, purpose, and self-deception are of a piece in a purposeless universe.

Turning his attention to a rock in the sea, Hughes uses the phrase "Stone likewise" to confer upon it the same symbolic status, with the dubious distinction that, as phenomenon, the rock is "imprisoned / Like nothing in the Universe." The rock's occasional "dream" that it is "the foetus of God" is yet another ironic subversion of the divine logos, a process continued by the wind that rushes over it as a parody of the divine afflatus. This

spiritus associated with the "blind" stone and "able to mingle with nothing" negates any hope of communion with the First Cause and of cosmic orientation amid the mere "fantasy of directions" that its arbitrary shiftings represent. Once again we are faced with an analogue of the invisible, boundless, aimless will.

The tree that is "Drinking the sea and eating the rock" is differentiated from both by that organic/inorganic boundary that Schopenhauer considered—as we have seen—the "most sharply drawn in the whole of nature." But, in keeping with the poem's atavistic thrust, the phenomenal blurs back into the noumenal in the image of the self-contradictory will feeding on itself as it generates a desperate and totally pointless "struggle" to survive in a barren, hostile environment. Similarly, the quasiconsciousness of the tree as a higher-order phenomenon is brutally diminished in its description as "An old woman, fallen from space," who "hangs on, because her mind's gone completely." It is not too much to say, in fact, that the cosmic status of human intellect itself is compromised by Hughes's metaphor, as it is by Schopenhauer's description of it vis-à-vis the will:

> the intellect is of a secondary character, and merely the organic function of a single part, a product of life; not the innermost kernel of our being, not the thing in itself, not metaphysical, incorporeal, eternal, like the will: the will never tires, never grows old, never learns, never improves by practice, is in infancy what it is in old age, eternally one and the same. . . . Being essential, moreover, it is likewise immutable, and therefore exists in animals as it does in us.
>
> ("Will" 247)

This passage reads like a philosophical gloss on the last stanza of **"Pibroch"**:

> Minute after minute, aeon after aeon,
> Nothing lets up or develops.
> And this is neither a bad variant nor a tryout.
> This is where the staring angels go through.
> This is where all the stars bow down.

The fundamental dynamic of nature, as presented here, is both normative and inexorable. It is also blindly unstinting, banally repetitive, and totally without telos. The angels, ostensibly the agents of God's will, can find no point of purchase in the nihilistic abyss of Schopenhauer's; and the stars, which Hughes follows William Blake in associating with rationalistic orderings, are forced to pay homage to an absolute irrationality at the very core of things.

Hughes forces us, as observers of this pointless, incessant process, to share in the angelic vertigo, and also—as he raises his focus to the sentient grades of matter—in the pathos of what Schopenhauer calls "the suffering animal world" (*World* 1: 379). At this level, consciousness itself becomes the prey of the perpetual restlessness and dissatisfaction that mark its ground:

The striving of matter can always be impeded only, never fulfilled or satisfied. But this is precisely the case with the striving of all the will's phenomena. Every attained end is at the same time the beginning of a new course, and so on *ad infinitum*. . . . Eternal becoming, endless flux, belong to the revelation of the essential nature of the will.

                                             (*World* 1: 164)

Schopenhauer refers specifically to the "life of birds," with its "endless needs and exertions" in the service of a "future that afterwards becomes bankrupt" (*World* 2: 353).

In his poem **"Poor Birds"** (*Moortown*), Hughes once again produces what we might call a poetic correlative of the philosopher's speculations:

> In the boggy copse. Blue
> Dusk presses into their skulls
> Electrodes of stars. All night
> Clinging to sodden twigs, with twiggy claws,
> They dream the featherless, ravenous
> Machinery of heaven. At dawn, fevered,
> They flee to the field. All day
> They try to get some proper sleep without
> Losing sight of the grass. Panics
> Fling them from hill to hill. They search everywhere
> For the safety that sleeps
> Everywhere in the closed faces
> Of stones.

The stars here are no longer avatars of a callow rationalism, but the poles of the will as galvanizing current, as the blind, seething, ubiquitous energy that burns without stint in the galaxies and relentlessly drives the creatures beneath them. The "machinery of heaven" *is* the will, unfeathered and unfleshed in its noumenal status. As the literally insatiable hunger at the heart of being, it is also the stuff that dreams are made on, and thus the subverter of all repose. Waking is nothing but a feverish flight from dream-hungers into the terrors of real ones—the unending needs to eat and to avoid being eaten. The linkage between an all-pervasive anxiety and the all-pervasive will is inherent in the etymology of the "panics" that constantly flush the birds from place to place. The word derives literally from the Greek god Pan, whose "presence or unseen appearance caused terror" in the woodlands, and whose name derives in turn from the Greek παν, meaning "all" (*Oxford* 646). This latter etymology was subsequently adopted by philosophers "who saw in the God the Universe, the Totality" (Grimal 341). Their search for safety "everywhere" is doomed to failure because the will that drives them is everywhere, decreeing that they—as organic phenomena—must stay in motion in order to constantly renew that matter the "sleeping" stone enjoys as a nonrenewable essence.

Even though the birds must "suffer" the will's relentless pressure in proportion to the grade of consciousness they possess, they obviously are incapable of formulat-

ing a notion such as "poor birds." This act is the prerogative of the human intellect, which is able to separate itself from the immediate demands of the will long enough to contemplate disinterestedly the essences of phenomena. In Schopenhauer's terms, we are able to relinquish considering things under the guidance of "the principle of sufficient reason," which involves considering them solely with regard to "the where, the when, the why, and the whither" as these relate to "our own will." Instead, we turn to the *what,* in which "the particular thing, at one stroke, becomes the *Idea* of its species, and the perceiving individual becomes the *pure subject of knowing*" (*World* 1: 178-79). This "Idea" is, for Schopenhauer, "the most *adequate objectivity* possible of the will" (*World* 1: 175). It occupies an intermediate status between the will, of which it is a *direct* objectification, and the particularized phenomena that are the will's *indirect* objectification.

Along these lines, Hughes's oblique, enigmatic poem **"Wodwo,"** from the volume of that title, can be profitably read as a drama of consciousness in which the evolving psyche struggles with the advent of a "pure" subjectivity that conjures "Ideas" along with the unsettling quest for whatness that they involve. The Middle English term *wodwo* is taken from a catalogue of fierce wilderness creatures in *Gawain and the Green Knight* and is variously translated as *satyr, troll,* and *wild man of the woods,* according to Keith Sagar, who goes on to cite Hughes's own gloss: "Introducing a reading of the poem Hughes described his wodwo as 'some sort of satyr or half-man or half-animal, half all kinds of elemental things, just a little larval being without shape or qualities who suddenly finds himself alive in this world at any time'" (*Art* 98). Elsewhere, Hughes says that he imagines this "half-man, half-animal spirit of the forests" as something that "does not know what it is and is full of questions. It is quite bewildered to know what is going on" (*Poetry* 62).

Leonard Scigaj, in a particularly useful observation, places the poem itself in a group that presents

> nature as benevolent, transfigured by a newly won sense of freedom wherein the psyche of the persona is not subject to an emotional dependency or ego dependency upon either the environment or cultural givens, but is rather a bemused spectator who can view nature as a soothing companion because of an already achieved calmness of mind.
>
>   (110)

Though one might question whether the wodwo finds nature "soothing," this commentary is quite in the spirit of the Schopenhauerian dynamic by which consciousness temporarily triumphs over the unremitting pressure of the will and conceptualizes the will's phenomena—including itself—in a spirit of objective curiosity. As a "half-man" just emerging from the tyranny of the animal's pure survival-focus, the wodwo is driven into a peculiarly intellectual ferment by having "been given the freedom of this place." Its question "What am I?" leads it to examine its position vis-à-vis the rest of nature not in self-defense, but as a matter of classifying itself and of orienting itself within a sort of conceptual geography:

> I enter water. What am I to split
> The glassy grain of water looking upward I see the
>   bed
> Of the river above me upside down very clear
> What am I doing here in mid-air? Why do I find
> this frog so interesting as I inspect its most secret
> interior and make it my own?

The last question has a three-fold resonance. It not only foregrounds for contemplation what Schopenhauer calls "the Idea" of another "species"; it suggests the mental assimilation of one phenomenon by another involved in the contemplation process, and it calls up as a second-order abstraction the Idea of the process itself—the wonderment that one is involved in such an enterprise. This layered self-consciousness, with its awareness of awareness, is more evidence for Keith Sagar's assertion that Hughes himself "is a wodwo in all his poems, asking these same questions of the world in which he finds himself" and thereby "expressing the idea of the poet" (*Art* 98). Schopenhauer underwrites such an identification in singling out the artist as the ultimate purveyor of the "knowledge of the Ideas," as the practitioner of a process that "plucks the object of its contemplation from the stream of the world's course and holds it isolated before it" (*World* 1: 185).

Elaborating on this artist-Idea nexus, the philosopher describes a particular mode of aesthetic response to nature that bears even more specifically on the case of Hughes:

> But these very objects, whose significant forms invite us to a pure contemplation of them, may have a hostile relation to the human will in general, as manifested in its objectivity, the human body. They may be opposed to it; they may threaten it by their might that eliminates all resistance, or their immeasurable greatness may reduce it to nought. Nevertheless, the beholder may not direct his attention to this relation to his will which is so pressing and hostile, but although he perceives and acknowledges it, he may consciously turn away from it, forcibly tear himself from his will and its relations, and, giving himself up entirely to knowledge, may quietly contemplate, as pure, will-less subject of knowing, those very objects so terrible to the will . . . he is then filled with the feeling of the *sublime*.

> (*World* 1: 201)

Since the wodwo/poet is "half-animal" and "half-man," he is at once a creature in the grip of blind, will-driven instincts unmitigated by reason and a detached psyche capable of contemplating from the inside the will's inexorable urgencies. The essential power of Hughes's poetry derives, it seems to me, from its struggle to render comprehensible the ineffable immediacies of will from which its images and formulations are—in Schopenhauer's figure—"forcibly" *torn*. The awe and terror evoked by the Hughesian sublime are produced not so much by the hawk, the jaguar, the predatory landscape on which a particular poem centers, as by the sense of close encounter with the primal energy—rapacious, unstinting, and totally indifferent to human concerns—that fuels existence.

It is in the stark, unsettling nature poems of *Wodwo* that Hughes finally perfects this mode, so that the evocations of the will as primal energy seem somehow informed by that energy, and always on the verge of dissolving back into its inscrutable vortex. His development to this point might itself be construed in Schopenhauerian terms as one of more and more immediate representations of the will, starting from his first volume, *The Hawk in the Rain* (1957), where the power that energizes nature seems more argumentatively and abstractly conceived, emerging indirectly from the strenuous and somewhat rigid dialectics of particular poems. In the title poem of that volume, for instance, the hawk is depicted—in counterpoint to its slogging, bemired observer—as "The diamond point of will that polestars / The sea drowner's endurance." By the time of **"Still Life," "Sugar Loaf,"** and **"Pibroch,"** however, a new immediacy is evident in representations that appear to partake of the generative (and destructive) flux they embody.

This mode persists in Hughes's work, it should be pointed out, long past the 1967 publication of *Wodwo*. In *Wolfwatching* (1989), for instance, we find the sparrow hawk with eyes "still wired to the nuclear core" (**"A Sparrow Hawk"**) and the fierce macaw in the fiercer grip of "the dancing stars / Who devised this / Trembling degradation and prison" (**"Macaw"**). It is true that in this interval another aspect of Hughes has emerged, the seeker of larger harmonies and reconciliations in the teachings of Eastern religions. But here too we find the shadow of Schopenhauer, who sought along some of the same paths for means of negating the will's relentless pressures. In the last analysis, it is hard to locate a point in Hughes's development where his profound affinity with Schopenhauer is not evident, and where it does not illuminate a poetry that explores more intrepidly than any other the nightmare of ravening cosmic energies—what Hughes in the poem **"Pike"** calls "the dream / Darkness beneath night's darkness had freed, / That rose slowly towards me, watching."

Notes

1. On Hardy's and Lawrence's links with Schopenhauer, see, respectively, Seymour-Smith (329-31) and Montgomery (43-72).

2. Keith Sagar mentions Schopenhauer as one of those we may wish to study in the quest to "seek out new coordinates" for reading Hughes ("Introduction" xiv-xv).

Works Cited

Bell, Michael. *D. H. Lawrence: Language and Being.* Cambridge: Cambridge UP, 1992.

Cooper, Anthony Ashley, third Earl of Shaftesbury. *Characteristics of Men, Manners, Opinions, and Times.* Ed. John M. Robertson. 2 vols. New York: Dutton, 1900.

Faas, Ekbert. *Ted Hughes: The Unaccommodated Universe.* Santa Barbara: Black Sparrow, 1980.

Grimal, Pierre. *The Dictionary of Classical Mythology.* Trans. A. R. Maxwell-Hyslop. Oxford: Blackwell, 1986.

Hobbes, Thomas. *Leviathan.* Ed. Richard Tuck. Cambridge: Cambridge UP, 1991.

Hughes, Ted. *The Hawk in the Rain.* London: Faber, 1968.

————. *Lupercal.* London: Faber, 1970.

————. *Moortown.* New York: Harper, 1979.

————. *Poetry in the Making.* London: Faber, 1967.

————. *Wodwo.* London: Faber, 1971.

————. *Wolfwatching.* London: Faber, 1989.

Magee, Bryan. *The Philosophy of Schopenhauer.* New York: Oxford UP, 1983.

Montgomery, Robert E. *The Visionary D. H. Lawrence: Beyond Philosophy and Art.* New York: Cambridge UP, 1994.

The Oxford Dictionary of English Etymology. Oxford: Clarendon, 1966.

Sagar, Keith. *The Art of Ted Hughes.* 2nd ed. New York: Cambridge UP, 1978.

————. "Introduction." *The Challenge of Ted Hughes.* Ed. Keith Sagar. New York: St. Martin's, 1994.

Schopenhauer, Arthur. "The Will in Nature." *Two Essays by Arthur Schopenhauer.* Trans. Mme. Karl Hillebrand. London: Bell, 1889.

————. *The World as Will and Representation.* Trans. E. F. J. Payne. 2 vols. New York: Dover, 1969.

Scigaj, Leonard. *The Poetry of Ted Hughes: Form and Imagination.* Iowa City: U of Iowa P, 1986.

Seymour-Smith, Martin. *Hardy.* London: Bloomsbury, 1994.

Tennyson, Alfred Lord. *In Memoriam.* Ed. Robert H. Ross. New York: Norton, 1973.

Sarah Annes Brown (essay date 1999)

SOURCE: Brown, Sarah Annes. "*Carmen perpetuum*: Ovid today." In *The Metamorphosis of Ovid: From Chaucer to Ted Hughes,* pp. 217-27. London: Duckworth, 1999.

[*In the following essay, Brown discusses Hughes's* Tales from Ovid, *noting that Hughes considered Ovid's poetry relevant to the late twentieth century.*]

It would be possible to trace the Ovidian line's continuation into a great deal of twentieth-century culture—such a project might include the discourses of psychoanalysis and postmodernism as well as artistic developments such as surrealism and magic realism. The *Metamorphoses* has been described as a cinematic text, and there is certainly room for an investigation of Ovid and film, which might focus on works with an avowed debt to myth, such as Cocteau's *Orphée,* or perhaps on more diffused Ovidian motifs—Pygmalion as a subtext in *Vertigo* for example. Until very recently such an approach, continuing the move away from direct influence already initiated in the previous chapters, might have provided the most obvious conclusion to this study; however the last decade has produced an unexpected flowering of fully conscious Ovidianism. Christoph Ransmayr's dreamlike novel of exile *The Last World,* a (very) free translation of the *Metamorphoses* by David Slavitt, *After Ovid*—a modern Garth—and, most recently, Ted Hughes' **Tales from Ovid,** are among the most notable examples of this development.

Critics and teachers may take some of the credit for this welcome resurgence of interest in the *Metamorphoses* among creative writers. Long marginalised by the academy, Ovid has finally been reabsorbed into the mainstream. The rehabilitation of the *Metamorphoses* can be traced back to L. P. Wilkinson's *Ovid Recalled* (1955), and then to a steadily increasing number of important critical studies, including such diverse volumes as Galinsky's *Ovid's Metamorphoses* and Solodow's *The World of Ovid's Metamorphoses.* Critics whose concerns might loosely be termed 'theoretical' have responded with particular enthusiasm to Ovid, having discovered that the poet who could be allegorised, euhemerised and moralised is equally amenable to being politicised, psychoanalysed and deconstructed—or indeed received.

Hughes celebrates Ovid's 'relevance' to a twentieth-century audience in his introduction to **Tales from Ovid.** He reminds us that the *Metamorphoses* was written at the time of Christ's birth, when Rome was waiting for a new religion to fill the gap left by the decay of the old Pantheon:

For all its Augustan stability, it was at sea in hysteria and despair, at one extreme wallowing in the bottomless appetites and sufferings of the gladiatorial arena, and at the other searching higher and higher for a spiritual transcendence—which eventually did take form, on the crucifix.

(p. xi)

Hughes then invites us to align this state of mind with the imminent millennium, implying a special bond between our own age and Ovid's—for gladiators and crucifixes read Tarantino and the X Files. Such a claim is dubious; it is debatable how much impact the death of an obscure Jew would have had on a sophisticated Roman. And although Hughes implies that ours is an age with a peculiar affinity with Ovid his translations continually remind us that he comes at the end of a venerable Ovidian tradition.

The modern reader may be inclined to overestimate Hughes' daring, for reasons which are implicit in a thoughtful review of the volume by Allan Massie:

> All this is admirably Ovidian. If he fails, for me anyway, where Dryden and Golding succeed, it is for a reason that has nothing to do with his rendering. The truth is that, although they translate Ovid into the poetic language of their own day, just as Hughes does, time has given their versions a sheen of age which makes them more like Ovid than any translation into modern idiom can.

(*The Daily Telegraph,* 24 May, 1997)

There is a telling slippage in Massie's claim that Dryden and Golding are 'more like Ovid' than Hughes. Obviously the glamour of antiquity was itself once absent from Ovid—as Pope's 'The First Epistle of the Second Book of Horace Imitated' would remind us. There is certainly plenty in Hughes to jar on the reader in search of classical remoteness. When Jove prepares to destroy Phaethon rather than allow the earth to be incinerated, 'He soared to the top of heaven, / Into the cockpit of thunder' (p. 42). Still more strikingly anachronistic is Hughes' description of Jove's appearance before Semele in his full divine glory:

> He chose
> A slighter manifestation
> Fashioned, like the great bolts, by the Cyclops
> But more versatile—known in heaven
> As the general deterrent. . . .
>
> In that splinter of a second,
> Before her blazing shape
> Became a silhouette of sooty ashes
> The foetus was snatched from her womb.

(p. 99)

The vocabulary of nuclear warfare—'general deterrent' is reinforced by the evocation of Semele's ghostly trace, the silhouette of a Hiroshima victim.

But as we saw in this book's very first example of Ovidianism, Chaucer's *House of Fame,* to depart from the letter of the *Metamorphoses* can bring one closer to its spirit. The precise details used by Hughes were obviously not available to Ovid, but the effect is directly paralleled in various anachronistic touches in the *Metamorphoses,* such as when Venus is described consulting the 'archive office' (XV 810), a ploy which was not lost on Ovid's earlier translators, and particularly the contributors to Garth's edition of the *Metamorphoses.*

Indeed many of Hughes' stylistic quirks would, one feels, have appealed to Ovid. The inappropriately jaunty zeugma of Venus' punishment of the Propoetides—'She stripped off their good names / And their undergarments' (p. 145)—has a parallel at an equally 'serious' moment in the original. When Apollo begs Phaethon to reconsider his choice of boon he pleads that he should 'take my counsel, not my chariot', 'consiliis, non curribus utere nostris!' (II 146). The punning description of Callisto's fear of Diana after being seduced by Jove will make the same readers who are alienated by Keats' wordplay in the last stanza of 'Ode on a Grecian Urn' squirm with annoyance:

> Callisto's
> Jumpy terror of Diana's likeness
> Grabbed with electric hands, and she bolted—

(p. 48)

In another uneasy pun Adonis (the son of Cinyras and Myrrha) is described as 'the meaty fruit her father implanted' (p. 129). This is just one of a number of unpleasant touches from the author of **Crow** which might seem to owe little to Ovid's famous urbanity and elegance. Yet 'implanted' performs precisely the same function as *medulla,* invoking Myrrha both as tree and woman. In a similarly ingenious vein Hughes' Venus cautions Adonis not to 'stake my heart in a fool's gamble' (p. 131)—the pun is absent in the original of course, but is in many ways typical of a poet often censured for his self-consciously clever wordplay. For Hughes as well as for Ovid, words, not just objects, are subject to metamorphosis.

In his creative fidelity to the original Hughes is guilty of some inconsistency. In the introduction to *Shakespeare's Ovid,* an earlier volume containing a selection of the later **Tales,** Hughes suggests that he subscribes to an outmodedly limited view of Ovid, ascribing to his work the epithets 'romantic' and 'superficial' and concluding that 'the outline of the mural cartoon is Ovid's, and I stick to it: the colouring is my own' (Hughes 1995, p. ix). But if Hughes underestimates the degree to which he has been influenced by the spirit of Ovid, he is at least in good company, for we may remember that an earlier Poet Laureate was equally scornful of Ovid's 'boyisms' and yet did them more than justice in his own translations. In a more specific instance Hughes may be said to resemble Dryden, for both poets appear to have responded with particular intensity to the tale of Pygmalion.

Pygmalion's misogynism, subtly tainted by Dryden and made more decidedly problematic in Beddoes' version (which omits the Propoetides), is here unambiguously pathological:

> The spectacle of these cursed women sent
> Pygmalion the sculptor slightly mad.
> He adored woman, but he saw
> The wickedness of these particular women
> Transform, as by some occult connection,
> Every woman's uterus to a spider.
>
> (p. 145)

As in Beddoes' 'Pygmalion' (and unlike in Ovid) the sculptor has a vision of the statue which predates the carving itself. But whereas Beddoes' Galatea comes to him like a beautiful if mysterious epiphany, inspiring his greatest work of art, Hughes describes a disembodied shade, as dubious as Keats' Lamia:

> a spectre, sick of unbeing,
> That had taken possession of his body
> To find herself a life.
>
> (p. 146)

In a further negative intensification of a process begun by Beddoes, the statue's creation is itself controlled by this vampiric female. We may recall that in Beddoes the sculptor seemed in the grip of a nameless external force, whereas Ovid emphasises his conscious artistry:

> She moved into his hands,
> She took possession of his fingers
> And began to sculpt a perfect woman.
>
> (p. 146)

Like Pope's Belinda and H. D., this is a Galatea in at least partial control of her own creation.

Hughes' Pygmalion is less unequivocally solicitous than Ovid's, who is anxious lest he has bruised the statue; he 'half wanted to bruise her / into a proof of life' (147). The line ending is poised so that we must wait to learn that his strange wish is in some way justified, and the hint of sadism still lingers. Similarly the sculptor's placing of the statue on his bed, a tender if erotic moment in Ovid, gains an additional salaciousness in Hughes through the sexual force of two ambiguous verbs—'He *laid* her on his couch, / *Bedded* her in pillows' (p. 148).

As we saw in Chapter 7, Dryden was particularly alert to the connections between the stories of Pygmalion and Myrrha, his great-granddaughter. Significantly,

when Hughes describes the latter's metamorphosis, he allows a third possible form to hover between the obvious ones of woman and tree, 'she swayed / Living statuary on a tree's foundations' (p. 128). This curious detail might seem designed to remind us of Galatea, and perhaps nudge the reader into reflecting that both Pygmalion and Myrrha fall in love with their 'creations'. Certainly Hughes, like so many Ovidian writers before him, seems attuned to all the more disturbing possibilities within this ostensibly positive tale.

Michael Longley offers a still more unusual version of the story in 'Ivory and Water'. The retelling remains reasonably faithful—though truncated—up to the vital moment of animation when the metamorphosis is itself metamorphosed:

> And her veins pulse under your thumb to the end of the dream
> When she breaks out in a cold sweat that trickles into pools
> And drips from her hair dissolving it and her fingers and toes,
> Watering down her wrists, shoulders, rib-cage, breasts until
> There is nothing left of her for anyone to hug or hold.
>
> (*After Ovid,* p. 240)

Galatea's mollification doesn't stop at flesh; she softens further into water. Although we might expect a certain amount of similarity between quite independent accounts of girls changing into streams, it does seem possible to discover traces of both Cyane and Arethusa's metamorphoses in Longley's poem—the former is changed into a fountain out of shock at Proserpina's rape, and the latter is herself metamorphosed to avoid being ravished:

> post haec umeri tergusque latusque
> pectoraque in tenues abeunt evanida rivos . . .
> restatque nihil, quod prendere possis.

Next after these, her shoulders, back and sides and breasts vanish into thin watery streams . . . and nothing is left that you can touch. (V 434-5, 437)

> occupat obsessos sudor mihi frigidus artus,
> caeruleaeque cadunt toto de corpore guttae,
> quaque pedem movi, manat lacus, eque capillis
> ros cadit

> Cold sweat poured down my beleaguered limbs and the dark drops rained down from my whole body. Wherever I put my foot a pool trickled out, and from my hair fell the drops . . .
>
> (V 632-5)

These troubling intertexts invite us to view Pygmalion's attraction to the statue as predatory and rapacious rather than loving and miraculous. Even if the transformation into a stream did not recall other victims of male lust, the picture is still a negative one, suggesting disintegration and a loss of stable selfhood rather than, as we might expect, a dawning personality. Longley's treatment of Pygmalion thus seems to align itself with H. D.'s similarly barbed response to the legend. Alternatively, if we recall that Pygmalion can be seen as a Narcissus figure and the statue as an extension of his fantasy life, the pulsing veins under his thumb and subsequent dreamy liquefaction might lead the reader to a rather more mundane interpretation of the poem. Unpleasantly twentieth-century as such a reading might seem, it should be remembered that Beddoes' Pygmalion also appears almost to ejaculate Galatea into being.

* * *

It is difficult to respond in an entirely novel way to a poem which has been read, imitated and appropriated constantly for two thousand years. David Slavitt certainly tries to inject fresh life into his recent translation of the *Metamorphoses,* giving us plenty of reminders that his is a response grounded in the late twentieth century: Jove uses a 'thick duvet of cloud' (I 600) to conceal his liaison with Io from Juno, and Actaeon's dogs include 'Valley Girl', 'Tenzing' and 'Damned Spot (who always wants to go out)'. For sheer breathtaking banality it is hard to beat Slavitt's fancy that a gouged out eyeball sticks on an antler tine 'like a cocktail cherry' (XII 262)—unless of course we turn to Ovid's account of the same incident (the battle between the lapiths and the centaurs) when he likens brains oozing through a shattered skull to sieved cottage cheese (XII 436-8).

Still more audacious are Slavitt's own comments and interjections, which are incorporated seamlessly into the body of the text. After introducing the story of Byblis and Caunus for example:

> This story, a somewhat mannered performance,
> is one of those nice rhetorical set pieces Ovid loved
> To dazzle with. He could put his lawyer's training to use
> as he made up elaborate speeches for his characters to declaim.
>
> (IX 441-4)

He takes even greater liberties with the story of Medea, alluding briefly to her dealings with Creusa, not mentioned by Ovid, and then continuing:

> But the point is that Ovid avoids it,
> gives us
> instead a bizarre catalogue in the effete Alexandrian style
> of references we're supposed to get and respond to, pointless
> except for the way they obscure what is uppermost in his mind

and ours, too. In dreams, we find ourselves sometimes engaged
in this kind of repression, distortion, transmogrification . . .

> (VII 369-74)

But we might align this daring, postmodern metatranslation with one of the earliest and (to modern eyes) least attractive treatments of Ovid, the *Ovide Moralisé* which also incorporates comment, interpretation and judgment within the translation itself. Slavitt himself acknowledges the influence of mediating Ovidians upon his work. His two acknowledged debts are perhaps surprising, for they are not derived from the most fashionable or revered Ovidians—Eliot and Shakespeare for example—but from Sandys and Gay. Slavitt reproduces Gay's rendition of Polyphemus' song verbatim in Book XIII and uses the same rhyme scheme as Sandys for the last dozen lines of his poem. With this act of homage we may compare Kenneth Koch's bizarre *Io,* written (apparently in tribute to Golding) in rebarbative fourteeners—the redundant padding in the following couplet, if not the diction, is certainly authentic:

> The King of Gods espying her, in her bodacious tresses,
> Desired for to fuck with her beside the watercresses
> . . .
>
> (*After Ovid*, p. 59)

Slavitt responds sensitively to Ovid's interest in the ontology, the psychology of metamorphosis. As Actaeon begins to metamorphose:

> His ears are sharpening into pointed excrescences, while his hands are pointing, becoming hoofs,
> and his arms are turning to forelegs. His skin is a hide,
> and his heart
> is cold with terror.
>
> (III 184-7)

The catalogue of change cheats us into expecting that Actaeon's heart has also become something different. The line ending intensifies the shock of remembering that his consciousness remains that of a suffering human. This is the key to the tale's horror—the hunter fully shares the reader's awareness of his fate's terrible irony. A line break is used to similar effect in Slavitt's account of Pygmalion:

> One, especially lovely,
> he fashioned out of a piece of snowy ivory flesh
> could never have duplicated. No skin was as smooth and clear . . .
>
> (X 246-8)

We are reminded of the resemblance between Pygmalion's statue and a poet's *scripta puella*—each equally a construct. Ivory might as easily be an adjective qualifying flesh as a noun, and only as our eye travels to the next line do we realize we have been wrongfooted. We may remember that Dryden played precisely the same trick on his readers in his translation of the Wife of Bath's tale. A suggestive refinement, hinting at the idea of nature imitating art, is introduced in the way Slavitt translates 'formamque dedit, qua femina nasci / nulla potest', 'giving it a beauty more perfect than that of any woman ever born' (X 248-9). Slavitt's version implies that the statue sets the standard which mere flesh can only aspire to duplicate, and thus draws out the unnatural, fetishising aspect of Pygmalion's love. Again, this modification of Ovid was anticipated by Dryden:

> And carved in ivory such a maid, so fair,
> As nature could not with his art compare,
> Were she to work; but in her own defence
> Must take her pattern here and copy hence.
>
> (7-10)

Beddoes also describes souls as mere 'dross' compared to beautiful statues.

Hughes is equally engaged by the idea of being two things at once. Of Actaeon he writes, 'Human tears shone on his stag's face' (p. 108). As well as evoking the split between mind and body, Hughes replicates the impression of a metamorphosis taking place even as we read, discussed at the end of the previous chapter. The tears which left his eyes when they were human have not yet dried although his metamorphosis is now complete. Sometimes Hughes provides us with an extra reminder of a character's double identity. Arethusa, the nymph who is transformed into a stream, describes to Ceres how she became aware of Proserpina's presence in the underworld:

> As I slid through the Stygian pool
> In the underworld, I felt myself
> Reflecting a face that looked down on me.
>
> (p. 62)

In the original Arethusa simply sees Proserpina; the embellishment is, however, entirely in keeping with Ovid's own acute awareness of the phenomenology of metamorphosis.

* * *

Strictly speaking Christoph Ransmayr's *The Last World* falls outside this book's brief, being the work of an Austrian rather than an English Ovidian; nevertheless this complexly textured and richly imaginative response to the *Metamorphoses* deserves some attention. Once again we have come full circle, for Ransmayr's subject is Ovid's banishment to Tomi refracted through the distorting lens of his *Metamorphoses*—a move anticipated by Ovid in the metamorphic world of his own exile poetry.[1] The poet is presumed dead at the begin-

ning of the novel, which is narrated by his friend Cotta who arrives in Tomi to find it peopled by characters from the *Metamorphoses,* albeit strangely altered—Tereus is the local butcher and Fama keeps a grocery store. Ransmayr's Philomela does not weave her dreadful tidings but points to Tereus' house, 'a blank wall framed in ivy and wild grape' (p. 169), as though creating, if not a picture, a kind of *tabula rasa* on which Procne can project her own worst fears—only the border is yet in place. Like Hughes, Ransmayr seeks to bring our world closer to Ovid's, for the decaying Roman outpost is arbitrarily infected by twentieth-century paraphernalia to produce a confusing montage of anachronisms; the effect is typical of late twentieth-century fiction—of magic realism, for example—but at the same time true to the spirit of Ransmayr's original source, for Ovid also combines the remote and miraculous with practical, humdrum detail. Even in metamorphosing Ovid, Ransmayr replicates his effects; the process which transforms Arachne, for example, into the deaf-mute weaver of Tomi, engages the reader in the same identification of sameness and difference as does one of Ovid's metamorphoses. The eventual metamorphosis of Tomi itself as it becomes overrun with unruly vegetation mirrors the contest between art and nature fought over Diana's grotto:

> It was impossible to tell if a weather-cock or a gable ornament was still in place or had long since fallen apart under the embracing branches. The rioting green mimicked the forms it enclosed, playfully, mockingly at first, but then, obeying its own law of form and beauty, went on relentlessly to obliterate all signs of human handiwork.
>
> (p. 165)

The evocation of nature initially imitating the forms of art—or architecture—might be compared with Stanley Spenser's *The Resurrection in Cookham Churchyard* where the vegetation similarly follows the precise lines of the church gable.

Much of what seems new and daring in these postmodern—or even millennial—*Metamorphoses* can be traced back either to Ovid's many imitators or to Ovid himself. The erotic charge of Fred D'Aguiar's 'Thisbe to Pyramus' might read like a modern accretion:

> Your wet blade's sweet tip
> Is hardly in me;
> Already the fruit
> Turn red on the tree.
>
> (*After Ovid,* p. 113)

but the imagery of penetration is matched by Ovid's own ejaculatory evocation of Pyramus' wound:

> ut iacuit resupinus humo, cruor emicat alte,
> non aliter quam cum vitiato fistula plumbo

scinditur et tenui stridente foramine longas
eiaculatur aquas atque ictibus aera rumpit.

As he lay stretched upon the earth the spouting blood
leaped high; just as when a pipe has broken at a weak
spot in the lead and through the small hissing aperture
sends spurting forth long streams of water, cleaving the
air with its jets.

(IV 121-4)

Some of the contributors to *After Ovid* opt for full-scale
modernisations. Lawrence Joseph recasts Pyreneus (who
offered the Muses shelter from the rain and then tried to
rape them) as an American gangster:

Two of his boys drove up, told us
to get in out of the rain. Took us

to the villa. Into an inner room.
From his rococo chair upholstered

with silk he arose, arms extended,
to greet us. Designer blue jeans,

T-shirt, yellow linen jacket.

(p. 138)

And William Logan offers a strange version of Niobe,
where Apollo and Diana are transformed into inbred
homicidal rednecks, and Niobe herself into the wife of
a Wall Street banker with a Hermès handbag and a
brownstone off Park Avenue. But even these Ovidian
improvisations are merely the latest in a line of modernised Ovids. At the beginning of the tradition we find
Chaucer's Manciple's Tale, a retelling of Apollo's
revenge on the unfaithful Coronis (II 542-632),
reinventing the god as a cuckold straight out of fabliau
tradition. The tell tale crow who betrays Coronis is a
free agent in Ovid but a domestic caged bird in Chaucer, and Coronis herself is described as Apollo's 'wyf';
like May and Alisoun, she knows how to take advantage
of a husband's absence:

And so bifel, when Phebus was absent,
His wyf anon hath for hir lemman sent.

(203-4)

Even this rather vague circumstantial detail, suggesting
the need to plan an intrigue within defined spatial and
temporal constraints, is missing in Ovid's more lofty
version.

Matthew Prior's 1715 version of Apollo and Daphne is
just as freely and irreverently modernised. It takes the
form of a dialogue between god and nymph; whereas
the former's speeches uphold the subtitle's claim to
have 'faithfully translated' from *Metamorphoses* I,
Daphne has been metamorphosed from a trembling
victim into a pert Augustan miss:

A.

What is to come by certain art I know.

D.

Pish, Partridge has as fair pretence as thou.

A.

Behold the beauties of my locks—[D] a fig,
That may be counterfeit a Spanish wig . . .

A.

I sing—[D] that never shall be Daphne's choice.
Syphacio had an admirable voice.

(15-18, 21-2)

(Partridge was a well known astrologer, Syphacio a
castrato.) Daphne does soften so far as to suggest that
Apollo might like to amuse her father by reading the
'Courant' with him—this was a contemporary newspaper, but Prior is also making a punning reference to Pe-
neus' watery provenance.

Modernisation seems to be one of the many constants
running through the Ovidian tradition—although it
would certainly be dangerous to assume that Chaucer
and Prior wrote with precisely the same intentions or
achieved the same effect as today's modernisers, or that
the same impulses which drove Medieval illuminators
to present Narcissus and Apollo *et al.* in the costume of
their own day inspired Cocteau to substitute a posse of
hit-and-run bikers for the snake which killed Eurydice.

To end this book with a study of the last decade's Ovidianism emphasises the way the reception of the *Metamorphoses,* as well as the poem itself, is a *carmen perpetuum,* not only because Ovid's influence on English
literature is an ongoing process, but also because, like
Finnegans Wake, the end of the story in a sense takes
us right back to where we started—and indeed to
everywhere we've been along the way:

In nova fert animus mutatas dicere formas
corpora; di, coeptis (nam vos mutastis et illas)
adspirate meis primaque ab origine mundi
ad mea perpetuum deducite tempora carmen!

My mind is bent to tell of bodies changed into new
forms. Ye gods, for you yourselves have wrought the
changes, breathe on these my undertakings, and bring
down my song in unbroken strains from the world's
very beginning even unto the present time.

(I 1-4)

Note

1. Ovid's exile is also the inspiration for David Mal-
   ouf's *An Imaginary Life,* although his handling of
   the subject is far less interestingly 'Ovidian' (in
   my opinion) than Ransmayr's.

Bibliography

This is a bibliography of items cited in the text, as well as a selection of other items consulted in the preparation of this book, rather than an exhaustive bibliography of the topic.

Beddoes, T. L., *The Poetical Works,* 2 vols (London: J. M. Dent and Co.) 1890.

Chaucer, Geoffrey, *The Riverside Chaucer,* ed. Larry D. Benson (Oxford: Oxford University Press) 1988.

Dryden, John, *The Poems of John Dryden,* 4 vols, ed. James Kinsley (Oxford: Clarendon Press) 1980.

Galinsky, G. K., *Ovid's Metamorphoses: An Introduction to the Basic Aspects* (Berkely & Los Angeles: University of California Press) 1975.

H. D., *Her* (London: Virago Press) 1984.

H. D., *Collected Poems 1912-44,* ed. Louis L. Martz (Manchester: Carcanet Press) 1984.

Hofmann, Michael & Lasdun, James, *After Ovid* (London: Faber & Faber) 1994.

Hughes, Ted, *Shakespeare's Ovid* (London: Enitharmon Press) 1995.

Hughes, Ted, *Tales from Ovid* (London: Faber & Faber) 1997.

Ovid, *Ovid's Metamorphoses in fifteen books translated by the most eminent hands,* ed. Sir Samuel Garth (London: Jacob Tonson) 1717.

Ovid, *Metamorphoses,* trans. by F. J. Miller (London: Heinemann) 1984.

Pope, Alexander, *The Poems,* ed. John Butt (London: Methuen & Co) 1963.

Prior, Matthew, *The Literary Works,* 2 vols (Oxford: Clarendon Press) 1971.

Ransmayr, Christoph, *The Last World,* trans. John Woods (London: Chatto & Windus) 1990.

Sandys, George, *Ovid's Metamorphoses Englished* (Oxford, 1632).

Slavitt, David, *The Metamorphoses of Ovid* (Baltimore & London: Johns Hopkins University Press) 1994.

Solodow, J. B., *The World of Ovid's Metamorphoses* (Chapel Hill, NC: University of North Carolina Press) 1988.

Wilkinson, L. P., *Ovid Recalled* (Cambridge: Cambridge University Press) 1955.

Lynda K. Bundtzen (essay date summer 2000)

SOURCE: Bundtzen, Lynda K. "Mourning Eurydice: Ted Hughes as Orpheus in *Birthday Letters.*" *Journal of Modern Literature* 23, no. 3/4 (summer 2000): 455-69.

[*In the following essay, Bundtzen discusses the verse-letters of Hughes's* Birthday Letters, *addressed to Sylvia Plath more than three decades after her suicide.*]

The task is now carried through bit by bit . . . while all the time the existence of the lost object is continued in the mind. Each single one of the memories and hopes which bound the libido to the object is brought up . . . and the detachment of the libido from it accomplished. Why this process of carrying out the behest of reality bit by bit . . . should be so extraordinarily painful is not at all easy to explain. . . . The fact is, however, that when the work of mourning is completed the ego becomes free and uninhibited again.[1]

> I see you there, clearer, more real
> Than in any of the years in its shadow—
> As if I saw you that once, then never again.

(p. 15)[2]

Reviewers of Ted Hughes's **Birthday Letters** have understandably been absorbed with biographical issues. Addressed to his American poet-wife Sylvia Plath thirty-five years after her death, these verse-letters hold the promise of providing answers to the many questions that biographers and critics have asked about the circumstances of their marriage, his desertion of her and their children for another woman in October 1962, and her suicide on 11 February 1963. Why, after a prolonged and obdurate silence about these matters has Hughes suddenly decided to tell what is presumably his side of the story—what A. Alvarez calls "scenes from a marriage, Hughes's take on the life they shared?"[3] Are the poems, as Jacqueline Rose suggests, "calling for a response. Of understanding? Of sympathy?"[4] and assuredly not from Plath, but more likely, from her readers and admirers who have found his silence "another sign of callousness"[5] and his handling of her estate—the writing which she left unpublished when she committed suicide in 1963—highly suspect. His editing of her journals, his reconstruction of her *Ariel* volume, and his infamous disclosures about losing or destroying her final journals and an unfinished novel have all been seen as self-serving in one way or another. For many critics, Hughes censored those parts of Plath's journals which implicate him as a domineering husband; he mutilated her artistic intentions in *Ariel* to obscure his role as a villain in its poetic narrative; he destroyed valuable information about her final months in the journal which he burned; and he carelessly lost another journal and an unfinished novel because these works accuse him, point to him as the unfaithful one, the philandering and unfeeling husband.[6] Are Hughes's **Birthday Letters** a confession? an apology? a catharsis? Do they provide information about Plath's final months and days? These are the questions initially raised in critical responses to their publication.

Symptomatic of reviewers' preoccupation with biographical accuracy is Katha Pollitt's description of the dilemma for Hughes's readers: "Inevitably, given the claims that these poems set the record straight, the question of truth arises."[7] And Pollitt, with several other reviewers, is not convinced that Hughes is capable of objectivity and impartiality, or even of a modest and limited personal truth, especially not over the stretch of eighty-eight poems and two hundred pages of verse:

> that intimate voice . . . is overwhelmed by others: ranting, self-justifying, rambling, flaccid, bombastic. Incident after incident makes the same point: she was the sick one, I was the "nurse and protector." I didn't kill her—poetry, Fate, her obsession with her dead father killed her." The more Hughes insists on his own good intentions and the inevitability of Plath's suicide, the less convincing he becomes.[8]

In a blistering review for the *New Republic* titled "Muck Funnel," James Wood likewise denounces *Birthday Letters* as boringly repetitious minor tantrums: "His poems are little epidemics of blame"[9] that endlessly rebuke the dead Plath and her poems, and it's "like listening to one half of a telephone call."[10] The other side of the conversation is missing.

Even when a reviewer offers a more positive view of *Birthday Letters* as poetry rather than biographical evidence, as in Jack Kroll's praise of Hughes's "masterly arsenal of forms, rhythms and images," the laurel is quickly withdrawn because Hughes has not been as "merciless to himself" as he should have, has not submitted himself to the "deep self-examination" which would have provided answers to biographers who want to know, "Why did he leave? And what happened to drive Assia [Wevill, the other woman in the love triangle with his wife] to exactly the same self-destruction as Plath?"[11] Similarly, even as Jacqueline Rose forgives the portent-laden plot of *Birthday Letters* that other reviewers have derided as evasive and "borrowed from the most familiar dirty magics,"[12] she reminds her reader of her own and other feminists' famous battles with Hughes and his sister, Olwyn, over interpreting Plath's work. She ends her review by asking him to end this feud with Plath's partisan women readers and to retract his wrong-headed and self-righteous "caricature" of feminists in *Birthday Letters* as, for example, hyenas feeding on Plath's corpse in **"The Dogs Are Eating Your Mother."**[13]

As all this suggests, *Birthday Letters* has received very little interpretation based primarily on its literary values. He is a husband addressing his tragically dead wife, and this is why we have come to eavesdrop—to discover whether he wants belatedly to share his guilt for her suicide or to offer intimate glimpses into what seemed to be a closed chapter in his life. As Pollitt notes, "The storm of publicity surrounding *Birthday Letters* has turned into a kind of marital spin contest, an episode in the larger war between the sexes";[14] A. Alvarez complains that the volume is on the best-seller list "'for all the wrong reasons. It's the Oprah Winfrey element.'"[15] Critics do not wish to interpret the poetry

so much as inquiring minds want to know all the gruesome and scandalous details.

Hughes's letters, however, are not simply the utterances of a bereaved husband invoking the haunting presence of a beloved spouse, but also poems addressed by one poet to another. In **"Sam,"** for example, Hughes speculates that when Plath survived a ride on a runaway horse, it was the genius of poetry that saved her:

> What saved you? Maybe your poems
> Saved themselves, slung under that plunging neck,
> Hammocked in your body over the switchback road.

> (p. 10)

The poems which she wrote in her final months, Hughes suggests here, needed her to live long enough for them to be written, and by saving her, "saved themselves" from oblivion. She "couldn't have done it. / Something in you not you did it for itself" (p. 10). "It" was poetic destiny at work. Similarly, in **"Flounders,"** he claims, "we / Only did what poetry told us to do" (p. 66), as if their lives were predetermined and their agency governed entirely by the Muse of their poetic marriage. Such assertions have no claim to factual truth, and, indeed, have been castigated as strategies for "fate playing"—manipulations by Hughes throughout *Birthday Letters* to escape responsibility and culpability for what happened in his marriage to Plath.

An alternative critical strategy begins by simply acknowledging the fictive nature of such assertions and then looks for a consistent patterning of poetic statements that offers an invented truth about what happened in their marriage. Hughes's "birthday letters" are embedded with myth, superstition, and folklore, with references to other poems, many of them by Plath, and they display an inordinate degree of literary self-consciousness. Further, when Hughes is not borrowing titles directly from Plath's poems—for example, **"The Rabbit Catcher," "Totem," "Apprehensions"**—he is engaging his wife's preoccupations with honeybees and Otto Plath, with the figure of Ariel and the other *dramatis personae* from Shakespeare's *Tempest,* and with Plath's overarching themes of death and rebirth, mourning and melancholia. *Birthday Letters* are both companion poems and adversarial poems, in conversation and argument with Plath as a fellow poet of grief and as the irretrievable wife, Eurydice, to Hughes's Orpheus.

* * *

> ". . . the life you begged / To be given again, you would never recover, ever."

> (**"18 Rugby Street,"** p. 21)

Throughout *Birthday Letters,* there is an implicit analogy between Hughes and Orpheus as the poet who mourns for his lost wife Plath-Eurydice, who repeatedly fails to retrieve her from "Inside that numbness of the earth / [for] Our future trying to happen" (p. 9), and who eventually challenges Plath's grieving verse with his own poetry of loss. By opposing her, he also releases himself from the melancholic and doomed poetic identity of Orpheus to complete a normal mourning process, simultaneously bidding final farewell to his dead wife. In **"A Picture of Otto,"** one of the final "letters," Hughes gives Plath back to her father, thereby lifting the mask that Plath imposed on him in her verse, in which the "ghost" of Otto Plath is

. . . inseparable from my shadow
As long as your daughter's words can stir a candle.
She could hardly tell us apart in the end.

(p. 193)

At least one of Hughes's motives for writing **Birthday Letters** is to "tell" himself "apart" from Otto Plath in his poetic version of their marriage. Instead of joining his dead wife in the underworld, as Orpheus joins Eurydice in Ovid's *Metamorphoses,* Hughes descends to make peace with Otto Plath, meeting him "face to face in the dark adit / Where I have come looking for your daughter" (p. 193). The ghost of Orpheus in Ovid

. . . found Eurydice
And took her in his arms with leaping heart.
There hand in hand they stroll, the two together;
Sometimes he follows as she walks in front,
Sometimes he goes ahead and gazes back—
No danger now—at his Eurydice.[16]

The figure of Otto Plath, however, stands between Hughes and Plath, making such a reunion impossible, except on Plath's poetic terms, which deny Hughes an identity separate from her father. What Hughes has come to understand and accept is that she will always be her father's daughter:

. . . you [Otto Plath] never could have released her.
I was a whole myth too late to replace you.
This underworld, my friend, is her heart's home.
Inseparable, here we must remain.

Everything forgiven and in common—

(p. 193)

To hold his wife "in common" with her father is the fate that Plath's verse imposes on Hughes. Hughes's final line in **"A Picture of Otto"** compares the dead Plath with Wilfrid Owen in Owen's poem, "Strange Meeting," like Owen "Sleeping with his German as if alone" (p. 193).[17] Plath, too, sleeps with her German father—her only company the supposed enemy whom she kills in her verse. The cold comfort of her poetic immortality is an eternity "as if alone" with presences she herself created for imaginary battles. As Owen is forever identified as the poet who died too young, a

casualty of the Germans in World War I, so Plath is remembered as another poet who died too young, a casualty of her own obsession with the German daddy, Otto Plath.

Two Classical texts interwoven within the narrative of **Birthday Letters** further suggest that Hughes has appropriated an Orpheus-like identity for himself: these are the *Metamorphoses* of Ovid and Book 4 of Virgil's *Georgics.* Hughes does not translate Ovid's version of the Orpheus and Eurydice myth for his own 1997 *Tales from Ovid,* but the elaborate narrative in **Birthday Letters** often seems ruled by mythic powers of transformation, inspired by an Ovidian "ether" invoked by the poet Hughes to explain his wife's poetic immortality. Even Plath's face is described in **"18 Rugby Street"** as continually metamorphosing, a shapeshifting shell for the restless spirit inside:

A device for elastic extremes,
A spirit mask transfigured every moment
In its own seance, its own ether.

(p. 23)

Plath's face is elementally protean—"a stage / For weathers and currents, the sun's play and the moon's"— and does not assume its final mask, "the face of a child—its scar / Like a Maker's flaw," until her death, "that final morning" (p. 23).

In the glossary for Hughes's *Tales,* Orpheus is described as the "Thracian bard, whose music could rouse emotion in wild beasts, trees, and mountains; son of the Muse Calliope by either Apollo or Oeagrus, a king of Thrace; husband of Eurydice; after her death he wandered through the mountains of Thrace, playing his lyre."[18] The wildness associated with Thrace has a parallel in the rough countryside and moors of Yorkshire, just as Orpheus' musical affinity for animals and nature may recall Yorkshire's native son, Hughes, also a poet of nature. In **"The Owl,"** a "letter" remembering an early episode in his marriage to Plath, Hughes fascinates her with his Orpheus-like gifts: he rouses a predatory owl to swoop down on him by sucking "the throaty thin woe of a rabbit / Out of my wetted knuckle" (p. 33). Perhaps like Orpheus wooing Eurydice, Hughes "made my world perform its utmost for you" (p. 33).

Finally, while Hughes does not appropriate Ovid's framing narrative (Book X of the *Metamorphoses* opens with the story of Orpheus and Eurydice and ends, as we move into Book XI, with the story of Orpheus' death), he does rework the Thracian bard's longer tales as they appear in Ovid: the stories of Pygmalion, Myrrha, Venus and Adonis, and Atalanta also form a group in Hughes's *Tales from Ovid.* The story of Myrrha's attempted suicide and incestuous affair with her father, Cinyras, is especially pertinent to Hughes's understanding of

Plath's suicide and her incestuous love for her father, Otto Plath. Myrrha's metamorphosis into a tree, a weeping myrrh, converges with Hughes's response to Plath's poem, "Elm," in which she assumes the voice of the tree in order to give figurative expression to her experience with shock treatments:

> I have suffered the atrocity of sunsets.
> Scorched to the root
> My red filaments burn and stand, a hand of wires.[19]

Her anxiety "petrifies the will": "I am terrified by this dark thing / That sleeps in me."[20] Akin to Hughes's narration of the birth of Adonis from the bole of his tree-mother Myrrha—"It heaves to rive a way out of its mother"[21]—is his description of Plath's giving birth to *Ariel*'s voice out of the process of composing "Elm": "the voice of *Ariel* emerges, fully-fledged, as a bird, 'a cry'":

> Nightly it flaps out
> Looking, with its hooks, for something to love.[22]

Like Hughes's Adonis in the *Tales*, conceived by Myrrha after spending several nights with her father, Cinyras, Plath's Ariel-*persona* is, in his interpretation, the fruit of an incestuous bonding with her father in a classical underworld, followed by a strange metamorphosis:

> . . . between the second of April [1962], when she entered her father's coffin under the Yew Tree [in the poem **"Little Fugue"**], and the nineteenth when she emerged as a terrible bird of love up through the "taproot" of the Elm Tree, she has made a journey of self-transformation from the Tree in the West to the Tree in the East. From a tree at one of the gates of the underworld in the sunset to a tree at another of the gates of the underworld in the dawn. As if she had travelled underground, like the sun in the night, from one to the other.[23]

Hughes further describes this transformative journey by Plath as "the bereft love returning to life,"[24] as if Plath had revivified her dead father, but only by disinterring an erotic attachment that leads inevitably to her own suffering and sacrifice. As Hughes understands Plath's plight in "Elm," "The unalterable truth to this reality is the voice's deeper negative story. It explains why the bird in the Elm 'terrified' her with its 'malignity'."[25] Perhaps this also explains why Hughes's own mourning poems for Plath will enact a counter-ritual for expressing grief, at times anti-Ovidian in their handling of metamorphosis.

Another influence on Hughes's *Birthday Letters* may be Book 4 of Virgil's *Georgics,* a text commonly read by English schoolboys of his generation and one that specifically intertwines the craft of beekeeping with the myth of Orpheus and Eurydice.[26] Here Virgil implicates Aristaeus, the classical patron of bees and beekeeping, in Orpheus' loss of Eurydice. As Hughes, in **"The Bee God"** and several other poems, blames Plath's father, Otto, the entomologist and expert on bees, for taking his wife away from him, so in the *Georgics* Orpheus' wrath is directed at the shepherd Aristaeus, whose lusty pursuit of Eurydice inadvertently causes her death. Aristaeus is punished when he loses all of his bees through famine and disease. Baffled at his misfortune, Aristaeus seeks oracular advice from Proteus, who explains why he has suffered this loss:

> "The anger that pursues you is divine,
> Grievous the sin you pay for. Piteous Orpheus
> It is that seeks to invoke this penalty
> Against you—did the Fates not interpose—
> Far less than you deserve, for bitter anguish
> At the sundering of his wife. You were the cause:
> To escape from your embrace across a stream
> Headlong she fled, nor did the poor doomed girl
> Notice before her feet, deep in the grass,
> The watcher on the bank, a monstrous serpent."[27]

Aristaeus is advised by Proteus to make a sacrifice to "'The nymphs with whom [Eurydice] used to dance her rounds'," who sent "'this wretched blight'" on his bees.[28] From the "putrid flesh" of a bull which Aristaeus batters with a mallet until dead, a swarm of bees emerges to refurbish the ravaged hives of Aristaeus.[29] Sacrifice reverses his misfortune and renews the life of his hives. Hughes reiterates this configuration of symbols and characters in *Birthday Letters,* adding to it an incestuous bond between Plath/Eurydice and Otto Plath/Aristaeus. Like Orpheus, the poet-husband must contend with another maestro of bees, who comes between him and his youthful wife, as well as with a "monstrous serpent" that appears as a "great snake" and "a mamba, fatal" (p. 137) at their marriage ceremony in **"The Rag Rug."** In other poems, Otto Plath is a roaring minotaur, recalling the bull sacrificed by Aristaeus to renew his beehives. Otto Plath is also a "German cuckoo," like the bird which usurps another's nest to lay the egg that will hatch into the voice of *Ariel*—"fully-fledged, as a bird," or, as Hughes goes on to describe the father who cuckolds him in **"The Table,"** "While I slept he snuggled / Shivering between us" (p. 138), a cold dead figure who robs their marriage bed of warmth and Hughes of his wife's body. Finally, in **"Fairy Tale,"** he is an "Ogre" and once again Plath is a fledgling who "died each night to be with him. / As if you flew off into death" (p. 159).

Throughout *Birthday Letters,* Hughes reiterates and refashions the Virgilian theme of sacrifice to placate and appease. The figure of Orpheus-Hughes, however, stands in stark contrast to Aristaeus, to Plath's poetry of sacrifice, to her father's portrayal as a bellowing minotaur demanding human victims, and, finally, to the women who advised Plath in her final days—like the nymphs who were Eurydice's friends and wanted Aristaeus to be punished. Whereas for all of these figures in Hughes's narrative, sacrifice is a form of reparation—even an exchange of death for new life—Orpheus-Hughes's loss is depicted as irreparable, his grief implacable, and his longing unappeased by sacrifice. Only through the historical process of remembering important moments in their marriage and then permitting them to fade does *Birthday Letters* complete the process of healing grief.

* * *

> "Step for step / I walked in the sleep / You tried to
> wake from."
>
> **("The Bird,"** p. 77)

The early poems in *Birthday Letters,* even as they move forward temporally—love at first sight, a whirlwind courtship, marriage, and honeymoon—are also frequently embedded both with narrative strands belonging to the Orpheus-Eurydice myth and freeze-frames or snapshots arresting motion and reminding readers of Orpheus' final, impulsive gaze at Eurydice. Memory and loss are conceived of as moments of backward-looking, briefly and stunningly vivid, then fading. Hence, in **"St. Botolph's,"** Hughes remembers their first meeting:

> . . .—suddenly you.
> First sight. First snapshot isolated
> Unalterable, stilled in the camera's glare.
>
> (pp. 14-15)

Almost immediately, however, Hughes leaps forward to the "years in its shadow— / As if I saw you that once, then never again" (p. 15), in which "its shadow" must be her death, the darkness that enfolds his "clearer, more real" poetic imagining of his first sight of her. As with so many moments of Plath's evocation in *Birthday Letters,* Hughes works with paradox, with absence that is palpable, with a "once" that is so real that its "never again" seems impossible—as impossible to accept as Orpheus' loss of Eurydice.

Another early "letter," **"Caryatids (I),"** plays with the frozen animation of Greek statuary—the young virgins who are simultaneously supporting columns. Hughes is also looking backward at the first poem by Plath which he read, in which these maidens make their appearance. Because he "disliked" the poem "through the eyes of a stranger" (p. 4), he "missed everything" that he now recognizes he was meant to see. He foolishly

> . . . made nothing
> Of that massive, starless, mid-fall, falling
> Heaven of granite
>
>   stopped, as if in a snapshot,
> By their hair.
>
> (p. 4)

In these artificed maids, he might have discerned the ghostly aura of his future wife, "Fragile, like the mantle of a gas-lamp" (p. 4), where "mantle" alludes to the caryatids' streaming hair as an architectural framing support, and also to the mantle of a gas lamp, a mesh bag that holds the burning gas of a gas lamp, yet instantly crumbles to powdery ash at the slightest touch.[30] With his friends, too "careless / Of grave life" (p. 5), he saw "No stirring / Of omen" (p. 4) in the "Heaven of granite" held up by such "friable" creatures: a forewarning of the terrible fate also awaiting Plath. The pun in "grave life" alludes simultaneously to Plath's extraordinary posthumous life, the poetic immortality which Hughes has taken care of, and also to the seriousness and preciousness of life and the carelessness of youth about it. Neither Orpheus nor Hughes anticipated how brief their marriages would be.

"Fate Playing" deals with an incident in Hughes's courtship of Plath—a planned rendezvous in London that almost went awry—and may also be read as a warning. The poem ominously enacts a version of the Orpheus-Eurydice myth. Fate disguises its oracular content by playfully reversing the roles of Hughes and Plath. As he emerges from a train at King's Cross, it is as if he has been pulled out of a dark underworld by the force of his wife's desire, suggested by Hughes's repeated use of "molten" to describe the intensity of Plath's inner fire. On their wedding day, he will see her "Wrestling to contain your flames" (p. 35), and here, in "the flow of released passengers," he sees her

> . . . molten face, your molten eyes
> And your exclamations, your flinging arms
> Your scattering tears
> As if I had come back from the dead
> Against every possibility, against
> Every negative but your own prayer
> To your own gods.
>
> (p. 31)

Even the taxi she has hired is a "chariot" driven by a "small god," and her "frenzied chariot ride" may recall Persephone's kidnapping by Hades in a wagon, her descent as a young maiden, like Eurydice, into premature death. The poem ends with a miraculous thunderstorm, and Plath's joy at being reunited with her 'lost' husband is

> Like the first thunder cloudburst engulfing
> The drought in August
> When the whole cracked earth seems to quake
> And every leaf trembles
> And everything holds up its arms weeping.
>
> (p. 32)

The epic simile here invites us to read—to exaggerate—this minor skirmish with "fate playing" as artifice, equal to mythic Demeter's restoration of fertility to the earth when she is joyfully reunited with her daughter, Persephone, or to the mingled tears of joy and sorrow in Shakespearean recognition scenes. Hughes as Orpheus may well feel comfortable using the expansive epic simile, since Orpheus' mother was Calliope, the muse of epic poetry. He deploys this technique similarly to describe Plath's emotional response to Spain, too, much of an underworld like the one that envelops Eurydice, a nightmare world of insubstantial spirits:

> . . . you tried to wake up from
> And could not. I see you, in moonlight,
> Walking the empty wharf at Alicante
> Like a soul waiting for the ferry,
> A new soul, still not understanding,
> Thinking it is still your honeymoon
> In the happy world, with your whole life waiting,
> Happy, and all your poems still to be found.
>
> (pp. 39-40)

Plath's Spain mimics Eurydice's limbo, that region between the world of the living and the world of shades, to which she will be ferried after all memories fade. Indeed, in **"Moonwalk,"** Plath sleepwalks on their honeymoon through a landscape resembling a charnel house and speaks a language belonging only to the dead. In her sleep, she mouths hieroglyphs from "tomb-Egyptian" that are "Like bits of beetles and spiders / Retched out by owls. Fluorescent, / Blue-black, splintered. Bat-skulls" (p. 41). Hughes, like Orpheus gazing at his wife from the dimension of life and vital color, watches Plath wander through "a day pushed inside out. / Everything in negative" (p. 41). He dares not wake her and "could no more join you / Than on the sacrificial slab / That you were looking for" (p. 42). Plath's search in sleep for an altar—the "sacrificial slab"—presages her later desperate search for a god to whom she can dedicate her writing and, finally, her life.

The mythic Orpheus, famed for his ability to animate what is dead, to imbue nature with his song, is also famed as the poet who fails, who looks back at the crucial moment and loses Eurydice, who then fades, loses corporeality, and becomes a shade. Indeed, Orpheus might be defined as the poet who fails, whose verse is dedicated to a compulsion to repeat this failure, fixated as he is on the lyric moment when desire comes into being as longing and regret for what may never be. As Eurydice dies twice, so Plath figuratively dies many times in **Birthday Letters,** as if retreating from the vividly realized life which Hughes as poet-Orpheus briefly restores to her, fading again into a dark underworld, dematerializing as Eurydice did into shadows. Hence, in **"The Blue Flannel Suit,"** Hughes relives her appearance and still concentration on the first morning when Plath teaches at Smith College, only to lose the memory of her in the shade of her loss: "as I am stilled / Permanently now, permanently / Bending so briefly at your open coffin" (p. 68). The paradoxical

rocking between "permanently" and "briefly," between a "now" and an implicit forever, is commensurate to the realization of loss as a brief moment, even while its trauma is lasting. Even more moving is the ending to **"Daffodils,"** a poem that returns to the first and only spring they would enjoy in their English home:

> We had not learned
> What a fleeting glance of the everlasting
> Daffodils are. Never identified
> The nuptial flight of the rarest ephemera—
> Our own days!
>
> (p. 127)

As with **"The Blue Flannel Suit,"** his memory of this lost moment is at once fleeting and everlasting, ephemeral and eternal.

In an Orpheus-like reversal of a trope that conventionally celebrates spring rebirth, the "everlasting daffodils" come to haunt Hughes with her death and his loss, as "On that same groundswell of memory, fluttering / They return to forget" (pp. 128-129) her every year. Only the "wedding-present scissors," which they lost while cutting daffodils in the garden, remember, but what they remember is her death: "April by April / Sinking deeper / Through the sod—an anchor, a cross of rust" (p. 129). For Plath, as for Eurydice, there is no Christlike resurrection; the scissors are a rusting anchor pulling her down and a symbol for a life prematurely cut short. As a symbol of the Plath-Hughes marriage, too, the scissors both contrast and complement the meaning of the daffodils. The scissors manifest the burial of memory, its gradual submergence, and the healing of an old wound, while the daffodils are "Wind-wounds, spasms from the dark earth" (p. 128), keeping Plath's loss fresh in the poet's heart. Indeed, many of Hughes's **Birthday Letters** may be read as "wind-wounds," with the winds as a familiar trope for poetic inspiration and wounds reminding the reader of lyric poetry's conventional relief of anguish through its expression.

This final phrase to capture daffodils also echoes Hughes's description of the birth of the windflower from Adonis' bloody wounds in **Tales from Ovid**: "His blood began to seethe—as bubbles thickly / Bulge out of hot mud."[31] In the *Metamorphoses,* the "minstrel's songs" of Ovid's Orpheus end with this tale of Venus and Adonis and her mourning tribute to her lover, another life prematurely cut short, but immortalized by her in the spring return of a flower blooming from his blood:

> "Memorials of my sorrow,
> Adonis, shall endure; each passing year
> Your death repeated in the hearts of men
> Shall re-enact my grief and my lament.
> But now your blood shall change into a flower."[32]

As Hughes renders this episode in his **Tales,** Venus promises, "'The circling year itself shall be your mourner,'" along with the "bright-blooded" windflower and its brief bloom: "Its petals cling so weakly, so ready to fall / Under the first light wind that kisses it."[33] In contrast, the Orpheus of **Birthday Letters** wants to memorialize nature's forgetfulness in the daffodils, as if Hughes were engaged in a type of mourning that seeks release rather than Venus' enduring attachment to her loss—or, perhaps, Sylvia Plath's enduring attachment to her dead father. The pathetic fallacy of Venus' wind-flowers is painfully acknowledged as a failure.

While Hughes may be adopting an Orpheus identity for many of his lyrics, then, he does not seek Orpheus' fate. Indeed, it is precisely here that Hughes and Orpheus may be said to part ways. In Ovid, the melancholic Orpheus retreats from human company, especially women's, and ultimately incurs their wrath for ignoring their attentions:

> . . . a frenzied band
> Of Thracian women, wearing skins of beasts,
> From some high ridge of ground caught sight of him.
> "Look!" shouted one of them, tossing her hair
> That floated in the breeze, "Look, there he is,
> The man who scorns us!" and she threw her lance
> Full in Apollo's minstrel's face. . . .[34]

Orpheus is sacrificed to the frenzy of these Maenads, his limbs torn apart, his voice "that held the rocks entranced" having no persuasive power over the scorned women. While Hughes has not escaped the wrath of feminists over the years, he portrays himself in **Birthday Letters** as at last freeing himself from a scene of sacrifice conceived originally by Plath.

* * *

"Your Aztec, Black Forest / God of the euphemism Grief." (**"The God,"** p. 191)

The Orpheus disguise, then, is sustained long enough for Hughes to mourn Plath with an extravagance derived from ancient literary sources, to remember all of the key moments in his marriage to Plath with mythic embellishment; but, finally, he moves toward catharsis and dissolution of grief. As Freud describes normal mourning, "Each single one of the memories and hopes which bound the libido to the object is brought up and hyper-cathected, and the detachment of the libido from it accomplished."[35] The term *cathexis* denotes an investment of emotional significance, while a hyper-cathexis is an exertion of counter-energy, an effort to dis-invest and take back the energy given to the lost love object. In **Birthday Letters,** counter-energy is exerted most strongly in poems in which Hughes engages Plath's own mourning verse. In **"The God,"** he describes her muse as evolving out of her "panic of emptiness" (p. 188) as a writer, her anxiety over having no tale to tell, no story "that has to be told" (p. 188). To this "dead

God / With a terrible voice" (p. 188), she first offers "Little phials of the emptiness" and "Oblations to an absence. / Little sacrifices" (p. 189). Gradually, however, this terrible God wants more substantial and larger offerings, and, as Hughes describes this process in several poems, nothing will satiate Plath's fiery God but "blood gobbets of me" (p. 189) until,

> You fed the flames with the myrrh of your mother
> The frankincense of your father
> And your own amber and the tongues
> Of fire told their tale.
>
> (p. 190)

Only by giving up her father, mother, husband, and finally herself to this roaring beast of a god does Plath find her poetic narrative. Hughes can only watch

> . . . everything go up
> In the flames of your sacrifice
> That finally caught you too till you
> Vanished, exploding
> Into the flames
> Of the story of your God
> Who embraced you
> And your Mummy and your Daddy—
> Your Aztec, Black Forest
> God of the euphemism Grief.
>
> (p. 191)

Here Hughes indicts Plath for her inability to discriminate between grief and self-flagellation, between a normal mourning that gradually accepts loss and suicidal depression with its inevitable component of murderous aggression.

As Hughes portrays Plath's so-called **"Grief,"** it is born out of her fear that she has no story to tell but the one given to her by her psychiatrist Ruth Beuscher about an Electra-complex:

> Beutscher [sic]
> Twanging the puppet strings
> That waltzed you in air out of your mythical grave
> To jig with your Daddy's bones on a kind of tight-
>   rope. . . .
>
> (p. 174)[36]

Hughes accuses Plath of making **"Grief"** her excuse for relinquishing her agency and voice as a writer in order to perform and to please—even to pander to—others. In **"Blood and Innocence,"** she willingly endures shock treatments because "They demanded it. Oh, no problem" (p. 168); then "they" want her to come back from her suicide attempt so long as she does not mind a poetic reconstructive surgery that is monstrous: "Yourself by Frankenstein, stiff-kneed, / Matricidal, mask in swollen plaster" (p. 168). Still, "they" want more—the corpse of her father—and she is eager to oblige: "Why on earth didn't you say. / Daddy unearthed" (p. 168) in order for her to "howl" her childhood loss and then to avenge it by killing him again and dancing on his grave. "They" are never identified but at times resemble the doctors who, in Hughes's view, mismanaged her electroshock therapy and then patched her back together with Freudian theory, who encouraged her to 'kill' her mother and father so that she might be "born again." At others, "they" are Plath's audience, the "peanut-crunching crowd" of "Lady Lazarus"[37] who await the show which she is willing to put on for the sake of "some acknowledgement" (p. 169); and they are Maenads, the feminists who are content only with finding someone to blame, who revel in dismemberment and sacrifice. They are "Grinning squabbling overjoyed" (p. 169) at the carnage that she performs, the rage against husband and father that she enacts in her poems.

The Maenad-feminists who have hounded him over the years find their inspiration in a Plath described by Hughes as "Catastrophic, arterial, doomed" (p. 197). His final poem, **"Red,"** describes the bedroom that he shared with Plath in Court Green as "A judgement chamber" and "A throbbing cell. Aztec altar-temple" (p. 197). It is another scene of sacrifice from which he seeks release not only for himself, but also, in some ways, for Plath as she is remembered in literary history. His revulsion against Plath's poetic identity as a priestess of blood is evident in his description of the impact of her ghoulish appearance:

> Your velvet long full skirt, a swathe of blood
> A lavish burgundy.
> Your lips a dipped, deep crimson.
> You revelled in red.
> I felt it raw—like the crisp gauze edges
> Of a stiffening wound. I could touch
> The open vein in it, the crusted gleam.
>
> (pp. 197-198)

Hughes ends *Birthday Letters* in flight from this portrait, mourning her adoption of a muse that needs to be fed with bloody sacrifice, when "Blue was your kindly spirit—not a ghoul / But electrified, a guardian, thoughtful" (p. 198). He prefers to remember Plath's genial spirit as fertile and forgiving, a guardian who is a healer, not an "open vein" and "stiffening wound," and a muse for a poet who chooses forgiveness over vengeance. Instead of the Aztec goddess bathed in red, Plath is pictured as a nurturing Madonna, whose "Kingfisher blue silks from San Francisco / Folded your pregnancy / In crucible caresses" (p. 198). Plath's true muse was a winged creature ("Blue was wings") like Shakespeare's "dainty" Ariel, an agent for executing Prospero's revenge who also inspires the magician-artist to pity the enemies in his power. Prospero might easily punish them, but, in response to Ariel's empathy, he muses:

> Hast thou, which art but air, a touch, a feeling
> Of their afflictions, and shall not myself,

> One of their kind, that relish all as sharply
> Passion as they, be kindlier mov'd than thou art?[38]

Like Prospero, who knows that "The rarer action is / In virtue than in vengeance,"[39] Hughes bids farewell to his wife with tenderness and regret, because "the jewel you lost was blue" (p. 198). Instead of rage and accusation, then—often regarded as the predominant emotions of Plath's grieving verse—Hughes doubles the loss, gazing backward at his wife and fellow poet, knowing that she herself was a jewel which he failed to keep safe.[40] Instead of a "bereft love returning to life," described by Hughes as Plath's inspiration for the *Ariel* poems,[41] *Birthday Letters* ends with a "bereft love" being laid to final rest.

Notes

1. Sigmund Freud, "Mourning and Melancholia" (1917), trans. Joan Riviere, in *General Psychological Theory,* ed. Philip Rieff (Macmillan, 1963), p. 166.

2. Passages from the poetry of Ted Hughes, cited parenthetically, are taken from *Birthday Letters* (Farrar, Strauss, & Giroux, 1998).

3. "Your Story, My Story," review of *Birthday Letters,* by Ted Hughes, *New Yorker,* 2 February 1998, p. 58.

4. Review of *Birthday Letters,* by Ted Hughes, *The Observer Review,* 1 February 1998, p. 15.

5. Alvarez, "Your Story, My Story," p. 58.

6. For a review of the many questions raised about Hughes's handling of Plath's literary estate and his vexed relationship with biographers and critics, see Mary Lynn Broe's "Plathologies: The 'Blood Jet' Is Bucks, Not Poetry," *Belles Lettres* 10 (1994): pp. 48-62.

7. "Peering Into the Bell Jar," review of *Birthday Letters,* by Ted Hughes, *New York Times Book Review,* Sunday, 1 Mar. 1998, p. 6.

8. "Peering Into the Bell Jar," p. 4.

9. *New Republic,* 30 March 1998, p. 31. Wood's title is taken from a poem by Plath titled "Words heard, by accident, over the phone," composed in July of 1962. The poem is based on a conversation which she overheard between Hughes and Assia Wevill that provoked Plath to tear the phone out of the wall in the home she still shared with Hughes. The phone is a "muck funnel" for shared intimacies between Hughes and his lover. Plath compares their conspiratorial whisperings to a "bowel-pulse" of words "plopping like mud"—plopping like feces, in fact, out of the phone and soiling the phone table (Sylvia Plath, *The Collected Poems,* ed. Ted Hughes [Harper, 1981], p. 202.).

10. Wood, pp. 30-31.

11. "Answering Ariel," review of *Birthday Letters,* by Ted Hughes, *Newsweek* 2 February 1998, p. 59; Kroll, "Answering Ariel," p. 59.

12. Wood, p. 33.

13. *The Observer Review,* p. 15.

14. Pollitt, p. 6.

15. Quoted in Rebecca Mead, "Poesy Department: For better and for worse, it's the Ted and Sylvia show," *New Yorker* 16 March 1998, p. 27.

16. Ovid, *The Metamorphoses,* trans. A. D. Melville (Oxford University Press, 1986), Bk. XI, ll. 63-68, pp. 250-251.

17. M. H. Abrams *et al.,* eds., *The Norton Anthology of English Literature,* vol. 2, 6th ed. (W. W. Norton, 1993), pp. 1846-1847.

18. *Tales from Ovid* (Farrar, Strauss, & Giroux, 1997), p. 252.

19. Sylvia Plath, *The Collected Poems,* p. 192.

20. *The Collected Poems,* p. 193.

21. *Tales from Ovid,* p. 119.

22. "Sylvia Plath's *Collected Poems* and *The Bell Jar,*" in *Winter Pollen: Occasional Prose,* by Ted Hughes, ed. William Scammell (Picador, 1994), p. 475.

23. *Winter Pollen,* p. 475.

24. *Winter Pollen,* p. 475.

25. *Winter Pollen,* pp. 480-81.

26. My colleague in the Classics Department at Williams, Meredith Hoppin, is the source for this observation. She also provided invaluable assistance in my working through of the Classical sources for Hughes's *Birthday Letters.*

27. *The Georgics,* trans. L. P. Wilkinson (Penguin, 1982), Bk. 4, ll. 452-461, pp. 139-140.

28. Wilkinson, p. 142, ll. 534-535.

29. Wilkinson, p. 143, l. 554.

30. I am indebted to an anonymous reader at the *Journal of Modern Literature* as the source for this definition of a mantle to a gas lamp. The definition supports the many flame-like images Hughes devotes to Plath's ephemeral spirit in *Birthday Letters.*

31. *Tales from Ovid,* p. 132.

32. Book X. ll. 27-31, Melville, p. 248.

33. *Tales from Ovid,* pp. 131-132.

34. *Metamorphoses,* Book XI, ll. 7-13, Melville, p. 249.

35. "Mourning and Melancholia," p. 166.

36. In a Public Symposium on *Birthday Letters* sponsored by the Academy of American Poets, 28 February 1998, Cooper Union, New York City, Fran McCullough and I agreed that Hughes's misspelling of Ruth Beuscher's last name may well be a conflation of her with Edward Butscher, whose unauthorized biography of Plath enraged both Hughes and his sister, Olwyn. There is also a pun on "butcher," suggesting the psychic carnage—in Hughes's view—created by the women who advised Plath in her final days.

37. *The Collected Poems,* p. 245.

38. William Shakespeare, *The Tempest,* Act v, Scene 1, ll. 21-24, in *The Riverside Shakespeare,* ed. G. Blakemore Evans et al, 2nd ed. (Houghton Mifflin, 1997), p. 1682.

39. *The Tempest,* Act 5, Scene 1, ll. 27-28, *The Riverside Shakespeare,* p. 1682.

40. In "Robbing Myself," pp. 165-67, Hughes remembers his clandestine return to the Devon home that he shared with Plath before their separation. After she and the children have moved to London, he drives back in the winter and "listened to our absence." He describes the house as a "plush-lined casket," "From which (I did not know) / I had already lost the treasure." As in the final poem, "Red," he describes the aura through which he moves as "snowblue twilight, / So precise and tender, a dark sapphire" and contrasts it with "our crimson chamber."

41. *Winter Pollen,* p. 475.

Ben Sonnenberg (essay date spring 2002)

SOURCE: Sonnenberg, Ben. "Ted's Spell." *Raritan* 21, no. 4 (spring 2002): 240-44.

[*In the following essay, Sonnenberg briefly recalls his personal friendship with Hughes.*]

Our friendship began in 1959 at Bill and Dido Merwin's house in London. Ted Hughes was twenty-eight years old and I was twenty-two. I had never met anyone I admired so much who was at the same time so approachable. Ted's voice was a level baritone with overtones of his birthplace in the Northwest of England. I listened to him so intently, literally on the edge of my seat, that I fell off my chair. When he helped me up from the floor, he didn't stop talking and I felt the vibration of his voice running down his arm. To borrow words from his poem **"Pike,"** his voice seemed to come from a "Stilled legendary depth: / It was as deep as England."

We took long walks together, Ted with his daughter, Frieda, in a baby carriage, gossiping some (quite a lot, actually) but talking of poetry mostly. He would declaim long passages of Chesterton and Kipling. He would quote at length from Lawrence and the poets of the First World War. His quotations from Shakespeare, by contrast, were short. "As the Clown says in *Measure for Measure. . . .*" I remember that last quotation. I remember his voice as he spoke it. I wish I could remember of what it was apropos. "Groping for trouts in a peculiar river."

* * *

We were good friends in those days. Not close friends exactly, not intimate friends; but good friends nonetheless. I remember encountering him in Marylebone Road one fine fall day. I was in a jaunty mood. "Where are you off to?" I asked him. He told me he was heading for the bookseller Bertram Rota, then in Vigo Street, to sell him some manuscript pages. I said, "How much does he give you for them?" "Five pounds," Ted said. I said, "I'll give you ten." I enjoyed transactions like that. I also gave him money to help start up *Modern Poetry in Translation.* I was quite the debonair young patron of the arts at that time of my life.

There were two main obstacles to a deeper friendship between us. One was geography. Ted moved to North Tawton in Devon in 1961; for most of the 1960s, I was living in London and in the south of Spain. The other was Sylvia. I didn't take to Sylvia. We were cordial to one another at first, but after she discovered that I knew people in New York who had once known her, she became distinctly cold to me. And yet, in his letters to me from Devon, he sends me her love and tells me of her interest in my work.

I never doubted Ted's feelings for me. Like an ideal older brother, he showed real interest in my work, always overpraising it and encouraging me to write more. Not only did he pay attention to my writing, he also asked my opinions about his own. In his foreword to *Difficulties of a Bridegroom,* he tells of showing me his story "The Suitor" and of me saying "You should have called it 'Death and the Maiden.'" That would have been during the winter of 1962, after his son, Nicholas, was born. "Your signsake," he wrote of Nicholas, born under Capricorn. At times Ted's belief in astrology seemed almost medieval to me. At other times it seemed of a piece with his scholarly interest in spirits, witches, magic, alchemy: elements of under-

standing the Elizabethan world picture. It was different with Sylvia. Or so I gathered from Ted. "She *witched* herself into that building," he said one day as we passed 27 Fitzroy Road, the house where Sylvia died (and where, as has often been noted, William Butler Yeats once lived).

He could be teased about his beliefs. (I doubt you could tease Yeats.) When he offered to cast the horoscope of my daughter Susanna, who was born in London in September 1965, I said, "You really believe in that stuff, don't you, Ted?"

"Sometimes it's a useful way of focusing one's attention on a person."

"So is a kiss, Ted."

"Well, you've got me there, haven't you, Ben?" he said.

* * *

I moved back to New York City in January 1966, and we kept up our friendship primarily by letters. His are fitful, apologetic, often beginning with phrases like "Long time since I wrote you" or "Sorry for the long delay." As always he expresses interest in my work in the theater. He writes me explications of **Wodwo, Crow** and *Orghast,* and, more needfully, of *Shakespeare and the Goddess of Complete Being.* Most of his letters are handwritten on both sides of the paper, sometimes extending up the left-hand margin and ending upside down on the top. Rereading them, I hear his voice: energetic, hypnotic, unstoppable.

Ted came to New York in September of 1986. Except for a brief visit in 1984, this was the first time I'd seen him in almost twenty years. He was here representing the Plath estate in an action concerning the 1979 movie of *The Bell Jar.* The action was brought by Dr. Jane V. Alexander, a psychiatrist in Brookline, Massachusetts, who figured in both the movie and the book as a character called Joan Gilling. A scene in the movie shows Gilling making homosexual advances toward Esther Greenwood, as the Plath character was named. Dr. Alexander claimed that her reputation had been damaged by the movie and she was asking $6,000,000 in compensation, not only from the Plath estate but also from fourteen other defendants, including Harper, the publisher of *The Bell Jar,* Avco Embassy Pictures, and various other corporations. The trial was expected to last six weeks.

Ted arrived with his sister, Olwyn, at about four in the afternoon. We had tea in my living room, a long bright room on the Upper West Side with an oblique view of the Hudson. Ted and Olwyn were in New York in order to find a lawyer. Before them was the prospect of a long, expensive trial. Both were under strain, Ted the more visibly so. His complexion was pale and his long hair unkempt. In the States, he explained, more even than in England, he had to contend with the "maenads," his term for those devotées of the cult of Sylvia Plath who blamed him for her suicide. I said I was sorry to see him so beleaguered. He said, "And I'm sad to see you in a wheelchair, Ben." At our last meeting, three years before, the symptoms of my multiple sclerosis had not been so advanced.

He was back in New York in January of 1987. The whole affair was over almost before it began. There was to be a settlement of $150,000. "All that the doctor wanted, Ben, was to have her day in court," Ted said. None of the judgment was chargeable to the Plath estate. Nevertheless, he told me, the costs to the estate had been considerable. "One year's earnings," he said. The amount was large. I forget how much. It astonished me, though.

Olwyn wasn't present that afternoon. A disappointment to me. I feel a bond with Olwyn. Ted came with the aptly named John Springer, a New York publicist. Christopher Hitchens was also there. Ted spoke of the lawyer Victor Kovner who'd represented the Plath estate. "Very good lawyer, wonderful man." I asked him how much trouble the "maenads" had been. "No more than usual," he said. "I've got John to thank for that." Then he told me of Ted Cornish, a healer in Oke-hampton, Devon. "He has helped people over long distances," he said. "I'll give you his telephone number." Nobody spoke for a moment. My wife, Dorothy, gave me a skeptical glance. I fancied I saw Christopher making a scornful mental note. Not for the first time in my friendship with Ted, I thought of that passage in *Henry IV, Part I* when Glendower says, "I can call spirits from the vasty deep" and Hotspur replies:

> Why, so can I, or so can any man;
> But will they come when you do call for them?

I promised I'd call Ted Cornish.

* * *

In 1990 I gave up the magazine *Grand Street,* which I'd started in 1981. Rising costs, declining health. . . . Ted wrote that he was sorry to hear that the magazine was folding. He went on to write: "In retrospect, I see I have submitted very little. Partly out of the wish to spare you having to turn down work from a friend." But his contribution of three poems to the first issue of *Grand Street* had been exceedingly important. It helped set the tone of the magazine, and his second contribution, "Sylvia Plath and Her Journals," in the third issue, made me feel that the magazine was indeed established.

He had blessed the magazine, which was exactly the kind of privilege I had from him from our first meeting, through our correspondence, up to the time he died: a beneficence, a blessing on everything I did.

* * *

After Ted died, his widow, Carol, sent me many photographs: Ted with the Poet Laureate's stipulated cask of fortified wine; Ted fishing in Cuba, in Scotland; Ted with an aged Leonard Baskin; Ted with Carol over the years. . . . My favorite shows him holding the case containing the Order of Merit as the Queen looks on with a genial smile. He smiles too like a small boy who's gotten the Christmas present he wants. Physically, he looks strong. In twelve days he was dead. Olwyn wrote: "It's almost as though he was suddenly shot."

On 11 October 1999, about a year after his death, I went with my wife to a tribute to Ted Hughes at the Ninety-second Street Y. Here is where I first saw him, in the winter of 1956. He read then from *The Hawk in the Rain,* which had been given a prize that year for the best first book of poems. Now several famous poets were reading from his numerous books and a famous actress was reading from his dramatic works. When they were done, the lights came down, and, over the sound system of the auditorium, we heard his spellbinding voice. He read **"The Thought Fox,"** from *The Hawk in the Rain,* with its last line, "The page is printed."

Michael Hofmann (essay date Feb. 2004)

SOURCE: Hofmann, Michael. "Stare at the Monster." *Poetry* 183, no. 5 (Feb. 2004): 278-89.

[*In the following essay, Hofmann examines Hughes's literary legacy, praising the poetry of the 2003 volume of collected poems.*]

I have a dim sense of how Ted Hughes may be perceived here in America. ("Stare at the monster," he wrote in a poem, **"Famous Poet,"** from the 1950s.) I have a slightly clearer sense of how Hughes has fared in the UK, at least over the last twenty years. Neither is the slightest use in preparing one for—a word I certifiably use for the first time in print!—an awesome collection of poems. Hughes is at least arguably the greatest English poet since Shakespeare; what's the competition? Milton, Pope, Keats, Wordsworth, Tennyson, Hardy, (maybe) Larkin. I think such a view can be advanced. This is indeed the man with the lifelong obsession with Beethoven. The poet whose voice Seamus Heaney described as "longer and deeper and rougher." Of whom the late Gavin Ewart wrote his one-line poem, "Folk Hero": "The one the foreign students call 'Ted Huge.'" Unscientific though it certainly is, people who bought Ted Hughes books on Amazon UK also bought Dante, Homer, Chaucer, Shakespeare, and Heaney. Match me that.

Of course, once poets die, there's some fun cutting them down to size. *Nihil de mortuis,* unless it cuts them off at the knees. British poets particularly, because what do the British know about scale? It'll fit on a postage stamp; albeit, a stamp that isn't obliged to declare its provenance. Ask Derek Walcott about the state of British poetry, he starts brabbling about Larkin (this was when Hughes was alive, but Larkin already safely dead). Ask James Schuyler for the last really good British poet, he would've sent you rooting back to Swinburne, or even earlier. I have a feeling, though, that Hughes will be spared this rather Australian ("tall poppy") treatment. Not only because at above 1,300 pages (1,200 of them poems), his book handily pips even Lowell's, published just a couple of months before, but because so many of the poems are wonderful, and practically unknown. And also, because at a time when appearance and presentation are getting to be almost everything, this one-time poet laureate (a label whose potential for comedy and obloquy has gone strangely unrecognized in the Po-Faced States) carried himself superbly. "All this, too," it says in **"October Salmon,"** "is stitched into the torn richness, / The epic poise / That holds him so steady in his wounds, so loyal to his doom, so patient / In the machinery of heaven."

Some of it is sheer industry. Hughes applied himself to poetry for the best part of fifty years, and with barely an intermission. The list of his poetry books alone covers a large, closely set page. (I suppose there are some nonentities who manage a big product, but on such a scale, one would have to be an acute graphomaniac, not merely a persistent hack, to compete). But there was much more: plays, translated from Aeschylus, Euripides, Seneca, Racine, Wedekind; Poetry International at the Albert Hall in 1970; the magazine *Modern Poetry in Translation,* founded and edited with his friend of fifty years, Daniel Weissbort; translations of Janos Pilinzky and Yehuda Amichai; poetry for children, and books to stimulate children to write (a lifelong commitment); editions of Plath (Hughes wasn't an exemplary editor in this case, for the simple reason that one wouldn't wish anyone to be in that position, but I think he's hard to fault); selections from Dickinson and Whitman and Keith Douglas and Shakespeare; two wonderful anthologies with Seamus Heaney, *The Rattle Bag* and then *The School Bag*; work with the theater director Peter Brook as a dramaturge, and deviser of the language called "Orghast"; the huge experimental book on deep narrative structures in Shakespeare, *Shakespeare and the Goddess of Complete Being*; a big selection of essays

and reviews called *Winter Pollen* (when he got the cancer that killed him, he blamed it, typically, on writing too much prose). And Hughes did all this not in some dusty monkish solitude or supportive college eyrie, but from a life in which he farmed, fished, traveled very widely, was several times honored by the Queen of England, with whom he was reputed to have got along well, and further, was—you won't need me to tell you—thrice married, and (before reading Elaine Feinstein's biography, I had no inkling of this) had many affairs, and also raised two children.

Ted Hughes's absence was one of the sad givens when I was in England in the 1980s and 1990s. One knew about him, and knew about his work, but never had any expectation of meeting him. He was both sanctioned—the schoolmaster's poet and under sanction. He dwelt simultaneously in a higher and a lower sphere; one thought of him as serving out some kind of punishment. Devonian relegation or house-arrest. It was one of a number of revelations in Feinstein's recent biography to learn that he was actually quite often in London, and lived not quite like Aung San Suu Kyi. I saw him just twice. Once at a Faber party, where our then-editor, Craig Raine, pushed us together and we shyly gulped at one another in silence like goldfish (I saw this happening with other baby-poets too), and once when he agreed to read with ten others at the London Festival Hall from the book of Ovid translations that James Lasdun and I brought out in 1992, to which he contributed four pieces.

A good outcome from this partly voluntary, partly imposed-seeming withdrawal was that he kept his freedom, his dignity, his time. This extended to his personal life, his illness and death, and his work. The successive poetry editors at Faber and Faber, Craig Raine, Christopher Reid, and Paul Keegan—the editor of this volume, who took the chair only after Hughes's death—were deeply impressed by their charge, and grew close to him. The rest of us may have thought we had him down, but he retained the capacity to surprise us with his every utterance. Whether it was his wholly unexpected *Paris Review* interview with Drue Heinz in 1995, or **Birthday Letters,** which floored us, or uncollected poems in his **Selected** like **"Remembering Teheran,"** or the last printed communication I remember from him, a long, eloquent piece in the *Guardian* in 1997 pleading for fox-hunting and stag-hunting to be allowed to continue—everything from him was considered and powerful and left-field. Nothing less would have allowed him to be poet laureate without a considerable diminution of his prestige. (That's how things work in England.)

And that's how it is with this **Collected Poems.** Paul Keegan has taken Hughes's **New Selected Poems** of 1995 as his model, and intercalated the expected and familiar Faber texts with uncollected or small press works like a Viennese layer cake—in astonishing quantity and quality. Most collected poems merely give us what we have already. Not this one, not unless you are a wealthy book-collector, with access to three continents. Hughes was assiduous in sending out individual poems all his life (his first publication outside Cambridge was in these illustrious pages, in August 1956, though the poem itself, **"Bawdry Embraced,"** is not terribly illustrious), and he had a lifelong affinity for small presses. He had the output, too, to command this double-issue. With Hughes's Hugheses, it's a little like Picasso's Picassos. Some don't fit whatever the large-press book happens to be; a few are rejects; some anticipate or trail along after preoccupations (there's a whole scatter-shot of **"Crow"** poems, for instance, before and after the 1970 volume); and some— especially late—are among his most personal. It's interesting that these were reserved for tiny, exclusive, luxurious publications, things I never suspected existed, let alone ever saw—*Capriccio* in 1990, *Howls and Whispers* of 1998, the year Hughes died. *Capriccio* was printed in an edition of fifty copies, selling at $4,000 apiece. Having these poems here is what gives this book some of its exceptional interest.

* * *

As I read through this huge book, I found all my provisional findings systematically overturned. Hughes's beginnings, half a dozen or so much-anthologized pieces aside—**"Wind," "Pike," "Thrushes," "View of a Pig"**—were, contrary to expectation (the perceived U-shape of his career), not especially impressive. Most of it was ordinary poetry of its time. After that, it seemed literary—diligently, strenuously literary. I had a sense of Hughes tinkering—it's a figure he would have liked—with the DNA of literature. Elements of Shakespeare (a lot), of Anglo-Saxon, of Donne, of Stevens, of Lawrence, of Hopkins. Of Plath. But when I got used to the literariness, and began looking for it, it lapsed. I felt—like Rimbaud alongside his river in *Le Bateau Ivre*—that I no longer had dependable guides. *Crow* (1970), then, I read as an Eastern European book. Analytical, diminished, distended, caricatured. Like something by Miroslav Holub or Zbigniew Herbert. Only for *Cogito* read Cuervo. Then a cosmic ferocity— always the least interesting part of Hughes to me: the hysterical, red-lit, gauge-busting style of "Death-orgasm supernovae // Flood from the bitten-away gills." *Prometheus on his Crag* (1973), no great development from its premise. (Curious, though, the number of male victim-figures in the poetry.) More series: birds, fish, flowers, insects, seasons, the majestic farm-diary of *Moortown* (from 1979). It's as if Rilke had written not two books of *New Poems,* but seven; or not one *Duino* but more than anyone cared to keep track of. Something magnificent and medieval and also workaday about

these catalogue-series: each one an illuminated letter, or one of the *Tres Riches Heures du Duc de Berry*. Occasional spurts of a thin but aggressive little vein of satire, like D. H. Lawrence's satire. Poems on Fay Godwin's landscape portraits of the North of England— humdrum, but suddenly sensational, two or three poems in a row. Wilderness a continual preoccupation, certainly—the last chronicler of wilderness on this shrinking McPlanet. "This is the Black Rhino, the elastic boulder, coming at a gallop. / The boulder with a molten core, the animal missile, / Enlarging towards you." Hughes would have known how many species and how many square miles were lost in his lifetime. He writes about things people now see on television, if at all; things whose existence we idly assume, and blithely imperil. But then the surprise of two beautiful poems on livestock auctions. Favor extended to rats. A long study, through the looking-glass, of spiders mating (another male victim). A tragic view of sex (like Lawrence, the tortoise), and of poetry.

A feeling that, whereas most of the best poetry of our time aims for and is distinguished by its speed (I think of Brodsky's phrase, "a highly economical form of mental acceleration"), Hughes often writes with heavy feet. Like Lawrence. Not just won't leap, but can't leap. A characteristic movement of his is the clanking, mired advance of bulldozer or caterpillar tracks. One plodding platelet at a time:

> I remember her hair as black
> Though I know it was brown.
> Dark brown. I first saw it as black.
> She was combing it. Probably it was wet.
> She was combing it out after washing it.
> Black, straight, shining hair down over her breasts.
> That's the memory.
>
> "Black Hair"

The sentences—often, like these, noun phrases—set themselves down, and the next one follows half in its print, barely an advance. The antithesis of speed. Weight. Method. Force. Brute or main. Instruction. Like someone writing a computer program. (And then one, three or four along, will contradict it: this isn't computer programming, it's poetry.) But so many wild exceptions to this. Astounding juxtapositions and swirling sentences that go miles. Perhaps one conclusion remains unoverturned: that the model and the repeated subject of Hughes's writing is Creation itself: "*Only birth matters* / Say the river's whorls. / And the river / Silences everything in a leaf-mouldering hush / Where sun rolls bare, and earth rolls, // And mind condenses on old haws."

* * *

When Hughes is described as a "nature poet," the effect—if not the intention—is drastically to limit him. That's what we were given at school, a vaguely reproachful litany of things with which we were unfamiliar, and in which we weren't greatly interested. We didn't live in *nature,* who on earth lived in nature? But if nature is the word one wants to use for Hughes, then one can only think of it as a sort of Tingueley-cum-Brueghel *Weltmaschine* of everything-that-is-the-case; a cartoonish vitalism that saw "the phenomenal technology" inside a fox's head; to which everything, *au fond,* was wild, even house-cats and daffodils, by virtue of its otherness; that outdid Marianne Moore by writing an ode to a sports car ("Flimsy-light, like a squid's funeral bone"); that offered a moorland tree as "A priest from a different land," who "Fulminated / Against heather, black stones, blown water"; that listened to a heron "cranking rusty abuse, / like an unwanted porter"; that showed us mannerly bears "Eating pierced salmon off their talons"; that was incapable of seeing crabs without a nightmarish Dix or Sutherland flashback of World War One ("Giant crabs, under flat skulls, staring inland / Like a packed trench of helmets"); that deconstructed a cranefly as "Her jointed bamboo fuselage, / Her lobster shoulders, and her face / Like a pinhead dragon, with its tender moustache, / And the simple colourless church windows of her wings."

Anything unhappy, ungainly, failed or doomed enlists the poet's sympathy, whether it's a baby swallow that can't fly ("the moustached goblin savage // Nested in a scarf . . . The inevitable balsa death"), or ugly, lumpy apple-blossom ("A straggle of survivors, nearly all ailing"), or a dirty river: "And the Okement, nudging her detergent bottles, tugging at her nylon stockings, starting to trundle her Pepsi-Cola cans." If this sympathy wasn't so universally extended, it might seem sentimental—a strange accusation to level at Hughes. Equally, when things work, they are celebrated for working. It is not "nature"—sky-blue and pink nature, schoolroom nature—so much as technology. A mother sheep "carries on investigating her new present and seeing how it works." A female spider's hands become cutting-edge: "Far from simple, / Though, were her palps, her boxing-glove nippers— / They were like the mechanical hands / That manipulate radioactive matter / On the other side of safe screen glass." A sparrow is read as a prole: "Pin-legged urchin, he's patient. / He bathes in smoke. He towels in soot, / And with his prematurely-aged hungry street-cry / Sells his consumptive sister." All this is drama, function, it takes us with an infra-red sensor to the sources of energy, character, identity. The descriptive resources of the writing match those of the creature or thing described. "The hills went on gently / Shaking their sieve." Hence the allowable comparison to Shakespeare. Who else—other than Shakespeare—would have dared the coda to **"Sing the Rat,"** where invention and anonymous folk-wit indistinguishably mingle:

> O sing
> Scupper-tyke, whip-lobber
> Smutty-guts, pot-goblin
> Garret-whacker, rick-lark
> Sump-swab, cupboard-adder
> Bobby-robin, knacker-knocker
> Sneak-nicker, sprinty-dinty
> Pintle-bum.

The corollary of the "nature-poet" label is that Hughes didn't "do" people. That his gift didn't extend to historical intelligence, to narrative, to psychology, to abstracting and inducing and contextualizing. It did, to all of those things—see *Birthday Letters,* see the *Tales from Ovid.* Like Lawrence though, Hughes often took animals as his way in. The *Metamorphoses* are god and man stories with animal outcomes. Animals challenged him, or commanded him unconditionally, as people only did if they struck him as exceptional, or in exceptional situations. (Old subjects, uncontemporary people, holdouts, veterans, drudges, people of a dandified strength, get his praise and attention: **"Sketching a Thatcher," "Dick Straightup," "Walt," "Sacrifice."**) There's any amount of human intelligence, and the slapstick of human incompetence ("O beggared eagle! O down-and-out falcon!"), in his poem **"Buzzard"**:

> When he treads, by chance, on a baby rabbit
> He looks like an old woman
> Trying to get her knickers off.
> In the end he lumbers away,
> To find some other buzzard, maybe older,
> To show him how.

It's not just the indignity of "old woman," the covertly sexual "treads," and the ribaldry of "knickers," it's the fact that an older buzzard might not necessarily be any more proficient. Sometimes a human subject will draw dignity and company from animal society, as in the early poem, **"The Retired Colonel"**:

> Here's his head mounted, though only in rhymes,
> Beside the head of the last English
> Wolf (those starved gloomy times!)
> And the last sturgeon of Thames.

Sometimes, it will draw further degradation, as in this short, uncollected poem, **"Gibraltar"**—where, I'm guessing, Hughes might have visited in 1956, at the time of his Spanish honeymoon with Plath:

> Empire has rotted back,
> Like a man-eater
> After its aeon of terror, to one fang.
>
> Apes on their last legs—
> Rearguard of insolence—
> Snapping at peanuts and defecating.
>
> The heirloom garrison's sold as a curio
> With a flare of Spanish hands
> And a two-way smile, wafer of insult,

Served in carefully-chipped English.
The taxi-driver talking broken American
Has this rock in his palm.

When the next Empire noses this way
Let it sniff here.

The "fang" is the Rock itself. There's a touch of Yeats about the poem, about the slightly squeamish deployment of slang. (You can't help looking for the word "slouch" somewhere!) "Carefully-chipped" is nice, doubling as crockery and mimicry. Overall, one might not necessarily have guessed it was Hughes, but it's very confident; had it been more widely circulated, it might have saved him from the laureateship.

"Remembering Teheran" is a terrific poem that I've written about elsewhere, full of heat and drought and static and theatricality and alienated intimations of pre-Revolutionary dread. It shows beyond a peradventure that Hughes could "do" abroad as well as anyone. **"Auction at Stanbury"** is a short and intense snapshot of the North of England, bleakly comic, sadly inward:

On a hillside, part farm, part stone rubble
Shitty bony cattle disconsolate
Rotten and shattered gear

Farmers resembling the gear, the animals
Resembling the strewn walls, the shabby slopes

Shivery Pakistanis
Wind pressing the whole scene towards ice

Thin black men wrapped in bits of Bradford
Waiting for a goat to come up

The auction is cleverly held off till the last two words; the scene is too miserably messy to deserve any more hierarchy or purpose than that. Shit / shat / shab / shiv. Waiting for a goat—a scapegoat, perhaps—waiting for Godot. It's a final, humbling indignity. Like the—roughly contemporaneous—devaluation of a currency.

The condition of England is always something Hughes is keen to infer, sometimes ceremonially, almost magically, as in the laureate poems, sometimes satirically, in more occasional pieces. It's one of the identifications that lends a cute cultural amplitude to his poems about Plath, the fact that she's America, and he's England, and much of the time he's on the receiving end: "It confirmed / Your idea of England: part / Nursing home, part morgue / For something partly dying, partly dead" (**"55 Eltisley"**). By the same metonymic token, one "J. R." is identified with Australia ("your firestick-naked, billabong spirit"), his second wife Assia Wevill with an unstable amalgam of German, Jewish, Levantine, and Russian, his father-in-law Jack Orchard with a gypsy Africa. It's ethnobotanical labeling.

* * *

Birthday Letters is mainly stunningly unbeautiful—it's mostly written in the bulldozer style with short, incremental sentences—but it's still Hardy by other means. I like to think Hughes couldn't have written it without writing the **Tales from Ovid** first, to draw him into the sphere of the human and the narrative, but I'm not so sure now. It's not known whether, as the title suggests, and as I think Hughes claimed, the poems were written steadily over many years, or if they were written pell-mell towards the end of his life. The latter seems likelier to me. There barely seems time to draw breath between one poem and the next; I can't imagine them being composed years apart, leisurely, or sharply, at so many separate promptings. The composition of the *Duino Elegies* seems to me a likely parallel, some glimmerings earlier and one or two poems (there were some in the **New Selected** of 1995), but basically an abrupt tumble at the end. In the case of the **Birthday Letters,** the very notion of such a project—the narrative and publication of his version of the years with Plath—might have been the last thing to emerge.

They're not all great, or even good, poems. Partly, I think, they are pulled apart by Hughes following different, and even contradictory, purposes at the same time: to celebrate, to explain, and to mourn. The simplicity and the heavy slowness of the style is almost forced upon the poet wanting to do so many different things. Third-person description, with its myriad revelations, exaggerations, and suggestions is abandoned for a simple "I-you" mode used by Hughes for the first time, though the rest of us have been flogging it for years. Dignity and reticence, I imagine, would have meant he abhorred it. The way he uses it, it's unexpectedly capable of holding and disclosing feeling. Sometimes, it's almost a style without words. I'm thinking especially of a poem—I think for Assia Wevill—called **"The Other,"** which it took me a while to "see," but which now looks drastic and original: "She had too much so with a smile you took some. / Of everything she had you had / Absolutely nothing, so you took some. / At first just a little." It's related to another poem from *Capriccio,* called **"Folktale,"** but it's even more bare. As in Lawrence, it seems to break every known rule. There's not a concrete noun in the place. Not a scene. Not a recognizable event. Nothing. A few clichés are allowed to disport themselves rather grimly, but basically it's naked arithmetic. Subtraction, to be precise. But something of the schematic style of that poem, the threadbare simplicity, an otherworldly point of view where memory and self-accusation, transgression and punishment, seem to become one thing, informs a lot of the poems of **Birthday Letters.** ("Birthday" perhaps in that rather British sense of "naked.") "Was that a happy day?" begins one poem, "Nearly happy," another. "What happened to Howard's portrait of you? / I wanted that painting." "Remember how we picked the daffodils? / Nobody else remembers, but I remember." It could hardly be any more straightforward. It's hard to think there could ever be a more successful narrative—not least because we all grew up on the story anyway. But then, "Nobody else remembers, but I remember." It's quite a card.

Some of the poems are more furnished than others, and they are the ones I prefer: **"Fever," "Flounders," "Daffodils," "The Beach."** I read Hughes with the grain—I've learned to do that, it's wasteful not to—and against. The one thing I'm loath to go along with is the doomed—not just predestined, but predestinarian—mode that he wraps a lot of the memories and episodes in. His celebrating and mourning, in other words, I allow; I jib a little at the explanations. Time and time again, he offers up the machinery of doom, whether it's ouija sessions, an offended gypsy, a dream, an illness, Otto, poetry. There's a tense—the opposite of the future-perfect, if you like, the posthumous future—where the poems like to take you, the tense of "I had no idea," of "if only I'd known then what I know now," the tense of dramatic irony. "We thought they were a windfall. / Never guessed they were a last blessing." This wears out, and it's my one serious reservation about ***Birthday Letters***. I much prefer it when Hughes coasts on the "present" of the simple past:

> You had a fever. You had a real ailment.
> You had eaten a baddie.
> You lay helpless and a little bit crazy
> With the fever. You cried for America
> And its medicine cupboard. You tossed
> On the immovable Spanish galleon of a bed
> In the shuttered Spanish house
> That the sunstruck outside glare peered into
> As into a tomb. "Help me," you whispered, "help
>   me."
>
>   **"FEVER"**

This painting over and over a scene and a situation is to me what Hughes does best in these poems; that "as into a tomb" I view as another intrusion from the dramatic-ironical department. I like "baddie," half-condescension, half-quotation. Hughes pits his own amusement and health and good intentions against the contagion of panic. "I bustled about. / I was nursemaid. I fancied myself at that. / I liked the crisis of the vital role." And the ending of that poem, though it has the right amplitude for an ending, is correctly deduced from the matter of the poem itself: "The stone man made soup. / The burning woman drank it."

So much of the personal drama is comic, and I bless it for that. It's the grandiloquent, posturing timing—riding for a fall—of "We are surrounded, I said, by magnificent beaches." It's riding the long wave of remembering Plath reading Chaucer to an audience of cows: "It must

have sounded lost. But the cows / Watched, then approached. They appreciated Chaucer." It's like a scene in Jerome K. Jerome, you wish it could go on for ever. It's his re-enactment of Plath's—justified and witty—tirades against England:

>   England
> Was so poor! Was black paint cheaper? Why
> Were English cars all black—to hide the filth?
> Or to stay respectable, like bowlers
> And umbrellas? Every vehicle a hearse.
> The traffic procession a hushing leftover
> Of Victoria's perpetual funeral Sunday—
> The funeral of colour and light and life!
> London a morgue of dinge—English dinge.
> Our sole indigenous art-form—depressionist!
> And why were everybody's
> Garments so deliberately begrimed?
> Grubby-looking, like a camouflage? "Alas!
> We have never recovered," I said, "from our fox-holes,
> Our trenches, our fatigues and our bomb-shelters."
>
>   **"THE BEACH"**

This, for all its apparent ease, is a miraculous balance of indirect and quoted speech, of question and answer, of expansive and pithy, of detailed and universal, of naïve and informed, of drama and editorial. To throw off a phrase like "a morgue of dinge" like that, in the middle of what the fiction writers call "a riff." There's life in the old country yet. Or there was.

Elizabeth Bergmann Loizeaux (essay date spring 2004)

SOURCE: Loizeaux, Elizabeth Bergmann. "Reading Word, Image, and the Body of the Book: Ted Hughes and Leonard Baskin's *Cave Birds*." *Twentieth-Century Literature* 50, no. 1 (spring 2004): 18-58.

[*In the following essay, Loizeaux examines Hughes's work done in collaboration with various visual artists, most especially Leonard Baskin, whose illustrations inspired the poems of* Crow *and* Cave Birds.]

> From Yeats and Pound to Stein and Williams and the writers of the Harlem Renaissance, fine-printing work, the small press, and the decorated book fashioned the bibliographical face of the modernist world.
>
>   —Jerome McGann (7)

When John Millington Synge declared "All art is collaboration" (vi), he anticipated by some 80 years the arguments such textual scholars as Jerome McGann have been making since the mid-1980s for the collaborative nature of literary production. Synge was thinking about the contributions the peasants he met on the Aran Islands made to his flamboyantly imaginative language; textual critics would add the whole panoply of those involved in all stages of literary production from initial drafts through print or electronic artifact. As recent material readings of modernism suggest, creative partnerships—both visible and not so visible—have especially contributed to the vitality and variety of twentieth-century literature: *The Waste Land* (Eliot and Pound), *Look Homeward, Angel* (Thomas Wolfe and Maxwell Perkins), *Paul Bunyan* (W. H. Auden and Benjamin Britten), and *Stones* (Frank O'Hara and Larry Rivers) are only some of the modern examples of the collaborations among writers, artists, composers, editors, publishers, and printers that have challenged what Jack Stillinger aptly calls "the myth of solitary genius."[1]

Such partnerships in the twentieth century often thrived at the small, innovative presses—themselves collaborative affairs—that encouraged and sometimes commissioned collaborations, ventured to publish their results, and created "the bibliographical face of the modernist world." The boom in small- and fine-press printing that began with William Morris's Kelmscott and continues through Hogarth and Cuala to Gehenna, Janus, Arion, Perishable, and Granary has been especially important in creating opportunities for collaborations between writers and visual artists.[2] Deriving from the European modernist tradition of the *livre d'artiste* as well as from Blake and Morris, the nexus of fine-press printing and verbal-visual collaboration made possible much experimental twentieth-century literature, especially poetry, that sought to cross the perceived boundaries of media. If the twentieth century can be characterized by a "pictorial turn" into our current culture of images, as W. J. T. Mitchell has argued (*Picture Theory* 11-34), poets participated in it from the start, both in an increasing awareness of the visual body of language itself (from Dada and Pound to Susan Howe) and in collaborative ventures in texts combining words and images. One thinks of such modernist work as the first three volumes of Pound's *Cantos* with decorated initials and headpieces by Henry Strater, Gladys Hines, and Dorothy Pound; of Laura Riding's *The Life of the Dead* with John Aldridge; of James Weldon Johnson and Aaron Douglas's *God's Trombones*; and of such postwar work as Thom Gunn's *Positives* with photographs by Ander Gunn, Susan Howe and Susan Bee's recent *Bed Hangings,* and numerous volumes by Robert Creeley including *Numbers* with Robert Indiana, *A Sight* with R. B. Kitaj, and *Signs* with Georg Baselitz.[3]

Though not often placed in the company of such poets as Howe and Creeley, Ted Hughes belongs to this tradition. A poet who produced much of his work for both adults and children in collaboration with visual artists, he frequently published that work with small and fine presses. Throughout his life, Hughes paid particular attention to the textual bodies of his poems, habitually working with such small presses as Gehenna, Bartholomew (at Exeter College of Art), Sceptre, and Janus.

Like many of Yeats's works that appeared in limited editions from his sister's Cuala Press before publication by his commercial publisher, in the 1970s many of Hughes's volumes first appeared in limited editions from the Rainbow Press, which he owned with his sister Olwyn.[4] Established in 1971, the press declared its lineage as a modern descendant of Blake's radical experiments in material textuality; Blake's picture of moon, dove, and rainbow served as its colophon. A money-making venture and an outlet for his own work and that of Plath and others, Rainbow was a collaborative effort.[5] Olwyn often planned the volumes and selected the designs and materials. Hughes took a hand in their production, suggesting the frequently used Bodoni type and the lushly decorated Japanese endpapers in some volumes (Sagar and Tabor 4). Under the imprint of Morrigu Press, his son Nicholas, as a teenager, printed broadsides of his father's poems on the Hugheses' Albion handpress (87-88, 93-94). Rainbow produced elegant, sensuous volumes, often small enough to hold intimately (the large goat-vellum-covered ***Moortown Elegies*** is a notable exception), with deeply colored, silky leather bindings stamped simply in silver or gold, contrasting with the heavy, cream-colored, rough Italian paper they favored on the inside.[6]

Hughes demonstrated his keen awareness of the physical aspects of texts and the signifying qualities of language as graphic marks on a page in the introduction to his 1968 selection of Emily Dickinson's poems, where he described her fascicles in language tuned to the particular sensual qualities of the poems, "copied in her headlong, simplified script, and sewn loosely together in little booklets" ("Emily Dickinson" 154). Dickinson's "eccentric dashes," he argued against the then-prevailing practice of regularizing her punctuation, "are an integral part of her method and style, and cannot be translated to commas, semicolons and the rest without deadening the wonderfully naked voltage of the poems." For Hughes, bibliographic normalizing stifled Dickinson's poems, which Hughes understood as having a kind of primitive physical life of their own, naked and electric. He conceived of his own poems as physically alive, akin to the animals he loved to catch as a boy in the Yorkshire countryside. "In a way," he said, "I suppose, I think of poems as a sort of animal" ("Poetry in the Making" 10).

Hughes developed his own sense of the animal physicality of his poems less by pursuing radical typographic innovation than by experimenting persistently with the interplay of words and images in the graphic field of the book. Many of Hughes's books from both commercial and private presses contain pictures, mostly of animals and landscapes. Some of the pictures are his own; most are done by others. In "Poetry in the Making," he recalls his pleasure as a child in "modelling and drawing," remembering in particular his satisfaction when he copied animals from a "thick green-backed" book of "glossy photographs" his aunt had given him for his fourth birthday: "I can remember very vividly the excitement with which I used to sit staring at my drawings, and it is a similar thing I feel nowadays with poems" (10-11). Bearing witness to the way the graphic marks of language and of the visual arts flow in and out of each other, some manuscript pages of his poems contain his drawings of animals, often fantastical. That relation is occasionally carried onto the printed page, where text and picture intermix, as in his own illustration in *Earth-moon.*

From the 1970s on, Hughes frequently collaborated on volumes of poems with visual artists, including photographers Fay Godwin (*Remains of Elmet,* 1979) and Peter Keen (*River,* 1983) and, most especially, with American graphic artist and sculptor Leonard Baskin. Hughes met Baskin during the year he and Plath spent in Northampton, Massachusetts (1957-58), where Baskin was a colleague of Plath's at Smith College. They began a lifelong friendship, important to them both. In 1942, as an undergraduate at Yale, Baskin had founded Gehenna Press, which was to become one of the most important fine presses of the century. In Baskin Hughes found a mythic thinker as obsessed with the ways of animals, especially birds, as he was. Baskin's work seemed to Hughes to derive from the written word, to be coextensive with the graphicality of language itself.[7] In his important introduction to *The Collected Prints of Leonard Baskin,* which he spent the first three months of 1983 writing, Hughes commented that Baskin's "style springs from Hebrew script itself—all those Alephs, Bets, Lameds, Yods, crammed in a basketry of nerves, growing heads, tails, feelers, hair, mouths" ("Hanged Man" 86). The seeds of *Crow* (1970), the volume that firmly placed Hughes on the map of modern poetry, were sown shortly after Plath's suicide in 1963, when, in an effort to "drive Hughes 'from despair into activity,'" Baskin asked him to write poems on some crow drawings, with the results to be printed at Gehenna.[8] In the troubled, unsettled years following Plath's death, Hughes was able to write little poetry, though he wrote much criticism, including the essay on Dickinson. In 1967 Baskin's drawings and Hughes's recent reading of Eastern European poets became the route back into poetry. They precipitated the major shift in style that enabled Hughes to write out of the tragedy of his life in the laconically cruel poems of *Crow.* In Baskin's drawings of birds—alert, predatory, intense, with "their tessera-like single-minded devotion to their ways of death" (Leonard Baskin 16)—Hughes clearly found images of his own dark and violent vision. *Crow* inaugurated a creative partnership with Baskin that lasted for more than 30 years and produced more than 10 collaborations including several children's books, *Cave Birds: An Alchemical Cave Drama* (1978), and *Capriccio* (1990).[9] Their last project,

Howls and Whispers, an illustrated edition of 11 poems on Hughes's relationship with Plath not included in *Birthday Letters,* appeared the year of Hughes's death (1998). Baskin redesigned Blake for the Rainbow Press's colophon. Hughes's collaboration with Baskin is arguably the most important sustained relationship of Hughes's literary career. The volumes they produced together comprise a sizable proportion of Hughes's work, and an essential part of his achievement as a poet.

If reading verbal-visual texts is, as Mary Ann Caws suggests, "stressed," it is especially so in the case of Hughes. While many studies speak to the power of images for Hughes and the importance of the collaborations in his life, many others do not mention them, and very few read them as part of the work.[10] As with most verbal-visual texts, there is with Hughes's texts the difficulty of articulating the word and image together or in relation. (How does one keep both arts simultaneously in view? How does one read doubly? Where is an adequate vocabulary?) This is complicated by the uncertain status of the image in a modern book for grown-ups: an illustration is usually understood as an incidental decoration merely. Further, with Hughes, sheer difficulty has kept critics focused on explication. Perhaps most importantly, attitudes toward Hughes's collaborations are curiously bound up in the dissension around his relationship with Plath. Efforts by admirers to defend Hughes against the charge of being an unwelcome collaborator as editor of Plath's *Ariel* (and as destroyer of her last journal) have often resulted in arguments that uncouple him from other partnerships as well. Leonard Scigaj, one of Hughes's most attentive critics and one sympathetic to his collaborations, voices explicitly the undercurrent in much Hughes criticism: "It would be untrue . . . to suggest that Hughes needs commissions [from Baskin], or myth or folklore texts to generate creative ideas . . ." (*Ted Hughes* 13). But Hughes's career suggests a different story. The relationship with Baskin is part of a larger pattern of interart collaborations that constantly fed his work, including that for the theater and cinema with Peter Brook (*Seneca's Oedipus* [1968], *King Lear* [1968], and *Orghast* [1970]) as well as that with Fay Godwin and Peter Keen.

In what follows, I'd like to look in detail at two textual incarnations of *Cave Birds,* Hughes's most extensive collaboration with Leonard Baskin, and focus on how we might read the three elements of Hughes's poetic that I've suggested here—words, images, and the body of the book—together in relation. Created in the 1970s, *Cave Birds* belongs to the controversial period of Hughes's career following Plath's suicide (1963) and the deaths of his lover Assia Wevill and their daughter Shura (1967), when the precise observations of nature that had given his early poems their astonishing vividness gave way to the need to see life and death in large, archetypal narratives in the volumes of his middle period—*Crow* (1970), *Gaudete* (1977), and *Cave Birds.* In her description of *Crow,* Elaine Feinstein suggests the desperate terms of these poems:

> Under the influence of Baskin, and Central European poets such as János Pilinszky and Vasko Popa, who understood the brutality of experience under totalitarian regimes, Hughes grappled with a darkness that few English poets of the time felt any necessity to allow into their poetry. His vision is comparable only to Beckett's in its bleakness.

(160-61)

In its fullest elaboration, *Cave Birds* is a series of narratively linked poems and black-and-white drawings that tells the tale of a guilty and suffering hero (sometimes cockerel, sometimes crow) who is judged, sentenced, sacrificed, and reborn. The poems are complex and allusive, an interweaving of pre-Christian (especially Egyptian) mythology with alchemy, shamanism, Blake, and Jung. Together the poems and pictures chart the hero's quest: after judgment in this world and purgation in the next, the disintegrated parts of the hero's being are, in a Lawrentian vision, united in an exchange with the neglected female and given new life.

In describing how we might read the constituent parts of *Cave Birds* (the poems, images, and the body of the book), I want to show, first, how these three elements work together to construct the volume's narrative. A multimedia book with a lively, often witty interplay of elements, *Cave Birds* pursues its argument—this *is* a didactic book—in several interrelated arenas at once. Reading the poems alone, we miss much of the interest, pleasure, and complexity of *Cave Birds.* Reading the images and poems in relation also brings into relief Hughes's and Baskin's negotiations with gender, opening them back into the history of gendered discourse about the arts and bringing us face to face with the gynophobic undertow of the volume's insistence on the importance of the female.

Second, I want to suggest that *Cave Birds* is, in part, about the process of its own making. Both the individual poems and the narrative as a whole self-reflexively comment on words and images, on seeing and saying. When the images and the body of the book are given their due along with the poems, the collaboration itself is displayed page by page and enters the volume's narrative. This has implications not only for how we might read the volume but also for how we might respond to Hughes's mythologizing. Graham Bradshaw expresses what has troubled many readers of Hughes: the possibility that Hughes's synthetic mythmaking is empty, that it is "a *tour de force* that might cast doubt on the authenticity of the experience the poetry conveys"

(237). But if Hughes's quest narrative can seem schematic and overblown in its epic ambitions, the drama of his crisis as a poet and his struggle to understand death, grief, suffering, and guilt in terms larger than himself nonetheless remain compelling. The active presence of the collaboration, once let into our field of reading, helps keep that struggle before us. On a local scale, the collaboration movingly embodies the desire for connection that the mythic narrative envisions.

THE COLLABORATION

Cave Birds is, in fact, not one text but several, the result of a complex compositional process. The *Cave Birds* that most readers encounter is the 1978 Faber & Faber trade edition (published by Viking in New York in 1979 from the same plates), whose narrative I've described above. Its bibliographic face disturbs. Baskin's weird anthropomorphic birds loom on all but one spread, filling the right-hand page, often threatening with their direct stares and blatant, if sometimes indeterminate, sexuality. On the left, across the gutter, appears a poem, complete on one page. On first approach, it is not clear exactly what this *Cave Birds* is. Shaped like a children's picture-book, though clearly nothing of the kind, it looks like an illustrated text— poems by Hughes to which Baskin has done pictures— and is talked of as such in the standard bibliography and by early commentators on the work (Sagar and Tabor 67).

Cave Birds, however, involves not only illustration (pictures on poems) but ekphrasis (poems on pictures), a different kind of collaborative relationship with a different history (Loizeaux 91-95). In 1974 Baskin, then living in Devon to be near Hughes, showed Hughes nine bird drawings; Hughes wrote nine poems on them (round A). Baskin then responded with 10 more drawings and Hughes with 10 more poems (round B). Hughes then wrote another 12 poems to which Baskin did 10 illustrations (round C). *Cave Birds* was composed, in other words, in three stages, two of ekphrasis and one of illustration.[11] But the division between ekphrasis and illustration is not so clear-cut. From the start, Baskin's images came with titles, his own acts of ekphrasis, so that Hughes's poems are both responses to Baskin's images and to his suggestive words about the images. As critics have noted, such titles as *A Hercules-in-the-Underworld Bird* (associated with the poem **"The summoner"**) and *A Tumbled Socratic Cock* (**"The accused"**) may well have set the initial direction for Hughes's epic anti-Socratic narrative. The same is true of round B. And round B is further complicated: Baskin's pictures were done in response to Hughes's poems of round A, and so may be viewed as a species of illustration, or at least a visual extension of the verbal narrative those first poems set in motion. The picture of a crow's skeleton encircled by the remaining ribbons of (perhaps) tendons, originally titled *The Stone of Death* (corresponding with **"The Knight,"** discussed below; carries on the enumeration of death's processes begun in such poems from the first round as **"The Risen."** And round C contains poems deeply rooted in both the verbal and visual texts already produced, poems that are ekphrastic as well as illustrated. Poem-and-picture pairs from all three rounds are intermixed in the trade edition's arrangement into a narrative of transformation. As in Anne Sexton's *Transformations* (illustrated by Barbara Swan) and Charles Simic's *Dime Story Alchemy* (on the work of Joseph Cornell), *Cave Birds'* interplay of word and image on the page, and the collaboration behind it, figure that transformation implicitly and explicitly. The transformation of word to image (illustration) and image to word (ekphrasis) enacts the metaphorical alchemy of the volume's subtitle, *An Alchemical Cave Drama.*[12]

Like Yeats's, Hughes's oeuvre is notoriously unstable. He frequently revised individual poems after initial publication and even more frequently revised the contents of his poetic volumes. *Cave Birds* has an especially diverse textual life. Along the way and subsequent to the collaboration, *Cave Birds* was offered to the public in various forms: a commissioned performance at the 1975 Ilkley Literature Festival, where the poems were read in front of the images projected on a screen; shortly after, a BBC radio broadcast on 26 May 1975 in which Hughes read 30 poems with brief, explanatory comments connecting the narrative; a limited-edition book of the 10 images and poems from round B produced by the Scolar Press for the Ilkley Literature Festival; and the 1978-79 Faber & Faber/Viking trade edition of 29 poems and images.[13] Some of the poems appeared in subsequent editions of Hughes's selected poems, in which the images and claims for their importance gradually leeched from the text.[14] The various incarnations contain various sets of the poems—some with images and some, as in the radio broadcast and selected poems, without—and in various orders. There is much to be said about the give and take as the poems were revised and recontextualized for presentation in different ways for different occasions, especially about the performative aspects of the Ilkley Literature Festival and the BBC broadcast. In terms of the dramatic interplay of word, image, and book, the trade edition and the magnificent Scolar Press limited edition are most suggestive.

THE SCOLAR PRESS LIMITED EDITION

Cave Birds was first presented to the world in print in a limited edition of 125 unbound books published by the Scolar Press in 1975. This edition contains only 10 poems, the round B poems, all ekphrastic. With some additions, these poems would form the central section of the trade edition three years later. It begins with the protagonist's death and tells the story of his progression through the tests and purgations of the afterlife and his rebirth into the world.[15] In the otherworld, the cockerel/crow hero is stripped bare, baptized in "winding waters" that dissolve him away "Like a hard-cornered grief, drop by drop" (**"The Baptist"**); his "soul is skinned, and the soul-skin laid out" (**"The Hall of Judgment"**); he confesses his guilt to heaven's gatekeeper ("yourself has confessed yourself"). This is not, for the most part, a gentle afterlife, but one, both pictures and poems tell us, inhabited by owls, eagles, and other predatory birds. It is an insistently physical place, bleak and threatening, alternately cold and hot: there are "the mountains of torment and mica," "the Arctic of stone," and "a red wind" and "the black wind, the longest wind / The head-wind // To scour you." In **"Incomparable Marriage,"** the hero's neglected, abused female partner—in Baskin's image, a huge eagle facing straight out at the viewer, filling the frame, screeching beak wide—confronts him:

> I meet you.
> For the audit. Your spellbound hours
> Were a summoning. I have come.
> Your creditor—even like water from the rock.
>
> It is too late to pray. Too late to cry.

In the final poem, full of the imagery of rebirth, **"Big Terror Descends,"** "A coffin spins on the torque. / Wounds flush with sap, headfull of pollen, / Wet with nectar" and the hero "Blinks at the source." "When everything that can fall has fallen / Something rises," as **"The Guide"** had earlier predicted.

One encounters this *Cave Birds* in a portfolio-style book, unbound pages set in a slim brown burlap-covered box secured by two sets of brown twill ties, thus joining the book form and the common carrying case for an artist's works on paper. It is huge (72.5 × 52.5 cm), the size of a kitchen table when open. One has to stand to heft the cover: reading it is a physical experience, in keeping with the volume's insistence on the physicality of all life, even after death. Photographs give little sense of how stunning this book is or what it feels like to read, using both hands, as one must, to lift and set aside page after page. Although the project had not yet acquired its subtitle, with its emphasis on drama (*An Alchemical Cave Drama*), the book requires one to read with large, theatrical gestures (especially stagey in the setting of the rare-book rooms where most copies are now housed). The images come first, as a group laid sideways in the volume. They must be lifted out and turned to be looked at, emphasizing their individual nature, their status as works of art separate from the poems. They seem to tease with the possibility of framing: should one want to break up the collection to display them so that they can be easily seen, they are ready. At £125, well beyond the later trade edition's cost of £5.95, though not exorbitant, this book is aimed at the collectors' market.

While the order of the contents showcases the images, it also emphasizes the process of collaboration: first Baskin's pictures, then the poems Hughes wrote on them. One peels away all the pictures one by one to reveal the poems beneath, printed on 10 separate sheets, each folded once to make a four-page signature. The unbound folded sheets are enclosed in a folder set into a well in the center of the book's back cover. The poem booklet is one-half the size of a drawing, the size of a large book (35.2 × 50 cm). Each poem, moreover, is accompanied by a copy of a holograph draft of the poem tipped in facing the printed poem on the inside of the folded sheet; some of the drafts, . . . contain, among the words and in the margins, Hughes's own sketches of fantastical and real animals, suggesting how intimately pictures were involved in the process of these poems' composition and reminding us of the way poems and animals and pictures keep, for Hughes, close company.

The volume's display of process highlights the very characteristic that makes this object valuable as art: it is the result of the handiwork of two artists. The book authenticates itself as having been made by hand by displaying part of the process of that making. The collaboration displayed thus advertises double value, an artistic twofer. But the book-as-object and the book-as-process also work against each other here: the display of process that produces the book's pieces undermines the idea of the whole, perfectly realized art object on which the art market is based. Word and image are not bound, nor are image and image or word and word. The reading process that the book enforces—standing, lifting the pages out, maybe walking to set them aside on another table—defies in exaggerated ways the "do not touch" dictum of fine-art viewing. And what it produces is not a whole but an assortment of fragments spread out around the reader, the result of reading as disassembling.

The book's tension between product and process may suggest the artist's and the poet's uneasiness with the ideological freight of the limited edition, so at odds with the scrappy, undecorative world of the poems. And one finds evidence that the book resists its own status as art object in other aspects of its bibliographic features as well: the antiart brown burlap cover, for example, whose color and texture underscore the poems' attention to the earthy physicality of the hero's disintegration. Hughes and Baskin try to walk the fine line, as did William Morris, between an art that brings the power of the handmade object into the daily world and the need to recoup the costs (and maybe even make some money on the venture) by selling to collectors. As with most

books from fine presses, the tension between the book as work of art and the book as common object, between what you shouldn't touch and what you must touch, between admiring and using, is part of the reading experience itself.

On another level, one can read the construction and arrangement of this *Cave Birds* as an embodiment of the book's concern with the halting process of decomposition that marks the transition from life into the uncertain state beyond. The volume opens with the cockerel hero's death in the collaboration's finest poem, which begins:

"The Knight"

Has conquered. He has surrendered everything.

Now he kneels. He is offering up his victory
And unlacing his steel.

In front of him are the common wild stones of the
  earth—
The first and last altar
Onto which he lowers his spoils.

And that is right. . . .

Identifying the cockerel's decaying body with the physical book, the poem shows how "the texts moulder" to reveal "the quaint courtly language / Of wingbones and talons," the language of the body itself. The disintegration of the cockerel's body, as "Skylines tug him apart, winds drink him, / Earth itself unravels him from beneath," suggestively echoes one's own reading of the book as one lifts and spreads out its pieces, sheets of pictures and of poems, disassembling the body of the book until only the case remains.

The texts may "moulder" in the poem, but disintegration does not produce complete decomposition, either in the narrative or the book. "His spine survives its religion," and among the ruins one finds "Here a bone, there a rag," recalling Yeats's "foul rag and bone shop of the heart" where all creation starts, and through that, the nineteenth-century shops that sold rags for the paper used in fine printing.[16] Out of old rags come new books. The detritus of the knight's body contains the material for a new body/book; "In the house of the dead are many cradles," says Hughes's **"Loyal Mother."** This is the hope Hughes holds out for the knight and also, perhaps, for himself as a poet. For readers of this book, the process of reading as disassembling will inevitably be followed by reassembling, though folding all back into the slipcase cannot be the radical reintegration Hughes has in mind for his hero.

Understanding the relation between word and image in this edition of *Cave Birds* is a particular challenge precisely because of the volume's fragmentation. But there is a list correlating the titles of the images with the titles of the poems, and its presence suggests that an effort is expected, perhaps even that the correlation of word and image has something to do with the narrative's insistence that the hero discover his relation to his neglected other half.

Throughout the volume, the words, written about the pictures (ekphrasis), establish an ever-shifting relation between the narrative and the images, keeping the reading unsettled, questioning. First-, second-, and third-person voices record the shifting relation and distance between reader, speaker, protagonist, and bird, playing out a drama of identification that implicates all in the passage through death. Sometimes the image is identified as the hero (**"The Knight"**) and described from a safe distance in the third person. Sometimes the image is identified as one of the agents of the otherworld (**"The Baptist," "The Gatekeeper"**). Sometimes, in an act of prosopopeia, the bird as agent of the otherworld speaks directly to us in the first person, identifying us with the flayed and guilty hero. And sometimes the bird is the hero himself and speaks in lyrical self-expression: "A blot has knocked me down. It clogs me. / A globe of blot, a drop of unbeing" (**"The Hall of Judgment"**). One might read these shifting relations both as the effort of the poet to keep the ekphrastic project fresh by approaching the image in a variety of ways and as part of the signifying work of the image-text. The constantly shifting distance among its terms suggests the psychological dance as the hero struggles to come to terms with death and embrace the female other. If in ekphrasis, as recent discussions of the poetic genre agree, the word confronts its visual semiotic other (Heffernan; Mitchell, *Picture Theory*), we might then read Hughes's ekphrasis here as a process that is analogous to that required of the volume's hero. The powerful effect of these shifts in relation cannot be felt in the absence of the images.

The poems and pictures of *Cave Birds* are, often wittily, interactive. In none of its textual incarnations does *Cave Birds* attempt a seamless verbal-visual textuality, for all that Blake's composite pages may lie behind the endeavor. Throughout, word and image occupy their own space. What interests Baskin and Hughes is relation across difference: words and images orbit each other, held in active tension, exchanging across the gap.

The poems are playfully aware of themselves as poems on images. "A blot has knocked me down," for example, describes the black oval, interpreted in the poem as an egg, in which Baskin's flayed crow is encased. "Or am I under attention?" he asks, which, of course, he is—from us and from Hughes. Hughes puns on the image: the crow calls what is at the center of the oval/egg "This yoke of afterlife." Light and darkness in the poems are deployed with their conventional associa-

tions of knowledge and ignorance but refer, of course, also to the black and white of the drawings. On one level these are, with a few dabs of color here and there, the colors of the afterworld presented in the poems as well, so that chromatically poem and picture together present an image of the afterlife. On another level the poems thematize looking, playing on the convention of sight as a way to knowledge. The necessary preparation for revelation is for the hero, as for other spiritual questers, a stripping bare of the self, until, in Hughes's version, "Nothing remains of the warrior but his weapons / / And his gaze." "His eyes darken bolder in their vigil" we're told, "As the chapel crumbles" (**"The Knight"**). In **"The Hall of Judgment," "Darkness,"** the state in which sight cannot happen, is the condition of "nothingness," the opposite of revelation. The compositional process of the poems themselves begins with looking; ekphrasis takes off from the knowledge attained by observation. While the reader cannot be said to become the quester of the narrative, in the difficult act of reading the limited-edition *Cave Birds,* he or she lives some of its confused searching.

THE TRADE EDITION

If the limited edition emphasizes fragmentation and reading as decomposition, the trade edition, binding word and image face to face in a codex volume, emphasizes reunion. The fullest elaboration of *Cave Birds,* the 1978-79 trade edition, contains all of the poems and drawings produced, except one each from rounds A and C. The poems and pictures are arranged narratively, not in order of composition. The three rounds are blended, ekphrasis and illustration interspersed throughout the volume, further complicating the shifts in relations suggested in the limited edition. With the exception of the first poem, which is not accompanied by a picture (more on this below), poems and pictures are paired, poem on the left, picture on the right. Bound on the short side, 28.25 cm × 22.5 cm, smaller than a coffee-table picture book but larger than the usual volume of poems, this book is a hybrid like the image-text itself and like the bird-humans of Baskin's drawings.

This *Cave Birds,* as the new subtitle suggests (*An Alchemical Cave Drama*), conceives of the volume as a stage. To the cast of characters in the limited edition (the knight, the baptist, etc.) have been added those who participate in the trial that leads up to the protagonist's death in **"The Knight"**: the summoner, the interrogator, the judge, the plaintiff, the executioner, and the accused himself. Eleven poems from rounds A and C precede **"The Knight"** and stage a revelation of the hero's guilt and his trial.[17] The poems from the limited edition dramatizing the hero's experiences in the afterlife are slightly reordered and augmented by six interspersed poems from round C. Two poems from round A conclude the volume: **"The Risen,"** in which the hero stands before us magnificently reborn as a falcon, and the two-line **"Finale,"** which impishly casts doubt on the hero's triumph: "At the end of the ritual / up comes a goblin." The cast of characters in this **Cave Birds,** the narrative makes clear, cannot be seen as external to the hero, as they might have been in the limited edition, but must be read as the fragmented parts of his inner psychic life who judge and condemn him to death as well as guide his remaking. This is an interior drama of transformation, a "cave drama."

The ekphrastic poems of round A, which often describe and interpret the image directly (a fact not apparent without the images) provide some of **Cave Birds'** greatest delights. Here is Hughes's satiric characterization of Baskin's comic plucked bird (originally titled *An Oven-Ready Piranha Bird*) as representative of Western justice (fig. 12):

"The Judge"

The pondering body of the law teeters across
A web-glistening geometry.

Lolling, he receives and transmits
Cosmic equipoise.

The garbage-sack of everything that is not
The Absolute onto whose throne he lowers his buttocks.

Clowning, half-imbecile,
A Nero of the unalterable.

(16)

Hughes's couplets teeter and loll, creating their own "cosmic equipoise" in each end-stopped couplet, comically echoing this grotesque bird's labored steps on the wide-planted, gnarled legs that support his immense body.

In much more obvious and complex ways in the trade edition, autobiographical concern is generalized into an analysis of Western culture and played out in mythological and historical terms. The purging and rebirth of the guilty hero from the limited edition are now set in the larger context of Hughes's cultural critique. The opening poem, **"The Scream,"** sets out the problem as manifested in the main character, the cockerel, who has led a life of complacent self-satisfaction:

Mountains lazed in their smoky camp.
Worms in the ground were doing a good job.

Flesh of bronze, stirred with a bronze thirst,
Like a newborn baby at the breast,
Slept in the sun's mercy.

And the inane weights of iron
That come suddenly crashing into people, out of nowhere,
Only made me feel brave and creaturely.

When I saw little rabbits with their heads crushed on roads
I knew I rode the wheel of the galaxy.

(7)

Dissociation of sensibility under the pressure of Western abstraction is for Hughes, as for Lawrence, the tragedy of modern man: the rational has suppressed the nonrational human capacities, the mind has gained ascendency over the body, empathy has given way to the exercise of power. "The psychological stupidity, the ineptitude, of the rigidly rationalist outlook—it's a form of hubris, and we're paying the traditional price," Hughes said (Fass 200). The hero of **Cave Birds** cracks under the strain of his own pride; he is brought up short at the end of the poem, suddenly unable to talk, bereft of the language that had allowed him to rationalize and so evade "the inane weights of iron," life's tragedies. He tries to speak, but "a silence wedged my gullet." He can voice only a primal cry: "The scream / Vomited itself."

As this poem suggests, language, for Hughes, has been the instrument of the rationality that distances feeling and suppresses the physical life of the body. In the anti-Socratic argument, central not only to **Cave Birds** but to his larger poetic project, "idealistic attempts to isolate abstract conceptual principles" have historically worked by "identifying Good with God as Logos," as Graham Bradshaw succinctly puts it (215). This is a familiar formulation, and throughout Western history it has been routinely accompanied, as scholars have shown (Mitchell, *Iconology*; Paulson; and Gilman, for example), with a valuation of the image as the word's challenging opposite. In the history of Western discourse about the arts, the image as present, replete, silent, and irrational contends with the logical, symbolic, and "civilizing" discipline of the word. "The history of culture," comments W. J. T. Mitchell, "is in part the story of a protracted struggle for dominance between pictorial and linguistic sign" (*Iconology* 43). Fear of the power of the image (and what it might make people do) underlies the periodic episodes of iconoclasm that mark Western history (see Freedberg), including, of course, the Reformation, the origin for Hughes of modern dissociation. In their bodiliness, images make men desert rationality in favor of base instinct. The dichotomy is routinely gendered: "Time [language] is a Man Space [image] is a Woman," Blake said (qtd. in Mitchell, *Iconology* 95), echoing the common cultural notions that lie behind the most influential attempt to delineate the differences between the arts, Gotthold Lessing's 1766 *Laocoön*. Such thinking is so pervasive that the conventional figuring of the image as female and subversive can be seen in the criticism of **Cave Birds** itself. Explaining what he finds the uneven quality of the poems in the volume, one critic remarks, "the story, seduced no doubt by Baskin's drawings, seems to lose its way, dissipating the energy" (Sagar, *Art* 179). "The decorum of the arts at bottom has to do with proper sex roles," explains Mitchell, glossing the underpinnings of Lessing's argument that words and images should stick to their own spheres (*Iconology* 109).

The terms in which the hero's problems are posed in the trade edition, and the insistent pairing that the layout and binding enforce, ask that we read the general relation of word and image in the context of this larger history of discourse about the arts. Baskin and Hughes pursue their narrative of modern humanity not by overturning the terms of the conventional dichotomies but by calling attention to and using them; the book itself dichotomizes—poems on the left, pictures on the right. Simultaneously, however, the binding and the layout urge the prescribed cure by setting word and image (mind and body, male and female) in relation and challenging us to read the exchange between them. Hughes's desire to join his words to images participates in a common sense among twentieth-century poets that images have an immediate embodied presence that language lacks. In **"The Scream,"** Hughes's victim is all words with no image because he is the logical conclusion to centuries of rationalizing language misguidedly valued as the good and powerful, and of the concomitant denigration of the image. The reader turns the page, the trial begins, and there stands Baskin's summoner on the right, a harsh corrective, "Spectral, gigantified, / Protozoic, blood-eating" (8), looking down on the reader, feathers stiffening into daggers, baroque talons menacing, demanding attention by his sheer physicality to the animal life the hero has criminally disregarded. As he calls the hero to account ("Sooner or later— / The grip"), the spread dramatizes the confrontation: image as body stands up to mind as word. In this *Cave Birds,* there is no turning aside from Baskin's often sexually charged, physically confrontational images. They dominate every subsequent spread. Sometimes Baskin manipulates the angle of vision to position us at groin level, staring straight at the genitals of his human birds, testing response to such blatant displays of the body.

Some of the poem-picture pairs thematize the opposition of thought and body. The image functions as concrete corrective to the hero's verbal rationalizing. When the protagonist gathers himself in the third poem, **"After the first fright,"** from round C—"I sat up and took stock of my options. / I argued my way out of every thought anybody could think" (10)—there is Baskin's bird as the body damaged by such rationalizing. The protagonist's linguistic evasions, full of the capitalized pieties of Enlightenment thought, are met by the illustration's insistence on physical torment as their price, the dismemberment of Baskin's bird.

When I said: "Civilization,"
He began to chop off his fingers and mourn.
When I said: "Sanity and again Sanity and above all
  Sanity,"
He disembowelled himself with a cross-shaped cut.

Later in the narrative, in **"The gatekeeper,"** when "remorse, promises, a monkey chatter" (32) blurt "from every orifice" of the hero, the play of word and image in the codex (unlike the limited edition) emphasizes his attempt to talk his way out of death as a last-ditch effort to make rationalizing logos work against the physicality of life insisted on by Baskin's bird (fig. 14).

The body's active presence also figures in other aspects of the volume's bibliographic features. Less dramatically than the limited edition, but nevertheless insistently, this book calls attention to its physicality. Awkwardly rectangular, bound on the short side, it flops open in the hands, is difficult to hold, and defies the usual physical balance of a modern open book. Like the spread-winged raptor on the frontispiece, its covers flap wide. The colors (deep cream paper, drawings and type in black ink, bound in black, covered with a paper-bag-brown dust jacket printed in black and blood red) insist on earthiness, as does the thick, matte texture of paper and jacket.

The trade edition develops the narrative of the female other in seven of the added poems, detailing most importantly (in two ekphrastic poems from round A) her roles as the wronged plaintiff and the interrogator who will make the case against the hero. But while the narrative urges union with the female other, Hughes's treatment of the images in these poems lays bare the volume's disturbing gynophobia. Exercising the license given ekphrasis to do what it will with the image, Hughes takes two of Baskin's most threatening images of raptors and genders them female, as he also did with two images from round B that appeared in the limited edition (**"A Loyal Mother," "Incomparable Marriage"**). Probably working off the original title of the image, *A Titled Vultress,* Hughes describes Baskin's vultress—solidly, implacably black on the page)—as carrying "a dripping bagful of evidence / Under her humped robe" (12). The witty description of her body as "the sun's key-hole" also suggests voyeurism and the vaginal threat that echoes back to **"Crow's First Lesson"**: "And woman's vulva dropped over man's neck and tightened" (*Crow* 20). Hughes's vultress makes clear that there is "Small hope now for the stare-boned mule of man / Lumped on the badlands." The forceful spondees convey the inevitability of her intentions:

With her prehensile goad of interrogation
Her eye on the probe

Her olfactory x-ray
She ruffles the light that chills the startled eyeball.

Turning the tables on the conventional male gaze, the vultress uses sight (so often the agent of knowledge in this book) with scientific precision to locate and drag up the truth: "Investigation / By grapnel."

In **"The plaintiff,"** Hughes turns Baskin's ambiguously gendered owl—spread out with breast feathers threateningly engorged—into the protagonist's suppressed other, come to claim her own:

> Her feathers are leaves, the leaves tongues,
> The mouths wounds, the tongues flames
>
> The feet
> Roots
> Buried in your chest, a humbling weight
> That will not let you breathe.
>
> Your heart's winged flower
> Come to supplant you.
>
> (18)

The sexual suggestiveness of Baskin's bird is heightened by Hughes into a fantasy of erotic asphyxiation. These poems seem to participate willfully and with sadomasochistic pleasure in the long ekphrastic tradition of fear of the (female) image most vividly played out in Shelley's "On the Medusa of Leonardo da Vinci in the Florentine Gallery," where the gorgon's image exercises such power that she "turns the gazer's spirit into stone."

The narrative of *Cave Birds* climaxes in **"Bride and groom lie hidden for three days,"** where the flayed and purified protagonist is reassembled in union with the neglected female in a ritual alchemical marriage. In Hughes's poem, the predatory female seems to have melted away, presumably because the hero has accepted her as part of himself, but in Baskin's illustration . . . her powerful legs and torso and impossibly pneumatic breasts pull against the poem's lyricism. The poem charts a dance of mutual remaking as male and female create each other out of the world's refuse:

> She gives him his eyes, she found them
> Among some rubble, among some beetles
>
> He gives her her skin
> He just seemed to pull it down out of the air
>   and lay it over her
>
> (56)

In a sexualizing of Yeats's vow to "lie down" in the "foul rag and bone shop of the heart," male creation reciprocates female as "they bring each other to perfection," "gasping with joy, with cries of wonderment." The sparsity of punctuation is as headlong as any of Dickinson's dashes. The visual pattern of urgently overlapping lines expresses the intertwining of their making, repeated in the horizontal reach of the bird man's outstretched leg across the thigh of the bird woman in Baskin's illustration, where their feathers are nearly all stripped away, showing the human features beneath, making explicit the volume's presiding anthropomorphism.

After 55 pages of poems and pictures, it is impossible not to read this climax as also a description of the volume's collaboration, of the mutual bringing to perfection of poet and artist, word and image constituting each other in a book whose binding proves their inextricability. Like other collaborators (Frank O'Hara and Larry Rivers in *Stones,* for example), Hughes and Baskin work self-reflexively. The reassembled body parts ("spine," "plates"), the stitching "with steely purple silk," and the inlaying with "scrolls" play off the art of bookmaking.

But Baskin's image makes evident the fact that the task he and Hughes set for themselves was formidable, and there are arguments to be made that the collaboration does not wholly succeed. Elsewhere powerfully responsive to the written word,[18] Baskin, in round C, produced some images that are, as Terry Gifford and Neil Roberts justly observe of **"Bride and groom,"** "inferior" (200). (See also "His legs ran about.") Ironically, the poem that celebrates the mutual creation of man and woman, word and image, inspired the least satisfying image in the volume. Fascination with the hybrid, with the results of unions of difference, can easily shade into the grotesque, as they do here.

And what are we to make of the extent of the mechanical metaphor of **"Bride and groom,"** so at odds, as critics have protested, with the celebration of a reunion with earthy physicality? While the art of the book echoes in the description, bride and groom emerge from their mutual making more like fine machines with "delicate cogs" and "newly wound coils, all shiningly oiled" (56). Such questions about the success of *Cave Birds* belong to a larger critique of the gap between Hughes's primitivist message and his ability to realize it himself. Graham Bradshaw's thoughtful reservations about Hughes's mythologizing are worth recalling here. He observes that it "can seem primitivistic in worrying ways, when the saving 'primitive' message depends, for its creative advancement, on a highly elaborate and 'intellectual' ideology of romantic retrospection" (237), but he concludes that Hughes was aware of the difficulties and writes that awareness into the self-reflexive closing poem of *Cave Birds*, **"Finale"** ("At the end of the ritual / up comes a goblin"). The poem

> reminds us that the problem confronts the poet as well
> as his protagonist; this suggests how Hughes has

avoided or at least contained the danger of romantic retrospection and sophisticated primitivism, by recognising it within his "alchemical cave drama."

(Bradshaw 237)

We might understand the cogs and coils in similar terms as another recognition within the narrative of the difficulties of recovering the body, specifically that it is hard to escape the methods and products of mechanical rationalism.

The volume's gender dynamics, however, resist such containment within the narrative. Even a sympathetic feminist reader like Nathalie Anderson finds the terms of the mystic marriage unsatisfying. "Perfection," she notes of **"Bride and groom,"** may "feel diminishing to a female reader": "'she' characteristically *finds* the parts of his body . . . while 'he' characteristically *devises* her parts" (106-07). Rarely in this volume does the main female character exist on her own: always she is understood as his victim and the necessary component of his redemption. Apart from her desire to end the victimization, her need (does she, too, require reunion?) is never an issue. In addition, there is no sense within the narrative that the erotic frisson that the predatory females provide their author (and maybe their reader/ viewers) might be a problem.

Although *Cave Birds* offers evidence that collaboration is not the panacea it is sometimes imagined to be, Hughes's repeated collaborations have the effect, in one aspect of his life, of bringing his mythologizing into the realm of practical activity, of giving it a small but real commitment to the collaboration itself and to the other artist, and of producing a tangible consequence in the collaborative book. Collaboration grounds Hughes's great theme—the integration of damaged, rational man with the other, the recovery of empathy—in a social commitment.

Now is a good time, as Hughes's life and achievements are being reconsidered following his death, to give his collaborative works the thoughtful readings they deserve and to undertake comparative studies placing them in the context of other modern experiments with words, images, and the body of the book. How would Hughes's collaborations appear compared with Creeley's or O'Hara's? Such defamiliarizing would, I think, prove suggestive in understanding and assessing Hughes's achievements by reshaping the field in which we see them. It would also help expand the current, growing effort to write the history of collaboration in twentieth-century poetry not only by adding Hughes to the account but also by demonstrating the extension of collaborative practice beyond avant-garde circles.

Notes

1. See for example Bornstein, Rainey, Dettmar and Watt, and McGann. For studies of literary col-laboration in addition to Stillinger, see for example Koestenbaum, Rabaté, and Laird.

2. I use the term *fine press* or *fine printing* in the broad sense Johanna Drucker describes: "The term 'fine printing' is generally associated with letterpress, handset type, and limited editions, but also can be used to describe carefully produced work in any print medium" (380). Most fine presses are small, but the reverse is not necessarily the case.

3. Most of these books were published only in limited editions. Some, like *Positives* and *God's Trombones,* are published only in trade editions. For an account of the rarely discussed collaboration on *God's Trombones,* see Carroll.

4. Among these volumes are *Poems* by Ted Hughes, Ruth Fainlight, and Alan Sillitoe (1971); *Eat Crow,* drawing by Leonard Baskin (1971); *Prometheus on His Crag,* drawing by Leonard Baskin (1973); *Season Songs* (1974); *Earth-Moon,* illustrated by Hughes (1976); *Orts,* drawing by Leonard Baskin (1978); *Moortown Elegies,* drawing by Leonard Baskin (1978); *Adam and the Sacred Nine,* drawing by Leonard Baskin (1979); and *Remains of Elmet,* photographs by Fay Godwin (1979).

5. Hughes hoped Rainbow could publish Plath's poems "quietly without drawing the attention of a readership he now thought to be hostile" (Feinstein 183). *Crossing the Water* and *Winter Trees* (both 1971) turned out to be financial successes, prompting further charges that Hughes was exploiting Plath.

6. Sagar and Tabor note that

the name of the Press is related to an original plan (unfortunately foiled by vagaries in the availability of materials) to have each publication bound in a different shade of leather, so that the books would form a 'spectrum' across the bookshelf.

(4)

7. Graphicality is discussed by Morris Eaves.

8. Scigaj, *Poetry* 144. Sagar suggests the invitation came in 1966 (*Laughter* xxii), and Feinstein suggests it came in 1967 (160), but Lisa Baskin confirms that 1963 is accurate.

9. The collaborations range from the coupling of their works, as in the numerous books by Hughes that contain a drawing by Baskin, to the more extensive give and take that is usually implied by the term *collaboration*. In addition to *Cave Birds, Capriccio,* and *Howls and Whispers,* these latter include the limited edition of *Crow* with 12 drawings by Baskin (London: Faber, 1973), *Season Songs* (New York: Viking, 1975), *Moon-Whales*

and Other Moon Poems (New York: Viking, 1976), *A Primer of Birds* (Devon: Gehenna, 1981), *Makomaki* (Leeds: Eremite, 1985); and *Flowers and Insects* (London: Faber, 1986).

10. Two studies that do read them as part of the work are Elizabeth Maslen's "Counterpoint" and, itself a collaboration, Terry Gifford and Neil Roberts's *Ted Hughes.* As Maslen pointed out more than 15 years ago, the "focus on Hughes' own achievements has tended to obscure the fact that collaborations with visual artists have been an integral part of his work for well over twenty years" (33). For example, Alexander Davis's interesting essay on visionary imagination in Hughes never mentions Leonard Baskin or his images in a long discussion of *Cave Birds.*

11. See Sagar, *The Art of Ted Hughes* 243-44, for an overview of the collaboration. Sagar counts only eight illustrations to the 12 Hughes poems in round C, but there seem to be 10.

12. For a summary and analysis of the volume's alchemical background and quest, see Timothy Materer 141-55. He does not discuss the pictures or the collaboration. Nick Bishop, in exploring the possibility of psychological criticism based not on Jung or Freud but on Sufism and Gurdjieff, notes the relation of the "principle of alchemy" to the "'layered' compositional process" of *Cave Birds* (178).

13. The Ilkley Literature Festival is especially interesting in terms of the volume's composition. Baskin and Hughes had originally planned an edition of the poems to be published by Baskin's Gehenna Press, but then the Ilkley Literature Festival invited Hughes (for a commission, not an insignificant motive in modern collaborative production) to stage a presentation of the poems. According to Scigaj, Hughes reworked the poems of round B with the performative nature of the occasion in mind (*Poetry of Ted Hughes* 207). The verbal-visual relation of this version of *Cave Birds* (dramatic reading with projected images) was conceived within the conventions of the theater's composite art.

In addition to the limited edition of *Cave Birds,* the Scolar Press also published a broadside (a single folded sheet) of "The Interrogator" with Baskin's drawing and a facsimile of a draft of the poem (Sagar and Tabor 65).

14. In *New Selected Poems* (1982), selections from *Cave Birds* appear without accompanying images but with a foreword by Hughes outlining the collaboration with Baskin, briefly describing the missing images, and asserting their importance:

"throughout the original sequence the interdependence between drawings and verses is quite close." In subsequent versions, reference to the images gradually shrinks, until in *New Selected Poems 1957-1994* there are not only no images but no contextualizing notes of any kind.

15. The 10 poems are, followed by their titles in the trade edition where different: "The Knight," "The Baptist," "The Hall of Judgment" ("A flayed crow in the hall of judgment"), "The Gatekeeper," "A Loyal Mother" ("A green mother"), "Incomparable Marriage" ("A riddle"), "The Culprit" ("The scapegoat"), "The Guide," "Walking Bare," and "The Good Angel" ("The owl flower").

16. See McGann for a reading of the final lines of "The Circus Animals' Desertion" as an allusion to the commerce of the paper industry. Rag and bone shops, he explains, sold rags

> either to stationers or to the great paper merchants, who would reprocess them to make paper. . . . The immediate historical allusion is not to papermaking in general, but to printers and publishers who used a certain kind of paper (rag paper) and made a certain kind of book (fine-press printing).
>
> (5)

17. The round A poems are: "The summoner," "The interrogator," "The judge," "The plaintiff," "The executioner," "The accused," "The risen," and "Finale." The round C poems are "The scream," "After the first fright," "She seemed so considerate," "In these fading moments I wanted to say," "First, the doubtful charts of skin," "Something was happening," "Only a little sleep, a little slumber," "As I came, I saw a wood," "After there was nothing there was a woman," "His legs ran about," and "Bride and groom lie hidden for three days."

18. Not only in other collaborations with Hughes but also in his numerous illustrations to other writers including Shakespeare, Euripides, Poe, Blake, Tennyson, and James Baldwin. See Baskin and Franklin.

Works Cited

Anderson, Nathalie. "Ted Hughes and the Challenge of Gender." Sagar, *Challenge* 91-115.

Baskin, Leonard. *Sculpture, Drawings, and Prints.* New York: Braziller, 1970.

Baskin, Lisa. Telephone conversation. 12 Aug. 2004.

Baskin, Lisa, and Colin Franklin. *The Gehenna Press: The Work of Fifty Years, 1942-1992.* Dallas: Gehenna, 1992.

Bishop, Nick. *Re-making Poetry: Ted Hughes and a New Critical Psychology.* New York: St. Martin's, 1991.

Bornstein, George. *Material Modernism: The Politics of the Page.* Cambridge: Cambridge UP, 2001.

Bradshaw, Graham. "Creative Mythology in *Cave Birds.*" *The Achievement of Ted Hughes.* Ed. Keith Sagar. Athens: U of Georgia P, 1983. 210-38.

Carroll, Anne. "Art, Literature, and the Harlem Renaissance: The Messages of *God's Trombones.*" *College Literature* 29.3 (Summer 2002): 57-82.

Caws, Mary Ann. *The Art of Interference: Stressed Readings in Verbal and Visual Texts.* Princeton: Princeton UP, 1989.

Davis, Alexander. "Romanticism, Existentialism, Patriarchy: Hughes and the Visionary Imagination." Sagar, *Challenge* 70-90.

Dettmar, Kevin, and Stephen Watt, eds. *Marketing Modernisms: Self-Promotion, Canonization, Rereading.* Ann Arbor: U of Michigan P, 1996.

Drucker, Johanna. "The Artist's Book as Idea and Form." *A Book of the Book: Some Works and Projections about the Book and Writing.* Ed. Jerome Rothenberg and Steven Clay. New York: Granary, 2000. 376-88.

Eaves, Morris. "Graphicality: Multimedia Fables for 'Textual' Critics." *Reimagining Textuality: Textual Studies in the Late Age of Print.* Ed. Elizabeth Bergmann Loizeaux and Neil Fraistat. Madison: U of Wisconsin P, 2002. 99-122.

Faas, Ekbert. *Ted Hughes: The Unaccommodated Universe.* Santa Barbara: Black Sparrow, 1980.

Feinstein, Elaine. *Ted Hughes: The Life of a Poet.* New York: Norton, 2001.

Freedberg, David. *The Power of Images: Studies in the History and Theory of Response.* Chicago: U of Chicago P, 1989.

Gifford, Terry, and Neil Roberts. *Ted Hughes: A Critical Study.* London: Faber, 1981.

Gilman, Ernest. *Iconoclasm and Poetry in the English Reformation: Down Went Dagon.* Chicago: U of Chicago P, 1986.

Heffernan, James A. W. *Museum of Words: The Poetics of Ekphrasis from Homer to Ashbery.* Chicago: U of Chicago P, 1993.

Hughes, Ted. *Earth-moon.* London: Rainbow, 1976.

———. "Emily Dickinson." 1968. Hughes, *Winter Pollen* 154-60.

———. "The Hanged Man and the Dragonfly." 1984. Hughes, *Winter Pollen* 84-102.

———. *New Selected Poems.* New York: Harper, 1982.

———. *New Selected Poems 1957-1994.* London: Faber, 1995.

———. "Poetry in the Making: Three Extracts." 1967. Hughes, *Winter Pollen* 10-24.

———. *Winter Pollen: Occasional Prose.* Ed. William Scammell. New York: Picador, 1995.

Hughes, Ted, and Leonard Baskin. *Cave Birds.* Ilkley: Scolar, 1975.

———. *Cave Birds: An Alchemical Cave Drama.* New York: Viking, 1978.

———. *Crow: From the Life and Songs of the Crow.* London: Faber, 1974.

Koestenbaum, Wayne. *Double Talk: The Erotics of Male Literary Collaboration.* New York: Routledge, 1989.

Laird, Holly. *Women Coauthors.* Urbana: U of Illinois P, 2000.

Loizeaux, Elizabeth Bergmann. "Ekphrasis and Textual Consciousness." *Word and Image* 15.1 (1999): 76-96.

Maslen, Elizabeth. "Counterpoint: Collaborations between Ted Hughes and Three Visual Artists." *Word and Image* 2.1 (1986): 33-44.

Materer, Timothy. *Modernist Alchemy: Poetry and the Occult.* Ithaca: Cornell, 1995.

McGann, Jerome. *Black Riders: The Visible Language of Modernism.* Princeton: Princeton UP, 1993.

Mitchell, W. J. T. *Iconology: Image, Text, Ideology.* Chicago: U of Chicago P, 1986.

———. *Picture Theory: Essays on Verbal and Visual Representation.* Chicago: U of Chicago P, 1994.

Paulson, Ronald. "English Iconoclasm in the Eighteenth Century." *Space, Time, Image, Sign: Essays on Literature and the Visual Arts.* Ed. James Heffernan. New York: Lang, 1987. 41-62.

Rabaté, Jean-Michel. *The Ghosts of Modernity.* Gainesville: UP of Florida, 1996.

Rainey, Lawrence. *Institutions of Modernism: Literary Elites and Public Culture.* New Haven: Yale UP, 1998.

Sagar, Keith. *The Art of Ted Hughes.* 2nd ed. Cambridge: Cambridge UP, 1978.

———, ed. *The Challenge of Ted Hughes.* New York: St. Martin's, 1994.

———. *The Laughter of Foxes: A Study of Ted Hughes.* Liverpool: Liverpool UP, 2000.

Sagar, Keith, and Stephen Tabor. *Ted Hughes: A Bibliography 1946-1980.* London: Mansell, 1983.

Scigaj, Leonard. *The Poetry of Ted Hughes: Form and Imagination.* Iowa City: U of Iowa P, 1986.

————. *Ted Hughes.* Boston: Twayne, 1991.

Stillinger, Jack. *Multiple Authorship and the Myth of Solitary Genius.* New York: Oxford UP, 1991.

Synge, John Millington. Preface. *Playboy of the Western World.* London: Maunsel, 1907.

Jeffrey Meyers (essay date spring 2004)

SOURCE: Meyers, Jeffrey. "Terminator: The Legacy of Ted Hughes." *The Virginia Quarterly Review* 80, no. 2 (spring 2004): 219-31.

[*In the following essay, Meyers examines Diane Middlebrook's 2003 book on the relationship between Hughes and Plath, and the 2003* Collected Poems.]

> The lunatic, the lover and the poet,
> Are of imagination all compact.
>
> *A Midsummer Night's Dream*

The liaisons and marriages of famous literary couples of the 20th century—H. G. Wells and Rebecca West, Leonard and Virginia Woolf, Ernest Hemingway and Martha Gellhorn, Edmund Wilson and Mary McCarthy, Robert Lowell and Jean Stafford, as well as Ted Hughes and Sylvia Plath—inevitably ended in a clash of egos, in recrimination and hatred, disaster or divorce. (Iris Murdoch and John Bayley are the notable exception.) A book on Hughes and Plath, two violently temperamental and death-obsessed poets, provokes some challenging questions. Was Plath impossible to live with? Was Hughes to blame for her death? Could her suicide have been avoided? What effect did it have on Hughes and their children?

Diane Middlebrook is the first scholar to troll through the vast Hughes archive at Emory University in Atlanta: "108,000 items in eighty-six boxes weighing 2½ tons, plus materials sealed in a trunk that is not to be opened until the year 2023." But she fatally weakened her book by failing to interview many crucial figures in the lives of her subjects: Plath's younger brother Warren and her early lover Richard Sassoon; Hughes' older brother Gerald; his widow, Carol Orchard; his children with Plath, the beautiful Frieda (a poet and writer of children's books) and Nicholas (a scientist, last sighted in Alaska); and David Wevill, husband of Hughes' lover Assia. (She broke up Plath's marriage and outdid her by killing her daughter by Hughes as well as herself.) Middlebrook's work, an even-handed portrait of their marriage rather than a biography, is like Elaine Feinstein's life of Hughes—competent but disappointingly familiar and thin. It wavers uneasily between a hyped-up and sometimes awkward style and rather pedantic explications of the poetry, with the most exiguous "fair use" quotations.

Middlebrook, with adjectival insistence, writes of a "wild party," "glamorous weekends," and "glamorous meetings," of "violent love" and a "ravishing performance." She also uses many banalities, slang expressions, and flat similes: Hughes "was in a profound dither about where his life was heading"; "marriage opens a joint account in the language bank"; they trod the "minefield of their differences"; "she knew where Hughes was coming from"; Plath's postcards to Hughes "were like discrete [discreet?] knocks with knuckles on doors that might be firmly shut." The narrative is padded with pointless details: "Plath's journal also indicates that she carried to [their honeymoon in Spain] a new pair of scissors, and a pair of sunglasses in a white plastic case with a green starfish on it." In an unintentional pun, she writes that Plath had "a good connection in the poet and magazine editor Peter Davison"—without mentioning that they'd been lovers. The structure is oddly unbalanced, and she treats the last fifteen years of Hughes' life, the period of his greatest fame, in only twenty pages. There are a number of typos—they (118), *Mousetrap* (178), title (226), and Marjorie (349), for example—as well as some factual errors. Byron's papers were burned (not shredded) by John Murray, and the Booker (not the Whitbread) is Britain's most prestigious literary prize.

Why, despite good looks and brilliant talent, is Plath so unappealing and Hughes at times so repulsive? At Cambridge University she seemed the crass "caricature of an American girl, overdressed, and gushy"—with a hard, metallic brightness. Though aggressively eager for literary fame, she cranked out trashy, formulaic stories for women's magazines. Suffused with self-pity, she flew into sudden rages, was intensely jealous, and was in constant need of reassurance. When Hughes was trying to write, she once interrupted him 104 times in one morning. Sexually sophisticated, voracious, and dominant, she claimed her vagina was an organ of perception. She demanded an orgasm and if she didn't have one, would confront her lovers with their pathetic inadequacy. Hughes, in a characteristically self-exculpatory mode, spoke of her "incandescent desperation" and "death-ray quality" and desperately confessed: "It was either her or me."

Hughes could be boorish, brutal, and cruel—and Plath was attracted to these very qualities. Middlebrook casually mentions that when they first met, Plath bit him on the cheek till the blood ran. But in this primitive rite she set out to shock, to mark him as her own, and to demonstrate her passion in his flesh. Though touted by Plath as a great lover—"We had a very good f'ing. Enormously good, perhaps the best yet"—Ted shocked and terrified Assia during their first sexual encounter "by tearing off [her expensive silk] negligee, and sweating profusely." His first connection with animals came from killing them; and his grisly private mausoleum included "tiger, leopard, python, kangaroo [pelts] . . . along with the skins and bones and skulls of foxes, stags, and badgers; and such shamanistic talismans as tigers' teeth and eagles' claws."

Always enraged by his poverty and eager for money, Hughes devised numerous get-rich schemes. As the recipient of Plath's substantial royalties, he later became one of the richest British poets of the century and left more than £1.4 million to his second wife. He also, as poet laureate, became a toady to the brainless nonentities of the royal family and allowed himself to be pampered by the Queen Mum. One almost expected him to write of savage beasts tearing at the entrails of the princess royal. Celebrating, instead, the wedding of Fergy and Andrew, he was caustically condemned for the embarrassingly inept effusions (not mentioned by Middlebrook) of **"The Honey Bee and the Thistle"**:

> Upon this day in Westminster
> That brings the Prince his Bride
> Out of the sun there sweeps a song
> That cannot be denied.

Hughes' work, like Yeats', was radically damaged by his lifelong obsession with spiritualism and the occult, with a trashy hodgepodge of Ouija boards and tarot cards, astrology and alchemy, black magic and witchcraft, psychic entities and minatory visions, hypnosis and séances, Shamanism and the Tibetan *Book of the Dead,* Rosicrucianism and Jungianism. This mystical freight threatened to obliterate the true source of his poetic power: the primordial legacy of our animal past, "a hurtling momentum . . . of gasps and howling cries."

There's also the problem of Hughes' irresponsible treatment of Plath's posthumous work. By killing herself, she turned her best material over to Hughes: her infants, her torments, and her poems. His triple authority as husband, poet, and critic—expressed in at least fourteen essays, introductions, notes, and letters—profoundly influenced our understanding of her life and art. He insisted that "any bit of evidence which corrects and clarifies our idea of what she really was is important," but he changed the order of the poems in *Ariel,* censored her published *Journals,* and destroyed her most important diaries, written shortly before her death. Middlebrook tells us almost nothing about Frances McCullough, the Harper & Row editor and Hughes' "most trusted ally," who collaborated in this massive disservice to Plath's readers.

Her Husband becomes painfully absorbing as their marriage disintegrates. Plath discovers Hughes' infidelity and throws him out of their house in Devon. As he leaves "with a strange little laugh," she accelerates toward self-inflicted catastrophe. Hughes complained of "the nervous strain of being suddenly quite famous"

and the need to find a hiding place. But the strain on Plath of *not* being famous was even greater. Middlebrook speaks of their "irreconcilable differences"—perhaps Hughes' need for other women and Plath's fury at his betrayal—without explaining what they were. Toward the end, Plath's poems sent out gasps and howling cries: "stark signals of distress" that were ignored (as Assia's were later on) by the brutally egoistic Hughes. He *knew,* better than anyone else, that she was mentally unstable and suicidal. Shortly before she killed herself, she felt her mind disintegrating and was overwhelmed by "the force of her rage and the pathos of her helplessness."

Middlebrook indulgently writes that Plath's "last written words concerned her children's safety." In fact, on February 11, 1963, she risked their lives with the gas that killed her. Middlebrook tersely concludes that "Depression killed Sylvia Plath," but she doesn't explain what caused the depression: heredity, body chemistry, improper medication, an unusually harsh winter, the strain of caring for two infants—and Hughes' betrayal. Five years later, on March 25, 1968, when Hughes became involved with yet another woman, Assia also took ghastly revenge. She "turned on the gas, and lay down with her daughter in her arms." She was forty-one and Shura had just turned four when both of them died. For the rest of his life the Terminator conducted a dialogue with the dead.

Middlebrook doesn't note that Hughes' regret at letting "my lovelies drift & die" echoed Macduff's agonizing lament: "All my pretty ones . . . and their dam / At one fell swoop." She does not explain Hughes' relations with Frieda and Nicholas, whether his early resentment of and hostility to his infant son persisted and harmed the boy, and what sort of life the children had; doesn't explain the sort of marriage he had with Carol Orchard, whether she was aware of his predatory love affairs and, if so, how she responded to them.

Middlebrook misses several important allusions and could have said a great deal more about the literary influences on Plath's poems. Their Court Green house in Devon, like the Brontë parsonage in Haworth (close to where Hughes grew up in Yorkshire), looks out onto a mournful cemetery. (Hughes stared out at the yews.) Middlebrook mentions "Hughes' belief that all art originates with a wound" without noting its origins in Edmund Wilson's influential essay "The Wound and the Bow" (1941). She quotes Hughes' statement that his emblematic "Crow is another word of course for the entrails, lungs, heart" without connecting it to Eliot's visceral pronouncement in "The Metaphysical Poets" (1921) that a poet must look not only into his heart but also "into the cerebral cortex, the nervous system, and the digestive tracts."

D. H. Lawrence had a profound impact on both Hughes and Plath. Hughes' sudden switch from English to anthropology at Cambridge was prompted by the dream, later described in **"The Thought-Fox,"** in which the animal placed its bloody paw on Hughes' blank page and said: "Stop this—you are destroying us." Middlebrook fails to see the influence of Lawrence's story "The Fox," in which a symbolic animal imparts feral wisdom to a man, or to link it to the fox cub episode of **"Epiphany"** in *Birthday Letters*. At the beginning of their marriage, after Plath had submitted Hughes' *Hawk in the Rain* to a poetry contest, it won first prize and was accepted for publication by Harper & Row. Hughes exclaimed, "Sylvia is my luck," echoing Lawrence's exclamation when his girlfriend Jessie Chambers successfully sent his early poems to Ford's *English Review*: "*You* are my luck."

Middlebrook discusses the influence of Lawrence's "Rabbit Snared in the Night" on Plath's condemnation of Hughes in "The Rabbit Catcher" but fails to note the even stronger influence of Lawrence's "Love on the Farm," which emphasizes the connection between the excited woman and the dead rabbit, between sex and death—the orgasmic "little deaths" in Plath's poem. Lawrence writes:

> The rabbit presses back her ears,
> Turns back her liquid, anguished eyes
> And crouches low; then with wild spring
> Spurts from the terror of his oncoming;
> To be choked back, the wire ring
> Her frantic effort throttling:
>   Piteous brown ball of quivering fears!
> Ah, soon in his large, hard hands she dies.

Middlebrook does not extract the richest meaning from several of Plath's most revealing poems. Plath's psychiatrist finally gave her "permission to hate" her self-sacrificing but ghoulish mother. Aurelia went on their honeymoon, witnessed the breakup of their marriage, and urged her daughter to get a divorce when Plath really wanted a reconciliation. After Plath's suicide, she even urged Hughes to surrender the children so she could bring them up in ultraconventional Wellesley, Massachusetts, and (as she had with Sylvia) burden them with her unbearable kindness. Sylvia's "Electra on the Azalea Path," about the horrific visit to her father's grave, is also a severe judgment of Electra on Aurelia Plath.

Middlebrook connects Esther Greenwood's dream in *The Bell Jar* of "sitting in the crotch of a fig tree amid branches loaded with ripe fruit" to Rupert Birkin peeling a fig in a major scene in Lawrence's *Women in Love* (1920). But she doesn't relate the dream to Plath's "Virgin in a Tree," inspired by Paul Klee's etching of 1903, which portrays the negative aspects of sex. The virgin, retreating from emotional and sexual entangle-ments, has become as warped and twisted as the barren tree that protects her from life in the real world. Plath sees the etching as a tart fable of a ruined life. The ugly spinster on her tortured rack is

> ripe and unplucked, 's
> Lain splayed too long in the tortuous boughs: overripe
> Now, dour-faced, her fingers
> Stiff as twigs, her body woodenly
> Askew, she'll ache and wake
> Though doomsday bud.

Middlebrook writes that Plath, early on, sent Hughes a postcard of Henri Rousseau's *The Snake Charmer* (1907) but doesn't mention that it inspired another poem of the same name by Plath. The flutist in his lush Eden, like God in Genesis, calls forth the serpents: "let there be snakes! / And snakes there were." But he finally yawns, tires of music, and sounds the snakes out of existence:

> Pipes the cloth of snakes
> To a melting of green waters, till no snake
> Shows its head, and those green waters, back to
> Water, to green, to nothing like a snake.

Plath's poem—like the postcard, freighted with meaning—extols the power of the artist to summon up his dreams and create his own world.

Finally, Middlebrook rather awkwardly calls Plath's "The Disquieting Muses" "the first poem in which her negative emotions toward her mother are given a symbolic relationship to her writing." But she doesn't connect the poem to De Chirico's painting of the same name. Plath uses De Chirico's menacing figures to express hostility to her mother, who'd brought equally frightening apparitions into her nursery. She associates these distressing muses with scary stories and frightening hurricanes and in the final stanza compares the depressing painting to the harsh world her mother forced her to endure:

> They stand their vigil in gowns of stone,
> Faces blank as the day I was born,
> Their shadows long in the setting sun
> That never brightens or goes down.
> And this is the kingdom you bore me to,
> Mother, mother.

Hughes' 1,332-page *Collected Poems* is not complete, for it does not include unpublished works. But this edition contains some juvenilia, nearly 150 uncollected poems, and many poems from fine press limited editions, especially *Howls and Whispers* (only 110 copies), which was omitted from his response to Plath in his last book, *Birthday Letters*. It also has 25 pages of Hughes' notes and prefaces and 75 pages of the editor's preface and notes. Some of the latter are explanatory, but most concern the publication history and textual variants of the poems.

This massive book provides an occasion to examine Hughes' best and most characteristic work. His early poems, written between 1957 and 1979, reveal his dominant themes and help establish his place in contemporary poetry. His subjects are wild creatures (pike, bull, hawk, and jaguars); a bloody stillbirth; violent jealousy; a bayonet charge; a fiery martyrdom; and his tragic marriage to Plath. His finest work belongs to the great tradition of animal poems, from Clare's "Badger" to Rilke's "Panther." They express the elemental power of the beasts and often portray malevolent predators locked in a fierce Darwinian struggle to kill and to survive. His aim is to capture and restore to man the primordial powers of the wild animals. In **"Pike,"** one fanged and clamp-jawed fish, captured and kept behind glass, devoured its two companions: one of them "jammed past its gills down the other's gullet." Silently casting in "the still splashes of the dark pond," Hughes, raw-nerved and in close touch with the feral world, hears with heightened sense,

> Owls hushing the floating woods
> Frail on my ear against the dream
> Darkness beneath night's darkness had freed,
> That rose slowly towards me, watching.

The bull Moses, enclosed but with explosive potential, is like a charged bomb ready for detonation. Alluding to the place of the bull in Mithraic religion and penetrating a nonhuman consciousness, Hughes suggests that the powerful but strangely passive animal deliberately allows the farmer to lead him out of and back into the dark primeval world. But the bull is also capable of sudden and dangerous revolt:

> He would raise
> His streaming muzzle and look out over the meadows,
> But the grasses whispered nothing awake, the fetch
> Of the distance drew nothing to momentum
> In the locked black of his powers.

The mystery of the bull's inner world seems closed to the farm boy who, when Moses returns to the byre, shuts in his mysterious perception and strength.

"Hawk Roosting," narrated in sinister diction by the hawk himself, portrays the evolutionary perfection of the predator and the egocentric horror of his worldview. He doesn't act, merely surveys the world between "hooked head and hooked feet" while pondering his past kills. But he also tyrannizes his prey and represents the deadliness of the natural world:

> I kill where I please because it is all mine. . . .
> My manners are tearing off heads—
> The allotment of death.
> For the one path of my flight is direct
> Through the bones of the living.

"The Jaguar," Hughes' early and perhaps most famous poem, contrasts the defiant fury of the caged wild animal with the human beings who try to contain him.

After the poet (a former zoo employee) takes a witty, vibrant tour of indolent apes, parrots who "shriek as if they were on fire" or "strut / Like cheap tarts," a coiled boa constrictor, and stinking cages, he reaches (as the diction intensifies and the verbs speed up) a South American leopard, hurrying and "enraged / Through prison darkness after the drills of his eyes / On a short fierce fuse." Driven by "the bang of blood in the brain," he remains untamed and free in his head. Despite his cage, he still sees a distant view of the jungle:

> His stride is wildernesses of freedom:
> The world rolls under the long thrust of his heel.
> Over the cage floor the horizons come.

"Second Glance at a Jaguar," but much more than a glance, has—like a vital animal drawing by Henri Gaudier-Brzeska—more physical detail and murderous intensity. Hughes begins with an exact observation of the ballbearing-like movement of this obsessively pacing "Aztec disemboweler" and ritualistic killer. He craftily captures the menace and persistent desire for revenge of the jaguar,

> Muttering some mantra, some drum-song of murder
> To keep his rage brightening, making his skin
> Intolerable, spurred by the rosettes, the cain-brands,
> Wearing the spots off from inside,
> Rounding some revenge.

Hughes' poem was influenced by the morbid Aztec-jaguar connection at the beginning of chapter 3 in Lawrence's Mexican novel, *The Plumed Serpent* (1926): "the undertone was like the low, angry, snarling purring of some jaguar spotted with night. There was a ponderous, down-pressing weight upon the spirit: the great folds of the dragon of the Aztecs. . . . It was all death! death! death! as insistent as the Aztec sacrifices. Something for ever gruesome and macabre."

Hughes explores the grim cycle of birth, love, and death in the next four poems. In **"February 17th"** a lamb, trying to get born too soon in the wintry weather, dies before it is born. "He had stuck his head out too early / And his feet could not follow." The desperate farmer, forced to become a gruesome obstetrician, slices the neck tendons and cuts the lamb's head off "to stare at its mother." Then, managing to force his hand past the corpse, he grasps the lamb's knee and saves the mother by pulling it out:

> And after it the long, sudden, yolk-yellow
> Parcel of life
> In a smoking slither of oils and soups and syrups—
> And the body lay born, beside the hacked-off head.

This shocking poem, about man's helplessness against nature, is charged with irony. The "parcel of life" is actually dead and the "born" body is stillborn. February was the month Hughes first met Plath and the month she killed herself. And **"February 17th,"** with its allusions to the severed head of John the Baptist and the Green Knight, can also be read as an allegory of their marriage: of his miscarried efforts to help her and his need to sacrifice her in order to save himself.

"Kreutzer Sonata" is more complex. It alludes to both Beethoven's sonata for violin and piano, Opus 47 (1803), dedicated to the French virtuoso Rodolphe Kreutzer, and Tolstoy's story of the same title (1889). In the story, the wife and her lover (based on the infatuated Sofya Tolstoy and her teacher S. I. Taneyev) express their sexual passion by playing the sonata that helps destroy her. The husband, Pozdnyshev, confesses that he stabbed his wife to death when he discovered her with the fiddler. The poem follows the three-part sonata form—theme, repetition and variations, finale—and opens as the speaker, addressing the insanely jealous Pozdnyshev, describes the wound that "Blooms wetly on her dress" and saps the life of the once-beloved victim. As the murderer expresses Tolstoy's late hatred of sex as the debaser of spiritual values, his "wife's sweet flesh"—sweet to her lover, but not to her husband—"goes off" her body, which turns to bone. The tormented, demented husband, who claims his evil wife drove him to commit the crime, calls it "A sacrifice, not a murder." In the final stanza Hughes—following Lawrence's assault on *Anna Karenina* in his essay "The Novel"—attacks Tolstoy's intrusive moralizing. Speaking directly to the novelist, Hughes condemns his life-denying vegetarianism and asceticism:

> Rest in peace, Tolstoy!
> It must have taken supernatural greed
> To need to corner all the meat in the world,
> Even from your own hunger.

In **"Bayonet Charge"** Hughes moves from a domestic crime to a massacre. His father was one of only seventeen survivors of an entire regiment destroyed by Turkish artillery in the 1915 campaign in Gallipoli. Hughes' description of the disastrous infantry assault captures the excitement, confusion, and terror of war. In the frantic, mindless, self-sacrificial charge, the soldier, literally running for his life, plunges toward the meager protection of a hedge:

> King, honour, human dignity, et cetera
> Dropped like luxuries in a yelling alarm
> To get out of that blue crackling air
> His terror's touchy dynamite

—which is about to explode, both within and without. Hughes' poem was strongly influenced by Wilfred Owen and by the famous passage in Hemingway's *A Farewell to Arms* (1929) where he rejects the patriotic lies and suggests that only the actual places where men had fought and died had any dignity and meaning:

"Abstract words such as glory, honor, courage, or hallow were obscene beside the concrete names of villages, the numbers of roads, the names of rivers, the numbers of regiments and the dates."

"The Martyrdom of Bishop Farrar" concerns another kind of death. Described in John Foxe's *Book of Martyrs* (1563), the ritual burning took place on March 30, 1555, during the reign of the Catholic queen, "Bloody Mary." Robert Farrar, Bishop of St. David's, refused to abjure the Protestant faith and was pronounced a heretic and excommunicated. He was then burnt at the Market Cross at Carmarthen, in Wales. In the poem, during the slow consumption of the bishop's body and of the blood that had once coursed comfortably through his veins, the shrewd townsfolk pocket his last words like coins of the realm. The willing martyr, who kept his spiritual vow to God and his parishioners, did not cry out in extremis—as Christ had done on the cross. As Farrar's eyes melted and fire shot out of his mouth, "smoke burned his sermons into the skies." The bishop defeats Mary. He dies, but his unflinching silence proclaims, as he'd predicted, the triumph of his doctrine. Hughes reminds our mild, ecumenical age that religious persecution once took place in Britain and that Bishop Farrar (a distant ancestor of his mother, *née* Farrar) was killed in the name of God by his fellow Christians.

In three revealing poems, written after her death, Hughes meditates on his agonizing relations with Plath. He was attracted by, Plath repelled by, the violence of the bullfight and the obsession with death in Spanish culture—though its morbidity matched the themes of her poems. She was drawn to the cruelty in the paintings of Bosch and Goya in the Prado. But, Hughes writes, echoing Auden's "Spain" (1937): "that arid square, that fragment nipped off from hot / Africa, soldered so crudely to inventive Europe"—

> The blood-raw light,
> The oiled anchovy faces, the African
> Black edges to everything, frightened you.

The bullfight they watched on their 1956 honeymoon in Benidorm, on the southeast Mediterranean coast, inspired Hughes' **"You Hated Spain,"** which emphasizes their fundamental differences and reappears in *Birthday Letters*. (Plath gave her version of the event in "The Goring.") The corrida was particularly repulsive: the matador vomited from fear and the picador was knocked off his horse and gored. Alluding to Joyce's "history . . . is a nightmare from which I am trying to awake" and to Charon carrying the dead across the Styx to Hades, Hughes exclaims:

> Spain was what you tried to wake up from
> And could not. I see you, in moonlight,
> Walking the empty wharf at Alicante
> Like a soul waiting for the ferry,

A new soul, still not understanding,
Thinking it is still your honeymoon
In the happy world, with your whole life waiting
Happy, and all your poems still to be found.

Though Plath's illusions helped shield her from the harsh reality of Spain, her confrontation with violence and death darkened her vision and helped inspire her future poems.

In the austere and agonizing **"The Rat's Dance,"** Hughes expresses his poetic reaction to Plath's suicide and his own Job-like disaster. He had imagined himself as a hawk, tearing his way through life, but now sees himself as the prey. He is the rat, unthinking, screeching (variants of this word are repeated four times), inextricably caught in the iron jaws of a trap. He rejects the soothing Christian response to human suffering: that God wills and man must endure this earthly trial. But after long suffering, the rat stops screeching and becomes silent:

> The rat understands suddenly.
>
> It bows and is still,
> With a little beseeching of blood on its nose end.

Bleeding out its life, the Hughes-rat, realizing that it's doomed and dead, stoically accepts its tragic fate.

Hughes' **"Lovesong,"** like Baudelaire's "Lethe," is really a hatesong and opposes the long tradition of English love poetry. This unsettling poem deceptively begins like a romance as he imagines himself Plath's only lover and makes her live only for their climactic sex. But his whole body becomes absorbed by and in her—swallowed, chewed, and devoured—as she bites, gnaws, and sucks him. During their wounding dialogue he can't escape, is crucified, and becomes a fallen colossus (the title of her first book). When the real world intrudes on their sadomasochistic lovemaking, she becomes the deadly female spider that mates with and then devours the male. Finally, alluding to her hidden mental illness, her Nazi imagery, their divorce, her orgasmic cries, and his deadly rat trap, he confesses:

> His words were occupying armies
> Her laughs were an assassin's attempts
> Her looks were bullets daggers of revenge
> Her glances were ghosts in the corner with horrible
>   secrets
> Her whispers were whips and jackboots
> Her kisses were lawyers steadily writing
> Her caresses were the last hooks of a castaway
> Her love-tricks were the grinding of locks
> And their deep cries crawled over the floors
> Like an animal dragging a great trap.

As "their heads fell apart" after sex, they parody Plato's explanation of sexual desire in *The Symposium* (also discussed in Lawrence's *Women in Love*): that primeval man and woman had originally been one being, were subsequently split apart, and forever sought to achieve their original union. Finally, they swap arms and legs, faces and brains in a total surrender of their identities. The unintentionally devouring Plath explained Hughes' fears when she wrote in her *Journal* of May 5, 1958: "I think I must live in his heat and presence, for his smells and words,—as if all my senses fed involuntarily on him and deprived for more than a few hours, I languish, wither, die to the world."

It's axiomatic that poets' wives have rotten lives. Plath—consumed by that which she was nourished by—might never have found the elemental energy and visceral imagery of *Ariel* poems like "Daddy" and "Lady Lazarus" without the formidable example of Hughes' *Hawk in the Rain.* The brutal power so admired by critics in Hughes' poetry was bitterly condemned by Plath's defenders in his character. But his poems transcend the deeply flawed man who wrote them. Despite his mystical rubbish and tendency to overkill, Hughes now stands—with Seamus Heaney, Philip Larkin, and Geoffrey Hill—among the outstanding English poets since the war.

Stephen Enniss (essay date 2004)

SOURCE: Enniss, Stephen. "Self-Revelation, Self-Concealment and the Making of the Ted Hughes Archive." In *Ted Hughes: Alternative Horizons,* edited by Joanny Moulin, pp. 67-75. London: Routledge, 2004.

[In the following essay, Enniss discusses the Hughes archive, now housed at Emory University, and notes that the restrictions placed on some of the material is in keeping with patterns of revelation and concealment represented in the poetry of Hughes's later years.]

When Emory University acquired the Ted Hughes archive in February 1997, journalists around the U.S. and abroad were quick to proclaim Ted Hughes's secrets revealed. "Hughes papers reveal agony and ecstasy of his love life" (Harlow) was one of the more sensational and, I would add, one of the more misleading. The truth is few journalists actually visited the archive itself, and those who did were ill-equipped for the time-consuming spade work necessary even to begin to grasp the extent or the nature of the archive's revelations. Nevertheless the presence of the archive evoked for them, as it often does for us, intimations of the deeply personal. Its very existence gave the newspaper stories that followed a new degree of credibility, simply through their invocation of the archive's authority.

Even as some were proclaiming Hughes's secrets revealed, however, others were approaching the archive with the opposite conclusion. A number of journalists were particularly interested in that small portion of the collection that remains under restriction.[1] In particular there was great interest in a single trunk that the library was asked to keep closed for twenty-five years. One reporter was particularly eager to get a photograph, not of any of the newly acquired papers, but of the sealed trunk itself (a request I'm happy to say I declined). Another chose to fill his newspaper's column space with his own unsupported speculation about the contents of the sealed trunk (Bone).[2]

The truth is an archive is many things. The Ted Hughes archive is as much a product of Hughes's inattention as it is his deliberate actions. Many decisions—most small but some large—give an archive its final character. The daily decisions over what to save and what to throw out offer ample opportunity for a self-conscious fashioning of the self that all of us engage in. The neatly numbered and cataloged boxes also have the power to blow the top off our carefully constructed notions of self.

What I wish to examine in the following essay are some of the ways these contrary impulses of self-revelation and self-concealment are expressed in the Ted Hughes archive now housed at Emory. I want to examine some of the decisions that have gone into the making of the Hughes archive but not in order to implicate one person or another for this or that lost artifact. All archives, after all, are a record of absences. The one figure we most want to find in the archive is, in the end, the figure that we are sure not to find. Instead, I wish to examine the making of the Ted Hughes archive for what it may tell us about Ted Hughes's own stance towards personal history and artistic creativity. The same contrary impulses of self-revelation and self-concealment that we see dramatized in his own actions towards the material archive reflect on a life-long pattern of self-presentation that informs his mature poetry as well.

As Ted Hughes recalled in his 1961 BBC radio program "Capturing Animals," some of his earliest and fondest childhood memories were of fishing and hunting in Yorkshire. In recalling the importance of those early experiences in his own development, he mentions the diaries that he kept at the time, diaries where he recorded "nothing but my catches" (3). While these childhood diaries have apparently not survived, his reference to them establishes an early preoccupation with capturing—not simply animals—but his own experience in some more permanent form. These early diaries, along with the sketches he began making at the time, point to a precocious self-expression on the blank page and hint at what would become for Hughes a life-long preoccupation.

The earliest surviving manuscripts in the Emory collection were not preserved by Hughes himself but, rather, were saved by the Mexborough Grammar School classmate to whom he gave them in 1947 or 1948. These two poems (one of which is reprinted here for the first time) are heavily derivative and offer little glimpse of the self that composed them. The one reprinted here seems less an expression of a distinctive personality than an expression of sheer will. Like Alexander whose conquests it relates, the poem casts the poet himself in a different kind of drama of conquest, one for the affections of a childhood classmate.

Among the earliest surviving manuscripts from the Hughes archive itself are drafts of poems that were collected in the early collection *Wodwo.* Examining these drafts now what one immediately notices is Hughes's habit of composing poems on any scrap paper at hand. Poems appear on envelopes, on the back of letters, on coarse brown wrapping paper, and, most strikingly, on the back of his own and Sylvia Plath's own discarded manuscripts.[3] On the one hand, the practice seems to reflect a disinterest—if not, in fact, a more active disdain—for the manuscript itself. Clean desk paper is not required. One can instead scribble on anything at hand, since the manuscript is temporary, a means to another end. Yet these drafts have survived in the hundreds. An early manuscript draft of **"Public Bar TV"** appears on the opposite side of a letter from his Faber & Faber editor Charles Monteith; drafts of **"Gog"** were written on a discarded typescript of his 1960 radio play *The House of Aries,* and an unpublished verse play (*Bardo Thodol*) is written on discarded pages of Sylvia Plath's lost novel *Falcon Yard.* Handling them now, they seem to have a power more charged with the current of Hughes's own daily life than do any clean, carefully scripted drafts. The dual-sided drafts evoke something of Hughes and Plath's shared life, even as they document each poet's own creative work.

The absence of any significant number of drafts from *The Hawk in the Rain* and *Lupercal* can be explained by Hughes's own early awareness of the commercial value of his manuscripts. While Emory purchased the bulk of his archive in 1997,[4] as early as 1960 he sold the manuscripts from his first two collections to a rare book and manuscript dealer for a mere £160 (*LH* [Plath, *Letters Home*] 388).[5] Two years later he was actively promoting his manuscripts to the London dealers Winifred Myers, Kyrle Fletcher, Bertram Rota, and Ben Sonnenberg, in effect, working them against one another. In a 1962 letter to Myers he holds out the prospect of a direct sale to the University of Texas bypassing the London dealers altogether. This was a period when Ted and Sylvia were struggling to meet their financial obligations. Ted's Guggenheim had come to an end immediately before the 1960 sale, and the following year they had purchased a home in Devon and were trying to live off of their writing. The sale of his manuscripts provided some modest help in facing these hardships, and, as for later, "he'll have other manuscripts then"

Sylvia noted in a letter to her mother (387). Thus began a life-long practice of cannibalizing his own manuscripts in order to supplement his irregular income.

We catch some glimpse of Hughes's own attitude towards this enforced stringency when he confides in a later letter that he has parted with the manuscript of **"Pike"** reluctantly, only because he was "exceedingly pressed for cash" (Hughes to Gold, 19 Mar 1964).⁶ Indeed, immediately after selling that particular manuscript, Hughes regretted the decision and took steps to recover it from the American collector who had subsequently purchased it. In an exchange of letters with this collector, Hughes acknowledges, "This last year I've lost a lot of stuff, manuscripts and so on. I've started locking [them] in a chest—ridiculous business" (Hughes to Gold, 7 Aug 1964).

The specific loss Hughes refers to is likely Sylvia's burning of an unknown quantity of his papers in July 1962 (recounted in her poem "Burning the Letters"), soon after learning of his affair with Assia Wevill. In a second fire, this one in 1971, Hughes's papers were again targeted, this time by someone who broke into his Yorkshire home and set them ablaze.⁷ A number of manuscripts in the Hughes archive bear evidence of one or the other of these fires, including a 1969 letter from Leonard Baskin which was badly singed in the second fire. In each case the manuscript stands in as a surrogate for the self that is the real target of anger.

While Hughes took steps to safeguard his manuscripts, he showed no awareness of the greater value that a larger archive might contain, indeed, just the opposite. He apparently made little effort to secure an institutional buyer (the earlier mention of the University of Texas came to nothing), but was content instead to let his early manuscripts be scattered among many different individual collectors. In the mid-1970s he was still selling manuscript material with his sole interest apparently being the price realized. A handwritten note from that period lists potential buyers for his manuscripts along with the prices he expected to get.⁸ "Market price of holograph of published poem—1 page—written out by author—£20 . . . Market price for manuscript pages of achieved poems—£35" ("Possible Buyers"). On at least one occasion in the mid-1970s, Hughes eliminated the step of converting his manuscripts into cash and instead used drafts of *Wodwo* as a kind of currency in a direct payment for a chest from a Devon antique dealer. Similarly when a friend once asked him for money, he sent instead fair copies of several poems which he copied for the purpose.

Letters that survive in the archive reflect Hughes's growing understanding of the value of such material and his active negotiation over prices. In the early 1960s he writes to one of his London dealers: "I am gradually

being forced to realize that in time to come my manuscripts are going to be worth quite a lot . . . I would be foolish, and so would you, if we were to go on almost giving these things away." (Letter to Myers) One element of this letter is of particular interest, that is the implication that the manuscript—the material artifact itself—has a greater inherent value than the published poem. "In the past, I've sold manuscripts for next to nothing," he writes, "for less than I was paid *merely* for the publication of the poems" (emphasis added). While the manuscript, as we have seen, clearly had a monetary value for Hughes, it also had a value unrelated to the marketplace and, indeed, unrelated to *mere* publication. Unlike the published poem, the manuscript draft retained some vestige of that creative power that first animated the poem. For some insight into the nature of that power, we need to look at the poems themselves; I'd like to consider briefly just two, one well-known, the other previously unpublished and unknown.

The early poems—those written at the time when he was beginning to sell his own manuscripts—return often to images of decay, whether that decay takes the form of "dust" (**"Song"**), "fragments" (**"The Horses"**), "muck" (**"Fallgrief's Girlfriends"**), or the broken jawbone and carapaces washed ashore in **"Relic."** Unpublished drafts from the time express a similarly bleak view of a broken and mutable world. "Dust has no memory whatsoever," is how he puts it in one unpublished fragment (**"Dust"**), while in another he acknowledges time's steady assault in the line, "Paper yellows, even without flame" (**"Concurrence"**). Such images dominate Hughes's poetry and suggest a familiar and characteristic stance towards human history and man's tenuous hold on it.

Against the broken fragments of these early poems there is, however, often a suggestion of some opposite movement. This latter poem, titled **"Concurrence"** in the surviving manuscript, continues: "Paper yellows, even without flame, / But in words carbon has already become diamond" (**"Concurrence"**). In these lines Hughes establishes a link between the carbon that is the result of time's slow fire and the carbon of the poet's own pencil. Even as the page slowly smoulders, the poet's own creative fire inscribes words on the page that have already become diamond. The poem is an affirmation of some counter movement against, what he calls it elsewhere, the "cold clockwork of the stars" (**HR** [**The Hawk in the Rain**] 53), and an expression of hope for that otherwise fleeting creative force.

We see such an affirmation of the creative moment many places in Hughes's poetry, but perhaps nowhere as familiarly as in his self-mythologizing account of writing a poem that we find in **"The Thought Fox"** (**HR** 15). In this well-known poem poetic inspiration is described as a midnight visit from a fox which slowly advances across a forest clearing. In his recent study, Keith Sagar takes exception to "the myth of unpremeditated art" that the poem seems to posit; however, we need to consider not the accuracy of its account so much as the importance of this myth of creativity to Hughes (2000 89). Early in his career the poem became a kind of signature piece for him. He gave it pride-of-place in his *New Selected,* and he commented on the circumstances of composition on more than one occasion, most fully in the same "Listening and Writing" radio broadcast where he described his childhood hunts. In his remarks, he did not qualify or otherwise retreat from the fictional elements of the analogy, but instead expanded them even further: "If I had not caught the real fox there in the words, I never would have saved the poem," he writes. "I would have thrown it into the wastepaper basket as I have thrown so many other hunts that did not get what I was after." More to the point, he then adds, "as long as a copy of the poem exists, every time anyone reads it the fox will get up somewhere out in the darkness and come walking towards them" ("Capturing Animals").

What Hughes is describing is the original moment of creative inspiration. The poem, if successful, reenacts that moment and gives us as readers access to the original experience that the poet serves. The reader's experience is not a new one but is, instead, a distant echo of that original inspiration. In Hughes's mind that moment is the final measure of value and is the end that the poet serves. As Ekbert Faas summarizes his position, "No craft, education, professional dedication and experimental ingenuity, not even the most thorough artistic conscience, will produce great poetry in default of this inspiration" (39).⁹ This chain of association which stretches back to the poet's original inspiration explains in large part the great value that Hughes came to place in the manuscript draft itself. The draft is always closer to that original inspiration than the final published poem. More than the achieved poem, the draft is for Hughes a reminder of the fox's first stirring and his slow movement towards us.

The poetic manuscript held a particular power for Hughes as evidenced as well by his early and frequent publication in special manuscript editions of his work. The first of these was the 1967 publication of *Animal Poems* in only one hundred copies, thirty-six of which include one or more of the poems in Hughes's own hand. This was followed by numerous other manuscript editions which incorporated either fair copies of his poems in his hand, cannibalized working drafts, or, in the case of *Cave Birds* and the broadside of **"Sky Furnace,"** facsimiles of the original manuscripts prepared for the purpose. The practice, begun in 1967 was one he returned to repeatedly over his lifetime, most recently in *Howls and Whispers* the fine press

companion volume to *Birthday Letters* published shortly before his death.¹⁰

Like his early sale of manuscript drafts, his decision to issue these manuscript editions was surely, in large part, a financial one. He could not only charge considerably more for these special editions, he could also issue them between the appearance of his major collections. We should not, however, let the economics of these publications obscure what they also convey about the special status he accorded the manuscript itself. These editions served a personal need as well and are consistent with Hughes's early critical statements privileging the original creative inspiration over any subsequent working out of a poem's final form. The manuscript edition quite literally contains the artifact of that otherwise elusive inspiration, which Ekbert Faas calls an "obsessive concern" of Hughes's early poetry (38).

Hughes's 1981 sale of the Sylvia Plath archive to Smith College offers further evidence of Hughes's own attitude toward the manuscript record. In a letter that anticipates this upcoming sale, Hughes comments on the wide fluctuations in prices paid for archives and on the impossibility of capturing their real value. "I know that Dylan Thomas' miraculous early notebooks, from which he drew all his major poems, went for a few pounds—even as late as the fifties. While in 1963 Roethke's papers went for [a] quarter of a million [dollars]." He then adds, "these things have no absolute value. They are simply priceless." While he recognizes their clear market value—and its fluctuations—he also attaches a value to manuscripts that is outside the marketplace altogether. Neither a few pounds nor a quarter million dollars can adequately measure the value of such materials. "The first drafts, in hand," he writes, "are astonishing documents of inspiration" (Letter to Prouty Smith).

It is important to note, however, the manuscript that he charges with such importance is the poem draft: "the first drafts in hand" and the "miraculous early notebooks." Indeed, in what is clearly the most commented on manuscript action of Hughes's life, his destruction of Sylvia Plath's last journal, we see him drawing a clear distinction between Plath's creative work (which he saw into print in five major collections) and a journal record of her personal life. What has escaped notice is that Hughes maintained the same distinction with regard to his own journals from the period. In a 1975 letter to Plath's mother, Aurelia, he mentions "my journal of that time" and later adds that the harsh view of his marriage to Plath "will only be corrected, probably, when somebody produces her journals of the time and mine" (Letter to Aurelia Plath).¹¹

Hughes's early insistence that the sources of his own inspiration lay outside the self explains, in large part, his very different stances towards the poem draft and towards personal documents such as letters or journals. In drawing a distinction between the public value of poetic manuscripts and the private nature of the journal, Hughes forces a split between the lived life and the creative imagination itself. Implicit in such a position is the notion that creative inspiration can be separated from the day-to-day details of the lived life, indeed, that its source lies somewhere outside the self altogether. The self-effacement implicit in such a split would later be construed by many readers as a defensive act of self-protection. In fact, the roots of this split lie in his early conception of the creative process itself.

In 1988 Roy Davids, the head of manuscripts at Sotheby's and a personal friend of Hughes's, asked Hughes if he could provide some notes on the surviving drafts of Plath's poem "Sheep in Fog" for a lecture that Davids was to give later that year. What began as only a series of notes quickly grew into a well-developed essay that now offers one of the most full statements by Hughes on the manuscript and poetic creativity itself. Hughes presents a view of the creative process remarkably consistent with his early views first articulated twenty-five years before. Repeatedly Hughes refers to "the amazing *inspiration*" (emphasis added) that produced Plath's major poems, in effect, giving agency to some force other than the self. Elsewhere in the original notes for the essay, Hughes suggests that the process of writing the *Ariel* poems was "a triumphant surmounting of all her personal difficulties" (Letter to Davids). In such statements, Hughes seems on the brink of an Eliot-like argument. about the impersonality of the poet, yet what he privileges in these statements is not so much a larger poetic tradition beyond the self as it is a kind of possession of the self. Thus, he writes of "the inner law of the poem," the poem that has been "persistently trying to emerge," and its "inevitable conclusion."

In a series of highly illuminating statements, Hughes describes three types of poetic composition, three degrees really of poetic inspiration.[12] In the first, the poem springs complete from its initial inspiration. As Hughes puts it "the poem seems to write itself, and takes the poet completely by surprise, as if he had no idea where it came from. Once here, it cannot be altered" (TH to Davids). The second type of process is one where "the poem can half rise" and the poet "struggles to help it, offering it words, images, anything from his bag of tricks, trying to anticipate it and take its slightest suggestions from the bits that have appeared." In the third, the initial inspiration offers the poet no more than an odd phrase or line, and the poet "goes after it" with deliberate skill. "The final work can often carry a strong poetic charge, it may well be rhetorically powerful and carry striking phrases, lines, felicities, and at the very least can be an admirable piece of craftmanship [sic]. But we have to ask: *what relation does it*

bear to the first inspiration (emphasis added), to the unique psychic materials that were pushing for expression?"

I am less interested in the application of this scheme to Plath's own poem than I am in the implications for Hughes's own poetics. These statements seem aimed at establishing the primacy of poetic inspiration. The drafts before him are important not for where they eventually lead, but for where they have come. They trace "the beginning, middle and end of a phenomenon to which no poem's final printed version can give any clue" (*WP* [*Winter Pollen*] 207). They are "a complementary revelation . . . the log-book of its real meanings."

This view of artistic creativity has wide implications. While it validates the initial impulse that animates the manuscript draft, it also diminishes the poet's own contribution to that creative process. Hughes attributes creativity not to any deliberate skill of the poet but, instead, to some fundamentally unknowable inspiration. In order to make such a claim Hughes had to ignore the considerable manuscript evidence of his own creative work. His own papers typically reveal extensive revision of draft upon draft. In the "Sheep in Fog" essay, however, he chose to emphasize not the artist's control over his materials but his role as a channel for that original inspiration. Implicit in this position is a certain denial of self that on some level Hughes found appealing.

What is most remarkable about the late collection **Birthday Letters** is the way the poems reunite that previously bifurcated self. When Hughes published the collection near the end of his life, reviewers were quick to proclaim, as the *New York Times* did, "Hughes Breaks His Silence on Sylvia Plath." Though he had written extensively about Plath, and had edited a considerable body of her work for publication, the **Birthday Letters** poems, for the first time, presented Hughes's own self as a register of events. No longer was he writing in a disinterested voice of a third party, as he had done in "The Chronological Order of Sylvia Plath's Poems," "Ariel by Sylvia Plath," "Sylvia Plath's Crossing the Water," his introduction to the **Collected Poems,** or in various other editorial notes and introductions. In **Birthday Letters** he once again placed himself in relation to the events the poems. He also did so in verse. That act, more than any other, reunited the two halves of the self that he had kept apart in his earlier critical statements regarding the sources of poetic inspiration. Here was a series of poems that sprang not from any impersonal and unknowable inspiration but quite directly from the journals, letters, poems, and photographs that are such a frequent point of reference of the poems. **Birthday Letters** sprang quite directly from the stuff of his own lived life. These poems are an effort towards the coherent reassembly of that personal past, a past that is by its very nature broken, fragmentary, and always receding into dim and irrecoverable memory.

In the end, the split that Hughes tried to claim between his personal experience and the sources of his own art was not one he was able to maintain with any consistency. The tensions between these two selves are most apparent in the contradictory actions towards his own material archive. While he valued the poem draft for its creative and talismanic properties, he also insisted that other elements of his archive were his alone and not for any public scrutiny. These contradictory impulses of self-revelation and self-concealment allow us a glimpse of Hughes's own conception of his art. The late synthesis of these opposing tendencies, most apparent in **Birthday Letters,** allows us a glimpse of a self restored by art.

Notes

1. Such restrictions are common in archives of contemporary materials. Often the restriction, as is the case in the Ted Hughes papers, protects the privacy of individuals whose letters are present among the papers but who was not a party to their disposition. The largest number of restrictions in the Hughes archive are of this kind and are on letters Hughes received from friends and colleagues. In each case, the restriction on these letters can be lifted with the permission of the copyright holder.

2. There is no evidence to support James Bone's speculation that the sealed trunk contains Sylvia Plath's lost journal. As the agent in the sale of the Ted Hughes archive made clear in a reply to Bone's article published in *The Times*: "I can satisfy the curiosity of scholars and others about the possibility of Sylvia Plath's missing journal being incarcerated in it. It is not" (Davids).

3. As a result of this practice, a number of previously lost works by Plath have surfaced in the Ted Hughes archive, among them a fragment of a short story titled "Runaway," based on the same incident as Hughes's *Birthday Letters* poem "Sam" and notes for her previously lost novel *Falcon Yard.*

4. Emory began buying Ted Hughes manuscripts in 1985 and had assembled a substantial Ted Hughes collection before the 1997 purchase of his own archive. Since that time, Emory has continued to make additions to the papers including a large number of early manuscript drafts from the collection of Joseph Gold, correspondence from Hughes to Lucas Myers, and an extensive correspondence (1950-1998) with his own brother, Gerald.

5. In a 1975 letter to Aurelia Plath, Hughes recalls the amount paid as $450 dollars (Ted Hughes to Aurelia Plath).

6. This element of regret for this early sale is captured as well in a 1975 letter to Mrs. Prouty Smith. He writes, "I sold my own early papers years ago for a couple of hundred pounds—parts of them I know have since changed hands for vastly greater sums, but they can't help me any more . . . They were probably my freshest best work" (Letter to Prouty Smith, 12 May 1975).

7. Hughes describes this fire in the Note to the Vintage Edition of Janet Malcolm's *The Silent Woman* (210).

8. Among the possible buyers were the well-known bookseller Bernard Stone, the London-based firm of Bernard Quaritch, and the American dealer Marjorie Cohen of the House of Books.

9. Hughes's insistence on a spontaneous and uncontrollable inspiration may have been, in part, a response to Sylvia Plath's far different manner of laboring over her poems with thesaurus in hand. In his "Notes on the Chronological Order of Sylvia Plath's Poems," he describes her method of composition this way: "She wrote her early poems very slowly, Thesaurus open on her knee, in her large, strange handwriting, like a mosaic, where every letter stands separate within the work, a hieroglyph to itself . . . Every poem grew complete from its own root, in that laborious inching way, as if she were working out a mathematical problem, chewing her lips, putting a thick ring of ink around each word that stirred for her on the page of the Thesaurus." (188)

10. *Howls and Whispers* was published in an edition of only 110 copies, ten of which included a single manuscript of one of the poems.

11. The Ted Hughes papers at Emory include several journal-like entries on widely scattered notebook pages but contain no sustained journal.

12. In the original letter to Roy Davids, Hughes describes three forms of poetic inspiration; in the published essay, he identifies four. The fourth, however, is a variation on the third; therefore, I do not consider it here.

Works Cited

Davids, R. (2000). Letter. *The Times* (11 April 2000).

Davids, R. (2000). Plath's Missing Journal. *The [London] Times* 11 April.

Hughes, T. Capturing Animals, radio script, Ted Hughes Papers, Robert W. Woodruff Library, Emory University.

Hughes, T. Introduction. (1981). *Collected Poems* by Sylvia Plath. Ed. Ted Hughes. London & New York: Faber & Faber.

Hughes, T. (1970). Notes on the Chronological Order of Sylvia Plath's Poems. *The Art of Sylvia Plath: A Symposium.* Ed. Charles Newman. Bloomington: Indiana Univ. Press.

Hughes, T. Possible Buyers, Ted Hughes Papers, Robert W. Woodruff Library, Emory University.

Hughes, T. (1966, Fall). The chronological order of Sylvia Plaths poems. *TriQuarterly,* 7.

Hughes, T. (1967). *Animal Poems.* Bow, Credition: Richard Gilbertson.

Hughes, T. (1998). *Birthday Letters,* London: Faber & Faber.

Hughes, T. (1978). *Cave Birds. An Alchemical Cave Drama.* London: Faber & Faber.

Hughes, T. (1975). *Cave Birds.* Ilkley: Scolar Press.

Hughes, T. (1998). *Howls & Whispers.* Illustrations by Leonard Baskin. Rockport, Me. The Gehenna Press.

Hughes, T. (1975, 12 January). Letter to Aurelia Plath. Ted Hughes Papers. Robert W. Woodruff Library, Emory.

Hughes, T. (1964, 19 March). Letter to Joseph Gold. Ted Hughes Papers. Robert W. Woodruff Library, Emory.

Hughes, T. (1964, 7 August). Letter to Joseph Gold. Ted Hughes Papers. Robert W. Woodruff Library, Emory.

Hughes, T. (1988, 25 February). Letter to Roy Davids, TL. Ted Hughes Papers, Robert W. Woodruff Library, Emory University.

Hughes, T. (1962, 14 August). Letter to Winifred Myers. Ted Hughes Papers, Robert W. Woodruff Library, Emory.

Hughes, T. (1995). *New Selected Poems 1957-1994.* London: Faber & Faber.

Hughes, T. (1994). *Winter Pollen* (Ed.) William Scammell, London: Faber & Faber.

Malcolm, J. (1994). *The Silent Woman: Sylvia Plath & Ted Hughes.* New York: Alfred A. Knopf.

Plath, S. (1973). Burning the Letters. *Pursuit.* London: The Rainbow Press.

Plath, S. (1975). *Letters Home, Correspondence 1950-1963.* Ed. Aurelia Schober Plath. New York: Harper & Row.

Sagar, K. (2000). *The Laughter of Foxes,* Liverpool: Liverpool University Press.

Axel Nesme (essay date 2004)

SOURCE: Nesme, Axel. "Drives & their Vicissitudes in the Poetry of Ted Hughes." In *Ted Hughes: Alternative Horizons,* edited by Joanny Moulin, pp. 77-85. London: Routledge, 2004.

[*In the following essay, Nesme approaches Hughes's poetry through the theories of Freud, Jung, and Lacan.*]

When I indicated to Joanny Moulin that I was considering working on "drives and their vicissitudes" in Ted Hughes's poetry, he wrote back suggesting that I do some checking on the concept of *enantiodromia* as introduced by Jung in his writings and further explored by Hughes in *Shakespeare and the Goddess of Complete Being.* I will therefore go back on this term, which I hope will permit me to situate differentially the more specifically Freudian concept of drive. In *Shakespeare and the Goddess of Complete Being* (40), Hughes defines the term with the formula: "Jung's term for the reversal of one dominant psychological attitude into its opposite." In his own use of the concept Jung acknowledges his debt towards Heraclitus:

> Old Heraclitus . . . discovered the most marvellous of all psychological laws: the regulative function of opposites. he called it *enantiodromia,* a running contrariwise, by which he meant that sooner or later everything runs into its opposite . . . Thus the rational attitude of culture necessarily runs into its opposite, namely the irrational devastation of culture . . . The enantiodromia that always threatens when a movement attains to undisputed power offers no solution of the problem, for it is just as blind in its disorganization as it was in its organization.

In *Psychology and Alchemy* Jung also writes: "an enantiodromia has obviously taken place: after being rejected the unconscious asserts itself even more strongly" (1970 112). Enantiodromia could thus be viewed roughly as a return of the repressed in the form of a dream or a symptom. It may also take on the shape of a reversal affecting the history of a subject or an entire culture. In any case, between enantiodromia and entropy or, to use a more Freudian terminology, homeostatic regulation, or even the life-drive / death-drive dialectic, the difference may seem minimal. However, while in Freud's theory this dynamic is as unavoidable as the very existence of the drive itself, Jung does not view it as a necessary condition: "The only person who escapes the grim law of enantiodromia is the man who knows how to separate himself from the unconscious, not by repressing it. but by putting it clearly before him as *that which he is not.*" (1966 72)

I would not therefore go as far as to assimilate enantiodromia to a "reversal of a drive into its opposite," for insofar as the drive is that which defines man as a linguistic being subjected to the Other's desire, there is no object which, being perfectly adequate to it as would be the object of the *need,* can put an end to it; there is only a succession of metonymic substitutes which temporarily fill the gap of the lost primal object[1] and which constantly reactivate the dynamics of the drive, whose aim is "but the return, as in a closed circuit. to its own source, which allows us to understand how a drive can be satisfied without reaching its goal." (Dorr 185) Following Hughes's own logic, the poet's writing is not only enantiodromic in relation to the culture whose repressed side it unveils, its shamanistic claim is also to offer its reader a way out of what Jung calls "the grim law of enantiodromia." On the contrary it seems to me there is no possible integration of the objects of the drive in Hughes's poetry; instead the drive can be seen as both constantly re-circulating and circumventing what Lacanian theory designates as *Objet Petit a.*

Whether in its in its vocal or phonemic manifestations on which I will primarily focus in this paper, the object of the drive defines itself partly by the space it delineates, the vacuum whose edges it maps out as does the curlew's flight in **"The Horses"** (**HR** [*The Hawk in the Rain*] 16): "I listened in emptiness on the moor-ridge. / The curlew's tear turned its edge on the silence."

Thus while insisting in **"Skylarks"** that "The sky lies blank open" (**W** [*Wodwo*] 168) and depicting in the poem **"Pibroch"** (177) the universe as the cradle of a persisting nothingness where his gnats will later be seen to fly, "at large in the nothing" (179), Hughes does not only create a vacuum in the sky the better to lodge there his new gods of survival, be they thrushes, larks, or "an almighty gnat," he also pins down the nothingness to which the object of the drive can be assimilated in the final analysis. For as Alain Juranville points out, "the object of the drive lends itself to infinite substitutions. It is nothing (*Il est le rien*)." It is, in Lacan's own terms, "the object that we confuse all too often with that upon which the drive closes—this object, which is in fact simply the presence of a hollow, a void, which can be occupied, Freud tells us, by any object, and whose agency we know only in the form of the lost object, the *petit a*" (1964 180).

The void central to the mechanism of the drive is apt to become resonant and turn into the oxymoronic "ringing nothing" which is heard at the end of **"The Contender"** (**C** [*Crow*] 41), "the one note of silence / To which the whole earth dances gravely" in the poem **"Fern"** (**W** 28), or conceivably the uncanny hieroglyphic silence of the bodies of the mute children described in **"Deaf School"** (**M** [*Moortown*] 105). The voice as object of what Lacanian theory calls *"pulsion invocante,"* i. e. "invoking drive," partakes of a similar paradox. Its truest expression might be the silent scream at the center of Munch's famous painting which carries the same title, the same scream Hughes presents as the origin of all things in **"Lineage"** and whose toned-down version we might trace for example to the rat's screeching in

"Song of a Rat" (**W** 162), an apt analogon of Hughes's writing insofar at least as it is the other of the metaphysical sophistries his poetry is fond of denouncing, but also more importantly the other of meaning itself.

In *Poetry in the Making* Hughes explains that a good poem may acquire the same solidity and unavoidable factuality as what he calls "some lovely solid thing" (*WP* [*Winter Pollen*] 19). In that case, its mode of presence in the world is not similar but identical to that of an animal: "I think of poems as a sort of animal . . . Maybe my concern has been to capture not animals particularly and not poems, but simply things which have a vivid life of their own, outside mine" (10). In other words, the poem does not exist as a linguistic artefact implicitly signalling to the subject's divorce from the Real. It is a thing among others, hence also consubstantial to *das Ding*, the Freudian Thing defined in Lacanian theory as "plenitude insofar as it is there located by the (verbal) signifier" (Juranville 253), or, following one of Lacan's many untranslatable formulas, *"ce qui, du réel primordial . . . pâtit du signifiant"* (1986 142), i. e. that part of the primal real of which the signifier necessarily falls short and whose quest leads the subject beyond the pleasure principle.

For lack of ever becoming one with the real of *das Ding*, however, a poem may at least convoke it by means of the scream which brings into play the vocal object as that which stands for *das Ding*, or rather, for the gap which its absence inscribes in each speaking subject:

The scream is not primarily a call, it brings silence into being. Not because silence sustains it, being in its background: quite the opposite. According to Lacan the scream creates a gulf into which silence rushes. He then mentions the knot that silence ties between something which exists just before it vanishes and the Other thing where speech may falter: it is this knot that becomes resonant when the scream carves a space inside it. The "gap the scream delineates" is internal, but it is also that of the Thing. The death drive penetrates this inner gap, then returns to its surface. The scream thus carves a hole within the body while at the same time resonating in the space where *das Ding* is lacking. It is at this level that the *Nebenmensch* (the Freudian Thing) appears as an unbridgeable gap delineated within ourselves and which we can barely approach. The death drive has no object, since the subject then becomes that nothing which is the Thing in its emptiness, and can trigger no desire. It is there that the lack of the Object is experienced as the lack of all objects. (Juranville 231-2)

The pure voice of the other thing where speech falters thus resonates in the scream with which the pure signifier Gulkana is equated in Hughes's poem by the same title **"The Gulkana"** (*R* [*River*] 78): "Gulkana— / Biblical, a deranging cry / From the wilderness—burst past us. / A stone voice that dragged at us." The utter nonsense of this river name isolates the voice as object, a petrified voice ("a stone voice that dragged at us") whose fate the gaze will later share ("Bliss had fixed their eyes"), a voice which therefore carries no meaningful speech and reduces the speaker's ear to a pure void; the voice of perversion perhaps also, since, as A. Juranville points out, it "ultimately refers to the voice of the threatening mother, of the seducing mother" (187) whose deadly power and force of attraction is expressed in the verb "dragged." The voice which thus makes itself heard is a voice from before the law, hence the denial attempt ("something I kept trying to deny") of the speaker, led by his transgressive desire to set foot on the locus of origins where the resurrection of the fish translates a primal scene fantasy in almost explicit terms. This experience necessarily triggers a sense of anxiety, as the speaker finds in the resurrected fish his own image, "A bodiless twin, some doppelgänger / Disinherited other, unliving," reflected in the frame of fantasy, here designated as "the windows of the express torrent."

Bearing witness to a dysfunctioning of the paternal metaphor which introduces the subject to the symbolic order, this erection of the voice as object is also the privileged medium of a questioning of the law of finitude, the law of symbolic castration partly challenged by the poetic subject in **"Anniversary"** (*CPH* [*Collected Poems*] 854). In this poem, as in a sonnet by Seamus Heaney called "In Memoriam M. K. H.," the use of grammatical tenses signals the incompletion of the mourning process, as does from the outset the fate inflicted on the page from the diary which mentions the death of the poet's mother. While the indication "Ma died today" inscribes this death in the linear temporality of the diary, the poem subtracts the vision of the mother from this order to maintain her in a perpetual present, in a fashion similar to the tearing off of the page mentioning her death from the diary. The text thus offers the maternal voice as object of the invoking drive a space where it can be heard from the grave and become the voice that is invoked, an evanescent and seductive object which, by drawing the outline of a void, turns it into the imaginary locus where the lack of *das Ding* designates itself: "Her voice comes, piping, / Down a deep gorge of woodland echoes" (292). Indeed, it is no accident if many poems in which Ted Hughes apostrophizes the departed, such as **"For the Duration"** (*Ww* [*Wolfwatching*] 22) or **"Old oats"** (*CPH* 852) or **"You Hated Spain"** (*BL* [*Birthday Letters*] 39) foreground the dimension of invocation, thus possibly manifesting the poet's difficulty in coming to terms with loss otherwise than via a return of the ghost of the object, that which all invocations aims at, and more specifically that which occurs in **"Anniversary."** For here the

voice which is invoked is precisely the object which, according to Juranville "lets the ear appear as a void" (186) where the drive involutes. This is at least the suggestion one may read in the lines, "She is using me to tune finer / Her weeping love for my brother" (*CPH* 855), where the speaker subjected to the mother's desire for fusion (be it presented as a mere con-fusion between the two brothers: "able for all that distance to think me him") becomes a tuning instrument, in other words, an ear for the voice of the mother who, having merged with the cosmos, is animated by the pure binary movement of the drive: "The work of the cosmos, / Creation and destruction of matter / And of anti-matter / Pulses and flares, shudders and fades / Like the Northern Lights in their feathers" (292). Central to the emergence of the voice as object is its withdrawal as the vehicle of meaningful speech, at times when selves are "no longer woven into a voice" as Hughes wrote once again in **"Deaf School"** (*M* 105) or when animals set in resonance the void in which their voices are heard: "the voices and frenzies of the larks, / Squealing and gibbering and cursing. / Like sacrifices set floating / The cruel earth's offerings / The mad earth's missionaries." These lines from **"Skylarks"** (*W* 168) are exemplary of the two contradictory forces at work in Hughes's poetry: on the one hand the fascination with the Other of articulate language as embodied by the larks' gibberish; on the other, the discursiveness which here substitutes a meaningful comparison for the nonsense of which the reader previously caught a glimpse. Given the line of questioning I have chosen, my focus will continue to bear primarily on the first term of this dichotomy, which I would now like to approach from a more metapoetic angle.

As meaningless as the scream in which the invoking drive opens onto the death drive which is the *primum mobile* of all partial drives in the essential vanity of their motion, is the writing that Hughes's gnats are seen to successively jot down and erase in mid air, "Writing on the air, rubbing out everything they write" (179). Animated by the pure alternating motion of the drive in their constant shifts from activity to passivity—"Ridden to death by your own bodies / Riding your bodies to death" (180)—the dancing gnats also follow the circular pattern of the drive circumscribing the central void which stands for the absence of *das Ding,* hence their being defined as "immense magnets fighting around a center." Hughes's insects thus offer an apt analogy for the initial moment of the writing process, preceding sublimation:

> The act of writing. is a pure act in which the signifier is produced, but as meaningless in and of itself. This appears quite clearly in the way one draws a letter on the page, then returns to where one started, in the same way as in the partial drive, one revolves around the object, i. e. always also the void of *das Ding.* The motion which inscribes a letter is the motion of the drive.

And this motion is bound to repetition in writing: once the letter has been produced, it calls for the production of another letter, without the second one being anymore than the first, with the same presence of meaninglessness (*non-sens*).

(Juranville 284)

Yet all this only applies to the initial logical moment of writing. As soon as a structure emerges, however, sublimation occurs, by virtue of which, in Lacanian theory, the object is elevated to the dignity of *das Ding*, which appears in lieu of the object, within the specific temporality of poetic speech. This scenario we can see at work in the poem from *River* **"Milesian Encounter on the Sligachan"** (44) with which I would like to conclude this paper. In his article entitled "The Subversion of the Subject and the Dialectic of Desire in the Freudian Unconscious" after listing the various objects of standard analytical theory Lacan adds: "An unthinkable list, if one adds, as I do, the phoneme, the gaze, the voice—the nothing" (1966 315). Following Lacan's suggestion I would like to show how in this poem, it is precisely through the agency of the phoneme that the object is elevated to the dignity of the Thing.

Despite the predominance of its narrative aspect, reinforced by the six prose paragraphs inserted after the third line, this poem presents a number of formal features which suggest from the start that the encounter in question will extend beyond the level of the plot and involve the dimension of the signifier. Indeed, besides the falling rhythms introduced by several dactyls and trochees—"tumblequag," "hairiness," "clatterbrook," "petrified scapulae, vertebrae," "underbank opposite," "something sinister about bogland rivers"—as a prelude to the fading "from the light of reality" undergone by the speaker at the end of the poem, one formal characteristic that stands out are the numerous alliterations which seem to take this poem back to the origins of English verse, perhaps as an echo of the primitivist longing for Beowulf days already expressed in **"Thistles"** (*W* 17).

Here are a few examples: "*s*omething *s*inister" (l. 2) "*c*rusty, *q*uaking *c*adaver and me *l*urching over it in e*l*ation *l*ike a daddy-*l*ong-*l*egs" (l. 6); "*c*rooked little *c*latterbrook" (l. 7); "The *sh*ock. / The *sh*eer *c*avern of current" (l. 5); "*cl*ear / *Cl*eansing" (ll. 8-9); "*gi*ddy / *G*hostly" (ll. 12-13); "*p*eering into that *s*uperabundance of *sp*irit" (l. 15) "Those *sh*uttles of love-*sh*adow" (l. 23) "*pr*ecious like a *pr*eservative" (l. 29).

This omnipresence of alliteration draws the reader's attention to what Laurent Jenny calls "plastic nuances" which "bring the weight of reality to bear on utterance," they belong to what the critic calls "that sensitive border which unfolds at the same time as utterance itself" and which can be seen as "a kind of "interface"

between discourse and the world" (17). Indeed, according to Jenny, not only "deictics and nouns act as shifters between language and its other. The sensitive materiality of discourse also functions "deictically" in that it is oriented towards the world" (18). This plasticity of poetic speech, this encoding of the real in the substance of the text to which alliteration contributes, may thus be seen as the exact counterpart of the symptom as the encoding of *jouissance* in the real of the body. In its primitivism, alliteration thus opens up a discursive space "made up of the substance of the world and unfolding together with it;" it fashions the poem as the locus where "this world divides within itself, tears itself away from itself while preserving its plasticity, thereby creating the possibility of a withdrawal, but not of an absolute separation." (Jenny 19). This last quote encapsulates, I believe, the transgressive dimension of Hughes's poetic undertaking in its problematic relationship to the law that posits the real as language's impossibility.

No wonder therefore, if in **"Milesian Encounter on the Sligachan,"** language is made subservient to the speaker's attempt at restoring a primal unity of sorts, notably by way of hyphenated words and compounds that stitch various nouns together[2], the most spectacular example being the *bog* which serves not only as the setting for poetic revelation, but also as an omnific signifier that lends itself to various transformations: "bogland" (line 2), "bog-cotton" (l. 11), "underbog" (l. 28), "boggart" (l. 65). By stressing the infinite malleability of words as he also does in suggesting the genesis of the word "whisker" (l. 54) from the merger of "whisky" (l. 51) and "whisper" (l. 52), Hughes thus reenacts in the materiality of the letter the imaginary scenario of the origins one of whose main protagonists is, if not the Freudian Thing, at least that which stands for it, call it the phallic mother or simply the legendary Gorgon whose presence in this text is made quite explicit by the mythological reference: "With a ram's skull there—magnified, a Medusa" (l. 30) bearing witness to the "Milesian" or picaresque aesthetic adopted by Hughes, but also conveniently assimilating the river to the Gorgon from whose veins legend has it that both a deadly poison and medicine to bring the dead back to life could be drawn.

There are thus, I would argue, two encounters in this poem: first, the imaginary confrontation—mediated by a scopic fantasy in which gazes are exchanged: "I . . . peering into . . ." (l. 14), "the loveliest ogress . . . watched me," (ll. 59-61)—with the "fellow aliens" (l. 16), whose oxymoron encapsulates the poem's strategy aiming to reduce alterity to similarity—"Those peculiar eyes / So like mine," (ll. 17-8)—the better to tone down the threat perceived in the landscape as locus of epiphany. The frame of fantasy does not however provide the only connection between the two agencies involved. Indeed the subject and the Other, being respectively compared to a "Daddy-long-legs" and to a "most-longed-for-ogress," i. e., both designated by hyphenated names, seem linguistically destined to meet, which transfers the stage of the encounter from the river's imaginary setting to the poem's linguistic make-up. In the same way as the various hyphens create a continuity between signifiers, the [ou] assonance and [l] consonance thus metonymically connect verbs predicated of the speaker with the Other of the encounter: "I str*ou*ked its thr*oa*t . . . I *l*icked the m*ou*lded h*o*l*l*ows / Of its c*o*l*l*arb*o*nes." But while a sexual meaning is deliberately suggested in lines 34-47 where the speaker portrays himself as successfully attempting to arouse the pool, an attempt which partially culminates in the climactic crash of line 47, the linguistic climax of the poem only occurs in lines 50-2, which define the text's second, and more specifically poetic, encounter. This apex is itself followed by the purely verbal anticlimax of "salmo salar" (71) where Latin taxonomy takes over from the more native capitalized nouns of lines 50-2.

The poem thus stages a love encounter with the signifiers of the mother tongue, the word "boggart," which is West Yorkshire dialect for "specter," and also with a specific *phoneme*. In **"Milesian Encounter"** the poet is not only fishing "the long pool-tail" for the tale of an encounter in a pool, but also for certain gutturals, be it at the cost of what Craig Robinson calls "deliberate exaggeration" (203-4). This, Hughes does most spectacularly in the apocopated internal rhyme of line 50 ("a Grua*gach* of the Sli*gach*an), where he extols those remnants of his language's Celtic prehistory as the privileged vehicles of the metaphor which veils the woman as imaginary bearer of the phallus, before staging their demise when denotative, scientific language takes over and the lack is revealed behind the linguistic veil that covered it. Yet through the mediation of Hughes's poetic narrative, the reader has had ample enough opportunity to relish the raucous charms of the voiceless velar fricative, previously repressed from the signifier which designates the setting of the poem, namely the Cuillins whose Promethean connotations ("asylum of eagles") were the only reminder of the hero Cu*ch*ullain after whom those mountains are also named.

While **"Thistles"** (*W* 17), one of Hughes's many explorations of the death and resurrection pattern, stages by way of a simile the resurrection of "the gutturals of dialects," **"A Milesian Encounter"** thus achieves a similar effect to that described by Hughes in the often-quoted passage from his "Notes on Shakespeare" (*WP* 105) where the poet explains how Shakespeare's use of the Latin word "aggravate" reactivates "the concrete Anglo-Saxon "gr" core of growl, grind, eager, grief, grate etc." Hughes's own brand of linguistic archaelogy not only unearthes the same sound combination set off by the chiasmatic ordering of the voiced and voiceless

velar plosives ("grabbed . . . crashed" / "crack . . . granite" [græ] / [kræ], [kræ] / [græ]), it also throws into relief a phoneme that takes us back to the Germanic roots of English.

This poem thus enacts a transition of sorts from linguistic innocence to experience as well as the speaker's exile from original light. As he implicitly did lines 35-6 in constructing a phonological chain that connected him with the Thing, the speaker finally suggests that such metonymic ruins of the (m)other are the only object of jouissance allotted to him as subjected to the signifier. While confining the other within the "*judas*-hole" of line 61, i. e. the frame of scopic fantasy necessarily perceived as a betrayal of the total truth that hides behind, the poem, by also letting through phonemic glimmers of what Hughes terms "the light of reality," elevates those to the dignity of the Thing

Does the poet emulate Perseus who defeated Medusa by trapping her image in the reflection of his shield, i. e. by interposing the imaginary order between himself and the Other's jouissance? This reading would be legitimate, but perhaps incomplete. It is worth remembering here that at the beginning of the poem, the origin of the encounter is located in directions provided by a third party—""up in the pools," *they'd* said," (l. 1)—a symbolic Other ensuring mediation between subject and object of the encounter. This fact, I would argue is to be related to the poem itself being addressed to "Hilary and Simon." Simultaneously to this inscription opposing the gift of the poem as symbolic artefact to the gift of the salmon's eye as imaginary object also thematized in the poem, knowledge of *jouissance* is located in the Other: "*you* know when it's coming" (l. 40). The phoneme as letter thus borders a gap in knowledge, the knowledge of *jouissance* as located in the unconscious, i. e., an Other which defines the subject of speech as the product of his splitting between his discourse and his speech as well as between his imaginary reflection and the real of his body. Which may explain why in the poem under scrutiny, alterity, initially located in a prehistoric other whose connection with the subject, although acknowledged, was of a primarily specular nature ("Those peculiar eyes / So like mine") is later on integrated in terms of an "altering" predicated of the speaker's body at the same time as the text undergoes the rather theatrical linguistic alteration I have been studying.

In a recent book psychoanalyst Henri Rey-Flaud propounds a vision of modernity as the moment when the ultimate Cause of all things, a signifier which incidentally shares the same root as Chose, the French word for *thing,* is elided. Previously, he adds, the world "was only thinkable as obeying a principle of causality whose founding signifier was located in the Other, designated by the expression "Heaven." In other words, the universe was thought as reasonable on the basis of the belief that the final reason of all things would be given one day and provide the meaning of meaning" (58). Rey-Flaud argues that the moment when "the chain of causes was broken and the founding signifier was lost is a decisive one in our culture, for it marks the birth of scientific thought which, by "eluding" and "eliding" the question of the ultimate cause, once and for all dismissed as pertaining to the impossibility of the real, lays down the foundation of reality as such." (58-9).

As for Ted Hughes's poetic project, it manifests a resurgence of a pre-scientific imaginary order which, in its iconoclastic guise, denounces metaphysical illusion the better to promote nature as a universal cause of creation and destruction. Hence his mimologism, which can be read as a refusal to accept the signifier's essential inadequacy to its meaning, or in other words, that for lack of an ultimate Cause, the only possible belief rests on the absence of the ultimate Cause and on the assumption of the arbitrariness of the sign. Perhaps therefore Ted Hughes falls short of what Rey-Flaud thus defines as "pure belief." I have tried to show how in his poetry meaningless objects occupy the space which this belief leaves vacant, and are convoked in lieu of the primal signifier (designated in Lacanian theory as S2, or the phallic symbol Φ) to function as substitutes of the Thing whose absence it proclaims.

Notes

1. "L'objet d'une pulsion. ne peut pas être l'objet du besoin. Le seul objet à même de répondre à cette propriété ne peut être que l'objet du désir, cet objet que Lacan désignera comme objet an objet du désir et objet cause du désir tout à la fois, objet perdu. A ce titre, l'objet a en tant qu''il est éternellement manquant, inscrira la présence d'un creux que n''importe quel objet pourra venir occuper (Dorr 185).

2. "Tumblequag," "Ice-Age hairiness" (ll. 4-5) "daddy-long-legs" (l. 7), "clatterbrook" (l. 7), "a razor-edged, blood-smeared grass, the flood-sucked swabs of bog-cotton, the dusty calico rip-up of snipe—" (l. 12), "the Cuillins . . . that were blue-silvered" (ll. 14-5), "up to my hip in a suck-hole . . . teetering over the broken-necked heath-bobs a good half-hour" (ll. 19-20), "So lonely-drowning deep, so drowned-hair silent" (l. 7); "the long pool-tail" (l. 14); "With an ushering-in of chills" (l. 43); "the tip of my heart-nerve" (l. 47); "the eye-pupil darkness? The loveliest, left-behind, most-longed-for ogress" (l. 59), "her time-warped judas-hole" (l. 61).

Works Cited

Dorr, J. (1985). *Introduction à la lecture de Lacan I.* Paris: Denoël.

Freud, S. (1964). *New Introductory Lectures on Psychoanalysis* (1933). *The Standard Edition of the Complete Psychological Works of Sigmund Freud,* vol. XXII. Ed. James Strachey. London: the Hogarth Press.

Heaney S. (1999). Speech at the Memorial Service for Ted Hughes (*The Observer* 16th May)

Hughes, T. (1998). *Birthday Letters.* London: Faber & Faber.

Hughes, T. (1972). *Crow. From the Life & Songs of the Crow.* London: Faber & Faber.

Hughes, T. (1979). *Moortown.* New York: Harper & Row.

Hughes, T. (1967). *Poetry in the Making. An Anthology of Poems & Programmes from Listening & Writing.* London: Faber & Faber.

Hughes, T. (1983). *River.* London: Faber & Faber.

Hughes, T. (1992). *Shakespeare & The Goddess of Complete Being,* London: Faber & Faber.

Hughes, T. (1957). *The Hawk in the Rain,* London: Faber & Faber.

Hughes, T. (1994). *Winter Pollen* (Ed.) William Scammell, London: Faber & Faber.

Jung, C. G. (1970). *Psychologie et alchimie.* Paris: Buchet/Chastel.

Jung, C. G. (1966). *Two Essays on Analytical Psychology.* Princeton (N.J.): Princeton University Press.

Juranville, A. (1984). *Lacan et la philosophie.* Paris: P. U. F.

Lacan, J. (1997). *Ecrits.* (1966). London: Routledge.

Lacan, J. (1971). *Ecrits II.* Paris: Seuil.

Lacan, J. (1986). *Le Séminaire VII. L'Ethique de la psychanalyse.* Paris: Seuil.

Lacan, J. (1978). *Le Séminaire. Livre II. Le moi dans la théorie de Freud et la technique de la psychanalyse.* Paris: Seuil.

Lacan, J. (1973). *Le Séminaire. Livre XI. Les quatre concepts fondamentaux de la psychanalyse.* Paris: Seuil.

Lacan, J. (1998). *The Four Fundamental Concepts of Psychoanalysis.* (1964). London: Vintage.

Rey-Flaud, H. (1996). *L'Eloge du rien.* Paris: Seuil.

Heather Clark (essay date winter 2005)

SOURCE: Clark, Heather. "Tracking the Thought-Fox: Sylvia Plath's Revision of Ted Hughes." *Journal of Modern Literature* 28, no. 2 (winter 2005): 100-12.

[*In the following essay, Clark discusses the poetry written by Sylvia Plath in direct response to Hughes's work, particularly his highly-acclaimed poem "The Thought-Fox."*]

In January of 1961, Ted Hughes and Sylvia Plath were interviewed by BBC commentator Owen Leeming about their marriage, and their poetry, in a radio broadcast entitled "Two of a Kind: Poets in Partnership." Plath and Hughes must have known that Leeming would question them about their influence on each other's poetry, yet, when he did so, both seemed caught off guard. When he asked them, for instance, whether there was anything in their collections "to" or "about" each other (apart from the dedications), Plath responded with an unusually muddled answer—one that reveals her deep ambivalence and anxiety about the very nature of poetic "partnership" itself:

> Well I think that all the poems that we wrote to each other and about each other were really before our marriage, and then something happened, I don't know what it was, I hope it was all to the good, but we began to be able to, well, somehow free ourselves for other subjects and I think the dedications, at least as far as mine goes, I feel that I'd never be writing as I am, and as much as I am, without Ted's understanding and cooperation, really.

(Hughes and Plath, 1961)

Plath here dismisses those poems she and Hughes wrote to each other before their marriage as somehow less substantial than the work that came later, after they were able to "free" themselves, and their poems, from the influence of the other. She is vague about how they were able to attain this freedom ("something happened, I don't know what"), and not entirely certain that it was for the best ("I hope it was all to the good"). When she says that her success is due to Hughes, she seems to contradict her earlier claim that the marriage was poetically liberating; it is as if she rushes in to credit Hughes's influence the moment she declares herself free of it. The two poets continue to send contradictory messages about their 'collaborative' relationship throughout the interview. Hughes says that he and Plath have "a single, shared mind," "a telepathic union" that was "a source of great deal" in his poetry, but then emphasizes that when they "happen" to write about the same thing, they always approach it differently. Plath says Hughes inspired her to become more interested in nature, but becomes defensive when Leeming remarks that she and Hughes write about nature in similar ways. Clearly uncomfortable with this observation, she says "this was true of our poems before we ever knew each other" and reiterates that their work is "really quite, quite different."

The fact that both Plath and Hughes at turns embrace and reject each other's influence should come as no surprise—both were wary of being, in Plath's words, "made by" the other (*Journals* 401).[1] Like the poets themselves, Plath and Hughes critics also disagree upon the extent to which the couple influenced one another. Margaret Dickie Uroff, the first to write a full-length

study of poetic influence between Plath and Hughes (1979), insists that their poems should be read "as parts of a continuing debate about the nature of the universe, in which Plath's reservations and Hughes's assertions play against each other" (12). She sees Plath's interest in "psychological states and extreme human experiences" as similar to Hughes's "concern with the non-human cosmos" (13), and argues that they influenced each other in equal measure, albeit at different stages of their poetic development. Yet Uroff's claims have been rejected by major Plath scholars such as Marjorie Perloff, Susan Van Dyne, Jacqueline Rose, and Lynda Bundtzen, all of whom have questioned Hughes's editorial decisions concerning Plath's posthumous publications—particularly his decision to rearrange Plath's *Ariel* manuscript, to burn her last journal, to label her pre-Cambridge work juvenilia, and to insist that her "real self" appeared only in the *Ariel* poems.

What is often missing from these scholars' compelling discussions is an analysis of the ways in which Plath looted Hughes's poetic corpus. This is not to say that Plath's plundering has gone unnoticed—Van Dyne, for example, has said that "Plath's dialogue with Hughes's poems is always competitive and her strategy revisionary" (40) while Diane Middlebrook has commented upon "the call and response manner of their productive collusion" (191). Yet few critics, apart from Uroff, have seriously examined the frequent allusions to *The Hawk in the Rain* and *Lupercal* in *Ariel*, nor speculated upon what these allusions might mean.[2] Such reluctance may be due to the fact that many Plath scholars, who regard Hughes with hostility, are uncomfortable with the idea that he may have influenced her remarkable late poems. For example, Van Dyne, a feminist critic, has claimed, "Plath's fondest fiction about her relationship with Hughes was that it was a mutually beneficial collaboration" (19). But to suggest that Plath borrowed from Hughes does not diminish her achievements; on the contrary, reading these poets side by side (indeed, they often wrote back to back) only deepens our understanding of the complexity of Plath's late work.

Van Dyne, Bundtzen, and Neil Roberts have recently commented upon the relationship between Plath's "Burning the Letters" and Hughes's **"The Thought-Fox,"** generally agreeing that Plath is "throwing down the gauntlet," arguing with Hughes about whether his "impersonal" lines or her "cri de coeur" (Bundtzen 55) will stand the test of time.[3] This interpretation rests on the fact that Plath wrote "Burning the Letters" on the other side of the page upon which she had typed Hughes's **"The Thought-Fox."** Van Dyne speculates that this was no accident (38), that Plath's image of dogs "tearing a fox" to death (Plath, *Collected Poems* 205) was a rebuttal of Hughes's feelings about **"The Thought-Fox,"** which he made public during a 1961 BBC broadcast:

Long after I am gone, as long as a copy of the poem
exists, every time anyone reads it the fox will get up
somewhere out in the darkness and come walking
towards them. So, you see, in some ways my fox is
better than an ordinary fox. It will live forever, it will
never suffer from hunger or hounds. And I made it.
And all through imagining it clearly enough and finding the living words.

(*Poetry in the Making* 20-21)

Van Dyne's assertion is convincing, for by the time
Plath wrote "Burning the Letters" in August 1962, **"The
Thought-Fox"** had become Hughes's most famous
poem. It was the piece that established his reputation as
an animal poet, as someone who tracked his creatures
through his poems with the surefooted instinct of a
hunter.[4] It makes sense, then, that in a poem about the
destruction of her husband's "letters," Plath would
choose to respond or "talk back" to the poem Hughes
held most dear, the poem most emblematic of his major
themes.[5]

Although "Burning the Letters" supposedly constitutes
"an end" to Hughes's "writing" (*Collected Poems* 204),
it inaugurates a phase in which Plath borrows from
Hughes's poems, distorting both his voice and images
to fashion her own art. She again answers back to
Hughes in "Ariel," a poem that has come to be associated with her struggle to achieve independence from the
many "fathers"—Ted Hughes, Otto Plath, the male
modernist tradition, the patriarchy, etc.—out of whose
shadow she struggled to emerge. Plath's "arrow" in
"Ariel," as Van Dyne has noted (123), is an inversion
of the same image mentioned in both *The Bell Jar* and
her *Journals,* in which man is the arrow, woman the
bow.[6] In "Ariel," the female speaker becomes the arrow,
ignoring her "child's cry" in her single-minded pursuit
of transcendence. Yet "Ariel" is less concerned with
"the fiery transubstantiation of the female subject," as
Van Dyne has suggested (119), than it is with the act of
writing itself. During this time, Plath awoke around 4
A.M., after her sleeping pills wore off, and wrote until
her two children awoke. "Ariel" is a record of those
inspired hours during which she was suddenly able to
write the poems that, as she told her mother, would
make her name (*Letters Home* 468). The fact that Plath
positions her speaker in a quiet room, presumably a
study, sitting before a window as the sun rises and her
child wakes, suggests that the poem is a comment upon
the imaginative ascent engendered by poetic inspiration:
her speaker's journey upon Ariel parallels Plath's
creation of the poem itself.

Much of the critical commentary regarding "Ariel"
emphasizes its "hurtling velocity" (Van Dyne 120), and
seems to insist that the poem somehow wrote itself, that
Plath is, in the words of Tim Kendall, "an oracular poet
writing as if taking dictation" (206). Yet there is reason

to believe that Plath's composition was as considered as
it was inspired. Plath's friends reported that Ariel, the
horse Plath rode at her local riding stable, was a far cry
from the svelte mare in the poem (Middlebrook 192);
Anne Stevenson went so far as to call the horse
"elderly" (272). Nor was Plath herself an experienced
rider—according to Kate Moses, who interviewed
Plath's riding teacher, she was not skilled enough to
gallop in October of 1962 (Middlebrook 327). Most
likely, then, Plath imagined, rather than recalled, her
wild ride upon Ariel. What she may have in fact recalled
as she sat down to compose was a poem by Hughes
entitled **"Phaetons,"** published five years before
"Ariel," in 1957:

Angrier, angrier, suddenly the near-madman
In mid-vehemence rolls back his eye
And lurches to his feet—

Under each sense the other four hurtle and thunder
Under the skull's front the horses of the sun

The gentle reader in his silent room
Loses the words in mid-sentence—

The world has burned away beneath his book
A tossing upside-down team drags him on fire
Among the monsters of the zodiac.

(***Collected Poems*** 33)

Hughes's poem, like Plath's, draws upon the myth of
Phaethon, mentioned (among other places) in Plato's
Timaeus. In the story, Phaethon asks his mother about
the identity of his father and discovers, to his amaze-
ment, that he is the son of the sun-god Helios. Doubtful
about his legitimacy, he immediately sets out to find
Helios in order to question him face to face. When Helios reassures him that they are, in fact, father and son,
Phaethon demands further proof and asks if he may ride
Helios's sun-chariot through the heavens. Helios, in a
moment of indulgence, agrees, only to realize suddenly
that Phaethon is not strong enough to control the powerful sun-horses who draw the chariot. He asks Phaethon
not to go, but when Phaethon refuses, Helios implores
him to take the middle path through the heavens so as
not to plunge the earth into fire or ice. Phaethon takes
off and discovers too late that his father was right: he is
not strong enough to control the chariot. The horses
veer from the middle path, scorching the earth with fire
when they ride too low, freezing the land and ocean
when they ride too high. A distressed Zeus looks on and
decides he must put an end to the catastrophic ride, and
so he destroys the chariot, and Phaethon, with a
thunderbolt.

Stylistically, "Ariel" and **"Phaetons"** are quite different, although it may be worth noting that both attempt
to build momentum through the frequent use of enjambment, while both also use dashes to halt that

momentum at times. Plath is more interested in responding to the Phaethon story itself, or at least to Hughes's version of it. Hughes's poem is about a reader who is presumably so engrossed in the tale of Phaethon's wild ride that he imagines himself being dragged away, into another realm, by the powerful sun-horses. In "Ariel," however, Plath's speaker *is* Phaethon. Indeed, she could not be more different than Hughes's "gentle" reader. She is in control of her own words, while Hughes's reader is swept away by someone else's. Plath's speaker focuses so intently on her journey that she ignores her child's cry; Hughes's reader, on the other hand, distractedly loses his words "in mid-sentence." Although both are transformed by the poem's end, those transformations are quite different: Hughes's speaker becomes disoriented and loses his grip on reality, while Plath's harnesses the energy of her imaginary "sun-horse" and uses that energy to propel her to the poem's conclusive end. Whereas Hughes's speaker resembles a victim, Plath's is more like a predator; where he is passive, she is active.

Why might Plath have chosen to echo Hughes's poem, and the Phaethon myth, in "Ariel"? Phaethon's story touches upon ideas of authority, legitimacy, rebellion, and hubris that may have interested Plath at this time. Phaethon takes the sun-chariot because he needs to prove to himself that he is indeed his father's son, and thus capable of steering the wild horses; however, he rebels from his father's authority when he refuses to acknowledge that he is too weak to control the chariot. Plath may have been toying with this idea in "Ariel," fashioning herself as the rebellious and unruly daughter determined to show off her poetic skill to her literary fathers, including Ted Hughes. Yet, unlike Phaethon, Plath's speaker remains in control of her metaphorical sun-horse even up to the moment of annihilation; importantly for Plath, that moment is "suicidal"—willed rather than ordained. She has, in fact, outwitted Zeus's thunderbolt. It seems as if Plath's speaker delights in veering from "the middle path" here, that she is in some way provoking her poetic fathers by writing poetry that will embrace extremity rather than moderation.

"Ariel" also alludes to Hughes's **"The Thought-Fox."** Indeed, "Ariel" borrows so much from Hughes's poem that one must, at least, indulge the idea that Plath is in some way answering back to her husband as she did in "Burning the Letters." Although Plath wrote "Ariel" quickly, there is no doubt that she thought carefully about its construction (*Letters Home* 466). As Van Dyne points out, there are three handwritten drafts in the Smith archive; in the first draft, she says, most of the poem is written out in full sentences, but by the third, Plath has cut the lines in half (126). Again, as in "Burning the Letters," Plath skillfully manipulates poetic technique, methodically constructing her lines to achieve the desired effect of speed, an effect, says Van

Dyne, through which Plath "progressively obliterates the distance and difference between the speaker and the animal energy of her horse" (119). Such "animal energy," as Plath well knew, was what characterized Hughes's greatest poems: in **"The Thought-Fox," "The Jaguar," "Hawk Roosting,"** and **"Thrushes,"** Hughes strives to use language that will reveal how animals are "triggered to stirrings beyond sense" (*Collected Poems* 82). His are poems in which the instincts of the animal are heightened by the sense that the poet, too, is acting upon instinct as he writes. This is how he described the writing process in a 1961 BBC broadcast: "The special kind of excitement, the slightly mesmerized and quite involuntary concentration with which you make out the stirrings of a new poem in your mind [. . .]. This is hunting and the poem is a new species of creature, a new specimen of the life outside your own" (*Poetry in the Making,* 17). Such an idea is, in fact, the basis of **"The Thought-Fox,"** in which the poet is led through the poem by the animal he tracks. Plath employed this same strategy in "Ariel" when she cut her lines to produce the illusion of speed and to emphasize the fusion of animal and poet; as in **"The Thought-Fox,"** the poet-speaker relies on the animal to guide her through the poem and ultimately lead her to its conclusion. Reading "Ariel" alongside **"The Thought-Fox"** strengthens the idea that Plath's signature poem is deeply concerned with poetic inspiration and the act of writing, rather than the destruction and creation of an unfettered (or ungendered) self.

From the outset of both "Ariel" and **"The Thought-Fox,"** Plath and Hughes invoke symbolic animals to guide them on their journey across the blank page. Ariel is both the name of Plath's horse and Shakespeare's mischievous spirit, while Hughes's thought-fox is a function of his imagination; both become linked, throughout the course of their respective poems, to creativity. It is also worth noting that each poem begins in darkness: Hughes's opens on "midnight's moment" (*Collected Poems* 21) while Plath's first line is "stasis in darkness" (*Collected Poems* 239). Although this darkness defines a natural landscape—for Hughes a forest, for Plath "tor and distances" (239)—the poets are not actually situated in these landscapes but inside a room, writing. This fact is made explicit in **"The Thought-Fox,"** in which the speaker describes himself "Beside the clock's loneliness / And this blank page where my fingers move" (21). In "Ariel" we do not discover this detail until Plath writes of the child's cry sounding through the wall, suggesting that the speaker has been, like Hughes's, alone in the act of writing—possibly also sitting before a "blank page" watching her fingers move.

The darkness in the first line of each poem is literal: Hughes's speaker writes at midnight, Plath's just before dawn. Yet this darkness is also figurative in that it represents for both poets the stasis of the imagination in the moment before creation. Hughes emphasizes this idea in his second stanza, in which the star, emblematic of celestial guidance, fails to appear and provide the poet with a clear sense of direction:

> Through the window I see no star:
> Something more near
> Though deeper within darkness
> Is entering the loneliness:
>
> (21)

The poet must look inward rather than outward in order to find direction for his words; this vague, enigmatic force that will guide the poet on his internalized journey is described in the first stanza as "something else" and in the second stanza as "something near." Plath uses the same word in "Ariel" to describe the mysterious force that sets her mind (as well as her body and horse) racing:

> Something else
> Hauls me through air—
>
> (239)

In both poems, the use of the word "something" relates both to poetic inspiration and to the imagined animal that leads the poet to the source of the poem deep inside the self. Both the fox and the horse, then, serve similar purposes—they represent "something else" that allows the poets to move beyond the "midnight's moment" or "stasis in darkness" in which there is "no star" to guide them. The phrase "something else" is noteworthy for its appropriate vagueness: it speaks to the impossibility of literally naming the force which drives the poem, and suggests that the protean nature of poetic inspiration can be captured only through metaphor. The force is a wild animal in motion, shape-shifting throughout the course of each poem (here a horse, there an arrow), eluding both reader and writer who seek to capture its essence. The poet is, in "Ariel," only along for the ride. That Plath, like Hughes, would also choose the words "something else" to describe the force that drives her speaker's writing seems more conscious than coincidental.

There are other ways in which Plath seems to be responding to **"The Thought Fox."** Like Hughes's fox, Plath's horse is "a body that is bold to come / Across clearings" (Hughes, *Collected Poems,* 21). Both poems follow similar trajectories: like **"The Thought Fox,"** which begins in a midnight forest, expands into a "widening, deepening greenness," then contracts again to a "hole of the head" (21), "Ariel" moves from stasis to the more expansive "tor and distances" to finally contract into the "red eye" of the rising sun (239). There is the sense in both poems that this trajectory has given the poets the momentum to break through a barrier: for

Hughes the moment occurs when the fox "enters the dark hole of the head," while Plath's speaker aims straight into the sun. In each case, the deepest corners of the imagination have been penetrated.

Both poets also play with the word "eye." In each poem, the eye stands outside the poet's domain, looking in, as it were. Hughes's speaker first imagines the "two eyes" of the thought-fox outside his window, then later spies "an eye" again as the fox comes into his room (21). Plath's red eye, the "cauldron of morning"—that is, the sun—also rises outside the writer's window (240). There is something almost oracular about these "eyes"— not only do they allow each speaker to see into the creative process, both lead the poet towards his or her ultimate vision. Hughes's speaker will follow the thought-fox to its end on the printed page, while Plath's finds fulfillment by aiming straight into the rising sun. In each case, the writer achieves his or her vision with the aid of this allseeing "eye," one which works in conjunction with the writer's self, that is, his or her "I." As symbols of the racing mind in the process of creation, these roving eyes stand in contrast to the "stasis in darkness" out of which each speaker struggles to emerge. It is perhaps no coincidence that both speakers position themselves before a window—another device that allows them to see beyond the confines of the room, and, by extension, the bounded self.

Plath's invocation of Lady Godiva may also have been a way of answering back to Hughes, since Lady Godiva's decision to ride naked on her horse through the streets of Coventry was prompted by her husband's dare. Plath may have imagined herself enacting a similar dare in "Ariel," stepping up to an imaginary poetic challenge from Hughes and proving to him that in her metaphoric nakedness she is empowered rather than humiliated. Such a move relates to Plath's decision to "bare all" in poems such as "Lady Lazarus" and "Daddy," where she subverts the power of her interrogators and torturers by confessing what she has suffered under their custody. Thus, like Lady Godiva, Plath dignifies what might otherwise be understood as humiliating—discussing a botched suicide attempt, for example, in "Lady Lazarus."

Plath's galloping horse also subtly mocks Hughes's slinking fox. Horses are larger, stronger, and faster than foxes; by analogy, Plath's poem will merit the same kind of comparison to Hughes's. Hers is the stronger of the two, the one with the more intensely rhythmic momentum, the more resounding final crescendo. Unlike Hughes's speaker, Plath's will not wait passively for the poem to sneak into the mind; she will ride after it (or ride with it) as an active participant in the creative process. Hers is the more daring of the two speakers, the one more willing to take physical risks. Whereas Hughes's fox displays what could crudely be called female characteristics—it is timid, quiet, moves "delicately" while setting "neat prints" on the snow (21)—Plath's horse, although referred to as "God's lioness," displays stereotypically male characteristics of strength, agility, speed, and recklessness (239). When we consider that Plath's self-identification with the shooting arrow was meant, at some level, to undermine the docile, sexist platitudes of women like Mrs. Willard in *The Bell Jar,* and that the speaker of "Ariel" is a working mother who ignores her child's cry in order to finish her poem, it seems likely that the galloping, jumping mare also works to mock the culturally imposed confines of gender. Plath's poems, as Marianne Moore lamented, were not decorous; at any moment they could rise up, throw the reader off, and pursue their own course. Hers were poems that could not be tamed. Plath's use of a horse, then, as opposed to a fox, was just one more way of suggesting that her poems were "indefatigable hoof-taps" (Plath, *Collected Poems* 270) as opposed to Hughes's "neat prints."

Finally, it is likely that "Ariel" was influenced by another Hughes poem, **"The Horses,"** from **The Hawk in the Rain.** Both poems begin at "the hour-before-dawn dark" (Hughes, **Collected Poems,** 23) in a formless landscape where the color of the air and sky are indistinguishable. The mood changes when the sun rises and Hughes's speaker sees the horses in the valley below, "steaming and glistening under the flow of light" (23). The speaker becomes exuberant and runs toward them, "Stumbling in the fever of a dark dream" (23). He has emerged out of darkness, into the light, out of stillness into motion. Such a progression may have influenced "Ariel," in which the speaker begins at a similar point of "stasis in darkness," then gathers momentum as the sun rises. In both poems, the rising sun is a catalyst for transcendence; both speakers are transformed in the moments between night and day. In **"The Horses,"** the speaker "erupts" as the sun emerges out of the dark—"Orange, red, red erupted" (23)—while the sunrise in "Ariel" causes the speaker to shape-shift into weightless, ethereal substances that allow her to ascend into "the red eye." And, needless to say, horses play a central role in each speaker's moment of transcendence, carrying them from one realm to another. Plath's horse, however, is a far cry from Hughes's horses, who "made no sound. / Not one snorted or stamped, / Their hung heads patient as the horizons" (23). Where Hughes's speaker hopes he will be able to recapture the moment ("In din of crowded streets . . . / May I still meet my memory in so lonely a place" [24]) Plath's speaker *becomes* the moment. Again, where Hughes is passive, Plath is active.

Not all of Plath's horses engage in one-upmanship with Hughes, however. Plath's "Sheep in Fog" also describes a horse ride, but here the speaker's mood is defeatist rather than triumphant; as Tim Kendall has written, "the

hope of rebirth has disappeared, to be replaced by resignation" (190). Like "Ariel," this poem was presumably inspired by an early morning ride on a horse over the North Tawton landscape, but this time the mood is deathly somber:

> The hills step off into whiteness.
> People or stars
> Regard me sadly, I disappoint them.
>
> (*Collected Poems* 262)

Plath introduced the poem on a BBC program in January 1963, saying, "In this poem, the speaker's horse is proceeding at a slow, cold walk down a hill of macadam to the stable at the bottom. It is December. It is foggy. In the fog there are sheep" (*Collected Poems* 295). Her emotionless description mirrors the benumbed state of the speaker, who has lost the will to live. Plath no longer uses enjambment to create the illusion of motion; here the horse's slow walk is emphasized by at least two end-pauses in every stanza. As Kendall has noted, the exuberant repetition that characterized the earlier *Ariel* poems is gone, as are the question marks and the exclamation points (192). The tone now is flat, dulled. The only striking use of internal assonance and consonance comes in the last line of the poem, in which the siren song of the soft vowels in "starless," "fatherless," "dark," and "water" tempts the speaker ever closer to the abyss (262).

One cannot help but notice that the tone of "Sheep in Fog" echoes the first few stanzas of Hughes's **"The Horses."** Plath's poem embraces a static world in which the speaker resists the imaginative leap of "Ariel"— vision, both literal and figurative, is shrouded in fog. Thus Hughes's depiction of a still, remote landscape where the air is "evil," the light is "iron," and the morning is "cast in frost" may have appealed to Plath that January—suddenly his "grey silent world" (Hughes, **Collected Poems,** 23) seemed much more hospitable than it had in October, when she had escaped "stasis in darkness" on Ariel. In "Sheep in Fog," however, Plath's dawn world is, like Hughes's, cold and desolate, the "flower left out" (262); the mention of rust suggests decay, while the train reminds one of other trains in *Ariel,* bound for a dark destination.[7] Likewise, "dolorous bells" and the double reference to "morning" (mourning) further prepare the reader for the final stanza, in which the speaker ponders the lure of her own death (262). Plath's line "My bones hold a stillness" (262), suggests Hughes's "frost-making stillness" (23), while Plath's second stanza—"The train leaves a line of breath. / O slow / Horse the color of rust" (262)—also seems to owe its imagery to Hughes's line, "Where my breath left tortuous statues in the iron light" (23). Plath's "All morning / The morning has been blackening" (262) echoes Hughes's "blackening dregs of the brightening grey" (23), while her "far fields" appear to be a version of Hughes's moors. Whereas in "Ariel" and **"The Horses"** the scene gradually brightens, the morning only blackens in "Sheep in Fog," the "heaven" at the poem's end suggesting none of the brightness or redemptive beauty of the sunrise in **"The Horses"** or "Ariel." Plath's speaker now resembles Hughes's in **"Phaetons,"** dragged into an equally dark "heaven" by forces beyond her control.

In a lecture originally delivered to the Wordsworth Trust in 1988, Hughes revealed that in earlier drafts of "Sheep in Fog" Plath had again made use of the Phaethon myth. In her first draft she had written, "The world rusts around us / Ribs, spokes, a scrapped chariot," and then, four lines later, "I am a scrapped chariot" (*Winter Pollen* 195); Plath also refers, in the same draft, to the body of the fallen Phaethon as "a dead man left out" (195). Such lines highlight the flight and fall trajectory from "Ariel" to "Sheep in Fog;" as Kendall has written, the movement from one poem to another "is the movement from the red heat of Phaethon's life-affirming, self-destructive adventure to its wrecked and somber aftermath" (192). Yet these lines, ultimately rejected, also reveal the extent to which Plath may have intended to comment upon her poetic rivalry with Hughes. The rebellious daughter who attempted to prove her legitimacy in "Ariel" now seems less confident about her ability to master the poetic forces she had harnessed so skillfully only a few months earlier. Hughes himself suggested as much when he described how "quite suddenly, the *Ariel* inspiration has changed. The astonishing, sustained, soaring defiance of the previous eight weeks has suddenly failed. Or rather has reversed" (*Winter Pollen* 198).

"Sheep in Fog" is a kind of anti-"Ariel," but not for the reasons Hughes suggests. Hughes says Plath's invocation of the Phaethon myth in "Ariel" was partly "an attempt to soar (plunge) into the inspirational form of her inaccessible father" (201). He emphasizes this claim in his analysis of "Sheep in Fog," in which he suggests that Plath's reference to Phaethon's dead body is also "the spirit that was also her resurrected father" (202). He touches upon this idea several times in this essay, writing that "In the poem 'Ariel' she had fused her heart—her whole being—into the sun's red eyes, as a triumphant Phaeton reaching her Father" (206) and, later, that "Sheep in Fog" was an attempt "to deal with terrible news about her father and her fateful bond with him (such as she feels stirring again here more frighteningly than ever)" (210). He even goes so far as to suggest that "the body of her father" was "the Chrysalis" of the *Ariel* voice (202). Hughes here makes clear (and would again make clear in **Birthday Letters**) that his interpretation of *Ariel* rested upon Plath's obsession with Otto Plath rather than her feelings of marital betrayal. "Sheep in Fog," with its dark vision of a "fatherless" heaven, supported Hughes's thesis; this is

why, as Bundtzen suggests, he chose to include it in his version of *Ariel* (103-4).[8]

Needless to say, Hughes did not interpret the reference to the father at the end of "Sheep in Fog" as a reference to himself, nor does he ever mention that Plath's images of Phaethon might allude to his own poem concerning the myth. Yet the image of Phaethon's wrecked chariot (uncovered by none other than Hughes himself) suggests that perhaps "Sheep in Fog" was Plath's way of saying that her attempt to prove her own legitimacy in the face of her poetic father (Hughes, not Otto Plath) came at too high a cost. Indeed, if we are to read the poem in the context of Plath's rivalry with Hughes, we might wonder whether Plath's image of Phaethon's dead body was a comment upon her perceived failure to achieve the poetic end she desired. The profound feeling of resignation that marks the poem may be due to Plath's anxieties that Hughes would forever remain ahead of her, poetically. Indeed, one of her frequent complaints to her mother in late 1962 and early 1963 is that Hughes's fame has skyrocketed while she has been left to languish in obscurity, on her own, with two babies. As Plath's mental health worsened, such resentment, which had earlier fueled her rage, now became a measure of defeat. For if "Ariel" is an attempt to forge a poetic self and a poetic method distinct from Hughes's, then "Sheep in Fog" suggests that for Plath the attempt has been futile, that the loss of the poetic father was not worth the wild ride upon his borrowed chariot.

Notes

1. "We are amazingly compatible. But I must be myself—make myself & not let myself be made by him" (*Journals,* 401).

2. Although Uroff has undertaken extensive intertextual analysis of Plath's and Hughes's work, she does not examine, as I do in this essay, Hughes's influence on Plath's "Ariel" and "Sheep in Fog." Middlebrook has also briefly addressed Hughes's influence, insisting that *Ariel* was "aimed at Hughes" (218). She recognizes that Plath's original *Ariel* manuscript contained forty-one poems, the same number in Hughes's *Lupercal,* and posits that the word "Ariel" was an echo of "Lupercal" (218). See also Paul Bentley's "'Hitler's Familiar Spirits': Negative Dialectics in Sylvia Plath's 'Daddy' and Ted Hughes's 'Hawk Roosting.'"

3. Van Dyne writes that Plath's poem "defies Hughes's visionary equation of his own poetic genius with the mysterious powers of nature" (41) while Roberts has claimed that Plath finds "something troubling about [. . .] [Hughes's] confidence that the poem is immortal" (167).

4. "The Thought-Fox" was published in the *New Yorker* in August 1957 (ten months before Plath's first *New Yorker* acceptance), and, in 1958, it received the Guinness Award, a substantial cash prize awarded to best poem published in Britain that year.

5. Lynda Bundtzen insists that in "Burning the Letters," Plath was writing a poetic manifesto, declaring that the (female) confessional cry ultimately trumps (male) modernist artifice. Yet it is debatable whether Plath was self-consciously reacting against the male modernist aesthetic in this poem, replacing Hughes's "'high' culture version of literary immortality with something literal, real, and downright low" (Bundtzen 55). On the contrary, it is clear Plath put much thought into the formal shape of this poem; she is deliberately playing with the sonnet form. Plath is not rejecting Hughes's 'high' formalism so much as she is responding with an artifice of her own, an artifice that seems very much at odds with the "crude and sensational" (53) confessionalism Bundtzen sees as both the poem's defining aesthetic and its ideological position.

6. Plath may also be slyly alluding to one of Hughes's early reviews, in which the reviewer referred to Hughes's poems "as direct as an arrow from a bow" (Seymour).

7. Kendall notes that "Daddy," "Metaphors," "Getting There," "Totem," and "Sheep in Fog" all employ "sinister" train metaphors (176).

8. Plath did not include "Sheep in Fog" in her final *Ariel* manuscript, a gesture which suggests she may have been aware that the poem undermined the collection's intended narrative of rebirth. She may in fact have agreed with Hughes's assessment that the poem was "the epitaph and funeral cortege of the whole extraordinary adventure dramatized in the poems of *Ariel*" (*Winter Pollen*, 207). For a detailed analysis of Plath's original *Ariel* manuscript see Marjorie Perloff's "The Two *Ariels*: The (Re)Making of the Sylvia Plath Canon."

Works Cited

Bentley, Paul. "'Hitler's Familiar Spirits': Negative Dialectics in Sylvia Plath's 'Daddy' and Ted Hughes's 'Hawk Roosting.'" *Critical Survey* 12.3 (2000): 27-38.

Bundtzen, Lynda K. *The Other Ariel*. Amherst: U of Massachusetts P, 2001.

Hughes, Ted. *Poetry in the Making: An Anthology of Poems and Programmes from* Listening and Writing. London: Faber & Faber, 1967.

———. *Collected Poems*. New York: Farrar, Straus & Giroux, 2003.

———. *Winter Pollen*. New York: Picador, 1995.

———, and Sylvia Plath. "Two of a Kind: Poets in Partnership." Interview with Owen Leeming. *Third Program*. British Broadcasting Corporation, London, England. 18 Jan. 1961. National Sound Archives, British Library.

Kendall, Tim. *Sylvia Plath: A Critical Study*. London: Faber & Faber, 2001.

Middlebrook, Diane. *Her Husband: Hughes and Plath—A Marriage*. New York: Viking Press, 2003.

Perloff, Marjorie. "The Two *Ariels*: The (Re)Making of the Sylvia Plath Canon." *Poems in Their Place: The Intertextuality and Order of Poetic Collections*. Ed. Neil Fraistat. Chapel Hill: U of North Carolina P, 1986. 308-33.

Plath, Sylvia. *Collected Poems*. Ed. Ted Hughes. London: Faber & Faber, 1981.

———. *The Journals of Sylvia Plath, 1950-1962*. Ed. Karen Kukil. London: Faber & Faber, 2000.

———. *Letters Home*. Ed. Aurelia Plath. 1978. London: Faber & Faber, 1999.

Roberts, Neil. "The Common Text of Sylvia Plath and Ted Hughes." *Symbiosis* 7.1 (2003): 157-173.

Rose, Jacqueline. *The Haunting of Sylvia Plath*. London: Virago, 1991.

Seymour, William Kean. "To Note and To Observe." *Poetry Review* January 1958. OP 103. Ted Hughes Papers. Special Collections Archive, Emory University.

Stevenson, Anne. *Bitter Fame: A Life of Sylvia Plath*. New York: Penguin, 1998.

Ryan Hibbett (essay date winter 2005)

SOURCE: Hibbett, Ryan. "Imagining Ted Hughes: Authorship, Authenticity, and the Symbolic Work of *Collected Poems*." *Twentieth Century Literature* 51, no. 4 (winter 2005): 414-36.

[*In the following essay, Hibbett recaps Hughes's ever-changing literary reputation and comments on the relationship between his tumultuous personal life and his legacy as a poet.*]

Ted Hughes's recently published ***Collected Poems*** runs 1331 pages, the table of contents alone taking 29. It sits impressively on your local Barnes and Noble or Borders poetry shelf, cover facing out—the British counterpart to another hefty 2003 publication by Farrar, Straus, and

Giroux, the *Collected Poems* of Robert Lowell.[1] On the cover, a cross-legged, semireclined Hughes gazes absently away from the camera. Whatever his concerns are, they do not appear to be his immediate surroundings; his slightly parted lips are those of one deep in thought, lost in his own world. He is the inaccessible subject, the mystified poet (how we'd like to know what he's thinking!). Near the bottom of the photograph, where Hughes's large hands gently commune, a wedding band catches a bit of light: Hughes the husband is here as well.

Today "Ted Hughes" is an extraordinarily loaded sign, the meaning of which will vary depending on the knowledge one brings to it. We might see the sexy, virile Hughes—the one reported by A. Alvarez to have made women "weak in the knees" on eye contact (qtd. in Malcolm 120), pictured here in open blazer, no tie, his thick head of hair swept haphazardly over and growing wildly around his ear. We might see the tortured artist, wrongly blamed for Sylvia Plath's death and demonized as the oppressive male—a callous brute in the Hemingway tradition, hyperbolized (again by Alvarez) as having gone "through swaths of women, like a guy harvesting corn" (212). We might see the warm and sympathetic figure from Elaine Feinstein's biography or the bloodsucking double of Plath's "Daddy." Not to mention Hughes the destroyer of Plath's journals, Hughes the unfaithful husband, or the powerless, star-crossed Hughes of *Birthday Letters.* We might even see England's former poet laureate, or the author of such well-known works as **"The Thought-Fox," "Thistles,"** and *Crow.* Even the academically invested, approaching the book with specialized knowledge, are likely to bring with them a set of associations, if not judgments and strong feelings, stemming from the popular discourse surrounding Hughes's personal life—things that academics are not supposed to be concerned with, though they have become such an inextricable part of Hughes's cultural legacy that even the most diplomatic explicator of his poetry cannot leave them unaccounted for.

It is a poetry collection's job, we might think, to suppress everything extraneous to the poetry itself, even when such things contribute to the book's market value.[2] The collection completes, confirms, and finalizes a writer's identity as a poet, promising not only that its contents all belong exclusively to the singular entity on its cover but also that the author's stature is such that it warrants their being collectively published. Nonetheless, the image on the cover of *Collected Poems* captures something of Hughes's split identity as a creator of poems on the one hand and a product of the popular imagination on the other. The photograph, taken in 1979 by Noel Chanan, renders neither the dashing young genius of the Sylvia Plath years nor the stouter, white-haired poet laureate. This Hughes falls somewhere

in between: he has the sobered, reflective look of one who has suffered and who possesses a special wisdom because of that suffering. The photo avoids the kind of humanizing, direct subject-to-viewer connection established when a subject looks straight into the camera. Hughes is not interacting with his public or with the medium that will publicly represent him but is held aloof from our gaze—aestheticized in black-and-white print, as another's subject matter. We look contemplatively at Hughes, who looks elsewhere, contemplating. The author is suspended somewhere in between, untouchable, with only his ring to ground him socially (and even that, for Hughes, is a mythically charged sign).

Approaching the author less as an individual personality than as a site where meaning is constructed, this essay will bear the influence of Michel Foucault. His highly influential critique of authorship, "What Is an Author?" hardly needs rehearsing, except to rearticulate that the way we understand authors and their works is historically and socially contingent, and necessarily implicated in negotiations of power and knowledge. The prevalence of these ideas as an intellectual phenomenon, however, does not necessarily translate into new practices.[3] Models of authorship based on collaboration and intertextuality, for example, remain largely at odds with the prevailing ideologies informing such regulatory and authoritative practices as copyright law and literary publication.[4] Certainly the field that we might call mainstream British poetry continues to elude the author-effacing measures of poststructural analysis, an approach well equipped for investigating the complex processes at work in Ted Hughes's erratic and sometimes volatile reception.

Equally important to this essay are Pierre Bourdieu's ideas concerning the circulation of literary knowledge as cultural capital, or the kind of specialized knowledge that may be used toward the ends of social classification and distinction, and which allows a set of culturally learned preferences to function as taste (*Distinction* 2). Bourdieu permits us to examine those places where Ted Hughes enters a preexisting cultural opposition, such as that between popular culture and high art, as a symbolic form of currency. Clearly more than one discursive formation lays claim to Hughes, in part because of his dramatically troubled life but also because his assimilation as a "great poet" coincides with an intellectual climate of skepticism regarding authorship in its conventional forms and uses. Currently suspended in a flux of posthumous publications, just seven years after the wave-making pronouncement of *Birthday Letters* and the poet's subsequent death, Hughes represents "the author" in an unusually heightened state of negotiation. As Bourdieu explains, "The literary or artistic field is a *field of forces,* but it is also a *field of struggles* tending to transform or conserve this field of forces" (*Field* 30); through Hughes we may encounter the tectonic rumblings of poetry itself as it responds to a changing and often unaccommodating environment, and *Collected Poems* is no doubt a major force in such phenomena. Finally, because Hughes is one of few (if any) candidates in line for a place among the undisputed giants of twentieth-century British poetry, what befalls him may tell us something about the future of British poetry.

While using *Collected Poems* as an occasion to rethink Hughes's place in English poetry, this article aims to shed light on the processes through which "great writers" are produced. Toward this end I have made the conversations about Hughes's creative work, not just the work itself, my object of analysis, and hope to reveal by navigating between the two a struggle for authenticity between competing yet interdependent structures of meaning. After providing an overview of Hughes's rather beleaguered career, this article will (1) examine the reviews and comments that greeted *Collected Poems* as an occasion for reestablishing cultural boundaries and reaffirming the "the poet" as a cultural authority, (2) consider Hughes's place in a lineage of "great English poets" to which he is currently being assimilated and for which he provides a measure of continuity, and (3) examine some of Hughes's publication practices and recent poetry as they figure into and are transformed by these larger contexts. At the intersection of these practices and negotiations, and in the face of the ordering tendencies of literary production, one can begin to see a Ted Hughes who is neither here nor there but disseminated across the various boundaries of literary production.

Hughes's career has been embattled by a grievous effort to separate his personal life from his creative work and to lend poetry an independent, even organic life. "I think of poems as a sort of animal," he writes.

> They have their own life, like animals, by which I mean that they seem quite separate from any person, even from their author, and nothing can be added to them or taken away without maiming and perhaps even killing them.
>
> (*Winter* 10)

In addition to giving poetry an animate, pretextual existence, this quotation, reprinted on the inside sleeve of *Collected Poems,* suggests that poems are willed into being exactly as they are, and, in that sense, are of the most sovereign authority. At the same time, it characterizes poetry as fragile—in danger of disappearing at the slightest intervention—and binds Hughes's exaltations to intense anxieties regarding the cultural status of his work. Like his modernist predecessors, Hughes bears a burden of self-validation; his entire career can be seen as a monumental effort to "prove poetry," not as the

institutionalized cultural practice he was in fact bound to but as a simultaneously mystical and biological energy which the poet aims to tap into. Everything else—author, reader, and text alike—is subordinated to this primal creative energy.

For Hughes, such an effort proved impossible to sustain. The nearly posthumous publication of *Birthday Letters* was largely a product of external pressures—the infiltration of popular discourse and autobiographical material into the sanctified space of poetry. The tragedies in Hughes's personal life have, in a roundabout way, spotlighted "the author" as an unstable concept where a host of communal myths and identities may be realized: in the demonstrative discourse surrounding Ted Hughes, among the various and often opposing efforts to represent him, we may begin to see the author as a free-floating signifier, the meaning of which is quite beyond Hughes's own or anyone else's control, the product of competing interests. In short, the myth maker has become the myth—and his own laggard participation in the conversation throws into question the autonomy of his creative work. Hughes's *Collected Poems,* which ostensibly acts as a neutralized site where poetry may transcend the circumstances of its production and is given sanctity from the corruptive influence of competing interests, can only pretend to exist independently of that other, equally mythic Ted Hughes, the very presence of which challenges the value of his poetry. It can, however, argue poetry as the proper testing ground, or resting place, of our conjectures: the cover image gives way to the text inside.

Reviews indicate that *Collected Poems* is, for many, a welcome counterthrust to what is perceived as a threatening and invasive interest in Hughes's personal life. In this sense, Farrar's massive collection snuffs out the hearsay and gossip, returning us to what Carol Bere calls "the real thing" ("Knot" 23), meaning the poetry, where Hughes's essence and value are genuinely located; distractions aside, it is hoped, we can get back to the proper business of appraising Hughes's talents and evaluating his place in the British literary tradition. "The effort in this volume," explains John Kinsella, "is to show Hughes's mastery over a lifetime, and to place him at the top of the first rank of poets."

In its still-fresh reception history, *Collected Poems* is repeatedly placed in direct contention with popular representations of Ted Hughes. Writes Simon Armitage:

> The story that this volume does not tell, mercifully, is the biography, and prior to the release in January [2003] of a film which casts Gwyneth Paltrow as Sylvia and some bloke you've never heard of as Ted, it is a blessed relief to think only of the work.

Similarly, James Parker remarks:

Collected Poems arrives in the same season as the biopic *Sylvia,* starring the rugged Daniel Craig as Hughes and Gwyneth Paltrow as Sylvia Plath, and Diane Middlebrook's *Her Husband* (Viking), an excavation of Ted and Sylvia's doomed marriage and poetic partnership.

"Can Hughes the poet escape these encrustations?" asks Parker; "The answer is yes." In all likelihood, those interested in *Sylvia* and Middlebrook's biographical work are among the same group interested in *Collected Poems,* but the commentary here would indicate a clear-cut cultural divide. It is as if the mere mention of a famous actress's name discredits the film as an authority on the subject, and points to a kind of cultural decline responsible for obscuring what really matters; citing Gwyneth Paltrow in an academic review suggests that something has gone wrong and positions *Collected Poems* as a badly needed corrective. The biographical industry, in turn, becomes a sphere in which the value of poetry is debased and misrepresented; popular or biographical representations are "encrustations"—limiting, fixing, and smothering the poet's identity—which the real Ted Hughes, restored by such a collection as that under review, may escape.

This dual sense of exasperation with a popular interest in Hughes and relief in being redirected to the poetry itself extends to other reviews as well. "Hughes," writes Bere, "risks being known for his biography rather than his poetry . . . but the recently published, excellent edition of his collected poems . . . should go some distance toward redressing the balance" ("Knot" 23). In his review, Sean O'Brien regrets that "gossip has displaced writing among the interests of many readers," but affirms, in Auden's phrase, that

> Hughes's gift "survived it all," and the *Collected Poems* demonstrates beyond reasonable doubt that Hughes was among the best English-language poets of the second half of the 20th century, vastly gifted and influential.

Thus *Collected Poems* represents an effort to fix Ted Hughes within the lineage of literary giants in a way that is unadulterated by his misdirected popularity.

But clearly more than Ted Hughes's reputation is at stake: important distinctions are being drawn between superior and inferior cultural practices, and arguments for cultural authority in the manufacturing of knowledge are being asserted. The reviews reflect at least a timidly pronounced sense of threat and serve as an opportunity to reaffirm not only an author's authenticity but that of an entire cultural institution. The same boundary lines were tended to following the publication of *Birthday Letters,* a text whose reception, more than its content, forced critics and scholars to either marginalize it from the corpus of Hughes's "legitimate" work, seeing its

popularity as a problem of taste,[5] or embrace it as a welcome change of pace in Hughes's otherwise monolithic oeuvre[6]—responses available, at least, to those not inclined to use it as new evidence in the case of Ted Hughes versus Sylvia Plath. Certainly its popularity created a problem for literature at the institutional level—an academically controlled field that relies, as Bourdieu would say, on a lack of popularity and economic reward to sustain its uniquely symbolic breed of value (*Field* 39-40). *Collected Poems* is less disruptive than *Birthday Letters* in this respect, as it appears clearly within one domain and not the other, and presents itself not as a marketed product but as an intellectual tool and cultural artifact—an effect achieved in part (as with any such collection) by crediting Hughes as author of a book whose contents are arranged by someone else, thus framing the collection as a presentation of what already exists rather than a construction of new knowledge and leading reviewers to comment appreciatively on the editor's unobtrusiveness.

Even while legitimizing Hughes's reputation, *Collected Poems* marks a transfer of agency from the author to the institutions responsible for and invested in maintaining that author's value. No longer at the receiving end of economic exchange, the author becomes a commodity serving the interests of others even as his work is further removed from any obvious relation to economic capital. Thus assimilated, Ted Hughes takes on a purely symbolic identity, secured within and serving the equally symbolic tradition of canonized literature. O'Brien's use of Auden is significant in that it links us to a tradition in which the representative poet of one generation (Yeats) is succeeded by another (Auden) and to a poem ("In Memory of W. B. Yeats") that symbolically transforms the dead poet into his poetry—the immortalized "it" that simply and independently "survives / In the valley of its making" (82). Auden's poem is as much a proof of poetry as an elegy for Yeats, and it hinges on a separation between the two: "Let the Irish vessel lie," he decrees, "Emptied of his poetry." While putting the poet to rest, Auden gives life to poetry as an autonomous and persevering essence free from the author's life and intentions ("You were silly like us" [81]), from political agency ("poetry makes nothing happen" [82]), from institutional meddling ("where executives / Would never want to tamper"), and from the social spaces that we "believe and die in." Free, even, of language itself, becoming finally a preverbal, biologically located essence, or "mouth." Auden's poem—ritualized in its final section by its incantatory meter and rhyme (a direct echo of Blake's "The Tiger")[7]—enacts a kind of sacrificial rite in which the poet is immortalized only by surrendering his identity to that of poetry itself; Yeats, so to speak, may persevere as "Yeats," a purely textual essence whose words, the poet half-laments, will be "modified in the guts of the living" (81). But what is naturalized by Auden as a kind of digestive process, through which the poet "becomes his admirers," also marks the less figurative consumption of a poet who has completed his transformation into a source of symbolic and economic capital.

It was T. S. Eliot who called Yeats "one of those few whose history is the history of their own time, who are part of the consciousness of an age which cannot be understood without them" (257). Already "Yeats," as Eliot austerely titles his essay, has assumed a stature of epic proportions; his history is history itself, and without him that history is incomprehensible. In commemorating Yeats, Auden betrays an awareness of his own position as next in line, and indeed becomes the cultural authority in Seamus Heaney's eulogy for Joseph Brodsky, "Audenesque." Heaney's simulation of Auden's (via Blake's) poem and meter places Heaney at the present end of a Yeats/Auden continuum and grounds that continuum in terms specific to poetic technique: "Joseph, yes, you know the beat. / Wystan Auden's metric feet / Marched to it, unstressed and stressed / Laying William Yeats to rest" (77). Auden's presence authorizes Heaney ("Do again what Auden said / Good poets do" [80]) to boldly undertake such tasks as addressing the deceased and defining a poet's job, just as Heaney's own growing prestige authorizes him to emulate Auden.

But Heaney, one might argue, has been situated more precisely than Yeats as an Irish, not necessarily British, writer, and Auden's departure to America opened a void in England's lineage of representative poets that neither Ted Hughes nor Philip Larkin (names with considerably less symbolic value than Yeats and Auden, especially in America) have adequately filled. Hughes and Larkin may in part have each other to thank for this, as neither has been able to shake the other from contention as "England's best,"[8] and each calls into question the other's form of poetry by offering a fundamentally opposed alternative to it. Additionally, the reputations of both have contended with shifting scholarly interests in which the discovery of new and marginalized voices takes priority over the maintenance of old ones, themselves approached more suspiciously than in the past. One might also argue, and some do, that the quality of British poetry has simply taken a nosedive since Auden.[9] But it seems likely that a lack of belief in what was once a stable and seemingly autonomous field of production has lessened the demand for literary "giants" and presented a set of conditions rendering Auden's vacated throne more or less unattainable.

Hughes's *Collected Poems* works against this trend. As a major collection from a major voice, it hooks us back into a tradition of literary greatness, beckoning us to see that tradition as a natural process by which such greatness achieves fruition. Auden's heir, so to speak, is made visible, given substance as a singular, complete, and collectible entity who in turn gives credence to an English tradition of great poets and provides evidence of that tradition's continuity. *Collected Poems* is the material with which one might resume construction of "British poetry," annexing Hughes to what is for many a crumbling structure, and begin to make order of that nebulous and unarticulated space beyond Auden. The concentration of Ted Hughes into a single artifact, unmatched in size (the moniker "Ted Huge" assumes new relevance), helps to extend one's mental configuration of British poetry, though not without narrowing its scope and potentially squeezing other writers from view. Its size alone separates Hughes from competitors, prompting Michael Hofmann to ask glibly, "What's the competition?" (278). Hofmann has swelled the stakes to "greatest English poet since Shakespeare," and in a list that includes Milton, Wordsworth, and Hardy, Larkin is added only with a parenthetical and skeptical "maybe." In O'Brien's review, the collection earns the distinction "essential" ("essential but unlovely" is O'Brien's exact phrase)—a designation that hints of ownership, of a text's or author's relevance to one's own cultural capital ("of the highest importance for achieving something," as the dictionary puts it) and characterizes the text as an essence, the pure embodiment or most basic element of something else, rather than a representation. The pretense is one of determining the relative importance and artistic merit of Ted Hughes's poetry—and O'Brien is in fact one of few reviewers to comment on the quantity of unimpressive poetry the collection makes available—but the very act of doing so is to substantiate an entire universe of belief: that there is a representable British poetic tradition, that its poets and their poems can be ranked; and beyond these, the assumptions that great poets are discovered not created, and that poetry itself is an authentic, autonomous, and ultimately necessary practice. Serious stuff, to be sure, and the unflinching seriousness that Ted Hughes brings to poetry makes him a champion of that universe of belief.

In his autobiographical essay "Poetry in the Making," Hughes speaks of poems as a mysterious "they" that possess a special knowledge that "we are very curious to learn" and have "a vivid life of their own, outside mine" (*Winter* 10). To endure as a reality, it would seem, poetry must be distinguished from the processes, people, and institutions that authorize and perpetuate it through discourse; even if no one reads it, writes it, or spends money on it, poetry must go on, we concede, secretly existing. Hughes has always presented himself as a protector of that secret life, more interested in poetry as a life force or energy than as a textual practice. When discussing poetry, his terminology is generally borrowed from some field of study—psychology, anthropology, mythology, physics, biology—not centered on language, taking particular care to set his own endeavors apart from what he sees as the destructive practice of literary criticism: "I have suspended scholarly disbelief," he writes, in what is actually a formally presented theory of Eliot's "poetic self," "and adopted the attitude of an interpretative, performing musician" (*Winter* 291).

Whether as music, animal, or part of the "elemental power circuit of the universe" (qtd. in Fass 9), poetry in Hughes's descriptions is always metaphorically transposed, made "real" through its manifestation as something else. Poetry for Hughes is hidden, submerged, antithetical to ordinary, conscious, or daily life, though in need of being reconciled with that life. His writing comprises an elaborate system of justification for poetry and poets, based less on pleasure than necessity. As did Larkin, Hughes struggled immensely to separate poetry from the institutions surrounding it and struggled with the hazards of identifying one's self above all else as a poet. In this light, any other potential role or identity was perceived as a threat. Having escaped college, where he learned to dissect poetry rather than write it, Hughes had to protect his calling (one gathers from *Birthday Letters,* in addition to other autobiographical material) against the demands of family life and, for a short time, against a culturally displaced life in America. Considering writers such as Hughes and Larkin, one cannot help but speculate that poetry remains since the romantic period bound to a desire for privacy and control, and that it supplies for some a means of self-protection if not self-preservation.

Despite his deferral to a muse in all things creative, Hughes put forth considerable effort to secure control over his work throughout the processes of production and distribution, exercising what Paul Keegan, referring to one of Hughes's small, family-run presses, calls a "Blakean version of ownership of the means of production" (v). As Keegan explains, Hughes published a considerable amount of material in this manner

> during the same decades in which the official canon of his poetry was established with Faber and Faber. Hughes's engagement with small press publication extended to the co-ownership of actual presses, as a collaborative, even familial mode of literary production—and as an alternative to the protocols of trade publishing, according to which an author might be expected not to contribute to the design of a book, or choose its endpapers, or propose the typeface (declaring an abiding preference for blackest Bodoni)—all of which counted among Hughes's concerns.

Paradoxically, the *Collected Poems* both calls attention to and erases this "alternative" practice of Hughes's, bringing his small-press, anticorporate publications into the fold of the very thing they were defined against. According to Keegan, "these practices were complementary rather than opposed, and one of the roles of the small press was as a tiring room or rehearsal space" (vi). But Hughes's intense concern with the appearance of his small-press publications, his valuing of the physical artifact, suggests more than a revision process leading to the "official" publication of poems. The plan for Rainbow Press, for example, was "to have each smaller-format title bound in a different shade of leather so that the book spines would form a 'rainbow' along the shelf" (Keegan v). These books, according to Elizabeth Bergmann Loizeaux, were "elegant, sensuous volumes, often small enough to hold intimately . . . with deeply colored, silky leather bindings stamped simply in silver or gold, contrasting with the heavy, cream-colored, rough Italian paper they favored on the inside" (20). This "sensuous" aspect of Hughes's texts, which in some cases circulate as rare and highly valuable collector's items, is among the things supplanted by *Collected Poems,* where all of Hughes's poems are in this respect leveled (presented with the same look, and of equal authority), and where Hughes's careful selections, based on a conscious distinction between private and public practices, are undone even as they are revealed in Keegan's introduction.

A considerable number of Hughes's large-format publications, Keegan reminds us, were originally of a collaborative and visual nature, either "set in motion by or [finding] . . . confirmation in the visual contributions of others" (x). Leonard Baskin's drawings, for example, both inspired and haunt the cover of *Crow* and are featured throughout *Cave Birds.* Likewise, Fay Godwin's black-and-white photographs of the Calder Valley inspired Hughes to write *Remains of Elmet* and appear opposite his poems throughout the collection. The implications are significant for material and aesthetic reasons alike. Foremost, Hughes's visually oriented books bear a different relation to their audience than does a text such as the *Collected Poems* or, for that matter, Faber's tiny "classroom" edition of *Crow.* Thin, hardcover books with broad dimensions and visually striking covers (Viking's *Season Songs,* with more illustrations by Baskin, fits this description as well), these books have a display value uncharacteristic of "serious" poetry and encourage a different, possibly more casual, method of reading. Tom Paulin comments similarly on Hughes's 1983 volume *River:*

> The glossy appearance . . . and the colour photographs it contains make it resemble a coffee-table book. Like the high-gloss pocket volume *Flowers and Insects,* it draws attention to its sale-ability, its existence as commodity.

(275)

Better fit for display than discreet shelving, these books would seem to locate poetry within the household rather than the library; they stand ready for observation by company. They also encourage a reader to flip through the book casually rather than study one poem at length, or perhaps to read poem and image in relation to each other. The effects of these altered reading practices vary. For *Remains of Elmet,* the visual element grounds the poetry in the particular region photographed by Godwin, spatially aligns reader and poet in a shared gaze, and presents poetry as a product of visual observation, bound to the natural landscape. With *Cave Birds,* Baskin's assortment of misshapen, grotesque, and comically disturbing creatures adds dimension to the poems' already dark and challenging investigation of bodily identity.[10] Hughes's singular, occupational titles—**"The summoner," "The judge," "The plaintiff"**—imply a direct correlation to the sketch opposite, which makes a monster of an otherwise human, though institutionalized, identity. The importance Hughes placed on the drawings is evident in his foreword to *New Selected Poems*:

> For the four poems printed here the drawings cannot be reproduced, so it might help to know that the Executioner is a giant raven; the Knight is a decomposing bird of the Crow type; Bride and Groom are human beings with bird attributes, and the Risen is a falcon, the full-fledged emergence of a Horus. Throughout the original sequence the interdependence between drawing and verse is quite close.
>
> (xi)

As visual accompaniments, or as means to entering the poems, these images help to package difficult poetry in a more accessible form and popularize an otherwise esoteric Ted Hughes by bringing him into domestic and visual space—a very different experience from that offered by *Collected Poems,* where each originally individual volume enters a new set of spatial and visual relations, surrendering to the foregrounded author its material existence as something self-contained and distinctly other and perhaps losing connections to other volumes forged previously through visual presentation.[11]

Hughes's collaboration suggest an interest on his part in contemporary visual art that rivals his well-known obsessions with classic writers such as Shakespeare and Ovid. Hughes's view of art is fundamentally Jungian, the best of it seen as hammering away at the same overarching mythic structures—mainly humanity's separation from and repression of nature. In this sense, the primal energy tapped into by poetry is available to other artistic genres as well, and while Hughes often seems to privilege poetry as the most authentic means of communication, his publications reveal a belief that poetry can work in conjunction with other genres toward a single vision. Like the artwork accompanying several volumes, Hughes's prose fiction is left out of *Collected Poems,* where the poetry assumes an independent life and presumably coheres without the visual images and prose texts that originally accompanied some of it.

Two of Hughes's major volumes, *Wodwo* and *Gaudete,* challenge traditional expectations by interspersing short stories, drama, and prose narrative with sections of poetry. In his author's note to *Wodwo*—a 1967 publication divided into three parts, the middle one consisting of five short stories and a short play—Hughes provides the following instructions:

> The stories and the play in this book may be read as notes, appendix, and universified episodes of the events behind the poems, or as chapters of a single adventure to which the poems are commentary or amplification. Either way, the verse and the prose are intended to be read together, as parts of a single work.
>
> (9)

The note betrays a concern that readers may not know how to approach such a work and assumes a valuing of the author's intention. Having a potentially confused audience in mind, Hughes offers two strategies for processing the work as a whole and assures us that its seemingly disparate parts are interrelated. He does not prioritize one form of writing over the other but gives his readers a choice of treating either the poetry or the fiction/drama as the book's foundation and the rest as supplementary material—though all of it is connected, he says, and should be "read together" as a "single work." He seems to be differentiating between a work and the various genres that may constitute one, represented here by his peculiar assortment of literary and scholarly terms. Approach the book this way or that, he seems to say, but remember that all the pieces are inherently related to one another, and the book's meaning exists independently of any one section or method. Poems here are valued less by Hughes as independent compositions than as part of a larger system of meaning, which may explain the recurrence of particular poems in different volumes. Keegan is aware of this when he writes of Hughes's "provisional view of what might be termed the unrepeatability of the poem, and its supposed fixity in place" (viii), and he concludes that for Hughes, "Making new poems was akin to making new habitats for old poems" (xi). If Hughes deemphasized the fixity of individual poems in this way, he redirected that emphasis toward the sequence—a form that emphasizes the whole over its individual parts, and which occupied Hughes almost exclusively from *Crow* to the end of his career.

But our belief in the unified work depends solely on our trust in the artist as a fixed and unifying presence; when and if that belief collapses, there is little reason to assume an inherent connection between the stories and the poems. Hughes, at least, felt the need to intervene, providing his readers with some sort of scheme, story, or theme to which the poetry might be comfortably fitted; one gathers from his efforts that poetry must emanate from or exist in relation to some other discursive structure or base text, whether that text is an author's note, another's artwork, or, as is the case with *Birthday Letters,* another's writing. To a large extent this remains a method for substantiating Hughes's work, as we turn, for example, to Sagar's reconstruction of the story of *Crow* (170-80)—gathered from bits and pieces of Hughes's own elucidations—in order to understand a sequence that by itself lacks any kind of overriding narrative structure, or to the story of *Birthday Letters* recreated by Erica Wagner to gain perspective on Hughes's more personally informed work. It is another paradox of *Collected Poems* to rid the poetry of such mediations, collaborations, and interventions—essentially denying, under the guise of a "purified" body of work, its intertextuality—while performing in its own way those very functions; as an institutionally authorized collection (not *a* collection of Hughes's poetry, but *the* collection) it consecrates the author, validating and unifying his body of work even as it displaces his agency and intentions.

Hughes's *Gaudete* originally presented the reader with a nine-page prologue (a prose/verse hybrid, having the appearance of one of William Carlos Williams's more ambitious projects), a long sequence of narrative poems (equally ambiguous in form), and a three-page prose epilogue before delivering its concluding sequence of lyrical poems—an arrangement undone by *Collected Poems,* where only the final section is reproduced. Both *Gaudete* and *Wodwo* show a Hughes straining to establish an organic relation between poetry and prose, where the former ultimately emerges as a kind of hard-earned achievement. *Gaudete* goes further than *Wodwo,* however, in its efforts to unite its disjointed fragments, contextualizing them within a mythic (and typically Hughesian) cycle of death, descent, and rebirth, and sustaining its protagonist, the Reverend Nicholas Lumb, throughout. Both publications of *Gaudete* include a prefatory "argument"—a plot summary, basically—the second of which appears more developed, specific, and reader-sensitive than the vaguely pretentious version from two years earlier. In fact, Hughes was regularly explaining his work, often developing his introductory notes for a second publication. This concern for audience and accessibility is not typically associated with Hughes, but it is an indication that he thought his poetry required such prosaic interventions to make sense.

Hughes's mediation of his more esoteric projects with explanatory narratives suggests a conflicted sense of audience and authorship consistent with his bifurcated publication practice. Among the surprising number of private-press collections appearing in *Collected Poems* are *Capriccio*—a 1990 sequence about the "other woman," Assia Wevil, who committed suicide six years after Plath, and *Howls and Whispers,* a group of 11 poems invoking Sylvia Plath in the manner of *Birthday Letters* but published separately from it. Both were published in expensive limited editions, and neither was reviewed by the press. Although the chronological ordering of *Collected Poems* distances *Capriccio* from the other two volumes, they form an autobiographical triad: not only do they share the same form and style, but the very poem that begins *Capriccio* ("Capriccios") appears, with minor alterations and a new title ("**Superstitions**"), at the end of *Howls and Whispers,* creating (in Bere's words) "a circular link or pattern among the three sequences" ("**Knot**" 25). In this way Hughes's contrasting methods of publication form a dialogue of knowledge and secrecy. If *Birthday Letters* represents a coming forth, a release of previously withheld information, the other two volumes signify a holding back—a way of simultaneously saying and not saying, as well as an assertion of the author's control over his work.

"To make *Howls and Whispers,*" Middlebrook explains, "Hughes had reserved eleven poems from the manuscripts that became *Birthday Letters,* as a winemaker sets aside the choicest vintage for special labeling" (xvii). As the comparatively expressive title would suggest, Hughes's feelings—of resentment and self-pity as well as guilt—seem at least slightly less guarded than they do in *Birthday Letters.* Hughes begins the sequence by distancing his present self from "that young man" oblivious to the "scream" that will "find his soul and tear it from him" ("**Paris 1954**," *Collected Poems* 1173). Similar poems can be found in *Birthday Letters,* where again Hughes makes a hapless character of his former self, though few of these poems ask quite so directly for the reader's sympathy or similarly recall a moment from the poet's life before Plath entered the picture. This particular moment, in which the young man, presumably on an early continental expedition, sips fine wine and nibbles "his first Gruyère," represents an alternative life, full of hope and possibility, that the vexed poet "will spend the rest of his life / Trying to recapture" (1173). Elsewhere in the sequence, Hughes lets loose his anger toward Plath's mother, who emerges more fully as a biographical presence than the mythologized, smothering Mummy of *Birthday Letters* and is depicted as a kind of Satanic informer ("She squatted at your ear") largely responsible for Plath's illness and eventual suicide (1178-79). Thus *Howls and Whispers* is Hughes's volume in a way that *Birthday Letters*—given over to a Plath-centered universe from start to finish—is not. It is clear that the poems, however good or bad they may be, are not far removed from the embittered contests over the authority to represent Plath's life and work—a struggle that surely favors Hughes's voice, sanctioned by the institution of poetry and his own literary and cultural prestige, over someone like Plath's mother, with whom he traded executorial blows.[12] The poems nonetheless reflect an overriding feeling of powerlessness, and "**The Offers**"—published in the London *Sunday Times* 10 days before Hughes's death—conveys more openly than any other of Hughes's poems his feelings of guilt and responsibility for Plath's death, as its dreaming speaker is chillingly cautioned by his dead wife, "This time / Don't fail me" (1183).

Hughes's use of Wevil and Plath as the interchangeable objects of what is virtually the same poem (**"Capriccios"** and **"Superstitions"**) displays, perhaps alarmingly, a tendency to fit all personal and historical events into a similar "mythic equation." A common poetic truth, it is suggested, underlies the individual realties of both women. Like Plath, Wevil is referred to simply as "you"—a controlling absence throughout the sequence—giving the impression that we are eavesdropping on a private and direct correspondence. Despite their autobiographical subject matter, the poems maintain a cryptic air, not so much telling the story as entering its key moments or dropping enigmatic references to things that carry little meaning for the biographically uninformed. In **"Chlorophyl,"** for example, Hughes begins, "She sent him a blade of grass, but no word" (*Collected Poems* 799). For those who have read Feinstein's biography[13] or are acquainted with the story through some other source, the line summons a store of shared knowledge before giving way to a purely symbolic and artfully structured investigation of that event. For those outside the loop, the poem might be dismissed as nonsensical or identified as the sort of biblically repetitive, widely allusive effort found throughout much of Hughes's earlier work.

This potential for vastly different reading experiences is shared by *Birthday Letters* and *Howls and Whispers*, the contents of which regulate and obstruct at least as much as they inform and invite: "while Hughes opens the gate," Bere comments in her review of *Birthday Letters,* "he still guards the entrance, and readers looking for true confessions will be disappointed" (**"Owning"**). While alluding to and interacting with a wide range of Plath's writing, and charged with Hughes's cognizance of what was being said in biographies and critical studies, the poems seek the authority of a traditional literary heritage. Middlebrook has demonstrated, for instance, how the opening poem **"Fulbright Scholars"**

> thread[s] the strands of *Birthday Letters* into a thick cable of twentieth-century texts that had figured in the literary educations of Hughes and Plath: W. B. Yeats and James Joyce and T. S. Eliot; and, of course, D. H. Lawrence.
>
> (87)

The poems therefore appeal to at least two kinds of insider knowledge: that of a basic Hughes/Plath narrative (his infidelity, her suicide, his silence) with all its surrounding controversy, and that of a canonical literary tradition called upon by Hughes's widespread allusions. If the first of these is responsible (regrettably, some

would say) for the poems' popularity, the second, replete with signs of sophistication, is more in keeping with traditional literary values.

What may seem surprising is the extent to which these poems reinforce rather than provide an alternative to existing narratives of the Hughes/Plath saga, at least in terms of its defining moments. For example, the rather sensational tale of their first encounter—which left Hughes with bite marks on his face and holding the earrings he had stripped from Plath—is validated in **"St Botolph's,"** where Hughes describes "the swelling ringmoat of tooth-marks / That was to brand my face for the next month" (1051). And stories that find affirmation in *Birthday Letters*—Plath's reading Chaucer to cows, Hughes's throwing clods of dirt at her Cambridge window—have in turn become primary sources for other accounts, such as the motion picture *Sylvia* and Wagner's synopsis in *Ariel's Gift*. Even while providing Hughes an opportunity to tell his side of the story, his poetry enters an active and mutually substantiating relationship with other sources, most of which work toward a tragic-romantic version of the poets' lives (as opposed to the less impressive, squabbling couple we encounter through much of Middlebrook's *Her Husband*) and which continue to rely heavily on Freud when it comes to explaining Plath's troubled existence.

It is not difficult to see Hughes's autobiographical poetry as a site of tension and conflict that extends well beyond Hughes and his critics. To what cultural domain do these poems belong, and for whom are they written? What accounts for their popularity, and how do we begin to assess their value? Hughes's late work not only confuses our distinctions between popular and high art, and between private and public discourse, but potentially upsets the place we may have reserved for him in our literary landscape. Does Hughes remain at a safe distance from the confessional school to which Plath is so often conscripted? Is he still a poet of the concrete particular, as he is often characterized, or does such a characterization collapse in the abstract meanderings and the toiling, almost willfully artless language of his more personal writing?[14] Given the intimate nature of this new material, does Hughes retain his characteristic toughness? Should he be considered an esoteric poet in the Blake/Yeats tradition, to be contrasted with Larkin and others, or a down-to-earth one, to be aligned with Larkin in opposition to, say, an abstruse Geoffrey Hill?

Strangely, perhaps, *Collected Poems* seems to diffuse such questions: among its myriad pages and poems, *Birthday Letters* and its companion volumes seem altogether less disorienting than they did by themselves—maybe because they now have a fixed material location, a shared context in which they form part of an author-centered narrative, conforming to Hughes's massive body of work rather than challenging it. In this new context, their emergence in the pressure cooker of public scrutiny and their attempt to establish dialogue between poetry and the institutions that threaten it (such as biography and literary criticism) are obscured.

Collected Poems provides more than an occasion for assessing an author's body of work. It is a means by which "the poet" may be reaffirmed as a genuine type, distinguishable, among other things, from those who merely write poetry. If epithetical review titles such as "King of the Beasts" (Armitage), "The Wild Poet" (Parker), and "The Master's Voice" (anonymous) are any indication, the collection has been successful in tidying up the messier aspects of Hughes's identity and practice, delivering instead a poet of singular voice and unified vision who is therefore worthy of elite company. His poems, meanwhile, enjoy a more stable context than ever before: they are officially Ted Hughes poems, with all the significance that name entails.

Notes

1. At Amazon.com the two collections are marketed as a set; a buyer interested in one is directed to the other and encouraged to buy both.

2. Paul Keegan, the editor of *Collected Poems,* regards it as an "interim edition," restricted to Hughes's published work. It foreshadows "the long-term project of a *Complete Poems*" (vii).

3. In accounting for some of the limitations in what is now a conventional use of Foucault, Rimi Khan asks "what it is actually possible to say and do in cultural studies' name" (par. 1). As Khan's analysis makes evident, the "Foucault phenomenon" has itself become a site of investigation, and one can no longer help but feel a little self-conscious when referencing Foucault's name. In my own study, I have found it less useful to match my findings with actual text from Foucault than to adopt what I understand to be a Foucauldian investigation of identity and discourse and to bind that investigation more firmly to social conditions with the supplemental use of Bourdieu.

4. For an in-depth discussion of authorship in terms of copyright law and literature, see Woodmansee and Jaszi (1-56).

5. Keith Sagar, a leading authority on Hughes, has this to say:

   > *Birthday Letters* sold ten times more copies than any other Hughes book in its first year, not because it is ten times better as poetry but because there are ten times as many voyeurs as poetry-lovers among book-buyers, and a hundred times as many among newspaper editors . . . [T]he claim that *Birthday Letters* is the summit of his achievement is as absurd as it would be to claim that the sonnets . . . are the pinnacle of Shakespeare's.
   >
   > (x)

Douglas Barbour qualifies his praise for the collection as follows: "whether or not *Birthday Letters* is good poetry, it is a fascinating book." Later, in a follow-up to that review (but now accessible at the same site) he retracts the praise altogether: "I can only wonder at a world of readers who throng to this book while continuing to ignore so many collections that give me much more pleasure and stimulation."

6. Margaret Reese, for example, is pleased to find in *Birthday Letters* a hope "that poetry has still untapped potential to find a broad audience," and Karl Miller is among those who feel that at least parts of *Birthday Letters* "are among the best poems Ted Hughes has written."

7. Compare "Earth, receive an honoured guest" to "Tiger, tiger burning bright," etc.

8. A *Guardian* article titled "Poets' Poll Crowns Larkin King of Verse" (Ezard), which reports that Larkin edged out Hughes and Plath as the favorite among poetry readers, indicates that the question of "England's best" is a lingering one.

9. There is considerable truth in Keith Tuma's thesis that British poetry is dead in America, and Tuma is among those actively reconstructing British poetry to reveal a living but suppressed modernist practice.

10. For an in-depth reading of Baskin's images in *Cave Birds* as well as some wonderful reproductions of Hughes's visual components, see Loizeaux.

11. For example, *Crow* and *Cave Birds* are visually connected through Baskin's artwork—a connection that apparently runs deeper, as (Keegan tells us) some poems published in *Cave Birds* were originally intended for *Crow* (viii).

12. In *The Silent Woman,* Janet Malcolm shows Hughes's publication of Plath's journals, which contain damaging characterizations of her mother, as a response to Aurelia Plath's publication of *Letters Home,* which present an unflattering portrait of Hughes.

13. Apparently Hughes had sent Assia a note that read: "I have come to see you, despite all marriages." Assia replied by sending Hughes "a red rose pressed between two sheets of paper"—an account that "does not accord with Hughes' own recollection" of a blade of grass (Feinstein 124).

14. Take, for example, these lines from "The Offers": "my brain's hemisphere / Seemed to have twisted slightly out of phase / To know you you yet realize that you / Were not you" (*Collected Poems* 1182).

Works cited

Armitage, Simon. "The King of the Beasts." Rev. of *Collected Poems,* by Ted Hughes. *Independent* 24 Oct. 2003: 25.

Auden, W. H. *Selected Poems.* New York: Vintage, 1989.

Barbour, Douglas. "Late Thoughts on Ted Hughes's *Birthday Letters.*" *Lynx: Poetry from Bath* 8 (1998). <http://www.dgdclynx.plus.com/lynx/lynx810.html>. 20 Jan. 2005.

Bere, Carol. "A Knot of Obsessions." Rev. of *Collected Poems,* by Ted Hughes. *Boston Review* 29.1 (2004): 23-25.

———. "Owning the Facts of His Life." Rev. of *Birthday Letters,* by Ted Hughes. *Literary Review* 41.4 (1998): 556.

Bourdieu, Pierre. *Distinction: A Social Critique of the Judgement of Taste.* Trans. Richard Nice. Cambridge: Harvard UP, 1984.

———. *The Field of Cultural Production.* Ed. Randal Johnson. Columbia: Columbia UP, 1993.

Eliot, T. S. *Selected Prose of T. S. Eliot.* Ed. Frank Kermode. New York: Harvest, 1988.

Ezard, John. "Poetry Lovers Poll Crowns Larkin King of Verse." *Guardian* 15 Oct. 2003: 8.

Fass, Ekbert. "Ted Hughes and *Crow.*" *London Magazine* Jan. 1971: 5-20.

Feinstein, Elaine. *Ted Hughes: The Life of a Poet.* New York: Norton, 2001.

Foucault, Michel. "What Is an Author?" *Textual Strategies: Perspectives in Post-Structuralist Criticism.* Ed. Josue V. Harari. Ithaca: Cornell UP, 1979. 141-60.

Heaney, Seamus. *Electric Light.* New York: Farrar, 2001.

Hofmann, Michael. "Stare at the Monster." Rev. of *Collected Poems,* by Ted Hughes. *Poetry* 183.5 (2004): 278-89.

Hughes, Ted. *Cave Birds: An Alchemical Cave Drama.* New York: Viking, 1978.

———. *Collected Poems.* Ed. Paul Keegan. New York: Farrar, 2003.

———. Foreword. *New Selected Poems.* By Hughes. New York: Harper, 1982. xi-xii.

———. *Gaudete.* London: Faber, 1977.

———. *Winter Pollen: Occasional Prose.* Ed. William Scammell. Boston: Faber, 1994.

———. *Wodwo.* London: Faber, 1967.

Keegan, Paul. Preface. *Collected Poems.* By Ted Hughes. New York: Farrar, 2003. v-xi.

Khan, Rimi. "Reading Cultural Studies, Reading Foucault." *Postmodern Culture* 15.1 (2004). 72 pars. <http://www.iath.virginia.edu/pmc/current.issue/15.1khan.html>. 6 Feb. 2005.

Kinsella, John. "Beguiled by the Wild." Rev. of *Collected Poems,* by Ted Hughes. *Guardian* 2 Nov. 2003: 15.

Loizeaux, Elizabeth Bergmann. "Reading Word, Image, and the Body of the Book: Ted Hughes and Leonard Baskin's *Cave Birds.*" *Twentieth-Century Literature* 50.1 (2004): 18-58.

Malcolm, Janet. *The Silent Woman: Sylvia Plath and Ted Hughes.* New York: Vintage, 1995.

"The Master's Voice." Rev. of *Collected Poems,* by Ted Hughes. *Economist* 8 Nov. 2003: 83.

Middlebrook, Diane. *Her Husband: Hughes and Plath—A Marriage.* New York: Viking, 2003.

Miller, Karl. Rev. of *Birthday Letters,* by Ted Hughes. *Times Literary Supplement* 6 Feb. 1998: 3.

O'Brien, Sean. "Essential but Unlovely." Rev. of *Collected Poems,* by Ted Hughes. *Guardian* 1 Nov. 2003: 25.

Parker, James. "The Wild Poet." Rev. of *Collected Poems,* by Ted Hughes. *Boston Globe* 21 Dec. 2003: 2.

Paulin, Tom. *Minotaur: Poetry and the Nation State.* Cambridge: Harvard UP, 1992.

Reese, Margaret. "Memories of Sylvia Plath." Rev. of *Birthday Letters,* by Ted Hughes. *World Socialist Web Site* 28 May 1998. <http://www.wsws.org/arts/1998/may1998/hugh-m28.shtml>. 8 Jan. 2005.

Sagar, Keith. *The Laughter of Foxes: A Study of Ted Hughes.* Liverpool: Liverpool UP, 2000.

Tuma, Keith. *Fishing by Obstinate Isles: Modern and Postmodern British Poetry and American Readers.* Evanston: Northwestern UP, 1998.

Wagner, Erica. *Ariel's Gift: Ted Hughes, Sylvia Plath, and the Story of "Birthday Letters."* New York: Norton, 2000.

Woodmansee, Martha, and Peter Jaszi. *The Construction of Authorship: Textual Appropriation in Law and Literature.* Durham: Duke UP, 1994.

Lissa Paul (essay date May/June 2005)

SOURCE: Paul, Lissa. "'Writing poetry for children is a curious occupation': Ted Hughes and Sylvia Plath." *The Horn Book Magazine* 81, no. 3 (May/June 2005): 257-67.

[In the following essay, Paul examines the children's verse produced by Hughes and Plath, noting that the

pair hoped their entry into the field of children's literature would be an important step in establishing themselves as professional writers.]

The flashy Ted and Sylvia story is the big-screen biopic—with Gwyneth Paltrow in the starring role. For more serious students of literature, there are other stories. There is Ted's version in his verse collection, **Birthday Letters** (1998), ostensibly written to Sylvia on birthdays long after her death. And there is Sylvia's version, in *The Unabridged Journals of Sylvia Plath* (2000). I'd like to tell a different Ted and Sylvia story. It's a literary story; it's an American story—and it has a Horn Book connection. For the most part, my story takes place in Massachusetts, in Northampton and Boston, between the summer of 1957 and December 1959. It was there and then, at the beginning of their intimate creative partnership, that Ted and Sylvia negotiated the hazardous transformation from promising to professional writers; where they began to acknowledge formally the possibilities of writing poetry and prose for children as well as for adults.

Because beginnings make most sense when viewed from endings, my story begins at the end, in the archives at Emory University in Atlanta, Georgia, where Ted's papers and books are now housed. There, among the two-and-a-half tons of archival material he gave to Emory, are two files classified as unidentified notes on "children's writing and teaching." They contain loose sheets of yellow scratch pad, unlined and undated (though they appear to be from a late stage in his career), on which Ted has written rough drafts for an apparently unproduced radio program. The rhythmically elegant phrase "writing poetry for children is a curious occupation" appears repeatedly as Ted tries out various ways of writing something that will resolve—as elegantly as the opening phrase—the inherent conflicts he sketches among producers, manufacturers, distributors, and consumers of children's poetry. Here's one version as Ted tries to articulate the problem:

> And the most curious thing about it is that we think children need a special kind of poetry. Each writer for children has his own idea of what that is. . . . Publishers, of course, know that poetry is not sold to children—it is sold to their parents or teachers. So this is the barrier to publishing children's poetry. The author thinks he knows what they want, or need, the teachers or parents think they know best. And the publisher thinks he knows best what poet & teacher think they know best. And we all think differently. Each author writing for children thinks the same—and all write differently.

Although Ted is talking about writing poetry for children, his remarks apply equally well to his prose. Poets always write as poets—tuned to rhythm, imagery, and feeling. Every phrase, every sentence, is carefully

balanced so that it is held in perfect tension with the structure as a whole. But the main concern of this passage, as Ted tries to explain, is the problem of audience relations: Who is the text for? Adults or children? Who publishes it? Who buys it? Who knows best?

One craftily simple way Ted resolved the audience problem was by publishing, without comment, the same poem in different collections—some marked as being for children, some not. But that was a partial solution at best. He cared deeply about nurturing imaginative life and was attracted to the idea that children "are more fluid and alert" than adults. He was also troubled by the speed with which that openness was closed down and sealed up, hidden, as he says, behind a "space helmet." That's one reason Ted was so concerned with audience-and characterized that audience much as traditional storytellers might have characterized their undifferentiated audiences of adults and children. In a 1984 letter to me, Ted described the kind of writing that might reach such an audience as a "lingua franca"—that is, "a style of communication for which children are the specific audience, but which adults can overhear . . . and listen, in a way secretly—as children." And it appears that Ted was attempting to compose in that style, that "lingua franca," as early as 1956, on his honeymoon in Spain with Sylvia. That's when he wrote the first drafts of little animal fables that ultimately grew into the collection *How the Whale Became.*

In that bright Spanish summer of 1956, Ted writes, enthusiastically, to his beloved older brother Gerald: "I have written a book of children's & grown up animal fables which surprised even me." Sylvia writes with equal enthusiasm in her journal:

> Yesterday Ted read me three new fables he'd just written for his fine animal book about how all the animals became: the Tortoise one was the funniest and dearest yet; the hyena, more serious about a bitter perverted character, and the fox and dog alive with plot and marvelous Sly-Look and Four-Square. I have great hopes for this as a children's classic. Even as I write, Ted is working at the main table on the elephant and the cricket stories. Living with him is like being told a perpetual story: his mind is the biggest, most imaginative, I have ever met. I could live in its growing countries forever.

The celebration was a little premature. Though Ted received initial encouragement from publishers, in 1957 his new creation fables (eventually published in 1963) were rejected as being "too sophisticated" for children. So, as questions of audience relations began to simmer for Ted, the fables were temporarily put on the back burner. But I'll return to them—Ted's stories about animals becoming themselves serve as a poignant counterpoint to the story about Ted and Sylvia becoming writers.

By early 1957, that brief Spanish interlude with its dedicated writing time had become a golden memory. Ted and Sylvia were back in the gray cold of England. Sylvia was completing her Fulbright-sponsored degree in English at Cambridge. Ted, having completed his degree there in anthropology in 1954 and a master's degree the following year, wrote and worked at odd jobs in the neighborhood. Among them was a stint, in the spring of 1957, teaching adolescents at what was called a secondary modern school—a school for the least able students, the ones putting in time between finishing elementary school and being legally able to leave. In the summer, Ted and Sylvia sailed for the United States. Sylvia began teaching freshman English at Smith College (her alma mater) that fall. In January 1958, Ted too took up an academic position, at the nearby University of Massachusetts, Amherst. By spring, both Ted and Sylvia knew that they'd had enough of teaching. Ted writes to Gerald: "Teaching is the deadly-friendly enemy of writing—so that while I am teaching I write nothing that's much good." Sylvia didn't like teaching much either, though she was, as she knew, fulfilling her academic destiny: star student to star professor. But teaching was strangling her writing, too. In **Birthday Letters** Ted writes about how trapped she appeared in her "blue flannel" teaching suit: "I watched / The strange dummy stiffness, the misery, / Of your blue flannel suit, its straitjacket, ugly / Half-approximation to your idea / Of the proprieties you hoped to ease into, / And your horror in it."

Ted's teaching experiences, both at the American university and at the British secondary modern, had alarmed him. Because he felt that the majority of the students he encountered had been "stupefied by mechanical entertainment, distraction," he began to formulate the idea (learned from his knowledge of myth and folklore) that imaginative stories could act as antidotes, that they could potentially counteract the stultifying effects of modern life. Ted exhorts his brother, repeatedly, to tell stories to his two young sons. "You should be telling them stories continually," says Ted, "the more ominous & frightful the better." So it came to pass that "some time in the spring," says Ted in his notes to Sylvia's *Collected Poems*, "they made the decision to leave teaching and attempt to live on their earnings as writers."

At that point several features that would shape their lives as writers—especially as writers for children and "secretly" listening adults—were already in place. Ted and Sylvia had saved scrupulously in order to afford the one crucial year they had allowed themselves to become full-time professional writers. They'd already recognized the contours of their mature writing lives and the role that children's literature could play in it. They knew that the core subjects of Ted's imaginative landscape—animals, nature, myth, fable, folktale, fairy tale, and ballad—were subjects considered suitable for children. Sylvia increasingly took on some of those subjects, which chimed, in a Wordsworthian way, with Romantic ideas of childhood as being in tune with imagination and the natural world. By 1957, both Ted and Sylvia had added writing for children to the growing repertoire of genres in which they were working. Sylvia, in fact, writes to her mother that year: "Ted wants to make children's books his other field."

Ted had taken to heart the criticism that his first animal fables were "too sophisticated" and started to work on ways of reconciling his imaginative landscape with the requirements of publishers. While on a brief writing holiday in Cape Cod, just before the teaching year began, Ted writes to Gerald:

> I am writing one children's story per day before 9 a.m. These are a sort that really should sell. The publishers showed such interest in my last year's attempt [the first *How the Whale Became* fables written in Spain]—which I wrote without having a notion of what children read at what age, and which were hopelessly abstract. Now I'm doing better. I am writing for about age six. A paragraph of simple story to each full page picture. Maybe if I practice a bit each day I could do the drawings too within a year or two. Now if I can keep this up—one a day—and I can, and if I can sell them—as I shall soon—either because they are good, or become good through practice, or both & my shortly-to-be-bandied name as a poet—then that will be quite a wage, and leave my whole day after 8:30 or so for more strenuous lofty attempts. These stories come to me absolutely naturally, so I'm not prostituting my imagination. I would like to produce a classic volume—about 5,000 children's stories. I shall bring in all the situations & characters etc. out of all the fairy tales, animal tales etc. that I have read & I have read millions in the last six years. Now, if I could do that it would be a classic because there would be so much in it for desperate parents. At present there are countless children's books, mostly bad, all different, very few that you want to read 2X—so parents don't know what to buy—they first buy one here & one there.

It's clear that Ted had been learning a lot about the children's book business. He and Sylvia had met the engraver and sculptor Leonard Baskin and his wife, Esther, who were both producing picture books for children. Another important source of information on writing for children is likely to have been Sylvia's 1956 edition of *The Writer's Handbook,* a collection of articles originally published in *The Writer.* (Sylvia's copy, heavily underlined and annotated, is housed in the archives in the rare book collection at Smith.) *The Writer's Handbook* contains several articles by children's authors (including Eleanor Estes), all filled with practical, commonsense advice about manuscript presentation, subject matter, and audience. Lee Wyndham, for example, in "Writing for the Look 'n' Listen Age," makes comments that Ted seems to have adapted. "The child's inner world," Wyndham says, "can be a subject." And here: "The young child wants the story in his book to reflect his everyday world because, familiar though it may be to us, to him it is still a thing of wonder, in each moment a new discovery." And finally: "As a writer for the young, train yourself to see, hear, feel, taste and smell in words."

Ted took those conventional instructions and transformed them into vital components in his own aesthetic. In *Poetry in the Making* (1967), Ted explains how a poem is like an animal, a living creature: "an assembly of living parts moved by a single spirit." He goes on to say that "as a poet, you have to make sure that all those parts over which you have control, the words and rhythms and images, are alive":

> Words that live are those which we hear, like "click" or "chuckle", or which we see, like "freckled" or "veined", or which we taste, like "vinegar" or "sugar", or touch, like "prickle" or "oily", or smell, like "tar" or "onion". Words which belong directly to one of the five senses.

The aesthetic sense Ted articulates here also reflects his deep understanding of the way traditional folktales link precise observation of the outer world with emotional response to the inner. In a letter to Gerald, he says, "The thing about imaginative stories is that they make an inner mind and activate it, populate it and become the brain with which the child lives."

July 1958. Ted publishes his first story for children. Sylvia writes in her journal: "Vicarious joy at Ted's writing which opens promise for me too: *New Yorker*'s 3rd poem acceptance & a short story for *Jack & Jill*. 1958: The year I stop teaching & start writing." Sylvia regarded the acceptance as a kind of talisman, confirmation of their "promise" as writers. When the story is published, Sylvia writes in her journal: "In the A & P I rushed to the magazine rack & there was Ted's story 'Billy Hook and the Three Souvenirs' in the July issue of *Jack & Jill*. The story was sumptuously presented: two fine lively color pictures & two half-tone drawings: gay & magic." Ted was less sanguine. In a letter to Gerald, he dismisses the story in a sentence: "The children's story I sold was so castrated when it finally came out that I don't want to send it to you." The story is a version of a famous Scottish border ballad, "Thomas Rymer," about a man who disappears forever into "Elfland" when he marries the fairy queen. Ted loved this ballad, and others of its I kind, famously collected in the nineteenth century by F. J. Child. My guess is that Ted's ballad ending was cut, as the *Jack and Jill* version ends in a conventional way, with Billy Hook returning to the everyday world with his bride.

Despite Ted's disappointment at the published version, it was still an important marker for Ted and Sylvia. Every story sold, every poem, every award, represented tangible proof that they could, in fact, support themselves as writers. When Sylvia typed up their combined earnings from writing for the period between June 1956 and June 1958, the total came to $2,100.34. The biggest sums were from prize money. Poems mostly sold by the line: nine dollars, ten dollars, fifteen dollars. *The New Yorker* paid Ted sixty-four dollars for **"The Thought-Fox,"** a sum significantly more than he received from poetry and literary magazines. And for "Billy Hook and the Three Souvenirs," *Jack and Jill* paid Ted fifty dollars.

Sylvia too tried her hand at the *Jack and Jill* genre. In a 1958 journal entry she sketches a plot for a domestic fantasy tentatively titled "Changeabout in Mrs. Cherry's Kitchen":

> Suddenly, Ted & I looked at things from our unborn children's point of view. Take gadgets: a modern pot & kettle story. Shiny modern gadgets are overspecialized-long to do others tasks. Toaster, iron, waffle-maker, refrigerator, egg beater, electric fry-pan, blender. One midnight fairies or equivalent grant wish to change-about. Iron wants to make waffles, dips point for dents; refrigerator tired of foods, decides to freeze clothes, toaster tired of toast, wants to bake fancy cake. . . .

The story is rejected and Sylvia is disheartened, although even in the sketch it's possible to glimpse the lost world of Sylvia's imagination at work in 1950s America. But Sylvia kept trying to break into publishing for children.

In a letter to her friend, author Ann Davidson, Sylvia writes bravely: "We are plugging our children's books. I go to see an editor at the Atlantic Press tomorrow, probably to get a rejection." The two long verse narratives Sylvia wrote for children in 1959, *The Bed Book* and *The It-Doesn't-Matter Suit,* were both rejected—and not published until long after her death. Yet Sylvia did make her debut in children's literature that year—in *The Horn Book Magazine.* In January 1959, then-editor Ruth Hill Viguers writes:

> Dear Mr. and Mrs. Hughes:
>
> Your names had been familiar to me for some time when our good friend Mel Culbrandsen [Viguers's neighbor] spoke of you. He knew of my interest in poetry and my wish to find unpublished poems for the magazine of which I am editor. Then this past week, my twin daughters in the Wellesley High School spoke of hearing Mr. Crockett [Sylvia's high school English teacher] read some poems by Sylvia Plath to their English class.

Later in her letter, Viguers explains the *Horn Book*'s mandate as "a literary magazine devoted to criticisms and evaluation of books and reading for children and young people. It is for adults—parents, librarians, teachers, artists, writers—anyone interested in the field of good children's books." In other words, she describes the way the *Horn Book* reaches children via adults—prefiguring the audience Ted later identifies as the one he wants to reach.

In February 1959, polite and enthusiastic young woman that she was, Sylvia writes a cheerful thank-you note to Ruth Viguers: "My husband and I enjoyed so much meeting you and having tea with you and your daughters when we were in Wellesley last." Then she adds: "Both of us enjoy writing poems about birds, beasts and fish, so we are enclosing one from each of us, about an otter and a goatsucker . . ." As an afterthought, Sylvia decides to include a few more, and in a postscript writes, "We're adding to the zoo a bull and a field of horses." What she's indicating to Viguers is that she and Ted have recognized that their animal poems, in keeping with Romantic nineteenth-century traditions, are suitable subjects for children's literature.

When published in the April 1959 issue of the *Horn Book,* Sylvia's "The Bull of Bendylaw" begins with an epigraph, a ballad fragment from F. J. Child's late-nineteenth-century collected *English and Scottish Popular Ballads*:

> The great bull of Bendylaw
> Has broken his band and run awa,
> And the king and a' his court
> Canna turn that bull about.

But Sylvia creates a much more complex creature and international creature in the poem she spins out of the Child ballad fragment. In her journal, Sylvia records the ideas she has in mind for the composition.

> The Bull of Bendylaw—King & court: ceremony & rule—tapestry meadow, dasies, marigolds-playing card
> King & queen
> Bull-Dionysiac force-inspiration
> Male virility
> unbindable
> Europa & bull
> color: versus black bull

The detailed, conscious construction of the mythic world of her verse was typical of Sylvia. The poem itself presents her dense, filigreed approach to the crush of experience she brought to making poems. The bull, for example, is not just the bull of the ballad fragment but also the mythic Dionysian bull—and the bull of the bullfights Ted and Sylvia saw in Spain during their honeymoon—reconfigured as an "unbindable" sea creature:

> The great bronze gate began to crack,
> The sea broke in at every crack,
> Pell-mell, blue-black.
> The bull surged up, the bull surged down . . .

It's a wonderful, mature poem, its first publication in the *Horn Book* hinting that her poems were to reach both adults and children. In Sylvia Plath: *Collected Poems,* edited by Ted and published in 1981, "The Bull of Bendylaw" leads off the publications for 1959, the year Ted marks as an important transitional period for Sylvia, when her first collection of "book" poems (as she liked to call the ones she considered good enough for books) began to take shape. For a time, she'd considered using "The Bull of Bendylaw" as the title poem of the collection ultimately published as *The Colossus* in 1960. Retrospectively, it's possible to see "The Bull of Bendylaw" as a potential locus of Sylvia's poems for both adults and children, poems redolent with mythic, ballad, and folkloric traditions. Sylvia never published formally for children during her lifetime, though there is a hint that she was developing such plans once she had children of her own. In a BBC broadcast produced in January 1963, just before her death, she identifies her poem "You're" as "one of a growing series about a baby." "You're" is a riddle poem, of a piece with other traditional forms with which Sylvia had been working, the ones that communicate to children and adults, the ones that connect observed experience with inner emotion.

In the author note that accompanies "The Bull of Bendylaw" in the *Horn Book,* Sylvia is identified as having studied at Cambridge and taught at Smith, as having published in *The Atlantic* and *The New Yorker,* and as living in Boston "with her husband, Ted Hughes, who is also a poet." That is, she appears promising. Ted does not appear again in the *Horn Book* until October 1964, when the influential children's literature critic Ethel L. Heins favorably reviews *How the Whale Became,* the creation fables born in that honeymoon summer of 1956: "A completely new kind of 'how' story," she says, "written by a young English poet with imagination, philosophical wisdom, and perceptive insight into the ways of animals and men." But even in 1959, Ted understood what kinds of stories he wanted to tell, what he wanted stories to communicate, and their value. In a letter to Gerald he writes:

> The thing about imaginative stories is that they make an inner mind and activate it, populate it and become the brain with which the child lives. Without this inner world the child then becomes a mechanical reflection of his environment & responds to it—which is exactly as if he had been lobotomized or had some part of his brain cut away. Life has less meaning for such people, and is less interesting. Hence the incredible boredom & mental vacuity of vast tracts of the American and English younger generation. The whole purpose of education—apart from the mechanical apprentice to certain necessary skills is in rousing mental activity, an inner world.

In the same letter, Ted explains that he had found that kind of vital inner life ("belatedly & remorsefully") in what he describes as "the better sort of folk tale," and offers a few for Gerald to try out on his sons. Ted explains the purpose:

> The aim isn't to turn them into writers or dreamers but to give them a bigger, stronger grasp of everything that comes up and a more flexible immunity and a supply of symbols to understand experience—explain it to themselves. Because these stories are composed of psychic symbols-unlike the run of nonsensical children's books which are unreal, essentially false and sentimental.

The four short fables Ted includes in the letter all are redolent with folktale traditions, though not identifiable as being from any single tradition. My favorite is a trickster tale of sorts, with apparently Russian antecedents. It's about a ploughman who unwisely wishes that a bear would eat his recalcitrant horse. When the bear appears, the ploughman is remorseful, but it's too late. A fox comes to the rescue with an idea to trick the bear into thinking he's being hunted. The bear falls for it:

> "Save me," [the bear] cried, "And I promise not to eat your horse." At that moment the fox, without showing himself, shouted from the forest: "Ploughman, what's that big dark thing beside you?" "Say it's a stump," whispered the bear. So the ploughman pushed the bear, and the bear kept very rigid, so that he seemed to topple over like a stump.

Ted's poet's eyes and ears are very much evident in the passage: the dramatic cry, "Save me," and the image of the bear toppling "like a stump."

The moral questions multiply. The bear, once in the cart pretending to be firewood, has his head smashed by the ploughman's axe. And the fox (whom the ploughman initially says he'll reward with a chicken) is tricked into a sack of chickens, supposedly to choose the best one. The ploughman smashes the sack "against a wall with all his strength."

For twenty-first century readers—conditioned to school rules of zero-tolerance and a ruthless exclusion of violent stories from children—the story may seem shocking. But it's supposed to. It provokes readers and listeners into thinking about moral actions and consequences. Ted explains to Gerald that "the sadistic element is very prominent in all genuine folk tales. They are a sort of therapy for it, they get it out of the system. It's where repressed that it's so dangerous. Unrepressed it can be converted to more useful ends." That's it. The story provides ideas to think with, tools for imaginative approaches to otherwise complex problems.

In the end, Ted was able to engage the therapeutic virtues of those tales. Besides *How the Whale Became,* he produced two more collections of creation fables: *Tales of the Early World* and *The Dreamfighter.* They stand alongside other important, mythic works (stories, poems, and plays) Ted wrote for children, including *The Iron Man* (called *The Iron Giant* in America), *The Tiger's Bones, The Iron Woman, Ffangs the Vampire Bat* and the *Kiss of Truth,* and *What Is the Truth?*—all reaching for children and secretly listening adults. Sylvia's death in 1963 necessarily precluded the fulfillment of her early promise as a children's author, so evident in her writings of the late 1950s. What remains is the knowledge that her poem "The Bull of Bendylaw" saw its first published life in the *Horn Book* and that it was produced in that intensely creative period with Ted. It was a crucible of poetic achievement for both of them: volatile, productive—and destructive. But, in the end, the works stand. The promise is kept.

Leslie Cahoon (essay date 2005)

SOURCE: Cahoon, Leslie. "Haunted Husbands: Orpheus's Song (Ovid, *Metamorphoses* 10-11) in Light of Ted Hughes's *Birthday Letters*." In *Defining Genre and Gender in Latin Literature: Essays Presented to William S. Anderson on His Seventy-Fifth Birthday,* edited by William W. Batstone & Garth Tissol, pp. 239-67. New York: Peter Lang, 2005.

[*In the following essay, Cahoon finds a number of similarities between Ovid's Orpheus and Hughes's poetic persona in* Birthday Letters.]

> I understand—you could never have released her.
>   I was a whole myth too late to replace you.
> This underworld, my friend, is her heart's home.
>   Inseparable, here we must remain. . . .
>
>   Hughes, **Birthday Letters, "A Picture of Otto"**[1]

In the opening lines of *Metamorphoses* 10, Ovid's narrator introduces the figure of Orpheus as one whose voice prays in vain to Hymenaeus, the god of weddings. After a strangely oblique, condensed, and unfeeling account (in only seven lines) of the ill-omened wedding of Orpheus and Eurydice, and of the subsequent double death of the bride, the narrator turns his attention and ours to the subject of Orpheus's mourning. The narrator emphasizes Orpheus's identity as a singer, first in the opening reference in line 3 to *Orphea . . . voce,* again in the description of the grief of the *Rhodopeius . . . vates* on earth, and then in the introduction to Orpheus's own song, where we see him with the lyre, *pulsis . . . ad carmina nervis.*[2]

Thus, even before he sings his short song in the underworld, and well before he unfolds eight tales in 600 lines of song (*Met.* [*Metamorphoses*] 10.143-739), Orpheus's credentials as poetic voice, sacred bard, and enchanting singer are carefully established. Many prominent critics (Charles Segal and J. Hillis Miller most notably) have therefore concluded that Orpheus is a kind of alter ego for Ovid and that his song provides a helpful microcosmic version of the whole poem, and so is a kind of window into Ovid's poetic technique and larger purposes.[3] The prevailing view then takes the Ovidian Orpheus as a celebration of the artist and of the poet-as-hero:

> [Ovid] presents the triumph of imagination, emotionality, the interior life over external reality. Victorious as both a poet and a lover, Orpheus vindicates the two realms that for Ovid form the surest and finest basis for human happiness: love and art . . .[4]

Challenges to such sanguine readings of Orpheus have appeared as well,[5] and these are always duly acknowledged; nevertheless, they have somehow had little effect on the mainstream view. In this essay, I build on Janan's argument in order to suggest a very different understanding of what Segal has described as the love-art-death triad in the story of, and in the song sung by, Ovid's Orpheus. Janan has argued that Orpheus is not only responsible for Eurydice's second death, but that he also gains from it a new poetic voice, a new sexual identity, and a new subject for his song:

> However loving his intentions may have been, Orpheus *is* responsible for sending his beloved, Eurydice, back to death. She loses everything because of his lack of self-control. He, on the other hand, mourns for no more than a week; he then takes up his lyre and diverts his sorrow into creative energy. He gains everything from her death: a new poetic identity, a new sexual identity, and new material for his verse.[6]

Moreover, Orpheus's mourning for Eurydice takes strange and disturbing forms in contrast to Proteus's treatment of the same myth in Virgil's *Georgics* 4; in the *Georgics* both Orpheus and Eurydice are poignant victims, issues of responsibility are blurred, and we are left with the sorrowful awareness of the *lacrimae rerum* and with the art of Orpheus's mournful song as a kind of therapy or solace for human suffering. In Ovid's narrator's treatment, on the other hand, Orpheus's story differs so strikingly from the Virgilian model as to raise numerous problematic questions about moral responsibility, about appropriate emotional response, and about the role of art in human experience.

In dealing with the comparable figure of Cephalus in Book 7, Anderson, Tissol, Ahl, and Johnson have variously shown how his story makes sense as the "confabulation" (Johnson) that results from Cephalus' elaborate denial of his guilt in Procris's death.[7] In his book, Stephen Wheeler similarly (but only in a passing reference) describes Orpheus as "caught in the loop of 'repetition compulsion' . . . telling stories that repeat and vary the theme of bringing the dead back to life" in the effort to "master his loss of Eurydice."[8] I wish to

push that point further in arguing, first, that, like Cephalus, Orpheus tries to deny his love and his responsibility for Eurydice in order to deflect his guilt; second, unlike Cephalus, who tells a story about himself, Orpheus uses his art to tell stories about others that obliquely justify his conduct and that attempt to celebrate his art. Orpheus's art thus becomes a complex strategy for evading feelings of guilt and love.

Indeed, a modern analogue may come even closer to Orpheus than the story of Cephalus in heightening our awareness of all the phenomena that are not saved in celebratory readings of Ovid's Orpheus such as Segal's. In a *New York Times* book review, Katha Pollitt reads Ted Hughes's **Birthday Letters,** his collection of poems about his marriage to Sylvia Plath, in ways that shed light, *mutatis mutandis,* on reading Ovid's narrator's story of Orpheus as well as Orpheus's own song within that story.[9] There is, of course, the critical difference that Hughes's poems are about historical, and even living, people, and the complication, furthermore, that Plath was a poet, too. Pollitt's reading is inevitably grounded in this complex mix of literary history, soap opera, and celebrity intrigue. Nevertheless, the following excerpts seem helpful in their unwitting suggestion of similarities between Ovid's Orpheus and Ted Hughes, with the added, if not directly relevant, attraction of the recent appearance of Ted Hughes's own translations from the *Metamorphoses,* his **Tales from Ovid.**[10] I cite here at length from Pollitt's review because numerous relevant parts are inseparable from less relevant ones:

> The mingled tenderness and pathos and bewilderment of [Hughes's verse] is quite moving, despite the low-energy writing. . . . It would be a hard heart and a tin ear that could remain impervious to [the best lines in **Birthday Letters**]. The trouble is, if you added them all up, you'd have a 20-page chapbook, instead of a volume of nearly 200 pages in which [his] intimate voice, insisting on its personal truth, is overwhelmed by others: ranting, self-justifying, rambling, flaccid, bombastic. Incident after incident makes the same point: she was the sick one, I was the "nurse and protector." I didn't kill her—poetry, Fate, her obsession with her dead father killed her. The more Hughes insists on his good intentions and the inevitability of Plath's suicide, the less convincing he becomes. One starts to wonder what it means to blame a suicide on Fate, or a father who died after all, when Plath was 8 years old, or on "fixed stars. . . ."

Throughout the book, Hughes depicts himself as a passive figure, a stand-in for Daddy in Plath's lurid psychodrama: "Your life / Was a liner I voyaged in." His own psyche is left curiously unexplored, as if nothing deep in his nature drew him to Plath, shaped their relationship, helped bring it to its disastrous end. Could this, however, really be the way it was? It may be that suicide only takes one—even if Plath had not attempted suicide and had a mental breakdown before she met

Hughes, it would be simple-minded to accuse him of causing her death—but surely marriage takes two. There's a striking lack of inward reflection here. . . .

Plath's poetry is one of intense compression and musicality, its imagery complex and ambiguous, whereas **Birthday Letters** is lax and digressive, the symbolism all on the surface, so these allusions, quotations and re-renderings serve mostly to remind us of what a great poet she was.

Inevitably, given the claims that these poems set the record straight, the question of truth arises. Plath's letters and journals present her as struggling hard to be a dutiful, literary wife—typing her husband's poems, promoting his work, rejoicing in his success and also resenting it. The difficulties—practical, social, and most of all, psychological—of being a woman of burning literary ambition preoccupied her from earliest adulthood. None of this struggle is reflected in **Birthday Letters,** nor does Hughes engage the fury that suffuses Plath's late poems—and with which so many women have identified—about being stuck at home with the babies and the housework and the boring neighbors. . . .

The storm of publicity surrounding **Birthday Letters** has turned into a kind of marital spin contest, an episode in the larger war between the sexes. Feminists have long been blamed for demonizing Hughes. . . . Hughes's partisans portray Plath as unsparingly and moralistically as Plath's partisans portray Hughes: One or the other is narcissistic, deceitful, impossibly demanding, oblivious, a user.

Here, however, is a thought: What if, as in many bad marriages, both partners were driven to the extremes of their personalities, did all sorts of awful things, including some that might look to outsiders like acts of saintly forbearance and others that might look totally mad but had a kind of intuitive rightness, and what if his poems and her poems each represent the limited, self-justifying perspective of a terribly injured and injuring spouse who wants all the friends to rally round and murmur their support? If we were friends, we might have to take sides. Because, however, we are readers, we can have both, whatever the biographers say, as long as the poems make the hair stand up on the back of our necks. Alas, with **Birthday Letters,** what is hair-raising is not the poetry, but the ghost of Sylvia Plath.

What seems fascinating to me about Hughes's take on Plath's suicide and poetry in Pollitt's reading is that it is a kind of *Tale from Ovid*: an unconscious re-working, almost, of Ovid's Orpheus and Eurydice, a story, which incidentally, is strikingly absent from Hughes's explicitly Ovidian sampler. Thus, like Hughes's poems as Pollitt describes them, Orpheus's collection of stories

includes resonant, elegant, and powerful moments to be sure, but these are complicated by much more extensive dissonances and illogicalities, even unacknowledged and bizarre contradictions, not to mention the embarrassment of the great *vates* singing his soulful compositions to an audience of flora and fauna with no humans in view.[11]

Like Hughes too, Orpheus blames the victim, only with even less clarity: Hughes knows that he is talking about Plath; by contrast, because he never discusses her explicitly we cannot hope to discover whether or not Orpheus realizes that his stories can be seen as variously demonizing Eurydice (albeit obliquely) and even proposing a counter-model to her in Pygmalion's statue woman. In addition, as Janan points out, Orpheus capitalizes on Eurydice's death both as poet and as lover, just as Hughes capitalizes on Plath's suicide, fame, and poetry in his own collection of poems. As with Hughes in Pollitt's shrewd assessment, we see no depth of character, no introspection, no self-awareness in Orpheus's song, or in the framing narrative about him, despite repeated assurances of his great stature as a sacred bard.

Another similarity is the use of the poems/stories to re-envision the beloved wife's death as justly deserved punishment combined with a cruel fate, but with no recognition of any responsibility or complicity on the husband's part. Of course, in Orpheus's case, this shifting of blame to the victim's moral dereliction and cursed fate is transferred to other characters, but it is my contention here that the bizarre inconsistencies that result most make sense as caused by unacknowledged guilt for the second death of Eurydice. Just as Pollitt, in her construction of a resisting reading,[12] uses her knowledge of Plath's life and poetry as a supplement to and intertext for Hughes's assertions of innocence, we can recall the Virgilian intertext and observe how Orpheus's odd fixations on the women of his stories and his own weird war between the sexes obliquely reflect his unresolved emotions about Eurydice, who is conspicuous by her silence and absence. In sum, I see striking resemblances between Hughes's (persona's) response to Plath's suicide and (Ovid's) Orpheus's responses to the second death of Eurydice, namely, in both cases: self-pity, denial, evasion of responsibility, bizarre deflections, and blaming the victim.

In fact, from the very beginning of Book 10, well before Orpheus's own song begins, Ovid's external narrator participates in Orpheus's guilt, denial, and evasion. His account is abrupt and condensed, yet, in a way, exaggerated as well. He takes the Virgilian elisions of Eurydice's speech and her evaporation into thin air in the *Georgics* to new extremes. His Eurydice dissolves first, then does not speak, and finally utters a farewell that is scarcely heard, if at all:

iamque iterum moriens non est de coniuge quicquam
questa suo (quid enim nisi se quereretur amatam?)
supremumque "vale," quod iam vix auribus ille
acciperet, dixit revolutaque rursus eodem est.

and now, dying yet again, she made no complaint about
her husband (for what would she have to complain
about, except that she was loved?) and uttered a final
"farewell" so faint that it scarcely reached his ears, and
turned back to the same place from which she had just
come.

(*Met.* 10.60-63)

Virgil's Proteus's Eurydice only speaks fleetingly, seeming to exonerate Orpheus by ambiguously blaming his
furor; Ovid's narrator's Eurydice, having already
vanished, blames no one and nothing. No ambiguity
remains, for Eurydice does not complain at all, and her
single word, *vale,* "farewell," at first seems to leave no
room for interpretation, no apparent gap in which to
make meaning.[13]

Far more radically than Virgil's Proteus, then, Ovid's
external narrator excises Eurydice. Proteus insists that
Orpheus is to be forgiven and is to be perceived as
forgivable, but the Ovidian narrator renders otiose any
issue of blame (which might then make forgiveness
possible or desirable) by the ingenious invocation of
love in the implied conditional clause of a contrary-to-
fact condition, in which the implied imperfect subjunctive makes the rhetorical question to the audience/reader
immediate and present, and with which the concluding
clause is merged: "for why, (if she were complaining,
but she isn't) would she complain now, unless (she
were complaining) that she has been loved?" The
extreme condensation of this intrusive appeal to the
audience rushes past all the problems it raises. Eurydice
has every reason, however, to complain of having been
loved, despite the narrator's cheery assumption that no
such reason is even imaginable. Moreover, the narrator
implies further that no reader could conceivably
disagree with his assumption that a woman (or perhaps
any human?) would always rather be loved, even at the
price of life itself, than never have been loved at all.
Whereas Proteus gently guides Virgil's reader, Ovid's
narrator is so confident and aggressive as potentially to
provoke his reader into resistance. In conjunction with
the silencing of Eurydice's voice (and also with the
omission of her rape by Aristaeus that then leads her to
her death in the *Georgics*), the narrator's complacent
conviction that being loved makes (a woman's) death
worthwhile may suggest to a resisting reader, especially
if she is a woman, that being loved by Orpheus (and
possibly even being loved by anyone at all) may (*pace*
Segal et al.) be essentially suicidal. Comparable to a
beloved *puella* in Roman elegy, Eurydice receives the
consolation of commemoration in song, but, alas, she is
not alive to enjoy it. The narrator ostentatiously draws
attention to Eurydice's vanishing and to her silence,[14]
particularly if the reader is recalling the *Georgics* as an
intertext.[15]

As a result, far more than in Proteus's account, the
Ovidian version of Eurydice invites the reader to *interrogate* the text, not just to mourn over it. Eurydice
herself is allowed to leave no gap, but the space from
which her body and voice are so conspicuously absent
can itself become the occasion for the reader to mediate
on the risks of being loved and on the value of art as
consolation for death. Producing meaning from silence
and from absence, we may choose to notice this exaggerated case of the conveniently vanishing and pleas-
ingly silent woman.[16] Such a Eurydice can become a
useful means to thinking about other compelling or
touching, but nevertheless convenient, deaths and van-
ishings in Roman texts: Creüsa, Dido, Lucretia, Cleopatra.[17] Certainly, her absence corresponds nicely to the
context of Hughes's ***Birthday Letters,*** where the shared
understanding between poet and reader is the knowledge
that Plath is dead and that the occasion of the poems is
her birthday (**"Freedom of Speech"**). This understanding, especially in light of the collection's dedication to
the couple's children, is potentially terribly disturbing,
as Hughes's various accusations against and criticisms
of Plath cannot receive her response, her self-defense,
or her own recriminations.

On the other hand, Eurydice's absence can be read as a
tribute to her feminine tact and to Orpheus's love: Segal contrasts Virgil's and Ovid's Eurydice's and favors
Ovid's (actually Orpheus's) sweet and forgiving
heroine:

> Virgil emphasized the bitterness of Eurydice's disap-
> pointment in Orpheus' failure. . . . Ovid has replaced
> bitterness with a womanly gentleness and sweetness.
> His Eurydice does not judge; she accepts. She under-
> stands, resignedly, that the very failure of her spouse is
> a proof, sadly, of his love. There is almost a tacit
> forgiveness, for the weakness of Orpheus is the pardon-
> able weakness of love. The emphatic *amatam* (*Met.*
> 10.61), echoing *amans* a few lines before (57) stresses
> the fact that the bond between them, the bond between
> "lover" and "beloved," is still unbroken.[18]

It seems to me, however, that Orpheus's stories make
much less sense if Orpheus simply receives this alleged
"tacit forgiveness" and accepts her unexpressed love as
his due. Rather, his too brief mourning and odd stories
suggest a failure to come to grips with her death and
with his role in it, resembling Hughes's poems in their
strenuous effort to deflect blame and to rationalize guilt.
For his tales are themselves not so much about "bringing the dead back to life"[19] as they are about art as a
poor substitute for life and love and a ludicrously
inadequate compensation for their lack: Hyacinthus,

somewhat like Daphne in Book 1, becomes both a memorial floral tribute to Apollo's sorrow and the material celebrated by Apollo's songs and lyre; tragic Myrrha, while pregnant, becomes a tree that not only gives birth in excruciating pain through its stiff bark, but also produces tears that are beautiful amber beads; in the crowning tour de force, of course, Pygmalion's beautiful statue becomes, by Venus's super-artistry, an ideal substitute for Eurydice, i.e., *mutatis mutandis,* a clone, a fembot android Barbie doll, a Stepford robot-wife, a perfect imitation of life, yet free of all annoying wifely encumbrances, such as a voice, a memory, a family, a history, a character.

Turning first to Hyacinthus (keeping in mind that the earlier story of Cyparissus was told by the external narrator, not by Orpheus), we see that Orpheus tells of Apollo's love for Hyacinthus and how that love mysteriously leads to Apollo's accidentally killing his beloved with an unlucky throw of a discus. Though Apollo the Great Healer tries desperately to heal Hyacinthus by applying herbs to the wound, it remains, alas, *inmedicabile*—incurable. For all his divine gifts of healing, Apollo cannot bring his love back to life. *Nil prosunt artes*; his arts do no good. In telling this particular tale, Orpheus goes to great lengths to emphasize Apollo's innocence, his heroic efforts to save Hyacinthus, and, finally, the poems (*carmina*), the flower, and the annual festival that Apollo establishes as memorials to his lost lover. Nevertheless, Apollo himself takes, at least fleetingly, some sort of responsibility for the death of Hyacinthus, initially calling the mortal wound *mea crimina* at 10.197 and calling Hyacinthus both *dolor* and *facinus meum*. Moreover, Apollo actually says at 10.198-99 that his own hand should be noted (*inscribenda*) with the death (that is, formally acknowledged as guilty of the death), and even that he is the source, the author, of his beloved's death:

> . . . mea dextera leto
> inscribenda tuo est. ego sum tibi funeris auctor.

> . . . my right hand ought to be inscribed with (publicly proclaimed as responsible for) your death. I am the author of your death.

(10.198-99)

No sooner, however, does the issue of moral responsibility emerge than Apollo hastens to banish it:

> quae mea culpa tamen? nisi si lusisse vocari
> culpa potest, nisi culpa potest et amasse vocari.

> yet what fault is it of mine? Unless having played around can be called a fault, unless having loved also can be called a fault.

(10.200-1)

Although these questions rhetorically deflect blame from Apollo, they also recall the question whereby the external narrator earlier deflected blame from Orpheus

(who is now singing about Apollo): *quid enim nisi se quereretur amatam?* (10.61). Whereas the narrator asked (and now, in light of Orpheus and Apollo, the question seems defensive) how Eurydice could reasonably complain about being loved, Orpheus has Apollo conclude that "playing around" (*lusisse*)—at games, with lovers, with words—involves no *culpa* whatsoever. Even more directly parallel to the external narrator's question is Apollo's second (and even more problematic) implied question: Can it be called a fault to have loved? Of course, the negative condition leaves the question implicit and less open, for the rhetorical goal is gently to coerce the reader or the members of an audience into muttering to themselves that, naturally, loving can never be wrong. Clearly, however, it is enormously to Orpheus's advantage in dealing with his betrayal of Eurydice to persuade himself that, as it was all for love, he was in no way culpable. So too Hughes often describes himself as passively watching Plath undo herself, the while making caustic and distanced observations at her expense (e.g., **"The Fever," "Ouija"**), intimating again and again that internal demons and fate destroyed her, forces altogether beyond his control.

Similarly, in the story of Myrrha, Orpheus presumably sets out to show (judging by his mini-proem at 10.148-54) that hers is a story of a girl who gets the punishment she deserves for her passion (and so here, it seems, it can be a fault to have loved, after all). Even though Myrrha tries to commit suicide rather than acknowledge her incestuous desire for her father Cinyras, even though her nurse eggs her on, even though her father expresses sexual interest particularly for a girl of his daughter's age, and even though she hesitates and wants to change her mind just before her nurse hands her over to her father, Orpheus blames her exclusively and describes Cinyras as the wronged and innocent victim. Like Hughes, Orpheus adds an atmosphere of general doom that somehow seems to be Myrrha's fault, too:

> ter pedis offensi signo est revocata, ter omen
> funereus bubo letali carmine fecit:
> it tamen. . . .

> three times has she been called back because of the omen of tripping on something, three times has the deadly owl caused a bad omen with its lethal song. All the same, she continues on her way. . . .

(10.452-54)

Orpheus blames Myrrha repeatedly for the incest that follows, from the very beginning of his song. He blames the nurse once explicitly as *male sedula,* and many details thereafter implicitly corroborate that judgment, although Orpheus never recommends any alternatives to the incestuous union, not even commending, for instance, the nobility of the plan of suicide. He seems to favor denunciation ("just say no") over any deeper understanding or alternative resolution. On the other hand, for all the blame he assigns, in keeping with his unexplained postmarital misogyny, he never acknowledges any fault on the part of Cinyras.

We have already seen Cinyras, however, in two questionable positions. Least offensive, by itself, at least, and most understandable, is his failure to notice something wrong in Myrrha's preference for a husband who resembles her father. Flattered and pleased, he is quick to attribute Myrrha's signs of hysteria to virginal fears. Then, with his next appearance, we learn that he feels no obligation to be faithful to his wife or to honor her religious obligations with any parallel abstinence of his own. Orpheus seems to attribute this lapse to the nurse's taking advantage of Cinyras's being *gravem vino,* but even though he has already heard that a beauty has conceived a serious passion (*veros amores*) for him, Cinyras is not immediately moved, wine notwithstanding. He does not, however, reject the question out of hand, as Myrrha's sense of his great *pietas* and *memoria moris* (10.354-55) might lead us to expect.

Rather, he is sober enough to ask a pointed question about the girl's age, and, upon hearing that she is just the same age as Myrrha, immediately commands that she be brought to him. Thus, although Orpheus has almost ostentatiously avoided blaming him, Cinyras' easy willingness to betray his wife and his special interest in young girls of his daughter's age are part of the problematic background that we bear in mind as we come to the consummation scene:

> accipit obsceno genitor sua viscera lecto
> virgineosque metus levat hortaturque timentem.
> forsitan aetatis quoque nomine "filia" dixit:
> dixit et illa "pater," sceleri ne nomina desint.

> her father receives his own flesh and blood in the obscene bed and relieves her virginal fears and encourages her since she is so frightened. Perhaps he even called her 'daughter,' as a name befitting her age, and she said 'father,' lest explicit names be missing from the crime.

> (10.465-68)

For almost two hundred lines, this moment is the one that Orpheus has led us on both to look forward to and to dread. The deed itself is not actually mentioned, however, and this passage is far more disturbing even than the incestuous act. For one thing, Cinyras suddenly takes control and becomes an active participant in the story as subject of active verbs and as centrally placed *genitor* in line 465. That line appears to be on the verge of plunging us into depths of horror at the act itself, with the early appearance of *obsceno* and the vivid concreteness of *sua viscera.* Yet *lecto* deferred to the end of the line mocks prurient expectation, as the line turns out only to say, really, that she got into bed with him, an idea already far more blatantly expressed by

the nurse's action of joining their bodies (*devota . . . corpora iunxit,* 10.464). The only additional contribution, besides a lewd atmosphere, that the line makes is to enclose the couple verbally as well as physically in the obscene bed.

What do they do there in the *obsceno . . . lecto*? They talk. He soothes her virginal fears, but how? By especially gentle foreplay? No, by exhortation, by encouraging speech: *hortatur . . . timentem.* However difficult it may be to imagine a father so distant that he does not recognize his daughter's body (and hair, facial structure, smell) at close proximity, even in the darkest of dark rooms, it is vastly more difficult to imagine his not recognizing her voice in conversation. Of course, *he* exhorts *her;* perhaps she only murmurs to avoid detection. But no, or at least, *maybe* not, because now Orpheus adds a speculation of his own to what has seemed to be an authoritative account: *forsitan aetatis quoque nomine "filia" dixit: / dixit et illa "pater."*

The intrusion of *forsitan* at this crucial point exacerbates the problem of narrative authority that has lurked in the margins of the story at least because the nurse's encounter with Myrrha was attributed to unknown sources. Hitherto, the story has fluctuated throughout between two modes: on the one hand, a more self-effacing reporting that, explicitly because of its knowledge of intimate or completely private detail (Myrrha's secret feelings, Myrrha's monologue), seems to draw on authoritative sources; on the other hand, authorial intrusions of foreboding, condemnation, opinion, and so on, that seem likely to represent Orpheus's own perspective on the story he has inherited.

Forsitan goes far beyond those intrusions in its suggestion that Orpheus has an even greater investment in the incest plot than his earlier remarks so much as hinted at, for all their strong conviction. Not only are we now asked to imagine that Cinyras and Myrrha used normal father-daughter terms of endearment to each other in bed without Cinyras's recognizing his only daughter's voice, but the prurient interest that Orpheus feels is captured by his openly speculating on the bedroom conversation that is somehow so much more horrifying than the incest itself, a kind of speaking forth of the unspeakable *nefas.* One horrible aspect is the corroboration of the sense that has been building because Cinyras told Myrrha to choose a suitor (without understanding her tears, but attributing them to virginal fear, *virginei Cinyras haec credens esse timoris* ["Cinyras believing these to be signs of virginal fear"], 10.361) that he does not really know his daughter at all.

Now he soothes her actual virgin fears but does not understand her or know her well enough to recognize her. Moreover, the sweet comfort and encouragement that he tenderly offers now to a stranger, to the girl unknown to him, are, *mutatis mutandis* of course, exactly what she needed then. Had he been truly fatherly to Myrrha when she needed it, conceivably the passion could have been diffused, defused, sublimated, even redeemed. Orpheus's *forsitan* suggests, however, what we might have expected. In spite of his moral posturings, Orpheus has been leading up to this outcome and would surely have been disappointed had Myrrha been helped early on, or if she had successfully pulled back from the *scelus* at the last minute. *Forsitan* brings him into the act with his hopeful guesses at the horrible verbal pre-enactment. As he finishes speaking the unspeakable, he quickly adds a moral note: "maybe they actually called each other father and daughter! . . . oh, yes, of course, so as to confirm the crime in name as well as in deed."

In oral recitation for an audience,[20] this section would be even more powerful, with Orpheus speaking in four different tones: as I see it, distant and judgmental in line 465, fatherly and tender in line 466, salacious and eager in 467 and the first half of 468, and then rational and condemning in the remaining half line. Of course, these would be punctuated by the voice of Myrrha and the voice of Cinyras calling to each other, *pater!*, *filia!* Possibly, too, in performance the voice of Cinyras would be hard or impossible to differentiate from the tender fatherly tone of Orpheus in line 466. If so, the similarity could reinforce the growing sense that Orpheus has so carefully avoided blaming Cinyras (although it almost slips out in line 465) because he in fact takes vicarious pleasure in the *scelus* that he carefully assigns to Myrrha throughout. Thus, he can safely identify with Cinyras as the innocent victim of Myrrha's evil machinations, while enjoying a vicarious participation in the *obsceno . . . lecto.*[21]

In light of Orpheus's responsibility for Eurydice's death and of his subsequent alleged predilection for young boys, followed by his prolonged fantasy about a sexually cooperative statute-doll, one can readily understand the appeal of a young virgin daughter whom one can control as both father and lover, while comfortably blaming her for the sexual involvement; all this too in her mother's absence and enabled by a servant who can easily be scapegoated along with the *virgo* herself. Similar to Pygmalion, Cinyras has, at least temporarily, complete control over a completely vulnerable beloved, by combining the roles of creator and lover in absolute, incontestable possession. Like Jupiter and Apollo, too, Cinyras can possess and dominate (and even destroy) the beloved with impunity.

Thus, Orpheus's stories come to share thematic continuities even more profound than the explicit ones of the initial program: misogyny, a preference for boys, and a vindictive pleasure in the punishment of sexual passion. Connecting these apparent incongruities is the consistent pattern of pleasure in the complete subjection of the beloved through various combinations of ownership, reification, death, and scapegoating. Because these all seem to grow out of guilt and anxiety and unfinished mourning in connection with the death of Eurydice, they surely make most sense to us as a complex mix of denial, projection, and transference. The stories are like symptoms of the inevitable failure of repression, as Eurydice haunts Orpheus's mind out of having been loved too much.

In such a view of the effects of Orpheus's song, it is oddly fitting that, before embarking on his extensive account of anguish and cruelty in the story of Myrrha, Orpheus offers his *pièce de résistance* in the glorification of the aesthetic by way of the story of Pygmalion and his ivory girl.[22] The transitional tales that lead up to Pygmalion remind us of Orpheus's early promise to sing not only of boys beloved by the gods, but also of girls deservedly punished for their illicit passions. Orpheus introduces the story of the Propoetides as a contrast to that of Hyacinthus, but he quickly digresses to the *gens inpia* (10.232) of the Cerastae in order, apparently, to rejoice in *alma* (10.230) Venus's swift punishment of their alleged violation of the code of hospitality in the brutal sacrifice of guests. In the absence of more information and of fuller versions of this story, we can only observe the *Schadenfreude* with which Orpheus tells of the punishment and his concomitant ability to describe Venus as *alma* as she nicely calculates the perfect punishment. Returning to the Propoetides, Orpheus connects the vindictive wrath of Venus to the theme of women being punished as they deserve:

> Sunt tamen obscenae Venerem Propoetides ausae
> esse negare deam; pro quo sua, numinis ira,
> corpora cum forma primae vulgasse feruntur:
> utque pudor cessit sanguisque induruit oris,
> in rigidum parvo silicem discrimine versae.

> But the obscene Propoetides dared to say that Venus was no goddess—for which, because of her divine wrath, they are said to have been the first to prostitute their bodies along with their beauty; and as their modesty waned and the blood hardened in their faces, they were turned into rigid rock with only a slight difference from their previous condition.

(10.238-42)

When Pygmalion enters Orpheus's song, he reinforces Orpheus's position, and indeed takes the misogyny a step further:

> Quas [Propoetides] quia Pygmalion aevum per crimen agentis
> viderat, offensus vitiis, quae plurima menti
> femineae natura dedit, sine coniuge caelebs
> vivebat thalamique diu consorte carebat.

> since Pygmalion had seen the Propoetides spending their days in crime, he was outraged at their faults,

which nature gave so plentifully to the female mind, and he was living as a celibate without a spouse and for a long time was lacking a partner for his bed.

(10.243-46)

Outrage piled upon outrage here makes it difficult to sort out the cumulative effect of this passage. First of all, Pygmalion may not know, but in any case certainly does not acknowledge, that the Propoetides have been compelled to the *crimen* and *vitia* that so offend him. Furthermore, the *crimen* and *vitia,* such as they are, do not affect him directly at all. Assuming with Orpheus that prostitution is a shameless preference for promiscuity, rather than (generally) an economic necessity for survival or (as in this case) a divine punishment, Pygmalion concludes from the particular case of the Propoetides that a general application obtains: nature (not Venus) has given such faults to all women's minds. Finally, from the *vitia* of a particular group of women, and from the universal condemnation of the nature of all women, Pygmalion shifts to a priggish rejection of marriage. That any whores ever existed anywhere requires celibacy! (Why Pygmalion does not therefore embrace the much touted pederasty of the larger narrative context, we cannot, apparently, be told.) Orpheus seems to imply that Pygmalion (and there is a suggestion of some universal norm as well) very much wants a wife, but that no real woman will do. Thus, in an extreme displacement, perhaps, Orpheus dismisses his *culpa* for returning Eurydice to Hades; after all, if Pygmalion is right about women's minds, no man should want or keep a wife at all.

Pygmalion, however, actually has an alternative to a real woman as wife:

interea niveum mira feliciter arte
sculpsit ebur formamque dedit, qua femina nasci
nulla potest, operisque sui concepit amorem.

meanwhile he has sculpted snowy ivory with marvelous art, and has given it a shape from which (in which?) no woman can be born, and he has conceived a passion for his own *opus.*

(10.247-49)

The first word, *interea,* makes the transition loose, casual, and temporal; Pygmalion was living without a wife, celibate, and without a bedmate (three versions, just in case we might not grasp the idea), and *meanwhile* he just happened to sculpt some ivory and give it the shape of a non-woman (*femina . . . nulla*) with wondrous skill (*mira . . . arte*). This skill, this marvelous art (along with the misogyny that presumably produces it) links Orpheus and Pygmalion, who has generally been taken as "the creative artist *par excellence.*" Pygmalion is then to be equated with "Ovid himself," and is often seen as a parallel to Orpheus, so that Ovid thereby "provides a metaphorical reflection of

the creative and restorative power of his own art. . . . In myths like those of Pygmalion and Orpheus, the poet—Ovid himself—finds his artistic life confirmed and its highest aspirations clarified."[23]

Alison Sharrock has also equated "Ovid himself" with Pygmalion, but in more guarded and potentially pejorative terms. For Sharrock, Pygmalion's story, "by foregrounding the lover as artist / artist as lover, . . . exposes the workings of gendered power relations in erotic and specifically elegiac discourse."

If Pygmalion is subliminally a metaphor for the elegist, he is perhaps *quite precisely Ovid,* the elegist writing epic. . . . As *Ovid / Pygmalion* falls in love with his own art, he breathes the life of flawed elegy into the frozen beauty of epic.[24]

Sharrock emphasizes the lover's love of his own creation in *Amores* 1.2 and in the Pygmalion story (*operisque sui concepit amorem,* 10.249) and so conflates Ovid/Pygmalion with minimal reference to the go-between Orpheus, except in connection with his ties to the genre of elegy. As Leach pointed out in 1964, however, Orpheus is least in control of his material in telling the story of Pygmalion and deviates wildly from his expressed programmatic intentions with a story in which no boys are loved by gods or bad girls punished for their illicit loves:

. . . The puzzling discrepancy suggests that Orpheus' thoughts and purpose wander as he sings. The relationship of the tales to the mind of the singer becomes much closer and more intricate than [a] simple outline suggests. . . . In all of [Orpheus's] tales save that of Pygmalion, love is presented as a fatal impulse verging on death. The Pygmalion story stands out by contrast for it is the least closely related to Orpheus' two categories, but rather, as a tale of love and an artist, comes closest to the experiences of the teller himself.[25]

Pygmalion's "happy" (*feliciter*) substitution of flawless ivory beauty for any actual woman follows close upon Venus's transformation of the Propoetides into *rigidum . . . silicem* (10.242). There, Orpheus regards as negligible (*parvo . . . discrimine*) the difference between these *obscenae* (as they lose their *pudor*) and the rock that they become. Only six lines later, however, Orpheus finds Pygmalion's equally rigid ivory creation fortunate and marvelous, of a shape unlike that of any woman who can be born. Although neither Orpheus nor Pygmalion articulates this point, it is consistent with Orpheus's negligences and misogynies hitherto that, for a real woman to be born, it would regrettably be necessary that yet another real woman be involved in order to give her birth. Thus, hard rock and snowy ivory are both, ironically, more tractable, more bearable than any engagement with actual flesh, both in the eyes of Orpheus the teller and of Pygmalion the hero of the tale. As a result, Pygmalion himself creates the statue and gives birth himself *ex nihilo* to his own passion for his own *opus.*

The ivory itself, too, seems to come conveniently out of nowhere. Whereas Orpheus's gifts and history as a singer are carefully (if strangely) established by the external narrator, Pygmalion's previous circumstances, apart from the bizarre and condensed genealogy of his misogyny, go untold. Is he a sculptor by profession? Does he just happen to sculpt the ivory non-woman (and just happen to have the ivory available) on a whim? As a hobby? The lack of at least some concrete detail of the kind provided by the narrators of the earlier stories of artists heightens the sense of unreality, of a fairy-tale world of pure fantasy.[26] Thus, the amazing non-woman occurs without apparent effort (consider, by way of contrast, all the details about weaving in the Arachne story, or the artful laying on of wax and feathers to produce the wings of Icarus and Daedalus). Though not a woman, the statue manages to look just like one:

> virginis est verae facies, quam vivere credas
> et, si non obstet reverentia, velle moveri:
> ars adeo latet arte sua . . .

> It is the likeness of a real maiden, whom you would suppose to be alive and who, if modesty did not forbid it, you would think was wishing to get some action. Art is hidden by its own art.

> (10.250-52)

The ivory simulacrum (pod-girl) looks exactly like a real girl (and a true virgin) and as such manages to serve as the nexus for a number of fantasies of impossible wish-fulfillment.

The Ivory Robot is, first of all, unlike any real woman who can be born and yet still manages to seem like a real woman. It is an authentic virgin in every conceivable sense: unpolluted by carnal birth, family ties, personal history, social class, political context; indeed, it has no flesh and no mind with which to be unvirginal. It is the artist's own possession and creation, his *opus* (both artistic achievement and sexual, procreative prowess), yet it seems to be human, alive because it is the acme of mimetic perfection. With the "if you should happen to be there" implied by the subjunctive *credas,* Orpheus assumes an eager complicity with Pygmalion's artistic project on the part of each individual reader or member of the audience because the "you" of the expressed part of his condition, *credas,* is singular. "You" would recognize Pygmalion's self-concealing art in "your" belief that the statue was alive. "You" would also conclude that the statue wanted to be moved (*velle moveri*), or perhaps merely to move around (taking *moveri* as a middle rather than as a passive) if modesty/awe/reverence should not prevent it.

The muddle of my paraphrase here is intended to capture how unclear this passage is, how unusually heavily it relies on a complicit reader to fill in the

blanks, to complete the articulation of one impossible fantasy after another. Whose modesty or reverence might prevent exactly what here at line 251 is not at all clear. Is the reader too sexually modest to allow him-(probably not her-) self to envision the ivory as moving or too awestruck or religiously reverent to imagine such a possibility? Could it be that the ivory *opus* too modest to wish to be moved, or too reverent before its creator to wish to move? In light of these uncertainties, the vague *qua* of line 248 comes to seem (retrospectively) equally puzzling, especially in conjunction with the unequivocal present and presumably universalizing indicative, *potest.* Bömer assimilates the line to an Ovidian *Lieblingsmotiv* of opposing *ars* to *natura* (citing *Met.* 11.235-36, where such an opposition does indeed occur):

> Ovid benutzt die Gelegenheit, hier eines seiner Lieblingsmotive in einer besonderen Variation vorzuführen, den Gegensatz *ars-natura* ([*forma*], *qua femina nasci nulla potest*), in X 252 ist die *ars* so kunstvoll, dass man sie nicht bemerkt. . . .[27]

It is, of course, the task of commentaries to clarify and inevitably to simplify as well. Nevertheless, Bömer's characteristic desire to remove a difficulty and to make a passage comfortably comparable to other passages here makes him seem particularly anxious and quick to leap ahead of himself to the more accessible though paradoxical formulation of 10.252: *ars adeo latet arte sua.* Commentaries and most translations seem overinvested in clearing up the complexities and ambiguities that are striking features of 10.247-52. By contrast, for instance, Elsner explores the punning possibilities of *reverentia,* which etymologically "inscribes the term *re vere* ('in reality') and thus asserts the whole problematic of the 'real' woman which the image cannot be."[28]

Thus, it seems to me, Orpheus has been exceptionally successful in luring modern scholarly readers into participating in voyeuristic delight in the revelation of the ivory *opus.*[29] For we do not know at this point that the statue is a nude, and the vague *qua* has generally been processed as an ablative of comparison implying the statue's superiority to any possible human female *in the absence of any expressed comparative form.* Modern critics have generally desired, then, before the fact, that there be at least a sublimely lovely naked virginal artificial girl, and probably also the goddess-whore suggested by Sharrock,[30] for them to fall in love with along with Pygmalion. The Orpheus who could bring in the trees in groves can take in the human (male?) audience quite as effectively (though what the effect on the wild animals and birds would be is hard to imagine).

After all, the *si non obstet reverentia* clause might quite as easily imply *tibi* as *ei* and then mean (perhaps more easily, because imputing emotions to the statue within the indirect statement set up by *credas* is both syntactically and psychologically less likely) "if you weren't too awestruck/dazzled to think of it" or "if you weren't too respectful (of vulnerable youth? or virginity? or beauty in art?) to allow yourself to think of such a thing." Similarly, if *qua* is taken as an ablative of comparison (and not as an odd and awkward ablative of place where or from which, either of which it may just as easily be), then any comparative adjective could go with *formam*: e.g., he gave the ivory a shape more lumpy/elongated/emaciated than that of any woman ever born (I have replaced the Loeb's "perfect" with possible alternatives and retained all the rest of the sentence). If, on the other hand, *qua* is not comparative, the phrase seems more plausibly to mean "he has given to the ivory a shape / beauty in which (from which?) no woman can be born." On this reading, because women are born as lumpy babies from distended mothers, Orpheus only says at this point that the ivory *opus* in no way resembles a new baby girl (or a woman giving birth). The previous triple assurance of Pygmalion's having no wife or bedmate, however, combined with the suggestive adjective *niveum* and the hope held out by *mira arte,* has presumably encouraged readers to supply the desired object, to create it themselves, before the details of its existence emerge clearly in the text.

The epigram that Orpheus sums up with—*ars adeo latet arte sua*—is thus an exceptionally apt one for describing much of the modern critical reception of, and recorded reader response to, the Pygmalion story. So deeply do the hints given correspond to many readers' fantasies that they (the readers) are manipulated into an engagement sufficiently intense to enable them to anticipate the story as it unfolds without their realizing how artfully they have been drawn in. The matchless mimesis in the visual arts has been verbally replicated/reflected/represented in Orpheus's song. Unresisting readers have been implicitly revealed as sharing Pygmalion's obsession with virginity (his fear that all real women are whores); with flawless, untouchable, and rigid beauty; with mimetic perfection in art; with a perfect virgin goddess who even, paradoxically, seems eager to move in unwifelike fashion. Readers who share such obsessions are likely to understand as well, if only implicitly, the strange ambivalence toward Eurydice that allowed Orpheus to turn back, to lose her, and to mourn so briefly. After all, she was a wife, a woman (and so probably given to complaining, as *quereretur* and even *non est de coniuge quicquam / questa suo* at 10.60-61 subtly hint ["unless she were complaining she did not complain at all about her husband"]). How lovely, by contrast, the speechless ivory beauty!

Whereas Orpheus's blaming Myrrha corresponds nicely to Hughes's blaming Plath, the **Birthday Letters** provide no analogue to the story of Pygmalion and the Statue, except perhaps very loosely in the poem, **"Fidelity,"** where Hughes cherishes the memory of a "lovely girl" whom he knew during his courtship of Plath:

> She and I slept in each other's arms,
> Naked and easy as lovers, a month of nights,
> Yet never once made love. A holy law
> Had invented itself, somehow, for me.
> But she too served it, like a priestess,
> Tender, kind, and stark naked behind me.

In contrast to the dead Plath, this "sisterly comforting" becomes an eternal possession:

> . . . What
> Knighthood possessed me there? I think of it
> As a kind of time that cannot pass,
> That I never used, so still possess.

The unused beloved lasts forever; the used one dies. It will come as no great surprise, then, that Pygmalion does appear in Hughes's **Tales from Ovid,** and in a tortured version much augmented: the Propoetides undergo a second transformation "as by some occult connection, every woman's uterus to a spider;" a dream woman, "a spectre, sick of unbeing" possesses Pygmalion and through him sculpts the statue. Hughes thus makes Pygmalion the victim of occult forces through the medium of a ghostly woman linked somehow to the bite of a horrible spider-woman, a picture not unlike his view of himself as a victim of Plath's demons.

Even in Orpheus's less tortured account, Pygmalion is possessed, but only *after* making his statue; he responds to his own achievements in a kind of attenuated narcissism, adding to the *amor* he conceived for his own *opus* at 10.249:

> . . . miratur et haurit
>   pectore Pygmalion simulati corporis ignes.

> Pygmalion marvels and drinks in the flames of passion
> from the heart of the body he has simulated (or: in his
> heart drinks in flames of passion for the body he has
> simulated).

> (10.252-53)

He is deceived by his own success, marvels at his marvelous art (*miratur* echoes *mira arte*), and then the syntax is potentially confusing again at line 253. Bömer helpfully assures us that *pectore* is locative and that *haurire ignes* is equivalent to *concipere amorem*, in which case, of course, the text is merely repeating itself. Although *pectore* certainly can mean "in Pygmalion's heart," it could surely also seem to mean "from the heart of the simulated body he drinks in fires (of passion)" which would capture perfectly the way in which he has been deceived by his own art, has ceased to know it as art, and has moved from a self-contained *amor* to *ignes* emanating (in his mind) from the statue, which Orpheus himself reminds us here is but a simulated body, with *simulati* strategically placed at the center of the line.

Hughes's augmented Pygmalion resembles a thinly veiled version of his own sense of having been seized by Plath's demons; Orpheus's Pygmalion is possessed by the passion that he perceives as emanating from his own statue. The (very slight) gap between Orpheus's perceptions and Pygmalion's allows for the reader's participation in a way that Hughes's more monolithic treatment cannot. Readers can choose to participate in Pygmalion's perspective, or, as Orpheus does, though only fleetingly and presumably inadvertently, can distance themselves from it. Many readers have, as we have seen, chosen to identify with Pygmalion, eagerly anticipating the miracle of the statue's transformation. In so doing, they share in Orpheus's larger purpose (again, one assumes, inadvertent) of replacing with an extended erotic fantasy the unpleasant complexities of a real wife with legitimate complaints and of real responsibility for her. Segal, Sharrock, and J. Hillis Miller all read Pygmalion as standing for Ovid, either occluding Orpheus or including him as sharing without differentiation in the merged perspective of both Pygmalion and Ovid; moreover, the possibility of there being any external narrator between Orpheus and Ovid does not occur to them.

Another point of view, however, is not only possible but is actually inscribed in Book 11, where, after having addressed himself throughout Book 10 to audiences of gods, trees, wild animals, and rocks, Orpheus finally confronts a human audience of real women, the Thracian *matres* who quickly identify him as a *feminarum contemptor* (cf.11.6-9). Perhaps familiar with the powerful misogynies of his song and perhaps unwilling to be replaced by animated ivory dolls, these wives break the power of Apollonian song to subdue and oppress by dismembering Orpheus in a Bacchic revel. As Joseph Farrell has pointed out, such confrontations in the *Metamorphoses* between pluralistic and monologic forces clearly stand "at the center of the poem's meaning . . . this type of confrontation . . . was also, as Ovid's personal experience tragically attests, a crucial issue in the increasingly authoritarian climate of the late Augustan principate."[31] For all their rabid violence against Orpheus and his animal train, as the narrator so indignantly describes it, the women retaliate in their own indignation and overturn however strange a form of Roman military triumph (I use the reading *triumphi* at the end of 11.22)[32] with a feminist populist uprising. The narrator uses a series of accusative participles to make Orpheus's victimization vivid and pathetic, but unwisely emphasizes that this is the first time Orpheus has ever spoken in vain and the first time that his voice has affected and effected *nothing*. The narrator fails to realize that the women's view of the bard's eloquence is not the same as his own: that Orpheus's main affected audience hitherto has been the gods of the underworld, who rewarded him for moving them with his song by restoring Eurydice, only that he might kill

her off again; moreover, he has moved or at least numbed and thunderstruck (*attonitas*) a crowd of animals and insensate things; finally, he has indeed moved the women as they listened in, moved them precisely to destroy him for reasons that make simply dismissing them as *sacrilegae* seem far too one-sided.

The narrator is horrified, however, at the sacrilege against Apollo's *vates,* calls on Jupiter for sympathy, and laments the passing of a voice that rocks and wild animals appreciated, but not humans. No sense of Dionysus' power or of women's power touches the narrator as he grieves over the exhalation of *anima* from the sacred mouth of the bard. Like Adonis, one of the most minor characters of his own song, Orpheus is lost to the winds, as ephemeral and fragmented as the frail anemone. The narrator in full seriousness recounts the mourning of birds, rocks and trees:

> te maestae volucres, Orpheu, te turba ferarum,
> te rigidi silices, tua carmina saepe secutae
> fleverunt silvae; positis te frondibus arbor
> tonsa comas luxit. . . .
>
> For you, O Orpheus!, did the grieving birds weep; for you a whole crowd of wild beasts wept. For you, the hard rocks, and even the forests that had often followed your singing, wept also; a tree that had lost its leaves in grief mourned for you too with its head thus shorn in sorrow. . . .
>
> (11.44-47)

In the *Amores,* Ovid's *amator-poeta* laments the death of Corinna's parrot in an elegy that has funny elements because the deceased is only a bird, but also has a sweet and tender quality one would not expect in such a poem. Conversely, in another lament in the same collection, he mourns the death of the poet Tibullus in a poem that is far more preposterous because of its inflated and disproportionate extravagance in praising Tibullus and in describing the grief of (and competition among) his mourners.[33] Both poems seem to be part of the background to the violations of decorum with which the narrator earnestly mourns the death of Orpheus. In particular, the detail of the tree putting aside its leaves as a shearing off of hair in a gesture of mourning is so extravagant as to verge on the ludicrous, and the repetition of *te* in fivefold apostrophe, to a man whom no humans mourn at all, becomes funny by its excess as well.

Inadvertently producing something more like the implicit near-ridicule of the poet Tibullus than like the affectionate tribute to the parrot, the narrator moves now to new categories of non-human groupies of the dead star:

> . . . lacrimis quoque flumina dicunt
> increvisse suis, obstrusaque carbasa pullo
> naides et dryades passosque habuere capillos.

. . . they say that even the rivers expanded with the addition of their own tears, and the naiads and dryads wore the dark outer garment of mourning and let their hair fall loose and disheveled in their grief.

(11.47-49)

In contrast to the naiads and nymphs, who, in Book 9, gently comfort Byblis and help her to weep as she turns into a fountain of her own tears, the naiads and dryads here follow the tree's example and go into human modes of mourning, the dark clothing being especially *gauche,* again reminding us of the absence of humans to mourn the great artist's passing. (Of course, Orpheus's story traditionally emphasizes his ability to charm nature, but the idea is surely that, so great is his vatic power, he even moves inanimate objects and animals as well as, rather than to the exclusion of, gods and mortals; for a similar *topos,* compare the last lines of the Anglican hymn, "When Jesus left His Father's throne:" "should we forget our Saviour's praise, the stones themselves would sing," where the future less vivid condition suggests the unlikelihood of such forgetting in a hymn that is specifically about the children singing "Hosanna" when Jesus enters Jerusalem on Palm Sunday. Similarly, of course, Orpheus succeeds in moving the gods to restore Eurydice at the beginning of Book 10. In the external narrator's inept treatment, Orpheus's magical powers are subsumed in a *reductio ad absurdum,* most notably here in Book 11[34] and in the extravagant and interminable catalogue of trees at 10.86-105 that follows close upon the arrestingly brief account of Orpheus's arrestingly brief period of mourning for Eurydice.) The narrator confines himself to the birds, stones, trees, and animals of his earlier account; others report that rivers weep as well and swell as a result. Returning to Orpheus himself, the sympathetic narrator reports a miracle:

> membra iacent diversa locis, caput, Hebre, lyramque
> excipis, et (mirum!), medio dum labitur amne,
> flebile nescio quid queritur lyra, flebile lingua
> murmurat exanimis, respondent flebile ripae.

> His limbs he scattered all about; O Hebrus, you receive both his head and his lyre, and (o wondrous portent!) as it floats along midstream, his lyre makes some sad complaint or other; his lifeless tongue murmurs some sad something or other; and the shores themselves respond with some sad something or other.

(11.50-53)

In contrast to the delicacy of Adonis' floral disintegration, the scattered limbs of Orpheus are the grotesque residue of the *sparagmos,* and the equally grotesque and far more surreal murmuring head and lyre float along singing a vague dirge for themselves, with antiphonal responses from the riverbanks (once again, no humans notice or care). As Anderson has powerfully argued, the *flebile nescio quid* of the lyre and the cor-

responding *flebile* uttered by the dead tongue in the floating head are striking (to say the least) substitutes for Orpheus's sad cry of "Eurydice" in the *Georgics.*[35]

Critics have frequently found fault with Ovid's excess in portraying Philomela's writhing and quivering tongue in Book 6 as it returns to its mistress's feet, still trying to voice her indignation at the outrage of rape and betrayal, as well as of its own excision. Orpheus's devotees, however, ignore or downplay his surreal babbling head with its lifeless tongue that has nothing to say except that it is not happy. The *flebile nescio quid* suggests, in fact, that Orpheus's whole song, with its compulsive reinforcement of the power of Apollo and Venus has been a series of attempts at transference and denial of his own general unhappiness and an effort at shoring up his sense of his own importance through affiliation with ruthlessly powerful deities.

For when he finally returns to the beginning of Orpheus's story from the opening of Book 10, the narrator abandons the pursuit of Orpheus's scattered body parts in favor of rekindling lost romance; Orpheus is suddenly back in the underworld and knows where to find Eurydice, even though in their previous underworld encounter she was summoned from the spirits of the recently dead to his presence. Nevertheless, he somehow knows to seek her among the pious, a detail that suggests an implicit recognition on his part that he, not she, was to blame for their sorrow in the past. More important, he finds her and eagerly, lovingly embraces her. In vivid contrast to the reunion of Dido and Aeneas in Book 6 of the *Aeneid,* there is no suggestion that Eurydice resents Orpheus's presumptuous return or refuses his love; rather, they playfully reenact together, and even enjoy variations on, the now harmless movements that tragically separated them before:

> hic modo coniunctis spatiantur passibus ambo:
> nunc praecedentem sequitur, nunc praevius anteit
> Eurydicenque suam iam tuto respicit Orpheus.

> . . . here now they two amble about together with their footsteps closely linked: now he follows as she goes before; now he, ahead of her, goes first, and Orpheus this time looks safely back at his Eurydice.

(11.64-66)

Whereas his dead mouth did not call out her name, the narrator now joyfully repeats it at 66, shortly after its appearance at 63. Eurydice's own reaction is nowhere expressed, but the sweet playful games suggest her enthusiastic acceptance of her weirdly wayward husband: after all, *quid enim nisi se quereretur amatam?* (10.61).

It has often been pointed out that Pygmalion's proof of his art is lost when his statue brings to fruition his dreams of romantic and erotic bliss.[36] If Orpheus's song has been a long, elaborate, frustrated, and malevolent attempt to deny his love and his responsibility, then here too his art dies as his love is reborn. The horrible idea arises that his misogyny, and his support of cruel divinities, and his pleasure in blame and punishment have all been symptoms of the failed repression of his guilt and grief and loneliness. More than a sacred bard, that is, more than a representative of art and song and of the beauty-is-truth equation, Orpheus has been a study in numbness, repression, guilt, and denial. His art as a result is variously warped, twisted, confused, and even vindictive, lashing out at a world of unbearable pain, and he has only been able to depict love as various kinds of cruel control and selfish manipulation. When his shade is finally reunited with Eurydice in the underworld, his poetic voice seems to have evaporated, as he no longer needs it, preferring to play a lover's game of tag, endlessly performing a revisionist reenactment of the fatal moment when he prematurely looked back at his wife and caused her second death. Thus, ultimately, perhaps, like poor Ted Hughes and Sylvia Plath, Orpheus, in order for his love to be restored to him, has to be dead, no longer human and no longer an artist. Just as Pollitt's reading of **Birthday Letters** challenges the picture of Ted Hughes as sublime Poet Laureate, crowned with triumphant laurels by a grateful Empire, yet unjustly dogged by memories of his two wives' suicides, a resisting reading of Orpheus sees him not as victorious poet and lover, not as artist triumphant, but as haunted throughout his tale and his song (until this shadowy reunion) by his responsibility for the death of Eurydice. Such a reading also suggests that one of the major thematic concerns of Ovid's epic is to interrogate the very glorification of artistry for its own sake that has been supposed to be the poem's central theme and also suggests that it is the proper work of audiences and readers to scrutinize the motives of artists and narrators.[37]

> . . . On the black stream's dismay my vatic skull
> In fervent song floats to the sudden sun.
>
> W. Ralph Johnson, "Orpheus."[38]

Notes

1. Hughes (1998).

2. Quotations from the *Metamorphoses* are from Anderson (1982a); translations are my own. I have attached a chart of *Met.* 10-11.193 to help the reader to keep track of the various narrators and stories. Cf. Wheeler (1999); the corresponding part of Wheeler's chart appears on page 209 in his appendix on "Internal Narrators and Audiences in the *Metamorphoses*." See also Genette (1980) 244-45.

3. Segal (1989) and Miller (1990).

4. Segal (1989) 64.

5. Leach (1974a); Anderson (1982b and 1989); Janan (1988); Barchiesi (1989); and Heath (1996).

6. Janan (1988) 117.

7. Anderson (1990); Tissol (1997); Johnson (1999); and Ahl (1985) 204-8.

8. Wheeler (1999) 156.

9. Pollitt (1998).

10. Hughes (1997). For a penetrating review, see Johnson (1998).

11. Barchiesi (1989) 73.

12. Fetterley (1978).

13. Macherey (1978). I have described my theoretical stance *vis-à-vis* Ovid's *Metamorphoses* at some length in Cahoon (1996). In addition to Macherey, I have found the following works helpful: Bal (1985); Barthes (1986); Belsey (1980); Culler (1982); Flynn and Schweikart (1986); Noakes (1988); and Todorov (1970).

14. Heath (1996).

15. On the *Georgics,* see Miles (1985). See also Batstone (1988) and Farrell (1991).

16. On the significance of silences and gaps, see Macherey (1978).

17. See Desmond (1994). For the general theoretical position, see Fetterley (1978) and Flynn and Schweikart (1986).

18. Segal (1989) 65-66. By contrast, see the exemplary sensitivity of Van Nortwick (1996); I am greatly indebted to Mary-Kay Gamel for sending me a copy of this superb essay.

19. Wheeler (1999) 156.

20. Wheeler (1999) 34-65 *et passim.* For a powerful description (and useful bibliography) of how thinking about performance and focalization can inform and enrich our experience of Ovid, see Johnson (1997).

21. Anderson (1972b) *ad* 10.465-66.

22. As has often been noted (e.g., by Janan, 1988), Pygmalion's quasi-incestuous relations with his own creation lead genealogically to the unequivocally incestuous relations between Cinyras and Myrrha. For a good synopsis of the range of critical positions on the Pygmalion story, see Elsner (1991). My own favorites are Leach (1974a) and Ahl (1985) 246-60.

23. Segal (1989) 70-72.

24. Sharrock (1991a) 49.

25. Leach (1974a) 122.

26. Leach also notes the fairy-tale qualities of Orpheus's fantasy about Pygmalion.

27. F. Bömer (1969-86) *ad* 10.247-49.

28. Elsner (1991) 160.

29. For an excellent summary of the evidence from the critics, see Elsner (1991) 154 and 166 (n. 3-8).

30. Sharrock (1991b).

31. Farrell (1992).

32. Ac primum attonitas etiamnum voce canentis innumeras volucres anguesque agmenque ferarum Maenades Orphei titulum rapuere *triumphi*.

   First, even while they were still dumbstruck by the voice of Orpheus singing, the innumerable birds and the snakes and the array of wild animals that made up the glory of Orpheus's triumphal train were besieged by the Maenads.

   (11.20-22)

   Anderson follows the better manuscripts and reads *theatri*. I take *trumphi* (of which Bömer, 169-86, says "kaum richtig") from G. M. Murphy's edition of Book 11 (Oxford 1972); for bibliography and additional discussion, see Bömer (169-86) *ad* 11.22 and *ad* 11.25-26 where *theatro* occurs at the end of line 25 with a different meaning from that of 22.

33. I have discussed these poems and their critical reception in Cahoon (1984). For a more recent discussion, see Perkins (2000).

34. Anderson (1982b).

35. Anderson (1982b).

36. Elsner (1991) and Sharrock (1991b) both discuss this matter and provide bibliographical resources in their *Ramus* articles.

37. My thanks to the editors for their wisdom and generosity in conceiving of and in organizing this collection and for their kindness in encouraging my contribution. Thanks also for useful suggestions to Ralph Johnson and to the very helpful and benevolent anonymous reader; thanks as well to Sumathi Raghavan, to Margaret Gillespie Cahoon, and to Anne Thayer Cahoon for indispensable help with typing and editing. Many thanks to Sumathi Raghavan and to Garth Tissol for last minute bibliographical help. I am particularly indebted to the Pew Charitable Trusts for a fellowship in 1997-98 and to Gettysburg College for a leave of absence during the tenure of the fellowship. A preliminary outline of this essay was presented at the Claremont colleges for the Pacific Ancient and Modern Language Association in November 1998.

A much longer version was presented in February 1999 at NYU at the gracious invitation of the New York Classical Club (special thanks to Barbara McManus and David Murphy) where I offered it as a tribute to Professor W. S. Anderson's monumental and groundbreaking achievements as a classical scholar and especially as a pioneer in making fruitful contributions to the fields of classics and comparative literature. In that spirit still, I gratefully offer this, I hope improved, version. I had the great privilege of studying Roman satire and Roman elegy with Professor Anderson and the blessing of his directing my dissertation on Ovid's *Amores* (Berkeley, 1981). In the years since, he has been the most cordial and supportive of colleagues, generous beyond all conceivable expectation. My meager notes attest to only a few of his vast contributions in what is only one of his many areas of magisterial expertise; less obvious and possibly even more important is the large number of outstanding authors in these notes for whom he has been a principal teacher and mentor. Words cannot begin to express my own deep gratitude or my high esteem, so I close simply with heartfelt wishes for a happy birthday, many happy returns, and for many productive years yet to come!

38. Johnson (1986).

Abbreviations

AJP: American Journal of Philology

ANRW: Aufstieg und Niedergang der römischen Welt

BICS: Bulletin of the Institute of Classical Studies of the University of London

BMCR: Bryn Mawr Classical Review

CA: Classical Antiquity

CB: Classical Bulletin

CJ: Classical Journal

CP: Classical Philology

CQ: Classical Quarterly

CR: Classical Review

CSCA: California Studies in Classical Antiquity

CW: Classical World

GRBS: Greek, Roman, and Byzantine Studies

ICS: Illinois Classical Studies

JbAC: Jahrbuch für Antike und Christentum

JRS: Journal of Roman Studies

LLS: Papers of the Liverpool Latin Seminar

MD: Materiali e discussioni per l'analisi dei testi classici

PACA: Proceedings of the African Classical Association

PCPhS: Proceedings of the Cambridge Philological Society

PQ: Philological Quarterly

RPh: Revue de Philologie

RSC: Rivista di Studi Classici

SCO: Studi Classici e Orientali

SO: Symbolae Osloenses

SP: Studies in Philology

TAPA: Transactions of the American Philological Society

TLL: Thesaurus Linguae Latinae

WZRostock: Wissenschaftliche Zeitschrift der Universität Rostock, Gesellsch.- & sprach.-wiss. Reihe

YCS: Yale Classical Studies

ZPE: Zeitschrift für Papyrologie und Epigraphik

Works Cited

Ahl, Frederick M. 1985. *Metaformations: Soundplay and Wordplay in Ovid and Other Classical Poets.* Ithaca.

Anderson, William S. ed. 1972b. *Ovid's Metamorphoses Books 6-10.* Norman, OK.

————, ed. 1982a. *Ovid's Metamorphoses.* Stuttgart and Leipzig.

————. 1982b. "The Orpheus of Virgil and Ovid: *flebile nescio quid.*" In *Orpheus: The Metamorphoses of a Myth,* ed. John Warden. Toronto.

Bal, Mieke. 1985. *Narratology.* Translated by Christine van Boheemen. Toronto.

Barchiesi, Alessandro. 1989. "Voci e istanze narrative nelle *Metamorphosi* di Ovidio." *MD* 23: 55-97.

Barthes, Roland. 1986. *The Rustle of Language.* Translated by Richard Howard. New York.

Batstone, William W. 1988. "On the Surface of the *Georgics.*" *Arethusa* 21: 225-45.

Belsey, Catherine. 1980. *Critical Practice.* London and New York.

Bömer, F. 1969-86. *P. Ovidius Naso: Metamorphosen.* Heidelberg.

Cahoon, Leslie. 1984. "The Parrot and the Poet: The Function of Ovid's Funeral Elegies." *CJ* 80: 27-35.

————. 1996. "Calliope's Song: Shifting Narrators in Ovid, *Metamorphoses* 5." *Helios* 23.1: 43-66.

Culler, Jonathan. 1982. *On Deconstruction.* Ithaca.

Desmond, Marilynn. 1994. *Reading Dido: Gender, Textuality and the Medieval Aeneid.* Minneapolis.

Elsner, John. 1991. "Visual Mimesis and the Myth of the Real: Ovid's Pygmalion as Viewer." *Ramus* 20: 154-68.

Farrell, Joseph. 1991. *Vergil's Georgics and the Traditions of Epic: The Art of Allusion in Literary History.* New York.

————. 1992. "Dialogue of Genres in Ovid's 'Lovesong of Polyphemus' (*Metamorphoses* 13.719-897)." *AJP* 113: 235-68.

Fetterley, Judith. 1978. *The Resisting Reader: A Feminist Approach to American Fiction.* Bloomington, IN.

Flynn, Elizabeth, and Patrocinio Schweikart. 1986. *Gender and Reading.* Baltimore.

Heath, John. 1996. "The Stupor of Orpheus: Ovid's *Metamorphoses* 10.64-71." *CJ* 91.4: 353-70.

Hughes, Ted. 1997. *Tales From Ovid.* New York.

————. 1998. *Birthday Letters.* New York.

Janan, Micaela. 1988. "The Book of Good Love? Design versus Desire in *Metamorphoses* 10." *Ramus* 17: 110-37.

Johnson, W. Ralph. 1986. "Orpheus." *Poem.*

————. 1997. "Vertumnus in Love." *CP* 92.4: 367-74.

————. 1999. "Confabulating Cephalus." In *Literary Imagination: Ancient and Modern.* Edited by Todd Breyfogle. Chicago.

Leach, Eleanor Winsor. 1974a. "*Ekphrasis* and the Theme of Artistic Failure in Ovid's *Metamorphoses.*" *Ramus* 3: 102-42.

Macherey, Pierre. 1978. *A Theory of Literary Production.* Translated by Geoffrey Wall. London.

Miles, Gary. 1985. *Virgil's Georgics: A New Interpretation.* Berkeley and Los Angeles.

Miller, J. Hillis. 1990. *Versions of Pygmalion.* Cambridge and London.

Murphy, G. M. H. 1972. *Ovid, Metamorphoses, Book XI.* Oxford.

Noakes, Susan. 1988. *Timely Reading: Between Exegesis and Interpretation.* Ithaca.

Perkins, Caroline A. 2000. "Ovid's Erotic *Vates.*" *Helios* 27.1: 53-61.

Pollitt, Katha. March 1, 1998. "Peering into the Bell Jar." *New York Times Book Review*: 4-6.

Segal, Charles. 1989. "Ovid's Orpheus and Augustan Ideology." In *Orpheus: The Myth of the Past*. Baltimore.

Sharrock, Alison. 1991a. "Womanufacture." *JRS* 81: 36-49.

———. 1991b. "The Love of Creation." *Ramus* 20: 169-82.

Tissol, G. 1997. *The Face of Nature: Wit, Narrative, and Cosmic Origins in Ovid's Metamorphoses*. Princeton.

Todorov, Tzvetan. 1970. "Language and Literature." In *The Structuralist Controversy*. Edited by R. Macksey and E. Donato. Baltimore.

Van Nortwick, Thomas. 1996. "Eurydice is Dead." *North Dakota Quarterly* 63.2: 73-85.

Wheeler, Stephen M. 1999. *A Discourse of Wonders: Audience and Performance in Ovid's Metamorphoses*. Philadelphia.

Roger Craik (essay date winter 2006)

SOURCE: Craik, Roger. "'High and Dry and Dead': A Source for Ted Hughes's 'Pike.'" *ANQ* 19, no. 1 (winter 2006): 59-62.

[*In the following essay, Craik explores a possible source for the much-anthologized poem "Pike," suggesting that its inspiration was not from personal experience but rather from his reading.*]

In Ted Hughes's frequently anthologized poem **"Pike,"** the speaker describes two pike spectacularly dead, each having killed the other:

> Two, six pounds each, over two feet long,
> High and dry and dead in the willow-herb—
> One jammed past its gills down the other's gullet:
> The outside eye stared: as a vice locks—
> The same iron in this eye
> Though its film shrank in death.
>
> (23-28)

"Down," suggesting movement, makes clear that one pike is swallowing the other head-first (and being attacked from inside while doing so), and the struggle between the two fish has been so violent that they have thrashed themselves clear of their natural element, the water. Presumably seeing the lines as self-explanatory, critics have cited them as a second instance of the pike's cannibalistic ferocity; the adult pike are as eager to attack and eat their own kind as were the three baby pike kept by the speaker in the previous verse:

> Three we kept behind glass,
> Jungled in weed: three inches, four,
> And four and a half: fed fry to them—
> Suddenly there were two. Finally one [. . .]
>
> (17-20)

In her recent biography of Hughes, Elaine Feinstein reveals that, with his school friend John Wholey, the young Ted Hughes "put three baby pike into a fish-tank at school, feeding them regularly at first. The boys forgot about them over a school holiday, and returned to find the three fish reduced to one" (13). However, Feinstein finds no source from Hughes's life for the dead adult pike. Hughes himself characterized **"Pike"** as "charged with particular memories and a specific obsession" (Faas 209). Taking Hughes at his word, critics see the fighting pike as one of these "particular memories." Terry Gifford and Neil Roberts observe the "tone of personal narrative reminiscence" and "anecdotes [. . .] about pike kept behind glass that ate each other, and two found high and dry" (40), while Dennis Walden points out that the poem's narrator is "unable to avoid the memory of two of 'six pounds each,' dead in the willow-herb (a nicely English rural-domestic touch), jammed into each other with the merciless cannibalism of the species" (14). Alan Bold's view of the pike is that "even the dead ones he retrieves in a lust of possession" (66).

My suggestion in this note is that these fighting pike come neither from Hughes' own experience (had this been the case, Hughes, as a keen schoolboy fisherman, would surely have retrieved the pike, achieved boyhood fame as the finder of them, and would have mentioned the incident in interviews about **"Pike"**) nor from his power of invention, but from his reading. In 1891, in *Natural History of British Fishes: Their Structure, Economic Uses, and Capture by Net and Rod*, Francis Trevelyan Buckland refers to two pike found at the head of Loch Tay, in the Perthshire Highlands of Scotland, "fastened firmly together by the impact of the head of one within the mouth and jaws of the other" (160). He then cites a letter, dated 1870, from a Mr. Cramp, who sent them to him: "'you will observe that the head of one fish (weighing, perhaps, 9lb.) is tightly inserted up to the termination of the gill, and part of the first lower in the mouth and throat of the larger one'" (160).

Not surprisingly, the incident became famous. We cannot know for certain where Hughes read of it, but Elaine Feinstein provides a valuable clue in her discussion of the biographical origins of **"Pike."** As well as noting that Hughes's "interest in pike-fishing in his teens approached an obsession" and that the young Hughes "formed the habit of buying *The Shooting Times* and *The Gamekeeper*," she points out that Hughes's mother, Edith, "had brought a children's encyclopedia into the house" (14). Feinstein gives no source for this detail or any further information about the encyclopedia. My conjecture is that the encyclopedia was not merely "a children's encyclopedia" but *The Children's Encyclopedia,* edited by Arthur Mee from 1923 onward, and extremely popular in its day. There Hughes would have read of the pike:

> With its weight are associated great power, huge teeth in the lower jaw, and others in the upper part of the mouth which curve backwards to the throat, so admitting prey, but rendering it impossible for them to escape. This produces results like that we see when two snakes meet, mouth to mouth. Some Loch Tay fishermen found two pike of practically equal size engaged in a deadly grapple. One was swallowing the other alive, and had got it down as far as the shoulders.

> In its artful lurking in the shade, looking like a submerged log, the pike resembles the crocodile.

> ("Fishes of the Rivers" 4979)

There is more than Feinstein's unintended direction to point to this account as the one Hughes read. The encyclopedia writer's "like a submerged log" becomes in Hughes "logged to last year's black leaves" (11). Now, more than possessing camouflage and cunning in its choice of places to lurk, the pike itself (or perhaps some malevolent power) does the logging, which has the pike seeming to its prey (if they see it at all) as being at one with the leaves, a log of their own tree. Furthermore, the surrounding text of the encyclopedia account must also have resonated with Hughes. On the same page, immediately after the discussion of pike, a heading reads, in bold capitals that must have caught Hughes's attention, "The Living Submarines which come in from the Sea," meaning trout ("Fishes of the Rivers" 4979). On this detail, I suggest, Hughes drew for the line "Of submarine delicacy and horror" (7). Not only this, but in the previous column Hughes would have read, of carp:

> We know much about them from the fact that in the time of the monasteries the monks bred them in their ponds [. . .] So we inherit a store of facts about these slow, cunning loiterers through life. They eat well, and exhaust little energy, so like tortoises and turtles, they should live long. And they do. It is said that the great carp still swimming in the lake among the country cottages of Marie Antoinette at Versailles were put there by Marie Antoinette herself, and such a span of existence is not impossible, for carp are the longest lived of all fish concerning which we have any clear evidence.

> (4979)

These details, I suggest, pass into the poem's conclusion:

> A pond I fished, fifty yards across,
> Whose lilies and muscular tench
> Had outlasted every visible stone
> Of the monasteries that planted them—

> Stilled legendary depth
> It was as deep as England. It held
> Pike too immense to stir [. . .]

> (29-35)

In short, Hughes has made the Loch Tay pike his own. The scheme of the poem has the reader hearing first of pike generally, small and adult, and then of the three small pike kept by the speaker, pike that prove themselves cannibalistic. Then come the Loch Tay pike in the wild—observed, cannibalistic too, and dead—and, thus, they connect the small pike in captivity to the phantasmagoric unseen pike, terrifying to man and straining credibility, with which the poem ends. Hughes' adverbial phrase "in the willow-herb" (24) is perhaps his most masterful touch of all, keeping intact the point of the Loch Tay pike yet, at the same time, suggesting, through this homely reference to a common summer weed, the immediacy of personal experience.

Works Cited

Bold, Alan. *Thom Gunn and Ted Hughes.* Edinburgh: Oliver and Boyd, 1976.

Buckland, Francis Trevelyan. *Natural History of British Fishes: Their Structure, Economic Uses, and Capture by Net and Rod.* New York: E. and J. B. Young, 1891.

Faas, Ekbert. "Ted Hughes and Gaudete." *Ted Hughes: The Unaccommodated Universe.* Santa Barbara, CA: Black Sparrow Press, 1980. 208-11.

Feinstein, Elaine. *Ted Hughes: The Life of a Poet.* New York: Norton, 2001.

"Fishes of the Rivers." *The Children's Encyclopedia.* Vol. 7. London: Educational Book Company, 1923. 4975-82.

Gifford, Terry, and Neil Roberts. *Ted Hughes: A Critical Study.* London: Faber and Faber, 1981.

Hughes, Ted. "Pike." *New Selected Poems.* New York: Harper and Rowe, 1982. 47-48.

Walden, Dennis. *Ted Hughes.* Milton Keynes: Oxford UP, 1987.

Elizabeth Anderson Stansell (essay date spring 2006)

SOURCE: Stansell, Elizabeth Anderson. "'Somebody Else Will Have to Write Their Poems': Ted Hughes and the Evolution of 'Skylarks.'" *The South Carolina Review* 38, no. 2 (spring 2006): 72-85.

[*In the following essay, Stansell examines Hughes's notebooks in Emory University's archives and traces the development of his poem "Skylarks."*]

There are two particular manuscript notebooks within the Ted Hughes papers, stored in the Manuscript, Archives, and Rare Book Library at Emory University's Woodruff Library, that reveal the gradual metamorphosis of Hughes's poem **"Skylarks."** Notebook 1, containing handwritten drafts of poems written from 1949-66, includes unpublished lyrics entitled **"Ode to Indolence"** and **"Against Larks"**; the second notebook, Notebook 8, holds Hughes's drafts of poems from 1965-66, most of which later appear in his collection *Wodwo*. In this later notebook, Hughes continues to revise **"Ode to Indolence"** and begins work on another unpublished draft entitled **"Larks." "Skylarks,"** which first appears under this title in the second notebook, seems to be a combination of these three unpublished lyrics: **"Ode to Indolence," "Larks,"** and **"Against Larks."** Consequently, the evolution of **"Skylarks"**—from its individual components to a final hybrid manuscript version—is fascinating, as it reveals the various stages of thought that went into its creation. The earlier versions of the poem reveal a darker, more cynical side of Hughes than does the final version of **"Skylarks,"** but rather than casting negative shadows on the published poem, the manuscripts actually highlight the art of Hughes's creative process as one can trace his conscious efforts to clearly express poetic identification with the skylarks as well as demonstrate his view of poetry's ultimate purpose.

The **"Ode to Indolence"** is most likely Hughes's earliest version of **"Skylarks,"** and it makes several appearances in both Notebook 1 and Notebook 8. One of the most noticeable disparities between **"Ode to Indolence"** and **"Skylarks"** is that the former is written in irregular four-line stanzas, whereas the published version of **"Skylarks"** makes use of free verse, perhaps better to emulate the erratic flight of the skylark. (For clarity's sake, future references to **"Skylarks [P]"** will indicate the poem published in *Wodwo,* and **"Skylarks [M]"** will signify the final manuscript version of the poem if a differentiation between the two is needed. Use of the manuscripts is approved by the Ted Hughes Estate.) Though the stanzas of **"Ode to Indolence"** are unrhymed and irregular in rhythm, the lines are still much more formally structured than one might expect from a mid-1960s Hughes poem.

Aside from its structure, **"Ode to Indolence"** differs from **"Skylarks"** in that it focuses on the persona of the narrator much sooner and much more in depth than does the latter. The earliest versions of **"Ode to Indolence"** in Notebook 1 contain stanzas that divulge the narrator's thoughts directly, although Hughes seems to have difficulty deciding where to place these extremely revealing lines in the poem itself. For example, in what appears to be the earliest draft, two versions of an eight-line diatribe against larks are written separately at the top of the page, though neither of these makes it into

the following draft. Hughes tries hard to find the perfect wording. One version reads: "The trouble with the lark is / That I do not particularly like it / Otherwise, I suppose it is OK / But I can't get [roused?] about it / So I shall have to leave larks alone / Somebody else / Will have to write their poem / The truth is, they get on my nerves". His next try at the phrasing varies slightly: "For me, the trouble about larks / Is that I don't particularly like them. / Otherwise, I suppose they're alright [sic] / Lots of people don't agree with me / I can't get [roused] about the lark / Somebody else will have to sing them their praises / I can't. / I've tried and I can't." Hughes contemplates inserting yet another variation on this theme at the end of this draft of **"Ode to Indolence,"** but he scratches out the lines "Somebody else will have to write their poems / Not for me. / Somebody else's bird" from the final stanza. The next appearance of **"Ode to Indolence"** in Notebook I is an incomplete version of the poem. Hughes writes this page in two columns, turning the notebook 90°, apparently to compare different versions of his stanzas. There he provides two more variations of his anti-lark verse: "For me, the trouble concerning skylarks / Is that they get on my nerves. Yes, too bad. / Somebody else will have to write their poems. / I can't. I've tried and I can't" the second version changes only the word "trouble" to "grief" in the first line and amends "I've tried" to "I've tried *it*" [emphasis added] in the last line.

With the final occurrence of **"Ode to Indolence"** in Notebook 1, Hughes changes the poem's title to **"Against Larks."** This version has no reference to the long toyed-with cynical narrator stanzas, except in its very last line: "Somebody else will have to write their poems". However, the poem's new title and opening stanza do turn the focus directly on the narrator and his dislike of the larks: "When a skylark goes up, on a blue spring day, / Why is that so irritating?" **"Against Larks"** is almost identical to the version of **"Ode to Indolence"** that appears later in Notebook 8, although the ode begins not with the narrator but with the familiar description of the skylark's having a "barrel chest like an Indian of the Andes," as well as a "whippet head" and "leaden" body.

It is important to note that **"Skylarks [P]"** does not introduce the narrator's direct remarks at all until section III, after the bird has been described in depth. Even then, the narrator's first-person references are kept to a minimum. He asks the bird, "I suppose you just gape and let your gaspings / Rip in and out through your voicebox" (III.1-2); he admits that "My idleness curdles / Seeing the lark labour near its cloud" (IV.1-2); he stares at the birds until "my eye's gossamer snaps / and my hearing floats back widely to earth" (IV.12-13); and, finally, he observes, "Heads flung back, as I see them, / Wings almost torn off backwards" (V.5-6). In this version, the first-person voice is used just enough to alert the reader to the narrator's presence, but the focus nevertheless remains on the skylarks themselves. In fact, section VI, the final segment of **"Skylarks [P],"** is entirely free of the persona of the narrator.

"Against Larks" and **"Ode to Indolence,"** however, are quite different in their portrayal of the narrator. Obviously, the earliest versions of **"Ode to Indolence"** make great use of the narrator's intense dislike of the skylarks. Though this sentiment is toned down in **"Against Larks,"** it is still undeniably present. The version of **"Ode to Indolence"** in Notebook 8 subdues the narrator's presence even more, as he is introduced not in the first line but the tenth line, remarking on the skylarks: "But when they go up on a blue spring day, / Why is that so irritating? I wonder." He answers himself, saying, "Because that's what they are then, ir- ritations, / Tunnelling up through ~~your~~ skull, from ~~your~~ earhole—up." Hughes had crossed out both occurrences of the word "your" in that line, as if he were making a conscious effort to diminish the presence of the speaker. Hughes also leaves out the phrase "I write it down," present in **"Against Larks,"** which draws further atten- tion to the narrator in this earlier version. However, whether Hughes was attempting to temper the speaker's authority or not, the persona returns resurfaces just a few lines later, saying, "Maybe it's the thought of their [the skylarks'] effort hurts me, / Struggling away in this nightmare difficulty up through the nothing / While I'm lying on ~~a bank~~ looking from one to the other." In addi- tion, while the first-person references in **"Skylarks [P]"** stop after section V so that the last segment is devoted solely to the skylarks, **"Ode to Indolence"** contains two direct references to the narrator's persona in the last ten lines of the poem. In the first instance, the nar- rator is describing the skylarks' descent, after their long, laboring climb, when he says, "And they relax, drifting with changed notes— / They sound as thankful as I am / They dip & float." In this early version of the poem, the narrator deems his relief to be greater than that of the skylarks, whereas in the published version, the "relief, a cool breeze" (VI.6) is ambiguous and in fact appears to be equally applicable to both man (narrator) and beast.

The next direct mention of the narrator in the Notebook 8 version of **"Ode to Indolence"** occurs in the final line with the familiar refrain, "Somebody else will have to write their poems". Though Hughes has taken great strides to diminish the narrator's cynicism in Notebook 8, especially by changing the title back from **"Against Larks"** to the more subtle **"Ode to Indolence,"** the narrator's ambivalence toward the birds is apparent in the ode, and the last line completely shatters any illu- sion of poetic sympathy for the birds. In addition, the line's reference to writing draws direct attention to the speaker as the poet, as opposed to a mere spectator. Poetry itself is thus brought into the foreground as a

subject, but in a negative way, as the poet pronounces himself incapable of identification with the skylark.

It is actually more than a little ironic that Hughes would declare that "somebody else needs to write" poems for the skylark since several people had already done so, including William Wordsworth and Percy Shelley. In fact, one of the most well-known poems of the Romantic period is Shelley's "To a Skylark," in which the bird's song motivates the poet by giving rise to the poetic imagination (West 44). Indeed, in Romantic poetry a bird is often given to represent the poet himself, a lone singer (Oerlemans 6). Shelley's "To a Skylark" is less than subtle in its attempt to make the bird a human be- ing of sorts, but, even so, the song of the bird leads the poet to the "realization that there is Life beyond human life that is worth considering" (Oerlemans 17). The skylark's song is all the poet ever experiences from the bird; as Diana Hendry points out, Shelley's skylark is "famously bodiless," present only through the poet's sense of hearing (67). Unlike Hughes's skylarks for whom the act of singing is quite painful, Shelley's bird does not experience pain, nor "Shadow of annoyance," nor "love's sad satiety" (stanzas 15-16). While Shel- ley's skylark "of death must deem / Things more true and deep / Than we mortals dream" (lines 82-84), Hugh- es's birds are too preoccupied with "the struggle / Against / Earth's center" to philosophize on death (I.9- 11). While Shelley urges his skylark to "Teach me half the gladness / That thy brain must know" (101-102), Hughes describes his skylarks as residing in the "madhouse" of the heavens, "With the voices and frenzies of the larks, / Squealing and gibbering and cursing" (V. 3-4)—certainly nothing like the "harmoni- ous madness" of Shelley's skylark (103). Nothing is easy for Hughes's skylarks, whether they are singing, flying, or plummeting to earth.

However, Hughes's vivid description of the harshness of the skylark's life may not be so different from Shel- ley's version, after all: while Shelley is obviously using the skylark as a symbol for a poet, Hughes is doing the same thing but from the opposite direction. If Shelley's skylark is a bit glorified, Hughes's is likewise exagger- ated, but for the purpose of describing a different aspect of the poetic imagination. Unlike Shelley, who elevates the skylark almost to the point of absurdity, Hughes is interested in exploring the little considered hardships of both skylark and poet. Perhaps Hughes is making a direct comment on Shelley's poem, taking issue with "society's notion of the poet sent on his poetic flight of fancy to retrieve heavenly instructions (via a little divine madness)" in order to portray the true state of both skylark and poet: "Martyrs all" (Hendry 69).

Indeed, Hughes does admit in *Poetry in the Making* that words are "learned late and laboriously and easily forgotten" (19); in addition, a poet must always be aware of the "little goblin in a word," the "side-meanings" of each individual word that must be cross-checked with every other word in the poem to prevent the words from "kill[ing] each other" (13). Though Hughes says in the same breath that writing should not be a labor for a skilled poet, he makes it clear that there are certain considerations that every poet, good or bad, expert or novice, must acknowledge. Poetry, in other words, is not as simple as it may appear, even if it is in many ways a natural process.

Sylvia Plath, for instance, was born with a gift for poetry, but Hughes has often commented on how her early, painstakingly systematic poetic process differed from the furious storm of creativity during the months prior to her suicide that resulted in the *Ariel* poems. As Erica Wagner states, "Poetry, for Hughes, was animated by a shaping force whose energy was beyond the poet's control" (33). As seen in **Birthday Letters,** Hughes believed that once the *Ariel* voice—what Hughes referred to as "'the real thing'"—took over Plath, her pen became an instrument of destruction (qtd. in Wagner 38). She could not resist the wave of poetic inspiration that came over her at this time, but, ironically, her writing seemed only to heighten her despair. Hughes was initially pleased that Plath had overcome her terribly labored method of writing; he could not relate to her earlier process of composition. In **"The Earthenware Head,"** a poem in Hughes's **Birthday Letters,** he says to Plath, "You ransacked thesaurus in your poem about it [the earthenware head] / Veiling its mirror, rhyming yourself into safety" (lines 23-24). However, Hughes came to realize that though Plath's poetry improved when she discarded her old methods of writing, she was also necessarily tapping into dangerous psychological territory (much like the skylark's desperate dive after its laborious climb). In fact, Plath's suicide occurred in 1963, so she surely would have been in the forefront of Hughes's mind at the time he wrote and polished **"Skylarks."** Thus, in a transformation of Shelley's idea of the connection between poet and bird, **"Skylarks"** is an exploration of the idea that a bird's flight is about as easy as a poet's composing process.

Of course, in considering the evolution of **"Skylarks,"** one must realize that Shelley is not the only Romantic poet to whom Hughes alludes. The very title **"Ode to Indolence"** immediately conjures the image of John Keats, author of "Ode on Indolence." Perhaps by using this title, Hughes is simply intending to refer to the lines in this draft that point out the discrepancy between the active birds and his speaker's inactive self: "Maybe it's the thought of their effort hurts me, / Struggling away in the nightmare difficulty up through the nothing / While I'm lying on ~~a bank~~ looking from one to the other." And the theme of laziness does carry through the final version, as the narrator states, "My idleness curdles / Seeing the lark labour near its cloud" (IV.1-2),

and while the birds are frantically flying in a frenzy, the narrator is of course merely looking on.

However, in considering Keats's ode in conjunction with that of Hughes, one generates alternative interpretations. Just as a comparison to Shelley's skylark poem makes Hughes appear to be somewhat cynical and wary of poetic impulse, Keats's ode seems at first to be evidence of his turning his back on poetry. "Ode on Indolence" relates Keats's vision of three figures: Love, Ambition, and Poesy. He bemoans their appearance: "O, why did ye not melt, and leave my sense / Unhaunted quite of all but—nothingness?" (19-20). Keats continues to describe Poesy by saying that "she has not a joy— / At least for me,—so sweet as drowsy noon, / And evenings steep'd in honied indolence" (35-37), and by the end of the poem Keats is commanding: "Vanish, ye phantoms, from my idle spright, / Into the clouds, and never more return!" (60).

Despite initial appearances, Keats may not be as dismissive of the poetic imagination as he seems. After all, he is writing this very ode after he has supposedly renounced faith in poetry (just as Hughes asks someone else to write the skylarks' poem after he has already written one). A more positive interpretation emerges when one takes into account an 1818 letter in which Keats proposes that a poet must be idle to be receptive to any possible poetic fertilization, much like a flower waiting for a bee (Zak 58). In other words, "Keats links poetic productivity to the capacity for passivity and submission to time in a metaphor of organic growth" (58). Moreover, the three figures of love, ambition, and poetry are not graces, but sirens. William Zak explains that in this ode, the three figures are tempting the poet to test whether "the god within . . . truly possesses itself" (60). Therefore, the poet's refusal to follow poetry is not the result of his inability to do so; he is simply refusing to write poetry for mere effect. The poet thus becomes analogous to Christ in the wilderness when He refuses to do the tasks that Satan puts forth, such as turning stone into bread: it is not that Christ could not perform the miracles, it is that He refused to do it under Satan's direction (Zak). His refusal to act, then, is not evidence of weakness but evidence of strength to resist temptation and perform only for the right reasons.

Just as Keats's "Ode on Indolence" is easily interpreted in a negative, anti-poetic way, so the final version of **"Skylarks"** invites pessimistic interpretations. To be sure, skylarks do not seem to be inherently positive symbols for Hughes, especially if his fixation with the anti-lark stanzas in Notebook 1 was a personal rather than a poetic preoccupation. Moreover, in **"Skylarks [P],"** the birds are the "cruel earth's offerings" (V.8), beings destined to sing "incomprehensibly both ways— / Joy! Help! Joy! Help!" (III.5-6). In another, later

Hughes poem, **"Ravens,"** the skylarks mentioned are described as worried about nothing, but their carefree attitude does not indicate that they are "fancy-free"; rather, they are "incapable of sympathy" (Dilulio 40), ironically similar to the narrator of **"Ode to Indolence."**

However, though the birds in **"Skylarks [P]"** are not exactly free creatures, being "Obedient as to death a dead thing" (II.7), this lack of individual will is echoed in Hughes's description of his own life as a poet. In **"Flounders,"** another poem from *Birthday Letters,* Hughes admits that he and Plath "Only did what poetry told us to do" (66); they were, in a sense, incapable of thinking and acting for themselves. Therefore, the skylarks' inability to act independently of their instinct is analogous to Hughes's assertion that he is unable to ignore the poetic impulse when it strikes. This incapacity is not a weakness *per se*; rather, it seems to Hughes to be morally and ethically neutral, something that simply exists and cannot be changed. For Hughes, "[t]he mind of the poet . . . in the initial stages of poetic composition, is inert, non-reactive, Locke's *tabula rasa* . . . and for the time of writing he can do nothing but accept it" (Singh 59). In a way, this definition of a poet who cannot deny whatever comes to him is a fairly accurate description of the poet-narrator's persona in **"Ode to Indolence"**; he certainly does not seem pleased to be observing and writing about the skylarks, but he does it nonetheless.

In contrast, **"Larks,"** the second holograph poem that Hughes eventually incorporated into **"Skylarks,"** is surprisingly devoid of a self-conscious narrator. It actually bears very little resemblance to any of the versions of **"Ode to Indolence"** except that it continues the theme of the larks. This brief poem consists of approximately fourteen lines devoted to describing the lark, but at this point the poem shifts gears and launches an allusion to Cuchulain, "the Irish Hercules" (Raine 23). The poem is specifically referring to Cuchulain's death scene, during which he requests to be tied to a pole so as to die standing up (see Figure 6). Though the final version of **"Skylarks"** makes no direct reference to Cuchulain, Catherine Runcie manages to forge a connection from **"Skylarks"** to that mythical hero:

> In a nightmare narrative, a little myth, the heroic Cuchulain, proud enough to want to stand, is dying and cannot move, while the impossible birds move closer. . . . Their relentless forward movement toward the helpless, immobilized Cuchulain completes the pattern of trapped helplessness and trapped suffering established in the previous sections [of **"Skylarks"**] . . . sustaining and intensifying the horror, the existential dread.

(215)

It is significant that despite the absence of a direct allusion in the final version of **"Skylarks,"** Runcie could pick up on the poem's nightmarish overtones and the subsequent connection to Cuchulain's death scene, which is specifically referred to in **"Larks."** Indeed, **"Larks"** seems to contribute quite a bit to the final version of **"Skylarks."** For one thing, the lines "A towered bird shot through the crested head / With the command not die / But climb / Climb / Sing / Obedient as to death a dead thing" (in Appendix E) first appear in this short poem and are repeated in **"Skylarks."** The larks are also referred to as the "cruellest of birds" in **"Larks,"** which is only slightly altered to the skylark's being "Crueller than owl or eagle" in **"Skylarks [P]"** (II.1). In addition, the detached, impersonal tone of **"Larks"** helps to counteract the overly intrusive narrator of **"Ode to Indolence,"** resulting in the nicely controlled tone of **"Skylarks [P]."**

Though Runcie interprets the song of the birds in the Cuchulain legend as signaling death and thus being a rather terrifying symbol, in **"Larks"** Hughes associates the lark itself with being a Cuchulain-figure, "a flute tied to a [crackling?] stake." Hughes seems to be asserting that the lark and Cuchulain will be somehow merging together in a mystical, mysterious exchange. In *The Death of Cuchulain,* W. B. Yeats writes that his dying hero's soul will assume "a soft feathery shape" upon death (qtd. in Bjersby 55). (Yeats is, of course, the poet most associated with Cuchulain, as the poet wrote both verse and dramas devoted to various mythical events in Cuchulain's life.) In **"Larks,"** the crow's "blind song," serving to guide "the near lark nearer" to the dying Cuchulain, claims that something "more feeble and misguided than thyself / Take thy head / Thine ear / And thy life's career from thee." It is unclear in the context of the poem whether the crow's song is directed to Cuchulain or the lark, but this ambivalence actually emphasizes the apparent connection between the bird and Cuchulain. Moreover, according to Yeats's "Cuchulain Comforted," the birds that sing to the hero during his death are not actual animals; they are transformed dead cowards who "had changed their throats and had the throats of birds" (line 25, qtd. in Raine).

Cuchulain is thus established as a "hero among cowards" (Raine 37); unlike the birdmen who ran from death, Cuchulain chooses to die, chooses rebirth, because "to act is better than to dream" (40). Yeats himself identified with the character of Cuchulain and wondered whether he, as a poet, lived up to the heroic standards established by that hero (Bjersby). Perhaps Hughes too is making a comparison between himself as a poet and Cuchulain as a mythic hero: poets, after all, must embrace a kind of death when they succumb to identification with their subject matter, but they are then reborn in a way as their own identities re-emerge, enhanced. For Keats, negative capability does not require self-oblivion; on the contrary, it requires an extremely high awareness of self (Zak). Therefore, Hughes's connection of the larks and death is not an entirely negative association, for with death comes rebirth. According to Mercia Eliade's *Shamanism,* which Hughes had studied in depth, shamans believe that "only death restores men to their primordial condition; only then can they ascend to heaven, fly like birds" (qtd. in Singh 64). It would seem that for Hughes poetry, death, rebirth, flight, and birds are intricately connected.

Indeed, it is impossible to ignore the shamanistic overtones of **"Skylarks."** Thomas West, for instance, argues that for Hughes, "the task is to submit the mind, through something like a trance . . . to the physiological creature," the skylark (44). The poet-narrator must enter into this trance-like state in order for the bird and its "Conscience perfect" to truly exist outside of the realm of ideas (VI.22). Hughes is interested in the difference between merely *understanding* the word skylark—knowing with the mind the physical appearance and sounds of the bird—and *experiencing* the skylark via the imagination, a process by which the poet-narrator can somehow enter into the skylark's own consciousness.

Moreover, Leonard M. Scigaj reveals evidence of oriental mythology that he finds within the poem. Scigaj views the narrator as identifying with the skylark because he "recognizes . . . a metaphor for the entire joyous agony of life" ("Oriental" 143). The poet-narrator is a "bemused spectator" who sees all of "benevolent" (142) nature as "a soothing companion because of [the narrator's] already achieved calmness of mind" (143). Thus, rather than being unpleasant, the "nothing" (IV.5) into which the skylark flies is actually a positive thing, as temporality is, by its very nature, constantly changing and therefore incomplete. The "nothing" is a total negation that represents "unchanging, all-encompassing fullness, an allness of benign nature in an absolute present" (145). (Perhaps Hughes's "nothing" alludes to the "nothingness" that Keats yearns for in his "Ode on Indolence.") The narrator, through identification with the skylark, achieves a *satori* sense of ecstatic participatory involvement in the is-ness of all reality" (134). In other words, the narrator becomes one with the skylark and thus experiences a transient yet all-important connection with the universe itself. The skylark is the vehicle through which the poet-narrator can attain a glimpse of unity between the spiritual and physical worlds through the "necessary sacrifice of the ego" (Robinson 49). Moreover, the cost of "poetic vision" is a "suicidal dive," a dive much like the one on which the skylark embarks (Parker 45).

Scigaj's argument for the influence of oriental mythology is bolstered by the fact that Hughes was certainly deeply interested in shamanism, so it is not much of a stretch to see this fascination manifesting itself in **"Skylarks."** Hughes was greatly influenced by his reading *The Tibetan Book of the Dead* as well as the poetry of

Yeats, which "opened his eyes to his own system and to Indian mythology" (Singh 56). Scigaj explains Hughes's belief that one can "achieve an assured sense of selfhood . . . either through the 'objectless' asceticism of Oriental thought . . . where nature is perceived as a 'benign' extension of the self's interior serenity, or through the Western quest for an ideal, involving psychological rounds of nature's cycle of struggle, death, and rebirth—the world of the 'virtuoso bacteria'" ("Ophialatry" 381). **"Skylarks"** can certainly be interpreted as a kind of "regeneration through self-annihilation" (Parker 45), both for the bird as well as the poet. Hughes admired the sort of "unselfconscious expenditure of energy" that birds such as skylarks possess; he believed they would receive as much energy back from nature as they spent (Scigaj, *Ted Hughes* 69). A poet too must self-negate in order to identify with his subject, but in so doing he regains himself through the act of writing and reconciling the forces both within and outside himself.

Indeed, one of the qualities that Hughes requires of a great poet is that he be able to bring the physical world and the spiritual world into a sort of equilibrium:

> [T]he real problem comes from the fact that outer world and inner world are interdependent at every moment. We are simply the locus of their collision. Two worlds, with mutually contradictory laws, or laws that seem to us to be so, colliding afresh every second, struggling for peaceful coexistence. And whether we like it or not our life is what we are able to make of that collision and struggle. . . . So what we need, evidently, is a faculty that embraces both worlds simultaneously.
>
> ("Myth and Education" 150)

This faculty, according to Hughes, is the "imagination of great artists" (150). In *Poetry in the Making,* Hughes describes words as being able to "give some part of our experience a more or less permanent shape outside ourselves" (19). Hughes would most likely agree that by "seeing signs of subjectivity in animals, we are not necessarily projecting human qualities onto them, but recognizing in them natural attributes which we share with them" (Oerlemans 12).

Perhaps Hughes's interest in connecting inner and outer worlds is what drives him to write so many animal poems. John J. DiIulio claims that Hughes writes about animals because "he has the imagination to see, feel, smell their actuality as few of us ever do" (39). In *Poetry in the Making,* Hughes reveals that he had been an avid hunter as a child, but at age fifteen, he began seeing animals from their point of view (11); it was around this time that he began composing poetry, although it would be several years before he wrote his first animal poem, **"The Thought-Fox."** The connection for Hughes between animals and poetry is made even stronger when he refers to a poem as a type of animal: it is an "assembly of living parts moved by a single spirit," the parts of which the poet is responsible for keeping "alive" (12). He further complicates this metaphor when he compares the act of writing poetry to hunting, and the poem itself to "a new species of creature, a new specimen of the life outside your own" (12).

Perhaps this definition of a poet—hunter of the animal poem—helps explain some of the violence within Hughes's poetry. Certainly, **"Skylarks"** is no exception, as it is rife with violent images: the bird is "shot through the crested head" (II.2), its "gaspings / Rip in and out" of its voicebox (III.2), with its "wings almost torn off backwards" (V.6). However, despite this sort of violence, Thomas West sees **"Skylarks"** as a crucial element building up to the final poem, the title poem, in the collection, **"Wodwo."** Wodwo is a sort of primitive man who "wants all the world to be a part of him" (60); he cannot quite speak in complete sentences, but he has submitted himself to a certain "state of mind," namely, that of nature in its purest sense (60). West interprets the structure of **"Skylarks"**—in which the length of the lines forces the reader to speed up or pause accordingly, mimicking a pattern of flight—as evidence of the poet-narrator "[m]oving down to a wodwo standard of living," which, though primitive and somewhat simplistic, Hughes would consider a good thing (60). And it is evident from comparing **"Ode to Indolence"** and **"Larks"** to the final version of **"Skylarks"** that Hughes wished to emphasize the poet-narrator's identification with the skylark rather than any dissociation between man and beast.

Even the final manuscript version of **"Skylarks,"** though it differs from the published version in only a few ways, demonstrates Hughes's main concern that the poem should relate the narrator's affinity with the skylark rather than a perpetuation of his own separate identity. For instance, where the **"Skylarks [M]"** version states, "Suddenly they've had enough, they're burned out / And the sun's sucked them empty", the **"Skylarks [P]"** reads, "So it's a relief, a cool breeze / When they've had enough, when they're burned out" (VI.6-7). This subtle change demonstrates the narrator's empathy with the bird, being himself able to experience the relief felt in a "reciprocal transference of affect" from narrator to skylark and skylark to narrator (Runcie 205). Another noteworthy difference between the manuscript and published versions of **"Skylarks"** is that Hughes crosses out and later completely omits one three-line stanza in **"Skylarks [M]"**—a stanza describing the lark: "And it has to keep singing / Not to pleasure anybody / For no reason whatsoever." This omission seems to be further evidence that Hughes did not wish to attach any sort of pointlessness to the bird. While Hughes did not shy away from depicting the skylark's pain and difficulty in flying, he apparently does not want to diminish the significance of the bird,

and this attention is particularly legitimate since Hughes's skylark is directly related to the poet; in belittling the skylark, he would belittle poets as well.

The changes that take place in Hughes's notebooks—from the various iterations of **"Ode to Indolence," "Against Larks," "Larks,"** and even the manuscript version of **"Skylarks"** to the final published poem—reveal the poet's ultimate interest in maintaining the narrator's identification with the skylarks. Though both **"Larks"** and especially **"Ode to Indolence"** contain certain references that could be construed as hostility directed toward the skylarks, what is most important is not Hughes's personal feelings toward the birds, whether they were similar to those of the **"Ode to Indolence"** narrator or not; it is, rather, that Hughes made irrelevant any personal biases he might have had so that he might demonstrate what he considered to be the hallmark of a true poet: an expression of the commingling of physical and spiritual, of animal and human, of figurative death and poetic rebirth. **"Skylarks,"** in its final form, expresses not only the narrator's gradual identification with the skylark, but also Hughes's personal view of the poetic imagination as a whole. While **"Skylarks"** validates and, in some ways, reiterates the same Romantic ideology of Shelley and Keats, these ideals are expressed in terms that are entirely Hughes's own. Thus, Hughes is indeed the epitome of a neo-Romantic poet in that he is capable of transforming ideas from the nineteenth century according to his twentieth-century consciousness.

Works Cited

Bjersby, Birgit. *The Interpretation of the Cuchulain Legend in the Works of W. B. Yeats.* Dublin: Hodges, 1970.

DiIulio, John J., Jr. "Wolfwatching." *New Republic* 204.25 (1991): 36-41.

Hendry, Diana. "Up with the Lark(s)." *Critical Survey* 4.1 (1992): 67-69.

Hughes, Ted. *Birthday Letters.* New York: Farrar, 1998.

———. "Myth and Education." *Winter Pollen.* Hughes 136-153.

———. Notebook 1, Subseries 2.1, ms. Ted Hughes Papers. Emory U, Atlanta.

———. Notebook 8, Subseries 2.1, ms. Ted Hughes Papers. Emory U, Atlanta.

———. *Poetry in the Making. Winter Pollen.* Hughes 10-24.

———. "Skylarks." *Wodwo.* New York: Harper & Row, 1967. 169-72.

———. *Winter Pollen: Occasional Prose.* Ed. William Scammell. New York: Picador, 1994.

Keats, John. "Ode on Indolence." PoetryConnection-.Net. 1 April 2005 <www.poetryconnection.net/poets/John_Keats/1772>.

Oerlemans, Onno Dag. "'The Meanest Thing that Feels': Anthropomorphizing Animals in Romanticism." *Mosaic* 27.1 (March 1994): 1-32.

Parker, Michael. "Hughes and the Poets of Eastern Europe." *The Achievement of Ted Hughes.* Sagar 37-51.

Raine, Kathleen. *Death-in-Life and Life-in-Death: 'Cuchulain Comforted' and 'News for the Delphic Oracle.'* New Jersey: Humanities P, 1974.

Robinson, Craig. *Ted Hughes as Shepherd of Being.* New York: St. Martin's P, 1989.

Runcie, Catherine. "On Figurative Language: A Reading of Shelley's, Hardy's and Hughes's Skylark Poems." *Journal of the Australasian Universities Modern Language Association* 66 (Nov. 1986): 205-217.

Sagar, Keith, ed. *The Achievement of Ted Hughes.* Athens: U of Georgia P, 1983.

Scigaj, Leonard M. "The Ophiolatry of Ted Hughes." *Twentieth Century Literature* 31.4 (Winter 1985): 380-398.

———. "Oriental Mythology in *Wodwo.*" *The Achievement of Ted Hughes.* Sagar 126-153.

———. *Ted Hughes.* Twayne's English Author Series 486. Boston: Twayne, 1991.

Shelley, Percy Bysshe. "To a Skylark." Poetry Connection.Net. 1 April 2005 <www.poetryconnection.net/poets/Percy_Bysshe_Shelley/2610>.

Singh, Charu Steel. "The Poetics of Ted Hughes." *The Literary Criterion* 20.2 (1985): 56-69.

Wagner, Erica. *Ariel's Gift: Ted Hughes, Sylvia Plath, and the Story of* Birthday Letters. New York: Norton, 2000.

West, Thomas. *Ted Hughes.* Contemporary Writers Series. New York: Methuen, 1985.

Zak, William F. "The Confirmation of Keats's Belief in Negative Capability: The 'Ode on Indolence.'" *Keats-Shelley Journal* 25 (1976): 55-64.

Sarah Churchwell (essay date 2006)

SOURCE: Churchwell, Sarah. "'Your Sentence Was Mine Too': Reading Sylvia Plath in Ted Hughes's *Birthday Letters.*" In *Literary Couplings: Writing Couples, Collaborators, and the Construction of Authorship,* edited by Marjorie Stone and Judith Thompson, pp. 260-87. Madison, Wis.: University of Wisconsin Press, 2006.

[*In the following essay, Churchwell examines* Birthday Letters, *focusing in particular on Hughes's representation of Plath's poem "Daddy."*]

A secret! A secret!
How superior.
You are blue and huge, a traffic policeman,
Holding up one palm—. . .

You stumble out,

Dwarf baby,
The knife in your back.
"I feel weak."
The secret is out

Sylvia Plath, "A Secret" (1962)

The sudden publication of Ted Hughes's *Birthday Letters* in February 1998 made headlines on both sides of the Atlantic. This fact was no sooner noted than it was assimilated by the media back into the reception of the poems. Most considerations of *Birthday Letters* opened just as I began mine, namely, by registering the singularity of a collection of poems ever becoming front-page news in the first place. The media thus helped make the collection famous, remarked upon its fame with surprise, and reincorporated that surprising fame into its coverage. In this essay I want to argue that this feedback loop of writing, reading, and reception is the same one that produced *Birthday Letters* itself. Although it has consistently been represented in the popular press as a collection of "secret" poems that "directly" reveal Hughes's "private" memories of his life with Sylvia Plath—to whom he was married and from whom he was estranged when she killed herself in February 1963—*Birthday Letters* can also be read as a public response to disputes over the politics of publication, representation, and literary authority.[1] Ghosts of many other texts haunt *Birthday Letters,* which is not simply a "direct, private, inner" presentation of Hughes's memories of Plath but also a response to the problems of publication.

Birthday Letters was sold as Hughes's "unknown side" of a thirty-five-year battle of the sexes.[2] While it is certainly Hughes's only published chronicle of his marriage to Plath, *Birthday Letters* is also a citational, intertextual account that is ambivalent about its own status as a text. Kaleidoscopically reassembling particularly fraught moments in a long public controversy, *Birthday Letters* responds to many audiences: to Plath and to a shifting public that fought battles in and over her name for more than thirty-five years. Equivocal moves between revelation and concealment characterize this best-selling volume of poetry, which was always flanked by the words "secret," "private," and "direct" in a media that tirelessly mediated between it and its audience. *Birthday Letters,* too, can be read as a mediation, a collection that couples the poetic voices of Sylvia Plath and Ted Hughes. Less biography than biographical criticism, *Birthday Letters* entangles the woman and her work so that reading Plath is inextricably bound up with remembering her in *Birthday Letters.* Hughes plays on the idea of *revision* throughout the collection in order to read, remember, and correct Sylvia Plath.

In this essay I will sketch some of Hughes's "revisionary" strategies in melding his words with Plath's, focusing in particular on the intricacies of his representation of her poem "Daddy." These necessarily brief readings are not meant to be conclusive but rather suggestive of a method of interpretation. Ultimately I want to propose that **Birthday Letters** is best understood as an "open secret," a volume hesitating uneasily between disclosure and encryption, unsettled by its inability to fix the boundaries between life and art.

PUBLISHING SYLVIA PLATH

To begin with, it is necessary to recall some of the more familiar aspects of the controversies surrounding Plath and Hughes. In doing so, I do not wish to reconstitute what has been reductively misrepresented as a two-sided argument but rather to reconsider its stakes. Though admittedly selective, these examples culled from an immense history of dispute provide **Birthday Letters** not only with its themes but also with its very language; they are the conversation from which **Birthday Letters** is, so to speak, sampling. The more a given incident was rehearsed in competing accounts, the more it accrued sufficient citational intensity to warrant public response from Hughes.[3] Thus if readers familiar with Plath's reception encounter here some familiar, even stock, examples, that is precisely the point.

I opened this essay with an epigraph from Plath's poem "A Secret"[4] because it suggests, in condensed form, much of the strife, both public and private, to which **Birthday Letters** responds. Like most of the poems Plath intended for the collection she would entitle *Ariel*, "A Secret" was written in the fall of 1962, when she and Ted Hughes were separating as a result of his affair with Assia Gutman Wevill. It was composed the day after Plath finished "Wintering," the poem with which she would decide to close *Ariel*, and the day before Hughes moved out of Court Green, their home in Devon. That same day Sylvia Plath wrote "The Applicant," a biting satire of marriage, and the following day produced what would become probably her most famous poem, "Daddy."

"Wintering," "The Applicant," and "Daddy" were all published relatively quickly after Plath's death, and all have received substantial critical attention. But "A Secret," aptly enough, would be one of the last of Plath's poems to be published, despite her intention to include it in *Ariel*. "A Secret" was, so to speak, kept secret by Hughes, who became Plath's literary heir and executor when she died intestate. It would not be published by a mainstream press until *The Collected*

Poems appeared in 1981, nearly twenty years after it was composed, although in 1973 Hughes included it in *Pursuit*, an expensive limited edition (the limited edition itself could be seen as a kind of open secret, poised on the brink between public and private, silence and circulation). Furthermore, the poem is almost never discussed in detail in Plath criticism.[5] "A Secret," which is about the politics of betrayal, mocks the imaginary power with which some people imbue secrecy ("A secret! A secret! / How superior"), which is the Damoclean sword of potential exposure; the poem almost certainly derives directly from Hughes's affair with Wevill. Even within such a biographical context, however, "A Secret" remains one of Plath's more cryptic poems, finding its own "superiority" in the virtuosity of its rapid shifts among metaphors (one of Plath's most characteristic techniques). "A Secret" is implicitly about revealing secrets, about publishing them: the eponymous secret, by its very nature, seeks disclosure ("'But it wants to get out! / Look, look!' . . . My god, there goes the stopper!"). Although the secret is troped as treachery ("the knife in the back"), the poem is unclear about whether it is betrayer or betrayed. Such labile boundaries between assailant and victim, strength and weakness, suppression and exposure characterize not only much of Plath's late poetry but also the disputes surrounding Plath and Hughes, which converge on the theme of betrayal but differ over who betrayed whom.

The story of Sylvia Plath and Ted Hughes is unique in polarizing readers across both sexual and textual lines.[6] From the beginning, many Plath critics were suspicious of the way details of her private life seemed to affect considerations of her art. Hugh Kenner, an admirer of Plath's early poetry, saw in the late poems only a vulgar spectacle affording "Guignol fascination, like executions." He admonished that "such spectacles gather crowds and win plaudits for 'honesty' from critics who should know better. . . . The death poems—say a third of *Ariel*—are bad for anyone's soul. They give a look of literary respectability to voyeurist passions." Paul West went further, asking, "Had Sylvia Plath been ugly, and not died in so deliberate a manner, I wonder if she would have the standing she has."[7] The question for many readers is whether Plath's poetic authority is merited, or derived illegitimately on the basis of details from her personal life. Plath's authority—both authorship and power—hovers precariously between public and private, with many public accounts seeking to undermine her cultural status by locating it in the private, personal, feminine, and trivialized realms of her suicide, her looks, and her domestic drama.

But it is not only Plath's relationship to the private sphere that is vexed; the relationship of her writing to the public arena is even more complicated (as "A Secret" exemplifies). The conventional gendering of "publication" as a masculinized, active statement antipathetic to the feminized silence of the "private" sphere falters under the complexity of Plath's publications. Nor can biographical criticism of Plath be summarily dismissed as fallacious. The publication of Plath's poetry is intimately—and messily—bound up with the details of her private life, for the man who was at the very least the occasion for (if not reducible to the subject of) much of her writing was the man who also edited and published it after her death. The only volume published in Plath's name during her life was *The Colossus,* her first collection of poetry. *Winter Trees* and *Crossing the Water* were both posthumous collections, "arbitrarily" selected by Hughes and misleadingly described.[8] Plath published *The Bell Jar* pseudonymously in Britain to protect the feelings of her family. However, Hughes published it in the United States in 1971 under Plath's real name.[9] In 1975 Plath's *Letters Home: Correspondence, 1950-1963* appeared, officially edited by Aurelia Plath, Sylvia Plath's mother, but in actual fact edited at least three times since material was excised by Mrs. Plath, by Hughes, and by Harper & Row, the book's publisher. In 1977 Hughes published *Johnny Panic and the Bible of Dreams and Other Prose Writings* by Sylvia Plath, another arbitrary collection of published and unpublished stories, essays, and "excerpts" from her working notes.[10] In 1981 Hughes published the long-delayed *Collected Poems of Sylvia Plath,* but as Jacqueline Rose and others have argued, the editing of this collection also remains problematic, for it dismisses everything written before Plath met Hughes as "Juvenilia" and its concordances to "Plath's" earlier publications are confusing and misleading; it also surreptitiously eliminates some of her early poems. The following year Hughes published the heavily edited *The Journals of Sylvia Plath* in the United States.[11] In the original foreword (as well as in a revised version published as a separate article in *Grand Street*) Hughes made the (to many incredible) revelation that he had destroyed Plath's last volume of journals, that she had kept until her death, and that the next to last volume "had been lost."[12] Finally, one should note that all of these collected editions—letters, prose pieces, journals, and poems—were framed by introductions, all of which, with the exception of *Letters Home,* were written by Hughes. Thus, even lesser-known Plath texts were always already mediated, in their public form, by Ted Hughes.

The best-known Plath text, *Ariel,* is the one with the most complicated history, and it is often the controversies surrounding this collection that, unsurprisingly, reappear in **Birthday Letters.** When Plath died in 1963, she left behind the manuscript of a poetry collection entitled *Ariel,* which she had carefully arranged so that the first word of the collection was "love" and the last "spring." The latest poem Plath included was "Death & Co.," composed on November 11, 1962. Although she continued composing poems and seeking publication for most of them, she excluded these later poems from *Ariel.* In 1965 Hughes published a collection called *Ariel,* by Sylvia Plath, but as Marjorie Perloff has argued, he made several major changes to the collection. Hughes included fourteen (mostly later) poems Plath had excluded, cut out twelve poems she had included, and reorganized the whole.[13] The effect was twofold. First, it changed the volume's emphasis from rebirth and regeneration (Plath's ends with the rising of the bees at the close of "Wintering," who "taste the spring") to suicide (Hughes's ends with "Edge" and "Words"). Second, it also excluded many of the poems that Hughes later claimed were "aimed too nakedly," which is to say biographically.[14] Thus, as Perloff has argued, there are two *Ariels*—Plath's and Hughes's— and it is Hughes's that was published and continues to circulate.

Hughes was subsequently charged with "silencing Plath" (although he was also the person who published her writing), an accusation that is closely linked to other concomitant charges of censorship. Not only were some of Plath's poems withheld from publication, but critics and biographers found that what they were permitted to say was also controlled by the agent of the Plath estate, who for many years was Olwyn Hughes, Ted's sister. Unfortunately, Olwyn made little secret of her personal dislike of Plath.[15] Frequently permission to quote from Plath's poetry was withheld when "the Estate" did not agree with the point of view being expressed. This included not just biographers but journalists, critics, and scholars, who argued that copyright control was being abused as a tool of censorship.[16]

Hughes's reordering, editing, and control of virtually all of Plath's published writing renders questionable any claims that her poetry, journals, or letters tell her "version" of their story as she saw it or chose to make it public. When **Birthday Letters** is publicized as Hughes's long-withheld, answering "version" of their story, the implication that he had until then been the passive victim of Plath's prior "version" is equally dubious.[17] None of Plath's writing, with the exception of the "lost" and unfinished novel manuscript *Double Exposure,* proclaims itself as her "story" of her life with Hughes, and even *Double Exposure* was, she said, only semiautobiographical. In her poems Plath writes of isolated, fragmentary instances that are recognizably drawn from incidents in her life with Hughes, but that can easily be read figuratively in ways that transcend the personal (indeed, in the absence of biographical information they can *only* be read figuratively). Nowhere does she write what she declares a narrative of autobiographical poetry in the way Hughes does in **Birthday Letters.** Whereas **Birthday Letters** relies on a strong teleological narrative that emphasizes chronology, temporality, and memory—in other words, seeking temporal priority and closure—Plath did not choose to constitute such a chronicle in her late poems.

Thus, if Plath's position in the public sphere cannot be separated from sexual politics, neither can it be disentangled from what one might call the politics of publication. Many readers have interpreted Plath's "publication" of her "private" rage as an embryonic feminism, an active repudiation of the private-as-domestic ("writing like mad . . . as if domesticity had choked me," as she famously wrote in a letter).[18] However, as we have seen, Hughes helped put her writings in the public sphere, and her place there remains vexed for readers who see it as resulting from her "private" suicide rather than from the force of her published words. Nor are Plath's publications in any simple or easy sense triumphant evidence that her "voice" has been heard. Hughes is everywhere implicated in the history of her poems, at once their (apparent) subject, editor, publisher, and interpreter.

The boundary between Plath and Hughes continues to be erased in their public, published texts, as well as in the public disputes about those texts, which themselves blur the distinctions among author, text, and reader. For example, in 1971 Hughes wrote an essay entitled "Publishing Sylvia Plath," whose title does not distinguish the woman from the work. However, the article itself distinguishes among various audiences while sweepingly condemning their supposedly equivalent demands for an "anatomy of the birth of the poetry; and . . . her blood, hair, touch, smell, and a front seat in the kitchen where she died." Hughes declares that "the scholars may well inherit what they want, some day, and there are journalists supplying the other audience right now. But neither audience makes me feel she owes them anything" (*WP* [*Winter Pollen*], 164). Hughes's words, ostensibly uttered in defense of Plath, here camouflage a defense of himself. Plath's audience—always posthumous—from whom Hughes is defending "her," were not claiming that she owed them something but rather that he did. Furthermore, they were arguing that Hughes owed them—Plath's audience—because he owed her. Whereas some argued that he owed her because of his public (textual) relationship to her, others attributed the debt to his private (sexual) relationship. Many in Plath's audience did collapse the difference between the two, and then further collapsed the difference between themselves and Plath, as if a debt were owed them as Plath's proxy. Metaphors of obligation—both moral and economic—permeate the history, as implicit contracts between reader and writer, husband and wife, executor and deceased can be interchanged in a long chain of displacement. Hughes elides his own

role in admitting the public into the story; he also implicitly denies the ways in which he, too, is a member of Plath's "public," insofar as he is part of her audience.

Instead, he consistently figured himself as fact checker, arbiter of truth, and coauthor. Janet Malcolm quotes Hughes as complaining in a letter that what biographers failed to realize was "that the most interesting & dramatic part of S. P.'s life is only 1/2 S. P.—the other 1/2 is *me*. They can caricature & remake S. P. in the image of their foolish fantasies, & get away with it—and assume, in their brainless way, that it's perfectly O.K. to give me the same treatment. Apparently forgetting that I'm still here, to check." And in another letter, also quoted by Malcolm, he attacked both the accuracy and the motives of A. Alvarez's memoir of Plath on the grounds that Alvarez hadn't collaborated on it with Hughes: "If your intentions had been documentary style, if your respect had been for what really happened, and the way things really went, you would have asked me to be co-author."[19] What Hughes objected to, more often than not, were interpretations, warning biographers "to avoid interpreting my feelings and actions for me, and to beware how they interpreted Sylvia's."[20] Biographers were, of course, not interpreting his feelings and actions for Hughes but for the public—accounts that Hughes then read, since he was, after all, also part of the public. He objected, in other words, to becoming an unwilling audience to his "own story"—to becoming reader rather than author.

Hughes maintained that his right to a monopoly over the "truth" about Plath's life was based on his having married her. This equation of marriage with consummate knowledge is, to say the least, arguable. (Plath, for one, wrote letters around the time of the breakup of her marriage in which she pointed to the difference between who she had thought Hughes was and who she felt he turned out to be.) In his foreword to the 1982 edited *Journals,* Hughes uses his marriage to the woman metonymically to cement his authoritative interpretation of the poetry, declaring that Plath found her "voice" when the "real poet" became the same as the woman he married: "Her real self had showed itself in her writing, just for a moment, three years earlier, and when I heard it—the self I had married, after all, and lived with and knew well—in that brief moment, three lines recited as she went out through a doorway, I knew that what I had always felt must happen had now begun to happen, that her real self, being the real poet, would now speak for itself."[21] The real self, the real poet, and the woman he married are all the same. Having been unfairly accused of neglecting Plath's headstone, in 1989 Hughes complained in an oft-quoted letter to *The Guardian* that he had been "accused of trying to suppress Free Speech" every time he attempted to "correct some fantasy" about Plath.[22] He further objected to the fact that where his "correction" was "accepted, it rarely displaced a fantasy. More often, it was added to the repertoire, as a variant hypothesis. . . . The truth simply tends to produce more lies."[23] In trying to partition public accounts neatly into "truth" and "lies," Hughes is objecting to the fact that there *is* a repertoire, that there are other versions, indeed, that the story keeps reproducing itself, so that (his) "truth" can produce (others') "lies."

Even if one were to translate these divisive (and reductive) terms and argue that what Hughes really objected to was the way his account of his private experience could produce alternative public accounts, he was still protesting against the process of reception itself, against the feedback loop in which he was participating. In another oft-quoted letter cited by Malcolm, he wrote of his "simple wish to recapture for myself, if I can, the privacy of my own feelings and conclusions about Sylvia, and to remove the contamination of everyone else's." Representation becomes a virus: readers and stories are "contaminated" by what is implicitly promiscuous intertextuality, a "contagious," messy disorder. The existence of uncontrollable other versions infects an implicitly prelapsarian private experience before the fall into publicity occasioned by Plath's original sin of misrepresentation. But where Olwyn Hughes would blame Plath as the authorial source of what she calls a "contagion" of literary scurrilousness,[24] Ted Hughes would blame academics as readers, who have "indoctrinated" students with "tainted"— because fallacious—ideas about Plath.[25] The problem was that Hughes wanted his private experience to be acknowledged and authorized by readers without being "infected" by their mistaken interpretations. However, as soon as private experience is admitted into the public sphere, it is subject to the forces of reception and interpretation.

Over the years this complex of issues about gender and power, authority and reception, privacy and publication, writing and reading has been reduced and fixed by the popular press into a battle between Ted Hughes and "the feminists." *Birthday Letters* emerged as always already flanked by caricatures of this contest and is only fully intelligible when contextualized within a larger battle over the sovereignty of the literary patriarch. The "calumny," "vilification," "reviling," and "abuse" offered by feminists appeared in nearly all of the popular press's reportage concerning *Birthday Letters,* an aggressive "calumny" opposed to the myth of Hughes's noble "silence."[26] However, it needs to be remembered that the distinguished career Hughes mounted while supposedly maintaining his silence was precisely that of a public voice. The argument has been inverted. Feminists' earlier accusations that Hughes silenced Plath have undergone a complete transformation—thanks to Malcolm's reading of Plath as the "silent woman" whose deathly silence is her ultimate

weapon—into a reading of all feminists as aggressive, masculinized speakers who attack the nobly silent Hughes. More remarkable than the low repute in which the popular press holds feminism is the way in which an intensely public (and published) male poet—the poet laureate of Great Britain—is mythologized as victimized and "silent" in a powerfully politicized version of the reciprocal charges in Plath's and Hughes's poetry. Silence becomes a triumphal strategy in a battle over publication. Feminists are written (off) as hysterically screaming, a transposition of earlier accusations about Plath's "shrill" hysteria, the background noise against which Hughes, ironically, can be (not) heard as the heroically feminized suffering, silent man.[27] Hughes's "silence" paved the way for the suddenly vocal *Birthday Letters,* which the *New York Times* declared a "definitive and authoritative statement."[28] The popular press does not seem to find the authority of this definitive "statement" at odds with the prior authority of Hughes's definitive "silence." Indeed, that silence was also interpreted as a definitive and authoritative statement. That is, silence functions on a sliding scale in this story, its weight depending upon an acknowledgment by its audience that effectively renders it not silent but heard.

(Re-)Reading Sylvia Plath

While its reception reconstituted the "privacy" of this collection in order to sell it as a volume that broke secrets, only a few reviewers noted that although the existence of the book itself might have been a "revelation," its narrative told us little we didn't already know.[29] In fact, not much about *Birthday Letters* is private. These are voluntarily published poems by a poet laureate (*the* public poet of Great Britain) reacting as much to the storm of publicity surrounding Plath as to Plath herself. If what Hughes wanted was to "remove the contamination of everyone else's" ideas about Plath, *Birthday Letters* demonstrates the impossibility of "removing" the infection of intertextuality that was caught through reading and publication.

Hughes's liminal position between author and reader, mediating text and interpretation, standing between Plath and her audience (like her "blue and huge . . . traffic policeman / Holding up one palm"), remains at issue throughout *Birthday Letters,* which continually stages scenes of reading that show the way her "book [was] becoming a map" for his interpretations.[30] Plath's death risks rendering Hughes as just another reader of her story, for *Birthday Letters* locates Plath's personal truths not in Hughes's memories but in the "secrets" and "truths" he later discovered in her journals (and, less frequently, in *The Bell Jar*). For the British Hughes "revision" means studying as well as editing: to revise Plath means simultaneously to reread her and to rewrite her. In *Birthday Letters* Hughes revises his own prior experiences, "re-visioning" it all again through the prism of later information. "Now, I see, I saw, sitting, the lonely / Girl who was going to die" (*BL* [*Birthday Letters*], 68). Most of this revisionary information is gleaned from her journals. For example, in **"Your Paris"** Hughes implicitly uses his later reading of Plath's journals to locate her "actual" experience and viewpoint, by means of which he can correct his own memories:

> Your practised lips
> Translated the spasms to what you excused
> As your gushy burblings—which I decoded
> Into a language, utterly new to me
> With conjectural, hopelessly wrong meanings—
> You gave me no hint how, at every corner,
> My fingers linked in yours, you expected
> The final face-to-face revelation
> To grab your whole body.

(*BL,* 37-38)

Having read her journals, Hughes no longer "decodes" her words into "hopelessly wrong meanings"— implicitly the journals have offered the truth of what Plath was thinking. In *Birthday Letters* Hughes now rereads his own experience in light of Plath's texts; he also revises her poems in light of her (implicitly "truer") prose.

The "re-vision" that Hughes undertakes of Plath's words and his memories means that he tropes memory in visual terms as snapshots, photographs, pictures, seeing, and re-seeing ("now, I see, I saw"). But these "pictures" also undermine truth and accuracy with doubts about representation, interpretation, and mediation. Thus, **"Fulbright Scholars,"** the very first poem of *Birthday Letters,* was often described in reviews as a memory of "the day Hughes first caught sight of Plath's picture," or, slightly less inaccurately, as "the first time he became aware of Plath in a photograph he saw."[31] But the poem actually depicts the speaker remembering himself, at twenty-five, seeing a photograph in a newspaper in which, he now knows, Plath's face *might* have appeared. Like most of the memories in *Birthday Letters,* it is a memory laden with doubts, retrospectively undermined by questions later knowledge would prompt; in other words, it is not a direct recollection. "Were you among them?" he asks. He remembers the photograph and what he thought but not whether she was there: "I remember that thought. Not / Your face," adding, "Maybe I noticed you." From its opening page, that is, *Birthday Letters* responds not to a first memory of Plath but to a retroactively imagined, publicly mediated, possible viewing of her picture: it is a memory of perhaps forgetting a published representation. "Then I forgot," he says. "Yet I remember / The picture" (*BL,* 3). This confusion of memory over the difference between representation and reality will characterize many of the poems in the collection, which move uneasily between remembering and forgetting, seeking a direct access

they cannot recreate. Thus, Hughes's actual first memory of Plath is also likened to a photograph: "First sight. First snapshot isolated / Unalterable, stilled in the camera's glare" (*BL,* 15). Memory is troped as a "snapshot" throughout the poems, a trite association complicated by Hughes's further association of these pictures with stillness, snares, and death: "Remembering it, I see it all in a bubble," Hughes writes. "A rainy wedding picture / On a foreign grave" (*BL,* 123).

Birthday Letters represents the "truth" about Sylvia Plath in terms of direct speech and first readings. (The difference between speech and writing may be the real Derridean ghost of *Birthday Letters.*) In Hughes's rendering, Plath's words sometimes intervene between him and "direct, private, inner" access to her, whereas at other times they provide precisely that direct, private, inner truth. In several poems Hughes remembers reading Plath's journals following her death. In **"18 Rugby Street"** he discovers from the journal the "real" narrative she was constructing, a story he now knows is "the story of [her] torture" (*BL,* 21-22). Similarly, in **"Visit"** Hughes describes what it was like to "meet on a page" for the first time her reactions to him when they first met: "Suddenly I read all this— / Your actual words" (*BL,* 8). The image suggests direct access to Plath, rediscovering her "actual words," and yet he is reading them in her journals, like the rest of Plath's audience, having been rendered only another reader (albeit a privileged, "original" reader). Reading is imagined as an act of introduction: he "meets" Plath's words on the page. Hughes opposes looking forward—under the illusion that he might "meet your voice / With all its urgent future"—to the need to "look back / At the book of printed words" to rediscover the past (*BL,* 9). The inadequacy of both memory and writing is clear: the "book of printed words" not only alters memory but seems proleptically to substitute the published ("printed") journals for Plath's handwritten journals, which are what Hughes remembers himself reading. This moment of direct access to "actual words" is a fantasy, as the poem acknowledges. He is discovering her through printed words, but as the poem ends she is "ten years dead. It is only a story. / Your story. My story."

Although some readers objected to this line's equation of their two stories, his story *is* the same as her story, according to his interpretation. Reviewers focused a great deal of attention on the narrative of *Birthday Letters,* which repetitively insists that Plath died in order to "rejoin" her father, who died as a result of untreated diabetes when she was eight. Readers argued over the ethics of this narrative (was it an evasion of responsibility?) and over its plausibility (was this really the reason she died?).[32] But no one asked what seems a begged question: If *Birthday Letters* is Hughes's long-delayed "version," the counter to Plath's previous version, why does "Hughes's" story retell Sylvia Plath's most famous poem? In *Birthday Letters* Hughes lifts the plot of Plath's poem "Daddy" and offers it as the "true story" of her death. Critics like James Fenton argued for the virtue of what I call the "'Daddy' plot," for *Birthday Letters* as family romance, because, they said, it was Plath's own view, and thus Hughes was doing her the honor of taking "her view of herself" seriously.[33] Fenton's explanation authorizes Hughes's poetic claim on the basis of Plath's prior interpretation, which, he argues, Hughes is simply ratifying. But Plath offered many other poetic versions of suicide; among dozens of Plath's poems that imagine self-destruction, only five are also elegies for her father ("Full Fathom Five," "Electra on Azalea Path," "The Colossus," "Little Fugue," and "Daddy"), and of those only "Daddy" and "Full Fathom Five" explicitly suggest that a suicide would reunite the speaker with her dead father. Furthermore, after Plath wrote "Daddy" on October 12, 1962, her father never figured in another poem.[34] The vast majority of Plath's supposedly "suicidal poems" imagine the death of the speaker without reference to any father at all.[35] Furthermore, as Fenton acknowledges, these kinds of "autobiographical" (literal) readings have been "the source of Hughes's misfortunes." If that is so, then Hughes also performs the kinds of readings that are the source of his own misfortunes. All of these arguments take the "Daddy" plot extremely literally, but when Plath worked out this construction in her journals, even she asked herself: "Is this a plausible interpretation?"[36] *Birthday Letters,* purportedly "Hughes's version," his side of the story, repeats her side of the story in order to revise it.[37]

"Daddy" is a poem in which the speaker identifies her husband with her father and angrily rejects both for betraying and abandoning her: "I knew what to do," the speaker tells "Daddy." "I made a model of you / A man in black with a meinkampf look // And a love of the rack and the screw. / And I said, I do, I do" (*CP* [*Collected Poems*], 224). For almost forty years that "man in black" has been read reductively and literally as Ted Hughes. If the poet's husband and the speaker's husband are one and the same, then Hughes is the real-life villain in the tale, implicated in Plath's death. Whether "Daddy" really led Plath to kill herself, whether either Plath or Hughes—or both—really believed in the "Daddy" plot is, finally, a moot point. Given that *Birthday Letters* consistently responds to Plath's writing, and given its own overwhelmingly symbolic structure, one might well read Hughes's invocation of "Daddy" more figuratively.

The overwhelming presence of "Daddy" in *Birthday Letters* can also be read metatextually as Hughes's response to Plath's poem. In Hughes's poems "Daddy" functions as *both* (Plath's image of) Otto Plath and as her poem. The "Daddy" plot gives Hughes his own "model" for an erotics—and politics—of identification. Revealing a persistent anxiety over questions of originality and influence, *Birthday Letters* returns final consequence to the symbolic patriarch, upon whom Hughes blames Plath's suicide. In "accepting" what he writes as Plath's phantasmic identification of himself with her father, Hughes can identify, in a mediated way, with the symbolic authority of the father, but he can also distance himself from that father in order to displace blame onto him. Simultaneously, Hughes denies the *poem* final consequence, insisting upon its "erroneous" interpretations.

In Hughes's version of the "Daddy" plot, Plath ceases to be its author—one even willing to question the plausibility of the plot itself—instead becoming its subject and passive victim. In **"The Shot"** Hughes imagines Plath as "a high-velocity bullet" that killed "the elect / More or less . . . on impact." "You were undeflected," he writes. "You were gold-jacketed, solid silver / Nickel-tipped. Trajectory perfect," and then describes himself standing hapless in front of her "real target," "Your Daddy, / The god with the smoking gun" (*BL,* 17). Returning to the secret cause of the dead father reveals a crisis in authority, a fight for the position of author of the dead female body and of the story it symbolizes. A particularly bitter irony seems to linger in the fact that even her suicide, that most solitary of acts, is not Plath's (to) own in Hughes's representation of her in *Birthday Letters.* I emphatically do not want to imply (idiotically) that Plath's suicide was or ought to be read as a triumphant feminist gesture. But Hughes transforms Plath from vengeful, triumphant author of a story—in which she knows "If I've killed one man / I've killed two"—into the mere bullet in her father's gun. If she is murderous, it is not her fault: Hughes leaves it to patriarchs to pull the trigger.

Given Plath's vilification of the "man in black" in "Daddy," and given Hughes's subsequent opposition to the poem's publication—he admitted that he "would have cut 'Daddy' [from *Ariel*] if I'd been in time (there are quite a few things more important than giving the world great poems" (*WP,* 167)—it seems even more noteworthy that *Birthday Letters* relies on "Daddy"'s plot. Hughes's interpretation accepts the poem's apparent association of himself with the man in black. Certainly any claim to maintain an absolute separation between the husband in the poem and the poet's husband must be considered a dubious one, as difficult for Hughes to maintain as for his audience. But, at the same time, when Hughes renders himself in *Birthday Letters* as the "he" in Plath's poetry, he traps himself in a double bind that makes him predominant in her story yet also the subject of her vilification. (This is the double logic of defamation, which says that one recognizably is and isn't the person being represented.)[38] In this collection Hughes seeks to revise his own public identity, which was erroneously defined in Plath's earlier representation of (what he interprets as) him. However, he must accept the terms set by her writing in order to do so.[39] Thus, in **Birthday Letters** Hughes must continually reconstitute the characterization of "himself" that he would dispute, mis-recognizing himself, so to speak, in Plath's representations.

In **"Black Coat"** Hughes negates Plath's identification of him with her father as an "error" that results from her pathology, error-as-disease, which is specifically an error in the gaze.[40] Hughes responds in **"Black Coat"** to Plath's poem "Man in Black," in which she writes to a "you" she watches emerging from the sea. Hughes masters this representation by reinscribing himself as author, not audience, writing a poem in which he watches Plath watching him. Hughes imagines that while watching him Plath was creating a "double image / [Her] eye's inbuilt double exposure / . . . the projection of [her] two-way heart's diplopic error" (**BL,** 103). Diplopia means double vision, a "disorder of the sight." Hughes imagines himself, being watched, standing like a "decoy" and a "target" beside the sea "[f]rom which [her] dead father had just crawled." At that moment, Hughes imagines, "I did not feel" when "[h]e slid into me." Hughes remembers and imagines what (he thinks) she must have seen at the time but he did not feel at the time.

Hughes literalizes her poem, remembering being there and then reinterpreting the scene according to the knowledge later afforded him by reading not her poem (which itself makes not a single mention of the "Daddy" figure) but rather her journal—and only selectively. In the journal Plath first describes the poem's occasion—the walk on the beach she and Hughes took together—without mentioning the poem. She describes their walk immediately after recounting a visit to her father's grave, yet she interprets neither scene. Five pages later she alludes to the poem she has since composed, calling it the "only 'love' poem in my book." She then writes, "must do justice to my father's grave," before musingly adding (following two paragraphs about her literary ambitions and anxieties), "the 'dead black' in my poem may be a transference from the visit to my father's grave."[41] This passing interpretation is one Hughes has elected to accept and reinforce (choosing not to interpret the poem alternatively as "the only 'love' poem" in *The Colossus*). He then blames Plath for what he construes as *her* erroneous vision, comparing her eye to a "paparazzo sniper" and proleptically imagining the fatal effect her famous "picture" of Hughes will have in the media. Thus, his memory of the scene is filtered through his interpretation of her poem's representation of him via his selective reading of her journal. Her double vision would seem the obverse of his re-vision.

By the end of **"Black Coat,"** Hughes has declared Plath's viewpoint to be an "error," one of "double exposure." *Double Exposure* was the title of Plath's unfinished last novel, which Hughes said he lost. In an unpublished letter Plath described her last novel (at that time titled *Doubletake*) as a story structured around the idea that a "double take," a second look, is necessary to see a hidden truth. She said it was semiautobiographical, about a woman betrayed by a husband whom she had once idealized but who would turn out to be a cheat who abandoned her.[42] Plath had always been interested in the metaphor of the double: she wrote her undergraduate honor's thesis as Smith on the role of the double in Dostoyevsky; *The Bell Jar* is constructed around a running pun on doubles and double standards; and *Double Exposure* was clearly arranged around a similar play on words about duplicity. What Plath imagined as a woman's critical reinterpretation of her life Hughes rewrites as a medicalized disorder of Plath's "double vision," her mistakenly blurred viewpoint. Hughes corrects Plath's description of "him" in *Double Exposure* as an adulterer and traitor to make that novel's portrait, by intertextual association, part of Plath's "two-way heart's diplopic error." Her error is excused as part of her "disorder," her "double vision," but the "view" (of Hughes) she presented in her poetry and in her last, lost novel is nonetheless erroneous.[43]

Hughes's **"A Picture of Otto"** begins with a rewritten line from "Daddy." Plath wrote: "You stand at the blackboard, Daddy, / In the picture I have of you." Hughes opens his poem by adding only the idea of failure to Plath's line: "You stand there at the blackboard: Lutheran / Minister *manqué*" (**BL,** 193). Whereas on the one hand Hughes's representation here literalizes Plath's, on the other hand it is a poem very much about the force of representation itself. Hughes repeatedly emphasizes that he is "inseparable" from Plath's depiction of both of them in "Daddy": "Your ghost inseparable from my shadow / As long as your daughter's words can stir a candle. / She could hardly tell us apart in the end." He moves from her "words" to her "self" without a pause: her poem, read in conjunction with her journals, is taken as evidence of what she really believed. Hughes writes that Plath's lingering words are what render him inseparable from her father, but ironically Hughes's words here do the same: "Inseparable here we must remain / / Everything forgiven and in common." The fatalism of this statement mystifies Hughes's own agency in agreeing that they must both remain "here," inseparable on *his* page. But Hughes knows that what he is inseparable from is a "picture of Otto," a representation that appeared in another poem. Like "Daddy," the phrase **"Picture of Otto"** both refers to the poem itself and to the representation within the poem. Hughes's poem is a picture of a poem about a picture of a person; that is, Hughes's **"Picture of Otto"** interprets Plath's portrait in "Daddy" of a photograph of her father.

Representations themselves become culpable third parties, mediating between the "truth" of Hughes's and Plath's direct relationship. Indeed, triangles provide *Birthday Letters* with its geometry, for Hughes will consistently triangulate his relationship with Plath over a variously identified third party. The reiterated pivotal, figurative triangle of Hughes, Plath, and Daddy would seem to supplant the more literal and tragic erotic triangle of Hughes, Plath, and Wevill, which appears explicitly only in the poem "Dreamers." But there is another key triangle as well consisting of Hughes, Plath, and other readers that emerges in poems like **"Caryatids (2),"** **"God Help the Wolf After Whom the Dogs Do Not Bark,"** **"The Literary Life,"** and **"The Dogs Are Eating Your Mother,"** to name just a few. Finally— and most ambivalently—there is a triangle composed of Hughes, Plath, and Plath's writing that recurs throughout the collection. The triangles in *Birthday Letters* suggest the "error" of introducing any mediating figure into their relationship, since that mediation will inevitably destroy them all. These mistaken triangles are all associated with Plath and her writing (bringing Daddy or the public into their lives) rather than with Hughes's more obvious—and more obviously destructive— triangle with Wevill.

Many of Hughes's poems use Plath's titles to revisit texts—not all of which are poems—in which she has been interpreted by other readers as having criticized "him." ("The 59th Bear," for example, is a Plath short story about a wife willing the death of her husband; this story is frequently interpreted as revealing Plath's repressed hostility toward Hughes.) In revising these texts, Hughes can simultaneously correct Plath and "her critics," many of whom criticized him. Plath's poem "The Rabbit Catcher" is an obvious example: Hughes fought a very public battle with Jacqueline Rose and other Plath critics over the poem's interpretation, and the "snares" from Plath's "Rabbit Catcher" recur throughout the poems in *Birthday Letters,* suggesting the traps her representations would set for Hughes.[44] However, some of the most interesting re-visions in *Birthday Letters* of Hughes's role in Plath's writing are more oblique, not overtly advertising themselves as responses to Plath but sampling and correcting her words nonetheless.[45] For example, if read biographically, Plath's poem "The Jailer" is, like "Daddy," one of the most vituperative of Plath's attacks against Hughes, accusing "him" of imprisoning, torturing, raping, murdering, and (unkindest cut of all) "forgetting" her. *Birthday Letters* replies to "The Jailer" by adopting and then transposing all of these images in different poems. In **"The Blackbird"** Hughes retaliates against Plath's accusations by writing himself back into "The Jailer" not as Plath's torturer but as her victim, similarly imprisoned and unable to imagine being free. Yet he also represents their relationship while commenting metatextually on the imprisonment of that very represen-

tation: "You were the jailer of your murderer— / Which imprisoned you. / And since I was your nurse and your protector / Your sentence was mine too" (**BL,** 162). The revising and revisioning that Hughes undertakes here depends upon misrecognizing himself in Plath's poem "The Jailer," just as he misrecognized himself as the "man in black." Revising Plath means that she is both right and wrong ("a pen already writing / Wrong is right, right wrong"). Thus, he inverts her judgment: he was both her prisoner and her "nurse" and "protector," roles that, like Hughes's ambiguous "silence," combine the feminine with the masculine to create a new locus of power and victimization. This ambiguous position is finally that of "coauthor": he may share her punishment, but he also writes her "sentences." By arguing within inverted terms throughout the poem, Hughes suggests that the inescapability of representation may be the real "prison" here, for he never gets out of the "sentence" of publication, of being part of her sentence.

Coda: Open Secrets

Birthday Letters won the Forward Poetry Prize in October 1998, just a few weeks before Ted Hughes would die of cancer. Because of his illness, Hughes could not attend the ceremony, but he wrote a letter to the judges thanking them for the prize, a letter widely quoted in the press. *Birthday Letters,* Hughes explained, "is a gathering of the occasions—written with no plan over about 25 years—in which I tried to open a direct, private, inner contact with my first wife . . . thinking mainly to evoke her presence to myself, and to feel her there listening. Except for a handful, I never thought of publishing these pieces until last year, when quite suddenly I realized I had to publish them, no matter what the consequences."[46] Hughes's description of his decision to publish these poems strikingly resembles what D. A. Miller has characterized as the logic of the "open secret." Hughes describes the poems as "direct, private, inner," implying that they are by definition never to be published—never, that is, until an unspecified moment when he "suddenly realized he had to" make them public. In retrospect the motive seems obvious: Hughes's knowledge that he was dying is the "secret" cause of his decision to publish and, implicitly, to vindicate or at least justify himself. However, the formulation of his letter is worth commenting on because it is the grammar of the volume itself: the grammar of the open secret.

For Miller the open secret inheres in the ambivalent relationship of the subject to the social (what in Hughes's case I have been calling the "public"). The open secret is expressed in "odd compromises between expression and repression," gestures toward secrets that will not be fully revealed. Miller describes the logic as follows: "I have had to intimate my secret, if only *not to tell it*; and conversely, in theatrically continuing to keep my secret, I have already rather given it away. But if I don't tell my secret, why can't I keep it better? And if I can't keep it better, why don't I just tell it?"[47] The open secret characterizes the fundamental mechanism of *Birthday Letters,* making moves between what (again following Miller) one can call allusion and elision. Hughes's description of his decision to publish negotiates between public and private in exactly this way, gesturing toward the centrality of his "sudden realization" that he "had" to publish, a motive to which he alludes and then elides.

One might also note the highly mediated nature of this explanation for Hughes's publication of *Birthday Letters.* It appeared as a letter that presumably would be quoted in the press. This letter was necessitated by Hughes's illness, but it is not the only time Hughes used a letter to discuss his attitudes toward writing about Plath. There has been some speculation as to why Hughes chose to entitle the book *Birthday Letters.* (Some assumed the poems were composed on Plath's birthdays over the years, but only **"Freedom of Speech"** marks its occasion as Plath's birthday.) It seems appropriate that they are letters, however, since letters were always Hughes's preferred mode for negotiating his ambivalent relationship with the public while objecting to others' writings about Plath's life. Hughes not only consistently "corrected" errors in letters to the British press but also allowed Janet Malcolm to quote from several of his letters in *The Silent Woman,* although he refused to be interviewed directly. Through the indirect mediation of Malcolm's book *about* biographers, Hughes maintained his right not to be "pricked and goaded into vomiting up details" of his life *to* biographers.[48] That Hughes consistently discussed the privacy of his feelings for Plath in letters seems apt since letters themselves ambivalently bridge the public and the private. Indeed, letters might be said to literalize the move from the private to the public, as they move from the sender "out" into the world. But they are also a "private" form, which may or may not be intended for publication. Finally, the poems in *Birthday Letters* seem to be "dead letters": letters that have not arrived and are left unread by their intended recipient.

In poems like **"Freedom of Speech"** and **"Costly Speech"** falling toward the end of *Birthday Letters* Hughes brings the mechanism of the open secret into the open, so to speak, by opposing speech to writing. **"Costly Speech"** repeatedly refers to a mysterious "it" that has been forbidden by Plath's words and by Hughes's "own airier words":

> . . . your own words
> Irrevocably given to your brother,
> Hostage guarantors,

> And my own airier words, conscripted, reporting for duty,
> Forbade it and forbade it.

> (**BL,** 170)

The poem will not say what crime "it" is, but "it" has something to do with "US Copyright Law," which her "dead fingers so deftly unpicked." Thus, the crime involves publication and presumably alludes to the defamation trial in which the film version of *The Bell Jar* embroiled Hughes. Not only will the crime go unnamed, but so will the crucial spoken "words / Irrevocably given" to her brother. They will be "costly" but never, ironically, published in the poem that will maintain their definitional status as speech, that which is not written.

Likewise, in **"Brasilia,"** one of the poems that shares a title with a Plath poem, Hughes describes being "dragged into court," which he calls Plath's "arena," where she

> delivered
> The three sentences. Not a whisper
> In the hush.
> Your great love had spoken.

> (**BL,** 178)

These "three sentences" have the same consequences as "the most horrible crime," but what they expressed is also never revealed. Given the "court" setting, this would clearly seem to be another pun on prison "sentences," but this statement may also allude to and doubly encrypt the already oblique reference in Hughes's introduction to Plath's edited *Journals,* in which Hughes describes the emergence of Plath's "real" voice. Hughes, it will be remembered, proffers as "evidence" of the emergence of Plath's real self "three lines recited as she walked through the door," but he never relates what that real self said that was so revealing, so essential, merely gesturing toward the importance of a revelation whose content will be concealed. The tropes remained consistent: speech versus silence; real versus false; memory bleeding into inaccurate representation: "Your portraits, tearlessly, / Weep in the books" as **"Brasilia"** closes. But whether Plath is speaker or spoken still remains ambiguous. Are these tearlessly weeping textual portraits the ones she drew or portraits of her?

Direct speech and direct representation recede farther away as the volume draws to a close. The climactic moment of Plath's death is the most open secret of all: *Birthday Letters* never names it. Instead, the moment of Plath's suicide stretches across two poems, which become so cryptic as to be unintelligible to anyone unfamiliar with the facts of her life or with Plath's poetry. The first, **"Night-Ride on Ariel,"** ends with allusions to Plath's last two poems, the famous "Edge" and the never discussed "Balloons," both of which were composed on February 5, 1963. (Since "Balloons" is about a baby boy popping a balloon and being left with a "red shred" in his "fist," and "Edge" is about a dead woman, it is always assumed that "Edge" was Plath's last poem, but this is an unverifiable—and problematic—assumption.) As **"Night-Ride on Ariel"** comes to a close, Hughes lifts Plath's phrase "crackling and dragging their blacks" from "Edge." He then ends the poem with an allusion to "Balloons," describing Plath left with a "shred of the exploded dawn / In your fist / / That Monday." The reader can only infer Plath's death from extratextual (biographical) or intertextual knowledge that these allusions point to her last two poems. The next poem, **"Telos,"** evades direct discussion of Plath's death by attributing it to her notorious ambition. It imagines Plath attempting to hide from "The Furies of Alpha" (the British equivalent of the American grade "A") by "hurdl[ing] every letter in the Alphabet / And hurling [her]self beyond Omega" only to fall "Into a glittering Universe of Alpha" (**BL**, 176-77). The poem here mimics the movement of the larger narrative, hurling itself beyond the telos of Plath's death and leaping right to the academic response to Plath's death in a "Universe of Alpha." Both poems are in a code keyed to extratextual knowledge. Hughes is assuming that the reader knows the open secret of their story.

Birthday Letters jumps over the "climax" of Plath's death to its denouement, keeping Plath's death private, just as Hughes had always insisted it should be. The poems that, from their place in the sequence, might be expected to reveal Hughes's reaction to Plath's death instead become reactions to the public carnival—to the "peanut-crunching crowd" Plath named in "Lady Lazarus" and Hughes sneers at more than once in **Birthday Letters,** coupling his hostility toward real audiences with her notional crowd. The penultimate poem in **Birthday Letters, "The Dogs Are Eating Your Mother,"** attacks Plath's audience—and, by extension, Hughes's own—for "tearing" at what Hughes tells his children, in classic negation, is "not your mother but her body." At the end of his collection Hughes leaves scholars to "[j]erk their tail-stumps, bristle and vomit / Over their symposia" (**BL**, 196). The tables have turned: now it is not scholars "goading" Hughes to "vomit" out details of his life but rather the scholars (like me) who will "vomit" out their interpretations of his book.

Not publishing was not an option: the rest could not be silence. Hughes felt he had to publish these poems "no matter what the consequences," perhaps because, as he explained in a 1995 interview, he felt he shared with Plath a view of poetry as definitionally "a secret confession," the obliquity of which—its metaphorical, coded nature—was precisely a consequence of the dual need to reveal and to conceal this "secret." "The real mystery," Hughes mused, "is this strange need. Why

can't we just hide it and shut up?"[49] Ultimately Hughes could not leave readers out of it all together because reading is the heart of **Birthday Letters.**

Notes

A longer version of the present essay entitled "Secrets and Lies: Plath, Privacy, Publication and Ted Hughes's *Birthday Letters*" has appeared in *Contemporary Literature* (winter 2001). Both essays have benefited enormously from the careful suggestions of readers (some anonymous) and even more from discussions with Paul Kelleher, who makes everything smarter.

1. Elizabeth Lund offers a characteristic example: "The man often accused of stifling Plath and pushing her toward suicide is breaking his self-imposed silence. In his new book, 'Birthday Letters'—which made front-page news on both sides of the Atlantic and was an immediate bestseller in Britain and the U.S.—Hughes offers a collection of 88 poems written secretly over 25 years. In it, he speaks as if directly to Plath." "Breaking the Long Silence: Ted Hughes on Sylvia Plath," 14. See also the following: Alvarez, "Your Story, My Story"; Gray, "Poet's License"; Kakutani, "A Portrait of Plath in Poetry for Its Own Sake"; Kroll, "Answering Ariel"; Lyall, "In Poetry, Ted Hughes Breaks His Silence on Sylvia Plath"; Moseley, "Sylvia Plath's Former Husband Ends 35 Years of Silence"; Motion, "A Thunderbolt from the Blue"; Stothard, "Revealed: The Most Tragic Literary Love Story of Our Time."

2. Erica Wagner has written that these poems "set out the unknown side of the 20th-century's most tragic literary love story." "Poet Laureate Breaks Decades of Silence," 18. Katha Pollitt has written that "the storm of publicity surrounding 'Birthday Letters' has turned into a kind of marital spin contest, an episode in the larger war between the sexes. Feminists have long been blamed for demonizing Hughes." "Peering into the Bell Jar," 7.

3. Let me say a word about intentions (mine and Hughes's). At no point am I claiming the ability to distinguish clearly Hughes's conscious from his unconscious intentions. I can surmise, but then so can the reader. My intention here is to try, as much as possible, to read the effects of the texts backward to their publicly known sources, which will necessarily blur neat critical boundaries between text and biography. Several effects—or intentions—can be found in *Birthday Letters*: some self-serving; some critical of Plath and what she did to him; others expressions of real grief or anger whose justifiability changed according to circumstances. (For example, his anger at poets

who accuse him of having "real blood on real hands" seems justifiable to me, but not his anger at readers who love Plath's writings for reasons that may differ from his.) The expressions of grief should be self-evident. It is the complexity of Hughes's conversations with Plath and the critics that concerns me here, being the most encrypted and most misrepresented aspect of the collection. With the exception of one unpublished letter by Plath, which I have paraphrased (see n. 42), I have also refrained from introducing archival material in an effort to keep the conversation focused on "public" controversies.

4. Plath, *The Collected Poems,* 219-20. Subsequent references appear parenthetically as *CP* in the text.

5. This has gradually begun to change. See Britzolakis, *Sylvia Plath and the Theatre of Mourning,* and Brain, *The Other Sylvia Plath.*

6. It is something of a cliché, in writing about Plath and Hughes, that entering the fray inevitably makes one a target for floating accusations. Certainly the polarization of opinion continues: an earlier version of this essay received simultaneous and contradictory anonymous readers' reports: the first complained that I "bent over backward to avoid mentioning" Hughes's "self-serving" relationship to Plath's writing, while the second disliked the fact that the "tone of the piece" was "often very hostile toward Hughes" because I felt that he always wanted "the last word" and sought to make this "nefarious intention absolutely clear."

7. Kenner, "Sincerity Kills," 43; West, "Crossing the Water," 157.

8. The term appears in Hughes's prefatory note to Plath's *Winter Trees*: "The poems in this volume are all out of the batch from which the *Ariel* poems were more or less arbitrarily chosen." For a good discussion of the problems with the editing of *Winter Trees* and *Crossing the Water,* see Perloff, "On the Road to *Ariel*: The 'Transitional' Poetry of Sylvia Plath."

9. For a discussion of the complicated political aspects surrounding the publication of *The Bell Jar,* see Malcolm, *The Silent Woman: Sylvia Plath and Ted Hughes,* 39-41, 210-13.

10. Hughes also divided these writings (some said officiously) into "the more successful short stories and prose pieces" and "other stories." See J. Rose, *The Haunting of Sylvia Plath,* 73.

11. Hughes authorized the publication of Plath's unabridged journals just before he died; they were published in 2000, two years after *Birthday Letters* appeared.

12. See Malcolm, *The Silent Woman: Sylvia Plath and Ted Hughes,* 3-7; see also Rose, *The Haunting of Sylvia Plath,* 65-113.

13. Perloff, "The Two Ariels: The (Re)making of the Sylvia Plath Canon." In 1971 Hughes defended these decisions in an essay offering several explanations for the *Ariel* that appeared and concluding: "But I no longer remember why I did many things—why the U.S. edition is different from the English, for example. But again, I think most of it was concern for certain people." *Winter Pollen: Occasional Prose,* 166-67.

14. Hughes, *Winter Pollen: Occasional Prose,* 167. Subsequent references appear parenthetically as *WP* in the text.

15. For example, in 1986 she wrote the following to one of Plath's friends: "You liked her. I think she was pretty straight poison." Quoted in Thomson, "Under the Bell Jar," 21. Here is how Olwyn countered complaints about her role as "agent" for the Plath estate: "The myth of the Plath estate is fast becoming as unpleasant and artificial as the Plath myth itself." Letter dated June 17-23, 1988, 677.

16. This practice apparently continued after Hughes's death, as Lynda Bundtzen explains in her preface to *The Other Ariel.* Faber & Faber denied Bundtzen permission to quote both Plath and Hughes on the grounds that "if we agreed to the quotations being published then we would be seen as giving our seal of approval to the comments you make." Bundtzen wryly observes: "I did not know that I needed to 'reflect' anyone else's views in order to express my own in print." Bundtzen, *The Other Ariel,* ix-x.

17. For example, Alvarez has written that the poems in *Birthday Letters* are "scenes from a marriage; Hughes's take on the life they shared. Plath had written her own version." Alvarez, "Your Story," 59.

18. Plath, *Letters Home: Correspondence, 1950-1963,* 466.

19. Quoted in Malcolm, *The Silent Woman: Sylvia Plath and Ted Hughes,* 201, 129.

20. Hughes, "Where Research Becomes Intrusion," 47.

21. Hughes, foreword to *The Journals of Sylvia Plath,* xiv.

22. Hughes, "Sylvia Plath: The Facts of Her Life and the Desecration of Her Grave."

23. Hughes, "The Place Where Sylvia Plath Should Rest in Peace," 22.

24. Quoted in Malcolm, *The Silent Woman: Sylvia Plath and Ted Hughes,* 141. According to Olwyn Hughes, "[Because Sylvia's] work seems to take cruel and poetically licensed aim at those nearest to her, journalists feel free to do the same. Whether such writings are the result of this kind of contagion . . . I do not know." Letter dated September 30, 1976, 43.

25. Hughes, "Where Research Becomes Intrusion," 47.

26. Hughes's "silence" was omnipresent in the book's reception (see n. 1). Here is a representative example of the way Hughes's battle with feminism was figured: "Hughes's brief privileged marriage to Sylvia Plath, her suicide and his subsequent silence, turned him into a horned creature at whose character and reputation the feminist dogs have been baying and biting during the thirty-five years since her death." McClatchy, "Old Myths in New Versions," 159.

27. Stephen Spender saw Sylvia Plath as a "priestess cultivating her hysteria," saved from "shrillness" by her "form," arguing that "with Sylvia Plath, her femininity is that her hysteria comes completely out of herself, and yet seems about all of us. And she has turned our horrors and our achievements into the same witches' brew. . . . As with all visionary poetry, one can sup here on horror even with enjoyment." "Warnings from the Grave," 202-3. Richard Dyson has commented on the "depth of derangement" in Plath's "personal experience." "On Sylvia Plath," 209. George Steiner accused Plath of a "brokenness" that is "sharply feminine." "Dying Is an Art," *Sylvia Plath: A Symposium,* 215.

28. Lyall, "A Divided Response to Hughes Poems," E1.

29. Two reviewers who did note the familiarity of the story Hughes was telling were Pollitt ("Peering into the Bell Jar") and Logan ("Soiled Desire").

30. Hughes, *Birthday Letters,* 59. Subsequent references appear parenthetically as *BL* in the text.

31. Davison, "Dear Sylvia," G1; Pastan, "Scenes from a Marriage," 5.

32. Cf. Elaine Showalter: "I'm seeing how much [Hughes] mythologized the relationship and how much he takes a very determinist view of her, that it [the suicide] was because of her father, and that she was doomed to die and there was nothing he could do to stop her. I don't believe in this kind of determinism. I don't believe she was doomed to die. I don't believe that for a minute." Quoted in Lyall, "A Divided Response to Hughes Poems," E1.

33. Cf. Fenton: "Hughes's view of Plath is not far from Plath's of herself." "A Family Romance," 79. Davison has written: "Hughes does Plath the honor of respecting her demons as profoundly as she did herself." "Dear Sylvia," G1.

34. I am indebted to Susan R. Van Dyne for this observation.

35. Among the best known, see "A Birthday Present," "The Detective," "The Bee Meeting," "Fever 103°," "Ariel," "Lady Lazarus," "Getting There," "Death & Co.," and "Edge."

36. In a long passage in the unabridged journals Plath discusses the "psychodrama" that she is exploring. Her tone is cool and analytical, self-conscious about the story as an interpretation. The passage is full of qualifications, insisting that the identification is neither literal nor absolute. Plath is determined to "manipulate" the idea sufficiently to employ it in her writing: "How fascinating all this is. Why can't I master it and manipulate it . . . ?" *The Unabridged Journals of Sylvia Plath,* 447.

37. Only a few reviewers noted the triteness of the explanation. One who did was Logan, who was also the only reviewer I have come across who relates the "secrets" in this volume to the unintelligibility of the final poems. See the concluding section of this essay.

38. This logic mirrors Rose's reading of the defamation trial over *The Bell Jar.* See *The Haunting of Sylvia Plath,* 105-11.

39. Diane Wood Middlebrook noted in her review that in Hughes's "response to the challenge laid down most powerfully in his consort's greatest work," he no longer "resist[s] the role written for him by her work." "Poetic Justice for Sylvia Plath," A19.

40. A poem about Plath called "Error" mirrors a poem not included in the volume called "The Error," the biographical details of which clearly suggest it is addressed to Assia Wevill (or her avatar). It appeared in Hughes's *New Selected Poems* in 1995.

41. Plath, *Unabridged Journals,* 477-78.

42. This unpublished letter is in the Plath archive at Smith College. It has accrued its own intertextual existence in Plath criticism and has been paraphrased by many biographers and critics who were denied the right to publish archival material. Its contents are thus something of an "open secret." See the concluding section of this essay.

43. When my essay had been accepted for publication, Lynda Bundtzen was making a similar observation in her book *The Other Ariel.* However, she certifies Hughes's interpretation of "Man in

Black" via his reading of Plath's journals, quoting Plath's one sentence suggesting transference and adding an even more explicitly literalizing interpretation by claiming that "what Plath does here is to dress Hughes in her father's coat" (94). What Plath actually does is visit her father's grave, watch her husband at the beach, write a poem about a figure in black at the beach that neither names Hughes nor alludes to her father, and subsequently muse on the possibility of its having been a moment of transference.

44. The other poems in *Birthday Letters* that borrow a Plath title include: "The Owl," "Ouija," "Wuthering Heights," "Apprehensions," "Totem," and "Brasilia." In addition, one might include the obvious rewritings of Hughes's "Earthenware Head" for Plath's "The Lady and the Earthenware Head"; Hughes's "Black Coat" for Plath's "Man in Black"; "Fever" for "Fever 103°"; "A Picture of Otto" for "Daddy"; and perhaps his poem "A Dream" for Plath's early poem "The Dream" (though it is such a common title as to be unremarkable). Furthermore, not all of these shared titles share incidents. "Fever" and "Fever 103°," for example, take their source from Plath's various illnesses; she suffered throughout her life from sinusitis.

45. For a discussion of some of the other oblique revisions in *Birthday Letters,* see Churchwell, "Secrets and Lies: Plath, Privacy, Publication and Ted Hughes's *Birthday Letters.*"

46. Quoted in Gentleman, "Accolade for Hughes's Poems of Love and Loss, 4.

47. Miller, D. A. "Secret Subjects, Open Secrets," 194.

48. Malcolm, *The Silent Woman,* 141-42.

49. Hughes, "The Art of Poetry," 54-94.

Bibliography

Alvarez, A. "Your Story, My Story." *The New Yorker,* February 2, 1998, 58-65.

Brain, Tracy. *The Other Sylvia Plath.* London: Longman, 2001.

Britzolakis, Christina. *Sylvia Plath and the Theatre of Mourning.* Oxford: Clarendon Press, 1999.

Bundtzen, Lynda. *The Other Ariel.* Amherst: University of Massachusetts Press, 2001.

Churchwell, Sarah. "Secrets and Lies: Plath, Privacy, Publication and Ted Hughes's Birthday Letters." *Contemporary Literature* 42 (2001): 102-48.

Davison, Peter. "Dear Sylvia." *Boston Globe,* February 8, 1998, G1.

Dyson, Richard. "On Sylvia Plath." *Sylvia Plath: A Symposium,* edited by Charles Newman, London: Faber and Faber, 1970.

Fenton, James. "A Family Romance." *New York Review of Books,* March 5, 1998, 7-9.

Gentleman, Amelia. "Accolade for Hughes's Poems of Love and Loss." *The Guardian,* October 8, 1998, 4.

Gray, Paul. "Poet's License." *Time,* February 16, 1998.

Hughes, Olwyn. Letter. *New York Review of Books,* September 30, 1976, 42-43.

———. Letter. *Times Literary Supplement,* June 17-23, 1988, 677.

Hughes, Ted. "Ted Hughes: The Art of Poetry." Interview with Drue Heinz. *The Paris Review* 37 (1995): 54-94.

———. *Birthday Letters.* New York: Farrar, Straus, & Giroux, 1998.

———. "Where Research Becomes Intrusion." *The Observer,* October 29, 1989, 47.

Kakutani, Michiko. "A Portrait of Plath in Poetry for Its Own Sake." *New York Times,* February 13, 1998.

Kenner, Hugh. "Sincerity Kills." In *Sylvia Plath: New Views on the Poetry,* edited by Gary Lane, 33-44. Baltimore, Md.: Johns Hopkins University Press, 1979.

Kroll, Jack. "Answering Ariel." *Newsweek,* February 2, 1998, 58-59.

Logan, William. "Soiled Desire." *New Criterion* 16 (June 1998): 61-69.

Lund, Elizabeth. "Breaking the Long Silence: Ted Hughes on Sylvia Plath." *The Christian Science Monitor,* March 11, 1998, 14.

Lyall, Sarah. "A Divided Response to Hughes Poems." *New York Times,* January 27, 1998, 1.

———. "In Poetry, Ted Hughes Breaks His Silence on Sylvia Plath." *New York Times,* January 17, 1998, A1.

Malcolm, Janet. *The Silent Woman: Sylvia Plath and Ted Hughes.* New York: Knopf, 1993.

McClatchy, J. D. "Old Myths in New Versions." *Poetry* (June 1998): 154-65.

Middlebrook, Diane Wood. "Poetic Justice for Sylvia Plath." *New York Times,* January 27, 1998, A19.

Miller, D. A. "Secret Subjects, Open Secrets." In *The Novel and the Police*. Berkeley: University of California Press, 1988.

Moseley, Ray. "Sylvia Plath's Former Husband Ends 35 Years of Silence." *Chicago Tribune,* January 28, 1998, A1.

Motion, Andrew. "A Thunderbolt from the Blue." *Times* (London) January 17, 1998, 22.

Pastan, Linda. "Scenes from a Marriage." *Washington Post Book World,* March 8, 1998, 5.

Perloff, Marjorie G. "On the Road to *Ariel*: The 'Transitional' Poetry of Sylvia Plath." *Iowa Review* 4 (1973): 94-110.

————. "The Two Ariels: The (Re)Making of the Sylvia Plath Canon." *American Poetry Review* (November 1984): 10-18.

Plath, Sylvia. *The Collected Poems.* Edited by Ted Hughes. London: Faber and Faber, 1981.

————. *Letters Home: Correspondence, 1950-1963.* Edited by Aurelia Schober Plath. New York: Harper & Row, 1975.

————. *The Unabridged Journals of Sylvia Plath.* Edited by Karen V. Kukil. London: Faber and Faber, 2000.

————. *Winter Trees.* Edited by Ted Hughes. London: Faber and Faber, 1975.

Pollitt, Katha. "Peering into the Bell Jar." *New York Times Book Review,* March 1, 1998, 7.

Rose, Jacqueline. *The Haunting of Sylvia Plath.* Cambridge, Mass.: Harvard University Press, 1991.

Showalter, Elaine. *A Literature of Their Own: British Women Novelists from Brontë to Lessing.* Princeton, N.J.: Princeton University Press, 1977.

————. *Sexual Anarchy: Gender and Culture at the Fin de Siècle.* London: Penguin, 1990.

Spender, Stephen. "Warnings from the Grave." In *Sylvia Plath: A Symposium,* edited by Charles Newman, 199-203. London: Faber and Faber, 1970.

Steiner, George. "Dying Is an Art." In *Sylvia Plath: A Symposium,* edited by Charles Newman, 211-18. London: Faber and Faber, 1970.

Stothard, Peter. "Revealed: The Most Tragic Literary Love Story of Our Time." *Times* (London) January 17, 1998, A1.

Thomson, Ian. "Under the Bell Jar." *The Independent,* March 12, 1988, 21.

Wagner, Erica. "Poet Laureate Breaks Decades of Silence." *Times* (London), January 17, 1998, 18.

West, Paul. "Crossing the Water." In *Sylvia Plath: The Critical Heritage,* edited by Linda Wagner, 157-61. London: Routledge, 1988.

FURTHER READING

Bibliography

Sagar, Keith and Stephen Tabor. *Ted Hughes: A Bibliography: Second Edition 1946-1995,* 470 p. London: Mansell, 1998.
> Comprehensive bibliography of Hughes's writings, including translations, broadcasts, recordings, and manuscripts.

Criticism

Beer, John. "Coleridge, Ted Hughes, and Sylvia Plath: Mythology and Identity." In *The Monstrous Debt: Modalities of Romantic Influence in Twentieth-Century Literature,* edited by Damian Walford Davies and Richard Marggraf Turley, pp. 123-41. Detroit: Wayne State University Press, 2006.
> Examines affinities between Hughes's poetry and the mythological work of Samuel Taylor Coleridge.

Bentley, Paul. "Depression and Ted Hughes's *Crow,* or Through the Looking Glass and What Crow Found There." *Twentieth Century Literature* 43, no. 1 (spring 1997): 27-40.
> Discussion of the critical reception of *Crow,* and an attempt to look beyond the violence and brutality apparent in the poem's language and imagery.

————. "Introduction" and "Early Hughes." In *The Poetry of Ted Hughes: Language, Illusion and Beyond,* pp. 1-38. London: Longman, 1998.
> Concentrates on Hughes's use of language in his poems rather than on the works' themes or referential content.

Berry, David. "Ted Hughes and the Minotaur Complex." *The Modern Language Review* 97, no. 3 (July 2002): 539-52.
> Exploration of Hughes's use of minotaur imagery in *Birthday Letters* and the translation of Racine's *Phedre.*

Bradshaw, Graham. "Hughes and Shakespeare: Visions of the Goddess." In *The Achievement of Ted Hughes,* edited by Keith Sagar, pp. 52-69. Athens, Ga.: The University of Georgia Press, 1983.

Examines Hughes's engagement with the work of Shakespeare and its implications for Hughes's own poetry.

Davison, Peter. "Predators and Prey." *New York Times Book Review* (December 1 2002): 8.

Notes the preponderance of violence in the poetry included in *Selected Poems, 1957-1994.*

Roberts, Neil. *Ted Hughes: A Literary Life,* 256 p. Houndmills, England: Palgrave Macmillan, 2006.

Study of the major literary works and a discussion of the way they were informed by the events of Hughes's life.

Rowland, Antony. "Peephole Metaphysics in the Poetry of Ted Hughes." *Critical Survey* 14, no. 2 (2002): 49-60.

Discusses the poems "Pike," "The Thought-Fox," and "Lines about Elias."

Additional coverage of Hughes's life and career is contained in the following sources published by Gale: *British Writers: The Classics,* **Vol. 2;** *British Writers Retrospective Supplement,* **Vol. 2;** *British Writers Supplement,* **Vol. 1;** *Children's Literature Review,* **Vol. 3;** *Concise Major 21st-Century Writers,* **Ed. 1;** *Contemporary Authors,* **Vols. 1-4R;** *Contemporary Authors—Obituary,* **Vol. 171;** *Contemporary Authors New Revision Series,* **Vols. 1, 33, 66, 108;** *Contemporary Literary Criticism,* **Vols. 2, 4, 9, 14, 37, 119;** *Contemporary Poets,* **Eds. 1, 2, 3, 4, 5, 6;** *Dictionary of Literary Biography,* **Vols. 40, 161;** *Discovering Authors: British Edition; Discovering Authors: Canadian Edition; Encyclopedia of World Literature in the 20th Century,* **Ed. 3;** *Exploring Poetry; Literature Resource Center; Major Authors and Illustrators for Children and Young Adults,* **Eds. 1, 2;** *Major 20th-Century Writers,* **Eds. 1, 2;** *Major 21st-Century Writers* **(eBook), Ed. 2005;** *Modern British Literature,* **Ed. 2;** *Poetry Criticism,* **Vol. 7;** *Poetry for Students,* **Vols. 4, 19;** *Poets: American and British; Reference Guide to English Literature,* **Ed. 2;** *St. James Guide to Young Adult Writers; Something About the Author,* **Vol. 49;** *Something About the Author—Brief,* **Vol. 27;** *Something About the Author—Obituary,* **Vol. 107; and** *Twayne's English Authors.*

Venus and Adonis

William Shakespeare

English narrative poem, 1593.

INTRODUCTION

The erotically-charged *Venus and Adonis* is one of Shakespeare's two nondramatic narrative poems—the other being the tragic and somber *The Rape of Lucrece,* published in 1594. A highly successful poem among Renaissance readers, *Venus and Adonis* has as its source Book Ten of Ovid's mythological *Metamorphoses,* which was written in the first century C. E. and which contains the story of the goddess Venus and her seduction of the beautiful, mortal Adonis. Shakespeare's version was dedicated to Henry Wriothesley, the nineteen-year-old Earl of Southampton who favored Ovidian poetry; it is considered by some critics to be Shakespeare's first published work, and perhaps his first poem. Most historians agree that Shakespeare wrote the poem in the years 1592 to 1593, during an epidemic of the plague that shut down London theaters. By this time Shakespeare had acquired a reputation as a renowned playwright, but may have turned his attention to poetry—a genre associated with gentlemen—in a deliberate attempt to command greater literary respect. Totaling more than one thousand words, *Venus and Adonis* consists of six-line stanzas, in the rhyme scheme *ababcc.* Regarded as Shakespeare's most popular publication during his lifetime, the poem was read primarily by male university students and young men at the inns of court; it was considered too scandalous for women readers.

TEXTUAL HISTORY

Venus and Adonis was probably printed from Shakespeare's own carefully edited text, by Stratford-born friend and printer Robert Field. The First Quarto edition was released in the summer of 1593, and is regarded by scholars as a highly reliable text, with few errors. *Venus and Adonis* marked the first time Shakespeare's name had been recorded as the author of a printed piece of writing, giving Elizabethan audiences their first opportunity to read his work in book form. The poem quickly became one of the most popular literary compositions of the Renaissance period, undergoing sixteen printings before Shakespeare's death in 1616.

PLOT AND MAJOR CHARACTERS

Venus and Adonis tells the story of Venus, the mythological goddess of love, and her passionate desire for Adonis, a human. A young man who takes pleasure in hunting, Adonis resists Venus's advances, even when she lifts him bodily from his horse. She is unrelenting in her kisses and attempts at verbal persuasion, to no avail. Adonis implores her to let him go, insisting on his desire to go hunting the next morning. When Venus faints, Adonis attempts to revive her by kissing her. Night begins to fall as she awakens, engaging Adonis in a passionate embrace and expressing her joy at what she sees as his change of heart. To her dismay, however, Adonis reiterates his refusal and his wish to hunt boars the following day. She begs him to choose less dangerous game; he disregards her admonitions and departs, leaving her to spend the night in lamentation. The next morning Venus discovers Adonis dead, having been fatally gored by a wild boar. She mourns his death, divining that thereafter all human love will be tainted by sadness, jealousy, and distrust. Adonis's body disintegrates, and a sweet flower emerges from the blood that remains. Venus carries the withered bloom away in her chariot, promising that "There shall not be one minute in an hour / Wherein I will not kiss my sweet love's flower."

MAJOR THEMES

A main theme of *Venus and Adonis* is the power and limitations of rhetoric, especially as it applies to persuasion. The representation of sexual desire constitutes another major area of interest, as Shakespeare explored the consequences and often violent results of unbridled lust. To this end, several scholars suggest that the poem implies that lust deforms by destroying what is beautiful and natural. This distortion extends to the narrative's treatment of love, as the poem examines an aggressive and domineering approach to passion and desire, and the subsequent rejection of these erotic advances. The Christian debate of vice versus virtue is identified as a motif as well, with some critics seeing Adonis's choice of the more virtuous path of sexual purity and innocence as symbolizing the Christian doctrine of chastity. Nevertheless, Adonis succumbs to a violent death, which has led some historians to discern in the text a criticism of Catholic martyrdom. Among the numerous other themes identified by scholars is Shakespeare's portrayal of gender ambiguities, since he casts Venus as the sexual aggressor, traditionally a male role.

CRITICAL RECEPTION

Extremely popular in Shakespeare's day, *Venus and Adonis* was admired for its wit, erotic imagery, and bawdy subject matter. As the seventeenth century progressed, however, the poem virtually disappeared from discussions of Shakespeare's body of work. Considered marginal at best until the late eighteenth century and into the early nineteenth century, the poem enjoyed a slight revival with the Romantics, especially Samuel Taylor Coleridge, who favored its combination of passion and classicism. According to Anthony Mortimer, *Venus and Adonis* was long ignored for a variety of reasons, including its diminished literary status based on the erroneous belief that it had been written to follow the popular literary fashion of the day. Also prevalent was the idea that the work was flawed because of inconsistencies in tone and its lack of clear purpose. A revival in scholarly interest did not occur until the latter half of the twentieth century, when scholars began focusing on the poem's formal and ornate rhetorical style, a device that had long deterred critics, who dismissed it as simple artifice—a common Renaissance literary conceit.

This emphasis on rhetoric in the poem has prompted a surge of critical interest, with most pointing out that it is Shakespeare's portrayal of an Adonis who resists Venus—a major departure from Ovid—that provided the poet with the narrative foundation upon which to display his masterful command of rhetoric. The poem is unique because, despite the use of a range of oratorical styles, neither party succeeds in persuading the other. In this way, according to many critics, Shakespeare dramatically explored both the strengths and weaknesses of language and the obstruction of verbal perception between two individuals. Venus's extensive use of language in particular continues to interest scholars. Noting a conflict between her speech and her gender, critics have seen Venus in the traditionally male role of Petrarchan lover, attempting to persuade Adonis by imploring him to participate in the natural act of reproduction and to take pleasure in his youth while time allows. In a further reversal of gender roles, Shakespeare endowed Adonis with what scholars view as the typically idealistic attributes commonly reserved for the female recipients of such entreaties.

A number of critics focus on the political subtext of the poem, particularly its possible references to Queen Elizabeth. Richard Wilson examines the poem's treatment of Catholic martyrdom in light of the "Bloody Question" of 1588. This "deadly test" subjected English Catholics to the question of whether their loyalties resided with the pope or with the queen. In his analysis, Wilson cites the first published appraisal of *Venus and Adonis,* written by Robert Southwell, a Jesuit and England's foremost Catholic poet, who claimed that Shakespeare's poem constituted a political and religious betrayal by its author. According to Wilson—who agrees that beneath the poem's eroticism lay political undertones—Shakespeare refuted Southwell's celebration of martyrdom and instead argued that Catholics who had been executed for their faith had died in vain. Shakespeare further claimed that history would not revere Catholic martyrs but would see Queen Elizabeth—i.e., the masculine and aggressive Venus—as the hero. Other critics speculate that the poem reveals Shakespeare's conflicted feelings about the manipulative and powerful queen.

PRINCIPAL WORKS

Poetry

Venus and Adonis 1593
Sonnets 1593-94
The Rape of Lucrece 1594
The Phoenix and Turtle 1601
A Lover's Complaint 1609

Other Major Works

The Tragedy of Richard the Third (play) 1592-93
The Taming of the Shrew (play) 1593-94
A Midsummer Night's Dream (play) 1595-96
The Tragedy of Romeo and Juliet (play) 1595-96
The Merchant of Venice (play) 1596-97
The Tragedy of Julius Caesar (play) 1599
The Tragedy of Hamlet, Prince of Denmark (play) 1600-01
The Tragedy of Othello, the Moor of Venice (play) 1604
The Tragedy of King Lear (play) 1605
The Tragedy of Macbeth (play) 1606
The Tempest (play) 1611

CRITICISM

A. D. Cousins (essay date 1994)

SOURCE: Cousins, A. D. "Venus Reconsidered: The Goddess of Love in *Venus and Adonis.*" *Studia Neophilologica* 66, no. 2 (1994): 197-207.

[*In the essay below, Cousins examines the various characterizations of Venus depicted in the poem, focus-*

ing on how Shakespeare subverted the traditional conceptions of the mythological goddess and claiming that Venus's experience of the pain of rejection constitutes a major and transforming aspect of her character.]

The how and what of Venus' presentation have been studied from mainly two angles. Sometimes she has been looked at as if a character in a play—appropriate enough given that her creator was a playwright and that he gave her speech after speech. As a result, the consistencies, fluctuations and contradictions in her characterization have been often discussed, with a good deal of agreement but by no means with unanimity.[1] Sometimes she has been studied in connection with particular aspects of Renaissance symbolism or thinking about ancient myths. Critical commentary adopting that angle of approach has occasionally interpreted Venus as a simple, symbolic figure but, more usually, as an evocatively allegorical one (especially, of course, in the context of some Renaissance interpretations of the Venus and Adonis story).[2] Here, employing both well established ways of approach, I want to offer a new account of Venus' presentation in the poem. First it will be argued that the characterization of Venus, although often acknowledged to be various, is in fact far more diverse than has been recognized. Most of the manifold aspects of her, it will be suggested at the same time, accord with (maybe derive from, partly or wholly) ancient representations of her that were still known and studied in Shakespeare's time, as can be seen from a range of contemporary books about the meanings of ancient myths.[3] The main points of that first argument will be: that even if most of the different aspects of Venus' characterization seem conventional, frequently they are treated ironically—their conventionality is subverted; that, in presenting the goddess of love as having a great variety of aspects, Shakespeare's narrator implies not merely love's many-sidedness but its often incongruous multiplicity. The second argument put forward will be that one of the more important aspects of Venus' characterization is her discovering the familiar, human experience of loving another in vain.[4] It will be suggested that her experiencing the misery of unrequited human love has significance for a couple of reasons. She comes to know something of not only the unhappiness to be found in human love but, as well, of how love can usurp control over a human consciousness.[5] Therefore the goddess of love comes experientially to know—to a degree—a phenomenon that she has necessarily seen yet never felt. For her, the experience of loving Adonis both in vain and obsessively is a new, alien experience: ultimately, the experience of love as otherness. The third and last major argument proposed in what follows will be that Venus, herself partly transformed by her unrequited love for Adonis, offers him her love as a means for his achieving self-transformation. To be more specific, it will be argued

that, in offering Adonis her love, Venus simultaneously offers him metamorphosis, a redefined subjectivity, in which self-perfection and safety will be supposedly gained but a loss of self will be inevitable.

Venus had been seen since ancient times as having a wide range of aspects; there were, as various writers had demonstrated, many Venuses. Early in her initial wooing of Adonis (lines 7-12), Venus uses a tactically considered, schematic language of sexual seduction, and it characterizes her as a goddess of physical desire, wise in the techniques of enticement. That characterization is developed when she goes on to say:

> "Vouchsafe, thou wonder, to alight thy steed,
> And rein his proud head to the saddle-bow;
> If thou wilt deign this favour, for thy meed
> A thousand honey secrets shalt thou know.
> Here come and sit, where never serpent hisses,
> And being set, I'll smother thee with kisses.
>
> "And yet not cloy thy lips with loath'd satiety,
> But rather famish them amid their plenty,
> Making them red, and pale, with fresh variety:
> Ten kisses short as one, one long as twenty.
>   A summer's day will seem an hour but short,
>   Being wasted in such time-beguiling sport."

(II.13-24)

The rest of Venus' opening speech suggests both the mingling of imagination with sensuality in her attempt to seduce Adonis and how intensely, almost boundlessly physical her desire for him is. The speech as a whole, then, shows, the goddess of love to be skilled in the deceptive language/rhetoric of seduction and obsessive in her desire, in effect seeking infinite physical enjoyment of Adonis who, in his physicality, is finite.

Yet while Venus' opening speech vigorously characterizes her, it does so in accord with two ancient versions of the goddess which were still current in the sixteenth century. Insofar as she is the calculating rhetorician of love, Shakespeare's Venus recalls the *Venus Mechanitis* of the ancient world, the Venus practised in love's verbal and other artifices.[6] Insofar as she is the goddess of virtually limitless physical desire, she recalls *Venus Vulgaris,* the ancient representation of Venus as the goddess of wholly sensual love.[7] Venus' opening speech at once forcefully presents her and offers what can be seen as a conventional representation of her. It seems clear, however, that whether Shakespeare's Venus merely harmonizes with or actually derives from convention, the conventional elements in her characterization are treated ironically and thus subverted. For a start, Venus fails as a rhetorician of love. Her language and tactics of seduction are problematic because some of their main images for praising Adonis' exceptional beauty also highlight its transience and (or) vulnerability ("flower," "doves," "roses"). But a far more important problem is that in trying to seduce Adonis she uses the wrong language—the wrong language and rhetoric for her particular audience.[8] Maybe Venus does not fully recognize that Adonis is not only very young and inexperienced but very reluctant as well; it seems likelier, though, that in her urgency she just pays too little attention to those things. Whatever the case, her speech implies that she is both a connoisseur of the erotic ("A thousand honey secrets shalt thou know") and smothering ("I'll smother thee with kisses"), greedy (see lines 19-24, *passim*) in her passion. Adonis, clearly enough, has no wish to be smothered by Venus' greedy passion, something the introductory stanza has indicated and that the rest of the poem makes explicit. Therefore her words of love repel him—and failing to express her desire persuasively in words, she gets no chance to express it physically to her satisfaction. In effect, she fails as *Venus Mechanitis* and so is frustrated as *Venus Vulgaris.* It could be suggested that her opening speech even has the result of turning her into a parodic *Venus Verticordia,* the Venus who promotes chastity in women (and Adonis is described as having some female attributes).

Perhaps two other features of Venus' presentation here might be briefly considered before further aspects of her in the poem are discussed. When Venus tries to seduce Adonis she acts, according to the poem's introductory stanza, like an assertive, male lover. Some of the words she chooses and her tactics of persuasion distinctly suggest that. For example, her insistence that the beauty of her beloved is unique, though justified by its actually being so, is of course conventional in sixteenth-century English love verse written in imitation of Petrarch's, and by men to or about women. No less conventional in that love verse are celebrations of female beauty in terms of emphatic images of white-ness and redness, such as appear in Venus' praise of Adonis' beauty.[9] Likewise, the male speakers in that love verse sometimes offer their ladies gifts in order to win their affections. To cite a pair of obvious instances, Marlowe's speaker in "Come live with me and be my love" offers gifts to his beloved; Damon, in Marvell's "Damon the Mower," tells of the gifts with which he has wooed his beloved Juliana.[10] Venus, too, offers Adonis a gift, an elaborate enticement in order to bring him physically close to her ("A thousand honey secrets . . ."). As those examples reveal, Venus uses a predominantly male, assertive (Petrarchan) language and rhetoric of love. The outcome is, though, that when Venus acts "like a bold-fac'd suitor" in using such a language/rhetoric she uses it inappropriately (after the fashion described above) and appears comic. Shakespeare's Venus seems, as it were, to be a *Venus Mechanitis* who simultaneously fails and acts out a comedy of gender-reversal. And that doubly ironic presentation of her is immediately developed. Having misemployed language in her initial attempt to make Adonis love her,

she then successfully persuades herself of his sexual inclinations by misreading the body language of his "sweating palm" (line 25). She cannot or will not read his "sweating palm" as signifying physical discomfort and (or) emotional distress. Moreover, the comedy of gender-reversal becomes almost grotesque when Venus subsequently "pluck[s]" (line 30) Adonis from his horse, tucks him under her arm (line 32) and finally "thrust[s]" (line 41) him to the ground. The comedy of gender-reversal is, nonetheless, more sophisticated than such an instance of it might indicate, and that more interest-ing dimension to it will be considered later in this discussion.

The final feature of Venus' presentation here that I wish to glance at is this: in her attempt to seduce Adonis she offers him a heightening of his beauty, to be achieved through transformation. Assuring Adonis that when "smother[ing him] with kisses" (line 18) she will "not cloy [his] lips with loath'd satiety" (line 19), Venus goes on to assert that in fact she will enhance their beauty, "[m]aking them red, and pale, with fresh variety" (line 21). She will add, that is, to the "white and red" (line 10) of Adonis' natural beauty—and specifically to the natural beauty of his (red) lips—through her art of sexuality, making his lips startlingly change in colour and thus into instances of the Renais-sance aesthetic principle of *varietà* (connected with the principle, or ideal, of *grazia*—an elegance delightful to the observer/reader).[11] To receive that heightening of his beauty, Adonis must allow himself to be transformed from an asexual to a sexual being. For his beauty to be transformed, in other words, he must allow himself to be metamorphosed. The "time-beguiling sport" (line 24) of sexual play will involve at once his superficial aesthetic transformation and a metamorphosis of his identity. Venus' offer of metamorphosis will be repeat-edly made to Adonis throughout the poem. One of those offers, in particular, is both challenging and complex. The motif's introduction, however, occurs in her first speech; its initial, witty appearance suggests the aesthetic element in Venus' connoisseurship of the erotic and Adonis' presentation in the rest of the poem as an aesthetic/sexual object.

It seems reasonable to argue that the aspects of Venus so far discussed (*Venus Mechanitis* and *Venus Vulgaris,* to put it briefly) recur more often throughout Shakes-peare's poem than do virtually any of the others contributing to her many-sided characterization, and hence their elaborate, foundational encoding has been examined in some detail. It is not necessary, I think, that the subsequent treatment of those aspects be completely traced since in that initial encoding their defining features seem to be indicated. Some of the modifications to them, nonetheless, do have to be looked at and now will be—in the context of an account of Venus' other guises in the poem.

Another major aspect of Venus in the poem is that of *Venus Genetrix*: the Venus, from ancient times to those of Shakespeare, associated with the generative power in nature, fertility and the desire to reproduce beauty through offspring (to take the most obvious illustration, the beauty of one's beloved). There has often been mention of Shakespeare's Venus in that role but the question remains as to how the role functions.[12] Insofar as Shakespeare's Venus resembles *Venus Genetrix,* she does so problematically. When Adonis' stallion breaks away from where it has been tied and runs after "[a] breeding jennet" (line 260), it forcefully displays the generative impulse. Venus, turning the horse into an *exemplum* for its master, suggests that he too should do, with her, what comes naturally:

> "Let me excuse thy courser, gentle boy,
> And learn of him, I heartily beseech thee,
> To take advantage on presented joy;
> Though I were dumb, yet his proceedings teach thee.
> O learn to love. . . .

(lines 403-407)

But in fact Venus argues there that Adonis, in acting "naturally," should imitate merely animal desire: that his natural love for her should be solely of and for the body. Her love for him is certainly of that kind, what Pico called "Bestial . . . Love" as distinct from human or divine love.[13] It is natural and obsessively physical, as the image of the "glutton eye" in her immediately preceding words makes startlingly clear:

> "Who see his true-love in her naked bed,
> Teaching the sheets a whiter hue than white,
> But when his glutton eye so full hath fed,
> His other agents aim at like delight?"

(lines 397-400)

That "glutton eye" image, moreover, connects with other images in the poem that insistently imply Venus' devouring sexuality (see, for instances: lines 18-22, in her first speech, and especially lines 445-450, 543-552). And all those link with the images suggesting that her desire is predatory as well as natural, the best known of which are probably the simile of the "empty eagle . . . devouring all in haste, / Till either gorge be stuff'd or prey be gone" (lines 55-58, a comparison made by the narrator), and the metaphor likening her to the boar (lines 1117-1118, a comparison made by Venus herself). If she resembles *Venus Genetrix,* she is a parodic, brutally "natural" version of that divinity. That being granted, the problematics of Venus as *Venus Genetrix* do not, even so, end there.

The similarity between Shakespeare's Venus and *Venus Genetrix* also seems ironic in at least a couple of other ways. First, when Venus speaks in effect as *Venus Genetrix*—celebrating the generative impulse in nature, urging Adonis to reproduce his unique beauty through offspring (on his supposed duty to breed, see lines 163-174)—she speaks primarily to seduce him. What could be called the *Venus Genetrix* aspect of her characterization is subordinate to the (*de facto*) *Venus Mechanitis* and *Venus Vulgaris* aspects.[14] Second, when Venus searches desperately for Adonis after she has gone to hunt the boar, there occurs this description of nature impeding the preoccupied goddess:

> And as she runs, the bushes in the way
> Some catch her by the neck, some kiss her face,
>   Some twine about her thigh to make her stay:
>   She wildly breaketh from their strict embrace,
>   Like a milch doe, whose swelling dugs do ache,
>   Hasting to feed her fawn hid in some brake.

(lines 871-876)

The elision of the sexual and the maternal in that description of Venus (lines 875-876) incongruously mingles her *Vulgaris* and *Genetrix* aspects. However it is ironic, too, that the goddess whose love almost smothered Adonis now finds herself almost imprisoned by a sexually assertive natural world with which, as *Venus Genetrix,* she is associated. She comes to experience something of what Adonis appears to have been undergoing throughout much of the poem, and "wildly breaketh" indicates her response.[15] The final function of Venus as *Venus Genetrix* may, then, be twofold. First, in that particular role she seems to imply the natural brutality and reductiveness, rather than the natural, creative beneficence, of sexual desire. Second, in that role she seems also to help make problematic the nature of "nature" in Shakespeare's poem. In trying to seduce Adonis she appeals recurrently to "nature"; Adonis appeals to "nature" in rejecting her. But if she is, at least in part, a nature/fertility divinity, and incomplete as well as self-divided in being so, while Adonis' perception of "nature" differs in important respects from hers, her role as *Venus Genetrix* seems to emphasize the ambiguity of "nature" in her fictional world (and also in ours), its openness to appropriation for the justifying of quite opposite ends.

There are a great many further aspects to Shakespeare's Venus. For a start, she is also a deceiver. Just after telling Adonis that even Mars the god of war has wooed her (lines 97-102), she reassures him that, if he makes love to her, no one will find out and that therefore secrecy will preserve his honour (lines 121-126). She omits to tell Adonis that Vulcan, her husband, not only caught Mars and her in bed but added to their embarrassment by calling in the other gods to share his discovery, an omission all too obvious to the reader. In trying to trick Adonis—and she tries more than once in the course of the tale—she bears a clear likeness to the conventional *Venus Apaturia* (Venus the Deceiver).[16] The poem reveals, though, that Venus has most success in unwittingly deceiving herself (as when, for example, she persuades herself that Adonis' "sweating palm" indicates his amorous disposition). Venus the deceived Deceiver is, additionally, a prophet. She uncertainly foresees Adonis' death at the hunt (lines 661-666). Soon after his death she deliberately and formally foretells what the experience of love will thenceforward be, always and everywhere (lines 1135-1164). Again, an old convention seems to underlie this aspect of her characterization: that of Venus as *Magistra Divinandi* (Mistress of/Instructor in Prophesying).[17] However, Shakespeare's Venus again parodically refigures convention. Jealousy (line 657) prompts her first, accurate, hesitant foretelling. Her second is anachronistic, for—as the myths show—love had already and widely been what she announces it will become. Her wholly negative vision of love's future seems, moreover, open to query since the reader could object that its truth is incomplete. The mock-explanatory prophecy, that is to say, actually tells more about Venus' bitterness, and selfishness, than it does about the nature of love supposedly since Adonis' death.

Although other aspects of Shakespeare's Venus in relation to conventional representations of the goddess still remain to be examined, for example, the link between her and *Venus Meretrix* (Venus the Prostitute; see lines 511-522), there is space for study of only one more of her guises: her pervasive guise as *Venus Victrix* (Venus the Conqueror). The ancient title Venus the Conqueror referred, as is fairly well known, to Venus' overcoming of Mars, the god of war, through the power of her beauty and of his desire for her. In the sixteenth century that title was often interpreted as signifying Love's capacity to overcome Strife, even, Love's capacity to bind the conflicting elements of the universe into a harmonious discord.[18] The connection between Shakespeare's Venus and *Venus Victrix* is made explicit in the poem. Venus boasts to Adonis:

> "I have been woo'd as I entreat thee now,
> Even by the stern and direful god of war,
> Whose sinewy neck in battle ne'er did bow,
> Who conquers where he comes in every jar;
>   Yet hath he been my captive and my slave,
>   And begg'd for that which thou unask'd shalt have.
>
> "Over my altars hath he hung his lance,
> His batter'd shield, his uncontrolled crest;
> And for my sake hath learn'd to sport and dance,
> To toy, to wanton, dally, smile and jest,
>   Scorning his churlish drum and ensign red,
>   Making my arms his field, his tent my bed.
>
> "Thus he that overrul'd I oversway'd,
> Leading him prisoner in a red rose chain:
> Strong-temper'd steel his stronger strength obey'd,
> Yet was he servile to my coy disdain."

(lines 97-112)

But of what kind is that connection? Shakespeare's Venus seems to be a failed *Venus Victrix*; more important, the *Venus Victrix* motif itself—as an emblem of Love's salutary power—seems to be dismantled throughout the poem.

When Venus has finished recounting her victory over Mars, she immediately says to Adonis: "O! be not proud, nor brag not of thy might, / For mastering her that foil'd the god of fight" (lines 113-114). Her point is, of course, that Adonis has made her love him (simply by being irresistible) and in doing so has conquered Venus the Conqueror, who overcame even the god of war. She consciously inverts the *Venus Victrix* motif and identifies herself as a now-failed, now-parodic Venus the Conqueror. Obviously enough, her admission is partly true because she has indeed been overcome by Adonis' beauty. Yet it is also disingenuous, flattery to seduce Adonis: she reveals herself as a failed/parodic *Venus Victrix* so that she can subsequently conquer him and re-enact her role as victor. At this moment of the poem, that is to say, she puts her role as *Venus Victrix* in the service of her roles as *Venus Mechanitis* and *Venus Vulgaris* so that, ultimately, the first and third of those roles can be fused. Her failure to seduce Adonis, however, means that she remains just the failed and parodic *Venus Victrix* she disingenuously claims to be.

Nonetheless Venus does have her moments of victory. She "pluck[s]" (line 30) Adonis from his horse, for example, walks off with him under her arm and then pushes him to the ground (lines 32-42). To take another example, she forces (cf. line 61) her kisses on him with the greed and dominance of an "empty eagle" (line 55) devouring its prey (lines 57-58). Again, Adonis when imprisoned "in her arms" (line 68) is as helpless as a "bird . . . tangled in a net" (line 67). Likewise, her hand imprisons his as "a gaol of snow" might "a lily" or as "an alabaster band" might a piece of "ivory" (lines 362-363). Her lips "conquer" (line 549) his and she preys on him like a "vulture" (line 551) or a plunderer (lines 553-558). Those are indeed moments of victory but they are all flawed.[19] The reader sees Venus as a ludicrous, bestial, predatory or, at the least, visually perfect yet wholly undesired Conqueror. The narrator's ironic imaging of her as a Victor seems relentless: as the examples above indicate, he subverts the *Venus Victrix* motif not only once in the poem but throughout it. The implication would appear to be that, in the world of the poem, the *Venus Victrix* motif cannot function as an emblem of Love's overcoming Strife, or of Love's making the universe into an harmonious discord. The motif, as a signifier of love's benignly invincible power, is pervasively, comically, vehemently dismantled.

Those aspects of Venus' characterization which seem to accord with, and often to refigure, conventional representations of her suggest love to be not one thing, nor merely a number of things, but a great range of things. They emphasize love's multiplicity—both within and outside the fictive world of *Venus and Adonis*—and imply how unstable, protean, how incongruous and dangerous love can be in its manifold variety. In doing so they seem as well to imply the inadequacy of a single definition to encompass love. Notably absent among them, and therefore foregrounded by its absence, is a connection between Shakespeare's Venus and the conventional *Venus Urania,* the Venus of Divine Love. Certainly it is true that Venus asserts: "Love is a spirit all compact of fire, / Not gross to sink, but light, and will aspire" (lines 149-150). Even so, her description of love as a fiery "spirit" receives little, if any, confirmation in the rest of the poem, the "gross" physicality of her love for Adonis instead being stressed. And Adonis, just after he has associated her with *Venus Vulgaris* (line 790; in the next he associates her with *Venus Genetrix*), complains—accurately enough given his encounter with the goddess: "[L]ove to heaven is fled, / Since sweating lust on earth usurp'd his name" (lines 793-794). As far as the conventional/(often) refigured aspects of Shakespeare's Venus reveal, love in its manifold variety may be unstable, protean, incongruous and dangerous—insistent, self-demeaning and frequently comic, one could add—but it is not divine, although Venus is of course a goddess.

Although the different aspects of Shakespeare's Venus that are related, directly or otherwise, to the conventions of ancient religious practice or to those of mythography seem to form the major part of her characterization, there appears to be at least one further, important element in her portrayal: her personal discovery, as it were, of the way humans experience unrequited love—a greatly disorientating discovery for her, even though one necessarily limited by the fact that she is a goddess. That element of Venus' characterization often makes her look comic, adding to the ludic treatment of her throughout the tale. However the main point to be emphasized here is that, in partly discovering human experience of unrequited love, Venus also discovers, to a degree, the experience of love as otherness, as partly and disturbingly "outside the system of normality or convention to which [she] belongs [herself]."[20]

It was argued earlier in this discussion that Venus uses a predominantly male, in fact chiefly Petrarchan, language/rhetoric of love in order to seduce Adonis. She is given that form of erotic speech, of course, to involve her in simple (human) gender-reversal—to make her sexual assertiveness look clearly and oddly like male sexual assertiveness. Yet there is arguably another reason as well, namely, to suggest that in trying to seduce Adonis she comes personally to know how humans experience loving in vain. Venus' speech between lines 187-216 provides brief, sample evidence of this. There Venus speaks to Adonis in what are obviously and mostly Petrarchan terms. "Thine eye darts

forth the fire that burneth me . . . ," she says early on (line 196), adding almost at once: "Art thou obdurate, flinty, hard as steel? / Nay more than flint, for stone at rain relenteth; / Art thou a woman's son and canst not feel / What 'tis to love, how want of love tormenteth?" (lines 199-202). Those words suggest that the predominantly male form of erotic speech Venus uses can function not just to show her incongruously resembling "a bold-fac'd [male] suitor" (line 6) in her sexual aggressiveness but also, and simultaneously, to stress how human is her whole experience of loving Adonis in vain. To be more exact, those words suggest this: the Petrarchan language and rhetoric used so recurrently by Venus are able to involve her in (human) gender-reversal which is not merely a matter of narrowly limited analogy, for they at times function to confer on her many features of a primarily male, human, love psychology. Predictably, those features include angry, bewildered frustration and loss of self-control—the case in the passage quoted above—vulnerability, anguish, self-division, and so on, in keeping with the usual descriptions of male lovers in Petrarch-derived verse. And Venus' climactic words at this moment of the text, like her early ones, reveal that distinctly. A series of Petrarchan paradoxes recalls anachronistically/anticipates a multitude of fictional, male lovers' complaints to their disdainful beloveds: "Fie, lifeless picture, cold and senseless stone, / Well-painted idol, image dull and dead, / Statue contenting but the eye alone . . ." (lines 211-213). In short, the reader can see a more than superficial gender-reversal at work in some of Venus's speeches—but working to make her appear recognizably (if *not* completely) human, rather than specifically male, in her experience of unrequited love.

The same process can sometimes be seen when Venus the would-be seducer is described in Petrarchan terms, whether or not she herself uses them. For example, just after Adonis has failed to recover his horse and has sat angrily down, Venus softly approaches him. The narrator remarks: "O what a sight it was, wistly to view / How she came stealing to the wayward boy! / To note the fighting conflict of her hue, / How white and red each other did destroy!" (lines 343-346). The Petrarchan images of "white and red" imply Venus' alternating timidity and boldness or, as is also possible, bashfulness.[21] That emotional conflict is often ascribed in Petrarchan love poems (by means either of those images or of ones closely related to them) to a male lover cautiously approaching his disdainful beloved, as readers then and now would readily perceive. Venus' recurrent sexual assertiveness seems here to be modified by her knowledge that Adonis does not return her love. Consequently she draws near to him as might a wary human lover. Now it may be that her apparent wariness is merely a ploy to conceal her hitherto unsuccessful aggressiveness: that it is, in fact, a reinscription of her aggressiveness. Whatever the case, in the speech by her looked at a moment ago she appears comically petulant in her human, sexual frustration; at this moment of the text, however, her human experience of unrequited love makes her appear comically hesitant but also pathetic (even if she may be falsely evoking pathos).

Much that is suggested by Venus' being repeatedly attributed with a Petrarchan love psychology seems to be summed up when the narrator compares her with Tantalus (see lines 91-94 and 599-600). Those comparisons imply that her personal discovery of how humans experience unrequited love, even though limited, puts her in hell: for Venus, in effect, to feel how mortals experience loving in vain is to enter a hell of obsessive, frustrated desire. Her love for Adonis can therefore be seen as involving her in a second and simultaneous personal discovery, that of love as a new and alien experience.[22] The second discovery is limited because the first is also; nonetheless, it is significant because it means that, in loving Adonis, the goddess of love herself comes experientially to know something of love as otherness. She is led into human intensities of emotion: human yearning, frustration, misery and false hope.

A final point should be quickly added here. What might be called the Petrarchan humanizing of Venus contributes not only to the portrayal of her as would-be seducer but, as well, to the portrayal of her after Adonis has left (lines 811ff.). In that latter part of the poem, however, it does not primarily indicate Venus' continued, personal discovery of how humans experience unrequited love; rather, it chiefly suggests her personal discovery of how humans experience separation from, and the death of, a beloved.[23] (Thus it also suggests development and intensification in her coming to know love as otherness). For example, just after mentioning Adonis' departure from Venus, the narrator indicates her confusion, anxiety and misery by a series of motifs that recur throughout Petrarchan love verse (the lamenting lover's grief being echoed by nature, and so on; see lines 823-846). Likewise, when he tells of her meeting with the boar (lines 901-912) he describes her horrified response to the creature in Petrarchan terms (a sequence of paradoxes suggests her self-division and paralysis; see lines 907-912). He accounts for her sudden change from belief to disbelief in Adonis' death by means of Petrarchan love psychology (there, too, the paradoxical is emphasized; see lines 985-990). He partly describes her grieving for the dead Adonis, moreover, in Petrarchan terms (again, a paradoxical rhetoric indicates her self-division—and confusion, and loss of self-control; see, for example, lines 1057-1074). Unsurprisingly enough, for it was the case earlier in the poem, pathos is interwoven with comedy in those presentations of Venus humanized.[24]

A Venus humanized, even if only to a degree, is of course a Venus transformed. It was suggested above that self-transformation seems to be an enticement of-

fered to Adonis when the goddess tries to seduce him. To repeat what was specifically suggested: in offering Adonis her love, Venus simultaneously offers him metamorphosis, a redefined subjectivity, in which self-perfection and safety will be supposedly gained but a loss of self will be inevitable. One instance of her putting that proposition to him has already been examined. In that particular instance, Venus implicitly promises Adonis self-perfection as a result of his sexual initiation. I want now to consider the most direct and elaborate offer of self-transformation that she makes to him (lines 229-240), an offer in which she appears to envisage her own transformation.

At once embracing and imprisoning Adonis in her arms, Venus tells him: "Within the circuit of this ivory pale [the fence, as it were, of her white arms] / I'll be a park, and thou shalt be my deer: / Feed where thou wilt . . ." (lines 230-232). The goddess's serio-comic offer of transformation seems variously problematic. To begin with, her projection of her body as metamorphosed into a site for Adonis to inhabit and enjoy, in fact, into a type of the "ideal landscape," implies that to him she will be at once sentient and insentient, passive yet active, in her sexuality (active because, as she apparently sees it, she will in effect own Adonis: "my deer/[dear]" she hopefully calls him in lines 231-239).[25] More important, her projection of Adonis as metamorphosed into her "deer/[dear]" offers him a comprehensively redefined subjectivity—a new and ambiguous personal identity. Venus' "deer" image suggests that, when sexually involved with her, he will be her beloved ("dear"); it also suggests, as she probably does not recognize, that in becoming her lover he will become less than human because primarily concupiscent. His former identity as someone committed to the active life will vanish. No longer a hunter, instead a captured creature of the hunt of love—the "deer" image of course connecting with the motif of Venus as a predator—he will be both a new person and a lost one, safe from the consequences of his planned boar hunt (about which Venus does not yet know) but himself a hunter's prize. Venus' fantastic, sophisticated offer of metamorphosis to Adonis indicates that her desire for him necessitates his loss of self, his gaining of a new, incongruously diminished identity. On the other hand, her imagined self-transformation does not so much imply change to her as it does change to his perception of her. Venus' disregard for Adonis' independent selfhood, which pervades her offer(s) of metamorphosis to him and indeed all her attempt to seduce him, is emblematized at the poem's end by her plucking the flower sprung from his blood and carrying it away.

The intricate characterization of Shakespeare's Venus represents her as a diverse and unstable yet not as an incoherent identity. If the goddess of love appears to be, for example, tender and callous, compassionate and predatory, sophisticated and naive, pathetic and comic, alluring but also at times repellent, her almost infinite variety is nonetheless held together by the force of her self-centred sexual desire. One Renaissance view of love, mentioned above, was that love's power draws into coherence the various and conflicting elements of the world, compelling them into an harmonious discord, or *discordia concors*. It seems reasonable to suggest that in **Venus and Adonis** the reader sees the goddess of love, and so erotic love itself, as a *discordia concors*, centred upon desire's selfishness. Venus' characterization implies love's often incongruous multiplicity and its inability to be encompassed by a single definition. Her experience of love as otherness, co-existent with her humanized experience of love's frustration, implies human love's extremes of misery and of obsession (as well, momentarily, of elation)—a Petrarchan humanizing of the goddess being Shakespeare's recreation of Ovid's anthropomorphic refashioning of his divinities. Her offer of metamorphosis to Adonis indicates love's capacity to transform the lover and, chiefly, the unresponsive beloved should he (she) become in turn a lover. That transformation, it appears to be suggested, may involve uncertain gain but will involve unavoidable loss of self. Yet, as has just been proposed, the insistent pulsing of egocentric desire within the many aspects of Shakespeare's Venus seems a sign of what remains constant amid her inconstancies and those of human passion.

Notes

1. All reference to the poem is from William Shakespeare, *The Poems,* ed. F. T. Prince (1960; rpt. London: Methuen, 1976). There has been general agreement, for example, about Venus' predatoriness, dishonesty, maternalism and so on—though with varying emphases. Among the commentaries on *Venus and Adonis,* see especially: D. N. Beauregard, "*Venus and Adonis*: Shakespeare's Representation of the Passions," *Shakespeare Studies,* 8 (1975), 83-98; W. A. Rebhorn, "Mother Venus: Temptation in Shakespeare's *Venus and Adonis,*" *Shakespeare Studies,* 11 (1978), 1-19; L. J. Daigle, "*Venus and Adonis*: Some Traditional Contexts," *Shakespeare Studies,* 13 (1980), 31-46; J. Doebler, "The Many Faces of Love: Shakespeare's *Venus and Adonis,*" *Shakespeare Studies,* 16 (1983), 33-43; H. Dubrow, *Captive Victors: Shakespeare's Narrative Poems and Sonnets* (Ithaca and London: Cornell University Press, 1987), pp. 21-79; Gunnar Sorelius, *Shakespeare's Early Comedies: Myth, Metamorphosis, Mannerism* (Uppsala: Almqvist & Wiksell Intern., 1993), pp. 111-117. I am indebted to Heather Dubrow for her helpful comments on an earlier draft of this essay.

2. See, for example: T. W. Baldwin, *On the Literary Genetics of Shakespeare's Poems and Sonnets* (Urbana: University of Illinois Press, 1950), pp. 1-93; D. C. Allen, *Image and Meaning: Metaphoric Traditions in Renaissance Poetry* (1960; rpt. Baltimore: Johns Hopkins Press, 1968), pp. 42-57; W. Keach, *Elizabethan Erotic Narratives* (New Brunswick: Rutgers University Press, 1977), pp. 52-84; C. Hulse, *Metamorphic Verse: The Elizabethan Minor Epic* (Princeton, N.J.: Princeton University Press, 1981), pp. 141-175.

3. The mythographers drawn on in this discussion are chiefly Natalis Comes and Vincenzo Cartari, respectively in their *Mythologiae* (Venice, 1567) and *Le Imagini . . . Degli Dei* (Venice, 1571)—both in the Garland reprints of 1976, introduced by S. Orgel.

4. Whether or not other myths or tales depict or suggest that as having happened to the goddess prior to her loving Adonis, the discovery seems new to her in Shakespeare's narrative—as she indicates in her speech about Mars. See lines 91-114. But were this not, in fact, her personal discovery, it would still be so forceful an experience of love as otherness that it almost completely disorientates the goddess of love herself.

5. Even if Venus has been previously obsessed with love for another divinity, love between immortals cannot be equated with love between mortals; hence the humanized experience of obsessive love she seems newly to undergo *in this tale* would have to be qualitatively different from any other experience she may have had of Love's power to preoccupy the consciousness.

6. See Cartari, *Le Imagini . . .*, p. 543.

7. On *Venus Vulgaris,* see: Comes, *Mythologiae,* 120(a); Pico, *Commento sopra una canzona de amore . . .* trans. Thomas Stanley, *A Platonick Discourse upon Love,* in *The Poems and Translations,* ed. G. M. Crump (Oxford: Clarendon Press, 1962), 2, 7-22. Filarete, *Treatise on Architecture,* trans J. R. Spencer (New Haven and London: Yale University Press, 1965), Bk 18, fol. 148v. Venus as *Venus Vulgaris* thus aptly perceives Adonis as her "banquet of sense."

8. Heather Dubrow, in *Captive Victors,* notes that "*Venus and Adonis* is concerned with faulty or failed communication . . ." (p. 38), and I would wholly agree; however, her reading of Venus' opening speech and of its context differs significantly from my own (see pp. 31-37 of her study). My main point here is that Venus' speech subverts her role as *Venus Mechanitis.*

9. The images have immediately Petrarchan associations, though in fact they can be traced much further back. Cf. T. W. Baldwin, *On the Literary Genetics . . .*, pp. 9-10.

10. On parody of this in "Damon the Mower," see my "Marvell's;'Upon Appleton House to my Lord Fairfax' and the Regaining of Paradise," in *The Political Identity of Andrew Marvell,* edited by C. Conden and myself (Aldershot: Scolar Press, 1990), 53-84, at p. 73.

11. On *varietà* and its link to *grazia,* see David Summers, *Michelangelo and the Language of Art* (Princeton, N.J.: Princeton University Press, 1981), pp. 82, 166, 172.

12. On *Venus Genetrix* see: Comes, *Mythologiae,* 122(a); Cartari, *Le Imagini . . . ,* p. 530; Ficino, *Commentary on the Symposium,* 1, 5.

13. Pico, *Commento,* trans. Stanley, 2, 20, 323. Ficino, in his *Commentary on the Symposium,* of course also calls such love "bestial love" (*"amor ferinus"*).

14. That is, Venus' celebration of the generative impulse and her urging Adonis to breed are merely ploys in an attempt at seduction.

15. For further discussion of Venus' maternalism, see Rebhorn, "Mother Venus . . . ," cited in note 1.

16. On *Venus Apaturia,* see Comes' allusion in *Mythologiae,* 121(a). The goddess's role of *Venus Apaturia* naturally links to her role as *Venus Mechanitis.*

17. On Venus as *Magistra Divinandi,* see Comes, *Mythologiae,* 121(a).

18. Here I follow Edgar Wind, *Pagan Mysteries in the Renaissance,* rev. edn (1958; rpt. Harmondsworth: Penguin, 1967), pp. 91-96. Clark Hulse also discusses the motif, though differently. See his *Metamorphic Verse,* pp. 166-173.

19. There seems no need to give further examples, as they clearly tend the same way. It could be added, however, that if the *Venus Victrix* motif is dismantled, so too is that of *Venus Basilea* (Queen of Love).

20. Jeremy Hawthorne, *A Concise Glossary of Contemporary Literary Theory* (London: Arnold, 1992), p. 124.

21. Cf. Ficino, *Commentary,* 1, 6.

22. Again, seemingly new and alien within the confines of the tale.

23. Of course, secondarily it *is* continued experience for Venus of how humans may experience unrequited love.

24. As regards the comic: exaggeration generates it—but then Venus actually is larger than human life, and Adonis, likewise, is perfect; the Petrarchan comedy, as it were, contributes to other comic elements—such as Venus' questioning the dogs and scolding the boar. As regards the pathetic: Venus disorientation and misery are, despite all their comic features, nonetheless recognizably and familiarly human, evoking sympathy.

25. On the "ideal landscape" See E. R. Curtius, *European Literature and the Latin Middle Ages* (1953; rpt. New York and Evanston: Harper and Row, 1963), pp. 183-202. Her self-description seems a recreation of Claudian's famous set-piece in his *Epithalamium de Nuptis Honorii Augusti,* lines 49-96.

David-Everett Blythe (essay date winter 1995)

SOURCE: Blythe, David-Everett. "Shakespeare's *Venus and Adonis.*" *The Explicator* 53, no. 2 (winter 1995): 68-70.

[*In the essay that follows, Blythe analyzes Shakespeare's use of the term "vailing" as it pertains to Adonis's stallion.*]

The stallion in Shakespeare's **Venus and Adonis** "vails his tail" in the specific action—

> Then, like a melancholy malcontent,
> He vails his tail, that, like a falling plume,
> Cool shadow to his melting buttock lent.

(312-15)

The image is commonly taken to mean "to lower" (Riverside) [*The Riverside Shakespeare*], even though horsetails naturally hang in an already lowered position.

Shakespeare's vailing can signify lowering in only an exact anatomical way: That is, the *dock,* or cartilage, of the tail must first be lifted in order to let down the *plume* of hair. It is a highly distinctive horsetail movement as likewise depicted by Robert Frost in the lines, "with whited eyes / And all his tail that isn't hair up straight" ("The Runaway")—where the horsetail is divided into "isn't hair" and "hair."

Tails consist of hair and cartilage, and when the solid tissue (dock) is held up in fright or excitation (as precisely imaged of Adonis's rebellious horse), strands of hair sweep aloft and droop down as profiled in "vail" and "falling plume." The *OED* [*Oxford English Dictionary*] also defines this vailing action as "to lower" or "to hang," but horses cannot hang/lower their tails in this unique sense until the dock ("isn't hair") is first hoisted, for then only will horsehair cascade vertically over the croup in resemblance of a "plume" on its pole of cartilage.

From that toplofty place, horsehair that ordinarily reaches the knees will now lend "cool shadow" to that "buttock" above, where "melting" images the foamy sweat of the hind quarters. The swaying upright plume and this yeasty perspiration underneath also signify a fear and arousal that is restated in the "high desire" (276) and the "fury" (318) of Adonis's unmanageable stallion.

There are many other instances in the plays of vailing "eyelids" (*Venus and Adonis* 956) and clouds (*Love's Labor's Lost* V.ii.297), or a "lofty-plumed crest" (*Henry VI, Part I* V.iii.25), where vailing means simply to let down—much like the picturesque ship run aground in *The Merchant of Venice*: "And see my wealthy Andrew dock'd in sand, / Vailing her high top lower than her ribs / To kiss her burial" (I.i.27-29). But when horses "vail" their tails, they raise to lower by lifting the dock that then "lowers" the plume in Shakespeare's prancing, vailing runaway.

The entire action of horses in this characteristic excitement is a commonplace of equine lore first noted by Xenophon, who explains how stallions run toward mares, head high, neck arched, lifting legs in free motion, and raising the tail (56), much like Adonis's steed. For according to R. H. Smythe, flying the tail in this manner is a "graceful arching . . . at the dock" admired for centuries and "characterized in many old prints and . . . pre-historic cave drawings" (88). The figure Shakespeare presents is an expression that would not require a note for anyone who has seen horses either actually, or so rendered, in this state; and where, for those who have not, the correct image is certainly not "to lower" but "to lift"—in this phenomenal sense of vailing.

Works Cited

Smythe, R. H. *The Mind of the Horse*. London: J. A. Allen, 1965.

Xenophon. *The Art of Horsemanship*. Trans. Morris H. Morgan. London: J. A. Allen and Co., 1962.

Anthony Mortimer (essay date 2000)

SOURCE: Mortimer, Anthony. "Rhetoric, Myth and the Descent of Venus." In *Variable Passions: A Reading of Shakespeare's* Venus and Adonis, pp. 1-35. New York: AMS Press, 2000.

[*In the excerpt below, Mortimer discusses Shakespeare's use of rhetoric in* Venus and Adonis, *claiming that the poet explores both the power and the limitations of a number of rhetorical strategies used by both characters in their attempts to persuade the other.*]

It is difficult nowadays to imagine anyone making their first acquaintance with Shakespeare through the narrative poems. In 1593, however, although Shakespeare had already achieved a certain notoriety in the theater, the publication of *Venus and Adonis* gave an Elizabethan public their first opportunity to actually read his work. For the young dramatist the change of genre and the move from stage to page involved an appeal to the judgment of a more literate and sophisticated audience who, after Greene's virulent pamphlet, would be curious to see whether, in the cooler medium of print, there was more to the "upstart Crow" than resounding theatrical bombast.[1] The epigraph (from Ovid, *Amores*, I. xv. 35-36) is perfectly appropriate to the situation: *Vilia miretur vulgus: mihi flavus Apollo / Pocula Castalia plena ministret acqua* ("Let what is cheap excite the marvel of the crowd; for me may golden Apollo minister full cups from the Castalian fount"). Shakespeare, to Greene's disgust, had already demonstrated his capacity to "excite the marvel of the crowd," and was now set to challenge the University Wits on their own social and literary ground with an Ovidian poem that would be learned and copious, erotically and rhetorically sophisticated. From readers who knew their Ovid he might hope for recognition of the precise context of his quotation: concluding the first book of the *Amores,* the Latin poet defies "biting envy" and proclaims the immortality of poetry with a list that includes Homer, Hesiod, Sophocles, Menander, Virgil, Lucretius and Tibullus. Shakespeare, by recalling that context, lays implicit claim to the same distinguished ancestry; but transmitted to him, as it were, by a single mediator, the most protean of poets and the master of many moods.

Everything suggests a carefully calculated career-move. The printer was Richard Field, a Stratford fellow-citizen, who had brought out an impressive edition of the *Metamorphoses* in 1589. The dedicatee is the young Henry Wriothesley, Earl of Southampton, a patron of poets and already a faintly sulfurous figure. Shakespeare may or may not have found the germ of a recalcitrant Adonis in Southampton's aversion to marriage with Lord Burghley's granddaughter, Lady Elizabeth Vere.[2] The poem obviously develops in a way that leaves any such occasion far behind, but one need only think of the way Sidney teases his readers with hints of the "real story" behind *Astrophil and Stella* to see that the whiff of scandal would have done no harm to the popularity of *Venus and Adonis.* Taken together, the epigraph and the dedication steer a prudent middle course between self-advertisement and humility, making an ambitious claim to the inheritance of Ovid and at the same time demanding indulgence for "unpolished lines." The relation between poet and patron is given a conventionally feudal coloring with Southampton as the lord who stands "godfather" to the "first heir" of his vassal. Shakespeare, as one of the new and socially insecure class of professional writers, is making a discreet but unequivocal plea for admission to the court circle which was the source of patronage and the arbiter of literary reputation.

Shakespeare would have had no reason to be dissatisfied with his success. With ten printings during the poet's lifetime (more than for any of the plays), *Venus and Adonis* became a byword or touchstone for the kind of witty and erotic Ovidian narrative that went on to flourish well into the seventeenth century.[3] Indeed, with the possible exception of *The Faerie Queene,* it may be doubted whether any other poem of the period was quite so widely read.[4] It then practically disappeared from circulation for about a hundred and fifty years and neither the bardolatry of the nineteenth century nor the massive critical industry of our own times has been able to grant it much more than a marginal place in the Shakespearean canon. Even Coleridge's powerful advocacy was probably in the long run counter-productive insofar as he was more concerned to find evidence of Shakespeare's nascent poetic powers than to make sense of the poem as a whole. He offers some brilliantly suggestive comment on specific passages such as the flight of Adonis in the dusk and he celebrates, as critics have done ever since, "the affectionate love of nature and natural objects" and the skill in painting "the very minutest beauties of the external world;"[5] but this emphasis on details of imagery could only encourage what became the standard Victorian view of the poem as essentially apprentice work, a mass of unrefined ore from which a few shining nuggets might be extracted by the discerning reader. In recent years *Venus and Adonis* has attracted substantial and appreciative attention from William Keach, Richard Lanham, Coppelia Kahn, Heather Dubrow and Jonathan Bate, but even as late as 1986, in a book that is otherwise almost painfully fashionable, we can still find Gary Waller complaining that the poem is too static, "with just too much argument and insufficient flowing sensuality to make it pleasurable reading."[6]

The initial obstacle to any appreciation of what *Venus and Adonis* has to offer is the sheer magnitude of Shakespeare's reputation. Is this a minor poem that would scarcely merit our attention if it were not by Shakespeare? Or is it a work that we would regard far more highly if it happened to be by someone else? The fact is that we simply cannot put ourselves back in 1593 and read the text without an awareness of Shakespeare's subsequent achievement. The continuities between the narrative poem and the *Sonnets* have long been recognized and go far beyond the common presence of a lovely boy or the shared arguments for procreation.[7] Nor would one want to deny that the confusion of gender roles in the poem prefigures, in a different key, the exploitation of crossdressing and sexual ambivalence in the comedies. There is, however, a danger that we shall end up by seeing these continu-

ities as more interesting than the poem itself. On the one hand, the poem is subtly diminished if we approach it with expectations created by the dramatist or the sonneteer: on the other hand, not much is to be gained by such an inversion of the process as the eccentric attempt of Ted Hughes to make *Venus and Adonis* the mythological key that unlocks the whole of Shakespeare.[8] To accept the complete Shakespeare as a relevant and inevitable context for interpretation need not become a pretext for neglecting to read the poem on its own terms as an accomplished and mature performance in a genre to which the poet never returned.

As a preliminary to any interpretation or commentary, it may be as well to clear the ground by looking at some of the common prejudices or misconceptions that have got in the poem's way. One of these derives, strangely enough, from the very fact of its initial success. For many readers, a cloud of suspicion must hang over a work that was apparently so deliberately designed to establish a literary reputation and to satisfy a specifically Elizabethan taste. Behind the repeated assertions that the poem is cold, unfeeling, a mere sideline, an exercise in convention or a self-conscious display of virtuosity lies the unmistakable implication that *Venus and Adonis* is not "the real Shakespeare," that the poet was working against his natural grain in a pardonable but misguided attempt to jump on the fashionable Ovidian bandwagon. This is, however, a rather unconvincing way of escaping from the challenge of a poem that is both obviously Shakespearean and rather unlike anything else by Shakespeare. Shakespeare certainly was making a bid for the kind of literary respectability that the theatre alone could not provide, but neither he nor any other Renaissance poet would have seen such a move as other than a perfectly normal and laudable professional ambition. Moreover, the whole idea of a Shakespeare momentarily seduced by the Ovidian fashion will not stand up to examination. As Jonathan Bate has demonstrated, Shakespeare's engagement with Ovid lasts throughout his career; it shows up not only in the proliferation of Ovidian allusions, but also in the extraordinary range of his empathy, in his awareness of the provisional and flexible nature of sexual identity, in all those qualities that Bate so aptly describes as "mercurial."[9] Shakespeare is so deeply Ovidian that there is no justification for regarding *Venus and Adonis* as an opportunistic response to some specifically Ovidian moment. Not without reason did Francis Meres see Shakespeare as the reincarnation of the "sweet witty soul of Ovid": Shakespeare at his most Ovidian is most emphatically himself.[10]

One may also question whether in the England of 1593 the Ovidian epyllion was really such a fashionable genre as literary history has led us to believe.[11] Shakespeare used Arthur Golding's influential translation of the *Metamorphoses* (1565-67) and he may possibly have been aware of such insignificant adaptations as the anonymous *Fable of Ovid treting of Narcissus* (1560) or Thomas Peend's *Pleasant fable of Salmacis and Hermaphroditus* (1565), but it takes a drastic foreshortening of literary history to see texts that were already twenty-five or thirty years old as constituting the fashion in the 1590s. Shakespeare may have heard of Marlowe's *Hero and Leander* which was entered in the Stationers' Register in the same year as *Venus and Adonis*; there is, however, no solid evidence that he was influenced by it.[12] This leaves us with Thomas Lodge's *Scillaes Metamorphosis* (1589) as the only notable English epyllion before *Venus and Adonis.* On the other hand, the rapid development of the epyllion after 1593 is clearly marked by Shakespeare's example and the basic situation of sexually aggressive female and reluctant or inexperienced youth recurs in such poems as Michael Drayton's *Endimion and Phoebe* (1595), Francis Beaumont's *Salmacis and Hermaphroditus* (1602) and Phineas Fletcher's *Venus and Anchises* (1628). In this light *Venus and Adonis* appears less as an exercise in a conventional genre than as one of the two or three poems that promoted the genre and created its characteristic themes and manner. Shakespeare, on this occasion, did more than jump on a bandwagon; he set the wagon rolling.

More serious than the prejudice against *Venus and Adonis* as a concession to fashionable taste is the objection that it fails to establish any consistent atmosphere and lacks any unifying intention. C. S. Lewis' remark that "as we read on we become more and more doubtful how the work should be taken" is, at least, a comprehensible reaction to the poem's rapid and disturbing shifts in tone.[13] Sexual desire is represented both with highflown Petrarchan imagery and in terms of earthy physicality; Venus is both the grotesquely large and smothering female who can tuck Adonis under her arm and the lightfooted goddess whose passage leaves no trace in the sand; Adonis appears now as a petulant self-obsessed adolescent and now as an innocent victim of attempted rape before emerging in his final speech as a spokesman for ideal love; the narrator may express his sympathy with one protagonist or the other and then distance himself in a way that accounts for Coleridge's comment on "the utter aloofness of the poet's own feelings from those of which he is at once the painter and the analyst."[14] At times the poem seems to nudge us towards an allegory of Lust and Chastity or Love and Death and then again we are brought back to an ironic psychological comedy where such large abstractions appear remote if not quite irrelevant. And no sooner have we opted for comedy than we are threatened with a flood of pathos. Unable or unwilling to cope with this bewildering display of legerdemain, Lewis concludes that *Venus and Adonis* falls between two stools, being neither genuinely erotic in its presentation of the sexual appetite nor clearly didactic as a warning against lust.

Lewis may have an unduly sanitized view of what constitutes the erotic (he cannot forgive Shakespeare for making Venus sweat), but he does have the real merit of recognizing that the poem cannot be read either as a coherent moral allegory or as straightforward eroticism. Too many attempts to rescue the reputation of *Venus and Adonis* have ended with interpretations that fail to acknowledge the elements that generate Lewis' perplexed reaction. To take one extreme tendency, attempts to read the poem in the light of *Ovide moralisé* obviously fall apart. Both *Ovide moralisé* and Golding see the fate of Adonis as illustrating what happens to a young man who gives way to lust; but it is hard to see what moral lesson is being taught by Shakespeare's version where Adonis resists the advances of Venus and gets killed just the same. Can we, instead, see the poem as a simple story of offended innocence with Venus, like Tarquin, as a figure of destructive lust and Adonis, like Lucrece, as a martyr of chastity or reason in love?[15] Shakespeare's sullen youth seems an unlikely candidate for canonization and his Venus can be tender as well as aggressive; but the real problem with such readings is that they depend so heavily on the idea that the boar is "Venus in her most horrible symbol."[16] Venus has, in fact, warned Adonis against the boar and it is a pretty confused allegory that asks us to hold her responsible for the destructive act that she has done everything to prevent.

Rather more promising in that it accounts for the narrator's blend of balanced sympathy and amused neutrality might be Donald Watson's argument that the poem is an unresolved debate between the Concupiscible (Venus) and the Irascible (Adonis) and that it is the failure to reconcile these opposed but necessary temperaments that provokes the final catastrophe. Adonis, however, is surely too self-controlled to represent the Irascible (compare Pyrochles in *Faerie Queene,* Book II), and it seems an unduly cerebral and flattening approach that sees Venus and Adonis "more as psychological dispositions than as dramatic characters"[17]. One suspects that any reading which needs to call on Aristotle, Augustine and Aquinas has become rather remote from the book that the undergraduate Gullio placed under his pillow and from the "luscious marrow-bone pie" that Middleton's Harebrain feared might corrupt his bride.[18] It is not that allegory and eroticism are mutually exclusive but that the eroticism of *Venus and Adonis* simply does not raise—except, as we shall see, in a provisional and ironic fashion—the kind of issues that allegory is equipped to handle. The depth of the poem is not philosophical or theological and the subtlety of its sexual psychology goes well beyond anything that can be expressed in terms of conventional Renaissance "dispositions." It is, after all, a characteristic of the Ovidian epyllion and a probable cause of its popularity that, by its recourse to stories that combined the dignity of classical ancestry with the license granted to entertaining fables, it allowed not just eroticism but also a more free, dispassionate and investigative approach to sexuality than was possible in official discourse on the topic. When Gary Waller objects that *Venus and Adonis* relies too much "upon heavy moralizing allegory" one suspects that he has been reading not the poem itself but some of the many critical attempts to reduce its content to the platitudes of Renaissance orthodoxy.[19]

The most seductive allegorical readings are probably those that look to Neoplatonism. Since the days of Kristeller, Gombrich and Wind we have grown less inclined to see Neoplatonism as the dominant current in Renaissance thought as a whole, but it was certainly a pervasive element in the sixteenth-century rhetoric of love. Its total absence would be surprising in a poem where rhetoric turns out to be a central issue. T. W. Baldwin brings massive erudition to support his claim that "the argument of *Venus and Adonis* is all worked through in proper Platonic order to a proper Platonic conclusion, as interpreted by Ficino and his followers"—which turns out to mean that Adonis is "Beauty or true Love refusing to be won by Venus-Lust to propagation."[20] And yet, though the Neoplatonic echoes that Baldwin documents so thoroughly can hardly be denied, this reading takes little account of the problematic context in which they are placed by Shakespeare's characterization of Adonis. To make Adonis an embodiment of true love rather than of chastity involves taking his final speech (769-810) at its face value and it still leaves us with an ideal figure that we fail to recognize in the complex (and complexed) youth of the text. Using Neoplatonism to redeem Venus, Heather Asals sees in her development from comedy to pathos a version of the ascension from sensual love to the contemplation of pure beauty and truth that we find in the treatises of Ficino, Bembo and Castiglione;[21] but this "education of a goddess" is no more convincing than the ideal Adonis. Though there certainly is a difference between the sexually aggressive Venus of the opening and the mourning maternal Venus of the end, it is by no means clear that the poem invites us to see this change as progress from a lower to a higher stage. Venus' repeated claims that Adonis embodies the ideal beauty towards which nature strives or the source of harmony without which the world will return to chaos (11-12, 727-32, 953-54, 1015-20, 1079-80) may suggest a Neoplatonic program, but they are constantly undermined by her own demands for immediate physical satisfaction. For her, as for Sidney's Astrophil, "Desire still cries, give me some food" (*Astrophil and Stella*, 71). When she complains that the death of Adonis has deprived the world of a prelapsarian harmony or of "true sweet beauty" (1080), the reader cannot be sure whether to take this as the final recognition of a Neoplatonic ideal or as a vindictive hyperbole designed to justify the curse on love that will follow. Nor can we think of Venus as having achieved

any culminating vision of the truth when her own account of her relationship with Adonis (1069-1120, 1177-88) is so self-indulgently expurgated as to give no hint of her aggression or his resistance. The fact is that Shakespeare is careful to avoid any facile contrast between the old Venus and the new. There is no sense of conversion or enlightenment. It is, if anything, the continuities that are striking. Her desire for Adonis has, from the start, co-existed with maternal protective elements and her transformation into a *mater dolorosa* remains erotic. The final incestuous image of the Adonis-flower as a son who takes his father's place in the mother's bed is a fitting conclusion to the story of a passion where the erotic and the maternal are so intricately woven that the movement from one to the other must be seen less as an ascent than as a shift of emphasis.

More circumspectly, Lennet Daigle argues that *Venus and Adonis* confronts two systems of value. In one of these Venus stands condemned as the personification of lust; in the other she is the Neoplatonic heavenly goddess who, as the source of generation (Venus Genitrix), ensures the continuation of a divinely established order of nature. It is, he believes, in the latter terms that the poem finally vindicates the demands of Venus.[22] This, however, begs more questions than it answers. Why, if she is to be seen as the beneficent patroness of a natural order, does she end by placing a curse on all future lovers? Why does she depart and leave the world to its own devices? How seriously are we supposed to take arguments for procreation that are the traditional stock-in-trade of seducers? John Roe comes much nearer to defining the role of Neoplatonism in *Venus and Adonis* when he remarks that "the Neoplatonic vision, which is glimpsed sporadically and, in the main, comically earlier in the poem, functions seriously at the close not as its own triumphant principle but as an enhancement of tragic pathos."[23] One would only want to add that even at the close the pathos generated by that Neoplatonic vision is still veined with the irony that one would expect in a poem where Neoplatonism is viewed critically as one source of a rhetoric that is always in excess of or inadequate to the reality of a sexual situation.

For a robust counter to the solemnities of allegory and a release from Lewis' erotic-didactic dilemma, we might turn to Rufus Putney who stresses the poem's comic dimension to the exclusion of almost everything else.[24] Unfortunately, Putney's approach is woefully heavy-handed. He underestimates the pathos and the psychological insight that prevent the poem from becoming a Renaissance version of Fielding's Lady Booby and Joseph Andrews; his useful recognition that the rhetoric is sometimes parodic is vitiated by his tendency to reduce the whole issue of rhetoric to mere debunking. His frequent recourse to the term "farce" should warn us that he has lost sight of the sophisticated erotic comedy that the Elizabethans enjoyed. Eroticism and comedy are perfectly compatible; eroticism and farce are certainly not. There may be passages when the poem does, indeed, teeter on the edge of slapstick ("He on her belly falls, she on her back," 594), but it is worth noting how rapidly Shakespeare draws back from the brink as if he is repeatedly trying to test how far he can push the extremes of comedy and pathos without breaking the link between them. That kind of tension is as absent from Putney's reading as it is from the straitjackets of the allegory-mongers.

In the long run, most of the debate about "how the work should be taken" boils down to the central issue of its flamboyant rhetoric. Lewis' failure to appreciate *Venus and Adonis* may be traced back to his conviction that "rhetoric is the greatest barrier between us and our ancestors"[25] and Douglas Bush takes a similar line when, in extenuation of a text where "action bears to rhetoric much the same proportion as bread to sack in Falstaff's bill," he pleads that "the conceited style was instinctive with most Elizabethans as it cannot be with us." Like Victorian readers of the poem, Bush insists that "Shakespeare's best bits of imagery are fresh pictures of nature," but neither these crumbs of comfort nor his grudging admiration for the rhetoric's "inexhaustible energy" are enough to save a "soulless" poem where the occasional flashes of "truth and actuality" only draw attention to the bookish artificiality of the rest.[26]

The fact is that Bush and Lewis, with all their feeling for Renaissance poetry, still inherit the Romantic distrust of rhetoric that we find so vigorously expressed in Hazlitt's essay of 1817:

> The two poems of Venus and Adonis and of Tarquin and Lucrece appear to us like a couple of ice-houses. They are about as hard, as glittering, and as cold. The author seems all the time to be thinking of his verses, and not of his subject,—not of what his characters would feel, but of what he shall say; and as it must happen in all such cases, he always puts into their mouths those things which they would be the last to think of, and which it shows the greatest ingenuity in him to find out. The whole is laboured, up-hill work. The poet is perpetually singling out the difficulties of the art to make an exhibition of his strength and skill in wrestling with them. He is making perpetual trials of them as if his mastery over them were doubted. The images, which are often striking, are generally applied to things which they are the least like: so that they do not blend with the poem, but seem stuck upon it, like splendid patch-work, or remain quite distinct from it, like detached substances, painted and varnished over. A beautiful thought is bound to be lost in an endless commentary upon it. The speakers are like persons who have both leisure and inclination to make riddles on their own situation, and to twist and turn every object or incident into acrostics or anagrams. Everything is spun out into an allegory; and a digression is always preferred to the main story. Sentiment is built up upon

plays of words; the hero or heroine feels, not from the impulse of passion, but from the force of dialectics.[27]

The attack on Shakespeare's rhetoric is mounted with formidable rhetorical energy. Hazlitt, like Dr. Johnson, has the capacity to force one's admiration at the very moment when he provokes the strongest disagreement. He puts his finger unerringly upon the basic problem by recognizing that rhetorical display is central to the way the narrative poems function. If we cannot come to terms with that display, then no amount of striking imagery will serve to acquit *Venus and Adonis* of being "splendid patch-work." Where Bush and others have seen the rhetoric as the "instinctive" linguistic excess of a young Elizabethan, Hazlitt's comment that the poet singles out and wrestles with "the difficulties of the art" points to the way the poem deliberately highlights rhetoric as a problem. If "a digression is always preferred to the main story," it may well be that the main story is, in some sense, unspeakable. It will not do to see the rhetoric as a husk to be peeled away in order to get at the poem's kernel. The statement that "sentiment is built up upon plays of words" and that the protagonists feel "from the force of dialectics" may be taken without the irony that Hazlitt intended. Venus and Adonis exist in and not behind their rhetoric as surely as the characters of an opera exist in and not behind their music.

To understand the way rhetoric works in *Venus and Adonis* we need to start from Shakespeare's crucial modification of the Ovidian story (*Met.* [*Metamorphoses,* with translation by Frank Justus Miller, 1977], X. 519-59, 705-39). In Ovid there is no suggestion that Adonis resists Venus or that the goddess has to resort to any extraordinary eloquence. For the Adonis of Ovid and of all sixteenth-century versions of the myth apart from Shakespeare's, Venus' own physical attractions are a more than sufficient argument. It is through his creation of an Adonis who resists that Shakespeare compensates for the myth's lack of action by turning the poem into a debate, thus restoring rhetoric to its primary function as persuasion. This is surely the major reason why the rhetoric of Venus does not pall like the rhetoric of Lucrece. When F. T. Prince remarks that "the greatest weakness of Shakespeare's Lucrece is her remorseless eloquence"[28] we might be tempted to say the same of Venus; but there is an essential difference. The eloquence of Lucrece, after a dozen stanzas of pleading with Tarquin, expands into an interminable post-rape soliloquy; the eloquence of Venus, for two thirds of the poem, is addressed to an antagonist and is, therefore, public in the sense of being geared to an audience within the text. Here, indeed, lies part of the answer to Hazlitt's objection that Shakespeare is always "thinking of his verses" and "not of what his characters would feel." Venus and Adonis do not primarily speak in order to express their feelings, but in order to win an argument which has immediate and practical consequences. They are, that is to say, in an essentially rhetorical situation. It is not that Shakespeare is uninterested in what his characters feel or that he reduces them to mere vehicles of the conventional arguments for and against sexual intercourse. The feelings emerge, as it were, through the shadings and interstices of the rhetoric, through incomplete analogies, metaphors that fail to fit the case, gaps in the argument, contradictions and changes in strategy. Venus and Adonis fall into what might be called the double trap of rhetoric which controls the speaker who thinks it can be neglected and betrays the speaker who tries to exploit it, revealing something more or other than was intended. Thus, to take only a few examples that will be discussed more fully later on, Venus cannot argue that Adonis should take the male initiative without effectively appropriating the male role for herself; and her advocacy of procreation (in keeping with her mythical status as Venus Genitrix) fails to mask the underlying truth that one aspect of her passion is not to have a child by Adonis but to have Adonis as her child. Adonis seizes on this disjunction between motive and argument to condemn the rhetoric of Venus as both ineffective ("Your treatise makes me like you worse and worse," 774) and dishonest ("reason is the bawd to lust's abuse," 792), but lays himself open to the same accusations when he embarks on a series of conventional and aphoristic distinctions between lust and love that have nothing to do with his own need "to grow unto himself" (1180) or with his crippling fear of sexual experience as something that would damage his fragile and immature sense of autonomy.

It is, therefore, a basic mistake to think of *Venus and Adonis* as a poem where Shakespeare or his characters indulge in rhetoric as an end in itself. Venus may derive some wry satisfaction from her own rhetorical skills, but there is no justification for Tita French Baumlin's insistence on seeing Venus as a budding poet, a figure for the apprentice bard.[29] The fact that Venus (like so many Shakespearean characters) uses rhetoric in a self-conscious fashion need not mean that rhetorical brilliance is her main preoccupation. Shakespeare himself is undoubtedly concerned with the nature of rhetoric, but one may doubt whether he would even have understood a concept like "rhetoric as an end in itself." What matters to him in *Venus and Adonis* is rhetoric as functional and dysfunctional, the ways in which it succeeds or fails in producing a concrete result. Richard Lanham's observation that "far from being infatuated with rhetoric, he fashions a mature satire in which it becomes the principal target"[30] is perceptive enough, but could be misleading if it leads us to think that *Venus and Adonis* takes a straightforwardly anti-rhetorical stance. The satire is "mature" precisely because the poem accepts rhetoric as inevitable and demonstrates both its power and its limits. To grasp this one need

only look at Venus' plea for procreation as the "law of nature" (171) or at Adonis' reply that sexual initiation should wait upon ripeness and self-knowledge (415-20, 523-28). Both arguments are advanced with considerable rhetorical efficiency and the reader surely realizes that they are not, in the long run, irreconcilable. That Venus is more interested in copulation than in procreation or that Adonis is only looking for a pretext to get off the hook may indeed underline their rhetorical dexterity in finding arguments to suit their respective predicaments. The gap between underlying motive and explicit argument makes the rhetoric ineffective for its audience within the poem (its addressee) without totally undermining its effect on the audience outside the poem. We are led to a heightened awareness that the efficacy of rhetoric depends upon context and that it is perfectly possible for rhetoric to exist in two contexts at the same time. The reader, whatever his instinctive sympathies, can hardly avoid comparing his own reactions with those of the poem's protagonists and he is free to find the rhetoric of Venus highly persuasive while recognizing that it is inappropriate for persuading Adonis.

Venus and Adonis is a poem that draws our attention to the complex implications of the Renaissance obsession with rhetoric. Seen from one angle, Renaissance rhetoric functions as an instrument of social control. With its listing of tropes and figures from *ablatio* to *zeugma*, it seems to impose order on the chaos of language; with its emphasis on decorum and levels of discourse, it reinforces hierarchical divisions; as the basis of a humanist education, it is a competence that distinguishes the rulers from the ruled. Seen from another angle, the centrality of rhetoric may appear as potentially subversive. To be trained to argue *in utramque partem*, to regard arguments in terms of their immediate effectiveness rather than their abstract validity, to cultivate the skills of the debater rather than those of the logician—all these aspects of a rhetorical education might encourage a relativist outlook that would place any orthodoxy at risk. It is in this light that we can look yet again at the "law of nature" which provides Venus with her basic arguments. Natural analogies always come in handy for ideologies which seek to appear as the reflection of some timeless order; but, as David Norbrook points out, by the sixteenth century natural analogies in political discourse were increasingly "attended with an awareness that they were rhetorical constructs with evident palpable designs on their audience."[31] The same is obviously true of sexual discourse in *Venus and Adonis*—not only because Venus uses natural analogies with a literally "palpable" end in view, but because the analogies themselves (the natural behavior of the horses, the ripe fruit that must be plucked) turn out to be double-edged. When Adonis also appeals to nature, the text surely invites the "resisting reader" (Norbrook's phrase) to conclude that the natural analogies in which rhetoric delights can be used to justify more or less anything. That the poem's most elaborate rhetoric should be uttered by a woman (even one who is a goddess) is also, of course, potentially subversive. How are we to distinguish between the *copia* that is the result of the male's rhetorical training and the garrulity which is a traditional mark of female inferiority? Is the practice of rhetoric diminished when it can be "mastered" by a woman or is the woman revalued by her demonstration of competence in a supposedly male domain?

However ethically dubious we may find the practice of rhetoric, it remains necessary in a fallen world if only because it can achieve practical results where purely rational arguments are likely to fail. It is, however, a powerful instrument rather than a precision tool and its functioning is anything but automatic. Venus, in the course of the poem, moves from a situation where she uses rhetoric in traditional humanist fashion as a means of persuasion to one where, after the death of Adonis, it becomes a way of reinventing experience. As she does so, she discovers to her cost that rhetoric can neither guarantee desired results in a real world nor detach itself from experience to create a world of its own. To become embroiled in the indirections and approximations of rhetoric is part of the penalty that a goddess pays for descending to a human condition.

If the barrier of the poem's rhetoric dissolves as soon as we see that rhetoric itself is being subjected to a witty and critical appraisal, the same can be said of the poem's approach to myth. What myth and rhetoric have in common is that, while we seem unable to speak of ourselves without them, there is no myth and no rhetoric that is ever perfectly adapted to a specific human situation. *Venus and Adonis* investigates the functions and dysfunctions of rhetoric; it also investigates the relevance and irrelevance of myth.

It should hardly be necessary to demonstrate that Shakespeare, unlike the Spenser of *Faerie Queene,* Book III, has little interest in exploiting the story of Venus and Adonis as a cosmic or vegetative myth. Venus, when it serves her own interests, may assume the traits of Venus Genitrix, but Adonis bears no relation to the "Father of all forms," and the ending of the poem, as I shall argue in Chapter Four, seems expressly designed to defeat any hope of rebirth or any attempt to see Adonis as the sacrificial young victim whose blood regenerates the world. The Venus who makes her body into a deer-park (229-40) and who addresses Adonis as an "earthly sun" (198) certainly recalls the tradition that reads Venus as the upper hemisphere of the earth, Adonis as the sun and the boar as winter,[32] but these allusions serve more as an ironic counterpoint to the theme of frustrated copulation than as a recognition that the protagonists have a truly mythical dimension. Must

we, therefore, assume that Shakespeare is using the myth only as a pretext for what turns out to be a very human drama? It is, no doubt, very tempting to see Venus as "a forty-year-old countess with a taste for Chapel Royal altos"[33] or as a sixteenth-century Erica Jong for whom "feisty" would be the only appropriate adjective. The problem is that Shakespeare does not allow us to forget that Venus is, after all, a goddess. The narrator is usually careful to acknowledge her regal title and even Adonis, in a rare moment of courtesy, addresses her as "Fair queen" (523). Venus herself is highly conscious of her own divinity, reminding Adonis that she is immortal ("And were I not immortal, life were done," 197), that she is perennially youthful ("My beauty as the spring doth yearly grow," 141) and that, despite his experience of her weight, she can defy the laws of gravity ("Two strengthless doves will draw me through the sky," 153). Thus we are repeatedly made aware of the gap between Venus' status as the goddess of love and the all-too-human condition to which she has been reduced by Adonis' resistance. The narrator stresses the point with pungent formulae ("Being judge in love, she cannot right her cause," 220; "Poor queen of love, in thine own law forlorn," 251), and it is not only the reader but Venus herself who discovers that on this occasion the goddess can no longer perform the role assigned to her by the mythographers. *Venus and Adonis* is not simply a poem about a mature woman's frustrated desire for a younger man; it is also and equally a poem about a goddess who finds out what it is like to be human.

Among the many things that must have struck Shakespeare in his reading of Ovid is the fact that when the gods are seized with desire for mortals the first casualty is usually their own dignity: *non bene conveniunt nec in una sede morantur / maiestas et amor* ("Majesty and love do not go well together, nor tarry long in the same dwelling place," *Met,* II. 846-47). In Book VI of the *Metamorphoses* the weaving contest between Minerva and Arachne offers two sharply contrasting pictures of the relations between the Olympians and their human subjects. Minerva predictably portrays the heavenly gods in statuesque poses, decked with the emblems of their authority as the guardians of law and order: in the four corners of her tapestry audacious mortals are punished for their presumption with a variety of unpleasant metamorphoses. Arachne also portrays metamorphoses, but now at the center of the web. And they are those in which the gods themselves, no longer awesome and statuesque, indulge to seduce innocent mortal women—Jove as a bull, an eagle or a swan, Neptune as a ram or a dolphin, Phoebus as a hawk and Saturn as a horse. Ovid makes it clear that Arachne does not lose the contest; she is, indeed, only too successful:

Non illud Pallas, non illud carpere Livor
possit opus: doluit successu flava virago
et rupit pictas, caelestia crimina, vestes.

(*Met,* VI. 129-31)

Not Pallas, nor Envy himself, could find a flaw in that
work. The golden-haired goddess was indignant at her
success, and rent the embroidered web with its heavenly
crimes.

What provokes Minerva's rage is not only Arachne's
unsurpassable skill but the very subject-matter of her
work which shows the gods as both criminal and comic,
descending below the human into animal forms in order
to satisfy their lusts. It is no wonder that Minerva, by
transforming Arachne into a spider, condemns her to
non-figurative art.[34]

Ovid's own poem (apart from the last book) takes a
distinctly Arachnean line and for poets of Shakespeare's
generation it was this irreverent and ironic portrayal of
the gods, with its opportunities for eroticism and
comedy, that proved irresistible. Marlowe's *Hero and
Leander* sets the tone when in an ecphrasis that recalls
Arachne's tapestry, it presents the pictures that adorn
the pavement of the temple of Venus:

There might you see the gods in sundry shapes
Committing heady riots, incest, rapes:
For know that underneath this radiant floor
Was Danae's statue in a brazen tower,
Jove slyly stealing from his sister's bed,
To dally with Idalian Ganymede,
Or for his love Europa bellowing loud,
And tumbling with the Rainbow in a cloud.

(*HL* [*Hero and Leander*], I. 143-50)[35]

The self-inflicted indignity of Jove's behavior, neatly
suggested by the verbs ("slyly stealing," "bellowing,"
"tumbling"), provides us with one set of expectations
that Shakespeare's Venus will obviously fulfill. Reduced
to blatant self-advertisement, sweating with passion and
wrestling with Adonis, the ethereal goddess will be
brought heavily down to earth.

There is, however, more to Ovid's presentation of the
gods in love than mere ridicule and we should beware
of adopting an approach that would lead us back to Putney's view of *Venus and Adonis* as unadulterated
comedy. Ovid's humor is more subtle than broad and it
is held in check by a recurrent vein of violence and terror. The behavior of the Olympians in Arachne's
tapestry is, we are told, criminal; when a mortal virgin
is chosen by a god, her sexual initiation usually takes
the form of a rape. To the initial metamorphosis of the
immortal aggressor corresponds the final metamorphosis
of the mortal victim—as an unjustified punishment
(Juno's transformation of Callisto into a bear), as a
strategy to avoid detection (Jupiter turning Io into a
cow) or as an answer to the victim's own prayer

(Daphne becoming a laurel to escape Apollo). This may
sometimes function as an aesthetic solution that
distances the real violence of the episode, but more
often Ovid draws our attention to the pain involved in
the gradual loss of human faculties and to the horror of
imprisonment in a non-human shape. When the gods
impose their lust on mortals they do more than violate
the physical integrity of their victims; they end by
depriving them of a recognizable human identity. Here
then is another and darker aspect of Shakespeare's
Ovidian inheritance. His violent Venus and virginal
Adonis conform, at least in part, to the Ovidian pattern
of lustful gods and innocent human victims. *Venus and
Adonis* is Ovidian not least in the way it achieves a balance between the comedy and the terror of sexual initiation.

The complexity of Shakespeare's relation to Ovid can
be seen in the fact that the direct source for his poem in
the *Metamorphoses,* Book X, turns out to be an exception from the pattern described above. Ovid's Venus is,
for a start, the only female divinity who descends to
love a mortal and his Adonis is a willing partner rather
than a victim. There is no animal disguise and no brutality; on the contrary, Venus does her best to please
Adonis by adopting his way of life and accompanying
him as a huntress, even if this means imitating the dress
of her arch-rival Diana. The death of Adonis does not
result from any divine vindictiveness and his metamorphosis is without pain. In this light it would seem that
Shakespeare, by creating a more aggressive goddess,
goes some way towards forcing Ovid's exception back
into the more habitual Ovidian mold.

What we ultimately get in Shakespeare's poem is a version that stands midway between the dominant Ovidian
pattern and what Ovid actually makes of the story of
Venus and Adonis. The crucial factor is not simply that
Adonis resists, but that his resistance is successful. Allowing for some important homosexual variations, the
prevailing formula for Ovid's tales of gods and mortals
can be presented schematically as follows: immortal,
male, active, powerful vs mortal, female, passive,
powerless. Shakespeare's startling and seminal innovation is to keep these attributes but reshuffle them so that
we have a Venus who is immortal, female, active and
powerless opposed to an Adonis who is mortal, male,
passive and powerful. It is this redistribution that
transforms the relation between divine and mortal into a
real contest rather than a mere invasion and that creates
in the reader a current of sympathy that can alternate
between the two protagonists. Venus' demonstration of
physical and rhetorical power is undermined by her
biological status as a woman who cannot command
Adonis' will—with all the sexual connotations that
Shakespeare so often gives that term. Adonis, for all his
mortal vulnerability and weakness, still has the power
to withhold the one thing that Venus wants.

For an immortal to be frustrated by a mortal is already a humiliation, but for the goddess of love the defeat is a more personal affront than it would be for any other Olympian. She fails in the very domain from which she takes her celestial title and prestige: "She's Love; she loves; and yet she is not loved" (610). The situation that seems on the surface so paradoxical can also be seen as perfectly logical: "Being judge in love, she cannot right her cause" (220). By falling in love with a mortal Venus momentarily loses her authority to control the loves of mortals; the judge has become a plaintiff. From what we might call the Arachnean perspective the spectacle offers the acid satisfaction of seeing the biter bit. Ovid tells us that Adonis, in attracting the love of Venus, took revenge for his mother's fate (the incestuous passion of Myrrha),[36] and Shakespeare's narrator makes a similar point in more general fashion when he addresses Venus as "Poor queen of love, in thine own law forlorn" (251). The sympathetic tone is not without a touch of *Schadenfreude* as we are reminded that the goddess is now suffering the pains she habitually inflicts on others. Any reader of the *Metamorphoses* or the *Heroides* would know that Venus has rarely exercised her powers in a benevolent manner and would recognize in her final prophetic curse on lovers only a confirmation of the capricious way she has always behaved towards her unfortunate human subjects. Venus argues that because love has been bitter for her it will henceforth prove bitter for everyone else; the whole Ovidian tradition suggests that we should invert the proposition.

Despite the knowledge that we would expect her to have, Shakespeare's Venus seems to start with naively optimistic expectations of what love on earth should be. She encourages Adonis to accept his sexual initiation as the key to a new world of pleasure in a prelapsarian Eden "where never serpent hisses" (17) and as conformity with the "law of nature" that imposes procreation (171). On the one hand, by speaking of a "time-beguiling sport" (24), she suggests that lovemaking is an innocent pastime that Adonis need not take too seriously; on the other hand, she argues that it is man's most momentous activity as his only defense against mortality ("And so in spite of death thou dost survive," 173) and as a moral imperative ("Thou wast begot; to get it is thy duty," 168). What these two contrasting arguments have in common is that they both present love as an essentially unproblematic affair for which men require no guidance beyond that of their own natural inclinations ("For men will kiss even by their own direction," 216) and of nature itself. As Venus tells Adonis when she urges him to follow the example of his horse, the situation is so simple that words should not be needed.

> "Though I were dumb, yet his proceedings teach thee.
>   O, learn to love! the lesson is but plain,

> And, once made perfect, never lost again."

> (406-08)

Unfortunately for the goddess, the lesson of nature is by no means as plain as she would like to believe. The horses communicate through an elaborate language of gesture that reflects more than it contradicts the conventions and complexities of human courtship (259-324). Moreover, if the horses do indeed follow the law of nature, then Venus has been the first to break that law by appropriating the male initiative. She loses on both counts: either the law of nature is not as simple as she assumes or she herself is responsible for creating an unnatural situation.

It is the complexities of Venus' own desire, her "variable passions" (967), that most radically undermine her plea for natural simplicity. If nature dictates mutual attraction between the sexes, what are we to make of the fact that Venus is attracted to Adonis by his feminine qualities ("Stain to all nymphs, more lovely than a man," 9)? If sexual intercourse is, as she argues, the fruit of maturity, how do we take her own admission that she wishes to taste Adonis while he is still "unripe" (127-28)? And, if it is an initiation into manhood, how does this fit with her repeated attempts to reduce him to the level of a child to be tempted with "honey secrets" and protected from the dangerous world by the playpen of a maternal body? Ambivalence reigns—nowhere more obviously than in the goddess's account of her affair with Mars (97-114) where what purports to be an invitation to imitate a virile conquest ends up as a demonstration of her own power to reduce the male to a state of unmanly and humiliating servitude.

Venus's profuse and ingenious rhetoric is not, therefore, just means in excess of matter. With all its elaborations, expansions, contradictions and shifts in strategy, it stands at odds with her basic argument that love is naturally simple. It gets her into a hole where she cannot stop digging. Through it she excites herself more than she excites Adonis and the result is a potentially endless rhythm of frustration where eloquence repeatedly topples over into physical aggression and where the defeat of that aggression provokes a new bout of eloquence. The physical entanglement of Adonis ("Look how a bird lies tangled in a net, / So fastened in her arms Adonis lies," 67-68) is analogous to the rhetorical entanglement of Venus herself. And Venus is entangled precisely because all her arguments in favor of simplicity keep revealing the complexity of motive which she cannot afford to acknowledge and from which she cannot escape.

The desire of Venus defies definition because it knows no limits. She sees Adonis not so much as a type who excites a specific kind of sexual appetite, but as an empty space, a blank page on which all forms of desire can be inscribed. Thus, by turns, she constructs him as an effeminate beauty who provides relief from male roughness, as a passive partner who allows her to assume the male role, as the virile rider who will manage her and take back that initiative for himself and as an eroticized child whose feeding (232-34) might grant her a variety of oral and incestuous satisfactions. Shakespeare's Venus unites in herself most of the varieties of desire that we find in the *Metamorphoses* where they proliferate to such an extent that we lose sight of any norm dictated by nature. Like Shakespeare's narrator who reproaches Venus for "Forgetting shame's pure blush and honor's wrack" (558), Ovid may at times throw up his hands in official horror and urge his chaste readers to proceed no further; but the overall direction of his poem is to challenge the idea that sexual desire has any preordained "natural" object. Desire in Ovid is naturally transgressive and this is surely part of the appeal of Renaissance Ovidian fictions in which, as Bruce Smith suggests, the reader "is invited, for a limited season, to give free play to desires that must ordinarily be held in check."[37] What we have already said of the poem's rhetoric is also true of its mythological content: both work against the idea of a normative nature.

It is, of course, entirely appropriate that the goddess of love should experience all those "variable passions" which assume the name of love. "She's Love; she loves," and it would be a limitation of her divinity to restrict her to any single version of desire. "And yet she is not loved": it is the very range of her desires that prevents them from being realized in a specific and human sexual situation. Adonis is presented with lovemaking as an agreeable pastime and also as a moral duty, urged to lie back and let it happen and then reproached for not taking the initiative, offered the female body as a safe haven from the dangerous world and also incited to possess it as a manly conquest. If the abundance of Venus' arguments reflects the range of her passions, then she must be truly insatiable since no single lover could respond to such multifarious demands. Readers who join too easily with Venus in condemning Adonis' refusal "To take advantage on presented joy" (405) underestimate the threat posed by the sheer profusion and incoherence of her persuasions. If Adonis replies "I know not love [. . .] nor will not know it" (409), this is partly because Venus has proved incapable of presenting love as something knowable. Love, in her rhetoric, is so riddled with contradictions as to justify Adonis' conclusion that it has no real substance: "For I have heard it is a life in death, / That laughs and weeps, and all but with a breath" (413-14). The love proposed by Venus appears so protean and so unstable, so much all and therefore nothing, that it can only threaten to dissolve rather than define the fragile identity of a youth who pleads "Before I know myself, seek not to know me" (525). Coppelia Kahn may be right to read **Venus and Adonis** as the story of a failed initiation, but the failure is not entirely to be blamed on Adonis.[38] Venus gives him every reason to believe that, in this case, carnal knowledge and self-knowledge are incompatible.

The opposition between the two protagonists is reinforced by a marked difference in rhetorical styles. The rhetoric of Venus is opportunistic and infinitely flexible, short on logic but strong on invention, expansive, all-embracing, taking whatever offers as grist to her mill. The flora and fauna inhabit her imagination, the landscape becomes her body, the sun participates in her inflamed passion and the behavior of the horses justifies her own sexual energy. Even when the death of Adonis finally destroys the illusion of a nature that mirrors and supports her intentions, the old habit dies hard and she makes a last desperate effort to read her own erotic motives into the mindless violence of the boar "Who did not whet his teeth at him again, / But by a kiss thought to persuade him there" (1113-14). Something of the same expansive quality can be observed in the mastery of tone that enables her to move from the seductive and the reassuring to the pathetic and the reproachful, or again in the astonishing variety of register that encompasses visionary Neoplatonism, sophisticated Petrarchism, libertine Ovidian wit and earthy sexual proverbs. She is, in short (or rather, at length), an anthology of love poetry.[39] Adonis speaks a good deal less—89 lines as against 384 for Venus in the debate that ends with his departure (811). He says enough, however, to embody a very different brand of rhetoric which, despite some revealing lapses into self-pity, is relatively even in tone, tightly organized, antithetical and aphoristic—the opposite of expansive, concerned with making rather than blurring distinctions.

> "Love comforteth, like sunshine after rain,
> But lust's effect is tempest after sun;
> Love's gentle spring doth always fresh remain;
> Lust's winter comes ere summer half be done:
>   Love surfeits not; lust like a glutton dies.
>   Love is all truth, lust full of forgèd lies."
>
>   (799-804)

Critics have been quick to hear the voice of a diligent and priggish schoolboy reciting a well-learned lesson and there is certainly a hint of parody. But there is more to it than that. The clipped and rigorous symmetries of the syntax and the predictability of the antitheses convey Adonis' need to find security in a scheme of moral certainties, rigid boundaries and mutually absolute exclusions. The tidy, self-contained quality of the rhetoric is mimetic of his yearning for the "quiet closure" (782) and solitary "bedchamber" (784) where he can escape from the turbulent and chaotic emotions of Venus.

These two rhetorical styles can be seen as reflecting two opposed versions of the self. For Venus, with her blurring of distinctions, the self is asserted by reaching out to invade, incorporate and digest the world. For Adonis the self is created by the erection of barriers, by a refusal to let the world impinge on one's precious identity. We should, however, resist the temptation to oppose a Venus who is generous, creative, and life-enhancing to an Adonis who is selfish, sterile and life-denying. The truth is that both versions of the self are equally selfish and equally destructive of love. If Venus fails to persuade Adonis, it is because she refuses to recognize him as Other, because she cannot conceive of anything that resists absorption into the self. If Adonis cannot be persuaded, it is because he cannot conceive of the Other as anything but a threat to the self. Neither protagonist has any vision of the "mutual render" celebrated in the **Sonnets,** but they differ insofar as Adonis makes exclusion of the Other into a conscious principle whereas Venus seems quite unaware of the threat posed to Adonis by her own contrasting urge to absorb and incorporate. Thus she will, at times, use the metaphors of exchange, while instinctively developing them to suggest a very unequal bargain.[40] It is not just that the one kiss she proposes to Adonis as the price of his freedom (84) soon becomes two thousand (522), but that who gives and who takes a kiss depends on context and perspective. "Take" can mean either "seize" or "accept;" "give" may be either "inflict" or "donate." Venus exploits the ambiguity of give and take in a way that is not so much dishonest as deeply self-regarding and pathetically self-deceptive.

That Venus should display this ignorance of her own motives is perfectly consistent with her status as a goddess. It is only humans who need to create and define an identity; the gods, immortal and immutable, are what they are. Since the identity of Venus as goddess of love is beyond question, self-knowledge is not her concern and she is, therefore, incapable of appreciating that concern in Adonis. Placed in a position where her biological status as woman prevents the automatic imposition of her will, she needs to persuade and she fails to grasp that persuasion cannot be effective without some recognition of the otherness of the addressee, of the obstinate selfhood that mortals hold so dear. Her rhetoric, after all, exemplifies the ambiguity of her status in the poem. In its profusion, exuberance and inventiveness, it is the reflection of her divinely creative powers as Venus Genitrix; in its confusions and revisions—or even by the simple fact that she needs rhetoric at all—it becomes the measure of her humiliation, a demonstration of how far she has fallen.

Venus sees no difference between lust and love; Adonis refuses to recognize the continuities between them.[41] Venus seeks to incorporate the world into the self; Adonis tries to construct a self in isolation from the world. Both the goddess who blurs all distinctions and the youth who makes them hard and fast are victims of their own radical and self-centered simplification of

experience. The poem does not adjudicate between them and neither does the boar. Readers who demand that the poem deliver a tidy moral package may see the boar as an embodiment of natural justice, punishing Venus for her destructive lust or Adonis for his self-imposed sterility; yet this is to miss the essential point that the boar represents not some offended natural law but nature's arbitrary violence. Though it is certainly in keeping with the theme of the poem that the death of Adonis should resemble a rape or a castration, the event in itself has no obvious or inevitable connection with Venus' desire or Adonis' resistance. To argue that Adonis is punished for not making love is much like saying that the victim of an aircrash has been punished for not staying at home. Venus herself, though she warns Adonis that hunting the boar is mortally dangerous, never suggests that death will be the punishment for his chastity. Her argument is only that, since accidents are always waiting to happen, Adonis should make love before death prevents him from doing so. Ovid's Adonis, we remember, does make love to Venus and gets killed just the same. For Shakespeare, as for Ovid, the death of Adonis remains an accident or, in the words of Venus, one of those "mad mischances" (738) which always lurk to "cross the curious workmanship of nature" (734).

As that line suggests, Venus fears the boar because his very existence gives the lie to her self-indulgent vision of a natural order that is in harmony with her own amorous and/or procreative inclinations: he represents that aspect of the world which stubbornly resists her rhetoric of incorporation. Already undermined by her own confused motives and challenged by Adonis' refusal to conform, her idea of the "law of nature" is finally destroyed by the boar's mindless brutality and by nature's manifest indifference to the beauty it produces but neglects to preserve. By descending to the human level Venus experiences both the human urge to discover order in the world and the world's resistance. Her reaction is a blend of impotence and vindictiveness. Reconstructing her own story as an etiological myth, she ordains that love shall henceforth be as unlucky for others as it has been for her (1135-64). Imitating the boar who "would root these beauties as he roots the mead" (636), she deprives the world of the flower that is the last and only legacy of Adonis. It is not just Adonis but the world that has defeated her, and she leaves it in disgust.

I shall argue later that the poem's ending is not quite as depressing as this bald account makes it sound. The vindictiveness of Venus is balanced by her impotence. She leaves the world because she is obviously incapable of changing it—incapable not just of seducing Adonis but even of granting him the limited form of immortality that he receives in Ovid. Lovers need not fear the curses of a goddess who is so powerless. If the descent of Venus has not changed the world for the better, her departure will not make it any worse. We may, like Adonis, be the victims of nature's meaningless violence, but at least we shall not be the victims of the gods. Above all, the ending, with its goddess flying off into the sky and its youth transformed into a flower, reminds us that the myth, even in Shakespeare's untraditional version, has a partial and problematic relevance to any genuinely human situation. However convincingly Venus and Adonis may have acted human roles, they retain a fabulous dimension, existing outside history and outside society, abstracted in a theater of human passions without a human context. It is as if we have viewed ourselves not as we are in the world that is ours, but in a laboratory experiment through a glass that, because it enlarges and intensifies, also isolates and distorts. As mythical characters, Venus and Adonis are both like and unlike us—entangled in rhetoric as we all are and rhetorically constructed as the saner of us know that we are not. Coleridge remarked that **Venus and Adonis** seems "at once the characters themselves, but more, the representations of those characters by the most consummate actors."[42] Perhaps that is why, in the long run, we can contemplate the poem with the serenity that comes from an awareness that it illuminates but does not reproduce our own condition.

Notes

1. "There is an upstart Crow, beautified with our feathers, that with his *Tygers hart wrapt in a Players hyde,* supposes he is as well able to bombaste out a blank verse as the best of you." Robert Greene, *Groats-worth of witte, bought with a million of Repentance* (London, 1592), sig. A3v. See Muriel C. Bradbrook, "Beasts and Gods: Greene's *Groats-Worth of Witte* and the Social Purpose of *Venus and Adonis,*" ShS [*Shakespeare Survey*] 15 (1962), 62-72.

2. In 1591 John Clapham, one of Burghley's secretaries, had addressed to Southampton a moralistic Latin poem entitled *Narcissus,* and Shakespeare's Venus, in her turn, uses the example of Narcissus to warn Adonis against the dangers of self-love (157-62). Self-love, however, seems to be the only link between the chaste Adonis and the promiscuous Southampton. See Charles Martindale and Colin Burrow, "Clapham's *Narcissus*: A Pre-Text for Shakespeare's *Venus and Adonis* (text, translation, commentary)," ELR [*English Literary Renaissance*] 22 (1992), 147-75. On the more general issue of Southampton's relations with Shakespeare see G. P. V. Akrigg, *Shakespeare and the Earl of Southampton* (London, 1968).

3. The standard anthology is *Elizabethan Minor Epics,* ed. Elizabeth Story Donno (New York, 1963) which begins with Thomas Lodge, *Scillaes Meta-*

morphosis (1589), and ends with James Shirley, *Narcissus or The Self-Lover* (1646).

4. For "The Vogue of *Venus and Adonis* and *Lucrece*" see Rollins, 447-75. See also Katherine Duncan-Jones, "Much Ado with Red and White: The Earliest Readers of Shakespeare's *Venus and Adonis* (1593)," *RES* [*Review of English Studies*] New Series XLIV, No. 176 (1993), 480-501. This is a fascinating and witty account of the "open responsiveness" of the poem's first readers, beginning with the eccentric William Reynolds who saw Venus as Queen Elizabeth and Adonis as himself.

5. *Coleridge's Shakespearean Criticism,* ed. T. M. Raysor, 2 vols. (London, 1960), 1. 188-93 (p. 188).

6. Gary Waller, *English Poetry in the Sixteenth Century* (London, 1986), 217.

7. The most stimulating discussion of the continuities between the narrative poems and the *Sonnets* is in Heather Dubrow, *Captive Victors: Shakespeare's Narrative Poems and Sonnets* (Ithaca, NY, 1987).

8. Ted Hughes, *Shakespeare and the Goddess of Complete Being* (London, 1992).

9. Jonathan Bate, *Shakespeare and Ovid* (Oxford, 1993), 270.

10. Francis Meres, *Palladis Tamia* (1598) in *Elizabethan Critical Essays* ed. G. Gregory Smith, 2 vols. (Oxford, 1904), ii. 317.

11. "Epyllion" (little epic) is a convenient if anachronistic shorthand for the Ovidian erotic narrative poem. On the origins of the term see Walter Allen, Jr., "The Non-Existent Classical Epyllion," *SP* [*Studies in Philology*] 55 (1958), 515-18. As my last chapter will suggest, I am tempted by the Italian *idillio,* but "idyll" would have inappropriate Tennysonian echoes.

12. We have ample evidence that *Hero and Leander* was widely read before its earliest extant edition in 1598. It may seem to echo or foreshadow Shakespeare by presenting Adonis as "careless and disdainful" (I. 13) and by describing him as "rose-cheeked" (I. 93); but there is nothing here that need strain our belief in coincidence.

13. C. S. Lewis, *English Literature in the Sixteenth Century, Excluding Drama* (London, 1954), 498.

14. S. T. Coleridge, *Biographia Literaria,* 2 vols., ed. J. Shawcross (London, 1954), ii. 15-16.

15. "Venus is shown as the destructive agent of sensual love; Adonis as reason in love. The one sullies whatever it touches: the other honors and

makes it beautiful. The one is false and evil; the other is all truth, all good. [. . .] This is the teaching of *Venus and Adonis,* as didactic a piece of work, perhaps, as Shakespeare ever wrote." L. E. Pearson, *Elizabethan Love Conventions* (New York, 1933), 285.

16. Hereward T. Price, "The Function of Imagery in *Venus and Adonis,*" *Papers of the Michigan Academy of Science, Arts and Letters* 31 (1945), 275-97 (p. 292).

17. Donald G. Watson, "The Contrarieties of *Venus and Adonis,*" *SP* 75 (1978), 32-63 (p. 54).

18. *The Return from Parnassus, Part I* (1600); Thomas Middleton, *A Mad World, my Masters* (1608). Both cited in Rollins, 455.

19. Waller, 217.

20. T. W. Baldwin, *On the Literary Genetics of Shakspere's Poems and Sonnets* (Urbana, Ill., 1943), 83-84.

21. Heather Asals, "*Venus and Adonis*: The Education of a Goddess," *SEL* [*Studies in English Literature, 1500-1900*] 13 (1973), 31-51.

22. Lennet J. Daigle, "*Venus and Adonis*: Some Traditional Contexts," *Shakespeare Studies* 13 (1980), 31-46.

23. Roe, 21.

24. Rufus Putney, "*Venus and Adonis*: Amour with Humor," *PQ* [*Philological Quarterly*] 20 (1941), 533-48; "Venus Agonistes," *University of Colorado Studies* 4 (1953), 52-66.

25. Lewis, 61.

26. Douglas Bush, *Mythology and the Renaissance Tradition in English Poetry* (1932, rev. edn., New York, 1963), 137-55.

27. William Hazlitt, *Characters of Shakespeare's Plays* (London, 1906), 264-65.

28. Prince, xxxvi.

29. Tita French Baumlin, "The Birth of the Bard: *Venus and Adonis* and Poetic Apotheosis," *Southern Illinois Papers on Language and Literature* 26 (1990), 191-211.

30. Richard Lanham, *The Motives of Eloquence: Literary Rhetoric in the Renaissance* (New Haven, Conn., 1976), 90.

31. David Norbrook, "Rhetoric, Ideology and the Elizabethan World Picture," in *Renaissance Rhetoric,* ed. Peter Mack (London, 1994), 140-64 (p. 147).

32. See Abraham Fraunce, *The Third part of the Countess of Pembrokes Yvychurch* (London, 1592). The cosmological reading of the myth was a Renaissance commonplace which Fraunce could have picked up from Boccaccio's *Genealogia Deorum* or from a number of popular manuals such as those of Natalis Comes (1551) and Vincenzo Cartari (1556) or, in England, Thomas Cooper (1565).

33. Don Cameron Allen, "On *Venus and Adonis,*" in *Elizabethan and Jacobean Studies Presented to F. P. Wilson,* ed. H. Davis and H. Gardner (Oxford, 1959), 100-11 (p. 101).

34. For an illuminating discussion of the Arachne episode see the opening chapter of Leonard Barkan, *The Gods Made Flesh: Metamorphosis and the Pursuit of Paganism* (New Haven, Conn., 1986).

35. Christopher Marlowe, *The Complete Poems and Translations,* ed. Stephen Orgel (Harmondsworth, 1971). All subsequent quotations of *Hero and Leander* are from this edition, followed by line reference in my text.

36. *iam placet et Veneri matrisque ulciscitur ignes* (*Met,* X. 524).

37. Bruce R. Smith, *Homosexual Desire in Shakespeare's England: A Cultural Poetics* (Chicago, 1991), 132.

38. Coppelia Kahn, "Self and Eros in *Venus and Adonis,*" *Centennial Review* 4 (1976), 351-71.

39. Rob Maslen notes that "the language she uses is a giddyingly inventive display of familiar Petrarchan tropes," but this is a simplification. Petrarchism is only one ingredient in a very heady brew. See Rob Maslen, "*Venus and Adonis* and the Death of Orpheus," *Glasgow Review. Renaissance* 1 (1993), 70.

40. Dubrow (35-37) points out Venus' characteristic reliance on the conditional mode and relates it to her propensity for offering bargains where what is on offer is not something that Adonis wants. The same self-centredness is revealed by the rhetorical questions that assume answers Adonis would not in fact give.

41. Catherine Belsey has noted that the narrator uses both "love" and "lust" as synonymous terms to indicate the passion of Venus. She argues that this reflects older attitudes, whereas Protestantism's positive revaluation of marriage created the need for rigid distinctions of the kind that Adonis makes at 793-804. Catherine Belsey, "Love as Trompe-l'oeil: Taxonomies of Desire in *Venus and Adonis,*" *Shakespeare Quarterly* 40 (1995), 257-76.

42. *Shakespearean Criticism,* ii. 64.

Bibliography

TEXTS OF THE POEM

Prince, F. T., *The Poems,* Arden Shakespeare (London, 1960).

Roe, John, *The Poems,* New Cambridge Shakespeare (Cambridge, 1992).

Rollins, Hyder Edward, *The Poems: A New Variorum Edition of Shakespeare* (Philadelphia, 1938).

Wells, Stanley, and Gary Taylor, *The Oxford Shakespeare* (London, 1986).

[For all poems and plays by Shakespeare I have used the *Oxford Shakespeare* (1986) edited by Stanley Wells and Gary Taylor. Line reference after citation is always to this edition. Where they were needed to indicate direct speech I have preserved quotation marks round indented citations.]

SECONDARY MATERIAL

Akrigg, G. P. V., *Shakespeare and the Earl of Southampton* (London, 1968).

Allen, D. C., "On Venus and Adonis" in *Elizabethan and Jacobean Studies, Presented to F. P. Wilson,* ed. H. Davis and H. Gardner (Oxford, 1959), 100-11.

Allen, Walter, Jr., "The Non-Existent Classical Epyllion", *SP* [*Studies in Philology*] 55 (1958), 515-18.

Asals, Heather, "*Venus and Adonis*: The Education of a Goddess," *SEL* [*Studies in English Literature, 1500-1900*] 13 (1973), 31-51.

Baldwin, T. W., *On the Literary Genetics of Shakspere's Poems and Sonnets* (Urbana, Ill., 1950).

Barkan, Leonard, *The Gods Made Flesh: Metamorphosis and the Pursuit of Paganism* (New Haven, Conn., 1986).

Bate, Jonathan, *Shakespeare and Ovid* (Oxford, 1993).

Baumlin, Tita French, "The Birth of the Bard: *Venus and Adonis* and Poetic Apotheosis," *Southern Illinois Papers on Language and Literature* 26 (1990), 191-211.

Belsey, Catherine, "Love as Trompe-l'oeil: Taxonomies of Desire in *Venus and Adonis,*" *Shakespeare Quarterly* 40 (1995), 257-76.

Bradbrook, M. C., "Beasts and Gods: Greene's *Groats-Worth of Witte* and the Social Purpose of *Venus and Adonis,*" *Shakespeare Survey* 15 (1962), 62-72.

Bush, Douglas, *Mythology and the Renaissance Tradition in English Poetry* (1932, rev. edn., New York, 1963).

Coleridge, S. T., *Coleridge's Shakespearean Criticism,* ed. T. M. Raysor, (2 vols., London, 1960).

————, *Biographia Literaria,* ed. J. Shawcross (2 vols, London, 1954).

Daigle, Lennet, "*Venus and Adonis*: some traditional contexts," *Shakespeare Studies* 13 (1980), 31-46.

Donno, Elizabeth Story (ed.), *Elizabethan Minor Epics* (London, 1963).

Dubrow, Heather, *Captive Victors: Shakespeare's Narrative Poems and Sonnets* (Ithaca, NY, 1987).

Duncan-Jones, Katherine, "Much Ado with Red and White: the Earliest Readers of Shakespeare's *Venus and Adonis,*" *RES* [*Review of English Studies*] New Series, XLIV, No 176 (1993), 480-501.

Fraunce, Abraham, *The Third Part of the Countesse of Pembrokes Yvychurch* (London, 1592). Garland reprint, 1976).

Golding, Arthur, *Shakespeare's Ovid being Arthur Golding's Translation of the Metamorphoses,* ed. W. H. D. Rouse (1904, reprint, London, 1961).

Hazlitt, William, *Characters of Shakespeare's Plays* (London, 1906).

Hughes, Ted, *Shakespeare and the Goddess of Complete Being* (London, 1992).

Kahn, Coppelia, "Self and Eros in *Venus and Adonis,*" *Centennial Review* 4 (1976), 351-71.

Lanham, R. A., *The Motives of Eloquence: Literary Rhetoric in the Renaissance* (New Haven, Conn., 1976).

Lewis, C. S., *English Literature in the Sixteenth Century, Excluding Drama* (Oxford, 1954).

Martindale, Charles, and Colin Burrow, "Clapham's *Narcissus*: A Pre-Text for Shakespeare's *Venus and Adonis,*" *ELR* [*English Literary Renaissance*] 22 (1992), 147-75.

Maslen, Rob, "*Venus and Adonis* and the Death of Orpheus," *The Glasgow Review. Renaissance* 1 (1993).

Ovid, *Metamorphoses,* with translation by Frank Justus Miller, Loeb Classical Library (2 vols, London, 1977).

Ovide moralisé, Poème du commencement du quatorzième siècle, ed C. de Boer, *Verhandelingen der Koninklijke Akademie van Wetenschappen* (Amsterdam), Afd. Letterkunde, new series XV (1915), XXI (1920), XXX (1931), XXXVII (1936), XLIII (1938). Sändig reprint (Vaduz, 1988).

Price, Hereward T., "The Function of Imagery in *Venus and Adonis,*" *Papers of the Michigan Academy of Science, Arts, and Letters* 31 (1945), 275-97.

Putney, Rufus, "*Venus and Adonis*: Amour with Humor," *PQ* [*Philological Quarterly*] 20 (1941), 533-48.

Smith, Bruce, *Homosexual Desire in Shakespeare's England* (Chicago, 1991).

Smith, G. Gregory, *Elizabethan Critical Essays* (2 vols., Oxford, 1904).

Smith, Hallett, *Elizabethan Poetry: A Study in Conventions, Meaning and Expression* (Cambridge, Mass., 1952).

Watson, D. G., "The Contrarieties of *Venus and Adonis*," *SP* 75 (1978), 32-63.

Richard Wilson (essay date 2001)

SOURCE: Wilson, Richard. "A Bloody Question: The Politics of *Venus and Adonis*."[1] *Religion and the Arts* 5, no. 3 (2001): 297-316.

[*In the following essay, Wilson uses historical evidence, including Catholic poet Robert Southwell's early critique of the poem, to argue that* Venus and Adonis *is a veiled criticism of Catholic martyrdom.*]

Venus and Adonis was Shakespeare's most instantaneous success, with sixteen editions printed before 1640. Yet the earliest recorded commentary on the poem was one of bitter disappointment, and it came from a writer whom Ben Jonson rated so highly he said "he would have been content to destroy many of his poems" to have written just one of his.[2] Jonson of course was referring to the Jesuit poet Robert Southwell, and Southwell's criticism must have stung Shakespeare. In the last days before his arrest in June 1592, Southwell responded to the circulated manuscript of **Venus and Adonis** with a poem of his own in identical stanzas, entitled *Saint Peter's Complaint*, which he prefaced with a dedication deploring the waste of Shakespeare's gifts:

> This makes my mourning Muse resolve in tears,
> This themes my heavy pen to plain in prose:
> Christ's thorn is sharp, no head his garland wears,
> Still finest wits are stilling Venus' rose,
> In paynim toys the sweetest veins are spent,
> To Christian works few have their talents lent.
>
> (*Complaint* A4)

Southwell's dismissal of **Venus and Adonis** as a "pagan toy" has been ignored by almost all Shakespeareans, and this may be because the implications are so sensational. For not only is this the first critical reaction to Shakespeare's work, it is also the clearest indication of how the "finest wit" and "sweetest vein" of his generation had been expected to produce "Christian works" that "lent his talent" to the Catholic cause. At the end of his career Shakespeare would be publicly exposed with the Jesuit leader Robert Parsons by the

historian John Speed, as "this papist and his poet, of like conscience for lies, the one ever feigning, the other ever falsifying the truth" (224). Southwell's belief that the young writer would have been better employed weaving a martyr's crown of thorns for himself than distilling a lover's rose confirms that the Society of Jesus did indeed look to him as one of its brightest potential stars. As Gary Taylor has observed, "It is a short step from Parsons and Southwell to Shakespeare" (306). But just how short a step was only revealed in the 1616 edition of the priest's poem published by the Jesuit press in Belgium, where the text was capped by a prose-letter "To my worthy good cousin, Master W. S.," signed "Your loving cousin, R. S." (*Complaint* A2). In fact, William Shakespeare was actually a distant relative of Robert Southwell through his mother, Mary Arden; and the martyr's secret handshake pulled him firmly within the tight family circle of aristocratic Elizabethan Catholicism, where, as Antonia Fraser writes, "everyone was related to everyone else" (35). And if, as Southwell claimed in the letter, it had been "Master W. S." himself who "importuned" the publication of *Peter's Plaint,* "and therefore must beare parte of the pennance, when it shall please sharpe censures to impose it" (*Poems* 2), the Jesuit poem can be read both as a guide to the politics of **Venus and Adonis,** and a pass into that dangerous company where the "first heir" of Shakespeare's invention was composed. Punning on Shakespeare's name at the end of the verse dedication, his cousin suggested, in any case, that this "sweetest" Ovidian poet would be a worthy peer and partner on the martyr's road:

> Licence my single pen to seek a peer;
> You heavenly sparks of wit show native light,
> Cloud not with misty loves your orient clear;
> Sweet flights you shoot, learn once to level right.
> Favour my wish, well-wishing works no ill;
> I move the suit, the grant rests in your will.

Southwell's punning challenge to "seek a peer" (or "phere," meaning a soul-mate) evokes the ardour with which Shakespeare's "pagan toy" was received when it was published in 1593. And Southwell confirms the hopes with which **Venus and Adonis** was scanned by its readership, when he opens *St. Peter's Complaint* by comparing the exile of a seminarian upon a sea of tears—with "Torment thy haven, shipwreck thy best reward"—to the plain-sailing of "Ambitious heads . . . plung'd in Folly's tide," who "Fill volumes with your forged goddess' praise," or "Devote your fabling wits to lovers' lays" (stanzas 1, 6). What follows is a scalding sermon on betrayal, in which the poet's choice of profane over sacred verse—"Writing in works lessons of ill advice; / The doing-tale that eye in practise reads" (stanza 40)—is equated with Saint Peter's denial of Christ. As the Oxford editors note, Southwell revised his account of Peter's desertion several times, with the effect of heightening the role of the "damsel" who, in the Gospels, "kept the door" of the court where Jesus was on trial, and said "unto Peter, Art thou not also one of this man's disciples? [And] He saith, I am not" (John 18:16-17). Thus, in the final version, it is the seductiveness with which this woman poses her question that compels Peter to drop his sword, and the misogyny of his railing then leaves no doubt that what is implied is a parallel, as the editors observe, "between her questions and the actions of the Queen, whose demands for an Oath of Supremacy and show of allegiance tempted Catholics to deny their loyalty to Rome" (*Poems* lxxxix). More specifically, if the porteress figures Queen Elizabeth, Southwell seems to interpret *Venus and Adonis* as an example of the craven capitulation to the Crown that followed the introduction of the notorious "Bloody Question" in 1588, when all English Catholics were confronted with a deadly test: "If the Pope were to send over an army . . . whose side would you be on: the Pope's or the Queen's?" (quoted in Devlin 166). For in *Peter's Plaint* those "words . . . delivered from a woman's tongue" (stanza 49) are likewise a trap to catch an entire generation of the soldiers of Christ:

> O port'ress of the door of my disgrace,
>   Whose tongue unlock'd the truth of vowed mind;
> Whose words from coward's heart did courage chase,
>   And let in deathful fears my soul to blind;
> O had thou been the port'ress of my tomb,
> When thou wert port'ress to that cursed room!
>
> (stanza 36)

"And the servants and officers stood there," in the words of the Gospel, "who had made a fire of coals, for it was cold; and they warmed themselves: and Peter stood with them and warmed himself" (John 18:18). Southwell's exclamation that he "rather had congeal'd to ice, / Than bought my warmth at such a damning price!" (43) condenses, in his favourite imagery of fire and snow, contempt for all those Catholic intellectuals who answered the "Bloody Question" by defecting to "so ill a Court" (39). In fact, Burghley had expressly drafted the Question, according to a memorandum, so as to split militants from such deserters, who could then be neutralised "by a process of guile and attrition: by inciting their tenants against them . . . taking their children hostage under colour of education . . . or stripping them of armour so that twenty thousand will be helpless before one thousand Protestants" (quoted in Devlin 330-31). This letter to "Master W. S." is heavy with disappointment that his cousin was one who had warmed himself at court. The reproof may date from late in the priest's imprisonment, as it misquotes Theseus' line, in *A Midsummer Night's Dream,* that the lunatic, lover and poet "Are of imagination all compact" (5.1.8), which it refutes with the "authority of God, Who delivering many parts of Scripture in verse, and willing us to exercise devotion in hymns and spiritual sonnets, warranteth the art good, and the use allowable." Against Theseus's idea of art for art's sake, therefore, Southwell

insists that poetry "hath been used by men of greatest piety in matters of most devotion," and that the morality of literature has been attested by Christ, who, by staging His Last Supper and Passion as a "pageant," gave to dramatists "a method to imitate . . . and . . . a pattern to know the true use of this measured style." The inference is unavoidable that, like Saint Peter, the author of the *A Midsummer Night's Dream* and *Venus and Adonis* has "quailed at words . . . delivered from a woman's tongue," and sold himself, in "fear of woman's breath," for "Hire of a hireling mind" (stanzas 49, 53, 34):

> Poets, by abusing their talent, and making the follies and fayninges of love, the customary subject of their base endeavours, have so discredited this faculty, that a Poet, a Lover, and a Liar, are by many reckoned but three wordes of one signification. . . . [For] the Divell as hee affecteth Deity, and seeketh to have all complements of Divine honour applied to his service, so hath he among the rest possessed most Poets with his idle fansies. For in lieu of solemne and devout matter, to which in duety they owe their abilities, they now busy themselves in expressing such passions, as onely serve for testimonies to how unwoorthy affections they have wedded their wils.
>
> (*Poems* 1)

Written more in sorrow than anger, Southwell's appeal to his literary kinsman ends with the wish that his own "few ditties" will inspire the "skilfuller wit," who does not fear "Of mirth to make a trade," to "begin some finer piece, wherein it may be shown how well verse and virtue suit together . . . add you the tunes, and let the Mean, I pray you, be still a part in all your music." The martyr's biographer infers that Shakespeare, "pricked by Southwell's example," did indeed "try his hand at tapping a loftier, more metaphysical vein" than *Venus and Adonis,* and so devised *The Rape of Lucrece* as the "graver labour" he had pledged in the dedication to his earlier poem (Devlin 273). But the question this begs is why Shakespeare's "unpolished lines" should have provoked such a sad rebuke from England's leading Catholic poet, and why an unashamedly erotic text should have been construed as such a *political* betrayal by the recusant community.

The answer lies, of course, in the similarity of Southwell's temptress and Shakespeare's Venus, who both sweeten their coercion with what the Jesuit calls "These Syrens' sugared tunes" (stanza 52), and offer "A thousand honey secrets" if their men disarm (*Venus* l. 16). Read with the hindsight of the poem it prompted, *Venus and Adonis* is Ovid moralised, as Shakespeare's Queen herself says, with painful relevance to its occasion: "Applying this to that, and so to so, / For love can comment upon every woe" (ll. 713-4). This was the type of Aesopian allegory that Southwell himself trusted "the better sort" of reader would not confuse with "idle fancy. . . . For in fables are often figured moral truths, covertly uttered to a common good, which without mask would not find so free a passage." The priest excused the "inconvenience" of such fables, he wrote, "if the drift of their discourse levelled at any virtuous mark" (quoted in Devlin 268-69); but what evidently shocked him in his cousin's work was that it so missed the mark of papist virtue. For compared to *Peter's Plaint*, **Venus and Adonis** presents the worst possible prospectus for martyrdom:

> The picture of an angry chafing boar,
> Under whose sharp fangs on his back doth lie
> An image like thyself, all stain'd with gore;
> Whose blood upon the fresh flowers being shed,
> Doth make them droop with grief and hang their
> head.
>
> (662-6)

"This looks like the last stage before the expected end," Southwell had exulted, when the government introduced its Bloody Question, "and it puts us, as some fear and others hope, very close to martyrdom" (quoted in Devlin 167). The poems that he then wrote, between 1588 and 1592, with their imagery of "hunting, falconry, trapping birds, fishing and coursing," but, above all, their euphoria "in shedding blood: / The whips, the thorns, the nails, the spear, and rod," created a discourse of sacrifice for a generation of Catholics living in expectation of imminent massacre (Brown 198). And it was in the context of this fatalistic cult of the Christian hero as a "young flower" who, "with flowers in flower . . . may . . . hang on a tree,"[3] that Shakespeare's fable of the purple flower springing from a boy's blood would have been immediately interpreted. For what this iconography clarifies, with a sharpness lost to modern critics, is that, at its core, **Venus and Adonis** is a critique of martyrdom. The poet-priest's disenchantment with his lay-brother becomes explicable, therefore, once the poem is reinserted into the masochistic semiotics of Catholic martyrology, where the slaughter of the chase affirms—as it does in Southwell's lyrics—that the massacre of innocents will not be in vain: "The merlin cannot ever soar on high, / Nor the greedy greyhound still pursue the chase; / The tender lark will find a time to fly, / And fearful hare to run a quiet race."[4] The Jesuit had adopted this hunting metaphor, according to his biographers, whilst hiding at Baddesley Clinton in the Warwickshire Forest of Arden;[5] and it was in such Catholic houses, with their hidden chambers and secret passageways, that Venus's enticement of Adonis to escape his death by turning against "the timorous flying hare" (674) would indeed have been moralised for its contemporary relevance: as the invitation made to Elizabeth's Catholic subjects, to save their skins by betraying their "earth-delving" (687) co-religionists to the "hot scent-snuffing hounds" (692) of the pursuivants and priest-finders:

> And when thou hast on foot the purblind hare,
> Mark the poor wretch, to overshoot his troubles,
> How he outruns the wind, and with what care
> He cranks and crosses with a thousand doubles;
> The many musits through which he goes
> Are like a labyrinth to amaze his foes . . .
>
> Then shalt thou see the dew-bedabbled wretch
> Turn, and return, indenting with the way.
> Each envious briar his weary legs do scratch,
> Each shadow makes him stop, each murmur stay:
> For misery is trodden on by many,
> And being low, never reliev'd of any.
>
> (679-84; 703-8)

Itself constructed like one of those secret "musits" or priest-holes through which outlawed Catholics evaded capture, **Venus and Adonis** conceals politics beneath erotics; yet behind the false facade of an erotic narrative the text discloses its topicality as nothing less than a "Bloody Question" of loyalty or betrayal, when the boy is warned that Cynthia will "obscure her silver shine" from him until his own mother-goddess, "nature," is "condemn'd of treason" (**Venus** ll. 728-9).

In her study of the multi-faceted "Gloriana," Frances Yates explains how Cynthia, the moon, was a name for Elizabeth in Protestant guise, as "The virgin of imperial reform who withstood the claims of the Papacy [by] shedding beams of pure religion"; whereas the Queen could be opportunistically aligned with Venus, or even the Virgin Mary, in her other mask as "a nursing mother" to her erstwhile Catholics. Yet what Yates also notes is that Shakespeare's treatment of this ambivalent symbolism—in episodes like the one in *Titus Andronicus* where the sign of Virgo is shot to pieces with arrows—was "so surprising and unconventional . . . so remote from the stock-in-trade of a court poet," as to "leave an eternal question-mark against his name" (75-80). Certainly, the moon of his poem is quite unlike the "Queen and huntress, chaste and fair," worshipped in court festivities,[6] being "cloudy and forlorn," and the authoress of

> . . . the tyranny
> Of mad mischances and much misery:
> As burning feavers, agues pale and faint,
> Life-poisoning pestilence and frenzies wood,
> The marrow-eating sickness whose attaint
> Disorder breeds by heating of the blood.
>
> (737-42)

With "Surfeits, imposthumes, grief and damned despair" her malign effects, this jealous despot plots "nature's death" because Adonis is "so fair" (743-4); and the insinuation seems obvious, as it is in *A Midsummer Night's Dream*, that while her people remain with "no hymn or carol blest," the writer will not be deceived by moonshine into love for this Queen of the Night:

> Therefore the moon, the governess of floods,
> Pale in her anger, washes all the air,

That rheumatic diseases do abound.
And thorough this distemperature we see
The seasons alter . . .

(Dream, 1.1.73)

Shakespeare's caricature, in **Venus and Adonis,** of a suspicious, vindictive and self-pitying moon, who provokes rebellion when she "attaints" for treason those suffering "The marrow-eating sickness" of despair, prefigures the "cold," "fruitless," "wandering," "wat'ry" planet of the *Midsummer Night's Dream* (1.1.73; 2.1.156-162; 4.1.98), whose decrepitude prompts such impatience in the land:

> But O, methinks, how slow
> This old moon wanes! She lingers my desires,
> Like to a step-dame or a dowager,
> Long withering-out a young man's revenue.

(1.1.3-6)

The wicked crone of the comedy, who spies through windows pretending a "maiden meditation, fancy free" (2.1.164), shows how far Aesopian satire could go "to disfigure . . . the person of Moonshine" (3.1.60-1) on the public stage; but the oppositional politics of the **Venus and Adonis** are already blatant when Adonis is assured that "one minute's fight" with Cynthia will "bring [his] beauty under; / Both favour, savour, hue and qualities, / Whereat th'impartial gazer late did wonder" (746-8). It is a chilling prophecy, which connects the text to "The place of death and sorry execution / Behind the ditches" of Holywell that is the terminus of *The Comedy of Errors* (5.1.121-2). In that optimistic scenario an Abbess emerges from her convent as if to rescue martyrdom from hanging, disembowelling and quartering; but in the poem the tender mercies of the Queen seem equally pitiless, as Venus "murders" resistance "with a kiss," like a ravenous eagle tearing "with her beak on feathers, flesh and bone, / Shaking her wings, devouring all in haste, / Till either gorge be stuff'd or prey be gone" (54-8). A Jove with Ganymede, this "vulture" kills the "yielding prey" she claims to love: "Her lips are conquerors," as "With blindfold fury she begins to forage" (549-54). So, if this is allegory, its desperation seems close to that of the *Humble Supplication* Southwell wrote in December 1591, begging his "most merciful and best beloved Princess" to own up to the executions, tortures and extortions inflicted on the Catholics in her care:

> We presume that your Majesty never heareth the truth of our persecutions, your lenity and tenderness being known to be so professed an enemy to these cruelties that you would never permit their continuance, if they were expressed to your Highness as they are practised upon us. Yet, since we can bring the ruin of our houses . . . the poverty of our estates, and the weeping eyes of our desolate families for witnesses of the truth of these complaints, let us not be so far exiled out of all

> compassion, as besides all other evils, to have it confirmed under your Majesty's hand, *that we suffer no punishments for Religion*—suffering in proof all punishments for nothing else.

(Quoted in Devlin 252)

It is in light of the regime's hypocritical denial of persecution, and disingenuous claim that "Our gaolers are guilty of felony . . . if they torment any prisoner committed to their custody,"[7] that the irony of Shakespeare's portrait of the "Queen of Love" (251) can best be read. For if the whorishness of the "love-sick Queen" (175) towards her helpless victim analogises Elizabeth's exploitation of loyal papists, the police state she mobilises against suspected enemies is also starkly recognizable. As Venus herself admits, "where Love reigns, disturbing Jealousy / Doth call himself Affection's sentinel," and surveillance depends on the "sour informer," "bate-breeding spy," "carry-tale" and "dissentious" *agent-provocateur,* who "Gives false alarms, suggesteth mutiny, / And in a peaceful hour doth cry, 'Kill, kill!'" (649-60). This is the paranoid system operated by the infamous priest-hunter, Richard Topcliffe, that involved planting in all Catholic "houses and chambers, traitors, spies, intelligencers, and promoters that take watch for all their ways, words, and writings,"[8] and which gave him, as the poem records, a sinister hold on Elizabeth: "For who hath she to spend the night withal, / But . . . parasites, / Like shrill-tongu'd tapsters answering every call . . . She says, ''Tis so,' they answer all, ''Tis so,' / And would say after her, if she said 'No.'" (847-52).

In fact, Shakespeare's anatomy of the court—where the Queen berates her security chief, Death, as a "Grim-grinning ghost . . . ugly, meagre, lean" (931-3), but then "adds honours to his hateful name . . . Tells him of trophies, statues, tombs" (994, 1113)—accurately reports the duplicity of this reign of terror, which Elizabeth was liable to disown (as she did the execution of Mary Stuart) by setting one faction against another: "''Tis not my fault, the boar provok'd my tongue: / Be wreak'd on him, invisible commander'" (1003-4). In 1592 this is surely the limit of comment on a monarch whose "sick heart commands her [eyes] to watch" with such suspicion (584), though it does provide the possibility of a startlingly negative picture of the "ageless" Eliza:

> Were I ill-favour'd, foul, or wrinkled old,
> Ill-nurtur'd, crooked, churlish, harsh of voice,
> O'erworn, despised, rheumatic and cold,
> Thick-sighted, barren, lean, and lacking juice,
> > Then mightst thou pause, for then I were not for thee;
> > But having no defects, why dost abhor me?
>
> Thou canst not see one wrinkle in my brow . . .
> My beauty as the spring doth yearly grow . . .

(133-41)

Romantic critics have sentimentalised Shakespeare's relations with his monarch, but the sceptical portrait that emerges from **Venus and Adonis** in fact corresponds to the irreverence of the circle in which it was composed, typified by Swithin Wells, a tutor to the Earl of Southampton, when he praised the Bull excommunicating Elizabeth with the jest to his hangman, "Better a roaring bull than a diseased cow" (quoted in Devlin 238-9). For it is the Dedication "To the Right Honourable Henry Wriothesley" which places the poem firmly at the heart of recusant England. Wriothesley's papist sympathies have always been downplayed by Shakespeareans, but by 1592 the nineteen-year-old Earl had replaced Philip Howard, the imprisoned Earl of Arundel, as the great hope of Catholic resistance. He inherited his religion from his father, who had solved the problem whether "subjects of this land may, with safe conscience, obey the Queen as our Righteous Princess," by deciding that "it were better to lose all he had," and paid with his life, dying suddenly in suspicious circumstances soon after aiding the Jesuit Edmund Campion (Akrigg 9-10). Southampton's mother was a Montagu, however, and in her widowhood sustained the Montagu tradition of piety by keeping sanctuaries for priests at Cowdray Park in Sussex and Southampton House in Holborn. So, though it was often raided for massing books and missionaries, the Wriothesley's London home survived as a London headquarters of the Old Religion, and a counterweight to Cecil House, where the Earl was held hostage, from the age of nine to twelve, in the guardianship of Burghley. As he approached maturity, therefore, this son of "the most illustrious and leading Catholic in England,"[9] became the prize in a fierce ideological struggle, which reached a crisis when Burghley commanded him to marry his own granddaughter. Instead, the boy pleaded for time and conferred with a priest. Years later, Topcliffe discovered that Southampton's spiritual adviser at this turning-point had been a cousin: young "Father Robert"—the Jesuit, Southwell.[10]

"The young Earl of Southampton refusing the Lady de Vere," reported the Jesuit Henry Garnet in 1594, "payeth £5,000 of present payment" (Rowse 103). The minute is important as a record not only of the colossal cost of thwarting the Lord Treasurer, but of the interest invested by Rome in Wriothesley's resistance. This was, perhaps, what the poet meant by inscribing **Venus and Adonis** to "so noble a godfather," and commending the Earl "to your heart's content, which I wish may always answer your own wish, and the world's hopeful expectation." As critics long ago noted, Shakespeare's poem is the only version of the Adonis story in which the boy resists the goddess, and in diverging so radically from the sources, it may have "functioned as a form of advice literature which enabled Southampton to avoid complicity" with his guardian (Murphy 323-40). Thus, G. P. V. Akrigg has argued that in **Venus and**

Adonis Shakespeare is "discreetly excusing his lordship's aversion to marriage . . . knowing how Southampton had begged old Burghley for more time before taking a bride." Akrigg sees the poem as a reply, therefore, to the first work dedicated to the teenage patron: *Narcissus,* written in 1591 by John Clapham, a clerk in Burghley's office (195-6). But the trouble with this reading, as recent editors point out, is that *Narcissus* is hardly an argument for marriage, since it consists of a diatribe against Cupid that shifts into an attack on self-love (Martindale 151). Nor is the grisly fate of Shakespeare's Adonis a compelling advertisement for bachelorhood. Read alongside Southwell's poem, however, the texts do form a sequence, in which Peter glories in the martyrdom that annihilates Adonis and Narcissus. As a group, then, they suggest the young Earl may have contemplated a choice far more subversive than misogamy, when he talked with "Father Robert" in the chapel of the Montagues. Venus spells it out, when she says that worse than infanticide, suicide or civil war is the calling to the Roman Church:

> Therefore despite of fruitless chastity,
> Love-lacking vestals and self-loving nuns,
> That on the earth would breed a scarcity
> And barren dearth of daughters and of sons,
>   Be prodigal; the lamp that burns by night
>   Dries up his oil to lend the world his light.
>
> (751-56)

In Clapham's poem, Narcissus, "nurtured with the warm milk of Error," joins the young men who throng, "as massed crows seek dead bodies," to the temple of Cupid, enthroned in the clouds. Struck in the heart with an arrow, the boy says: "I am yours . . . I will be Love's slave," and bends his knee. Then Love addresses him from the throne: "As you are to others, be always loveable to yourself. Thus your opinion of yourself will allure you until you are caught by a shadow and perish." So saying, Love plucks a branch steeped in the water of Lethe and sprinkling it over his brow, says, "Henceforth, Narcissus, you will not know yourself" (Martindale 159-63). With its black "massed crows" and incense clouds, this seems such a transparent skit on the Jesuits at Saint Peter's that the surprise is that it has never been decoded; but it does offer an intriguing new perspective on the lesson that "Narcissus so himself forsook, / And died to kiss his shadow in the brook" (161-2), not only as it appears in **Venus and Adonis,** but also in the Sonnets on the "Sin of self-love" (**Sonnets** 62). It had been Southwell, after all, who perfected what Louis Martz calls the "sacred parody" of sexual love (186), by arguing that "If on thy beauty God enamoured be, / Base is thy love of any less than he";[11] and when Burghley's secretary scorned such sublimation, he may have been cued by the fervent homoeroticism in which the Jesuit moved. Famous himself, in his black satin, as "The beauteous English youth," Southwell taught that God made a seminarian handsome so that "who so viewed his person might desire like comeliness of soul"; but when he was escorted round Cambridge by a "bevy of aristocratic youths" (which may have included Southampton) the "boy priest" was asking for his self-fashioning to be misconstrued.[12] As Robert Ellrodt remarks, in this Counter-Reformation culture care of the self quickly hardened into egotism as "self-centredness became self-display" (12). Shakespeare may be closer to the Protestant clerk, therefore, than the Catholic cleric, when he has Venus castigate self-love:

> Is thine own heart to thine own face affected?
> Can thy right hand seize love upon thy left?
> Then woo thyself, be of thyself rejected;
> Steal thine own freedom, and complain on theft.

(157-60)

"To grow unto himself was his desire" (1180): Adonis' epitaph acquires a tragic urgency if it refers to the recusant doctrine of conscience, and if the techniques of self-examination taught by Southwell inspire his plea: "Before I know myself, seek not to know me" (525). Then, this doomed youth would no longer figure selfish adolescence, but the self-immolation of an entire generation of Catholic emigres, lost to the Queen as "a bright star shooteth from the sky," and mourned by the England they abandoned: "as one on shore / Gazing upon a late embarked friend, / Till the wild waves will have him seen no more, / Whose ridges with the meeting clouds contend" (815-20). In 1592 this was exactly the exile beckoning Southampton, as he weighed the "Bloody Question" and the order to dismount the "trampling courser" of "imperious" Spain (261-5). For when Venus woos Adonis to "alight [his] steed . . . rein his proud head to the saddle-bow," and "come and sit, where never serpent hisses" (13-17), she not only talks in the language of resistance (where Hapsburg warhorses conventionally trampled the Tudor snake), but poses the choice between St. George and the Dragon as a dilemma that would have been acutely relevant to the Earl. Thus, while his grandfather, Lord Montagu, was a model of loyal compliance, who entertained the Queen at Cowdray in 1591, his brother-in-law, Thomas Arundell, actually enlisted in the imperial army of Rudolf II. On a knife-edge, therefore, between treason and betrayal, Southampton was uniquely placed to grasp how for his generation "the question" was indeed (as Hamlet says) whether "to suffer / The slings and arrows of outrageous fortune, / Or to take arms against a sea of troubles / And by opposing end them" (*Hamlet* 3.1.56-9). So, when he read **Venus and Adonis,** Shakespeare's patron can have had no doubt about the political implications of the boy's decision, when he spurns the Queen's embrace, "And homeward through the dark laund runs apace" (813).

If the Earl's surname was pronounced "Rosely," as historians confirm, his journey home would have carried this "Rose-cheek'd Adonis" (3) to an equally evocative place, since Boarhunt is the name of the wooded region between his mansion at Titchfield and the sea. Here Southampton would have returned to the hunting country that was the last hideaway of Catholicism in southern England, and to a chain of safe-houses which ran from Titchfield along the Channel coast. And here he would have been welcomed back into "a tightly-knit clan of recusant families who provided Catholic leadership in Sussex and Hampshire," and "preserved their faith in face of persecution by quasi-feudal marital alliances and economic interdependence" (Manning 156). All his father's executors were from this papist ring; his "earthly mother" was determined (as the poem hints) to restore him to its "light" (863-4); and, like Adonis, he was keenly "expected of his friends" (718). The text almost begs us to identify the group, when the boy excuses his absence from the Queen: "He tells her no, tomorrow he intends / To hunt the boar with certain of his friends" (587-8). And if these hunting friends are those said in the Dedication to have such "hopeful expectation," it is tempting to guess their identity, as they might have been the poem's first reading community. "Certain friends" of Southampton, then, meant the Montagu, Copley, Shelley, and Gage families, who formed "a particularly strategic link between the continental seminaries and London," by operating "a communication network that smuggled priests from south-coast ports" to the capital (Manning 156). When Topcliffe cracked this system, he discovered that the route led up to Southampton House via Cowdray, with missionaries disguised in the Montagu livery, but that its orchestrator was imprisoned in the Marshalsea. He was Southampton's uncle, Thomas Pound, whose mansion in the woods near Boarhunt was a vital entry-point from France. For a haven of Catholic relief, this house also carried a suggestive name, as it was called Belmont.

"Come ho! And wake Diana with a hymn": the sacred music that rouses Belmont in *Merchant of Venice,* while its owner "doth stray about / By holy crosses where she kneels and prays," is sung expressly to dissociate the household from all "treasons, stratagems, and spoils" against a Protestant Queen (*Merchant* 5.1.30-1.66, 85); but under the mantle of Southampton's mother and grandmother the Montagu houses in Sussex and Hampshire sustained, even after the death of the old Lord in 1592, a freedom of worship "not seen in all England besides," and astonished visitors by the size of their chapels and the boldness with which Mass was celebrated "with singing and musical instruments."[13] Likewise, the master of Belmont continued to operate in prison as "a great maintainer of priests,"[14] and made his cell a port of call for priests. The importance of Southampton's uncle was that he funded the Sodality of young aristocrats formed in 1580 to imitate the French Catholic League which may have recruited the teenage

Shakespeare. Moreover, he could have been the link-man between the poet and his patron, as it was he who converted to the priesthood the London schoolteacher, Thomas Cottam, who was the brother of John Cottam, the Master of Stratford Grammar School and a protege of Shakespeare's first Lancashire benefactors. In fact, Thomas Pound might be considered a guardian angel of the poet's world, since he not only connected Midland recusancy to the southern network through his South-wark base, but exercised that restraint over his "race of youthful and unhandled colts" which Shakespeare attributes to the influence of Belmont (*Merchant* 5.1.72). By always drawing "a careful distinction between what they considered to be legitimate means of preserving their faith and what could be construed as treason" (Manning 161), Pound and the Montagues saved their kinsmen from decimation; but moving between them, smuggled into some hunting party, slipped Father Robert, preaching, by contrast, the politics of refusal coded in his poems: that the Queen of Love is a "tyrant cruel" and "Lewd Love is Loss" compared to "True love in Heav'n."[15] It cannot be chance, therefore, that when Adonis finally rejects Venus, he does so in what sounds exactly like a parody of the homely similes of Southwell:

> Call it not love, for love to heaven is fled,
> Since sweating lust on earth usurp'd his name;
> Under whose simple semblance she hath fed
> Upon fresh beauty, blotting it with blame;
>   Which the hot tyrant stains and soon bereaves,
>   As caterpillars do the tender leaves.
>
> Love comforteth like sunshine after rain,
> But lust's effect is tempest after sun;
> Love's gentle spring doth always fresh remain,
> Lust's winter comes ere summer half be done;
>   Love surfeits not, lust like a glutton dies;
>   Love is all truth, lust full of forged lies.
>
> (793-804)

"Hunting he lov'd, but love he laughed to scorn" (l. 4): from its opening lines, the politics of *Venus and Adonis* are expressed in the oppositional terms of the recusant culture that promoted the poet from the heartland of the Old Religion, in Warwickshire, to feudal Lancashire, and then to the clan around the Earl of Southampton, in the other bulwark of Catholic resistance. It was Ted Hughes who noticed that Shakespeare's first poem is, in fact, a version of Catholicism's founding myth, "of the Mother Goddess and her dying son." Hughes saw the Bard as "the shaman of Old Catholicism," who wrote, "from a secret and passionate (even fanatic) cell of illicit religious loyalty," a lament over "the threatened extermination of the Catholic tribe"; but he then deciphered the text as a nightmare in which the Puritan Adonis spurns "the Catholic Church, personified . . . by the Great Goddess of Love."[16] In other words, Hughes overlooked the historic irony that a Protestant

Queen had usurped the Virgin Mary, even as her Catholic sons had adopted the Counter-Reformation's puritanical clothes. Shakespeare carried this irony over from Narcissus, however (where Venus is expressly identified as the Virgin Queen who rules "the Fortunate Island" in the West),[17] and made it the reason for his dire alteration when, for the first time ever, Love is refused. *Venus and Adonis* is thus more topical than even Hughes supposed, because it presents the "Bloody Question" confronting Shakespeare's generation as a catastrophic ultimatum not from some "Goddess of Complete Being," but a Queen of Hell. For if Adonis and his friends do make up a group portrait of the knot of Catholic nobles in league against Elizabeth, there can be no doubt that the creature who is their nemesis is the Queen's own thing of darkness: in reality, the arch-priest-hunter and grand inquisitor who would drag them down to ruin, and whose very name was as much an omen as the Earl's: the "boar"—or Burghley himself:

> But this foul, grim, and urchin-snouted boar
> Whose downward eye still looketh for a grave,
> Ne'er saw the beauteous livery that he wore
> Witness the entertainment that he gave.
>
> 'Tis true, 'tis true, thus was Adonis slain:
> He ran upon the boar with his sharp spear,
> Who did not whet his teeth at him again,
> But by a kiss thought to persuade him there;
>   And nuzzling in his flank, the loving swine
>   Sheath'd unaware the tusk in his soft groin.
>
> (1105-16)

"His courage, nobility, gentleness, and the beauty of his face and form, so won the hearts of all," recalled Father Garnet of Southwell's execution, "that even the mob gave their verdict that this was the properest man that ever came to Tyburn for hanging." The "beautiful English youth" had gone to the gallows protesting that "I never intended, God Almighty knows, to commit any treason to the Queen" (quoted in Devlin 320-21); but in *Venus and Adonis* his cousin had predicted how, if he refused her embrace, Burghley would still be content to "nuzzle in his flank" to mutilate and castrate him, "Like to a mortal butcher bent to kill" (618). Shakespeare knew enough about the erotics of martyrdom to foretell how, like Campion, a "boy priest" would be amorously "entertained" by the "swine" who tortured and killed him; and sure enough, the hangman "took him down with great reverence and carried him in his own arms, assisted by his companions, to the place where he was to be quartered. . . . [And] when he was being disembowelled, his heart leapt into the hands of the executioner. All who stood around spoke of him with respect and there was none to cry "Traitor" according to custom" (quoted in Marotti 52). There was even a coda to confirm the poem's final perverted *pieta*, when Elizabeth was visited by one of the witnesses. He was a friend of Southampton, Lord Mountjoy, who had asked

Southwell on his last night "whether it was true that he had come to detach subjects from obedience to the Queen. To [which] the Father replied that his intention had never been anything but the good of their souls." Next day, Mountjoy had stepped forward to prevent the hangman from cutting the rope before the victim had died; and now he had come to the Queen, he explained, to prove to her that the young man had been innocent of politics:

> When the Queen had heard him, she replied that they had all deceived her with calumnies telling her that the Father had come to raise sedition; and she showed signs of grief for his death, especially when she saw the book he had composed in the English tongue on different topics, pious and devout . . . a book designed to teach Poets how to safeguard their talent and employ it as befitted.

> (Quoted in Devlin 317-18)

"She bows her head, the new-sprung flower to smell, / Comparing it to her Adonis' breath, / And says within her bosom it shall dwell" (1171-3): if Elizabeth wept over Southwell's book, it must have been a performance of the crocodile tears she had already shed for so many other "bright stars," such as Campion. Like Venus, however, she was also careful to "crop the stalk" (1175) of martyrdom, by burning all remains, so as to deprive Catholics of those "handkerchiefs dipped in blood" or "pieces of bone and hair" for which they begged (Devlin 324). So, when she read Southwell's criticism of *Venus and Adonis,* was she sincerely persuaded that, compared to other poets, it proved the martyr an innocent? And was this why Shakespeare had "importuned" his cousin to publish it? If so, the Queen may have had a shrewder insight than the Jesuit into the real oppositional politics of Shakespeare's poem. For there, the young Earl had been confronted not with a glorification of martyrdom, but with a parable of its futility in the sadistic arms of a "hard-favour'd tyrant" (931) and a state "most deceiving when it seems most just" (1156). The playwright, it appears, understood better than the priest the "Bloody Question" of loyalty and treason. Though he was happy to celebrate his patron's own later escape from execution—and to rejoice at the death of the old "tyrant" herself when "the mortal moon her eclipse endured" (*Sonnets* 107)—he clearly had no illusions either that his "loving cousin" and the other martyrs were anything but what he called them—after history had turned the traitors into heroes—"the fools of time, / Which die for goodness, who have liv'd for crime" (*Sonnets* 124).

Notes

1. This is a revised version of an essay published in *William Shakespeare, Venus and Adonis: nouvelles perspectives critiques,* ed. Jean-Marie Maguin and Charles Walters Whitworth (Montpellier: Université Paul-Valéry, 1999).

2. Cited in James H. McDonald, *The Poems and Prose Writings of Robert Southwell* 134. See also Richard Dutton, *Ben Jonson: Authority: Criticism* 134. The poem admired so much by Jonson was "The Burning Babe."

3. "Christ's Return out of Egypt," ll. 17-18 in *Poems* 10.

4. "Scorn not the least," ll. 13-16, in *Poems* 69.

5. Devlin 208-9.

6. Ben Jonson, "Hymn to Diana," from *Cynthia's Revels,* in *Poems of Ben Jonson* 261.

7. Harrison's *Description of England* (1587), quoted in Devlin 212.

8. William Allen, *Admonition to the Nobility and People of England* (1588), quoted in Lacey Baldwin Smith, *Treason in Tudor England* 159-60.

9. Letter of Thomas Stephens (page to Thomas Pounde), Stonyhurst MSS., *Collectio Cardwelli,* f. 16; quoted Devlin 14.

10. Devlin 219. Southwell's connection with Southampton—he was twice a cousin by marriage—meant that Shakespeare was also distantly related to the Earl.

11. Southwell, "At Home in Heaven," 29-30, in *Poems* 56.

12. Southwell, unpublished ms. quoted, *Poems,* xxii; Devlin 26, 185-6.

13. Devlin 159-60.

14. Government informer quoted in Thomas Graves Law, *Jesuits and Seculars in the Reign of Elizabeth* 137.

15. Southwell, "Love's Servile Lot," 41; "Lewd Love is Loss," 12, in *Poems* 60-3.

16. Ted Hughes, *Shakespeare and the Goddess of Complete Being* 12, 57, 86, 90, et passim.

17. Martindale and Burrow 159, 173.

Works Cited

Akrigg, G. P. V. *Shakespeare and the Earl of Southampton.* London: Hamish Hamilton, 1968.

Allen, William. *Admonition to the Nobility and People of England* (1588), quoted in Lacey Baldwin Smith, *Treason in Tudor England.* London: Jonathan Cape, 1986.

Brown, Nancy Pollard. "Robert Southwell: The Mission of the Written Word," in *The Reckoned Expense: Edmund Campion and the Early English Jesuits,* ed. Thomas M. McCoog. Woodbridge England: Boydell Press, 1996.

Devlin, Christopher. *The Life of Robert Southwell, Poet and Martyr.* London: Longmans, 1956.

Dutton, Richard. *Ben Jonson: Authority: Criticism.* London: Macmillan, 1996.

Ellrodt, Robert. "The Search for Identity: Montaigne to Donne." *Confluences* XI. Paris: Centre de recherches sur les origines de la modernite et les pays anglophones, 1995. 12.

Fraser, Antonia. *The Gunpowder Plot.* London: Weidenfeld & Nicolson, 1995.

Hughes, Ted. *Shakespeare and the Goddess of Complete Being.* London: Faber & Faber, 1992.

Jonson, Ben. *Poems of Ben Jonson,* ed. George Burke Johnston. London: Routledge, 1954.

Law, Thomas Graves. *Jesuits and Seculars in the Reign of Elizabeth.* London: David Nutt, 1889.

McDonald, James H. *The Poems and Prose Writings of Robert Southwell, S.J., A Bibliographical Study.* Oxford England: Clarendon Press, 1937.

Manning, Roger B. *Religion and Society in Elizabethan Sussex.* Leicester England: Leicester University Press, 1969.

Marotti, Arthur. "Southwell's Remains: Catholicism and Anti-Catholicism in Early Modern England." In *Texts and Cultural Change in Early Modern England,* ed. Cedric Brown & Arthur Marotti. Basingstoke: Macmillan, 1997.

Martindale, Charles, and Colin Burrow. "Clapham's *Narcissus*: A Pre-Text for Shakespeare's *Venus and Adonis?*" *English Literary Renaissance* 22:2 (Spring 1992): 147-75.

Martz, Louis. *The Poetry of Meditation.* New Haven CT: Yale University Press, 1962.

Murphy, Patrick M. "Wriothesley's Resistance: Wardship Practices and Ovidian Narratives in Shakespeare's *Venus and Adonis.*" In *Venus and Adonis: Critical Essays,* ed. Philip Kohn. New York: Garland, 1997. 323-40.

Rowse, A. L. *Shakespeare's Southampton.* London: Macmillan, 1965.

Shakespeare, William. *The Riverside Shakespeare.* Ed. G. Blakemore Evans, with the assistance of J. J. M. Tobin. 2nd ed. Boston MA: Houghton Mifflin, 1997.

Southwell, Robert. *The Poems of Robert Southwell, S.J.* Ed. James H. McDonald and Nancy Pollard Brown. Oxford England: Clarendon Press, 1967.

———. *Saint Peter's Complaint and Saint Mary Magdalen's Funeral Tears.* St. Omer: Society of Jesus, 1616.

Speed, John. *The History of Great Britain* (London, 1611). In *The Shakespeare Allusion Book,* ed. John Munro. London: Chatto & Windus, 1909. Vol. 1.

Taylor, Gary. "Forms of Opposition: Shakespeare and Middleton." *English Literary Renaissance* 24 (Spring 1994): 283-314.

Yates, Frances A. *Astraea: The Imperial Theme in the Sixteenth Century.* Harmondsworth: Penguin, 1977.

Signe Hansen (essay date 2001)

SOURCE: Hansen, Signe. "Shakespeare's Un(w)holy Trinities: Female Identity in *Venus and Adonis* and *The Rape of Lucrece*." *Shakespeare in Southern Africa* 13 (2001): 65-75.

[*In the essay that follows, Hansen posits that Venus and Lucrece can each be viewed as being comprised of three separate parts, and that, based on Renaissance notions of feminine morality and sexuality, these different aspects conflict with one another.*]

Shakespeare's **Venus and Adonis** and **The Rape of Lucrece** both figure a woman as one of two central characters. In the first, Venus tries to seduce Adonis; in the second, Lucrece is raped by Tarquin. Structurally then, these female characters are cast in opposite roles as, respectively, subject and object of desire. Despite these contrary positions, however, a consistency exists between the female identities in the two poems: both are represented as being essentially tripartite. The following discussion will examine this representation of female identity as consisting of three—at times conradictory—qualities, each of which is, as we shall see, grounded in Renaissance conceptions of gender. It is therefore important to stress that 'female identity' is not synonymous with 'femininity'; I will argue that 'femininity' constitutes but a part of the whole that is female identity. The contradictions that arise between the three parts are, precisely, due to that which is not 'feminine,' that is, I suggest, due to the discordance between Renaissance virtues of femininity and the more threatening (to males) aspect of female identity: sexuality.

In **Venus and Adonis,** Venus demonstrates qualities of lover and mother, as well as occupying the structurally masculine position of seducer. Following Ted Hughes, I maintain that this masculinity finally manifests itself in the form of the boar,[1] which, by killing Adonis, signifies the danger that female sexual desire poses to men. There is, then, a clear disparity between Venus's nurturing qualities as lover and mother and her destructive capabilities as desiring woman. Moreover, Shakespeare's recourse to a boar to depict this final aspect of

Venus's character intimates the unrepresentability of female sexuality and thus stresses its incongruousness with 'femininity.'

In *Lucrece,* the dividedness of female identity—represented externally in *Venus and Adonis*—is internalised in the separation of Lucrece's blood into three colours. This is not to say that a simplistic parallel exists between the two poems, or to assert, as Hughes does, that "*Lucrece* is the same event as *Venus and Adonis* on a different level; it is . . . the second half of a binary whole" (1992, 82). The aim of this discussion is not to impose structural or thematic unity on the two poems; it is, rather, to examine the similarities that exist between the representations of two female characters that are cast in radically differing roles, that undergo radically different experiences, that themselves have radically different perspectives on femininity and female sexuality. Lucrece is depicted as the ideally beautiful and virtuous wife and mother who embraces and embodies the Neoplatonic belief in the harmony between body and soul. Her experience of rape disrupts this belief by introducing aggressive sexuality to the equation. Granted, it is not originally her sexuality, but her tri-coloured blood testifies to the fact that, despite her virtuosity, this sexuality has, indeed, become intrinsic to her conclusive identity. Finally, in light of the unrepresentability of female sexuality, I contend that it is of crucial importance that the sexualised component of Lucrece's identity is revealed at her death. This suggests that Shakespeare is ultimately unable to consolidate the three aspects of female identity that he represents. The moment sexuality is introduced to complete a (realistic) portrayal of female identity, it is diverted: in *Venus and Adonis,* to the boar; in *Lucrece,* to suicide and a (male) republican revolution. So, in these two poems Shakespeare at once alludes to the tripartite unity of female identity and dismantles that unity by disallowing the threatening sexual component to remain in place.

To initiate the action of *Venus and Adonis,* we are told that Venus, "like a bold-faced suitor 'gins to woo" (6) Adonis. The word "like" stresses that the role of suitor can only be used as a simile to describe Venus—she cannot be a suitor, because she is not a man. This is an important indicator of Renaissance conceptions of gender that maintained quite definitive ideas about what was expected of men and women. Sir Thomas Elyot's *The Book Named the Governor* provides an instructive example:

> A man in his natural perfection is fierce, hardy, strong in opinion, covetous of glory, desirous of knowledge, appetiting by generation to bring forth his semblable. The good nature of a woman is to be mild, timorous, tractable, benign, of sure remembrance, and shamefast.
>
> (580)

In this context, Venus's behaviour is undeniably masculine: she threatens Adonis ("If thou wilt chide, thy lips will never open" (48); he accuses her of being "immodest" (53); she boasts of having had Mars, the "stern and direful god of war" (98), as her "captive and . . . slave" (101); she is likened to bird of prey ("as an empty eagle, sharp by fast" (55), whereas Adonis is merely a bird "tangled in a net" (68). And, on a rhetorical level, she idealises him in the familiar male voice of *Sonnets 1-126,* but now from a woman's perspective ("The field's chief flower, sweet above compare, / Stain to all nymphs, more lovely than a man, / more white or red than doves or roses are—Nature that made thee with herself at strife / Saith that the world has ending with thy life" (7-12).)

These masculine qualities and behaviour do not, however, unproblematically confer 'femininity' on Adonis. He is, on one level, in the female position of being wooed, and "burns with bashful shame" (49) at Venus's advances. Assuming that the stallion and mare represent the 'natural' course of male-female desire, Adonis's timidity can, at first, be read like that of the jennet: "Being proud, as females are, to see him woo her, / She puts on outward strangeness, seems unkind" (309). But, as it turns out, Adonis is not playing hard-to-get; he has no sexual desire. And this lack of desire, as Venus articulates it, implies, precisely, the lack of a female quality:

> Art thou a woman's son, and canst not feel
> What 'tis to love, how want of love tormenteth?
>
> (201-2)

> Fie, lifeless picture, cold and senseless stone
> Well painted idol, image dull and dead,
> Statue contenting but the eye alone,
> Thing like a man, but of no woman bred.
>
> (211-14)

This paradoxically suggests that Adonis is not responding to sexual advances as would be expected of a man, but that this expectation is fundamentally based on the man's identity as the son of a woman. That is, man's desire is predicated on his 'female side.' Or, put more simply, desire—and thus the desiring subject—is feminine. In this light, Adonis's lack of desire can be read as a rejection of his femininity. In her discussion of *The Merchant of Venice,* Catherine Belsey proposes a similar argument: "Passion . . . renders men effeminate, incapable of manly pursuits; it threatens identity, arousing fears that subjectivity itself is unstable" (1995, 199). This statement is suggestive of the fear underlying Adonis's cynical declaration that his "love to love is love but to disgrace it" (412)[2]: the stability of his (one-dimensional) masculine identity is based on the exclusion of desire. Venus's appellation of Adonis as a "well painted idol" and a "statue" implies that his lack of desire renders him unnatural; not unlike, I would suggest, the effect of Petrarchan idealism that places woman on a figurative pedestal. This similarity emphasises the non-sexual nature of the ideal woman (and man) and at the same time sets Venus apart in her complex role as masculine/feminine desiring subject.

These contradictions of female identity are not easily reconcilable. On the contrary, Venus's lament that she is not a man underscores, again, the one-dimensionality of Adonis's male identity[3] as opposed to the complexities she experiences as a woman:

> O fairest mover on this mortal round,
>   Would thou wert as I am, and I a man,
>   My heart as whole as thine, thy heart my wound
> For one sweet look thy help I would assure thee
> Though nothing but my body's bane would cure thee.
>
>   (368-72; my emphasis)

Doreen Feitelberg's comment that what is "particularly arresting about Venus is that even though she is a goddess with supernatural powers, there is no doubt about the fact that she is essentially a woman" (1994, 55) is pertinent in this context, because what the passage underlines is precisely her limitations as a woman and as a goddess. She cannot force Adonis to want her, but she is willing to forfeit her body for "one sweet look." This readiness to sacrifice herself posits Venus as one of Sir Elyot's "tractable" women, a desired quality that is reiterated in her wish that her heart remain impressionable ("O, give it me, lest thy heart do steel it, / And, being steeled, soft sighs can never grave it" (375-76)) and that Adonis "stamp" her with his kiss ("Set thy seal manual on my wax-red lips" (516)).[4]

Even so, there is a darker undercurrent to Venus's proclamations of submissiveness. After she states that she will do anything for him, Adonis counters her with, "I know not love . . . nor will not know it, / Unless it be a boar, and then I chase it" (409-10). This is, in my opinion, a pivotal moment in the poem: it initiates the manifestation of Venus's female desire in the external, male form of the boar. It is noteworthy that Hughes' interpretation of the boar as Venus's 'alter-ego' is primarily based on Shakespeare's possible sources for the narrative.[5] In my reading, however, the relationship between the two is textually evident in the affiliation between the boar and Venus's jealousy and, furthermore, in Venus's ambivalence towards the animal. When Adonis states that he will hunt the following day rather than meet Venus again (587-88), she turns "a sudden pale" (589), and explains her reaction as follows:

> Didst thou not mark my face? Was it not white?
>   Saw'st thou not signs of fear lurk in mine eye?
>
>   . . . . .
>
> My boding heart pants, beats, and takes no rest,
> But like an earthquake shakes thee on my breast.

> For where love reigns, disturbing jealousy
> Doth call himself affection's sentinel,
> Gives false alarms, suggesteth mutiny,
> And in a peaceful hour doth cry, 'Kill, kill!'
> Distemp'ring gentle love in his desire,
> As air and water do abate the fire.
>
>   (643-54)

In this way, an undeniable parallel is drawn between jealousy as a murderous quality (born of love) and the boar, "Like to a mortal butcher, sent to kill" (618). This affiliation between love and death—or Venus and the boar—is finally connoted in her prophetic words: "This sour informer / . . . / Knocks at my heart, and whispers in mine ear / That if I love, I thy death should fear" (655-60). This reading depends on an emphasis on the causal relationship between love and death, that is, that Adonis will die because Venus loves/desires him and he does not heed the destructive potential of female desire.

The appearance of the animal with a "frothy mouth, be-painted all with red, / Like milk and blood being mingled all together" (901-2) ironically conveys the conventional red-white colour imagery of adulatory rhetoric (previously used by Venus to describe Adonis) to the figure of the boar. The sight, portending that Adonis is dead, fuels Venus's rage and her subsequent tirade against death (931-54). But when she "hears some huntsman hollo" (973) and suspects that he is, after all, alive, she is quick to absolve herself:

> Tis not my fault, the boar provoked my tongue.
>   Be wreaked on him, invisible commander.
>   'Tis he, foul creature, that hath done thee wrong.
> I did but act; he's the author of thy slander.
>   Grief hath two tongues, and never woman yet
>   Could rule them both, without ten women's wit.
>
>   (1003-8)

This passage is highly indicative of the conflicting nature of Venus's identity. In the very act of blaming the boar to extricate herself, she asserts an uncanny relationship to the animal; a connection that enables her to 'act' on the boar's behalf, so to speak.[6] These two agents—actor and author—are then compounded in the word "grief," suggesting that they constitute two parts ("tongues") of a whole, and that in a woman, these two parts remain fundamentally irreconcilable. This ambivalence in Venus's identity is finally insinuated in her naming the boar a "foul, grim, and urchin-snouted" (1105) creature, only to call him "the loving swine" (1115) ten lines on. Speaking of either the boar or Venus, we might then, at this point, appropriate Troilus's phrase and say, in summary, "This is, and is not, Venus."

But the final image of Venus is neither that of masculine wooer nor of murderously jealous woman. It is of a mother:

Here was thy father's bed, here in my breast.
 Thou art the next of blood, and 'tis thy right.
 Lo, in this hollow cradle take thy rest:
 My throbbing heart shall rock thee day and night.

(1183-86)

Jonathan Bate uses this maternal imagery to relate *Venus and Adonis* to its Ovidian source, in which Adonis is conceived incestuously. Based on this, Bate suggests that the poem essentially concerns itself with what he terms "transgressive sexuality" (1993, 88) and, he goes on, "since it is supposed to be an etiology of sexual love—the goddess of love's own experience of desire sets the tone for everybody else's—there is a strong implication that sexual love is always at some level transgressive" (ibid.). My own reading of this maternal aspect of Venus's character is not that it signifies sexual transgression—a view that seems to me to partake in a mentality that deems female sexuality disreputable—but that it represents a fundamental component of the female self. As William Keach states: "What Shakespeare suggests with the implicitly incestuous maternal-filial imagery applied to *Venus and Adonis* is not a scandalous unnatural-ness, but a connection between the erotic and maternal aspects of the feminine psyche" (1977, 77). So, to conclude the discussion on *Venus and Adonis,* it is, by now, evident that the female identity represented in the poem is, variously—but not harmoniously—seductive, destructive and mothering, the complexity of which is thrown into relief by Adonis's one-dimensional character.

Whereas the initial description of Adonis's ideal beauty is delivered through Venus's direct speech, the first description of Lucrece is twice removed: the narrator reports on Collatine's words ("When Collatine unwisely did not let / To praise the clear unmatched red and white / Which triumphed in that sky of his delight / Where mortal stars as bright as heaven's beauties / With pure aspects did him peculiar duties," (10-14). This rhetoric stresses Lucrece's structural position in a male world where honour and beauty in a woman are qualities that belong to her husband ("Honour and beauty, in the owner's arms, / Are weakly fortressed from a world of harms," (27); "I'll beg her love—but she is not her own" (239). This fact of 'ownership' means that Collatine's praise of his wife is, in fact, him boasting about a possession that other men do not have. In a society informed by male power structures, Collatine's speech thus induces Tarquin's covetousness:

Perchance his boast of Lucrece' sov'reignty
 Suggested this proud issue of a king,
 For by our ears our hearts oft tainted be.
 Perchance that envy of so rich a thing
 Braving compare, disdainfully did sting
 His high-pitched thought, that meaner men should vaunt
 That golden hap which their superiors want.

(36-42)

Rape as the result of this envy sets up an intricate relationship between language, power and eroticism,[7] and helps to explain Nancy Vicker's chilling phrase: "Rape is the price Lucrece pays for having been described" (1999, 353).

The limitations of description are intimated when Tarquin actually sees Lucrece and reflects that "her husband's shallow tongue, / The niggard prodigal that praised her so, / In that high task hath done her beauty wrong" (78-80). This does not, however, signify a rejection of Petrarchan idealism (as in, for example, *Sonnet 130*). Quite the reverse: the image of Lucrece as seen by Tarquin and reported by the narrator simply exacerbates this form of idealism. In her face, we are told, "When virtue bragged, beauty would blush for shame; / When beauty boasted blushes, in despite / Virtue would stain that or with silver white" (54-6), resulting in a "silent war of lilies and roses" (71). Moreover, her external beauty reflects an inner sanctity:

This earthly saint adored by this devil
 Little suspecteth the false worshipper,
 For unstained thoughts do seldom dream on evil.

(85-87)

In this way, Lucrece is represented as an embodiment of the duality between body and soul. She is, so far, the ideal woman/wife. But it is important to note that the narrator implies that this duality is basically naive. Given her own purity, the "holy-thoughted Lucrece" (384) not only does not suspect Tarquin, but tries to restrain him with a tellingly weak argument: "Thou look'st not like deceit; do not deceive me" (585).

Lucrece's naivety and her exemplary looks and behaviour combine to provide a curious resemblance to Adonis's character. Lucrece is, like Adonis, compared to a statue ("like a virtuous monument she lies / To be admired of lewd unhallowed eyes" (391-92)), the lifelessness of which complements the narrator's remark, "Pure thoughts are dead and still" (167).[8] I have argued that Adonis's one-dimensionality is hinged on the elimination of (feminine) sexuality. Lucrece can, I maintain, be viewed in the same light: the naivety that results from her beauty and chastity is, precisely, ignorance about sexuality. In stark contrast to this ignorance is Tarquin, who, "madly tossed between desire and dread" (171), is fully aware of the complexities of his actions. He recognises the perplexing quality of lust that causes him to him to risk losing his own honour (also explored in *Sonnet 129*):

And die, unhallowed thoughts, before you blot
 With your uncleanness that which is divine.
 Offer pure incense to so pure a shrine.
 Let fair humanity abhor the deed
 That spots and stains love's modest snow-white weed.

> O shame to knighthood and to shining arms!
> O foul dishonour to my household's grave!
> O impious act including all foul harms!
> A martial man to be soft fancy's slave!'
>
> (192-200)

This acute awareness of the consequences of desiring the ideal (non-sexual) woman anticipates Angelo in *Measure for Measure*: "Shall we desire to raze the sanctuary, / And pitch our evils there? O, fie, fie! / What dost thou, or what an thou, Angelo? / Dost thou desire her foully for those things / That make her good?" (2.3.175-79). According to one Renaissance conception of love and desire, the virtue of the beloved is, indeed, indispensable. As Leone Ebreo's Philo states, "Prior to loving or desiring, we must know that the object of love or desire is good" (1967, 176). So, Tarquin and Angelo are thrown into sexual desire because of the "goodness" of Lucrece and Isabella, and they both experience this desire as a threat to their masculine identities, affirming Belsey's comment that passion "renders men effeminate." But Tarquin succeeds in reconciling desire with his masculinity by invoking a military metaphor:

> Affection is my captain, and he leadeth,
>   And when his gaudy banner is displayed;
>   The coward fights, and will not be dismayed.
>
> (271-73)

> Desire my pilot is, beauty my prize.
> Then who fears sinking where such treasure lies?
>
> (279-80)

Rape is thus figured as intrinsic to the construction of masculinity and is, thereby, justified in Tarquin's mind. Richard Lanham's opinion is dangerously close to this mentality: "Politics, war, love, they all amount to the same thing in this world—attack. Tarquin does what he does because that is all anyone in such a world can do, and this includes every allegorical personification in the poem—fight" (342; my emphases). True, a strong connection exists between power (or politics and war) and eroticism (or love),[9] a connection that enables Tarquin to threaten Lucrece into sexual submission (526-35). Yet the blatant exclusion of Lucrece—and women in general—from Lanham's collective 'anyone' renders this critical perspective symptomatic of the very same patriarchal configuration that relegates women to structural positions. In other words, by justifying Tarquin's behaviour, Lanham denies the existence of female subjecthood.

But Lucrece is there, and she is not able to fight; instead, "surfeit-taking Tarquin" (698) rapes her. The narrator's remark immediately following the rape provides, in my view, a crucial key to understanding the imminent division of her blood:

> O, that prone lust should stain so pure a bed,
>   The spots whereof could weeping purify,
>   Her tears should drop on them perpetually!
>
> (684-86)

The fact that only perpetual tears can reclaim the purity of Lucrece's bed (and body), implies that there is, finally, nothing to be done.[10] No matter how she behaves or thinks about her experience, she is no longer the ideal mother/wife, but a "spotted princess" (721). In other words, Lucrece's identity has been fundamentally changed by the imposition of (aggressive) sexuality. The main consequence of this change is that she is forced to revise her perception of the relationship between body and soul. This is not only evident in her complicated attempts to find some method of cleansing herself and her family of Tarquin's violation—attempts which are, as the narrator has already suggested, futile—but, more importantly, in the way in which she perceives others. This altered perception materialises at the sight of Sinon in the painting of Troy:

> 'It cannot be,' quoth she, 'that so much guile'—
> She would have said 'can lurk in such a look',
> But Tarquin's shape came in her mind the while,
> And from her tongue 'can lurk' from 'cannot' took.
> 'It cannot be' she in that seine forsook,
>   And turned it thus: 'It cannot be, I find,
>   But such a face should bear a wicked mind'
>
> (1534-40)

What she is about to say recalls the reasoning—informed by a perceived equality between body and soul—that she used to try to dissuade Tarquin from raping her ("Thou look'st not like deceit; do not deceive me" (585). That line of reasoning was based on (sexual) naivety. What she says instead implies that her naivety has been replaced by suspicion. This suspicion is based on (sexual) experience and thus implies that her thoughts are no longer "unstained" (85), in spite of her declaration that her mind is "Immaculate and spotless" (1656).

On one level, this could, then, suggest that some unity does still exist between her body and soul and thereby explain her assumption of guilt. It is not, however, my intention to justify or try to come to terms with why Lucrece commits suicide. My interest lies, rather, in the representation of her identity as tripartite at the moment of her death, a representation that has, in the end, nothing to do with Lucrece's perception of herself. Let us turn to the episode in question:

> And bubbling from her chest it doth divide
>   In two slow rivers, that the crimson blood
>   Circles her body in on every side,
>   Who like a late-sacked island vastly stood,
>   Bare and unpeopled in this fearful flood.
>   Some of her blood still pure and red remained,

And some looked black, and that false Tarquin-
stained.

About the mourning and congealed face
Of that black blood a wat'ry rigol goes,
Which seems to weep upon the tainted place;
And ever since, as pitying Lucrece' woes,
Corrupted blood some watery token shows;
And blood untainted still doth red abide,
Blushing at that which is so putrefied.

(1737-50)

The three colours of her blood prove, I believe, that Lucrece, her husband and father are all wrong in their assumption that the sexuality that has been imposed on
her can in some way be removed ("'The poisoned
fountain clears itself again, / Why not I from this
compelled stain?' / With this they all at once began to
say / Her Body's stain her mind untainted clears,"
(1707-10).) Joyce MacDonald suggests that "in death
[Lucrece's] body is mysteriously and multiply voiced:
. . . vindicating her innocence and proving Tarquin's
guilt" (79). The first part of this contention is aptly
phrased—the blood does, indeed, render Lucrece's body
"voiced" in a way she was unable to in life, but the
suggestion that this voice proves her innocence is
somewhat problematic. Surely the fact that only "some"
of her blood is "pure and red" means that her innocence
is not simplistically asserted by the narrator. How can
she remain wholly pure when a third of her blood is "so
putrefied"? She cannot, became she is, precisely,
"multiply voiced," that is, there is more than one voice.
To exploit MacDonald's metaphor, the concurrent red
and black blood streams represent the contradictory
"voices" of chastity and sexuality. The "wat'ry rigol"
recalls and represents the perpetual tears that are needed
to purify Lucrece. But the presence of this clear stream
does not signal her purity. Rather, it ironically reiterates
the fact that she is powerless; her blood may contain
the tears that could purify her, but these tears, which
"seem to weep upon the tainted place," cannot exist
without the stain. In this way, the "wat'ry rigol" functions as a continuous reminder, the perpetual "voice" of
Lucrece's shame. The division of her blood thus signifies that Lucrece—and, by extension, Shakespeare—
proves unable to resolve the internal contradictions
generated by the rape into a sustainable unity. The result
is, instead, a death that displays, in Katherine Maus's
terms, a "tragic dividedness" (72).

It is, at this point, evident that **Venus and Adonis** and
The Rape of Lucrece represent female identities that
are far from one-dimensional. In the context of Renaissance theories of gender, Venus is, at first, cast in the
structurally and rhetorically masculine position of
seducer. Yet her role as desiring subject is, paradoxically, a feminine one. The destructive quality of her
female desire then manifests itself in the male boar that
kills Adonis. And to complicate matters further, she is
finally represented as a nurturing mother. Her identity
thus ranges from lover to murderer to mother. It is
significant that these divergent qualities are represented
sequentially and not simultaneously: the (unthreatening)
mother figure can only emerge once the aspect of
threatening sexuality (the boar)—who emerges from the
unsatisfied lover—has left the scene. By regarding the
poem as a whole, then, all three facets of Venus's self
emerge. But they are never represented as a sustainable
unity; the one exists at the expense of the other two.

In **The Rape of Lucrece,** these contrasts are rendered in
a subtler but ultimately more disturbing manner. Lucrece is, through the idealising rhetoric of her husband,
Tarquin, and the narrator, represented as an embodiment of physical and spiritual perfection, that is, the
ideally 'feminine' wife/mother figure. The violent
sexuality of her rape functions as a catalyst for the
development of contradictions in—or, obscuring of—
this otherwise transparent identity. These incongruities
are finally revealed at the moment of her suicide, when
Lucrece's blood separates into three different colours,
each representative of a different aspect of her (post-
rape) self. The simultaneous depiction of these conflicting features represents the unity that Shakespeare does
not portray in **Venus and Adonis.** But the expense of
this representation is Lucrece's life. So, while the
female identities of Venus and Lucrece in the two poems
are essentially comprised of three parts. Shakespeare
finally, I conclude, refuses (or remains unable) to
reconcile the contra-dictions that inform this tripartition
into an operational whole.

Notes

1. See Hughes's argument that the boar represents
   Venus's "alter-ego" (58).

2. Adonis's cynicism and eventual death by goring
   provides a tragic parallel to Benedick in *Much
   Ado About Nothing,* whose challenge to Don Pedro
   ("if ever the sensible Benedick bear it [the yoke],
   pluck off the bull's horns and set them in my
   forehead" (1.1.215-17)) ironically anticipates his
   marriage and revised opinion that "There is no
   staff more reverend than one tipped with horn"
   (5.4.118).

3. See also William Keach, who suggests that
   Shakespeare treats Adonis with "Extreme external-
   ity . . . in order to bring out his thematic significance as an embodiment of ideal but unresponsive
   beauty" (68).

4. Although imagery of impression is also used with
   reference to Adonis ("His tend'rer cheek receives
   her soft hand's print / As apt as new fall'n snow
   takes any dint" (353-54); "What wax so frozen
   but dissolves with temp'ring / And yields at last to
   every last impression" (565-67); Shakespeare later

develops it as a characteristically chauvinist metaphor. Examples can be found in *Lucrece* ("For men have marble, women waxen minds, / And therefore are they formed as marble will" (240-41), as well as in Theseus's speech suggesting that women should be "but as a form in wax, / By him imprinted, and within his power / To leave the figure or to disfigure it" (*A Midsummer Night's Dream* (1.1.48-51).

5. See Hughes (58).

6. And, by extension, for the boar to act on Venus's behalf, which is one possible reading of her final ambiguous admission: "Had I been toothed like him, I must confess / With kissing him I should have killed him first" (1117-18).

7. See also Stephen Greenblatt's discussion of language as a means to eroticism in Shakespeare's comedies. He argues that "For Shakespeare friction is specifically associated with verbal wit; indeed at moments the plays seem to imply that erotic friction originates in the wantonness of language and thus that the body itself is a tissue of metaphors or, conversely, that language is perfectly embodied" (89).

8. Joyce MacDonald interprets the comparison of Lucrece to a statue as an indication that "Tarquin escalates the abstraction inherent in Roman languages of female behaviour by seeing her as more closely resembling a graven image than a living being" (79). While the comment is indicative of the effect of idealising rhetoric, it is, in my view, too simplistic in its conflation of the narrator and Tarquin; it is the narrator who describes Lucrece in this manner.

9. Rene Girard's comment about *Troilus and Cressida* articulates this relationship succinctly: "The politics of eroticism and the politics of power are really one and the same" (206).

10. For an illuminating discussion of the subtext of revenge represented by the reference to Philomela and the ideological implications of a revenge option not being available to Lucrece, see Jane Newman, 1994.

Works Cited

Bate, Jonathan. 1993. "Sexual Perversity in *Venus and Adonis*." *Yearbook of English Studies* 13.

Belsey, Catherine. 1995. "Love in Venice." *Shakespeare and Gender: A History*. Ed. Ivo Kamps and Deborah E. Barker. London: Verso.

Ebreo, Leone. 1967. "On Love and Desire." *Renaissance Philosophy of English Literature*. Vol. 1. *The Italian Philosophers*. Ed. Arturo B. Fallico and Herman Shapiro. New York: The Modern Library.

Elyot, Thomas. [1973]. *The Book Named the Governor. The Oxford Anthology of English Literature Vol. 1*. New York: OUP.

Feitelberg, Doreen. 1994. "The Theme of Love and Wooing and the Consequences of Seduction in Shakespeare's Poems *Venus and Adonis* and *The Rape of Lucrece*." *Shakespeare in Southern Africa* Vol. 7.

Girard, Rene. 1985. "The Politics of Desire in *Troilus and Cressida*." *Shakespeare and the Question of Theory*. Ed. Patricia Parker and Geoffrey Hartman. London: Methuen.

Greenblatt, Stephen. 1988. "Fiction and Friction." *Shakespearean Negotiations*. Berkeley: Berkeley UP.

Hughes, Ted. 1992. "Conception and Gestation of the Equation's Tragic Myth: *The Sonnets, Venus and Adonis, Lucrece*." *Shakespeare and the Goddess of Complete Being*. London: Faber.

Keach, William. 1977. *"Venus and Adonis." Elizabethan Erotic Narratives: Irony and Pathos in the Ovidian Poetry of Shakespeare, Marlowe and Their Contemporaries*. Sussex: The Harvester Press.

Lanham, Richard A. 1999. "The Politics of *Lucrece*." *Shakespeare's Poems*. Ed. Stephen Orgel and Sean Keilen. New York: Garland.

MacDonald, Joyce Green. 1994. "Speech, Silence, and History in *The Rape of Lucrece*." *Shakespeare Studies* XXII.

Maus, Katharine Eisaman. 1986. "Taking Tropes Seriously: Language and Violence in Shakespeare's *Rape of Lucrece*." *Shakespeare Quarterly* 37.1.

Newman, Jane. 1994. "'And Let Mild Women to Him Lose Their Mildness': Philomela, Female Violence and Shakespeare's *The Rape of Lucrece*." *Shakespeare Quarterly* 45.3.

Vickers, Nancy J. 1999. "'This Heraldry in Lucrece' Face'." *Shakespeare's Poems*. Ed. Stephen Orgel and Sean Keilen. New York: Garland.

Peter Hyland (essay date 2001)

SOURCE: Hyland, Peter. "Praising the Vile for Recompense: Shakespeare and Patronage Poetry." *The Upstart Crow* 21 (2001): 41-7.

[*In this essay, Hyland explores the reasons why Shakespeare returned to playwriting despite having secured the literary patronage of the Earl of Southampton and having enjoyed considerable success with the nondramatic poems* Venus and Adonis *and* The Rape of Lucrece.]

I think that it is of more than passing interest that the first reference to Shakespeare's presence in London, Robert Greene's sneering attack on him as a parvenu and perhaps a plagiarist in the theatrical profession, should have appeared in the year in which Shakespeare temporarily diverted his literary energies from plays to poems:

> there is an upstart crow, beautified with our feathers, that with his *Tiger's heart wrapt in a player's hide,* supposes he is as well able to bombast out a blank verse as the best of you; and being an absolute *Johannes Factotum,* is in his own conceit the only Shakescene in a country.[1]

Greene's words have been exhaustively analyzed, and they probably tell us more about Greene than about his victim. Nevertheless, it is worth considering what effect they might have had on the neophyte playwright, presumably still unsure about the wisdom of trying to make a living with his pen in a city where a university-educated man like Greene, a versatile and not inconsiderable writer of plays, poems, pamphlets and prose romances, could come to the embittered end that is shadowed in Greene's deathbed book. If the world of professional writing had so little to offer Greene, what could it offer Shakespeare?

Documentation of Shakespeare's theatrical career prior to Greene's reference to him remains a blank, but it is reasonable to assume that he had by that time written the three parts of *Henry VI* (as Greene's own words suggest), and perhaps *Richard III, The Comedy of Errors, The Two Gentlemen of Verona,* and *Titus Andronicus.* These had clearly brought him some celebrity, or there would have been no reason for Greene's resentment. The profession of playwright was not a lucrative one, however, and no matter what success he was beginning to experience, when in 1592 the theatres were closed because of a severe outbreak of the plague, Shakespeare did not have enough money to sit around waiting for them to re-open. The writing for publication of non-dramatic poetry was itself not a way of making much money, since the market for volumes of verse was necessarily small. The penurious writer had to find a patron, as Shakespeare did in the Earl of Southampton, to whom he dedicated *Venus and Adonis* and *The Rape of Lucrece* (1594). Despite the many romantic theories that have been built around this connection we do not know how Shakespeare came into contact with Southampton, nor do we know how intimate their relationship was. What we do know is that as soon as it became possible for Shakespeare to get back to the playhouse he did so, and he seems to have shown no further interest in writing for the more prestigious market represented by his patron.

This, on the face of it, is odd, because numerous editions of both poems were printed in Shakespeare's lifetime, which attest to their great popularity. While no kind of professional writing was respectable, there was a difference, measured in social legitimacy, between writing for the tiny sophisticated (or would-be sophisticated) minority who bought volumes of poetry, and writing for the rowdy masses who frequented the public playhouses. For the whole of his career Ben Jonson resented having to write for the "loathed stage"; he got away from it whenever he could find a patron, and when he was forced back into it by financial need he tried to elevate his plays into poems by giving their printing and publication the same detailed attention that he gave his poems and by blurring the distinction between the two by calling them "Works." Even so, as he told William Drummond, "Of all his plays he never gained two hundred pounds."[2] It is clear that Shakespeare was no less ambitious than Jonson, and in 1592 he had not yet had the chance to discover in himself the business acumen that would eventually allow him to make much more money out of the theatre than writing for it could have done. He could not have known, either, that he was going to become a universal genius and the "inventor of the human." Why, then, did he not pursue, as Jonson would certainly have done, the possibilities he had opened up for himself with the contact he had made with Southampton and the popular success of these two poems? Why did he return to the undeniably risky business of writing plays?

First, it is necessary to be clear about the widespread assumption that Elizabethans placed "poems" above "plays," because much has been made of Shakespeare's claim in his dedication to **Venus and Adonis** that it is the first heir of his invention, and to the fact that he apparently carefully supervised the printing of both narrative poems but showed no interest whatever in the publication of his plays. As David Kay puts it:

> We have to remember the low status accorded to play texts in this period, and recognize that Shakespeare, as a man of his time, saw scripts as inescapably transient and collaborative efforts; they were to be distinguished from a work of art, an altogether loftier enterprise and something grounded upon the idea, the "foreconceit," the concetto, the "invention" of the poet.[3]

It seems to me that this statement conflates two different things. We cannot take Shakespeare's lack of involvement in the publication of his scripts as an indication that he did not think of them as "works of art." His relationship to his play-texts was limited by the realities of his profession: once a play was written it became the property of the acting company that staged it, and was usually released for publication only when it no longer had the power to bring an audience into the theatre or in circumstances when the acting company was in dire need, or when a pirated version had been printed. In any case this usually happened some years after the play's composition. The dramatist no longer had a financial stake in its publication, and was probably sufficiently distanced from it to have no aesthetic stake in it either. Not until Ben Jonson conceived the idea of recuperating his plays by reconstructing them as literary texts for his 1616 Folio did any dramatist find a way to reassert control over his work. Since Shakespeare died in that year he could hardly profit from the example, but there is no reason to believe that he would not have been delighted by the publication by Heminges and Condell of his happy imitations of Nature in his own First Folio, whether or not their primary motives were commercial.

Indeed, the hierarchization of poems over plays implied by Jonson's struggle to give his plays the dignity of poems is not as clear a matter as it appears. While it is certainly true that Jonson was far more aware of aesthetic issues than were most of his contemporaries, it is often difficult to separate his artistic theories from his social hunger. His main reason for loathing the stage was that it forced him to cater to the tastes of what he called the "vulgar" or the "world," the broad public audience. His printed works reached a different, smaller and more affluent market of readers (he called them "understanders"), a social and intellectual elite that he desperately wanted to join. But many of these wealthier understanders also attended theatres and probably would not have drawn the distinction between poems and plays as clearly as Jonson did, though they might have been flattered by Jonson's characterization of them. While I have no doubt that Jonson believed in his literary theories, I think also that they fitted with his social ambition.

For most of Shakespeare's contemporaries the term "poetry" meant roughly what the term "literature" means today. A decade before Shakespeare made his brief shift to non-dramatic poetry Sir Philip Sidney had struggled with the problem of raising the reputation of poetry, by which he clearly means something broader than the term implies today. Indeed, he labors to distinguish poetry from history and philosophy, which do not depend on fancy or imagination, but when he surveys literary genres as reflected in the then-contemporary English canon he includes plays, which he condemns not because plays are not literature, but because these particular plays do not observe generic conventions; he makes an exception of Gorboduc, however, which "obtain[s] the very end of poesy."[4] In spite of this effort to make poetry more respectable, Sidney himself did not differ from other aristocratic poets in his attitude toward publication. In court circles more writing circulated in manuscripts than as printed books; some courtiers themselves wrote poetry that was intended for small coteries of their friends, and for them the idea of the widespread publication of their work would have been offensive. Indeed, such manuscript circulation kept elite culture exclusive, one of the means whereby aristocratic power was preserved.

What really was a contentious issue was the idea of publication itself, and it made little difference whether this was of poems or plays. "Literature" as a profession barely existed at all, and those who wished to make a profession of it were all, in effect, upstart crows, from Spenser through to Jonson. They were intelligent and ambitious men from the margins and the provinces for most of whom writing was a means rather than an end, an activity that could get them into service in the court through the patronage system, but the circles of the privileged did not make such breaches easy. Most writers depended upon patronage. In return for some degree (usually not large) of financial support writers provided their patrons with poems or dedicated writings to them. The obvious demand for flattery limited what we might think of as the writer's "artistic freedom," but it did provide him with an income. The writer who depended on patronage was trapped in a paradox, in that many in these court circles who were avid consumers of literature nevertheless had contempt for those who produced it.

Only a year before Shakespeare turned to writing the kind of poetry that needed a patron, Edmund Spenser had published "Mother Hubberd's Tale," with its bitter account of the realities of existence for those who needed to seek preferment at court:

> Full little knowest thou that hast not tride,
> What hell it is, in suing long to bide:
> To loose good dayes, that might be better spent;
> To waѕt long nights in pensive discontent;
> To speed today, to be put back tomorrow;
> To feed on hope, to pine with feare and sorrow;
> To have thy Princes grace, yet want her Peeres;
> To have thy asking, yet waite manie yeeres;
> To fret thy soule with crosses and with cares;
> To eate thy heart through comfortlesse dispaires;
> To fawne, to crowche, to waite, to ride, to ronne,
> To spend, to give, to want, to be undonne.
> Unhappie Wight, borne to desastrous end,
> That doth his life in so long tendance spend.
>
> (895-908)[5]

The usual assumption, arising from the myths built out of Shakespeare's relationship with Southampton, is that Shakespeare found a patron easily. I find this hard to credit, however. By 1592 he was developing a reputation as a playwright (though the absence of any reference to him prior to Greene's makes it reasonable to assume that it was not yet great). As far as is known he had no reputation at all as a poet. There is no reason to believe that Shakespeare did not suffer the frustration and humiliation described by Spenser, the suing and waiting, the fawning and running, particularly as Spenser's experience came in spite of his having far more powerful connections than Shakespeare could have had. If Shakespeare did suffer any of this, it would not be surprising if he got out of the patronage trap as quickly as he could.

Unlike Jonson, Shakespeare left no explicit statements about his attitude to the various aspects of his profession, but there are poet-figures in a number of his plays. We might reasonably ask what can be derived from his treatment of them, but this leads us into problematic territory, since any statement in a play must be identified primarily with the character who utters it rather than with the dramatist who wrote it. What we find, however, is what Ekbert Faas has characterized as a "consistently negative portrayal of poets in his work."[6] Now of course, our judgement of any such portrayal will depend on the context in which it is presented. Nevertheless, this insistent hostility has been apparent to others: Katherine Duncan-Jones in her recent edition of the Sonnets asks, "How do we reconcile Shakespeare's consistently scornful allusions to sonnets and sonneteering in his plays with the fact of his having composed one of the longest sonnet sequences of the period?"[7] There is, of course, more than one possible answer to this question, but one thing that should be noted is that Faas simplifies through generalization, for while it is (fairly) consistently negative, they are treated in different ways, and the greatest mockery is directed at fashionable, courtly poets.

With the possible exception of *The Two Gentlemen of Verona,* Shakespeare's poets appear in plays written after his own experience as a poet. His best known statement about poets and poetry is the speech by Duke Theseus in the last act of *A Midsummer Night's Dream,* and the hostility is surely there. Having listened to the strange story told by the young lovers, Theseus weighs it with "cool reason," and dismisses it, on the grounds that love generates the same delusions, the same "shaping fantasies," as madness. He then goes on, perhaps rather arbitrarily, to lump the poet in with the lunatic and the lover, condemning him for indulging in the same excesses. Theseus tells us:

> The poet's eye, in a fine frenzy rolling,
> Doth glance from heaven to earth, from earth to
>   heaven,
> And as imagination bodies forth
> The forms of things unknown, the poet's pen
> Turns them to shapes, and gives to airy nothing
> A local habitation and a name.
> Such tricks hath strong imagination
> That if it would but apprehend some joy;
> It comprehends some bringer of that joy;
> Or in the night, imagining some fear,
> How easy is a bush supposed a bear!

(5.1.12-22)

We might respond that Theseus is here confusing two different operations of the imagination, confounding illusion with delusion, since the poet actively uses his imagination to give shape to airy nothing, while the lunatic and the lover are passive victims of theirs. Furthermore, as audience, we have seen the things that

he is denying in the name of his conception of "reality." Theseus has often been taken as the authoritative voice in *A Midsummer Night's Dream,* but the context of this speech seems to prevent us from uncritically accepting his view of things, and we might (using our own "cool reason") conclude that Shakespeare expects us to reject this dismissal of the poet as a manifestation of aristocratic arrogance.

I think that this is indeed the response that Shakespeare expects of us, if for no other reason than that Theseus's words would condemn *A Midsummer Night's Dream* itself. Nevertheless, if we place his comments in the context of Shakespeare's treatment of poet characters in other plays, the distance of the dramatist's position from the Thesean attitude is not quite so evident as we might wish to suppose. Any praise of poetry is usually undercut through being located in an ironic context, and poets themselves are always mocked, sometimes harshly. For example, in *Two Gentlemen of Verona* poetry is described as "heaven-bred," its magical powers originating in the figure of Orpheus, "Whose golden touch could soften steel and stones, / Make tigers tame, and huge leviathans / Forsake unsounded deeps to dance on sands" (3.2.78-80). This, however, is an attempt to persuade the fool Thurio to write a sonnet with the hope of winning Sylvia, bringing "heaven-bred" poesy sharply down to earth. As a type of the gentleman amateur (albeit a sham one) Thurio stands as a sort of mock version of the courtly poet who by Shakespeare's time had made Petrarchan love poetry fashionable to the point where it had effectively been emptied of meaning. In *As You Like It* the young gentleman Orlando is also entrapped by Petrarchanism in an artificial view of love. He hangs poems on trees to express his love for Rosalind, and is only freed to win her after she has shown him how far divorced from reality his literary understanding of love is: "Men have died from time to time, and worms have eaten them, but not for love" (4.1.91-92). This play appears to suggest, perhaps more gently, that poetry can be dangerous if it prevents us from seeing what is really there. Of course, we have to remember that the plays themselves are poetry, and presumably Shakespeare is not mounting a serious attack on the source of his own livelihood. Perhaps his laughter is really directed against the aristocratic concept of the amateur poet rather than against poetry itself.

Shakespeare's most extensive treatment of this kind of poet comes in *Love's Labour's Lost,* in which four young aristocrats try to use poetry as a means of wooing four young women. Their endeavor ends in failure, and they are mocked by the women whom they seek to impress. The main reason for this is the extreme affectation of their language, in which display has taken the place of substance. Biron, the lover whose scepticism puts him closest to "reality," is eventually led to renounce the linguistic ornamentation that the young men have believed to be the essence of poetry:

> O, never will I trust to speeches penned,
> Nor to the motion of a schoolboy's tongue,
> Nor never come in visor to my friend,
> Nor woo in rhyme, like a blind harper's song.
> Taffeta phrases, silken terms precise,
> Three-piled hyperboles, spruce affectation,
> Figures pedantical—these summer flies
> Have blown me full of maggot ostentation.
> I do forswear them, and I here protest,
> By this white glove—how white the hand, God
>   knows—
> Henceforth my wooing mind shall be expressed
> In russet yeas, and honest kersey noes
> And to begin, wench, so God help me, law!
> My love to thee is sound, sans crack or flaw.

(5.2.402-15)

There are many ironies here. Although these lines are part of a slightly longer speech, they constitute a sonnet: Biron expresses his renunciation of literary artifice in one of the most elaborately artificial of verse forms. There are other blatant rhetorical devices—the conscious patterning of the first four lines, the linguistic affectation, the Petrarchan cliche of the white hand. Biron claims to recognize them as a disease, yet he is unable to cure himself of them. At best, we can take from the treatment of the four young aristocrats the idea that an interest in poetry is a sign of an immature and incomplete approach to life.

In the same play, however, there are "poets" whose treatment cannot be quite so easily interpreted. Nathaniel and Holofernes present a play for their noble superiors which in its ineptitude rivals Peter Quince's most lamentable comedy. The aristocrats, like those in *A Midsummer Night's Dream,* provide a mocking and disruptive commentary, but the purpose of the scene seems less to mock the two "dramatists" than to expose the callow attitudes of their supposedly well-bred audience, and when Holofernes chides them with "This is not generous, not gentle, not humble" (5.2.617) we are inclined to agree with him. *Love's Labour's Lost* can be seen not so much as presenting a negative portrayal of poets as mocking poetic amateurism and revealing the humiliations of those at the receiving end of the patronage system. It foreshadows the frustrations of Quince and Bottom and their friends as they try to reflect refined values back to their aristocratic audience.

There are two other plays in which poets make a significant appearance, *Julius Caesar* and *Timon of Athens.* In *Julius Caesar* Shakespeare gives us two poets. In the first case the poet Cinna, a supporter of Julius Caesar, is mistaken by the Roman mob for the conspirator Cinna. The mob threatens to tear him to pieces; when he tries to defend himself by insisting on his identity as Cinna the poet, they instead decide to "Tear him for his bad verses" (3.3.29). It might be that Shakespeare merely wished to show the undiscriminating ugliness of mob violence here, but the tone of the scene, dark as it is, is nevertheless comic: Cinna falls victim to an extreme act of literary criticism. Two scenes later a different poet, labeled "cynic" by Cassius, approaches Brutus and Cassius, who have just reconciled after a bitter quarrel. His marginal position seems to make him a "professional," even a Jonsonian poet, and he has come as healer, offering the wisdom of his years, to beg them to "Love and be friends" (4.2.183). The response of the two generals is to dismiss him with mockery and contempt. Shakespeare gives these two characters together hardly more than a dozen lines, and we might want to ask why he bothered to include them at all. In the case of the cynic-poet, Brutus and Cassius have already made up their quarrel, so his presence appears particularly redundant. Perhaps this is Shakespeare's point, however. The question asked by Brutus, "What should the wars do with these jigging fools?" (4.2.189), indicates the political ineffectuality of poets, and in this play they are scorned at both ends of the social hierarchy, by the plebeian mob and by the aristocratic conspirators.

The one play that unquestionably presents a "professional" poet is *Timon of Athens.* Here, the Poet seeks patronage from Timon for his living, selling his dedications as the Jeweller and the Merchant sell their wares, while acknowledging the duplicity that betrays his art: "When we for recompense have praised the vile, / It stains the glory in that happy verse / Which aptly sings the good" (1.1.15-17). On the one hand, he presents himself as a satirist, a single honest voice predicting that Timon will fall and be abandoned by his suitors; on the other, he is revealed by Apemantus and finally dismissed by Timon as a mere flatterer, an alchemist whose art is directed only at the making of gold and therefore no different from the "infinite flatteries that follow youth and opulency" (5.1.33-34) that he purports to reveal. While Timon's rage is partially explained by a misanthropy that finally collapses into madness, the Poet's honesty is certainly compromised by his involvement in the general materialism.

If, however, we set this Poet and the second Poet in *Julius Caesar* (it is perhaps significant that neither is given an identity beyond his professional one) alongside the various aristocratic poets of the earlier plays, we might see that while it is true, as Faas and Duncan-Jones argue, that the treatment of all poets is negative or scornful, there is an important difference here. Most of the poets who are mocked are courtly amateurs who play at being poets. These two Poets have a different relationship to their work; one hesitates to call it "serious", given the way in which they are treated, but underlying it is a sense of frustration at the position of the professional poet within the class-dominated social system that made it difficult for him to be heard, and impossible for him to earn a living and retain integrity at the same time. The play's mockery, that is, is directed at the whole situation in which poetry is dominated by the self-absorbed amateurism of the courtly poet; the obverse of this is the contempt in which the professional poet is held by those from whom he needs to seek patronage—a contempt that appears justified in that the dependent writer is forced into "infinite flatteries" if he is to avoid starvation. Perhaps Shakespeare's brief experience in the toils of the patronage system was, in spite of the success of the poems he produced, sufficient to repel him from continuing in it once he could escape it. The comparative freedom of the public stage also allowed for a comparative honesty of self-expression.

Such a reading allows us to question the view, far too frequently expressed, that Shakespeare is an apologist for aristocratic values. On the contrary, most of his plays offer us a position, like that of Holofernes, that resists elitist narrowness and contempt. It might, like Thersites, counter contempt with contempt, but it must be understood for what it is. In this light we can see that it is entirely appropriate that both Shakespeare's narrative poems expose the destructiveness of aristocratic arrogance and irresponsible self-love. His views on poetry, it appears, cannot be divorced from a skeptical ideological position, a position, we can hardly doubt, that was painfully earned.

Notes

1. *Greene's Groats-worth of Wit* (1592), reprinted in E. K. Chambers, *William Shakespeare: A Study of Facts and Problems* (Oxford: Oxford University Press, 1930) Vol. 2, p. 188.

2. George Parfitt (ed.). *Ben Jonson: The Complete Poems* (Harmondsworth: Penguin Books; 1975) p. 476.

3. Dennis Kay. *Shakespeare: His Life, Work, and Era* (New York: Quill, 1992) p. 156.

4. Sir Philip Sidney. *An Apology for Poetry* in David Kalstone (ed.) *The Selected Poetry and Prose of Sidney* (New York: New American Library, 1970), p. 260.

5. Quotations from Spenser are from *Spenser: Poetical Works,* ed. J. C. Smith and E. DeSelincourt (London: Oxford University Press, 1912).

6. Ekbert Faas. *Shakespeare's Poetics.* Cambridge: Cambridge UP, 1986. p. xii.

7. Katherine Duncan-Jones (ed). *Shakespeare's Sonnets.* London: Thomas Nelson and Sons Ltd., 1997. p. 45.

Lauren Shohet (essay date winter 2002)

SOURCE: Shohet, Lauren. "Shakespeare's Eager Adonis." *Studies in English Literature, 1500-1900* 42, no. 1 (winter 2002): 85-102.

[*In the essay below, Shohet investigates the distinct poetic modes Shakespeare used to express the characters' contradictory views on sexual desire, representation, and language.*]

In Shakespeare's *Venus and Adonis,* when Venus solicits Adonis, he famously turns away. Venus entreats:

> "Vouchsafe, thou wonder, to alight thy steed,
> And rein his proud head to the saddle-bow;
> If thou wilt deign this favor, for thy meed
> A thousand honey secrets shalt thou know."[1]

Adonis rebuffs her, because "Hunting he lov'd, but love he laugh'd to scorn" (line 4). The critical tradition has discussed in great detail Adonis's refusal to love.[2] But, importantly, this line does *not* begin with a refusal. Rather, it introduces Adonis with a positive predicate: he "loves" hunting. Moreover, the "but" that conjoins his predilection for hunting with his antipathy to love has dialectical overtones: Adonis would seem to scorn "love" more as an alternative to the hunt than as an independent proposition.

The two characters thus articulate distinct forms of "love" that present competing models of desire. Furthermore, the poem provocatively interrelates models of desire and language. In the stanza cited above, if Adonis alights, Venus will reward him with "'a thousand honey secrets.'" Not only does Venus promise the linguistic reward of "'secrets'" for erotic surrender, but her proposal of "'honey secrets'" as "'meed'" ("reward," punning on "mead" [honey liquor]) also intertwines these linguistic treats with the honeyed sexual "'secrets'" also on offer ("'honey'" denoting moreover sexual bliss).[3] And while Adonis straightforwardly "loves" hunting, he does not simply "scorn" Venus—as grammatical parallelism would have him do—but rather "*laugh[s] to* scorn" her (my emphasis). Metrical contingency aside, this doubled verb adds a layer of complexity to Adonis's response to "love." Whereas hunting elicits an unmediated affective response ("hunting he loved"), the poem's evocation of eros emphasizes the mode *through which* Adonis (unlike Venus) distinctively expresses his response of affective withdrawal.

Such intersections of desire and discourse have been remarked in various literary contexts—commentators include Michel de Montaigne and Michel Foucault—and have occasioned innumerable provocative analyses in criticism of the last two decades. Relatively less explored in Shakespeare studies have been the questions of whether different kinds of desire require different poetics, and whether, conversely, different modes of discourse produce different kinds of desire.[4] I propose that we might fruitfully read Shakespeare's **Venus and Adonis** as addressing just these questions: as considering multiple and competing discourses of desire, and exploring how different poetic and erotic modes might inflect one another.

Previous criticism of **Venus and Adonis** certainly has remarked on the poem's engagement with love on the one hand and language on the other. But most scholarship on **Venus and Adonis** focuses *either* on questions of desire and subjectivity *or* on issues of language and representation.[5] More significantly, the limited number of analyses that bring these areas together tend to take only one of the two categories as a complex and multiple field. In considering the poem's "taxonomy of desire," for example, Catherine Belsey argues that the poem innovatively distinguishes between the concepts of love and lust. But while her focus on the difference between these terms has discursive implications, Belsey's interest lies in contrasting modes of desire, not modes of representation. Similarly, Heather Dubrow connects Venus's "linguistic" and "psychological" "habits," but relies on a unified notion of "language itself," whereas I would propose that the poem encompasses multiple and competing notions of what language is.[6] In one further example, James Schiffer remarks (in passing) that the poem illustrates the interdependence of economies of language and desire in Lacanian analysis ("Venus' prophecy-curse also reminds us of the relationship throughout the poem between language and desire"), but Schiffer distinguishes neither among *kinds* of desire (as Belsey does) nor *kinds* of language.[7]

In this essay, by contrast, I want to focus particularly on the *range* of disagreements between Venus and Adonis—sexual, linguistic, and representational—to explore how these contrasting views come together into distinct (if asymmetrically articulated) discursive models of poetic subjectivity. Venus's amorous eagerness is met with Adonis's disdainful withdrawal; Venus's heteroerotic desire for Adonis with his homoerotic desire for the hunt; Venus's invocations of a mythic realm of abstraction, personification, and analogy with Adonis's emphasis on the historical realm of particular experience; Venus's reliance on literary convention with the narrative innovation of Adonis's erotic refusal. Wryly dissociating the seduction and "venery" ("hunting") linked in traditional puns and mythography, the poem distinguishes between Venus's views of language, desire, and selfhood—largely consonant with the dominant Elizabethan models Jane Hedley characterizes as "static, synchronistic, and centripetal"—and Adonis's desires, which sketch out a tentative exploration of alternatives.[8] The vagueness of my last locution reflects the difficulty of definitively

discerning Adonis's desires in a text largely controlled by the opposition. For Shakespeare's poem rearticulates the traditionally fecund *venus genetrix* in Venus's extraordinary volubility: she gushes forth stanza after stanza of erotic desire, hampering intrusions by her interlocutor or even, it seems, the narrator. Rather like the copious production of panegyric by Elizabeth's court, Venus's linguistic facility leaves little room for alternatives, effectively preventing Adonis's admittedly rather inchoate desires from coming fully into focus. Yet, as I shall argue below, the open-endedness of Adonis's aims is an important part of what makes them distinctive.

For Adonis *does* formulate positive aims. To be sure, Adonis's first direct speech in the poem (not granted him until line 185) is "'Fie, no more of love!'"; the next line adds to this wholesale rejection the intransitively negative "'I must remove'" (line 186). Adonis is, however, fleeing *toward* something as well. He actively "'removes'"—re-*moves*—to the homosocial alternative of the boar hunt. He prefers keeping faith with his male hunting band to tarrying with Venus: "'I am,' quoth he, 'expected of my friends'" (line 718). And, as we have seen, the poem's very first claim about Adonis reports, "Hunting he lov'd" (line 4). Although it might be possible to interpret "hunt-love" here as an ironic aggregation opposed to the second phrase's "love" ("love he laugh'd to scorn"), Adonis protests in other lines as well that he does indeed "love" hunting, or perhaps the hunt, or even the deadly boar himself: "'I know not love,' quoth he, 'nor will not know it, / Unless it be a boar, and then I chase it'" (lines 409-10).[9]

Adonis's desire differs from Venus's both in its target and in the way it relates subject to object. Whereas Venus desires an eros that merges lover and beloved. Adonis desires the hunt, which depends upon boundaries between subject and object (albeit contingent and perhaps temporary ones). Adonis's desire fits somewhere along a homosocial-homoerotic continuum that is distinct in both its ends and its means from Venus's desires, as shown by three elements of his preference: Adonis's attraction to the boar itself, his allegiance to the masculine hunting band, and the ways in which the hunt suggests patriarchal order. The poem's presentation of the boar is, of course, quite phallic. Unlike Venus's suggested alternatives of foxes, hares, and roes (which Adonis spurns), the boar has tusks, a "'battle set / Of bristly pikes'" (lines 619-20), and a grave-digging snout. Adonis's keen interest in the boar hunt and simultaneous disdain for innocuous quarries betray some attraction to the deadly possibility of being penetrated by the boarish tusk.[10] More significant than this genitally suggestive imagery are the abstract qualities linking the boar not merely to the penis but to the phallus, with the full weight of cultural privilege which that term connotes. For the poem emphasizes the boar's powers of intention, resolution, invulnerability, and efficacy. As Venus fearfully describes him,

> "Being mov'd, he strikes, what e'er is in his way,
> And whom he strikes his crooked tushes slay.
>
> "His brawny sides, with hairy bristles armed,
> Are better proof than thy spear's point can enter;
> His short thick neck cannot be easily harmed;
> Being ireful, on the lion he will venter.
> The thorny brambles and embracing bushes,
> As fearful of him, part, through whom he rushes."
>
> (lines 623-30)

Moreover, Adonis's desire draws him to the more abstractly phallic *order* of the hunt: an activity that develops identity—what Lacan calls the "social I"—by projecting the power, knowledge, and autonomy that the subject hopes to gain onto the ever-receding Other who putatively commands this mastery (who, in Lacanian terms, possesses the phallus).[11] Hence, whereas in discussing the boar as the "locus of the missing phallic impulse" William Sheidley uses "phallus" more or less synonymously with "penis," the Lacanian notion that the "phallus" is always illusory would suggest that the hunt itself, rather than the boar, embodies the "phallic *impulse*" that constitutes masculine self-realization.[12] In the poem (as in culture generally), the compensation for the impossibility of these young men ever attaining full mastery—because no subject ever realizes complete autonomy—is nothing other than patriarchy: a fraternal band, excluding women and children by the nature of its mission, linked in the bonds of a common purpose made all the more permanent because the goal never can be definitively accomplished (*i.e.,* because patriarchy operates without authentic patriarchs). "'Expected of my friends,'" Adonis is not only awaited *by* his friends, but also, partitively, expected to become "'of'" his friends: part of a masculine order based on perpetual quest.[13]

Significantly, the poem articulates Adonis's desire not as finding, overcoming, or killing the boar, but rather as "chasing" him: "'I know not love,' quoth he, 'nor will not know it, / Unless it be a boar, and then I chase it'" (lines 409-10). It is pursuit itself that attracts Adonis: a relation that depends upon preserving distance between desirer and object. By its nature, the ever-receding object of his desire is constitutively ungraspable. By contrast, Venus's erotics specifically seek to vanquish this distance; as Coppélia Kahn notes, Venus desires the "blurring of boundaries, an anonymous merging of eyes and lips."[14] Merging and boundlessness characterize Venus's version of erotic idyll: "'My smooth moist hand, were it with thy hand felt, / Would in thy palm dissolve, or seem to melt'" (lines 143-4).[15] Significantly, these same qualities prove fatal to Adonis, culminating in the images of commingling surrounding his death. The boar's mouth is painted with red, "Like milk and

blood being mingled both together" (line 902); as the wound breaches Adonis's bodily boundaries, "No flow'r was nigh, no grass, herb, leaf, or weed, / But stole his blood, and seem'd with him to bleed" (lines 1055-6). Congruently, whereas Venus's erotics suspend time at the moment of consummation, pursuit rather than capture is endless in Adonis's "chase." (Accordingly, one of Adonis's two moments of erotic engagement with Venus comes at a point when he believes her to be similarly unattainable, in her deathlike swoon [lines 475-80]; in the other, he teases Venus with a kiss proffered and retracted [lines 88-90]). The proximity and the breaching of boundaries that constitute infinite and ecstatic fulfillment for Venus are inherently fatal in the hunt, an opposition emphasized by Venus's use of "'kiss[ing]'" to describe the boar's mortally wounding Adonis (line 1114). Indeed, the successful approach of hunter to quarry necessarily signals the end of the hunt, usually accompanied by the death of one or more participants.

Associated with these different modes of desire are different modes of *poeisis*. Venus's hermeneusis relies on mythic/conventional presentation; Adonis tends toward the palpable and the particular. Venus seeks to inscribe Adonis into an archetypal tale of seduction, speaking as the goddess of love who advocates eros and procreation as general principles:

> "Upon the earth's increase why shouldst thou feed,
> Unless the earth with thy increase be fed?
> By law of nature thou art bound to breed,
> That thine may live, when thou thyself art dead."
>
> (lines 169-72)

Near silent for most of the poem and dead at the end, Adonis struggles less than articulately to assert a character whose volition is undetermined by tradition or myth. Venus serves, perhaps, as the "straight" reader of Ovid, following the mythic script. Adonis resists this, but the sophisticated, ironic, self-reflective Ovid of the elite Elizabethan reader does not seem fully available to him either. Instead, eschewing both elegant rhetoric and erotic action, Adonis refuses to be written into the timeless seduction scene and insists on his present, idiosyncratic discomfort and lack of interest: "'Fie, no more of love! / The sun doth burn my face, I must remove'" (lines 185-6). In Adonis's narrative, particularity makes Venus and Adonis into personae with some degree of agency, rather than inherited figures whose desires are determined by the metatextual drama they enact.

The poem renders the mythic and realistic modes emphatically incompatible; indeed, the pointedly ridiculous effect of realistically narrating mythic action creates the poem's humor.[16] Comically, the mythic/conventional narrative relishes a poetic eloquence that the realistic eschews. The meter of the poem's opening lines is unapologetically elegant:

Even as the sun with purple-color'd face
Had ta'en his last leave of the weeping morn,
Rose-cheek'd Adonis hied him to the chase;
Hunting he lov'd, but love he laugh'd to scorn.

(lines 1-4)

The stanza's concluding couplet, on the other hand, introduces the seduction theme in a burlesque rhyme: "Sick-thoughted Venus makes amain unto him, / And like a bold-fac'd suitor gins to woo him" (lines 5-6). The second stanza reverts to the stylishness of the first four lines, but in the third stanza, when Venus ceases lauding Adonis and begins soliciting him, singsong meter and comically overblown feminine rhyme return ("'Here come and sit, where never serpent hisses, / And being set, I'll smother thee with kisses'" [lines 17-8]). When Venus finally takes decisive action, in couplet lines, the metrical reinforcement of the plot is farcically pat: "Being so enrag'd, desire doth lend her force / Courageously to pluck him from his horse" (lines 29-30). The caesura trumpets dramatic suspense; the iambic regularity of the fast-reading, five-foot, mostly monosyllabic line 30 underlines the physical ease with which Venus accomplishes her kidnap, the melodramatic acceleration in tempo pointing up the ludicrousness of sweatily embodying the Goddess of Love.

More significantly, the poetic and narrative effects of the two discourses work to opposite ends. Venus's linguistic and erotic initiatives alike impede the diegetic progress of the suspended hunt narrative that Adonis desires to resume. For, although language serves many needs for Venus, narrative momentum is not one of them. Her discourse winds along digressive paths shaped by the figurative logic of her images or the forensic logic of her conventional arguments, interrupting the progression of the plot. In the opening stanzas discussed above, Venus addresses Adonis for three and a half figure-laden stanzas before seizing him. By contrast, the poem's so-called "action"—Adonis's sporadic bursts of motion away from Venus and toward the hunt—moves briskly forward precisely whenever Venus stops talking. Even Adonis's most extended speech, the seven stanzas that culminate in his narratively decisive departure,

With this he breaketh from the sweet embrace
Of those fair arms which bound him to her breast,
And homeward through the dark laund runs apace,

(lines 811-3)

seems terse and active in comparison to the preceding twenty-five stanzas of Venus's attempts to dissuade him—a passage that confuses even Venus, who must ask in the middle "'Where did I leave?'" (line 715).

As judged by capaciousness, poetic versatility, facility, and claims on the reader's attention—i.e., by the standards of humanist *sprezzatura*—it is Venus who

owns language in the poem.[17] The poem associates Adonis's silences with his refusal of Venus's erotics; inverting this link, Venus's language is inextricably intertwined with the passion governing and governed by the goddess. Language and desire produce and magnify one another:

That all the neighbor caves, as seeming troubled,
Make verbal repetition of her [Venus's] moans;
Passion on passion deeply is redoubled:
    "Ay me!" she cries, and twenty times, "Woe, woe!"
    And twenty echoes twenty times cry so.

(lines 830-4)

Kissing, speaking, the refracting and multiplying of Venus's speech, and the silencing of Adonis are simultaneous effects of a single gesture:

                    now doth he frown.
And gins to chide, but soon she stops his lips,
And kissing speaks, with lustful language broken.
"If thou wilt chide, thy lips shall never open."

(lines 45-8)

Even the ruptures in Venus's speech—the kisses that render her "'lustful language broken'"—do not impede language so much as disperse it. Greedily inserting itself everywhere, Venus's language operates in an economy of lust that utterly overcomes Adonis's volition. When Adonis tries to articulate his refusal of Venus's arguments, her kiss prevents him: "He saith she is immodest, blames her miss; / What follows more, she murthers with a kiss" (lines 53-4). "Murthers" figuratively realizes the earlier threat that disobedient lips "'shall never open'" (line 48); "'smother[ing]'" Adonis (line 18), her kisses deny him both oxygen and argument.

Through conventional rhetorical strategies, Venus's discourse blurs temporal and rhetorical boundaries as well, to ends equally antipathetic to Adonis. Substitution of the figurative for the literal permeates Venus's arguments. She assures Adonis:

"The kiss shall be thine own as well as mine.
What seest thou in the ground? hold up thy head,
Look in mine eyeballs, there thy beauty lies;
Then why not lips on lips, since eyes in eyes?"

(lines 117-20)

Departing from the Neoplatonic axiom that beauty lies in the beholder's eye, Venus advances a formal argument for acknowledging through action the commensurability between lips and eyes already established by conventional logic and by analogy. Erasing substantive difference between gazes and kisses, Venus's argument—like Scholastic or indeed Petrarchan reasoning—treats "'eyes'" and "'lips'" as interchangeable subjects of formal manipulation. This congruence rhetorically anticipates concession, further eroding distinctions between logic and volition, suggestion and acquiescence, wish and fulfillment. Furthermore, love's language propels its speakers out of narrative temporality into the timelessness of the mythic: "copious stories, oftentimes begun, / End without audience, and are never done" (lines 845-6). Accordingly, Venus's first declaration of passion for Adonis violates temporal boundaries by serving as prophecy, articulating the future in the present. The floral—and, incongruously, also apocalyptic—images she addresses to Adonis prefigure his eventual transformation in death: he is, ominously, "'more lovely than a man'" (line 9). Furthermore, "'Nature, that made thee with herself at strife, / Saith that the world hath ending with thy life'" (lines 11-2). As metaphoric comparison that also serves as literal prediction, this language of desire likewise dissolves the semantic distinction between vehicle and tenor.[18]

Venus's reasoning from analogy, together with her characteristic equation of distinct categories, thus exemplifies what Foucault calls "analogical" thought, distinct from the "modern" disjunctions between words and things and among kinds of things. "Analogic" thought ponders a world that "fold[s] in upon itself, duplicate[s] itself, reflect[s] itself, or form[s] a chain with itself so that things can resemble one another"; this language "partakes in the world-wide dissemination of similitudes and signatures."[19] Whereas Venus's discourse is predicated on proximity and analogy, Adonis's is more invested in separation and substitution—in Foucault's terms, with "modern" signification: that is, the "ordering of things by means of . . . *fabricated* signs" for a "knowledge based upon identity and difference."[20] The poem figures Venus's affect through pathetic fallacies: her thoughts leach into nature as troubled "neighbor caves" murmur her longing (line 830) and "shrill-tongu'd tapsters" share her anxiety (line 849). Adonis's death, by contrast, is represented by *signifiers* requiring *interpretation*: the "sad signs" (line 929) the narrator associates with "apparitions . . . and prodigies" (line 926). Adonis's hunting hounds are saddened by his death, but not with the same kind of pathetic sorrow that Venus's caves express. Whereas the caves *iconically* participate in Venus's affect (in Roman Jakobson's sense of "icons" as signifiers that represent a signified by sharing its essence), the hounds suggest a signifying *narrative*.[21] In their silence, wound licking, and scowling (lines 914-7), the hounds present information that is interpretable but not transparent, emphasizing disjunctions and incommensurabilities where the caves and tapsters emphasize contiguities. Hence the hunting hounds do not share a language with Venus, but rather preserve distinctions among species of discourse: "here she meets another sadly scowling, / To whom she *speaks,* and he replies with *howling*" (lines 917-8, my emphasis).

Adonis's death and metamorphosis further link him to semiotic habits associated with separation, distinction, and mediated "signification," as opposed to comparison, analogy and iconicity. The flower that Adonis becomes functions not as an icon but as a sign. To be more precise, it is a sign in the terms of *his* story; the meanings of the metamorphosis—indeed of metamorphosis in general—diverge significantly in the two logical frameworks. Venus attempts rather desperately to impose an analogical likeness onto the blossom: in her vision of the dead Adonis, the flower "Resembl[es] well his pale cheeks" (line 1169), and Venus informs the flower that it shares a kinship tie with Adonis: "'Here was thy father's bed'" (line 1183). But despite her insistence on the filial continuity between bloom and man, the point of view we can infer from Adonis's words as well as his representation in the poem makes the flower function as an incommensurable stand-in—like a sign—for the young man made absent by death. For existence as a flower, immobile and delicate, is utterly incompatible with existence as a hunter. Despite herself, Venus betrays the gap between Adonis and the flower by disingenuously suggesting that she has won the amorous contest. Claiming that her breast was "'thy father's bed'" and announcing with a certain compensatory triumph that "'There shall not be one minute in an hour / Wherein I will not kiss my sweet love's flow'r'" (lines 1187-8), Venus glosses over a crucial inversion of agency: she had begged for the live Adonis to kiss *her*. The conventional association of flowering with completion or fulfillment casts further ironic light on the phrase "'my sweet love's flower'"; Adonis's transformation hardly constitutes Venus's love come to flower, but rather its final frustration. Soon to wither, deprived of the potential to grant the acquiescence Venus craves, the blossom escapes Venus's erotics despite its imprisonment in the "'hollow cradle'"—we might emphasize "'hollow'"—of her breasts (line 1185).

Metamorphosis directly engages questions of contiguity and separation, sameness and difference, the object as *Ding an sich* and the object as contingent and mutable manifestation of first matter, ideal form, or similar early modern notions of the cosmic relatedness of all things. In its play on form as stable, autonomous identity versus form as signifier of other potential or erstwhile states, metamorphosis provides the poem another arena for working through the differences between the mythic/conventional and the historical/particular modes of narrative, desire, and subjectivity. Like the actual metamorphosis that closes the tale, other metamorphoses figuratively invoked earlier in the poem provide double interpretative possibilities. These transformations contrast metamorphosis as the transcendent instantiation of analogy (similarity among things) to metamorphosis as destruction (the annihilation of a thing, alienated when a profoundly different form overcomes it). As part of her seduction argument, for example, Venus suggests an extended analogy between Adonis and a deer:

"since I have hemm'd thee here
Within the circuit of this ivory pale,
I'll be a park, and thou shalt be my deer:
Feed where thou wilt, on mountain, or in dale;
  Graze on my lips, and if those hills be dry,
  Stray lower, where the pleasant fountains lie."

(lines 229-34)

Within the logic of Venus's poetics, the deer figure allows Adonis to be both himself and something else. That is, Venus proposes a metaphor that provides an alternative lexical framework for actions—whether grazing or caressing—that are equally possible for a man or a deer. The easy continuity in Venus's discourse between vehicle and tenor underlines the full congruence between Venus-as-body and Venus-as-park, conveying the wholesomeness, the delightful variety, and the naturalness of habitat (she maintains) for hart and lover alike. Adonis's transformation into a fragile flower, whose inevitable demise Venus rudely hastens, retroactively suggests a dissenting view of this same image: the deer metamorphosis that Adonis refuses would transform the young man into an entity inimical and fatal to his self—in fact, into quarry for his proper self. The echoes of Actaeon in the metamorphosis Venus offers heighten the opposition Adonis seems to see between heteroerotic seduction and hunting. Such alienation would certainly follow from a deer grazing/gazing on a goddess: Actaeon's transformation turned him from hunter to hunted, and Adonis wants no part of it.

Adonis's metamorphosis simultaneously realizes and frustrates both Venus's and Adonis's aims. Adonis escapes Venus's logic only to be returned helplessly to her bosom; Venus finally sees Adonis's scrupulously defended boundaries breached only to render him incapable of satisfying her passion. In its traditionally tragic end, the myth of Venus and Adonis explores the impossibility of erotic satisfaction when mortals are involved; Shakespeare's text distills this aspect of the tale into Venus's version of the story. This poem's reluctant Adonis renders another kind of fulfillment impossible—a pleasure that depends on escaping Venus. The entire narrative has shown the two figures' desires to be incompatible; analyzing Adonis's metamorphosis shows that the mere existence of each desire undermines the other's conditions of possibility. On one side, Adonis's distaste for Venus's proposals, together with the ways the poem pokes fun at Venus's excesses, suggests her limitations. On the other, Venus's use of mythic logic, her assertions of infinite analogy, and her own identity as the personification of love operate as inherently self-evident and universal: hence, they can-

not accommodate compromise.[22] Notably, however, Adonis offers objections rather than alternatives: Venus's poetic dominance makes positively articulating other erotics, poetics, or values impossible.

Thus, whereas Peter Erickson and Patrick Murphy have interpreted the poem's cautiousness in representing alternatives to Venus's views as mere political circumspection, I would argue that the poem's recourse to indirect suggestions of vaguely delineated choices indicates more than strategic self-censorship.[23] Adonis's hesitations also gesture toward emergent paradigms of subjectivity and semiotics that are not sufficiently manifest to be clearly represented: something akin to what Francis Barker characterizes as the *"incipient modernity"* of Hamlet's "anachronistic" longing for a more modern subject position than his historical moment permits.[24] If we were to characterize the poem's competing modes of desire and representation historically, then, my understanding of Adonis's (proto) subjectivity would lead in the opposite direction from Nona Fienberg's conclusions. Fienberg associates Adonis with an aristocratic "fixity," "absoluteness," and "patriarchy" that she characterizes as essentially medieval, while her Venus evidences a "mutability and diversity" that "provid[e] . . . a way to reevaluate patriarchy."[25] While I agree to an extent that the poem associates Adonis's desires with "fixity" and "patriarchy," I would argue that these do not, as Fienberg claims, constitute the *status quo* in the poem—nor, entirely, in its historical context. Rather, the Venus whom Fienberg argues to be fluid and "dynamic" uses this "flexibility" only instrumentally, within traditional humanist rhetorical practice, to ingeniously and irrefutably perpetuate paradigms based on rhetorical analogy, ontological continuity, and the authority of mythic and literary-conventional tradition. Whereas Fienberg (in a move medievalists might find oversimplifying) characterizes Adonis as "a relic of the time before the commercial and humanist revolutions, when value was a given"[26] who "holds on to his old ways of measuring time, growth, maturity, and value," I would argue that through inclining in both his desires and his semiotics toward deferral, separation, and idiosyncrasy, Adonis emerges as something of a figure for protomodernity, or at least for resistance to the values Venus espouses.[27] It is semiotic absoluteness, autonomous identity, and social patriarchy, I think, that the poem presents as constituting a departure.[28]

The poem's simultaneous representation of different discursivities and subjectivities might, however, give pause to the project of firmly historicizing these modes (a Foucauldean version of the Whiggish march to modernity). It might be more fruitful, and more accurate, to consider what I have called the poem's protomodern and nonmodern modes as simultaneous aspects of a typically mixed cultural moment. Indeed, particularly intriguing about this poem (and its milieu) are the differences between the modes and interests here aligned as congruent (femininity/*status quo*/speech, for example, versus masculinity/marginality/silence) with our more expected aggregations. This is not to say that the poem celebrates a happy heteroglossia of Elizabethan culture. By confining its represented action to what Venus witnesses, and by demonstrating the limitations of her practices, the poem thematizes the difficulty of representing competing models (whether we trace this difficulty to an authoritarian queen, the poetic demands of generic convention, a watershed moment in the history of subjectivity, covert cultural contests between masculinist poetic culture and propagandists for the Cult of Elizabeth—or concede it to be overdetermined). The hunting band provides the locus for alternatives to Venus's authority, in a way that may have been particularly satisfying for the primary 1590s (male) readership at the Inns of Court or indeed the royal court—but precisely what these alternatives would be remains pointedly oblique.[29] In the end, the poem draws much of its energy from this obliqueness, creating an epyllion about what Ovidian poetry cannot represent—a gushing epideictic on an overbearing queen, a camp triangulation of a Venus who does not realize she is in a poem, an Adonis who half realizes and does not want to be, and a reader who smugly knows the score. And in this obliqueness, I suggest, Adonis's positions come closest to a kind of realization, insofar as the poem's silences draw the reader into fleshing out what the text occludes. Venus argues her familiar positions all too thoroughly, leaving the reader no task but assent. But drawing the reader into chasing an alternative that is not fully visible, traceable from two steps behind through prints left between the lines, does not the poem invite the reader into the oppositional hunting band?

Notes

For their help with various versions of this essay, I would like to thank the anonymous panel of Shakespeare Association of America judges who gave me the opportunity to present a version of this argument at the SAA conference, and Stephen M. Foley, Coppélia Kahn, William Keach, Karen Newman, and Evan Radcliffe.

1. William Shakespeare, *Venus and Adonis,* in *The Riverside Shakespeare,* ed. G. Blakemore Evans (Boston: Houghton Mifflin, 1974), pp. 1705-19, lines 13-6. All subsequent references to *Venus and Adonis* will be to this edition and will appear parenthetically in the text by line number.

2. For the range of interpretations particularly focused on Adonis's reluctance, see T. W. Baldwin's Neoplatonic reading in *On the Literary Genetics of Shakespeare's Poems and Sonnets* (Urbana: Univ. of Illinois Press, 1950); S. Clark Hulse's and John Doebler's discussions of iconography in, respectively, "Shakespeare's Myth of Venus and Adonis," *PMLA* 93, 1 (January 1978): 95-105, and "The Reluctant Adonis: Titian and Shakespeare," *SQ* [*Shakespeare Quarterly*] 33, 4 (Winter 1982): 480-90; J. D. Jahn's analysis of Adonis's moral failings in "The Lamb of Lust: The Role of Adonis in Shakespeare's *Venus and Adonis,*" *ShakS* [*Shakespeare Studies*] 6 (1970): 11-25; Coppélia Kahn's psychoanalytic account of Adonis's hesitation in *Man's Estate: Masculine Identity in Shakespeare* (Berkeley: Univ. of California Press, 1981); Catherine Belsey's taxonomy of desire in "Love as Trompe-l'oeil: Taxonomies of Desire in *Venus and Adonis,*" *SQ* 46, 3 (Fall 1995): 257-76; Patrick M. Murphy's discussion of the poem as advice literature on negotiating competing obligations in "Wriothesley's Resistance: Wardship Practices and Ovidian Narratives in Shakespeare's *Venus and Adonis,*" in *Venus and Adonis: Critical Essays,* ed. Philip C. Kolin (New York: Garland Publishing, 1997), pp. 323-40; and A. D. Cousins's argument that Adonis is feminized by his refusal, in "Towards a Reconsideration of Shakespeare's Adonis: Rhetoric, Narcissus, and the Male Gaze," *SN* [*Studia Neophilologica*] 68, 2 (1996): 195-204. Although Karen Newman argues for a "shift in perspective from Adonis's unwillingness to Venus's desire" (p. 254), she shares these critics' understanding of a reluctant Adonis: see the important but seldom cited "Myrrha's Revenge: Ovid and Shakespeare's Reluctant Adonis," *Illinois Classical Studies* 9, 2 (Fall 1984): 251-65.

Recently, Robert P. Merrix and, briefly, Bruce R. Smith have considered what *does* interest Adonis as well as what repels him, in Smith's *Homosexual Desire in Shakespeare's England: A Cultural Poetics* (Chicago: Univ. of Chicago Press, 1991) and Merrix's "'Lo, in This Hollow Cradle Take Thy Rest': Sexual Conflict and Resolution in *Venus and Adonis,*" in Kolin, pp. 341-58. An unusual earlier reading that acknowledges Adonis's desire is A. Robin Bowers, "'Hard Armours' and 'Delicate Amours' in Shakespeare's *Venus and Adonis,*" *ShS* [*Shakespeare Survey*] 12 (1979): 1-23. However, Bowers bases this argument on Adonis's single kiss, failing to account for the distaste Adonis demonstrates in the rest of the poem.

3. See Frankie Rubinstein, *A Dictionary of Shakespeare's Sexual Puns and Their Significance,* 2d edn. (New York: St. Martin's Press, 1995).

4. An important exception here is Joel Fineman's *Shakespeare's Perjured Eye: The Invention of Poetic Subjectivity in the Sonnets* (Berkeley: Univ. of California Press, 1986).

5. Influential examples of the former include Kahn, *Man's Estate,* and Nona Fienberg, "Thematics of Value in *Venus and Adonis,*" *Criticism* 31, 1 (Winter 1989): 21-32. On the latter, see particularly Lucy Gent, "'Venus and Adonis': The Triumph of Rhetoric," *MLR* [*Modern Language Review*] 69, 4 (October 1974): 721-9; Hulse; and Jonathan Hart, "'Till Forging Nature Be Condemned of Treason': Representational Strife in *Venus and Adonis,*" *Cahiers Élisabéthains: Études sur la Pré-Renaissance et la Renaissance Anglaises* 36 (1989): 37-48.

6. Heather Dubrow, *Captive Victors: Shakespeare's Narrative Poems and Sonnets* (Ithaca: Cornell Univ. Press, 1987), p. 27. Conversely, Goran Stanivukovic examines rhetoric "as a cognitive mode which suggests *the* early modern conceptualisation of desire in *Venus and Adonis,*" in "Troping Desire in Shakespeare's *Venus and Adonis,*" *FMLS* [*Forum for Modern Language Studies*] 33, 4 (October 1997): 289-301, 290 (my emphasis).

7. James Schiffer, "Shakespeare's *Venus and Adonis*: A Lacanian Tragicomedy of Desire," in Kolin, pp. 359-76, 372.

8. Jane Hedley, *Power in Verse: Metaphor and Metonymy in the Renaissance Lyric* (University Park: Pennsylvania State Univ. Press, 1988), p. 22.

9. Most interpretations of Adonis's Venus/boar opposition pair "love" and Venus together as an alternative to the boar hunt, rather than following the verse's syntactically implied opposition of Venus-love and boar-love. See D. C. Allen on hunting and love as alternative but complementary forms of pursuit ("On *Venus and Adonis,*" in *Elizabethan and Jacobean Studies Presented to F. P. Wilson,* ed. Herbert Davis and Helen Gardner [Oxford: Clarendon Press, 1959], pp. 100-11), and Norman Rabkin on the characters' arguments for and against sensual love, in *Shakespeare and the Common Understanding* (New York: Free Press, 1967). Exceptions to the tendency of opposing hunting and love include A. T. Hatto's "*Venus and Adonis*—and the Boar," *MLR* 41, 4 (October 1946): 353-61, which depicts the boar as "overbearing masculinity" that rivals Venus, and Kahn's notion of the boar as the repository of Adonis's projected fantasy/fears about Venus. Other interpretations making substantial use of this line include William E. Sheidley, "'Unless It Be a Boar': Love and Wisdom in Shakespeare's *Venus and Adonis,*" *MLQ* [*Modern Language Quarterly*] 35, 1 (March 1974): 3-15, and William Keach, *Elizabethan Erotic Narratives: Irony and Pathos in the Ovidian Poetry of Shakespeare, Marlowe, and Their Contemporaries* (New Brunswick NJ: Rutgers Univ. Press, 1977).

10. J. W. Lever notes the relevance here of Theocritus's idyll, translated in 1588, in which the boar declares his love for the young shepherd; see "The Poems," *ShS* 15 (1962): 18-22, 21.

11. See Jacques Lacan, "The Signification of the Phallus," in *Écrits: A Selection,* trans. Alan Sheridan (New York: W. W. Norton, 1977), pp. 281-92.

12. Sheidley, p. 10.

13. As this discussion indicates, I disagree with Peter Erickson's claim that the dynamics of the hunting band are entirely opaque and thus irrelevant ("In theory, Adonis's hunt is not a solitary activity, as his allusions to his [male] friends . . . indicate . . . [but] . . . since they never actually appear, they are for practical purposes nonexistent"); see Erickson's *Rewriting Shakespeare, Rewriting Ourselves* (Berkeley: Univ. of California Press, 1991), p. 43.

14. Kahn, p. 36.

15. Likewise, Fienberg cites "The sea hath bounds, but deep desire hath none" (line 389) to illustrate that "Venus's desire is unlimited, multiple" (p. 25).

16. The contrast fails to amuse some commentators; for instance, Hallett Smith remarks that "the celebrated description of the horse, the account of the coursing of the hare, and the images of the dive-dapper, the snail, and the lark . . . [are] difficult to harmonize with the elements of classical myth" (introduction to *Venus and Adonis,* p. 1704). Others contend that the realistic and mythic modes are compatible; for example, Douglas Bush comments that rare "natural" images "heighten" the overall effect of Ovidian artifice; see *Mythology and the Renaissance Tradition in English Poetry* (Minneapolis: Univ. of Minnesota Press, 1932), p. 147. A more recent take on the same problem comes in Hart's claim that the work foregrounds the "friction between mimetic and supplemental art" (p. 37). Dubrow provides an important counterargument to these kinds of binary analyses, arguing against "an absolute split between the rhetorical and the mimetic" (p. 16).

17. In remarks relevant to my linking Venus's discourse with specifically humanist mastery, Dubrow notes the poem's association of Venus with Elizabethan aesthetic convention; M. L. Stapleton intriguingly casts Venus as a rhetorical pedagogue ("Venus as *Praeceptor*: The *Ars Amatoria* in *Venus and Adonis,*" in Kolin, pp. 309-21); Sheidley identifies Venus's language as that of the sonneteer; and Christy Desmet notes that "Venus is an orator . . . [whose] weapons are those commonly found in the schoolboy's arsenal" (*Reading*

Shakespeare's Characters: Rhetoric, Ethics, and Identity [Amherst: Univ. of Massachusetts Press, 1992], p. 138).

18. Dubrow emphasizes a different aspect of this tendency in her discussion of Venus "renaming the world" by "transform[ing] the material into the spiritual" (p. 29); Gent discusses the same habit as "hyberbole," and Katharine Eisaman Maus notes the consistently violent results of collapsing metaphor in "Taking Tropes Seriously: Language and Violence in Shakespeare's *Rape of Lucrece*," SQ 37, 1 (Spring 1986): 66-82.

19. Michel Foucault, *The Order of Things: An Archaeology of the Human Sciences* (1966; rprt. New York: Vintage Books, 1973), pp. 25-6, p. 35.

20. Foucault, pp. 59, 63 (my emphasis).

21. See particularly Roman Jakobson's "A Glance at the Development of Semiotics," in *Selected Writings,* ed. Stephen Rudy, 8 vols.—(Gravenhage: Mouton, 1962-), 7:199-218.

22. Logically enough, psychoanalytic as well as archetypal interpretations of the poem reproduce Venus's reasoning. To give a twentieth-century psychoanalytic example: for Kahn, Venus is love, heterosexual erotics provide a requisite rite of passage, and Adonis's reluctance constitutes a refusal to embrace mature male identity. Ovidian commentators of late antiquity, who associate the myth with seasonal change and ritual renewal, work in a similarly definite framework.

23. Erickson remarks—and I would agree—that "Venus's domination evokes Elizabeth's control, and this undercurrent helps to account for the poem's unstable tonal mixture of defensive jocularity and general alarm" (p. 41). Murphy argues that the poem offers Henry Wriothesley counsel on his negotiations with the crown.

24. Francis Barker, *The Tremulous Private Body: Essays on Subjection* (London: Methuen, 1984), pp. 27, 37 (my emphasis).

25. Fienberg, p. 21.

26. Fienberg, p. 23.

27. Fienberg, p. 27.

28. Like mine, Belsey's argument aligns Adonis's position with historical change, insofar as Adonis is the figure who articulates the distinction between love and lust. This distinction "brings an emergent taxonomy into conjunction—and conflict—with a residual indeterminacy" (p. 275). Without making historical claims, Merrix and Smith both associate Venus with the fixity of social proscription and domestic confinement. Merrix argues that "[t]he conflict between Venus and Adonis . . . concerns conflicting lifestyles, one domestic, fruitful and secure, and the other exotic, sterile, and dangerous" (p. 343). Smith addresses the poem's participation in an Elizabethan paradigm shared by romance narratives and folk plays, which "strike . . . [a balance] . . . between positive and negative controls . . . Both, for a season, 'valorize' polymorphous passion. Both, in the end, take that value away" (p. 127).

29. Detailing the dynamics of these readerships lies beyond the scope of the present paper. Briefly, both these venues constitute circles of male power, subject to the greater authority of the queen, but internally exclusively male. Significantly, both the Inns of Court and the royal court are subject to far more frequent and regular assertion of the queen's authority—particularly, of course, the latter—than such analogous male bastions as the universities or the church, since they operate in such geographic proximity to Elizabeth's quotidian routines. Exploring how this poem functions in these circles would perhaps serve to flesh out what might be entailed in the "homosocial style" Richard Halpern enigmatically invokes without specification: "The English tradition of Ovidian poetry was fostered in . . . exclusively male bastions that cultivated a homosocial style" ("'Pining Their Maws': Female Readers and the Erotic Ontology of the Text in Shakespeare's *Venus and Adonis*," in Kolin, pp. 377-88, p. 378).

On Inns of Court readership of *Venus and Adonis,* see Keach; Philip J. Finkelpearl, *John Marston of the Middle Temple: An Elizabethan Dramatist in His Social Setting* (Cambridge MA: Harvard Univ. Press, 1969); and Arthur F. Marotti, *John Donne, Coterie Poet* (Madison: Univ. of Wisconsin Press, 1986). On Venus and Elizabeth, see also Kirby Farrell, *Play, Death, and Heroism in Shakespeare* (Chapel Hill: Univ. of North Carolina Press, 1989), pp. 125-30.

Katherine Duncan-Jones (essay date 2003)

SOURCE: Duncan-Jones, Katherine. "Playing Fields or Killing Fields: Shakespeare's Poems and *Sonnets*." *Shakespeare Quarterly* 54, no. 2 (2003): 127-41.

[*In the essay that follows, Duncan-Jones contends that in what is ostensibly love poetry—particularly* Venus and Adonis *and the* Sonnets—*Shakespeare emphasized the inevitability of death.*]

In a chorus for his 1935 play *The Dog Beneath the Skin,* W. H. Auden explored the differences between human beings and animals, and the differences between privileged human beings, on the one hand, and, on the other, everyone else:

> Happy the hare at morning, for she cannot read
> The Hunter's waking thoughts. Lucky the leaf
> Unable to predict the fall . . .
> But what shall men do, who can whistle tunes by heart,
> Knows to the bar when death shall cut him short like the cry of the shearwater?
> We will show you what he has done.
> How comely are his places of refuge and the tabernacles of his peace,
> The new books upon the morning table, the lawns and the afternoon terraces!
> Here are the playing-fields where he may forget his ignorance . . .[1]

Humankind's "playing-fields" are, for Auden, places of refuge from the knowledge of death, and of death's proximity. For the privileged and the literate, such playing fields have always included "new books," and especially, perhaps, new books of amorous literature, such as Shakespeare's poems and *Sonnets* proclaimed themselves to be. The epigraph to *Venus and Adonis* labels it as a poem not for the vulgar "general," those playgoing multitudes who had recently flocked to Edward Alleyn's Rose Theatre in Southwark to see John Talbot's battles against the French, but for the learned and knowledgeable. The poem's title page is a door leading to an elite site of high inspiration drawn from pure Castalian springs:

> *Vilia miretur vulgus: mihi flauus Apollo*
> *Pocula Castalia plena ministret aqua.*

—translated from Ovid by Marlowe as

> Let base-conceited witts admire vilde things,
> Faire *Phoebus* lead me to the Muses springs.[2]

Educated readers, sporting themselves within such carefully fenced playing fields as *Venus and Adonis, The Rape of Lucrece,* and *Shake-speares Sonnets,* could for a while forget their own painful "ignorance" of the proximity of death.

For the earliest readers of these poems, it was particularly desirable to find escape, for death was all around them. They must have hoped to forget the severe plague in London that closed the playhouses and compromised the economic and social life of the City. The years in which Shakespeare's three volumes of non-dramatic verse were published—1593, 1594, and 1609—were marked by outbreaks of plague, and all three publications in this sense relate to "love in time of plague." Yet plague is mentioned very little in any of them. There are barely more than half a dozen occurrences of the word in the sum total of over 6,000 lines. Almost

incidentally, it appears, Venus claims that the freshness of Adonis's lips ought to have the power "To drive infection from the dangerous year: / That the star-gazers, having writ on death, / May say, the plague is banish'd by thy breath" (ll. 508-10). Yet this is no more than an amorous play of fancy, just one among the many hyperboles with which the goddess of love attempts to beguile the mortal boy by means of flattering rhetoric, while signally failing to do so. Venus's later allusion to "Life-poisoning pestilence" (l. 740) is slipped almost unnoticed into a catalogue of the "maladies" that she claims have been visited on mortals by her fellow goddess Diana out of spite against human beauty. In Shakespeare's poem, Adonis was not merely a character in classical mythology but a primitive pagan deity identified with vegetation and the seasonal cycles of death and rebirth. In the poem's conclusion it would have been possible for Shakespeare to draw on the classical tradition of pastoral elegy and to celebrate the apotheosis of Adonis as a spirit of renewal and fecundity. Adonis's tutelary status could have been explicitly applied to the topical theme of plague. But this was not the treatment Shakespeare chose.

Two allusions to plague in a single stanza of *Lucrece* have a good deal more force, using the infectiousness of plague to illustrate the way in which the sexual transgression of a single individual—such as Tarquin—has the power to cause suffering to huge numbers of innocent people:

> 'Why should the private pleasure of some one
> Become the public plague of many moe? . . .
> For one's offence why should so many fall,
> To plague a private sin in general?'

(ll. 1478-79, 1483-84)

Many believed that plague was sent from heaven as a punishment for the sins of a few individuals, and especially for sexual sins, committed in pursuit of "private pleasure." For readers of these poems when they were "new books upon the morning table," in the summers of 1593 and 1594, images of driving "infection from the dangerous year," or else of the capacity of private vices to trigger public suffering, were a good deal more compelling than they can be for us. Yet even in *Lucrece* the allusions are glancing and transient.

The four occurrences of the word *plague* in *Shake-speares Sonnets* are even more transient than those in the narrative poems and invite even less consideration of the external reality of infection. Only the first, in a line of **"Sonnet 14"** concerning subjects for divination, "Of plagues, of dearths, or seasons' quality" (l. 4), bears any literal reference to plague. In the other three (114.2, 137.14, and 141.13) it seems that the word *plague* is used merely as a rhetorical metonym for something deeply unpleasant.

On 12 June 1593, Shakespeare's *Venus and Adonis* became "a new book upon the morning table" for an elderly Teller of the Exchequer, Richard Stonley, whose diaries are [now housed/preserved] in the Folger Shakespeare Library.[3] He seems to have paid sixpence for it. As a man living in the heart of London, in Aldersgate Street, Stonley must have been acutely conscious of the plague's effects on the City's residents. According to Thomas Nashe, deaths this summer were running at more than sixteen hundred a week in London as a whole.[4] Nor was a visit to a bookshop a pleasant or hygienic experience—though Stonley may have sent one of his servants—for virtually all of the supplying bookshops were situated in and around Paul's Churchyard. As Peter Blayney has shown, the primary supplier of *Venus and Adonis,* John Harrison, had premises to the northeast of the cathedral, on the site of the former charnel house and just to the south of Paternoster Row.[5] At least five other London parishes buried their dead in Paul's Churchyard at this time, and the shops to the northeast overlooked the cathedral's largest burial ground. This was an improvement: ten years earlier as many as twenty-three London parishes had all crammed their dead into Paul's Churchyard. Nashe offers an exaggerated, but probably not wholly fanciful, account of his enemy Gabriel Harvey's residence at the house of the printer and publisher John Wolfe during the plague-ridden summer of 1593. Wolfe's shop was on the opposite side of the cathedral from Harrison's, "right against the great South door."[6] According to Nashe, Gabriel Harvey was scarcely able, during this warm summer, to open either window or door for fear of infection from the newly interred plague victims:

> he was so barricadoed vp with graues, which besiedged and vndermined his verie threshold; nor to open his window euening or morning, but a damp . . . from the fat manured earth with contagion (being the buriall place of fiue parishes) in thick rouling clowds would strugglingly funnell vp, & with a full blast puffe in at his casements.[7]

We should remember that odors were thought to be agents of infection, rather than just its disagreeable by-product. Perfumes were presumed, therefore, to act as antidotes. In this sense *Venus and Adonis,* with its outdoor setting and its sustained evocation of sweet smells and tastes, may have offered some imaginative solace to readers who, like Richard Stonley and Gabriel Harvey, were unfortunate enough to live in or near the plague-stricken parishes. Early on in the poem, Venus feasts on the breath of Adonis as if it were a therapeutic vapor:

> Panting he lies and breatheth in her face.
> She feedeth on the steam as on a prey,
> And calls it heavenly moisture, air of grace,
>   Wishing her cheeks were gardens full of flowers,
>   So they were dew'd with such distilling showers.

(ll. 62-66)

Nearly four hundred lines further on, she imagines how much she would still adore Adonis even if she had been deprived of all senses except that of smell:

> And nothing but the very smell were left me,
> Yet would my love to thee be still as much;
>   For from the stillitory of thy face excelling
>   Comes breath perfum'd, that breedeth love by smelling.

(ll. 441-44)

Yet only in a strained and peripheral sense can the poem's pervasive imagery of succulent smells and sweet tastes be connected with measures against infection. Neither *Venus and Adonis* nor any of Shakespeare's other published poems can be said to be explicitly "about" plague. Though it is historically and bibliographically important to be aware that all the poems were published, and to some extent also written, during plague outbreaks, the sense in which they are about places of death as well as places of entertainment is a much broader one.

Their central preoccupation is, rather, the one that Sir Philip Sidney summed up in the phrase "What may words say, and what may words not say?"[8] All of the nondramatic poems at once showcase rhetorical power and adopt the ultimate limitations of such power as part of their subject matter. Like most major works, they push the possibilities of art up to its limits and beyond. As Anthony Mortimer has recently shown, Shakespeare's Venus deploys a marvelously varied and ingenious range of rhetorical tropes and registers of language to woo the "lovely" boy Adonis.[9] Many of the poem's earliest readers, such as Gullio in the second *Parnassus* play,[10] admired Venus's rhetoric so much that they appropriated it for their own private purposes, using Shakespeare's poem as a kind of handbook for wooers. Yet this was paradoxical, for Venus's rhetoric, though it has such a huge effect on the poem's readers, has only negative effects on Adonis. Adonis is first annoyed, then bored, and finally disgusted by it. The "graver" *Lucrece* offers an opposite scenario.[11] Against the brilliant and ample rhetoric of the goddess of love, which is so notably unsuccessful in enabling her to encompass her desire, may be set the all-too-successful rhetoric of the Roman lord Collatine in praise of his wife's chastity. His speech is first tersely summarized in the prose Argument—"Collatinus extolled the incomparable chastity of his wife Lucretia"—and then fleshed out rather more fully, but in indirect speech, in the poem's second stanza: "When Collatine unwisely did not let / To praise the clear unmatched red and white / Which triumph'd in that sky of his delight . . ." (ll. 10-12). In acting as "the publisher / Of that rich jewel he should keep unknown" (ll. 33-34), Lucrece's husband spells its doom. Shakespeare does not put as much stress as Thomas Heywood was to do in his dramatic version of *The Rape of Lucrece* on the culpability of Collatine in putting his wife at risk. In Heywood's play Collatine gives Tarquin a ring as a token to Lucrece to admit the unexpected guest, for which Lucrece ultimately rebukes him in front of all the Roman lords: "This Ring, oh Collatine, this Ring you sent / Is cawse of all my woe, our discontent."[12] However, within Shakespeare's extremely long poem Collatine's "unwise" praise of his wife occupies very few lines and is readily overlooked or forgotten in what follows. Only in *Cymbeline,* written sixteen or seventeen years later, did Shakespeare make it fully apparent that it is not only tasteless but irresponsible for a husband to boast in male company about his wife's virtue, since such a boast may be taken as a challenge by other young men. But even in *Lucrece* it is clear that Collatine's incautious rhetoric has been too potent, triggering the sequence of events that leads first to Tarquin's destruction of Lucretia's chastity, then to her death, and finally to the ending of monarchical rule in Rome.

Unlike Collatine, the speaker in the *Sonnets* is fully aware of the danger that eulogistic rhetoric may attract the wrong kind of attention. It may function as cheap sales-talk rather than as the disinterested discourse of affection. At the end of **"Sonnet 21,"** he promises that "I will not praise, that purpose not to sell" (l. 14). Yet the poet-speaker does not refrain from praising his love object; he merely refrains from praising him in what he feels to be trite and outworn language. But like Collatine's, his rhetorical efforts backfire. In the so-called "Rival Poet" sonnets (**"Sonnets 78-86"**), it appears that his rhetoric of praise has indeed attracted unwanted attention from other poet-lovers:

> So oft have I invoked thee for my Muse,
> And found such fair assistance in my verse,
> As every alien pen hath got my use,
> And under thee their poesy disperse.
>
> (78.1-4)

He acknowledges that the pen of the Rival Poet is "worthier" (79.6); he calls him a "better spirit" (80.2); and he indicates that the style of the other man's writing is more fashionable, offering "Some fresher stamp of the time-bettering days" (82.8). Eventually, however, the speaker reveals that what he feels most threatened by is not so much the other poet's status and stylistic sophistication as his success in winning the favorable regard, or the "countenance," of the fair youth: "when your countenance filled up his line, / Then lacked I matter, that enfeebled mine" (86.13-14). Like Venus and Collatine, the *Sonnets*' speaker discovers to his cost that all his most brilliant rhetorical efforts have produced unforeseen outcomes. Language designed to articulate and nourish private devotion may be either misconstrued or abused by its intended audience, or, as in the case of the *Sonnets*' speaker, it may reach an audience for whom it was never meant. In all three cases, words originally spoken out of love or private affection miss their mark, reach other auditors, and produce unwelcome results.

Readers who turned to Shakespeare's narrative poems and sonnets as an escape would, at this point, be in for an unpleasant surprise, as the poems caught them up in the processes that lead inexorably from the failed rhetoric of love to the death of the love object, and the playing field becomes a killing field. Though these early readers may have turned from the pressing threat of infection toward what promised to be a sensuous arena of amorous delight, if they persevered to the end of these books, they discovered that the playing field is a bloody place. Even in Arcadia, death is. This is obvious at the outset in the case of the explicitly tragic *Lucrece,* and I shall say little more about the poem. A few naive male readers in 1594 may have hoped, given the prominence of the word *rape* in the running title, that the poem would offer some sort of pornographic thrill, but they would soon have realized their mistake. According to Gabriel Harvey, it was the "wiser," not the younger, "sort" who most relished this work.

It is in *Venus and Adonis* that the metamorphosis of playing field to killing field can be seen most clearly. This is not simply because the story is so familiar that most readers know in advance that Adonis is destined to be killed by the boar that he tries to hunt. It's true that even the poem's opening words foreshadow loss and the abandonment of a languishing female lover by an active male one, "as the sun with purple-colour'd face / Had ta'en his last leave of the weeping morn" (ll. 1-2). This is a sunrise that feels rather like a sunset, and the weeping and vanishing goddess Aurora poignantly foreshadows the weeping and vanishing goddess Venus of the poem's closing stanza. But Shakespeare encourages us for much of the first two-thirds of the poem to forget that the story will be a tragedy. He does so partly by adopting a comic, at times almost farcical, tone and partly by encouraging us to forget another important point: the fact that Venus is divine. His strategy is so effective that many critics also seem quickly to forget it. Anthony Mortimer, for instance, immediately after remarking that "the identity of Venus as goddess of love is beyond question," alludes to "her biological status as a woman."[13] Yet, strictly speaking, she is *not* biologically a woman, however much her visible and tangible humanoid body, evoked in all its warmth, steam, and aroma, makes her appear to be one. She is a magical, shape-changing deity who attempts to win Adonis with the promise of magic tricks:

> 'Bid me discourse, I will enchant thine ear,
> Or like a fairy trip upon the green,
> Or like a nymph, with long dishevell'd hair,
> Dance on the sands, and yet no footing seen.
>
> (ll. 145-49)

A goddess was proverbially to be identified by "her gait," as in **"Sonnet 130"**: "I grant I never saw a goddess go; / My mistress when she walks treads on the ground" (ll. 11-12). Unlike the so-called Dark Lady, the goddess Venus does not "walk on the ground" in the plodding manner of a mortal woman. She can run on sand without leaving footprints, and she can step or even lie on primroses without making these delicate flowers bend.

The lines I've just quoted made a great impression on one of the poem's earliest readers, the paranoid soldier William Reynolds. He commented on them in a letter dated 21 September 1593, seeing Shakespeare's poem as an ingenious trap sprung for him by the Privy Council. He identified Venus with the queen and Adonis with himself. He summarized the passage from which I've quoted thus:

> the queen represents the person of Venus, and greatly desires to kiss him, and she woos him most entirely, telling him although she be old yet she is lusty, fresh and moist . . . and she can trip it as lightly as a fairy nymph upon the sands and her footsteps not seen.[14]

Like some modern readers, Reynolds was so transported by the physical naturalism of Shakespeare's Venus that he forgot about her divine status. He gave her Queen Elizabeth's attribute of being "old"—the queen had just turned sixty that month—while the Venus of the poem is, as a goddess, ageless and immortal. She is not, as Reynolds implies, a well-preserved older woman but a supernatural being. Though she has a "past"—she boasts about her love affair with Mars—she is physically of no age; nor is she subject to physical aging.

At a key moment in the poem, it is Venus herself, deploying rhetoric in the normal human manner, to cajole, persuade, and threaten, who fatally forgets her own divine status. In her desperate anxiety to persuade Adonis to hunt only harmless prey, she delivers a threat whose terms she has not properly thought through: "I prophesy thy death, my living sorrow, / If thou encounter with the boar tomorrow" (ll. 671-72). In the mouth of a goddess, this formula is not merely a pressuring admonition, comparable to a worried mother warning a child of the consequences of running out into a busy road. Rashly, forgetting her own strength, Venus has used the word *prophesy,* and as a goddess, she has the power not merely to foresee future events but to shape them. Trapped in the web of her own desires, however, she seems immediately to overlook what she has just said, proceeding to her next strategy, that of "selling" Adonis the alternative sport of hunting the hare. In a play, this prophecy would be identified as a moment of dramatic irony. But even when she moves into her virtuoso evocation of the hunted hare, the vatic force of that couplet beginning "I prophesy thy death"

may resonate in the mind of the attentive reader. For the hare was of course associated with lust. Venus's picture of the "grief" of the hare, that "may be compared well / To one sore sick, that hears the passing bell" (ll. 701-2—this *is* for once a topical reference, for the passing bell was much heard in London in 1593), prefigures her own sufferings only a few hours later. Just as the hunted hare, "the dew-bedabbled wretch," will have his legs scratched by "Each envious briar," so Venus herself, running to find Adonis, will be tightly caught by "the bushes in the way" (ll. 703, 705, 871).

The word *prophesy* occurs only twice in the poem. But the next time Venus uses it, she means business and is fully cognizant of her own divine power: "'Since thou art dead, lo here I prophesy, / Sorrow on love hereafter shall attend" (ll. 1135-36). This is a passage that I think Anthony Mortimer seriously—or rather comically—misreads by failing to take into account Venus's divine status. According to Mortimer, Venus "leaves the world because she is obviously incapable of changing it"; "lovers," says Mortimer comfortingly, "need not fear the curses of a goddess who is so powerless."[15] Here I think he fails to confront the poem's generic status as an aetiological fable. In this sense the five stanzas in which Venus prophesies that all human love will in future be blighted are the poem's generic climax. They explain the way the world is now with reference to the story we have just read. I'm tempted to rebut Mortimer's claim that Venus's curse doesn't have to be feared with reference to that philosophically slippery concept, real life. For wouldn't most of us assent to her proposition "That all love's pleasure shall not match his [i.e., its] woe" (l. 1140)? However, I don't think I need to take a vote on this, since Shakespeare's own writings testify overwhelmingly that he expected his readers to accept this proposition. Any early readers who doubted "That all love's pleasure shall not match his woe" would find ample affirmation of it only a year later in **Lucrece.** While deliberating about the rape, Tarquin presents the brevity of love's pleasure as a truism: "'What win I if I gain the thing I seek? / A dream, a breath, a froth of fleeting joy" (ll. 211-12). Looking a little further into Shakespeare's work immediately after the narrative poems, the affirmations are even stronger. In what quickly became his most popular play, *Romeo and Juliet,* two young lovers are, like Adonis, killed in their "prime," having enjoyed only one single night of bliss. The closely connected *Midsummer Night's Dream* explores the proposition in Lysander's speech that "The course of true love never did run smooth" (1.1.134), which echoes Venus's prophecy. Only by treating the star-crossed lovers Pyramus and Thisbe in a wholly farcical manner can the play persuade us that, at least for the six courtly lovers at the end of the comedy, the general curse on love may have been suspended. The seeds of many of Shakespeare's subsequent writings on love's pains can be discerned in those five stanzas on blighted love in Venus's prophecy, reaching forward as far as *Othello, Antony and Cleopatra,* and *Cymbeline.* While such hindsight from Shakespeare's later writings was not available to readers in 1593, they would immediately have recognized the lines "'It shall be cause of war and dire events, / And set dissension 'twixt the son and sire" (ll. 1159-60) as foretelling one of the central events in Western cultural history. This passage alludes most obviously to the Trojan War, brought about by Paris's love for Helen. What is never made quite explicit in *Venus and Adonis,* however, is that, in Oscar Wilde's aphorism, "each man kills the thing he loves."[16] Though Venus herself, through her first prophecy, can be seen as inadvertently bringing about the very outcome she is trying to prevent, neither she nor the poet draws attention to this. Instead, it is in the *Sonnets* that the Wildean paradox is more fully explored and in which amorous play is quickly lost in the arena of death and decay.

There are three sonnets in which the paradox is particularly clear. My first example is **"126,"** which is technically not a sonnet but a poem of six couplets. It forms an envoi or coda to the preceding **"125"** "Fair Youth" sonnets, many of which explore methods by which the young man's beauty and worth may be preserved. This poem takes up just where *Venus and Adonis* left off, rapidly reaching a tragic conclusion that, though analogous to that of the longer poem, is much bleaker:

> O thou my lovely Boy, who in thy power
> Dost hold time's fickle glass, his sickle hour,
> Who hast by waning grown, and therein show'st
> Thy lover's withering, as thy sweet self grow'st;
> If nature, sovereign mistress over wrack,
> As thou goest onwards still will pluck thee back,
> She keeps thee to this purpose: that her skill
> May time disgrace, and wretched minute kill.
> Yet fear her, O thou minion of her pleasure:
> She may detain, but not still keep, her treasure!
> Her audit, though delayed, answered must be,
> And her quietus is to render thee.
>   (   )
>   (   )

In this brutal meditation on death and judgment, Shakespeare was thinking intently about the closing book of the Bible. This is made clear in the unprecedented phrase "his sickle hour" in line 2, suggesting "that hour when death cuts down every life," for the image is used in chapter 14 of *Revelation:*

> And I looked, and beholde, a white cloud, and upon the cloud one sate like unto the sonne of man, having on his head a golden crowne, and in his hand a sharp sickle.

> And another Angel came out of the Temple crying with a loud voice to him that sate on the cloud: Thrust in thy sickle and reape, for the time is come for thee to reape, for the harvest of the earth is ripe.

> And he that sate on the cloude thrust in his sickle on the earth, and the earth was reaped.[17]

Brief though the poem is, it's clear that **"Sonnet 126"** looks forward not merely to a single death but to the end of all human history and the period of apocalypse.

In the first line of the sonnet, the speaker's address to his "lovely Boy" echoes Venus's opening address to Adonis as "more lovely than a man" (l. 9). The next three lines of the sonnet, however, in which the addressee is seen as growing even while the speaker, "Thy lover," withers, relate more specifically to such preceding sonnets as **"63"** and **"73,"** in which the double process has already been traced. And this "lovely Boy" has a different patroness from the boy Adonis, not Venus but Nature. However, the relationship with Nature does have connections with the earlier poem, where Venus says, "Nature that made thee with herself at strife, / Saith that the world hath ending with thy life" (ll. 11-12). These lines in *Venus and Adonis* also prepare for the notion in **"Sonnet 126"** that Nature has invested all her ambition to compete with Time in the "lovely Boy." She has attempted to conquer "wrack," or destruction, and to create a being so beautiful that when he is dead, Nature will be—as anticipated in **"Sonnet 67"**— "bankrupt" (l. 9).

The phrase "sovereign mistress" in line 5 inevitably evokes that long-lived monarch to whom the phrase was so often applied, Elizabeth I. Such associations lend sinister tones of admonition to line 9: "Yet fear her, O thou minion of her pleasure." Just as the "sovereign mistress" Elizabeth eventually rendered up her much loved "minion" Essex to the scaffold for the sake of the "quiet" of her realm, so Dame Nature will sooner or later hand over *her* "minion," the speaker's "lovely Boy," in order to settle her accounts. The dominant metaphor here is still the financial one, however, with the day of judgment or reckoning seen as a final "audit" or "hearing" of accounts. Like all human beings, the speaker's "Boy" "owes God a death," in the popular phrase.

The poem seems to end suddenly, leaving something unsaid, and those two pairs of empty parentheses give a chilling sense that "the rest is silence." Here, too, there is a parallel to *Venus and Adonis,* which also seems, after all the amplitude of Venus's rhetoric, to end very suddenly and to leave something unsaid. Venus takes flight through the "empty skies," her chariot drawn by silver doves—"Holding their course to Paphos, where their queen / Means to immure herself and not be seen" (ll. 1193-94). When mortals get caught up in disputes between divinities, whether Venus and Diana or Nature and Time, sooner or later they will always come off worse. The divinities hold the winning cards, for they are immortal. And there are severe restrictions on what a mortal poet can either know or say about the thoughts and actions of such remote beings.

There are equally severe restrictions on the poet's power to defy Time on behalf of the beloved. The supposed capacity of verse to counteract aging is revealed as weak and impotent, as we see, for example, in **"Sonnet 63"**:

> Against my love shall be as I am now,
> With time's injurious hand crushed and o'erworn;
> When hours have drained his blood, and filled his
>   brow
> With lines and wrinkles; when his youthful morn
> Hath travailed on to age's steepy night,
> And all those beauties whereof now he's king
> Are vanishing, or vanished out of sight,
> Stealing away the treasure of his spring;
> For such a time do I now fortify
> Against confounding age's cruel knife,
> That he shall never cut from memory
> My sweet love's beauty, though my lover's life.
>   His beauty shall in these black lines be seen,
>   And they shall live, and he in them still green.

This is one of the clearest instances of a sonnet in which the poet-speaker attempts to bestow immortality yet succeeds only in impressing on the reader the inescapability of the beloved's decline and death.

The whole of the sonnet's octave is dedicated to setting up a powerful defense "Against" the cruel process that the speaker has already undergone, and which has left him "as I am now," bloodless and withered. Though the octave closes on the youthful word *spring,* this hardly comes across as positive, since the focus is on the future time, perhaps not even very far distant, when spring's "treasure" will have been stolen away. The sestet marks a fresh rally on the poet's part—"For such a time do I now fortify. . . ." But the poet has only five lines left within which to construct his bastion against the processes of decay, and his attempts to "fortify," or build a fortification, are continually undercut by slippery language. We should remember that in Shakespeare's period a sharp knife, as well as pen and ink, was a regular part of a writer's equipment, for quill pens constantly required to be trimmed and shaped. We should remember also that a penknife was sometimes used to scrape away unwanted or erroneous passages in a manuscript or book. Almost as fast as the poet can write of his "sweet love's beauty," age, it seems, will inscribe "lines and wrinkles" on the young man's brow; and age may even cut from the page the very words that the poet has just written.

The couplet, where we expect to encounter the climactic affirmation of the power of art to preserve human beauty, is instead pitifully weak. In contrast to those "eternal lines" so confidently promised in line 12 of **"Sonnet 18,"** the phrase "these black lines" is worryingly ambiguous. Obviously there is a clever play on words here, with the poet's "black lines" of verse supposedly canceling out the "lines and wrinkles" inscribed

by the passage of "hours." But "black lines" do not present a very positive image—facial "lines" are hard to forget—and the image is hardly sufficient to counteract the final acknowledgment that "my lover's life" will inevitably be "cut" from the world. And in what sense can the beloved's "beauty" be "seen" in this sonnet's "black lines," which offer several vivid images of physical decay but none of florescence? At the close, the attempt to preserve the beloved's beauty relies on a single word, the word *green.* But that word is too ambiguous for the task, for *green* connotes unripeness, callowness, sourness. In line 805 of **Venus and Adonis,** for instance, "The text is old, the orator too green." In *Antony and Cleopatra,* Cleopatra looks back contemptuously to her "salad days, / When I was green in judgement" (1.5.76-77). Girls who were "green-sick" suffered from a kind of festering chastity; and a "green wound" was an injury that had not yet begun to heal. In trying to counter one greatly feared point of the human lifespan, terminal aging, it appears that the poet has overcompensated, allowing his imaginative pendulum to rest not on the point at which the beloved's beauty is at its most perfect but on a phase of immaturity and callowness. If the beloved is indeed "seen" in the "black lines" of **"Sonnet 63,"** he is seen either as one who must inevitably age, as the speaker has done, or else as one who is remembered best as being raw and unripe.

Finally, in **"Sonnet 104"** the speaker scarcely claims that his poetic art can preserve the young man's beauty:

> To me, fair friend, you never can be old;
> For as you were when first your eye I eyed,
> Such seems your beauty still: three winters cold
> Have from the forests shook three summers' pride;
> Three beauteous springs to yellow autumn turned
> In process of the seasons have I seen;
> Three April perfumes in three hot Junes burned,
> Since first I saw you fresh, which yet art green.
> Ah, yet doth beauty, like a dial hand,
> Steal from his figure, and no pace perceived;
> So your sweet hue, which methinks still doth stand,
> Hath motion, and mine eye may be deceived;
>   For fear of which, hear this, thou age unbred,
>   Ere you were born was beauty's summer dead.

This is one of the most blatant examples in *Shakespeares Sonnets* of what might now be described as emotional blackmail. The "fair friend" should feel obliged to return the speaker's affection because in the older man's doting eyes he still looks as young as when they first met, even though in the eyes of himself and others he may have aged. It reminds one of old married couples who say affectionately of each other, "In my eyes she/he doesn't look a day older than when we got married." But someone who had been married for a mere three years would hardly be likely to invoke such a formula. The three-year time scheme, which, as I argue in the introduction to my edition of the *Sonnets,* is likely to be a fictive construction, seems ironically or even satirically to undercut the speaker's claim that his friend's beauty "seems" the same as when he first saw him.[18] How much visible change would we expect after a mere three years? We might expect to see quite a lot of change in the appearance of a pre-pubertal child but very little, I think, in a fully developed young adult. Following on **"103,"** at the end of which the addressee was told to "look" in his glass (l. 14), **"Sonnet 104"** gives a sense that the "fair friend" is being nudged into worrying about subtle tokens of aging of which he might otherwise have been unaware. There are also touches of exaggeration and stiltedness in the sonnet's style. The threefold iteration of *i* sounds in "your eye I eyed" is extremely awkward. The ponderousness of lines 3 through 8, "three winters cold . . . / Three beauteous springs . . . / Three April perfumes" recalls the speech by the Player King which opens the play-within-the-play in *Hamlet*: "Full thirty times hath Phoebus' cart gone round . . . / And thirty dozen moons with borrow'd sheen . . ." (3.2.157, 159). Just where we might hope for confident affirmation, the speaker insinuates doubt: "Such *seems* your beauty still. . . ." Some of Shakespeare's earliest readers will have learned from Spenser's *Faerie Queene* to be on the lookout for the word *seems,* which is virtually always a warning of speciousness. And, as in **"Sonnet 63,"** much rests on that very dubious epithet "green," here closing the octave.

In the sestet we encounter, in line 11, the even more doubt-inducing word *methinks.* Gazing intently on his friend's face, the speaker can't actually see it losing its beauty, or having beauty "stolen" from it, as the dial hand "steals" moment by moment from the young man's allotted "figure" of hours of life. Yet such a process probably is under way—"mine eye may be deceived."

The closing couplet has some clumsy stylistic touches, such as the internal rhyme *fear/hear.* Ostensibly addressing "thou age unbred," a posterity of persons yet unborn, unconceived, and also perhaps lacking in "breeding" or refinement, the speaker informs them that they are born too late to view true beauty, since "Ere you were born was beauty's summer dead." But this statement resonates uncomfortably in several ways. Its final word, *dead,* echoes like a tolling bell that sounds the fair friend's extinction. Furthermore, the line itself is ambiguous. It can be read in just the opposite sense: beauty's summer (embodied in the "fair friend") was dead until you (person or persons yet "unbred") were born to bring it back to life. If the friend can be seen as a reincarnation of consummate beauties of the past, as he frequently is, as for instance in **"Sonnet 53,"** so presumably can other beautiful young persons in the future.

The collection entitled **Shake-speares Sonnets** is in many respects astonishingly original and unlike the work of any previous Renaissance sonneteer. It marks a boldly decisive abandonment of the entire courtly love tradition within which poets celebrated the worth of an unattainable mistress. The major part of the collection is focused, in extremely complex ways, on a young male addressee, and even the so-called "Dark Lady" of **"Sonnets 127"** through **"154"** is no typical Petrarchan mistress. But the *Sonnets* also flout a tradition that goes even further back, to such classical poets as Horace: the affirmation of the poet's power to immortalize a patron or lover through his enduring art. While an attempt to immortalize through verse is frequently envisaged or affirmed by Shakespeare's speaker, it is also subtly but powerfully undercut. Thanks to print publication, it's true these sonnets may be read by future generations, "So long as men can breathe or eyes can see" (18.13). But the beautiful love object does not live in the poet's "eternal lines" (18.12), he dies in them. He has been embalmed like a corpse or speared like a butterfly. The freshness of his beauty will never be preserved in language, for it is essentially mobile. Such love poetry does not conquer death but reaffirms it. As we close each book of Shakespeare's nondramatic poetry, what we most remember about Adonis, about Lucrece, and about the "lovely Boy" of the *Sonnets'* speaker is that they have died or will die. "THAT.ETERNITIE.PROMISED.BY.OVER.EVERLIVING.POET" is in this sense an eternity of death.[19] The playing field has become a battlefield on which human beauty can never be victorious.

Notes

This essay derives from the 2002 annual Shakespeare Birthday Lecture delivered at the Folger Shakespeare Library on 9 April 2002 and dedicated to the memory of Susan Snyder.

1. W. H. Auden, *Plays and Other Dramatic Writings by W. H. Auden 1928-1938,* ed. Edward Mendelson (Princeton, NJ: Princeton UP, 1988), 240-41.

2. See *Venvs and Adonis* (London, 1593) and *Ouids Elegies: Three Bookes,* trans. C[hristopher] M[arlowe] (Middlebourgh, 1603), sig. B7r. Quotations from Shakespeare follow *The Arden Shakespeare Complete Works,* ed. Richard Proudfoot, Ann Thompson, and David Scott Kastan (Walton-on-Thames, UK: Thomas Nelson and Sons, 1998).

3. MS Folger V.a. 460, fol. 9a.

4. See *The Works of Thomas Nashe,* ed. Ronald B. McKerrow, 5 vols. (London: Sidgwick and Jackson, 1904-10), 3:87.

5. See Peter W. M. Blayney, *The Bookshops in Paul's Cross Churchyard,* Occasional Papers of the Bibliographical Society 5 (London: The Bibliographical Society, 1990), 25-29.

6. This wording appears on the title pages of books printed by Wolfe from 1590.

7. Nashe, 3:87.

8. *The Poems of Sir Philip Sidney,* ed. W. A. Ringler (Oxford: Clarendon Press, 1962), 182 (*Astrophil and Stella,* 35.1).

9. See Anthony Mortimer, *Variable Passions: A Reading of Shakespeare's* Venus and Adonis (New York: AMS Press, 2000).

10. See *The Three Parnassus Plays (1598-1601),* ed. J. B. Leishman (London: Nicholson and Watson, 1949), 183-84.

11. In his dedication of *Venus and Adonis* to Henry Wriothesley, Shakespeare vows to honor his patron "with some graver labour" at a future date, a promise he fulfilled a year later with *Lucrece.*

12. Thomas Heywood, *The Rape of Lucrece. A True Romaine Tragedie* (London, 1608), sig. H2v.

13. Mortimer, 32.

14. BL MS Lansdowne 99, fol. 87; quoted more fully in Katherine Duncan-Jones, "Much Ado with Red and White: The Earliest Readers of Shakespeare's *Venus and Adonis* (1593)," *Review of English Studies,* n.s., 44.176 (1993): 479-501, esp. 488.

15. Mortimer, 34.

16. Oscar Wilde, "The Ballad of Reading Gaol" in *The Complete Works of Oscar Wilde,* ed. Bobby Fong and Karl Beckson, 1 vol. (Oxford and New York: Oxford UP, 2000-), 1:196 (l. 37).

17. *The Holy Bible: 1611,* ed. A. W. Pollard (Oxford: Oxford UP, 1911), Revelation 14:14-16.

18. Katherine Duncan-Jones, ed., *Shakespeare's Sonnets* ([London]: Thomas Nelson, 1997), 21.

19. *Shake-speares Sonnets* (London, 1609), sig. A2ʳ.

Jim Ellis (essay date 2003)

SOURCE: Ellis, Jim. "'More Lovely Than a Man': The Metamorphosis of the Youth." In *Sexuality and Citizenship: Metamorphosis in Elizabethan Erotic Verse,* pp. 65-108. Toronto, Canada: University of Toronto Press, 2003.

[*In the excerpt below, Ellis posits that in* Venus and Adonis *Shakespeare sought to caution his patron, Henry Wriothesley, against the perils of narcissism and to warn him, given his youthful beauty, of the dangers of becoming an object of sexual desire.*]

Venus and Adonis

In one of his more famous marginal notations, Gabriel Harvey recorded sometime in 1599 that 'the younger sort takes much delight in Shakespeares **Venus, &** *Adonis*.'[1] Katherine Duncan-Jones suggests that among the 'younger sort' thus entranced were Thomas Edwards, author of *Cephalus and Procris* and *Narcissus;* Michael Drayton, author of *Piers Gaveston;* and Thomas Heywood, author of *Oenone and Paris;* all of them wrote poems indebted to Shakespeare's.[2] Beyond newly emerging writers, however, there is another group of readers that may also have taken delight in the poem: the younger sort who attended the Inns of Court. While Shakespeare did not himself attend the Inns (as far as we know), he was certainly acquainted with that world and its literary tastes. For example, his friend and 'cousin,' Thomas Greene, transferred to the Middle Temple in 1595 after a stay at Staple Inn, one of the Inns of Chancery (this stay would normally last about two years).[3] In 1594, a year after the publication of the poem, *The Comedy of Errors* would be performed at Gray's Inn. Most relevant to the present discussion, however, is the fact that Shakespeare's poem is dedicated to Henry Wriothesley, the earl of Southampton, who was admitted to Gray's Inn on 29 February 1588; G. P. V. Akrigg argues that it was likely in the company of Inns of Court men that Shakespeare first met his patron.[4]

This was not, in fact, the first poem of this sort dedicated to Southampton. Two years earlier John Clapham, a secretary to Lord Burghley, dedicated his neo-Latin poem *Narcissus* to Southampton, and scholars have identified a number of similarities between Clapham's and Shakespeare's poem.[5] Clapham's poem, in turn, seems to have been influenced by early epyllia written in English; Charles Martindale and Colin Burrow argue that the poem makes a nod towards Marlowe's epyllion in the ecphrasis,[6] and in its relocation of the mythological action to England Clapham's poem follows Lodge's *Scillaes Metamorphosis* (and in this it will be followed to some degree by Shakespeare). And like almost all examples of the genre, the poem is most interested in youths.

Clapham's poem starts with a description of the palace of Love, to which many young men flock (57). Among them is Narcissus, accompanied by Liberty and Youth (65), who is embraced by Venus on his arrival. Narcissus is subsequently shot by Cupid and then instructed on the finer points of love and the psychology of women. He gallops off on a horse named Libido (151), falls in love with his reflection, and drowns himself in the pond at dusk when his image disappears. Akrigg argues of Shakespeare's and Clapham's poems that 'the basic pattern is the same: the meeting with Venus, the departure of the young man, Venus's lamentation, and the final metamorphosis';[7] Martindale and Burrow similarly note, 'There are signs that Shakespeare, rather than just taking allegorical or mythographic materials from *Narcissus* (as earlier commentators believed), absorbed the poem's shape and, especially in the early part of *Venus and Adonis,* filled the stiffly allegorical forms of Clapham with luxurious vitality.'[8]

While it is important to note the similarities between Clapham's and Shakespeare's poems, particularly the ways in which Adonis is indebted to the portrayal of Narcissus, it is equally important to note how both poems participate in a particular literary and cultural milieu, one centred around the Inns of Court. Whereas the earliest epyllia are admonitory tales directed towards the young men of the Inns, these poems offer warnings to a particular young man, Wriothesley.[9] Considering Shakespeare's poem within the context of the epyllion brings certain aspects of the poem, such as the interest in Venus's rhetoric, the rhetorical education of Adonis, and the poem's use of Petrarchanisms, into sharper focus. It also helps us to see in a different light Shakespeare's innovation of having a resistant Adonis, whose resistance may have less to do with morality than it does with a dangerous narcissism. As we have already noted, while the genre has a number of different candidates for positive exempla of masculine subjectivity, it is virtually unanimous in holding up Narcissus as the chief example of failure. As we shall see in more detail in our reading of Edwards's *Narcissus,* the beauty of youths is perceived both by the genre and arguably by the culture at large as somehow dangerous. While the story of Adonis traditionally figures the fleeting nature of beauty, within the genre Adonis represents not so much beauty as more specifically the beauty of the youth. Indeed, in its parade of surpassingly beautiful young men such as Leander, Cephalus, and Narcissus, the genre suggests that youth *is* beauty, an attitude reflected in the Sonnets as well, where the beloved is both Narcissus and Adonis. But the beauty of youths is at the same time dangerous, both to themselves and to those around them. This is a particular concern of the genre, and negotiating this perilous transitional phase becomes a recurrent theme.

In *Venus and Adonis,* the dangers posed by the beauty of the youth are told though the genre's most popular narrative, that of the reluctant youth and the ardent female wooer. Bearing in mind the other poems' reactions against Petrarchanisms and their sometimes ambiguous gender coding, it is not too extreme to read the reluctant youth as the Petrarchan mistress and the ardent goddess as the frustrated lover. Reading the gender of the goddess as male could be supported by noting the similarities between the Petrarchan code and Platonic pederasty. In both, sex is nominally disallowed, and in the latter, the youth is bound by honour to resist, or at least not to enjoy, the advances of his adult lover. This scenario can be seen in play in *Hero and Leander* in the various references to Ganymede, in the relation of the poet to Leander, and most clearly in the encounter between Neptune and Leander. The very category of 'youth' or 'boy' must be considered in relation to the

more capacious category of 'not-man,' which at least in classical cultures and arguably in early modern England, denoted a proper or at least possible object of desire. Indeed, Will Fisher argues that boys 'were quite literally a different gender from men during the early modern period.'[10] At the same time, youths are a very special subset of the category 'not-man,' in that they will possibly become men. It is precisely this possibility that provides much of the erotic interest in a number of the poems, and it is certainly at the heart of the most central metamorphoses of the genre.

If the youths of the epyllion are not men, it is worth noting that the goddesses are generally not women either. They frequently insist that they are not mortal, and that their powers are far greater than their beloveds'. Structurally speaking, they could be read as phallic mothers, or more simply as men. This confusion of genders is supported within the poems by the ambiguous gender coding of the characters. Venus, for example, when she first sees Adonis, woos him in the following manner:

'Thrice fairer than myself,' thus she began,
'The field's chief flower, sweet above compare,
Stain to all nymphs, more lovely than a man,
More white and red than doves or roses are . . .'

(7-10)

As Lucy Gent observes, Venus 'out-Petrarchs the most Petrarchan sonneteer.'[11] Adonis, for his part, 'burns with bashful shame, she with her tears / Doth quench the maiden burning of his cheeks' (49-50). Venus, in a move that would no doubt please Marston, plucks Adonis from his horse: 'Over one arm the lusty courser's rein, / Under her other was the tender boy' (31-2). She sets him down, and then 'Backward she push'd him, as she would be thrust, / And govern'd him in strength, though not in lust' (41-2). Superior in strength and driven by lust, Venus plays the man when Adonis will not and pushes him into the position she wishes to occupy. Adonis, by being so thrust, is thrown into the position of the female.[12] Venus brags to Adonis of her sexual conquests, saying that she has led 'the stern and direful god of war . . . prisoner in a red rose chain' (98, 110), thus presenting herself as the erotic version of Hercules and his golden chain of rhetoric. Through the early part of the poem Adonis continues to play the role of the reluctant mistress, leading to Venus's exasperation:

'Fie, liveless picture, cold and senseless stone,
Well-painted idol, image dull and dead,
Statue contenting but the eye alone,
Thing like a man, but of no woman bred!
Thou art no man, though of a man's complexion,
For men will kiss even by their own direction.'

(211-16)

Adonis, in a manner similar to Pygmalion's statue, is the shade but not the substance of man. If Venus is temporarily acting the part of Pygmalion in this scenario, showing the ridiculous side of Petrarchan desire, Adonis shows the 'danger' to the beloved youth that Marston only hinted at.

The comparisons between Adonis and Pygmalion's statue make sense within a critique of Petrarchan verse, but they also make sense within the Ovidian universe, as Adonis is the descendent of Pygmalion and his statue, and his tale is part of the linked series of stories told by Orpheus in Book 10. It is thus appropriate that Adonis not only resembles the statue but also its creator; significantly, both he and Pygmalion begin their tales by scorning love and women. More to the point, as Lynn Enterline points out in her discussions of both Petrarch's and Marston's treatments of the myth, Pygmalion's attachment to his statue is fundamentally narcissistic.[13] In both Shakespeare's and Marston's poems, then, we see a strange potential for reversability in the central character: from subject to object, and male to female. This instability is also a characteristic both of the position of the Petrarchan author and of the youth.

Because Adonis is a male youth, he is at least literally an acceptable object of desire in the early modern world. What these poems stress, however, is the danger for the male of being the object of (male) desire, even if this warning is refracted through the figure of the female wooer. The heterosexualization of desire is here partially accomplished through an incomplete heterosexualization of the pederastic couple. It is clear enough in these poems that this form of coupling is not acceptably heterosexual, even if it is nominally so. One of the ways by which this condemnation is accomplished is similar to the way in which Marston condemns Petrarchan love: by associating this scenario with the Imaginary, and by condemning it as sterile, immature, or infantile.

This regressive fantasy scene is clear in Venus's erotic proposal to Adonis:

'Fondling,' she saith, 'since I have hemmed thee here
Within the circuit of this ivory pale,
I'll be a park, and thou shalt be my deer:
Feed where thou wilt, on mountain or in dale;
Graze on my lips, and if those hills be dry,
Stray lower, where the pleasant fountains lie.

'Within this limit is relief enough,
Sweet bottom-grass and high delightful plain,
Round rising hillocks, brakes obscure and rough,
To shelter thee from tempest and from rain;
Then be my deer, since I am such a park,
No dog shall rouse thee, though a thousand bark.'

(229-40)

Venus's body threatens to swallow Adonis's being, trapping him in an infantilizing dyadic relation. The metaphor clearly evokes the relation of mother and child, hinted at occasionally throughout the poem. This relation is made explicit later in the poem when Venus frantically searches for Adonis, 'Like a milch doe, whose swelling dugs do ache, / Hasting to feed her fawn hid in some brake' (875-6). She later recaptures this relation when she plucks the flower that springs up from Adonis's blood, knowing full well that it will 'wither in [her] breast' (1182):

'Here was thy father's bed, here in my breast;
Thou art the next of blood, and 'tis thy right.
Lo in this hollow cradle take thy rest,
My throbbing heart shall rock thee day and
night. . . .'

(1183-6)

The relation of mother and child is posited within the poem as a smothering one, something which the youth must escape in order to become a man. C. S. Lewis responds to this presentation when he comments, 'I have never read [the poem] through without feeling that I am being suffocated.'[14] But this mother is also persistently figured as vampiric: 'Panting he lies, and breatheth in her face. / She feedeth on the steam, as on a prey' (62-3); 'Look how a bird lies tangled in a net, / So fast'ned in her arms Adonis lies' (67-8); 'Now quick desire hath caught the yielding prey, / And glutton-like she feeds, yet never filleth' (547-8).

The course of the seduction runs through the various possibilities that Grosz sees in the Lacanian Imaginary:

The unmediated two-person structure of imaginary identifications leaves only two possibilities for the child, between which it vacillates but cannot definitively choose: being overwhelmed by the other, crowded out, taken over (the fantasy of the devouring mother/ voracious child); and the wretched isolation and abandonment of all self-worth by the other's absence or neglect (the fantasy of the bad or selfish mother/child).[15]

The vacillations between subject and object and male and female that we have noted in the poem are clearly characteristic of the register of the Imaginary. Further, the scenarios Grosz mentions of isolation and abandonment are acted out in the deaths, imagined and real, of Venus and Adonis. The former scenarios are far more central: in the genre, for a male to be the object of desire is to be trapped in the arms of the mother. In Michael Drayton's *Endimion and Phoebe*, Endimion gives in to the desire of his goddess, and is condemned to a form of suspended animation. Phoebe

layd Endimion on a grassy bed,
With sommers Arras ritchly over-spred
Where from her sacred Mantion next above,
She might descend and sport her with her love,
Which thirty yeeres the Sheepheards safely kept,
Who in her bosom soft and soundly slept.

(983-8)

Adonis says of love, 'I have heard it is a life in death' (413), which seems a fairly accurate description of Endimion's fate. This suspended state is enacted by the poem itself, which is curiously static until Adonis breaks away from Venus's arms. Lewis notes that even 'the stanza of *Venus and Adonis* is unprogressive.'[16] Linked to this unproductive scenario of desire is the similarly unproductive position of narcissism, against which Adonis is warned (157-62).

Part of Adonis's education, both sexual and rhetorical, comes from the poem's two digressions. In the first, Adonis (and the reader) are witness to a 'natural' example of proper gender relations when Adonis's horse is spied by a 'breeding jennet, lusty, young, and proud' (260) and desire causes him to break free of his reins:

> He looks upon his love, and neighs unto her,
> She answers him, as if she knew his mind;
> Being proud as females are, to see him woo her,
> She puts on outward strangeness, seems unkind,
> Spurns at his love, and scorns the heat he feels,
> Beating his kind embracements with her heels.
>
> Then like a melancholy malcontent,
> He vails his tail that like a falling plume
> Cool shadow to his melting buttock lent;
> He stamps, and bites the poor flies in his fume.
> His love, perceiving how he was enrag'd,
> Grew kinder, and his fury was assuag'd.
>
> (307-18)

The lessons offered here by the natural world are remarkably similar to the gender ideologies of the other epyllia. The female horse only ever reacts, and her brief attempt at playing the disdainful Petrarchan mistress is only meant to excite her lover into more masculine shows of force. Venus urges Adonis to read the horses as an example: 'learn of him, I heartily beseech thee, / To take advantage on presented joy' (404-5). Her reading of the parallels is only a partial one, however, as the mare's actions amount to nothing more than simply presenting herself to view, certainly far less than Venus herself does. Nonetheless, the poem, like Venus, sees the horse as an example to be followed, and promotes this by persistently pairing horse and man, as when Venus initially abducts them both: 'Over one arm the lusty courser's rein, / Under her other was the tender boy' (31-2). Venus's praise of Adonis's beauty is paralleled by the narrator's longer blazon of the horse; both for their beauty are compared to works of art, but whereas the metaphor is used to accuse Adonis of being less than a man ('Fie, liveless picture, cold and senseless stone' [211]), the horse becomes the ideal horse ('So did this horse excel a common one' [293]). The horse is, in short, an equine equivalent of Adonis, and stands as an example of a more proper masculinity, a piece of natural rhetoric that Adonis should aim to emulate.

The other major foray into the rhetoric of the natural world is Venus's tale of Wat the hare (679-708). This replaces the story in Ovid of Atalanta and Hippomenes, which Venus tells for similar reasons, namely, to warn Adonis from the hunt.[17] In Ovid, Hippomenes and Atalanta are ungrateful to Venus for her assistance and ignore the clear warnings of the gods; as a consequence they are turned into lions. Both failings—ingratitude and inattention—are also characteristic of Adonis. Venus pleads with Adonis not to pursue the boar, and to hunt the hare or the fox or the roe instead. This segues into a story of the hare trying to elude the hunters and the hounds. The story is distinctly Ovidian in its interest in the darker side of desire: the hare relentlessly pursued and the cruel fate that awaits it provide a contrast to the previous lightness of the poem but foreshadow Adonis's end a little later. But the Hippomenes myth is not the only one invoked here. Through the tale of Wat, Adonis also becomes Acteon: 'And now his grief may be compared well / To one sore sick that hears the passing bell' (701-2). Even more so than Hippomenes, Acteon is an appropriate model for Adonis, particularly because of the reversal that occurs as the hunter becomes the hunted, which is, of course, the central narrative of the poem. While Venus's hunting of Adonis is comic, it will be perversely reprised in the boar's turning of the tables at the end of the poem. But the Acteon myth has a further significance in that it is also a tale of rhetoric, which is why Acteon becomes for so many poets a compelling model for their own vocation.

The story of the hare breaks off before it reaches its conclusion, when Venus loses her place: '"Where did I leave?" "No matter where," quoth he, / "Leave me, and then the story aptly ends"' (715-16). Is Adonis's death partly attributable to his failure to listen well to this story? He has had more obvious warnings, of course, but is this a test of the reception of rhetoric? Venus does mention that she is uncharacteristically interested in morals at this moment—'Unlike myself thou hear'st me moralize / Applying this to that, and so to so' (712-13)—but he refuses to listen to her explication of the tale. While his own rhetoric may have improved over the course of the poem, we can see that he is not yet skilled in attending to the rhetoric of others, which includes, in Hoskyns's terms, the rhetoric of the natural world.

Hallet Smith, in his introduction to the poem in the *Riverside Shakespeare,* argues that 'the celebrated description of the horse, the account of the coursing of the hare, and the images of the dive-dapper, the snail, and the lark . . . [are] difficult to harmonize with the elements of classical myth.'[18] In fact, as we have seen, the digressions are very much of a piece with the rest of the poem, and this disjuncture between the mythological material and Shakespeare's 'country taste and outlook' may also be working as part of the genre's rejection of the Petrarchan code as sterile literary cliché. The poem's counterposing of a 'natural' narrative of desire (that is at the same time heavily cultural), works precisely to make the central narrative of Venus's seduction and Adonis's rejection of her seem unnatural. At the same time, the use of the English countryside as backdrop is similar to Lodge's Oxford setting, Clapham's lightly allegorized English setting for the Narcissus myth, or Edwards's Spenserian additions to his poems. All of these participate in what might be called an Englishing of the muse, part of an attempt, as we shall see in later chapters, to claim a classical heritage for England, while at the same time rewriting the script of normative desire.

As with the youths in other epyllia, if Adonis is to become a man, he must reject the position of object of desire. What might have enabled him to do this is the education in rhetoric he receives over the course of the poem. As a number of critics have observed, Shakespeare's major change to the myth is 'the creation of an Adonis who resists [Venus's attractions] . . . Shakespeare compensates for the myth's lack of action by turning the poem into a debate, thus restoring rhetoric to its primary function.'[19] Initially Adonis is as silent as Pygmalion's statue, confining himself to mostly struggling against Venus and blushing. When he finally does speak, 185 lines into the poem, he blurts out a mere line and a half: 'Fie, no more of love! / The sun doth burn my face, I must remove' (185-6). Venus slyly notes the insufficiency of this immature ejaculation, remarking: 'young and so unkind, / What bare excuses mak'st thou to be gone!' (187-8). He speaks again almost two hundred lines later, offering only slightly more plausible excuses to be gone. We are over four hundred lines into the poem before Adonis offers any substantial speech (409-26), or attempts to counter any of Venus's logic, at which point she mutters, 'What, canst thou talk? . . . hast thou a tongue?' (427). He offers his lengthiest speech, lasting thirty-nine lines, just before he leaves both the poem and Venus for the last time, and by this point he has become something of an orator:

> What have you urg'd that I cannot reprove?
> The path is smooth that leadeth on to danger.
> I hate not love but your device in love,
> That lends embracements unto every stranger.
> You do it for increase: O strange excuse!
> When reason is the bawd to lust's abuse.
>
> (787-92)

It is only when Adonis has begun to learn rhetoric that he can break out of Venus's arms, and reject the form of desire that she represents. At the same time he shows himself to be resistant to her rhetoric: 'know, my heart stands armed in mine ear, / And will not let a false sound enter there' (779-80). He declares that he will no more be the object of rhetorical persuasion than he will

be the object of desire, and he makes it clear that the one often involves the other. But while his rhetorical ability may have improved (even if it consists largely of clichés), we have seen in the Wat episode that he is far from sensitive to the rhetoric of others and is completely unable to recognize even the simplest of allegories.

In spite of his rhetorical shortcomings ('the text is old, the orator too green' [806], as he himself recognizes), it is worth looking at the arguments that Adonis makes against Venus. Not surprisingly, given the connections between language and the exchange of women, and given that this poem is by Shakespeare, the thematics of their discussions turn out to be principally economic. Venus's arguments often echo those made by the sonneteer to the young man, especially when the conversation turns to begetting. This leads Nona Fienberg to remark, 'So often in *Venus and Adonis* does Venus employ the language of the marketplace as language of seduction, that she seems to have come to earth to learn to speak commercial jargon.'[20] It is as a commodity, in turn, that Adonis speaks of himself, a dangerous position in the sexual economy, as Irigaray points out, for a man to be in:

> 'Fair queen,' quoth he, 'if any love you owe me,
> Measure my strangeness with my unripe years;
> Before I know myself, seek not to know me,
> No fisher but the ungrown fry forbears;
> The mellow plum doth fall, the green sticks fast,
> Or being early pluck'd, is sour to taste.'
>
> (523-8)

Adonis is perhaps being a little dishonest here: given that he is a youth he is ripe for the picking, according to both Venus and the Platonic theory of desire. In fact, if Venus waits too long, the fry will develop not into a fish but a fisher, not a commodity but an exchanger of commodities. The anxiety underlying Adonis's argument seems to be that if he allows himself to become the object of desire he will be forever condemned to that position. While this particular plum might be sour, we can see in *Hero and Leander* and in other poems that invoke the Ganymede myth that youths were not, at least in some contemporary literary works, forbidden fruit. However, Adonis's reluctance to be a commodity is not unusual. It is, as I have suggested, the most typical narrative in the epyllia. It is only his disingenuous argument that is out of place, the protest that he was never a suitable object of desire.

How does the boar figure in this scenario? This has been a problem for critics, especially because of Shakespeare's decision to make Adonis reject Venus in favour of the hunt. In older versions of the story, such as Robert Greene's retelling of the myth in *Perimedes the Blacke-Smithe* (1588), Adonis gives in to Venus, and his killing by the boar can then be read as a punishment for succumbing to lust: 'So Long he followed flattering *Venus* lore, / Till seely Lad, he perisht by a bore.'[21] Venus's recognition that she would have killed Adonis in a similar way is perhaps an indication that Shakespeare knew well this tradition, and was specifically avoiding it. Shakespeare's alteration of the poem spoils the moral reading of the poem, so that whatever the meaning of the boar is, argues A. C. Hamilton, 'it cannot be simply "moral." Since Adonis does not yield to Venus, the poem's center becomes a mystery.'[22] Although he grapples with the issue, Hamilton does not get any closer to pinning down the boar than to argue that it 'expresses all those forces which seek to pluck the flower of Beauty.'[23] William Sheidley points out that it is difficult to read the boar as punishment for anything, as is the tradition, but then goes on to suggest that Adonis is somehow being punished for being imperfectly or incompletely phallic: 'The dislocation of phallic potency predicates the frustration of Venus and brings about the destruction of Adonis. Properly placed, in Adonis, if that were possible, it might have rendered all well. How can Adonis deal with the suffocations of Venus's advances and free himself from her constricting embrace? Slice through them with the phallic tusk.'[24] Sheidley's interpretation of the boar is to a certain extent persuasive, but unfortunately he does not pursue his own arguments to their conclusion. Why does Adonis choose the boar over Venus? That is to say, what if, as Gordon Williams argues, 'Adonis's death, far from being a punishment, is a consummation devoutly to be wished'?[25] What does the boar's goring of Adonis say about 'phallic energy'? One conclusion, writes Sheidley, is that 'the properly ordered male must accept and realize his phallic potential.'[26] What exactly does this say about Adonis then? And what precisely is an improperly ordered male? Further, argues Sheidley, 'Shakespeare's Boar is ugly and destructive, and, by extension, the phallic energy he embodies may be ungentle, violent, and even painful, but it is also clearly necessary and productive.'[27] Necessary for and productive of what? Heterosexuality? Phallic masculinity? I do not want to suggest that these are not conclusions one can draw from the poem: indeed, part of the argument of this [essay] is that epyllia work to install precisely that version of phallic masculinity that Sheidley finds there. We must, however, be careful not to confuse the imperatives or norms of a particular cultural order with universal prescriptions. In other words, Shakespeare's poem might be participating in the inauguration of a new mode of phallic masculinity, a shift in the dominant fiction, rather than simply showing how Adonis falls short of a timeless masculine ideal.

Venus is clearly terrified by the boar, fainting when Adonis mentions it. She describes it as an avatar of death, correctly predicting the outcome of the hunt: 'I prophesy thy death, my living sorrow, / If thou encounter with the boar to-morrow' (671-2). Heather

Asals argues that 'to the reader familiar with the most basic elements of Neoplatonism, it would have been clear that the blindness of the boar identified him as unadulterated lust.'[28] Reading the boar this way would make him something of a counterpart to Venus, which could account for the appearance of Jealousy at this point in the poem (649). Jealousy presents to Venus 'The picture of an angry chafing boar, / Under whose sharp fangs, on his back doth lie / An image like [Adonis]' (662-4). This reproduces the positions that Venus and Adonis occupy earlier in the poem, and which at this point in the poem is being parodied with Adonis ineffectually on top: 'He will not manage her, although he mount her' (598). Venus does not fear the boar for her own sake but rather for its potential to take Adonis away from her. This reading of the rivalry between Venus and the boar could be supported by Adonis's earlier pronouncement: '"I know not love," quoth he, "nor will not know it, / Unless it be a boar, and then I chase it"' (409-10). Finally, when Venus sees Adonis dead she draws something of a parallel between herself and the boar, and rewrites the killing in a specifically erotic way:

> He ran upon the boar with his sharp spear,
> Who did not whet his teeth at him again,
> But by a kiss thought to persuade him there;
> And nousling in his flank, the loving swine
> Sheath'd unaware the tusk in his soft groin.
> 'Had I been tooth'd like him, I must confess,
> With kissing him I should have kill'd him first.'

(1112-18)

Although these parallels do exist between Venus and the boar, clearly the boar has got something that Venus has not, something which, moreover, Adonis apparently wants. If the desires of Venus and the boar are both figured in the poem as dangerous, clearly they are dangerous in different ways. Hunting and the boar are both persistently gendered masculine in the poem: Adonis chooses this world of vigour and hardness over the soft, effeminizing arms of Venus, or, as tradition has it, he chooses between the soft hunt and the hard hunt, erotics and heroics.[29] In that regard, the boar is more of a stand-in for Mars than Venus: 'On his bow-back he hath a battle set / Of bristly pikes that ever threat his foes' (619-20).

The boar's connections with Mars should prompt us as well to see him as in some way a reflection of Adonis, which would help to clarify why Venus seems to equate Adonis's interest in the hunt with a dangerous narcissism. Certainly the exchange of roles between hunter and hunted, a literalization of the figure of chiasmus that persistently accompanies Adonis, would suggest some kind of reciprocity or reversibility between the two characters. The association of the hunt with narcissism is one of the chief consequences of Shakespeare's innovation of a resistant Adonis, a consequence that is perhaps attributable to the poem's precursor, Clapham's *Narcissus.* The equation between narcissism and the hunt is suggested early on in the opening chiasmus— 'Hunting he lov'd, but love he laugh'd to scorn' (4)— and in Adonis's later objection to Venus—'"I know not love," quoth he, "nor will not know it, / Unless it be a boar, and then I chase it"' (409-10). His later objections to Venus, especially his banal, priggishly idealistic opposition of love and lust, are attributable more to his literary origins as Petrarchan mistress, and to the narcissism of Petrarchanisms in general, than they are to any interest in morality. This is, after all, an Ovidian poem at heart.

If the ending of the poem has been a puzzle to critics, it is probably because Adonis seems to be embracing vigorous, masculine activity over Venus's effeminizing charms. That is, the hunt is typically seen as productive rather than sterile and narcissistic. However, the horse episode, the poem's chief example of an Ovidian, adult masculinity, should steer us away from such a reading. Moreover, the boar in this version is, quite unusually, portrayed as a lover, and it is not only Venus who characterizes it as a figure of desire. The one fleeting image we have of the boar that is not mediated through Venus is of his 'frothy mouth bepainted all with red, / Like milk and blood being mingled both together' (901-2). Because of the poem's very careful use of colour, the mingling of red and white, and in particular on his mouth, makes the boar a perverse figure of Petrarchanisms, and thus some kind of reflection of Adonis ('More white and red than doves or roses are' [10]) and of Venus as Petrarchan poet. Seen in this light, Adonis's death is an ironically appropriate Ovidian punishment. Because he scorns love and rejects her counsel, preferring instead to play the Petrachan mistress, Adonis meets death in the form of a monstrous Petrarchan lover, the boar. As with other versions of the myth, Adonis's death can still be read as a punishment, but in this case for the opposite reason, for rejecting Venus rather than for embracing sexual pleasure. And further, for rejecting Ovidian desire in favour of perverse Petrarchanisms.

An anonymous poem published in 1597, *The Legend of Orpheus and Euridice,* characterizes the boar in a similar fashion.[30] The poem is written using the **Venus and Adonis** stanza, devoting six of them to outrage over Orpheus's introduction of pederasty to Thrace. It culminates by characterizing Orpheus's sin as:

> The *Calidonian* Boare which Gods have sent
> For to destroy the gardens of the blest,
> Whose bloody tuskes in shivering pieces rent
> The daintie young brought up in beauties nest,
>   Virginities defrauder, Autumnes cold,
>   which hurts the bud ere it the leaves unfold.
>
> (sig. E7)

There can be little doubt here that the poet is thinking of Shakespeare's poem, objecting to Orpheus's seduc-

tion of youths in much the same terms that Adonis objects to Venus. If we read Shakespeare's boar in a similar light, as the poem encourages us to do, we see the connection between Petrarchan poetry and sodomy that surfaces frequently in the genre, a connection I will explore in greater detail in the following chapter.

While Venus does not avenge the insults to herself in as direct a fashion as she does in the Atalanta and Hippomenes story, she does not hesitate to kill Adonis a second time, metaphorically, when she plucks the flower that grows after his death. It is significant that in this version Venus does not cause Adonis's transformation. In Ovid, Venus decides that 'From yeere to yeere shall growe / A thing that of my heavinesse and of thy death shall showe / The lively likenesse. In a flowre thy blood I will bestowe' (10. 849-51). In Shakespeare's version it is much less clear how Adonis is transformed, or even whether he is transformed, except in Venus's rhetoric:

> By this the boy that by her side lay kill'd
> Was melted like a vapor from her sight,
> And in his blood that on the ground lay spill'd,
> A purple flow'r sprung up, check'red with white,
> Resembling well his pale cheeks and the blood
> Which in round drops upon their whiteness stood.
>
> She bows her head, the new-sprung flow'r to smell,
> Comparing it to her Adonis' breath . . .
>
> (1165-72)

The flower's origins are ambiguous, and Venus transforms it into Adonis only through a series of comparisons, most of which return him to the position of Petrarchan mistress.

Venus's early aggression towards Adonis is reprised by her plucking of the flower, demonstrating for at least the second time in the poem the fleeting nature of beauty. She of course recognizes this, but as is her wont, rationalizes it away:

> 'Poor flow'r,' quoth she, 'this was thy father's guise—
> Sweet issue of a more sweet-smelling sire—
> For every little grief to wet his eyes;
> To grow unto himself was his desire,
> And so 'tis thine, but know it is as good
> To wither in my breast as in his blood.'
>
> (1177-82)

Venus's final words on Adonis, made to the flower, evoke both common satires of Petrarchan poets ('For every little grief to wet his eyes') and narcissism ('To grow unto himself was his desire'). At the same time they reprise Venus's economic complaints about Adonis's narcissism, arguing that the flower might as well be plucked, since Adonis's blood is not a source of life.

It is important to note that Adonis's transformation takes place only in the sphere of Venus's rhetoric. In the poem, rhetoric is connected with creation and vitality. As Richard Lanham observes, 'To talk well is to be alive, to see, hear, feel. To all of these, serious, inarticulate Adonis is insensitive. Venus really creates with her own praise the Adonis who can represent beauty. She creates herself with her own praise. She creates the significance of Adonis's death by her descriptive sorrow. Only she can give meaning, not only to her desire for Adonis, but to his for the boar.'[31] Adonis's failure to 'take advantage on presented joy' (405) is linked to both his rhetorical shortcomings and his inability to apprehend in a sophisticated way either Venus's rhetoric or the rhetoric of the natural world. Adonis does not even understand the implications of his own rhetoric—'Hunting he lov'd, but love he laugh'd to scorn' (4)—and Venus attempts throughout the poem to teach him both the truth of the metaphor—love is a hunt—and the force of chiasmus in order to coax him into becoming an adult masculine subject rather than a narcissistic Petrarchan youth. While Adonis recognizes the dangers of being the object of desire, he nonetheless cannot break out of the circuit of narcissism to become a desiring subject. Tone-deaf to the last, Adonis is felled by his own metaphor.

Adonis's transformation changes irrevocably the script of desire. Venus announces that sorrow will hereafter always wait on love (1136), that love will be untimely, unsuitable, and unseemly, and that desire 'shall be fickle, false, and full of fraud' (1141). Venus's catalogue of unsuitable lovers is reminiscent of Freud's comment that heterosexual love is always one generation out of sync. One of the more interesting of Venus's prophecies is that desire 'shall be cause of war and dire events, / And set dissension 'twixt the son and sire' (1159-60). Adonis's encounter with the boar can thus be said to institute the Oedipus complex, the very story of heterosexuality itself, the means by which sons are separated from mothers, and homosexuality is disallowed.[32] If the poem does end with the institution of heterosexuality, it is on rather unstable ground. As with the earlier poems, the homoerotic desire that underwrites the encounter of the boar and Adonis certainly troubles the narrative, and it is by no means certain how long Venus will remain immured. . . .

Notes

1. Stern, *Gabriel Harvey,* 127.

2. Duncan-Jones, 'Much Ado with Red and White,' 490-7.

3. Taylor, 'Shakespeare's Cousin, Thomas Greene, and his Kin,' 81.

4. 'Often of an afternoon groups of young Inns of Court men would head for the public playhouses in the London suburbs, where a personal acquaintance with the players helped to distinguish the real bloods among them. Probably it was on some such excursion that William Shakespeare and the young Earl of Southampton first saw each other' (Akrigg, *Shakespeare and the Earl of Southampton,* 31).

5. Akrigg, *Shakespeare and the Earl of Southampton,* 195-7; Martindale and Burrow, 'Clapham's *Narcissus.*'

6. Martindale and Burrow, 'Clapham's *Narcissus,*' 150. A. L. Rowse's argument that Leander is modelled on Southampton suggests a further connection between Clapham's and Marlowe's poems (*Shakespeare's Southampton,* 78-80).

7. Akrigg, *Shakespeare and the Earl of Southampton,* 195.

8. Martindale and Burrow, 'Clapham's *Narcissus,*' 152.

9. On *Venus and Adonis* as an admonitory fiction, see Akrigg, *Shakespeare and the Earl of Southampton,* 33-4, 194-5 and, more recently, Murphy, 'Wriothesley's Resistance.'

10. Fisher, 'The Renaissance Beard,' 175.

11. Gent, 'Venus and Adonis,' 726.

12. See, for example, the Nurse's speech in *Romeo and Juliet,* 1.3.16-48, 50-7.

13. Enterline, *The Rhetoric of the Body from Ovid to Shakespeare,* 129.

14. Lewis, *English Literature in the Sixteenth Century, Excluding Drama,* 236-7.

15. Grosz, *A Feminist Introduction to Jacques Lacan,* 50-1.

16. Lewis, *English Literature in the Sixteenth Century,* 238.

17. Don Cameron Allen argues that the horse narrative is the replacement for the Atalanta/Hippomenes tale. As Venus does not narrate that particular part of the poem, and as it has as its likely source Clapham's *Narcissus,* it makes more sense that this episode be seen as the substitution ('On Venus and Adonis,' 100).

18. Smith in Evans, *Riverside Shakespeare,* 1704.

19. Mortimer, *Variable Passions,* 15.

20. Fienberg, 'Thematics of Value in *Venus and Adonis,*' 26.

21. Quoted in Hamilton, 'Venus and Adonis,' 7.

22. Hamilton, 'Venus and Adonis,' 7.

23. Ibid., 13.

24. Sheidley, "'Unless It Be a Boar,'" 11.

25. Williams, 'The Coming of Age of Shakespeare's Adonis,' 770.

26. Sheidley, "'Unless It Be a Boar,'" 13.

27. Ibid., 14.

28. Asals, 'Venus and Adonis,' 46.

29. Hulse, *Metamorphic Verse,* 166.

30. *The Legend of Orpheus and Euridice* in *[. . .] Loues Complai[nts]* London: 1597. For a discussion of the poem in relation to R. B.'s *Orpheus His Journey to Hell,* see Kenneth Borris, 'R[ichard] B[arnfield]'s Homosocial Engineering,' 346-8. Borris speculates that the anonymous author wrote this homophobic poem in direct response to R. B.'s homoerotic verses.

31. Lanham, *The Motives of Eloquence,* 88.

32. In a parallel argument, Catherine Belsey writes that the poem participates in the emergence of family values in the period. 'The family promises gratification in exchange for submission to the rules: true love is desire that is properly regulated; it is for an appropriate (heterosexual) object; and its story is told in Shakespearean comedy' ('Taxonomies of Desire,' 275). . . .

Works Cited

1. EDITIONS OF EPYLLIA

Shakespeare, William. *The Riverside Shakespeare.* Edited by G. Blakemore Evans. Boston: Houghton Mifflin, 1974.

2. SECONDARY SOURCES

Akrigg, G. P. V. *Shakespeare and the Earl of Southampton.* Cambridge, MA: Harvard University Press, 1968.

Allen, Don Cameron. 'On Venus and Adonis.' In *Elizabethan and Jacobean Studies Presented to Frank Percy Wilson,* 100-11. Oxford: Clarendon Press, 1959.

Asals, Heather. '*Venus and Adonis*: The Education of a Goddess.' *Studies in English Literature* 13 (1973): 31-51.

Belsey, Catherine. 'Love as Trompe-l'oeil: Taxonomies of Desire in *Venus and Adonis.*' *Shakespeare Quarterly* 40 (1995): 257-76.

Borris, Kenneth. 'R[ichard] B[arnfield]'s Homosocial Engineering in *Orpheus His Journey to Hell,*' in Borris and Klawitter, eds, 332-60.

Duncan-Jones, Katherine. 'Much Ado with Red and White: The Earliest Readers of Shakespeare's *Venus and Adonis* (1593).' *Review of English Studies* 44 (1993): 479-501.

Enterline, Lynn. *The Rhetoric of the Body from Ovid to Shakespeare.* Cambridge: Cambridge University Press, 2000.

Fienberg, Nona. 'Thematics of Value in *Venus and Adonis.*' *Criticism* 31 (1989): 21-32.

Fisher, Will. 'The Renaissance Beard: Masculinity in Early Modern England.' *Renaissance Quarterly* 54 (2001): 155-87.

Gent, Lucy. 'Venus and Adonis: The Triumph of Rhetoric.' *Modern Language Review* 69 (1974): 721-9.

Grosz, Elizabeth. *Jacques Lacan: A Feminist Introduction.* London: Routledge, 1990.

Hamilton, A. C. 'Venus and Adonis.' *Studies in English Literature* 1 (1961): 1-15.

Hulse, Clark. *Metamorphic Verse: The Elizabethan Minor Epic.* Princeton, NJ: Princeton University Press, 1981.

Lanham, Richard. *The Motives of Eloquence: Literary Rhetoric in the Renaissance.* New Haven, CT: Yale University Press, 1976.

Lewis, C. S. *English Literature in the Sixteenth Century, Excluding Drama.* Oxford: Clarendon Press, 1954.

Martindale, Charles, and Colin Burrow. 'Clapham's *Narcissus*: A Pre-Text for Shakespeare's *Venus and Adonis*? (text, translation, and commentary).' *English Literary Renaissance* 22.2 (1992): 147-76.

Mortimer, Anthony. *Variable Passions: A Reading of Shakespeare's* Venus and Adonis. New York: AMS Press, 2000.

Murphy, Patrick M. 'Wriothesley's Resistance: Wardship Practices and Ovidian Narratives in Shakespeare's *Venus and Adonis.*' In Venus and Adonis: *Critical Essays,* edited by Philip C. Kolin, 323-40. New York: Garland, 1997.

Rowse, A. L. *Shakespeare's Southampton.* London: Macmillan, 1965.

Sheidley, William E. "'Unless It Be a Boar": Love and Wisdom in Shakespeare's *Venus and Adonis.*' *Modern Language Quarterly* 35 (1974): 3-15.

Stern, Virginia F. *Gabriel Harvey: His Life, Marginalia and Library.* Oxford: Clarendon Press, 1979.

Taylor, Rupert. 'Shakespeare's Cousin, Thomas Greene, and his Kin: Possible Light on the Shakespeare Family Background.' *PMLA* 60 (1945): 81-94.

Williams, Gordon. 'The Coming of Age of Shakespeare's Adonis.' *Modern Language Review* 78 (1983): 769-76.

Madhavi Menon (essay date 2005)

SOURCE: Menon, Madhavi. "Spurning Teleology in *Venus and Adonis*." *Gay and Lesbian Quarterly* 11, no. 4 (2005): 491-519.

[*In the essay below, Menon considers Venus's unsuccessful seduction of Adonis as the failure of sexuality as well as the failure of teleology.*]

Even as it marketed itself as the show about the often surprising sexual urges of single women, *Sex and the City* went the way of all flesh in its finale. That is to say, it returned us, after the promise of freedom, to a location that looked remarkably familiar: where lust matures into love and the single woman finds her man. One reviewer hailed the show for finally getting "around the issue of sex to the more basic concern . . . of finding love," while another was relieved that the finale "made good on its pledge to resolve the love life of New York sex columnist Carrie Bradshaw."[1] The 10.6 million viewers who tuned in to watch *Sex and the City*—a record for the show's six-season run—presumably had mixed responses to the finale, but most reports suggested deep satisfaction with the way in which it "nicely tied up some loose ends," revealing, for example, the name of Carrie's big lover.[2] But the anticlimax of this last revelation—his name is John—also marked the rest of the episode, in which the choices of the conventional Charlotte suddenly became the things that all women want. This is not to suggest that Carrie should not fall in love, or that Miranda should not forfeit her independence to move to Brooklyn and give her mother-in-law a sponge bath, but what made the finale of *Sex and the City* so satisfying to several million viewers was a sense of closure, a sense that everything—all the suffering, all the humiliation, all the raunchiness, all the sexual adventures—had a point, and that point was monogamous, consummated love. Nor were these millions wrong; after all, most successful books and films trace the same trajectory. Perhaps even more interestingly, much literary criticism follows the same path, in which the ends justify the means and reveal them to have been purposeful all along.

These unlikely allies of *Sex and the City* are to be found in the dust of academic archives and the catalogs of publishing presses. Current studies of Renaissance sexuality, for instance, which read texts written more than four hundred years before Carrie Bradshaw burst onto the HBO scene, adhere strictly to the notion of a consummated ending tying together sexual threads of the past. This fantasy of consummated endings is found less in the literary texts of the Renaissance, however, than in the hegemonic critical-historical narratives about the movement from "early modern" to "modern" regimes of sexuality. According to these narratives, the divide between sexual regimes follows a curve of increasing legibility in which the regime we currently inhabit is anticipated in the Renaissance, though not fully developed until the nineteenth century at the earliest. Such an understanding of sexuality depends on the existence of a developmental curve from the proto-gay to the gay, from the sodomite to the homosexual, in which the latter provides the settled term, transparent in its meaning and identifiable in its physiognomy.[3] This insistence on a progressive curve has also been terminologically institutionalized—and the Renaissance is now more "correctly" and commonly known—as the *early* modern period, the precursor to the modern period (which in turn has been ousted by the postmodern). The emphasis of such a movement is to arrive at an identifiable phenomenon and personality against which to oppose the lack of an identifiable phenomenon and personality. Uncertainty, lust, and fluidity belonged to the past, and their legacy to us is certainty, love, and fixity. Indeed, the very term *sexuality,* "as we use the word to designate a systematic organization and orientation of desire," indicates a fixing of desire that fixes also a groove for desire to follow.[4] Such a groove is marked by two features. First, there is progress made from an early point to a later one, in which the first point makes sense only in relation to its end point. As the literary field inhabiting the "early" node of a developmental curve, Renaissance studies is invested in assuring this movement from "pre" to "post," since the "pre" acquires importance only inasmuch as it results in an identifiable "post." Second, the realm of fluidity has to be located in the past: if the present were fluid, then there would be no ground from which to judge the past. In other words, the movement can never be from love to lust or from present to past; it always has to be the other way around.

The nominal term for this investment in conclusive progress is teleology. Defined as the doctrine of ends or final causes, teleology depends on a sequence leading to an end that can retrospectively be seen as having had a beginning. Issues of time and consequence are paramount for such narratives; this is why statements like Michel Foucault's "The sodomite *was* a temporary aberration; the homosexual is *now* a species" are read teleologically to posit a fixed end and a more fluid beginning.[5] Such a teleological reading of Foucault leaves no room for the failure of either (homo)sexuality or teleology, ensuring the success, if not of sex, then at least of developmental narratives about sex. This investment in teleology, however, owes less to Foucault than to a fascination with thinking about sexuality as a developmental movement from before to after, from prematurity (or early modernity) to maturity (or modernity), an investment that marks the historicist project of distinguishing between a distant past and a current present. This historicism does not follow David M. Halperin's strictures about sexual historiography, which, "far from installing [(homo)sexuality] as the goal to which all human societies strive, ought to have the effect of depriviledging it, enabling it to appear as one of many documented varieties of human social organization, reopening the question of its temporality, and thereby testifying to the heterogeneity of sexual life both past and present."[6] Halperin's description of historicism, in which past and present interact uneasily and neither is a fixed or fixable entity, is closer to Foucault's notion of an archaeology of knowledge than to a teleology of events.[7] Far from recognizing the fissures in the present, however, studies of Renaissance sexuality tend to locate such fissures only in the past so as to, one imagines, recover the Renaissance more fully as the period of the incipient "early modern." At the same time, these recognizable fissures of the past are not allowed to affect how we read that past. The Renaissance thus becomes both the time that is different from us and the time that is read by us as we like to read ourselves.

The fascination of studies of sexuality with teleology is based on a reading of the famous passage from volume 1 of Foucault's *History of Sexuality* or, as Halperin describes it, on a nonreading of that passage.[8] In his complex and careful analysis of Foucault's work, Halperin suggests that this nonreading has resulted in serious errors in understanding the history of sexuality. Toward the end of his essay Halperin discusses what he terms Foucault's resistance to a "theory" of sexuality. Inasmuch as a theory might be considered bounded and well defined, Halperin notes, it becomes the very opposite of Foucault's aim in the *History*. This lack of boundedness is where the problem lies:

> I believe it is our resistance to Foucault's resistance to this resistance to theory, our insistence on transforming Foucault's critical antitheory into a theory of sexuality, that has led us to mistake his discursive analysis for a historical assertion—and that has licensed us, on that basis, to remake his strategic distinction between the sodomite and the homosexual into a conceptual distinction between sexual acts and sexual identities, into a bogus theoretical doctrine, and into a patently false set of historical premises.

(111)

For Halperin, Foucault's aim is not to shut down inquiry into premodern sexual subjectivities or morphologies that might be understandable in modern terms; rather, it is to open up an area of inquiry in which distinctions can be understood rhetorically rather than literally, productively rather than judgmentally. In other words, Foucault may sound as if he were drawing a neat arc according to which what comes before the nineteenth century is merely preparatory for what comes after it, but there is nothing in his work to suggest that chronology and concept need to be fused teleologically. Indeed, the discursive idea of the homosexual may be productive for thinking also about Renaissance sexualities (Halperin does not go this far), because rather than

name "real" people and things, such categories name the slippages and fissures inherent in every age's attempt to represent its libido to itself.[9] As discursive terms that try to contain competing investments, then, categories of desire can only be relational and contingent, never absolute and never sequential. Homo- and heterosexuality, sodomy and homosexuality, may be different in degree, but they can never represent the end point for any one of the others. If *homosexuality* today names a problem in discursive understanding—or in understanding discourse—then that problem is being approached (citing "Foucauldian" teleology) in the most unproblematic manner possible.[10] The "almost ritual invocation of [Foucault's] name by academic practitioners . . . [has] reduce[d] the operative range of his thought to a small set of received ideas," transforming his challenge into a critical orthodoxy. Halperin notes that "it is a matter of considerable irony that Foucault's influential distinction between the discursive construction of the sodomite and the discursive construction of the homosexual, which had originally been intended to open up a domain of historical inquiry, has now become a major obstacle blocking further research into the rudiments of sexual identity formation in premodern and early modern European societies."[11] The range of operative ideas opened up by Foucault in his *History of Sexuality* has been constricted within well-policed boundaries between ages, peoples, and times. What is of interest for the present essay, however, are the misreadings of Foucault that share discursive space with the season finale of *Sex and the City,* and around which most studies of past sexualities gather.[12]

That discursive space, of course, is teleology. So-called practitioners of Foucault—including Halperin himself—largely focus on the teleological difference between the sodomite and the homosexual, according to which the sodomite marks a necessary first stage in the development of an individual we can now recognize as a homosexual. Despite his critique of literal Foucauldianism, there are significant ways in which Halperin reinscribes teleology as the marker of how to do the history of homosexuality. He suggests, for instance, that even though the distinction between the sodomite and the homosexual is not meant to be an empirical claim for Foucault, "ultimately, it is a heuristic device for foregrounding what is distinctive about modern techniques of social and sexual regulation." This distinctiveness implies an identifiable end point that can be differentiated from its tangled (and spurious) beginnings; Halperin suggests that "neither the sexual morphology of the *kinaidos* nor the sexual subjectivity of the fourteenth-century Italian sodomite should be understood as a sexual identity, or a sexual orientation in the modern sense—much less as equivalent to the modern formation known as homosexuality."[13] To depend on the fixity and transparency of "the modern formation known as homosexuality," as opposed to an earlier "subjectivity" that it nonetheless helps throw into recognizable relief, is to argue for a teleological progression of sexuality; indeed, it is to argue for sexuality *as* a teleological progression.

The trap of teleology, though, is by no means universal, and the argument of the present essay is indebted to several queer theorists who have formulated similar challenges to teleology, both in and out of the Renaissance. As an exemplar of the latter, Valerie Traub has critiqued the teleological paradigm shift—"I have not privileged alterity for its own sake"—and articulated the desire "to enjoy the pleasures of queering history, while appreciating a past that both is, and is not, our own."[14] Louise Fradenburg and Carla Freccero's important collection of essays on premodern sexualities makes the point that

> history—and not just family history—is an erogenous zone, and knowing this helps us understand sexuality itself a lot better. It might also help us better understand the kinds of ethical structures at stake in historical thinking. For example, the argument that modern desires and perspectives can and must be set aside if we are to read the past properly is itself revealing, for it suggests that historical knowledge is often founded on the renunciation, the *ascesis,* of "self." And to the degree that this renunciation tries to hide its own narcissistic investments, it begs for queer scrutiny.[15]

In her aptly titled study *Inconsequence,* Annamarie Jagose "foregrounds the risks for any reading of sexuality in naturalizing sequence as an interpretive mode."[16] Echoing the tension over tenses that powers the title of an earlier essay by Jonathan Goldberg, "The History That Will Be," Jagose warns against the illusion of "uncovering" lesbian history to invoke its primacy among sexualities.[17] "It might be more useful," she contends, "to explore how the cultural production of lesbianism as a perverse turn of some other sexual organization that can consequently lay an easier claim to authenticity might be read as a defense, a disavowal of precisely that derivativeness which, far from being the definitional bent of female homosexuality, is the heart of sexuality itself."[18]

Even as these studies of queer theory and history call into question the primacy of teleology in narrating the queerness of the past, the ideal of telos continues to shape even the least heteronormative studies of Renaissance sexuality. But my argument against teleology is not meant to suggest that Renaissance sexuality is the same as our own (such a suggestion, given our instant recoil from even the faintest hint of "narcissism," is impossible); rather, it asserts that the marker of teleology is stable consequence rather than difference. As such, an antiteleological argument can respect historical difference while militating against consequence; it can accept that no two ages will behave in an identical manner while it resists the argument that one (homogeneous) age always sets the stage for a later (homogeneous) age, especially in so ungrounded an arena as sexual desire. An antiteleological argument is thus not straightforwardly an argument against cultural and historical difference; if anything, it is an argument against straightforwardness as a mode of inquiry into sexuality. To stay within the register of Foucault's thought, an argument against teleology would be an argument for archaeology, in which different layers of desire overlapped and streamed messily into one another, and an argument for genealogy, in which homosexuality and sodomy were related but not exhibited as the fruition of each other's latency. It might well be argued, of course, that our current understanding of homosexuality is in itself not an end point but a placeholder in an ever-evolving continuum that could give rise to newer permutations of sexual taxonomies. No matter how appealing this argument might seem, it inhabits a framework of perfectibility in which the present provides an identity with which to contrast the aberrations of the past. In studies of Renaissance sexuality, desire in the sixteenth and seventeenth centuries is always compared to the fixed end point where we currently find ourselves. Even more, Renaissance desire is seen as essentially reproductive, giving birth to descendants who then return to the womb to understand from where they have come. The *Oxford English Dictionary* suggests that teleology is "the doctrine or study of ends or final causes, esp. as related to the evidences of design or purpose in nature."[19] This "natural" design is purposeful only to the extent that it is also reproductive; teleology names the causal link between two generational and generative moments in history when the child, though he may well be father to the man, is also the final design of his progenitor.

Defenders of teleology—mostly historians rather than literary critics, but whose ideas have been internalized by many of the latter—have much to say about its success as a historiographical method. In his essay on the so-called historical turn in literary studies, Glenn Burgess suggests that

> the difficulty with the idea of the open encounter with the past is that the past does not exist until reconstructed. If you do not reconstruct it non-anachronistically, you construct only a version of yourself, your prejudices, a version of the present. Your enriching encounter with the alien past becomes a cosy self-confirming fireside chat with yourself. To encounter the other, you must first grasp the nature of its otherness. And, for historians of the past, the *only* way of doing that is to attempt descriptions and accounts that avoid anachronism.[20]

Despite admitting to the reconstructed nature of "the past," Burgess makes it clear that there are two ways of doing that reconstruction: the proper way and the improper way. The proper way involves distancing the past adequately so that it does not become a version of the present, even as we might need the present to be the teleological end for the past that we have reconstructed. The improper way of doing history, the nonteleological way, involves a "cosy self-confirming fireside chat with yourself," which threatens to conflate past and present, ends and means. By not adequately recognizing the otherness of the other, such a chat feeds on itself, gorging on anachronism and spurning teleology. The improper mode, in other words, fatally affects the study of ends and may even imply the end of study. What may sound like a critique of the heterosexual investment in constructing reproductive versions of the self is neatly turned into a homophobic categorization of anachronous narcissism. The passage suggests that the existence of an other is crucial to the formation of a self: without an other, there can be no self; without something that has come before, we cannot be said to come after. It is therefore not "the past [that] does not exist until reconstructed" but the present that needs teleological cords with which to connect itself to a past that must be seen as having a version of what has eventually become the present. Thus the "you" in the passage—presumably the historian currently alive—is the stable point of reference in it and also the measure against which the blur of the past might be seen to be in need of reconstruction. The very project of reconstruction, however, implies knowledge of what is being reconstructed, and this knowledge works backward to uncover a past that can be understood as having conceived of the present. In other words, there is no method for reconstructing the past that is not anachronistic. In Burgess's case, however, anachronism is anathema to the project of allowing the past to speak in its "own" terms; the relation between past and present is a causal one in which the well-being of the present is predicated on the past's being a certain way.

This approach to history, in which everything has a purpose and the purpose is enrichment, is teleologically invested in the idea of consequence: an "early" form of desire, now alien to us, will lead to a later form of sexuality, now stable, and they will occupy different positions on the same continuum. Teleology thus becomes the paradigm within which to study the past, but this paradigm dominates at the expense of alternative paradigms found in prominent Renaissance texts. If we take seriously not the project of teleology itself so much as the investment in the alterity of the past, then it seems that the alterity of the past has been allowed to take only one form: that of occupying the node of teleological incipience in relation to the present. I argue that the alterity of the past can be equally well served by expanding the palette of differences. Such an expansion would involve taking seriously modes of inquiry that might differ from our own investment in historicist imperatives. That is, we need to focus less on the dif-

ferent objects of inquiry—sodomy and homosexuality name far too simplistic modes of difference—and more on the *method* of that inquiry, whether teleological or not, developmental or its opposite. Such methods can redefine what we understand by historical periods and the objects by which we define them. Studying such texts and such methods, then, takes the project of "queering the Renaissance" in a different direction, where the focus is more on methodology than on object.[21] Ignoring such methods only perpetuates the heteronormative mode of sexual analysis in which teleology governs our understanding, not only of the early modern period but also of its libidinal desires.

I would like to consider one instance of such a text, well known in its time as a sexual text, reprinted in its author's lifetime, and evidently popular among whores: Shakespeare's erotic epyllion, *Venus and Adonis.*[22] Not only does this poem describe in some detail erotic pleasures of the flesh, but it also provides us with an astonishingly well-articulated approach to an alternative mode of doing Renaissance sexuality. Instead of focusing on the success of a teleological approach to desire, the poem ponders what it might mean for such studies to fail, or rather, what it might mean for studies of sexuality to take seriously not the idea of teleological success but that of failure. This investment in failure as a theoretical paradigm marks the antiteleological success of Shakespeare's poem. By shifting the focus of studies of Renaissance sexuality from objects to methods, it also counters the divisions between peoples and times that stifle our own intellectual creativity and that enable teleological studies to flourish in the first place.

THE FAILURE OF TELEOLOGY

In his introduction to the *Riverside* edition of the poem, Hallett Smith criticizes *Venus and Adonis* for being "an Ovidian poem that does not fully succeed."[23] He dismisses it as a stylistic failure, worthy of neither its source in Ovid's *Metamorphoses* nor its contemporary in Marlowe's *Hero and Leander*. But even as Smith notes the poem's stylistic failure, he himself fails to remark on the most crucial component of that failure, a component that defies a central tenet of Ovidian poetry and represents Shakespeare's most significant rewriting of Ovid. While in the *Metamorphoses* Adonis lustily capitulates to Venus, in Shakespeare's rendition he firmly resists the goddess's overtures. In the Ovidian text Adonis is transformed after his death into an annually renewing flower, but in the Shakespearean poem he is transformed into a flower that withers away almost immediately, with no promise of renewal. In Ovid, Adonis both has sex and lives on after his death to remind Venus of the pleasures of fulfilled desire; in Shakespeare, he both spurns her and fails to leave behind a recurrent image of himself. In *Venus and*

Adonis, then, the idea of failure is bound up with the idea of sexual failure.

This double failure—of narrative style and of sexual climax—militates against what is often considered the poem's most important function: as Shakespeare's first published work, *Venus and Adonis* inaugurates the developmental thrust of the Shakespearean canon. It provides a starting point from which to measure various ends: for instance, the dates of Shakespeare's "later" works, his departure from Stratford, his arrival in London, his interests at the time, his interaction with the Earl of Southampton. Without *Venus and Adonis* and the circumstantial biographical evidence it offers about its author, Shakespeareans would not know where to begin. The originality of *Venus and Adonis* (which is also, of course, its lack of originality) marks the first step in a narrative of Shakespearean progress.

The poem itself pays homage to such a progression, most notably in its epigraph, taken from Ovid's *Amores,* which announces at the start, *"Vilia miretur vulgus: mihi flauus Apollo / Pocula Castalia plena ministret aqua,"* or in Marlowe's translation, "Let base-conceited wits admire vile things, / Fair Phoebus lead me to the Muses' springs."[24] This epigraph sets up a teleological narrative in which the movement is from "vile things" to inspired "springs," from base "wits" to divine tits. This narrative both marks and praises its own success by announcing the transfer from a suspicious beginning to a desirable conclusion, or rather, from a beginning that should have ended to an ending that is just beginning. Despite its investment in teleological progress, this movement never arrives at its destination: it is only able to point elsewhere, to the poem, as the fulfillment it is itself unable to deliver. The poem stands as "proof" of the teleological move from vileness to fairness that the epigraph promises. Even as it sets up a narrative of before and after, however, the epigraph cannot make good on its promise and remains stuck in the realm of before and before: after the end of the beginning is a chronological point to which the epigraph cannot transport us, so it stops before the beginning of the end. Its investment in a historical sequence of before and after thus becomes mired in the uncomfortable position of two befores with no after (as yet). The epigraph attempts to set up a sense of linearity by giving us the illusion of beginning and end, fact and consequence, neatly coexisting on a teleological continuum, but as both epigraph and poem suggest, this illusion may never follow through on its own desire. Or rather, desire may never follow through, and that may be its most significant characteristic.

Venus and Adonis thus opens as a historical poem in which the teleological underpinnings of historical consciousness are set out for the historically conscious. Not only is the poem the starting point of Shakespeare's

published career, but it starts out with a comment on the virtue of good starts and better endings. If teleology is the basis of history, then *Venus and Adonis* is a historical poem, a poem that validates current critical methodologies of reading literature from the past. In its epigraph, in its providing a taste of things to come, *Venus and Adonis* upholds the desirability of such a plan of historical action, setting up a teleological framework into which it will presumably slot its own poetic aftermath. Except that it does not. Rather, the before and after of teleology—the sequence so necessary to establish success—are explicitly denied in a poem in which Adonis does not succumb to Venus at all. The movement forward, what we might call a "sequence," is clearly elusive in the poem, where Venus never achieves what she most desires: to fuck Adonis. The poem, as Smith so aptly notes, does *not* fully succeed. And this lack of success has resounding consequences, not just for the sequence suggested by the epigraph and seized on eagerly by the teleological imperative, but also for history itself.

Venus and Adonis is thus far less important as Shakespeare's first publication than as his first published word on teleology, in which failure fundamentally disrupts the flow of progress and the text seems far more interested in the relationship between sexuality and failure than in the teleological success of sex. The before and after of teleology are converted—in this paradigmatic tale of the historical process, of the passing of time, and of the change wrought by this passing—into a narrative device doomed to failure. Widely acknowledged as a poem about sexual desire, *Venus and Adonis* is also a narrative that denies us a consummated end toward which we can read its beginning; it provides no consummation to the tale of sexual desire that it has been plotting. Unlike the Ovidian narrative in which Adonis turns into a flower that will be resurrected annually through Venus's mediation, the Shakespearean text leads to Adonis's spontaneous transformation into a pansy that is immediately plucked up and withers, with no mention of rebirth. In Shakespeare's rendition, the death of Adonis really is the end of Adonis; at the end Venus appropriates Adonis's stem, but the bud of his desire—of their desire, of desire itself—rather than bloom into a teleological flower, remains stubbornly blasted.

Defined as the opposite of success, this blast of "failure" denotes a kink in the chain of consequence; it marks the end of a sequence and withholds the promise of succession, and also, therefore, of what we might call "success." If "success" is understood as the expectation of ends, issues, and sequels,[25] then "failure" insists on the lack of an end, issue, and sequel; the inability to provide an end lies entirely in failure's insistence on endings. These truncated definitions join success and sequence at the hip; there can be no success without a sense of sequence, and sequence itself can be measured only by its success, its outcome, its issue. Success rests on an after that can testify to the success of what came before, and the after depends on a narrative structure that confers on it the status of coming after and therefore of being able to pronounce authoritatively on what has passed before. Both success and sequence— event and judgment—rely heavily on the idea of teleology. After all, without a determinable sequence, there can be no measure of success, let alone measurable, or even measured, success. In Shakespeare's poem, the Adonis who dies, the Adonis flower that withers, the Venus whose desire remains unconsummated are all markers of failure precisely because they have no remainder—no reminder—to show either for or of themselves. Their desire has no tangible witness, no material residue. Their longing does not ensure future trysts. The "failure" of sexuality in **Venus and Adonis,** then, is not only a failure of sexuality but, more fundamentally, a failure of teleology, marked forever by the absence of an act and an issue of consequence.

Venus plays on this fear of failure in her attempts to woo Adonis. After pleading and physical seduction have failed, the goddess of love tries to induce teleological guilt in her prey:

> Is thine own heart to thine own face affected?
> Can thy right hand seize love upon thy left?
> Then woo thyself, be of thyself rejected;
> Steal thine own freedom, and complain on theft.
> Narcissus so himself himself forsook,
> And died to kiss his shadow in the brook.

> (157-62)

What is clearly at issue is the question of issue itself— the question of a successful succession taken up variously in the sonnets and **Venus and Adonis.**[26] In fact, this poem anticipates some of the sonnets when Venus says soon after these lines, "Seeds spring from seeds, and beauty breedeth beauty; / Thou wast begot, to get it is thy duty" (167-68). The stanza thus becomes the staging ground for a battle between the proponents of different historiographies: Venus speaks for a "straight" history, in which what is begotten must in turn beget, while Adonis, though silent in this passage, represents a swerving from the course of nature. As the reference to Narcissus makes clear, Venus accuses Adonis of self-love—of affecting his own face. For Venus, his narcissistic love marks the failure of sequence, because it precludes consequence. Rather than set in motion a narrative whose end can reference, without being identical to, its beginning, Adonis is criticized for letting things slide, for being self-contained, for being self-referential, and, even worse, for allowing his death to be his end. Venus, although agitated by this idea of death, expresses her fear by dwelling not on the fact of death but on its cause: Adonis, like Narcissus, will die trying to "kiss his shadow in the brook."

This investment in causality is not new to Venus. A few lines earlier, while upbraiding Adonis for picking *on* her, rather than picking her, she states:

> Were I hard-favor'd, foul, or wrinkled old,
> Ill-nurtur'd, crooked, churlish, harsh in voice,
> O'erworn, despised, rheumatic, and cold,
> Thick-sighted, barren, lean, and lacking juice,
>   Then mightst thou pause, for then I were not for thee,
>   But having no defects, why dost abhor me?

> (133-38)

None of the reasons Venus lists for possible dismissal applies to her. In other words, she can understand effects that are related to causes, but in Adonis she is faced with an effect without a cause, which breaches the teleological network. Venus's rhetoric describes a historical investment in consequence: if a legitimate cause exists, then the effect can be understood. To Venus, Adonis's problem is not simply that he does not pick her but that his choice makes no sense; it departs from a historical paradigm that functions according to the logic of causality. Adonis's narcissism partakes of the logic of illogic, in which effects occur without causes and befores double up at the expense of afters. Adonis thinks only of himself, not of his consequence. Spurning Venus again, he flounces off after dismissing her plea for love: "Fie, no more of love! / The sun doth burn my face, I must remove" (185-86).

For Venus, this removal from consequence is intimately connected with Adonis's narcissism. As Burgess's comment makes evident, narcissism bears the burden of an indulgence that registers as the opposite of propriety, both historical and sexual. Idealized historicism poses as an ideal sexuality, and the movement of both is forward rather than backward. Adonis's narcissism, then, marks the end not of teleological history but of teleological progress toward the (proper) end of history. This particular equation of narcissism with regression has given rise to one of the most abiding slurs about homosexual desire; as Michael Warner points out, homosexuality as associated with narcissism is understood to be a "developmental misdirection,"[27] and Venus's lament over Adonis voices an idea that persists in our own cultural formation. Yet the poem's invocation of narcissism also produces it as the only resistance to such a cultural imperative: unending desire counters the desire for consummated endings and clarifies the stakes of such a repudiation of consequence. The text's privileging of narcissism is directly related to its de-privileging of teleology and inversely related to historical and sexual "correctness"; it is, in fact, directly related to inversion, which is endemic to the very concept of narcissism. Despite his obsession with himself, Adonis is characterized as taking *insufficient* care of himself: "Narcissus so himself himself *forsook*" (my emphasis).[28] The explicit association with Narcissus condemns Adonis for hindering the creation of a consequential self even as this hindrance is achieved by a preoccupation with the self; the "himself" Adonis forsakes is the one that might exist reproductively in the future. This resistance to reproducing his image despite a narcissistic investment in that image points to the impossibility of reading narcissism univocally.

Thus narcissism becomes a useful tool with which to oppose the normative insistence of both heterosexuality and teleology. As Lee Edelman argues in a different context, the fantasy of an "escape" from narcissism—the fantasy of "Narci-schism"—is impossible, because "it is never . . . a question of leaving the mirror. It is a question, rather, of which mirror we choose to reflect the image we will recognize as ours."[29] In the case of **Venus and Adonis,** the teleological mirror is cracked by the poem's narcissistic image. Such a naked investment in narcissism is so disturbing to both the goddess of love and the poem's readers that Adonis's unresponsiveness to Venus is squarely cast—in order to contain the spread of narcissistic infection and to defend her honor—as *his* problem. Adonis, it is argued, is stuck in a chronological and psychological "phase" that renders him immune to Venus's charms: he has yet to blossom into (hetero)sexual "maturity"; the goddess of love fails to have her way with him, not for lack of trying but because he proves too trying.[30] Adonis has an apocalyptic effect on Venus and the reader alike, because he does much more than spurn sex; he also spurns teleology in relation to sex and embraces narcissism instead.[31]

Not satisfied with his own resistance to sexual teleology, Adonis insists that everyone around him be equally resistant to it. Indeed, the only sexual course taken with the hope of consummation in this poem is that of Adonis's courser, who breaks free from his restraint to pursue a saucy jennet emerging from a copse (259-64). The horses enact a love ritual more traditionally coded from the perspective of heterosexuality: the courser is enamored of the jennet, the jennet acts coy to heighten his interest, the courser becomes frenzied with anxiety, and the jennet relents. Just then, however, Adonis steps into the picture, determined to seize his horse, and so interrupts their tryst:

> His testy master goeth about to take him,
> When lo the unback'd breeder, full of fear,
> Jealous of catching, swiftly doth forsake him,
> With her the horse, and left Adonis there.
> As they were mad unto the woods they hie them,
> Outstripping crows that strive to overfly them.
>
> (319-24)

Adonis once again stands in the way of sex; even more, he is the instrument by which consummation is actively excluded from the poem. He manages to chase his horse out of the picture, and by running away to escape "his

testy master," the courser takes the heat of sex with him into the woods. Presumably the courser mounts the jennet, but only after leaving the poem, never to return. These horses embody a relation to desire in which teleological consummation is achieved, though never within the visible frame. In other words, they embody what Venus wants from Adonis, and she attempts to initiate him into the wonders of love: "O, learn to love, the lesson is but plain, / And once made perfect, never lost again" (407-8). But the very perfection of the lesson renders it unpalatable to Adonis; unlike the comparison with Narcissus, which Adonis's narrative space can accommodate, the parallel with the horses would entail his leaving the poem altogether. It would also entail eliding one of the poem's most profound insights into sexuality: that desire cannot be coupled with sexual consummation.[32] In this as in so much else, **Venus and Adonis** undermines itself theoretically. In the end, the poem is not about "Venus and Adonis"; indeed, it pivots on how Venus and Adonis can never be "Venus and Adonis," on how the conjunctive kiss can never translate into conjugal bliss.

This undermining is perhaps most evident when the not-lovers are in the very "throes of love." Alarmed by Adonis's plans "to-morrow . . . / To hunt the boar," Venus pulls him down on top of her (587-88, 592-94). "Now is she in the very lists of love, / Her champion mounted for the hot encounter," but alas, "all is imaginary she doth prove, / He will not manage her, although he mount her" (595-98). So she interrupts her seduction to counsel him against such an undertaking; she urges him at some length to hunt the hare instead. In Ovid's text, this warning is bolstered by appeal to the tale of the princess Atalanta and Hippomenes. It has been prophesied that for Atalanta marriage will result in death. In fear for her life, she institutes a rule whereby her suitors must race against her to win her hand and must die if they fail to outrun her. Atalanta's swiftness guarantees the failure of every suitor until Hippomenes arrives on the scene. Knowing that he cannot outrun the princess on his own, he prays to Venus for help. The goddess gives him golden apples to throw down at crucial moments in the race to distract Atalanta, who loses and so must marry Hippomenes. However, he fails to express his gratitude adequately, and Venus, displeased, possesses them with such lust that they have sex in a temple: "He entered here and with forbidden sin / Defiled the sanctuary."[33] Cybele, the matron goddess of the temple, punishes Hippomenes and Atalanta by turning them into lions, and Venus, who might have come to Hippomenes' aid, does nothing to prevent his metamorphosis. Because of her reluctance to protect Hippomenes, Venus fears that wild animals now seek to avenge themselves on her and her loved ones.

Even though the Venus of Shakespeare's poem does not refer to the Ovidian tale, she seems to be modeled on

Atalanta, while Adonis, despite his lack of interest in sexual consummation, uncannily resembles Hippomenes. These resemblances first strike us when we read about Atalanta's initial encounter with Hippomenes, during which the steel-hearted maiden shows a curious softening toward men:

> And as [Hippomenes] spoke King Schoenus' daughter gazed
> With tender eyes and doubted in her heart
> Whether this time she wished to win or lose.
> "What god," she thought, "who envies beauty's charms,
> Desires his death and bids him seek a bride
> At hazard of his own dear life? So much
> Is more than I am worth. It's not his beauty
> That touches me (though that could touch me too);
> But he is still a boy; it's not himself
> That moves me but his tender years, his youth."
>
> (10.64-73)

Like Shakespeare's Venus, Atalanta is drawn to a lover whose beauty is emblematized by his boyishness. Like Hippomenes, Adonis is a brash, beautiful young man willing to wager all for the gratification of his senses, but beyond this similarity the two diverge. Unlike Hippomenes, whose ardor is directed at winning and fucking Atalanta, Adonis is not interested in the heterosexual aim of desire; indeed, he is not invested in sexual victory at all. Unlike Atalanta, Venus is unwilling to see her predicament as a lose-lose situation. For Atalanta, losing the race will mean losing her life, while winning the race will mean losing the man. The inevitability of loss is in keeping with the oracle's prophecy:

> "No husband,
> Fair Atalanta, is for you; refuse
> A husband's kisses; yet you'll not refuse,
> And you, whilst still you live, yourself shall lose."
>
> (10.7-10)

For Atalanta, desire and dissatisfaction are relentlessly juxtaposed; Venus, however, dwells in the myth that seducing Adonis will be a significant victory and losing him a failure. Venus overlooks the link between desire and loss, while Adonis reinforces it. Thus Adonis comes to resemble not the boyish Hippomenes but the swift Atalanta—the attractive person fleeing sexuality for fear of losing her life. In spite of their mutual imbrication in loss and desire, however, Ovid's heroine and Shakespeare's hero follow different teleological trajectories: Atalanta is tricked into sexual consummation before being deprived of her humanity, while Adonis is allowed stubbornly to refuse the lure of sexual success.

In Shakespeare's poem Venus pauses in her seduction of Adonis to warn him against hunting the boar, but she does so without the narrative enlargement on Atalanta and Hippomenes. After delivering the warning, she then returns to her original discourse on desire:

> "Where did I leave?" "No matter where," quoth he,
> "Leave me, and then the story aptly ends;
> The night is spent." "Why, what of that?" quoth she.
> "I am," quoth he, "expected of my friends,
>   And now 'tis dark, and going I shall fall."
>   "In night," quoth she, "desire sees best of all."
>
> (715-20)

When Venus tries to pick up the thread of her narrative on desire, Adonis dismisses strings entirely, claiming both that he is not tied to Venus and that their story does not hang together. A successful end to the story of Venus and Adonis, for him, would not be a sexual end at all. Rather, it would have everything to do with the lack of success in sex: there is an inverse, perhaps even a perverse, relationship between sexual climax and narrative climax. The farther Venus and Adonis are from consummating their relationship, the sooner their story will end. "Leave me," Adonis insists, "and then the story aptly ends."

Unable to accept this ending, Venus tries to prevent Adonis's desire from blooming elsewhere, and she does so by shifting from the object of desire to desire itself. When Adonis protests that "now 'tis dark, and going I shall fall," Venus deftly retorts, "In night . . . desire sees best of all." Her assertion may suggest that desire can *see* best at night because it cannot itself *be seen,* or that it flourishes most when it *cannot* see beyond its own fulfillment, or even that it is always the thing banished to the margins of a narrative, because it can be represented only as a rupture of representation. The question of what desire "sees" or whose desire can be seen is thus profoundly complicated by the fact that desire thrives in a lack rather than an abundance of light and sight. Darkness not only captures the "pitchiness" that Shakespeare elsewhere associates with desire but also implies the uncertainty of Venus's very use of the word *desire.*[34] Whose desire? For whom? And, most crucially, to what end? Venus may be suggesting that the night is the perfect time for Adonis to consummate his relationship with her. Or she may be referring to his desire to be rid of her. In the latter case, she may mean that his desire—to go forth and be with his friends—is desire at its most clear-sighted or that this desire, though it can see clearly, will not be seen because of the dark night. Indeed, this second possibility turns out to be literally true, since we never see Adonis with either the boar or his friends. In the visible space Venus and Adonis do not have sex, and if sex takes place somewhere else, or in the dark, then it is not seen.

Thinking through the cultural implications of such darkness in relation to lesbianism, Jagose suggests that "the familiar figure of the invisible lesbian is animated by a structuring paradox. The persistent rhetorical figuration of lesbianism as unrepresentable, invisible, and impossible brings to representation the very thing that, this figuration claims, remains outside the visual field. Because lesbian invisibility is precisely, if paradoxically, a strategy of representation—even a strategy of visualization—lesbian visibility cannot be imagined as its redress."[35] In a related essay Celia R. Daileader speaks of the relationships among epistemology, darkness, and desire: "The point . . . is, of course, that in the dark, you cannot tell. And it may well be that the problem of anal sex is related to the figurative (or literal) darkness which accompanies it—that is, the darkness of/in the anus itself; the darkness of the matter it emits; the darkness in which it should remain shrouded; the darkness which enables its (mis)use; the darkness (moral and physical) of those who [misuse it]."[36]

"Darkness" is more than a literal absence of light, a nonspace whose coordinates are unpredictable, dangerous, erotic, and messy; it is also that which continues, like the Baudrillardian obscene—the seamy underbelly of the seen—to mold the limits of visibility.[37] It is the visible sign of invisibility; it is the lack of light that, to use John Milton's famous phrase, makes "darkness visible."[38] If one "cannot tell" in the dark, then the consequences of a dark encounter are unfathomable. Equally, however, the dark is what posits for us the limits of possibility. It is presumably this twin notion of darkness to which Venus refers in her assurance to Adonis that "in night . . . desire sees best of all." Desire operates in the dark, not because desire does not seek to see its object or to be seen by it but because the condition of desire is itself dark: it is something both obscene and, to use a term coined by Linda Williams, "on/scene." Explaining the etymology of this scenic turn, Williams states:

> In Latin, the accepted meaning of the term *obscene* is quite literally "offstage," or that which should be kept "out of public view" (*OED* [*Oxford English Dictionary*]). On/scene is one way of signaling not just that pornographies are proliferating but that once off (*ob*) scene sexual scenarios have been brought onto the public sphere. . . .
>
> If *obscenity* is the term given to those sexually explicit acts that once seemed unspeakable, and were thus permanently kept off-scene, *on/scenity* is the more conflicted term with which we can mark the tension between the speakable and the unspeakable.[39]

In her insistence on seeing desire in the dark, Venus too points to the relationship between obscenity and on/scenity, between what is not seen and what is visible, between Adonis's desire and his resistance to Venus. The desire that swells in the darkness of this poem is not Venus's desire for Adonis, which is entirely in the open, but Adonis's desire for the shadowy world of the hunt. Although—indeed, because—we do not see them, Adonis's friends, along with the boar, form an alternative focus of desire, illuminating the limits of the vis-

ible in the poem. Interestingly, Shakespeare's rhyme suggests that Adonis's "friends" contain his "ends." Since the pursuit of ends is also the essence of teleology, what would a teleological study make of rhymes in which "he" and "she" both "fall" and the "ends" are found with "friends" who are never seen at "all"? If Adonis's dark end lies with his friends, then their nonpresence—and therefore their inability to provide a visible locus of desire—registers a failure of teleology. It also registers the failure of desire to either see or be seen. Sexuality in this poem fails not only to perform but also to register; it operates stubbornly in the dark. This darkness is, of course, the very space of sexual success, not in the sense of consummation—this more common understanding of success is exemplified by the horses that leave the light of the text to fuck at its margins—but in the sense of making desire visible without waiting for teleological light to herald the break of day.

Thus even as the poem gives us a narrative climax—after spurning Venus, Adonis hunts and is killed by the boar—it fails to give us a sexual climax. This is not to suggest that desire is invisible in the poem, or even that it is ineffable; it is to assert that desire in *Venus and Adonis* lacks an object by which either its presence or its success can be measured—desire exists offstage even as it is itself insistently theatrical. The poem suggests that desire dwells in the dark and that the teleological clarity of daylight quells the erotic aspects of not seeing and being unseen. In Shakespeare's narrative, then, sexuality occupies a register where its manifestations cannot be enumerated or tabulated but from where it nonetheless dictates how its province of darkness is to be read. Fulfilled desire—desire that can be seen as progress either to or from a goal, as either act or identity—is outside the realm of poetic speculation, and this is the poem's contribution to what we might call a theory—with its never-presupposed object—as opposed to a history of sexuality.[40] Such a theory of sexuality divests itself from a study of ends that Morrison terms "at once heterosexual and heterosexualizing."[41] *Venus and Adonis* theorizes sexuality inasmuch as it refuses to bend to the ends of teleological pressure.

In Blackwell's *Companion to Shakespeare's Works*, Richard Rambuss suggests that we read the burying of the boar's tusk in Adonis's groin as the sexual climax in the poem, a climax that allows us to articulate a nonheteronormative paradigm in which to approach the text.[42] Although I agree with this expansion of sexual possibility—indeed, Adonis's investment in his unseen friends bolsters a nonheteronormative interpretation—I would caution against a conflation of sexual success and narrative success. Instead, I would suggest that the gaping wound in Adonis's groin—the only sign of bodily penetration in the poem—resists our desire for a narrative account of sexuality. Since we never see the boar charge Adonis, the wound furnishes no act from which to formulate sexual identity; like Adonis himself, it stubbornly refuses to reveal a primary and identifiable thing on which to base a definition of sexuality. Instead, both Adonis and *Venus and Adonis* give us a text in which sexuality resists consequence even as this resistance is termed by some critics, without irony, the poem's most abiding failure.

However, this resistance is also punishable by death, and Adonis is killed at the end of Shakespeare's poem, just as he is in Ovid's. This death has been interpreted as retribution for Adonis's denial of the heterosexuality proffered by Venus; such an assertion has been made by critics like Coppélia Kahn, whose reading of the poem receives sustained comment in Rambuss's essay:

> Why does Shakespeare's Adonis die? Or, "since all Adonises must die," as Don Cameron Allen reminds us . . . , what does his death here mean? Surely there is more to his death on the point of the boar's tusk than simply a scoring of the familiar Renaissance pun on dying as climax, as orgasm. Indeed, the meaning of Adonis's death has puzzled many of *Venus and Adonis*'s readers, especially the poem's most moralizing allegorists. We expect Adonis to die in Ovid (so the moralist accounts go) because there we find that beauty has succumbed to lust. There, Adonis's death is a form of punishment for the youth and the goddess both. But here, in Shakespeare's poem, Adonis does no more than sample Venus's lips, that kiss ultimately serving only to confirm his decided indifference. So why should Shakespeare's Adonis, who ultimately spurns Venus, and with her what he censures as "sweating lust" (794), have to die? According to Coppélia Kahn, this is precisely the reason that he does, and deservedly so. . . . she argues that Adonis meets his death because he refuses Venus, precisely because he "scornfully rejects the easier, more overtly pleasurable and normal course for the fatal one." . . . Kahn sees Adonis as caught between the poles of adulthood and youth, between "intimacy with Venus, which constitutes entry into manhood, and the emotional isolation of narcissism, which constitutes a denial of growth."[43]

While Rambuss is right to point to the pathologization of nonheterosexuality in readings of the poem, the root of the problem, I suggest, lies not only in the cultural equation of homosexuality, narcissism, and death but also, and perhaps more insidiously, in the cultural imperative to read teleologically—an imperative repeatedly questioned in the poem. While the plot allows us to read Adonis's death homophobically as punishment for his rejection of Venus, the poem's rhetorical thrust suggests another interpretation. Neither Venus nor Adonis nor the horses nor the friends have sex in the poem, but everyone desires something. The thing that is desired, however, can never be reached, and that is the condition of desire in the poem. Paradoxical though it may seem, to read Adonis's death in the poem as homophobic, or indeed, to read the poem as either ho-

mophobic or not, is to read heteronormatively. The question we avoid asking the text is the one that Ellis Hanson warns against in relation to Hollywood cinema—"[Is it] good for the gays or bad for the gays[?]"—because it presumes in advance to limit the possibilities of the text to a heteronormative either-or schema.[44] Rather, the poem allows its possible homophobic reading—Adonis dies because he rejects Venus—to exist only by simultaneously calling it into question: Adonis forever escapes Venus; desire forever evades capture. The gaze we train on the poem is sustained by a strategy of desire in which death is not (only) a homophobic punishment for the rejection of teleology but (also) a serious inquiry into nonteleological desire. Adonis's death is almost beside the point, because the point is what the poem can never reach. His death marks the only alternative locus of desire in the text: a desire without end. Adonis's death in Shakespeare does not renew his life, as it does in Ovid, but heralds an end to desired endings. This is the poem's final word on the need to decouple desire from telos and the necessity to read failure successfully.

THEORETICAL ENDS

The resistance to such failure, however, is itself unfailing. Studies of Renaissance sexuality continue to operate within a teleological paradigm in which homosexuality not only is knowable and different from heterosexuality but is antecedent to it. This model assumes the fixity of the two ends of a continuum and provides variations only in the middle; thus it tends to focus on identifiable ends that relate to each other in the mode of familiar difference. Rarely, if ever, does it suggest that the idea of a consequential continuum might be problematic, that in fact it might be the biggest roadblock to thinking about sexuality as a disruptive figure, as a challenger of hierarchy. Studying Renaissance sexuality within the current historicist orthodoxy perpetuates the safe containment encouraged by such a paradigm. Teleology can be a useful tool for studying various cultural, social, historical, and literary phenomena, but if we understand sexuality to be unsafe, uncontained, and unfinished, then teleology is not conducive to a study of its effects.

The temptation to dress desire in teleological garb, despite its resistance to being fixed, fixing, and fixable, is often overpowering. In an incisive essay on *Venus and Adonis,* Catherine Belsey notes that

> nothing very much happens in this narrative of desire. Tantal-ized as she is, Venus cajoles and entreats, Adonis resists, rejects, and finally escapes her; he is killed by the boar, and Venus laments. The poem, exceptionally popular in its own period, prompts in the reader a desire for action that it fails to gratify. Meanwhile, the critical tradition in its turn, tantalized by the poem's lack of closure, has sought to make something happen, at least

at the thematic level, by locating a moral center that would furnish the work with a final meaning, a conclusion, a definitive statement. . . . I propose that it is precisely in its lack of closure that Shakespeare's poem may be read as marking a specific moment in the cultural history of love. A literary trompe-l'oeil, a text of and about desire, *Venus and Adonis* promises a definitive account of love but at the same time withholds the finality that such a promise might lead us to expect. Instead, it tantalizes and, in so doing, throws into relief the difference between its historical moment and our own.[45]

This passage provides a perceptive analysis of the poem's many tantalizing moments that fail to materialize in any one concrete thing. But the passage is astonishing for its simultaneous unsettling and recuperation of an investment in teleology. Belsey describes the poem's lack of closure as its most tantalizing feature, yet *Venus and Adonis* remains a text that "throws into relief the difference between its historical moment and our own." She recuperates the poem's lack of "action" as having a historical function; elsewhere in the essay she suggests that Adonis is an early spokesman for the value of love, as opposed to the villainy of lust, and this valorization of love is precedent to the sentimental tendencies we currently inhabit. Even though Belsey rightly notes that readers rush to fill the text with meaning when faced with its lack of closure, she is guilty of the same crime. She fills the vacuity of the poem with the teleological development of an identifiable, fixed set of family values; *Venus and Adonis* may tantalize without ever delivering the goods, but that very tantalization can be made teleologically productive. While the interrogation of "love" is a worthwhile end in itself, its commitment to providing a historical narrative also ensures its reliance on teleology; this reliance must in turn cause us to forget the poem's lack of closure so *Venus and Adonis* can mark a specific point in a historical continuum.

Belsey's essay seemingly gives up on the project of stable signification, only to return to it on the coattails of teleology. For every assertion she makes about voided desire in the poem, there are several others that endow desire with a historical role in the development of "love" as the basis and framework of romantic relationships. For every statement like "At the moment when the desiring subject takes possession of the object, something slips away, eludes the lover's grasp, and is lost," another adds that "true love is identifiable in terms of a set of norms produced in the early modern period, norms now so familiar that they pass for nature."[46] To list these statements is not in any way to diminish the brilliance of Belsey's essay, but it is to point out that until their methodology is beyond question, inquiries into Renaissance sexuality will only repeat the problems they set out to repudiate. Even as Belsey recognizes the inability of *Venus and Adonis* to provide consequential

certainty in its own narrative, the lure of that certainty in the narration of history is too great for her to resist. Teleology strikes through the critic even as it is spurned by the poem; thus it is that through its lack of closure the text is able to throw "into relief the difference between its historical moment and our own."

The difference between the moment of *Venus and Adonis* and our moment of writing about *Venus and Adonis,* however, lies entirely in our need for "a definitive account of love," an account that the poem can never provide definitively. Belsey's project lies in unearthing the production of the "family values" that people take for granted in current political discourse. As an attempt to show how naturalness is never itself, Belsey's essay would remove our stigmas against, say, homosexuality by suggesting that heterosexuality has not always been the norm. What is gained by such a denaturalization of the norm, however, is immediately lost in the methodology by which one undertakes it: to say that history is always meaningful and consequential is to participate implicitly in the heterosexualizing of history. So instead of scrutinizing the framework in which nonheteronormative sexuality seeks to assert itself, Belsey's project provides yet another indicator of the worth of teleological success. By investing in what Morrison, quoting Freud, terms "end pleasure," Belsey merely reproduces the mechanism by which heteronormativity reproduces itself. Despite her insistence on the failure of all attempts to provide a successful sexual sequence for the poem, she fits *Venus and Adonis* into a teleological frame in which the specter of such failure is kept at bay and even recuperated for a teleological study nominally grounded in the text's lack of signification. Belsey's essay does not consider—and thus it is symptomatic of the field—that a definitive account of desire fails precisely because it demands finitude. Instead, the poem's rejection of teleological closure is itself subsumed by a discourse on Renaissance sexuality that takes as axiomatic "the difference between its historical moment and our own." This difference sustains the teleological thrust of studies of Renaissance sexuality and is predicated on our discomfort with the idea of nonteleological desire.

For *Venus and Adonis,* however, sex is both less than it is made out to be and more than we make it out to be. By uncoupling itself from a system of teleological difference that valorizes early and late, "pre" and "post," the poem suggests that in writing the history of sexuality we might dispense with defining distinctions between acts and identities, subjects and their issue. Such a process of writing history would be, properly speaking, narcissistic rather than teleological, Adonaic rather than Venereal, and its use value, its productivity, would lie precisely in its inability to reach an end, in its inevitable lack of success. For *Venus and Adonis,* then, an alternative to teleology is not historical if by history we understand what Karl Marx once described as "the activity of man in pursuit of his ends."[47] An alternative to teleology is not methodological, since method constrains what might otherwise be a lively exchange across lines, texts, and centuries. An alternative to teleology, according to this poem, is the study of failure, a study that works archaeologically, to use Foucault's term, rather than progressively, a study that does not take teleology as the basis of history and that is unable to posit a developmental model as the basis of theory. In such a realm, desire does not correspond to an end by whose progress it can be measured. In such a realm, **Venus and Adonis** would be praised for being an *un*successful poem: a poem about sex in which no one has sex, in which sex produces no succession, and in which sexual desire does not succeed either at being identified or at being contained, in people or in categories. In such a realm, we would stop having successful sex. Or perhaps more pleasurably, we would have sex endlessly.

Notes

With thanks to Jonathan Gil Harris, Lee Edelman, and Rick Rambuss.

1. R. D. Heldenfels, "Finally, 'Sex and the City' Beginning Its Final Season," *Beacon Journal,* January 4, 2004, www.ohio.com/mld/ohio/entertainment/7624947.htm; Frazier Moore, "Carrie Ends Up with Big in 'Sex' Finale," *Advocate,* February 23, 2004, www.stamfordadvocate.com/entertainment/tv/sns-ap-tv-sex-and-the-city-finale,0,5039826.story?coll=sns-at-tv-headlines.

2. Moore, "Carrie Ends Up with Big."

3. This developmental curve has persisted despite the early assertion by Eve Kosofsky Sedgwick, in *Epistemology of the Closet* (Berkeley: University of California Press, 1990), about the "overlap" between regimes of sexual desire such that one model cannot "replace" an earlier one without being irretrievably marked by it (44), and the more recent nuancing of the notion of sexual and historical difference by David M. Halperin in his breathtaking book *How to Do the History of Homosexuality* (Chicago: University of Chicago Press, 2002).

4. Lee Edelman posits and argues against the fixity of this definition of sexuality in *Homographesis: Essays in Gay Literary and Cultural Theory* (New York: Routledge, 1994), 8.

5. Michel Foucault, *The History of Sexuality,* trans. Robert Hurley, vol. 1 (Harmondsworth: Penguin, 1981), 43; emphasis mine.

6. David M. Halperin, "Forgetting Foucault," in *How to Do the History of Homosexuality,* 22-23.

7. Inasmuch as it revolves around questions of historical and chronological difference, archaeology always runs the risk of being teleological. In Foucault's case, however, these kinds of difference are never posited as mutually exclusive or definitionally fixed. Foucault would probably not have any difficulty with the coexistence of the sodomite and the homosexual; in any case, for him the latter does not represent the distillation of pervious discourses of desire even as one discourse might, at any given point, overwhelm another. Halperin suggests that Foucault's "approach to the history of the present was also too searching, too experimental, and too open-ended to tolerate converting a heuristic analytic distinction into an ill-founded historical [or teleological] dogma, as his more forgetful epigones have not hesitated to do" ("Forgetting Foucault," 44).

8. Ibid., esp. 27.

9. "As almost always in *The History of Sexuality,*" Halperin asserts, "Foucault is speaking about discursive and institutional practices, not about what people really did in bed or what they thought about it" ("Forgetting Foucault," 29).

10. Paul Morrison returns to this nexus between signification and homosexuality at the end of his essay "End Pleasure," *GLQ* [*Gay and Lesbian Quarterly*] 1 (1993): 53-78. Speaking of the protagonist of Paul Monette's *Halfway Home,* Morrison analyzes the safe ending of that novel in these terms: "Our culture allows Tom and his kind to want only in accordance with a rigid binarism: choose between a sexuality that works toward its own effacement, the erotic pessimism that calls itself love, and a sexuality that issues in death, the erotic excess that is called perversion. Refuse the terms of the opposition and you are committed, willingly or not, to forcing what all the deaths have not yet occasioned: a crisis in signification" (74). The refusal of a historicist teleology in studies of Renaissance sexuality might well occasion just such a crisis where its acceptance currently allows for contained reinscription.

11. Halperin, "Forgetting Foucault," 93-94, 109.

12. Studies of Renaissance sexuality that tend toward the teleological include Mario DiGangi, *The Homoerotics of Early Modern Drama* (Cambridge: Cambridge University Press, 1997); and Harriette Andreadis, *Sappho in Early Modern England* (Chicago: University of Chicago Press, 2001). However, teleology for these studies is not a celebratory formula; the way in which the present has allegedly distilled and fixed the past is a matter of some sadness, and these works thus are

political attempts to change the current status quo. As I argue below in relation to Catherine Belsey's essay "Love as Trompe-l'oeil: Taxonomies of Desire in *Venus and Adonis,*" in *Venus and Adonis: Critical Essays,* ed. Philip C. Kolin (New York: Garland, 1997), 261-85, such attempts at change repeat, ironically, the terms by which the sexual status quo is maintained.

13. Halperin, "Forgetting Foucault," 32, 42.

14. Valerie Traub, *The Renaissance of Lesbianism in Early Modern England* (Cambridge: Cambridge University Press, 2002), 32, 354.

15. Louise Fradenburg and Carla Freccero, eds., *Premodern Sexualities* (New York: Routledge, 1996), viii. In their introduction Fradenburg and Freccero make explicit the difficulties inherent in reading Foucault literally: "Alterity is too often used now to stabilize periods or epistemes. . . . the academic reception of Foucault has tended to emphasize the radical difference of one episteme from another, and to de-emphasize those aspects of Foucauldian thought engaged with multiple timelines" (xx).

16. Annamarie Jagose, *Inconsequence: Lesbian Representation and the Logic of Sexual Sequence* (Ithaca: Cornell University Press, 2002), xii. Valerie Traub reads the Shakespearean sonnet sequence "for what it can tell us about the interarticulation of sequence and sexuality," noting that "the problem of narrative sequence and the problem of 'same-sex love' are often closely related" ("Sequence, Sexuality, and Shakespeare's Two Loves," in *A Companion to Shakespeare's Works,* ed. Richard Dutton and Jean E. Howard, 4 vols. [Oxford: Blackwell, 2003], 4:280, 278). Judith Roof poses "the question of how to break narrative and sexuality apart, entwined as they are (and we with them) like tragically doomed lovers whirling around Dante's third circle" (*Come as You Are: Sexuality and Narrative* [New York: Columbia University Press, 1996], xiv).

17. Jonathan Goldberg, "The History That Will Be," in Fradenburg and Freccero, *Pre-modern Sexualities,* 3-21. The sense of a futurity that is, and should be recognized as, alien to the province of queerness is explored in Lee Edelman, *No Future: Queer Theory and the Death Drive* (Durham: Duke University Press, 2004).

18. Jagose, *Inconsequence,* x.

19. *Oxford English Dictionary,* 2nd ed. (1989), s.v. "teleology."

20. Glenn Burgess, "The 'Historical Turn' and the Political Culture of Early Modern England:

Towards a Postmodern History?" in *Neo-historicism: Studies in Renaissance Literature, History, and Politics,* ed. Robin Headlam Wells, Glenn Burgess, and Rowland Wymer (Woodbridge, UK: Brewer, 2000), 36.

21. See Jonathan Goldberg, ed., *Queering the Renaissance* (Durham: Duke University Press, 1994).

22. Sixteen editions of this poem were printed before 1640, and several of them allegedly found their way into bawdy houses.

23. *The Riverside Shakespeare,* ed. G. Blakemore Evans, 2nd ed. (Boston: Houghton Mifflin, 1997), 1798. All quotations from Shakespeare are taken from this edition.

24. *The Riverside Shakespeare,* 1799 and n.

25. *Oxford English Dictionary,* s.v. "success."

26. In several early sonnets, the young man is urged to reproduce his kind to stave off the end signified by death: "From fairest creatures we desire increase, / That thereby beauty's rose might never die" (1.1-2); "And nothing 'gainst Time's scythe can make defense / Save breed, to brave him when he takes thee hence" (12.13-14); "Who will believe my verse in time to come / If it were fill'd with your most high deserts? / . . . But were some child of yours alive that time, / You should live twice, in it and in my rhyme" (17.1-2, 13-14).

27. Michael Warner, "Homo-narcissism; or, Heterosexuality," in *Engendering Men: The Question of Male Feminist Criticism,* ed. Joseph A. Boone and Michael Cadden (New York: Routledge, 1990), 194.

28. In certain early sonnets, the poet similarly chides the "fair youth" for not reproducing: "No love toward others in that bosom sits / That on himself such murd'rous shame commits" (9.13-14); "of thy beauty do I question make / That thou among the wastes of time must go, / Since sweets and beauties do themselves forsake, / And die as fast as they see others grow, / And nothing 'gainst Time's scythe can make defense / Save breed, to brave him when he takes thee hence" (12.9-14).

29. Lee Edelman, "The Mirror and the Tank," in *Homographesis,* 109. Fradenburg and Freccero make a similar argument in the introduction to *Premodern Sexualities*: "In struggling against cultural demonizations of certain kinds of sameness, queer perspectives can usefully call into question the historiographical status of concepts of alterity and sameness" (xviii).

30. Several critics, regardless of their theoretical inclination, blame Adonis for spurning Venus's

sexual advances. For Coppélia Kahn, this spurning is cause enough for his violent death (*Man's Estate: Masculine Identity in Shakespeare* [Berkeley: University of California Press, 1981], 44). Maurice Evans blames Adonis for choosing "the sterile chase of the boar in preference to the kiss of Venus" (introduction to William Shakespeare, *The Narrative Poems* [London: Penguin, 1989], 14). Heather Dubrow suggests that we see signs of Adonis's immaturity when "we begin to suspect subterranean motives that he cannot or will not face, such as the narcissism of which Venus accuses him" ("'Upon Misprision Growing': *Venus and Adonis*," in Kolin, *Venus and Adonis*, 240). See also Richard Rambuss's magisterial reading of the poem, "What It Feels Like for a Boy: Shakespeare's *Venus and Adonis*," in Dutton and Howard, *A Companion to Shakespeare's Works*, 4:240-58.

31. Not that Adonis is uninvested in teleology. In fact, as Belsey makes clear ("Love as Trompe-l'oeil"), Adonis clearly outlines his belief in teleological growth: "'Fair queen,' quoth he, 'if any love you owe me, / Measure my strangeness with my unripe years; / Before I know myself, seek not to know me, / No fisher but the ungrown fry forbears; / The mellow plum doth fall, the green sticks fast, / Or being early pluck'd, is sour to taste'" (523-28). Even as he becomes a vehicle for teleology, however, his teleological yearnings are not articulated in response to Venus's desire; in the lines quoted here, he holds out firmly against the desire for consummation and sketches the poem's resistance to final endings in relation to desire.

32. Morrison suggests that "where the well-made narrative is, the pervert is not" ("End Pleasure," 63). *Venus and Adonis* complicates this assertion, since it is a complete and polished narrative *about* incompletion; its perversion lies equally in the narrative and sexual realms.

33. Ovid, *Metamorphoses,* trans. A. D. Melville (Oxford: Oxford University Press, 1986), 10.697-98. All quotations from Ovid are taken from this edition.

34. In *Love's Labor's Lost,* for instance, Berowne states: "The King he is hunting the deer: I am coursing myself. They have pitch'd a toil: I am toiling in a pitch—pitch that defiles—defile! a foul word" (4.3.1-3). In *1 Henry IV* Falstaff, playing the king, rebukes Hal by saying, "There is a thing, Harry, which thou hast often heard of, and it is known to many in our land by the name of pitch. This pitch (as ancient writers do report) doth defile, so doth the company thou keepest" (2.4.410-14).

35. Jagose, *Inconsequence,* 2.

36. Celia R. Daileader, "Renaissance Gynosodomy, Aretino, and the Erotic," *ELH* 69 (2002): 323.

37. "Many things are obscene," Jean Baudrillard postulates, "because they have too much meaning, because they occupy too much space. They thus attain an exorbitant representation of the truth, that is to say the apogee of simulation" (*Revenge of the Crystal: Selected Writings on the Modern Object and Its Destiny, 1968-1983* [London: Pluto, 1999], 187). Baudrillard's notion of obscenity, then, provides the very framework within which a scene can be made sense of. The obscene contains the excess that threatens to overwhelm the scene's ability to produce meaning but that simultaneously provides the conditions in which the scene can mean.

38. John Milton, *Paradise Lost,* ed. Christopher Ricks (New York: Signet, 1968), 1.63.

39. Linda Williams, introduction to *Porn Studies,* ed. Linda Williams (Durham: Duke University Press, 2004), 3-4.

40. While I see a fixing of ideas as the defining attribute of "history," Halperin considers it the basis of "theory." Thus he suggests that Foucault in fact does not offer a theory of sexuality: "*The History of Sexuality,* volume I, . . . does not contain an original theory of sexuality. If anything, its theoretical originality lies in its refusal of existing theory and its consistent elaboration of a critical anti-theory. It offers a model demonstration of how to dismantle theories of sexuality, how to deprive them of their claims to legitimate authority. . . . As a theory of sexuality, however, *The History of Sexuality,* volume I, is unreadable. That may in fact be its greatest virtue" ("Forgetting Foucault," 45).

41. Morrison, "End Pleasure," 68.

42. After quoting Venus's acknowledgment of the sexual nature of Adonis's encounter with the boar—"And, nousling in his flank, the loving swine / Sheath'd unaware the tusk in his soft groin" (1115-16)—Rambuss suggests in "What It Feels Like for a Boy" that, "as rendered by Venus in such palpable, voluptuous detail, the coupling of the boar and the boy stands as one of the most graphically sexual figurations in Renaissance poetry of male/male penetration, of tusk in groin, of male body 'rooting' male body" (249). However, Rambuss never suggests that *Venus and Adonis* is a homoerotic poem in any easy sense. Rather, he argues that "Adonis's eschewal of

Venus—the pivotal feature of Shakespeare's rendering of the story—points in the direction of another kind of love. . . . Adonis's desire—to the extent that it finds expression in the poem . . .—flows in only one direction: towards the boar" (251-52). The essay ends, then, not with an embrace of teleology but with an understanding of the rhetorical complications of desire: "What a boy like Adonis wants remains gestural, allegorical in Shakespeare's poem" (255). While making a compelling case for a nonheterosexual reading of the poem, Rambuss manages not to cast it in a teleological light, despite his hope of evoking a sexual climax for Adonis.

43. Ibid., 249-50. Rambuss quotes Kahn, *Man's Estate,* 44, 21; and Don Cameron Allen, "On *Venus and Adonis,*" in *Elizabethan and Jacobean Studies: Presented to Frank Percy Wilson in Honour of His Seventieth Birthday* (Oxford: Clarendon, 1959), 111.

44. Ellis Hanson, introduction to *Out Takes: Essays on Queer Theory and Film,* ed. Ellis Hanson (Durham: Duke University Press, 1999), 5.

45. Belsey, "Love as Trompe-l'oeil," 262-63.

46. Ibid., 265, 280.

47. Karl Marx and Friedrich Engels, *The Holy Family; or, Critique of Critical Criticism: Against Bruno Bauer and Company* (Moscow: Progress, 1956), 110.

FURTHER READING

Criticism

Burrow, Colin. Introduction to *The Complete Sonnets and Poems,* by William Shakespeare, edited by Colin Burrow, pp. 1-158. Oxford: Oxford University Press, 2002.

Presents a detailed account of several aspects of *Venus and Adonis,* including its printing history, its critical reception among Renaissance readers and imitators, its source in Ovid, and its use of rhetoric.

Cousins, A. D. "Towards a Reconsideration of Shakespeare's Adonis: Rhetoric, Narcissus, and the Male Gaze." *Studia Neophilologica* 68, no. 2 (1996): 195-204.

Character analysis that focuses on Adonis's rhetorical counter-arguments to Venus, his dissimilarity to Narcissus, and his role as the poem's beautiful and youthful object of sexual longing.

Dubrow, Heather. "'Upon misprision growing': *Venus and Adonis.*" In *Captive Victors: Shakespeare's Narrative Poems and Sonnets,* pp. 21-79. Ithaca, N.Y.: Cornell University Press, 1987.

Detailed examination of Shakespeare's use of the epyllion structure, focusing on the poet's emphasis on characterization and how the poem influenced later writers of Ovidian narratives.

Enterline, Lynn. "Psychoanalytic Criticisms." In *Shakespeare: An Oxford Guide,* edited by Stanley Wells and Lena Cowen Orlin, pp. 451-71. Oxford: Oxford University Press, 2003.

Takes a psychoanalytical approach to discussing the use of rhetoric in the poem, focusing on the revisions Shakespeare made to his source document, his indebtedness to Petrarchan love poetry, and the poem's ambiguous representations of gender, desire, and sexuality.

Fletcher, Loraine. "Animal Rites: A Reading of *Venus and Adonis.*" *Critical Survey* 17, no. 3 (2005): 1-14.

Concentrates on the depiction of the animal world in the poem, demonstrating how Shakespeare contrasted the animals—who are able to communicate even without the gift of words—with the "human" Venus and Adonis, who fail in their repeated and powerful attempts to persuade one another through the use of language.

Kiernan, Pauline. "*Venus and Adonis* and Ovidian Indecorous Wit." In *Shakespeare's Ovid: The* Metamorphoses *in the Plays and Poems,* edited by A. B. Taylor, pp. 81-95. Cambridge: Cambridge University Press, 2000.

Demonstrates the influence of Ovid on the poem, specifically how Shakespeare subverted and mocked Venus's divine status with his depiction of her as sexually insatiable, aggressive, and prone to rhetorical excess.

Roberts, Sasha. "Ladies Reading 'bawdy geare': Shakespeare, *Venus and Adonis* and the Early Modern Woman Reader." In *Reading Shakespeare's Poems in Early Modern England,* pp. 20-61. Houndmills, England: Palgrave Macmillan, 2003.

Outlines the discrepancies between common seventeenth-century perceptions of the "dangers" associated with women reading the sexually explicit poem and actual reactions to the work from seventeenth-century English women readers.

Stanivukovic, Goran V. "'Kissing the Boar': Queer Adonis and Critical Practice." In *Straight with a Twist: Queer Theory and the Subject of Heterosexuality,* edited by Calvin Thomas, pp. 87-108. Urbana, Ill.: University of Illinois Press, 2000.

> Focuses on Adonis's death, exploring the issue of homoerotic desire in relation both to twentieth-century critical views on the poem's emphasis on sexuality and to commonly held ideologies and social beliefs of the Renaissance.

Additional coverage of *Venus and Adonis* is contained in the following sources published by Gale: *Literature Resource Center*; *Reference Guide to English Literature*, Ed. 2; *Shakespearean Criticism*, Vols. 10, 33, 51, 67, 79; and *Shakespeare for Students*, Vol. 2

How to Use This Index

The main references

Calvino, Italo
1923-1985 .... CLC 5, 8, 11, 22, 33, 39,
73; SSC 3, 48

list all author entries in the following Gale Literary Criticism series:

AAL = *Asian American Literature*
BG = *The Beat Generation: A Gale Critical Companion*
BLC = *Black Literature Criticism*
BLCS = *Black Literature Criticism Supplement*
CLC = *Contemporary Literary Criticism*
CLR = *Children's Literature Review*
CMLC = *Classical and Medieval Literature Criticism*
DC = *Drama Criticism*
FL = *Feminism in Literature: A Gale Critical Companion*
GL = *Gothic Literature: A Gale Critical Companion*
HLC = *Hispanic Literature Criticism*
HLCS = *Hispanic Literature Criticism Supplement*
HR = *Harlem Renaissance: A Gale Critical Companion*
LC = *Literature Criticism from 1400 to 1800*
NCLC = *Nineteenth-Century Literature Criticism*
NNAL = *Native North American Literature*
PC = *Poetry Criticism*
SSC = *Short Story Criticism*
TCLC = *Twentieth-Century Literary Criticism*
WLC = *World Literature Criticism, 1500 to the Present*
WLCS = *World Literature Criticism Supplement*

The cross-references

See also CA 85-88, 116; CANR 23, 61;
DAM NOV; DLB 196; EW 13; MTCW 1, 2;
RGSF 2; RGWL 2; SFW 4; SSFS 12

list all author entries in the following Gale biographical and literary sources:

AAYA = *Authors & Artists for Young Adults*
AFAW = *African American Writers*
AFW = *African Writers*
AITN = *Authors in the News*
AMW = *American Writers*
AMWR = *American Writers Retrospective Supplement*
AMWS = *American Writers Supplement*
ANW = *American Nature Writers*
AW = *Ancient Writers*
BEST = *Bestsellers*
BPFB = *Beacham's Encyclopedia of Popular Fiction: Biography and Resources*
BRW = *British Writers*
BRWS = *British Writers Supplement*
BW = *Black Writers*
BYA = *Beacham's Guide to Literature for Young Adults*
CA = *Contemporary Authors*
CAAS = *Contemporary Authors Autobiography Series*
CABS = *Contemporary Authors Bibliographical Series*
CAD = *Contemporary American Dramatists*
CANR = *Contemporary Authors New Revision Series*
CAP = *Contemporary Authors Permanent Series*
CBD = *Contemporary British Dramatists*
CCA = *Contemporary Canadian Authors*
CD = *Contemporary Dramatists*
CDALB = *Concise Dictionary of American Literary Biography*

CDALBS = *Concise Dictionary of American Literary Biography Supplement*
CDBLB = *Concise Dictionary of British Literary Biography*
CMW = *St. James Guide to Crime & Mystery Writers*
CN = *Contemporary Novelists*
CP = *Contemporary Poets*
CPW = *Contemporary Popular Writers*
CSW = *Contemporary Southern Writers*
CWD = *Contemporary Women Dramatists*
CWP = *Contemporary Women Poets*
CWRI = *St. James Guide to Children's Writers*
CWW = *Contemporary World Writers*
DA = *DISCovering Authors*
DA3 = *DISCovering Authors 3.0*
DAB = *DISCovering Authors: British Edition*
DAC = *DISCovering Authors: Canadian Edition*
DAM = *DISCovering Authors: Modules*
  DRAM: *Dramatists Module;* **MST:** *Most-studied Authors Module;*
  MULT: *Multicultural Authors Module;* **NOV:** *Novelists Module;*
  POET: *Poets Module;* **POP:** *Popular Fiction and Genre Authors Module*
DFS = *Drama for Students*
DLB = *Dictionary of Literary Biography*
DLBD = *Dictionary of Literary Biography Documentary Series*
DLBY = *Dictionary of Literary Biography Yearbook*
DNFS = *Literature of Developing Nations for Students*
EFS = *Epics for Students*
EXPN = *Exploring Novels*
EXPP = *Exploring Poetry*
EXPS = *Exploring Short Stories*
EW = *European Writers*
FANT = *St. James Guide to Fantasy Writers*
FW = *Feminist Writers*
GFL = *Guide to French Literature,* Beginnings to 1789, 1798 to the Present
GLL = *Gay and Lesbian Literature*
HGG = *St. James Guide to Horror, Ghost & Gothic Writers*
HW = *Hispanic Writers*
IDFW = *International Dictionary of Films and Filmmakers: Writers and Production Artists*
IDTP = *International Dictionary of Theatre: Playwrights*
LAIT = *Literature and Its Times*
LAW = *Latin American Writers*
JRDA = *Junior DISCovering Authors*
MAICYA = *Major Authors and Illustrators for Children and Young Adults*
MAICYAS = *Major Authors and Illustrators for Children and Young Adults Supplement*
MAWW = *Modern American Women Writers*
MJW = *Modern Japanese Writers*
MTCW = *Major 20th-Century Writers*
NCFS = *Nonfiction Classics for Students*
NFS = *Novels for Students*
PAB = *Poets: American and British*
PFS = *Poetry for Students*
RGAL = *Reference Guide to American Literature*
RGEL = *Reference Guide to English Literature*
RGSF = *Reference Guide to Short Fiction*
RGWL = *Reference Guide to World Literature*
RHW = *Twentieth-Century Romance and Historical Writers*
SAAS = *Something about the Author Autobiography Series*
SATA = *Something about the Author*
SFW = *St. James Guide to Science Fiction Writers*
SSFS = *Short Stories for Students*
TCWW = *Twentieth-Century Western Writers*
WLIT = *World Literature and Its Times*
WP = *World Poets*
YABC = *Yesterday's Authors of Books for Children*
YAW = *St. James Guide to Young Adult Writers*

Literary Criticism Series
Cumulative Author Index

Author Index

Alexander, Lloyd 1924-2007 .... **CLC 35**
See also AAYA 1, 27; BPFB 1; BYA 5, 6, 7, 9, 10, 11; CA 1-4R; 260; CANR 1, 24, 38, 55, 113; CLR 1, 5, 48; CWRI 5; DLB 52; FANT; JRDA; MAICYA 1, 2; MAIC-YAS 1; MTCW 1; SAAS 19; SATA 3, 49, 81, 129, 135; SATA-Obit 182; SUFW; TUS; WYA; YAW

Alexander, Lloyd Chudley
See Alexander, Lloyd

Alexander, Meena 1951- .... **CLC 121**
See also CA 115; CANR 38, 70, 146; CP 5, 6, 7; CWP; DLB 323; FW

Alexander, Samuel 1859-1938 .... **TCLC 77**

Alexeiev, Konstantin
See Stanislavsky, Constantin

Alexeyev, Constantin Sergeivich
See Stanislavsky, Constantin

Alexeyev, Konstantin Sergeyevich
See Stanislavsky, Constantin

Alexie, Sherman 1966- .... **CLC 96, 154; NNAL; PC 53; SSC 107**
See also AAYA 28; BYA 15; CA 138; CANR 65, 95, 133, 174; CN 7; DA3; DAM MULT; DLB 175, 206, 278; LATS 1:2; MTCW 2; MTFW 2005; NFS 17; SSFS 18

Alexie, Sherman Joseph, Jr.
See Alexie, Sherman

al-Farabi 870(?)-950 .... **CMLC 58**
See also DLB 115

Alfau, Felipe 1902-1999 .... **CLC 66**
See also CA 137

Alfieri, Vittorio 1749-1803 .... **NCLC 101**
See also EW 4; RGWL 2, 3; WLIT 7

Alfonso X 1221-1284 .... **CMLC 78**

Alfred, Jean Gaston
See Ponge, Francis

Alger, Horatio, Jr. 1832-1899 .... **NCLC 8, 83**
See also CLR 87; DLB 42; LAIT 2; RGAL 4; SATA 16; TUS

Al-Ghazali, Muhammad ibn Muhammad 1058-1111 .... **CMLC 50**
See also DLB 115

Algren, Nelson 1909-1981 ..... **CLC 4, 10, 33; SSC 33**
See also AMWS 9; BPFB 1; CA 13-16R; 103; CANR 20, 61; CDALB 1941-1968; CN 1, 2; DLB 9; DLBY 1981, 1982, 2000; EWL 3; MAL 5; MTCW 1, 2; MTFW 2005; RGAL 4; RGSF 2

al-Hamadhani 967-1007 .... **CMLC 93**
See also WLIT 6

al-Hariri, al-Qasim ibn 'Ali Abu Muhammad al-Basri 1054-1122 .... **CMLC 63**
See also RGWL 3

Ali, Ahmed 1908-1998 .... **CLC 69**
See also CA 25-28R; CANR 15, 34; CN 1, 2, 3, 4, 5; DLB 323; EWL 3

Ali, Tariq 1943- .... **CLC 173**
See also CA 25-28R; CANR 10, 99, 161

Alighieri, Dante
See Dante
See also WLIT 7

al-Kindi, Abu Yusuf Ya'qub ibn Ishaq c. 801-c. 873 .... **CMLC 80**

Allan, John B.
See Westlake, Donald E.

Allan, Sidney
See Hartmann, Sadakichi

Allan, Sydney
See Hartmann, Sadakichi

Allard, Janet CLC 59

Allen, Edward 1948- .... **CLC 59**

Allen, Fred 1894-1956 .... **TCLC 87**

Allen, Paula Gunn 1939- .... **CLC 84, 202; NNAL**
See also AMWS 4; CA 112; 143; CANR 63, 130; CWP; DA3; DAM MULT; DLB 175; FW; MTCW 2; MTFW 2005; RGAL 4; TCWW 2

Allen, Roland
See Ayckbourn, Alan

Allen, Sarah A.
See Hopkins, Pauline Elizabeth

Allen, Sidney H.
See Hartmann, Sadakichi

Allen, Woody 1935- .... **CLC 16, 52, 195**
See also AAYA 10, 51; AMWS 15; CA 33-36R; CANR 27, 38, 63, 128, 172; DAM POP; DLB 44; MTCW 1; SSFS 21

Allende, Isabel 1942- ... **CLC 39, 57, 97, 170; HLC 3; SSC 65; WLCS**
See also AAYA 18, 70; CA 125; 130; CANR 51, 74, 129, 165; CDWLB 3; CLR 99; CWW 2; DA3; DAM MULT, NOV; DLB 145; DNFS 1; EWL 3; FL 1:5; FW; HW 1, 2; INT CA-130; LAIT 5; LAWS 1; LMFS 2; MTCW 1, 2; MTFW 2005; NCFS 1; NFS 6, 18; RGSF 2; RGWL 3; SATA 163; SSFS 11, 16; WLIT 1

Alleyn, Ellen
See Rossetti, Christina

Alleyne, Carla D. CLC 65

Allingham, Margery (Louise) 1904-1966 .... **CLC 19**
See also CA 5-8R; 25-28R; CANR 4, 58; CMW 4; DLB 77; MSW; MTCW 1, 2

Allingham, William 1824-1889 ...... **NCLC 25**
See also DLB 35; RGEL 2

Allison, Dorothy E. 1949- .... **CLC 78, 153**
See also AAYA 53; CA 140; CANR 66, 107; CN 7; CSW; DA3; FW; MTCW 2; MTFW 2005; NFS 11; RGAL 4

Alloula, Malek CLC 65

Allston, Washington 1779-1843 .... **NCLC 2**
See also DLB 1, 235

Almedingen, E. M. CLC 12
See Almedingen, Martha Edith von
See also SATA 3

Almedingen, Martha Edith von 1898-1971
See Almedingen, E. M.
See also CA 1-4R; CANR 1

Almodovar, Pedro 1949(?)- .... **CLC 114, 229; HLCS 1**
See also CA 133; CANR 72, 151; HW 2

Almqvist, Carl Jonas Love 1793-1866 .... **NCLC 42**

al-Mutanabbi, Ahmad ibn al-Husayn Abu al-Tayyib al-Jufi al-Kindi 915-965 .... **CMLC 66**
See Mutanabbi, Al-
See also RGWL 3

Alonso, Damaso 1898-1990 .... **CLC 14**
See also CA 110; 131; 130; CANR 72; DLB 108; EWL 3; HW 1, 2

Alov
See Gogol, Nikolai (Vasilyevich)

al'Sadaawi, Nawal
See El Saadawi, Nawal
See also FW

al-Shaykh, Hanan 1945- .... **CLC 218**
See Shaykh, al- Hanan
See also CA 135; CANR 111; WLIT 6

Al Siddik
See Rolfe, Frederick (William Serafino Austin Lewis Mary)
See also GLL 1; RGEL 2

Alta 1942- .... **CLC 19**
See also CA 57-60

Alter, Robert B. 1935- .... **CLC 34**
See also CA 49-52; CANR 1, 47, 100, 160

Alter, Robert Bernard
See Alter, Robert B.

Alther, Lisa 1944- .... **CLC 7, 41**
See also BPFB 1; CA 65-68; CAAS 30; CANR 12, 30, 51; CN 4, 5, 6, 7; CSW; GLL 2; MTCW 1

Althusser, L.
See Althusser, Louis

Althusser, Louis 1918-1990 .... **CLC 106**
See also CA 131; 132; CANR 102; DLB 242

Altman, Robert 1925-2006 .... **CLC 16, 116, 242**
See also CA 73-76; 254; CANR 43

Alurista HLCS 1; PC 34
See Urista (Heredia), Alberto (Baltazar)
See also CA 45-48R; DLB 82; LLW

Alvarez, A. 1929- .... **CLC 5, 13**
See also CA 1-4R; CANR 3, 33, 63, 101, 134; CN 3, 4, 5, 6; CP 1, 2, 3, 4, 5, 6, 7; DLB 14, 40; MTFW 2005

Alvarez, Alejandro Rodriguez 1903-1965
See Casona, Alejandro
See also CA 131; 93-96; HW 1

Alvarez, Julia 1950- .... **CLC 93; HLCS 1**
See also AAYA 25; AMWS 7; CA 147; CANR 69, 101, 133, 166; DA3; DLB 282; LATS 1:2; LLW; MTCW 2; MTFW 2005; NFS 5, 9; SATA 129; WLIT 1

Alvaro, Corrado 1896-1956 .... **TCLC 60**
See also CA 163; DLB 264; EWL 3

Amado, Jorge 1912-2001 ... **CLC 13, 40, 106, 232; HLC 1**
See also CA 77-80; 201; CANR 35, 74, 135; CWW 2; DAM MULT, NOV; DLB 113, 307; EWL 3; HW 2; LAW; LAWS 1; MTCW 1, 2; MTFW 2005; RGWL 2, 3; TWA; WLIT 1

Ambler, Eric 1909-1998 .... **CLC 4, 6, 9**
See also BRWS 4; CA 9-12R; 171; CANR 7, 38, 74; CMW 4; CN 1, 2, 3, 4, 5, 6; DLB 77; MSW; MTCW 1, 2; TEA

Ambrose, Stephen E. 1936-2002 .... **CLC 145**
See also AAYA 44; CA 1-4R; 209; CANR 3, 43, 57, 83, 105; MTFW 2005; NCFS 2; SATA 40, 138

Amichai, Yehuda 1924-2000 .. **CLC 9, 22, 57, 116; PC 38**
See also CA 85-88; 189; CANR 46, 60, 99, 132; CWW 2; EWL 3; MTCW 1, 2; MTFW 2005; PFS 24; RGHL; WLIT 6

Amichai, Yehudah
See Amichai, Yehuda

Amiel, Henri Frederic 1821-1881 .... **NCLC 4**
See also DLB 217

Amis, Kingsley 1922-1995 . **CLC 1, 2, 3, 5, 8, 13, 40, 44, 129**
See also AAYA 77; AITN 2; BPFB 1; BRWS 2; CA 9-12R; 150; CANR 8, 28, 54; CDBLB 1945-1960; CN 1, 2, 3, 4, 5, 6; CP 1, 2, 3, 4; DA; DA3; DAB; DAC; DAM MST, NOV; DLB 15, 27, 100, 139, 326; DLBY 1996; EWL 3; HGG; INT CANR-8; MTCW 1, 2; MTFW 2005; RGEL 2; RGSF 2; SFW 4

Amis, Martin 1949- ... **CLC 4, 9, 38, 62, 101, 213; SSC 112**
See also BEST 90:3; BRWS 4; CA 65-68; CANR 8, 27, 54, 73, 95, 132, 166; CN 5, 6, 7; DA3; DLB 14, 194; EWL 3; INT CANR-27; MTCW 2; MTFW 2005

Amis, Martin Louis
See Amis, Martin

Ammianus Marcellinus c. 330-c. 395 .... **CMLC 60**
See also AW 2; DLB 211

Appelfeld, Aron
See Appelfeld, Aharon
Apple, Max (Isaac) 1941- .... **CLC 9, 33; SSC 50**
See also AMWS 17; CA 81-84; CANR 19, 54; DLB 130
Appleman, Philip (Dean) 1926- .... **CLC 51**
See also CA 13-16R; CAAS 18; CANR 6, 29, 56
Appleton, Lawrence
See Lovecraft, H. P.
Apteryx
See Eliot, T(homas) S(tearns)
Apuleius, (Lucius Madaurensis) c. 125-c. 164 .... **CMLC 1, 84**
See also AW 2; CDWLB 1; DLB 211; RGWL 2, 3; SUFW; WLIT 8
Aquin, Hubert 1929-1977 .... **CLC 15**
See also CA 105; DLB 53; EWL 3
Aquinas, Thomas 1224(?)-1274 ..... **CMLC 33**
See also DLB 115; EW 1; TWA
Aragon, Louis 1897-1982 .... **CLC 3, 22; TCLC 123**
See also CA 69-72; 108; CANR 28, 71; DAM NOV, POET; DLB 72, 258; EW 11; EWL 3; GFL 1789 to the Present; GLL 2; LMFS 2; MTCW 1, 2; RGWL 2, 3
Arany, Janos 1817-1882 .... **NCLC 34**
Aranyos, Kakay 1847-1910
See Mikszath, Kalman
Aratus of Soli c. 315B.C.-c. 240B.C. .... **CMLC 64**
See also DLB 176
Arbuthnot, John 1667-1735 .... **LC 1**
See also DLB 101
Archer, Herbert Winslow
See Mencken, H(enry) L(ouis)
Archer, Jeffrey 1940- .... **CLC 28**
See also AAYA 16; BEST 89:3; BPFB 1; CA 77-80; CANR 22, 52, 95, 136; CPW; DA3; DAM POP; INT CANR-22; MTFW 2005
Archer, Jeffrey Howard
See Archer, Jeffrey
Archer, Jules 1915- .... **CLC 12**
See also CA 9-12R; CANR 6, 69; SAAS 5; SATA 4, 85
Archer, Lee
See Ellison, Harlan
Archilochus c. 7th cent. B.C.- .... **CMLC 44**
See also DLB 176
Ard, William
See Jakes, John
Arden, John 1930- .... **CLC 6, 13, 15**
See also BRWS 2; CA 13-16R; CAAS 4; CANR 31, 65, 67, 124; CBD; CD 5, 6; DAM DRAM; DFS 9; DLB 13, 245; EWL 3; MTCW 1
Arenas, Reinaldo 1943-1990 .. **CLC 41; HLC 1; TCLC 191**
See also CA 124; 128; 133; CANR 73, 106; DAM MULT; DLB 145; EWL 3; GLL 2; HW 1; LAW; LAWS 1; MTCW 2; MTFW 2005; RGSF 2; RGWL 3; WLIT 1
Arendt, Hannah 1906-1975 .... **CLC 66, 98; TCLC 193**
See also CA 17-20R; 61-64; CANR 26, 60, 172; DLB 242; MTCW 1, 2
Aretino, Pietro 1492-1556 .... **LC 12**
See also RGWL 2, 3
Arghezi, Tudor **CLC 80**
See Theodorescu, Ion N.
See also CA 167; CDWLB 4; DLB 220; EWL 3
Arguedas, Jose Maria 1911-1969 .... **CLC 10, 18; HLCS 1; TCLC 147**
See also CA 89-92; CANR 73; DLB 113; EWL 3; HW 1; LAW; RGWL 2, 3; WLIT 1

Argueta, Manlio 1936- .... **CLC 31**
See also CA 131; CANR 73; CWW 2; DLB 145; EWL 3; HW 1; RGWL 3
Arias, Ron 1941- .... **HLC 1**
See also CA 131; CANR 81, 136; DAM MULT; DLB 82; HW 1, 2; MTCW 2; MTFW 2005
Ariosto, Lodovico
See Ariosto, Ludovico
See also WLIT 7
Ariosto, Ludovico 1474-1533 ... **LC 6, 87; PC 42**
See Ariosto, Lodovico
See also EW 2; RGWL 2, 3
Aristides
See Epstein, Joseph
Aristophanes 450B.C.-385B.C. .... **CMLC 4, 51; DC 2; WLCS**
See also AW 1; CDWLB 1; DA; DA3; DAB; DAC; DAM DRAM, MST; DFS 10; DLB 176; LMFS 1; RGWL 2, 3; TWA; WLIT 8
Aristotle 384B.C.-322B.C. .... **CMLC 31; WLCS**
See also AW 1; CDWLB 1; DA; DA3; DAB; DAC; DAM MST; DLB 176; RGWL 2, 3; TWA; WLIT 8
Arlt, Roberto (Godofredo Christophersen) 1900-1942 .... **HLC 1; TCLC 29**
See also CA 123; 131; CANR 67; DAM MULT; DLB 305; EWL 3; HW 1, 2; IDTP; LAW
Armah, Ayi Kwei 1939- . **BLC 1:1, 2:1; CLC 5, 33, 136**
See also AFW; BRWS 10; BW 1; CA 61-64; CANR 21, 64; CDWLB 3; CN 1, 2, 3, 4, 5, 6, 7; DAM MULT, POET; DLB 117; EWL 3; MTCW 1; WLIT 2
Armatrading, Joan 1950- .... **CLC 17**
See also CA 114; 186
Armin, Robert 1568(?)-1615(?) .... **LC 120**
Armitage, Frank
See Carpenter, John (Howard)
Armstrong, Jeannette (C.) 1948- .... **NNAL**
See also CA 149; CCA 1; CN 6, 7; DAC; DLB 334; SATA 102
Arnette, Robert
See Silverberg, Robert
Arnim, Achim von (Ludwig Joachim von Arnim) 1781-1831 .. **NCLC 5, 159; SSC 29**
See also DLB 90
Arnim, Bettina von 1785-1859 ...... **NCLC 38, 123**
See also DLB 90; RGWL 2, 3
Arnold, Matthew 1822-1888 ..... **NCLC 6, 29, 89, 126; PC 5; WLC 1**
See also BRW 5; CDBLB 1832-1890; DA; DAB; DAC; DAM MST, POET; DLB 32, 57; EXPP; PAB; PFS 2; TEA; WP
Arnold, Thomas 1795-1842 .... **NCLC 18**
See also DLB 55
Arnow, Harriette (Louisa) Simpson 1908-1986 ...... **CLC 2, 7, 18; TCLC 196**
See also BPFB 1; CA 9-12R; 118; CANR 14; CN 2, 3, 4; DLB 6; FW; MTCW 1, 2; RHW; SATA 42; SATA-Obit 47
Arouet, Francois-Marie
See Voltaire
Arp, Hans
See Arp, Jean
Arp, Jean 1887-1966 .... **CLC 5; TCLC 115**
See also CA 81-84; 25-28R; CANR 42, 77; EW 10
Arrabal
See Arrabal, Fernando
Arrabal (Teran), Fernando
See Arrabal, Fernando
See also CWW 2

Arrabal, Fernando 1932- ... **CLC 2, 9, 18, 58**
See Arrabal (Teran), Fernando
See also CA 9-12R; CANR 15; DLB 321; EWL 3; LMFS 2
Arreola, Juan Jose 1918-2001 .... **CLC 147; HLC 1; SSC 38**
See also CA 113; 131; 200; CANR 81; CWW 2; DAM MULT; DLB 113; DNFS 2; EWL 3; HW 1, 2; LAW; RGSF 2
Arrian c. 89(?)-c. 155(?) .... **CMLC 43**
See also DLB 176
Arrick, Fran **CLC 30**
See Gaberman, Judie Angell
See also BYA 6
Arrley, Richmond
See Delany, Samuel R., Jr.
Artaud, Antonin (Marie Joseph) 1896-1948 .... **DC 14; TCLC 3, 36**
See also CA 104; 149; DA3; DAM DRAM; DFS 22; DLB 258, 321; EW 11; EWL 3; GFL 1789 to the Present; MTCW 2; MTFW 2005; RGWL 2, 3
Arthur, Ruth M(abel) 1905-1979 ..... **CLC 12**
See also CA 9-12R; 85-88; CANR 4; CWRI 5; SATA 7, 26
Artsybashev, Mikhail (Petrovich) 1878-1927 .... **TCLC 31**
See also CA 170; DLB 295
Arundel, Honor (Morfydd) 1919-1973 .... **CLC 17**
See also CA 21-22; 41-44R; CAP 2; CLR 35; CWRI 5; SATA 4; SATA-Obit 24
Arzner, Dorothy 1900-1979 .... **CLC 98**
Asch, Sholem 1880-1957 .... **TCLC 3**
See also CA 105; DLB 333; EWL 3; GLL 2; RGHL
Ascham, Roger 1516(?)-1568 .... **LC 101**
See also DLB 236
Ash, Shalom
See Asch, Sholem
Ashbery, John 1927- ... **CLC 2, 3, 4, 6, 9, 13, 15, 25, 41, 77, 125, 221; PC 26**
See also AMWS 3; CA 5-8R; CANR 9, 37, 66, 102, 132, 170; CP 1, 2, 3, 4, 5, 6, 7; DA3; DAM POET; DLB 5, 165; DLBY 1981; EWL 3; GLL 1; INT CANR-9; MAL 5; MTCW 1, 2; MTFW 2005; PAB; PFS 11, 28; RGAL 4; TCLE 1:1; WP
Ashbery, John Lawrence
See Ashbery, John
Ashbridge, Elizabeth 1713-1755 .... **LC 147**
See also DLB 200
Ashdown, Clifford
See Freeman, R(ichard) Austin
Ashe, Gordon
See Creasey, John
Ashton-Warner, Sylvia (Constance) 1908-1984 .... **CLC 19**
See also CA 69-72; 112; CANR 29; CN 1, 2, 3; MTCW 1, 2
Asimov, Isaac 1920-1992 ..... **CLC 1, 3, 9, 19, 26, 76, 92**
See also AAYA 13; BEST 90:2; BPFB 1; BYA 4, 6, 7, 9; CA 1-4R; 137; CANR 2, 19, 36, 60, 125; CLR 12, 79; CMW 4; CN 1, 2, 3, 4, 5; CPW; DA3; DAM POP; DLB 8; DLBY 1992; INT CANR-19; JRDA; LAIT 5; LMFS 2; MAICYA 1, 2; MAL 5; MTCW 1, 2; MTFW 2005; RGAL 4; SATA 1, 26, 74; SCFW 1, 2; SFW 4; SSFS 17; TUS; YAW
Askew, Anne 1521(?)-1546 .... **LC 81**
See also DLB 136
Assis, Joaquim Maria Machado de
See Machado de Assis, Joaquim Maria
Astell, Mary 1666-1731 .... **LC 68**
See also DLB 252, 336; FW

Astley, Thea (Beatrice May)
1925-2004 .... **CLC 41**
See also CA 65-68; 229; CANR 11, 43, 78; CN 1, 2, 3, 4, 5, 6, 7; DLB 289; EWL 3

Astley, William 1855-1911
See Warung, Price

Aston, James
See White, T(erence) H(anbury)

Asturias, Miguel Angel 1899-1974 .... **CLC 3, 8, 13; HLC 1; TCLC 184**
See also CA 25-28; 49-52; CANR 32; CAP 2; CDWLB 3; DA3; DAM MULT, NOV; DLB 113, 290, 329; EWL 3; HW 1; LAW; LMFS 2; MTCW 1, 2; RGWL 2, 3; WLIT 1

Atares, Carlos Saura
See Saura (Atares), Carlos

Athanasius c. 295-c. 373 .... **CMLC 48**

Atheling, William
See Pound, Ezra (Weston Loomis)

Atheling, William, Jr.
See Blish, James (Benjamin)

Atherton, Gertrude (Franklin Horn)
1857-1948 .... **TCLC 2**
See also CA 104; 155; DLB 9, 78, 186; HGG; RGAL 4; SUFW 1; TCWW 1, 2

Atherton, Lucius
See Masters, Edgar Lee

Atkins, Jack
See Harris, Mark

Atkinson, Kate 1951- .... **CLC 99**
See also CA 166; CANR 101, 153; DLB 267

Attaway, William (Alexander)
1911-1986 .... **BLC 1:1; CLC 92**
See also BW 2, 3; CA 143; CANR 82; DAM MULT; DLB 76; MAL 5

Atticus
See Fleming, Ian; Wilson, (Thomas) Woodrow

Atwood, Margaret 1939- . **CLC 2, 3, 4, 8, 13, 15, 25, 44, 84, 135, 232, 239, 246; PC 8; SSC 2, 46; WLC 1**
See also AAYA 12, 47; AMWS 13; BEST 89:2; BPFB 1; CA 49-52; CANR 3, 24, 33, 59, 95, 133; CN 2, 3, 4, 5, 6, 7; CP 1, 2, 3, 4, 5, 6, 7; CPW; CWP; DA; DA3; DAB; DAC; DAM MST, NOV, POET; DLB 53, 251, 326; EWL 3; EXPN; FL 1:5; FW; GL 2; INT CANR-24; LAIT 5; MTCW 1, 2; MTFW 2005; NFS 4, 12, 13, 14, 19; PFS 7; RGSF 2; SATA 50, 170; SSFS 3, 13; TCLE 1:1; TWA; WWE 1; YAW

Atwood, Margaret Eleanor
See Atwood, Margaret

Aubigny, Pierre d'
See Mencken, H(enry) L(ouis)

Aubin, Penelope 1685-1731(?) .... **LC 9**
See also DLB 39

Auchincloss, Louis 1917- ..... **CLC 4, 6, 9, 18, 45; SSC 22**
See also AMWS 4; CA 1-4R; CANR 6, 29, 55, 87, 130, 168; CN 1, 2, 3, 4, 5, 6, 7; DAM NOV; DLB 2, 244; DLBY 1980; EWL 3; INT CANR-29; MAL 5; MTCW 1; RGAL 4

Auchincloss, Louis Stanton
See Auchincloss, Louis

Auden, W(ystan) H(ugh) 1907-1973 . **CLC 1, 2, 3, 4, 6, 9, 11, 14, 43, 123; PC 1; WLC 1**
See also AAYA 18; AMWS 2; BRW 7; BRWR 1; CA 9-12R; 45-48; CANR 5, 61, 105; CDBLB 1914-1945; CP 1, 2; DA; DA3; DAB; DAC; DAM DRAM, MST, POET; DLB 10, 20; EWL 3; EXPP; MAL 5; MTCW 1, 2; MTFW 2005; PAB; PFS 1, 3, 4, 10, 27; TUS; WP

Audiberti, Jacques 1899-1965 .... **CLC 38**
See also CA 252; 25-28R; DAM DRAM; DLB 321; EWL 3

Audubon, John James 1785-1851 . **NCLC 47**
See also AAYA 76; AMWS 16; ANW; DLB 248

Auel, Jean M(arie) 1936- .... **CLC 31, 107**
See also AAYA 7, 51; BEST 90:4; BPFB 1; CA 103; CANR 21, 64, 115; CPW; DA3; DAM POP; INT CANR-21; NFS 11; RHW; SATA 91

Auerbach, Berthold 1812-1882 .... **NCLC 171**
See also DLB 133

Auerbach, Erich 1892-1957 .... **TCLC 43**
See also CA 118; 155; EWL 3

Augier, Emile 1820-1889 .... **NCLC 31**
See also DLB 192; GFL 1789 to the Present

August, John
See De Voto, Bernard (Augustine)

Augustine, St. 354-430 .... **CMLC 6, 95; WLCS**
See also DA; DA3; DAB; DAC; DAM MST; DLB 115; EW 1; RGWL 2, 3; WLIT 8

Aunt Belinda
See Braddon, Mary Elizabeth

Aunt Weedy
See Alcott, Louisa May

Aurelius
See Bourne, Randolph S(illiman)

Aurelius, Marcus 121-180 .... **CMLC 45**
See Marcus Aurelius
See also RGWL 2, 3

Aurobindo, Sri
See Ghose, Aurabinda

Aurobindo Ghose
See Ghose, Aurabinda

Ausonius, Decimus Magnus c. 310-c. 394 .... **CMLC 88**
See also RGWL 2, 3

Austen, Jane 1775-1817 ...... **NCLC 1, 13, 19, 33, 51, 81, 95, 119, 150; WLC 1**
See also AAYA 19; BRW 4; BRWC 1; BRWR 2; BYA 3; CDBLB 1789-1832; DA; DA3; DAB; DAC; DAM MST, NOV, DLB 116; EXPN; FL 1:2; GL 2; LAIT 2; LATS 1:1; LMFS 1; NFS 1, 14, 18, 20, 21; TEA; WLIT 3; WYAS 1

Auster, Paul 1947- .... **CLC 47, 131, 227**
See also AMWS 12; CA 69-72; CANR 23, 52, 75, 129, 165; CMW 4; CN 5, 6, 7; DA3; DLB 227; MAL 5; MTCW 2; MTFW 2005; SUFW 2; TCLE 1:1

Austin, Frank
See Faust, Frederick (Schiller)

Austin, Mary (Hunter) 1868-1934 . **SSC 104; TCLC 25**
See also ANW; CA 109; 178; DLB 9, 78, 206, 221, 275; FW; TCWW 1, 2

Averroes 1126-1198 .... **CMLC 7**
See also DLB 115

Avicenna 980-1037 .... **CMLC 16**
See also DLB 115

Avison, Margaret 1918-2007 .... **CLC 2, 4, 97**
See also CA 17-20R; CANR 134; CP 1, 2, 3, 4, 5, 6, 7; DAC; DAM POET; DLB 53; MTCW 1

Avison, Margaret Kirkland
See Avison, Margaret

Axton, David
See Koontz, Dean

Ayckbourn, Alan 1939- ...... **CLC 5, 8, 18, 33, 74; DC 13**
See also BRWS 5; CA 21-24R; CANR 31, 59, 118; CBD; CD 5, 6; DAB; DAM DRAM; DFS 7; DLB 13, 245; EWL 3; MTCW 1, 2; MTFW 2005

Aydy, Catherine
See Tennant, Emma

Ayme, Marcel (Andre) 1902-1967 ... **CLC 11; SSC 41**
See also CA 89-92; CANR 67, 137; CLR 25; DLB 72; EW 12; EWL 3; GFL 1789 to the Present; RGSF 2; RGWL 2, 3; SATA 91

Ayrton, Michael 1921-1975 .... **CLC 7**
See also CA 5-8R; 61-64; CANR 9, 21

Aytmatov, Chingiz
See Aitmatov, Chingiz (Torekulovich)
See also EWL 3

Azorin CLC 11
See Martinez Ruiz, Jose
See also DLB 322; EW 9; EWL 3

Azuela, Mariano 1873-1952 .. **HLC 1; TCLC 3, 145**
See also CA 104; 131; CANR 81; DAM MULT; EWL 3; HW 1, 2; LAW; MTCW 1, 2; MTFW 2005

Ba, Mariama 1929-1981 ...... **BLC 2:1; BLCS**
See also AFW; BW 2; CA 141; CANR 87; DNFS 2; WLIT 2

Baastad, Babbis Friis
See Friis-Baastad, Babbis Ellinor

Bab
See Gilbert, W(illiam) S(chwenck)

Babbis, Eleanor
See Friis-Baastad, Babbis Ellinor

Babel, Isaac
See Babel, Isaak (Emmanuilovich)
See also EW 11; SSFS 10

Babel, Isaak (Emmanuilovich)
1894-1941(?) . **SSC 16, 78; TCLC 2, 13, 171**
See Babel, Isaac
See also CA 104; 155; CANR 113; DLB 272; EWL 3; MTCW 2; MTFW 2005; RGSF 2; RGWL 2, 3; TWA

Babits, Mihaly 1883-1941 .... **TCLC 14**
See also CA 114; CDWLB 4; DLB 215; EWL 3

Babur 1483-1530 .... **LC 18**

Babylas 1898-1962
See Ghelderode, Michel de

Baca, Jimmy Santiago 1952- . **HLC 1; PC 41**
See also CA 131; CANR 81, 90, 146; CP 6, 7; DAM MULT; DLB 122; HW 1, 2; LLW; MAL 5

Baca, Jose Santiago
See Baca, Jimmy Santiago

Bacchelli, Riccardo 1891-1985 .... **CLC 19**
See also CA 29-32R; 117; DLB 264; EWL 3

Bach, Richard 1936- .... **CLC 14**
See also AITN 1; BEST 89:2; BPFB 1; BYA 5; CA 9-12R; CANR 18, 93, 151; CPW; DAM NOV, POP; FANT; MTCW 1; SATA 13

Bach, Richard David
See Bach, Richard

Bache, Benjamin Franklin
1769-1798 .... **LC 74**
See also DLB 43

Bachelard, Gaston 1884-1962 ...... **TCLC 128**
See also CA 97-100; 89-92; DLB 296; GFL 1789 to the Present

Bachman, Richard
See King, Stephen

Bachmann, Ingeborg 1926-1973 ..... **CLC 69; TCLC 192**
See also CA 93-96; 45-48; CANR 69; DLB 85; EWL 3; RGHL; RGWL 2, 3

Bacon, Francis 1561-1626 ..... **LC 18, 32, 131**
See also BRW 1; CDBLB Before 1660; DLB 151, 236, 252; RGEL 2; TEA

Bacon, Roger 1214(?)-1294 .... **CMLC 14**
See also DLB 115

Beattie, James 1735-1803 .... **NCLC 25**
  See also DLB 109

Beauchamp, Kathleen Mansfield 1888-1923
  See Mansfield, Katherine
  See also CA 104; 134; DA; DA3; DAC;
  DAM MST; MTCW 2; TEA

Beaumarchais, Pierre-Augustin Caron de
  1732-1799 .... **DC 4; LC 61**
  See also DAM DRAM; DFS 14, 16; DLB
  313; EW 4; GFL Beginnings to 1789;
  RGWL 2, 3

Beaumont, Francis 1584(?)-1616 .. **DC 6; LC
  33**
  See also BRW 2; CDBLB Before 1660;
  DLB 58; TEA

Beauvoir, Simone de 1908-1986 .... **CLC 1, 2,
  4, 8, 14, 31, 44, 50, 71, 124; SSC 35;
  WLC 1**
  See also BPFB 1; CA 9-12R; 118; CANR
  28, 61; DA; DA3; DAB; DAC; DAM
  MST, NOV; DLB 72; DLBY 1986; EW
  12; EWL 3; FL 1:5; FW; GFL 1789 to the
  Present; LMFS 2; MTCW 1, 2; MTFW
  2005; RGSF 2; RGWL 2, 3; TWA

**Beauvoir, Simone Lucie Ernestine Marie
  Bertrand de**
  See Beauvoir, Simone de

Becker, Carl (Lotus) 1873-1945 ..... **TCLC 63**
  See also CA 157; DLB 17

Becker, Jurek 1937-1997 .... **CLC 7, 19**
  See also CA 85-88; 157; CANR 60, 117;
  CWW 2; DLB 75, 299; EWL 3; RGHL

Becker, Walter 1950- .... **CLC 26**

Becket, Thomas a 1118(?)-1170 .... **CMLC 83**

Beckett, Samuel 1906-1989 ... **CLC 1, 2, 3, 4,
  6, 9, 10, 11, 14, 18, 29, 57, 59, 83; DC
  22; SSC 16, 74; TCLC 145; WLC 1**
  See also BRWC 2; BRWR 1; BRWS 1; CA
  5-8R; 130; CANR 33, 61; CBD; CDBLB
  1945-1960; CN 1, 2, 3, 4; CP 1, 2, 3, 4;
  DA; DA3; DAB; DAC; DAM MST,
  NOV; DFS 2, 7, 18; DLB 13, 15,
  233, 319, 321, 329; DLBY 1990; EWL 3;
  GFL 1789 to the Present; LATS 1:2;
  LMFS 2; MTCW 1, 2; MTFW 2005;
  RGSF 2; RGWL 2, 3; SSFS 15; TEA;
  WLIT 4

Beckford, William 1760-1844 .... **NCLC 16**
  See also BRW 3; DLB 39, 213; GL 2; HGG;
  LMFS 1; SUFW

Beckham, Barry (Earl) 1944- .... **BLC 1:1**
  See also BW 1; CA 29-32R; CANR 26, 62;
  CN 1, 2, 3, 4, 5, 6; DAM MULT; DLB 33

Beckman, Gunnel 1910- .... **CLC 26**
  See also CA 33-36R; CANR 15, 114; CLR
  25; MAICYA 1, 2; SAAS 9; SATA 6

Becque, Henri 1837-1899 .... **DC 21; NCLC 3**
  See also DLB 192; GFL 1789 to the Present

Becquer, Gustavo Adolfo
  1836-1870 .... **HLCS 1; NCLC 106**
  See also DAM MULT

Beddoes, Thomas Lovell 1803-1849 .. **DC 15;
  NCLC 3, 154**
  See also BRWS 11; DLB 96

Bede c. 673-735 .... **CMLC 20**
  See also DLB 146; TEA

Bedford, Denton R. 1907-(?) .... **NNAL**

Bedford, Donald F.
  See Fearing, Kenneth (Flexner)

Beecher, Catharine Esther
  1800-1878 .... **NCLC 30**
  See also DLB 1, 243

Beecher, John 1904-1980 .... **CLC 6**
  See also AITN 1; CA 5-8R; 105; CANR 8;
  CP 1, 2, 3

Beer, Johann 1655-1700 .... **LC 5**
  See also DLB 168

Beer, Patricia 1924- .... **CLC 58**
  See also CA 61-64; 183; CANR 13, 46; CP
  1, 2, 3, 4, 5, 6; CWP; DLB 40; FW

Beerbohm, Max
  See Beerbohm, (Henry) Max(imilian)

Beerbohm, (Henry) Max(imilian)
  1872-1956 .... **TCLC 1, 24**
  See also BRWS 2; CA 104; 154; CANR 79;
  DLB 34, 100; FANT; MTCW 2

Beer-Hofmann, Richard
  1866-1945 .... **TCLC 60**
  See also CA 160; DLB 81

Beg, Shemus
  See Stephens, James

Begiebing, Robert J(ohn) 1946- .... **CLC 70**
  See also CA 122; CANR 40, 88

Begley, Louis 1933- .... **CLC 197**
  See also CA 140; CANR 98, 176; DLB 299;
  RGHL; TCLE 1:1

Behan, Brendan (Francis)
  1923-1964 .... **CLC 1, 8, 11, 15, 79**
  See also BRWS 2; CA 73-76; CANR 33,
  121; CBD; CDBLB 1945-1960; DAM
  DRAM; DFS 7; DLB 13, 233; EWL 3;
  MTCW 1, 2

Behn, Aphra 1640(?)-1689 .. **DC 4; LC 1, 30,
  42, 135; PC 13, 88; WLC 1**
  See also BRWS 3; DA; DA3; DAB; DAC;
  DAM DRAM, MST, NOV, POET; DFS
  16, 24; DLB 39, 80, 131; FW; TEA;
  WLIT 3

Behrman, S(amuel) N(athaniel)
  1893-1973 .... **CLC 40**
  See also CA 13-16; 45-48; CAD; CAP 1;
  DLB 7, 44; IDFW 3; MAL 5; RGAL 4

Bekederemo, J. P. Clark
  See Clark Bekederemo, J.P.
  See also CD 6

Belasco, David 1853-1931 .... **TCLC 3**
  See also CA 104; 168; DLB 7; MAL 5;
  RGAL 4

Belcheva, Elisaveta Lyubomirova
  1893-1991 .... **CLC 10**
  See Bagryana, Elisaveta

Beldone, Phil "Cheech"
  See Ellison, Harlan

Beleno
  See Azuela, Mariano

Belinski, Vissarion Grigoryevich
  1811-1848 .... **NCLC 5**
  See also DLB 198

Belitt, Ben 1911- .... **CLC 22**
  See also CA 13-16R; CAAS 4; CANR 7,
  77; CP 1, 2, 3, 4, 5, 6; DLB 5

Belknap, Jeremy 1744-1798 .... **LC 115**
  See also DLB 30, 37

Bell, Gertrude (Margaret Lowthian)
  1868-1926 .... **TCLC 67**
  See also CA 167; CANR 110; DLB 174

Bell, J. Freeman
  See Zangwill, Israel

Bell, James Madison 1826-1902 ..... **BLC 1:1;
  TCLC 43**
  See also BW 1; CA 122; 124; DAM MULT;
  DLB 50

Bell, Madison Smartt 1957- ..... **CLC 41, 102,
  223**
  See also AMWS 10; BPFB 1; CA 111; 183;
  CAAE 183; CANR 28, 54, 73, 134, 176;
  CN 5, 6, 7; CSW; DLB 218, 278; MTCW
  2; MTFW 2005

Bell, Marvin (Hartley) 1937- ...... **CLC 8, 31;
  PC 79**
  See also CA 21-24R; CAAS 14; CANR 59,
  102; CP 1, 2, 3, 4, 5, 6, 7; DAM POET;
  DLB 5; MAL 5; MTCW 1; PFS 25

Bell, W. L. D.
  See Mencken, H(enry) L(ouis)

Bellamy, Atwood C.
  See Mencken, H(enry) L(ouis)

Bellamy, Edward 1850-1898 ..... **NCLC 4, 86,
  147**
  See also DLB 12; NFS 15; RGAL 4; SFW
  4

Belli, Gioconda 1948- .... **HLCS 1**
  See also CA 152; CANR 143; CWW 2;
  DLB 290; EWL 3; RGWL 3

Bellin, Edward J.
  See Kuttner, Henry

Bello, Andres 1781-1865 .... **NCLC 131**
  See also LAW

**Belloc, (Joseph) Hilaire (Pierre Sebastien
  Rene Swanton)** 1870-1953 .... **PC 24;
  TCLC 7, 18**
  See also CA 106; 152; CLR 102; CWRI 5;
  DAM POET; DLB 19, 100, 141, 174;
  EWL 3; MTCW 2; MTFW 2005; SATA
  112; WCH; YABC 1

Belloc, Joseph Peter Rene Hilaire
  See Belloc, (Joseph) Hilaire (Pierre Sebastien Rene Swanton)

Belloc, Joseph Pierre Hilaire
  See Belloc, (Joseph) Hilaire (Pierre Sebastien Rene Swanton)

Belloc, M. A.
  See Lowndes, Marie Adelaide (Belloc)

Belloc-Lowndes, Mrs.
  See Lowndes, Marie Adelaide (Belloc)

Bellow, Saul 1915-2005 ...... **CLC 1, 2, 3, 6, 8,
  10, 13, 15, 25, 33, 34, 63, 79, 190, 200;
  SSC 14, 101; WLC 1**
  See also AITN 2; AMW; AMWC 2; AMWR
  2; BEST 89:3; BPFB 1; CA 5-8R; 238;
  CABS 1; CANR 29, 53, 95, 132; CDALB
  1941-1968; CN 1, 2, 3, 4, 5, 6, 7; DA;
  DA3; DAB; DAC; DAM MST, NOV,
  POP; DLB 2, 28, 299, 329; DLBD 3;
  DLBY 1982; EWL 3; MAL 5; MTCW 1,
  2; MTFW 2005; NFS 4, 14, 26; RGAL 4;
  RGHL; RGSF 2; SSFS 12, 22; TUS

Belser, Reimond Karel Maria de 1929-
  See Ruyslinck, Ward
  See also CA 152

Bely, Andrey .... **PC 11; TCLC 7**
  See Bugayev, Boris Nikolayevich
  See also DLB 295; EW 9; EWL 3

Belyi, Andrei
  See Bugayev, Boris Nikolayevich
  See also RGWL 2, 3

Bembo, Pietro 1470-1547 .... **LC 79**
  See also RGWL 2, 3

Benary, Margot
  See Benary-Isbert, Margot

Benary-Isbert, Margot 1889-1979 .... **CLC 12**
  See also CA 5-8R; 89-92; CANR 4, 72;
  CLR 12; MAICYA 1, 2; SATA 2; SATA-
  Obit 21

Benavente (y Martinez), Jacinto
  1866-1954 .... **DC 26; HLCS 1; TCLC 3**
  See also CA 106; 131; CANR 81; DAM
  DRAM, MULT; DLB 329; EWL 3; GLL
  2; HW 1, 2; MTCW 1, 2

Benchley, Peter 1940-2006 .... **CLC 4, 8**
  See also AAYA 14; AITN 2; BPFB 1; CA
  17-20R; 248; CANR 12, 35, 66, 115;
  CPW; DAM NOV, POP; HGG; MTCW 1,
  2; MTFW 2005; SATA 3, 89, 164

Benchley, Peter Bradford
  See Benchley, Peter

Benchley, Robert (Charles)
  1889-1945 .... **TCLC 1, 55**
  See also CA 105; 153; DLB 11; MAL 5;
  RGAL 4

Benda, Julien 1867-1956 .... **TCLC 60**
  See also CA 120; 154; GFL 1789 to the
  Present

Berryman, John 1914-1972 ... **CLC 1, 2, 3, 4, 6, 8, 10, 13, 25, 62; PC 64**
See also AMW; CA 13-16; 33-36R; CABS 2; CANR 35; CAP 1; CDALB 1941-1968; CP 1; DAM POET; DLB 48; EWL 3; MAL 5; MTCW 1, 2; MTFW 2005; PAB; PFS 27; RGAL 4; WP

Bertolucci, Bernardo 1940- ...... **CLC 16, 157**
See also CA 106; CANR 125

Berton, Pierre (Francis de Marigny)
1920-2004 .... **CLC 104**
See also CA 1-4R; 233; CANR 2, 56, 144; CPW; DLB 68; SATA 99; SATA-Obit 158

Bertrand, Aloysius 1807-1841 ...... **NCLC 31**
See Bertrand, Louis oAloysiusc

Bertrand, Louis oAloysiusc
See Bertrand, Aloysius
See also DLB 217

Bertran de Born c. 1140-1215 .... **CMLC 5**

Besant, Annie (Wood) 1847-1933 ..... **TCLC 9**
See also CA 105; 185

Bessie, Alvah 1904-1985 .... **CLC 23**
See also CA 5-8R; 116; CANR 2, 80; DLB 26

Bestuzhev, Aleksandr Aleksandrovich
1797-1837 .... **NCLC 131**
See also DLB 198

Bethlen, T.D.
See Silverberg, Robert

Beti, Mongo BLC 1:1; CLC 27
See Biyidi, Alexandre
See also AFW; CANR 79; DAM MULT; EWL 3; WLIT 2

Betjeman, John 1906-1984 ...... **CLC 2, 6, 10, 34, 43; PC 75**
See also BRW 7; CA 9-12R; 112; CANR 33, 56; CDBLB 1945-1960; CP 1, 2, 3; DA3; DAB; DAM MST, POET; DLB 20; DLBY 1984; EWL 3; MTCW 1, 2

Bettelheim, Bruno 1903-1990 .... **CLC 79; TCLC 143**
See also CA 81-84; 131; CANR 23, 61; DA3; MTCW 1, 2; RGHL

Betti, Ugo 1892-1953 .... **TCLC 5**
See also CA 104; 155; EWL 3; RGWL 2, 3

Betts, Doris (Waugh) 1932- ..... **CLC 3, 6, 28; SSC 45**
See also CA 13-16R; CANR 9, 66, 77; CN 6, 7; CSW; DLB 218; DLBY 1982; INT CANR-9; RGAL 4

Bevan, Alistair
See Roberts, Keith (John Kingston)

Bey, Pilaff
See Douglas, (George) Norman

Beyala, Calixthe 1961- .... **BLC 2:1**
See also EWL 3

Bialik, Chaim Nachman
1873-1934 .... **TCLC 25, 201**
See Bialik, Hayyim Nahman
See also CA 170; EWL 3

Bialik, Hayyim Nahman
See Bialik, Chaim Nachman
See also WLIT 6

Bickerstaff, Isaac
See Swift, Jonathan

Bidart, Frank 1939- .... **CLC 33**
See also AMWS 15; CA 140; CANR 106; CP 5, 6, 7; PFS 26

Bienek, Horst 1930- .... **CLC 7, 11**
See also CA 73-76; DLB 75

Bierce, Ambrose (Gwinett)
1842-1914(?) ..... **SSC 9, 72; TCLC 1, 7, 44; WLC 1**
See also AAYA 55; AMW; BYA 11; CA 104; 139; CANR 78; CDALB 1865-1917; DA; DA3; DAC; DAM MST; DLB 11, 12, 23, 71, 74, 186; EWL 3; EXPS; HGG; LAIT 2; MAL 5; RGAL 4; RGSF 2; SSFS 9; SUFW 1

Biggers, Earl Derr 1884-1933 .... **TCLC 65**
See also CA 108; 153; DLB 306

Billiken, Bud
See Motley, Willard (Francis)

Billings, Josh
See Shaw, Henry Wheeler

Billington, (Lady) Rachel (Mary)
1942- .... **CLC 43**
See also AITN 2; CA 33-36R; CANR 44; CN 4, 5, 6, 7

Binchy, Maeve 1940- .... **CLC 153**
See also BEST 90:1; BPFB 1; CA 127; 134; CANR 50, 96, 134; CN 5, 6, 7; CPW; DA3; DAM POP; DLB 319; INT CA-134; MTCW 2; MTFW 2005; RHW

Binyon, T(imothy) J(ohn)
1936-2004 .... **CLC 34**
See also CA 111; 232; CANR 28, 140

Bion 335B.C.-245B.C. .... **CMLC 39**

Bioy Casares, Adolfo 1914-1999 ... **CLC 4, 8, 13, 88; HLC 1; SSC 17, 102**
See Casares, Adolfo Bioy; Miranda, Javier; Sacastru, Martin
See also CA 29-32R; 177; CANR 19, 43, 66; CWW 2; DAM MULT; DLB 113; EWL 3; HW 1, 2; LAW; MTCW 1, 2; MTFW 2005

Birch, Allison CLC 65

Bird, Cordwainer
See Ellison, Harlan

Bird, Robert Montgomery
1806-1854 .... **NCLC 1, 197**
See also DLB 202; RGAL 4

Birdwell, Cleo
See DeLillo, Don

Birkerts, Sven 1951- .... **CLC 116**
See also CA 128; 133, 176; CAAE 176; CAAS 29; CANR 151; INT CA-133

Birney, (Alfred) Earle 1904-1995 .. **CLC 1, 4, 6, 11; PC 52**
See also CA 1-4R; CANR 5, 20; CN 1, 2, 3, 4; CP 1, 2, 3, 4, 5, 6; DAC; DAM MST, POET; DLB 88; MTCW 1; PFS 8; RGEL 2

Biruni, al 973-1048(?) .... **CMLC 28**

Bishop, Elizabeth 1911-1979 ... **CLC 1, 4, 9, 13, 15, 32; PC 3, 34; TCLC 121**
See also AMWR 2; AMWS 1; CA 5-8R; 89-92; CABS 2; CANR 26, 61, 108; CDALB 1968-1988; CP 1, 2, 3; DA; DA3; DAC; DAM MST, POET; DLB 5, 169; EWL 3; GLL 2; MAL 5; MBL; MTCW 1, 2; PAB; PFS 6, 12, 27; RGAL 4; SATA-Obit 24; TUS; WP

Bishop, John 1935- .... **CLC 10**
See also CA 105

Bishop, John Peale 1892-1944 ..... **TCLC 103**
See also CA 107; 155; DLB 4, 9, 45; MAL 5; RGAL 4

Bissett, Bill 1939- .... **CLC 18; PC 14**
See also CA 69-72; CAAS 19; CANR 15; CCA 1; CP 1, 2, 3, 4, 5, 6, 7; DLB 53; MTCW 1

Bissoondath, Neil 1955- .... **CLC 120**
See also CA 136; CANR 123, 165; CN 6, 7; DAC

Bissoondath, Neil Devindra
See Bissoondath, Neil

Bitov, Andrei (Georgievich) 1937- ... **CLC 57**
See also CA 142; DLB 302

Biyidi, Alexandre 1932-
See Beti, Mongo
See also BW 1, 3; CA 114; 124; CANR 81; DA3; MTCW 1, 2

Bjarme, Brynjolf
See Ibsen, Henrik (Johan)

Bjoernson, Bjoernstjerne (Martinius)
1832-1910 .... **TCLC 7, 37**
See also CA 104

Black, Benjamin
See Banville, John

Black, Robert
See Holdstock, Robert

Blackburn, Paul 1926-1971 .... **CLC 9, 43**
See also BG 1:2; CA 81-84; 33-36R; CANR 34; CP 1; DLB 16; DLBY 1981

Black Elk 1863-1950 .... **NNAL; TCLC 33**
See also CA 144; DAM MULT; MTCW 2; MTFW 2005; WP

Black Hawk 1767-1838 .... **NNAL**

Black Hobart
See Sanders, (James) Ed(ward)

Blacklin, Malcolm
See Chambers, Aidan

Blackmore, R(ichard) D(oddridge)
1825-1900 .... **TCLC 27**
See also CA 120; DLB 18; RGEL 2

Blackmur, R(ichard) P(almer)
1904-1965 .... **CLC 2, 24**
See also AMWS 2; CA 11-12; 25-28R; CANR 71; CAP 1; DLB 63; EWL 3; MAL 5

Black Tarantula
See Acker, Kathy

Blackwood, Algernon 1869-1951 .... **SSC 107; TCLC 5**
See also CA 105; 150; CANR 169; DLB 153, 156, 178; HGG; SUFW 1

Blackwood, Algernon Henry
See Blackwood, Algernon

Blackwood, Caroline (Maureen)
1931-1996 .... **CLC 6, 9, 100**
See also BRWS 9; CA 85-88; 151; CANR 32, 61, 65; CN 3, 4, 5, 6; DLB 14, 207; HGG; MTCW 1

Blade, Alexander
See Hamilton, Edmond; Silverberg, Robert

Blaga, Lucian 1895-1961 .... **CLC 75**
See also CA 157; DLB 220; EWL 3

Blair, Eric (Arthur) 1903-1950 .... **TCLC 123**
See Orwell, George
See also CA 104; 132; DA; DA3; DAB; DAC; DAM MST, NOV; MTCW 1, 2; MTFW 2005; SATA 29

Blair, Hugh 1718-1800 .... **NCLC 75**

Blais, Marie-Claire 1939- .... **CLC 2, 4, 6, 13, 22**
See also CA 21-24R; CAAS 4; CANR 38, 75, 93; CWW 2; DAC; DAM MST; DLB 53; EWL 3; FW; MTCW 1, 2; MTFW 2005; TWA

Blaise, Clark 1940- .... **CLC 29**
See also AITN 2; CA 53-56, 231; CAAE 231; CAAS 3; CANR 5, 66, 106; CN 4, 5, 6, 7; DLB 53; RGSF 2

Blake, Fairley
See De Voto, Bernard (Augustine)

Blake, Nicholas
See Day Lewis, C(ecil)
See also DLB 77; MSW

Blake, Sterling
See Benford, Gregory

Blake, William 1757-1827 . **NCLC 13, 37, 57, 127, 173, 190; PC 12, 63; WLC 1**
See also AAYA 47; BRW 3; BRWR 1; CD-BLB 1789-1832; CLR 52; DA; DA3; DAB; DAC; DAM MST, POET; DLB 93, 163; EXPP; LATS 1:1; LMFS 1; MAI-CYA 1, 2; PAB; PFS 2, 12, 24; SATA 30; TEA; WCH; WLIT 3; WP

Blanchot, Maurice 1907-2003 .... **CLC 135**
See also CA 117; 144; 213; CANR 138; DLB 72, 296; EWL 3

Blasco Ibanez, Vicente 1867-1928 . **TCLC 12**
See Ibanez, Vicente Blasco
See also BPFB 1; CA 110; 131; CANR 81; DA3; DAM NOV; EW 8; EWL 3; HW 1, 2; MTCW 1

Borne, Ludwig 1786-1837 .... **NCLC 193**
 See also DLB 90

Borowski, Tadeusz 1922-1951 .... **SSC 48; TCLC 9**
 See also CA 106; 154; CDWLB 4; DLB 215; EWL 3; RGHL; RGSF 2; RGWL 3; SSFS 13

Borrow, George (Henry) 1803-1881 .... **NCLC 9**
 See also BRWS 12; DLB 21, 55, 166

Bosch (Gavino), Juan 1909-2001 ..... **HLCS 1**
 See also CA 151; 204; DAM MST, MULT; DLB 145; HW 1, 2

Bosman, Herman Charles 1905-1951 .... **TCLC 49**
 See Malan, Herman
 See also CA 160; DLB 225; RGSF 2

Bosschere, Jean de 1878(?)-1953 ... **TCLC 19**
 See also CA 115; 186

Boswell, James 1740-1795 ... **LC 4, 50; WLC 1**
 See also BRW 3; CDBLB 1660-1789; DA; DAB; DAC; DAM MST; DLB 104, 142; TEA; WLIT 3

Bottomley, Gordon 1874-1948 ..... **TCLC 107**
 See also CA 120; 192; DLB 10

Bottoms, David 1949- .... **CLC 53**
 See also CA 105; CANR 22; CSW; DLB 120; DLBY 1983

Boucicault, Dion 1820-1890 .... **NCLC 41**

Boucolon, Maryse
 See Conde, Maryse

Bourdieu, Pierre 1930-2002 .... **CLC 198**
 See also CA 130; 204

Bourget, Paul (Charles Joseph) 1852-1935 .... **TCLC 12**
 See also CA 107; 196; DLB 123; GFL 1789 to the Present

Bourjaily, Vance (Nye) 1922- .... **CLC 8, 62**
 See also CA 1-4R; CAAS 1; CANR 2, 72; CN 1, 2, 3, 4, 5, 6, 7; DLB 2, 143; MAL 5

Bourne, Randolph S(illiman) 1886-1918 .... **TCLC 16**
 See also AMW; CA 117; 155; DLB 63; MAL 5

Bova, Ben 1932- .... **CLC 45**
 See also AAYA 16; CA 5-8R; CAAS 18; CANR 11, 56, 94, 111, 157; CLR 3, 96; DLBY 1981; INT CANR-11; MAICYA 1, 2; MTCW 1; SATA 6, 68, 133; SFW 4

Bova, Benjamin William
 See Bova, Ben

Bowen, Elizabeth (Dorothea Cole) 1899-1973 . **CLC 1, 3, 6, 11, 15, 22, 118; SSC 3, 28, 66; TCLC 148**
 See also BRWS 2; CA 17-18; 41-44R; CANR 35, 105; CAP 2; CDBLB 1945-1960; CN 1; DA3; DAM NOV; DLB 15, 162; EWL 3; EXPS; FW; HGG; MTCW 1, 2; MTFW 2005; NFS 13; RGSF 2; SSFS 5, 22; SUFW 1; TEA; WLIT 4

Bowering, George 1935- .... **CLC 15, 47**
 See also CA 21-24R; CAAS 16; CANR 10; CN 7; CP 1, 2, 3, 4, 5, 6, 7; DLB 53

Bowering, Marilyn R(uthe) 1949- .... **CLC 32**
 See also CA 101; CANR 49; CP 4, 5, 6, 7; CWP; DLB 334

Bowers, Edgar 1924-2000 .... **CLC 9**
 See also CA 5-8R; 188; CANR 24; CP 1, 2, 3, 4, 5, 6, 7; CSW; DLB 5

Bowers, Mrs. J. Milton 1842-1914
 See Bierce, Ambrose (Gwinett)

Bowie, David **CLC 17**
 See Jones, David Robert

Bowles, Jane (Sydney) 1917-1973 ..... **CLC 3, 68**
 See Bowles, Jane Auer
 See also CA 19-20; 41-44R; CAP 2; CN 1; MAL 5

Bowles, Jane Auer
 See Bowles, Jane (Sydney)
 See also EWL 3

Bowles, Paul 1910-1999 ..... **CLC 1, 2, 19, 53; SSC 3, 98**
 See also AMWS 4; CA 1-4R; 186; CAAS 1; CANR 1, 19, 50, 75; CN 1, 2, 3, 4, 5, 6; DA3; DLB 5, 6, 218; EWL 3; MAL 5; MTCW 1, 2; MTFW 2005; RGAL 4; SSFS 17

Bowles, William Lisle 1762-1850 . **NCLC 103**
 See also DLB 93

Box, Edgar
 See Vidal, Gore

Boyd, James 1888-1944 .... **TCLC 115**
 See also CA 186; DLB 9; DLBD 16; RGAL 4; RHW

Boyd, Nancy
 See Millay, Edna St. Vincent
 See also GLL 1

Boyd, Thomas (Alexander) 1898-1935 .... **TCLC 111**
 See also CA 111; 183; DLB 9; DLBD 16, 316

Boyd, William 1952- .... **CLC 28, 53, 70**
 See also CA 114; 120; CANR 51, 71, 131, 174; CN 4, 5, 6, 7; DLB 231

Boyesen, Hjalmar Hjorth 1848-1895 .... **NCLC 135**
 See also DLB 12, 71; DLBD 13; RGAL 4

Boyle, Kay 1902-1992 .... **CLC 1, 5, 19, 58, 121; SSC 5, 102**
 See also CA 13-16R; 140; CAAS 1; CANR 29, 61, 110; CN 1, 2, 3, 4, 5; CP 1, 2, 3, 4, 5; DLB 4, 9, 48, 86; DLBY 1993; EWL 3; MAL 5; MTCW 1, 2; MTFW 2005; RGAL 4; RGSF 2; SSFS 10, 13, 14

Boyle, Mark
 See Kienzle, William X.

Boyle, Patrick 1905-1982 .... **CLC 19**
 See also CA 127

Boyle, T. C.
 See Boyle, T. Coraghessan
 See also AMWS 8

Boyle, T. Coraghessan 1948- ..... **CLC 36, 55, 90; SSC 16**
 See Boyle, T. C.
 See also AAYA 47; BEST 90:4; BPFB 1; CA 120; CANR 44, 76, 89, 132; CN 6, 7; CPW; DA3; DAM POP; DLB 218, 278; DLBY 1986; EWL 3; MAL 5; MTCW 2; MTFW 2005; SSFS 13, 19

Boz
 See Dickens, Charles (John Huffam)

Brackenridge, Hugh Henry 1748-1816 .... **NCLC 7**
 See also DLB 11, 37; RGAL 4

Bradbury, Edward P.
 See Moorcock, Michael
 See also MTCW 2

Bradbury, Malcolm (Stanley) 1932-2000 .... **CLC 32, 61**
 See also CA 1-4R; CANR 1, 33, 91, 98, 137; CN 1, 2, 3, 4, 5, 6, 7; CP 1; DA3; DAM NOV; DLB 14, 207; EWL 3; MTCW 1, 2; MTFW 2005

Bradbury, Ray 1920- ... **CLC 1, 3, 10, 15, 42, 98, 235; SSC 29, 53; WLC 1**
 See also AAYA 15; AITN 1, 2; AMWS 4; BPFB 1; BYA 4, 5, 11; CA 1-4R; CANR 2, 30, 75, 125; CDALB 1968-1988; CN 1, 2, 3, 4, 5, 6, 7; CPW; DA; DA3; DAB; DAC; DAM MST, NOV, POP; DLB 2, 8; EXPN; EXPS; HGG; LAIT 3, 5; LATS 1:2; LMFS 2; MAL 5; MTCW 1, 2;

MTFW 2005; NFS 1, 22; RGAL 4; RGSF 2; SATA 11, 64, 123; SCFW 1, 2; SFW 4; SSFS 1, 20; SUFW 1, 2; TUS; YAW

Braddon, Mary Elizabeth 1837-1915 .... **TCLC 111**
 See also BRWS 8; CA 108; 179; CMW 4; DLB 18, 70, 156; HGG

Bradfield, Scott 1955- .... **SSC 65**
 See also CA 147; CANR 90; HGG; SUFW 2

Bradfield, Scott Michael
 See Bradfield, Scott

Bradford, Gamaliel 1863-1932 .... **TCLC 36**
 See also CA 160; DLB 17

Bradford, William 1590-1657 .... **LC 64**
 See also DLB 24, 30; RGAL 4

Bradley, David, Jr. 1950- ...... **BLC 1:1; CLC 23, 118**
 See also BW 1, 3; CA 104; CANR 26, 81; CN 4, 5, 6, 7; DAM MULT; DLB 33

Bradley, David Henry, Jr.
 See Bradley, David, Jr.

Bradley, John Ed 1958- .... **CLC 55**
 See also CA 139; CANR 99; CN 6, 7; CSW

Bradley, John Edmund, Jr.
 See Bradley, John Ed

Bradley, Marion Zimmer 1930-1999 .... **CLC 30**
 See Chapman, Lee; Dexter, John; Gardner, Miriam; Ives, Morgan; Rivers, Elfrida
 See also AAYA 40; BPFB 1; CA 57-60; 185; CAAS 10; CANR 7, 31, 51, 75, 107; CPW; DA3; DAM POP; DLB 8; FANT; FW; MTCW 1, 2; MTFW 2005; SATA 90, 139; SATA-Obit 116; SFW 4; SUFW 2; YAW

Bradshaw, John 1933- .... **CLC 70**
 See also CA 138; CANR 61

Bradstreet, Anne 1612(?)-1672 .... **LC 4, 30, 130; PC 10**
 See also AMWS 1; CDALB 1640-1865; DA; DA3; DAC; DAM MST, POET; DLB 24; EXPP; FW; PFS 6; RGAL 4; TUS; WP

Brady, Joan 1939- .... **CLC 86**
 See also CA 141

Bragg, Melvyn 1939- .... **CLC 10**
 See also BEST 89:3; CA 57-60; CANR 10, 48, 89, 158; CN 1, 2, 3, 4, 5, 6, 7; DLB 14, 271; RHW

Brahe, Tycho 1546-1601 .... **LC 45**
 See also DLB 300

Braine, John (Gerard) 1922-1986 . **CLC 1, 3, 41**
 See also CA 1-4R; 120; CANR 1, 33; CD-BLB 1945-1960; CN 1, 2, 3, 4; DLB 15; DLBY 1986; EWL 3; MTCW 1

Braithwaite, William Stanley (Beaumont) 1878-1962 ...... **BLC 1:1; HR 1:2; PC 52**
 See also BW 1; CA 125; DAM MULT; DLB 50, 54; MAL 5

Bramah, Ernest 1868-1942 .... **TCLC 72**
 See also CA 156; CMW 4; DLB 70; FANT

Brammer, Billy Lee
 See Brammer, William

Brammer, William 1929-1978 .... **CLC 31**
 See also CA 235; 77-80

Brancati, Vitaliano 1907-1954 .... **TCLC 12**
 See also CA 109; DLB 264; EWL 3

Brancato, Robin F(idler) 1936- .... **CLC 35**
 See also AAYA 9, 68; BYA 6; CA 69-72; CANR 11, 45; CLR 32; JRDA; MAICYA 2; MAICYAS 1; SAAS 9; SATA 97; WYA; YAW

Brand, Dionne 1953- .... **CLC 192**
 See also BW 2; CA 143; CANR 143; CWP; DLB 334

Brand, Max
See Faust, Frederick (Schiller)
See also BPFB 1; TCWW 1, 2
Brand, Millen 1906-1980 .... **CLC 7**
See also CA 21-24R; 97-100; CANR 72
Branden, Barbara 1929- .... **CLC 44**
See also CA 148
Brandes, Georg (Morris Cohen)
1842-1927 .... **TCLC 10**
See also CA 105; 189; DLB 300
Brandys, Kazimierz 1916-2000 .... **CLC 62**
See also CA 239; EWL 3
Branley, Franklyn M(ansfield)
1915-2002 .... **CLC 21**
See also CA 33-36R; 207; CANR 14, 39;
CLR 13; MAICYA 1, 2; SAAS 16; SATA
4, 68, 136
Brant, Beth (E.) 1941- .... **NNAL**
See also CA 144; FW
Brant, Sebastian 1457-1521 .... **LC 112**
See also DLB 179; RGWL 2, 3
Brathwaite, Edward Kamau
1930- ..... **BLC 2:1; BLCS; CLC 11; PC
56**
See also BRWS 12; BW 2, 3; CA 25-28R;
CANR 11, 26, 47, 107; CDWLB 3; CP 1,
2, 3, 4, 5, 6, 7; DAM POET; DLB 125;
EWL 3
Brathwaite, Kamau
See Brathwaite, Edward Kamau
Brautigan, Richard (Gary)
1935-1984 .... **CLC 1, 3, 5, 9, 12, 34, 42;
TCLC 133**
See also BPFB 1; CA 53-56; 113; CANR
34; CN 1, 2, 3; CP 1, 2, 3, 4; DA3; DAM
NOV; DLB 2, 5, 206; DLBY 1980, 1984;
FANT; MAL 5; MTCW 1; RGAL 4;
SATA 56
Brave Bird, Mary
See Crow Dog, Mary
Braverman, Kate 1950- .... **CLC 67**
See also CA 89-92; CANR 141; DLB 335
Brecht, (Eugen) Bertolt (Friedrich)
1898-1956 ..... **DC 3; TCLC 1, 6, 13, 35,
169; WLC 1**
See also CA 104; 133; CANR 62; CDWLB
2; DA; DA3; DAB; DAC; DAM DRAM,
MST; DFS 4, 5, 9; DLB 56, 124; EW 11;
EWL 3; IDTP; MTCW 1, 2; MTFW 2005;
RGHL; RGWL 2, 3; TWA
Brecht, Eugen Berthold Friedrich
See Brecht, (Eugen) Bertolt (Friedrich)
Bremer, Fredrika 1801-1865 .... **NCLC 11**
See also DLB 254
Brennan, Christopher John
1870-1932 .... **TCLC 17**
See also CA 117; 188; DLB 230; EWL 3
Brennan, Maeve 1917-1993 ... **CLC 5; TCLC
124**
See also CA 81-84; CANR 72, 100
Brenner, Jozef 1887-1919
See Csath, Geza
See also CA 240
Brent, Linda
See Jacobs, Harriet A(nn)
Brentano, Clemens (Maria)
1778-1842 .... **NCLC 1, 191**
See also DLB 90; RGWL 2, 3
Brent of Bin Bin
See Franklin, (Stella Maria Sarah) Miles
(Lampe)
Brenton, Howard 1942- .... **CLC 31**
See also CA 69-72; CANR 33, 67; CBD;
CD 5, 6; DLB 13; MTCW 1
Breslin, James 1930-
See Breslin, Jimmy
See also CA 73-76; CANR 31, 75, 139;
DAM NOV; MTCW 1, 2; MTFW 2005

Breslin, Jimmy **CLC 4, 43**
See Breslin, James
See also AITN 1; DLB 185; MTCW 2
Bresson, Robert 1901(?)-1999 .... **CLC 16**
See also CA 110; 187; CANR 49
Breton, Andre 1896-1966 .. **CLC 2, 9, 15, 54;
PC 15**
See also CA 19-20; 25-28R; CANR 40, 60;
CAP 2; DLB 65, 258; EW 11; EWL 3;
GFL 1789 to the Present; LMFS 2;
MTCW 1, 2; MTFW 2005; RGWL 2, 3;
TWA; WP
Breton, Nicholas c. 1554-c. 1626 .... **LC 133**
See also DLB 136
Breytenbach, Breyten 1939(?)- .. **CLC 23, 37,
126**
See also CA 113; 129; CANR 61, 122;
CWW 2; DAM POET; DLB 225; EWL 3
Bridgers, Sue Ellen 1942- .... **CLC 26**
See also AAYA 8, 49; BYA 7, 8; CA 65-68;
CANR 11, 36; CLR 18; DLB 52; JRDA;
MAICYA 1, 2; SAAS 1; SATA 22, 90;
SATA-Essay 109; WYA; YAW
Bridges, Robert (Seymour)
1844-1930 .... **PC 28; TCLC 1**
See also BRW 6; CA 104; 152; CDBLB
1890-1914; DAM POET; DLB 19, 98
Bridie, James **TCLC 3**
See Mavor, Osborne Henry
See also DLB 10; EWL 3
Brin, David 1950- .... **CLC 34**
See also AAYA 21; CA 102; CANR 24, 70,
125, 127; INT CANR-24; SATA 65;
SCFW 2; SFW 4
Brink, Andre 1935- .... **CLC 18, 36, 106**
See also AFW; BRWS 6; CA 104; CANR
39, 62, 109, 133; CN 4, 5, 6, 7; DLB 225;
EWL 3; INT CA-103; LATS 1:2; MTCW
1, 2; MTFW 2005; WLIT 2
Brinsmead, H. F.
See Brinsmead, H(esba) F(ay)
Brinsmead, H. F(ay)
See Brinsmead, H(esba) F(ay)
Brinsmead, H(esba) F(ay) 1922- ...... **CLC 21**
See also CA 21-24R; CANR 10; CLR 47;
CWRI 5; MAICYA 1, 2; SAAS 5; SATA
18, 78
Brittain, Vera (Mary) 1893(?)-1970 . **CLC 23**
See also BRWS 10; CA 13-16; 25-28R;
CANR 58; CAP 1; DLB 191; FW; MTCW
1, 2
Broch, Hermann 1886-1951 ... **TCLC 20, 204**
See also CA 117; 211; CDWLB 2; DLB 85,
124; EW 10; EWL 3; RGWL 2, 3
Brock, Rose
See Hansen, Joseph
See also GLL 1
Brod, Max 1884-1968 .... **TCLC 115**
See also CA 5-8R; 25-28R; CANR 7; DLB
81; EWL 3
Brodkey, Harold (Roy) 1930-1996 .. **CLC 56;
TCLC 123**
See also CA 111; 151; CANR 71; CN 4, 5,
6; DLB 130
Brodsky, Iosif Alexandrovich 1940-1996
See Brodsky, Joseph
See also AITN 1; CA 41-44R; 151; CANR
37, 106; DA3; DAM POET; MTCW 1, 2;
MTFW 2005; RGWL 2, 3
Brodsky, Joseph **CLC 4, 6, 13, 36, 100; PC 9**
See Brodsky, Iosif Alexandrovich
See also AAYA 71; AMWS 8; CWW 2;
DLB 285, 329; EWL 3; MTCW 1
Brodsky, Michael 1948- .... **CLC 19**
See also CA 102; CANR 18, 41, 58, 147;
DLB 244
Brodsky, Michael Mark
See Brodsky, Michael
Brodzki, Bella **CLC 65**

Brome, Richard 1590(?)-1652 .... **LC 61**
See also BRWS 10; DLB 58
Bromell, Henry 1947- .... **CLC 5**
See also CA 53-56; CANR 9, 115, 116
Bromfield, Louis (Brucker)
1896-1956 .... **TCLC 11**
See also CA 107; 155; DLB 4, 9, 86; RGAL
4; RHW
Broner, E(sther) M(asserman)
1930- .... **CLC 19**
See also CA 17-20R; CANR 8, 25, 72; CN
4, 5, 6; DLB 28
Bronk, William (M.) 1918-1999 .... **CLC 10**
See also CA 89-92; 177; CANR 23; CP 3,
4, 5, 6, 7; DLB 165
Bronstein, Lev Davidovich
See Trotsky, Leon
Bronte, Anne
See Bronte, Anne
Bronte, Anne 1820-1849 ..... **NCLC 4, 71, 102**
See also BRW 5; BRWR 1; DA3; DLB 21,
199, 340; NFS 26; TEA
Bronte, (Patrick) Branwell
1817-1848 .... **NCLC 109**
See also DLB 340
Bronte, Charlotte
See Bronte, Charlotte
Bronte, Charlotte 1816-1855 ...... **NCLC 3, 8,
33, 58, 105, 155; WLC 1**
See also AAYA 17; BRW 5; BRWC 2;
BRWR 1; BYA 2; CDBLB 1832-1890;
DA; DA3; DAB; DAC; DAM MST, NOV;
DLB 21, 159, 199, 340; EXPN; FL 1:2;
GL 2; LAIT 2; NFS 4; TEA; WLIT 4
Bronte, Emily
See Bronte, Emily (Jane)
Bronte, Emily (Jane) 1818-1848 ... **NCLC 16,
35, 165; PC 8; WLC 1**
See also AAYA 17; BPFB 1; BRW 5;
BRWC 1; BRWR 1; BYA 3; CDBLB
1832-1890; DA; DA3; DAB; DAC; DAM
MST, NOV, POET; DLB 21, 32, 199, 340;
EXPN; FL 1:2; GL 2; LAIT 1; TEA;
WLIT 3
Brontes
See Bronte, Anne; Bronte, (Patrick) Bran-
well; Bronte, Charlotte; Bronte, Emily
(Jane)
Brooke, Frances 1724-1789 .... **LC 6, 48**
See also DLB 39, 99
Brooke, Henry 1703(?)-1783 .... **LC 1**
See also DLB 39
Brooke, Rupert (Chawner)
1887-1915 .. **PC 24; TCLC 2, 7; WLC 1**
See also BRWS 3; CA 104; 132; CANR 61;
CDBLB 1914-1945; DA; DAB; DAC;
DAM MST, POET; DLB 19, 216; EXPP;
GLL 2; MTCW 1, 2; MTFW 2005; PFS
7; TEA
Brooke-Haven, P.
See Wodehouse, P(elham) G(renville)
Brooke-Rose, Christine 1926(?)- ..... **CLC 40,
184**
See also BRWS 4; CA 13-16R; CANR 58,
118; CN 1, 2, 3, 4, 5, 6, 7; DLB 14, 231;
EWL 3; SFW 4
Brookner, Anita 1928- . **CLC 32, 34, 51, 136,
237**
See also BRWS 4; CA 114; 120; CANR 37,
56, 87, 130; CN 4, 5, 6, 7; CPW; DA3;
DAB; DAM POP; DLB 194, 326; DLBY
1987; EWL 3; MTCW 1, 2; MTFW 2005;
NFS 23; TEA
Brooks, Cleanth 1906-1994 . **CLC 24, 86, 110**
See also AMWS 14; CA 17-20R; 145;
CANR 33, 35; CSW; DLB 63; DLBY
1994; EWL 3; INT CANR-35; MAL 5;
MTCW 1, 2; MTFW 2005

Brooks, George
See Baum, L(yman) Frank

Brooks, Gwendolyn 1917-2000 .... **BLC 1:1, 2:1; CLC 1, 2, 4, 5, 15, 49, 125; PC 7; WLC 1**
See also AAYA 20; AFAW 1, 2; AITN 1; AMWS 3; BW 2, 3; CA 1-4R; 190; CANR 1, 27, 52, 75, 132; CDALB 1941-1968; CLR 27; CP 1, 2, 3, 4, 5, 6, 7; CWP; DA; DA3; DAC; DAM MST, MULT, POET; DLB 5, 76, 165; EWL 3; EXPP; FL 1:5; MAL 5; MBL; MTCW 1, 2; MTFW 2005; PFS 1, 2, 4, 6; RGAL 4; SATA 6; SATA-Obit 123; TUS; WP

Brooks, Mel 1926-
See Kaminsky, Melvin
See also CA 65-68; CANR 16; DFS 21

Brooks, Peter (Preston) 1938- .... **CLC 34**
See also CA 45-48; CANR 1, 107

Brooks, Van Wyck 1886-1963 .... **CLC 29**
See also AMW; CA 1-4R; CANR 6; DLB 45, 63, 103; MAL 5; TUS

Brophy, Brigid (Antonia)
1929-1995 .... **CLC 6, 11, 29, 105**
See also CA 5-8R; 149; CAAS 4; CANR 25, 53; CBD; CN 1, 2, 3, 4, 5, 6; CWD; DA3; DLB 14, 271; EWL 3; MTCW 1, 2

Brosman, Catharine Savage 1934- ..... **CLC 9**
See also CA 61-64; CANR 34, 46, 149

Brossard, Nicole 1943- .... **CLC 115, 169; PC 80**
See also CA 122; CAAS 16; CANR 140; CCA 1; CWP; CWW 2; DLB 53; EWL 3; FW; GLL 2; RGWL 3

Brother Antoninus
See Everson, William (Oliver)

Brothers Grimm
See Grimm, Jacob Ludwig Karl; Grimm, Wilhelm Karl

The Brothers Quay
See Quay, Stephen; Quay, Timothy

Broughton, T(homas) Alan 1936- ..... **CLC 19**
See also CA 45-48; CANR 2, 23, 48, 111

Broumas, Olga 1949- .... **CLC 10, 73**
See also CA 85-88; CANR 20, 69, 110; CP 5, 6, 7; CWP; GLL 2

Broun, Heywood 1888-1939 .... **TCLC 104**
See also DLB 29, 171

Brown, Alan 1950- .... **CLC 99**
See also CA 156

Brown, Charles Brockden
1771-1810 .... **NCLC 22, 74, 122**
See also AMWS 1; CDALB 1640-1865; DLB 37, 59, 73; FW; GL 2; HGG; LMFS 1; RGAL 4; TUS

Brown, Christy 1932-1981 .... **CLC 63**
See also BYA 13; CA 105; 104; CANR 72; DLB 14

Brown, Claude 1937-2002 ..... **BLC 1:1; CLC 30**
See also AAYA 7; BW 1, 3; CA 73-76; 205; CANR 81; DAM MULT

Brown, Dan 1964- .... **CLC 209**
See also AAYA 55; CA 217; MTFW 2005

Brown, Dee 1908-2002 .... **CLC 18, 47**
See also AAYA 30; CA 13-16R; 212; CAAS 6; CANR 11, 45, 60, 150; CPW; CSW; DA3; DAM POP; DLBY 1980; LAIT 2; MTCW 1, 2; MTFW 2005; NCFS 5; SATA 5, 110; SATA-Obit 141; TCWW 1, 2

Brown, Dee Alexander
See Brown, Dee

Brown, George
See Wertmueller, Lina

Brown, George Douglas
1869-1902 .... **TCLC 28**
See Douglas, George
See also CA 162

Brown, George Mackay 1921-1996 ... **CLC 5, 48, 100**
See also BRWS 6; CA 21-24R; 151; CAAS 6; CANR 12, 37, 67; CN 1, 2, 3, 4, 5, 6; CP 1, 2, 3, 4, 5, 6; DLB 14, 27, 139, 271; MTCW 1; RGSF 2; SATA 35

Brown, James Wllie
See Komunyakaa, Yusef

Brown, James Wllie, Jr.
See Komunyakaa, Yusef

Brown, Larry 1951-2004 .... **CLC 73**
See also CA 130; 134; 233; CANR 117, 145; CSW; DLB 234; INT CA-134

Brown, Moses
See Barrett, William (Christopher)

Brown, Rita Mae 1944- .... **CLC 18, 43, 79**
See also BPFB 1; CA 45-48; CANR 2, 11, 35, 62, 95, 138; CN 5, 6, 7; CPW; CSW; DA3; DAM NOV, POP; FW; INT CANR-11; MAL 5; MTCW 1, 2; MTFW 2005; NFS 9; RGAL 4; TUS

Brown, Roderick (Langmere) Haig-
See Haig-Brown, Roderick (Langmere)

Brown, Rosellen 1939- .... **CLC 32, 170**
See also CA 77-80; CAAS 10; CANR 14, 44, 98; CN 6, 7

Brown, Sterling Allen 1901-1989 ...... **BLC 1; CLC 1, 23, 59; HR 1:2; PC 55**
See also AFAW 1, 2; BW 1, 3; CA 85-88; 127; CANR 26; CP 3, 4; DA3; DAM MULT, POET; DLB 48, 51, 63; MAL 5; MTCW 1, 2; MTFW 2005; RGAL 4; WP

Brown, Will
See Ainsworth, William Harrison

Brown, William Hill 1765-1793 .... **LC 93**
See also DLB 37

Brown, William Larry
See Brown, Larry

Brown, William Wells 1815-1884 ... **BLC 1:1; DC 1; NCLC 2, 89**
See also DAM MULT; DLB 3, 50, 183, 248; RGAL 4

Browne, Clyde Jackson
See Browne, Jackson

Browne, Jackson 1948(?)- .... **CLC 21**
See also CA 120

Browne, Sir Thomas 1605-1682 .... **LC 111**
See also BRW 2; DLB 151

Browning, Robert 1812-1889 . **NCLC 19, 79; PC 2, 61; WLCS**
See also BRW 4; BRWC 2; BRWR 2; CD-BLB 1832-1890; CLR 97; DA; DA3; DAB; DAC; DAM MST, POET; DLB 32, 163; EXPP; LATS 1:1; PAB; PFS 1, 15; RGEL 2; TEA; WLIT 4; WP; YABC 1

Browning, Tod 1882-1962 .... **CLC 16**
See also CA 141; 117

Brownmiller, Susan 1935- .... **CLC 159**
See also CA 103; CANR 35, 75, 137; DAM NOV; FW; MTCW 1, 2; MTFW 2005

Brownson, Orestes Augustus
1803-1876 .... **NCLC 50**
See also DLB 1, 59, 73, 243

Bruccoli, Matthew J(oseph) 1931- ... **CLC 34**
See also CA 9-12R; CANR 7, 87; DLB 103

Bruce, Lenny CLC 21
See Schneider, Leonard Alfred

Bruchac, Joseph 1942- .... **NNAL**
See also AAYA 19; CA 33-36R; 256; CAAE 256; CANR 13, 47, 75, 94, 137, 161; CLR 46; CWRI 5; DAM MULT; JRDA; MAI-CYA 2; MAICYAS 1; MTCW 2; MTFW 2005; SATA 42, 89, 131, 176; SATA-Essay 176

Bruin, John
See Brutus, Dennis

Brulard, Henri
See Stendhal

Brulls, Christian
See Simenon, Georges (Jacques Christian)

Brunetto Latini c. 1220-1294 .... **CMLC 73**

Brunner, John (Kilian Houston)
1934-1995 .... **CLC 8, 10**
See also CA 1-4R; 149; CAAS 8; CANR 2, 37; CPW; DAM POP; DLB 261; MTCW 1, 2; SCFW 1, 2; SFW 4

Bruno, Giordano 1548-1600 .... **LC 27**
See also RGWL 2, 3

Brutus, Dennis 1924- ...... **BLC 1:1; CLC 43; PC 24**
See also AFW; BW 2, 3; CA 49-52; CAAS 14; CANR 2, 27, 42, 81; CDWLB 3; CP 1, 2, 3, 4, 5, 6, 7; DAM MULT, POET; DLB 117, 225; EWL 3

Bryan, C(ourtlandt) D(ixon) B(arnes)
1936- .... **CLC 29**
See also CA 73-76; CANR 13, 68; DLB 185; INT CANR-13

Bryan, Michael
See Moore, Brian
See also CCA 1

Bryan, William Jennings
1860-1925 .... **TCLC 99**
See also DLB 303

Bryant, William Cullen 1794-1878 . **NCLC 6, 46; PC 20**
See also AMWS 1; CDALB 1640-1865; DA; DAB; DAC; DAM MST, POET; DLB 3, 43, 59, 189, 250; EXPP; PAB; RGAL 4; TUS

Bryusov, Valery Yakovlevich
1873-1924 .... **TCLC 10**
See also CA 107; 155; EWL 3; SFW 4

Buchan, John 1875-1940 .... **TCLC 41**
See also CA 108; 145; CMW 4; DAB; DAM POP; DLB 34, 70, 156; HGG; MSW; MTCW 2; RGEL 2; RHW; YABC 2

Buchanan, George 1506-1582 .... **LC 4**
See also DLB 132

Buchanan, Robert 1841-1901 .... **TCLC 107**
See also CA 179; DLB 18, 35

Buchheim, Lothar-Guenther
1918-2007 .... **CLC 6**
See also CA 85-88; 257

Buchner, (Karl) Georg
1813-1837 .... **NCLC 26, 146**
See also CDWLB 2; DLB 133; EW 6; RGSF 2; RGWL 2, 3; TWA

Buchwald, Art 1925-2007 .... **CLC 33**
See also AITN 1; CA 5-8R; 256; CANR 21, 67, 107; MTCW 1, 2; SATA 10

Buchwald, Arthur
See Buchwald, Art

Buck, Pearl S(ydenstricker)
1892-1973 .... **CLC 7, 11, 18, 127**
See also AAYA 42; AITN 1; AMWS 2; BPFB 1; CA 1-4R; 41-44R; CANR 1, 34; CDALBS; CN 1; DA; DA3; DAB; DAC; DAM MST, NOV; DLB 9, 102, 329; EWL 3; LAIT 3; MAL 5; MTCW 1, 2; MTFW 2005; NFS 25; RGAL 4; RHW; SATA 1, 25; TUS

Buckler, Ernest 1908-1984 .... **CLC 13**
See also CA 11-12; 114; CAP 1; CCA 1; CN 1, 2, 3; DAC; DAM MST; DLB 68; SATA 47

Buckley, Christopher 1952- .... **CLC 165**
See also CA 139; CANR 119

Buckley, Christopher Taylor
See Buckley, Christopher

Buckley, Vincent (Thomas)
1925-1988 .... **CLC 57**
See also CA 101; CP 1, 2, 3, 4; DLB 289

Buckley, William F., Jr. 1925-2008 ... **CLC 7, 18, 37**
See also AITN 1; BPFB 1; CA 1-4R; 269; CANR 1, 24, 53, 93, 133; CMW 4; CPW; DA3; DAM POP; DLB 137; DLBY 1980; INT CANR-24; MTCW 1, 2; MTFW 2005; TUS

Buckley, William Frank
See Buckley, William F., Jr.

Buckley, William Frank, Jr.
See Buckley, William F., Jr.

Buechner, Frederick 1926- ..... **CLC 2, 4, 6, 9**
See also AMWS 12; BPFB 1; CA 13-16R; CANR 11, 39, 64, 114, 138; CN 1, 2, 3, 4, 5, 6, 7; DAM NOV; DLBY 1980; INT CANR-11; MAL 5; MTCW 1, 2; MTFW 2005; TCLE 1:1

Buell, John (Edward) 1927- .... **CLC 10**
See also CA 1-4R; CANR 71; DLB 53

Buero Vallejo, Antonio 1916-2000 ... **CLC 15, 46, 139, 226; DC 18**
See also CA 106; 189; CANR 24, 49, 75; CWW 2; DFS 11; EWL 3; HW 1; MTCW 1, 2

Bufalino, Gesualdo 1920-1996 .... **CLC 74**
See also CA 209; CWW 2; DLB 196

Bugayev, Boris Nikolayevich
1880-1934 .... **PC 11; TCLC 7**
See Bely, Andrey; Belyi, Andrei
See also CA 104; 165; MTCW 2; MTFW 2005

Bukowski, Charles 1920-1994 ... **CLC 2, 5, 9, 41, 82, 108; PC 18; SSC 45**
See also CA 17-20R; 144; CANR 40, 62, 105; CN 4, 5; CP 1, 2, 3, 4, 5; CPW; DA3; DAM NOV, POET; DLB 5, 130, 169; EWL 3; MAL 5; MTCW 1, 2; MTFW 2005; PFS 28

Bulgakov, Mikhail 1891-1940 .... **SSC 18; TCLC 2, 16, 159**
See also AAYA 74; BPFB 1; CA 105; 152; DAM DRAM, NOV; DLB 272; EWL 3; MTCW 2; MTFW 2005; NFS 8; RGSF 2; RGWL 2, 3; SFW 4; TWA

Bulgakov, Mikhail Afanasevich
See Bulgakov, Mikhail

Bulgya, Alexander Alexandrovich
1901-1956 .... **TCLC 53**
See Fadeev, Aleksandr Aleksandrovich; Fadeev, Alexandr Alexandrovich; Fadeyev, Alexander
See also CA 117; 181

Bullins, Ed 1935- ...... **BLC 1:1; CLC 1, 5, 7; DC 6**
See also BW 2, 3; CA 49-52; CAAS 16; CAD; CANR 24, 46, 73, 134; CD 5, 6; DAM DRAM, MULT; DLB 7, 38, 249; EWL 3; MAL 5; MTCW 1, 2; MTFW 2005; RGAL 4

Bulosan, Carlos 1911-1956 .... **AAL**
See also CA 216; DLB 312; RGAL 4

Bulwer-Lytton, Edward (George Earle Lytton) 1803-1873 .... **NCLC 1, 45**
See also DLB 21; RGEL 2; SFW 4; SUFW 1; TEA

Bunin, Ivan
See Bunin, Ivan Alexeyevich

Bunin, Ivan Alekseevich
See Bunin, Ivan Alexeyevich

Bunin, Ivan Alexeyevich 1870-1953 ... **SSC 5; TCLC 6**
See also CA 104; DLB 317, 329; EWL 3; RGSF 2; RGWL 2, 3; TWA

Bunting, Basil 1900-1985 ...... **CLC 10, 39, 47**
See also BRWS 7; CA 53-56; 115; CANR 7; CP 1, 2, 3, 4; DAM POET; DLB 20; EWL 3; RGEL 2

Bunuel, Luis 1900-1983 ... **CLC 16, 80; HLC 1**
See also CA 101; 110; CANR 32, 77; DAM MULT; HW 1

Bunyan, John 1628-1688 .. **LC 4, 69; WLC 1**
See also BRW 2; BYA 5; CDBLB 1660-1789; CLR 124; DA; DAB; DAC; DAM MST; DLB 39; RGEL 2; TEA; WCH; WLIT 3

Buravsky, Alexandr CLC 59

Burchill, Julie 1959- .... **CLC 238**
See also CA 135; CANR 115, 116

Burckhardt, Jacob (Christoph)
1818-1897 .... **NCLC 49**
See also EW 6

Burford, Eleanor
See Hibbert, Eleanor Alice Burford

Burgess, Anthony CLC 1, 2, 4, 5, 8, 10, 13, 15, 22, 40, 62, 81, 94
See Wilson, John (Anthony) Burgess
See also AAYA 25; AITN 1; BRWS 1; CD-BLB 1960 to Present; CN 1, 2, 3, 4, 5; DAB; DLB 14, 194, 261; DLBY 1998; EWL 3; RGEL 2; RHW; SFW 4; YAW

Buridan, John c. 1295-c. 1358 ...... **CMLC 97**

Burke, Edmund 1729(?)-1797 .... **LC 7, 36, 146; WLC 1**
See also BRW 3; DA; DA3; DAB; DAC; DAM MST; DLB 104, 252, 336; RGEL 2; TEA

Burke, Kenneth (Duva) 1897-1993 ... **CLC 2, 24**
See also AMW; CA 5-8R; 143; CANR 39, 74, 136; CN 1, 2; CP 1, 2, 3, 4, 5; DLB 45, 63; EWL 3; MAL 5; MTCW 1, 2; MTFW 2005; RGAL 4

Burke, Leda
See Garnett, David

Burke, Ralph
See Silverberg, Robert

Burke, Thomas 1886-1945 .... **TCLC 63**
See also CA 113; 155; CMW 4; DLB 197

Burney, Fanny 1752-1840 .... **NCLC 12, 54, 107**
See also BRWS 3; DLB 39; FL 1:2; NFS 16; RGEL 2; TEA

Burney, Frances
See Burney, Fanny

Burns, Robert 1759-1796 ... **LC 3, 29, 40; PC 6; WLC 1**
See also AAYA 51; BRW 3; CDBLB 1789-1832; DA; DA3; DAB; DAC; DAM MST, POET; DLB 109; EXPP; PAB; RGEL 2; TEA; WP

Burns, Tex
See L'Amour, Louis

Burnshaw, Stanley 1906-2005 ..... **CLC 3, 13, 44**
See also CA 9-12R; 243; CP 1, 2, 3, 4, 5, 6, 7; DLB 48; DLBY 1997

Burr, Anne 1937- .... **CLC 6**
See also CA 25-28R

Burroughs, Edgar Rice 1875-1950 . **TCLC 2, 32**
See also AAYA 11; BPFB 1; BYA 4, 9; CA 104; 132; CANR 131; DA3; DAM NOV; DLB 8; FANT; MTCW 1, 2; MTFW 2005; RGAL 4; SATA 41; SCFW 1, 2; SFW 4; TCWW 1, 2; TUS; YAW

Burroughs, William S. 1914-1997 . **CLC 1, 2, 5, 15, 22, 42, 75, 109; TCLC 121; WLC 1**
See Lee, William; Lee, Willy
See also AAYA 60; AITN 2; AMWS 3; BG 1:2; BPFB 1; CA 9-12R; 160; CANR 20, 52, 104; CN 1, 2, 3, 4, 5, 6; CPW; DA; DA3; DAB; DAC; DAM MST, NOV,

POP; DLB 2, 8, 16, 152, 237; DLBY 1981, 1997; EWL 3; HGG; LMFS 2; MAL 5; MTCW 1, 2; MTFW 2005; RGAL 4; SFW 4

Burroughs, William Seward
See Burroughs, William S.

Burton, Sir Richard F(rancis)
1821-1890 .... **NCLC 42**
See also DLB 55, 166, 184; SSFS 21

Burton, Robert 1577-1640 .... **LC 74**
See also DLB 151; RGEL 2

Buruma, Ian 1951- .... **CLC 163**
See also CA 128; CANR 65, 141

Busch, Frederick 1941-2006 .. **CLC 7, 10, 18, 47, 166**
See also CA 33-36R; 248; CAAS 1; CANR 45, 73, 92, 157; CN 1, 2, 3, 4, 5, 6, 7; DLB 6, 218

Busch, Frederick Matthew
See Busch, Frederick

Bush, Barney (Furman) 1946- .... **NNAL**
See also CA 145

Bush, Ronald 1946- .... **CLC 34**
See also CA 136

Busia, Abena, P. A. 1953- .... **BLC 2:1**

Bustos, F(rancisco)
See Borges, Jorge Luis

Bustos Domecq, H(onorio)
See Bioy Casares, Adolfo; Borges, Jorge Luis

Butler, Octavia E. 1947-2006 .... **BLC 2:1; BLCS; CLC 38, 121, 230, 240**
See also AAYA 18, 48; AFAW 2; AMWS 13; BPFB 1; BW 2, 3; CA 73-76; 248; CANR 12, 24, 38, 73, 145, 240; CLR 65; CN 7; CPW; DA3; DAM MULT, POP; DLB 33; LATS 1:2; MTCW 1, 2; MTFW 2005; NFS 8, 21; SATA 84; SCFW 2; SFW 4; SSFS 6; TCLE 1:1; YAW

Butler, Octavia Estelle
See Butler, Octavia E.

Butler, Robert Olen, (Jr.) 1945- ...... **CLC 81, 162**
See also AMWS 12; BPFB 1; CA 112; CANR 66, 138; CN 7; CSW; DAM POP; DLB 173, 335; INT CA-112; MAL 5; MTCW 2; MTFW 2005; SSFS 11, 22

Butler, Samuel 1612-1680 .... **LC 16, 43**
See also DLB 101, 126; RGEL 2

Butler, Samuel 1835-1902 .... **TCLC 1, 33; WLC 1**
See also BRWS 2; CA 143; CDBLB 1890-1914; DA; DA3; DAB; DAC; DAM MST, NOV; DLB 18, 57, 174; RGEL 2; SFW 4; TEA

Butler, Walter C.
See Faust, Frederick (Schiller)

Butor, Michel (Marie Francois)
1926- .... **CLC 1, 3, 8, 11, 15, 161**
See also CA 9-12R; CANR 33, 66; CWW 2; DLB 83; EW 13; EWL 3; GFL 1789 to the Present; MTCW 1, 2; MTFW 2005

Butts, Mary 1890(?)-1937 .... **TCLC 77**
See also CA 148; DLB 240

Buxton, Ralph
See Silverstein, Alvin; Silverstein, Virginia B(arbara Opshelor)

Buzo, Alex
See Buzo, Alexander (John)
See also DLB 289

Buzo, Alexander (John) 1944- .... **CLC 61**
See also CA 97-100; CANR 17, 39, 69; CD 5, 6

Buzzati, Dino 1906-1972 .... **CLC 36**
See also CA 160; 33-36R; DLB 177; RGWL 2, 3; SFW 4

Byars, Betsy 1928- .... **CLC 35**
  See also AAYA 19; BYA 3; CA 33-36R,
    183; CAAE 183; CANR 18, 36, 57, 102,
    148; CLR 1, 16, 72; DLB 52; INT CANR-
    18; JRDA; MAICYA 1, 2; MAICYAS 1;
    MTCW 1; SAAS 1; SATA 4, 46, 80, 163;
    SATA-Essay 108; WYA; YAW

Byars, Betsy Cromer
  See Byars, Betsy

Byatt, Antonia Susan Drabble
  See Byatt, A.S.

Byatt, A.S. 1936- .... **CLC 19, 65, 136, 223;**
  SSC 91
  See also BPFB 1; BRWC 2; BRWS 4; CA
    13-16R; CANR 13, 33, 50, 75, 96, 133;
    CN 1, 2, 3, 4, 5, 6; DA3; DLB 14, 194, 319, 326; EWL 3;
    POP; DLB 14, 194, 319, 326; EWL 3;
    MTCW 1, 2; MTFW 2005; RGSF 2;
    RHW; TEA

Byrd, William II 1674-1744 .... **LC 112**
  See also DLB 24, 140; RGAL 4

Byrne, David 1952- .... **CLC 26**
  See also CA 127

Byrne, John Keyes 1926-
  See Leonard, Hugh
  See also CA 102; CANR 78, 140; INT CA-
    102

Byron, George Gordon (Noel)
  1788-1824 ..... **DC 24; NCLC 2, 12, 109,**
  149; PC 16; WLC 1
  See also AAYA 64; BRW 4; BRWC 2; CD-
    BLB 1789-1832; DA; DA3; DAB; DAC;
    DAM MST, POET; DLB 96, 110; EXPP;
    LMFS 1; PAB; PFS 1, 14; RGEL 2; TEA;
    WLIT 3; WP

Byron, Robert 1905-1941 .... **TCLC 67**
  See also CA 160; DLB 195

C. 3. 3.
  See Wilde, Oscar

Caballero, Fernan 1796-1877 .... **NCLC 10**

Cabell, Branch
  See Cabell, James Branch

Cabell, James Branch 1879-1958 .... **TCLC 6**
  See also CA 105; 152; DLB 9, 78; FANT;
    MAL 5; MTCW 2; RGAL 4; SUFW 1

Cabeza de Vaca, Alvar Nunez
  1490-1557(?) .... **LC 61**

Cable, George Washington
  1844-1925 .... **SSC 4; TCLC 4**
  See also CA 104; 155; DLB 12, 74; DLBD
    13; RGAL 4; TUS

Cabral de Melo Neto, Joao
  1920-1999 .... **CLC 76**
  See Melo Neto, Joao Cabral de
  See also CA 151; DAM MULT; DLB 307;
    LAW; LAWS 1

Cabrera Infante, G. 1929-2005 ... **CLC 5, 25,**
  45, 120; HLC 1; SSC 39
  See also CA 85-88; 236; CANR 29, 65, 110;
    CDWLB 3; CWW 2; DA3; DAM MULT;
    DLB 113; EWL 3; HW 1, 2; LAW; LAWS
    1; MTCW 1, 2; MTFW 2005; RGSF 2;
    WLIT 1

Cabrera Infante, Guillermo
  See Cabrera Infante, G.

Cade, Toni
  See Bambara, Toni Cade

Cadmus and Harmonia
  See Buchan, John

Caedmon fl. 658-680 .... **CMLC 7**
  See also DLB 146

Caeiro, Alberto
  See Pessoa, Fernando (Antonio Nogueira)

Caesar, Julius CMLC 47
  See Julius Caesar
  See also AW 1; RGWL 2, 3; WLIT 8

Cage, John (Milton), (Jr.)
  1912-1992 .... **CLC 41; PC 58**
  See also CA 13-16R; 169; CANR 9, 78;
    DLB 193; INT CANR-9; TCLE 1:1

Cahan, Abraham 1860-1951 .... **TCLC 71**
  See also CA 108; 154; DLB 9, 25, 28; MAL
    5; RGAL 4

Cain, G.
  See Cabrera Infante, G.

Cain, Guillermo
  See Cabrera Infante, G.

Cain, James M(allahan) 1892-1977 .. **CLC 3,**
  11, 28
  See also AITN 1; BPFB 1; CA 17-20R; 73-
    76; CANR 8, 34, 61; CMW 4; CN 1, 2;
    DLB 226; EWL 3; MAL 5; MSW; MTCW
    1; RGAL 4

Caine, Hall 1853-1931 .... **TCLC 97**
  See also RHW

Caine, Mark
  See Raphael, Frederic (Michael)

Calasso, Roberto 1941- .... **CLC 81**
  See also CA 143; CANR 89

Calderon de la Barca, Pedro
  1600-1681 . **DC 3; HLCS 1; LC 23, 136**
  See also DFS 23; EW 2; RGWL 2, 3; TWA

Caldwell, Erskine 1903-1987 ... **CLC 1, 8, 14,**
  50, 60; SSC 19; TCLC 117
  See also AITN 1; AMW; BPFB 1; CA 1-4R;
    121; CAAS 1; CANR 2, 33; CN 1, 2, 3,
    4; DA3; DAM NOV; DLB 9, 86; EWL 3;
    MAL 5; MTCW 1, 2; MTFW 2005;
    RGAL 4; RGSF 2; TUS

Caldwell, (Janet Miriam) Taylor (Holland)
  1900-1985 .... **CLC 2, 28, 39**
  See also BPFB 1; CA 5-8R; 116; CANR 5;
    DA3; DAM NOV, POP; DLBD 17;
    MTCW 2; RHW

Calhoun, John Caldwell
  1782-1850 .... **NCLC 15**
  See also DLB 3, 248

Calisher, Hortense 1911- ..... **CLC 2, 4, 8, 38,**
  134; SSC 15
  See also CA 1-4R; CANR 1, 22, 117; CN
    1, 2, 3, 4, 5, 6, 7; DA3; DAM NOV; DLB
    2, 218; INT CANR-22; MAL 5; MTCW
    1, 2; MTFW 2005; RGAL 4; RGSF 2

Callaghan, Morley Edward
  1903-1990 ..... **CLC 3, 14, 41, 65; TCLC**
  145
  See also CA 9-12R; 132; CANR 33, 73;
    CN 1, 2, 3, 4; DAC; DAM MST; DLB
    68; EWL 3; MTCW 1, 2; MTFW 2005;
    RGEL 2; RGSF 2; SSFS 19

Callimachus c. 305B.C.-c.
  240B.C. .... **CMLC 18**
  See also AW 1; DLB 176; RGWL 2, 3

Calvin, Jean
  See Calvin, John
  See also DLB 327; GFL Beginnings to 1789

Calvin, John 1509-1564 .... **LC 37**
  See Calvin, Jean

Calvino, Italo 1923-1985 .... **CLC 5, 8, 11, 22,**
  33, 39, 73; SSC 3, 48; TCLC 183
  See also AAYA 58; CA 85-88; 116; CANR
    23, 61, 132; DAM NOV; DLB 196; EW
    13; EWL 3; MTCW 1, 2; MTFW 2005;
    RGHL; RGSF 2; RGWL 2, 3; SFW 4;
    SSFS 12; WLIT 7

Camara Laye
  See Laye, Camara
  See also EWL 3

Camden, William 1551-1623 .... **LC 77**
  See also DLB 172

Cameron, Carey 1952- .... **CLC 59**
  See also CA 135

Cameron, Peter 1959- .... **CLC 44**
  See also AMWS 12; CA 125; CANR 50,
    117; DLB 234; GLL 2

Camoens, Luis Vaz de 1524(?)-1580
  See Camoes, Luis de
  See also EW 2

Camoes, Luis de 1524(?)-1580 . **HLCS 1; LC**
  62; PC 31
  See Camoens, Luis Vaz de
  See also DLB 287; RGWL 2, 3

Camp, Madeleine L'Engle
  See L'Engle, Madeleine

Campana, Dino 1885-1932 .... **TCLC 20**
  See also CA 117; 246; DLB 114; EWL 3

Campanella, Tommaso 1568-1639 .... **LC 32**
  See also RGWL 2, 3

Campbell, Bebe Moore 1950-2006 . **BLC 2:1;**
  CLC 246
  See also AAYA 26; BW 2, 3; CA 139; 254;
    CANR 81, 134; DLB 227; MTCW 2;
    MTFW 2005

Campbell, John Ramsey
  See Campbell, Ramsey

Campbell, John W(ood, Jr.)
  1910-1971 .... **CLC 32**
  See also CA 21-22; 29-32R; CANR 34;
    CAP 2; DLB 8; MTCW 1; SCFW 1, 2;
    SFW 4

Campbell, Joseph 1904-1987 .... **CLC 69;**
  TCLC 140
  See also AAYA 3, 66; BEST 89:2; CA 1-4R;
    124; CANR 3, 28, 61, 107; DA3; MTCW
    1, 2

Campbell, Maria 1940- .... **CLC 85; NNAL**
  See also CA 102; CANR 54; CCA 1; DAC

Campbell, Ramsey 1946- ... **CLC 42; SSC 19**
  See also AAYA 51; CA 57-60, 228; CAAE
    228; CANR 7, 102, 171; DLB 261; HGG;
    INT CANR-7; SUFW 1, 2

Campbell, (Ignatius) Roy (Dunnachie)
  1901-1957 .... **TCLC 5**
  See also AFW; CA 104; 155; DLB 20, 225;
    EWL 3; MTCW 2; RGEL 2

Campbell, Thomas 1777-1844 .... **NCLC 19**
  See also DLB 93, 144; RGEL 2

Campbell, Wilfred TCLC 9
  See Campbell, William

Campbell, William 1858(?)-1918
  See Campbell, Wilfred
  See also CA 106; DLB 92

Campbell, William Edward March
  1893-1954
  See March, William
  See also CA 108

Campion, Jane 1954- .... **CLC 95, 229**
  See also AAYA 33; CA 138; CANR 87

Campion, Thomas 1567-1620 . **LC 78; PC 87**
  See also CDBLB Before 1660; DAM POET;
    DLB 58, 172; RGEL 2

Camus, Albert 1913-1960 ...... **CLC 1, 2, 4, 9,**
  11, 14, 32, 63, 69, 124; DC 2; SSC 9,
  76; WLC 1
  See also AAYA 36; AFW; BPFB 1; CA 89-
    92; CANR 131; DA; DA3; DAB; DAC;
    DAM DRAM, MST, NOV; DLB 72, 321,
    329; EW 13; EWL 3; EXPN; EXPS; GFL
    1789 to the Present; LATS 1:2; LMFS 2;
    MTCW 1, 2; MTFW 2005; NFS 6, 16;
    RGHL; RGSF 2; RGWL 2, 3; SSFS 4;
    TWA

Canby, Vincent 1924-2000 .... **CLC 13**
  See also CA 81-84; 191

Cancale
  See Desnos, Robert

Canetti, Elias 1905-1994 .. **CLC 3, 14, 25, 75,**
  86; TCLC 157
  See also CA 21-24R; 146; CANR 23, 61,
    79; CDWLB 2; CWW 2; DA3; DLB 85,
    124, 329; EW 12; EWL 3; MTCW 1, 2;
    MTFW 2005; RGWL 2, 3; TWA

Canfield, Dorothea F.
  See Fisher, Dorothy (Frances) Canfield

Canfield, Dorothea Frances
See Fisher, Dorothy (Frances) Canfield
Canfield, Dorothy
See Fisher, Dorothy (Frances) Canfield
Canin, Ethan 1960- .... **CLC 55; SSC 70**
See also CA 131; 135; DLB 335; MAL 5
Cankar, Ivan 1876-1918 .... **TCLC 105**
See also CDWLB 4; DLB 147; EWL 3
Cannon, Curt
See Hunter, Evan
Cao, Lan 1961- .... **CLC 109**
See also CA 165
Cape, Judith
See Page, P(atricia) K(athleen)
See also CCA 1
Capek, Karel 1890-1938 .... **DC 1; SSC 36;**
TCLC 6, 37, 192; WLC 1
See also CA 104; 140; CDWLB 4; DA;
DA3; DAB; DAC; DAM DRAM, MST,
NOV; DFS 7, 11; DLB 215; EW 10; EWL
3; MTCW 2; MTFW 2005; RGSF 2;
RGWL 2, 3; SCFW 1, 2; SFW 4
Capella, Martianus fl. 4th cent. - .. **CMLC 84**
Capote, Truman 1924-1984 . **CLC 1, 3, 8, 13,**
19, 34, 38, 58; SSC 2, 47, 93; TCLC
164; WLC 1
See also AAYA 61; AMWS 3; BPFB 1; CA
5-8R; 113; CANR 18, 62; CDALB 1941-
1968; CN 1, 2, 3; CPW; DA; DA3; DAB;
DAC; DAM MST, NOV, POP; DLB 2,
185, 227; DLBY 1980, 1984; EWL 3;
EXPS; GLL 1; LAIT 3; MAL 5; MTCW
1, 2; MTFW 2005; NCFS 2; RGAL 4;
RGSF 2; SATA 91; SSFS 2; TUS
Capra, Frank 1897-1991 .... **CLC 16**
See also AAYA 52; CA 61-64; 135
Caputo, Philip 1941- .... **CLC 32**
See also AAYA 60; CA 73-76; CANR 40,
135; YAW
Caragiale, Ion Luca 1852-1912 ...... **TCLC 76**
See also CA 157
Card, Orson Scott 1951- .... **CLC 44, 47, 50**
See also AAYA 11, 42; BPFB 1; BYA 5, 8;
CA 102; CANR 27, 47, 73, 102, 106, 133;
CLR 116; CPW; DA3; DAM POP; FANT;
INT CANR-27; MTCW 1, 2; MTFW
2005; NFS 5; SATA 83, 127; SCFW 2;
SFW 4; SUFW 2; YAW
Cardenal, Ernesto 1925- .... **CLC 31, 161;**
HLC 1; PC 22
See also CA 49-52; CANR 2, 32, 66, 138;
CWW 2; DAM MULT, POET; DLB 290;
EWL 3; HW 1, 2; LAWS 1; MTCW 1, 2;
MTFW 2005; RGWL 2, 3
Cardinal, Marie 1929-2001 .... **CLC 189**
See also CA 177; CWW 2; DLB 83; FW
Cardozo, Benjamin N(athan)
1870-1938 .... **TCLC 65**
See also CA 117; 164
Carducci, Giosue (Alessandro Giuseppe)
1835-1907 .... **PC 46; TCLC 32**
See also CA 163; DLB 329; EW 7; RGWL
2, 3
Carew, Thomas 1595(?)-1640 . **LC 13; PC 29**
See also BRW 2; DLB 126; PAB; RGEL 2
Carey, Ernestine Gilbreth
1908-2006 .... **CLC 17**
See also CA 5-8R; 254; CANR 71; SATA
2; SATA-Obit 177
Carey, Peter 1943- .... **CLC 40, 55, 96, 183**
See also BRWS 12; CA 123; 127; CANR
53, 76, 117, 157; CN 4, 5, 6, 7; DLB 289,
326; EWL 3; INT CA-127; MTCW 1, 2;
MTFW 2005; RGSF 2; SATA 94
Carleton, William 1794-1869 .... **NCLC 3**
See also DLB 159; RGEL 2; RGSF 2
Carlisle, Henry (Coffin) 1926- .... **CLC 33**
See also CA 13-16R; CANR 15, 85

Carlsen, Chris
See Holdstock, Robert
Carlson, Ron 1947- .... **CLC 54**
See also CA 105, 189; CAAE 189; CANR
27, 155; DLB 244
Carlson, Ronald F.
See Carlson, Ron
Carlyle, Jane Welsh 1801-1866 ... **NCLC 181**
See also DLB 55
Carlyle, Thomas 1795-1881 ..... **NCLC 22, 70**
See also BRW 4; CDBLB 1789-1832; DA;
DAB; DAC; DAM MST; DLB 55, 144,
254, 338; RGEL 2; TEA
Carman, (William) Bliss 1861-1929 ... **PC 34;**
TCLC 7
See also CA 104; 152; DAC; DLB 92;
RGEL 2
Carnegie, Dale 1888-1955 .... **TCLC 53**
See also CA 218
Carossa, Hans 1878-1956 .... **TCLC 48**
See also CA 170; DLB 66; EWL 3
Carpenter, Don(ald Richard)
1931-1995 .... **CLC 41**
See also CA 45-48; 149; CANR 1, 71
Carpenter, Edward 1844-1929 .... **TCLC 88**
See also BRWS 13; CA 163; GLL 1
Carpenter, John (Howard) 1948- ... **CLC 161**
See also AAYA 2, 73; CA 134; SATA 58
Carpenter, Johnny
See Carpenter, John (Howard)
Carpentier (y Valmont), Alejo
1904-1980 . **CLC 8, 11, 38, 110; HLC 1;**
SSC 35; TCLC 201
See also CA 65-68; 97-100; CANR 11, 70;
CDWLB 3; DAM MULT; DLB 113; EWL
3; HW 1, 2; LAW; LMFS 2; RGSF 2;
RGWL 2, 3; WLIT 1
Carr, Caleb 1955- .... **CLC 86**
See also CA 147; CANR 73, 134; DA3
Carr, Emily 1871-1945 .... **TCLC 32**
See also CA 159; DLB 68; FW; GLL 2
Carr, John Dickson 1906-1977 .... **CLC 3**
See Fairbairn, Roger
See also CA 49-52; 69-72; CANR 3, 33,
60; CMW 4; DLB 306; MSW; MTCW 1,
2
Carr, Philippa
See Hibbert, Eleanor Alice Burford
Carr, Virginia Spencer 1929- .... **CLC 34**
See also CA 61-64; CANR 175; DLB 111
Carrere, Emmanuel 1957- .... **CLC 89**
See also CA 200
Carrier, Roch 1937- .... **CLC 13, 78**
See also CA 130; CANR 61, 152; CCA 1;
DAC; DAM MST; DLB 53; SATA 105,
166
Carroll, James Dennis
See Carroll, Jim
Carroll, James P. 1943(?)- .... **CLC 38**
See also CA 81-84; CANR 73, 139; MTCW
2; MTFW 2005
Carroll, Jim 1951- .... **CLC 35, 143**
See also AAYA 17; CA 45-48; CANR 42,
115; NCFS 5
Carroll, Lewis **NCLC 2, 53, 139; PC 18, 74;**
WLC 1
See Dodgson, Charles L(utwidge)
See also AAYA 39; BRW 5; BYA 5, 13; CD-
BLB 1832-1890; CLR 2, 18, 108; DLB
18, 163, 178; DLBY 1998; EXPN; EXPP;
FANT; JRDA; LAIT 1; NFS 27; PFS 11;
RGEL 2; SUFW 1; TEA; WCH
Carroll, Paul Vincent 1900-1968 ...... **CLC 10**
See also CA 9-12R; 25-28R; DLB 10; EWL
3; RGEL 2

Carruth, Hayden 1921- ..... **CLC 4, 7, 10, 18,**
84; PC 10
See also AMWS 16; CA 9-12R; CANR 4,
38, 59, 110, 174; CP 1, 2, 3, 4, 5, 6, 7;
DLB 5, 165; INT CANR-4; MTCW 1, 2;
MTFW 2005; PFS 26; SATA 47
Carson, Anne 1950- .... **CLC 185; PC 64**
See also AMWS 12; CA 203; CP 7; DLB
193; PFS 18; TCLE 1:1
Carson, Ciaran 1948- .... **CLC 201**
See also BRWS 13; CA 112; 153; CANR
113; CP 6, 7; PFS 26
Carson, Rachel
See Carson, Rachel Louise
See also AAYA 49; DLB 275
Carson, Rachel Louise 1907-1964 .... **CLC 71**
See Carson, Rachel
See also AMWS 9; ANW; CA 77-80; CANR
35; DA3; DAM POP; FW; LAIT 4; MAL
5; MTCW 1, 2; MTFW 2005; NCFS 1;
SATA 23
Carter, Angela 1940-1992 ...... **CLC 5, 41, 76;**
SSC 13, 85; TCLC 139
See also BRWS 3; CA 53-56; 136; CANR
12, 36, 61, 106; CN 3, 4, 5; DA3; DLB
14, 207, 261, 319; EXPS; FANT; FW; GL
2; MTCW 1, 2; MTFW 2005; RGSF 2;
SATA 66; SATA-Obit 70; SFW 4; SSFS
4, 12; SUFW 2; WLIT 4
Carter, Angela Olive
See Carter, Angela
Carter, Martin (Wylde) 1927- .... **BLC 2:1**
See also BW 2; CA 102; CANR 42; CD-
WLB 3; CP 1, 2, 3, 4, 5, 6; DLB 117;
EWL 3
Carter, Nick
See Smith, Martin Cruz
Carver, Raymond 1938-1988 ..... **CLC 22, 36,**
53, 55, 126; PC 54; SSC 8, 51, 104
See also AAYA 44; AMWS 3; BPFB 1; CA
33-36R; 126; CANR 17, 34, 61, 103; CN
4; CPW; DA3; DAM NOV; DLB 130;
DLBY 1984, 1988; EWL 3; MAL 5;
MTCW 1, 2; MTFW 2005; PFS 17;
RGAL 4; RGSF 2; SSFS 3, 6, 12, 13, 23;
TCLE 1:1; TCWW 2; TUS
Cary, Elizabeth, Lady Falkland
1585-1639 .... **LC 30, 141**
Cary, (Arthur) Joyce (Lunel)
1888-1957 .... **TCLC 1, 29, 196**
See also BRW 7; CA 104; 164; CDBLB
1914-1945; DLB 15, 100; EWL 3; MTCW
2; RGEL 2; TEA
Casal, Julian del 1863-1893 .... **NCLC 131**
See also DLB 283; LAW
Casanova, Giacomo
See Casanova de Seingalt, Giovanni Jacopo
See also WLIT 7
Casanova, Giovanni Giacomo
See Casanova de Seingalt, Giovanni Jacopo
Casanova de Seingalt, Giovanni Jacopo
1725-1798 .... **LC 13, 151**
See Casanova, Giacomo
Casares, Adolfo Bioy
See Bioy Casares, Adolfo
See also RGSF 2
Casas, Bartolome de las 1474-1566
See Las Casas, Bartolome de
See also WLIT 1
Case, John
See Hougan, Carolyn
Casely-Hayford, J(oseph) E(phraim)
1866-1903 .... **BLC 1:1; TCLC 24**
See also BW 2; CA 123; 152; DAM MULT
Casey, John (Dudley) 1939- .... **CLC 59**
See also BEST 90:2; CA 69-72; CANR 23,
100

Casey, Michael 1947- .... **CLC 2**
    See also CA 65-68; CANR 109; CP 2, 3;
    DLB 5
Casey, Patrick
    See Thurman, Wallace (Henry)
Casey, Warren (Peter) 1935-1988 .... **CLC 12**
    See also CA 101; 127; INT CA-101
Casona, Alejandro **CLC 49; TCLC 199**
    See Alvarez, Alejandro Rodriguez
    See also EWL 3
Cassavetes, John 1929-1989 .... **CLC 20**
    See also CA 85-88; 127; CANR 82
Cassian, Nina 1924- .... **PC 17**
    See also CWP; CWW 2
Cassill, R(onald) V(erlin)
    1919-2002 .... **CLC 4, 23**
    See also CA 9-12R; 208; CAAS 1; CANR
    7, 45; CN 1, 2, 3, 4, 5, 6, 7; DLB 6, 218;
    DLBY 2002
Cassiodorus, Flavius Magnus c. 490(?)-c.
    583(?) .... **CMLC 43**
Cassirer, Ernst 1874-1945 .... **TCLC 61**
    See also CA 157
Cassity, (Allen) Turner 1929- .... **CLC 6, 42**
    See also CA 17-20R, 223; CAAE 223;
    CAAS 8; CANR 11; CSW; DLB 105
Cassius Dio c. 155-c. 229 .... **CMLC 99**
    See also DLB 176
Castaneda, Carlos (Cesar Aranha)
    1931(?)-1998 .... **CLC 12, 119**
    See also CA 25-28R; CANR 32, 66, 105;
    DNFS 1; HW 1; MTCW 1
Castedo, Elena 1937- .... **CLC 65**
    See also CA 132
Castedo-Ellerman, Elena
    See Castedo, Elena
Castellanos, Rosario 1925-1974 .... **CLC 66;**
    HLC 1; SSC 39, 68
    See also CA 131; 53-56; CANR 58; CD-
    WLB 3; DAM MULT; DLB 113, 290;
    EWL 3; FW; HW 1; LAW; MTCW 2;
    MTFW 2005; RGSF 2; RGWL 2, 3
Castelvetro, Lodovico 1505-1571 .... **LC 12**
Castiglione, Baldassare 1478-1529 ...... **LC 12**
    See Castiglione, Baldesar
    See also LMFS 1; RGWL 2, 3
Castiglione, Baldesar
    See Castiglione, Baldassare
    See also EW 2; WLIT 7
Castillo, Ana 1953- .... **CLC 151**
    See also AAYA 42; CA 131; CANR 51, 86,
    128, 172; CWP; DLB 122, 227; DNFS 2;
    FW; HW 1; LLW; PFS 21
Castillo, Ana Hernandez Del
    See Castillo, Ana
Castle, Robert
    See Hamilton, Edmond
Castro (Ruz), Fidel 1926(?)- .... **HLC 1**
    See also CA 110; 129; CANR 81; DAM
    MULT; HW 2
Castro, Guillen de 1569-1631 .... **LC 19**
Castro, Rosalia de 1837-1885 ... **NCLC 3, 78;**
    PC 41
    See also DAM MULT
Cather, Willa (Sibert) 1873-1947 . **SSC 2, 50;**
    TCLC 1, 11, 31, 99, 132, 152; WLC 1
    See also AAYA 24; AMW; AMWC 1;
    AMWR 1; BPFB 1; CA 104; 128; CDALB
    1865-1917; CLR 98; DA; DA3; DAB;
    DAC; DAM MST, NOV; DLB 9, 54, 78,
    256; DLBD 1; EWL 3; EXPN; EXPS; FL
    1:5; LAIT 3; LATS 1:1; MAL 5; MBL;
    MTCW 1, 2; MTFW 2005; NFS 2, 19;
    RGAL 4; RGSF 2; RHW; SATA 30; SSFS
    2, 7, 16; TCWW 1, 2; TUS
Catherine II
    See Catherine the Great
    See also DLB 150

Catherine, Saint 1347-1380 ..... **CMLC 27, 95**
Catherine the Great 1729-1796 .... **LC 69**
    See Catherine II
Cato, Marcus Porcius
    234B.C.-149B.C. .... **CMLC 21**
    See Cato the Elder
Cato, Marcus Porcius, the Elder
    See Cato, Marcus Porcius
Cato the Elder
    See Cato, Marcus Porcius
    See also DLB 211
Catton, (Charles) Bruce 1899-1978 . **CLC 35**
    See also AITN 1; CA 5-8R; 81-84; CANR
    7, 74; DLB 17; MTCW 2; MTFW 2005;
    SATA 2; SATA-Obit 24
Catullus c. 84B.C.-54B.C. .... **CMLC 18**
    See also AW 2; CDWLB 1; DLB 211;
    RGWL 2, 3; WLIT 8
Cauldwell, Frank
    See King, Francis (Henry)
Caunitz, William J. 1933-1996 .... **CLC 34**
    See also BEST 89:3; CA 125; 130; 152;
    CANR 73; INT CA-130
Causley, Charles (Stanley)
    1917-2003 .... **CLC 7**
    See also CA 9-12R; 223; CANR 5, 35, 94;
    CLR 30; CP 1, 2, 3, 4, 5; CWRI 5; DLB
    27; MTCW 1; SATA 3, 66; SATA-Obit
    149
Caute, (John) David 1936- .... **CLC 29**
    See also CA 1-4R; CAAS 4; CANR 1, 33,
    64, 120; CBD; CD 5, 6; CN 1, 2, 3, 4, 5,
    6, 7; DAM NOV; DLB 14, 231
Cavafy, C(onstantine) P(eter) **PC 36; TCLC**
    2, 7
    See Kavafis, Konstantinos Petrou
    See also CA 148; DA3; DAM POET; EW
    8; EWL 3; MTCW 2; PFS 19; RGWL 2,
    3; WP
Cavalcanti, Guido c. 1250-c.
    1300 .... **CMLC 54**
    See also RGWL 2, 3; WLIT 7
Cavallo, Evelyn
    See Spark, Muriel
Cavanna, Betty **CLC 12**
    See Harrison, Elizabeth (Allen) Cavanna
    See also JRDA; MAICYA 1; SAAS 4;
    SATA 1, 30
Cavendish, Margaret Lucas
    1623-1673 .... **LC 30, 132**
    See also DLB 131, 252, 281; RGEL 2
Caxton, William 1421(?)-1491(?) .... **LC 17**
    See also DLB 170
Cayer, D. M.
    See Duffy, Maureen (Patricia)
Cayrol, Jean 1911-2005 .... **CLC 11**
    See also CA 89-92; 236; DLB 83; EWL 3
Cela (y Trulock), Camilo Jose
    See Cela, Camilo Jose
    See also CWW 2
Cela, Camilo Jose 1916-2002 .... **CLC 4, 13,**
    59, 122; HLC 1; SSC 71
    See Cela (y Trulock), Camilo Jose
    See also BEST 90:2; CA 21-24R; 206;
    CAAS 10; CANR 21, 32, 76, 139; DAM
    MULT; DLB 322; DLBY 1989; EW 13;
    EWL 3; HW 1; MTCW 1, 2; MTFW
    2005; RGSF 2; RGWL 2, 3
Celan, Paul **CLC 10, 19, 53, 82; PC 10**
    See Antschel, Paul
    See also CDWLB 2; DLB 69; EWL 3;
    RGHL; RGWL 2, 3
Celine, Louis-Ferdinand **CLC 1, 3, 4, 7, 9,**
    15, 47, 124
    See Destouches, Louis-Ferdinand
    See also DLB 72; EW 11; EWL 3; GFL
    1789 to the Present; RGWL 2, 3

Cellini, Benvenuto 1500-1571 .... **LC 7**
    See also WLIT 7
Cendrars, Blaise **CLC 18, 106**
    See Sauser-Hall, Frederic
    See also DLB 258; EWL 3; GFL 1789 to
    the Present; RGWL 2, 3; WP
Centlivre, Susanna 1669(?)-1723 .... **DC 25;**
    LC 65
    See also DLB 84; RGEL 2
Cernuda (y Bidon), Luis
    1902-1963 .... **CLC 54; PC 62**
    See also CA 131; 89-92; DAM POET; DLB
    134; EWL 3; GLL 1; HW 1; RGWL 2, 3
Cervantes, Lorna Dee 1954- ..... **HLCS 1; PC**
    35
    See also CA 131; CANR 80; CP 7; CWP;
    DLB 82; EXPP; HW 1; LLW
Cervantes (Saavedra), Miguel de
    1547-1616 .... **HLCS; LC 6, 23, 93; SSC**
    12, 108; WLC 1
    See also AAYA 56; BYA 1, 14; DA; DAB;
    DAC; DAM MST, NOV; EW 2; LAIT 1;
    LATS 1:1; LMFS 1; NFS 8; RGSF 2;
    RGWL 2, 3; TWA
Cesaire, Aime 1913-2008 .... **BLC 1:1; CLC**
    19, 32, 112; DC 22; PC 25
    See also BW 2, 3; CA 65-68; CANR 24,
    43, 81; CWW 2; DA3; DAM MULT,
    POET; DLB 321; EWL 3; GFL 1789 to
    the Present; MTCW 1, 2; MTFW 2005;
    WP
Chaadaev, Petr Iakovlevich
    1794-1856 .... **NCLC 197**
    See also DLB 198
Chabon, Michael 1963- ... **CLC 55, 149; SSC**
    59
    See also AAYA 45; AMWS 11; CA 139;
    CANR 57, 96, 127, 138; DLB 278; MAL
    5; MTFW 2005; NFS 25; SATA 145
Chabrol, Claude 1930- .... **CLC 16**
    See also CA 110
Chairil Anwar
    See Anwar, Chairil
    See also EWL 3
Challans, Mary 1905-1983
    See Renault, Mary
    See also CA 81-84; 111; CANR 74; DA3;
    MTCW 2; MTFW 2005; SATA 23; SATA-
    Obit 36; TEA
Challis, George
    See Faust, Frederick (Schiller)
Chambers, Aidan 1934- .... **CLC 35**
    See also AAYA 27; CA 25-28R; CANR 12,
    31, 58, 116; JRDA; MAICYA 1, 2; SAAS
    12; SATA 1, 69, 108, 171; WYA; YAW
Chambers, James 1948-
    See Cliff, Jimmy
    See also CA 124
Chambers, Jessie
    See Lawrence, D(avid) H(erbert Richards)
    See also GLL 1
Chambers, Robert W(illiam)
    1865-1933 .... **SSC 92; TCLC 41**
    See also CA 165; DLB 202; HGG; SATA
    107; SUFW 1
Chambers, (David) Whittaker
    1901-1961 .... **TCLC 129**
    See also CA 89-92; DLB 303
Chamisso, Adelbert von
    1781-1838 .... **NCLC 82**
    See also DLB 90; RGWL 2, 3; SUFW 1
Chance, James T.
    See Carpenter, John (Howard)
Chance, John T.
    See Carpenter, John (Howard)

Chandler, Raymond (Thornton)
1888-1959 .... **SSC 23; TCLC 1, 7, 179**
See also AAYA 25; AMWC 2; AMWS 4;
BPFB 1; CA 104; 129; CANR 60, 107;
CDALB 1929-1941; CMW 4; DA3; DLB
226, 253; DLBD 6; EWL 3; MAL 5;
MSW; MTCW 1, 2; MTFW 2005; NFS
17; RGAL 4; TUS
Chang, Diana 1934- .... **AAL**
See also CA 228; CWP; DLB 312; EXPP
Chang, Eileen 1920-1995 .... **AAL; SSC 28;
TCLC 184**
See also CA 166; CANR 168; CWW 2;
DLB 328; EWL 3; RGSF 2
Chang, Jung 1952- .... **CLC 71**
See also CA 142
Chang Ai-Ling
See Chang, Eileen
Channing, William Ellery
1780-1842 .... **NCLC 17**
See also DLB 1, 59, 235; RGAL 4
Chao, Patricia 1955- .... **CLC 119**
See also CA 163; CANR 155
Chaplin, Charles Spencer
1889-1977 .... **CLC 16**
See Chaplin, Charlie
See also CA 81-84; 73-76
Chaplin, Charlie
See Chaplin, Charles Spencer
See also AAYA 61; DLB 44
Chapman, George 1559(?)-1634 . **DC 19; LC
22, 116**
See also BRW 1; DAM DRAM; DLB 62,
121; LMFS 1; RGEL 2
Chapman, Graham 1941-1989 .... **CLC 21**
See Monty Python
See also CA 116; 129; CANR 35, 95
Chapman, John Jay 1862-1933 .... **TCLC 7**
See also AMWS 14; CA 104; 191
Chapman, Lee
See Bradley, Marion Zimmer
See also GLL 1
Chapman, Walker
See Silverberg, Robert
Chappell, Fred (Davis) 1936- .... **CLC 40, 78,
162**
See also CA 5-8R, 198; CAAE 198; CAAS
4; CANR 8, 33, 67, 110; CN 6; CP 6, 7;
CSW; DLB 6, 105; HGG
Char, Rene(-Emile) 1907-1988 .... **CLC 9, 11,
14, 55; PC 56**
See also CA 13-16R; 124; CANR 32; DAM
POET; DLB 258; EWL 3; GFL 1789 to
the Present; MTCW 1, 2; RGWL 2, 3
Charby, Jay
See Ellison, Harlan
Chardin, Pierre Teilhard de
See Teilhard de Chardin, (Marie Joseph)
Pierre
Chariton fl. 1st cent. (?)- .... **CMLC 49**
Charlemagne 742-814 .... **CMLC 37**
Charles I 1600-1649 .... **LC 13**
Charriere, Isabelle de 1740-1805 .. **NCLC 66**
See also DLB 313
Chartier, Alain c. 1392-1430 .... **LC 94**
See also DLB 208
Chartier, Emile-Auguste
See Alain
Charyn, Jerome 1937- .... **CLC 5, 8, 18**
See also CA 5-8R; CAAS 1; CANR 7, 61,
101, 158; CMW 4; CN 1, 2, 3, 4, 5, 6, 7;
DLBY 1983; MTCW 1
Chase, Adam
See Marlowe, Stephen
Chase, Mary (Coyle) 1907-1981 .... **DC 1**
See also CA 77-80; 105; CAD; CWD; DFS
11; DLB 228; SATA 17; SATA-Obit 29

Chase, Mary Ellen 1887-1973 .... **CLC 2;
TCLC 124**
See also CA 13-16; 41-44R; CAP 1; SATA
10
Chase, Nicholas
See Hyde, Anthony
See also CCA 1
Chase-Riboud, Barbara (Dewayne Tosi)
1939- .... **BLC 2:1**
See also BW 2; CA 113; CANR 76; DAM
MULT; DLB 33; MTCW 2
Chateaubriand, Francois Rene de
1768-1848 .... **NCLC 3, 134**
See also DLB 119; EW 5; GFL 1789 to the
Present; RGWL 2, 3; TWA
Chatelet, Gabrielle-Emilie Du
See du Chatelet, Emilie
See also DLB 313
Chatterje, Sarat Chandra 1876-1936(?)
See Chatterji, Saratchandra
See also CA 109
Chatterji, Bankim Chandra
1838-1894 .... **NCLC 19**
Chatterji, Saratchandra TCLC 13
See Chatterje, Sarat Chandra
See also CA 186; EWL 3
Chatterton, Thomas 1752-1770 .... **LC 3, 54**
See also DAM POET; DLB 109; RGEL 2
Chatwin, (Charles) Bruce
1940-1989 .... **CLC 28, 57, 59**
See also AAYA 4; BEST 90:1; BRWS 4;
CA 85-88; 127; CPW; DAM POP; DLB
194, 204; EWL 3; MTFW 2005
Chaucer, Daniel
See Ford, Ford Madox
See also RHW
Chaucer, Geoffrey 1340(?)-1400 .. **LC 17, 56;
PC 19, 58; WLCS**
See also BRW 1; BRWC 1; BRWR 2; CD-
BLB Before 1660; DA; DA3; DAB;
DAC; DAM MST, POET; DLB 146;
LAIT 1; PAB; PFS 14; RGEL 2; TEA;
WLIT 3; WP
Chavez, Denise 1948- .... **HLC 1**
See also CA 131; CANR 56, 81, 137; DAM
MULT; DLB 122; FW; HW 1, 2; LLW;
MAL 5; MTCW 2; MTFW 2005
Chaviaras, Strates 1935-
See Haviaras, Stratis
See also CA 105
Chayefsky, Paddy CLC 23
See Chayefsky, Sidney
See also CAD; DLB 7, 44; DLBY 1981;
RGAL 4
Chayefsky, Sidney 1923-1981 .... **CLC 23**
See Chayefsky, Paddy
See also CA 9-12R; 104; CANR 18; DAM
DRAM
Chedid, Andree 1920- .... **CLC 47**
See also CA 145; CANR 95; EWL 3
Cheever, John 1912-1982 ..... **CLC 3, 7, 8, 11,
15, 25, 64; SSC 1, 38, 57; WLC 2**
See also AAYA 65; AMWS 1; BPFB 1; CA
5-8R; 106; CABS 1; CANR 5, 27, 76;
CDALB 1941-1968; CN 1, 2, 3; CPW;
DA; DA3; DAB; DAC; DAM MST, NOV,
POP; DLB 2, 102, 227; DLBY 1980,
1982; EWL 3; EXPS; INT CANR-5;
MAL 5; MTCW 1, 2; MTFW 2005;
RGAL 4; RGSF 2; SSFS 2, 14; TUS
Cheever, Susan 1943- .... **CLC 18, 48**
See also CA 103; CANR 27, 51, 92, 157;
DLBY 1982; INT CANR-27
Chekhonte, Antosha
See Chekhov, Anton (Pavlovich)

Chekhov, Anton (Pavlovich)
1860-1904 .... **DC 9; SSC 2, 28, 41, 51,
85, 102; TCLC 3, 10, 31, 55, 96, 163;
WLC 2**
See also AAYA 68; BYA 14; CA 104; 124;
DA; DA3; DAB; DAC; DAM DRAM,
MST; DFS 1, 5, 10, 12; DLB 277; EW 7;
EWL 3; EXPS; LAIT 3; LATS 1:1; RGSF
2; RGWL 2, 3; SATA 90; SSFS 5, 13, 14;
TWA
Cheney, Lynne V. 1941- .... **CLC 70**
See also CA 89-92; CANR 58, 117; SATA
152
Chernyshevsky, Nikolai Gavrilovich
See Chernyshevsky, Nikolay Gavrilovich
See also DLB 238
Chernyshevsky, Nikolay Gavrilovich
1828-1889 .... **NCLC 1**
See Chernyshevsky, Nikolai Gavrilovich
Cherry, Carolyn Janice CLC 35
See Cherryh, C.J.
See also AAYA 24; BPFB 1; DLBY 1980;
FANT; SATA 93; SCFW 2; SFW 4; YAW
Cherryh, C.J. 1942-
See Cherry, Carolyn Janice
See also CA 65-68; CANR 10, 147; SATA
172
Chesler, Phyllis 1940- .... **CLC 247**
See also CA 49-52; CANR 4, 59, 140; FW
Chesnutt, Charles W(addell)
1858-1932 .... **BLC 1; SSC 7, 54; TCLC
5, 39**
See also AFAW 1, 2; AMWS 14; BW 1, 3;
CA 106; 125; CANR 76; DAM MULT;
DLB 12, 50, 78; EWL 3; MAL 5; MTCW
1, 2; MTFW 2005; RGAL 4; RGSF 2;
SSFS 11
Chester, Alfred 1929(?)-1971 .... **CLC 49**
See also CA 196; 33-36R; DLB 130; MAL
5
Chesterton, G(ilbert) K(eith)
1874-1936 . **PC 28; SSC 1, 46; TCLC 1,
6, 64**
See also AAYA 57; BRW 6; CA 104; 132;
CANR 73, 131; CDBLB 1914-1945;
CMW 4; DAM NOV, POET; DLB 10, 19,
34, 70, 98, 149, 178; EWL 3; FANT;
MSW; MTCW 1, 2; MTFW 2005; RGEL
2; RGSF 2; SATA 27; SUFW 1
Chettle, Henry 1560-1607(?) .... **LC 112**
See also DLB 136; RGEL 2
Chiang, Pin-chin 1904-1986
See Ding Ling
See also CA 118
Chief Joseph 1840-1904 .... **NNAL**
See also CA 152; DA3; DAM MULT
Chief Seattle 1786(?)-1866 .... **NNAL**
See also DA3; DAM MULT
Ch'ien, Chung-shu 1910-1998 .... **CLC 22**
See Qian Zhongshu
See also CA 130; CANR 73; MTCW 1, 2
Chikamatsu Monzaemon 1653-1724 ... **LC 66**
See also RGWL 2, 3
Child, Francis James 1825-1896 . **NCLC 173**
See also DLB 1, 64, 235
Child, L. Maria
See Child, Lydia Maria
Child, Lydia Maria 1802-1880 .. **NCLC 6, 73**
See also DLB 1, 74, 243; RGAL 4; SATA
67
Child, Mrs.
See Child, Lydia Maria
Child, Philip 1898-1978 .... **CLC 19, 68**
See also CA 13-14; CAP 1; CP 1; DLB 68;
RHW; SATA 47
Childers, (Robert) Erskine
1870-1922 .... **TCLC 65**
See also CA 113; 153; DLB 70

Childress, Alice 1920-1994 .... **BLC 1:1; CLC 12, 15, 86, 96; DC 4; TCLC 116**
See also AAYA 8; BW 2, 3; BYA 2; CA 45-48; 146; CAD; CANR 3, 27, 50, 74; CLR 14; CWD; DA3; DAM DRAM, MULT, NOV; DFS 2, 8, 14; DLB 7, 38, 249; JRDA; LAIT 5; MAICYA 1, 2; MAICYAS 1; MAL 5; MTCW 1, 2; MTFW 2005; RGAL 4; SATA 7, 48, 81; TUS; WYA; YAW

Chin, Frank (Chew, Jr.) 1940- .... **AAL; CLC 135; DC 7**
See also CA 33-36R; CAD; CANR 71; CD 5, 6; DAM MULT; DLB 206, 312; LAIT 5; RGAL 4

Chin, Marilyn (Mei Ling) 1955- .... **PC 40**
See also CA 129; CANR 70, 113; CWP; DLB 312; PFS 28

Chislett, (Margaret) Anne 1943- ...... **CLC 34**
See also CA 151

Chitty, Thomas Willes 1926- .... **CLC 11**
See Hinde, Thomas
See also CA 5-8R; CN 7

Chivers, Thomas Holley
1809-1858 .... **NCLC 49**
See also DLB 3, 248; RGAL 4

Choi, Susan 1969- .... **CLC 119**
See also CA 223

Chomette, Rene Lucien 1898-1981
See Clair, Rene
See also CA 103

Chomsky, Avram Noam
See Chomsky, Noam

Chomsky, Noam 1928- .... **CLC 132**
See also CA 17-20R; CANR 28, 62, 110, 132; DA3; DLB 246; MTCW 1, 2; MTFW 2005

Chona, Maria 1845(?)-1936 .... **NNAL**
See also CA 144

Chopin, Kate SSC 8, 68, 110; TCLC 127; WLCS
See Chopin, Katherine
See also AAYA 33; AMWR 2; AMWS 1; BYA 11, 15; CDALB 1865-1917; DA; DAB; DLB 12, 78; EXPN; EXPS; FL 1:3; FW; LAIT 3; MAL 5; MBL; NFS 3; RGAL 4; RGSF 2; SSFS 2, 13, 17; TUS

Chopin, Katherine 1851-1904
See Chopin, Kate
See also CA 104; 122; DA3; DAC; DAM MST, NOV

Chretien de Troyes c. 12th cent. - . **CMLC 10**
See also DLB 208; EW 1; RGWL 2, 3; TWA

Christie
See Ichikawa, Kon

Christie, Agatha (Mary Clarissa)
1890-1976 .. **CLC 1, 6, 8, 12, 39, 48, 110**
See also AAYA 9; AITN 1, 2; BPFB 1; BRWS 2; CA 17-20R; 61-64; CANR 10, 37, 108; CBD; CDBLB 1914-1945; CMW 4; CN 1, 2; CPW; CWD; DA3; DAB; DAC; DAM NOV; DFS 2; DLB 13, 77, 245; MSW; MTCW 1, 2; MTFW 2005; NFS 8; RGEL 2; RHW; SATA 36; TEA; YAW

Christie, Philippa CLC 21
See Pearce, Philippa
See also BYA 5; CANR 109; CLR 9; DLB 161; MAICYA 1; SATA 1, 67, 129

Christine de Pisan
See Christine de Pizan
See also FW

Christine de Pizan 1365(?)-1431(?) ...... **LC 9, 130; PC 68**
See Christine de Pisan; de Pizan, Christine
See also DLB 208; FL 1:1; RGWL 2, 3

Chuang-Tzu c. 369B.C.-c.
286B.C. .... **CMLC 57**

Chubb, Elmer
See Masters, Edgar Lee

Chulkov, Mikhail Dmitrievich
1743-1792 .... **LC 2**
See also DLB 150

Churchill, Caryl 1938- .... **CLC 31, 55, 157; DC 5**
See Churchill, Chick
See also BRWS 4; CA 102; CANR 22, 46, 108; CBD; CD 6; CWD; DFS 25; DLB 13, 310; EWL 3; FW; MTCW 1; RGEL 2

Churchill, Charles 1731-1764 .... **LC 3**
See also DLB 109; RGEL 2

Churchill, Chick
See Churchill, Caryl
See also CD 5

Churchill, Sir Winston (Leonard Spencer)
1874-1965 .... **TCLC 113**
See also BRW 6; CA 97-100; CDBLB 1890-1914; DA3; DLB 100, 329; DLBD 16; LAIT 4; MTCW 1, 2

Chute, Carolyn 1947- .... **CLC 39**
See also CA 123; CANR 135; CN 7

Ciardi, John (Anthony) 1916-1986 . **CLC 10, 40, 44, 129; PC 69**
See also CA 5-8R; 118; CAAS 2; CANR 5, 33; CLR 19; CP 1, 2, 3, 4; CWRI 5; DAM POET; DLB 5; DLBY 1986; INT CANR-5; MAICYA 1, 2; MAL 5; MTCW 1, 2; MTFW 2005; RGAL 4; SAAS 26; SATA 1, 65; SATA-Obit 46

Cibber, Colley 1671-1757 .... **LC 66**
See also DLB 84; RGEL 2

Cicero, Marcus Tullius
106B.C.-43B.C. .... **CMLC 3, 81**
See also AW 1; CDWLB 1; DLB 211; RGWL 2, 3; WLIT 8

Cimino, Michael 1943- .... **CLC 16**
See also CA 105

Cioran, E(mil) M. 1911-1995 .... **CLC 64**
See also CA 25-28R; 149; CANR 91; DLB 220; EWL 3

Cisneros, Sandra 1954- .... **CLC 69, 118, 193; HLC 1; PC 52; SSC 32, 72**
See also AAYA 9, 53; AMWS 7; CA 131; CANR 64, 118; CLR 123; CN 7; CWP; DA3; DAM MULT; DLB 122, 152; EWL 3; EXPN; FL 1:5; FW; HW 1, 2; LAIT 5; LATS 1:2; LLW; MAICYA 2; MAL 5; MTCW 2; MTFW 2005; NFS 2; PFS 19; RGAL 4; RGSF 2; SSFS 3, 13; WLIT 1; YAW

Cixous, Helene 1937- .... **CLC 92, 253**
See also CA 126; CANR 55, 123; CWW 2; DLB 83, 242; EWL 3; FL 1:5; FW; GLL 2; MTCW 1, 2; MTFW 2005; TWA

Clair, Rene CLC 20
See Chomette, Rene Lucien

Clampitt, Amy 1920-1994 .... **CLC 32; PC 19**
See also AMWS 9; CA 110; 146; CANR 29, 79; CP 4, 5; DLB 105; MAL 5; PFS 27

Clancy, Thomas L., Jr. 1947-
See Clancy, Tom
See also CA 125; 131; CANR 62, 105; DA3; INT CA-131; MTCW 1, 2; MTFW 2005

Clancy, Tom CLC 45, 112
See Clancy, Thomas L., Jr.
See also AAYA 9, 51; BEST 89:1, 90:1; BPFB 1; BYA 10, 11; CANR 132; CMW 4; CPW; DAM NOV, POP; DLB 227

Clare, John 1793-1864 .. **NCLC 9, 86; PC 23**
See also BRWS 11; DAB; DAM POET; DLB 55, 96; RGEL 2

Clarin
See Alas (y Urena), Leopoldo (Enrique Garcia)

Clark, Al C.
See Goines, Donald

Clark, Brian (Robert)
See Clark, (Robert) Brian
See also CD 6

Clark, (Robert) Brian 1932- .... **CLC 29**
See Clark, Brian (Robert)
See also CA 41-44R; CANR 67; CBD; CD 5

Clark, Curt
See Westlake, Donald E.

Clark, Eleanor 1913-1996 .... **CLC 5, 19**
See also CA 9-12R; 151; CANR 41; CN 1, 2, 3, 4, 5, 6; DLB 6

Clark, J. P.
See Clark Bekederemo, J.P.
See also CDWLB 3; DLB 117

Clark, John Pepper
See Clark Bekederemo, J.P.
See also AFW; CD 5; CP 1, 2, 3, 4, 5, 6, 7; RGEL 2

Clark, Kenneth (Mackenzie)
1903-1983 .... **TCLC 147**
See also CA 93-96; 109; CANR 36; MTCW 1, 2; MTFW 2005

Clark, M. R.
See Clark, Mavis Thorpe

Clark, Mavis Thorpe 1909-1999 ...... **CLC 12**
See also CA 57-60; CANR 8, 37, 107; CLR 30; CWRI 5; MAICYA 1, 2; SAAS 5; SATA 8, 74

Clark, Walter Van Tilburg
1909-1971 .... **CLC 28**
See also CA 9-12R; 33-36R; CANR 63, 113; CN 1; DLB 9, 206; LAIT 2; MAL 5; RGAL 4; SATA 8; TCWW 1, 2

Clark Bekederemo, J.P. 1935- .... **BLC 1:1; CLC 38; DC 5**
See Bekederemo, J. P. Clark; Clark, J. P.; Clark, John Pepper
See also BW 1; CA 65-68; CANR 16, 72; DAM DRAM, MULT; DFS 13; EWL 3; MTCW 2; MTFW 2005

Clarke, Arthur C. 1917-2008 .. **CLC 1, 4, 13, 18, 35, 136; SSC 3**
See also AAYA 4, 33; BPFB 1; BYA 13; CA 1-4R; CANR 2, 28, 55, 74, 130; CLR 119; CN 1, 2, 3, 4, 5, 6, 7; CPW; DA3; DAM POP; DLB 261; JRDA; LAIT 5; MAICYA 1, 2; MTCW 1, 2; MTFW 2005; SATA 13, 70, 115; SCFW 1, 2; SFW 4; SSFS 4, 18; TCLE 1:1; YAW

Clarke, Arthur Charles
See Clarke, Arthur C.

Clarke, Austin 1896-1974 .... **CLC 6, 9**
See also CA 29-32; 49-52; CAP 2; CP 1, 2; DAM POET; DLB 10, 20; EWL 3; RGEL 2

Clarke, Austin C. 1934- .... **BLC 1:1; CLC 8, 53; SSC 45**
See also BW 1; CA 25-28R; CAAS 16; CANR 14, 32, 68, 140; CN 1, 2, 3, 4, 5, 6, 7; DAC; DAM MULT; DLB 53, 125; DNFS 2; MTCW 2; MTFW 2005; RGSF 2

Clarke, Gillian 1937- .... **CLC 61**
See also CA 106; CP 3, 4, 5, 6, 7; CWP; DLB 40

Clarke, Marcus (Andrew Hislop)
1846-1881 .... **NCLC 19; SSC 94**
See also DLB 230; RGEL 2; RGSF 2

Clarke, Shirley 1925-1997 .... **CLC 16**
See also CA 189

Clash, The
See Headon, (Nicky) Topper; Jones, Mick; Simonon, Paul; Strummer, Joe

Colum, Padraic 1881-1972 .... **CLC 28**
See also BYA 4; CA 73-76; 33-36R; CANR 35; CLR 36; CP 1; CWRI 5; DLB 19; MAICYA 1, 2; MTCW 1; RGEL 2; SATA 15; WCH

Colvin, James
See Moorcock, Michael

Colwin, Laurie (E.) 1944-1992 .... **CLC 5, 13, 23, 84**
See also CA 89-92; 139; CANR 20, 46; DLB 218; DLBY 1980; MTCW 1

Comfort, Alex(ander) 1920-2000 .... **CLC 7**
See also CA 1-4R; 190; CANR 1, 45; CN 1, 2, 3, 4; CP 1, 2, 3, 4, 5, 6, 7; DAM POP; MTCW 2

Comfort, Montgomery
See Campbell, Ramsey

Compton-Burnett, I(vy) 1892(?)-1969 .... **CLC 1, 3, 10, 15, 34; TCLC 180**
See also BRW 7; CA 1-4R; 25-28R; CANR 4; DAM NOV; DLB 36; EWL 3; MTCW 1, 2; RGEL 2

Comstock, Anthony 1844-1915 ...... **TCLC 13**
See also CA 110; 169

Comte, Auguste 1798-1857 .... **NCLC 54**

Conan Doyle, Arthur
See Doyle, Sir Arthur Conan
See also BPFB 1; BYA 4, 5, 11

Conde (Abellan), Carmen 1901-1996 .... **HLCS 1**
See also CA 177; CWW 2; DLB 108; EWL 3; HW 1

Conde, Maryse 1937- .... **BLC 2:1; BLCS; CLC 52, 92, 247**
See also BW 2, 3; CA 110; 190; CAAE 190; CANR 30, 53, 76, 171; CWW 2; DAM MULT; EWL 3; MTCW 2; MTFW 2005

Condillac, Etienne Bonnot de 1714-1780 .... **LC 26**
See also DLB 313

Condon, Richard 1915-1996 ...... **CLC 4, 6, 8, 10, 45, 100**
See also BEST 90:3; BPFB 1; CA 1-4R; 151; CAAS 1; CANR 2, 23, 164; CMW 4; CN 1, 2, 3, 4, 5, 6; DAM NOV; INT CANR-23; MAL 5; MTCW 1, 2

Condon, Richard Thomas
See Condon, Richard

Condorcet LC 104
See Condorcet, marquis de Marie-Jean-Antoine-Nicolas Caritat
See also GFL Beginnings to 1789

Condorcet, marquis de Marie-Jean-Antoine-Nicolas Caritat 1743-1794
See Condorcet
See also DLB 313

Confucius 551B.C.-479B.C. .... **CMLC 19, 65; WLCS**
See also DA; DA3; DAB; DAC; DAM MST

Congreve, William 1670-1729 ... **DC 2; LC 5, 21; WLC 2**
See also BRW 2; CDBLB 1660-1789; DA; DAB; DAC; DAM DRAM, MST, POET; DFS 15; DLB 39, 84; RGEL 2; WLIT 3

Conley, Robert J(ackson) 1940- .... **NNAL**
See also CA 41-44R; CANR 15, 34, 45, 96; DAM MULT; TCWW 2

Connell, Evan S., Jr. 1924- .... **CLC 4, 6, 45**
See also AAYA 7; AMWS 14; CA 1-4R; CAAS 2; CANR 2, 39, 76, 97, 140; CN 1, 2, 3, 4, 5, 6; DAM NOV; DLB 2, 335; DLBY 1981; MAL 5; MTCW 1, 2; MTFW 2005

Connelly, Marc(us Cook) 1890-1980 . **CLC 7**
See also CA 85-88; 102; CAD; CANR 30; DFS 12; DLB 7; DLBY 1980; MAL 5; RGAL 4; SATA-Obit 25

Connolly, Paul
See Wicker, Tom

Connor, Ralph TCLC 31
See Gordon, Charles William
See also DLB 92; TCWW 1, 2

Conrad, Joseph 1857-1924 ..... **SSC 9, 67, 69, 71; TCLC 1, 6, 13, 25, 43, 57; WLC 2**
See also AAYA 26; BPFB 1; BRW 6; BRWC 1; BRWR 2; BYA 2; CA 104; 131; CANR 60; CDBLB 1890-1914; DA; DA3; DAB; DAC; DAM MST, NOV; DLB 10, 34, 98, 156; EWL 3; EXPN; EXPS; LAIT 2; LATS 1:1; LMFS 1; MTCW 1, 2; MTFW 2005; NFS 2, 16; RGEL 2; RGSF 2; SATA 27; SSFS 1, 12; TEA; WLIT 4

Conrad, Robert Arnold
See Hart, Moss

Conroy, Pat 1945- .... **CLC 30, 74**
See also AAYA 8, 52; AITN 1; BPFB 1; CA 85-88; CANR 24, 53, 129; CN 7; CPW; CSW; DA3; DAM NOV, POP; DLB 6; LAIT 5; MAL 5; MTCW 1, 2; MTFW 2005

Constant (de Rebecque), (Henri) Benjamin 1767-1830 .... **NCLC 6, 182**
See also DLB 119; EW 4; GFL 1789 to the Present

Conway, Jill K. 1934- .... **CLC 152**
See also CA 130; CANR 94

Conway, Jill Kathryn Ker
See Conway, Jill K.

Conybeare, Charles Augustus
See Eliot, T(homas) S(tearns)

Cook, Michael 1933-1994 .... **CLC 58**
See also CA 93-96; CANR 68; DLB 53

Cook, Robin 1940- .... **CLC 14**
See also AAYA 32; BEST 90:2; BPFB 1; CA 108; 111; CANR 41, 90, 109; CPW; DA3; DAM POP; HGG; INT CA-111

Cook, Roy
See Silverberg, Robert

Cooke, Elizabeth 1948- .... **CLC 55**
See also CA 129

Cooke, John Esten 1830-1886 .... **NCLC 5**
See also DLB 3, 248; RGAL 4

Cooke, John Estes
See Baum, L(yman) Frank

Cooke, M. E.
See Creasey, John

Cooke, Margaret
See Creasey, John

Cooke, Rose Terry 1827-1892 ...... **NCLC 110**
See also DLB 12, 74

Cook-Lynn, Elizabeth 1930- .... **CLC 93; NNAL**
See also CA 133; DAM MULT; DLB 175

Cooney, Ray CLC 62
See also CBD

Cooper, Anthony Ashley 1671-1713 .. **LC 107**
See also DLB 101, 336

Cooper, Dennis 1953- .... **CLC 203**
See also CA 133; CANR 72, 86; GLL 1; HGG

Cooper, Douglas 1960- .... **CLC 86**

Cooper, Henry St. John
See Creasey, John

Cooper, J. California (?)- .... **CLC 56**
See also AAYA 12; BW 1; CA 125; CANR 55; DAM MULT; DLB 212

Cooper, James Fenimore 1789-1851 .... **NCLC 1, 27, 54**
See also AAYA 22; AMW; BPFB 1; CDALB 1640-1865; CLR 105; DA3; DLB 3, 183, 250, 254; LAIT 1; NFS 25; RGAL 4; SATA 19; TUS; WCH

Cooper, Susan Fenimore 1813-1894 .... **NCLC 129**
See also ANW; DLB 239, 254

Coover, Robert 1932- .. **CLC 3, 7, 15, 32, 46, 87, 161; SSC 15, 101**
See also AMWS 5; BPFB 1; CA 45-48; CANR 3, 37, 58, 115; CN 1, 2, 3, 4, 5, 6, 7; DAM NOV; DLB 2, 227; DLBY 1981; EWL 3; MAL 5; MTCW 1, 2; MTFW 2005; RGAL 4; RGSF 2

Copeland, Stewart (Armstrong) 1952- .... **CLC 26**

Copernicus, Nicolaus 1473-1543 .... **LC 45**

Coppard, A(lfred) E(dgar) 1878-1957 .... **SSC 21; TCLC 5**
See also BRWS 8; CA 114; 167; DLB 162; EWL 3; HGG; RGEL 2; RGSF 2; SUFW 1; YABC 1

Coppee, Francois 1842-1908 .... **TCLC 25**
See also CA 170; DLB 217

Coppola, Francis Ford 1939- ... **CLC 16, 126**
See also AAYA 39; CA 77-80; CANR 40, 78; DLB 44

Copway, George 1818-1869 .... **NNAL**
See also DAM MULT; DLB 175, 183

Corbiere, Tristan 1845-1875 .... **NCLC 43**
See also DLB 217; GFL 1789 to the Present

Corcoran, Barbara (Asenath) 1911- .... **CLC 17**
See also AAYA 14; CA 21-24R; 191; CAAE 191; CAAS 2; CANR 11, 28, 48; CLR 50; DLB 52; JRDA; MAICYA 2; MAIC-YAS 1; RHW; SAAS 20; SATA 3, 77; SATA-Essay 125

Cordelier, Maurice
See Giraudoux, Jean(-Hippolyte)

Corelli, Marie TCLC 51
See Mackay, Mary
See also DLB 34, 156; RGEL 2; SUFW 1

Corinna c. 225B.C.-c. 305B.C. ...... **CMLC 72**

Corman, Cid CLC 9
See Corman, Sidney
See also CAAS 2; CP 1, 2, 3, 4, 5, 6, 7; DLB 5, 193

Corman, Sidney 1924-2004
See Corman, Cid
See also CA 85-88; 225; CANR 44; DAM POET

Cormier, Robert 1925-2000 .... **CLC 12, 30**
See also AAYA 3, 19; BYA 1, 2, 6, 8, 9; CA 1-4R; CANR 5, 23, 76, 93; CDALB 1968-1988; CLR 12, 55; DA; DAB; DAC; DAM MST, NOV; DLB 52; EXPN; INT CANR-23; JRDA; LAIT 5; MAICYA 1, 2; MTCW 1, 2; MTFW 2005; NFS 2, 18; SATA 10, 45, 83; SATA-Obit 122; WYA; YAW

Corn, Alfred (DeWitt III) 1943- .... **CLC 33**
See also CA 179; CAAE 179; CAAS 25; CANR 44; CP 3, 4, 5, 6, 7; CSW; DLB 120, 282; DLBY 1980

Corneille, Pierre 1606-1684 .. **DC 21; LC 28, 135**
See also DAB; DAM MST; DFS 21; DLB 268; EW 3; GFL Beginnings to 1789; RGWL 2, 3; TWA

Cornwell, David
See le Carre, John

Cornwell, David John Moore
See le Carre, John

Cornwell, Patricia 1956- .... **CLC 155**
See also AAYA 16, 56; BPFB 1; CA 134; CANR 53, 131; CMW 4; CPW; CSW; DAM POP; DLB 306; MSW; MTCW 2; MTFW 2005

Cornwell, Patricia Daniels
See Cornwell, Patricia

Corso, Gregory 1930-2001 .... **CLC 1, 11; PC 33**
See also AMWS 12; BG 1:2; CA 5-8R; 193; CANR 41, 76, 132; CP 1, 2, 3, 4, 5, 6, 7; DA3; DLB 5, 16, 237; LMFS 2; MAL 5; MTCW 1, 2; MTFW 2005; WP

Crommelynck, Fernand 1885-1970 .. **CLC 75**
  See also CA 189; 89-92; EWL 3
Cromwell, Oliver 1599-1658 .... **LC 43**
Cronenberg, David 1943- .... **CLC 143**
  See also CA 138; CCA 1
Cronin, A(rchibald) J(oseph)
  1896-1981 .... **CLC 32**
  See also BPFB 1; CA 1-4R; 102; CANR 5;
  CN 2; DLB 191; SATA 47; SATA-Obit 25
Cross, Amanda
  See Heilbrun, Carolyn G(old)
  See also BPFB 1; CMW; CPW; DLB 306;
  MSW
Crothers, Rachel 1878-1958 .... **TCLC 19**
  See also CA 113; 194; CAD; CWD; DLB
  7, 266; RGAL 4
Croves, Hal
  See Traven, B.
Crow Dog, Mary (?)- .... **CLC 93; NNAL**
  See also CA 154
Crowfield, Christopher
  See Stowe, Harriet (Elizabeth) Beecher
Crowley, Aleister TCLC 7
  See Crowley, Edward Alexander
  See also GLL 1
Crowley, Edward Alexander 1875-1947
  See Crowley, Aleister
  See also CA 104; HGG
Crowley, John 1942- .... **CLC 57**
  See also AAYA 57; BPFB 1; CA 61-64;
  CANR 43, 98, 138; DLBY 1982; FANT;
  MTFW 2005; SATA 65, 140; SFW 4;
  SUFW 2
Crowne, John 1641-1712 .... **LC 104**
  See also DLB 80; RGEL 2
Crud
  See Crumb, R.
Crumarums
  See Crumb, R.
Crumb, R. 1943- .... **CLC 17**
  See also CA 106; CANR 107, 150
Crumb, Robert
  See Crumb, R.
Crumbum
  See Crumb, R.
Crumski
  See Crumb, R.
Crum the Bum
  See Crumb, R.
Crunk
  See Crumb, R.
Crustt
  See Crumb, R.
Crutchfield, Les
  See Trumbo, Dalton
Cruz, Victor Hernandez 1949- ... **HLC 1; PC
  37**
  See also BW 2; CA 65-68; CAAS 17;
  CANR 14, 32, 74, 132; CP 1, 2, 3, 4, 5,
  6, 7; DAM MULT, POET; DLB 41; DNFS
  1; EXPP; HW 1, 2; LLW; MTCW 2;
  MTFW 2005; PFS 16; WP
Cryer, Gretchen (Kiger) 1935- .... **CLC 21**
  See also CA 114; 123
Csath, Geza TCLC 13
  See Brenner, Jozef
  See also CA 111
Cudlip, David R(ockwell) 1933- .... **CLC 34**
  See also CA 177
Cullen, Countee 1903-1946 ..... **BLC 1:1; HR
  1:2; PC 20; TCLC 4, 37; WLCS**
  See also AFAW 2; AMWS 4; BW 1; CA
  108; 124; CDALB 1917-1929; DA; DA3;
  DAC; DAM MST, MULT, POET; DLB 4,
  48, 51; EWL 3; EXPP; LMFS 2; MAL 5;
  MTCW 1, 2; MTFW 2005; PFS 3; RGAL
  4; SATA 18; WP
Culleton, Beatrice 1949- .... **NNAL**
  See also CA 120; CANR 83; DAC

Cum, R.
  See Crumb, R.
Cumberland, Richard
  1732-1811 .... **NCLC 167**
  See also DLB 89; RGEL 2
Cummings, Bruce F(rederick) 1889-1919
  See Barbellion, W. N. P.
  See also CA 123
Cummings, E(dward) E(stlin)
  1894-1962 .. **CLC 1, 3, 8, 12, 15, 68; PC
  5; TCLC 137; WLC 2**
  See also AAYA 41; AMW; CA 73-76;
  CANR 31; CDALB 1929-1941; DA;
  DA3; DAB; DAC; DAM MST, POET;
  DLB 4, 48; EWL 3; EXPP; MAL 5;
  MTCW 1, 2; MTFW 2005; PAB; PFS 1,
  3, 12, 13, 19; RGAL 4; TUS; WP
Cummins, Maria Susanna
  1827-1866 .... **NCLC 139**
  See also DLB 42; YABC 1
Cunha, Euclides (Rodrigues Pimenta) da
  1866-1909 .... **TCLC 24**
  See also CA 123; 219; DLB 307; LAW;
  WLIT 1
Cunningham, E. V.
  See Fast, Howard
Cunningham, J(ames) V(incent)
  1911-1985 .... **CLC 3, 31**
  See also CA 1-4R; 115; CANR 1, 72; CP 1,
  2, 3, 4; DLB 5
Cunningham, Julia (Woolfolk)
  1916- .... **CLC 12**
  See also CA 9-12R; CANR 4, 19, 36; CWRI
  5; JRDA; MAICYA 1, 2; SAAS 2; SATA
  1, 26, 132
Cunningham, Michael 1952- .... **CLC 34, 243**
  See also AMWS 15; CA 136; CANR 96,
  160; CN 7; DLB 292; GLL 2; MTFW
  2005; NFS 23
Cunninghame Graham, R. B.
  See Cunninghame Graham, Robert
  (Gallnigad) Bontine
**Cunninghame Graham, Robert (Gallnigad)
  Bontine** 1852-1936 .... **TCLC 19**
  See Graham, R(obert) B(ontine) Cunning-
  hame
  See also CA 119; 184
Curnow, (Thomas) Allen (Monro)
  1911-2001 .... **PC 48**
  See also CA 69-72; 202; CANR 48, 99; CP
  1, 2, 3, 4, 5, 6, 7; EWL 3; RGEL 2
Currie, Ellen 19(?)- .... **CLC 44**
Curtin, Philip
  See Lowndes, Marie Adelaide (Belloc)
Curtin, Phillip
  See Lowndes, Marie Adelaide (Belloc)
Curtis, Price
  See Ellison, Harlan
Cusanus, Nicolaus 1401-1464 .... **LC 80**
  See Nicholas of Cusa
Cutrate, Joe
  See Spiegelman, Art
Cynewulf c. 770- .... **CMLC 23**
  See also DLB 146; RGEL 2
Cyrano de Bergerac, Savinien de
  1619-1655 .... **LC 65**
  See also DLB 268; GFL Beginnings to
  1789; RGWL 2, 3
Cyril of Alexandria c. 375-c. 430 . **CMLC 59**
Czaczkes, Shmuel Yosef Halevi
  See Agnon, S(hmuel) Y(osef Halevi)
Dabrowska, Maria (Szumska)
  1889-1965 .... **CLC 15**
  See also CA 106; CDWLB 4; DLB 215;
  EWL 3
Dabydeen, David 1955- .... **CLC 34**
  See also BW 1; CA 125; CANR 56, 92; CN
  6, 7; CP 5, 6, 7

Dacey, Philip 1939- .... **CLC 51**
  See also CA 37-40R, 231; CAAE 231;
  CAAS 17; CANR 14, 32, 64; CP 4, 5, 6,
  7; DLB 105
Dacre, Charlotte c. 1772-1825(?) . **NCLC 151**
Dafydd ap Gwilym c. 1320-c. 1380 ..... **PC 56**
Dagerman, Stig (Halvard)
  1923-1954 .... **TCLC 17**
  See also CA 117; 155; DLB 259; EWL 3
D'Aguiar, Fred 1960- ..... **BLC 2:1; CLC 145**
  See also CA 148; CANR 83, 101; CN 7;
  CP 5, 6, 7; DLB 157; EWL 3
Dahl, Roald 1916-1990 ...... **CLC 1, 6, 18, 79;
  TCLC 173**
  See also AAYA 15; BPFB 1; BRWS 4; BYA
  5; CA 1-4R; 133; CANR 6, 32, 37, 62;
  CLR 1, 7, 41, 111; CN 1, 2, 3, 4; CPW;
  DA3; DAB; DAC; DAM MST, NOV,
  POP; DLB 139, 255; HGG; JRDA; MAI-
  CYA 1, 2; MTCW 1, 2; MTFW 2005;
  RGSF 2; SATA 1, 26, 73; SATA-Obit 65;
  SSFS 4; TEA; YAW
Dahlberg, Edward 1900-1977 .. **CLC 1, 7, 14**
  See also CA 9-12R; 69-72; CANR 31, 62;
  CN 1, 2; DLB 48; MAL 5; MTCW 1;
  RGAL 4
Daitch, Susan 1954- .... **CLC 103**
  See also CA 161
Dale, Colin TCLC 18
  See Lawrence, T(homas) E(dward)
Dale, George E.
  See Asimov, Isaac
d'Alembert, Jean Le Rond
  1717-1783 .... **LC 126**
Dalton, Roque 1935-1975(?) ..... **HLCS 1; PC
  36**
  See also CA 176; DLB 283; HW 2
Daly, Elizabeth 1878-1967 .... **CLC 52**
  See also CA 23-24; 25-28R; CANR 60;
  CAP 2; CMW 4
Daly, Mary 1928- .... **CLC 173**
  See also CA 25-28R; CANR 30, 62, 166;
  FW; GLL 1; MTCW 1
Daly, Maureen 1921-2006 .... **CLC 17**
  See also AAYA 5, 58; BYA 6; CA 253;
  CANR 37, 83, 108; CLR 96; JRDA; MAI-
  CYA 1, 2; SAAS 1; SATA 2, 129; SATA-
  Obit 176; WYA; YAW
Damas, Leon-Gontran 1912-1978 ... **CLC 84;
  TCLC 204**
  See also BW 1; CA 125; 73-76; EWL 3
Dana, Richard Henry Sr.
  1787-1879 .... **NCLC 53**
Dangarembga, Tsitsi 1959- .... **BLC 2:1**
  See also BW 3; CA 163; WLIT 2
Daniel, Samuel 1562(?)-1619 .... **LC 24**
  See also DLB 62; RGEL 2
Daniels, Brett
  See Adler, Renata
Dannay, Frederic 1905-1982 .... **CLC 11**
  See Queen, Ellery
  See also CA 1-4R; 107; CANR 1, 39; CMW
  4; DAM POP; DLB 137; MTCW 1
D'Annunzio, Gabriele 1863-1938 ... **TCLC 6,
  40**
  See also CA 104; 155; EW 8; EWL 3;
  RGWL 2, 3; TWA; WLIT 7
Danois, N. le
  See Gourmont, Remy(-Marie-Charles) de
Dante 1265-1321 .... **CMLC 3, 18, 39, 70; PC
  21; WLCS**
  See Alighieri, Dante
  See also DA; DA3; DAB; DAC; DAM
  MST, POET; EFS 1; EW 1; LAIT 1;
  RGWL 2, 3; TWA; WP
d'Antibes, Germain
  See Simenon, Georges (Jacques Christian)

Desai, Anita 1937- .... **CLC 19, 37, 97, 175**
See also BRWS 5; CA 81-84; CANR 33, 53, 95, 133; CN 1, 2, 3, 4, 5, 6, 7; CWRI 5; DA3; DAB; DAM NOV; DLB 271, 323; DNFS 2; EWL 3; FW; MTCW 1, 2; MTFW 2005; SATA 63, 126

Desai, Kiran 1971- .... **CLC 119**
See also BYA 16; CA 171; CANR 127

de Saint-Luc, Jean
See Glassco, John

de Saint Roman, Arnaud
See Aragon, Louis

Desbordes-Valmore, Marceline
1786-1859 .... **NCLC 97**
See also DLB 217

Descartes, Rene 1596-1650 .... **LC 20, 35, 150**
See also DLB 268; EW 3; GFL Beginnings to 1789

Deschamps, Eustache 1340(?)-1404 .. **LC 103**
See also DLB 208

De Sica, Vittorio 1901(?)-1974 .... **CLC 20**
See also CA 117

Desnos, Robert 1900-1945 .... **TCLC 22**
See also CA 121; 151; CANR 107; DLB 258; EWL 3; LMFS 2

Destouches, Louis-Ferdinand
1894-1961 .... **CLC 9, 15**
See Celine, Louis-Ferdinand
See also CA 85-88; CANR 28; MTCW 1

de Tolignac, Gaston
See Griffith, D(avid Lewelyn) W(ark)

Deutsch, Babette 1895-1982 .... **CLC 18**
See also BYA 3; CA 1-4R; 108; CANR 4, 79; CP 1, 2, 3; DLB 45; SATA 1; SATA-Obit 33

Devenant, William 1606-1649 .... **LC 13**

Devkota, Laxmiprasad 1909-1959 . **TCLC 23**
See also CA 123

De Voto, Bernard (Augustine)
1897-1955 .... **TCLC 29**
See also CA 113; 160; DLB 9, 256; MAL 5; TCWW 1, 2

De Vries, Peter 1910-1993 ..... **CLC 1, 2, 3, 7, 10, 28, 46**
See also CA 17-20R; 142; CANR 41; CN 1, 2, 3, 4, 5; DAM NOV; DLB 6; DLBY 1982; MAL 5; MTCW 1, 2; MTFW 2005

Dewey, John 1859-1952 .... **TCLC 95**
See also CA 114; 170; CANR 144; DLB 246, 270; RGAL 4

Dexter, John
See Bradley, Marion Zimmer
See also GLL 1

Dexter, Martin
See Faust, Frederick (Schiller)

Dexter, Pete 1943- .... **CLC 34, 55**
See also BEST 89:2; CA 127; 131; CANR 129; CPW; DAM POP; INT CA-131; MAL 5; MTCW 1; MTFW 2005

Diamano, Silmang
See Senghor, Leopold Sedar

Diamant, Anita 1951- .... **CLC 239**
See also CA 145; CANR 126

Diamond, Neil 1941- .... **CLC 30**
See also CA 108

Diaz del Castillo, Bernal c.
1496-1584 .... **HLCS 1; LC 31**
See also DLB 318; LAW

di Bassetto, Corno
See Shaw, George Bernard

Dick, Philip K. 1928-1982 ... **CLC 10, 30, 72; SSC 57**
See also AAYA 24; BPFB 1; BYA 11; CA 49-52; 106; CANR 2, 16, 132; CN 2, 3; CPW; DA3; DAM NOV, POP; DLB 8; MTCW 1, 2, MTFW 2005; NFS 5, 26; SCFW 1, 2; SFW 4

Dick, Philip Kindred
See Dick, Philip K.

Dickens, Charles (John Huffam)
1812-1870 .... **NCLC 3, 8, 18, 26, 37, 50, 86, 105, 113, 161, 187; SSC 17, 49, 88; WLC 2**
See also AAYA 23; BRW 5; BRWC 1, 2; BYA 1, 2, 3, 13, 14; CDBLB 1832-1890; CLR 95; CMW 4; DA; DA3; DAB; DAC; DAM MST, NOV; DLB 21, 55, 70, 159, 166; EXPN; GL 2; HGG; JRDA; LAIT 1, 2; LATS 1:1; LMFS 1; MAICYA 1, 2; NFS 4, 5, 10, 14, 20, 25; RGEL 2; RGSF 2; SATA 15; SUFW 1; TEA; WCH; WLIT 4; WYA

Dickey, James (Lafayette)
1923-1997 .... **CLC 1, 2, 4, 7, 10, 15, 47, 109; PC 40; TCLC 151**
See also AAYA 50; AITN 1, 2; AMWS 4; BPFB 1; CA 9-12R; 156; CABS 2; CANR 10, 48, 61, 105; CDALB 1968-1988; CP 1, 2, 3, 4, 5, 6; CPW; CSW; DA3; DAM NOV, POET, POP; DLB 5, 193; DLBD 7; DLBY 1982, 1993, 1996, 1997, 1998; EWL 3; INT CANR-10; MAL 5; MTCW 1, 2; NFS 9; PFS 6, 11; RGAL 4; TUS

Dickey, William 1928-1994 .... **CLC 3, 28**
See also CA 9-12R; 145; CANR 24, 79; CP 1, 2, 3, 4; DLB 5

Dickinson, Charles 1951- .... **CLC 49**
See also CA 128; CANR 141

Dickinson, Emily (Elizabeth)
1830-1886 ..... **NCLC 21, 77, 171; PC 1; WLC 2**
See also AAYA 22; AMW; AMWR 1; CDALB 1865-1917; DA; DA3; DAB; DAC; DAM MST, POET; DLB 1, 243; EXPP; FL 1:3; MBL; PAB; PFS 1, 2, 3, 4, 5, 6, 8, 10, 11, 13, 16, 28; RGAL 4; SATA 29; TUS; WP; WYA

Dickinson, Mrs. Herbert Ward
See Phelps, Elizabeth Stuart

Dickinson, Peter (Malcolm de Brissac)
1927- .... **CLC 12, 35**
See also AAYA 9, 49; BYA 5; CA 41-44R; CANR 31, 58, 88, 134; CLR 29, 125; CMW 4; DLB 87, 161, 276; JRDA; MAICYA 1, 2; SATA 5, 62, 95, 150; SFW 4; WYA; YAW

Dickson, Carr
See Carr, John Dickson

Dickson, Carter
See Carr, John Dickson

Diderot, Denis 1713-1784 .... **LC 26, 126**
See also DLB 313; EW 4; GFL Beginnings to 1789; LMFS 1; RGWL 2, 3

Didion, Joan 1934- . **CLC 1, 3, 8, 14, 32, 129**
See also AITN 1; AMWS 4; CA 5-8R; CANR 14, 52, 76, 125, 174; CDALB 1968-1988; CN 2, 3, 4, 5, 6, 7; DA3; DAM NOV; DLB 2, 173, 185; DLBY 1981, 1986; EWL 3; MAL 5; MBL; MTCW 1, 2; MTFW 2005; NFS 3; RGAL 4; TCLE 1:1; TCWW 2; TUS

di Donato, Pietro 1911-1992 .... **TCLC 159**
See also CA 101; 136; DLB 9

Dietrich, Robert
See Hunt, E. Howard

Difusa, Pati
See Almodovar, Pedro

Dillard, Annie 1945- ...... **CLC 9, 60, 115, 216**
See also AAYA 6, 43; AMWS 6; ANW; CA 49-52; CANR 3, 43, 62, 90, 125; DA3; DAM NOV; DLB 275, 278; DLBY 1980; LAIT 4, 5; MAL 5; MTCW 1, 2; MTFW 2005; NCFS 1; RGAL 4; SATA 10, 140; TCLE 1:1; TUS

Dillard, R(ichard) H(enry) W(ilde)
1937- .... **CLC 5**
See also CA 21-24R; CAAS 7; CANR 10; CP 2, 3, 4, 5, 6, 7; CSW; DLB 5, 244

Dillon, Eilis 1920-1994 .... **CLC 17**
See also CA 9-12R, 182; 147; CAAE 182; CAAS 3; CANR 4, 38, 78; CLR 26; MAICYA 1, 2; MAICYAS 1; SATA 2, 74; SATA-Essay 105; SATA-Obit 83; YAW

Dimont, Penelope
See Mortimer, Penelope (Ruth)

Dinesen, Isak CLC 10, 29, 95; SSC 7, 75
See Blixen, Karen (Christentze Dinesen)
See also EW 10; EWL 3; EXPS; FW; GL 2; HGG; LAIT 3; MTCW 1; NCFS 2; NFS 9; RGSF 2; RGWL 2, 3; SSFS 3, 6, 13; WLIT 2

Ding Ling CLC 68
See Chiang, Pin-chin
See also DLB 328; RGWL 3

Diodorus Siculus c. 90B.C.-c.
31B.C. .... **CMLC 88**

Diphusa, Patty
See Almodovar, Pedro

Disch, Thomas M. 1940- .... **CLC 7, 36**
See Disch, Tom
See also AAYA 17; BPFB 1; CA 21-24R; CAAS 4; CANR 17, 36, 54, 89; CLR 18; CP 5, 6, 7; DA3; DLB 8; HGG; MAICYA 1, 2; MTCW 1, 2; MTFW 2005; SAAS 15; SATA 92; SCFW 1, 2; SFW 4; SUFW 2

Disch, Tom
See Disch, Thomas M.
See also DLB 282

d'Isly, Georges
See Simenon, Georges (Jacques Christian)

Disraeli, Benjamin 1804-1881 ... **NCLC 2, 39, 79**
See also BRW 4; DLB 21, 55; RGEL 2

Ditcum, Steve
See Crumb, R.

Dixon, Paige
See Corcoran, Barbara (Asenath)

Dixon, Stephen 1936- .... **CLC 52; SSC 16**
See also AMWS 12; CA 89-92; CANR 17, 40, 54, 91, 175; CN 4, 5, 6, 7; DLB 130; MAL 5

Dixon, Thomas, Jr. 1864-1946 ..... **TCLC 163**
See also RHW

Djebar, Assia 1936- .... **BLC 2:1; CLC 182**
See also CA 188; CANR 169; EWL 3; RGWL 3; WLIT 2

Doak, Annie
See Dillard, Annie

Dobell, Sydney Thompson
1824-1874 .... **NCLC 43**
See also DLB 32; RGEL 2

Doblin, Alfred TCLC 13
See Doeblin, Alfred
See also CDWLB 2; EWL 3; RGWL 2, 3

Dobroliubov, Nikolai Aleksandrovich
See Dobrolyubov, Nikolai Alexandrovich
See also DLB 277

Dobrolyubov, Nikolai Alexandrovich
1836-1861 .... **NCLC 5**
See Dobroliubov, Nikolai Aleksandrovich

Dobson, Austin 1840-1921 .... **TCLC 79**
See also DLB 35, 144

Dobyns, Stephen 1941- .... **CLC 37, 233**
See also AMWS 13; CA 45-48; CANR 2, 18, 99; CMW 4; CP 4, 5, 6, 7; PFS 23

Doctorow, Edgar Laurence
See Doctorow, E.L.

Doctorow, E.L. 1931- . **CLC 6, 11, 15, 18, 37, 44, 65, 113, 214**
See also AAYA 22; AITN 2; AMWS 4; BEST 89:3; BPFB 1; CA 45-48; CANR 2, 33, 51, 76, 97, 133, 170; CDALB 1968-1988; CN 3, 4, 5, 6, 7; CPW; DA3; DAM NOV, POP; DLB 2, 28, 173; DLBY 1980;

EWL 3; LAIT 3; MAL 5; MTCW 1, 2;
MTFW 2005; NFS 6; RGAL 4; RGHL;
RHW; TCLE 1:1; TCWW 1, 2; TUS

Dodgson, Charles L(utwidge) 1832-1898
See Carroll, Lewis
See also CLR 2; DA; DA3; DAB; DAC;
DAM MST, NOV, POET; MAICYA 1, 2;
SATA 100; YABC 2

Dodsley, Robert 1703-1764 .... **LC 97**
See also DLB 95; RGEL 2

Dodson, Owen (Vincent)
1914-1983 .... **BLC 1:1; CLC 79**
See also BW 1; CA 65-68; 110; CANR 24;
DAM MULT; DLB 76

Doeblin, Alfred 1878-1957 .... **TCLC 13**
See Doblin, Alfred
See also CA 110; 141; DLB 66

Doerr, Harriet 1910-2002 .... **CLC 34**
See also CA 117; 122; 213; CANR 47; INT
CA-122; LATS 1:2

Domecq, H(onorio) Bustos
See Bioy Casares, Adolfo; Borges, Jorge
Luis

Domini, Rey
See Lorde, Audre
See also GLL 1

Dominique
See Proust, (Valentin-Louis-George-Eugene)
Marcel

Don, A
See Stephen, Sir Leslie

Donaldson, Stephen R. 1947- ... **CLC 46, 138**
See also AAYA 36; BPFB 1; CA 89-92;
CANR 13, 55, 99; CPW; DAM POP;
FANT; INT CANR-13; SATA 121; SFW
4; SUFW 1, 2

Donleavy, J(ames) P(atrick) 1926- .... **CLC 1,
4, 6, 10, 45**
See also AITN 2; BPFB 1; CA 9-12R;
CANR 24, 49, 62, 80, 124; CBD; CD 5,
6; CN 1, 2, 3, 4, 5, 6, 7; DLB 6, 173; INT
CANR-24; MAL 5; MTCW 1, 2; MTFW
2005; RGAL 4

Donnadieu, Marguerite
See Duras, Marguerite

Donne, John 1572-1631 ... **LC 10, 24, 91; PC
1, 43; WLC 2**
See also BRW 67; BRW 1; BRWC 1;
BRWR 2; CDBLB Before 1660; DA;
DAB; DAC; DAM MST, POET; DLB
121, 151; EXPP; PAB; PFS 2, 11; RGEL
3; TEA; WLIT 3; WP

Donnell, David 1939(?)- .... **CLC 34**
See also CA 197

Donoghue, Denis 1928- .... **CLC 209**
See also CA 17-20R; CANR 16, 102

Donoghue, Emma 1969- .... **CLC 239**
See also CA 155; CANR 103, 152; DLB
267; GLL 1; SATA 101

Donoghue, P.S.
See Hunt, E. Howard

Donoso (Yanez), Jose 1924-1996 ... **CLC 4, 8,
11, 32, 99; HLC 1; SSC 34; TCLC 133**
See also CA 81-84; 155; CANR 32, 73; CD-
WLB 3; CWW 2; DAM MULT; DLB 113;
EWL 3; HW 1, 2; LAW; LAWS 1; MTCW
1, 2; MTFW 2005; RGSF 2; WLIT 1

Donovan, John 1928-1992 .... **CLC 35**
See also AAYA 20; CA 97-100; 137; CLR
3; MAICYA 1, 2; SATA 72; SATA-Brief
29; YAW

Don Roberto
See Cunninghame Graham, Robert
(Gallnigad) Bontine

Doolittle, Hilda 1886-1961 . **CLC 3, 8, 14, 31,
34, 73; PC 5; WLC 3**
See H. D.
See also AAYA 66; AMWS 1; CA 97-100;
CANR 35, 131; DA; DAC; DAM MST,

POET; DLB 4, 45; EWL 3; FW; GLL 1;
LMFS 2; MAL 5; MBL; MTCW 1, 2;
MTFW 2005; PFS 6, 28; RGAL 4

Doppo, Kunikida **TCLC 99**
See Kunikida Doppo

Dorfman, Ariel 1942- .... **CLC 48, 77, 189;
HLC 1**
See also CA 124; 130; CANR 67, 70, 135;
CWW 2; DAM MULT; DFS 4; EWL 3;
HW 1, 2; INT CA-130; WLIT 1

Dorn, Edward (Merton)
1929-1999 .... **CLC 10, 18**
See also CA 93-96; 187; CANR 42, 79; CP
1, 2, 3, 4, 5, 6, 7; DLB 5; INT CA-93-96;
WP

Dor-Ner, Zvi **CLC 70**

Dorris, Michael 1945-1997 .... **CLC 109;
NNAL**
See also AAYA 20; BEST 90:1; BYA 12;
CA 102; 157; CANR 19, 46, 75; CLR 58;
DA3; DAM MULT, NOV; DLB 175;
LAIT 5; MTCW 2; MTFW 2005; NFS 3;
RGAL 4; SATA 75; SATA-Obit 94;
TCWW 2; YAW

Dorris, Michael A.
See Dorris, Michael

Dorsan, Luc
See Simenon, Georges (Jacques Christian)

Dorsange, Jean
See Simenon, Georges (Jacques Christian)

Dorset
See Sackville, Thomas

Dos Passos, John (Roderigo)
1896-1970 ... **CLC 1, 4, 8, 11, 15, 25, 34,
82; WLC 2**
See also AMW; BPFB 1; CA 1-4R; 29-32R;
CANR 3; CDALB 1929-1941; DA; DA3;
DAB; DAC; DAM MST, NOV; DLB 4,
9, 274, 316; DLBD 1, 15; DLBY 1996;
EWL 3; MAL 5; MTCW 1, 2; MTFW
2005; NFS 14; RGAL 4; TUS

Dossage, Jean
See Simenon, Georges (Jacques Christian)

Dostoevsky, Fedor Mikhailovich
1821-1881 .. **NCLC 2, 7, 21, 33, 43, 119,
167; SSC 2, 33, 44; WLC 2**
See Dostoevsky, Fyodor
See also AAYA 40; DA; DA3; DAB; DAC;
DAM MST, NOV; EW 7; EXPN; NFS 3,
8; RGSF 2; RGWL 2, 3; SSFS 8; TWA

Dostoevsky, Fyodor
See Dostoevsky, Fedor Mikhailovich
See also DLB 238; LATS 1:1; LMFS 1, 2

Doty, Mark 1953(?)- .... **CLC 176; PC 53**
See also AMWS 11; CA 161, 183; CAAE
183; CANR 110, 173; CP 7; PFS 28

Doty, Mark A.
See Doty, Mark

Doty, Mark Alan
See Doty, Mark

Doty, M.R.
See Doty, Mark

Doughty, Charles M(ontagu)
1843-1926 .... **TCLC 27**
See also CA 115; 178; DLB 19, 57, 174

Douglas, Ellen **CLC 73**
See Haxton, Josephine Ayres; Williamson,
Ellen Douglas
See also CN 5, 6, 7; CSW; DLB 292

Douglas, Gavin 1475(?)-1522 .... **LC 20**
See also DLB 132; RGEL 2

Douglas, George
See Brown, George Douglas
See also RGEL 2

Douglas, Keith (Castellain)
1920-1944 .... **TCLC 40**
See also BRW 7; CA 160; DLB 27; EWL
3; PAB; RGEL 2

Douglas, Leonard
See Bradbury, Ray

Douglas, Michael
See Crichton, Michael

Douglas, (George) Norman
1868-1952 .... **TCLC 68**
See also BRW 6; CA 119; 157; DLB 34,
195; RGEL 2

Douglas, William
See Brown, George Douglas

Douglass, Frederick 1817(?)-1895 .. **BLC 1:1;
NCLC 7, 55, 141; WLC 2**
See also AAYA 48; AFAW 1, 2; AMWC 1;
AMWS 3; CDALB 1640-1865; DA; DA3;
DAC; DAM MST, MULT; DLB 1, 43, 50,
79, 243; FW; LAIT 2; NCFS 2; RGAL 4;
SATA 29

Dourado, (Waldomiro Freitas) Autran
1926- .... **CLC 23, 60**
See also CA 25-28R, 179; CANR 34, 81;
DLB 145, 307; HW 2

Dourado, Waldomiro Freitas Autran
See Dourado, (Waldomiro Freitas) Autran

Dove, Rita 1952- . **BLC 2:1; BLCS; CLC 50,
81; PC 6**
See also AAYA 46; AMWS 4; BW 2; CA
109; CAAS 19; CANR 27, 42, 68, 76, 97,
132; CDALBS; CP 5, 6, 7; CSW; CWP;
DA3; DAM MULT, POET; DLB 120;
EWL 3; EXPP; MAL 5; MTCW 2; MTFW
2005; PFS 1, 15; RGAL 4

Dove, Rita Frances
See Dove, Rita

Doveglion
See Villa, Jose Garcia

Dowell, Coleman 1925-1985 .... **CLC 60**
See also CA 25-28R; 117; CANR 10; DLB
130; GLL 2

Downing, Major Jack
See Smith, Seba

Dowson, Ernest (Christopher)
1867-1900 .... **TCLC 4**
See also CA 105; 150; DLB 19, 135; RGEL
2

Doyle, A. Conan
See Doyle, Sir Arthur Conan

Doyle, Sir Arthur Conan
1859-1930 ..... **SSC 12, 83, 95; TCLC 7;
WLC 2**
See Conan Doyle, Arthur
See also AAYA 14; BRWS 2; CA 104; 122;
CANR 131; CDBLB 1890-1914; CLR
106; CMW 4; DA; DA3; DAB; DAC;
DAM MST, NOV; DLB 18, 70, 156, 178;
EXPS; HGG; LAIT 2; MSW; MTCW 1,
2; MTFW 2005; RGEL 2; RGSF 2; RHW;
SATA 24; SCFW 1, 2; SFW 4; SSFS 2;
TEA; WCH; WLIT 4; WYA; YAW

Doyle, Conan
See Doyle, Sir Arthur Conan

Doyle, John
See Graves, Robert

Doyle, Roddy 1958- .... **CLC 81, 178**
See also AAYA 14; BRWS 5; CA 143;
CANR 73, 128, 168; CN 6, 7; DA3; DLB
194, 326; MTCW 2; MTFW 2005

Doyle, Sir A. Conan
See Doyle, Sir Arthur Conan

Dr. A
See Asimov, Isaac; Silverstein, Alvin; Silverstein, Virginia B(arbara Opshelor)

Drabble, Margaret 1939- ...... **CLC 2, 3, 5, 8,
10, 22, 53, 129**
See also BRWS 4; CA 13-16R; CANR 18,
35, 63, 112, 131, 174; CDBLB 1960 to
Present; CN 1, 2, 3, 4, 5, 6, 7; CPW; DA3;
DAB; DAC; DAM MST, NOV, POP;
DLB 14, 155, 231; EWL 3; FW; MTCW
1, 2; MTFW 2005; RGEL 2; SATA 48;
TEA

Endo, Shusaku 1923-1996 ..... **CLC 7, 14, 19, 54, 99; SSC 48; TCLC 152**
See Endo Shusaku
See also CA 29-32R; 153; CANR 21, 54, 131; DA3; DAM NOV; MTCW 1, 2; MTFW 2005; RGSF 2; RGWL 2, 3
Endo Shusaku
See Endo, Shusaku
See also CWW 2; DLB 182; EWL 3
Engel, Marian 1933-1985 .... **CLC 36; TCLC 137**
See also CA 25-28R; CANR 12; CN 2, 3; DLB 53; FW; INT CANR-12
Engelhardt, Frederick
See Hubbard, L. Ron
Engels, Friedrich 1820-1895 .. **NCLC 85, 114**
See also DLB 129; LATS 1:1
Enquist, Per Olov 1934- .... **CLC 257**
See also CA 109; 193; CANR 155; CWW 2; DLB 257; EWL 3
Enright, D(ennis) J(oseph) 1920-2002 .... **CLC 4, 8, 31**
See also CA 1-4R; 211; CANR 1, 42, 83; CN 1, 2; CP 1, 2, 3, 4, 5, 6, 7; DLB 27; EWL 3; SATA 25; SATA-Obit 140
Ensler, Eve 1953- .... **CLC 212**
See also CA 172; CANR 126, 163; DFS 23
Enzensberger, Hans Magnus 1929- .... **CLC 43; PC 28**
See also CA 116; 119; CANR 103; CWW 2; EWL 3
Ephron, Nora 1941- .... **CLC 17, 31**
See also AAYA 35; AITN 2; CA 65-68; CANR 12, 39, 83, 161; DFS 22
Epicurus 341B.C.-270B.C. .... **CMLC 21**
See also DLB 176
Epinay, Louise d' 1726-1783 .... **LC 138**
See also DLB 313
Epsilon
See Betjeman, John
Epstein, Daniel Mark 1948- .... **CLC 7**
See also CA 49-52; CANR 2, 53, 90
Epstein, Jacob 1956- .... **CLC 19**
See also CA 114
Epstein, Jean 1897-1953 .... **TCLC 92**
Epstein, Joseph 1937- .... **CLC 39, 204**
See also AMWS 14; CA 112; 119; CANR 50, 65, 117, 164
Epstein, Leslie 1938- .... **CLC 27**
See also AMWS 12; CA 73-76, 215; CAAE 215; CAAS 12; CANR 23, 69, 162; DLB 299; RGHL
Equiano, Olaudah 1745(?)-1797 ..... **BLC 1:2; LC 16, 143**
See also AFAW 1, 2; CDWLB 3; DAM MULT; DLB 37, 50; WLIT 2
Erasmus, Desiderius 1469(?)-1536 ..... **LC 16, 93**
See also DLB 136; EW 2; LMFS 1; RGWL 2, 3; TWA
Erdman, Paul E. 1932-2007 .... **CLC 25**
See also AITN 1; CA 61-64; 259; CANR 13, 43, 84
Erdman, Paul Emil
See Erdman, Paul E.
Erdrich, Karen Louise
See Erdrich, Louise
Erdrich, Louise 1954- .... **CLC 39, 54, 120, 176; NNAL; PC 52**
See also AAYA 10, 47; AMWS 4; BEST 89:1; BPFB 1; CA 114; CANR 41, 62, 118, 138; CDALBS; CN 5, 6, 7; CP 6, 7; CPW; CWP; DA3; DAM MULT, NOV, POP; DLB 152, 175, 206; EWL 3; EXPP; FL 1:5; LAIT 5; LATS 1:2; MAL 5; MTCW 1, 2; MTFW 2005; NFS 5; PFS 14; RGAL 4; SATA 94, 141; SSFS 14, 22; TCWW 2

Erenburg, Ilya (Grigoryevich)
See Ehrenburg, Ilya (Grigoryevich)
Erickson, Stephen Michael
See Erickson, Steve
Erickson, Steve 1950- .... **CLC 64**
See also CA 129; CANR 60, 68, 136; MTFW 2005; SFW 4; SUFW 2
Erickson, Walter
See Fast, Howard
Ericson, Walter
See Fast, Howard
Eriksson, Buntel
See Bergman, Ingmar
Eriugena, John Scottus c. 810-877 .... **CMLC 65**
See also DLB 115
Ernaux, Annie 1940- .... **CLC 88, 184**
See also CA 147; CANR 93; MTFW 2005; NCFS 3, 5
Erskine, John 1879-1951 .... **TCLC 84**
See also CA 112; 159; DLB 9, 102; FANT
Erwin, Will
See Eisner, Will
Eschenbach, Wolfram von
See von Eschenbach, Wolfram
See also RGWL 3
Eseki, Bruno
See Mphahlele, Ezekiel
Esenin, S.A.
See Esenin, Sergei
See also EWL 3
Esenin, Sergei 1895-1925 .... **TCLC 4**
See Esenin, S.A.
See also CA 104; RGWL 2, 3
Esenin, Sergei Aleksandrovich
See Esenin, Sergei
Eshleman, Clayton 1935- .... **CLC 7**
See also CA 33-36R, 212; CAAE 212; CAAS 6; CANR 93; CP 1, 2, 3, 4, 5, 6, 7; DLB 5
Espada, Martin 1957- .... **PC 74**
See also CA 159; CANR 80; CP 7; EXPP; LLW; MAL 5; PFS 13, 16
Espriella, Don Manuel Alvarez
See Southey, Robert
Espriu, Salvador 1913-1985 .... **CLC 9**
See also CA 154; 115; DLB 134; EWL 3
Espronceda, Jose de 1808-1842 ..... **NCLC 39**
Esquivel, Laura 1950(?)- ... **CLC 141; HLCS 1**
See also AAYA 29; CA 143; CANR 68, 113, 161; DA3; DNFS 2; LAIT 3; LMFS 2; MTCW 2; MTFW 2005; NFS 5; WLIT 1
Esse, James
See Stephens, James
Esterbrook, Tom
See Hubbard, L. Ron
Esterhazy, Peter 1950- .... **CLC 251**
See also CA 140; CANR 137; CDWLB 4; CWW 2; DLB 232; EWL 3; RGWL 3
Estleman, Loren D. 1952- .... **CLC 48**
See also AAYA 27; CA 85-88; CANR 27, 74, 139; CMW 4; CPW; DA3; DAM NOV, POP; DLB 226; INT CANR-27; MTCW 1, 2; MTFW 2005; TCWW 1, 2
Etherege, Sir George 1636-1692 . **DC 23; LC 78**
See also BRW 2; DAM DRAM; DLB 80; PAB; RGEL 2
Euclid 306B.C.-283B.C. .... **CMLC 25**
Eugenides, Jeffrey 1960(?)- .... **CLC 81, 212**
See also AAYA 51; CA 144; CANR 120; MTFW 2005; NFS 24
Euripides c. 484B.C.-406B.C. .... **CMLC 23, 51; DC 4; WLCS**
See also AW 1; CDWLB 1; DA; DA3; DAB; DAC; DAM DRAM, MST; DFS 1, 4, 6, 25; DLB 176; LAIT 1; LMFS 1; RGWL 2, 3; WLIT 8

Evan, Evin
See Faust, Frederick (Schiller)
Evans, Caradoc 1878-1945 ... **SSC 43; TCLC 85**
See also DLB 162
Evans, Evan
See Faust, Frederick (Schiller)
Evans, Marian
See Eliot, George
Evans, Mary Ann
See Eliot, George
See also NFS 20
Evarts, Esther
See Benson, Sally
Evelyn, John 1620-1706 .... **LC 144**
See also BRW 2; RGEL 2
Everett, Percival
See Everett, Percival L.
See also CSW
Everett, Percival L. 1956- .... **CLC 57**
See Everett, Percival
See also BW 2; CA 129; CANR 94, 134; CN 7; MTFW 2005
Everson, R(onald) G(ilmour) 1903-1992 .... **CLC 27**
See also CA 17-20R; CP 1, 2, 3, 4; DLB 88
Everson, William (Oliver) 1912-1994 .... **CLC 1, 5, 14**
See Antoninus, Brother
See also BG 1:2; CA 9-12R; 145; CANR 20; CP 2, 3, 4, 5; DLB 5, 16, 212; MTCW 1
Evtushenko, Evgenii Aleksandrovich
See Yevtushenko, Yevgeny (Alexandrovich)
See also CWW 2; RGWL 2, 3
Ewart, Gavin (Buchanan) 1916-1995 .... **CLC 13, 46**
See also BRWS 7; CA 89-92; 150; CANR 17, 46; CP 1, 2, 3, 4, 5, 6; DLB 40; MTCW 1
Ewers, Hanns Heinz 1871-1943 ..... **TCLC 12**
See also CA 109; 149
Ewing, Frederick R.
See Sturgeon, Theodore (Hamilton)
Exley, Frederick (Earl) 1929-1992 .... **CLC 6, 11**
See also AITN 2; BPFB 1; CA 81-84; 138; CANR 117; DLB 143; DLBY 1981
Eynhardt, Guillermo
See Quiroga, Horacio (Sylvestre)
Ezekiel, Nissim (Moses) 1924-2004 .. **CLC 61**
See also CA 61-64; 223; CP 1, 2, 3, 4, 5, 6, 7; DLB 323; EWL 3
Ezekiel, Tish O'Dowd 1943- .... **CLC 34**
See also CA 129
Fadeev, Aleksandr Aleksandrovich
See Bulgya, Alexander Alexandrovich
See also DLB 272
Fadeev, Alexandr Alexandrovich
See Bulgya, Alexander Alexandrovich
See also EWL 3
Fadeyev, A.
See Bulgya, Alexander Alexandrovich
Fadeyev, Alexander TCLC 53
See Bulgya, Alexander Alexandrovich
Fagen, Donald 1948- .... **CLC 26**
Fainzil'berg, Il'ia Arnol'dovich
See Fainzilberg, Ilya Arnoldovich
Fainzilberg, Ilya Arnoldovich 1897-1937 .... **TCLC 21**
See Il'f, Il'ia
See also CA 120; 165; EWL 3
Fair, Ronald L. 1932- .... **CLC 18**
See also BW 1; CA 69-72; CANR 25; DLB 33
Fairbairn, Roger
See Carr, John Dickson

Fairbairns, Zoe (Ann) 1948- .... **CLC 32**
See also CA 103; CANR 21, 85; CN 4, 5, 6, 7
Fairfield, Flora
See Alcott, Louisa May
Fairman, Paul W. 1916-1977
See Queen, Ellery
See also CA 114; SFW 4
Falco, Gian
See Papini, Giovanni
Falconer, James
See Kirkup, James
Falconer, Kenneth
See Kornbluth, C(yril) M.
Falkland, Samuel
See Heijermans, Herman
Fallaci, Oriana 1930-2006 .... **CLC 11, 110**
See also CA 77-80; 253; CANR 15, 58, 134; FW; MTCW 1
Faludi, Susan 1959- .... **CLC 140**
See also CA 138; CANR 126; FW; MTCW 2; MTFW 2005; NCFS 3
Faludy, George 1913- .... **CLC 42**
See also CA 21-24R
Faludy, Gyoergy
See Faludy, George
Fanon, Frantz 1925-1961 ...... **BLC 1:2; CLC 74; TCLC 188**
See also BW 1; CA 116; 89-92; DAM MULT; DLB 296; LMFS 2; WLIT 2
Fanshawe, Ann 1625-1680 .... **LC 11**
Fante, John (Thomas) 1911-1983 .... **CLC 60; SSC 65**
See also AMWS 11; CA 69-72; 109; CANR 23, 104; DLB 130; DLBY 1983
Far, Sui Sin SSC 62
See Eaton, Edith Maude
See also SSFS 4
Farah, Nuruddin 1945- .. **BLC 1:2, 2:2; CLC 53, 137**
See also AFW; BW 2, 3; CA 106; CANR 81, 148; CDWLB 3; CN 4, 5, 6, 7; DAM MULT; DLB 125; EWL 3; WLIT 2
Fargue, Leon-Paul 1876(?)-1947 .... **TCLC 11**
See also CA 109; CANR 107; DLB 258; EWL 3
Farigoule, Louis
See Romains, Jules
Farina, Richard 1936(?)-1966 .... **CLC 9**
See also CA 81-84; 25-28R
Farley, Walter (Lorimer) 1915-1989 .... **CLC 17**
See also AAYA 58; BYA 14; CA 17-20R; CANR 8, 29, 84; DLB 22; JRDA; MAICYA 1, 2; SATA 2, 43, 132; YAW
Farmer, Philip Jose 1918- .... **CLC 1, 19**
See also AAYA 28; BPFB 1; CA 1-4R; CANR 4, 35, 111; DLB 8; MTCW 1; SATA 93; SCFW 1, 2; SFW 4
Farquhar, George 1677-1707 .... **LC 21**
See also BRW 2; DAM DRAM; DLB 84; RGEL 2
Farrell, J(ames) G(ordon) 1935-1979 .... **CLC 6**
See also CA 73-76; 89-92; CANR 36; CN 1, 2; DLB 14, 271, 326; MTCW 1; RGEL 2; RHW; WLIT 4
Farrell, James T(homas) 1904-1979 . **CLC 1, 4, 8, 11, 66; SSC 28**
See also AMW; BPFB 1; CA 5-8R; 89-92; CANR 9, 61; CN 1, 2; DLB 4, 9, 86; DLBD 2; EWL 3; MAL 5; MTCW 1, 2; MTFW 2005; RGAL 4
Farrell, Warren (Thomas) 1943- ...... **CLC 70**
See also CA 146; CANR 120
Farren, Richard J.
See Betjeman, John
Farren, Richard M.
See Betjeman, John

Fassbinder, Rainer Werner 1946-1982 .... **CLC 20**
See also CA 93-96; 106; CANR 31
Fast, Howard 1914-2003 .... **CLC 23, 131**
See also AAYA 16; BPFB 1; CA 1-4R, 181; 214; CAAE 181; CAAS 18; CANR 1, 33, 54, 75, 98, 140; CMW 4; CN 1, 2, 3, 4, 5, 6, 7; CPW; DAM NOV; DLB 9; INT CANR-33; LATS 1:1; MAL 5; MTCW 2; MTFW 2005; RHW; SATA 7; SATA-Essay 107; TCWW 1, 2; YAW
Faulcon, Robert
See Holdstock, Robert
Faulkner, William (Cuthbert) 1897-1962 .... **CLC 1, 3, 6, 8, 9, 11, 14, 18, 28, 52, 68; SSC 1, 35, 42, 92, 97; TCLC 141; WLC 2**
See also AAYA 7; AMW; AMWR 1; BPFB 1; BYA 5, 15; CA 81-84; CANR 33; CDALB 1929-1941; DA; DA3; DAB; DAC; DAM MST, NOV; DLB 9, 11, 44, 102, 316, 330; DLBD 2; DLBY 1986, 1997; EWL 3; EXPN; EXPS; GL 2; LAIT 2; LATS 1:1; LMFS 2; MAL 5; MTCW 1, 2; MTFW 2005; NFS 4, 8, 13, 24; RGAL 4; RGSF 2; SSFS 2, 5, 6, 12; TUS
Fauset, Jessie Redmon 1882(?)-1961 ...... **BLC 1:2; CLC 19, 54; HR 1:2**
See also AFAW 2; BW 1; CA 109; CANR 83; DAM MULT; DLB 51; FW; LMFS 2; MAL 5; MBL
Faust, Frederick (Schiller) 1892-1944 .... **TCLC 49**
See also Brand, Max; Dawson, Peter; Frederick, John
See also CA 108; 152; CANR 143; DAM POP; DLB 256; TUS
Faust, Irvin 1924- .... **CLC 8**
See also CA 33-36R; CANR 28, 67; CN 1, 2, 3, 4, 5, 6, 7; DLB 2, 28, 218, 278; DLBY 1980
Fawkes, Guy
See Benchley, Robert (Charles)
Fearing, Kenneth (Flexner) 1902-1961 .... **CLC 51**
See also CA 93-96; CANR 59; CMW 4; DLB 9; MAL 5; RGAL 4
Fecamps, Elise
See Creasey, John
Federman, Raymond 1928- .... **CLC 6, 47**
See also CA 17-20R, 208; CAAE 208; CAAS 8; CANR 10, 43, 83, 108; CN 3, 4, 5, 6; DLBY 1980
Federspiel, J.F. 1931-2007 .... **CLC 42**
See also CA 146; 257
Federspiel, Juerg F.
See Federspiel, J.F.
Federspiel, Jurg F.
See Federspiel, J.F.
Feiffer, Jules 1929- .... **CLC 2, 8, 64**
See also AAYA 3, 62; CA 17-20R; CAD; CANR 30, 59, 129, 161; CD 5, 6; DAM DRAM; DLB 7, 44; INT CANR-30; MTCW 1; SATA 8, 61, 111, 157
Feiffer, Jules Ralph
See Feiffer, Jules
Feige, Hermann Albert Otto Maximilian
See Traven, B.
Feinberg, David B. 1956-1994 .... **CLC 59**
See also CA 135; 147
Feinstein, Elaine 1930- .... **CLC 36**
See also CA 69-72; CAAS 1; CANR 31, 68, 121, 162; CN 3, 4, 5, 6, 7; CP 2, 3, 4, 5, 6, 7; CWP; DLB 14, 40; MTCW 1
Feke, Gilbert David CLC 65
Feldman, Irving (Mordecai) 1928- ..... **CLC 7**
See also CA 1-4R; CANR 1; CP 1, 2, 3, 4, 5, 6, 7; DLB 169; TCLE 1:1

Felix-Tchicaya, Gerald
See Tchicaya, Gerald Felix
Fellini, Federico 1920-1993 .... **CLC 16, 85**
See also CA 65-68; 143; CANR 33
Felltham, Owen 1602(?)-1668 .... **LC 92**
See also DLB 126, 151
Felsen, Henry Gregor 1916-1995 ..... **CLC 17**
See also CA 1-4R; 180; CANR 1; SAAS 2; SATA 1
Felski, Rita CLC 65
Fenelon, Francois de Pons de Salignac de la Mothe- 1651-1715 .... **LC 134**
See also DLB 268; EW 3; GFL Beginnings to 1789
Fenno, Jack
See Calisher, Hortense
Fenollosa, Ernest (Francisco) 1853-1908 .... **TCLC 91**
Fenton, James 1949- .... **CLC 32, 209**
See also CA 102; CANR 108, 160; CP 2, 3, 4, 5, 6, 7; DLB 40; PFS 11
Fenton, James Martin
See Fenton, James
Ferber, Edna 1887-1968 .... **CLC 18, 93**
See also AITN 1; CA 5-8R; 25-28R; CANR 68, 105; DLB 9, 28, 86, 266; MAL 5; MTCW 1, 2; MTFW 2005; RGAL 4; RHW; SATA 7; TCWW 1, 2
Ferdowsi, Abu'l Qasem 940-1020(?) .... **CMLC 43**
See Firdawsi, Abu al-Qasim
See also RGWL 2, 3
Ferguson, Helen
See Kavan, Anna
Ferguson, Niall 1964- .... **CLC 134, 250**
See also CA 190; CANR 154
Ferguson, Niall Campbell
See Ferguson, Niall
Ferguson, Samuel 1810-1886 .... **NCLC 33**
See also DLB 32; RGEL 2
Fergusson, Robert 1750-1774 .... **LC 29**
See also DLB 109; RGEL 2
Ferling, Lawrence
See Ferlinghetti, Lawrence
Ferlinghetti, Lawrence 1919(?)- .... **CLC 2, 6, 10, 27, 111; PC 1**
See also AAYA 74; BG 1:2; CA 5-8R; CAD; CANR 3, 41, 73, 125, 172; CDALB 1941-1968; CP 1, 2, 3, 4, 5, 6, 7; DA3; DAM POET; DLB 5, 16; MAL 5; MTCW 1, 2; MTFW 2005; PFS 28; RGAL 4; WP
Ferlinghetti, Lawrence Monsanto
See Ferlinghetti, Lawrence
Fern, Fanny
See Parton, Sara Payson Willis
Fernandez, Vicente Garcia Huidobro
See Huidobro Fernandez, Vicente Garcia
Fernandez-Armesto, Felipe CLC 70
See Fernandez-Armesto, Felipe Fermin Ricardo
See also CANR 153
Fernandez-Armesto, Felipe Fermin Ricardo 1950-
See Fernandez-Armesto, Felipe
See also CA 142; CANR 93
Fernandez de Lizardi, Jose Joaquin
See Lizardi, Jose Joaquin Fernandez de
Ferre, Rosario 1938- ...... **CLC 139; HLCS 1; SSC 36, 106**
See also CA 131; CANR 55, 81, 134; CWW 2; DLB 145; EWL 3; HW 1, 2; LAWS 1; MTCW 2; MTFW 2005; WLIT 1
Ferrer, Gabriel (Francisco Victor) Miro
See Miro (Ferrer), Gabriel (Francisco Victor)
Ferrier, Susan (Edmonstone) 1782-1854 .... **NCLC 8**
See also DLB 116; RGEL 2

Ferrigno, Robert 1948(?)- .... **CLC 65**
See also CA 140; CANR 125, 161

Ferron, Jacques 1921-1985 .... **CLC 94**
See also CA 117; 129; CCA 1; DAC; DLB
60; EWL 3

Feuchtwanger, Lion 1884-1958 .... **TCLC 3**
See also CA 104; 187; DLB 66; EWL 3;
RGHL

Feuerbach, Ludwig 1804-1872 ..... **NCLC 139**
See also DLB 133

Feuillet, Octave 1821-1890 .... **NCLC 45**
See also DLB 192

Feydeau, Georges (Leon Jules Marie)
1862-1921 .... **TCLC 22**
See also CA 113; 152; CANR 84; DAM
DRAM; DLB 192; EWL 3; GFL 1789 to
the Present; RGWL 2, 3

Fichte, Johann Gottlieb
1762-1814 .... **NCLC 62**
See also DLB 90

Ficino, Marsilio 1433-1499 .... **LC 12**
See also LMFS 1

Fiedeler, Hans
See Doeblin, Alfred

Fiedler, Leslie A(aron) 1917-2003 ..... **CLC 4,
13, 24**
See also AMWS 13; CA 9-12R; 212; CANR
7, 63; CN 1, 2, 3, 4, 5, 6; DLB 28, 67;
EWL 3; MAL 5; MTCW 1, 2; RGAL 4;
TUS

Field, Andrew 1938- .... **CLC 44**
See also CA 97-100; CANR 25

Field, Eugene 1850-1895 .... **NCLC 3**
See also DLB 23, 42, 140; DLBD 13; MAI-
CYA 1, 2; RGAL 4; SATA 16

Field, Gans T.
See Wellman, Manly Wade

Field, Michael 1915-1971 .... **TCLC 43**
See also CA 29-32R

Fielding, Helen 1958- .... **CLC 146, 217**
See also AAYA 65; CA 172; CANR 127;
DLB 231; MTFW 2005

Fielding, Henry 1707-1754 .... **LC 1, 46, 85,
151; WLC 2**
See also BRW 3; BRWR 1; CDBLB 1660-
1789; DA; DA3; DAB; DAC; DAM
DRAM, MST, NOV; DLB 39, 84, 101;
NFS 18; RGEL 2; TEA; WLIT 3

Fielding, Sarah 1710-1768 .... **LC 1, 44**
See also DLB 39; RGEL 2; TEA

Fields, W. C. 1880-1946 .... **TCLC 80**
See also DLB 44

Fierstein, Harvey (Forbes) 1954- ..... **CLC 33**
See also CA 123; 129; CAD; CD 5, 6;
CPW; DA3; DAM DRAM, POP; DFS 6;
DLB 266; GLL; MAL 5

Figes, Eva 1932- .... **CLC 31**
See also CA 53-56; CANR 4, 44, 83; CN 2,
3, 4, 5, 6, 7; DLB 14, 271; FW; RGHL

Filippo, Eduardo de
See de Filippo, Eduardo

Finch, Anne 1661-1720 ..... **LC 3, 137; PC 21**
See also BRWS 9; DLB 95

Finch, Robert (Duer Claydon)
1900-1995 .... **CLC 18**
See also CA 57-60; CANR 9, 24, 49; CP 1,
2, 3, 4, 5, 6; DLB 88

Findley, Timothy (Irving Frederick)
1930-2002 .... **CLC 27, 102**
See also CA 25-28R; 206; CANR 12, 42,
69, 109; CCA 1; CN 4, 5, 6, 7; DAC;
DAM MST; DLB 53; FANT; RHW

Fink, William
See Mencken, H(enry) L(ouis)

Firbank, Louis 1942-
See Reed, Lou
See also CA 117

Firbank, (Arthur Annesley) Ronald
1886-1926 .... **TCLC 1**
See also BRWS 2; CA 104; 177; DLB 36;
EWL 3; RGEL 2

Firdawsi, Abu'l-Qasim
See Ferdowsi, Abu'l Qasem
See also WLIT 6

Fish, Stanley
See Fish, Stanley Eugene

Fish, Stanley E.
See Fish, Stanley Eugene

Fish, Stanley Eugene 1938- .... **CLC 142**
See also CA 112; 132; CANR 90; DLB 67

Fisher, Dorothy (Frances) Canfield
1879-1958 .... **TCLC 87**
See also CA 114; 136; CANR 80; CLR 71;
CWRI 5; DLB 9, 102, 284; MAICYA 1,
2; MAL 5; YABC 1

Fisher, M(ary) F(rances) K(ennedy)
1908-1992 .... **CLC 76, 87**
See also AMWS 17; CA 77-80; 138; CANR
44; MTCW 2

Fisher, Roy 1930- .... **CLC 25**
See also CA 81-84; CAAS 10; CANR 16;
CP 1, 2, 3, 4, 5, 6, 7; DLB 40

Fisher, Rudolph 1897-1934 ...... **BLC 1:2; HR
1:2; SSC 25; TCLC 11**
See also BW 1, 3; CA 107; 124; CANR 80;
DAM MULT; DLB 51, 102

Fisher, Vardis (Alvero) 1895-1968 .... **CLC 7;
TCLC 140**
See also CA 5-8R; 25-28R; CANR 68; DLB
9, 206; MAL 5; RGAL 4; TCWW 1, 2

Fiske, Tarleton
See Bloch, Robert (Albert)

Fitch, Clarke
See Sinclair, Upton

Fitch, John IV
See Cormier, Robert

Fitzgerald, Captain Hugh
See Baum, L(yman) Frank

FitzGerald, Edward 1809-1883 ...... **NCLC 9,
153; PC 79**
See also BRW 4; DLB 32; RGEL 2

Fitzgerald, F(rancis) Scott (Key)
1896-1940 ... **SSC 6, 31, 75; TCLC 1, 6,
14, 28, 55, 157; WLC 2**
See also AAYA 24; AITN 1; AMW; AMWC
2; AMWR 1; BPFB 1; CA 110; 123;
CDALB 1917-1929; DA; DA3; DAB;
DAC; DAM MST, NOV; DLB 4, 9, 86,
219, 273; DLBD 1, 15, 16; DLBY 1981,
1996; EWL 3; EXPN; EXPS; LAIT 3;
MAL 5; MTCW 1, 2; MTFW 2005; NFS
2, 19, 20; RGAL 4; RGSF 2; SSFS 4, 15,
21, 25; TUS

Fitzgerald, Penelope 1916-2000 . **CLC 19, 51,
61, 143**
See also BRWS 5; CA 85-88; 190; CAAS
10; CANR 56, 86, 131; CN 3, 4, 5, 6, 7;
DLB 14, 194, 326; EWL 3; MTCW 2;
MTFW 2005

Fitzgerald, Robert (Stuart)
1910-1985 .... **CLC 39**
See also CA 1-4R; 114; CANR 1; CP 1, 2,
3, 4; DLBY 1980; MAL 5

FitzGerald, Robert D(avid)
1902-1987 .... **CLC 19**
See also CA 17-20R; CP 1, 2, 3, 4; DLB
260; RGEL 2

Fitzgerald, Zelda (Sayre)
1900-1948 .... **TCLC 52**
See also AMWS 9; CA 117; 126; DLBY
1984

Flanagan, Thomas (James Bonner)
1923-2002 .... **CLC 25, 52**
See also CA 108; 206; CANR 55; CN 3, 4,
5, 6, 7; DLBY 1980; INT CA-108; MTCW
1; RHW; TCLE 1:1

Flaubert, Gustave 1821-1880 .... **NCLC 2, 10,
19, 62, 66, 135, 179, 185; SSC 11, 60;
WLC 2**
See also DA; DA3; DAB; DAC; DAM
MST, NOV; DLB 119, 301; EW 7; EXPS;
GFL 1789 to the Present; LAIT 2; LMFS
1; NFS 14; RGSF 2; RGWL 2, 3; SSFS
6; TWA

Flavius Josephus
See Josephus, Flavius

Flecker, Herman Elroy
See Flecker, (Herman) James Elroy

Flecker, (Herman) James Elroy
1884-1915 .... **TCLC 43**
See also CA 109; 150; DLB 10, 19; RGEL
2

Fleming, Ian 1908-1964 ... **CLC 3, 30; TCLC
193**
See also AAYA 26; BPFB 1; CA 5-8R;
CANR 59; CDBLB 1945-1960; CMW 4;
CPW; DA3; DAM POP; DLB 87, 201;
MSW; MTCW 1, 2; MTFW 2005; RGEL
2; SATA 9; TEA; YAW

Fleming, Ian Lancaster
See Fleming, Ian

Fleming, Thomas 1927- .... **CLC 37**
See also CA 5-8R; CANR 10, 102, 155;
INT CANR-10; SATA 8

Fleming, Thomas James
See Fleming, Thomas

Fletcher, John 1579-1625 . **DC 6; LC 33, 151**
See also BRW 2; CDBLB Before 1660;
DLB 58; RGEL 2; TEA

Fletcher, John Gould 1886-1950 .... **TCLC 35**
See also CA 107; 167; DLB 4, 45; LMFS
2; MAL 5; RGAL 4

Fleur, Paul
See Pohl, Frederik

Flieg, Helmut
See Heym, Stefan

Flooglebuckle, Al
See Spiegelman, Art

Flora, Fletcher 1914-1969
See Queen, Ellery
See also CA 1-4R; CANR 3, 85

Flying Officer X
See Bates, H(erbert) E(rnest)

Fo, Dario 1926- .... **CLC 32, 109, 227; DC 10**
See also CA 116; 128; CANR 68, 114, 134,
164; CWW 2; DA3; DAM DRAM; DFS
23; DLB 330; DLBY 1997; EWL 3;
MTCW 1, 2; MTFW 2005; WLIT 7

Foden, Giles 1967- .... **CLC 231**
See also CA 240; DLB 267; NFS 15

Fogarty, Jonathan Titulescu Esq.
See Farrell, James T(homas)

Follett, Ken 1949- .... **CLC 18**
See also AAYA 6, 50; BEST 89:4; BPFB 1;
CA 81-84; CANR 13, 33, 54, 102, 156;
CMW 4; CPW; DA3; DAM NOV, POP;
DLB 87; DLBY 1981; INT CANR-33;
MTCW 1

Follett, Kenneth Martin
See Follett, Ken

Fondane, Benjamin 1898-1944 ..... **TCLC 159**

Fontane, Theodor 1819-1898 . **NCLC 26, 163**
See also CDWLB 2; DLB 129; EW 6;
RGWL 2, 3; TWA

Fonte, Moderata 1555-1592 .... **LC 118**

Fontenelle, Bernard Le Bovier de
1657-1757 .... **LC 140**
See also DLB 268, 313; GFL Beginnings to
1789

Fontenot, Chester CLC 65

Fonvizin, Denis Ivanovich
1744(?)-1792 .... **LC 81**
See also DLB 150; RGWL 2, 3

Foote, Horton 1916- .... **CLC 51, 91**
See also CA 73-76; CAD; CANR 34, 51,
110; CD 5, 6; CSW; DA3; DAM DRAM;
DFS 20; DLB 26, 266; EWL 3; INT
CANR-34; MTFW 2005

Foote, Mary Hallock 1847-1938 .. **TCLC 108**
See also DLB 186, 188, 202, 221; TCWW
2

Foote, Samuel 1721-1777 .... **LC 106**
See also DLB 89; RGEL 2

Foote, Shelby 1916-2005 .... **CLC 75, 224**
See also AAYA 40; CA 5-8R; 240; CANR
3, 45, 74, 131; CN 1, 2, 3, 4, 5, 6, 7;
CPW; CSW; DA3; DAM NOV, POP;
DLB 2, 17; MAL 5; MTCW 2; MTFW
2005; RHW

Forbes, Cosmo
See Lewton, Val

Forbes, Esther 1891-1967 .... **CLC 12**
See also AAYA 17; BYA 2; CA 13-14; 25-
28R; CAP 1; CLR 27; DLB 22; JRDA;
MAICYA 1, 2; RHW; SATA 2, 100; YAW

Forche, Carolyn 1950- .. **CLC 25, 83, 86; PC
10**
See also CA 109; 117; CANR 50, 74, 138;
CP 4, 5, 6, 7; CWP; DA3; DAM POET;
DLB 5, 193; INT CA-117; MAL 5;
MTCW 2; MTFW 2005; PFS 18; RGAL
4

Forche, Carolyn Louise
See Forche, Carolyn

Ford, Elbur
See Hibbert, Eleanor Alice Burford

Ford, Ford Madox 1873-1939 ... **TCLC 1, 15,
39, 57, 172**
See Chaucer, Daniel
See also BRW 6; CA 104; 132; CANR 74;
CDBLB 1914-1945; DA3; DAM NOV;
DLB 34, 98, 162; EWL 3; MTCW 1, 2;
RGEL 2; TEA

Ford, Henry 1863-1947 .... **TCLC 73**
See also CA 115; 148

Ford, Jack
See Ford, John

Ford, John 1586-1639 .... **DC 8; LC 68**
See also BRW 2; CDBLB Before 1660;
DA3; DAM DRAM; DFS 7; DLB 58;
IDTP; RGEL 2

Ford, John 1895-1973 .... **CLC 16**
See also AAYA 75; CA 187; 45-48

Ford, Richard 1944- .... **CLC 46, 99, 205**
See also AMWS 5; CA 69-72; CANR 11,
47, 86, 128, 164; CN 5, 6, 7; CSW; DLB
227; EWL 3; MAL 5; MTCW 2; MTFW
2005; NFS 25; RGAL 4; RGSF 2

Ford, Webster
See Masters, Edgar Lee

Foreman, Richard 1937- .... **CLC 50**
See also CA 65-68; CAD; CANR 32, 63,
143; CD 5, 6

Forester, C(ecil) S(cott) 1899-1966 . **CLC 35;
TCLC 152**
See also CA 73-76; 25-28R; CANR 83;
DLB 191; RGEL 2; RHW; SATA 13

Forez
See Mauriac, Francois (Charles)

Forman, James
See Forman, James D.

Forman, James D. 1932- .... **CLC 21**
See also AAYA 17; CA 9-12R; CANR 4,
19, 42; JRDA; MAICYA 1, 2; SATA 8,
70; YAW

Forman, James Douglas
See Forman, James D.

Forman, Milos 1932- .... **CLC 164**
See also AAYA 63; CA 109

Fornes, Maria Irene 1930- .... **CLC 39, 61,
187; DC 10; HLCS 1**
See also CA 25-28R; CAD; CANR 28, 81;
CD 5, 6; CWD; DFS 25; DLB 7, 341; HW
1, 2; INT CANR-28; LLW; MAL 5;
MTCW 1; RGAL 4

Forrest, Leon (Richard)
1937-1997 .... **BLCS; CLC 4**
See also AFAW 2; BW 2; CA 89-92; 162;
CAAS 7; CANR 25, 52, 87; CN 4, 5, 6;
DLB 33

Forster, E(dward) M(organ)
1879-1970 ...... **CLC 1, 2, 3, 4, 9, 10, 13,
15, 22, 45, 77; SSC 27, 96; TCLC 125;
WLC 2**
See also AAYA 2, 37; BRW 6; BRWR 2;
BYA 12; CA 13-14; 25-28R; CANR 45;
CAP 1; CDBLB 1914-1945; DA; DA3;
DAB; DAC; DAM MST, NOV; DLB 34,
98, 162, 178, 195; DLBD 10; EWL 3;
EXPN; LAIT 3; LMFS 1; MTCW 1, 2;
MTFW 2005; NCFS 1; NFS 3, 10, 11;
RGEL 2; RGSF 2; SATA 57; SUFW 1;
TEA; WLIT 4

Forster, John 1812-1876 .... **NCLC 11**
See also DLB 144, 184

Forster, Margaret 1938- .... **CLC 149**
See also CA 133; CANR 62, 115, 175; CN
4, 5, 6, 7; DLB 155, 271

Forsyth, Frederick 1938- .... **CLC 2, 5, 36**
See also BEST 89:4; CA 85-88; CANR 38,
62, 115, 137; CMW 4; CN 3, 4, 5, 6, 7;
CPW; DAM NOV, POP; DLB 87; MTCW
1, 2; MTFW 2005

Forten, Charlotte L. 1837-1914 ..... **BLC 1:2;
TCLC 16**
See Grimke, Charlotte L(ottie) Forten
See also DLB 50, 239

Fortinbras
See Grieg, (Johan) Nordahl (Brun)

Foscolo, Ugo 1778-1827 .... **NCLC 8, 97**
See also EW 5; WLIT 7

Fosse, Bob 1927-1987
See Fosse, Robert L.
See also CA 110; 123

Fosse, Robert L. **CLC 20**
See Fosse, Bob

Foster, Hannah Webster
1758-1840 .... **NCLC 99**
See also DLB 37, 200; RGAL 4

Foster, Stephen Collins
1826-1864 .... **NCLC 26**
See also RGAL 4

Foucault, Michel 1926-1984 . **CLC 31, 34, 69**
See also CA 105; 113; CANR 34; DLB 242;
EW 13; EWL 3; GFL 1789 to the Present;
GLL 1; LMFS 2; MTCW 1, 2; TWA

**Fouque, Friedrich (Heinrich Karl) de la
Motte** 1777-1843 .... **NCLC 2**
See also DLB 90; RGWL 2, 3; SUFW 1

Fourier, Charles 1772-1837 .... **NCLC 51**

Fournier, Henri-Alban 1886-1914
See Alain-Fournier
See also CA 104; 179

Fournier, Pierre 1916-1997 .... **CLC 11**
See Gascar, Pierre
See also CA 89-92; CANR 16, 40

Fowles, John 1926-2005 .... **CLC 1, 2, 3, 4, 6,
9, 10, 15, 33, 87; SSC 33**
See also BPFB 1; BRWS 1; CA 5-8R; 245;
CANR 25, 71, 103; CDBLB 1960 to
Present; CN 1, 2, 3, 4, 5, 6, 7; DA3; DAB;
DAC; DAM MST; DLB 14, 139, 207;
EWL 3; HGG; MTCW 1, 2; MTFW 2005;
NFS 21; RGEL 2; RHW; SATA 22; SATA-
Obit 171; TEA; WLIT 4

Fowles, John Robert
See Fowles, John

Fox, Paula 1923- .... **CLC 2, 8, 121**
See also AAYA 3, 37; BYA 3, 8; CA 73-76;
CANR 20, 36, 62, 105; CLR 1, 44, 96;
DLB 52; JRDA; MAICYA 1, 2; MTCW
1; NFS 12; SATA 17, 60, 120, 167; WYA;
YAW

Fox, William Price (Jr.) 1926- .... **CLC 22**
See also CA 17-20R; CAAS 19; CANR 11,
142; CSW; DLB 2; DLBY 1981

Foxe, John 1517(?)-1587 .... **LC 14**
See also DLB 132

Frame, Janet 1924-2004 ...... **CLC 2, 3, 6, 22,
66, 96, 237; SSC 29**
See also CA 1-4R; 224; CANR 2, 36, 76,
135; CN 1, 2, 3, 4, 5, 6, 7; CP 2, 3, 4;
CWP; EWL 3; MTCW 1,2; RGEL 2;
RGSF 2; SATA 119; TWA

France, Anatole **TCLC 9**
See Thibault, Jacques Anatole Francois
See also DLB 123, 330; EWL 3; GFL 1789
to the Present; RGWL 2, 3; SUFW 1

Francis, Claude **CLC 50**
See also CA 192

Francis, Dick
See Francis, Richard Stanley
See also CN 2, 3, 4, 5, 6

Francis, Richard Stanley 1920- ... **CLC 2, 22,
42, 102**
See Francis, Dick
See also AAYA 5, 21; BEST 89:3; BPFB 1;
CA 5-8R; CANR 9, 42, 68, 100, 141; CD-
BLB 1960 to Present; CMW 4; CN 7;
DA3; DAM POP; DLB 87; INT CANR-9;
MSW; MTCW 1, 2; MTFW 2005

Francis, Robert (Churchill)
1901-1987 .... **CLC 15; PC 34**
See also AMWS 9; CA 1-4R; 123; CANR
1; CP 1, 2, 3, 4; EXPP; PFS 12; TCLE
1:1

Francis, Lord Jeffrey
See Jeffrey, Francis
See also DLB 107

Frank, Anne(lies Marie)
1929-1945 .... **TCLC 17; WLC 2**
See also AAYA 12; BYA 1; CA 113; 133;
CANR 68; CLR 101; DA; DA3; DAB;
DAC; DAM MST; LAIT 4; MAICYA 2;
MAICYAS 1; MTCW 1, 2; MTFW 2005;
NCFS 2; RGHL; SATA 87; SATA-Brief
42; WYA; YAW

Frank, Bruno 1887-1945 .... **TCLC 81**
See also CA 189; DLB 118; EWL 3

Frank, Elizabeth 1945- .... **CLC 39**
See also CA 121; 126; CANR 78, 150; INT
CA-126

Frankl, Viktor E(mil) 1905-1997 ...... **CLC 93**
See also CA 65-68; 161; RGHL

Franklin, Benjamin
See Hasek, Jaroslav (Matej Frantisek)

Franklin, Benjamin 1706-1790 .. **LC 25, 134;
WLCS**
See also AMW; CDALB 1640-1865; DA;
DA3; DAB; DAC; DAM MST; DLB 24,
43, 73, 183; LAIT 1; RGAL 4; TUS

Franklin, Madeleine
See L'Engle, Madeleine

Franklin, Madeleine L'Engle
See L'Engle, Madeleine

Franklin, Madeleine L'Engle Camp
See L'Engle, Madeleine

**Franklin, (Stella Maria Sarah) Miles
(Lampe)** 1879-1954 .... **TCLC 7**
See also CA 104; 164; DLB 230; FW;
MTCW 2; RGEL 2; TWA

Franzen, Jonathan 1959- .... **CLC 202**
See also AAYA 65; CA 129; CANR 105,
166

Fraser, Antonia 1932- .... **CLC 32, 107**
See also AAYA 57; CA 85-88; CANR 44, 65, 119, 164; CMW; DLB 276; MTCW 1, 2; MTFW 2005; SATA-Brief 32

Fraser, George MacDonald
1925-2008 .... **CLC 7**
See also AAYA 48; CA 45-48, 180; 268; CAAE 180; CANR 2, 48, 74; MTCW 2; RHW

Fraser, Sylvia 1935- .... **CLC 64**
See also CA 45-48; CANR 1, 16, 60; CCA 1

Frayn, Michael 1933- .... **CLC 3, 7, 31, 47, 176; DC 27**
See also AAYA 69; BRWC 2; BRWS 7; CA 5-8R; CANR 30, 69, 114, 133, 166; CBD; CD 5, 6; CN 1, 2, 3, 4, 5, 6, 7; DAM DRAM, NOV; DFS 22; DLB 13, 14, 194, 245; FANT; MTCW 1, 2; MTFW 2005; SFW 4

Fraze, Candida (Merrill) 1945- .... **CLC 50**
See also CA 126

Frazer, Andrew
See Marlowe, Stephen

Frazer, J(ames) G(eorge)
1854-1941 .... **TCLC 32**
See also BRWS 3; CA 118; NCFS 5

Frazer, Robert Caine
See Creasey, John

Frazer, Sir James George
See Frazer, J(ames) G(eorge)

Frazier, Charles 1950- .... **CLC 109, 224**
See also AAYA 34; CA 161; CANR 126, 170; CSW; DLB 292; MTFW 2005; NFS 25

Frazier, Charles R.
See Frazier, Charles

Frazier, Charles Robinson
See Frazier, Charles

Frazier, Ian 1951- .... **CLC 46**
See also CA 130; CANR 54, 93

Frederic, Harold 1856-1898 ... **NCLC 10, 175**
See also AMW; DLB 12, 23; DLBD 13; MAL 5; NFS 22; RGAL 4

Frederick, John
See Faust, Frederick (Schiller)
See also TCWW 2

Frederick the Great 1712-1786 .... **LC 14**

Fredro, Aleksander 1793-1876 .... **NCLC 8**

Freeling, Nicolas 1927-2003 .... **CLC 38**
See also CA 49-52; 218; CAAS 12; CANR 1, 17, 50, 84; CMW 4; CN 1, 2, 3, 4, 5, 6; DLB 87

Freeman, Douglas Southall
1886-1953 .... **TCLC 11**
See also CA 109; 195; DLB 17; DLBD 17

Freeman, Judith 1946- .... **CLC 55**
See also CA 148; CANR 120; DLB 256

Freeman, Mary E(leanor) Wilkins
1852-1930 .... **SSC 1, 47, 113; TCLC 9**
See also CA 106; 177; DLB 12, 78, 221; EXPS; FW; HGG; MBL; RGAL 4; RGSF 2; SSFS 4, 8; SUFW 1; TUS

Freeman, R(ichard) Austin
1862-1943 .... **TCLC 21**
See also CA 113; CANR 84; CMW 4; DLB 70

French, Albert 1943- .... **CLC 86**
See also BW 3; CA 167

French, Antonia
See Kureishi, Hanif

French, Marilyn 1929- .. **CLC 10, 18, 60, 177**
See also BPFB 1; CA 69-72; CANR 3, 31, 134, 163; CN 5, 6, 7; CPW; DAM DRAM, NOV, POP; FL 1:5; FW; INT CANR-31; MTCW 1, 2; MTFW 2005

French, Paul
See Asimov, Isaac

Freneau, Philip Morin 1752-1832 .. **NCLC 1, 111**
See also AMWS 2; DLB 37, 43; RGAL 4

Freud, Sigmund 1856-1939 .... **TCLC 52**
See also CA 115; 133; CANR 69; DLB 296; EW 8; EWL 3; LATS 1:1; MTCW 1, 2; MTFW 2005; NCFS 3; TWA

Freytag, Gustav 1816-1895 .... **NCLC 109**
See also DLB 129

Friedan, Betty 1921-2006 .... **CLC 74**
See also CA 65-68; 248; CANR 18, 45, 74; DLB 246; FW; MTCW 1, 2; MTFW 2005; NCFS 5

Friedan, Betty Naomi
See Friedan, Betty

Friedlander, Saul 1932- .... **CLC 90**
See also CA 117; 130; CANR 72; RGHL

Friedman, B(ernard) H(arper)
1926- .... **CLC 7**
See also CA 1-4R; CANR 3, 48

Friedman, Bruce Jay 1930- ...... **CLC 3, 5, 56**
See also CA 9-12R; CAD; CANR 25, 52, 101; CD 5, 6; CN 1, 2, 3, 4, 5, 6, 7; DLB 2, 28, 244; INT CANR-25; MAL 5; SSFS 18

Friel, Brian 1929- .. **CLC 5, 42, 59, 115, 253; DC 8; SSC 76**
See also BRWS 5; CA 21-24R; CANR 33, 69, 131; CBD; CD 5, 6; DFS 11; DLB 13, 319; EWL 3; MTCW 1; RGEL 2; TEA

Friis-Baastad, Babbis Ellinor
1921-1970 .... **CLC 12**
See also CA 17-20R; 134; SATA 7

Frisch, Max 1911-1991 ...... **CLC 3, 9, 14, 18, 32, 44; TCLC 121**
See also CA 85-88; 134; CANR 32, 74; CD-WLB 2; DAM DRAM, NOV; DFS 25; DLB 69, 124; EW 13; EWL 3; MTCW 1, 2; MTFW 2005; RGHL; RGWL 2, 3

Fromentin, Eugene (Samuel Auguste)
1820-1876 .... **NCLC 10, 125**
See also DLB 123; GFL 1789 to the Present

Frost, Frederick
See Faust, Frederick (Schiller)

Frost, Robert 1874-1963 . **CLC 1, 3, 4, 9, 10, 13, 15, 26, 34, 44; PC 1, 39, 71; WLC 2**
See also AAYA 21; AMW; AMWR 1; CA 89-92; CANR 33; CDALB 1917-1929; CLR 67; DA; DA3; DAB; DAC; DAM MST, POET; DLB 54, 284; DLBD 7; EWL 3; EXPP; MAL 5; MTCW 1, 2; MTFW 2005; PAB; PFS 1, 2, 3, 4, 5, 6, 7, 10, 13; RGAL 4; SATA 14; TUS; WP; WYA

Frost, Robert Lee
See Frost, Robert

Froude, James Anthony
1818-1894 .... **NCLC 43**
See also DLB 18, 57, 144

Froy, Herald
See Waterhouse, Keith (Spencer)

Fry, Christopher 1907-2005 ... **CLC 2, 10, 14**
See also BRWS 3; CA 17-20R; 240; CAAS 23; CANR 9, 30, 74, 132; CBD; CD 5, 6; CP 1, 2, 3, 4, 5, 6, 7; DAM DRAM; DLB 13; EWL 3; MTCW 1, 2; MTFW 2005; RGEL 2; SATA 66; TEA

Frye, (Herman) Northrop
1912-1991 .... **CLC 24, 70; TCLC 165**
See also CA 5-8R; 133; CANR 8, 37; DLB 67, 68, 246; EWL 3; MTCW 1, 2; MTFW 2005; RGAL 4; TWA

Fuchs, Daniel 1909-1993 .... **CLC 8, 22**
See also CA 81-84; 142; CAAS 5; CANR 40; CN 1, 2, 3, 4, 5; DLB 9, 26, 28; DLBY 1993; MAL 5

Fuchs, Daniel 1934- .... **CLC 34**
See also CA 37-40R; CANR 14, 48

Fuentes, Carlos 1928- .. **CLC 3, 8, 10, 13, 22, 41, 60, 113; HLC 1; SSC 24; WLC 2**
See also AAYA 4, 45; AITN 2; BPFB 1; CA 69-72; CANR 10, 32, 68, 104, 138; CDWLB 3; CWW 2; DA; DA3; DAB; DAC; DAM MST, MULT, NOV; DLB 113; DNFS 2; EWL 3; HW 1, 2; LAIT 3; LATS 1:2; LAW; LAWS 1; LMFS 2; MTCW 1, 2; MTFW 2005; NFS 8; RGSF 2; RGWL 2, 3; TWA; WLIT 1

Fuentes, Gregorio Lopez y
See Lopez y Fuentes, Gregorio

Fuertes, Gloria 1918-1998 .... **PC 27**
See also CA 178, 180; DLB 108; HW 2; SATA 115

Fugard, (Harold) Athol 1932- . **CLC 5, 9, 14, 25, 40, 80, 211; DC 3**
See also AAYA 17; AFW; CA 85-88; CANR 32, 54, 118; CD 5, 6; DAM DRAM; DFS 3, 6, 10, 24; DLB 225; DNFS 1, 2; EWL 3; LATS 1:2; MTCW 1; MTFW 2005; RGEL 2; WLIT 2

Fugard, Sheila 1932- .... **CLC 48**
See also CA 125

Fujiwara no Teika 1162-1241 .... **CMLC 73**
See also DLB 203

Fukuyama, Francis 1952- .... **CLC 131**
See also CA 140; CANR 72, 125, 170

Fuller, Charles (H.), (Jr.) 1939- ..... **BLC 1:2; CLC 25; DC 1**
See also BW 2; CA 108; 112; CAD; CANR 87; CD 5, 6; DAM DRAM, MULT; DFS 8; DLB 38, 266; EWL 3; INT CA-112; MAL 5; MTCW 1

Fuller, Henry Blake 1857-1929 .... **TCLC 103**
See also CA 108; 177; DLB 12; RGAL 4

Fuller, John (Leopold) 1937- .... **CLC 62**
See also CA 21-24R; CANR 9, 44; CP 1, 2, 3, 4, 5, 6, 7; DLB 40

Fuller, Margaret
See Ossoli, Sarah Margaret (Fuller)
See also AMWS 2; DLB 183, 223, 239; FL 1:3

Fuller, Roy (Broadbent) 1912-1991 ... **CLC 4, 28**
See also BRWS 7; CA 5-8R; 135; CAAS 10; CANR 53, 83; CN 1, 2, 3, 4, 5; CP 1, 2, 3, 4, 5; CWRI 5; DLB 15, 20; EWL 3; RGEL 2; SATA 87

Fuller, Sarah Margaret
See Ossoli, Sarah Margaret (Fuller)

Fuller, Sarah Margaret
See Ossoli, Sarah Margaret (Fuller)

Fuller, Thomas 1608-1661 .... **LC 111**
See also DLB 151

Fulton, Alice 1952- .... **CLC 52**
See also CA 116; CANR 57, 88; CP 5, 6, 7; CWP; DLB 193; PFS 25

Furphy, Joseph 1843-1912 .... **TCLC 25**
See Collins, Tom
See also CA 163; DLB 230; EWL 3; RGEL 2

Furst, Alan 1941- .... **CLC 255**
See also CA 69-72; CANR 12, 34, 59, 102, 159; DLBY 01

Fuson, Robert H(enderson) 1927- .... **CLC 70**
See also CA 89-92; CANR 103

Fussell, Paul 1924- .... **CLC 74**
See also BEST 90:1; CA 17-20R; CANR 8, 21, 35, 69, 135; INT CANR-21; MTCW 1, 2; MTFW 2005

Futabatei, Shimei 1864-1909 .... **TCLC 44**
See Futabatei Shimei
See also CA 162; MJW

Futabatei Shimei
See Futabatei, Shimei
See also DLB 180; EWL 3

Futrelle, Jacques 1875-1912 .... **TCLC 19**
See also CA 113; 155; CMW 4

Gaboriau, Emile 1835-1873 .... **NCLC 14**
See also CMW 4; MSW

Gadda, Carlo Emilio 1893-1973 ...... **CLC 11;
TCLC 144**
See also CA 89-92; DLB 177; EWL 3;
WLIT 7

Gaddis, William 1922-1998 ... **CLC 1, 3, 6, 8,
10, 19, 43, 86**
See also AMWS 4; BPFB 1; CA 17-20R;
172; CANR 21, 48, 148; CN 1, 2, 3, 4, 5,
6; DLB 2, 278; EWL 3; MAL 5; MTCW
1, 2; MTFW 2005; RGAL 4

Gage, Walter
See Inge, William (Motter)

Gaiman, Neil 1960- .... **CLC 195**
See also AAYA 19, 42; CA 133; CANR 81,
129; CLR 109; DLB 261; HGG; MTFW
2005; SATA 85, 146; SFW 4; SUFW 2

Gaiman, Neil Richard
See Gaiman, Neil

Gaines, Ernest J. 1933- ..... **BLC 1:2; CLC 3,
11, 18, 86, 181; SSC 68**
See also AAYA 18; AFAW 1, 2; AITN 1;
BPFB 2; BW 2, 3; BYA 6; CA 9-12R;
CANR 6, 24, 42, 75, 126; CDALB 1968-
1988; CLR 62; CN 1, 2, 3, 4, 5, 6, 7;
CSW; DA3; DAM MULT; DLB 2, 33,
152; DLBY 1980; EWL 3; EXPN; LAIT
5; LATS 1:2; MAL 5; MTCW 1, 2;
MTFW 2005; NFS 5, 7, 16; RGAL 4;
RGSF 2; RHW; SATA 86; SSFS 5; YAW

Gaitskill, Mary 1954- .... **CLC 69**
See also CA 128; CANR 61, 152; DLB 244;
TCLE 1:1

Gaitskill, Mary Lawrence
See Gaitskill, Mary

Gaius Suetonius Tranquillus
See Suetonius

Galdos, Benito Perez
See Perez Galdos, Benito
See also EW 7

Gale, Zona 1874-1938 .... **DC 30; TCLC 7**
See also CA 105; 153; CANR 84; DAM
DRAM; DFS 17; DLB 9, 78, 228; RGAL
4

Galeano, Eduardo 1940- ... **CLC 72; HLCS 1**
See also CA 29-32R; CANR 13, 32, 100,
163; HW 1

Galeano, Eduardo Hughes
See Galeano, Eduardo

Galiano, Juan Valera y Alcala
See Valera y Alcala-Galiano, Juan

Galilei, Galileo 1564-1642 .... **LC 45**

Gallagher, Tess 1943- .... **CLC 18, 63; PC 9**
See also CA 106; CP 3, 4, 5, 6, 7; CWP;
DAM POET; DLB 120, 212, 244; PFS 16

Gallant, Mavis 1922- ..... **CLC 7, 18, 38, 172;
SSC 5, 78**
See also CA 69-72; CANR 29, 69, 117;
CCA 1; CN 1, 2, 3, 4, 5, 6, 7; DAC; DAM
MST; DLB 53; EWL 3; MTCW 1, 2;
MTFW 2005; RGEL 2; RGSF 2

Gallant, Roy A(rthur) 1924- .... **CLC 17**
See also CA 5-8R; CANR 4, 29, 54, 117;
CLR 30; MAICYA 1, 2; SATA 4, 68, 110

Gallico, Paul (William) 1897-1976 ..... **CLC 2**
See also AITN 1; CA 5-8R; 69-72; CANR
23; CN 1, 2; DLB 9, 171; FANT; MAI-
CYA 1, 2; SATA 13

Gallo, Max Louis 1932- .... **CLC 95**
See also CA 85-88

Gallois, Lucien
See Desnos, Robert

Gallup, Ralph
See Whitemore, Hugh (John)

Galsworthy, John 1867-1933 .... **SSC 22;
TCLC 1, 45; WLC 2**
See also BRW 6; CA 104; 141; CANR 75;
CDBLB 1890-1914; DA; DA3; DAB;
DAC; DAM DRAM, MST, NOV; DLB
10, 34, 98, 162, 330; DLBD 16; EWL 3;
MTCW 2; RGEL 2; SSFS 3; TEA

Galt, John 1779-1839 .... **NCLC 1, 110**
See also DLB 99, 116, 159; RGEL 2; RGSF
2

Galvin, James 1951- .... **CLC 38**
See also CA 108; CANR 26

Gamboa, Federico 1864-1939 .... **TCLC 36**
See also CA 167; HW 2; LAW

Gandhi, M. K.
See Gandhi, Mohandas Karamchand

Gandhi, Mahatma
See Gandhi, Mohandas Karamchand

Gandhi, Mohandas Karamchand
1869-1948 .... **TCLC 59**
See also CA 121; 132; DA3; DAM MULT;
DLB 323; MTCW 1, 2

Gann, Ernest Kellogg 1910-1991 ..... **CLC 23**
See also AITN 1; BPFB 2; CA 1-4R; 136;
CANR 1, 83; RHW

Gao Xingjian 1940- .... **CLC 167**
See Xingjian, Gao
See also MTFW 2005

Garber, Eric 1943(?)-
See Holleran, Andrew
See also CANR 89, 162

Garber, Esther
See Lee, Tanith

Garcia, Cristina 1958- .... **CLC 76**
See also AMWS 11; CA 141; CANR 73,
130, 172; CN 7; DLB 292; DNFS 1; EWL
3; HW 2; LLW; MTFW 2005

Garcia Lorca, Federico 1898-1936 ...... **DC 2;
HLC 2; PC 3; TCLC 1, 7, 49, 181,
197; WLC 2**
See Lorca, Federico Garcia
See also AAYA 46; CA 104; 131; CANR
81; DA; DA3; DAB; DAC; DAM DRAM,
MST, MULT, POET; DFS 4, 10; DLB
108; EWL 3; HW 1, 2; LATS 1:2; MTCW
1, 2; MTFW 2005; TWA

Garcia Marquez, Gabriel 1928- .... **CLC 2, 3,
8, 10, 15, 27, 47, 55, 68, 170, 254; HLC
1; SSC 8, 83; WLC 3**
See also AAYA 3, 33; BEST 89:1, 90:4;
BPFB 2; BYA 12, 16; CA 33-36R; CANR
10, 28, 50, 75, 82, 128; CDWLB 3; CPW;
CWW 2; DA; DA3; DAB; DAC; DAM
MST, MULT, NOV, POP; DLB 113, 330;
DNFS 1, 2; EWL 3; EXPN; EXPS; HW
1, 2; LAIT 2; LATS 1:2; LAW; LAWS 1;
LMFS 2; MTCW 1, 2; MTFW 2005;
NCFS 3; NFS 1, 5, 10; RGSF 2; RGWL
2, 3; SSFS 1, 6, 16, 21; TWA; WLIT 1

Garcia Marquez, Gabriel Jose
See Garcia Marquez, Gabriel

Garcilaso de la Vega, El Inca
1539-1616 .... **HLCS 1; LC 127**
See also DLB 318; LAW

Gard, Janice
See Latham, Jean Lee

Gard, Roger Martin du
See Martin du Gard, Roger

Gardam, Jane 1928- .... **CLC 43**
See also CA 49-52; CANR 2, 18, 33, 54,
106, 167; CLR 12; DLB 14, 161, 231;
MAICYA 1, 2; MTCW 1; SAAS 9; SATA
39, 76, 130; SATA-Brief 28; YAW

Gardam, Jane Mary
See Gardam, Jane

Gardner, Herb(ert George)
1934-2003 .... **CLC 44**
See also CA 149; 220; CAD; CANR 119;
CD 5, 6; DFS 18, 20

Gardner, John, Jr. 1933-1982 ... **CLC 2, 3, 5,
7, 8, 10, 18, 28, 34; SSC 7; TCLC 195**
See also AAYA 45; AITN 1; AMWS 6;
BPFB 2; CA 65-68; 107; CANR 33, 73;
CDALBS; CN 2, 3; CPW; DA3; DAM
NOV, POP; DLB 2; DLBY 1982; EWL 3;
FANT; LATS 1:2; MAL 5; MTCW 1, 2;
MTFW 2005; NFS 3; RGAL 4; RGSF 2;
SATA 40; SATA-Obit 31; SSFS 8

Gardner, John 1926-2007 .... **CLC 30**
See also CA 103; 263; CANR 15, 69, 127;
CMW 4; CPW; DAM POP; MTCW 1

Gardner, John Edmund
See Gardner, John

Gardner, Miriam
See Bradley, Marion Zimmer
See also GLL 1

Gardner, Noel
See Kuttner, Henry

Gardons, S. S.
See Snodgrass, W.D.

Garfield, Leon 1921-1996 .... **CLC 12**
See also AAYA 8, 69; BYA 1, 3; CA 17-
20R; 152; CANR 38, 41, 78; CLR 21;
DLB 161; JRDA; MAICYA 1, 2; MAIC-
YAS 1; SATA 1, 32, 76; SATA-Obit 90;
TEA; WYA; YAW

Garland, (Hannibal) Hamlin
1860-1940 .... **SSC 18; TCLC 3**
See also CA 104; DLB 12, 71, 78, 186;
MAL 5; RGAL 4; RGSF 2; TCWW 1, 2

Garneau, (Hector de) Saint-Denys
1912-1943 .... **TCLC 13**
See also CA 111; DLB 88

Garner, Alan 1934- .... **CLC 17**
See also AAYA 18; BYA 3, 5; CA 73-76,
178; CAAE 178; CANR 15, 64, 134; CLR
20, 130; CPW; DAB; DAM POP; DLB
161, 261; FANT; MAICYA 1, 2; MTCW
1, 2; MTFW 2005; SATA 18, 69; SATA-
Essay 108; SUFW 1, 2; YAW

Garner, Hugh 1913-1979 .... **CLC 13**
See Warwick, Jarvis
See also CA 69-72; CANR 31; CCA 1; CN
1, 2; DLB 68

Garnett, David 1892-1981 .... **CLC 3**
See also CA 5-8R; 103; CANR 17, 79; CN
1, 2; DLB 34; FANT; MTCW 2; RGEL 2;
SFW 4; SUFW 1

Garnier, Robert c. 1545-1590 .... **LC 119**
See also DLB 327; GFL Beginnings to 1789

Garrett, George 1929-2008 ... **CLC 3, 11, 51;
SSC 30**
See also AMWS 7; BPFB 2; CA 1-4R, 202;
CAAE 202; CAAS 5; CANR 1, 42, 67,
109; CN 1, 2, 3, 4, 5, 6, 7; CP 1, 2, 3, 4,
5, 6, 7; CSW; DLB 2, 5, 130, 152; DLBY
1983

Garrett, George Palmer
See Garrett, George

Garrick, David 1717-1779 .... **LC 15**
See also DAM DRAM; DLB 84, 213;
RGEL 2

Garrigue, Jean 1914-1972 .... **CLC 2, 8**
See also CA 5-8R; 37-40R; CANR 20; CP
1; MAL 5

Garrison, Frederick
See Sinclair, Upton

Garrison, William Lloyd
1805-1879 .... **NCLC 149**
See also CDALB 1640-1865; DLB 1, 43,
235

Garro, Elena 1920(?)-1998 .. **HLCS 1; TCLC
153**
See also CA 131; 169; CWW 2; DLB 145;
EWL 3; HW 1; LAWS 1; WLIT 1

Garth, Will
See Hamilton, Edmond; Kuttner, Henry

Garvey, Marcus (Moziah, Jr.)
1887-1940 ..... **BLC 1:2; HR 1:2; TCLC 41**
See also BW 1; CA 120; 124; CANR 79; DAM MULT

Gary, Romain CLC 25
See Kacew, Romain
See also DLB 83, 299; RGHL

Gascar, Pierre CLC 11
See Fournier, Pierre
See also EWL 3; RGHL

Gascoigne, George 1539-1577 .... **LC 108**
See also DLB 136; RGEL 2

Gascoyne, David (Emery)
1916-2001 .... **CLC 45**
See also CA 65-68; 200; CANR 10, 28, 54; CP 1, 2, 3, 4, 5, 6, 7; DLB 20; MTCW 1; RGEL 2

Gaskell, Elizabeth Cleghorn
1810-1865 .... **NCLC 5, 70, 97, 137; SSC 25, 97**
See also BRW 5; CDBLB 1832-1890; DAB; DAM MST; DLB 21, 144, 159; RGEL 2; RGSF 2; TEA

Gass, William H. 1924- . **CLC 1, 2, 8, 11, 15, 39, 132; SSC 12**
See also AMWS 6; CA 17-20R; CANR 30, 71, 100; CN 1, 2, 3, 4, 5, 6, 7; DLB 2, 227; EWL 3; MAL 5; MTCW 1, 2; MTFW 2005; RGAL 4

Gassendi, Pierre 1592-1655 .... **LC 54**
See also GFL Beginnings to 1789

Gasset, Jose Ortega y
See Ortega y Gasset, Jose

Gates, Henry Louis, Jr. 1950- ... **BLCS; CLC 65**
See also BW 2, 3; CA 109; CANR 25, 53, 75, 125; CSW; DA3; DAM MULT; DLB 67; EWL 3; MAL 5; MTCW 2; MTFW 2005; RGAL 4

Gatos, Stephanie
See Katz, Steve

Gautier, Theophile 1811-1872 .. **NCLC 1, 59; PC 18; SSC 20**
See also DAM POET; DLB 119; EW 6; GFL 1789 to the Present; RGWL 2, 3; SUFW; TWA

Gay, John 1685-1732 .... **LC 49**
See also BRW 3; DAM DRAM; DLB 84, 95; RGEL 2; WLIT 3

Gay, Oliver
See Gogarty, Oliver St. John

Gay, Peter 1923- .... **CLC 158**
See also CA 13-16R; CANR 18, 41, 77, 147; INT CANR-18; RGHL

Gay, Peter Jack
See Gay, Peter

Gaye, Marvin (Pentz, Jr.)
1939-1984 .... **CLC 26**
See also CA 195; 112

Gebler, Carlo 1954- .... **CLC 39**
See also CA 119; 133; CANR 96; DLB 271

Gee, Maggie 1948- .... **CLC 57**
See also CA 130; CANR 125; CN 4, 5, 6, 7; DLB 207; MTFW 2005

Gee, Maurice 1931- .... **CLC 29**
See also AAYA 42; CA 97-100; CANR 67, 123; CLR 56; CN 2, 3, 4, 5, 6, 7; CWRI 5; EWL 3; MAICYA 2; RGSF 2; SATA 46, 101

Gee, Maurice Gough
See Gee, Maurice

Geiogamah, Hanay 1945- .... **NNAL**
See also CA 153; DAM MULT; DLB 175

Gelbart, Larry
See Gelbart, Larry (Simon)
See also CAD; CD 5, 6

Gelbart, Larry (Simon) 1928- .... **CLC 21, 61**
See Gelbart, Larry
See also CA 73-76; CANR 45, 94

Gelber, Jack 1932-2003 ...... **CLC 1, 6, 14, 79**
See also CA 1-4R; 216; CAD; CANR 2; DLB 7, 228; MAL 5

Gellhorn, Martha (Ellis)
1908-1998 .... **CLC 14, 60**
See also CA 77-80; 164; CANR 44; CN 1, 2, 3, 4, 5, 6 7; DLBY 1982, 1998

Genet, Jean 1910-1986 .. **CLC 1, 2, 5, 10, 14, 44, 46; DC 25; TCLC 128**
See also CA 13-16R; CANR 18; DA3; DAM DRAM; DFS 10; DLB 72, 321; DLBY 1986; EW 13; EWL 3; GFL 1789 to the Present; GLL 1; LMFS 2; MTCW 1, 2; MTFW 2005; RGWL 2, 3; TWA

Genlis, Stephanie-Felicite Ducrest
1746-1830 .... **NCLC 166**
See also DLB 313

Gent, Peter 1942- .... **CLC 29**
See also AITN 1; CA 89-92; DLBY 1982

Gentile, Giovanni 1875-1944 .... **TCLC 96**
See also CA 119

Geoffrey of Monmouth c.
1100-1155 .... **CMLC 44**
See also DLB 146; TEA

George, Jean
See George, Jean Craighead

George, Jean Craighead 1919- .... **CLC 35**
See also AAYA 8, 69; BYA 2, 4; CA 5-8R; CANR 25; CLR 1; 80; DLB 52; JRDA; MAICYA 1, 2; SATA 2, 68, 124, 170; WYA; YAW

George, Stefan (Anton) 1868-1933 . **TCLC 2, 14**
See also CA 104; 193; EW 8; EWL 3

Georges, Georges Martin
See Simenon, Georges (Jacques Christian)

Gerald of Wales c. 1146-c. 1223 ... **CMLC 60**

Gerhardi, William Alexander
See Gerhardie, William Alexander

Gerhardie, William Alexander
1895-1977 .... **CLC 5**
See also CA 25-28R; 73-76; CANR 18; CN 1, 2; DLB 36; RGEL 2

Gerson, Jean 1363-1429 .... **LC 77**
See also DLB 208

Gersonides 1288-1344 .... **CMLC 49**
See also DLB 115

Gerstler, Amy 1956- .... **CLC 70**
See also CA 146; CANR 99

Gertler, T. CLC 34
See also CA 116; 121

Gertsen, Aleksandr Ivanovich
See Herzen, Aleksandr Ivanovich

Ghalib NCLC 39, 78
See Ghalib, Asadullah Khan

Ghalib, Asadullah Khan 1797-1869
See Ghalib
See also DAM POET; RGWL 2, 3

Ghelderode, Michel de 1898-1962 ..... **CLC 6, 11; DC 15; TCLC 187**
See also CA 85-88; CANR 40, 77; DAM DRAM; DLB 321; EW 11; EWL 3; TWA

Ghiselin, Brewster 1903-2001 .... **CLC 23**
See also CA 13-16R; CAAS 10; CANR 13; CP 1, 2, 3, 4, 5, 6, 7

Ghose, Aurabinda 1872-1950 .... **TCLC 63**
See Ghose, Aurobindo
See also CA 163

Ghose, Aurobindo
See Ghose, Aurabinda
See also EWL 3

Ghose, Zulfikar 1935- .... **CLC 42, 200**
See also CA 65-68; CANR 67; CN 1, 2, 3, 4, 5, 6, 7; CP 1, 2, 3, 4, 5, 6, 7; DLB 323; EWL 3

Ghosh, Amitav 1956- .... **CLC 44, 153**
See also CA 147; CANR 80, 158; CN 6, 7; DLB 323; WWE 1

Giacosa, Giuseppe 1847-1906 .... **TCLC 7**
See also CA 104

Gibb, Lee
See Waterhouse, Keith (Spencer)

Gibbon, Edward 1737-1794 .... **LC 97**
See also BRW 3; DLB 104, 336; RGEL 2

Gibbon, Lewis Grassic TCLC 4
See Mitchell, James Leslie
See also RGEL 2

Gibbons, Kaye 1960- .... **CLC 50, 88, 145**
See also AAYA 34; AMWS 10; CA 151; CANR 75, 127; CN 7; CSW; DA3; DAM POP; DLB 292; MTCW 2; MTFW 2005; NFS 3; RGAL 4; SATA 117

Gibran, Kahlil 1883-1931 ..... **PC 9; TCLC 1, 9, 205**
See also CA 104; 150; DA3; DAM POET, POP; EWL 3; MTCW 2; WLIT 6

Gibran, Khalil
See Gibran, Kahlil

Gibson, Mel 1956- .... **CLC 215**

Gibson, William 1914- .... **CLC 23**
See also CA 9-12R; CAD; CANR 9, 42, 75, 125; CD 5, 6; DA; DAB; DAC; DAM DRAM, MST; DFS 2; DLB 7; LAIT 2; MAL 5; MTCW 2; MTFW 2005; SATA 66; YAW

Gibson, William 1948- .... **CLC 39, 63, 186, 192; SSC 52**
See also AAYA 12, 59; AMWS 16; BPFB 2; CA 126; 133; CANR 52, 90, 106, 172; CN 6, 7; CPW; DA3; DAM POP; DLB 251; MTCW 2; MTFW 2005; SCFW 2; SFW 4

Gibson, William Ford
See Gibson, William

Gide, Andre (Paul Guillaume)
1869-1951 ...... **SSC 13; TCLC 5, 12, 36, 177; WLC 3**
See also CA 104; 124; DA; DA3; DAB; DAC; DAM MST, NOV; DLB 65, 321, 330; EW 8; EWL 3; GFL 1789 to the Present; MTCW 1, 2; MTFW 2005; NFS 21; RGSF 2; RGWL 2, 3; TWA

Gifford, Barry (Colby) 1946- .... **CLC 34**
See also CA 65-68; CANR 9, 30, 40, 90

Gilbert, Frank
See De Voto, Bernard (Augustine)

Gilbert, W(illiam) S(chwenck)
1836-1911 .... **TCLC 3**
See also CA 104; 173; DAM DRAM, POET; RGEL 2; SATA 36

Gilbert of Poitiers c. 1085-1154 .... **CMLC 85**

Gilbreth, Frank B(unker), Jr.
1911-2001 .... **CLC 17**
See also CA 9-12R; SATA 2

Gilchrist, Ellen (Louise) 1935- .. **CLC 34, 48, 143; SSC 14, 63**
See also BPFB 2; CA 113; 116; CANR 41, 61, 104; CN 4, 5, 6, 7; CPW; CSW; DAM POP; DLB 130; EWL 3; EXPS; MTCW 1, 2; MTFW 2005; RGAL 4; RGSF 2; SSFS 9

Gildas fl. 6th cent. - .... **CMLC 99**

Giles, Molly 1942- .... **CLC 39**
See also CA 126; CANR 98

Gill, Eric TCLC 85
See Gill, (Arthur) Eric (Rowton Peter Joseph)

Gill, (Arthur) Eric (Rowton Peter Joseph)
1882-1940
See Gill, Eric
See also CA 120; DLB 98

Gill, Patrick
See Creasey, John

Gillette, Douglas CLC 70

Gilliam, Terry 1940- .... **CLC 21, 141**
See Monty Python
See also AAYA 19, 59; CA 108; 113; CANR
35; INT CA-113
Gilliam, Terry Vance
See Gilliam, Terry
Gillian, Jerry
See Gilliam, Terry
Gilliatt, Penelope (Ann Douglass)
1932-1993 .... **CLC 2, 10, 13, 53**
See also AITN 2; CA 13-16R; 141; CANR
49; CN 1, 2, 3, 4, 5; DLB 14
Gilligan, Carol 1936- .... **CLC 208**
See also CA 142; CANR 121; FW
Gilman, Charlotte (Anna) Perkins (Stetson)
1860-1935 ...... **SSC 13, 62; TCLC 9, 37,
117, 201**
See also AAYA 75; AMWS 11; BYA 11;
CA 106; 150; DLB 221; EXPS; FL 1:5;
FW; HGG; LAIT 2; MBL; MTCW 2;
MTFW 2005; RGAL 4; RGSF 2; SFW 4;
SSFS 1, 18
Gilmore, Mary (Jean Cameron)
1865-1962 .... **PC 87**
See also CA 114; DLB 260; RGEL 2; SATA
49
Gilmour, David 1946- .... **CLC 35**
Gilpin, William 1724-1804 .... **NCLC 30**
Gilray, J. D.
See Mencken, H(enry) L(ouis)
Gilroy, Frank D(aniel) 1925- .... **CLC 2**
See also CA 81-84; CAD; CANR 32, 64,
86; CD 5, 6; DFS 17; DLB 7
Gilstrap, John 1957(?)- .... **CLC 99**
See also AAYA 67; CA 160; CANR 101
Ginsberg, Allen 1926-1997 .... **CLC 1, 2, 3, 4,
6, 13, 36, 69, 109; PC 4, 47; TCLC
120; WLC 3**
See also AAYA 33; AITN 1; AMWC 1;
AMWS 2; BG 1:2; CA 1-4R; 157; CANR
2, 41, 63, 95; CDALB 1941-1968; CP 1,
2, 3, 4, 5, 6; DA; DA3; DAB; DAC; DAM
MST; POET; DLB 5, 16, 169, 237; EWL
3; GLL 1; LMFS 2; MAL 5; MTCW 1, 2;
MTFW 2005; PAB; PFS 5; RGAL 4;
TUS; WP
Ginzburg, Eugenia CLC 59
See Ginzburg, Evgeniia
Ginzburg, Evgeniia 1904-1977
See Ginzburg, Eugenia
See also DLB 302
Ginzburg, Natalia 1916-1991 .... **CLC 5, 11,
54, 70; SSC 65; TCLC 156**
See also CA 85-88; 135; CANR 33; DFS
14; DLB 177; EW 13; EWL 3; MTCW 1,
2; MTFW 2005; RGHL; RGWL 2, 3
Gioia, (Michael) Dana 1950- .... **CLC 251**
See also AMWS 15; CA 130; CANR 70,
88; CP 6, 7; DLB 120, 282; PFS 24
Giono, Jean 1895-1970 .... **CLC 4, 11; TCLC
124**
See also CA 45-48; 29-32R; CANR 2, 35;
DLB 72, 321; EWL 3; GFL 1789 to the
Present; MTCW 1; RGWL 2, 3
Giovanni, Nikki 1943- ... **BLC 1:2; CLC 2, 4,
19, 64, 117; PC 19; WLCS**
See also AAYA 22; AITN 1; BW 2, 3; CA
29-32R; CAAS 6; CANR 18, 41, 60, 91,
130, 175; CDALBS; CLR 6, 73; CP 2, 3,
4, 5, 6, 7; CSW; CWP; CWRI 5; DA;
DA3; DAB; DAC; DAM MST, MULT,
POET; DLB 5, 41; EWL 3; EXPP; INT
CANR-18; MAICYA 1, 2; MAL 5;
MTCW 1, 2; MTFW 2005; PFS 17, 28;
RGAL 4; SATA 24, 107; TUS; YAW
Giovanni, Yolanda Cornelia
See Giovanni, Nikki
Giovanni, Yolande Cornelia
See Giovanni, Nikki

Giovanni, Yolande Cornelia, Jr.
See Giovanni, Nikki
Giovene, Andrea 1904-1998 .... **CLC 7**
See also CA 85-88
Gippius, Zinaida (Nikolaevna) 1869-1945
See Hippius, Zinaida (Nikolaevna)
See also CA 106; 212
Giraudoux, Jean(-Hippolyte)
1882-1944 .... **TCLC 2, 7**
See also CA 104; 196; DAM DRAM; DLB
65, 321; EW 9; EWL 3; GFL 1789 to the
Present; RGWL 2, 3; TWA
Gironella, Jose Maria (Pous)
1917-2003 .... **CLC 11**
See also CA 101; 212; EWL 3; RGWL 2, 3
Gissing, George (Robert)
1857-1903 .... **SSC 37, 113; TCLC 3, 24,
47**
See also BRW 5; CA 105; 167; DLB 18,
135, 184; RGEL 2; TEA
Gitlin, Todd 1943- .... **CLC 201**
See also CA 29-32R; CANR 25, 50, 88
Giurlani, Aldo
See Palazzeschi, Aldo
Gladkov, Fedor Vasil'evich
See Gladkov, Fyodor (Vasilyevich)
See also DLB 272
Gladkov, Fyodor (Vasilyevich)
1883-1958 .... **TCLC 27**
See Gladkov, Fedor Vasil'evich
See also CA 170; EWL 3
Glancy, Diane 1941- .... **CLC 210; NNAL**
See also CA 136, 225; CAAE 225; CAAS
24; CANR 87, 162; DLB 175
Glanville, Brian (Lester) 1931- .... **CLC 6**
See also CA 5-8R; CAAS 9; CANR 3, 70;
CN 1, 2, 3, 4, 5, 6, 7; DLB 15, 139; SATA
42
Glasgow, Ellen (Anderson Gholson)
1873-1945 .... **SSC 34; TCLC 2, 7**
See also AMW; CA 104; 164; DLB 9, 12;
MAL 5; MBL; MTCW 2; MTFW 2005;
RGAL 4; RHW; SSFS 9; TUS
Glaspell, Susan 1882(?)-1948 ..... **DC 10; SSC
41; TCLC 55, 175**
See also AMWS 3; CA 110; 154; DFS 8,
18, 24; DLB 7, 9, 78, 228; MBL; RGAL
4; SSFS 3; TCWW 2; TUS; YABC 2
Glassco, John 1909-1981 .... **CLC 9**
See also CA 13-16R; 102; CANR 15; CN
1, 2; CP 1, 2, 3; DLB 68
Glasscock, Amnesia
See Steinbeck, John (Ernst)
Glasser, Ronald J. 1940(?)- .... **CLC 37**
See also CA 209
Glassman, Joyce
See Johnson, Joyce
Gleick, James (W.) 1954- .... **CLC 147**
See also CA 131; 137; CANR 97; INT CA-
137
Glendinning, Victoria 1937- .... **CLC 50**
See also CA 120; 127; CANR 59, 89, 166;
DLB 155
Glissant, Edouard (Mathieu)
1928- .... **CLC 10, 68**
See also CA 153; CANR 111; CWW 2;
DAM MULT; EWL 3; RGWL 3
Gloag, Julian 1930- .... **CLC 40**
See also AITN 1; CA 65-68; CANR 10, 70;
CN 1, 2, 3, 4, 5, 6
Glowacki, Aleksander
See Prus, Boleslaw
Gluck, Louise 1943- .... **CLC 7, 22, 44, 81,
160; PC 16**
See also AMWS 5; CA 33-36R; CANR 40,
69, 108, 133; CP 1, 2, 3, 4, 5, 6, 7; CWP;
DA3; DAM POET; DLB 5; MAL 5;
MTCW 2; MTFW 2005; PFS 5, 15;
RGAL 4; TCLE 1:1

Glyn, Elinor 1864-1943 .... **TCLC 72**
See also DLB 153; RHW
Gobineau, Joseph-Arthur
1816-1882 .... **NCLC 17**
See also DLB 123; GFL 1789 to the Present
Godard, Jean-Luc 1930- .... **CLC 20**
See also CA 93-96
Godden, (Margaret) Rumer
1907-1998 .... **CLC 53**
See also AAYA 6; BPFB 2; BYA 2, 5; CA
5-8R; 172; CANR 4, 27, 36, 55, 80; CLR
20; CN 1, 2, 3, 4, 5, 6; CWRI 5; DLB
161; MAICYA 1, 2; RHW; SAAS 12;
SATA 3, 36; SATA-Obit 109; TEA
Godoy Alcayaga, Lucila 1899-1957 .. **HLC 2;
PC 32; TCLC 2**
See Mistral, Gabriela
See also BW 2; CA 104; 131; CANR 81;
DAM MULT; DNFS; HW 1, 2; MTCW 1,
2; MTFW 2005
Godwin, Gail 1937- ...... **CLC 5, 8, 22, 31, 69,
125**
See also BPFB 2; CA 29-32R; CANR 15,
43, 69, 132; CN 3, 4, 5, 6, 7; CPW; CSW;
DA3; DAM POP; DLB 6, 234; INT
CANR-15; MAL 5; MTCW 1, 2; MTFW
2005
Godwin, Gail Kathleen
See Godwin, Gail
Godwin, William 1756-1836 .. **NCLC 14, 130**
See also CDBLB 1789-1832; CMW 4; DLB
39, 104, 142, 158, 163, 262, 336; GL 2;
HGG; RGEL 2
Goebbels, Josef
See Goebbels, (Paul) Joseph
Goebbels, (Paul) Joseph
1897-1945 .... **TCLC 68**
See also CA 115; 148
Goebbels, Joseph Paul
See Goebbels, (Paul) Joseph
Goethe, Johann Wolfgang von
1749-1832 . **DC 20; NCLC 4, 22, 34, 90,
154; PC 5; SSC 38; WLC 3**
See also CDWLB 2; DA; DA3; DAB;
DAC; DAM DRAM, MST, POET; DLB
94; EW 5; GL 2; LATS 1; LMFS 1:1;
RGWL 2, 3; TWA
Gogarty, Oliver St. John
1878-1957 .... **TCLC 15**
See also CA 109; 150; DLB 15, 19; RGEL
2
Gogol, Nikolai (Vasilyevich)
1809-1852 .... **DC 1; NCLC 5, 15, 31,
162; SSC 4, 29, 52; WLC 3**
See also DA; DAB; DAC; DAM DRAM,
MST; DFS 12; DLB 198; EW 6; EXPS;
RGSF 2; RGWL 2, 3; SSFS 7; TWA
Goines, Donald 1937(?)-1974 .... **BLC 1:2;
CLC 80**
See also AITN 1; BW 1, 3; CA 124; 114;
CANR 82; CMW 4; DA3; DAM MULT,
POP; DLB 33
Gold, Herbert 1924- ... **CLC 4, 7, 14, 42, 152**
See also CA 9-12R; CANR 17, 45, 125; CN
1, 2, 3, 4, 5, 6, 7; DLB 2; DLBY 1981;
MAL 5
Goldbarth, Albert 1948- .... **CLC 5, 38**
See also AMWS 12; CA 53-56; CANR 6,
40; CP 3, 4, 5, 6, 7; DLB 120
Goldberg, Anatol 1910-1982 .... **CLC 34**
See also CA 131; 117
Goldemberg, Isaac 1945- .... **CLC 52**
See also CA 69-72; CAAS 12; CANR 11,
32; EWL 3; HW 1; WLIT 1
Golding, Arthur 1536-1606 .... **LC 101**
See also DLB 136

Golding, William 1911-1993 . **CLC 1, 2, 3, 8, 10, 17, 27, 58, 81; WLC 3**
See also AAYA 5, 44; BPFB 2; BRWR 1; BRWS 1; BYA 2; CA 5-8R; 141; CANR 13, 33, 54; CD 5; CDBLB 1945-1960; CLR 94, 130; CN 1, 2, 3, 4; DA; DA3; DAB; DAC; DAM MST, NOV; DLB 15, 100, 255, 326, 330; EWL 3; EXPN; HGG; LAIT 4; MTCW 1, 2; MTFW 2005; NFS 2; RGEL 2; RHW; SFW 4; TEA; WLIT 4; YAW

Golding, William Gerald
See Golding, William

Goldman, Emma 1869-1940 .... **TCLC 13**
See also CA 110; 150; DLB 221; FW; RGAL 4; TUS

Goldman, Francisco 1954- .... **CLC 76**
See also CA 162

Goldman, William 1931- .... **CLC 1, 48**
See also BPFB 2; CA 9-12R; CANR 29, 69, 106; CN 1, 2, 3, 4, 5, 6, 7; DLB 44; FANT; IDFW 3, 4

Goldman, William W.
See Goldman, William

Goldmann, Lucien 1913-1970 .... **CLC 24**
See also CA 25-28; CAP 2

Goldoni, Carlo 1707-1793 .... **LC 4**
See also DAM DRAM; EW 4; RGWL 2, 3; WLIT 7

Goldsberry, Steven 1949- .... **CLC 34**
See also CA 131

Goldsmith, Oliver 1730(?)-1774 .... **DC 8; LC 2, 48, 122; PC 77; WLC 3**
See also BRW 3; CDBLB 1660-1789; DA; DAB; DAC; DAM DRAM, MST, NOV, POET; DFS 1; DLB 39, 89, 104, 109, 142, 336; IDTP; RGEL 2; SATA 26; TEA; WLIT 3

Goldsmith, Peter
See Priestley, J(ohn) B(oynton)

Goldstein, Rebecca 1950- .... **CLC 239**
See also CA 144; CANR 99, 165; TCLE 1:1

Goldstein, Rebecca Newberger
See Goldstein, Rebecca

Gombrowicz, Witold 1904-1969 .... **CLC 4, 7, 11, 49**
See also CA 19-20; 25-28R; CANR 105; CAP 2; CDWLB 4; DAM DRAM; DLB 215; EW 12; EWL 3; RGWL 2, 3; TWA

Gomez de Avellaneda, Gertrudis 1814-1873 .... **NCLC 111**
See also LAW

Gomez de la Serna, Ramon 1888-1963 .... **CLC 9**
See also CA 153; 116; CANR 79; EWL 3; HW 1, 2

Goncharov, Ivan Alexandrovich 1812-1891 .... **NCLC 1, 63**
See also DLB 238; EW 6; RGWL 2, 3

Goncourt, Edmond (Louis Antoine Huot) de 1822-1896 .... **NCLC 7**
See also DLB 123; EW 7; GFL 1789 to the Present; RGWL 2, 3

Goncourt, Jules (Alfred Huot) de 1830-1870 .... **NCLC 7**
See also DLB 123; EW 7; GFL 1789 to the Present; RGWL 2, 3

Gongora (y Argote), Luis de 1561-1627 .... **LC 72**
See also RGWL 2, 3

Gontier, Fernande 19(?)- .... **CLC 50**

Gonzalez Martinez, Enrique
See Gonzalez Martinez, Enrique
See also DLB 290

Gonzalez Martinez, Enrique 1871-1952 .... **TCLC 72**
See Gonzalez Martinez, Enrique
See also CA 166; CANR 81; EWL 3; HW 1, 2

Goodison, Lorna 1947- .... **BLC 2:2; PC 36**
See also CA 142; CANR 88; CP 5, 6, 7; CWP; DLB 157; EWL 3; PFS 25

Goodman, Allegra 1967- .... **CLC 241**
See also CA 204; CANR 162; DLB 244

Goodman, Paul 1911-1972 ..... **CLC 1, 2, 4, 7**
See also CA 19-20; 37-40R; CAD; CANR 34; CAP 2; CN 1; DLB 130, 246; MAL 5; MTCW 1; RGAL 4

Goodweather, Hartley
See King, Thomas

GoodWeather, Hartley
See King, Thomas

Googe, Barnabe 1540-1594 .... **LC 94**
See also DLB 132; RGEL 2

Gordimer, Nadine 1923- ...... **CLC 3, 5, 7, 10, 18, 33, 51, 70, 123, 160, 161; SSC 17, 80; WLCS**
See also AAYA 39; AFW; BRWS 2; CA 5-8R; CANR 3, 28, 56, 88, 131; CN 1, 2, 3, 4, 5, 6, 7; DA; DA3; DAB; DAC; DAM MST, NOV; DLB 225, 326, 330; EWL 3; EXPS; INT CANR-28; LATS 1:2; MTCW 1, 2; MTFW 2005; NFS 4; RGEL 2; RGSF 2; SSFS 2, 14, 19; TWA; WLIT 2; YAW

Gordon, Adam Lindsay 1833-1870 .... **NCLC 21**
See also DLB 230

Gordon, Caroline 1895-1981 . **CLC 6, 13, 29, 83; SSC 15**
See also AMW; CA 11-12; 103; CANR 36; CAP 1; CN 1, 2; DLB 4, 9, 102; DLBD 17; DLBY 1981; EWL 3; MAL 5; MTCW 1, 2; MTFW 2005; RGAL 4; RGSF 2

Gordon, Charles William 1860-1937
See Connor, Ralph
See also CA 109

Gordon, Mary 1949- .. **CLC 13, 22, 128, 216; SSC 59**
See also AMWS 4; BPFB 2; CA 102; CANR 44, 92, 154; CN 4, 5, 6, 7; DLB 6; DLBY 1981; FW; INT CA-102; MAL 5; MTCW 1

Gordon, Mary Catherine
See Gordon, Mary

Gordon, N. J.
See Bosman, Herman Charles

Gordon, Sol 1923- .... **CLC 26**
See also CA 53-56; CANR 4; SATA 11

Gordone, Charles 1925-1995 .... **BLC 2:2; CLC 1, 4; DC 8**
See also BW 1, 3; CA 93-96, 180; 150; CAAE 180; CAD; CANR 55; DAM DRAM; DLB 7; INT CA-93-96; MTCW 1

Gore, Catherine 1800-1861 .... **NCLC 65**
See also DLB 116; RGEL 2

Gorenko, Anna Andreevna
See Akhmatova, Anna

Gorky, Maxim SSC 28; TCLC 8; WLC 3
See Peshkov, Alexei Maximovich
See also DAB; DFS 9; DLB 295; EW 8; EWL 3; TWA

Goryan, Sirak
See Saroyan, William

Gosse, Edmund (William) 1849-1928 .... **TCLC 28**
See also CA 117; DLB 57, 144, 184; RGEL 2

Gotlieb, Phyllis (Fay Bloom) 1926- .. **CLC 18**
See also CA 13-16R; CANR 7, 135; CN 7; CP 1, 2, 3, 4; DLB 88, 251; SFW 4

Gottesman, S. D.
See Kornbluth, C(yril) M.; Pohl, Frederik

Gottfried von Strassburg fl. c. 1170-1215 .... **CMLC 10, 96**
See also CDWLB 2; DLB 138; EW 1; RGWL 2, 3

Gotthelf, Jeremias 1797-1854 .... **NCLC 117**
See also DLB 133; RGWL 2, 3

Gottschalk, Laura Riding
See Jackson, Laura (Riding)

Gould, Lois 1932(?)-2002 .... **CLC 4, 10**
See also CA 77-80; 208; CANR 29; MTCW 1

Gould, Stephen Jay 1941-2002 .... **CLC 163**
See also AAYA 26; BEST 90:2; CA 77-80; 205; CANR 10, 27, 56, 75, 125; CPW; INT CANR-27; MTCW 1, 2; MTFW 2005

Gourmont, Remy(-Marie-Charles) de 1858-1915 .... **TCLC 17**
See also CA 109; 150; GFL 1789 to the Present; MTCW 2

Gournay, Marie le Jars de
See de Gournay, Marie le Jars

Govier, Katherine 1948- .... **CLC 51**
See also CA 101; CANR 18, 40, 128; CCA 1

Gower, John c. 1330-1408 .... **LC 76; PC 59**
See also BRW 1; DLB 146; RGEL 2

Goyen, (Charles) William 1915-1983 .... **CLC 5, 8, 14, 40**
See also AITN 2; CA 5-8R; 110; CANR 6, 71; CN 1, 2, 3; DLB 2, 218; DLBY 1983; EWL 3; INT CANR-6; MAL 5

Goytisolo, Juan 1931- ... **CLC 5, 10, 23, 133; HLC 1**
See also CA 85-88; CANR 32, 61, 131; CWW 2; DAM MULT; DLB 322; EWL 3; GLL 2; HW 1, 2; MTCW 1, 2; MTFW 2005

Gozzano, Guido 1883-1916 .... **PC 10**
See also CA 154; DLB 114; EWL 3

Gozzi, (Conte) Carlo 1720-1806 .... **NCLC 23**

Grabbe, Christian Dietrich 1801-1836 .... **NCLC 2**
See also DLB 133; RGWL 2, 3

Grace, Patricia Frances 1937- .... **CLC 56**
See also CA 176; CANR 118; CN 4, 5, 6, 7; EWL 3; RGSF 2

Gracian y Morales, Baltasar 1601-1658 .... **LC 15**

Gracq, Julien 1910-2007 .... **CLC 11, 48**
See also CA 122; 126; 267; CANR 141; CWW 2; DLB 83; GFL 1789 to the present

Grade, Chaim 1910-1982 .... **CLC 10**
See also CA 93-96; 107; DLB 333; EWL 3; RGHL

Grade, Khayim
See Grade, Chaim

Graduate of Oxford, A
See Ruskin, John

Grafton, Garth
See Duncan, Sara Jeannette

Grafton, Sue 1940- .... **CLC 163**
See also AAYA 11, 49; BEST 90:3; CA 108; CANR 31, 55, 111, 134; CMW 4; CPW; CSW; DA3; DAM POP; DLB 226; FW; MSW; MTFW 2005

Graham, John
See Phillips, David Graham

Graham, Jorie 1950- .... **CLC 48, 118; PC 59**
See also AAYA 67; CA 111; CANR 63, 118; CP 4, 5, 6, 7; CWP; DLB 120; EWL 3; MTFW 2005; PFS 10, 17; TCLE 1:1

Graham, R(obert) B(ontine) Cunninghame
See Cunninghame Graham, Robert (Gallnigad) Bontine
See also DLB 98, 135, 174; RGEL 2; RGSF 2

20; JRDA; LAIT 5; MAICYA 1, 2; MAI-
CYAS 1; MTCW 1, 2; MTFW 2005;
SATA 4, 56, 79, 123; SATA-Obit 132;
WYA; YAW

Hammett, (Samuel) Dashiell
1894-1961 .... CLC 3, 5, 10, 19, 47; SSC
17; TCLC 187
See also AAYA 59; AITN 1; AMWS 4;
BPFB 2; CA 81-84; CANR 42; CDALB
1929-1941; CMW 4; DA3; DLB 226, 280;
DLBD 6; DLBY 1996; EWL 3; LAIT 3;
MAL 5; MSW; MTCW 1, 2; MTFW
2005; NFS 21; RGAL 4; RGSF 2; TUS

Hammon, Jupiter 1720(?)-1800(?) . **BLC 1:2;**
NCLC 5; PC 16
See also DAM MULT, POET; DLB 31, 50

Hammond, Keith
See Kuttner, Henry

Hamner, Earl (Henry), Jr. 1923- ...... **CLC 12**
See also AITN 2; CA 73-76; DLB 6

Hampton, Christopher 1946- .... **CLC 4**
See also CA 25-28R; CD 5, 6; DLB 13;
MTCW 1

Hampton, Christopher James
See Hampton, Christopher

Hamsun, Knut TCLC 2, 14, 49, 151, 203
See Pedersen, Knut
See also DLB 297, 330; EW 8; EWL 3;
RGWL 2, 3

Handke, Peter 1942- .... **CLC 5, 8, 10, 15, 38,**
134; DC 17
See also CA 77-80; CANR 33, 75, 104, 133;
CWW 2; DAM DRAM, NOV; DLB 85,
124; EWL 3; MTCW 1, 2; MTFW 2005;
TWA

Handy, W(illiam) C(hristopher)
1873-1958 .... **TCLC 97**
See also BW 3; CA 121; 167

Hanley, James 1901-1985 ..... **CLC 3, 5, 8, 13**
See also CA 73-76; 117; CANR 36; CBD;
CN 1, 2, 3; DLB 191; EWL 3; MTCW 1;
RGEL 2

Hannah, Barry 1942- .. **CLC 23, 38, 90; SSC**
94
See also BPFB 2; CA 108; 110; CANR 43,
68, 113; CN 4, 5, 6, 7; CSW; DLB 6, 234;
INT CA-110; MTCW 1; RGSF 2

Hannon, Ezra
See Hunter, Evan

Hansberry, Lorraine (Vivian)
1930-1965 ... BLC 1:2, 2:2; CLC 17, 62;
DC 2; TCLC 192
See also AAYA 25; AFAW 1, 2; AMWS 4;
BW 1, 3; CA 109; 25-28R; CABS 3;
CAD; CANR 58; CDALB 1941-1968;
CWD; DA; DA3; DAB; DAC; DAM
DRAM, MST, MULT; DFS 2; DLB 7, 38;
EWL 3; FL 1:6; FW; LAIT 4; MAL 5;
MTCW 1, 2; MTFW 2005; RGAL 4; TUS

Hansen, Joseph 1923-2004 .... **CLC 38**
See Brock, Rose; Colton, James
See also BPFB 2; CA 29-32R; 233; CAAS
17; CANR 16, 44, 66, 125; CMW 4; DLB
226; GLL 1; INT CANR-16

Hansen, Karen V. 1955- .... **CLC 65**
See also CA 149; CANR 102

Hansen, Martin A(lfred)
1909-1955 .... **TCLC 32**
See also CA 167; DLB 214; EWL 3

Hanson, Kenneth O(stlin) 1922- .... **CLC 13**
See also CA 53-56; CANR 7; CP 1, 2, 3, 4,
5

Hardwick, Elizabeth 1916-2007 .... **CLC 13**
See also AMWS 3; CA 5-8R; 267; CANR
3, 32, 70, 100, 139; CN 4, 5, 6; CSW;
DA3; DAM NOV; DLB 6; MBL; MTCW
1, 2; MTFW 2005; TCLE 1:1

Hardwick, Elizabeth Bruce
See Hardwick, Elizabeth

Hardwick, Elizabeth Bruce
See Hardwick, Elizabeth

Hardy, Thomas 1840-1928 . **PC 8; SSC 2, 60,**
113; TCLC 4, 10, 18, 32, 48, 53, 72,
143, 153; WLC 3
See also AAYA 69; BRW 6; BRWC 1, 2;
BRWR 1; CA 104; 123; CDBLB 1890-
1914; DA; DA3; DAB; DAC; DAM MST,
NOV, POET; DLB 18, 19, 135, 284; EWL
3; EXPN; EXPP; LAIT 2; MTCW 1, 2;
MTFW 2005; NFS 3, 11, 15, 19; PFS 3,
4, 18; RGEL 2; RGSF 2; TEA; WLIT 4

Hare, David 1947- . **CLC 29, 58, 136; DC 26**
See also BRWS 4; CA 97-100; CANR 39,
91; CBD; CD 5, 6; DFS 4, 7, 16; DLB
13, 310; MTCW 1; TEA

Harewood, John
See Van Druten, John (William)

Harford, Henry
See Hudson, W(illiam) H(enry)

Hargrave, Leonie
See Disch, Thomas M.

Hariri, Al- al-Qasim ibn 'Ali Abu
Muhammad al-Basri
See al-Hariri, al-Qasim ibn 'Ali Abu Mu-
hammad al-Basri

Harjo, Joy 1951- ..... **CLC 83; NNAL; PC 27**
See also AMWS 12; CA 114; CANR 35,
67, 91, 129; CP 6, 7; CWP; DAM MULT;
DLB 120, 175; EWL 3; MTCW 2; MTFW
2005; PFS 15; RGAL 4

Harlan, Louis R(udolph) 1922- .... **CLC 34**
See also CA 21-24R; CANR 25, 55, 80

Harling, Robert 1951(?)- .... **CLC 53**
See also CA 147

Harmon, William (Ruth) 1938- .... **CLC 38**
See also CA 33-36R; CANR 14, 32, 35;
SATA 65

Harper, F. E. W.
See Harper, Frances Ellen Watkins

Harper, Frances E. W.
See Harper, Frances Ellen Watkins

Harper, Frances E. Watkins
See Harper, Frances Ellen Watkins

Harper, Frances Ellen
See Harper, Frances Ellen Watkins

Harper, Frances Ellen Watkins
1825-1911 .. BLC 1:2; PC 21; TCLC 14
See also AFAW 1, 2; BW 1, 3; CA 111; 125;
CANR 79; DAM MULT, POET; DLB 50,
221; MBL; RGAL 4

Harper, Michael S(teven) 1938- ..... **BLC 2:2;**
CLC 7, 22
See also AFAW 2; BW 1; CA 33-36R, 224;
CAAE 224; CANR 24, 108; CP 2, 3, 4, 5,
6, 7; DLB 41; RGAL 4; TCLE 1:1

Harper, Mrs. F. E. W.
See Harper, Frances Ellen Watkins

Harpur, Charles 1813-1868 .... **NCLC 114**
See also DLB 230; RGEL 2

Harris, Christie
See Harris, Christie (Lucy) Irwin

Harris, Christie (Lucy) Irwin
1907-2002 .... **CLC 12**
See also CA 5-8R; CANR 6, 83; CLR 47;
DLB 88; JRDA; MAICYA 1, 2; SAAS 10;
SATA 6, 74; SATA-Essay 116

Harris, Frank 1856-1931 .... **TCLC 24**
See also CA 109; 150; CANR 80; DLB 156,
197; RGEL 2

Harris, George Washington
1814-1869 .... **NCLC 23, 165**
See also DLB 3, 11, 248; RGAL 4

Harris, Joel Chandler 1848-1908 ..... **SSC 19,**
103; TCLC 2
See also CA 104; 137; CANR 80; CLR 49,
128; DLB 11, 23, 42, 78, 91; LAIT 2;
MAICYA 1, 2; RGSF 2; SATA 100; WCH;
YABC 1

Harris, John (Wyndham Parkes Lucas)
Beynon 1903-1969
See Wyndham, John
See also CA 102; 89-92; CANR 84; SATA
118; SFW 4

Harris, MacDonald CLC 9
See Heiney, Donald (William)

Harris, Mark 1922-2007 .... **CLC 19**
See also CA 5-8R; 260; CAAS 3; CANR 2,
55, 83; CN 1, 2, 3, 4, 5, 6, 7; DLB 2;
DLBY 1980

Harris, Norman CLC 65

Harris, (Theodore) Wilson 1921- ... **BLC 2:2;**
CLC 25, 159
See also BRWS 5; BW 2, 3; CA 65-68;
CAAS 16; CANR 11, 27, 69, 114; CD-
WLB 3; CN 1, 2, 3, 4, 5, 6, 7; CP 1, 2, 3,
4, 5, 6, 7; DLB 117; EWL 3; MTCW 1;
RGEL 2

Harrison, Barbara Grizzuti
1934-2002 .... **CLC 144**
See also CA 77-80; 205; CANR 15, 48; INT
CANR-15

Harrison, Elizabeth (Allen) Cavanna
1909-2001
See Cavanna, Betty
See also CA 9-12R; 200; CANR 6, 27, 85,
104, 121; MAICYA 2; SATA 142; YAW

Harrison, Harry (Max) 1925- .... **CLC 42**
See also CA 1-4R; CANR 5, 21, 84; DLB
8; SATA 4; SCFW 2; SFW 4

Harrison, James
See Harrison, Jim

Harrison, James Thomas
See Harrison, Jim

Harrison, Jim 1937- .... **CLC 6, 14, 33, 66,**
143; SSC 19
See also AMWS 8; CA 13-16R; CANR 8,
51, 79, 142; CN 5, 6; CP 1, 2, 3, 4, 5, 6;
DLBY 1982; INT CANR-8; RGAL 4;
TCWW 2; TUS

Harrison, Kathryn 1961- .... **CLC 70, 151**
See also CA 144; CANR 68, 122

Harrison, Tony 1937- .... **CLC 43, 129**
See also BRWS 5; CA 65-68; CANR 44,
98; CBD; CD 5, 6; CP 2, 3, 4, 5, 6, 7;
DLB 40, 245; MTCW 1; RGEL 2

Harriss, Will(ard Irvin) 1922- .... **CLC 34**
See also CA 111

Hart, Ellis
See Ellison, Harlan

Hart, Josephine 1942(?)- .... **CLC 70**
See also CA 138; CANR 70, 149; CPW;
DAM POP

Hart, Moss 1904-1961 .... **CLC 66**
See also CA 109; 89-92; CANR 84; DAM
DRAM; DFS 1; DLB 7, 266; RGAL 4

Harte, (Francis) Bret(t)
1836(?)-1902 ... SSC 8, 59; TCLC 1, 25;
WLC 3
See also AMWS 2; CA 104; 140; CANR
80; CDALB 1865-1917; DA; DA3; DAC;
DAM MST; DLB 12, 64, 74, 79, 186;
EXPS; LAIT 2; RGAL 4; RGSF 2; SATA
26; SSFS 3; TUS

Hartley, L(eslie) P(oles) 1895-1972 ... **CLC 2,**
22
See also BRWS 7; CA 45-48; 37-40R;
CANR 33; CN 1; DLB 15, 139; EWL 3;
HGG; MTCW 1, 2; MTFW 2005; RGEL
2; RGSF 2; SUFW 1

Hartman, Geoffrey H. 1929- .... **CLC 27**
See also CA 117; 125; CANR 79; DLB 67

Hartmann, Sadakichi 1869-1944 ... **TCLC 73**
See also CA 157; DLB 54

Hartmann von Aue c. 1170-c.
1210 .... **CMLC 15**
See also CDWLB 2; DLB 138; RGWL 2, 3

Heliodorus fl. 3rd cent. - .... **CMLC 52**
　　See also WLIT 8
Hellenhofferu, Vojtech Kapristian z
　　See Hasek, Jaroslav (Matej Frantisek)
Heller, Joseph 1923-1999 . **CLC 1, 3, 5, 8, 11,**
　　36, 63; TCLC 131, 151; WLC 3
　　See also AAYA 24; AITN 1; AMWS 4;
　　BPFB 2; BYA 1; CA 5-8R; 187; CABS 1;
　　CANR 8, 42, 66, 126; CN 1, 2, 3, 4, 5, 6;
　　CPW; DA; DA3; DAB; DAC; DAM MST,
　　NOV, POP; DLB 2, 28, 227; DLBY 1980,
　　2002; EWL 3; EXPN; INT CANR-8;
　　LAIT 4; MAL 5; MTCW 1, 2; MTFW
　　2005; NFS 1; RGAL 4; TUS; YAW
Hellman, Lillian 1906-1984 . **CLC 2, 4, 8, 14,**
　　18, 34, 44, 52; DC 1; TCLC 119
　　See also AAYA 47; AITN 1, 2; AMWS 1;
　　CA 13-16R; 112; CAD; CANR 33; CWD;
　　DA3; DAM DRAM; DFS 1, 3, 14; DLB
　　7, 228; DLBY 1984; EWL 3; FL 1:6; FW;
　　LAIT 3; MAL 5; MBL; MTCW 1, 2;
　　MTFW 2005; RGAL 4; TUS
Helprin, Mark 1947- .... **CLC 7, 10, 22, 32**
　　See also CA 81-84; CANR 47, 64, 124;
　　CDALBS; CN 7; CPW; DA3; DAM NOV,
　　POP; DLB 335; DLBY 1985; FANT;
　　MAL 5; MTCW 1, 2; MTFW 2005; SSFS
　　25; SUFW 2
Helvetius, Claude-Adrien 1715-1771 .. **LC 26**
　　See also DLB 313
Helyar, Jane Penelope Josephine 1933-
　　See Poole, Josephine
　　See also CA 21-24R; CANR 10, 26; CWRI
　　5; SATA 82, 138; SATA-Essay 138
Hemans, Felicia 1793-1835 ...... **NCLC 29, 71**
　　See also DLB 96; RGEL 2
Hemingway, Ernest (Miller)
　　1899-1961 .... **CLC 1, 3, 6, 8, 10, 13, 19,**
　　30, 34, 39, 41, 44, 50, 61, 80; SSC 1, 25,
　　36, 40, 63; TCLC 115, 203; WLC 3
　　See also AAYA 19; AMW; AMWC 1;
　　AMWR 1; BPFB 2; BYA 2, 3, 13, 15; CA
　　77-80; CANR 34; CDALB 1917-1929;
　　DA; DA3; DAB; DAC; DAM MST, NOV;
　　DLB 4, 9, 102, 210, 308, 316, 330; DLBD
　　1, 15, 16; DLBY 1981, 1987, 1996, 1998;
　　EWL 3; EXPN; EXPS; LAIT 3, 4; LATS
　　1:1; MAL 5; MTCW 1, 2; MTFW 2005;
　　NFS 1, 5, 6, 14; RGAL 4; RGSF 2; SSFS
　　17; TUS; WYA
Hempel, Amy 1951- .... **CLC 39**
　　See also CA 118; 137; CANR 70, 166;
　　DA3; DLB 218; EXPS; MTCW 2; MTFW
　　2005; SSFS 2
Henderson, F. C.
　　See Mencken, H(enry) L(ouis)
Henderson, Sylvia
　　See Ashton-Warner, Sylvia (Constance)
Henderson, Zenna (Chlarson)
　　1917-1983 .... **SSC 29**
　　See also CA 1-4R; 133; CANR 1, 84; DLB
　　8; SATA 5; SFW 4
Henkin, Joshua 1964- .... **CLC 119**
　　See also CA 161
Henley, Beth CLC 23, 255; DC 6, 14
　　See Henley, Elizabeth Becker
　　See also AAYA 70; CABS 3; CAD; CD 5,
　　6; CSW; CWD; DFS 2, 21; DLBY 1986;
　　FW
Henley, Elizabeth Becker 1952-
　　See Henley, Beth
　　See also CA 107; CANR 32, 73, 140; DA3;
　　DAM DRAM, MST; MTCW 1, 2; MTFW
　　2005
Henley, William Ernest 1849-1903 .. **TCLC 8**
　　See also CA 105; 234; DLB 19; RGEL 2
Hennissart, Martha 1929-
　　See Lathen, Emma
　　See also CA 85-88; CANR 64

Henry VIII 1491-1547 .... **LC 10**
　　See also DLB 132
Henry, O. SSC 5, 49; TCLC 1, 19; WLC 3
　　See Porter, William Sydney
　　See also AAYA 41; AMWS 2; EXPS; MAL
　　5; RGAL 4; RGSF 2; SSFS 2, 18; TCWW
　　1, 2
Henry, Patrick 1736-1799 .... **LC 25**
　　See also LAIT 1
Henryson, Robert 1430(?)-1506(?) ..... **LC 20,**
　　110; PC 65
　　See also BRWS 7; DLB 146; RGEL 2
Henschke, Alfred
　　See Klabund
Henson, Lance 1944- .... **NNAL**
　　See also CA 146; DLB 175
Hentoff, Nat(han Irving) 1925- .... **CLC 26**
　　See also AAYA 4, 42; BYA 6; CA 1-4R;
　　CAAS 6; CANR 5, 25, 77, 114; CLR 1,
　　52; INT CANR-25; JRDA; MAICYA 1,
　　2; SATA 42, 69, 133; SATA-Brief 27;
　　WYA; YAW
Heppenstall, (John) Rayner
　　1911-1981 .... **CLC 10**
　　See also CA 1-4R; 103; CANR 29; CN 1,
　　2; EWL 3
Heraclitus c. 540B.C.-c. 450B.C. ... **CMLC 22**
　　See also DLB 176
Herbert, Frank 1920-1986 ... **CLC 12, 23, 35,**
　　44, 85
　　See also AAYA 21; BPFB 2; BYA 4, 14;
　　CA 53-56; 118; CANR 5, 43; CDALBS;
　　CPW; DAM POP; DLB 8; INT CANR-5;
　　LAIT 5; MTCW 1, 2; MTFW 2005; NFS
　　17; SATA 9, 37; SATA-Obit 47; SCFW 1,
　　2; SFW 4; YAW
Herbert, George 1593-1633 . **LC 24, 121; PC**
　　4
　　See also BRW 2; BRWR 2; CDBLB Before
　　1660; DAB; DAM POET; DLB 126;
　　EXPP; PFS 25; RGEL 2; TEA; WP
Herbert, Zbigniew 1924-1998 ..... **CLC 9, 43;**
　　PC 50; TCLC 168
　　See also CA 89-92; 169; CANR 36, 74; CD-
　　WLB 4; CWW 2; DAM POET; DLB 232;
　　EWL 3; MTCW 1; PFS 22
Herbst, Josephine (Frey)
　　1897-1969 .... **CLC 34**
　　See also CA 5-8R; 25-28R; DLB 9
Herder, Johann Gottfried von
　　1744-1803 .... **NCLC 8, 186**
　　See also DLB 97; EW 4; TWA
Heredia, Jose Maria 1803-1839 .... **HLCS 2**
　　See also LAW
Hergesheimer, Joseph 1880-1954 ... **TCLC 11**
　　See also CA 109; 194; DLB 102, 9; RGAL
　　4
Herlihy, James Leo 1927-1993 .... **CLC 6**
　　See also CA 1-4R; 143; CAD; CANR 2;
　　CN 1, 2, 3, 4, 5
Herman, William
　　See Bierce, Ambrose (Gwinett)
Hermogenes fl. c. 175- .... **CMLC 6**
Hernandez, Jose 1834-1886 .... **NCLC 17**
　　See also LAW; RGWL 2, 3; WLIT 1
Herodotus c. 484B.C.-c. 420B.C. ... **CMLC 17**
　　See also AW 1; CDWLB 1; DLB 176;
　　RGWL 2, 3; TWA; WLIT 8
Herr, Michael 1940(?)- .... **CLC 231**
　　See also CA 89-92; CANR 68, 142; DLB
　　185; MTCW 1
Herrick, Robert 1591-1674 .. **LC 13, 145; PC**
　　9
　　See also BRW 2; BRWC 2; DA; DAB;
　　DAC; DAM MST, POP; DLB 126; EXPP;
　　PFS 13; RGAL 4; RGEL 2; TEA; WP
Herring, Guilles
　　See Somerville, Edith Oenone

Herriot, James 1916-1995 .... **CLC 12**
　　See Wight, James Alfred
　　See also AAYA 1, 54; BPFB 2; CA 148;
　　CANR 40; CLR 80; CPW; DAM POP;
　　LAIT 3; MAICYA 2; MAICYAS 1;
　　MTCW 2; SATA 86, 135; TEA; YAW
Herris, Violet
　　See Hunt, Violet
Herrmann, Dorothy 1941- .... **CLC 44**
　　See also CA 107
Herrmann, Taffy
　　See Herrmann, Dorothy
Hersey, John 1914-1993 .. **CLC 1, 2, 7, 9, 40,**
　　81, 97
　　See also AAYA 29; BPFB 2; CA 17-20R;
　　140; CANR 33; CDALBS; CN 1, 2, 3, 4,
　　5; CPW; DAM POP; DLB 6, 185, 278,
　　299; MAL 5; MTCW 1, 2; MTFW 2005;
　　RGHL; SATA 25; SATA-Obit 76; TUS
Hervent, Maurice
　　See Grindel, Eugene
Herzen, Aleksandr Ivanovich
　　1812-1870 .... **NCLC 10, 61**
　　See Herzen, Alexander
Herzen, Alexander
　　See Herzen, Aleksandr Ivanovich
　　See also DLB 277
Herzl, Theodor 1860-1904 .... **TCLC 36**
　　See also CA 168
Herzog, Werner 1942- .... **CLC 16, 236**
　　See also CA 89-92
Hesiod fl. 8th cent. B.C.- .... **CMLC 5, 102**
　　See also AW 1; DLB 176; RGWL 2, 3;
　　WLIT 8
Hesse, Hermann 1877-1962 ... **CLC 1, 2, 3, 6,**
　　11, 17, 25, 69; SSC 9, 49; TCLC 148,
　　196; WLC 3
　　See also AAYA 43; BPFB 2; CA 17-18;
　　CAP 2; CDWLB 2; DA; DA3; DAB;
　　DAC; DAM MST, NOV; DLB 66, 330;
　　EW 9; EWL 3; EXPN; LAIT 1; MTCW
　　1, 2; MTFW 2005; NFS 6, 15, 24; RGWL
　　2, 3; SATA 50; TWA
Hewes, Cady
　　See De Voto, Bernard (Augustine)
Heyen, William 1940- .... **CLC 13, 18**
　　See also CA 33-36R; 220; CAAE 220;
　　CAAS 9; CANR 98; CP 3, 4, 5, 6, 7; DLB
　　5; RGHL
Heyerdahl, Thor 1914-2002 .... **CLC 26**
　　See also CA 5-8R; 207; CANR 5, 22, 66,
　　73; LAIT 4; MTCW 1, 2; MTFW 2005;
　　SATA 2, 52
Heym, Georg (Theodor Franz Arthur)
　　1887-1912 .... **TCLC 9**
　　See also CA 106; 181
Heym, Stefan 1913-2001 .... **CLC 41**
　　See also CA 9-12R; 203; CANR 4; CWW
　　2; DLB 69; EWL 3
Heyse, Paul (Johann Ludwig von)
　　1830-1914 .... **TCLC 8**
　　See also CA 104; 209; DLB 129, 330
Heyward, (Edwin) DuBose
　　1885-1940 .... **HR 1:2; TCLC 59**
　　See also CA 108; 157; DLB 7, 9, 45, 249;
　　MAL 5; SATA 21
Heywood, John 1497(?)-1580(?) .... **LC 65**
　　See also DLB 136; RGEL 2
Heywood, Thomas 1573(?)-1641 . **DC 29; LC**
　　111
　　See also DAM DRAM; DLB 62; LMFS 1;
　　RGEL 2; TEA
Hiaasen, Carl 1953- .... **CLC 238**
　　See also CA 105; CANR 22, 45, 65, 113,
　　133, 168; CMW 4; CPW; CSW; DA3;
　　DLB 292; MTCW 2; MTFW 2005

Hofmannsthal, Hugo von 1874-1929 ... **DC 4; TCLC 11**
See also CA 106; 153; CDWLB 2; DAM DRAM; DFS 17; DLB 81, 118; EW 9; EWL 3; RGWL 2, 3

Hogan, Linda 1947- ..... **CLC 73; NNAL; PC 35**
See also AMWS 4; ANW; BYA 12; CA 120, 226; CAAE 226; CANR 45, 73, 129; CWP; DAM MULT; DLB 175; SATA 132; TCWW 2

Hogarth, Charles
See Creasey, John

Hogarth, Emmett
See Polonsky, Abraham (Lincoln)

Hogarth, William 1697-1764 .... **LC 112**
See also AAYA 56

Hogg, James 1770-1835 .... **NCLC 4, 109**
See also BRWS 10; DLB 93, 116, 159; GL 2; HGG; RGEL 2; SUFW 1

Holbach, Paul-Henri Thiry
1723-1789 .... **LC 14**
See also DLB 313

Holberg, Ludvig 1684-1754 .... **LC 6**
See also DLB 300; RGWL 2, 3

Holcroft, Thomas 1745-1809 .... **NCLC 85**
See also DLB 39, 89, 158; RGEL 2

Holden, Ursula 1921- .... **CLC 18**
See also CA 101; CAAS 8; CANR 22

Holderlin, (Johann Christian) Friedrich
1770-1843 .... **NCLC 16, 187; PC 4**
See also CDWLB 2; DLB 90; EW 5; RGWL 2, 3

Holding, James (Clark Carlisle, Jr.)
1907-1997
See Queen, Ellery
See also CA 25-28R; SATA 3

Holdstock, Robert 1948- .... **CLC 39**
See also CA 131; CANR 81; DLB 261; FANT; HGG; SFW 4; SUFW 2

Holdstock, Robert P.
See Holdstock, Robert

Holinshed, Raphael fl. 1580- .... **LC 69**
See also DLB 167; RGEL 2

Holland, Isabelle (Christian)
1920-2002 .... **CLC 21**
See also AAYA 11, 64; CA 21-24R; 205; CAAE 181; CANR 10, 25, 47; CLR 57; CWRI 5; JRDA; LAIT 4; MAICYA 1, 2; SATA 8, 70; SATA-Essay 103; SATA-Obit 132; WYA

Holland, Marcus
See Caldwell, (Janet Miriam) Taylor (Holland)

Hollander, John 1929- .... **CLC 2, 5, 8, 14**
See also CA 1-4R; CANR 1, 52, 136; CP 1, 2, 3, 4, 5, 6, 7; DLB 5; MAL 5; SATA 13

Hollander, Paul
See Silverberg, Robert

Holleran, Andrew CLC 38
See Garber, Eric
See also CA 144; GLL 1

Holley, Marietta 1836(?)-1926 .... **TCLC 99**
See also CA 118; DLB 11; FL 1:3

Hollinghurst, Alan 1954- .... **CLC 55, 91**
See also BRWS 10; CA 114; CN 5, 6, 7; DLB 207, 326; GLL 1

Hollis, Jim
See Summers, Hollis (Spurgeon, Jr.)

Holly, Buddy 1936-1959 .... **TCLC 65**
See also CA 213

Holmes, Gordon
See Shiel, M(atthew) P(hipps)

Holmes, John
See Souster, (Holmes) Raymond

Holmes, John Clellon 1926-1988 ...... **CLC 56**
See also BG 1:2; CA 9-12R; 125; CANR 4; CN 1, 2, 3, 4; DLB 16, 237

Holmes, Oliver Wendell, Jr.
1841-1935 .... **TCLC 77**
See also CA 114; 186

Holmes, Oliver Wendell
1809-1894 .... **NCLC 14, 81; PC 71**
See also AMWS 1; CDALB 1640-1865; DLB 1, 189, 235; EXPP; PFS 24; RGAL 4; SATA 34

Holmes, Raymond
See Souster, (Holmes) Raymond

Holt, Victoria
See Hibbert, Eleanor Alice Burford
See also BPFB 2

Holub, Miroslav 1923-1998 .... **CLC 4**
See also CA 21-24R; 169; CANR 10; CD-WLB 4; CWW 2; DLB 232; EWL 3; RGWL 3

Holz, Detlev
See Benjamin, Walter

Homer c. 8th cent. B.C.- .... **CMLC 1, 16, 61; PC 23; WLCS**
See also AW 1; CDWLB 1; DA; DA3; DAB; DAC; DAM MST, POET; DLB 176; EFS 1; LAIT 1; LMFS 1; RGWL 2, 3; TWA; WLIT 8; WP

Hongo, Garrett Kaoru 1951- .... **PC 23**
See also CA 133; CAAS 22; CP 5, 6, 7; DLB 120, 312; EWL 3; EXPP; PFS 25; RGAL 4

Honig, Edwin 1919- .... **CLC 33**
See also CA 5-8R; CAAS 8; CANR 4, 45, 144; CP 1, 2, 3, 4, 5, 6, 7; DLB 5

Hood, Hugh (John Blagdon) 1928- . **CLC 15, 28; SSC 42**
See also CA 49-52; CAAS 17; CANR 1, 33, 87; CN 1, 2, 3, 4, 5, 6, 7; DLB 53; RGSF 2

Hood, Thomas 1799-1845 .... **NCLC 16**
See also BRW 4; DLB 96; RGEL 2

Hooker, (Peter) Jeremy 1941- .... **CLC 43**
See also CA 77-80; CANR 22; CP 2, 3, 4, 5, 6, 7; DLB 40

Hooker, Richard 1554-1600 .... **LC 95**
See also BRW 1; DLB 132; RGEL 2

Hooker, Thomas 1586-1647 .... **LC 137**
See also DLB 24

hooks, bell 1952(?)- .... **BLCS; CLC 94**
See also BW 2; CA 143; CANR 87, 126; DLB 246; MTCW 2; MTFW 2005; SATA 115, 170

Hooper, Johnson Jones
1815-1862 .... **NCLC 177**
See also DLB 3, 11, 248; RGAL 4

Hope, A(lec) D(erwent) 1907-2000 .... **CLC 3, 51; PC 56**
See also BRWS 7; CA 21-24R; 188; CANR 33, 74; CP 1, 2, 3, 4, 5; DLB 289; EWL 3; MTCW 1, 2; MTFW 2005; PFS 8; RGEL 2

Hope, Anthony 1863-1933 .... **TCLC 83**
See also CA 157; DLB 153, 156; RGEL 2; RHW

Hope, Brian
See Creasey, John

Hope, Christopher (David Tully)
1944- .... **CLC 52**
See also AFW; CA 106; CANR 47, 101; CN 4, 5, 6, 7; DLB 225; SATA 62

Hopkins, Gerard Manley
1844-1889 .... **NCLC 17, 189; PC 15; WLC 3**
See also BRW 5; BRWR 2; CDBLB 1890-1914; DA; DA3; DAB; DAC; DAM MST, POET; DLB 35, 57; EXPP; PAB; PFS 26; RGEL 2; TEA; WP

Hopkins, John (Richard) 1931-1998 .. **CLC 4**
See also CA 85-88; 169; CBD; CD 5, 6

Hopkins, Pauline Elizabeth
1859-1930 .... **BLC 1:2; TCLC 28**
See also AFAW 2; BW 2, 3; CA 141; CANR 82; DAM MULT; DLB 50

Hopkinson, Francis 1737-1791 .... **LC 25**
See also DLB 31; RGAL 4

Hopley-Woolrich, Cornell George 1903-1968
See Woolrich, Cornell
See also CA 13-14; CANR 58, 156; CAP 1; CMW 4; DLB 226; MTCW 2

Horace 65B.C.-8B.C. .... **CMLC 39; PC 46**
See also AW 2; CDWLB 1; DLB 211; RGWL 2, 3; WLIT 8

Horatio
See Proust, (Valentin-Louis-George-Eugene) Marcel

Horgan, Paul (George Vincent O'Shaughnessy) 1903-1995 .. **CLC 9, 53**
See also BPFB 2; CA 13-16R; 147; CANR 9, 35; CN 1, 2, 3, 4, 5; DAM NOV; DLB 102, 212; DLBY 1985; INT CANR-9; MTCW 1, 2; MTFW 2005; SATA 13; SATA-Obit 84; TCWW 1, 2

Horkheimer, Max 1895-1973 .... **TCLC 132**
See also CA 216; 41-44R; DLB 296

Horn, Peter
See Kuttner, Henry

Hornby, Nick 1957(?)- .... **CLC 243**
See also AAYA 74; CA 151; CANR 104, 151; CN 7; DLB 207

Horne, Frank (Smith) 1899-1974 ...... **HR 1:2**
See also BW 1; CA 125; 53-56; DLB 51; WP

Horne, Richard Henry Hengist
1802(?)-1884 .... **NCLC 127**
See also DLB 32; SATA 29

Hornem, Horace Esq.
See Byron, George Gordon (Noel)

Horne Tooke, John 1736-1812 ..... **NCLC 195**

Horney, Karen (Clementine Theodore Danielsen) 1885-1952 .... **TCLC 71**
See also CA 114; 165; DLB 246; FW

Hornung, E(rnest) W(illiam)
1866-1921 .... **TCLC 59**
See also CA 108; 160; CMW 4; DLB 70

Horovitz, Israel 1939- .... **CLC 56**
See also CA 33-36R; CAD; CANR 46, 59; CD 5, 6; DAM DRAM; DLB 7, 341; MAL 5

Horton, George Moses
1797(?)-1883(?) .... **NCLC 87**
See also DLB 50

Horvath, odon von 1901-1938
See von Horvath, Odon
See also EWL 3

Horvath, Oedoen von -1938
See von Horvath, Odon

Horwitz, Julius 1920-1986 .... **CLC 14**
See also CA 9-12R; 119; CANR 12

Horwitz, Ronald
See Harwood, Ronald

Hospital, Janette Turner 1942- .... **CLC 42, 145**
See also CA 108; CANR 48, 166; CN 5, 6, 7; DLB 325; DLBY 2002; RGSF 2

Hosseini, Khaled 1965- .... **CLC 254**
See also CA 225; SATA 156

Hostos, E. M. de
See Hostos (y Bonilla), Eugenio Maria de

Hostos, Eugenio M. de
See Hostos (y Bonilla), Eugenio Maria de

Hostos, Eugenio Maria
See Hostos (y Bonilla), Eugenio Maria de

Hostos (y Bonilla), Eugenio Maria de
1839-1903 .... **TCLC 24**
See also CA 123; 131; HW 1

Houdini
See Lovecraft, H. P.

Kinsella, W.P. 1935- .... **CLC 27, 43, 166**
See also AAYA 7, 60; BPFB 2; CA 97-100, 222; CAAE 222; CAAS 7; CANR 21, 35, 66, 75, 129; CN 4, 5, 6, 7; CPW; DAC; DAM NOV, POP; FANT; INT CANR-21; LAIT 5; MTCW 1, 2; MTFW 2005; NFS 15; RGSF 2

Kinsey, Alfred C(harles) 1894-1956 .... **TCLC 91**
See also CA 115; 170; MTCW 2

Kipling, (Joseph) Rudyard 1865-1936 . **PC 3; SSC 5, 54, 110; TCLC 8, 17, 167; WLC 3**
See also AAYA 32; BRW 6; BRWC 1, 2; BYA 4; CA 105; 120; CANR 33; CDBLB 1890-1914; CLR 39, 65; CWRI 5; DA; DA3; DAB; DAC; DAM MST, POET; DLB 19, 34, 141, 156, 330; EWL 3; EXPS; FANT; LAIT 3; LMFS 1; MAICYA 1, 2; MTCW 1, 2; MTFW 2005; NFS 21; PFS 22; RGEL 2; RGSF 2; SATA 100; SFW 4; SSFS 8, 21, 22; SUFW 1; TEA; WCH; WLIT 4; YABC 2

Kircher, Athanasius 1602-1680 .... **LC 121**
See also DLB 164

Kirk, Russell (Amos) 1918-1994 .. **TCLC 119**
See also AITN 1; CA 1-4R; 145; CAAS 9; CANR 1, 20, 60; HGG; INT CANR-20; MTCW 1, 2

Kirkham, Dinah
See Card, Orson Scott

Kirkland, Caroline M. 1801-1864 . **NCLC 85**
See also DLB 3, 73, 74, 250, 254; DLBD 13

Kirkup, James 1918- .... **CLC 1**
See also CA 1-4R; CAAS 4; CANR 2; CP 1, 2, 3, 4, 5, 6, 7; DLB 27; SATA 12

Kirkwood, James 1930(?)-1989 .... **CLC 9**
See also AITN 2; CA 1-4R; 128; CANR 6, 40; GLL 2

Kirsch, Sarah 1935- .... **CLC 176**
See also CA 178; CWW 2; DLB 75; EWL 3

Kirshner, Sidney
See Kingsley, Sidney

Kis, Danilo 1935-1989 .... **CLC 57**
See also CA 109; 118; 129; CANR 61; CDWLB 4; DLB 181; EWL 3; MTCW 1; RGSF 2; RGWL 2, 3

Kissinger, Henry A(lfred) 1923- ..... **CLC 137**
See also CA 1-4R; CANR 2, 33, 66, 109; MTCW 1

Kittel, Frederick August
See Wilson, August

Kivi, Aleksis 1834-1872 .... **NCLC 30**

Kizer, Carolyn 1925- ..... **CLC 15, 39, 80; PC 66**
See also CA 65-68; CAAS 5; CANR 24, 70, 134; CP 1, 2, 3, 4, 5, 6, 7; CWP; DAM POET; DLB 5, 169; EWL 3; MAL 5; MTCW 2; MTFW 2005; PFS 18; TCLE 1:1

Klabund 1890-1928 .... **TCLC 44**
See also CA 162; DLB 66

Klappert, Peter 1942- .... **CLC 57**
See also CA 33-36R; CSW; DLB 5

Klausner, Amos
See Oz, Amos

Klein, A(braham) M(oses) 1909-1972 .... **CLC 19**
See also CA 101; 37-40R; CP 1; DAB; DAC; DAM MST; DLB 68; EWL 3; RGEL 2; RGHL

Klein, Joe
See Klein, Joseph

Klein, Joseph 1946- .... **CLC 154**
See also CA 85-88; CANR 55, 164

Klein, Norma 1938-1989 .... **CLC 30**
See also AAYA 2, 35; BPFB 2; BYA 6, 7, 8; CA 41-44R; 128; CANR 15, 37; CLR 2, 19; INT CANR-15; JRDA; MAICYA 1, 2; SAAS 1; SATA 7, 57; WYA; YAW

Klein, T.E.D. 1947- .... **CLC 34**
See also CA 119; CANR 44, 75, 167; HGG

Klein, Theodore Eibon Donald
See Klein, T.E.D.

Kleist, Heinrich von 1777-1811 .... **DC 29; NCLC 2, 37; SSC 22**
See also CDWLB 2; DAM DRAM; DLB 90; EW 5; RGSF 2; RGWL 2, 3

Klima, Ivan 1931- .... **CLC 56, 172**
See also CA 25-28R; CANR 17, 50, 91; CDWLB 4; CWW 2; DAM NOV; DLB 232; EWL 3; RGWL 3

Klimentev, Andrei Platonovich
See Klimentov, Andrei Platonovich

Klimentov, Andrei Platonovich 1899-1951 .... **SSC 42; TCLC 14**
See Platonov, Andrei Platonovich; Platonov, Andrey Platonovich
See also CA 108; 232

Klinger, Friedrich Maximilian von 1752-1831 .... **NCLC 1**
See also DLB 94

Klingsor the Magician
See Hartmann, Sadakichi

Klopstock, Friedrich Gottlieb 1724-1803 .... **NCLC 11**
See also DLB 97; EW 4; RGWL 2, 3

Kluge, Alexander 1932- .... **SSC 61**
See also CA 81-84; CANR 163; DLB 75

Knapp, Caroline 1959-2002 .... **CLC 99**
See also CA 154; 207

Knebel, Fletcher 1911-1993 .... **CLC 14**
See also AITN 1; CA 1-4R; 140; CAAS 3; CANR 1, 36; CN 1, 2, 3, 4, 5; SATA 36; SATA-Obit 75

Knickerbocker, Diedrich
See Irving, Washington

Knight, Etheridge 1931-1991 .... **BLC 1:2; CLC 40; PC 14**
See also BW 1, 3; CA 21-24R; 133; CANR 23, 82; CP 1, 2, 3, 4, 5; DAM POET; DLB 41; MTCW 2; MTFW 2005; RGAL 4; TCLE 1:1

Knight, Sarah Kemble 1666-1727 .... **LC 7**
See also DLB 24, 200

Knister, Raymond 1899-1932 .... **TCLC 56**
See also CA 186; DLB 68; RGEL 2

Knowles, John 1926-2001 ... **CLC 1, 4, 10, 26**
See also AAYA 10, 72; AMWS 12; BPFB 2; BYA 3; CA 17-20R; 203; CANR 40, 74, 76, 132; CDALB 1968-1988; CLR 98; CN 1, 2, 3, 4, 5, 6, 7; DA; DAC; DAM MST, NOV; DLB 6; EXPN; MTCW 1, 2; MTFW 2005; NFS 2; RGAL 4; SATA 8, 89; SATA-Obit 134; YAW

Knox, Calvin M.
See Silverberg, Robert

Knox, John c. 1505-1572 .... **LC 37**
See also DLB 132

Knye, Cassandra
See Disch, Thomas M.

Koch, C(hristopher) J(ohn) 1932- .... **CLC 42**
See also CA 127; CANR 84; CN 3, 4, 5, 6, 7; DLB 289

Koch, Christopher
See Koch, C(hristopher) J(ohn)

Koch, Kenneth 1925-2002 .... **CLC 5, 8, 44; PC 80**
See also AMWS 15; CA 1-4R; 207; CAD; CANR 6, 36, 57, 97, 131; CD 5, 6; CP 1, 2, 3, 4, 5, 6, 7; DAM POET; DLB 5; INT CANR-36; MAL 5; MTCW 2; MTFW 2005; PFS 20; SATA 65; WP

Kochanowski, Jan 1530-1584 .... **LC 10**
See also RGWL 2, 3

Kock, Charles Paul de 1794-1871 . **NCLC 16**

Koda Rohan
See Koda Shigeyuki

Koda Rohan
See Koda Shigeyuki

Koda Shigeyuki 1867-1947 .... **TCLC 22**
See also CA 121; 183; DLB 180

Koestler, Arthur 1905-1983 ... **CLC 1, 3, 6, 8, 15, 33**
See also BRWS 1; CA 1-4R; 109; CANR 1, 33; CDBLB 1945-1960; CN 1, 2, 3; DLBY 1983; EWL 3; MTCW 1, 2; MTFW 2005; NFS 19; RGEL 2

Kogawa, Joy Nozomi 1935- ...... **CLC 78, 129**
See also AAYA 47; CA 101; CANR 19, 62, 126; CN 6, 7; CP 1; CWP; DAC; DAM MST, MULT; DLB 334; FW; MTCW 2; MTFW 2005; NFS 3; SATA 99

Kohout, Pavel 1928- .... **CLC 13**
See also CA 45-48; CANR 3

Koizumi, Yakumo
See Hearn, (Patricio) Lafcadio (Tessima Carlos)

Kolmar, Gertrud 1894-1943 .... **TCLC 40**
See also CA 167; EWL 3; RGHL

Komunyakaa, Yusef 1947- . **BLC 2:2; BLCS; CLC 86, 94, 207; PC 51**
See also AFAW 2; AMWS 13; CA 147; CANR 83, 164; CP 6, 7; CSW; DLB 120; EWL 3; PFS 5, 20; RGAL 4

Konigsberg, Alan Stewart
See Allen, Woody

Konrad, George
See Konrad, Gyorgy

Konrad, George
See Konrad, Gyorgy

Konrad, Gyorgy 1933- .... **CLC 4, 10, 73**
See also CA 85-88; CANR 97, 171; CDWLB 4; CWW 2; DLB 232; EWL 3

Konwicki, Tadeusz 1926- .... **CLC 8, 28, 54, 117**
See also CA 101; CAAS 9; CANR 39, 59; CWW 2; DLB 232; EWL 3; IDFW 3; MTCW 1

Koontz, Dean 1945- .... **CLC 78, 206**
See also AAYA 9, 31; BEST 89:3, 90:2; CA 108; CANR 19, 36, 52, 95, 138, 176; CMW 4; CPW; DA3; DAM NOV, POP; DLB 292; HGG; MTCW 1; MTFW 2005; SATA 92, 165; SFW 4; SUFW 2; YAW

Koontz, Dean Ray
See Koontz, Dean

Kopernik, Mikolaj
See Copernicus, Nicolaus

Kopit, Arthur (Lee) 1937- ...... **CLC 1, 18, 33**
See also AITN 1; CA 81-84; CABS 3; CAD; CD 5, 6; DAM DRAM; DFS 7, 14, 24; DLB 7; MAL 5; MTCW 1; RGAL 4

Kopitar, Jernej (Bartholomaus) 1780-1844 .... **NCLC 117**

Kops, Bernard 1926- .... **CLC 4**
See also CA 5-8R; CANR 84, 159; CBD; CN 1, 2, 3, 4, 5, 6, 7; CP 1, 2, 3, 4, 5, 6, 7; DLB 13; RGHL

Kornbluth, C(yril) M. 1923-1958 .... **TCLC 8**
See also CA 105; 160; DLB 8; SCFW 1, 2; SFW 4

Korolenko, V.G.
See Korolenko, Vladimir G.

Korolenko, Vladimir
See Korolenko, Vladimir G.

Korolenko, Vladimir G. 1853-1921 .... **TCLC 22**
See also CA 121; DLB 277

Korolenko, Vladimir Galaktionovich
See Korolenko, Vladimir G.

LaForet, Carmen 1921-2004 .... **CLC 219**
See also CA 246; CWW 2; DLB 322; EWL
3

LaForet Diaz, Carmen
See LaForet, Carmen

Laforgue, Jules 1860-1887 . **NCLC 5, 53; PC
14; SSC 20**
See also DLB 217; EW 7; GFL 1789 to the
Present; RGWL 2, 3

Lagerkvist, Paer (Fabian)
1891-1974 ..... **CLC 7, 10, 13, 54; TCLC
144**
See Lagerkvist, Par
See also CA 85-88; 49-52; DA3; DAM
DRAM, NOV; MTCW 1, 2; MTFW 2005;
TWA

Lagerkvist, Par SSC 12
See Lagerkvist, Paer (Fabian)
See also DLB 259, 331; EW 10; EWL 3;
RGSF 2; RGWL 2, 3

**Lagerloef, Selma (Ottiliana Lovisa) TCLC 4,
36**
See Lagerlof, Selma (Ottiliana Lovisa)
See also CA 108; MTCW 2

Lagerlof, Selma (Ottiliana Lovisa)
1858-1940
See Lagerloef, Selma (Ottiliana Lovisa)
See also CA 188; CLR 7; DLB 259, 331;
RGWL 2, 3; SATA 15; SSFS 18

La Guma, Alex 1925-1985 .. **BLCS; CLC 19;
TCLC 140**
See also AFW; BW 1, 3; CA 49-52; 118;
CANR 25, 81; CDWLB 3; CN 1, 2, 3;
CP 1; DAM NOV; DLB 117, 225; EWL
3; MTCW 1, 2; MTFW 2005; WLIT 2;
WWE 1

Lahiri, Jhumpa 1967- .... **SSC 96**
See also AAYA 56; CA 193; CANR 134;
DLB 323; MTFW 2005; SSFS 19

Laidlaw, A. K.
See Grieve, C(hristopher) M(urray)

Lainez, Manuel Mujica
See Mujica Lainez, Manuel
See also HW 1

Laing, R(onald) D(avid) 1927-1989 . **CLC 95**
See also CA 107; 129; CANR 34; MTCW 1

Laishley, Alex
See Booth, Martin

Lamartine, Alphonse (Marie Louis Prat) de
1790-1869 .... **NCLC 11, 190; PC 16**
See also DAM POET; DLB 217; GFL 1789
to the Present; RGWL 2, 3

Lamb, Charles 1775-1834 ..... **NCLC 10, 113;
SSC 112; WLC 3**
See also BRW 4; CDBLB 1789-1832; DA;
DAB; DAC; DAM MST; DLB 93, 107,
163; RGEL 2; SATA 17; TEA

Lamb, Lady Caroline 1785-1828 ... **NCLC 38**
See also DLB 116

Lamb, Mary Ann 1764-1847 ...... **NCLC 125;
SSC 112**
See also DLB 163; SATA 17

Lame Deer 1903(?)-1976 .... **NNAL**
See also CA 69-72

Lamming, George (William)
1927- . **BLC 1:2, 2:2; CLC 2, 4, 66, 144**
See also BW 2, 3; CA 85-88; CANR 26,
76; CDWLB 3; CN 1, 2, 3, 4, 5, 6, 7; CP
1; DAM MULT; DLB 125; EWL 3;
MTCW 1, 2; MTFW 2005; NFS 15;
RGEL 2

L'Amour, Louis 1908-1988 .... **CLC 25, 55**
See also AAYA 16; AITN 2; BEST 89:2;
BPFB 2; CA 1-4R; 125; CANR 3, 25, 40;
CPW; DA3; DAM NOV, POP; DLB 206;
DLBY 1980; MTCW 1, 2; MTFW 2005;
RGAL 4; TCWW 1, 2

Lampedusa, Giuseppe (Tomasi) di TCLC 13
See Tomasi di Lampedusa, Giuseppe
See also CA 164; EW 11; MTCW 2; MTFW
2005; RGWL 2, 3

Lampman, Archibald 1861-1899 .. **NCLC 25,
194**
See also DLB 92; RGEL 2; TWA

Lancaster, Bruce 1896-1963 .... **CLC 36**
See also CA 9-10; CANR 70; CAP 1; SATA
9

Lanchester, John 1962- .... **CLC 99**
See also CA 194; DLB 267

Landau, Mark Alexandrovich
See Aldanov, Mark (Alexandrovich)

Landau-Aldanov, Mark Alexandrovich
See Aldanov, Mark (Alexandrovich)

Landis, Jerry
See Simon, Paul

Landis, John 1950- .... **CLC 26**
See also CA 112; 122; CANR 128

Landolfi, Tommaso 1908-1979 .... **CLC 11, 49**
See also CA 127; 117; DLB 177; EWL 3

Landon, Letitia Elizabeth
1802-1838 .... **NCLC 15**
See also DLB 96

Landor, Walter Savage
1775-1864 .... **NCLC 14**
See also BRW 4; DLB 93, 107; RGEL 2

Landwirth, Heinz
See Lind, Jakov

Lane, Patrick 1939- .... **CLC 25**
See also CA 97-100; CANR 54; CP 3, 4, 5,
6, 7; DAM POET; DLB 53; INT CA-97-
100

Lane, Rose Wilder 1887-1968 ...... **TCLC 177**
See also CA 102; CANR 63; SATA 29;
SATA-Brief 28; TCWW 2

Lang, Andrew 1844-1912 .... **TCLC 16**
See also CA 114; 137; CANR 85; CLR 101;
DLB 98, 141, 184; FANT; MAICYA 1, 2;
RGEL 2; SATA 16; WCH

Lang, Fritz 1890-1976 .... **CLC 20, 103**
See also AAYA 65; CA 77-80; 69-72;
CANR 30

Lange, John
See Crichton, Michael

Langer, Elinor 1939- .... **CLC 34**
See also CA 121

Langland, William 1332(?)-1400(?) .... **LC 19,
120**
See also BRW 1; DA; DAB; DAC; DAM
MST, POET; DLB 146; RGEL 2; TEA;
WLIT 3

Langstaff, Launcelot
See Irving, Washington

Lanier, Sidney 1842-1881 . **NCLC 6, 118; PC
50**
See also AMWS 1; DAM POET; DLB 64;
DLBD 13; EXPP; MAICYA 1; PFS 14;
RGAL 4; SATA 18

Lanyer, Aemilia 1569-1645 .... **LC 10, 30, 83;
PC 60**
See also DLB 121

Lao-Tzu
See Lao Tzu

Lao Tzu c. 6th cent. B.C.-3rd cent.
B.C. .... **CMLC 7**

Lapine, James (Elliot) 1949- .... **CLC 39**
See also CA 123; 130; CANR 54, 128; DFS
25; DLB 341; INT CA-130

Larbaud, Valery (Nicolas)
1881-1957 .... **TCLC 9**
See also CA 106; 152; EWL 3; GFL 1789
to the Present

Larcom, Lucy 1824-1893 .... **NCLC 179**
See also AMWS 13; DLB 221, 243

Lardner, Ring
See Lardner, Ring(gold) W(ilmer)
See also BPFB 2; CDALB 1917-1929; DLB
11, 25, 86, 171; DLBD 16; MAL 5;
RGAL 4; RGSF 2

Lardner, Ring W., Jr.
See Lardner, Ring(gold) W(ilmer)

Lardner, Ring(gold) W(ilmer)
1885-1933 .... **SSC 32; TCLC 2, 14**
See Lardner, Ring
See also AMW; CA 104; 131; MTCW 1, 2;
MTFW 2005; TUS

Laredo, Betty
See Codrescu, Andrei

Larkin, Maia
See Wojciechowska, Maia (Teresa)

Larkin, Philip (Arthur) 1922-1985 ... **CLC 3,
5, 8, 9, 13, 18, 33, 39, 64; PC 21**
See also BRWS 1; CA 5-8R; 117; CANR
24, 62; CDBLB 1960 to Present; CP 1, 2,
3, 4; DA3; DAB; DAM MST, POET;
DLB 27; EWL 3; MTCW 1, 2; MTFW
2005; PFS 3, 4, 12; RGEL 2

La Roche, Sophie von
1730-1807 .... **NCLC 121**
See also DLB 94

La Rochefoucauld, Francois
1613-1680 .... **LC 108**
See also DLB 268; EW 3; GFL Beginnings
to 1789; RGWL 2, 3

**Larra (y Sanchez de Castro), Mariano Jose
de** 1809-1837 .... **NCLC 17, 130**

Larsen, Eric 1941- .... **CLC 55**
See also CA 132

Larsen, Nella 1893(?)-1963 ... **BLC 1:2; CLC
37; HR 1:3; TCLC 200**
See also AFAW 1, 2; BW 1; CA 125; CANR
83; DAM MULT; DLB 51; FW; LATS
1:1; LMFS 2

Larson, Charles R(aymond) 1938- ... **CLC 31**
See also CA 53-56; CANR 4, 121

Larson, Jonathan 1960-1996 .... **CLC 99**
See also AAYA 28; CA 156; DFS 23;
MTFW 2005

La Sale, Antoine de c. 1386-1460(?) . **LC 104**
See also DLB 208

Las Casas, Bartolome de
1474-1566 .... **HLCS; LC 31**
See Casas, Bartolome de las
See also DLB 318; LAW

Lasch, Christopher 1932-1994 .... **CLC 102**
See also CA 73-76; 144; CANR 25, 118;
DLB 246; MTCW 1, 2; MTFW 2005

Lasker-Schueler, Else 1869-1945 ... **TCLC 57**
See Lasker-Schuler, Else
See also CA 183; DLB 66, 124

Lasker-Schuler, Else
See Lasker-Schueler, Else
See also EWL 3

Laski, Harold J(oseph) 1893-1950 . **TCLC 79**
See also CA 188

Latham, Jean Lee 1902-1995 .... **CLC 12**
See also AITN 1; BYA 1; CA 5-8R; CANR
7, 84; CLR 50; MAICYA 1, 2; SATA 2,
68; YAW

Latham, Mavis
See Clark, Mavis Thorpe

Lathen, Emma CLC 2
See Hennissart, Martha; Latsis, Mary J(ane)
See also BPFB 2; CMW 4; DLB 306

Lathrop, Francis
See Leiber, Fritz (Reuter, Jr.)

Latsis, Mary J(ane) 1927-1997
See Lathen, Emma
See also CA 85-88; 162; CMW 4

Lattany, Kristin
See Lattany, Kristin (Elaine Eggleston)
Hunter

Lee, Willy
See Burroughs, William S.
See also GLL 1

Lee-Hamilton, Eugene (Jacob)
1845-1907 .... **TCLC 22**
See also CA 117; 234

Leet, Judith 1935- .... **CLC 11**
See also CA 187

Le Fanu, Joseph Sheridan
1814-1873 .... **NCLC 9, 58; SSC 14, 84**
See also CMW 4; DA3; DAM POP; DLB
21, 70, 159, 178; GL 3; HGG; RGEL 2;
RGSF 2; SUFW 1

Leffland, Ella 1931- .... **CLC 19**
See also CA 29-32R; CANR 35, 78, 82;
DLBY 1984; INT CANR-35; SATA 65;
SSFS 24

Leger, Alexis
See Leger, (Marie-Rene Auguste) Alexis
Saint-Leger

Leger, (Marie-Rene Auguste) Alexis
Saint-Leger 1887-1975 .. **CLC 4, 11, 46;**
PC 23
See Perse, Saint-John; Saint-John Perse
See also CA 13-16R; 61-64; CANR 43;
DAM POET; MTCW 1

Leger, Saintleger
See Leger, (Marie-Rene Auguste) Alexis
Saint-Leger

Le Guin, Ursula K. 1929- ...... **CLC 8, 13, 22,**
45, 71, 136; SSC 12, 69
See also AAYA 9, 27; AITN 1; BPFB 2;
BYA 5, 8, 11, 14; CA 21-24R; CANR 9,
32, 52, 74, 132; CDALB 1968-1988; CLR
3, 28, 91; CN 2, 3, 4, 5, 6, 7; CPW; DA3;
DAB; DAC; DAM MST, POP; DLB 8,
52, 256, 275; EXPS; FANT; FW; INT
CANR-32; JRDA; LAIT 5; MAICYA 1,
2; MAL 5; MTCW 1, 2; MTFW 2005;
NFS 6, 9; SATA 4, 52, 99, 149; SCFW 1,
2; SFW 4; SSFS 2; SUFW 1, 2; WYA;
YAW

Lehmann, Rosamond (Nina)
1901-1990 .... **CLC 5**
See also CA 77-80; 131; CANR 8, 73; CN
1, 2, 3, 4; DLB 15; MTCW 2; RGEL 2;
RHW

Leiber, Fritz (Reuter, Jr.)
1910-1992 .... **CLC 25**
See also AAYA 65; BPFB 2; CA 45-48; 139;
CANR 2, 40, 86; CN 2, 3, 4, 5; DLB 8;
FANT; HGG; MTCW 1, 2; MTFW 2005;
SATA 45; SATA-Obit 73; SCFW 1, 2;
SFW 4; SUFW 1, 2

Leibniz, Gottfried Wilhelm von
1646-1716 .... **LC 35**
See also DLB 168

Leino, Eino TCLC 24
See Lonnbohm, Armas Eino Leopold
See also EWL 3

Leiris, Michel (Julien) 1901-1990 ..... **CLC 61**
See also CA 119; 128; 132; EWL 3; GFL
1789 to the Present

Leithauser, Brad 1953- .... **CLC 27**
See also CA 107; CANR 27, 81, 171; CP 5,
6, 7; DLB 120, 282

le Jars de Gournay, Marie
See de Gournay, Marie le Jars

Lelchuk, Alan 1938- .... **CLC 5**
See also CA 45-48; CAAS 20; CANR 1,
70, 152; CN 3, 4, 5, 6, 7

Lem, Stanislaw 1921-2006 ..... **CLC 8, 15, 40,**
149
See also AAYA 75; CA 105; 249; CAAS 1;
CANR 32; CWW 2; MTCW 1; SCFW 1,
2; SFW 4

Lemann, Nancy (Elise) 1956- .... **CLC 39**
See also CA 118; 136; CANR 121

Lemonnier, (Antoine Louis) Camille
1844-1913 .... **TCLC 22**
See also CA 121

Lenau, Nikolaus 1802-1850 .... **NCLC 16**

L'Engle, Madeleine 1918-2007 .... **CLC 12**
See also AAYA 28; AITN 2; BPFB 2; BYA
2, 4, 5, 7; CA 1-4R; 264; CANR 3, 21,
39, 66, 107; CLR 1, 14, 57; CPW; CWRI
5; DA3; DAM POP; DLB 52; JRDA;
MAICYA 1, 2; MTCW 1, 2; MTFW 2005;
SAAS 15; SATA 1, 27, 75, 128; SATA-
Obit 186; SFW 4; WYA; YAW

L'Engle, Madeleine Camp Franklin
See L'Engle, Madeleine

Lengyel, Jozsef 1896-1975 .... **CLC 7**
See also CA 85-88; 57-60; CANR 71;
RGSF 2

Lenin 1870-1924
See Lenin, V. I.
See also CA 121; 168

Lenin, V. I. TCLC 67
See Lenin

Lennon, John (Ono) 1940-1980 .. **CLC 12, 35**
See also CA 102; SATA 114

Lennox, Charlotte Ramsay
1729(?)-1804 .... **NCLC 23, 134**
See also DLB 39; RGEL 2

Lentricchia, Frank, Jr.
See Lentricchia, Frank

Lentricchia, Frank 1940- .... **CLC 34**
See also CA 25-28R; CANR 19, 106, 148;
DLB 246

Lenz, Gunter CLC 65

Lenz, Jakob Michael Reinhold
1751-1792 .... **LC 100**
See also DLB 94; RGWL 2, 3

Lenz, Siegfried 1926- .... **CLC 27; SSC 33**
See also CA 89-92; CANR 80, 149; CWW
2; DLB 75; EWL 3; RGSF 2; RGWL 2, 3

Leon, David
See Jacob, (Cyprien-)Max

Leonard, Dutch
See Leonard, Elmore

Leonard, Elmore 1925- .... **CLC 28, 34, 71,**
120, 222
See also AAYA 22, 59; AITN 1; BEST 89:1,
90:4; BPFB 2; CA 81-84; CANR 12, 28,
53, 76, 96, 133, 176; CMW 4; CN 5, 6, 7;
CPW; DA3; DAM POP; DLB 173, 226;
INT CANR-28; MSW; MTCW 1, 2;
MTFW 2005; RGAL 4; SATA 163;
TCWW 1, 2

Leonard, Elmore John, Jr.
See Leonard, Elmore

Leonard, Hugh CLC 19
See Byrne, John Keyes
See also CBD; CD 5, 6; DFS 13, 24; DLB
13

Leonov, Leonid (Maximovich)
1899-1994 .... **CLC 92**
See Leonov, Leonid Maksimovich
See also CA 129; CANR 76; DAM NOV;
EWL 3; MTCW 1, 2; MTFW 2005

Leonov, Leonid Maksimovich
See Leonov, Leonid (Maximovich)
See also DLB 272

Leopardi, (Conte) Giacomo
1798-1837 .... **NCLC 22, 129; PC 37**
See also EW 5; RGWL 2, 3; WLIT 7; WP

Le Reveler
See Artaud, Antonin (Marie Joseph)

Lerman, Eleanor 1952- .... **CLC 9**
See also CA 85-88; CANR 69, 124

Lerman, Rhoda 1936- .... **CLC 56**
See also CA 49-52; CANR 70

Lermontov, Mikhail Iur'evich
See Lermontov, Mikhail Yuryevich
See also DLB 205

Lermontov, Mikhail Yuryevich
1814-1841 .... **NCLC 5, 47, 126; PC 18**
See Lermontov, Mikhail Iur'evich
See also EW 6; RGWL 2, 3; TWA

Leroux, Gaston 1868-1927 .... **TCLC 25**
See also CA 108; 136; CANR 69; CMW 4;
MTFW 2005; NFS 20; SATA 65

Lesage, Alain-Rene 1668-1747 .... **LC 2, 28**
See also DLB 313; EW 3; GFL Beginnings
to 1789; RGWL 2, 3

Leskov, N(ikolai) S(emenovich) 1831-1895
See Leskov, Nikolai (Semyonovich)

Leskov, Nikolai (Semyonovich)
1831-1895 ... **NCLC 25, 174; SSC 34, 96**
See Leskov, Nikolai Semenovich

Leskov, Nikolai Semenovich
See Leskov, Nikolai (Semyonovich)
See also DLB 238

Lesser, Milton
See Marlowe, Stephen

Lessing, Doris 1919- .. **CLC 1, 2, 3, 6, 10, 15,**
22, 40, 94, 170, 254; SSC 6, 61; WLCS
See also AAYA 57; AFW; BRWS 1; CA
9-12R; CAAS 14; CANR 33, 54, 76, 122;
CBD; CD 5, 6; CDBLB 1960 to Present;
CN 1, 2, 3, 4, 5, 6, 7; CWD; DA; DA3;
DAB; DAC; DAM MST, NOV; DFS 20;
DLB 15, 139; DLBY 1985; EWL 3;
EXPS; FL 1:6; FW; LAIT 4; MTCW 1, 2;
MTFW 2005; NFS 27; RGEL 2; RGSF 2;
SFW 4; SSFS 1, 12, 20; TEA; WLIT 2, 4

Lessing, Doris May
See Lessing, Doris

Lessing, Gotthold Ephraim
1729-1781 .... **DC 26; LC 8, 124**
See also CDWLB 2; DLB 97; EW 4; RGWL
2, 3

Lester, Julius 1939- .... **BLC 2:2**
See also AAYA 12, 51; BW 2; BYA 3, 9,
11, 12; CA 17-20R; CANR 8, 23, 43, 129,
174; CLR 2, 41; JRDA; MAICYA 1, 2;
MAICYAS 1; MTFW 2005; SATA 12, 74,
112, 157; YAW

Lester, Richard 1932- .... **CLC 20**

Levenson, Jay CLC 70

Lever, Charles (James)
1806-1872 .... **NCLC 23**
See also DLB 21; RGEL 2

Leverson, Ada Esther
1862(?)-1933(?) .... **TCLC 18**
See Elaine
See also CA 117; 202; DLB 153; RGEL 2

Levertov, Denise 1923-1997 .. **CLC 1, 2, 3, 5,**
8, 15, 28, 66; PC 11
See also AMWS 3; CA 1-4R; 178; 163;
CAAE 178; CAAS 19; CANR 3, 29, 50,
108; CDALBS; CP 1, 2, 3, 4, 5, 6; CWP;
DAM POET; DLB 5, 165; EWL 3; EXPP;
FW; INT CANR-29; MAL 5; MTCW 1,
2; PAB; PFS 7, 17; RGAL 4; RGHL;
TUS; WP

Levi, Carlo 1902-1975 .... **TCLC 125**
See also CA 65-68; 53-56; CANR 10; EWL
3; RGWL 2, 3

Levi, Jonathan CLC 76
See also CA 197

Levi, Peter (Chad Tigar)
1931-2000 .... **CLC 41**
See also CA 5-8R; 187; CANR 34, 80; CP
1, 2, 3, 4, 5, 6, 7; DLB 40

Levi, Primo 1919-1987 ...... **CLC 37, 50; SSC**
12; TCLC 109
See also CA 13-16R; 122; CANR 12, 33,
61, 70, 132, 171; DLB 177, 299; EWL 3;
MTCW 1, 2; MTFW 2005; RGHL;
RGWL 2, 3; WLIT 7

Machado de Assis, Joaquim Maria
1839-1908 . **BLC 1:2; HLCS 2; SSC 24; TCLC 10**
See also CA 107; 153; CANR 91; DLB 307; LAW; RGSF 2; RGWL 2, 3; TWA; WLIT 1

Machaut, Guillaume de c.
1300-1377 .... **CMLC 64**
See also DLB 208

Machen, Arthur SSC 20; TCLC 4
See Jones, Arthur Llewellyn
See also CA 179; DLB 156, 178; RGEL 2; SUFW 1

Machiavelli, Niccolo 1469-1527 ... **DC 16; LC 8, 36, 140; WLCS**
See also AAYA 58; DA; DAB; DAC; DAM MST; EW 2; LAIT 1; LMFS 1; NFS 9; RGWL 2, 3; TWA; WLIT 7

MacInnes, Colin 1914-1976 .... **CLC 4, 23**
See also CA 69-72; 65-68; CANR 21; CN 1, 2; DLB 14; MTCW 1, 2; RGEL 2; RHW

MacInnes, Helen (Clark)
1907-1985 .... **CLC 27, 39**
See also BPFB 2; CA 1-4R; 117; CANR 1, 28, 58; CMW 4; CN 1, 2; CPW; DAM POP; DLB 87; MSW; MTCW 1, 2; MTFW 2005; SATA 22; SATA-Obit 44

Mackay, Mary 1855-1924
See Corelli, Marie
See also CA 118; 177; FANT; RHW

Mackay, Shena 1944- .... **CLC 195**
See also CA 104; CANR 88, 139; DLB 231, 319; MTFW 2005

Mackenzie, Compton (Edward Montague)
1883-1972 .... **CLC 18; TCLC 116**
See also CA 21-22; 37-40R; CAP 2; CN 1; DLB 34, 100; RGEL 2

Mackenzie, Henry 1745-1831 .... **NCLC 41**
See also DLB 39; RGEL 2

Mackey, Nathaniel 1947- .... **BLC 2:3; PC 49**
See also CA 153; CANR 114; CP 6, 7; DLB 169

Mackey, Nathaniel Ernest
See Mackey, Nathaniel

MacKinnon, Catharine A. 1946- .... **CLC 181**
See also CA 128; 132; CANR 73, 140; FW; MTCW 2; MTFW 2005

Mackintosh, Elizabeth 1896(?)-1952
See Tey, Josephine
See also CA 110; CMW 4

Macklin, Charles 1699-1797 .... **LC 132**
See also DLB 89; RGEL 2

MacLaren, James
See Grieve, C(hristopher) M(urray)

MacLaverty, Bernard 1942- ..... **CLC 31, 243**
See also CA 116; 118; CANR 43, 88, 168; CN 5, 6, 7; DLB 267; INT CA-118; RGSF 2

MacLean, Alistair (Stuart)
1922(?)-1987 .... **CLC 3, 13, 50, 63**
See also CA 57-60; 121; CANR 28, 61; CMW 4; CP 2, 3, 4, 5, 6, 7; CPW; DAM POP; DLB 276; MTCW 1; SATA 23; SATA-Obit 50; TCWW 2

Maclean, Norman (Fitzroy)
1902-1990 .... **CLC 78; SSC 13**
See also AMWS 14; CA 102; 132; CANR 49; CPW; DAM POP; DLB 206; TCWW 2

MacLeish, Archibald 1892-1982 ... **CLC 3, 8, 14, 68; PC 47**
See also AMW; CA 9-12R; 106; CAD; CANR 33, 63; CDALBS; CP 1, 2; DAM POET; DFS 15; DLB 4, 7, 45; DLBY 1982; EWL 3; EXPP; MAL 5; MTCW 1, 2; MTFW 2005; PAB; PFS 5; RGAL 4; TUS

MacLennan, (John) Hugh
1907-1990 .... **CLC 2, 14, 92**
See also CA 5-8R; 142; CANR 33; CN 1, 2, 3, 4; DAC; DAM MST; DLB 68; EWL 3; MTCW 1, 2; MTFW 2005; RGEL 2; TWA

MacLeod, Alistair 1936- .. **CLC 56, 165; SSC 90**
See also CA 123; CCA 1; DAC; DAM MST; DLB 60; MTCW 2; MTFW 2005; RGSF 2; TCLE 1:2

Macleod, Fiona
See Sharp, William
See also RGEL 2; SUFW

MacNeice, (Frederick) Louis
1907-1963 .... **CLC 1, 4, 10, 53; PC 61**
See also BRW 7; CA 85-88; CANR 61; DAB; DAM POET; DLB 10, 20; EWL 3; MTCW 1, 2; MTFW 2005; RGEL 2

MacNeill, Dand
See Fraser, George MacDonald

Macpherson, James 1736-1796 .... **LC 29**
See Ossian
See also BRWS 8; DLB 109, 336; RGEL 2

Macpherson, (Jean) Jay 1931- .... **CLC 14**
See also CA 5-8R; CANR 90; CP 1, 2, 3, 4, 6, 7; CWP; DLB 53

Macrobius fl. 430- .... **CMLC 48**

MacShane, Frank 1927-1999 .... **CLC 39**
See also CA 9-12R; 186; CANR 3, 33; DLB 111

Macumber, Mari
See Sandoz, Mari(e Susette)

Madach, Imre 1823-1864 .... **NCLC 19**

Madden, (Jerry) David 1933- .... **CLC 5, 15**
See also CA 1-4R; CAAS 3; CANR 4, 45; CN 3, 4, 5, 6, 7; CSW; DLB 6; MTCW 1

Maddern, Al(an)
See Ellison, Harlan

Madhubuti, Haki R. 1942- .... **BLC 1:2; CLC 6, 73; PC 5**
See Lee, Don L.
See also BW 2, 3; CA 73-76; CANR 24, 51, 73, 139; CP 6, 7; CSW; DAM MULT, POET; DLB 5, 41; DLBD 8; EWL 3; MAL 5; MTCW 2; MTFW 2005; RGAL 4

Madison, James 1751-1836 .... **NCLC 126**
See also DLB 37

Maepenn, Hugh
See Kuttner, Henry

Maepenn, K. H.
See Kuttner, Henry

Maeterlinck, Maurice 1862-1949 ..... **TCLC 3**
See also CA 104; 136; CANR 80; DAM DRAM; DLB 192, 331; EW 8; EWL 3; GFL 1789 to the Present; LMFS 2; RGWL 2, 3; SATA 66; TWA

Maginn, William 1794-1842 .... **NCLC 8**
See also DLB 110, 159

Mahapatra, Jayanta 1928- .... **CLC 33**
See also CA 73-76; CAAS 9; CANR 15, 33, 66, 87; CP 4, 5, 6, 7; DAM MULT; DLB 323

Mahfouz, Nagib
See Mahfouz, Naguib

Mahfouz, Naguib 1911(?)-2006 ..... **CLC 153; SSC 66**
See Mahfuz, Najib
See also AAYA 49; BEST 89:2; CA 128; 253; CANR 55, 101; DA3; DAM NOV; MTCW 1, 2; MTFW 2005; RGWL 2, 3; SSFS 9

Mahfouz, Naguib Abdel Aziz Al-Sabilgi
See Mahfouz, Naguib

Mahfouz, Najib
See Mahfouz, Naguib

Mahfuz, Najib CLC 52, 55
See Mahfouz, Naguib
See also AFW; CWW 2; DLB 331; DLBY 1988; EWL 3; RGSF 2; WLIT 6

Mahon, Derek 1941- .... **CLC 27; PC 60**
See also BRWS 6; CA 113; 128; CANR 88; CP 1, 2, 3, 4, 5, 6, 7; DLB 40; EWL 3

Maiakovskii, Vladimir
See Mayakovski, Vladimir (Vladimirovich)
See also IDTP; RGWL 2, 3

Mailer, Norman 1923-2007 ... **CLC 1, 2, 3, 4, 5, 8, 11, 14, 28, 39, 74, 111, 234**
See also AAYA 31; AITN 2; AMW; AMWC 2; AMWR 2; BPFB 2; CA 9-12R; 266; CABS 1; CANR 28, 74, 77, 130; CDALB 1968-1988; CN 1, 2, 3, 4, 5, 6; CPW; DA; DA3; DAB; DAC; DAM MST, NOV, POP; DLB 2, 16, 28, 185, 278; DLBD 3; DLBY 1980, 1983; EWL 3; MAL 5; MTCW 1, 2; MTFW 2005; NFS 10; RGAL 4; TUS

Mailer, Norman Kingsley
See Mailer, Norman

Maillet, Antonine 1929- .... **CLC 54, 118**
See also CA 115; 120; CANR 46, 74, 77, 134; CCA 1; CWW 2; DAC; DLB 60; INT CA-120; MTCW 2; MTFW 2005

Maimonides, Moses 1135-1204 ..... **CMLC 76**
See also DLB 115

Mais, Roger 1905-1955 .... **TCLC 8**
See also BW 1, 3; CA 105; 124; CANR 82; CDWLB 3; DLB 125; EWL 3; MTCW 1; RGEL 2

Maistre, Joseph 1753-1821 .... **NCLC 37**
See also GFL 1789 to the Present

Maitland, Frederic William
1850-1906 .... **TCLC 65**

Maitland, Sara (Louise) 1950- .... **CLC 49**
See also BRWS 11; CA 69-72; CANR 13, 59; DLB 271; FW

Major, Clarence 1936- ...... **BLC 1:2; CLC 3, 19, 48**
See also AFAW 2; BW 2, 3; CA 21-24R; CAAS 6; CANR 13, 25, 53, 82; CN 3, 4, 5, 6, 7; CP 2, 3, 4, 5, 6, 7; CSW; DAM MULT; DLB 33; EWL 3; MAL 5; MSW

Major, Kevin (Gerald) 1949- .... **CLC 26**
See also AAYA 16; CA 97-100; CANR 21, 38, 112; CLR 11; DAC; DLB 60; INT CANR-21; JRDA; MAICYA 1, 2; MAIC-YAS 1; SATA 32, 82, 134; WYA; YAW

Maki, James
See Ozu, Yasujiro

Makin, Bathsua 1600-1675(?) .... **LC 137**

Makine, Andrei 1957-
See Makine, Andrei

Makine, Andrei 1957- .... **CLC 198**
See also CA 176; CANR 103, 162; MTFW 2005

Malabaila, Damiano
See Levi, Primo

Malamud, Bernard 1914-1986 .. **CLC 1, 2, 3, 5, 8, 9, 11, 18, 27, 44, 78, 85; SSC 15; TCLC 129, 184; WLC 4**
See also AAYA 16; AMWS 1; BPFB 2; BYA 15; CA 5-8R; 118; CABS 1; CANR 28, 62, 114; CDALB 1941-1968; CN 1, 2, 3, 4; CPW; DA; DA3; DAB; DAC; DAM MST, NOV, POP; DLB 2, 28, 152; DLBY 1980, 1986; EWL 3; EXPS; LAIT 4; LATS 1:1; MAL 5; MTCW 1, 2; MTFW 2005; NFS 27; RGAL 4; RGHL; RGSF 2; SSFS 8, 13, 16; TUS

Malan, Herman
See Bosman, Herman Charles; Bosman, Herman Charles

FW; GLL 1; LAIT 3, 4; MAL 5; MBL;
MTCW 1, 2; MTFW 2005; NFS 6, 13;
RGAL 4; RGSF 2; SATA 27; SSFS 5;
TUS; YAW

McCulloch, John Tyler
See Burroughs, Edgar Rice

McCullough, Colleen 1937- ...... **CLC 27, 107**
See also AAYA 36; BPFB 2; CA 81-84;
CANR 17, 46, 67, 98, 139; CPW; DA3;
DAM NOV, POP; MTCW 1, 2; MTFW
2005; RHW

McCunn, Ruthanne Lum 1946- .... **AAL**
See also CA 119; CANR 43, 96; DLB 312;
LAIT 2; SATA 63

McDermott, Alice 1953- .... **CLC 90**
See also CA 109; CANR 40, 90, 126; CN
7; DLB 292; MTFW 2005; NFS 23

McElroy, Joseph 1930- .... **CLC 5, 47**
See also CA 17-20R; CANR 149; CN 3, 4,
5, 6, 7

McElroy, Joseph Prince
See McElroy, Joseph

McEwan, Ian 1948- ... **CLC 13, 66, 169; SSC 106**
See also BEST 90:4; BRWS 4; CA 61-64;
CANR 14, 41, 69, 87, 132; CN 3, 4, 5, 6,
7; DAM NOV; DLB 14, 194, 319, 326;
HGG; MTCW 1, 2; MTFW 2005; RGSF
2; SUFW 2; TEA

McFadden, David 1940- .... **CLC 48**
See also CA 104; CP 1, 2, 3, 4, 5, 6, 7; DLB
60; INT CA-104

McFarland, Dennis 1950- .... **CLC 65**
See also CA 165; CANR 110

McGahern, John 1934-2006 .... **CLC 5, 9, 48, 156; SSC 17**
See also CA 17-20R; 249; CANR 29, 68,
113; CN 1, 2, 3, 4, 5, 6, 7; DLB 14, 231,
319; MTCW 1

McGinley, Patrick (Anthony) 1937- . **CLC 41**
See also CA 120; 127; CANR 56; INT CA-
127

McGinley, Phyllis 1905-1978 .... **CLC 14**
See also CA 9-12R; 77-80; CANR 19; CP
1, 2; CWRI 5; DLB 11, 48; MAL 5; PFS
9, 13; SATA 2, 44; SATA-Obit 24

McGinniss, Joe 1942- .... **CLC 32**
See also AITN 2; BEST 89:2; CA 25-28R;
CANR 26, 70, 152; CPW; DLB 185; INT
CANR-26

McGivern, Maureen Daly
See Daly, Maureen

McGivern, Maureen Patricia Daly
See Daly, Maureen

McGrath, Patrick 1950- .... **CLC 55**
See also CA 136; CANR 65, 148; CN 5, 6,
7; DLB 231; HGG; SUFW 2

McGrath, Thomas (Matthew)
1916-1990 .... **CLC 28, 59**
See also AMWS 10; CA 9-12R; 132; CANR
6, 33, 95; CP 1, 2, 3, 4, 5; DAM POET;
MAL 5; MTCW 1; SATA 41; SATA-Obit
66

McGuane, Thomas 1939- .. **CLC 3, 7, 18, 45, 127**
See also AITN 2; BPFB 2; CA 49-52;
CANR 5, 24, 49, 94, 164; CN 2, 3, 4, 5,
6, 7; DLB 2, 212; DLBY 1980; EWL 3;
INT CANR-24; MAL 5; MTCW 1;
MTFW 2005; TCWW 1, 2

McGuane, Thomas Francis III
See McGuane, Thomas

McGuckian, Medbh 1950- .... **CLC 48, 174; PC 27**
See also BRWS 5; CA 143; CP 4, 5, 6, 7;
CWP; DAM POET; DLB 40

McHale, Tom 1942(?)-1982 .... **CLC 3, 5**
See also AITN 1; CA 77-80; 106; CN 1, 2,
3

McHugh, Heather 1948- .... **PC 61**
See also CA 69-72; CANR 11, 28, 55, 92;
CP 4, 5, 6, 7; CWP; PFS 24

McIlvanney, William 1936- .... **CLC 42**
See also CA 25-28R; CANR 61; CMW 4;
DLB 14, 207

McIlwraith, Maureen Mollie Hunter
See Hunter, Mollie
See also SATA 2

McInerney, Jay 1955- .... **CLC 34, 112**
See also AAYA 18; BPFB 2; CA 116; 123;
CANR 45, 68, 116, 176; CN 5, 6, 7; CPW;
DA3; DAM POP; DLB 292; INT CA-123;
MAL 5; MTCW 1, 2; MTFW 2005

McIntyre, Vonda N. 1948- .... **CLC 18**
See also CA 81-84; CANR 17, 34, 69;
MTCW 1; SFW 4; YAW

McIntyre, Vonda Neel
See McIntyre, Vonda N.

McKay, Claude **BLC 1:3; HR 1:3; PC 2; TCLC 7, 41; WLC 4**
See McKay, Festus Claudius
See also AFAW 1, 2; AMWS 10; DAB;
DLB 4, 45, 51, 117; EWL 3; EXPP; GLL
2; LAIT 3; LMFS 2; MAL 5; PAB; PFS
4; RGAL 4; WP

McKay, Festus Claudius 1889-1948
See McKay, Claude
See also BW 1, 3; CA 104; 124; CANR 73;
DA; DAC; DAM MST, MULT, NOV,
POET; MTCW 1, 2; MTFW 2005; TUS

McKuen, Rod 1933- .... **CLC 1, 3**
See also AITN 1; CA 41-44R; CANR 40;
CP 1

McLoughlin, R. B.
See Mencken, H(enry) L(ouis)

McLuhan, (Herbert) Marshall
1911-1980 .... **CLC 37, 83**
See also CA 9-12R; 102; CANR 12, 34, 61;
DLB 88; INT CANR-12; MTCW 1, 2;
MTFW 2005

McManus, Declan Patrick Aloysius
See Costello, Elvis

McMillan, Terry 1951- .. **BLCS; CLC 50, 61, 112**
See also AAYA 21; AMWS 13; BPFB 2;
BW 2, 3; CA 140; CANR 60, 104, 131;
CN 7; CPW; DA3; DAM MULT, NOV,
POP; MAL 5; MTCW 2; MTFW 2005;
RGAL 4; YAW

McMurtry, Larry 1936- .... **CLC 2, 3, 7, 11, 27, 44, 127, 250**
See also AAYA 15; AITN 2; AMWS 5;
BEST 89:2; BPFB 2; CA 5-8R; CANR
19, 43, 64, 103, 170; CDALB 1968-1988;
CN 2, 3, 4, 5, 6, 7; CPW; CSW; DA3;
DAM NOV, POP; DLB 2, 143, 256;
DLBY 1980, 1987; EWL 3; MAL 5;
MTCW 1, 2; MTFW 2005; RGAL 4;
TCWW 1, 2

McMurtry, Larry Jeff
See McMurtry, Larry

McNally, Terrence 1939- ... **CLC 4, 7, 41, 91, 252; DC 27**
See also AAYA 62; AMWS 13; CA 45-48;
CAD; CANR 2, 56, 116; CD 5, 6; DA3;
DAM DRAM; DFS 16, 19; DLB 7, 249;
EWL 3; GLL 1; MTCW 2; MTFW 2005

McNally, Thomas Michael
See McNally, T.M.

McNally, T.M. 1961- .... **CLC 82**
See also CA 246

McNamer, Deirdre 1950- .... **CLC 70**
See also CA 188; CANR 163

McNeal, Tom **CLC 119**
See also CA 252

McNeile, Herman Cyril 1888-1937
See Sapper
See also CA 184; CMW 4; DLB 77

McNickle, (William) D'Arcy
1904-1977 .... **CLC 89; NNAL**
See also CA 9-12R; 85-88; CANR 5, 45;
DAM MULT; DLB 175, 212; RGAL 4;
SATA-Obit 22; TCWW 1, 2

McPhee, John 1931- .... **CLC 36**
See also AAYA 61; AMWS 3; ANW; BEST
90:1; CA 65-68; CANR 20, 46, 64, 69,
121, 165; CPW; DLB 185, 275; MTFW
1, 2; MTFW 2005; TUS

McPhee, John Angus
See McPhee, John

McPherson, James Alan 1943- . **BLCS; CLC 19, 77; SSC 95**
See also BW 1, 3; CA 25-28R; CAAS 17;
CANR 24, 74, 140; CN 3, 4, 5, 6; CSW;
DLB 38, 244; EWL 3; MTCW 1, 2;
MTFW 2005; RGAL 4; RGSF 2; SSFS
23

McPherson, William (Alexander)
1933- .... **CLC 34**
See also CA 69-72; CANR 28; INT
CANR-28

McTaggart, J. McT. Ellis
See McTaggart, John McTaggart Ellis

McTaggart, John McTaggart Ellis
1866-1925 .... **TCLC 105**
See also CA 120; DLB 262

Mda, Zakes 1948- .... **BLC 2:3**
See also CA 205; CANR 151; CD 5, 6;
DLB 225

Mead, George Herbert 1863-1931 . **TCLC 89**
See also CA 212; DLB 270

Mead, Margaret 1901-1978 .... **CLC 37**
See also AITN 1; CA 1-4R; 81-84; CANR
4; DA3; FW; MTCW 1, 2; SATA-Obit 20

Meaker, Marijane 1927-
See Kerr, M. E.
See also CA 107; CANR 37, 63, 145; INT
CA-107; JRDA; MAICYA 1, 2; MAIC-
YAS 1; MTCW 1; SATA 20, 61, 99, 160;
SATA-Essay 111; YAW

Mechthild von Magdeburg c. 1207-c.
1282 .... **CMLC 91**
See also DLB 138

Medoff, Mark (Howard) 1940- .... **CLC 6, 23**
See also AITN 1; CA 53-56; CAD; CANR
5; CD 5, 6; DAM DRAM; DFS 4; DLB
7; INT CANR-5

Medvedev, P. N.
See Bakhtin, Mikhail Mikhailovich

Meged, Aharon
See Megged, Aharon

Meged, Aron
See Megged, Aharon

Megged, Aharon 1920- .... **CLC 9**
See also CA 49-52; CAAS 13; CANR 1,
140; EWL 3; RGHL

Mehta, Deepa 1950- .... **CLC 208**

Mehta, Gita 1943- .... **CLC 179**
See also CA 225; CN 7; DNFS 2

Mehta, Ved 1934- .... **CLC 37**
See also CA 1-4R; 212; CAAE 212; CANR
2, 23, 69; DLB 323; MTCW 1; MTFW
2005

Melanchthon, Philipp 1497-1560 .... **LC 90**
See also DLB 179

Melanter
See Blackmore, R(ichard) D(oddridge)

Meleager c. 140B.C.-c. 70B.C. ...... **CMLC 53**

Melies, Georges 1861-1938 .... **TCLC 81**

Melikow, Loris
See Hofmannsthal, Hugo von

Melmoth, Sebastian
See Wilde, Oscar

Melo Neto, Joao Cabral de
See Cabral de Melo Neto, Joao
See also CWW 2; EWL 3

Miller, Arthur 1915-2005 ..... **CLC 1, 2, 6, 10, 15, 26, 47, 78, 179; DC 1, 31; WLC 4**
See also AAYA 15; AITN 1; AMW; AMWC 1; CA 1-4R; 236; CABS 3; CAD; CANR 2, 30, 54, 76, 132; CD 5, 6; CDALB 1941-1968; DA; DA3; DAB; DAC; DAM DRAM, MST; DFS 1, 3, 8; DLB 7, 266; EWL 3; LAIT 1, 4; LATS 1:2; MAL 5; MTCW 1, 2; MTFW 2005; RGAL 4; RGHL; TUS; WYAS 1

Miller, Henry (Valentine) 1891-1980 .... **CLC 1, 2, 4, 9, 14, 43, 84; WLC 4**
See also AMW; BPFB 2; CA 9-12R; 97-100; CANR 33, 64; CDALB 1929-1941; CN 1, 2; DA; DA3; DAB; DAC; DAM MST, NOV; DLB 4, 9; DLBY 1980; EWL 3; MAL 5; MTCW 1, 2; MTFW 2005; RGAL 4; TUS

Miller, Hugh 1802-1856 .... **NCLC 143**
See also DLB 190

Miller, Jason 1939(?)-2001 .... **CLC 2**
See also AITN 1; CA 73-76; 197; CAD; CANR 130; DFS 12; DLB 7

Miller, Sue 1943- .... **CLC 44**
See also AMWS 12; BEST 90:3; CA 139; CANR 59, 91, 128; DA3; DAM POP; DLB 143

Miller, Walter M(ichael, Jr.) 1923-1996 .... **CLC 4, 30**
See also BPFB 2; CA 85-88; CANR 108; DLB 8; SCFW 1, 2; SFW 4

Millett, Kate 1934- .... **CLC 67**
See also AITN 1; CA 73-76; CANR 32, 53, 76, 110; DA3; DLB 246; FW; GLL 1; MTCW 1, 2; MTFW 2005

Millhauser, Steven 1943- ... **CLC 21, 54, 109; SSC 57**
See also AAYA 76; CA 110; 111; CANR 63, 114, 133; CN 6, 7; DA3; DLB 2; FANT; INT CA-111; MAL 5; MTCW 2; MTFW 2005

Millhauser, Steven Lewis
See Millhauser, Steven

Millin, Sarah Gertrude 1889-1968 ... **CLC 49**
See also CA 102; 93-96; DLB 225; EWL 3

Milne, A. A. 1882-1956 .... **TCLC 6, 88**
See also BRWS 5; CA 104; CLR 1, 26, 108; CMW 4; CWRI 5; DA3; DAB; DAC; DAM MST; DLB 10, 77, 100, 160; FANT; MAICYA 1, 2; MTCW 1, 2; MTFW 2005; RGEL 2; SATA 100; WCH; YABC 1

Milne, Alan Alexander
See Milne, A. A.

Milner, Ron(ald) 1938-2004 .. **BLC 1:3; CLC 56**
See also AITN 1; BW 1; CA 73-76; 230; CAD; CANR 24, 81; CD 5, 6; DAM MULT; DLB 38; MAL 5; MTCW 1

Milnes, Richard Monckton 1809-1885 .... **NCLC 61**
See also DLB 32, 184

Milosz, Czeslaw 1911-2004 .... **CLC 5, 11, 22, 31, 56, 82, 253; PC 8; WLCS**
See also AAYA 62; CA 81-84; 230; CANR 23, 51, 91, 126; CDWLB 4; CWW 2; DA3; DAM MST, POET; DLB 215, 331; EW 13; EWL 3; MTCW 1, 2; MTFW 2005; PFS 16; RGHL; RGWL 2, 3

Milton, John 1608-1674 ..... **LC 9, 43, 92; PC 19, 29; WLC 4**
See also AAYA 65; BRW 2; BRWR 2; CD-BLB 1660-1789; DA; DA3; DAB; DAC; DAM MST, POET; DLB 131, 151, 281; EFS 1; EXPP; LAIT 1; PAB; PFS 3, 17; RGEL 2; TEA; WLIT 3; WP

Min, Anchee 1957- .... **CLC 86**
See also CA 146; CANR 94, 137; MTFW 2005

Minehaha, Cornelius
See Wedekind, Frank

Miner, Valerie 1947- .... **CLC 40**
See also CA 97-100; CANR 59; FW; GLL 2

Minimo, Duca
See D'Annunzio, Gabriele

Minot, Susan (Anderson) 1956- ...... **CLC 44, 159**
See also AMWS 6; CA 134; CANR 118; CN 6, 7

Minus, Ed 1938- .... **CLC 39**
See also CA 185

Mirabai 1498(?)-1550(?) .... **LC 143; PC 48**
See also PFS 24

Miranda, Javier
See Bioy Casares, Adolfo
See also CWW 2

Mirbeau, Octave 1848-1917 .... **TCLC 55**
See also CA 216; DLB 123, 192; GFL 1789 to the Present

Mirikitani, Janice 1942- .... **AAL**
See also CA 211; DLB 312; RGAL 4

Mirk, John (?)-c. 1414 .... **LC 105**
See also DLB 146

Miro (Ferrer), Gabriel (Francisco Victor) 1879-1930 .... **TCLC 5**
See also CA 104; 185; DLB 322; EWL 3

Misharin, Alexandr CLC 59

Mishima, Yukio CLC 2, 4, 6, 9, 27; DC 1; SSC 4; TCLC 161; WLC 4
See Hiraoka, Kimitake
See also AAYA 50; BPFB 2; DLB 182; EWL 3; GLL 1; MJW; RGSF 2; RGWL 2, 3; SSFS 5, 12

Mistral, Frederic 1830-1914 .... **TCLC 51**
See also CA 122; 213; DLB 331; GFL 1789 to the Present

Mistral, Gabriela
See Godoy Alcayaga, Lucila
See also DLB 283, 331; DNFS 1; EWL 3; LAW; RGWL 2, 3; WP

Mistry, Rohinton 1952- ... **CLC 71, 196; SSC 73**
See also BRWS 10; CA 141; CANR 86, 114; CCA 1; CN 6, 7; DAC; DLB 334; SSFS 6

Mitchell, Clyde
See Ellison, Harlan; Silverberg, Robert

Mitchell, Emerson Blackhorse Barney 1945- .... **NNAL**
See also CA 45-48

Mitchell, James Leslie 1901-1935
See Gibbon, Lewis Grassic
See also CA 104; 188; DLB 15

Mitchell, Joni 1943- .... **CLC 12**
See also CA 112; CCA 1

Mitchell, Joseph (Quincy) 1908-1996 .... **CLC 98**
See also CA 77-80; 152; CANR 69; CN 1, 2, 3, 4, 5, 6; CSW; DLB 185; DLBY 1996

Mitchell, Margaret (Munnerlyn) 1900-1949 .... **TCLC 11, 170**
See also AAYA 23; BPFB 2; BYA 1; CA 109; 125; CANR 55, 94; CDALBS; DA3; DAM NOV, POP; DLB 9; LAIT 2; MAL 5; MTCW 1, 2; MTFW 2005; NFS 9; RGAL 4; RHW; TUS; WYAS 1; YAW

Mitchell, Peggy
See Mitchell, Margaret (Munnerlyn)

Mitchell, S(ilas) Weir 1829-1914 .... **TCLC 36**
See also CA 165; DLB 202; RGAL 4

Mitchell, W(illiam) O(rmond) 1914-1998 .... **CLC 25**
See also CA 77-80; 165; CANR 15, 43; CN 1, 2, 3, 4, 5, 6; DAC; DAM MST; DLB 88; TCLE 1:2

Mitchell, William (Lendrum) 1879-1936 .... **TCLC 81**
See also CA 213

Mitford, Mary Russell 1787-1855 ... **NCLC 4**
See also DLB 110, 116; RGEL 2

Mitford, Nancy 1904-1973 .... **CLC 44**
See also BRWS 10; CA 9-12R; CN 1; DLB 191; RGEL 2

Miyamoto, (Chujo) Yuriko 1899-1951 .... **TCLC 37**
See Miyamoto Yuriko
See also CA 170, 174

Miyamoto Yuriko
See Miyamoto, (Chujo) Yuriko
See also DLB 180

Miyazawa, Kenji 1896-1933 .... **TCLC 76**
See Miyazawa Kenji
See also CA 157; RGWL 3

Miyazawa Kenji
See Miyazawa, Kenji
See also EWL 3

Mizoguchi, Kenji 1898-1956 .... **TCLC 72**
See also CA 167

Mo, Timothy (Peter) 1950- .... **CLC 46, 134**
See also CA 117; CANR 128; CN 5, 6, 7; DLB 194; MTCW 1; WLIT 4; WWE 1

Modarressi, Taghi (M.) 1931-1997 ... **CLC 44**
See also CA 121; 134; INT CA-134

Modiano, Patrick (Jean) 1945- .... **CLC 18, 218**
See also CA 85-88; CANR 17, 40, 115; CWW 2; DLB 83, 299; EWL 3; RGHL

Mofolo, Thomas (Mokopu) 1875(?)-1948 .... **BLC 1:3; TCLC 22**
See also AFW; CA 121; 153; CANR 83; DAM MULT; DLB 225; EWL 3; MTCW 2; MTFW 2005; WLIT 2

Mohr, Nicholasa 1938- .... **CLC 12; HLC 2**
See also AAYA 8, 46; CA 49-52; CANR 1, 32, 64; CLR 22; DAM MULT; DLB 145; HW 1, 2; JRDA; LAIT 5; LLW; MAICYA 2; MAICYAS 1; RGAL 4; SAAS 8; SATA 8, 97; SATA-Essay 113; WYA; YAW

Moi, Toril 1953- .... **CLC 172**
See also CA 154; CANR 102; FW

Mojtabai, A(nn) G(race) 1938- ..... **CLC 5, 9, 15, 29**
See also CA 85-88; CANR 88

Moliere 1622-1673 ..... **DC 13; LC 10, 28, 64, 125, 127; WLC 4**
See also DA; DA3; DAB; DAC; DAM DRAM, MST; DFS 13, 18, 20; DLB 268; EW 3; GFL Beginnings to 1789; LATS 1:1; RGWL 2, 3; TWA

Molin, Charles
See Mayne, William (James Carter)

Molnar, Ferenc 1878-1952 .... **TCLC 20**
See also CA 109; 153; CANR 83; CDWLB 4; DAM DRAM; DLB 215; EWL 3; RGWL 2, 3

Momaday, N. Scott 1934- ...... **CLC 2, 19, 85, 95, 160; NNAL; PC 25; WLCS**
See also AAYA 11, 64; AMWS 4; ANW; BPFB 2; BYA 12; CA 25-28R; CANR 14, 34, 68, 134; CDALBS; CN 2, 3, 4, 5, 6, 7; CPW; DA; DA3; DAB; DAC; DAM MST, MULT, NOV, POP; DLB 143, 175, 256; EWL 3; EXPP; INT CANR-14; LAIT 4; LATS 1:2; MAL 5; MTCW 1, 2; MTFW 2005; NFS 10; PFS 2, 11; RGAL 4; SATA 48; SATA-Brief 30; TCWW 1, 2; WP; YAW

Monette, Paul 1945-1995 .... **CLC 82**
See also AMWS 10; CA 139; 147; CN 6; GLL 1

Monroe, Harriet 1860-1936 .... **TCLC 12**
See also CA 109; 204; DLB 54, 91

Monroe, Lyle
See Heinlein, Robert A.

Montagu, Elizabeth 1720-1800 .... **NCLC 7, 117**
See also FW

Montagu, Mary (Pierrepont) Wortley
1689-1762 .... **LC 9, 57; PC 16**
See also DLB 95, 101; FL 1:1; RGEL 2

Montagu, W. H.
See Coleridge, Samuel Taylor

Montague, John (Patrick) 1929- ..... **CLC 13, 46**
See also CA 9-12R; CANR 9, 69, 121; CP 1, 2, 3, 4, 5, 6, 7; DLB 40; EWL 3; MTCW 1; PFS 12; RGEL 2; TCLE 1:2

Montaigne, Michel (Eyquem) de
1533-1592 .... **LC 8, 105; WLC 4**
See also DA; DAB; DAC; DAM MST; DLB 327; EW 2; GFL Beginnings to 1789; LMFS 1; RGWL 2, 3; TWA

Montale, Eugenio 1896-1981 ... **CLC 7, 9, 18; PC 13**
See also CA 17-20R; 104; CANR 30; DLB 114, 331; EW 11; EWL 3; MTCW 1; PFS 22; RGWL 2, 3; TWA; WLIT 7

Montesquieu, Charles-Louis de Secondat
1689-1755 .... **LC 7, 69**
See also DLB 314; EW 3; GFL Beginnings to 1789; TWA

Montessori, Maria 1870-1952 ...... **TCLC 103**
See also CA 115; 147

Montgomery, (Robert) Bruce 1921(?)-1978
See Crispin, Edmund
See also CA 179; 104; CMW 4

Montgomery, L(ucy) M(aud)
1874-1942 .... **TCLC 51, 140**
See also AAYA 12; BYA 1; CA 108; 137; CLR 8, 91; DA3; DA3; DAM MST; DLB 92; DLBD 14; JRDA; MAICYA 1, 2; MTCW 2; MTFW 2005; RGEL 2; SATA 100; TWA; WCH; WYA; YABC 1

Montgomery, Marion, Jr. 1925- .... **CLC 7**
See also AITN 1; CA 1-4R; CANR 3, 48, 162; CSW; DLB 6

Montgomery, Marion H. 1925-
See Montgomery, Marion, Jr.

Montgomery, Max
See Davenport, Guy (Mattison, Jr.)

Montherlant, Henry (Milon) de
1896-1972 .... **CLC 8, 19**
See also CA 85-88; 37-40R; DAM DRAM; DLB 72, 321; EW 11; EWL 3; GFL 1789 to the Present; MTCW 1

Monty Python
See Chapman, Graham; Cleese, John (Marwood); Gilliam, Terry; Idle, Eric; Jones, Terence Graham Parry; Palin, Michael (Edward)
See also AAYA 7

Moodie, Susanna (Strickland)
1803-1885 .... **NCLC 14, 113**
See also DLB 99

Moody, Hiram 1961-
See Moody, Rick
See also CA 138; CANR 64, 112; MTFW 2005

Moody, Minerva
See Alcott, Louisa May

Moody, Rick CLC 147
See Moody, Hiram

Moody, William Vaughan
1869-1910 .... **TCLC 105**
See also CA 110; 178; DLB 7, 54; MAL 5; RGAL 4

Mooney, Edward 1951-
See Mooney, Ted
See also CA 130

Mooney, Ted CLC 25
See Mooney, Edward

Moorcock, Michael 1939- ...... **CLC 5, 27, 58, 236**
See Bradbury, Edward P.
See also AAYA 26; CA 45-48; CAAS 5; CANR 2, 17, 38, 64, 122; CN 5, 6, 7; DLB 14, 231, 261, 319; FANT; MTCW 1, 2; MTFW 2005; SATA 93, 166; SCFW 1, 2; SFW 4; SUFW 1, 2

Moorcock, Michael John
See Moorcock, Michael

Moorcock, Michael John
See Moorcock, Michael

Moore, Alan 1953- .... **CLC 230**
See also AAYA 51; CA 204; CANR 138; DLB 261; MTFW 2005; SFW 4

Moore, Brian 1921-1999 ... **CLC 1, 3, 5, 7, 8, 19, 32, 90**
See Bryan, Michael
See also BRWS 9; CA 1-4R; 174; CANR 1, 25, 42, 63; CCA 1; CN 1, 2, 3, 4, 5, 6; DAB; DAC; DAM MST; DLB 251; EWL 3; FANT; MTCW 1, 2; MTFW 2005; RGEL 2

Moore, Edward
See Muir, Edwin
See also RGEL 2

Moore, G. E. 1873-1958 .... **TCLC 89**
See also DLB 262

Moore, George Augustus
1852-1933 .... **SSC 19; TCLC 7**
See also BRW 6; CA 104; 177; DLB 10, 18, 57, 135; EWL 3; RGEL 2; RGSF 2

Moore, Lorrie CLC 39, 45, 68
See Moore, Marie Lorena
See also AMWS 10; CN 5, 6, 7; DLB 234; SSFS 19

Moore, Marianne (Craig)
1887-1972 .... **CLC 1, 2, 4, 8, 10, 13, 19, 47; PC 4, 49; WLCS**
See also AMW; CA 1-4R; 33-36R; CANR 3, 61; CDALB 1929-1941; CP 1; DA; DA3; DAB; DAC; DAM MST, POET; DLB 45; DLBD 7; EWL 3; EXPP; FL 1:6; MAL 5; MBL; MTCW 1, 2; MTFW 2005; PAB; PFS 14, 17; RGAL 4; SATA 20; TUS; WP

Moore, Marie Lorena 1957- .... **CLC 165**
See Moore, Lorrie
See also CA 116; CANR 39, 83, 139; DLB 234; MTFW 2005

Moore, Michael 1954- .... **CLC 218**
See also AAYA 53; CA 166; CANR 150

Moore, Thomas 1779-1852 ...... **NCLC 6, 110**
See also DLB 96, 144; RGEL 2

Moorhouse, Frank 1938- .... **SSC 40**
See also CA 118; CANR 92; CN 3, 4, 5, 6, 7; DLB 289; RGSF 2

Mora, Pat 1942- .... **HLC 2**
See also AMWS 13; CA 129; CANR 57, 81, 112, 171; CLR 58; DAM MULT; DLB 209; HW 1, 2; LLW; MAICYA 2; MTFW 2005; SATA 92, 134, 186

Moraga, Cherríe 1952- ... **CLC 126, 250; DC 22**
See also CA 131; CANR 66, 154; DAM MULT; DLB 82, 249; FW; GLL 1; HW 1, 2; LLW

Morand, Paul 1888-1976 .... **CLC 41; SSC 22**
See also CA 184; 69-72; DLB 65; EWL 3

Morante, Elsa 1918-1985 .... **CLC 8, 47**
See also CA 85-88; 117; CANR 35; DLB 177; EWL 3; MTCW 1, 2; MTFW 2005; RGHL; RGWL 2, 3; WLIT 7

Moravia, Alberto CLC 2, 7, 11, 27, 46; SSC 26
See Pincherle, Alberto
See also DLB 177; EW 12; EWL 3; MTCW 2; RGSF 2; RGWL 2, 3; WLIT 7

More, Hannah 1745-1833 ...... **NCLC 27, 141**
See also DLB 107, 109, 116, 158; RGEL 2

More, Henry 1614-1687 .... **LC 9**
See also DLB 126, 252

More, Sir Thomas 1478(?)-1535 ... **LC 10, 32, 140**
See also BRWC 1; BRWS 7; DLB 136, 281; LMFS 1; RGEL 2; TEA

Moreas, Jean TCLC 18
See Papadiamantopoulos, Johannes
See also GFL 1789 to the Present

Moreton, Andrew Esq.
See Defoe, Daniel

Morgan, Berry 1919-2002 .... **CLC 6**
See also CA 49-52; 208; DLB 6

Morgan, Claire
See Highsmith, Patricia
See also GLL 1

Morgan, Edwin 1920- .... **CLC 31**
See also BRWS 9; CA 5-8R; CANR 3, 43, 90; CP 1, 2, 3, 4, 5, 6, 7; DLB 27

Morgan, Edwin George
See Morgan, Edwin

Morgan, (George) Frederick
1922-2004 .... **CLC 23**
See also CA 17-20R; 224; CANR 21, 144; CP 2, 3, 4, 5, 6, 7

Morgan, Harriet
See Mencken, H(enry) L(ouis)

Morgan, Jane
See Cooper, James Fenimore

Morgan, Janet 1945- .... **CLC 39**
See also CA 65-68

Morgan, Lady 1776(?)-1859 .... **NCLC 29**
See also DLB 116, 158; RGEL 2

Morgan, Robin (Evonne) 1941- .... **CLC 2**
See also CA 69-72; CANR 29, 68; FW; GLL 2; MTCW 1; SATA 80

Morgan, Scott
See Kuttner, Henry

Morgan, Seth 1949(?)-1990 .... **CLC 65**
See also CA 185; 132

Morgenstern, Christian (Otto Josef Wolfgang) 1871-1914 .... **TCLC 8**
See also CA 105; 191; EWL 3

Morgenstern, S.
See Goldman, William

Mori, Rintaro
See Mori Ogai
See also CA 110

Mori, Toshio 1910-1980 .... **AAL; SSC 83**
See also CA 116; 244; DLB 312; RGSF 2

Moricz, Zsigmond 1879-1942 .... **TCLC 33**
See also CA 165; DLB 215; EWL 3

Morike, Eduard (Friedrich)
1804-1875 .... **NCLC 10**
See also DLB 133; RGWL 2, 3

Mori Ogai 1862-1922 .... **TCLC 14**
See Ogai
See also CA 164; DLB 180; EWL 3; RGWL 3; TWA

Moritz, Karl Philipp 1756-1793 .... **LC 2**
See also DLB 94

Morland, Peter Henry
See Faust, Frederick (Schiller)

Morley, Christopher (Darlington)
1890-1957 .... **TCLC 87**
See also CA 112; 213; DLB 9; MAL 5; RGAL 4

Morren, Theophil
See Hofmannsthal, Hugo von

Morris, Bill 1952- .... **CLC 76**
See also CA 225

Morris, Julian
See West, Morris L(anglo)

Morris, Steveland Judkins (?)-
See Wonder, Stevie

Morris, William 1834-1896 . **NCLC 4; PC 55**
See also BRW 5; CDBLB 1832-1890; DLB 18, 35, 57, 156, 178, 184; FANT; RGEL 2; SFW 4; SUFW

Morris, Wright (Marion) 1910-1998 . **CLC 1, 3, 7, 18, 37; TCLC 107**
See also AMW; CA 9-12R; 167; CANR 21, 81; CN 1, 2, 3, 4, 5, 6; DLB 2, 206, 218; DLBY 1981; EWL 3; MAL 5; MTCW 1, 2; MTFW 2005; RGAL 4; TCWW 1, 2

Morrison, Arthur 1863-1945 .... **SSC 40; TCLC 72**
See also CA 120; 157; CMW 4; DLB 70, 135, 197; RGEL 2

Morrison, Chloe Anthony Wofford
See Morrison, Toni

Morrison, James Douglas 1943-1971
See Morrison, Jim
See also CA 73-76; CANR 40

Morrison, Jim CLC 17
See Morrison, James Douglas

Morrison, John Gordon 1904-1998 ... **SSC 93**
See also CA 103; CANR 92; DLB 260

Morrison, Toni 1931- . **BLC 1:3, 2:3; CLC 4, 10, 22, 55, 81, 87, 173, 194; WLC 4**
See also AAYA 1, 22, 61; AFAW 1, 2; AMWC 1; AMWS 3; BPFB 2; BW 2, 3; CA 29-32R; CANR 27, 42, 67, 113, 124; CDALB 1968-1988; CLR 99; CN 3, 4, 5, 6, 7; CPW; DA; DA3; DAB; DAC; DAM MST, MULT, NOV, POP; DLB 6, 33, 143, 331; DLBY 1981; EWL 3; EXPN; FL 1:6; FW; GL 3; LAIT 2, 4; LATS 1:2; LMFS 2; MAL 5; MBL; MTCW 1, 2; MTFW 2005; NFS 1, 6, 8, 14; RGAL 4; RHW; SATA 57, 144; SSFS 5; TCLE 1:2; TUS; YAW

Morrison, Van 1945- .... **CLC 21**
See also CA 116; 168

Morrissy, Mary 1957- .... **CLC 99**
See also CA 205; DLB 267

Mortimer, John 1923- .... **CLC 28, 43**
See also CA 13-16R; CANR 21, 69, 109, 172; CBD; CD 5, 6; CDBLB 1960 to Present; CMW 4; CN 5, 6, 7; CPW; DA3; DAM DRAM, POP; DLB 13, 245, 271; INT CANR-21; MSW; MTCW 1, 2; MTFW 2005; RGEL 2

Mortimer, John Clifford
See Mortimer, John

Mortimer, Penelope (Ruth) 1918-1999 .... **CLC 5**
See also CA 57-60; 187; CANR 45, 88; CN 1, 2, 3, 4, 5, 6

Mortimer, Sir John
See Mortimer, John

Morton, Anthony
See Creasey, John

Morton, Thomas 1579(?)-1647(?) .... **LC 72**
See also DLB 24; RGEL 2

Mosca, Gaetano 1858-1941 .... **TCLC 75**

Moses, Daniel David 1952- .... **NNAL**
See also CA 186; CANR 160; DLB 334

Mosher, Howard Frank 1943- .... **CLC 62**
See also CA 139; CANR 65, 115

Mosley, Nicholas 1923- .... **CLC 43, 70**
See also CA 69-72; CANR 41, 60, 108, 158; CN 1, 2, 3, 4, 5, 6, 7; DLB 14, 207

Mosley, Walter 1952- .... **BLCS; CLC 97, 184**
See also AAYA 57; AMWS 13; BPFB 2; BW 2; CA 142; CANR 57, 92, 136, 172; CMW 4; CN 7; CPW; DA3; DAM MULT, POP; DLB 306; MSW; MTCW 2; MTFW 2005

Moss, Howard 1922-1987 . **CLC 7, 14, 45, 50**
See also CA 1-4R; 123; CANR 1, 44; CP 1, 2, 3, 4; DAM POET; DLB 5

Mossgiel, Rab
See Burns, Robert

Motion, Andrew 1952- .... **CLC 47**
See also BRWS 7; CA 146; CANR 90, 142; CP 4, 5, 6, 7; DLB 40; MTFW 2005

Motion, Andrew Peter
See Motion, Andrew

Motley, Willard (Francis) 1909-1965 .... **CLC 18**
See also AMWS 17; BW 1; CA 117; 106; CANR 88; DLB 76, 143

Motoori, Norinaga 1730-1801 .... **NCLC 45**

Mott, Michael (Charles Alston) 1930- .... **CLC 15, 34**
See also CA 5-8R; CAAS 7; CANR 7, 29

Mountain Wolf Woman 1884-1960 . **CLC 92; NNAL**
See also CA 144; CANR 90

Moure, Erin 1955- .... **CLC 88**
See also CA 113; CP 5, 6, 7; CWP; DLB 60

Mourning Dove 1885(?)-1936 .... **NNAL**
See also CA 144; CANR 90; DAM MULT; DLB 175, 221

Mowat, Farley 1921- .... **CLC 26**
See also AAYA 1, 50; BYA 2; CA 1-4R; CANR 4, 24, 42, 68, 108; CLR 20; CPW; DAC; DAM MST; DLB 68; INT CANR-24; JRDA; MAICYA 1, 2; MTCW 1, 2; MTFW 2005; SATA 3, 55; YAW

Mowat, Farley McGill
See Mowat, Farley

Mowatt, Anna Cora 1819-1870 ..... **NCLC 74**
See also RGAL 4

Mo Yan CLC 257
See Moye, Guan

Moye, Guan 1956(?)-
See Mo Yan
See also CA 201

Moyers, Bill 1934- .... **CLC 74**
See also AITN 2; CA 61-64; CANR 31, 52, 148

Mphahlele, Es'kia
See Mphahlele, Ezekiel
See also AFW; CDWLB 3; CN 4, 5, 6; DLB 125, 225; RGSF 2; SSFS 11

Mphahlele, Ezekiel 1919- ...... **BLC 1:3; CLC 25, 133**
See Mphahlele, Es'kia
See also BW 2, 3; CA 81-84; CANR 26, 76; CN 1, 2, 3; DA3; DAM MULT; EWL 3; MTCW 2; MTFW 2005; SATA 119

Mqhayi, S(amuel) E(dward) K(rune Loliwe) 1875-1945 .... **BLC 1:3; TCLC 25**
See also CA 153; CANR 87; DAM MULT

Mrozek, Slawomir 1930- .... **CLC 3, 13**
See also CA 13-16R; CAAS 10; CANR 29; CDWLB 4; CWW 2; DLB 232; EWL 3; MTCW 1

Mrs. Belloc-Lowndes
See Lowndes, Marie Adelaide (Belloc)

Mrs. Fairstar
See Horne, Richard Henry Hengist

M'Taggart, John M'Taggart Ellis
See McTaggart, John McTaggart Ellis

Mtwa, Percy (?)- .... **CLC 47**
See also CD 6

Mueller, Lisel 1924- .... **CLC 13, 51; PC 33**
See also CA 93-96; CP 6, 7; DLB 105; PFS 9, 13

Muggeridge, Malcolm (Thomas) 1903-1990 .... **TCLC 120**
See also AITN 1; CA 101; CANR 33, 63; MTCW 1, 2

Muhammad 570-632 .... **WLCS**
See also DA; DAB; DAC; DAM MST; DLB 311

Muir, Edwin 1887-1959 . **PC 49; TCLC 2, 87**
See Moore, Edward
See also BRWS 6; CA 104; 193; DLB 20, 100, 191; EWL 3; RGEL 2

Muir, John 1838-1914 .... **TCLC 28**
See also AMWS 9; ANW; CA 165; DLB 186, 275

Mujica Lainez, Manuel 1910-1984 ... **CLC 31**
See Lainez, Manuel Mujica
See also CA 81-84; 112; CANR 32; EWL 3; HW 1

Mukherjee, Bharati 1940- ..... **AAL; CLC 53, 115, 235; SSC 38**
See also AAYA 46; BEST 89:2; CA 107, 232; CAAE 232; CANR 45, 72, 128; CN 5, 6, 7; DAM NOV; DLB 60, 218, 323; DNFS 1, 2; EWL 3; FW; MAL 5; MTCW 1, 2; MTFW 2005; RGAL 4; RGSF 2; SSFS 7, 24; TUS; WWE 1

Muldoon, Paul 1951- .... **CLC 32, 72, 166**
See also BRWS 4; CA 113; 129; CANR 52, 91, 176; CP 2, 3, 4, 5, 6, 7; DAM POET; DLB 40; INT CA-129; PFS 7, 22; TCLE 1:2

Mulisch, Harry (Kurt Victor) 1927- .... **CLC 42**
See also CA 9-12R; CANR 6, 26, 56, 110; CWW 2; DLB 299; EWL 3

Mull, Martin 1943- .... **CLC 17**
See also CA 105

Muller, Wilhelm NCLC 73

Mulock, Dinah Maria
See Craik, Dinah Maria (Mulock)
See also RGEL 2

Multatuli 1820-1881 .... **NCLC 165**
See also RGWL 2, 3

Munday, Anthony 1560-1633 .... **LC 87**
See also DLB 62, 172; RGEL 2

Munford, Robert 1737(?)-1783 .... **LC 5**
See also DLB 31

Mungo, Raymond 1946- .... **CLC 72**
See also CA 49-52; CANR 2

Munro, Alice 1931- .... **CLC 6, 10, 19, 50, 95, 222; SSC 3, 95; WLCS**
See also AITN 2; BPFB 2; CA 33-36R; CANR 33, 53, 75, 114; CCA 1; CN 1, 2, 3, 4, 5, 6, 7; DA3; DAC; DAM MST, NOV; DLB 53; EWL 3; MTCW 1, 2; MTFW 2005; NFS 27; RGEL 2; RGSF 2; SATA 29; SSFS 5, 13, 19; TCLE 1:2; WWE 1

Munro, H(ector) H(ugh) 1870-1916
See Saki
See also AAYA 56; CA 104; 130; CANR 104; CDBLB 1890-1914; DA; DA3; DAB; DAC; DAM MST, NOV; DLB 34, 162; EXPS; MTCW 1, 2; MTFW 2005; RGEL 2; SSFS 15

Murakami, Haruki 1949- .... **CLC 150**
See Murakami Haruki
See also CA 165; CANR 102, 146; MJW; RGWL 3; SFW 4; SSFS 23

Murakami Haruki
See Murakami, Haruki
See also CWW 2; DLB 182; EWL 3

Murasaki, Lady
See Murasaki Shikibu

Murasaki Shikibu 978(?)-1026(?) .. **CMLC 1, 79**
See also EFS 2; LATS 1:1; RGWL 2, 3

Murdoch, Iris 1919-1999 .. **CLC 1, 2, 3, 4, 6, 8, 11, 15, 22, 31, 51; TCLC 171**
See also BRWS 1; CA 13-16R; 179; CANR 8, 43, 68, 103, 142; CBD; CDBLB 1960 to Present; CN 1, 2, 3, 4, 5, 6; CWD; DA3; DAB; DAC; DAM MST, NOV; DLB 14, 194, 233, 326; EWL 3; INT CANR-8; MTCW 1, 2; MTFW 2005; NFS 18; RGEL 2; TCLE 1:2; TEA; WLIT 4

Murfree, Mary Noailles 1850-1922 .. **SSC 22; TCLC 135**
See also CA 122; 176; DLB 12, 74; RGAL 4

Murglie
See Murnau, F.W.

Murnau, Friedrich Wilhelm
See Murnau, F.W.

Murnau, F.W. 1888-1931 .... **TCLC 53**
See also CA 112

Murphy, Richard 1927- .... **CLC 41**
See also BRWS 5; CA 29-32R; CP 1, 2, 3,
4, 5, 6, 7; DLB 40; EWL 3

Murphy, Sylvia 1937- .... **CLC 34**
See also CA 121

Murphy, Thomas (Bernard) 1935- ... **CLC 51**
See Murphy, Tom
See also CA 101

Murphy, Tom
See Murphy, Thomas (Bernard)
See also DLB 310

Murray, Albert 1916- .... **BLC 2:3; CLC 73**
See also BW 2; CA 49-52; CANR 26, 52,
78, 160; CN 7; CSW; DLB 38; MTFW
2005

Murray, Albert L.
See Murray, Albert

Murray, James Augustus Henry
1837-1915 .... **TCLC 117**

Murray, Judith Sargent
1751-1820 .... **NCLC 63**
See also DLB 37, 200

Murray, Les(lie Allan) 1938- .... **CLC 40**
See also BRWS 7; CA 21-24R; CANR 11,
27, 56, 103; CP 1, 2, 3, 4, 5, 6, 7; DAM
POET; DLB 289; DLBY 2001; EWL 3;
RGEL 2

Murry, J. Middleton
See Murry, John Middleton

Murry, John Middleton
1889-1957 .... **TCLC 16**
See also CA 118; 217; DLB 149

Musgrave, Susan 1951- .... **CLC 13, 54**
See also CA 69-72; CANR 45, 84; CCA 1;
CP 2, 3, 4, 5, 6, 7; CWP

Musil, Robert (Edler von)
1880-1942 .... **SSC 18; TCLC 12, 68**
See also CA 109; CANR 55, 84; CDWLB
2; DLB 81, 124; EW 9; EWL 3; MTCW
2; RGSF 2; RGWL 2, 3

Muske, Carol CLC 90
See Muske-Dukes, Carol (Anne)

Muske-Dukes, Carol (Anne) 1945-
See Muske, Carol
See also CA 65-68, 203; CAAE 203; CANR
32, 70; CWP; PFS 24

Musset, Alfred de 1810-1857 . **DC 27; NCLC
7, 150**
See also DLB 192, 217; EW 6; GFL 1789
to the Present; RGWL 2, 3; TWA

Musset, Louis Charles Alfred de
See Musset, Alfred de

Mussolini, Benito (Amilcare Andrea)
1883-1945 .... **TCLC 96**
See also CA 116

Mutanabbi, Al-
See al-Mutanabbi, Ahmad ibn al-Husayn
Abu al-Tayyib al-Jufi al-Kindi
See also WLIT 6

My Brother's Brother
See Chekhov, Anton (Pavlovich)

Myers, L(eopold) H(amilton)
1881-1944 .... **TCLC 59**
See also CA 157; DLB 15; EWL 3; RGEL
2

Myers, Walter Dean 1937- ...... **BLC 1:3, 2:3;
CLC 35**
See Myers, Walter M.
See also AAYA 4, 23; BW 2; BYA 6, 8, 11;
CA 33-36R; CANR 20, 42, 67, 108; CLR
4, 16, 35, 110; DAM MULT, NOV; DLB
33; INT CANR-20; JRDA; LAIT 5; MAI-

CYA 1, 2; MAICYAS 1; MTCW 2;
MTFW 2005; SAAS 2; SATA 41, 71, 109,
157; SATA-Brief 27; WYA; YAW

Myers, Walter M.
See Myers, Walter Dean

Myles, Symon
See Follett, Ken

Nabokov, Vladimir (Vladimirovich)
1899-1977 .... **CLC 1, 2, 3, 6, 8, 11, 15,
23, 44, 46, 64; SSC 11, 86; TCLC 108,
189; WLC 4**
See also AAYA 45; AMW; AMWC 1;
AMWR 1; BPFB 2; CA 5-8R; 69-72;
CANR 20, 102; CDALB 1941-1968; CN
1, 2; CP 2; DA; DA3; DAB; DAC; DAM
MST, NOV; DLB 2, 244, 278, 317; DLBD
3; DLBY 1980, 1991; EWL 3; EXPS;
LATS 1:2; MAL 5; MTCW 1, 2; MTFW
2005; NCFS 4; NFS 9; RGAL 4; RGSF
2; SSFS 6, 15; TUS

Naevius c. 265B.C.-201B.C. .... **CMLC 37**
See also DLB 211

Nagai, Kafu
See Nagai, Sokichi

Nagai, Sokichi 1879-1959 .... **TCLC 51**
See Kafu
See also CA 117; DLB 180; EWL 3

Nagai Kafu
See Nagai, Sokichi

Nagy, Laszlo 1925-1978 .... **CLC 7**
See also CA 129; 112

Naidu, Sarojini 1879-1949 .... **TCLC 80**
See also EWL 3; RGEL 2

Naipaul, Shiva 1945-1985 .... **CLC 32, 39;
TCLC 153**
See also CA 110; 112; 116; CANR 33; CN
2, 3; DA3; DAM NOV; DLB 157; DLBY
1985; EWL 3; MTCW 1, 2; MTFW 2005

Naipaul, V.S. 1932- .. **CLC 4, 7, 9, 13, 18, 37,
105, 199; SSC 38**
See also BPFB 2; BRWS 1; CA 1-4R;
CANR 1, 33, 51, 91, 126; CDBLB 1960
to Present; CDWLB 3; CN 1, 2, 3, 4, 5,
6, 7; DA3; DAB; DAC; DAM MST,
NOV; DLB 125, 204, 207, 326, 331;
DLBY 1985, 2001; EWL 3; LATS 1:2;
MTCW 1, 2; MTFW 2005; RGEL 2;
RGSF 2; TWA; WLIT 4; WWE 1

Nakos, Lilika 1903(?)-1989 .... **CLC 29**

Napoleon
See Yamamoto, Hisaye

Narayan, R.K. 1906-2001 ...... **CLC 7, 28, 47,
121, 211; SSC 25**
See also BPFB 2; CA 81-84; 196; CANR
33, 61, 112; CN 1, 2, 3, 4, 5, 6, 7; DA3;
DAM NOV; DLB 323; DNFS 1; EWL 3;
MTCW 1, 2; MTFW 2005; RGEL 2;
RGSF 2; SATA 62; SSFS 5; WWE 1

Nash, (Fredric) Ogden 1902-1971 . **CLC 23;
PC 21; TCLC 109**
See also CA 13-14; 29-32R; CANR 34, 61;
CAP 1; CP 1; DAM POET; DLB 11;
MAICYA 1, 2; MAL 5; MTCW 1, 2;
RGAL 4; SATA 2, 46; WP

Nashe, Thomas 1567-1601(?) .. **LC 41, 89; PC
82**
See also DLB 167; RGEL 2

Nathan, Daniel
See Dannay, Frederic

Nathan, George Jean 1882-1958 .... **TCLC 18**
See Hatteras, Owen
See also CA 114; 169; DLB 137; MAL 5

Natsume, Kinnosuke
See Natsume, Soseki

Natsume, Soseki 1867-1916 .... **TCLC 2, 10**
See Natsume Soseki; Soseki
See also CA 104; 195; RGWL 2, 3; TWA

Natsume Soseki
See Natsume, Soseki
See also DLB 180; EWL 3

Natti, (Mary) Lee 1919-
See Kingman, Lee
See also CA 5-8R; CANR 2

Navarre, Marguerite de
See de Navarre, Marguerite

Naylor, Gloria 1950- . **BLC 1:3; CLC 28, 52,
156; WLCS**
See also AAYA 6, 39; AFAW 1, 2; AMWS
8; BW 2, 3; CA 107; CANR 27, 51, 74,
130; CN 4, 5, 6, 7; CPW; DA; DA3;
DAC; DAM MST, MULT, NOV, POP;
DLB 173; EWL 3; FW; MAL 5; MTCW
1, 2; MTFW 2005; NFS 4, 7; RGAL 4;
TCLE 1:2; TUS

Neal, John 1793-1876 .... **NCLC 161**
See also DLB 1, 59, 243; FW; RGAL 4

Neff, Debra CLC 59

Neihardt, John Gneisenau
1881-1973 .... **CLC 32**
See also CA 13-14; CANR 65; CAP 1; DLB
9, 54, 256; LAIT 2; TCWW 1, 2

Nekrasov, Nikolai Alekseevich
1821-1878 .... **NCLC 11**
See also DLB 277

Nelligan, Emile 1879-1941 .... **TCLC 14**
See also CA 114; 204; DLB 92; EWL 3

Nelson, Willie 1933- .... **CLC 17**
See also CA 107; CANR 114

Nemerov, Howard 1920-1991 .... **CLC 2, 6, 9,
36; PC 24; TCLC 124**
See also AMW; CA 1-4R; 134; CABS 2;
CANR 1, 27, 53; CN 1, 2, 3; CP 1, 2, 3,
4, 5; DAM POET; DLB 5, 6; DLBY 1983;
EWL 3; INT CANR-27; MAL 5; MTCW
1, 2; MTFW 2005; PFS 10, 14; RGAL 4

Nepos, Cornelius c. 99B.C.-c.
24B.C. .... **CMLC 89**
See also DLB 211

Neruda, Pablo 1904-1973 .. **CLC 1, 2, 5, 7, 9,
28, 62; HLC 2; PC 4, 64; WLC 4**
See also CA 19-20; 45-48; CANR 131; CAP
2; DA; DA3; DAB; DAC; DAM MST,
MULT, POET; DLB 283, 331; DNFS 2;
EWL 3; HW 1; LAW; MTCW 1, 2;
MTFW 2005; PFS 11, 28; RGWL 2, 3;
TWA; WLIT 1; WP

Nerval, Gerard de 1808-1855 ... **NCLC 1, 67;
PC 13; SSC 18**
See also DLB 217; EW 6; GFL 1789 to the
Present; RGSF 2; RGWL 2, 3

Nervo, (Jose) Amado (Ruiz de)
1870-1919 .... **HLCS 2; TCLC 11**
See also CA 109; 131; DLB 290; EWL 3;
HW 1; LAW

Nesbit, Malcolm
See Chester, Alfred

Nessi, Pio Baroja y
See Baroja, Pio

Nestroy, Johann 1801-1862 .... **NCLC 42**
See also DLB 133; RGWL 2, 3

Netterville, Luke
See O'Grady, Standish (James)

Neufeld, John (Arthur) 1938- .... **CLC 17**
See also AAYA 11; CA 25-28R; CANR 11,
37, 56; CLR 52; MAICYA 1, 2; SAAS 3;
SATA 6, 81, 131; SATA-Essay 131; YAW

Neumann, Alfred 1895-1952 .... **TCLC 100**
See also CA 183; DLB 56

Neumann, Ferenc
See Molnar, Ferenc

Neville, Emily Cheney 1919- .... **CLC 12**
See also BYA 2; CA 5-8R; CANR 3, 37,
85; JRDA; MAICYA 1, 2; SAAS 2; SATA
1; YAW

Nowlan, Alden (Albert) 1933-1983 ... **CLC 15**
See also CA 9-12R; CANR 5; CP 1, 2, 3;
DAC; DAM MST; DLB 53; PFS 12

Noyes, Alfred 1880-1958 ...... **PC 27; TCLC 7**
See also CA 104; 188; DLB 20; EXPP;
FANT; PFS 4; RGEL 2

Nugent, Richard Bruce
1906(?)-1987 .... **HR 1:3**
See also BW 1; CA 125; DLB 51; GLL 2

Nunez, Elizabeth 1944- .... **BLC 2:3**
See also CA 223

Nunn, Kem CLC 34
See also CA 159

Nussbaum, Martha Craven 1947- .. **CLC 203**
See also CA 134; CANR 102, 176

Nwapa, Flora (Nwanzuruaha)
1931-1993 .... **BLCS; CLC 133**
See also BW 2; CA 143; CANR 83; CD-
WLB 3; CWRI 5; DLB 125; EWL 3;
WLIT 2

Nye, Robert 1939- .... **CLC 13, 42**
See also BRWS 10; CA 33-36R; CANR 29,
67, 107; CN 1, 2, 3, 4, 5, 6, 7; CP 1, 2, 3,
4, 5, 6, 7; CWRI 5; DAM NOV; DLB 14,
271; FANT; HGG; MTCW 1; RHW;
SATA 6

Nyro, Laura 1947-1997 .... **CLC 17**
See also CA 194

Oates, Joyce Carol 1938- .. **CLC 1, 2, 3, 6, 9,
11, 15, 19, 33, 52, 108, 134, 228; SSC 6,
70; WLC 4**
See also AAYA 15, 52; AITN 1; AMWS 2;
BEST 89:2; BPFB 3; BYA 11; CA 5-8R;
CANR 25, 45, 74, 113, 129, 165; CDALB
1968-1988; CN 1, 2, 3, 4, 5, 6, 7; CP 5,
6, 7; CPW; CWP; DA; DA3; DAB; DAC;
DAM MST, NOV, POP; DLB 2, 5, 130;
DLBY 1981; EWL 3; EXPS; FL 1:6; FW;
GL 3; HGG; INT CANR-25; LAIT 4;
MAL 5; MBL; MTCW 1, 2; MTFW 2005;
NFS 8, 24; RGAL 4; RGSF 2; SATA 159;
SSFS 1, 8, 17; SUFW 2; TUS

O'Brian, E. G.
See Clarke, Arthur C.

O'Brian, Patrick 1914-2000 .... **CLC 152**
See also AAYA 55; BRWS 12; CA 144; 187;
CANR 74; CPW; MTCW 2; MTFW 2005;
RHW

O'Brien, Darcy 1939-1998 .... **CLC 11**
See also CA 21-24R; 167; CANR 8, 59

O'Brien, Edna 1932- ..... **CLC 3, 5, 8, 13, 36,
65, 116, 237; SSC 10, 77**
See also BRWS 5; CA 1-4R; CANR 6, 41,
65, 102, 169; CDBLB 1960 to Present;
CN 1, 2, 3, 4, 5, 6, 7; DA3; DAM NOV;
DLB 14, 231, 319; EWL 3; FW; MTCW
1, 2; MTFW 2005; RGSF 2; WLIT 4

O'Brien, Fitz-James 1828-1862 ..... **NCLC 21**
See also DLB 74; RGAL 4; SUFW

O'Brien, Flann CLC 1, 4, 5, 7, 10, 47
See O Nuallain, Brian
See also BRWS 2; DLB 231; EWL 3;
RGEL 2

O'Brien, Richard 1942- .... **CLC 17**
See also CA 124

O'Brien, Tim 1946- .... **CLC 7, 19, 40, 103,
211; SSC 74**
See also AAYA 16; AMWS 5; CA 85-88;
CANR 40, 58, 133; CDALBS; CN 5, 6,
7; CPW; DA3; DAM POP; DLB 152;
DLBD 9; DLBY 1980; LATS 1:2; MAL
5; MTCW 2; MTFW 2005; RGAL 4;
SSFS 5, 15; TCLE 1:2

Obstfelder, Sigbjoern 1866-1900 .... **TCLC 23**
See also CA 123

O'Casey, Sean 1880-1964 .... **CLC 1, 5, 9, 11,
15, 88; DC 12; WLCS**
See also BRW 7; CA 89-92; CANR 62;
CBD; CDBLB 1914-1945; DA3; DAB;
DAC; DAM DRAM, MST; DFS 19; DLB

10; EWL 3; MTCW 1, 2; MTFW 2005;
RGEL 2; TEA; WLIT 4

O'Cathasaigh, Sean
See O'Casey, Sean

Occom, Samson 1723-1792 .... **LC 60; NNAL**
See also DLB 175

Occomy, Marita (Odette) Bonner
1899(?)-1971
See Bonner, Marita
See also BW 2; CA 142; DFS 13; DLB 51,
228

Ochs, Phil(ip David) 1940-1976 .... **CLC 17**
See also CA 185; 65-68

O'Connor, Edwin (Greene)
1918-1968 .... **CLC 14**
See also CA 93-96; 25-28R; MAL 5

O'Connor, (Mary) Flannery
1925-1964 .... **CLC 1, 2, 3, 6, 10, 13, 15,
21, 66, 104; SSC 1, 23, 61, 82, 111;
TCLC 132; WLC 4**
See also AAYA 7; AMW; AMWR 2; BPFB
3; BYA 16; CA 1-4R; CANR 3, 41;
CDALB 1941-1968; DA; DA3; DAB;
DAC; DAM MST, NOV; DLB 2, 152;
DLBD 12; DLBY 1980; EWL 3; EXPS;
LAIT 5; MAL 5; MBL; MTCW 1, 2;
MTFW 2005; NFS 3, 21; RGAL 4; RGSF
2; SSFS 2, 7, 10, 19; TUS

O'Connor, Frank 1903-1966 ... **CLC 23; SSC
5, 109**
See O'Donovan, Michael Francis
See also DLB 162; EWL 3; RGSF 2; SSFS
5

O'Dell, Scott 1898-1989 .... **CLC 30**
See also AAYA 3, 44; BPFB 3; BYA 1, 2,
3, 5; CA 61-64; 129; CANR 12, 30, 112;
CLR 1, 16, 126; DLB 52; JRDA; MAI-
CYA 1, 2; SATA 12, 60, 134; WYA; YAW

Odets, Clifford 1906-1963 ..... **CLC 2, 28, 98;
DC 6**
See also AMWS 2; CA 85-88; CAD; CANR
62; DAM DRAM; DFS 3, 17, 20; DLB 7,
26, 341; EWL 3; MAL 5; MTCW 1, 2;
MTFW 2005; RGAL 4; TUS

O'Doherty, Brian 1928- .... **CLC 76**
See also CA 105; CANR 108

O'Donnell, K. M.
See Malzberg, Barry N(athaniel)

O'Donnell, Lawrence
See Kuttner, Henry

O'Donovan, Michael Francis
1903-1966 .... **CLC 14**
See O'Connor, Frank
See also CA 93-96; CANR 84

Oe, Kenzaburo 1935- .. **CLC 10, 36, 86, 187;
SSC 20**
See Oe Kenzaburo
See also CA 97-100; CANR 36, 50, 74, 126;
DA3; DAM NOV; DLB 182, 331; DLBY
1994; LATS 1:2; MJW; MTCW 1, 2;
MTFW 2005; RGSF 2; RGWL 2, 3

Oe Kenzaburo
See Oe, Kenzaburo
See also CWW 2; EWL 3

O'Faolain, Julia 1932- .... **CLC 6, 19, 47, 108**
See also CA 81-84; CAAS 2; CANR 12,
61; CN 2, 3, 4, 5, 6, 7; DLB 14, 231, 319;
FW; MTCW 1; RHW

O'Faolain, Sean 1900-1991 ...... **CLC 1, 7, 14,
32, 70; SSC 13; TCLC 143**
See also CA 61-64; 134; CANR 12, 66; CN
1, 2, 3, 4; DLB 15, 162; MTCW 1, 2;
MTFW 2005; RGEL 2; RGSF 2

O'Flaherty, Liam 1896-1984 .... **CLC 5, 34;
SSC 6**
See also CA 101; 113; CANR 35; CN 1, 2,
3; DLB 36, 162; DLBY 1984; MTCW 1,
2; MTFW 2005; RGEL 2; RGSF 2; SSFS
5, 20

Ogai
See Mori Ogai
See also MJW

Ogilvy, Gavin
See Barrie, J(ames) M(atthew)

O'Grady, Standish (James)
1846-1928 .... **TCLC 5**
See also CA 104; 157

O'Grady, Timothy 1951- .... **CLC 59**
See also CA 138

O'Hara, Frank 1926-1966 .... **CLC 2, 5, 13,
78; PC 45**
See also CA 9-12R; 25-28R; CANR 33;
DA3; DAM POET; DLB 5, 16, 193; EWL
3; MAL 5; MTCW 1, 2; MTFW 2005;
PFS 8, 12; RGAL 4; WP

O'Hara, John (Henry) 1905-1970 . **CLC 1, 2,
3, 6, 11, 42; SSC 15**
See also AMW; BPFB 3; CA 5-8R; 25-28R;
CANR 31, 60; CDALB 1929-1941; DAM
NOV; DLB 9, 86, 324; DLBD 2; EWL 3;
MAL 5; MTCW 1, 2; MTFW 2005; NFS
11; RGAL 4; RGSF 2

O'Hehir, Diana 1929- .... **CLC 41**
See also CA 245

Ohiyesa
See Eastman, Charles A(lexander)

Okada, John 1923-1971 .... **AAL**
See also BYA 14; CA 212; DLB 312; NFS
25

Okigbo, Christopher 1930-1967 ..... **BLC 1:3;
CLC 25, 84; PC 7; TCLC 171**
See also AFW; BW 1, 3; CA 77-80; CANR
74; CDWLB 3; DAM MULT, POET; DLB
125; EWL 3; MTCW 1, 2; MTFW 2005;
RGEL 2

Okigbo, Christopher Ifenayichukwu
See Okigbo, Christopher

Okri, Ben 1959- .... **BLC 2:3; CLC 87, 223**
See also AFW; BRWS 5; BW 2, 3; CA 130;
138; CANR 65, 128; CN 5, 6, 7; DLB
157, 231, 319, 326; EWL 3; INT CA-138;
MTCW 2; MTFW 2005; RGSF 2; SSFS
20; WLIT 2; WWE 1

Olds, Sharon 1942- .. **CLC 32, 39, 85; PC 22**
See also AMWS 10; CA 101; CANR 18,
41, 66, 98, 135; CP 5, 6, 7; CPW; CWP;
DAM POET; DLB 120; MAL 5; MTCW
2; MTFW 2005; PFS 17

Oldstyle, Jonathan
See Irving, Washington

Olesha, Iurii
See Olesha, Yuri (Karlovich)
See also RGWL 2

Olesha, Iurii Karlovich
See Olesha, Yuri (Karlovich)
See also DLB 272

Olesha, Yuri (Karlovich) 1899-1960 . **CLC 8;
SSC 69; TCLC 136**
See Olesha, Iurii; Olesha, Iurii Karlovich;
Olesha, Yury Karlovich
See also CA 85-88; EW 11; RGWL 3

Olesha, Yury Karlovich
See Olesha, Yuri (Karlovich)
See also EWL 3

Oliphant, Mrs.
See Oliphant, Margaret (Oliphant Wilson)
See also SUFW

Oliphant, Laurence 1829(?)-1888 .. **NCLC 47**
See also DLB 18, 166

Oliphant, Margaret (Oliphant Wilson)
1828-1897 .... **NCLC 11, 61; SSC 25**
See Oliphant, Mrs.
See also BRWS 10; DLB 18, 159, 190;
HGG; RGEL 2; RGSF 2

Oliver, Mary 1935- ... **CLC 19, 34, 98; PC 75**
See also AMWS 7; CA 21-24R; CANR 9,
43, 84, 92, 138; CP 4, 5, 6, 7; CWP; DLB
5, 193; EWL 3; MTFW 2005; PFS 15

Pasternak, Boris 1890-1960 ... **CLC 7, 10, 18, 63; PC 6; SSC 31; TCLC 188; WLC 4**
See also BPFB 3; CA 127; 116; DA; DA3; DAB; DAC; DAM MST, NOV, POET; DLB 302, 331; EW 10; MTCW 1, 2; MTFW 2005; NFS 26; RGSF 2; RGWL 2, 3; TWA; WP

Patchen, Kenneth 1911-1972 .... **CLC 1, 2, 18**
See also BG 1:3; CA 1-4R; 33-36R; CANR 3, 35; CN 1; CP 1; DAM POET; DLB 16, 48; EWL 3; MAL 5; MTCW 1; RGAL 4

Patchett, Ann 1963- .... **CLC 244**
See also AAYA 69; AMWS 12; CA 139; CANR 64, 110, 167; MTFW 2005

Pater, Walter (Horatio) 1839-1894 . **NCLC 7, 90, 159**
See also BRW 5; CDBLB 1832-1890; DLB 57, 156; RGEL 2; TEA

Paterson, A(ndrew) B(arton) 1864-1941 .... **TCLC 32**
See also CA 155; DLB 230; RGEL 2; SATA 97

Paterson, Banjo
See Paterson, A(ndrew) B(arton)

Paterson, Katherine 1932- .... **CLC 12, 30**
See also AAYA 1, 31; BYA 1, 2, 7; CA 21-24R; CANR 28, 59, 111, 173; CLR 7, 50, 127; CWRI 5; DLB 52; JRDA; LAIT 4; MAICYA 1, 2; MAICYAS 1; MTCW 1; SATA 13, 53, 92, 133; WYA; YAW

Paterson, Katherine Womeldorf
See Paterson, Katherine

Patmore, Coventry Kersey Dighton 1823-1896 .... **NCLC 9; PC 59**
See also DLB 35, 98; RGEL 2; TEA

Paton, Alan 1903-1988 ..... **CLC 4, 10, 25, 55, 106; TCLC 165; WLC 4**
See also AAYA 26; AFW; BPFB 3; BRWS 2; BYA 1; CA 13-16; 125; CANR 22; CAP 1; CN 1, 2, 3, 4; DA; DA3; DAB; DAC; DAM MST, NOV; DLB 225; DLBD 17; EWL 3; EXPN; LAIT 4; MTCW 1, 2; MTFW 2005; NFS 3, 12; RGEL 2; SATA 11; SATA-Obit 56; TWA; WLIT 2; WWE 1

Paton Walsh, Gillian
See Paton Walsh, Jill
See also AAYA 47; BYA 1, 8

Paton Walsh, Jill 1937- .... **CLC 35**
See Paton Walsh, Gillian; Walsh, Jill Paton
See also AAYA 11; CA 262; CAAE 262; CANR 38, 83, 158; CLR 2, 65; DLB 161; JRDA; MAICYA 1, 2; SAAS 3; SATA 4, 72, 109; YAW

Patsauq, Markoosie 1942- .... **NNAL**
See also CA 101; CLR 23; CWRI 5; DAM MULT

Patterson, (Horace) Orlando (Lloyd) 1940- .... **BLCS**
See also BW 1; CA 65-68; CANR 27, 84; CN 1, 2, 3, 4, 5, 6

Patton, George S(mith), Jr. 1885-1945 .... **TCLC 79**
See also CA 189

Paulding, James Kirke 1778-1860 ... **NCLC 2**
See also DLB 3, 59, 74, 250; RGAL 4

Paulin, Thomas Neilson
See Paulin, Tom

Paulin, Tom 1949- .... **CLC 37, 177**
See also CA 123; 128; CANR 98; CP 3, 4, 5, 6, 7; DLB 40

Pausanias c. 1st cent. - .... **CMLC 36**

Paustovsky, Konstantin (Georgievich) 1892-1968 .... **CLC 40**
See also CA 93-96; 25-28R; DLB 272; EWL 3

Pavese, Cesare 1908-1950 .... **PC 13; SSC 19; TCLC 3**
See also CA 104; 169; DLB 128, 177; EW 12; EWL 3; PFS 20; RGSF 2; RGWL 2, 3; TWA; WLIT 7

Pavic, Milorad 1929- .... **CLC 60**
See also CA 136; CDWLB 4; CWW 2; DLB 181; EWL 3; RGWL 3

Pavlov, Ivan Petrovich 1849-1936 . **TCLC 91**
See also CA 118; 180

Pavlova, Karolina Karlovna 1807-1893 .... **NCLC 138**
See also DLB 205

Payne, Alan
See Jakes, John

Payne, Rachel Ann
See Jakes, John

Paz, Gil
See Lugones, Leopoldo

Paz, Octavio 1914-1998 . **CLC 3, 4, 6, 10, 19, 51, 65, 119; HLC 2; PC 1, 48; WLC 4**
See also AAYA 50; CA 73-76; 165; CANR 32, 65, 104; CWW 2; DA; DA3; DAB; DAC; DAM MST, MULT, POET; DLB 290, 331; DLBY 1990, 1998; DNFS 1; EWL 3; HW 1, 2; LAW; LAWS 1; MTCW 1, 2; MTFW 2005; PFS 18; RGWL 2, 3; SSFS 13; TWA; WLIT 1

p'Bitek, Okot 1931-1982 . **BLC 1:3; CLC 96; TCLC 149**
See also AFW; BW 2, 3; CA 124; 107; CANR 82; CP 1, 2, 3; DAM MULT; DLB 125; EWL 3; MTCW 1, 2; MTFW 2005; RGEL 2; WLIT 2

Peabody, Elizabeth Palmer 1804-1894 .... **NCLC 169**
See also DLB 1, 223

Peacham, Henry 1578-1644(?) .... **LC 119**
See also DLB 151

Peacock, Molly 1947- .... **CLC 60**
See also CA 103, 262; CAAE 262; CAAS 21; CANR 52, 84; CP 5, 6, 7; CWP; DLB 120, 282

Peacock, Thomas Love 1785-1866 .... **NCLC 22; PC 87**
See also BRW 4; DLB 96, 116; RGEL 2; RGSF 2

Peake, Mervyn 1911-1968 .... **CLC 7, 54**
See also CA 5-8R; 25-28R; CANR 3; DLB 15, 160, 255; FANT; MTCW 1; RGEL 2; SATA 23; SFW 4

Pearce, Philippa 1920-2006
See Christie, Philippa
See also CA 5-8R; 255; CANR 4, 109; CWRI 5; FANT; MAICYA 2; SATA-Obit 179

Pearl, Eric
See Elman, Richard (Martin)

Pearson, Jean Mary
See Gardam, Jane

Pearson, T. R. 1956- .... **CLC 39**
See also CA 120; 130; CANR 97, 147; CSW; INT CA-130

Pearson, Thomas Reid
See Pearson, T. R.

Peck, Dale 1967- .... **CLC 81**
See also CA 146; CANR 72, 127; GLL 2

Peck, John (Frederick) 1941- .... **CLC 3**
See also CA 49-52; CANR 3, 100; CP 4, 5, 6, 7

Peck, Richard 1934- .... **CLC 21**
See also AAYA 1, 24; BYA 1, 6, 8, 11; CA 85-88; CANR 19, 38, 129; CLR 15; INT CANR-19; JRDA; MAICYA 1, 2; SAAS 2; SATA 18, 55, 97, 110, 158; SATA-Essay 110; WYA; YAW

Peck, Richard Wayne
See Peck, Richard

Peck, Robert Newton 1928- .... **CLC 17**
See also AAYA 3, 43; BYA 1, 6; CA 81-84; 182; CAAE 182; CANR 31, 63, 127; CLR 45; DA; DAC; DAM MST; JRDA; LAIT 3; MAICYA 1, 2; SAAS 1; SATA 21, 62, 111, 156; SATA-Essay 108; WYA; YAW

Peckinpah, David Samuel
See Peckinpah, Sam

Peckinpah, Sam 1925-1984 .... **CLC 20**
See also CA 109; 114; CANR 82

Pedersen, Knut 1859-1952
See Hamsun, Knut
See also CA 104; 119; CANR 63; MTCW 1, 2

Peele, George 1556-1596 .... **DC 27; LC 115**
See also BRW 1; DLB 62, 167; RGEL 2

Peeslake, Gaffer
See Durrell, Lawrence (George)

Peguy, Charles (Pierre) 1873-1914 .... **TCLC 10**
See also CA 107; 193; DLB 258; EWL 3; GFL 1789 to the Present

Peirce, Charles Sanders 1839-1914 .... **TCLC 81**
See also CA 194; DLB 270

Pelecanos, George P. 1957- .... **CLC 236**
See also CA 138; CANR 122, 165; DLB 306

Pelevin, Victor 1962- .... **CLC 238**
See Pelevin, Viktor Olegovich
See also CA 154; CANR 88, 159

Pelevin, Viktor Olegovich
See Pelevin, Victor
See also DLB 285

Pellicer, Carlos 1897(?)-1977 .... **HLCS 2**
See also CA 153; 69-72; DLB 290; EWL 3; HW 1

Pena, Ramon del Valle y
See Valle-Inclan, Ramon (Maria) del

Pendennis, Arthur Esquir
See Thackeray, William Makepeace

Penn, Arthur
See Matthews, (James) Brander

Penn, William 1644-1718 .... **LC 25**
See also DLB 24

PEPECE
See Prado (Calvo), Pedro

Pepys, Samuel 1633-1703 ... **LC 11, 58; WLC 4**
See also BRW 2; CDBLB 1660-1789; DA; DA3; DAB; DAC; DAM MST; DLB 101, 213; NCFS 4; RGEL 2; TEA; WLIT 3

Percy, Thomas 1729-1811 .... **NCLC 95**
See also DLB 104

Percy, Walker 1916-1990 .... **CLC 2, 3, 6, 8, 14, 18, 47, 65**
See also AMWS 3; BPFB 3; CA 1-4R; 131; CANR 1, 23, 64; CN 1, 2, 3, 4; CPW; CSW; DA3; DAM NOV, POP; DLB 2; DLBY 1980, 1990; EWL 3; MAL 5; MTCW 1, 2; MTFW 2005; RGAL 4; TUS

Percy, William Alexander 1885-1942 .... **TCLC 84**
See also CA 163; MTCW 2

Perec, Georges 1936-1982 .... **CLC 56, 116**
See also CA 141; DLB 83, 299; EWL 3; GFL 1789 to the Present; RGHL; RGWL 3

Pereda (y Sanchez de Porrua), Jose Maria de 1833-1906 .... **TCLC 16**
See also CA 117

Pereda y Porrua, Jose Maria de
See Pereda (y Sanchez de Porrua), Jose Maria de

Peregoy, George Weems
See Mencken, H(enry) L(ouis)

Piozzi, Hester Lynch (Thrale)
1741-1821 .... **NCLC 57**
See also DLB 104, 142

Pirandello, Luigi 1867-1936 .. **DC 5; SSC 22;**
TCLC 4, 29, 172; WLC 4
See also CA 104; 153; CANR 103; DA;
DA3; DAB; DAC; DAM DRAM, MST;
DFS 4, 9; DLB 264, 331; EW 8; EWL 3;
MTCW 2; MTFW 2005; RGSF 2; RGWL
2, 3; WLIT 7

Pirsig, Robert M(aynard) 1928- ... **CLC 4, 6,**
73
See also CA 53-56; CANR 42, 74; CPW 1;
DA3; DAM POP; MTCW 1, 2; MTFW
2005; SATA 39

Pisan, Christine de
See Christine de Pizan

Pisarev, Dmitrii Ivanovich
See Pisarev, Dmitry Ivanovich
See also DLB 277

Pisarev, Dmitry Ivanovich
1840-1868 .... **NCLC 25**
See Pisarev, Dmitrii Ivanovich

Pix, Mary (Griffith) 1666-1709 ..... **LC 8, 149**
See also DLB 80

Pixerecourt, (Rene Charles) Guilbert de
1773-1844 .... **NCLC 39**
See also DLB 192; GFL 1789 to the Present

Plaatje, Sol(omon) T(shekisho)
1878-1932 .... **BLCS; TCLC 73**
See also BW 2, 3; CA 141; CANR 79; DLB
125, 225

Plaidy, Jean
See Hibbert, Eleanor Alice Burford

Planche, James Robinson
1796-1880 .... **NCLC 42**
See also RGEL 2

Plant, Robert 1948- .... **CLC 12**

Plante, David 1940- .... **CLC 7, 23, 38**
See also CA 37-40R; CANR 12, 36, 58, 82,
152; CN 2, 3, 4, 5, 6, 7; DAM NOV;
DLBY 1983; INT CANR-12; MTCW 1

Plante, David Robert
See Plante, David

Plath, Sylvia 1932-1963 ..... **CLC 1, 2, 3, 5, 9,**
11, 14, 17, 50, 51, 62, 111; PC 1, 37;
WLC 4
See also AAYA 13; AMWR 2; AMWS 1;
BPFB 3; CA 19-20; CANR 34, 101; CAP
2; CDALB 1941-1968; DA; DA3; DAB;
DAC; DAM MST, POET; DLB 5, 6, 152;
EWL 3; EXPN; EXPP; FL 1:6; FW; LAIT
4; MAL 5; MBL; MTCW 1, 2; MTFW
2005; NFS 1; PAB; PFS 1, 15, 28; RGAL
4; SATA 96; TUS; WP; YAW

Plato c. 428B.C.-347B.C. .... **CMLC 8, 75, 98;**
WLCS
See also AW 1; CDWLB 1; DA; DA3;
DAB; DAC; DAM MST; DLB 176; LAIT
1; LATS 1:1; RGWL 2, 3; WLIT 8

Platonov, Andrei
See Klimentov, Andrei Platonovich

Platonov, Andrei Platonovich
See Klimentov, Andrei Platonovich
See also DLB 272

Platonov, Andrey Platonovich
See Klimentov, Andrei Platonovich
See also EWL 3

Platt, Kin 1911- .... **CLC 26**
See also AAYA 11; CA 17-20R; CANR 11;
JRDA; SAAS 17; SATA 21, 86; WYA

Plautus c. 254B.C.-c. 184B.C. .... **CMLC 24,**
92; DC 6
See also AW 1; CDWLB 1; DLB 211;
RGWL 2, 3; WLIT 8

Plick et Plock
See Simenon, Georges (Jacques Christian)

Plieksans, Janis
See Rainis, Janis

Plimpton, George 1927-2003 .... **CLC 36**
See also AITN 1; AMWS 16; CA 21-24R;
224; CANR 32, 70, 103, 133; DLB 185,
241; MTCW 1, 2; MTFW 2005; SATA
10; SATA-Obit 150

Pliny the Elder c. 23-79 .... **CMLC 23**
See also DLB 211

Pliny the Younger c. 61-c. 112 ...... **CMLC 62**
See also AW 2; DLB 211

Plomer, William Charles Franklin
1903-1973 .... **CLC 4, 8**
See also AFW; BRWS 11; CA 21-22; CANR
34; CAP 2; CN 1; CP 1, 2; DLB 20, 162,
191, 225; EWL 3; MTCW 1; RGEL 2;
RGSF 2; SATA 24

Plotinus 204-270 .... **CMLC 46**
See also CDWLB 1; DLB 176

Plowman, Piers
See Kavanagh, Patrick (Joseph)

Plum, J.
See Wodehouse, P(elham) G(renville)

Plumly, Stanley (Ross) 1939- .... **CLC 33**
See also CA 108; 110; CANR 97; CP 3, 4,
5, 6, 7; DLB 5, 193; INT CA-110

Plumpe, Friedrich Wilhelm
See Murnau, F.W.

Plutarch c. 46-c. 120 .... **CMLC 60**
See also AW 2; CDWLB 1; DLB 176;
RGWL 2, 3; TWA; WLIT 8

Po Chu-i 772-846 .... **CMLC 24**

Podhoretz, Norman 1930- .... **CLC 189**
See also AMWS 8; CA 9-12R; CANR 7,
78, 135

Poe, Edgar Allan 1809-1849 ..... **NCLC 1, 16,**
55, 78, 94, 97, 117; PC 1, 54; SSC 1,
22, 34, 35, 54, 88, 111; WLC 4
See also AAYA 14; AMW; AMWC 1;
AMWR 2; BPFB 3; BYA 5, 11; CDALB
1640-1865; CMW 4; DA; DA3; DAB;
DAC; DAM MST, POET; DLB 3, 59, 73,
74, 248, 254; EXPP; EXPS; GL 3; HGG;
LAIT 2; LATS 1:1; LMFS 1; MSW; PAB;
PFS 1, 3, 9; RGAL 4; RGSF 2; SATA 23;
SCFW 1, 2; SFW 4; SSFS 2, 4, 7, 8, 16;
SUFW; TUS; WP; WYA

Poet of Titchfield Street, The
See Pound, Ezra (Weston Loomis)

Poggio Bracciolini, Gian Francesco
1380-1459 .... **LC 125**

Pohl, Frederik 1919- .... **CLC 18; SSC 25**
See also AAYA 24; CA 61-64, 188; CAAE
188; CAAS 1; CANR 11, 37, 81, 140; CN
1, 2, 3, 4, 5, 6; DLB 8; INT CANR-11;
MTCW 1, 2; MTFW 2005; SATA 24;
SCFW 1, 2; SFW 4

Poirier, Louis
See Gracq, Julien

Poitier, Sidney 1927- .... **CLC 26**
See also AAYA 60; BW 1; CA 117; CANR
94

Pokagon, Simon 1830-1899 .... **NNAL**
See also DAM MULT

Polanski, Roman 1933- .... **CLC 16, 178**
See also CA 77-80

Poliakoff, Stephen 1952- .... **CLC 38**
See also CA 106; CANR 116; CBD; CD 5,
6; DLB 13

Police, The
See Copeland, Stewart (Armstrong); Summers, Andy

Polidori, John William
1795-1821 .... **NCLC 51; SSC 97**
See also DLB 116; HGG

Poliziano, Angelo 1454-1494 .... **LC 120**
See also WLIT 7

Pollitt, Katha 1949- .... **CLC 28, 122**
See also CA 120; 122; CANR 66, 108, 164;
MTCW 1, 2; MTFW 2005

Pollock, (Mary) Sharon 1936- .... **CLC 50**
See also CA 141; CANR 132; CD 5; CWD;
DAC; DAM DRAM, MST; DFS 3; DLB
60; FW

Pollock, Sharon 1936- .... **DC 20**
See also CD 6

Polo, Marco 1254-1324 .... **CMLC 15**
See also WLIT 7

Polonsky, Abraham (Lincoln)
1910-1999 .... **CLC 92**
See also CA 104; 187; DLB 26; INT CA-104

Polybius c. 200B.C.-c. 118B.C. ...... **CMLC 17**
See also AW 1; DLB 176; RGWL 2, 3

Pomerance, Bernard 1940- .... **CLC 13**
See also CA 101; CAD; CANR 49, 134;
CD 5, 6; DAM DRAM; DFS 9; LAIT 2

Ponge, Francis 1899-1988 .... **CLC 6, 18**
See also CA 85-88; CANR 40, 86;
DAM POET; DLBY 2002; EWL 3; GFL
1789 to the Present; RGWL 2, 3

Poniatowska, Elena 1932- . **CLC 140; HLC 2**
See also CA 101; CANR 32, 66, 107, 156;
CDWLB 3; CWW 2; DAM MULT; DLB
113; EWL 3; HW 1, 2; LAWS 1; WLIT 1

Pontoppidan, Henrik 1857-1943 .... **TCLC 29**
See also CA 170; DLB 300, 331

Ponty, Maurice Merleau
See Merleau-Ponty, Maurice

Poole, Josephine **CLC 17**
See Helyar, Jane Penelope Josephine
See also SAAS 2; SATA 5

Popa, Vasko 1922-1991 . **CLC 19; TCLC 167**
See also CA 112; 148; CDWLB 4; DLB
181; EWL 3; RGWL 2, 3

Pope, Alexander 1688-1744 ...... **LC 3, 58, 60,**
64; PC 26; WLC 5
See also BRW 3; BRWC 1; BRWR 1; CD-BLB 1660-1789; DA; DA3; DAB; DAC;
DAM MST, POET; DLB 95, 101, 213;
EXPP; PAB; PFS 12; RGEL 2; WLIT 3;
WP

Popov, Evgenii Anatol'evich
See Popov, Yevgeny
See also DLB 285

Popov, Yevgeny **CLC 59**
See Popov, Evgenii Anatol'evich

Poquelin, Jean-Baptiste
See Moliere

Porete, Marguerite (?)-1310 .... **CMLC 73**
See also DLB 208

Porphyry c. 233-c. 305 .... **CMLC 71**

Porter, Connie (Rose) 1959(?)- .... **CLC 70**
See also AAYA 65; BW 2, 3; CA 142;
CANR 90, 109; SATA 81, 129

Porter, Gene(va Grace) Stratton **TCLC 21**
See Stratton-Porter, Gene(va Grace)
See also BPFB 3; CA 112; CWRI 5; RHW

Porter, Katherine Anne 1890-1980 ... **CLC 1,**
3, 7, 10, 13, 15, 27, 101; SSC 4, 31, 43,
108
See also AAYA 42; AITN 2; AMW; BPFB
3; CA 1-4R; 101; CANR 1, 65; CDALBS;
CN 1, 2; DA; DA3; DAB; DAC; DAM
MST, NOV; DLB 4, 9, 102; DLBD 12;
DLBY 1980; EWL 3; EXPS; LAIT 3;
MAL 5; MBL; MTCW 1, 2; MTFW 2005;
NFS 14; RGAL 4; RGSF 2; SATA 39;
SATA-Obit 23; SSFS 1, 8, 11, 16, 23;
TCWW 2; TUS

Porter, Peter (Neville Frederick)
1929- .... **CLC 5, 13, 33**
See also CA 85-88; CP 1, 2, 3, 4, 5, 6, 7;
DLB 40, 289; WWE 1

Porter, William Sydney 1862-1910
See Henry, O.
See also CA 104; 131; CDALB 1865-1917;
DA; DA3; DAB; DAC; DAM MST; DLB
12, 78, 79; MTCW 1, 2; MTFW 2005;
TUS; YABC 2

Salas, Floyd Francis 1931- .... **HLC 2**
See also CA 119; CAAS 27; CANR 44, 75, 93; DAM MULT; DLB 82; HW 1, 2; MTCW 2; MTFW 2005
Sale, J. Kirkpatrick
See Sale, Kirkpatrick
Sale, John Kirkpatrick
See Sale, Kirkpatrick
Sale, Kirkpatrick 1937- .... **CLC 68**
See also CA 13-16R; CANR 10, 147
Salinas, Luis Omar 1937- ... **CLC 90; HLC 2**
See also AMWS 13; CA 131; CANR 81, 153; DAM MULT; DLB 82; HW 1, 2
Salinas (y Serrano), Pedro
1891(?)-1951 .... **TCLC 17**
See also CA 117; DLB 134; EWL 3
Salinger, J.D. 1919- . **CLC 1, 3, 8, 12, 55, 56, 138, 243; SSC 2, 28, 65; WLC 5**
See also AAYA 2, 36; AMW; AMWC 1; BPFB 3; CA 5-8R; CANR 39, 129; CDALB 1941-1968; CLR 18; CN 1, 2, 3, 4, 5, 6, 7; CPW 1; DA; DA3; DAB; DAC; DAM MST, NOV, POP; DLB 2, 102, 173; EWL 3; EXPN; LAIT 4; MAICYA 1, 2; MAL 5; MTCW 1, 2; MTFW 2005; NFS 1; RGAL 4; RGSF 2; SATA 67; SSFS 17; TUS; WYA; YAW
Salisbury, John
See Caute, (John) David
Sallust c. 86B.C.-35B.C. .... **CMLC 68**
See also AW 2; CDWLB 1; DLB 211; RGWL 2, 3
Salter, James 1925- .. **CLC 7, 52, 59; SSC 58**
See also AMWS 9; CA 73-76; CANR 107, 160; DLB 130; SSFS 25
Saltus, Edgar (Everton) 1855-1921 . **TCLC 8**
See also CA 105; DLB 202; RGAL 4
Saltykov, Mikhail Evgrafovich
1826-1889 .... **NCLC 16**
See also DLB 238:
Saltykov-Shchedrin, N.
See Saltykov, Mikhail Evgrafovich
Samarakis, Andonis
See Samarakis, Antonis
See also EWL 3
Samarakis, Antonis 1919-2003 .... **CLC 5**
See Samarakis, Andonis
See also CA 25-28R; 224; CAAS 16; CANR 36
Sanchez, Florencio 1875-1910 .... **TCLC 37**
See also CA 153; DLB 305; EWL 3; HW 1; LAW
Sanchez, Luis Rafael 1936- .... **CLC 23**
See also CA 128; DLB 305; EWL 3; HW 1; WLIT 1
Sanchez, Sonia 1934- . **BLC 1:3, 2:3; CLC 5, 116, 215; PC 9**
See also BW 2, 3; CA 33-36R; CANR 24, 49, 74, 115; CLR 18; CP 2, 3, 4, 5, 6, 7; CSW; CWP; DA3; DAM MULT; DLB 41; DLBD 8; EWL 3; MAICYA 1, 2; MAL 5; MTCW 1, 2; MTFW 2005; PFS 26; SATA 22, 136; WP
Sancho, Ignatius 1729-1780 .... **LC 84**
Sand, George 1804-1876 .... **DC 29; NCLC 2, 42, 57, 174; WLC 5**
See also DA; DA3; DAB; DAC; DAM MST, NOV; DLB 119, 192; EW 6; FL 1:3; FW; GFL 1789 to the Present; RGWL 2, 3; TWA
Sandburg, Carl (August) 1878-1967 . **CLC 1, 4, 10, 15, 35; PC 2, 41; WLC 5**
See also AAYA 24; AMW; BYA 1, 3; CA 5-8R; 25-28R; CANR 35; CDALB 1865-1917; CLR 67; DA; DA3; DAB; DAC; DAM MST, POET; DLB 17, 54, 284; EWL 3; EXPP; LAIT 2; MAICYA 1, 2; MAL 5; MTCW 1, 2; MTFW 2005; PAB; PFS 3, 6, 12; RGAL 4; SATA 8; TUS; WCH; WP; WYA

Sandburg, Charles
See Sandburg, Carl (August)
Sandburg, Charles A.
See Sandburg, Carl (August)
Sanders, (James) Ed(ward) 1939- .... **CLC 53**
See Sanders, Edward
See also BG 1:3; CA 13-16R; CAAS 21; CANR 13, 44, 78; CP 1, 2, 3, 4, 5, 6, 7; DAM POET; DLB 16, 244
Sanders, Edward
See Sanders, (James) Ed(ward)
See also DLB 244
Sanders, Lawrence 1920-1998 .... **CLC 41**
See also BEST 89:4; BPFB 3; CA 81-84; 165; CANR 33, 62; CMW 4; CPW; DA3; DAM POP; MTCW 1
Sanders, Noah
See Blount, Roy, Jr.
Sanders, Winston P.
See Anderson, Poul
Sandoz, Mari(e Susette) 1900-1966 .. **CLC 28**
See also CA 1-4R; 25-28R; CANR 17, 64; DLB 9, 212; LAIT 2; MTCW 1, 2; SATA 5; TCWW 1, 2
Sandys, George 1578-1644 .... **LC 80**
See also DLB 24, 121
Saner, Reg(inald Anthony) 1931- .... **CLC 9**
See also CA 65-68; CP 3, 4, 5, 6, 7
Sankara 788-820 .... **CMLC 32**
Sannazaro, Jacopo 1456(?)-1530 .... **LC 8**
See also RGWL 2, 3; WLIT 7
Sansom, William 1912-1976 . **CLC 2, 6; SSC 21**
See also CA 5-8R; 65-68; CANR 42; CN 1, 2; DAM NOV; DLB 139; EWL 3; MTCW 1; RGEL 2; RGSF 2
Santayana, George 1863-1952 .... **TCLC 40**
See also AMW; CA 115; 194; DLB 54, 71, 246, 270; DLBD 13; EWL 3; MAL 5; RGAL 4; TUS
Santiago, Danny CLC 33
See James, Daniel (Lewis)
See also DLB 122
Santillana, Inigo Lopez de Mendoza, Marques de 1398-1458 .... **LC 111**
See also DLB 286
Santmyer, Helen Hooven
1895-1986 .... **CLC 33; TCLC 133**
See also CA 1-4R; 118; CANR 15, 33; DLBY 1984; MTCW 1; RHW
Santoka, Taneda 1882-1940 .... **TCLC 72**
Santos, Bienvenido N(uqui)
1911-1996 .... **AAL; CLC 22; TCLC 156**
See also CA 101; 151; CANR 19, 46; CP 1; DAM MULT; DLB 312; EWL; RGAL 4; SSFS 19
Sapir, Edward 1884-1939 .... **TCLC 108**
See also CA 211; DLB 92
Sapper TCLC 44
See McNeile, Herman Cyril
Sapphire 1950- .... **CLC 99**
See also CA 262
Sapphire, Brenda
See Sapphire
Sappho fl. 6th cent. B.C.- ... **CMLC 3, 67; PC 5**
See also CDWLB 1; DA3; DAM POET; DLB 176; FL 1:1; PFS 20; RGWL 2, 3; WLIT 8; WP
Saramago, Jose 1922- ..... **CLC 119; HLCS 1**
See also CA 153; CANR 96, 164; CWW 2; DLB 287, 332; EWL 3; LATS 1:2; NFS 27; SSFS 23
Sarduy, Severo 1937-1993 .... **CLC 6, 97; HLCS 2; TCLC 167**
See also CA 89-92; 142; CANR 58, 81; CWW 2; DLB 113; EWL 3; HW 1, 2; LAW

Sargeson, Frank 1903-1982 ..... **CLC 31; SSC 99**
See also CA 25-28R; 106; CANR 38, 79; CN 1, 2, 3; EWL 3; GLL 2; RGEL 2; RGSF 2; SSFS 20
Sarmiento, Domingo Faustino
1811-1888 .... **HLCS 2; NCLC 123**
See also LAW; WLIT 1
Sarmiento, Felix Ruben Garcia
See Dario, Ruben
Saro-Wiwa, Ken(ule Beeson)
1941-1995 .... **CLC 114; TCLC 200**
See also BW 2; CA 142; 150; CANR 60; DLB 157
Saroyan, William 1908-1981 ... **CLC 1, 8, 10, 29, 34, 56; DC 28; SSC 21; TCLC 137; WLC 5**
See also AAYA 66; CA 5-8R; 103; CAD; CANR 30; CDALBS; CN 1, 2; DA; DA3; DAB; DAC; DAM DRAM, MST, NOV; DFS 17; DLB 7, 9, 86; DLBY 1981; EWL 3; LAIT 4; MAL 5; MTCW 1, 2; MTFW 2005; RGAL 4; RGSF 2; SATA 23; SATA-Obit 24; SSFS 14; TUS
Sarraute, Nathalie 1900-1999 .... **CLC 1, 2, 4, 8, 10, 31, 80; TCLC 145**
See also BPFB 3; CA 9-12R; 187; CANR 23, 66, 134; CWW 2; DLB 83, 321; EW 12; EWL 3; GFL 1789 to the Present; MTCW 1, 2; MTFW 2005; RGWL 2, 3
Sarton, May 1912-1995 ... **CLC 4, 14, 49, 91; PC 39; TCLC 120**
See also AMWS 8; CA 1-4R; 149; CANR 1, 34, 55, 116; CN 1, 2, 3, 4, 5, 6; CP 1, 2, 3, 4, 5, 6; DAM POET; DLB 48; DLBY 1981; EWL 3; FW; INT CANR-34; MAL 5; MTCW 1, 2; MTFW 2005; RGAL 4; SATA 36; SATA-Obit 86; TUS
Sartre, Jean-Paul 1905-1980 . **CLC 1, 4, 7, 9, 13, 18, 24, 44, 50, 52; DC 3; SSC 32; WLC 5**
See also AAYA 62; CA 9-12R; 97-100; CANR 21; DA; DA3; DAB; DAC; DAM DRAM, MST, NOV; DFS 5; DLB 72, 296, 321, 332; EW 12; EWL 3; GFL 1789 to the Present; LMFS 2; MTCW 1, 2; MTFW 2005; NFS 21; RGHL; RGSF 2; RGWL 2, 3; SSFS 9; TWA
Sassoon, Siegfried (Lorraine)
1886-1967 .... **CLC 36, 130; PC 12**
See also BRW 6; CA 104; 25-28R; CANR 36; DAB; DAM MST, NOV, POET; DLB 20, 191; DLBD 18; EWL 3; MTCW 1, 2; MTFW 2005; PAB; PFS 28; RGEL 2; TEA
Satterfield, Charles
See Pohl, Frederik
Satyremont
See Peret, Benjamin
Saul, John (W. III) 1942- .... **CLC 46**
See also AAYA 10, 62; BEST 90:4; CA 81-84; CANR 16, 40, 81; CPW; DAM NOV, POP; HGG; SATA 98
Saunders, Caleb
See Heinlein, Robert A.
Saura (Atares), Carlos 1932-1998 .... **CLC 20**
See also CA 114; 131; CANR 79; HW 1
Sauser, Frederic Louis
See Sauser-Hall, Frederic
Sauser-Hall, Frederic 1887-1961 ...... **CLC 18**
See Cendrars, Blaise
See also CA 102; 93-96; CANR 36, 62; MTCW 1
Saussure, Ferdinand de
1857-1913 .... **TCLC 49**
See also DLB 242
Savage, Catharine
See Brosman, Catharine Savage
Savage, Richard 1697(?)-1743 .... **LC 96**
See also DLB 95; RGEL 2

Scott, Sir Walter 1771-1832 .... **NCLC 15, 69, 110; PC 13; SSC 32; WLC 5**
See also AAYA 22; BRW 4; BYA 2; CD-BLB 1789-1832; DA; DAB; DAC; DAM MST, NOV, POET; DLB 93, 107, 116, 144, 159; GL 3; HGG; LAIT 1; RGEL 2; RGSF 2; SSFS 10; SUFW 1; TEA; WLIT 3; YABC 2

Scribe, (Augustin) Eugene 1791-1861 . **DC 5; NCLC 16**
See also DAM DRAM; DLB 192; GFL 1789 to the Present; RGWL 2, 3

Scrum, R.
See Crumb, R.

Scudery, Georges de 1601-1667 .... **LC 75**
See also GFL Beginnings to 1789

Scudery, Madeleine de 1607-1701 .. **LC 2, 58**
See also DLB 268; GFL Beginnings to 1789

Scum
See Crumb, R.

Scumbag, Little Bobby
See Crumb, R.

Seabrook, John
See Hubbard, L. Ron

Seacole, Mary Jane Grant 1805-1881 .... **NCLC 147**
See also DLB 166

Sealy, I(rwin) Allan 1951- .... **CLC 55**
See also CA 136; CN 6, 7

Search, Alexander
See Pessoa, Fernando (Antonio Nogueira)

Sebald, W(infried) G(eorg) 1944-2001 .... **CLC 194**
See also BRWS 8; CA 159; 202; CANR 98; MTFW 2005; RGHL

Sebastian, Lee
See Silverberg, Robert

Sebastian Owl
See Thompson, Hunter S.

Sebestyen, Igen
See Sebestyen, Ouida

Sebestyen, Ouida 1924- .... **CLC 30**
See also AAYA 8; BYA 7; CA 107; CANR 40, 114; CLR 17; JRDA; MAICYA 1, 2; SAAS 10; SATA 39, 140; WYA; YAW

Sebold, Alice 1963(?)- .... **CLC 193**
See also AAYA 56; CA 203; MTFW 2005

Second Duke of Buckingham
See Villiers, George

Secundus, H. Scriblerus
See Fielding, Henry

Sedges, John
See Buck, Pearl S(ydenstricker)

Sedgwick, Catharine Maria 1789-1867 .... **NCLC 19, 98**
See also DLB 1, 74, 183, 239, 243, 254; FL 1:3; RGAL 4

Sedulius Scottus 9th cent. -c. 874 .. **CMLC 86**

Seebohm, Victoria
See Glendinning, Victoria

Seelye, John (Douglas) 1931- .... **CLC 7**
See also CA 97-100; CANR 70; INT CA-97-100; TCWW 1, 2

Seferiades, Giorgos Stylianou 1900-1971
See Seferis, George
See also CA 5-8R; 33-36R; CANR 5, 36; MTCW 1

Seferis, George CLC 5, 11; PC 66
See Seferiades, Giorgos Stylianou
See also DLB 332; EW 12; EWL 3; RGWL 2, 3

Segal, Erich (Wolf) 1937- .... **CLC 3, 10**
See also BEST 89:1; BPFB 3; CA 25-28R; CANR 20, 36, 65, 113; CPW; DAM POP; DLBY 1986; INT CANR-20; MTCW 1

Seger, Bob 1945- .... **CLC 35**

Seghers, Anna CLC 7
See Radvanyi, Netty
See also CDWLB 2; DLB 69; EWL 3

Seidel, Frederick (Lewis) 1936- .... **CLC 18**
See also CA 13-16R; CANR 8, 99; CP 1, 2, 3, 4, 5, 6, 7; DLBY 1984

Seifert, Jaroslav 1901-1986 . **CLC 34, 44, 93; PC 47**
See also CA 127; CDWLB 4; DLB 215, 332; EWL 3; MTCW 1, 2

Sei Shonagon c. 966-1017(?) ..... **CMLC 6, 89**

Sejour, Victor 1817-1874 .... **DC 10**
See also DLB 50

Sejour Marcou et Ferrand, Juan Victor
See Sejour, Victor

Selby, Hubert, Jr. 1928-2004 ..... **CLC 1, 2, 4, 8; SSC 20**
See also CA 13-16R; 226; CANR 33, 85; CN 1, 2, 3, 4, 5, 6, 7; DLB 2, 227; MAL 5

Selzer, Richard 1928- .... **CLC 74**
See also CA 65-68; CANR 14, 106

Sembene, Ousmane
See Ousmane, Sembene

Senancour, Etienne Pivert de 1770-1846 .... **NCLC 16**
See also DLB 119; GFL 1789 to the Present

Sender, Ramon (Jose) 1902-1982 ...... **CLC 8; HLC 2; TCLC 136**
See also CA 5-8R; 105; CANR 8; DAM MULT; DLB 322; EWL 3; HW 1; MTCW 1; RGWL 2, 3

Seneca, Lucius Annaeus c. 4B.C.-c. 65 .... **CMLC 6; DC 5**
See also AW 2; CDWLB 1; DAM DRAM; DLB 211; RGWL 2, 3; TWA; WLIT 8

Senghor, Leopold Sedar 1906-2001 .. **BLC 1:3; CLC 54, 130; PC 25**
See also AFW; BW 2; CA 116; 125; 203; CANR 47, 74, 134; CWW 2; DAM MULT, POET; DNFS 2; EWL 3; GFL 1789 to the Present; MTCW 1, 2; MTFW 2005; TWA

Senior, Olive (Marjorie) 1941- .... **SSC 78**
See also BW 3; CA 154; CANR 86, 126; CN 6; CP 6, 7; CWP; DLB 157; EWL 3; RGSF 2

Senna, Danzy 1970- .... **CLC 119**
See also CA 169; CANR 130

Serling, (Edward) Rod(man) 1924-1975 .... **CLC 30**
See also AAYA 14; AITN 1; CA 162; 57-60; DLB 26; SFW 4

Serna, Ramon Gomez de la
See Gomez de la Serna, Ramon

Serpieres
See Guillevic, (Eugene)

Service, Robert
See Service, Robert W(illiam)
See also BYA 4; DAB; DLB 92

Service, Robert W(illiam) 1874(?)-1958 ... **PC 70; TCLC 15; WLC 5**
See Service, Robert
See also CA 115; 140; CANR 84; DA; DAC; DAM MST, POET; PFS 10; RGEL 2; SATA 20

Seth, Vikram 1952- .... **CLC 43, 90**
See also BRWS 10; CA 121; 127; CANR 50, 74, 131; CN 6, 7; CP 5, 6, 7; DA3; DAM MULT; DLB 120, 271, 282, 323; EWL 3; INT CA-127; MTCW 2; MTFW 2005; WWE 1

Seton, Cynthia Propper 1926-1982 .. **CLC 27**
See also CA 5-8R; 108; CANR 7

Seton, Ernest (Evan) Thompson 1860-1946 .... **TCLC 31**
See also ANW; BYA 3; CA 109; 204; CLR 59; DLB 92; DLBD 13; JRDA; SATA 18

Seton-Thompson, Ernest
See Seton, Ernest (Evan) Thompson

Settle, Mary Lee 1918-2005 .... **CLC 19, 61**
See also BPFB 3; CA 89-92; 243; CAAS 1; CANR 44, 87, 126; CN 6, 7; CSW; DLB 6; INT CA-89-92

Seuphor, Michel
See Arp, Jean

Sevigne, Marie (de Rabutin-Chantal) 1626-1696 .... **LC 11, 144**
See Sevigne, Marie de Rabutin Chantal
See also GFL Beginnings to 1789; TWA

Sevigne, Marie de Rabutin Chantal
See Sevigne, Marie (de Rabutin-Chantal)
See also DLB 268

Sewall, Samuel 1652-1730 .... **LC 38**
See also DLB 24; RGAL 4

Sexton, Anne (Harvey) 1928-1974 ..... **CLC 2, 4, 6, 8, 10, 15, 53, 123; PC 2, 79; WLC 5**
See also AMWS 2; CA 1-4R; 53-56; CABS 2; CANR 3, 36; CDALB 1941-1968; CP 1, 2; DA; DA3; DAB; DAC; DAM MST, POET; DLB 5, 169; EWL 3; EXPP; FL 1:6; FW; MAL 5; MBL; MTCW 1, 2; MTFW 2005; PAB; PFS 4, 14; RGAL 4; RGHL; SATA 10; TUS

Shaara, Jeff 1952- .... **CLC 119**
See also AAYA 70; CA 163; CANR 109, 172; CN 7; MTFW 2005

Shaara, Michael 1929-1988 .... **CLC 15**
See also AAYA 71; AITN 1; BPFB 3; CA 102; 125; CANR 52, 85; DAM POP; DLBY 1983; MTFW 2005; NFS 26

Shackleton, C.C.
See Aldiss, Brian W.

Shacochis, Bob CLC 39
See Shacochis, Robert G.

Shacochis, Robert G. 1951-
See Shacochis, Bob
See also CA 119; 124; CANR 100; INT CA-124

Shadwell, Thomas 1641(?)-1692 .... **LC 114**
See also DLB 80; IDTP; RGEL 2

Shaffer, Anthony 1926-2001 .... **CLC 19**
See also CA 110; 116; 200; CBD; CD 5, 6; DAM DRAM; DFS 13; DLB 13

Shaffer, Anthony Joshua
See Shaffer, Anthony

Shaffer, Peter 1926- ... **CLC 5, 14, 18, 37, 60; DC 7**
See also BRWS 1; CA 25-28R; CANR 25, 47, 74, 118; CBD; CD 5, 6; CDBLB 1960 to Present; DA3; DAB; DAM DRAM, MST; DFS 5, 13; DLB 13, 233; EWL 3; MTCW 1, 2; MTFW 2005; RGEL 2; TEA

Shakespeare, William 1564-1616 . **PC 84, 89; WLC 5**
See also AAYA 35; BRW 1; CDBLB Before 1660; DA; DA3; DAB; DAC; DAM DRAM, MST, POET; DFS 20, 21; DLB 62, 172, 263; EXPP; LAIT 1; LATS 1:1; LMFS 1; PAB; PFS 1, 2, 3, 4, 5, 8, 9; RGEL 2; TEA; WLIT 3; WP; WS; WYA

Shakey, Bernard
See Young, Neil

Shalamov, Varlam (Tikhonovich) 1907-1982 .... **CLC 18**
See also CA 129; 105; DLB 302; RGSF 2

Shamloo, Ahmad
See Shamlu, Ahmad

Shamlou, Ahmad
See Shamlu, Ahmad

Shamlu, Ahmad 1925-2000 .... **CLC 10**
See also CA 216; CWW 2

Shammas, Anton 1951- .... **CLC 55**
See also CA 199

Shandling, Arline
See Berriault, Gina

Shuttle, Penelope (Diane) 1947- .... **CLC 7**
　　See also CA 93-96; CANR 39, 84, 92, 108;
　　CP 3, 4, 5, 6, 7; CWP; DLB 14, 40
Shvarts, Elena 1948- .... **PC 50**
　　See also CA 147
Sidhwa, Bapsi 1939-
　　See Sidhwa, Bapsy (N.)
　　See also CN 6, 7; DLB 323
Sidhwa, Bapsy (N.) 1938- .... **CLC 168**
　　See Sidhwa, Bapsi
　　See also CA 108; CANR 25, 57; FW
Sidney, Mary 1561-1621 .... **LC 19, 39**
　　See Sidney Herbert, Mary
Sidney, Sir Philip 1554-1586 .... **LC 19, 39,**
　　131; PC 32
　　See also BRW 1; BRWR 2; CDBLB Before
　　1660; DA; DA3; DAB; DAC; DAM MST,
　　POET; DLB 167; EXPP; PAB; RGEL 2;
　　TEA; WP
Sidney Herbert, Mary
　　See Sidney, Mary
　　See also DLB 167
Siegel, Jerome 1914-1996 .... **CLC 21**
　　See Siegel, Jerry
　　See also CA 116; 169; 151
Siegel, Jerry
　　See Siegel, Jerome
　　See also AAYA 50
Sienkiewicz, Henryk (Adam Alexander Pius)
　　1846-1916 .... **TCLC 3**
　　See also CA 104; 134; CANR 84; DLB 332;
　　EWL 3; RGSF 2; RGWL 2, 3
Sierra, Gregorio Martinez
　　See Martinez Sierra, Gregorio
Sierra, Maria de la O’LeJarraga Martinez
　　See Martinez Sierra, Maria
Sigal, Clancy 1926- .... **CLC 7**
　　See also CA 1-4R; CANR 85; CN 1, 2, 3,
　　4, 5, 6, 7
Siger of Brabant 1240(?)-1284(?) . **CMLC 69**
　　See also DLB 115
Sigourney, Lydia H.
　　See Sigourney, Lydia Howard (Huntley)
　　See also DLB 73, 183
Sigourney, Lydia Howard (Huntley)
　　1791-1865 .... **NCLC 21, 87**
　　See Sigourney, Lydia H.; Sigourney, Lydia
　　Huntley
　　See also DLB 1
Sigourney, Lydia Huntley
　　See Sigourney, Lydia Howard (Huntley)
　　See also DLB 42, 239, 243
Siguenza y Gongora, Carlos de
　　1645-1700 .... **HLCS 2; LC 8**
　　See also LAW
Sigurjonsson, Johann
　　See Sigurjonsson, Johann
Sigurjonsson, Johann 1880-1919 ... **TCLC 27**
　　See also CA 170; DLB 293; EWL 3
Sikelianos, Angelos 1884-1951 .... **PC 29;**
　　TCLC 39
　　See also EWL 3; RGWL 2, 3
Silkin, Jon 1930-1997 .... **CLC 2, 6, 43**
　　See also CA 5-8R; CAAS 5; CANR 89; CP
　　1, 2, 3, 4, 5, 6; DLB 27
Silko, Leslie 1948- ...... **CLC 23, 74, 114, 211;**
　　NNAL; SSC 37, 66; WLCS
　　See also AAYA 14; AMWS 4; ANW; BYA
　　12; CA 115; 122; CANR 45, 65, 118; CN
　　4, 5, 6, 7; CP 4, 5, 6, 7; CPW 1; CWP;
　　DA; DA3; DAC; DAM MST, MULT,
　　POP; DLB 143, 175, 256, 275; EWL 3;
　　EXPP; EXPS; LAIT 4; MAL 5; MTCW
　　2; MTFW 2005; NFS 4; PFS 9, 16; RGAL
　　4; RGSF 2; SSFS 4, 8, 10, 11; TCWW 1,
　　2
Sillanpaa, Frans Eemil 1888-1964 ... **CLC 19**
　　See also CA 129; 93-96; DLB 332; EWL 3;
　　MTCW 1

Sillitoe, Alan 1928- .. **CLC 1, 3, 6, 10, 19, 57,**
　　148
　　See also AITN 1; BRWS 5; CA 9-12R, 191;
　　CAAE 191; CAAS 2; CANR 8, 26, 55,
　　139; CDBLB 1960 to Present; CN 1, 2, 3,
　　4, 5, 6; CP 1, 2, 3, 4, 5; DLB 14, 139;
　　EWL 3; MTCW 1, 2; MTFW 2005; RGEL
　　2; RGSF 2; SATA 61
Silone, Ignazio 1900-1978 .... **CLC 4**
　　See also CA 25-28; 81-84; CANR 34; CAP
　　2; DLB 264; EW 12; EWL 3; MTCW 1;
　　RGSF 2; RGWL 2, 3
Silone, Ignazione
　　See Silone, Ignazio
Silver, Joan Micklin 1935- .... **CLC 20**
　　See also CA 114; 121; INT CA-121
Silver, Nicholas
　　See Faust, Frederick (Schiller)
Silverberg, Robert 1935- .... **CLC 7, 140**
　　See also AAYA 24; BPFB 3; BYA 7, 9; CA
　　1-4R, 186; CAAE 186; CAAS 3; CANR
　　1, 20, 36, 85, 140, 175; CLR 59; CN 6, 7;
　　CPW; DAM POP; DLB 8; INT CANR-
　　20; MAICYA 1, 2; MTCW 1, 2; MTFW
　　2005; SATA 13, 91; SATA-Essay 104;
　　SCFW 1, 2; SFW 4; SUFW 2
Silverstein, Alvin 1933- .... **CLC 17**
　　See also CA 49-52; CANR 2; CLR 25;
　　JRDA; MAICYA 1, 2; SATA 8, 69, 124
Silverstein, Shel 1932-1999 .... **PC 49**
　　See also AAYA 40; BW 3; CA 107; 179;
　　CANR 47, 74, 81; CLR 5, 96; CWRI 5;
　　JRDA; MAICYA 1, 2; MTCW 2; MTFW
　　2005; SATA 33, 92; SATA-Brief 27;
　　SATA-Obit 116
Silverstein, Virginia B(arbara Opshelor)
　　1937- .... **CLC 17**
　　See also CA 49-52; CANR 2; CLR 25;
　　JRDA; MAICYA 1, 2; SATA 8, 69, 124
Sim, Georges
　　See Simenon, Georges (Jacques Christian)
Simak, Clifford D(onald) 1904-1988 . **CLC 1,**
　　55
　　See also CA 1-4R; 125; CANR 1, 35; DLB
　　8; MTCW 1; SATA-Obit 56; SCFW 1, 2;
　　SFW 4
Simenon, Georges (Jacques Christian)
　　1903-1989 .... **CLC 1, 2, 3, 8, 18, 47**
　　See also BPFB 3; CA 85-88; 129; CANR
　　35; CMW 4; DA3; DAM POP; DLB 72;
　　DLBY 1989; EW 12; EWL 3; GFL 1789
　　to the Present; MSW; MTCW 1, 2; MTFW
　　2005; RGWL 2, 3
Simic, Charles 1938- .... **CLC 6, 9, 22, 49, 68,**
　　130, 256; PC 69
　　See also AMWS 8; CA 29-32R; CAAS 4;
　　CANR 12, 33, 52, 61, 96, 140; CP 2, 3, 4,
　　5, 6, 7; DA3; DAM POET; DLB 105;
　　MAL 5; MTCW 2; MTFW 2005; PFS 7;
　　RGAL 4; WP
Simmel, Georg 1858-1918 .... **TCLC 64**
　　See also CA 157; DLB 296
Simmons, Charles (Paul) 1924- .... **CLC 57**
　　See also CA 89-92; INT CA-89-92
Simmons, Dan 1948- .... **CLC 44**
　　See also AAYA 16, 54; CA 138; CANR 53,
　　81, 126, 174; CPW; DAM POP; HGG;
　　SUFW 2
Simmons, James (Stewart Alexander)
　　1933- .... **CLC 43**
　　See also CA 105; CAAS 21; CP 1, 2, 3, 4,
　　5, 6, 7; DLB 40
Simmons, Richard
　　See Simmons, Dan
Simms, William Gilmore
　　1806-1870 .... **NCLC 3**
　　See also DLB 3, 30, 59, 73, 248, 254;
　　RGAL 4
Simon, Carly 1945- .... **CLC 26**
　　See also CA 105

Simon, Claude 1913-2005 ... **CLC 4, 9, 15, 39**
　　See also CA 89-92; 241; CANR 33, 117;
　　CWW 2; DAM NOV; DLB 83, 332; EW
　　13; EWL 3; GFL 1789 to the Present;
　　MTCW 1
Simon, Claude Eugene Henri
　　See Simon, Claude
Simon, Claude Henri Eugene
　　See Simon, Claude
Simon, Marvin Neil
　　See Simon, Neil
Simon, Myles
　　See Follett, Ken
Simon, Neil 1927- .... **CLC 6, 11, 31, 39, 70,**
　　233; DC 14
　　See also AAYA 32; AITN 1; AMWS 4; CA
　　21-24R; CAD; CANR 26, 54, 87, 126;
　　CD 5, 6; DA3; DAM DRAM; DFS 2, 6,
　　12, 18,, 24; DLB 7, 266; LAIT 4; MAL 5;
　　MTCW 1, 2; MTFW 2005; RGAL 4; TUS
Simon, Paul 1941(?)- .... **CLC 17**
　　See also CA 116; 153; CANR 152
Simon, Paul Frederick
　　See Simon, Paul
Simonon, Paul 1956(?)- .... **CLC 30**
Simonson, Rick CLC 70
Simpson, Harriette
　　See Arnow, Harriette (Louisa) Simpson
Simpson, Louis 1923- ... **CLC 4, 7, 9, 32, 149**
　　See also AMWS 9; CA 1-4R; CAAS 4;
　　CANR 1, 61, 140; CP 1, 2, 3, 4, 5, 6, 7;
　　DAM POET; DLB 5; MAL 5; MTCW 1,
　　2; MTFW 2005; PFS 7, 11, 14; RGAL 4
Simpson, Mona 1957- .... **CLC 44, 146**
　　See also CA 122; 135; CANR 68, 103; CN
　　6, 7; EWL 3
Simpson, Mona Elizabeth
　　See Simpson, Mona
Simpson, N(orman) F(rederick)
　　1919- .... **CLC 29**
　　See also CA 13-16R; CBD; DLB 13; RGEL
　　2
Sinclair, Andrew (Annandale) 1935- . **CLC 2,**
　　14
　　See also CA 9-12R; CAAS 5; CANR 14,
　　38, 91; CN 1, 2, 3, 4, 5, 6, 7; DLB 14;
　　FANT; MTCW 1
Sinclair, Emil
　　See Hesse, Hermann
Sinclair, Iain 1943- .... **CLC 76**
　　See also CA 132; CANR 81, 157; CP 5, 6,
　　7; HGG
Sinclair, Iain MacGregor
　　See Sinclair, Iain
Sinclair, Irene
　　See Griffith, D(avid Lewelyn) W(ark)
Sinclair, Julian
　　See Sinclair, May
Sinclair, Mary Amelia St. Clair (?)-
　　See Sinclair, May
Sinclair, May 1865-1946 .... **TCLC 3, 11**
　　See also CA 104; 166; DLB 36, 135; EWL
　　3; HGG; RGEL 2; RHW; SUFW
Sinclair, Roy
　　See Griffith, D(avid Lewelyn) W(ark)
Sinclair, Upton 1878-1968 ...... **CLC 1, 11, 15,**
　　63; TCLC 160; WLC 5
　　See also AAYA 63; AMWS 5; BPFB 3;
　　BYA 2; CA 5-8R; 25-28R; CANR 7;
　　CDALB 1929-1941; DA; DA3; DAB;
　　DAC; DAM MST, NOV; DLB 9; EWL 3;
　　INT CANR-7; LAIT 3; MAL 5; MTCW
　　1, 2; MTFW 2005; NFS 6; RGAL 4;
　　SATA 9; TUS; YAW
Sinclair, Upton Beall
　　See Sinclair, Upton

T. O., Nik
See Annensky, Innokenty (Fyodorovich)
Tabori, George 1914-2007 .... **CLC 19**
See also CA 49-52; 262; CANR 4, 69;
CBD; CD 5, 6; DLB 245; RGHL
Tacitus c. 55-c. 117 .... **CMLC 56**
See also AW 2; CDWLB 1; DLB 211;
RGWL 2, 3; WLIT 8
Tadjo, Veronique 1955- .... **BLC 2:3**
See also EWL 3
Tagore, Rabindranath 1861-1941 .... **PC 8;**
SSC 48; TCLC 3, 53
See also CA 104; 120; DA3; DAM DRAM,
POET; DLB 323, 332; EWL 3; MTCW 1,
2; MTFW 2005; PFS 18; RGEL 2; RGSF
2; RGWL 2, 3; TWA
Taine, Hippolyte Adolphe
1828-1893 .... **NCLC 15**
See also EW 7; GFL 1789 to the Present
Talayesva, Don C. 1890-(?) .... **NNAL**
Talese, Gay 1932- .... **CLC 37, 232**
See also AITN 1; AMWS 17; CA 1-4R;
CANR 9, 58, 137; DLB 185; INT
CANR-9; MTCW 1, 2; MTFW 2005
Tallent, Elizabeth 1954- .... **CLC 45**
See also CA 117; CANR 72; DLB 130
Tallmountain, Mary 1918-1997 .... **NNAL**
See also CA 146; 161; DLB 193
Tally, Ted 1952- .... **CLC 42**
See also CA 120; 124; CAD; CANR 125;
CD 5, 6; INT CA-124
Talvik, Heiti 1904-1947 .... **TCLC 87**
See also EWL 3
Tamayo y Baus, Manuel
1829-1898 .... **NCLC 1**
Tammsaare, A(nton) H(ansen)
1878-1940 .... **TCLC 27**
See also CA 164; CDWLB 4; DLB 220;
EWL 3
Tam'si, Tchicaya U
See Tchicaya, Gerald Felix
Tan, Amy 1952- ..... **AAL; CLC 59, 120, 151,**
257
See also AAYA 9, 48; AMWS 10; BEST
89:3; BPFB 3; CA 136; CANR 54, 105,
132; CDALBS; CN 6, 7; CPW 1; DA3;
DAM MULT, NOV, POP; DLB 173, 312;
EXPN; FL 1:6; FW; LAIT 3, 5; MAL 5;
MTCW 2; MTFW 2005; NFS 1, 13, 16;
RGAL 4; SATA 75; SSFS 9; YAW
Tandem, Carl Felix
See Spitteler, Carl
Tandem, Felix
See Spitteler, Carl
Tanizaki, Jun'ichiro 1886-1965 ... **CLC 8, 14,**
28; SSC 21
See Tanizaki Jun'ichiro
See also CA 93-96; 25-28R; MJW; MTCW
2; MTFW 2005; RGSF 2; RGWL 2
Tanizaki Jun'ichiro
See Tanizaki, Jun'ichiro
See also DLB 180; EWL 3
Tannen, Deborah 1945- .... **CLC 206**
See also CA 118; CANR 95
Tannen, Deborah Frances
See Tannen, Deborah
Tanner, William
See Amis, Kingsley
Tante, Dilly
See Kunitz, Stanley
Tao Lao
See Storni, Alfonsina
Tapahonso, Luci 1953- .... **NNAL; PC 65**
See also CA 145; CANR 72, 127; DLB 175
Tarantino, Quentin (Jerome)
1963- .... **CLC 125, 230**
See also AAYA 58; CA 171; CANR 125
Tarassoff, Lev
See Troyat, Henri

Tarbell, Ida M(inerva) 1857-1944 . **TCLC 40**
See also CA 122; 181; DLB 47
Tardieu d'Esclavelles,
Louise-Florence-Petronille
See Epinay, Louise d'
Tarkington, (Newton) Booth
1869-1946 .... **TCLC 9**
See also BPFB 3; BYA 3; CA 110; 143;
CWRI 5; DLB 9, 102; MAL 5; MTCW 2;
RGAL 4; SATA 17
Tarkovskii, Andrei Arsen'evich
See Tarkovsky, Andrei (Arsenyevich)
Tarkovsky, Andrei (Arsenyevich)
1932-1986 .... **CLC 75**
See also CA 127
Tartt, Donna 1964(?)- .... **CLC 76**
See also AAYA 56; CA 142; CANR 135;
MTFW 2005
Tasso, Torquato 1544-1595 .... **LC 5, 94**
See also EFS 2; EW 2; RGWL 2, 3; WLIT
7
Tate, (John Orley) Allen 1899-1979 .. **CLC 2,**
4, 6, 9, 11, 14, 24; PC 50
See also AMW; CA 5-8R; 85-88; CANR
32, 108; CN 1, 2; CP 1, 2; DLB 4, 45, 63;
DLBD 17; EWL 3; MAL 5; MTCW 1, 2;
MTFW 2005; RGAL 4; RHW
Tate, Ellalice
See Hibbert, Eleanor Alice Burford
Tate, James (Vincent) 1943- ..... **CLC 2, 6, 25**
See also CA 21-24R; CANR 29, 57, 114;
CP 1, 2, 3, 4, 5, 6, 7; DLB 5, 169; EWL
3; PFS 10, 15; RGAL 4; WP
Tate, Nahum 1652(?)-1715 .... **LC 109**
See also DLB 80; RGEL 2
Tauler, Johannes c. 1300-1361 ...... **CMLC 37**
See also DLB 179; LMFS 1
Tavel, Ronald 1940- .... **CLC 6**
See also CA 21-24R; CAD; CANR 33; CD
5, 6
Taviani, Paolo 1931- .... **CLC 70**
See also CA 153
Taylor, Bayard 1825-1878 .... **NCLC 89**
See also DLB 3, 189, 250, 254; RGAL 4
Taylor, C(ecil) P(hilip) 1929-1981 .... **CLC 27**
See also CA 25-28R; 105; CANR 47; CBD
Taylor, Edward 1642(?)-1729 . **LC 11; PC 63**
See also AMW; DA; DAB; DAC; DAM
MST, POET; DLB 24; EXPP; RGAL 4;
TUS
Taylor, Eleanor Ross 1920- .... **CLC 5**
See also CA 81-84; CANR 70
Taylor, Elizabeth 1912-1975 .... **CLC 2, 4, 29;**
SSC 100
See also CA 13-16R; CANR 9, 70; CN 1,
2; DLB 139; MTCW 1; RGEL 2; SATA
13
Taylor, Frederick Winslow
1856-1915 .... **TCLC 76**
See also CA 188
Taylor, Henry (Splawn) 1942- .... **CLC 44**
See also CA 33-36R; CAAS 7; CANR 31;
CP 6, 7; DLB 5; PFS 10
Taylor, Kamala 1924-2004
See Markandaya, Kamala
See also CA 77-80; 227; MTFW 2005; NFS
13
Taylor, Mildred D. 1943- .... **CLC 21**
See also AAYA 10, 47; BW 1; BYA 3, 8;
CA 85-88; CANR 25, 115, 136; CLR 9,
59, 90; CSW; DLB 52; JRDA; LAIT 3;
MAICYA 1, 2; MTFW 2005; SAAS 5;
SATA 135; WYA; YAW
Taylor, Peter (Hillsman) 1917-1994 .. **CLC 1,**
4, 18, 37, 44, 50, 71; SSC 10, 84
See also AMWS 5; BPFB 3; CA 13-16R;
147; CANR 9, 50; CN 1, 2, 3, 4, 5; CSW;
DLB 218, 278; DLBY 1981, 1994; EWL
3; EXPS; INT CANR-9; MAL 5; MTCW
1, 2; MTFW 2005; RGSF 2; SSFS 9; TUS

Taylor, Robert Lewis 1912-1998 .... **CLC 14**
See also CA 1-4R; 170; CANR 3, 64; CN
1, 2; SATA 10; TCWW 1, 2
Tchekhov, Anton
See Chekhov, Anton (Pavlovich)
Tchicaya, Gerald Felix 1931-1988 .. **CLC 101**
See Tchicaya U Tam'si
See also CA 129; 125; CANR 81
Tchicaya U Tam'si
See Tchicaya, Gerald Felix
See also EWL 3
Teasdale, Sara 1884-1933 .... **PC 31; TCLC 4**
See also CA 104; 163; DLB 45; GLL 1;
PFS 14; RGAL 4; SATA 32; TUS
Tecumseh 1768-1813 .... **NNAL**
See also DAM MULT
Tegner, Esaias 1782-1846 .... **NCLC 2**
Teilhard de Chardin, (Marie Joseph) Pierre
1881-1955 .... **TCLC 9**
See also CA 105; 210; GFL 1789 to the
Present
Temple, Ann
See Mortimer, Penelope (Ruth)
Tennant, Emma 1937- .... **CLC 13, 52**
See also BRWS 9; CA 65-68; CAAS 9;
CANR 10, 38, 59, 88; CN 3, 4, 5, 6, 7;
DLB 14; EWL 3; SFW 4
Tenneshaw, S.M.
See Silverberg, Robert
Tenney, Tabitha Gilman
1762-1837 .... **NCLC 122**
See also DLB 37, 200
Tennyson, Alfred 1809-1892 ... **NCLC 30, 65,**
115; PC 6; WLC 6
See also AAYA 50; BRW 4; CDBLB 1832-
1890; DA; DA3; DAB; DAC; DAM MST,
POET; DLB 32; EXPP; PAB; PFS 1, 2, 4,
11, 15, 19; RGEL 2; TEA; WLIT 4; WP
Teran, Lisa St. Aubin de CLC 36
See St. Aubin de Teran, Lisa
Terence c. 184B.C.-c. 159B.C. ...... **CMLC 14;**
DC 7
See also AW 1; CDWLB 1; DLB 211;
RGWL 2, 3; TWA; WLIT 8
Teresa de Jesus, St. 1515-1582 .... **LC 18, 149**
Teresa of Avila, St.
See Teresa de Jesus, St.
Terkel, Louis CLC 38
See Terkel, Studs
See also AAYA 32; AITN 1; MTCW 2; TUS
Terkel, Studs 1912-
See Terkel, Louis
See also CA 57-60; CANR 18, 45, 67, 132;
DA3; MTCW 1, 2; MTFW 2005
Terry, C. V.
See Slaughter, Frank G(ill)
Terry, Megan 1932- .... **CLC 19; DC 13**
See also CA 77-80; CABS 3; CAD; CANR
43; CD 5, 6; CWD; DFS 18; DLB 7, 249;
GLL 2
Tertullian c. 155-c. 245 .... **CMLC 29**
Tertz, Abram
See Sinyavsky, Andrei (Donatevich)
See also RGSF 2
Tesich, Steve 1943(?)-1996 .... **CLC 40, 69**
See also CA 105; 152; CAD; DLBY 1983
Tesla, Nikola 1856-1943 .... **TCLC 88**
Teternikov, Fyodor Kuzmich 1863-1927
See Sologub, Fyodor
See also CA 104
Tevis, Walter 1928-1984 .... **CLC 42**
See also CA 113; SFW 4
Tey, Josephine TCLC 14
See Mackintosh, Elizabeth
See also DLB 77; MSW

Toer, Pramoedya Ananta
1925-2006 .... **CLC 186**
See also CA 197; 251; CANR 170; RGWL 3

Toffler, Alvin 1928- .... **CLC 168**
See also CA 13-16R; CANR 15, 46, 67; CPW; DAM POP; MTCW 1, 2

Toibin, Colm 1955- .... **CLC 162**
See also CA 142; CANR 81, 149; CN 7; DLB 271

Tolkien, John Ronald Reuel
See Tolkien, J.R.R

Tolkien, J.R.R 1892-1973 ...... **CLC 1, 2, 3, 8, 12, 38; TCLC 137; WLC 6**
See also AAYA 10; AITN 1; BPFB 3; BRWC 2; BRWS 2; CA 17-18; 45-48; CANR 36, 134; CAP 2; CDBLB 1914-1945; CLR 56; CN 1; CPW 1; CWRI 5; DA; DA3; DAB; DAC; DAM MST, NOV, POP; DLB 15, 160, 255; EFS 2; EWL 3; FANT; JRDA; LAIT 1; LATS 1:2; LMFS 2; MAICYA 1, 2; MTCW 1, 2; MTFW 2005; NFS 8, 26; RGEL 2; SATA 2, 32, 100; SATA-Obit 24; SFW 4; SUFW; TEA; WCH; WYA; YAW

Toller, Ernst 1893-1939 .... **TCLC 10**
See also CA 107; 186; DLB 124; EWL 3; RGWL 2, 3

Tolson, M. B.
See Tolson, Melvin B(eaunorus)

Tolson, Melvin B(eaunorus)
1898(?)-1966 .... **BLC 1:3; CLC 36, 105; PC 88**
See also AFAW 1, 2; BW 1, 3; CA 124; 89-92; CANR 80; DAM MULT, POET; DLB 48, 76; MAL 5; RGAL 4

Tolstoi, Aleksei Nikolaevich
See Tolstoy, Alexey Nikolaevich

Tolstoi, Lev
See Tolstoy, Leo (Nikolaevich)
See also RGSF 2; RGWL 2, 3

Tolstoy, Aleksei Nikolaevich
See Tolstoy, Alexey Nikolaevich
See also DLB 272

Tolstoy, Alexey Nikolaevich
1882-1945 .... **TCLC 18**
See Tolstoy, Aleksei Nikolaevich
See also CA 107; 158; EWL 3; SFW 4

Tolstoy, Leo (Nikolaevich)
1828-1910 . **SSC 9, 30, 45, 54; TCLC 4, 11, 17, 28, 44, 79, 173; WLC 6**
See Tolstoi, Lev
See also AAYA 56; CA 104; 123; DA; DA3; DAB; DAC; DAM MST, NOV; DLB 238; EFS 2; EW 7; EXPS; IDTP; LAIT 2; LATS 1:1; LMFS 1; NFS 10; SATA 26; SSFS 5; TWA

Tolstoy, Count Leo
See Tolstoy, Leo (Nikolaevich)

Tomalin, Claire 1933- .... **CLC 166**
See also CA 89-92; CANR 52, 88, 165; DLB 155

Tomasi di Lampedusa, Giuseppe 1896-1957
See Lampedusa, Giuseppe (Tomasi) di
See also CA 111; DLB 177; EWL 3; WLIT 7

Tomlin, Lily 1939(?)-
See Tomlin, Mary Jean
See also CA 117

Tomlin, Mary Jean CLC 17
See Tomlin, Lily

Tomline, F. Latour
See Gilbert, W(illiam) S(chwenck)

Tomlinson, (Alfred) Charles 1927- .... **CLC 2, 4, 6, 13, 45; PC 17**
See also CA 5-8R; CANR 33; CP 1, 2, 3, 4, 5, 6, 7; DAM POET; DLB 40; TCLE 1:2

Tomlinson, H(enry) M(ajor)
1873-1958 .... **TCLC 71**
See also CA 118; 161; DLB 36, 100, 195

Tonna, Charlotte Elizabeth
1790-1846 .... **NCLC 135**
See also DLB 163

Tonson, Jacob fl. 1655(?)-1736 .... **LC 86**
See also DLB 170

Toole, John Kennedy 1937-1969 ..... **CLC 19, 64**
See also BPFB 3; CA 104; DLBY 1981; MTCW 2; MTFW 2005

Toomer, Eugene
See Toomer, Jean

Toomer, Eugene Pinchback
See Toomer, Jean

Toomer, Jean 1894-1967 ... **BLC 1:3; CLC 1, 4, 13, 22; HR 1:3; PC 7; SSC 1, 45; TCLC 172; WLCS**
See also AFAW 1, 2; AMWS 3, 9; BW 1; CA 85-88; CDALB 1917-1929; DA3; DAM MULT; DLB 45, 51; EWL 3; EXPP; EXPS; LMFS 2; MAL 5; MTCW 1, 2; MTFW 2005; NFS 11; RGAL 4; RGSF 2; SSFS 5

Toomer, Nathan Jean
See Toomer, Jean

Toomer, Nathan Pinchback
See Toomer, Jean

Torley, Luke
See Blish, James (Benjamin)

Tornimparte, Alessandra
See Ginzburg, Natalia

Torre, Raoul della
See Mencken, H(enry) L(ouis)

Torrence, Ridgely 1874-1950 .... **TCLC 97**
See also DLB 54, 249; MAL 5

Torrey, E. Fuller 1937- .... **CLC 34**
See also CA 119; CANR 71, 158

Torrey, Edwin Fuller
See Torrey, E. Fuller

Torsvan, Ben Traven
See Traven, B.

Torsvan, Benno Traven
See Traven, B.

Torsvan, Berick Traven
See Traven, B.

Torsvan, Berwick Traven
See Traven, B.

Torsvan, Bruno Traven
See Traven, B.

Torsvan, Traven
See Traven, B.

Tourneur, Cyril 1575(?)-1626 .... **LC 66**
See also BRW 2; DAM DRAM; DLB 58; RGEL 2

Tournier, Michel 1924- .... **CLC 6, 23, 36, 95, 249; SSC 88**
See also CA 49-52; CANR 3, 36, 74, 149; CWW 2; DLB 83; EWL 3; GFL 1789 to the Present; MTCW 1, 2; SATA 23

Tournier, Michel Edouard
See Tournier, Michel

Tournimparte, Alessandra
See Ginzburg, Natalia

Towers, Ivar
See Kornbluth, C(yril) M.

Towne, Robert (Burton) 1936(?)- ..... **CLC 87**
See also CA 108; DLB 44; IDFW 3, 4

Townsend, Sue CLC 61
See Townsend, Susan Lilian
See also AAYA 28; CA 119; 127; CANR 65, 107; CBD; CD 5, 6; CPW; CWD; DAB; DAC; DAM MST; DLB 271; INT CA-127; SATA 55, 93; SATA-Brief 48; YAW

Townsend, Susan Lilian 1946-
See Townsend, Sue

Townshend, Pete
See Townshend, Peter (Dennis Blandford)

Townshend, Peter (Dennis Blandford)
1945- .... **CLC 17, 42**
See also CA 107

Tozzi, Federigo 1883-1920 .... **TCLC 31**
See also CA 160; CANR 110; DLB 264; EWL 3; WLIT 7

Tracy, Don(ald Fiske) 1905-1970(?)
See Queen, Ellery
See also CA 1-4R; 176; CANR 2

Trafford, F. G.
See Riddell, Charlotte

Traherne, Thomas 1637(?)-1674 .. **LC 99; PC 70**
See also BRW 2; BRWS 11; DLB 131; PAB; RGEL 2

Traill, Catharine Parr 1802-1899 .. **NCLC 31**
See also DLB 99

Trakl, Georg 1887-1914 .... **PC 20; TCLC 5**
See also CA 104; 165; EW 10; EWL 3; LMFS 2; MTCW 2; RGWL 2, 3

Trambley, Estela Portillo TCLC 163
See Portillo Trambley, Estela
See also CA 77-80; RGAL 4

Tranquilli, Secondino
See Silone, Ignazio

Transtroemer, Tomas Gosta
See Transtromer, Tomas

Transtromer, Tomas (Gosta)
See Transtromer, Tomas
See also CWW 2

Transtromer, Tomas 1931- .... **CLC 52, 65**
See also CA 117; 129; CAAS 17; CANR 115, 172; DAM POET; DLB 257; EWL 3; PFS 21

Transtromer, Tomas Goesta
See Transtromer, Tomas

Transtromer, Tomas Gosta
See Transtromer, Tomas

Transtromer, Tomas Gosta
See Transtromer, Tomas

Traven, B. 1882(?)-1969 .... **CLC 8, 11**
See also CA 19-20; 25-28R; CAP 2; DLB 9, 56; EWL 3; MTCW 1; RGAL 4

Trediakovsky, Vasilii Kirillovich
1703-1769 .... **LC 68**
See also DLB 150

Treitel, Jonathan 1959- .... **CLC 70**
See also CA 210; DLB 267

Trelawny, Edward John
1792-1881 .... **NCLC 85**
See also DLB 110, 116, 144

Tremain, Rose 1943- .... **CLC 42**
See also CA 97-100; CANR 44, 95; CN 4, 5, 6, 7; DLB 14, 271; RGSF 2; RHW

Tremblay, Michel 1942- .... **CLC 29, 102, 225**
See also CA 116; 128; CCA 1; CWW 2; DAC; DAM MST; DLB 60; EWL 3; GLL 1; MTCW 1, 2; MTFW 2005

Trevanian CLC 29
See Whitaker, Rod

Trevisa, John c. 1342-c. 1402 .... **LC 139**
See also BRWS 9; DLB 146

Trevor, Glen
See Hilton, James

Trevor, William CLC 7, 9, 14, 25, 71, 116; SSC 21, 58
See Cox, William Trevor
See also BRWS 4; CBD; CD 5, 6; CN 1, 2, 3, 4, 5, 6, 7; DLB 14, 139; EWL 3; LATS 1:2; RGEL 2; RGSF 2; SSFS 10; TCLE 1:2

Trifonov, Iurii (Valentinovich)
See Trifonov, Yuri (Valentinovich)
See also DLB 302; RGWL 2, 3

Trifonov, Yuri (Valentinovich)
1925-1981 .... **CLC 45**
See Trifonov, Iurii (Valentinovich); Trifonov, Yury Valentinovich
See also CA 126; 103; MTCW 1

Updike, John Hoyer
See Updike, John

Upshaw, Margaret Mitchell
See Mitchell, Margaret (Munnerlyn)

Upton, Mark
See Sanders, Lawrence

Upward, Allen 1863-1926 .... **TCLC 85**
See also CA 117; 187; DLB 36

Urdang, Constance (Henriette)
1922-1996 .... **CLC 47**
See also CA 21-24R; CANR 9, 24; CP 1, 2,
3, 4, 5, 6; CWP

Urfe, Honore d' 1567(?)-1625 .... **LC 132**
See also DLB 268; GFL Beginnings to
1789; RGWL 2, 3

Uriel, Henry
See Faust, Frederick (Schiller)

Uris, Leon 1924-2003 .... **CLC 7, 32**
See also AITN 1, 2; BEST 89:2; BPFB 3;
CA 1-4R; 217; CANR 1, 40, 65, 123; CN
1, 2, 3, 4, 5, 6; CPW 1; DA3; DAM NOV,
POP; MTCW 1, 2; MTFW 2005; RGHL;
SATA 49; SATA-Obit 146

Urista (Heredia), Alberto (Baltazar)
1947- .... **HLCS 1**
See Alurista
See also CA 182; CANR 2, 32; HW 1

Urmuz
See Codrescu, Andrei

Urquhart, Guy
See McAlmon, Robert (Menzies)

Urquhart, Jane 1949- .... **CLC 90, 242**
See also CA 113; CANR 32, 68, 116, 157;
CCA 1; DAC; DLB 334

Usigli, Rodolfo 1905-1979 .... **HLCS 1**
See also CA 131; DLB 305; EWL 3; HW 1;
LAW

Usk, Thomas (?)-1388 .... **CMLC 76**
See also DLB 146

Ustinov, Peter (Alexander)
1921-2004 .... **CLC 1**
See also AITN 1; CA 13-16R; 225; CANR
25, 51; CBD; CD 5, 6; DLB 13; MTCW
2

U Tam'si, Gerald Felix Tchicaya
See Tchicaya, Gerald Felix

U Tam'si, Tchicaya
See Tchicaya, Gerald Felix

Vachss, Andrew 1942- .... **CLC 106**
See also CA 118, 214; CAAE 214; CANR
44, 95, 153; CMW 4

Vachss, Andrew H.
See Vachss, Andrew

Vachss, Andrew Henry
See Vachss, Andrew

Vaculik, Ludvik 1926- .... **CLC 7**
See also CA 53-56; CANR 72; CWW 2;
DLB 232; EWL 3

Vaihinger, Hans 1852-1933 .... **TCLC 71**
See also CA 116; 166

Valdez, Luis (Miguel) 1940- ..... **CLC 84; DC
10; HLC 2**
See also CA 101; CAD; CANR 32, 81; CD
5, 6; DAM MULT; DFS 5; DLB 122;
EWL 3; HW 1; LAIT 4; LLW

Valenzuela, Luisa 1938- .... **CLC 31, 104;
HLCS 2; SSC 14, 82**
See also CA 101; CANR 32, 65, 123; CD-
WLB 3; CWW 2; DAM MULT; DLB 113;
EWL 3; FW; HW 1, 2; LAW; RGSF 2;
RGWL 3

Valera y Alcala-Galiano, Juan
1824-1905 .... **TCLC 10**
See also CA 106

Valerius Maximus CMLC 64
See also DLB 211

Valery, (Ambroise) Paul (Toussaint Jules)
1871-1945 .... **PC 9; TCLC 4, 15**
See also CA 104; 122; DA3; DAM POET;
DLB 258; EW 8; EWL 3; GFL 1789 to
the Present; MTCW 1, 2; MTFW 2005;
RGWL 2, 3; TWA

Valle-Inclan, Ramon (Maria) del
1866-1936 .... **HLC 2; TCLC 5**
See del Valle-Inclan, Ramon (Maria)
See also CA 106; 153; CANR 80; DAM
MULT; DLB 134; EW 8; EWL 3; HW 2;
RGSF 2; RGWL 2, 3

Vallejo, Antonio Buero
See Buero Vallejo, Antonio

Vallejo, Cesar (Abraham)
1892-1938 .... **HLC 2; TCLC 3, 56**
See also CA 105; 153; DAM MULT; DLB
290; EWL 3; HW 1; LAW; PFS 26;
RGWL 2, 3

Valles, Jules 1832-1885 .... **NCLC 71**
See also DLB 123; GFL 1789 to the Present

Vallette, Marguerite Eymery
1860-1953 .... **TCLC 67**
See Rachilde
See also CA 182; DLB 123, 192

Valle Y Pena, Ramon del
See Valle-Inclan, Ramon (Maria) del

Van Ash, Cay 1918-1994 .... **CLC 34**
See also CA 220

Vanbrugh, Sir John 1664-1726 .... **LC 21**
See also BRW 2; DAM DRAM; DLB 80;
IDTP; RGEL 2

Van Campen, Karl
See Campbell, John W(ood, Jr.)

Vance, Gerald
See Silverberg, Robert

Vance, Jack 1916-
See Queen, Ellery; Vance, John Holbrook
See also CA 29-32R; CANR 17, 65, 154;
CMW 4; MTCW 1

Vance, John Holbrook CLC 35
See Vance, Jack
See also DLB 8; FANT; SCFW 1, 2; SFW
4; SUFW 1, 2

**Van Den Bogarde, Derek Jules Gaspard
Ulric Niven** 1921-1999 .... **CLC 14**
See Bogarde, Dirk
See also CA 77-80; 179

Vandenburgh, Jane CLC 59
See also CA 168

Vanderhaeghe, Guy 1951- .... **CLC 41**
See also BPFB 3; CA 113; CANR 72, 145;
CN 7; DLB 334

van der Post, Laurens (Jan)
1906-1996 .... **CLC 5**
See also AFW; CA 5-8R; 155; CANR 35;
CN 1, 2, 3, 4, 5, 6; DLB 204; RGEL 2

van de Wetering, Janwillem 1931- ... **CLC 47**
See also CA 49-52; CANR 4, 62, 90; CMW
4

Van Dine, S. S. TCLC 23
See Wright, Willard Huntington
See also DLB 306; MSW

Van Doren, Carl (Clinton)
1885-1950 .... **TCLC 18**
See also CA 111; 168

Van Doren, Mark 1894-1972 .... **CLC 6, 10**
See also CA 1-4R; 37-40R; CANR 3; CN
1; CP 1; DLB 45, 284, 335; MAL 5;
MTCW 1, 2; RGAL 4

Van Druten, John (William)
1901-1957 .... **TCLC 2**
See also CA 104; 161; DLB 10; MAL 5;
RGAL 4

Van Duyn, Mona 1921-2004 .... **CLC 3, 7, 63,
116**
See also CA 9-12R; 234; CANR 7, 38, 60,
116; CP 1, 2, 3, 4, 5, 6, 7; CWP; DAM
POET; DLB 5; MAL 5; MTFW 2005;
PFS 20

Van Dyne, Edith
See Baum, L(yman) Frank

van Herk, Aritha 1954- .... **CLC 249**
See also CA 101; CANR 94; DLB 334

van Itallie, Jean-Claude 1936- .... **CLC 3**
See also CA 45-48; CAAS 2; CAD; CANR
1, 48; CD 5, 6; DLB 7

Van Loot, Cornelius Obenchain
See Roberts, Kenneth (Lewis)

van Ostaijen, Paul 1896-1928 .... **TCLC 33**
See also CA 163

Van Peebles, Melvin 1932- .... **CLC 2, 20**
See also BW 2, 3; CA 85-88; CANR 27,
67, 82; DAM MULT

van Schendel, Arthur(-Francois-Emile)
1874-1946 .... **TCLC 56**
See also EWL 3

Vansittart, Peter 1920- .... **CLC 42**
See also CA 1-4R; CANR 3, 49, 90; CN 4,
5, 6, 7; RHW

Van Vechten, Carl 1880-1964 ... **CLC 33; HR
1:3**
See also AMWS 2; CA 183; 89-92; DLB 4,
9, 51; RGAL 4

van Vogt, A(lfred) E(lton) 1912-2000 . **CLC 1**
See also BPFB 3; BYA 13, 14; CA 21-24R;
190; CANR 28; DLB 8, 251; SATA 14;
SATA-Obit 124; SCFW 1, 2; SFW 4

Vara, Madeleine
See Jackson, Laura (Riding)

Varda, Agnes 1928- .... **CLC 16**
See also CA 116; 122

Vargas Llosa, Jorge Mario Pedro
See Vargas Llosa, Mario

Vargas Llosa, Mario 1936- .. **CLC 3, 6, 9, 10,
15, 31, 42, 85, 181; HLC 2**
See Llosa, Jorge Mario Pedro Vargas
See also BPFB 3; CA 73-76; CANR 18, 32,
42, 67, 116, 140, 173; CDWLB 3; CWW
2; DA; DA3; DAB; DAC; DAM MST,
MULT, NOV; DLB 145; DNFS 2; EWL
3; HW 1, 2; LAIT 5; LATS 1:2; LAW;
LAWS 1; MTCW 1, 2; MTFW 2005;
RGWL 2; SSFS 14; TWA; WLIT 1

Varnhagen von Ense, Rahel
1771-1833 .... **NCLC 130**
See also DLB 90

Vasari, Giorgio 1511-1574 .... **LC 114**

Vasilikos, Vasiles
See Vassilikos, Vassilis

Vasiliu, George
See Bacovia, George

Vasiliu, Gheorghe
See Bacovia, George
See also CA 123; 189

Vassa, Gustavus
See Equiano, Olaudah

Vassilikos, Vassilis 1933- .... **CLC 4, 8**
See also CA 81-84; CANR 75, 149; EWL 3

Vaughan, Henry 1621-1695 .... **LC 27; PC 81**
See also BRW 2; DLB 131; PAB; RGEL 2

Vaughn, Stephanie CLC 62

Vazov, Ivan (Minchov) 1850-1921 . **TCLC 25**
See also CA 121; 167; CDWLB 4; DLB
147

Veblen, Thorstein B(unde)
1857-1929 .... **TCLC 31**
See also AMWS 1; CA 115; 165; DLB 246;
MAL 5

Vega, Lope de 1562-1635 ... **HLCS 2; LC 23,
119**
See also EW 2; RGWL 2, 3

Veldeke, Heinrich von c. 1145-c.
1190 .... **CMLC 85**

Vendler, Helen (Hennessy) 1933- ... **CLC 138**
See also CA 41-44R; CANR 25, 72, 136;
MTCW 1, 2; MTFW 2005

Venison, Alfred
See Pound, Ezra (Weston Loomis)

MST, NOV, POP; DLB 2, 8, 152; DLBD 3; DLBY 1980; EWL 3; EXPN; EXPS; LAIT 4; LMFS 2; MAL 5; MTCW 1, 2; MTFW 2005; NFS 3; RGAL 4; SCFW; SFW 4; SSFS 5; TUS; YAW

Von Rachen, Kurt
See Hubbard, L. Ron

von Sternberg, Josef
See Sternberg, Josef von

Vorster, Gordon 1924- .... **CLC 34**
See also CA 133

Vosce, Trudie
See Ozick, Cynthia

Voznesensky, Andrei (Andreievich)
1933- .... **CLC 1, 15, 57**
See Voznesensky, Andrey
See also CA 89-92; CANR 37; CWW 2; DAM POET; MTCW 1

Voznesensky, Andrey
See Voznesensky, Andrei (Andreievich)
See also EWL 3

Wace, Robert c. 1100-c. 1175 .... **CMLC 55**
See also DLB 146

Waddington, Miriam 1917-2004 .... **CLC 28**
See also CA 21-24R; 225; CANR 12, 30; CCA 1; CP 1, 2, 3, 4, 5, 6, 7; DLB 68

Wagman, Fredrica 1937- .... **CLC 7**
See also CA 97-100; CANR 166; INT CA-97-100

Wagner, Linda W.
See Wagner-Martin, Linda (C.)

Wagner, Linda Welshimer
See Wagner-Martin, Linda (C.)

Wagner, Richard 1813-1883 ..... **NCLC 9, 119**
See also DLB 129; EW 6

Wagner-Martin, Linda (C.) 1936- .... **CLC 50**
See also CA 159; CANR 135

Wagoner, David (Russell) 1926- .... **CLC 3, 5, 15; PC 33**
See also AMWS 9; CA 1-4R; CAAS 3; CANR 2, 71; CN 1, 2, 3, 4, 5, 6, 7; CP 1, 2, 3, 4, 5, 6, 7; DLB 5, 256; SATA 14; TCWW 1, 2

Wah, Fred(erick James) 1939- .... **CLC 44**
See also CA 107; 141; CP 1, 6, 7; DLB 60

Wahloo, Per 1926-1975 .... **CLC 7**
See also BPFB 3; CA 61-64; CANR 73; CMW 4; MSW

Wahloo, Peter
See Wahloo, Per

Wain, John (Barrington) 1925-1994 . **CLC 2, 11, 15, 46**
See also CA 5-8R; 145; CAAS 4; CANR 23, 54; CDBLB 1960 to Present; CN 1, 2, 3, 4, 5; CP 1, 2, 3, 4, 5; DLB 15, 27, 139, 155; EWL 3; MTCW 1, 2; MTFW 2005

Wajda, Andrzej 1926- .... **CLC 16, 219**
See also CA 102

Wakefield, Dan 1932- .... **CLC 7**
See also CA 21-24R, 211; CAAE 211; CAAS 7; CN 4, 5, 6, 7

Wakefield, Herbert Russell
1888-1965 .... **TCLC 120**
See also CA 5-8R; CANR 77; HGG; SUFW

Wakoski, Diane 1937- ...... **CLC 2, 4, 7, 9, 11, 40; PC 15**
See also CA 13-16R, 216; CAAE 216; CAAS 1; CANR 9, 60, 106; CP 1, 2, 3, 4, 5, 6, 7; CWP; DAM POET; DLB 5; INT CANR-9; MAL 5; MTCW 2; MTFW 2005

Wakoski-Sherbell, Diane
See Wakoski, Diane

Walcott, Derek 1930- . **BLC 1:3; 2:3; CLC 2, 4, 9, 14, 25, 42, 67, 76, 160; DC 7; PC 46**
See also BW 2; CA 89-92; CANR 26, 47, 75, 80, 130; CBD; CD 5, 6; CDWLB 3; CP 1, 2, 3, 4, 5, 6, 7; DA3; DAB; DAC;

DAM MST, MULT, POET; DLB 117, 332; DLBY 1981; DNFS 1; EFS 1; EWL 3; LMFS 2; MTCW 1, 2; MTFW 2005; PFS 6; RGEL 2; TWA; WWE 1

Waldman, Anne (Lesley) 1945- .... **CLC 7**
See also BG 1:3; CA 37-40R; CAAS 17; CANR 34, 69, 116; CP 1, 2, 3, 4, 5, 6, 7; CWP; DLB 16

Waldo, E. Hunter
See Sturgeon, Theodore (Hamilton)

Waldo, Edward Hamilton
See Sturgeon, Theodore (Hamilton)

Walker, Alice 1944- .... **BLC 1:3, 2:3; CLC 5, 6, 9, 19, 27, 46, 58, 103, 167; PC 30; SSC 5; WLCS**
See also AAYA 3, 33; AFAW 1, 2; AMWS 3; BEST 89:4; BPFB 3; BW 2, 3; CA 37-40R; CANR 9, 27, 49, 66, 82, 131; CDALB 1968-1988; CN 4, 5, 6, 7; CPW; CSW; DA; DA3; DAB; DAC; DAM MST, MULT, NOV, POET, POP; DLB 6, 33, 143; EWL 3; EXPN; EXPS; FL 1:6; FW; INT CANR-27; LAIT 3; MAL 5; MBL; MTCW 1, 2; MTFW 2005; NFS 5; RGAL 4; RGSF 2; SATA 31; SSFS 2, 11; TUS; YAW

Walker, Alice Malsenior
See Walker, Alice

Walker, David Harry 1911-1992 ...... **CLC 14**
See also CA 1-4R; 137; CANR 1; CN 1, 2; CWRI 5; SATA 8; SATA-Obit 71

Walker, Edward Joseph 1934-2004
See Walker, Ted
See also CA 21-24R; 226; CANR 12, 28, 53

Walker, George F(rederick) 1947- .. **CLC 44, 61**
See also CA 103; CANR 21, 43, 59; CD 5, 6; DAB; DAC; DAM MST; DLB 60

Walker, Joseph A. 1935-2003 .... **CLC 19**
See also BW 1, 3; CA 89-92; CAD; CANR 26, 143; CD 5, 6; DAM DRAM, MST; DFS 12; DLB 38

Walker, Margaret 1915-1998 .... **BLC 1:3; CLC 1, 6; PC 20; TCLC 129**
See also AFAW 1, 2; BW 2, 3; CA 73-76; 172; CANR 26, 54, 76, 136; CN 1, 2, 3, 4, 5, 6; CP 1, 2, 3, 4, 5, 6; CSW; DAM MULT; DLB 76, 152; EXPP; FW; MAL 5; MTCW 1, 2; MTFW 2005; RGAL 4; RHW

Walker, Ted CLC 13
See Walker, Edward Joseph
See also CP 1, 2, 3, 4, 5, 6, 7; DLB 40

Wallace, David Foster 1962- .. **CLC 50, 114; SSC 68**
See also AAYA 50; AMWS 10; CA 132; CANR 59, 133; CN 7; DA3; MTCW 2; MTFW 2005

Wallace, Dexter
See Masters, Edgar Lee

Wallace, (Richard Horatio) Edgar
1875-1932 .... **TCLC 57**
See also CA 115; 218; CMW 4; DLB 70; MSW; RGEL 2

Wallace, Irving 1916-1990 .... **CLC 7, 13**
See also AITN 1; BPFB 3; CA 1-4R; 132; CAAS 1; CANR 1, 27; CPW; DAM NOV, POP; INT CANR-27; MTCW 1, 2

Wallant, Edward Lewis 1926-1962 ... **CLC 5, 10**
See also CA 1-4R; CANR 22; DLB 2, 28, 143, 299; EWL 3; MAL 5; MTCW 1, 2; RGAL 4; RGHL

Wallas, Graham 1858-1932 .... **TCLC 91**

Waller, Edmund 1606-1687 .... **LC 86; PC 72**
See also BRW 2; DAM POET; DLB 126; PAB; RGEL 2

Walley, Byron
See Card, Orson Scott

Walpole, Horace 1717-1797 .... **LC 2, 49**
See also BRW 3; DLB 39, 104, 213; GL 3; HGG; LMFS 1; RGEL 2; SUFW 1; TEA

Walpole, Hugh (Seymour)
1884-1941 .... **TCLC 5**
See also CA 104; 165; DLB 34; HGG; MTCW 2; RGEL 2; RHW

Walrond, Eric (Derwent) 1898-1966 . **HR 1:3**
See also BW 1; CA 125; DLB 51

Walser, Martin 1927- .... **CLC 27, 183**
See also CA 57-60; CANR 8, 46, 145; CWW 2; DLB 75, 124; EWL 3

Walser, Robert 1878-1956 ..... **SSC 20; TCLC 18**
See also CA 118; 165; CANR 100; DLB 66; EWL 3

Walsh, Gillian Paton
See Paton Walsh, Jill

Walsh, Jill Paton CLC 35
See Paton Walsh, Jill
See also CLR 2, 65, 128; WYA

Walter, Villiam Christian
See Andersen, Hans Christian

Walters, Anna L(ee) 1946- .... **NNAL**
See also CA 73-76

Walther von der Vogelweide c.
1170-1228 .... **CMLC 56**

Walton, Izaak 1593-1683 .... **LC 72**
See also BRW 2; CDBLB Before 1660; DLB 151, 213; RGEL 2

Walzer, Michael (Laban) 1935- ...... **CLC 238**
See also CA 37-40R; CANR 15, 48, 127

Wambaugh, Joseph, Jr. 1937- ...... **CLC 3, 18**
See also AITN 1; BEST 89:3; BPFB 3; CA 33-36R; CANR 42, 65, 115, 167; CMW 4; CPW 1; DA3; DAM NOV, POP; DLB 6; DLBY 1983; MSW; MTCW 1, 2

Wambaugh, Joseph Aloysius
See Wambaugh, Joseph, Jr.

Wang Wei 699(?)-761(?) . **CMLC 100; PC 18**
See also TWA

Warburton, William 1698-1779 .... **LC 97**
See also DLB 104

Ward, Arthur Henry Sarsfield 1883-1959
See Rohmer, Sax
See also CA 108; 173; CMW 4; HGG

Ward, Douglas Turner 1930- .... **CLC 19**
See also BW 1; CA 81-84; CAD; CANR 27; CD 5, 6; DLB 7, 38

Ward, E. D.
See Lucas, E(dward) V(errall)

Ward, Mrs. Humphry 1851-1920
See Ward, Mary Augusta
See also RGEL 2

Ward, Mary Augusta 1851-1920 ... **TCLC 55**
See Ward, Mrs. Humphry
See also DLB 18

Ward, Nathaniel 1578(?)-1652 .... **LC 114**
See also DLB 24

Ward, Peter
See Faust, Frederick (Schiller)

Warhol, Andy 1928(?)-1987 .... **CLC 20**
See also AAYA 12; BEST 89:4; CA 89-92; 121; CANR 34

Warner, Francis (Robert Le Plastrier)
1937- .... **CLC 14**
See also CA 53-56; CANR 11; CP 1, 2, 3, 4

Warner, Marina 1946- .... **CLC 59, 231**
See also CA 65-68; CANR 21, 55, 118; CN 5, 6, 7; DLB 194; MTFW 2005

Warner, Rex (Ernest) 1905-1986 ...... **CLC 45**
See also CA 89-92; 119; CN 1, 2, 3, 4; CP 1, 2, 3, 4; DLB 15; RGEL 2; RHW

Warner, Susan (Bogert)
1819-1885 .... **NCLC 31, 146**
See also DLB 3, 42, 239, 250, 254

Warner, Sylvia (Constance) Ashton
See Ashton-Warner, Sylvia (Constance)

Warner, Sylvia Townsend
1893-1978 .. **CLC 7, 19; SSC 23; TCLC 131**
See also BRWS 7; CA 61-64; 77-80; CANR 16, 60, 104; CN 1, 2; DLB 34, 139; EWL 3; FANT; FW; MTCW 1, 2; RGEL 2; RGSF 2; RHW

Warren, Mercy Otis 1728-1814 ..... **NCLC 13**
See also DLB 31, 200; RGAL 4; TUS

Warren, Robert Penn 1905-1989 .. **CLC 1, 4, 6, 8, 10, 13, 18, 39, 53, 59; PC 37; SSC 4, 58; WLC 6**
See also AITN 1; AMW; AMWC 2; BPFB 3; BYA 1; CA 13-16R; 129; CANR 10, 47; CDALB 1968-1988; CN 1, 2, 3, 4; CP 1, 2, 3, 4; DA; DA3; DAB; DAC; DAM MST, NOV, POET; DLB 2, 48, 152, 320; DLBY 1980, 1989; EWL 3; INT CANR-10; MAL 5; MTCW 1, 2; MTFW 2005; NFS 13; RGAL 4; RGSF 2; RHW; SATA 46; SATA-Obit 63; SSFS 8; TUS

Warrigal, Jack
See Furphy, Joseph

Warshofsky, Isaac
See Singer, Isaac Bashevis

Warton, Joseph 1722-1800 ... **LC 128; NCLC 118**
See also DLB 104, 109; RGEL 2

Warton, Thomas 1728-1790 .... **LC 15, 82**
See also DAM POET; DLB 104, 109, 336; RGEL 2

Waruk, Kona
See Harris, (Theodore) Wilson

Warung, Price TCLC 45
See Astley, William
See also DLB 230; RGEL 2

Warwick, Jarvis
See Garner, Hugh
See also CCA 1

Washington, Alex
See Harris, Mark

Washington, Booker T(aliaferro)
1856-1915 .... **BLC 1:3; TCLC 10**
See also BW 1; CA 114; 125; DA3; DAM MULT; LAIT 2; RGAL 4; SATA 28

Washington, George 1732-1799 .... **LC 25**
See also DLB 31

Wassermann, (Karl) Jakob
1873-1934 .... **TCLC 6**
See also CA 104; 163; DLB 66; EWL 3

Wasserstein, Wendy 1950-2006 . **CLC 32, 59, 90, 183; DC 4**
See also AAYA 73; AMWS 15; CA 121; 129; 247; CABS 3; CAD; CANR 53, 75, 128; CD 5, 6; CWD; DA3; DAM DRAM; DFS 5, 17; DLB 228; EWL 3; FW; INT CA-129; MAL 5; MTCW 2; MTFW 2005; SATA 94; SATA-Obit 174

Waterhouse, Keith (Spencer) 1929- . **CLC 47**
See also BRWS 13; CA 5-8R; CANR 38, 67, 109; CBD; CD 6; CN 1, 2, 3, 4, 5, 6, 7; DLB 13, 15; MTCW 1, 2; MTFW 2005

Waters, Frank (Joseph) 1902-1995 .. **CLC 88**
See also CA 5-8R; 149; CAAS 13; CANR 3, 18, 63, 121; DLB 212; DLBY 1986; RGAL 4; TCWW 1, 2

Waters, Mary C. CLC 70

Waters, Roger 1944- .... **CLC 35**

Watkins, Frances Ellen
See Harper, Frances Ellen Watkins

Watkins, Gerrold
See Malzberg, Barry N(athaniel)

Watkins, Gloria Jean
See hooks, bell

Watkins, Paul 1964- .... **CLC 55**
See also CA 132; CANR 62, 98

Watkins, Vernon Phillips
1906-1967 .... **CLC 43**
See also CA 9-10; 25-28R; CAP 1; DLB 20; EWL 3; RGEL 2

Watson, Irving S.
See Mencken, H(enry) L(ouis)

Watson, John H.
See Farmer, Philip Jose

Watson, Richard F.
See Silverberg, Robert

Watts, Ephraim
See Horne, Richard Henry Hengist

Watts, Isaac 1674-1748 .... **LC 98**
See also DLB 95; RGEL 2; SATA 52

Waugh, Auberon (Alexander)
1939-2001 .... **CLC 7**
See also CA 45-48; 192; CANR 6, 22, 92; CN 1, 2, 3; DLB 14, 194

Waugh, Evelyn (Arthur St. John)
1903-1966 .. **CLC 1, 3, 8, 13, 19, 27, 44, 107; SSC 41; WLC 6**
See also BPFB 3; BRW 7; CA 85-88; 25-28R; CANR 22; CDBLB 1914-1945; DA; DA3; DAB; DAC; DAM MST, NOV, POP; DLB 15, 162, 195; EWL 3; MTCW 1, 2; MTFW 2005; NFS 13, 17; RGEL 2; RGSF 2; TEA; WLIT 4

Waugh, Harriet 1944- .... **CLC 6**
See also CA 85-88; CANR 22

Ways, C.R.
See Blount, Roy, Jr.

Waystaff, Simon
See Swift, Jonathan

Webb, Beatrice (Martha Potter)
1858-1943 .... **TCLC 22**
See also CA 117; 162; DLB 190; FW

Webb, Charles (Richard) 1939- .... **CLC 7**
See also CA 25-28R; CANR 114

Webb, Frank J. NCLC 143
See also DLB 50

Webb, James, Jr.
See Webb, James

Webb, James 1946- .... **CLC 22**
See also CA 81-84; CANR 156

Webb, James H.
See Webb, James

Webb, James Henry
See Webb, James

Webb, Mary Gladys (Meredith)
1881-1927 .... **TCLC 24**
See also CA 182; 123; DLB 34; FW; RGEL 2

Webb, Mrs. Sidney
See Webb, Beatrice (Martha Potter)

Webb, Phyllis 1927- .... **CLC 18**
See also CA 104; CANR 23; CCA 1; CP 1, 2, 3, 4, 5, 6, 7; CWP; DLB 53

Webb, Sidney (James) 1859-1947 .. **TCLC 22**
See also CA 117; 163; DLB 190

Webber, Andrew Lloyd CLC 21
See Lloyd Webber, Andrew
See also DFS 7

Weber, Lenora Mattingly
1895-1971 .... **CLC 12**
See also CA 19-20; 29-32R; CAP 1; SATA 2; SATA-Obit 26

Weber, Max 1864-1920 .... **TCLC 69**
See also CA 109; 189; DLB 296

Webster, John 1580(?)-1634(?) ...... **DC 2; LC 33, 84, 124; WLC 6**
See also BRW 2; CDBLB Before 1660; DA; DAB; DAC; DAM DRAM, MST; DFS 17, 19; DLB 58; IDTP; RGEL 2; WLIT 3

Webster, Noah 1758-1843 .... **NCLC 30**
See also DLB 1, 37, 42, 43, 73, 243

Wedekind, Benjamin Franklin
See Wedekind, Frank

Wedekind, Frank 1864-1918 .... **TCLC 7**
See also CA 104; 153; CANR 121, 122; CDWLB 2; DAM DRAM; DLB 118; EW 8; EWL 3; LMFS 2; RGWL 2, 3

Wehr, Demaris CLC 65

Weidman, Jerome 1913-1998 .... **CLC 7**
See also AITN 2; CA 1-4R; 171; CAD; CANR 1; CD 1, 2, 3, 4, 5; DLB 28

Weil, Simone (Adolphine)
1909-1943 .... **TCLC 23**
See also CA 117; 159; EW 12; EWL 3; FW; GFL 1789 to the Present; MTCW 2

Weininger, Otto 1880-1903 .... **TCLC 84**

Weinstein, Nathan
See West, Nathanael

Weinstein, Nathan von Wallenstein
See West, Nathanael

Weir, Peter (Lindsay) 1944- .... **CLC 20**
See also CA 113; 123

Weiss, Peter (Ulrich) 1916-1982 .. **CLC 3, 15, 51; TCLC 152**
See also CA 45-48; 106; CANR 3; DAM DRAM; DFS 3; DLB 69, 124; EWL 3; RGHL; RGWL 2, 3

Weiss, Theodore (Russell)
1916-2003 .... **CLC 3, 8, 14**
See also CA 9-12R, 189; 216; CAAE 189; CAAS 2; CANR 46, 94; CP 1, 2, 3, 4, 5, 6, 7; DLB 5; TCLE 1:2

Welch, (Maurice) Denton
1915-1948 .... **TCLC 22**
See also BRWS 8, 9; CA 121; 148; RGEL 2

Welch, James (Phillip) 1940-2003 ..... **CLC 6, 14, 52, 249; NNAL; PC 62**
See also CA 85-88; 219; CANR 42, 66, 107; CN 5, 6, 7; CP 2, 3, 4, 5, 6, 7; CPW; DAM MULT, POP; DLB 175, 256; LATS 1:1; NFS 23; RGAL 4; TCWW 1, 2

Weldon, Fay 1931- . **CLC 6, 9, 11, 19, 36, 59, 122**
See also BRWS 4; CA 21-24R; CANR 16, 46, 63, 97, 137; CDBLB 1960 to Present; CN 3, 4, 5, 6, 7; CPW; DAM POP; DLB 14, 194, 319; EWL 3; FW; HGG; INT CANR-16; MTCW 1, 2; MTFW 2005; RGEL 2; RGSF 2

Wellek, Rene 1903-1995 .... **CLC 28**
See also CA 5-8R; 150; CAAS 7; CANR 8; DLB 63; EWL 3; INT CANR-8

Weller, Michael 1942- .... **CLC 10, 53**
See also CA 85-88; CAD; CD 5, 6

Weller, Paul 1958- .... **CLC 26**

Wellershoff, Dieter 1925- .... **CLC 46**
See also CA 89-92; CANR 16, 37

Welles, (George) Orson 1915-1985 .. **CLC 20, 80**
See also AAYA 40; CA 93-96; 117

Wellman, John McDowell 1945-
See Wellman, Mac
See also CA 166; CD 5

Wellman, Mac CLC 65
See Wellman, John McDowell; Wellman, John McDowell
See also CAD; CD 6; RGAL 4

Wellman, Manly Wade 1903-1986 ... **CLC 49**
See also CA 1-4R; 118; CANR 6, 16, 44; FANT; SATA 6; SATA-Obit 47; SFW 4; SUFW

Wells, Carolyn 1869(?)-1942 .... **TCLC 35**
See also CA 113; 185; CMW 4; DLB 11

Wells, H(erbert) G(eorge) 1866-1946 . **SSC 6, 70; TCLC 6, 12, 19, 133; WLC 6**
See also AAYA 18; BPFB 3; BRW 6; CA 110; 121; CDBLB 1914-1945; CLR 64, 133; DA; DA3; DAB; DAC; DAM MST, NOV; DLB 34, 70, 156, 178; EWL 3; EXPS; HGG; LAIT 3; LMFS 2; MTCW

1, 2; MTFW 2005; NFS 17, 20; RGEL 2;
RGSF 2; SATA 20; SCFW 1, 2; SFW 4;
SSFS 3; SUFW; TEA; WCH; WLIT 4;
YAW

Wells, Rosemary 1943- .... **CLC 12**
See also AAYA 13; BYA 7, 8; CA 85-88;
CANR 48, 120; CLR 16, 69; CWRI 5;
MAICYA 1, 2; SAAS 1; SATA 18, 69,
114, 156; YAW

Wells-Barnett, Ida B(ell)
1862-1931 .... **TCLC 125**
See also CA 182; DLB 23, 221

Welsh, Irvine 1958- .... **CLC 144**
See also CA 173; CANR 146; CN 7; DLB
271

Welty, Eudora 1909-2001 .... **CLC 1, 2, 5, 14,**
22, 33, 105, 220; SSC 1, 27, 51, 111;
WLC 6
See also AAYA 48; AMW; AMWR 1; BPFB
3; CA 9-12R; 199; CABS 1; CANR 32,
65, 128; CDALB 1941-1968; CN 1, 2, 3,
4, 5, 6, 7; CSW; DA; DA3; DAB; DAC;
DAM MST, NOV; DLB 2, 102, 143;
DLBD 12; DLBY 1987, 2001; EWL 3;
EXPS; HGG; LAIT 3; MAL 5; MBL;
MTCW 1, 2; MTFW 2005; NFS 13, 15;
RGAL 4; RGSF 2; RHW; SSFS 2, 10;
TUS

Welty, Eudora Alice
See Welty, Eudora

Wen I-to 1899-1946 .... **TCLC 28**
See also EWL 3

Wentworth, Robert
See Hamilton, Edmond

Werfel, Franz (Viktor) 1890-1945 ... **TCLC 8**
See also CA 104; 161; DLB 81, 124; EWL
3; RGWL 2, 3

Wergeland, Henrik Arnold
1808-1845 .... **NCLC 5**

Werner, Friedrich Ludwig Zacharias
1768-1823 .... **NCLC 189**
See also DLB 94

Werner, Zacharias
See Werner, Friedrich Ludwig Zacharias

Wersba, Barbara 1932- .... **CLC 30**
See also AAYA 2, 30; BYA 6, 12, 13; CA
29-32R, 182; CAAE 182; CANR 16, 38;
CLR 3, 78; DLB 52; JRDA; MAICYA 1,
2; SAAS 2; SATA 1, 58; SATA-Essay 103;
WYA; YAW

Wertmueller, Lina 1928- .... **CLC 16**
See also CA 97-100; CANR 39, 78

Wescott, Glenway 1901-1987 .. **CLC 13; SSC**
35
See also CA 13-16R; 121; CANR 23, 70;
CN 1, 2, 3, 4; DLB 4, 9, 102; MAL 5;
RGAL 4

Wesker, Arnold 1932- .... **CLC 3, 5, 42**
See also CA 1-4R; CAAS 7; CANR 1, 33;
CBD; CD 5, 6; CDBLB 1960 to Present;
DAB; DAM DRAM; DLB 13, 310, 319;
EWL 3; MTCW 1; RGEL 2; TEA

Wesley, Charles 1707-1788 .... **LC 128**
See also DLB 95; RGEL 2

Wesley, John 1703-1791 .... **LC 88**
See also DLB 104

Wesley, Richard (Errol) 1945- .... **CLC 7**
See also BW 1; CA 57-60; CAD; CANR
27; CD 5, 6; DLB 38

Wessel, Johan Herman 1742-1785 .... **LC 7**
See also DLB 300

West, Anthony (Panther)
1914-1987 .... **CLC 50**
See also CA 45-48; 124; CANR 3, 19; CN
1, 2, 3, 4; DLB 15

West, C. P.
See Wodehouse, P(elham) G(renville)

West, Cornel 1953- .... **BLCS; CLC 134**
See also CA 144; CANR 91, 159; DLB 246

West, Cornel Ronald
See West, Cornel

West, Delno C(loyde), Jr. 1936- .... **CLC 70**
See also CA 57-60

West, Dorothy 1907-1998 ...... **HR 1:3; TCLC**
108
See also BW 2; CA 143; 169; DLB 76

West, (Mary) Jessamyn 1902-1984 ... **CLC 7,**
17
See also CA 9-12R; 112; CANR 27; CN 1,
2, 3; DLB 6; DLBY 1984; MTCW 1, 2;
RGAL 4; RHW; SATA-Obit 37; TCWW
2; TUS; YAW

West, Morris L(anglo) 1916-1999 ..... **CLC 6,**
33
See also BPFB 3; CA 5-8R; 187; CANR
24, 49, 64; CN 1, 2, 3, 4, 5, 6; CPW; DLB
289; MTCW 1, 2; MTFW 2005

West, Nathanael 1903-1940 .. **SSC 16; TCLC**
1, 14, 44
See also AAYA 77; AMW; AMWR 2; BPFB
3; CA 104; 125; CDALB 1929-1941;
DA3; DLB 4, 9, 28; EWL 3; MAL 5;
MTCW 1, 2; MTFW 2005; NFS 16;
RGAL 4; TUS

West, Owen
See Koontz, Dean

West, Paul 1930- .... **CLC 7, 14, 96, 226**
See also CA 13-16R; CAAS 7; CANR 22,
53, 76, 89, 136; CN 1, 2, 3, 4, 5, 6, 7;
DLB 14; INT CANR-22; MTCW 2;
MTFW 2005

West, Rebecca 1892-1983 ... **CLC 7, 9, 31, 50**
See also BPFB 3; BRWS 3; CA 5-8R; 109;
CANR 19; CN 1, 2, 3; DLB 36; DLBY
1983; EWL 3; FW; MTCW 1, 2; MTFW
2005; NCFS 4; RGEL 2; TEA

Westall, Robert (Atkinson)
1929-1993 .... **CLC 17**
See also AAYA 12; BYA 2, 6, 7, 8, 9, 15;
CA 69-72; 141; CANR 18, 68; CLR 13;
FANT; JRDA; MAICYA 1, 2; MAICYAS
1; SAAS 2; SATA 23, 69; SATA-Obit 75;
WYA; YAW

Westermarck, Edward 1862-1939 . **TCLC 87**

Westlake, Donald E. 1933- .... **CLC 7, 33**
See also BPFB 3; CA 17-20R; CAAS 13;
CANR 16, 44, 65, 94, 137; CMW 4;
CPW; DAM POP; INT CANR-16; MSW;
MTCW 2; MTFW 2005

Westlake, Donald Edwin
See Westlake, Donald E.

Westmacott, Mary
See Christie, Agatha (Mary Clarissa)

Weston, Allen
See Norton, Andre

Wetcheek, J. L.
See Feuchtwanger, Lion

Wetering, Janwillem van de
See van de Wetering, Janwillem

Wetherald, Agnes Ethelwyn
1857-1940 .... **TCLC 81**
See also CA 202; DLB 99

Wetherell, Elizabeth
See Warner, Susan (Bogert)

Whale, James 1889-1957 .... **TCLC 63**
See also AAYA 75

Whalen, Philip (Glenn) 1923-2002 .... **CLC 6,**
29
See also BG 1:3; CA 9-12R; 209; CANR 5,
39; CP 1, 2, 3, 4, 5, 6, 7; DLB 16; WP

Wharton, Edith (Newbold Jones)
1862-1937 ... **SSC 6, 84; TCLC 3, 9, 27,**
53, 129, 149; WLC 6
See also AAYA 25; AMW; AMWC 2;
AMWR 1; BPFB 3; CA 104; 132; CDALB
1865-1917; DA; DA3; DAB; DAC; DAM
MST, NOV; DLB 4, 9, 12, 78, 189; DLBD
13; EWL 3; EXPS; FL 1:6; GL 3; HGG;

LAIT 2, 3; LATS 1:1; MAL 5; MBL;
MTCW 1, 2; MTFW 2005; NFS 5, 11,
15, 20; RGAL 4; RGSF 2; RHW; SSFS 6,
7; SUFW; TUS

Wharton, James
See Mencken, H(enry) L(ouis)

Wharton, William (a pseudonym)
1925- .... **CLC 18, 37**
See also CA 93-96; CN 4, 5, 6, 7; DLBY
1980; INT CA-93-96

Wheatley (Peters), Phillis
1753(?)-1784 .... **BLC 1:3; LC 3, 50; PC**
3; WLC 6
See also AFAW 1, 2; CDALB 1640-1865;
DA; DA3; DAC; DAM MST, MULT,
POET; DLB 31, 50; EXPP; FL 1:1; PFS
13; RGAL 4

Wheelock, John Hall 1886-1978 .... **CLC 14**
See also CA 13-16R; 77-80; CANR 14; CP
1, 2; DLB 45; MAL 5

Whim-Wham
See Curnow, (Thomas) Allen (Monro)

Whisp, Kennilworthy
See Rowling, J.K.

Whitaker, Rod 1931-2005
See Trevanian
See also CA 29-32R; 246; CANR 45, 153;
CMW 4

White, Babington
See Braddon, Mary Elizabeth

White, E. B. 1899-1985 .... **CLC 10, 34, 39**
See also AAYA 62; AITN 2; AMWS 1; CA
13-16R; 116; CANR 16, 37; CDALBS;
CLR 1, 21, 107; CPW; DA3; DAM POP;
DLB 11, 22; EWL 3; FANT; MAICYA 1,
2; MAL 5; MTCW 1, 2; MTFW 2005;
NCFS 5; RGAL 4; SATA 2, 29, 100;
SATA-Obit 44; TUS

White, Edmund 1940- .... **CLC 27, 110**
See also AAYA 7; CA 45-48; CANR 3, 19,
36, 62, 107, 133, 172; CN 5, 6, 7; DA3;
DAM POP; DLB 227; MTCW 1, 2;
MTFW 2005

White, Edmund Valentine III
See White, Edmund

White, Elwyn Brooks
See White, E. B.

White, Hayden V. 1928- .... **CLC 148**
See also CA 128; CANR 135; DLB 246

White, Patrick (Victor Martindale)
1912-1990 ... **CLC 3, 4, 5, 7, 9, 18, 65,**
69; SSC 39; TCLC 176
See also BRWS 1; CA 81-84; 132; CANR
43; CN 1, 2, 3, 4; DLB 260, 332; EWL 3;
MTCW 1; RGEL 2; RGSF 2; RHW;
TWA; WWE 1

White, Phyllis Dorothy James 1920-
See James, P. D.
See also CA 21-24R; CANR 17, 43, 65,
112; CMW 4; CN 7; CPW; DA3; DAM
POP; MTCW 1, 2; MTFW 2005; TEA

White, T(erence) H(anbury)
1906-1964 .... **CLC 30**
See also AAYA 22; BPFB 3; BYA 4, 5; CA
73-76; CANR 37; DLB 160; FANT;
JRDA; LAIT 1; MAICYA 1, 2; RGEL 2;
SATA 12; SUFW 1; YAW

White, Terence de Vere 1912-1994 ... **CLC 49**
See also CA 49-52; 145; CANR 3

White, Walter
See White, Walter F(rancis)

White, Walter F(rancis)
1893-1955 ..... **BLC 1:3; HR 1:3; TCLC**
15
See also BW 1; CA 115; 124; DAM MULT;
DLB 51

White, William Hale 1831-1913
See Rutherford, Mark
See also CA 121; 189

Williams, Sherley Anne
1944-1999 .... **BLC 1:3; CLC 89**
See also AFAW 2; BW 2, 3; CA 73-76; 185;
CANR 25, 82; DAM MULT, POET; DLB
41; INT CANR-25; SATA 78; SATA-Obit
116

Williams, Shirley
See Williams, Sherley Anne

Williams, Tennessee 1911-1983 . **CLC 1, 2, 5,
7, 8, 11, 15, 19, 30, 39, 45, 71, 111; DC
4; SSC 81; WLC 6**
See also AAYA 31; AITN 1, 2; AMW;
AMWC 1; CA 5-8R; 108; CABS 3; CAD;
CANR 31, 132, 174; CDALB 1941-1968;
CN 1, 2, 3; DA; DA3; DAB; DAC; DAM
DRAM, MST; DFS 17; DLB 7, 341;
DLBD 4; DLBY 1983; EWL 3; GLL 1;
LAIT 4; LATS 1:2; MAL 5; MTCW 1, 2;
MTFW 2005; RGAL 4; TUS

Williams, Thomas (Alonzo)
1926-1990 .... **CLC 14**
See also CA 1-4R; 132; CANR 2

Williams, Thomas Lanier
See Williams, Tennessee

Williams, William C.
See Williams, William Carlos

Williams, William Carlos
1883-1963 .... **CLC 1, 2, 5, 9, 13, 22, 42,
67; PC 7; SSC 31; WLC 6**
See also AAYA 46; AMW; AMWR 1; CA
89-92; CANR 34; CDALB 1917-1929;
DA; DA3; DAB; DAC; DAM MST,
POET; DLB 4, 16, 54, 86; EWL 3; EXPP;
MAL 5; MTCW 1, 2; MTFW 2005; NCFS
4; PAB; PFS 1, 6, 11; RGAL 4; RGSF 2;
TUS; WP

Williamson, David (Keith) 1942- ..... **CLC 56**
See also CA 103; CANR 41; CD 5, 6; DLB
289

Williamson, Ellen Douglas 1905-1984
See Douglas, Ellen
See also CA 17-20R; 114; CANR 39

Williamson, Jack CLC 29
See Williamson, John Stewart
See also CAAS 8; DLB 8; SCFW 1, 2

Williamson, John Stewart 1908-2006
See Williamson, Jack
See also AAYA 76; CA 17-20R; 255; CANR
23, 70, 153; SFW 4

Willie, Frederick
See Lovecraft, H. P.

Willingham, Calder (Baynard, Jr.)
1922-1995 .... **CLC 5, 51**
See also CA 5-8R; 147; CANR 3; CN 1, 2,
3, 4, 5; CSW; DLB 2, 44; IDFW 3, 4;
MTCW 1

Willis, Charles
See Clarke, Arthur C.

Willis, Nathaniel Parker
1806-1867 .... **NCLC 194**
See also DLB 3, 59, 73, 74, 183, 250;
DLBD 13; RGAL 4

Willy
See Colette, (Sidonie-Gabrielle)

Willy, Colette
See Colette, (Sidonie-Gabrielle)
See also GLL 1

Wilmot, John 1647-1680 .... **LC 75; PC 66**
See Rochester
See also BRW 2; DLB 131; PAB

Wilson, A.N. 1950- .... **CLC 33**
See also BRWS 6; CA 112; 122; CANR
156; CN 4, 5, 6, 7; DLB 14, 155, 194;
MTCW 2

Wilson, Andrew Norman
See Wilson, A.N.

Wilson, Angus (Frank Johnstone)
1913-1991 . **CLC 2, 3, 5, 25, 34; SSC 21**
See also BRWS 1; CA 5-8R; 134; CANR
21; CN 1, 2, 3, 4; DLB 15, 139, 155;
EWL 3; MTCW 1, 2; MTFW 2005; RGEL
2; RGSF 2

Wilson, August 1945-2005 .... **BLC 1:3, 2:3;
CLC 39, 50, 63, 118, 222; DC 2, 31;
WLCS**
See also AAYA 16; AFAW 2; AMWS 8; BW
2, 3; CA 115; 122; 244; CAD; CANR 42,
54, 76, 128; CD 5, 6; DA; DA3; DAB;
DAC; DAM DRAM, MST, MULT; DFS
3, 7, 15, 17, 24; DLB 228; EWL 3; LAIT
4; LATS 1:2; MAL 5; MTCW 1, 2;
MTFW 2005; RGAL 4

Wilson, Brian 1942- .... **CLC 12**

Wilson, Colin (Henry) 1931- .... **CLC 3, 14**
See also CA 1-4R; CAAS 5; CANR 1, 22,
33, 77; CMW 4; CN 1, 2, 3, 4, 5, 6; DLB
14, 194; HGG; MTCW 1; SFW 4

Wilson, Dirk
See Pohl, Frederik

Wilson, Edmund 1895-1972 .. **CLC 1, 2, 3, 8,
24**
See also AMW; CA 1-4R; 37-40R; CANR
1, 46, 110; CN 1; DLB 63; EWL 3; MAL
5; MTCW 1, 2; MTFW 2005; RGAL 4;
TUS

Wilson, Ethel Davis (Bryant)
1888(?)-1980 .... **CLC 13**
See also CA 102; CN 1, 2; DAC; DAM
POET; DLB 68; MTCW 1; RGEL 2

Wilson, Harriet
See Wilson, Harriet E. Adams
See also DLB 239

Wilson, Harriet E.
See Wilson, Harriet E. Adams
See also DLB 243

Wilson, Harriet E. Adams
1827(?)-1863(?) ...... **BLC 1:3; NCLC 78**
See Wilson, Harriet; Wilson, Harriet E.
See also DAM MULT; DLB 50

Wilson, John 1785-1854 .... **NCLC 5**
See also DLB 110

Wilson, John (Anthony) Burgess 1917-1993
See Burgess, Anthony
See also CA 1-4R; 143; CANR 2, 46; DA3;
DAC; DAM NOV; MTCW 1, 2; MTFW
2005; NFS 15; TEA

Wilson, Katharina CLC 65

Wilson, Lanford 1937- .. **CLC 7, 14, 36, 197;
DC 19**
See also CA 17-20R; CABS 3; CAD; CANR
45, 96; CD 5, 6; DAM DRAM; DFS 4, 9,
12, 16, 20; DLB 7, 341; EWL 3; MAL 5;
TUS

Wilson, Robert M. 1941- .... **CLC 7, 9**
See also CA 49-52; CAD; CANR 2, 41; CD
5, 6; MTCW 1

Wilson, Robert McLiam 1964- .... **CLC 59**
See also CA 132; DLB 267

Wilson, Sloan 1920-2003 .... **CLC 32**
See also CA 1-4R; 216; CANR 1, 44; CN
1, 2, 3, 4, 5, 6

Wilson, Snoo 1948- .... **CLC 33**
See also CA 69-72; CBD; CD 5, 6

Wilson, William S(mith) 1932- .... **CLC 49**
See also CA 81-84

Wilson, (Thomas) Woodrow
1856-1924 .... **TCLC 79**
See also CA 166; DLB 47

Winchester, Simon 1944- .... **CLC 257**
See also AAYA 66; CA 107; CANR 90, 130

Winchilsea, Anne (Kingsmill) Finch
1661-1720
See Finch, Anne
See also RGEL 2

Winckelmann, Johann Joachim
1717-1768 .... **LC 129**
See also DLB 97

Windham, Basil
See Wodehouse, P(elham) G(renville)

Wingrove, David 1954- .... **CLC 68**
See also CA 133; SFW 4

Winnemucca, Sarah 1844-1891 .... **NCLC 79;
NNAL**
See also DAM MULT; DLB 175; RGAL 4

Winstanley, Gerrard 1609-1676 .... **LC 52**

Wintergreen, Jane
See Duncan, Sara Jeannette

Winters, Arthur Yvor
See Winters, Yvor

Winters, Janet Lewis CLC 41
See Lewis, Janet
See also DLBY 1987

Winters, Yvor 1900-1968 .. **CLC 4, 8, 32; PC
82**
See also AMWS 2; CA 11-12; 25-28R; CAP
1; DLB 48; EWL 3; MAL 5; MTCW 1;
RGAL 4

Winterson, Jeanette 1959- .... **CLC 64, 158**
See also BRWS 4; CA 136; CANR 58, 116;
CN 5, 6, 7; CPW; DA3; DAM POP; DLB
207, 261; FANT; FW; GLL 1; MTCW 2;
MTFW 2005; RHW

Winthrop, John 1588-1649 .... **LC 31, 107**
See also DLB 24, 30

Winton, Tim 1960- .... **CLC 251**
See also AAYA 34; CA 152; CANR 118;
CN 6, 7; DLB 325; SATA 98

Wirth, Louis 1897-1952 .... **TCLC 92**
See also CA 210

Wiseman, Frederick 1930- .... **CLC 20**
See also CA 159

Wister, Owen 1860-1938 ..... **SSC 100; TCLC
21**
See also BPFB 3; CA 108; 162; DLB 9, 78,
186; RGAL 4; SATA 62; TCWW 1, 2

Wither, George 1588-1667 .... **LC 96**
See also DLB 121; RGEL 2

Witkacy
See Witkiewicz, Stanislaw Ignacy

Witkiewicz, Stanislaw Ignacy
1885-1939 .... **TCLC 8**
See also CA 105; 162; CDWLB 4; DLB
215; EW 10; EWL 3; RGWL 2, 3; SFW 4

Wittgenstein, Ludwig (Josef Johann)
1889-1951 .... **TCLC 59**
See also CA 113; 164; DLB 262; MTCW 2

Wittig, Monique 1935-2003 .... **CLC 22**
See also CA 116; 135; 212; CANR 143;
CWW 2; DLB 83; EWL 3; FW; GLL 1

Wittlin, Jozef 1896-1976 .... **CLC 25**
See also CA 49-52; 65-68; CANR 3; EWL
3

Wodehouse, P(elham) G(renville)
1881-1975 . **CLC 1, 2, 5, 10, 22; SSC 2;
TCLC 108**
See also AAYA 65; AITN 2; BRWS 3; CA
45-48; 57-60; CANR 3, 33; CDBLB
1914-1945; CN 1, 2; CPW 1; DA3; DAB;
DAC; DAM NOV; DLB 34, 162; EWL 3;
MTCW 1, 2; MTFW 2005; RGEL 2;
RGSF 2; SATA 22; SSFS 10

Woiwode, L.
See Woiwode, Larry (Alfred)

Woiwode, Larry (Alfred) 1941- ... **CLC 6, 10**
See also CA 73-76; CANR 16, 94; CN 3, 4,
5, 6, 7; DLB 6; INT CANR-16

Wojciechowska, Maia (Teresa)
1927-2002 .... **CLC 26**
See also AAYA 8, 46; BYA 3; CA 9-12R;
183; 209; CAAE 183; CANR 4, 41; CLR
1; JRDA; MAICYA 1, 2; SAAS 1; SATA
1, 28, 83; SATA-Essay 104; SATA-Obit
134; YAW

PC Cumulative Nationality Index

PC-89 Title Index

ISBN-13: 978-0-7876-9886-7
ISBN-10: 0-7876-9886-5

90000
9 780787 698867